# SOVIET NATURAL RESOURCES
# IN THE WORLD ECONOMY

# SOVIET NATURAL RESOURCES IN THE WORLD ECONOMY

Edited by
Robert G. Jensen, Theodore Shabad, and Arthur W. Wright

The University of Chicago Press
Chicago and London

ROBERT G. JENSEN is professor and chairman of the
Geography Department at Syracuse University and the editor of
*Soviet Energy Policy and the Hydrocarbons: Comments and Rejoinder*.

THEODORE SHABAD, editor of *Soviet Geography: Review and
Translation* and lecturer in the Department of Geography at
Columbia University, is the author of *Basic Industrial Resources
of the USSR* and co-author of *Gateway to Siberian Resources*
and *The Soviet Energy System*.

ARTHUR W. WRIGHT is professor and chairman of the Department
of Economics at the University of Connecticut and the editor of
a collection of essays by Jerzy F. Karcz entitled *The Economics
of Communist Agriculture*.

The University of Chicago Press, Chicago 60637
The University of Chicago Press, Ltd., London

Library of Congress Cataloging in Publication Data
Main entry under title:

Soviet natural resources in the world economy.

   Includes index.
   1. Natural resources—Soviet Union.  I. Jensen,
Robert G.  II. Shabad, Theodore.  III. Wright, Arthur W.,
1938–
HC333.5.S68  1983      333.7'0947      82-17317
ISBN 0-226-39831-5

# CONTENTS

vi     Contents

# ILLUSTRATIONS

# TABLES

# EDITORS' PREFACE

The research upon which this volume is based had its origins in three congruent events of the early 1970s: the beginnings of East-West détente marked by President Richard M. Nixon's visit to Moscow in 1972, the Arab oil embargo during the Arab-Israeli war of 1973, and the Soviet leadership's decision in 1974 to proceed with the construction of the Baikal-Amur Mainline (BAM), a 2,000-mile railroad in Far Eastern Siberia. A common denominator in all three events was the potential of intensified economic relations between the Soviet Union and the rest of the world. Détente appeared to lay the basis for greater East-West trade; the 1973 oil embargo demonstrated the dependence of the advanced industrial countries on imports of fuels and raw materials; and the BAM project suggested new Soviet interest in developing previously inaccessible Siberian resources for export beyond the Socialist bloc.

The long-term prospect of greater Soviet involvement in the world economy, primarily as a purveyor of fuels, minerals, timber and other industrial raw materials, largely in exchange for Western technology, thus appeared as a subject worthy of careful investigation from a number of points of view. The subject was of interest to American geographers because of the potential implications of growing Soviet resource exports for the United States itself and because few studies were available that evaluated Soviet resource potential in a global context. The feasibility of undertaking such a study was enhanced by the availability of experienced Soviet area specialists within the American geographic community who were interested in problems of regional development within the Soviet Union, a set of problems that needed to be analyzed carefully in order to evaluate Soviet raw-material export potential through the 1980s.

A small working group of geographers, including Theodore Shabad, editor of *Soviet Geography: Review and Translation*, and George W. Hoffman of the University of Texas at Austin, made an initial approach to the Council of the Association of American Geographers (A.A.G.) in 1975 to seek endorsement of a geographically oriented study of the potential role of Soviet natural resources in the world economy. With the Council's encouragement, a preliminary project proposal was drafted by Hoffman and Shabad with input from Leslie Dienes of the University of Kansas and Arthur W. Wright of the University of

Connecticut, an economist with long experience in Soviet affairs. In 1976, the A.A.G. Council appointed Robert G. Jensen of Syracuse University as project director and Theodore Shabad and Arthur W. Wright as associate directors. A final proposal was then drafted, approved and sponsored by the A.A.G., and in 1977 funded by the National Science Foundation. After funding, an interdisciplinary research team of some 30 members was assembled from university faculties and other institutions both in the United States and abroad. Over the three-year period 1978–80 more than 30 discussion papers were written for limited circulation among specialists outside the project and, on the basis of their comments and subsequent developments, were revised and updated for publication in the present volume.

World conditions have changed in the years since the ideas for this project first germinated. The prospects for economic cooperation between the Soviet Union and the United States that were very much in the air during the early 1970s have not materialized, although greater interaction between the Soviet Union, on the one hand, and Western Europe and Japan, on the other hand, did develop. However, the objective basis for closer economic relations over the long term remains, both in the untapped resource potential of the Soviet Union, notably Siberia, and in the need for raw-material supplies in the developed industrial countries, including the United States. The basic theme of this research project thus remains valid, and its results are presented here in the hope that they may prove useful in future investigations and decision making relating to the role that Soviet natural resources may play in the world economy.

We wish to acknowledge the many organizations and individuals who have made major contributions to this project. Our long-term effort was made possible by a grant from the National Science Foundation and by support from the Central Office of the Association of American Geographers. At every stage the project received encouragement from the executive director of the A.A.G., Warren Nystrom and, his successor in that post, Patricia McWethy. The Kennan Institute for Advanced Russian Studies of the Woodrow Wilson International Center for Scholars in Washington, D.C., provided facilities and support for a conference on the project theme in April of 1980. To all those who participated in the conference, some fifty experts from industry, government, and banking, we again express our thanks for discussion that enriched our ongoing research and for insights that contributed directly to many individual studies. Our greatest debt, of course, belongs to our colleagues who contributed chapters to this volume. For their splendid cooperation in what turned out to be a "labor of love," we can only express our inadequate but heartfelt thanks. Finally, for their assistance in the preparation of discussion papers and final manuscript, we want to acknowledge the outstanding work of three members of the Geography Department at Syracuse University: D. Michael Kirchoff, Staff Cartographer, who supervised the production of maps and illustrations; Gary J. Hausladen, doctoral candidate, who served ably as project assistant for several years; and Pamela Walker, who performed as an extraordinarily skilled manuscript typist. Credit for the monumental task of indexing this book also belongs to Pamela Walker.

Though many individuals and organizations have contributed to our project, it should be clear to the reader that all views and statements in this volume are those of individual scholars. In no way should those views be attributed to the Association of American Geographers, the National Science Foundation, or any other organization.

# NOTE ON TRANSLITERATION

In rendering Soviet proper names, place names and bibliographical references, the editors sought to use a system of transliteration from the Russian that would be both consistent and easily assimilable by the reader. The choice fell on a system that is slightly nonstandard, having been modified from the one developed by the United States Board on Geographic Names (BGN) for use by government agencies, but differing from the system used by the Library of Congress (LC) and many other libraries in the United States. The modified system used in this volume is similar to the form in which Soviet names appear in American newspapers and are most familiar to the general reader. For the benefit of those who wish to transform bibliographical citations into the Library of Congress system or render place names in the Board on Geographic Names system, the three systems are presented in the following table.

Transliteration Table

| Russian | Present volume | BGN | LC |
|---------|---------------|-----|-----|
| А | a | a | a |
| Б | b | b | b |
| В | v | v | v |
| Г | g | g | g |
| Д | d | d | d |
| Е | e* | e* | e |
| Ж | zh | zh | zh |
| З | z | z | z |
| И | i | i | i |
| Й | i** | y | i |
| К | k | k | k |
| Л | l | l | l |
| М | m | m | m |
| Н | n | n | n |
| О | o | o | o |
| П | p | p | p |
| Р | r | r | r |
| С | s | s | s |
| Т | t | t | t |
| У | u | u | u |
| Ф | f | f | f |
| Х | kh | kh | kh |
| Ц | ts | ts | ts |
| Ч | ch | ch | ch |
| Ш | sh | sh | sh |
| Щ | shch | shch | shch |
| Ъ | omit | ″ | ″ |
| Ы | y | y | y |
| Ь | omit | ′ | ′ |
| Э | e | e | e |
| Ю | yu | yu | iu |
| Я | ya | ya | ia |

*Ye initially, after another vowel and after a soft or hard sign (′,″).

**Omitted in such BGN combinations as iy and yy, which are rendered as i and y, respectively.

# I
## INTRODUCTION

# SOVIET NATURAL RESOURCES
# IN A GLOBAL CONTEXT

ROBERT G. JENSEN
Syracuse University

## Introduction

By virtue of an extraordinary natural resource base, the Soviet Union holds an enviable position among the world's industrial powers. Whereas most countries are vitally concerned about the adequacy and cost of their domestic energy and raw-material supplies and about growing dependence on uncertain foreign sources, the Soviet Union remains virtually self-sufficient, although its development costs have also increased. During more than fifty years following the October Revolution of 1917, Soviet economic development advanced largely on the basis of autarkic policies made possible by a rich endowment of natural resources, the vigorous mobilization of capital and labor, and the channeling of all three into key areas of industrial production. The relative success of this strategy was demonstrated by high rates of economic growth, the rapid creation of a modern industrial base, and finally by the development of a military capacity rivaling that of the United States. Yet, despite the attainment of superpower status, Soviet participation in international economic affairs remained at minimal levels.

Developments over the last two decades, however, have prompted important shifts in the strategy of Soviet economic development and these shifts may portend significant long-term changes for the Soviet role in the world economy. Since the mid-1960s traditional growth strategy based on large inputs of raw materials and fixed capital, a central feature of earlier five-year plans, has been declining in effectiveness. And in contrast to many industrial economies, reduced capital effectiveness in the Soviet Union has not been offset by buoyant technological progress. Chronic difficulties in agriculture, moreover, have remained as a damper on economic growth and in recent years have necessitated large grain imports causing the USSR to divert scarce foreign-exchange resources from other pressing needs. A tightening labor supply during the 1980s will add to Soviet problems by eliminating a major source of past economic expansions. These difficulties are exacerbated by the fact that the Soviet Union must increasingly exploit fuel and raw-material resources in remote and inhospitable northern and eastern regions that require massive inputs of capital and advanced technology.

Soviet planners, although optimistic about their country's economic future, are concerned about these problems and have recognized the need to adjust traditional development strategy in the face of new circumstances. The emphasis in recent years, on what has been termed the "scientific-technical revolution," represents a growing appreciation by Soviet leaders of the critical role of qualitative factors and technological progress in the growth of complex economies. Consequently, they have recognized opportunities to reap large dividends not only from improvements in domestic technology but also from imports of foreign technology, primarily from the West. This perception was unmistakably one of the cornerstones of détente, so widely proclaimed in the early 1970s.

During the same period, increases in the relative prices of raw materials on world markets and new concerns about the cost and accessibility of natural resources among the Western industrial powers, dramatically underlined by the leaps in oil prices since 1973, put a premium on Soviet energy exports and generated widespread interest in the implications of the enormous Soviet resource potential for the world economy. Such interest was heightened by the increasing involvement of the USSR in trade beyond the Soviet bloc and by Soviet plans to move rapidly forward with heavy investment in resource development programs in virtually untapped areas of Siberia. The large capital and technological requirements of such programs encouraged the Soviets to seek assistance from Western countries (including Japan) through trade and various credit or compensation arrangements. These arrangements, directly or indirectly, involved an exchange of Soviet raw materials for Western technology and suggested that the rate and timing of resource development programs in the USSR would depend in some degree on economic and political judgments made by Western governments. On the surface, therefore, it seemed that the traditional characterization of the Soviet economy as essentially autarkic had become increasingly untenable. Instead, it was reasonable to argue that the enormous resource base of the Soviet Union, which in the past made autarky possible, might now be used to foster increasing Soviet integration in the world economy.

It is too early to determine the extent or permanence of what appears to be a shift in the Soviet economy from autarky toward global integration. The 11th Five-Year Plan (1981–85) represents expanded international trade as being in the interest of the Soviet economy. But the cloud that has darkened East-West relations since the Soviet military intervention in Afghanistan has made economic cooperation with the advanced industrial countries more difficult. Yet, despite the present political climate, there is little doubt that in the long run the Soviet Union has the resource potential to become a more important factor in the world market for some fossil fuels and other industrial raw materials. Certainly future increases in raw-material prices, if they materialize, will provide the Soviet Union with an attractive means of earning foreign exchange to pay for expanded imports of technology, especially as the quality of Soviet manufactured goods is not likely to be competitive on world markets during this century. Soviet energy resources, particularly oil and natural gas, are already outstanding examples of this possibility.

## The Association of American Geographers' Project on Soviet Natural Resources in the World Economy

It was against this background that the Association of American Geographers (A.A.G.), with support from the National Science Foundation, began an interdisciplinary research project designed to provide an independent analysis of the implications of Soviet resource potential for the world economy in the period to 1990. During the life of the project, July 1977 to December 1980, more than thirty papers were completed bearing on different aspects of the project theme. These included detailed studies of energy and industrial raw materials, analyses of the regional and environmental dimensions of Soviet resource development policy with special attention to Siberia and the Far East, and studies of Soviet foreign trade with a focus on the role of raw materials.

This book is based on work commissioned by the A.A.G. project. Since project research was conducted over a period of years, the studies were revised and updated for publication. The present volume thus stands as the final report of the Association of American Geographers' Project on Soviet Natural Resources in the World Economy.

## The Question of Soviet Resource Potential and Strategy

During the 1980s, Soviet resource potential and strategy and the implications of expanded or reduced exports of energy and industrial raw materials from the USSR are likely to be of increasing international interest. Western governments, with their economies vulnerable to disruptions of energy and raw-material supplies, are wary of dependence on Soviet resources, on the one hand, and concerned about Soviet influence and competition in the often unstable mineral-producing areas of the world, on the other. Soviet resource potential and strategy are also of concern to those third-world countries whose own export earnings depend on world energy and raw-material prices, to producer-nation cartels seeking to raise or maintain prices for their products, and perhaps most importantly to Eastern Europe, which is heavily dependent on Soviet energy and raw-material supplies.

Thus the global implications of Soviet resource potential and strategy merit careful consideration. The questions are clear. How extensive are Soviet industrial resources and what is their present and potential role in the world economy? Can the Soviets meet the energy and resource needs of the domestic economy while continuing to supply Eastern Europe and to a more limited extent the West? Or conversely, as some have suggested, will the USSR find it advantageous to seek greater access to certain resources from outside its national boundaries? Will the Soviet Union continue to pursue a course of global interdependence by exchanging raw materials for foreign technology or ultimately revert to a more traditional autarkic stance? And to what extent can it divert key energy goods and raw materials from its allies in Eastern Europe to the West in order to earn much needed hard currency? Finally, what should Western policy be, especially that of the United States, with respect to Soviet resource development? Should we encourage international cooperation in the development of Soviet resources and the opening up of Siberia, or should we remain neutral or perhaps even work to hinder Soviet efforts?

These are some of the important questions to which our work is relevant. The more limited purpose of this book, however, is to evaluate Soviet resource potential in selected energy and industrial raw materials with attention to possible implications for the world economy in the period to 1990. This date was originally selected because it coincided with a proposed 15-year plan (1976–90) commissioned by Gosplan USSR, the Soviet economic planning agency. At the time of writing, unfortunately, these long-term projections had not been published. Our research was further complicated by a decline, beginning in 1973 and especially after 1977, in Soviet publication of basic regional production and foreign trade data for a number of important commodities. Despite these and other difficulties inherent in the topic, we are confident that the relatively comprehensive nature of our research will provide a useful foundation for judging the reality of the Soviet resource potential and for assessing the domestic and international implications of Soviet resource development in the years ahead. As new data on production and reserves in the USSR become available as the decade unfolds, this volume can serve as a baseline against which future trends may be judged and in some cases, we hope, even anticipated.

The book is divided into four parts. Part I provides an introduction and background to the volume's basic theme. Part II focuses on the regional dimensions of Soviet resource development with special attention to

Siberia, the key to Soviet export potential in natural resources in the period to 1990 and beyond. Part III examines selected energy and industrial raw materials that are important or potentially important in world markets. Part IV evaluates the special role of raw materials in Soviet foreign trade. Finally, Part V assesses the implications of Soviet resource potential for the world economy during the 1980s based on the findings in the previous parts of the book.

Each chapter is an original contribution which, though linked to the book's overall theme, may be read and evaluated on its own merits. Moreover, while the three central parts of the volume (II, III, and IV) identify the major dimensions of our overall research, it will be apparent to the reader that many chapters contribute in a crosscutting fashion to all three dimensions. This is as it should be since regional factors, the potential in specific resources, and the role of raw materials in Soviet foreign trade are all complexly interrelated as they bear on Soviet export potential in the natural-resource industries.

## The Regional Factor
## in Soviet Resource Development

A basic premise of this book is that a careful analysis of regional problems and policy in the USSR is essential to an understanding of Soviet natural resource potentials. Soviet planners must match supplies and demands over a geographic area embracing more than a sixth of the earth's land surface. That area is characterized by extreme variability in resource endowments, extraction possibilities, levels of development, and general accessibility. Soviet Asia, twice the size of the continental United States, contains upward of nine-tenths of the country's resources of fuels and industrial raw materials, including most of the proven energy reserves, 70 percent of all standing timber and, except for iron ore and manganese, most of the nonfuel minerals as well. But the vast area of Soviet Asia remains relatively undeveloped and is occupied by 70 million people, including only 28 million in all of Siberia and the Far East. In contrast, the more compact area of the European USSR, with a population of 195 million, is faced with rising resource costs and large deficits in basic energy supplies. With the exception of a few resources abundant west of the Urals, Soviet Europe must increasingly look to the vast trans-Urals region for an ever larger proportion of its primary imports. As a result Siberian development is critical both to the domestic economy of the USSR and to its potential as a raw-material exporter.

Thus an examination of the regional dimensions of Soviet resource development in association with the more usual analysis of national aggregates provides insights, not otherwise gained, into the Soviet capacity and inclination to export, or perhaps even import, natural-resource products. In a conventional geopolitical sense the Soviet Union is virtually self-sufficient in energy and industrial raw materials. But, given the extreme geographic separation between resource supplies and domestic demands, the Soviet Union must pay a high price to make self-sufficiency an economic reality. In reaching out to tap resources in Siberia, far from the heartland of the European USSR, the Soviet economy frequently faces costs for transportation and regional development considerably higher than those which other nations incur in obtaining raw materials from foreign suppliers across the ocean. At the same time, the domestic use of Siberian resources may entail stiff opportunity costs in terms of forgone export revenues.

Part II of this volume, introduced more fully in Chapter 2, provides a detailed assessment of those regional policy issues, programs, and constraints that are of general significance for Soviet resource development and investment planning. The focus is on Siberia because it is there that Soviet export potential in the natural-resource industries will ultimately be determined.

## Soviet Energy and Industrial Raw Materials

The chapters in Part III provide a detailed analysis of the specific Soviet natural resources that are important or potentially important for the world market. The resources were selected by the joint application of two criteria: first, that the Soviet Union have the potential of exporting the resource in large enough quantities and at attractive enough prices to have an impact on the world market; and second, that the prospect of Soviet exports would bear on Western policy concerns because of potential implications for East-West trade, concern about resource dependence or depletion in the major industrial nations, or because of the existence of a functioning producer cartel. Resources selected for detailed analysis include oil, natural gas, iron ore, timber, nickel, platinum, manganese, chrome, and gold. Several additional commodities, for which detailed studies could not be made available in time for publication, are considered in Chapter 11 more briefly. Part III concludes with a general analysis of the problem of Soviet resource valuation and the efficiency of resource production and use. These are important considerations because price signals do not usually provide Soviet enterprises with incentives to economize on fuels and raw materials and thus major reforms in this area could conceivably free additional resources for export. In the foreseeable future, however, price reforms are not likely to be so profound as to cause a major shift in domestic or international trade patterns.

In assessing the potential role of Soviet natural resources in the world economy, the Soviet energy situation emerges as a central as well as a controversial variable. It is central not only because of fundamental linkages with other parts of the economic system but also because energy resources play a leading role in domestic regional development programs and in Soviet trade both with the CMEA nations and with countries of the industrial West, including Japan. The Soviet energy situation is controversial because data are at best limited and at worst just not available. And if the most recent Soviet statistical yearbooks are any indication, access to data will be increasingly difficult in the years ahead. Beyond the current plan period, 1981-85, even production goals are not clear and the extent of Soviet energy resources, as for the world at large, remains speculative. However, for the remainder of this century the question will not be so much the extent of Soviet energy resources (proven and potential reserves), but whether they can be prospected and developed in time to meet growing domestic requirements and commitments to Eastern Europe, and to maintain a surplus for export to hard-currency countries. It is in this relatively short-term context that controversy prevails.

The future of Soviet oil production, the most controversial case, has been the subject of a lively international debate that was sparked by two widely publicized reports from the U.S. Central Intelligence Agency. One report, "Prospects for Soviet Oil Production" (ER-10270, April 1977), concluded that Soviet oil production would peak by the early 1980s and that later in the decade the USSR might not only have to reduce its oil exports to Eastern Europe and the West but also import OPEC oil for domestic use. As the report notes, this would be a dramatic reversal from a situation in which oil exports to the West provided roughly half of total Soviet earnings of hard currency. The second report, "The International Energy Situation: Outlook to 1985" (ER-77-10240U, April 1977), estimated that by 1985 the Soviet Union and Eastern Europe might require 3.5 to 4.5 million barrels per day of imported oil. Such a turn of events would have grave economic and political implications for the CMEA countries and for world energy markets. The CIA reports, associated as they were with President Carter's plan for energy independence and later with the United States Government's view of Soviet intentions in Afghanistan and the Persian Gulf area, generated considerable and often critical reaction in America and abroad. West European experts especially held to a more optimistic view of Soviet oil production for the 1980s. An extreme example was a report by the PetroStudies consultants group in Malmö, Sweden, which predicted, in sharp contrast to the CIA reports, that Soviet oil exports to the West might triple by 1985. (These estimates and others are critically reviewed in Chapter 14.) According to *The New York Times*, 18 May 1981, the Central Intelligence Agency has revised its estimates of Soviet oil production and now believes that the USSR will be able to meet domestic energy needs without oil imports for some years to come.

This book does not provide a monolithic view of the Soviet energy future, but the range of opinion among the authors concerned with the topic, all leading experts, is reasonably narrow and there is considerable agreement on a number of key factors.

During the last decade, in contrast to most of the industrial West, the Soviet Union actually benefited substantially from the world energy crisis. Now, however, it is certain that Soviet energy production has entered a new and more difficult phase which has important implications for both the domestic and international economy. Analysis of the Soviet energy situation by Leslie Dienes and other authors in this volume makes it clear that the economic gains resulting from rapid additions of

relatively cheap oil and natural gas to the Soviet energy balance are unlikely to continue during the 1980s. Moreover, domestic energy requirements and energy exports have come into clear conflict, so that in the years ahead Soviet leaders will be faced with difficult decisions about the relative priority of domestic energy needs, exports to Eastern Europe, and exports to the West. The current 11th Five-Year Plan provides few hints about how this dilemma will be resolved.

There is no question that during the 1980s Soviet energy production will depend increasingly on resource development in the northern and eastern regions of the country. Production in these areas is not only remote from consuming centers but faced with problems of inhospitable environments and lack of basic local and regional infrastructure. Development costs are high and lead times necessarily long, even with the most advanced technology, which is not always available. Accordingly, production and delivery costs, especially for oil and natural gas, have risen steeply and are likely to rise more in the future. Soviet planners, while apparently confident that a decline in oil output can be avoided at least to 1985, have expressed concern about the energy situation over the longer term and are apparently looking to natural gas, nuclear power and ultimately coal to make up for any problems with oil production.

For these and other reasons, described by the authors in chapters 12 through 16, it is virtually certain that the Soviet Union will encounter serious problems in the energy sector between now and 1990. It is certainly not likely that Soviet authorities will be able to restrict domestic energy consumption significantly without slowing an already sluggish economic growth. Moreover, despite a diversity of energy supplies, it is also unlikely that the Soviet Union will be able to effect significant energy substitution to reduce the pressure on oil or free more than marginal quantities for export. It is agreed, however, that by 1990 natural gas will be playing an increasingly important role in the Soviet energy balance and in the energy balance of Eastern Europe. To the extent that Soviet gas exports are possible beyond CMEA, they will be concentrated in Western Europe. The implications of a growing West European reliance on Soviet natural gas, though defended in West Germany and among other European members of the Atlantic alliance, have become a matter of concern to the Reagan administration in the United States.

However, the overwhelming conclusion of our analysis of the Soviet energy situation is that, despite vast oil resource potential and, in the case of gas and coal, explored reserves as well, the output of the three major fossil fuels cannot be expanded at a pace sufficient to enable the USSR to become more than a minor factor in world energy markets. Because the Soviet Union cannot abandon Eastern Europe, allowing further stagnation in the economy and living standards, the CMEA energy supply situation will play a key role in determining the amount of Soviet energy resources that reach the non-Communist world market. This suggests that, with the exception of natural gas, the USSR will be exporting less energy to the world economy in 1990 than in 1980.

The remaining chapters in Part III investigate Soviet potential in nonenergy resources. As with energy, these chapters focus on domestic supplies, domestic demand, and export potentials through 1990, along with evaluations of constraints on future development such as environmental problems, transport capacities, technological problems, and institutional obstacles. With the exception of timber and the ferrous metals, data for these commodities are even more limited than for energy resources.

The Soviet Union claims self-sufficiency in most of the key nonenergy resources and many have been traditional export items. If total energy exports decline in the future, as appears likely, an important question will be whether the Soviet Union has the potential to maintain hard-currency earnings by expanding exports of nonenergy resources. As noted earlier, industrial resources were selected for analysis in this volume only if Soviet reserves were believed to be large and potentially significant for world markets. Thus our analyses of nonenergy resources provide a solid basis for evaluating future Soviet export possibilities in primary commodities that have received relatively little attention in the Western literature.

Finally, our investigation of Soviet resource potential sheds light on a possibility that is exactly opposite to the one posed in this volume: the prospect of a shift in Soviet policy from resource self-sufficiency to selective import dependence in the short run, in order to secure increased access to global resources in the long run. For the Western industrial countries, already dependent on unstable foreign supplies for a number of natural resources, such a policy shift could have serious geopolitical and economic consequences.

The strongest statement in support of this view was presented by Daniel Fine, a mineral resources analyst, in a 1980 study for the World Affairs Council of Pittsburgh entitled *The Resource War in 3-D—Dependency, Diplomacy, Defense*. Noting recent Soviet purchases of strategic metals for which self-sufficiency is usually assumed, Fine argues that it pays the USSR to import selected natural resources now, instead of developing high-cost Siberian sources. Eventually, according to this scenario, as the cheaper world resources are depleted, the Soviet Union not only would be able to better afford development of the Siberian sources, but also would be able to use its enormous reserves as leverage to exact strategic concessions from the West. The long-term benefits of this strategy for the Soviet Union, Fine argues, outweigh the risk of potential conflct over foreign supplies in the short run.

The logic of the "resource wars" theme is based on a series of assumptions and on empirical relationships that are not yet well established. The analysis of world natural-resource markets and Soviet participation in them in Part IV speaks to these assumptions. The detailed analyses of individual commodities in Part III provide at least

the foundations of the empirical relationships. Thus, we shall be in a good position to return to a fuller consideration of the "resource wars" theme in the concluding chapter of the volume.

## The Role of Raw Materials in Soviet Foreign Trade

Earlier, mention was made of the shift in Soviet policy from autarky to the increased use of foreign trade, as a means of obtaining new technology from the advanced capitalist countries. Precisely because of lagging industrial technology, Soviet manufactures sell poorly in those countries. As a result, to pay for technology imports, the USSR has had to return to the old Russian tradition of specializing in natural-resource exports. As Chapter 27 points out, well over three-quarters of total Soviet hard-currency earnings come from natural-resource exports, with fuels alone accounting for better than half of the total.

Part IV deals with Soviet foreign-trade policy as it applies to natural-resource exports. Of primary interest here is what economists call the supplies of Soviet natural-resource exports—the amounts they will offer on world markets at various world prices. To understand these supplies fully, it is necessary to look at four important factors: (1) the way export (and import) decisions are made in the Soviet centrally planned, command economy; (2) the efficiency of Soviet production and domestic use of natural-resource products; (3) the level of Soviet export costs even with efficient production and domestic use; and (4) the Soviets' foreign-trade relationship with the other members of the CMEA trading bloc.

In contrast to a market economy, Soviet imports and exports do not simply occur in response to relative prices of goods and national currencies. Rather, they must be explicitly incorporated into the central plan, item by item, so that consuming enterprises can count on receiving certain imported inputs and producing enterprises can be counted upon to produce the commodities designated for export, to cover the cost of the imports. Any imbalance between the value of imports and the value of exports in a given year requires a negotiated agreement (in the case of CMEA trade) or a conscious decision by the planners to draw down or add to foreign-exchange reserves (in the case of trade outside the Soviet bloc). For this reason, the common term "export surplus" may be misleading, because it connotes an amount that is somehow left over, perhaps by accident, after domestic uses are satisfied. Chapters 28 and 30 document that supplies of Soviet natural-resource exports are the result of deliberate, purposeful behavior.

The next question is how Soviet planners and policymakers go about organizing their foreign-trade behavior—a question that encompasses the remaining three factors for understanding Soviet supplies of natural-resource exports. The efficiency with which Soviet enterprises and households produce and use natural-resource products is addressed implicitly, in great detail and for both individual products and the natural-resource sector as a whole, in Part III. In Part IV the efficiency factor is addressed explicitly. It is argued that Soviet production methods and utilization of natural resources have long been downright wasteful by world standards. The main reasons for such inefficiency are distorted incentives inherent in Soviet central planning and the intense pressure from economic policymakers to expand production at rapid rates. The shift in foreign-trade policy that has put the spotlight on natural-resource exports, together with reduced growth in capital and labor inputs and increased world prices for fuels and other natural resources, provides a pronounced incentive to reduce such waste. As yet, however, we have scant evidence that Soviet planners have responded significantly to that incentive, although considerable exhortation to do so is readily evident in the political and economic press in the USSR.

The prospect of reduced input growth rates raises a question as to whether the Soviet Union can afford to increase its natural-resource exports substantially, even if better management incentives improve the overall efficiency of resource production and use. Put differently, does the USSR have a sufficient comparative advantage in natural-resource exports to justify their expansion, or is it simply too high-cost a producer to compete effectively? The difficulties of producing natural resources under Siberian conditions and transporting them great distances to domestic users or to borders for export are well documented in this volume. Similarly, the commitments of labor and capital required for sizeable expansions of natural-resource production will inevitably strain the ability of the Soviet economy to expand manufacturing and agricultural output. The final paper in Part IV suggests that domestic constraints like these will pose more serious problems for Soviet attempts to increase natural-resource exports than more often cited constraints such as foreign credits and trade restrictions.

The Soviet Union's trade relationship with its CMEA allies parallels the Soviet position in world trade. The USSR supplies natural resources whereas the resource-poor East Europeans supply manufactures. Soviet natural-resource export policies inevitably depend, then, not only on the relative prices obtainable on world markets, but also on Soviet obligations within the CMEA trade bloc. The issue is whether, and to what extent, Moscow will curtail its natural-resource shipments to its East European trading partners, thereby forcing them into world markets as importers—at higher real prices, with potentially disruptive side-effects. The focal point of this issue is the terms of intra-CMEA trade and the incentives implicit in those terms for the USSR to switch natural-resource exports away from Eastern Europe and into hard-currency markets. Chapter 28 demonstrates convincingly that the Soviets do indeed move their natural-resource exports between the East European and the world markets in response to shifts in incentives as world prices change and renegotiations of CMEA trade occur. Chapter 29 details the plight of the East European countries in trying to cope with Soviet behavior and the increased world prices for many natural resources that underlie that behavior. East European options are quite limited and this fact has potentially grave implications for the long-term stability of those countries.

### The Implications of Soviet Raw Materials for the World Economy

The concluding chapter assesses the main implications of Soviet natural-resource export potentials for the world economy during the 1980s based on the findings of Parts II through IV. We do not claim to provide easy answers because, in the final analysis, the future role of Soviet natural resources in the world economy is only partly dependent on the complex realities of the USSR's resource potential that are investigated in this volume. Whether that potential is realized will depend on unpredictable events and complex political judgments made in Moscow, Washington, and other capitals of the world economy. But it is equally clear that without a thorough assessment of Soviet resource potential of the kind we have attempted to provide, economic policymakers will be forced to rely on hurried estimates and questionable conclusions in attempting to comprehend Soviet resource strategies and their possible effects on world commodity markets. To the extent that this volume provides a basis for more reasoned judgment, our efforts will have been worthwhile.

# II

## SOVIET RESOURCE DEVELOPMENT: THE REGIONAL DIMENSION

# 2

# THE REGIONAL PERSPECTIVE IN
# SOVIET RESOURCE DEVELOPMENT

ROBERT G. JENSEN
Syracuse University

National economic development is inevitably accompanied by a marked degree of geographical imbalance among the regions of a country. In the process of industrialization the growth of a national economy is propelled by concentrations of activity in a few regions, leaving the remainder of the country relatively backward. And within regions specialization and agglomeration lead to pronounced spatial polarization, intensifying the dichotomy between center and periphery. During more advanced stages of development a combination of economic and technological forces may encourage integration and geographic dispersion thereby reducing regional inequalities. But even then, as the experience of postindustrial societies demonstrates, problems of regional inequality and regional-economic realignment are likely to remain as significant national concerns.

In a country as large and diverse as the Soviet Union it is hardly surprising that regional problems and regional policy decisions play a crucial role in the national economy. In the context of central planning, decisions must be made regarding the allocation of resources not only among sectors of the economy but also among specific regions and locations. Thus, Soviet authorities have been forced to articulate a design for the spatial structure of the country and the socioeconomic growth of its regions, in short a policy for regional development.

The basic determinants of Soviet regional development policy include a set of location principles (or doctrine) taken directly (or inferred) from the classic works of Marxism-Leninism, the practical requirements of dealing with the realities of the country's physical and human geography, and rather pragmatic responses to shifting domestic and international objectives. The stated social aims of Soviet regional policy, mainly to provide for greater equality in living standards and opportunity across the country by dispersing economic development, have been reasonably consistent because of their close link with basic ideology. But other aspects of Soviet regional policy, because of the ambiguous formulation of locational doctrine, have produced debate and conflict over issues such as whether regions should be highly specialized or essentially self-sufficient, whether population should be shifted to raw-material sources creating more balanced development in new areas, or whether priority should be given to development in established core areas.

The outcome of such debates, and thus the character of regional economic programs, often depends on internal power relationships as, for example, between those who advocate heavy industry over light industry, sectoral planning over regional planning, industry over agriculture, and so forth. The nature of these relationships has had a powerful influence on Soviet regional economic structure in the past and will continue to do so in the future. Even now, 50 years after the completion of the 1st Five-Year Plan, the Soviet Union is grappling with essentially the same array of regional problems that has confronted the country for decades.

## The Siberian Regional Development Challenge

The primary regional challenge stems from a basic geographical dichotomy in the location of population and natural resources. In general terms, the European part of the Soviet Union, with about one-quarter of the national territory, accounts for about 70 percent of the population, 80 percent of the industrial and agricultural production, and most of the USSR's economic infrastructure and markets. Siberia and the Soviet Far East, on the other hand, with over half the national territory and about 10 percent of the population, contain more than 50 percent of the country's natural resources of minerals and timber and perhaps as much as 90 percent of Soviet energy resources. Siberia, the main resource frontier of the Soviet Union and a mainspring of future Soviet development, is also one of the largest storehouses of industrial raw materials remaining on earth. However, because of remoteness from domestic markets and extremely harsh physical environments, Siberian development still presents a formidable challenge. Although Russian explorers reached the Pacific coast more than 300 years ago, Siberia, with the exception of a few outlying nodes of development, remains a frontier linked to the European USSR by a single railway, the Trans-Siberian, which has allowed only a narrow band of permanent settlement to be established along the southern reaches of the region. The Soviet presence on the Pacific, apart from the military, is still minimal and most of West Siberia, East Siberia, and the Far East remain extremely underdeveloped.

Yet, despite the region's relative backwardness, Siberian development has long been a featured aim of Soviet regional policy. The early notion that central planning under Communism should promote a more uniform distribution of population and economic activity across the country meant that Siberia, virtually a void on the economic map, was the ultimate regional development challenge and a highly visible index of Soviet economic achievement. Moreover, to avoid the colonial relationship that was said to prevail between the "center" and "periphery" in capitalist countries, Soviet planners argued that, in addition to primary resource exploitation, Siberian development should include related industrial and service activities to provide balance and integration in the regional economy as well as to insure Siberia's full participation in the mainstream of national economic life. Siberian development was also supported by Soviet locational doctrine, which called for moving industry closer to raw-material supplies and by the leadership's early commitment to a rapid expansion of heavy industry that greatly increased the demand for basic energy and industrial raw materials known to be abundant in Siberia. Finally, of course, Siberian development was attractive from a national security point of view in that it would disperse industry, provide defense in depth, and occupy territory adjacent to the USSR's Asian neighbors.

In the years since the 1st Five-Year Plan, Soviet accomplishments in Siberia have been substantial. But so long as there were alternatives in more hospitable regions, many plans for Siberia remained on the drawing boards. Thus the earlier vision of Siberia as a comprehensively developed region, fully integrated into the mainstream of national economic life, has not been achieved and to a certain extent in fact that objective appears to have been removed from the economic agenda. As noted above, Soviet planners today face much the same challenge in Siberia that confronted their predecessors. Indeed, the current emphasis, despite continued mention of comprehensive development for Siberia in five-year plans, including the current, 11th plan, appears to focus on regional specialization, with Siberia supplying energy and industrial raw materials to the more developed European part of the country. However, while the current Soviet vision of Siberian development may be less ambitious than in the past, this should not be interpreted to mean that the region will be de-emphasized or that its development will be neglected. On the contrary, since about 1970, Soviet plans have called for an accelerated development of Siberia perhaps embarking the nation on a new and more sober commitment to its vast eastern territory. A complex of domestic and international factors account for this new commitment to Siberia.

For the domestic economy, accelerated Siberian development is no longer a matter of planner's choice—it is an absolute national necessity. Natural resources in the European USSR have been rapidly depleted and, to maintain or expand production, the Soviets have been forced to turn to Siberia. This is especially true in the case of energy, where virtually all incremental supplies must come from Siberia. Currently, the European USSR can supply less than half its energy needs from local resources and by 1990 this share will decline even further. Thus the already heavy flow of oil, gas, and coal westward from Siberia to the European USSR will increase even more during the 1980s.

The exploitation of Siberian energy and raw materials, now essential to the domestic economy, has required heavy capital investment and also has generated a demand for the most advanced technology that is often available only in the West and Japan. This demand for Western technology and industrial equipment has in turn generated a need for hard currency to pay for Western imports. Thus, Siberian resource development, having prompted growing Soviet demands for Western technology, is also the means by which the Soviets hope to pay for imports from the West.

Siberian development, like that of the rest of the Soviet economy, therefore, can no longer be viewed in isolation from the world at large. During the 1970s, détente, increased interaction with the West, and rising raw-material prices in world markets combined to provide the Soviet Union with new opportunities for the development of Siberian resources for domestic use and for export. Though the region presents many challenges, Soviet authorities have held open the possibility that resource deficits elsewhere in the world may be met to an increasing degree by Siberia. This was nowhere more apparent than in the Soviet decision in 1974 to proceed with the long-projected construction of the Baikal-Amur Mainline (BAM) railroad, which, when completed in the mid-1980s, will extend from the northern tip of Lake Baikal to the Pacific coast. The BAM is ultimately expected to open up a vast resource-rich region that may well be significant for both domestic and international markets. The heightening of East-West tensions in the early 1980s has put a damper on international participation in Soviet resource development. But in the longer term, resource depletion in the West and the inexorable discovery of new resources in an underexplored and underdeveloped Siberia may provide significant opportunities for increased foreign trade. Thus Siberian resource development is crucial for the future of the domestic economy as well as for Soviet participation in the world economy.

## Regional Policy, Problems, and Constraints in Siberian Resource Development

The chapters in Part II of this book focus on the regional dimensions of Soviet resource development with special attention to Siberia and the Soviet Far East. They analyze a range of policy issues, programs, and constraints that will determine the course of development in these regions in the foreseeable future and, at the same time, will have major implications for national investment planning and for export potentials in Soviet natural-resource industries during the 1980s and beyond.

## Environmental Constraints

In Chapter 3, Victor L. Mote provides a detailed assessment of the environmental constraints to Siberian economic development. His analysis includes macroscale constraints such as permafrost, microscale constraints such as natural hazards, and a variety of technogenic constraints, such as pollution, that are the inevitable by-product of economic development. In all more than twenty interrelated environmental constraints are reviewed and their varied impacts are evaluated for Siberia as a whole as well as for the major regional centers of economic development. Siberian resource development, Mote argues, is frustrated more by severe environmental difficulties and related technical problems than by purely economic factors. Concern with environmental protection, moreover, adds to the already high cost of Siberian development. Thus, while the resource potential of Siberia is great, exploitation costs will be high and, if the relatively sensitive environment of the region is to be protected, development must proceed at a moderate pace, under strict control. Even in the absence of other problems, and there are many, the total impact of environmental constraints on Siberian development is such that many of the region's resources will not be competitive on world markets in this century, let alone by 1990.

## Manpower Constraints

In recent years, regional development problems in the Soviet Union have been exacerbated by a growing shortage of labor and a maldistribution of the working-age population. In Chapter 4, Robert Lewis analyzes the growth of total, urban, and rural populations of working-age between 1970 and 1990 in a regional perspective with attention to implications for resource development in Siberia and the Soviet Far East. During the 1980s, Lewis observes, the growth of working-age population will not only be less than in the previous decade, but also the geographic distribution of that growth will be increasingly unfavorable for economic development in that it will be concentrated in the rural areas of Central Asia. In Siberia and the Far East, the increase in the local working-age population, between 1980 and 1990, will be less than one-third that of the previous decade. This decline, coupled with the growing availability of jobs in the European USSR and a lack of propensity for out-migration from the labor-surplus regions of Central Asia, is likely to result in further intensification of the already difficult labor problem in Siberia. The extent to which impending labor shortages will constrain resource development is difficult to determine, for it depends on the priority given to development projects by Soviet authorities. Nonetheless, Lewis provides considerable evidence that manpower

problems will become an increasingly important factor in Soviet regional and resource development plans, particularly in Siberia and the Far East.

## Foreign Trade's Impact on Soviet Regional Development

Several chapters in this volume explore the relationship between regional development and Soviet export potential in the natural-resource industries. In Chapter 5, Robert North directs attention to the reverse relationship by analyzing the impact of Soviet foreign trade on regional economic development. In the European USSR, where most of the foreign-trade-based developments with a strong multiplier effect are located, he finds that foreign trade has modified the geography of transport and altered the patterns of comparative advantage in favor of ports and border regions. In Siberia, on the other hand, the heavy dependence of Soviet exports on energy and other raw materials has increased the already specialized orientation of the Siberian economy. CMEA integration, moreover, makes Siberian locations less attractive for manufacturing activities serving the joint market. These impacts, combined with the current emphasis on refitting old plants, which are mostly in the west, suggest that the desire for more comprehensive development in the eastern regions mentioned in the 11th Five-Year Plan will continue to be frustrated. However, because of the region's previously low level of development, North concludes, the impact of recent foreign-trade policy has been felt most strongly in the Soviet Far East. During the 1980s, as the BAM provides access to new resources, further impacts might be expected.

## Regional Planning Decisions

In Chapter 6, George Huzinec examines the relationship between regional and national planning as it bears on Soviet foreign trade, especially Siberian resource exports. During most of the Soviet period, he points out, when regional development decisions were made in the context of an essentially closed, autarkic economy, Siberian development was severely retarded by its peripheral location relative to more advanced regions in the European part of the country. As the national economy is opened to increased foreign trade, the regional decision-making context changes to include location relative to international trading partners. As a result, established patterns of regional comparative advantage may be altered. At the same time, the geographic system developed under more autarkic conditions in the past will continue to exert strong influence on the nature, direction, and cost of Soviet exports. Thus, if Siberia is to benefit from proximity to Pacific markets, the Soviets must contend with the long lead times and heavy capital investment required to overcome the past neglect of basic economic and social infrastructure in the region. Huzinec suggests that increased foreign trade might be used to support several development strategies in Siberia but that the most likely is the continued emphasis on development programs closely related to the region's primary economic activities.

## The Baikal-Amur Mainline

Among recent regional development projects in the Soviet Union, none has received more attention than the Baikal-Amur Mainline railroad. In Chapter 7, Victor Mote provides the most comprehensive analysis of this project currently available in any literature. In addition to reviewing the status and problems of construction, he gives a detailed assessment of BAM service area resources and evaluates the implications of the entire project for the domestic economy and for trade with the Pacific Basin. On a regional scale, the impact will be substantial and Soviet authorities envision that the railroad will eventually help to link more than a dozen local industrial complexes into a functioning economic region. However, despite the huge investment, Mote concludes, the BAM will have only a limited impact on the national economy and on international markets during the present decade. In the long run, after the year 2000, the potential impact of the BAM could be of wider significance, but during this century, Mote suggests, the project will not have decisive global implications.

## Regional Development in the Soviet Far East

In Chapter 8, Allan Rodgers reviews the changing patterns of economic development in the Soviet Far East since 1940 and evaluates likely changes in those patterns for the 1980s with attention to their implications for trade between the USSR and the Pacific Basin. In terms of Soviet export potential, Rodgers conceives of the Far East as a major intervening opportunity, a kind of spatial sponge, soaking up potential interactions between the USSR and trading partners in the Pacific. If the region's dependence on supplies from the European USSR and other areas could be reduced, then the resulting possibilities for increased transit movements combined with commodities from the Far East itself might constitute potential exports to the Pacific Basin, mainly to Japan and some of the Communist countries of East Asia. Although difficult to achieve, Rodgers suggests, greater regional self-sufficiency in the Far East may be of increasing strategic importance in light of Soviet concerns about China. In any event, according to Rodgers, during the 1980s the Soviet Far East will play a greater role in the production and export of basic raw materials such as coal, timber, and possibly natural gas. Overall, the 1980s will be a period of accelerated development for the Soviet Far East, especially with the completion of the BAM and

related developments in the railroad's hinterland. But growth will be related mainly to a drive to develop resources for local needs and foreign markets. Development for the broader domestic market of the USSR will be of secondary importance.

## The Japanese Perspective of Siberian Resource Development

The role of Japan in trade with the Soviet Union and the complimentarity of the Japanese and Siberian economies are explored from many vantage points in this volume. In Chapter 9, Richard Edmonds assesses the Japanese attitude toward Siberian development as it has been articulated by Japanese politicians, businessmen, and scholars. The Japanese, he finds, view Siberia as a potentially important supplier of industrial resources. Although deep-seated political differences and concerns about possible overdependence on the Soviet Union are significant issues, the Japanese are even more concerned that they may be unable to obtain desired amounts of raw materials for their industrial economy. The Japanese are currently enthusiastic about new possibilities for trade with China, but Edmonds reports that the government and business community feel that China will not be able to supply the quantity or quality of resources potentially available from Siberia.

## Siberian Development in a Strategic Perspective

The final chapter in Part II provides a broad assessment of the strategic implications of Siberian resource development for East Asia. To establish a basis for considering the strategic significance of development plans in Siberia, Allen Whiting first evaluates Soviet military capabilities in the region. On balance, he concludes that Siberian development will not enhance Soviet military capability much beyond that currently existing in the region. On the question of economic leverage accruing to the USSR as a result of Siberian development and related trade, Whiting suggests that in view of the reciprocal nature of foreign participation in these activities there are few if any situations wherein the Soviet Union would gain a clear advantage in East Asia. In the absence of serious, perhaps insurmountable, political problems, Siberian development could serve the mutual interests of the USSR and other countries including China, Japan, and the United States. But in any event, Whiting argues, the strategic implications of economic expansion in Siberia are alone not significant enough either to preclude the participation of foreign powers or to compel them to work against the region's development.

# 3

# ENVIRONMENTAL CONSTRAINTS TO THE ECONOMIC DEVELOPMENT OF SIBERIA

VICTOR L. MOTE
University of Houston

## Introduction

In a development context, northern regions are the frontier that until recently no one ever really wanted. Remote in distance and inhospitable in almost every conceivable way, they really are "on the margins of the good earth." Yet, with modern aviation, defense networks, and mineral-resource requirements, northern areas increasingly are strategic to humankind. Permanent settlements, though rare, have become more apparent in the Subarctic and Arctic as a result of these needs. As northern economic development has expanded, concern for the fragile environment of these places has increased as well. For instance, demands for "special regulations" to safeguard the North have become commonplace in both the Soviet Union and North America.[1]

Northern settlements depend not only on their economic relationships to domestic and international markets but also on the costs of their operation in extreme environments and the carrying capacity of the land they occupy. In most regions of the earth, man-nature relationships have become important because of resource scarcity. For most of human history, this scarcity has been due to limitations imposed by the absence of technologies of production, rather than to constraints in the availability of physical resources. In many ways, the economic development of the Soviet Union, and its Far North especially, continues to be constrained by technological scarcity in lieu of shortages of resources.

During this century, still another constraint to economic development has arisen. This is the realization that the resources ultimately available to humankind are limited and that the amount of disruption that may be sustained inconsequentially by the biosphere or one of its subsystems is also restricted.[2] This constraint is given a considerable amount of scientific lip-service in the USSR, and the fact is nowhere more relevant than in the newly developing regions of Siberia and the Far East, where genuine environmental-impact analyses have been carried out. These analyses are supposed to be incorporated into a new (for Soviet authorities) kind of planning procedure called "program-oriented planning" or "complex regional development planning," which is comprehensive of both human and natural requirements.[3]

The purpose of this chapter is to provide a general overview of the environmental constraints to Siberian development, some of which may be of more interest to certain readers than others. The chapter is not intended to be all-inclusive or "the last word" on the subject. It is probably impossible to cover adequately all the economic implications of the constraints surveyed. Readers interested in particulars, for instance, transport, oil and gas, technology, and so forth, are urged to consult the pertinent sources listed in footnotes and appendices. Ultimately, the aim of the examination is to help clarify some of the complex and problematic interrelationships that exist between economic development and the harsh physical geography of Siberia, particularly its northern reaches as well as those areas that are subject to a variety of specific natural hazards. The importance of operational costs in extreme environments and the related carrying capacities of those regions are considered as well.

## Siberia and the North

When Soviet geographers allude to Siberia, they may not agree on common boundaries. This fact has been highlighted recently in the work of N. I. Mikhailov.[4] There is similar disagreement over what constitutes the Soviet North.[5] This is especially true of persons who are involved in recommending or creating new technology for use in northern conditions. For purposes of this chapter, Siberia and most of the Soviet North are composed of the area defined by V. F. Burkhanov in the late 1960s. The European North is excluded from this definition; thus, the subject region includes most of Western Siberia and all of the economic regions of Eastern Siberia and the Soviet Far East (Figure 1).

Siberia in conventional terminology is a classic hinterland of the Soviet economy. Its vast expanse includes 57 percent of the Soviet land mass but only 10 percent of the people and less than 10 percent of Soviet manufacturing. Yet, it contains 60 percent of the country's coal resources, 75 percent of its natural gas, 60 percent of its hydroelectric

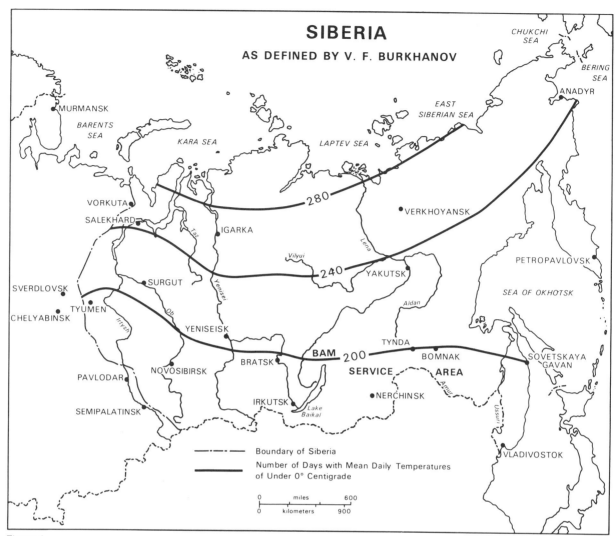

Figure 1
SOURCES: V. F. Burkhanov, "Criteria for Determining an Engineering-Geographic Boundary of the North of the USSR," *Soviet Geography: Review and Translation*, 11, no. 1 (January 1970): 30; Yu. M. Dogayev, *Ekonomicheskaya effektivnost novoi tekhniki na Severe* [The cost-effectiveness of new technology in the North], p. 23.

potential, 70 percent of its timber, and probably over half of its strategic minerals. Most of these resources remain untapped, and many more doubtlessly lie undiscovered.

Siberian resources and their potential exploitation thus represent a major concern of this book. If surplus raw materials exist in the Soviet Union, and there is no doubt they do, then most of them are likely to be found in Siberia. Siberian development is clearly the key factor in determining whether the Soviet Union will have a significant influence on world resource markets in the coming decades. Domestic energy shortage or glut, West Siberian oil production should have some measure of impact on energy costs everywhere. In the same way, provided they can be recovered, abundant Pacific Siberian raw materials should become a factor in international trade by the end of the century.[6] Both the 10th and now the 11th five-year plans have stressed the need for accelerated development of the resources of eastern regions.

It is necessary, therefore, to determine how much of a factor these resources represent. And, equally, we need to identify and analyze the elements that militate against the exploitation of Siberian minerals and the concomitant problems of permanent settlement in hostile environments. Thus, for every Siberian resource there is some kind of anti-resource, by which potential development plans are inhibited.

This study is limited to the physical and technological constraints to the human use of Siberian resources. Together with a host of natural constraints, there are counterconstraints that potentially can be unleashed by human mismanagement of exploitive activities. The problems inherent in scarce investment capital, concurrent competition for this capital in the developed western part of the USSR, and an impending, conceivably serious, labor shortage are touched upon but generally excluded from the study. Indeed, Siberian resource-development plans are frustrated more by severe environmental difficulties and associated technological problems than they are by purely economic factors. Physical and technological constraints present formidable obstacles to progress in Siberia. Until they are overcome and probably long thereafter, the region "will remain essentially a colony in the classical and modern meanings of the word: clumps of people sent out from, and still emotionally attached to, the mother country for the purpose of exploiting resources found there for the benefit of the motherland."[7]

The study is organized around three related sets of information. First, ubiquitous (in high-latitude regions), but diverse, macroscale limitations such as annual insolation deficits, consequent low temperatures, permafrost, and the like are analyzed in terms of their human and technological impacts. Second, unique and unpredictable microscale limitations, comprising natural hazards, are examined. Third, technogenic (technology-induced) hazards of pollution and disruptive land use are discussed. The constraints are interrelated and treated systematically. Wherever possible the data base is augmented by maps and/or flow diagrams.

## Review of the Literature

Soviet research on the environmental constraints to the economic development of Siberia, though certainly not exhaustive, is extensive and of generally high quality. The literature continues to increase because of the growing domestic requirement for raw materials that are no longer available or are in short supply in the more hospitable parts of the country.

In the forefront of applied geographic research on Siberia has been the work of Agranat, Gerasimov, Probst, Slavin, and Sochava among others.[8] V. F. Burkhanov and Yu. M. Dogayev have sought ways of classifying northern realms to match equipment properly with regionally specific physical-geographic characteristics.[9] The much-quoted work of S. V. Slavin focuses on the relationship between costs of development and hostile environments.[10] Lopatina and Nazarevsky have studied the effects of physical geography on human populations.[11] Related research has been carried out by economists and engineers.[12]

Natural hazards in the USSR have been investigated for many years. Soviet permafrost research is abundant and frequently is acclaimed the best in the world. This includes studies of ground ice and icings by V. R. Alekseyev.[13] Work on flows and slides has been coordinated by S. M. Fleishman, V. F. Perov, and G. K. Tushinsky.[14] The seismicity and vulcanism of Pacific Siberia have been inventoried and analyzed by V. P. Solonenko since the 1950s.[15] Recently, Gerasimov and his associates have attempted to map the hazard potential of the USSR, utilizing many of the above-mentioned studies.

During the past decade, Soviet ecological analyses have been conducted on a grand scale. This is especially true where the fragile environments of the arctic and subarctic are concerned. Research by Alekseyev, Vorobyev, Shotsky, Prokhorov, Kryuchkov, Izyumsky, Nefedova, and others reflects an extraordinary understanding of and sensitivity to the potential disruption that human beings can wreak on such environments.[16] Many of the ecological studies that have appeared recently are related to the construction of the Baikal-Amur Mainline (BAM) railroad and other major Siberian work projects.[17]

## Environmental Constraints to Siberian Development

In terms of the geographic extent of problematic environments, the physical-geographic constraints to the development of Siberia easily transcend those in Canada and Alaska. For example, the Siberian climate is commonly less conducive to human habitation, permafrost is more abundant, bogs are more prevalent, and the relief, at least with reference to Pacific Siberia, is more rugged.

The obstacles are so great that one wonders why Siberia should be developed for permanent settlement at all. In fact, in the USSR there has been a long-standing debate over the appropriate means to settle Siberia.[18] Initial investments are enormous and returns are limited. Construction costs range from two to three times the country average in the relatively developed areas near the Trans-Siberian Railroad to four to eight times the normal in remote centers of extraction accessible only by air, winter road, or summer boat.[19] One-third of the investment capital consists of infrastructural costs (communications, services, and amenities), which often exceed basic industrial outlays in temperate developed areas by a factor of 10.[20] Depending on the skills required and the sheer demand for the job as well as the geographical location of the enterprise, labor costs run 1.7 to 7 times above the norm.[21] Finally, with equipment costs well above the country average, repair and maintenance expenses are also high. According to Agranat and Loginov, the annual costs of all repairs are 25 to 30 percent of the total value of the equipment now utilized in the North. Capital repairs on some units actually exceed the value of the individual machines.[22]

One question, therefore, centers on whether the North should be developed as a place of permanent settlement in a social and economic sense or remain as a site of short-term exploitation. The Soviet answer is that either alternative should be employed, depending on the natural and economic constraints of the location of a given enterprise. Pro-Siberian planners say that the lack of returns over the short term should not prejudice people against the possibility of long-term benefits to Soviet society in general. Thus, high costs in northern environments, according to some Soviet geographers, should not be viewed as a liability, since cost-effectiveness models fail to include future economic opportunities, social improvements, political implications, and the like.

North American and Soviet experience in northern environments has produced similar settlement patterns. In the Soviet case, three labor operations are employed today: tour-of-duty (*ekspeditsiony*); work-shift (*vakhtenny*); and permanent (*statsionarny*).[23] Tour-of-duty and work-shift systems are utilized in remote, relatively inaccessible locations that exhibit the highest degree of physical-geographic harshness. In such areas, air transport is used extensively. The tour-of-duty method consists of work crews being flown into a job site for a season or more. These workers are fortunate to see their families for three months out of the year. The technique is used widely in the West Siberian oil and gas fields. The work-shift system is similar, except that individual shifts are only two to three weeks long. Work-shift labor is employed in northeast Siberian mining districts and in the Lower Ob gas fields. In both tour-of-duty and work-shift operations, the families of workers are accommodated in permanent cities and towns in economically developed areas. These latter are permanent settlements, which have most of the basic comforts and infrastructures.

Three types of permanent settlements exist in the Soviet North: rear support bases (*oporno-tylovye bazy*); advanced support bases (*opornye bazy*); and local bases or workers' settlements. Rear support bases are large, multipurpose cities with potential populations of 500,000 or more. Analogous to regional capitals in central place theory, modern Siberian examples of rear support bases are Krasnoyarsk, Irkutsk, Bratsk, Khabarovsk, and Komsomolsk. Advanced support bases are specialized service centers with existing or expected populations of 50,000 to 100,000, like Christaller's provincial capitals. These cities provide such functions as mining, transportation, and wood processing, modern Siberian instances of which are Novy Urengoi, Ust-Kut, Tynda, and Urgal. The populations of local bases, similar to district cities in central-place hierarchies, are not expected to exceed 15,000. Such towns are mining and logging centers that may ultimately develop some primary-processing functions.

With progressive resource development, the settlement forms evolve through four planning stages.[24] Stage I consists of development foci or "resource oases" that evolve independently of any serious attempt at regional planning. Such settlements arise on the basis of only the most valuable and, therefore, most transportable resources, for example, platinum, gold, and diamonds. Stage II is what Soviet authorities call the "stage of pioneer development,"[25] when, with the advent of reliable transportation systems (the BAM and Surgut-Urengoi railroads), planning and development acquire a broader scope. At this time, less valuable resources like hydrocarbons and iron ore can be extracted. All raw materials, including less valuable as well as precious resources, are shipped out of the pioneer region for processing in neighboring or more distant areas with better economic bases. In Stage III, some primary manufacturing and processing of local raw materials is introduced, principally to serve local needs. At this point along the continuum, the tour-of-duty and work-shift systems, which have been the chief modes of settlement and labor in the first two stages, may be abandoned. Workers' settlements, emphasizing small-scale manufacturing of construction materials and primary wood-processing, may arise. This is followed by Stage IV, during which

processing of raw materials becomes even more comprehensive and complex. Wood processing becomes multifarious, and, given the appropriate environment, metallurgy or petroleum refining may evolve. Initially, the products of this manufacturing are consumed locally; later, as the region becomes more specialized and settlements evolve into rear and advanced support bases (territorial-production complexes), the semi-processed and finished items may be distributed interregionally, nationally, or even internationally (Figure 2).

Between Stages II and IV, when orderly regional development is the primary aim of planning agencies, a complex system of supply and construction is required. On site in the developing local bases, the principal needs of civil engineering are satisfied by quarries, preventive maintenance facilities, machine shops, and prefabricated structural-assembly operations. Labor pools may be composed of tour-of-duty or work-shift personnel at this time. Advanced support bases are responsible for deliveries of lime or cement, some insulation materials, and small nonstandard construction requirements. Finally, the rear support bases supply crude and rolled steel, light wall and roofing materials, laminated aluminum panels, plywood sheeting, wood slab, and polymer insulation. In this regard, probably the most important present function of the rear support base is the organization of the light prefabricated components into modules for easier and faster assemblage in the local bases. The modular units are forwarded directly to the work sites by existing means of transportation, often by heavy cargo helicopters. All extensive overhauls and capital repairs of machinery and equipment are carried out in rear support bases.[26]

Program-oriented planning is a means of implementing the goal of complex regional development, which is similar to the Western concept of multipurpose planning. It combines the parameters of economic production, socioeconomic necessities, and appropriate ecological requirements. Variables intrinsic to the complex plans are: production; infrastructure, service, and amenities; utilization of natural and labor resources; settlement and demographic systems; conservation and renewal of the environment.

Implicit in these plans is the so-called "tree of goals," which represents an interrelated hierarchy of branches and subbranches of targeted projects.[27] In such a system, present construction programs are viewed simply as an extension of previously developed goals and serve concomitantly as springboards for future assimilation of underdeveloped territories. Thus, the Surgut-Urengoi railroad is merely a logical extension of the development of the Middle Ob oil fields and is a catalyst for future incorporation of the Lower Ob gas region. In the years ahead, it may be extended to Norilsk, providing that important minerals center with a reliable overland connection with the developed southern regions. The same kind of rationale applies to the BAM and its branch lines in Pacific Siberia.

Concern for the environment is expressed conspicuously throughout the planning process. Scientific studies are conducted in ostensibly adequate detail. Environmental-impact analyses include careful considera-

# MULTI-STAGE EVOLUTIONARY DEVELOPMENT OF A SIBERIAN TERRITORIAL PRODUCTION COMPLEX (T.P.C.)

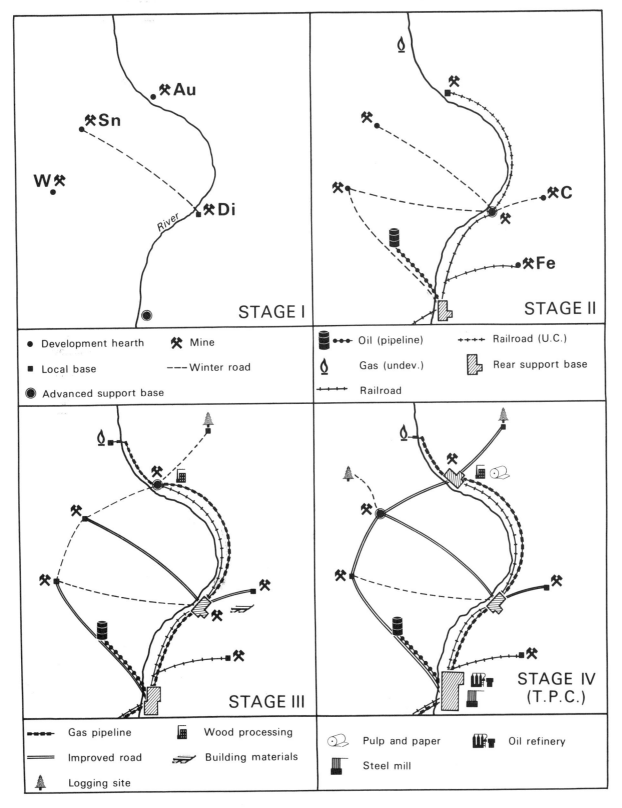

Figure 2
SOURCE: Adapted from O. A. Izyumsky, "The natural resources of the BAM zone and their rational utilization," in *Baikalo-Amurskaya Magistral*.

tion of the slow regenerative capacities of northern environments, the need to harmonize the system of "economy-population-environment," rational utilization of resources, regionally specific medical-geographical relationships, and preservation of unique natural areas and phenomena. Soviet planning officials insist that optimization of the man-nature balance should obtain highest priority during the first stage of economic development, since the most harmful environmental damage occurs at that time.[28]

The planning process is supposed to include the maximum use of stochastic models and computer analyses. However, persons responsible for carrying out this research complain that this service cannot be provided because appropriate data are not available. Thus, comprehensive planning for important construction projects like the BAM and Surgut-Urengoi railroads cannot be conducted because of insufficient information.

### Macroscale Physical Limitations

"Just because the land is unpopulated and unused does not mean that it . . . *should be* [author's emphasis] developed."[29] The fact is, though the number of relatively large cities like Norilsk and Yakutsk may increase, Siberia can never be densely populated. Among the world's great biomes, the taiga and tundra reflect some of the lowest carrying capacities based on gross primary production alone (Table 1). Species diversity steadily decreases poleward from the tropics. For instance, were it not for the Dahurian larch, most of Pacific Siberia would be treeless; but the taiga is a garden in comparison to the neighboring tundra, which on average environs three-quarters fewer plant species and fewer still of the animals. Animal communities, including those of human beings, require far more extensive habitats because of the lack of nourishment. Human densities would appear to be optimum at one to two persons per square kilometer.[30] Similarly, recommended recreational loads for northern environments should not exceed four to six people per hectare.[31]

The low carrying capacity of northern regions like Siberia is determined by at least a dozen variables, the

relative importance of which is not yet established. They range in description from the obvious to the unique.

Underpinning all of the obstacles is low-intensity insolation. The efficiency of insolation is affected by latitude, atmospheric thickness, degree of cloud cover, and albedo. Latitudinal position influences solar radiation in two ways. It determines the time of exposure to the sun and the intensity of that exposure (sun's angle). It is no mystery that days are longer in summer and shorter in winter in high latitudes than they are in low latitudes (Table 2). Moreover, although the atmosphere at high latitudes is richer in oxygen and ozone, freer of carbon dioxide, and generally cleaner than air at low latitudes, insolation is received at strongly oblique angles, meaning the radiation is less direct and therefore less effective. The low angle also implies that the sun's rays must pass through a thicker atmospheric layer in which many wavelengths are filtered by reflection and absorption. Depending on the degree of cloud cover, the remaining radiation reaches the earth's surface, which may in turn reflect or absorb the energy.[32] High-latitude locations, with their protracted periods of snow cover, possess higher surface albedos, that is, they reflect more of the radiant energy than they absorb. In fact, in northern Siberia from October to June, less than one-third of the available sunlight is absorbed.[33] The long periods of summer daylight somewhat restore the deficit, but albedo clearly takes its toll on annual insolation totals. Thus, in Salekhard on the Arctic Circle, of the total annual insolation of 81.6 kilocalories per cm², some 36 kilocalories are reflected back to the atmosphere.[34]

The long periods of winter darkness and summer daylight affect human beings and the use of their technology in strange, often bizarre, ways. As a result of the insolation deficit during the low-sun period, natural sources of vitamin D are at a premium. In order to prevent the occurrence of rickets and bone deformation, Soviet youngsters, who endure high-latitude winters, must undergo regular irradiation treatments. Vitamin-C deficiencies have also been noted.[35] Forms of blindness ("snow blindness"), headaches, and related discomforts may occur from sunlight that is reflected off snowfields. The lack of natural light during the winter leads to added expenditures of electric power for artificial illumination and the use of some machines. Driving during the polar night results in slower vehicular speeds because of im-

TABLE 1
Gross Primary Production of Biomass
(Annual Basis) by Ecosystems

| Ecosystem | Gross Primary Production (kilocalories per m² per year) |
| --- | --- |
| Wet Tropical and Subtropical Forest | 20,000 |
| Moist Temperate Forest | 8,000 |
| Northern Coniferous Forest (Taiga or Boreal Forest) | 3,000 |
| Grasslands and Pasture | 2,500 |
| Deserts and Tundra | 200 |

SOURCE: Eugene P. Odum, *Fundamentals of Ecology* (Philadelphia: W. B. Saunders, 1971), p. 51; thanks to Dennis Johnson, Department of Geography, University of Houston.

TABLE 2
Maximum Lengths of Day and Night at
Different Latitudes (Excluding Twilight)

| North Latitude | Daylight (in Days) | Darkness (in Days) |
| --- | --- | --- |
| 90°[a] | 189[b] | 176 |
| 85° | 163 | 150 |
| 80° | 137 | 123 |
| 75° | 107 | 93 |
| 70° | 70 | 55 |
| 67°38′ | 54 | under 24 hours[c] |

[a]SOURCE: Kryuchkov (n. 34).
[b]"Days" are continuously light or dark.
[c]Civil twilight exists even on shortest day.

paired visibility. A reduction of labor productivity of 10 to 15 percent is directly attributable to the polar night (November 30 to January 13) at Norilsk.[36] In contrast, long summer days frustrate regular sleep habits.

"Arctic hysteria" is a bizarre form of mental disorder that usually is defined as a reaction to long winter nights in the Subarctic and Arctic.[37] Actually, the affliction has been observed in several different geographical areas, including the tropics, and is known variously as *latah* (Malay), jumping disease (Maine, U.S.), and *windigo* or *wiitiko* psychosis (Canada). The syndrome comprises a wide range of symptoms: compulsive imitation (echopraxia or echolalia); extreme timidity, passivity, or fright; morbid depression; insomnia; suicidal inclinations; claustrophobia; and, historically among certain Indian tribes (Cree and Ojibwa of Canada), obsessive cannibalism.[38] In Siberia, elements of this behavior have been witnessed among the Yakuts, Tungus-Manchu, Buryats, Yukaghir, Kalmyks, and a few Russians. In most cases, the hysteria is a function of both geography and culture, but the monotony induced by the long periods of darkness (and daylight) is considered to be a contributing factor.

## Temperature and Harshness

The meager insolation that is absorbed in high-latitude locations is even less effective because the great majority of it is utilized to liquify snow and to vaporize the resultant meltwater. For instance, in Salekhard some 41 kilocalories of the annual insolation is utilized in fusion and vaporization; only 4.6 kilocalories of the original 81.6 is left to heat the soil and air. In other words, only 5.6 percent of the incoming energy is converted to terrestrial radiation![39]

Low amounts of effective radiation as at Salekhard are registered at stations throughout Siberia and are responsible for temperatures mainly below 0° Centigrade. (Table 3). Moreover, temperatures below 0°C. persist for protracted lengths of time—200 days or more—in all but the southernmost portions of the region (Figure 1). Thus, Siberian winters range from five months long in the southwest to over nine months in northeast Yakutia and average seven months over all.

The impact of the long periods of cold on human beings and machinery is considerable. At low temperatures, the skin becomes dry and chafed. The tear ducts are irritated. Skin blood vessels constrict, the blood thickens, and there is a tendency for increased movement. Consequent perspiration from the accelerated activity enhances conductive heat loss, especially at the bodily extremities. Urine volumes also expand. In subfreezing temperatures, any exposed part of the body is in danger of frostbite because of inadequate blood supply to those areas. If the skin tissue should freeze, cells are destroyed, and the constricted blood vessels become obstructed completely. Necrosis and gangrene may set in. Even brief exposures to severely low temperatures (−40°C) may damage lung tissue. Lethargy from cold discomfort may lead to neuroses and, in fact, may be more important than lack of sunlight in cases of Arctic hysteria.

There is a noticeable drop in labor productivity for

TABLE 3
Average Annual Temperatures at Selected
Siberian Stations (in °C)

| Station | Latitude (N) | Longitude (E) | Average Annual Temperature |
|---|---|---|---|
| Salekhard | 66°31′ | 66°35′ | − 6.6 |
| Surgut | 61°17′ | 72°30′ | − 4.0 |
| Tyumen | 57°10′ | 65°32′ | + 1.0 |
| Novosibirsk | 54°58′ | 82°56′ | − 0.4 |
| Igarka | 67°27′ | 86°35′ | − 8.5 |
| Yeniseisk | 58°27′ | 92°10′ | − 1.9 |
| Bratsk | 56°04′ | 101°50′ | − 2.7 |
| Irkutsk | 52°16′ | 104°19′ | − 1.1 |
| Verkhoyansk | 67°33′ | 133°25′ | −16.0 |
| Yakutsk | 62°01′ | 129°43′ | −10.3 |
| Bomnak | 54°43′ | 128°52′ | − 5.0 |
| Nerchinsk | 52°02′ | 116°31′ | − 3.8 |
| Anadyr | 64°27′ | 177°34′ | − 8.1 |
| Petropavlovsk | 52°33′ | 158°43′ | + 0.6 |
| Sovetskaya Gavan | 48°58′ | 140°17′ | − 0.5 |

SOURCE: M. Y. Nuttonson, *Agricultural Climatology of Siberia* (Washington: American Institute of Crop Ecology, 1950), appendices.

outdoor work when temperatures fall below 0°C. At relatively mild Yeniseisk (see Table 3), the average number of reduced-work days and nonwork days directly attributable to restrictions imposed by cold weather amounts to 30 percent of the total number of work days during the winter. Once the temperature drops to −20°C, warm-up breaks of 10 minutes per hour for each seven-hour work day are imposed, which may result in work losses of up to 73 percent. In an average year, total losses to cold comprise 33 percent of all possible working time in the Soviet North.[40]

It has been said that Russians are "connoisseurs of cold."[41] Yet, cold most certainly must be relative, for in research conducted in the 1960s, Siberian geographers discovered that 25 to 30 percent of the new arrivals in the Middle Ob oil fields found the physical environment too extreme and became chilled and "overchilled" in outdoor work for nine to ten months out of the year.[42] Even today 30 percent of the new migrants to the Middle and Lower Ob return to more hospitable climates before completing the first year on the job.[43] This rate of labor turnover has remained remarkably consistent during the last 15 years despite improvements in infrastructure and amenities in West Siberian cities.

Part of the discomfort apparently arises because of the clothing worn in the Arctic and Subarctic. Soviet clothiers continue to produce apparel that is more appropriate for the mid-latitudes than for Siberian conditions. According to Kryuchkov,[44]

wadded coats, jerseys, sweaters, sheepskin and fur coats are enormous and heavy; working in them is hot and uncomfortable. Sitting in them, without moving, is possible, but after a point, you begin to freeze. With their many buttons, slits, and fasteners, you feel the cold . . . as if the clothes were made of cheesecloth.

Many experts on cold have recommended that the Russians adopt designs patterned after the traditional native dress (long, seamless, buttonless parkas of reindeer hide with the fur on the inside; together with another reindeer-hide undergarment). However, these suggestions have not been taken seriously. In fact, the native Siberians themselves now purchase the more "fashionable" mid-latitude clothing because it is available and ready-made.

In the late 1960s, it was estimated that the replacement of a single basic laborer in the Soviet North by a machine would reduce the total number of workers by a factor of 10 (the laborer, his family, and the associated nonbasic service personnel).[45] At the time, northern environments reflected a comparatively high degree of mechanization, including 30 percent of all Soviet trucks, 37 percent of the bulldozers, 35 percent of the excavators, 33 percent of the tower cranes, 62 percent of the drilling equipment, and 64 percent of the tracked prime-movers. With expanded economic development and an unprecedented official interest in increasing sizes of the motor pools and equipment parks of Siberia, these percentages undoubtedly have gone up.[46] Unfortunately, much of the equipment still used in Siberia is of standard technology built to mid-latitude specifications.[47] In fact, 20 to 25 percent of all Soviet machinery functions in temperatures for which it was not designed. This situation persists despite the fact that new, "northern" technology has been improved and perfected by Soviet industry. Moreover, since 1972 Soviet contributions have been supplemented by imports of foreign equipment from North America, Japan, and Western Europe.[48] Even this supposedly superior equipment has been known to fail in Siberian conditions.

The continued use of standard Soviet equipment in the extreme cold of Siberia undoubtedly raises the cost of economic development there and increases the losses to the economy as a whole. The number of breakdowns of standard equipment, owing to rupturing and wear, is three to five times greater in the North than in the mid-latitudes. Low temperatures and the accompanying radical daily and seasonal ranges create a variety of prerequisites for machine design, lubrication, heating systems, materials' quality (frost resistance of steels; flexibility and strength of rubber and plastics; etc.), civil engineering, and other elements. Because of the cold, standard mining and excavation machinery may be used for only three to four months yearly in northern Siberian tin and gold operations. Even the much-vaunted Soviet rotary excavators may not be employed between November and March. Without appropriate garages and engine heaters, standard Soviet motor vehicles are left running in bitterly cold weather, even when not on the road. Lacking quality anti-freeze and hydraulic fluids, Siberian equipment operators often add vodka to the respective reservoirs and cylinders. Because of the cold temperatures, as well as darkness, surveying is curtailed sharply from October to March. Interestingly, for reasons to be introduced later, West Siberian pipelaying teams work in winter only.

Obviously, efficient residential heating systems are essential in cold weather. Soviet scientists have concluded

that central heat is the most effective utility alternative for the region.[49] This is in accord with a trend that is prevalent throughout the country. Yet, capital outlays for these systems may equal 10 percent of the total construction cost of a town the size of, let's say, 1,000 people. Many new towns in the BAM service area reportedly are without central heat. In some cases, the systems have not been incorporated into town plans. Centralized hot-water networks are practically unheard of, requiring each individual to heat his own water, which increases the need for fuel. The central heat and power plants that do exist are of low capacity, made of poor-quality construction materials, and lack appropriate insulation. Experi-

TABLE 4
Cold Thresholds for Human Beings
and Their Machinery in Siberia

| Temperature (°C) | Effects on Human Beings and Standard Soviet Machinery |
|---|---|
| 0 | Replace summer lubricants with winterized equivalents |
| −6 | Internal-combustion engines require pre-start engine heaters or starter pilots |
| −10 | Destruction of some standard-metal dredge components |
| −14 | Very cool to human beings; destruction of some standard excavator pushing axles |
| −15 | High-carbon steels break; car batteries must be heated; first critical threshold for standard equipment in general |
| −20 | Outdoor workers must take 10-minute breaks to warm up; standard compressors with internal combustion engines cease to operate; standard excavator hiltbeams break; destruction of some tower crane components, dredging buckets, and bulldozer blades |
| −25 to −30 | 7-hour work day reduced to 5 hours (warm-up breaks continue); unalloyed steels break; car-engine space, fuel tanks, and oil tanks must be insulated; frost-resistant rubber required; non-frost-resistant conveyor belts and standard pneumatic hoses break; some cranes fail |
| −30 | Minimum temperature for use of any standard equipment |
| −30 to −35 | Sailors in Arctic conditions stop outside work; trestle cranes fail; some tractor shoes break |
| −35 to −40 | Tin-alloyed steel (ballbearings, etc.) shatter; fuel entering carburetors and air entering filters must be heat-treated; tower cranes and lifters work at 50% capacity; saw frames and circular saws stop work; all compressors stop work; standard steels and structures rupture on mass scale; most standard equipment begins to deteriorate rapidly; standard motor oils must be replaced |
| −40 to −45 | All outdoor work ceases; very cold to human beings; tolerance limit for electrical circuits and some standard lubricants; all cranes work at half capacity; majority of other standard machinery ceases to operate |
| −45 to −50 | Cranes operate at quarter capacity |
| −50 | All cranes stop work; spot welds cease to hold |
| −60 | Tolerance limit for fuel oils of "northern" design |

SOURCE: Dogayev (n. 36, pages 29–31).

ence at Tynda indicates that total capital investments in heating systems of standard design are outstripped by yearly operational costs because of the above defects plus pipe corrosion and lack of preventive maintenance on the boilers.

This clearly argues for the development of boiler technologies of northern design. These include thicker boiler walls, heavy-duty pipe, fewer moving parts, and a simple method of chemo-mechanical purification of boiler water.

For all structures built in Siberia, insulation that is at least 50 percent thicker (or more effective, given modern synthetic fibers) than the national norm should be utilized despite higher initial construction costs.[50] Research from the early 1970s indicates that structures assembled with the right kind of northern insulation are more expensive by 10 rubles per average residence, but the added cost is recouped by savings of fuel within two years.

Research on thresholds of cold for human beings and their machinery has been carried out in the USSR for some time (Table 4). There are two critically low temperatures where Soviet technology is affected significantly. At −15°C there is a tendency for the metal parts and components of standard equipment to break. Minus 35°C is the point at which standard Soviet steels shatter *en masse*. Soviet engineers design northern technology to meet the stress of the latter threshold. Beyond −45°C work outdoors ceases for all practical purposes.

Cold and "harshness" have been correlated by Kolyago.[51] In the latter study, harshness was viewed as a function of temperature and machine breakages. By utilizing the −15°C threshold and −30°C, the minimum temperature for the usage of any standard equipment, Kolyago determined harshness subtypes. The subtypes were modified further by averages of absolute annual minima and mean January temperatures (Table 5).

Although explicated, several other important physical variables could not be incorporated into the Kolyago cold-harshness scale. These were rapid temperature changes; the mean number of days with winds of mean velocities of 6 meters per second or more in winter; the mean number of winter days with a relative humidity of 80 percent or more at 1 P.M.; and the mean absolute daily range. The reason for the exclusion of these variables was a lack of clear statistical relationships between them and machine breakages. Thus, Kolyago's system is really a direct reflection of harshness as measured by temperature alone and its effect on machinery. His Siberian harshness subtypes are illustrated in Figure 3.

Air Pressure

According to Griffiths, air pressure is not, strictly speaking, a climatological factor, "its variations only being experienced through other elements such as air movement."[52] In fact, the correlation between air pressure and its effects on technology has been studied insufficiently at this time. Concerning human beings, changes in atmospheric pressure appear to bear a relation to certain kinds of muscular pains and headaches.

The unequal distribution of temperature around the globe is responsible to a large degree for the unequal patterns of air pressure. High pressure, associated with subsiding air and relative coolness, is naturally frequent over most of Siberia during the cold months of winter. Apart from the record high of 1,084 mb that was registered at Agata (67°N 94°E) on 31 December 1968, standard sea level air pressure is exceeded by an average of at least two millibars virtually everywhere in Siberia on a mean annual basis (Table 6). In Eastern Siberia, pressures are in excess of 1,025 mb throughout the low-sun period. The air is so dense that sounds are magnified considerably out of proportion. "The creak of a sled can be distinguished for almost two miles, and the rumble of the ground and crackling of the ice, from cold, sounds like gunfire."[53] This magnification of sound augurs poorly for urban residents with respect to noise pollution. Moreover, high atmospheric pressure yields periods of calm and little wind: the higher the pressure, the stabler the calm. This, in turn, means lack of air turbulence, low limits of natural diffusion, and weak propensities for self-purification. Thus, industrial development should be planned carefully because of the high potential for air pollution.

Wind and Wind Chill

Differential air pressure induces air movement. After cold weather, probably the most serious climatic constraint to the economic development of Siberia is the impact of the wind, even though high-speed winds are predominantly limited to coastal locations. Siberian continental climates are not characterized by frequent storminess and gusts except during the brief summer months. Nevertheless, any wind at all during the cold season is a significant obstacle to human activity.

In contrast to the effects of air pressure, the influence of wind on human beings and their technology is well

TABLE 5
Subtypes of a Harsh Cold Climate and Basic Temperature Indices

| Subtypes | Number of Days with Mean Daily Temperatures Below −15°C | Number of Days with Mean Daily Temperatures Below −30°C | The Mean of Absolute Annual Minimum Temperatures | Mean January Temperature |
|---|---|---|---|---|
| I. Low Harshness | 60 to 90 | 1 to 21 | −32 to −48° | −18 to −20° |
| II. Medium Harshness | 90 to 120 | 4 to 50 | −36 to −54° | −24 to −26° |
| III. High Harshness | 120 to 150 | 30 to 95 | −39 to −57° | −30 to −32° |
| IV. Very High Harshness | over 150 | 45 to 130 | −46 to −64° | −36 to −38° |

SOURCE: Kolyago (n. 51).

**SUBZONES OF HARSH COLD IN SIBERIA**

LOW HARSHNESS
MEDIUM HARSHNESS
HIGH HARSHNESS
VERY HIGH HARSHNESS

−90  SUBZONE BOUNDARIES (FIGURE INDICATES NUMBER OF DAYS WITH MEAN DAILY TEMPERATURES OF LESS THAN −15° C)
------  Boundary of Siberia

Figure 3
Source: V. A. Kolyago, "A Classification and Regionalization of the Harsh, Cold Climate of Siberia and the Far East in Relation to Problems of Cold Resistance of Machines," *Soviet Geography: Review and Translation*, 11, no. 1 (January 1970): 38–47.

known. Siple, for instance, has correlated wind speed with temperature and has developed a wind-chill factor based on the rate at which the naked body would cool in the presence of low temperatures and winds of various speeds. For example, exposed parts of the body will become frostbitten in air of −12°C when coupled with a wind of 8 meters per second (18 mph) (Figure 4). A person freezes to death in temperatures of −20 to −24°C with winds of 3 to 4 m/sec (7–9 mph), when exposed to those conditions for 15 to 20 minutes.

The influence of the wind and wind chill is less clear with reference to their effect on technology. However, by speeding the freezing process, wind increases the heat exchange between any object and the atmosphere at low temperatures. In so doing, it rapidly disrupts the operational efficiency of motors, freezes different components, and lowers the frost-resistance of metal in general. Besides rendering obvious physical damage in high-velocity winds, air movement augments other limiting factors, such as precipitation, snowstorms, and

visibility. For example, snowstorms (*meteli*) and blizzards (*purgi*) are the combination of fallen or falling snow and winds in excess of 4 m/sec.[54]

Wind-tolerance levels have been established for technology by Soviet scientists. Winds up to 4 m/sec generally cause few problems for machinery except at very low temperatures (below −30°C), but winds of more than 4 m/sec in subfreezing temperatures are harmful to internal-combustion engines.[55] During winds of 10 m/sec (22 mph) the use of construction equipment like tower cranes should be curtailed by 50 percent. And, in winds of 12 m/sec (26 mph), all work should stop. This threshold is enforced because blizzards normally occur in winds of this speed. In blizzards, visibility is reduced sharply, and the blowing snow melts upon contact with any heated surface. The latter is the more important reason for deadlining standard equipment in blizzard conditions. In Norilsk, the hardiest of Soviet standard equipment, cranes (see Table 4), stand idle because of excessive wind for 45 days out of the year, 35 of them coming in winter.

TABLE 6
Average Annual Deviations from Standard Sea Level
Air Pressure in Siberia (in mb)

| Station | Average Annual Deviation |
|---|---|
| Salekhard | −1.6 |
| Surgut | +0.6 |
| Tyumen | — |
| Novosibirsk | +6.1 |
| Igarka | — |
| Yeniseisk | +4.9 |
| Bratsk | — |
| Irkutsk | +7.3 |
| Verkhoyansk | +3.7 |
| Yakutsk | +2.6 |
| Bomnak | +1.5 |
| Nerchinsk | — |
| Anadyr | +0.9 |
| Petropavlovsk | −5.3 |
| Sovetskaya Gavan | — |

SOURCE: Lydolph (n. 62, pp. 364–427).

Thus, in the USSR, winds are distinguished as weak, dangerous, or very dangerous to people and equipment depending on the following velocity ranges (technological wind tolerance levels): weak, up to 4 m/sec; dangerous, 4 to 12 m/sec; very dangerous, over 12 m/sec.[56]

Siberian wind regions as determined by Dogayev are illustrated in Figure 5. Shown as well are minimum sensible temperatures (wind chill) as reported by Lydolph. The probability of surface wind speed occurring with air temperatures below 0°C. in each wind region can be expressed as a percentage of all days during the winter.[57] In Wind Region I, 48 percent of the days in winter with winds are considered dangerous, and 24 percent very dangerous; in Wind Region II, 45 percent are considered dangerous and 14 percent very dangerous.

Prevailing wind direction is a constraining factor where the orientation and operation of technology and the requirements for human comfort are concerned. Parts and components on the windward side of equipment are observed to break down more often than those on the leeward side. Fuel storage tanks and above-ground pipelines are especially susceptible to ruptures in the sector exposed to the wind. In recent northern settlement plans, Soviet architects have been more concerned with wind speed and direction in their designs. For instance, streets are sheltered from the prevailing winds by parallel elongated multi-story buildings placed at right angles to the wind direction.

In the Soviet North, labor schedules are governed by wind-chill tables as developed by a number of state agencies.[58] For example, authorities at the Institute of Worker Hygiene and Occupational Disease of the USSR urge cancellation of all work when the wind reaches velocities of 15 m/sec (34 mph) in temperatures of −10° to −15°C (Table 7). Such precautions are necessary not only because of the danger from frostbite and freezing but also because of the danger from illness in general. On any given January day in Norilsk, the illness rate for selected occupations is 3 to 11 percent. The illnesses include in-

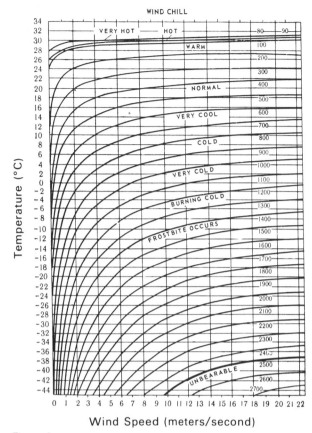

Figure 4
SOURCE: V. V. Kryuchkov, *Kraini Sever: Problemy ratsionalnogo ispolzovaniya prirodnykh resursov* [The extreme North: Problems of rational utilization of natural resources], p. 22. The figures on the right-hand side of the chart represent the heat loss in kilocalories per square meter of unprotected body during an hour's exposure time.

fluenza, tonsillitis, and bronchitis, all of them exacerbated by wind and wind chill.

Temperature Inversion, Humidity, and Fog

Because of the persistent high pressure, resultant air stillness, long nights, and snow-covered surfaces, Siberia is noted for frequent temperature inversions. Radiation (surface) inversions are especially prevalent, being observed for 60 to 90 percent of the year. In winter, northeastern Siberia may record inversion frequencies as high as 95 percent. Most of these inversions are above-surface types related to the intense anticyclonic subsidence that occurs within the Asiatic High. Inversions of weaker intensity are witnessed over West Siberia during summer.

Siberia in general is more likely to have inversions than is European Russia, with the exception of the Ural Mountains and the Ufa Plateau.[59] From the Ob River east and the China border north, January inversion layers range from 0.6 to 2 km thick between the earth's surface and the inversion lid, reaching a maximum over Yakutia. Beneath the inversions, temperatures increase with increasing altitude by more than −8°C, and wind speeds average less than 4 m/sec.

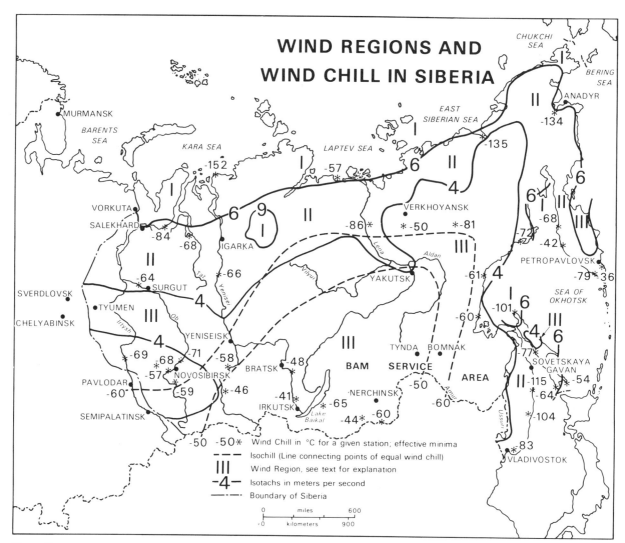

Figure 5
SOURCE: Yu. M. Dogayev, *Ekonomicheskaya effectivnost novoi tekhniki na Severe* [The cost-effectiveness of new technology in the North], p. 161.

Hills and mountains commonly have high inversion frequencies because of the phenomenon of air drainage. The magnitude of this problems is so great in certain intermontane basins of Siberia that there is actually an inversion of vegetation, with frost-tolerant species on the valley floors and warmth-loving plants on the slopes and peaks. In the Chara Lowland (57°N 118°E), 600 m above sea level, temperatures are often 15°C cooler than the adjacent mountains at 2,500 m. In the vicinity of the Yenisei Ridge, the Eldorado mine (60°N 93°E) at 750 m has experienced temperatures 44°C warmer than those simultaneously recorded in contiguous lowlands (150 m). Differences of 18° or more have persisted there for four

consecutive days.[60] Inversions caused by air drainage in the mountains and basins of Siberia endure all winter. Even passing air masses and fronts have little impact, literally skimming across the mountain tops.[61]

Siberian inversions are said to be just as effective in trapping air pollutants as those over London. Because of this, Soviet planners have advised against the location of heavy industry, such as copper smelters, in places like the Chara Lowland. Even Norilsk, situated in a region of relatively high wind speeds (6 to 9 m/sec) and comparatively light inversions, is so heavily polluted that the larch tree no longer grows there. Although by nature a wooded tundra, the Norilsk area has become what Soviet

TABLE 7
Soviet Work Loads and the Wind Chill Factor (Institute of Worker Hygiene and Occupational Disease USSR)

| Negative Ambient Air Temperature, °C | Warm-Up Periods* | Wind Speed, Meters per Second Necessitating: | |
|---|---|---|---|
| | | Reduction of Work Day by 30% | Cessation of Work |
| 5.1–10 | 8–15 | 15–20 | Over 20 |
| 10.1–15 | 3–12 | 12–15 | Over 15 |
| 15.1–20 | 0–8 | 8–12 | Over 12 |
| 20.1–25 | 0–5 | 5–8 | Over 8 |
| 30.1–35 | 0–3 | 3–5 | Over 5 |
| 40.1–45 | 0 | 0–1 | Over 1 |
| Below 45 | 0 | 0 | 0 |

*10 minutes per hour for up to 7 hours.
SOURCE: Dogayev (n. 36, p. 39).

scientists call a "technogenic tundra," and it begins where the streets of Norilsk end. Soviet planners would hope to avoid such gloomy scenarios in the regions south and east of Norilsk, even more likely to be affected by inversions and air pollution.

Throughout Siberia, humidity, like air pressure, is not so much a direct constraint to economic development as it is an harbinger of other more serious obstacles: fog, glaze ice, and rime. In winter, relative humidities average 80 percent or more, except in Magadan Oblast, western Kamchatka, and Maritime Krai, where they fall to 70 percent and below. In summer, the situation is reversed owing to the Pacific monsoon. Yakutian humidities equal 60 percent or less during high sun; where, coastal means are 80 to 90 percent. Simultaneously, readings of 70 to 80 percent are recorded in the swamps and bogs of West Siberia.

Where relative humidities are high, sensible temperatures are increased in summer and decreased in winter. Since the most comfortable values of relative humidity lie in the range of 30 to 70 percent, a relatively high degree of discomfort can be expected in most Siberian stations (Table 8). The high relative humidities have a deleterious effect on construction materials, preservatives, and paints. Under conditions of high humidity, metal corrodes, paints deteriorate, and masonry disintegrates more rapidly then when the air is dry. Low humidities, which occur in the taiga of Yakutia and the BAM service area in spring, summer, and fall, raise forest fire potential.

When high humidities and temperature inversions occur together, radiation or barometric fog may result. The frequency of fog is encouraged by atmospheric stagnation. In regions of relatively high concentrations of people and animals, as in the Yakutian Lowland, extremely localized "mixing fogs," based chiefly on the activity of humans and livestock, are common in winter. When temperatures plunge below −30°C, such fogs may be composed entirely of ice crystals, giving vent to "ice fogs" or "diamond dust." On the Arctic and Pacific coasts, where fog frequencies are highest (over 70 to 90 days per annum), advection fog occurs in summer and fall. In contrast, radiation fogs associated with air drain-

age exist in the continental interiors for only 30 to 50 days, mainly during winter.

A fog subtype, particularly characteristic of Siberia, is steam fog, which is caused by intense evaporation from still-warm rivers and lakes into already-saturated cool or cold air. The city of Irkutsk on the Angara River is plagued by dense steam fogs for two-thirds of its winter-days. Ironically, Lake Baikal, a short distance away, is relatively fog-free (7 to 25 days per year).[62]

Obviously, fog is an environmental deterrent because of what it portends for visibility. It is a handicap to transportation, principally aviation. In regions reliant on air transport as the sole means of supply and delivery, as in development foci and workers settlements, fog can be a significant disruptive element. In places like Norilsk, with fog 65 to 75 days per year, mainly in winter, fog thresholds are utilized even for surface operations. When

TABLE 8
Mean Annual Relative Humidity and Number of Days with Fog at Selected Siberian Stations[a]

| Station | Mean Annual Relative Humidity (%) | Fog (Annual No. of Days) |
|---|---|---|
| Salekhard | 80 | 43 (W: 15–20%)* |
| Surgut | 76[b] | — |
| Tyumen | 73[b] | — |
| Novosibirsk | 75 | 27 (F; 12%) |
| Igarka | — | 45[c] |
| Yeniseisk | 74 | 37 (F, W) |
| Bratsk | — | — |
| Irkutsk | 73 | 103 (W; 67%) |
| Verkhoyansk | 70 | 52 (W; 25–30%) |
| Yakutsk | 68 | 59 (W; 50%) |
| Bomnak | 68 | 16 (S; 10%) |
| Nerchinsk | 68[b] | — |
| Anadyr | 82 | 33 (even distrib.) |
| Petropavlovsk | 72 | 46 (S; 33%) |
| Sovetskaya Gavan | — | — |

[a]Lydolph (n. 62, pp. 364–427).
[b]M. Y. Nuttonson, *Agricultural Climatology of Siberia* (Washington: American Institute of Crop Ecology, 1950), appendices.
[c]Kryuchkov (n. 34, p. 49).
*Chief season of occurrence (W = winter; F = fall; S = summer) and percentage of days during that season with fog.

visibility is 20 meters or less, excavator and crane operations cease. This increases idle time and lowers productivity almost as much as the polar night, cold weather, and wind. "Diamond dust" is a significant constraint to drilling operations because it speeds the weakening of the steel drilling pipe.

Although much less of a factor in Siberia than in European Russia—even to the extent that they do not occur every year—glaze ice and rime can pose significant technological problems. Glaze ice is especially troublesome for lines of communication and equipment stored outdoors. Glaze ice, caused by freezing rain and/or alternative freezing and thawing of snow, is rarely observed in cold, dry Siberia. Only West Siberia and the Arctic Coast experience glaze for more than two to three days per year.

Rime ice is more frequent, being created by saturated air blown against objects with surface temperatures below freezing. Thus, rime accumulates most spectacularly in Wind Region I (see Figure 5). Rime thicknesses of 50 cm or more have been observed on telephone poles and other objects on the Arctic Coast. On a linear meter of electric or telephone wiring of 5 mm in diameter, it is possible to accumulate up to 9 kg of rime or glaze.[63] This may be sufficient to snap the line or to bring down the supports.

## Clouds, Rain, and Snow

Cloud cover is hardly a constraint except as it affects aviation and visibility. However, cloudiness does reduce potential oxygenation by surface water bodies. In a year's time, Siberia as a whole experiences far less cloud cover than European Russia because of distance from maritime influences. West Siberia, (closer to the Atlantic Ocean) and the Pacific Coast area have the highest degree of cloud cover among Siberian regions. On a larger scale, Lydolph has noted an anomalous lack of cloud cover along the course of the middle Amur River. Simultaneously, he has reported relatively greater cloudiness over the Aldan Upland.[64] North and south of that physiographic province, in Yakutia and the BAM service area, cloudiness diminishes.

Seasonally, cloud cover is more extensive in winter than in summer over West Siberia because of frequent cyclonic passages at that time. In contrast, Pacific Siberia is cloudiest, as one would expect, during the summer monsoon. The Arctic Coast likewise experiences a summer maximum of cloud cover.

Aviation obviously is influenced by heavy cloud banks, particularly mature cumulonimbus types, which develop in the Far East and along the Arctic coast in summer. As with fog, dense stratus clouds impede visibility and encourage the phenomenon of "whiteout." The latter problem is explained variously as the result of blowing powder snow or a kind of optical illusion brought about by the diffuse illumination that occurs under overcast skies on a uniformly snow-covered surface.[65] The former happens in blizzards, the latter on cloudy winter days in the tundra. During whiteout, all depth perception is lost to the human eye. Hence, all forms of mobility—from the simple act of walking to the sensitive act of landing an aircraft—are made more difficult. Such conditions also facilitate the inducement of snow blindness. Fortunately for most Siberian residents, overcast skies are far more frequent at night during winter than they are during the brief daylight hours, which reduces the potential for whiteout.

Rainfall is a constraint to economic development when it occurs in sufficient quantities, at the wrong time, or in catastrophic amounts.

Throughout most of Siberia annual precipitation varies from light (200 to 500 mm) to moderate (500 to 800 mm), some 10 to 25 percent of it in snow. Precipitation totals decline steadily from the Ural Mountains (500 to 600 mm) to the Lena River, only to rise again from there to the Pacific. The Pacific fringe, including Kamchatka, coastal ranges, and offshore islands, reflects moderate to wet levels.

The regime of precipitation, both in terms of annual marches and in terms of variability, is more important to human habitation and use than sheer quantity. Befitting its continental interior position, Siberia presents distinct summer maxima of precipitation. Rainfall clusters symmetrically above the middle and late summer months. These July or August maxima serve as a constraint to agriculture, expecially in the fertile parklands and grasslands of West Siberia, for it means that drought often occurs in the sensitive sprouting and maturing phases of crop growth followed by wetness during ripening and harvest seasons. Lydolph has pointed out the severity of this limitation:[66]

> The shortness and wetness of the harvest season necessitate the harvesting of grain in two stages, first cutting and allowing it to lie on the ground to cure and then picking it up with combines and threshing it. *It also requires costly airlifts of men and equipment to follow the harvest.* [Italics mine]

The month of maximum rainfall lags later and later into the year all the way to the Pacific, where late summer and autumn monsoons are the rule.

The variability of precipitation usually increases with decreasing quantities of rainfall. Thus, rains become more unpredictable in the directions of the Kazakhstan border, the Arctic coast, and northeast Siberia. The probability of drought between May and July also correlates well with this belt, which begins in the Virgin Lands and extends northeastward at a width of 1,000 km to the Arctic coast and Kamchatka. Within this belt, drought probabilities are 5 to 20 percent, with increasingly high percentages of 40 percent or more near the Kazakhstan border. Susceptibility to drought is also high in the Yakutian lowland, the upper Yana, and the Kolyma basin. An exclave of high-drought potential is found in Transbaikalia, with the greatest probabilities in the Shilka-Argun watershed.[67] Variations of annual precipitation in the wooded steppe of West Siberia run as high as 600 mm and as low as 200 mm; in the western taiga, 600 mm to 300 mm; in the upper Yana area, 230 mm to 50 mm; in the BAM service area, 480 mm to 180 mm; and in Maritime Krai, the difference between one year and the next may be as much as 700 mm.[68] Such extreme variability and droughtiness obviously impose limits on crop yields (by as much as 25 percent), river transport, domestic water supply, and hydropower regimes.

Heavy rains, either as downpours or prolonged forms, associated with thunderstorms and fronts are constraining factors, where floods, mudflows, and dirt roads are concerned. Few thunderstorms and downpours occur in Pacific Siberia, these being more common in West Siberia. East of the Yenisei the rain originates chiefly as a result of prolonged inflows of maritime Pacific air masses. In Maritime Krai between June and September, rain falls continuously for 10 to 20 days at a time. Occasionally, there are intense downpours that persist from one to four days, causing floods, destroying crops, uprooting trees, and eroding topsoil. Downpours in this region may coincide with whole gales or hurricane-like storms, with winds of 60 mph or more, which are often the result of Pacific typhoons in late summer or early fall. Throughout Pacific Siberia, summer rains in any form bring the threat of mudflows in the mountains.[69] Summer is also the season of impassable roads in a region where most roads are of the unimproved, dirt type. Ordinary wheeled vehicles are rendered immobile at this time of year; they are more readily maneuverable on winter ice or snow roads. Finally, during the steamy summers of the southern Far East, mildew and wet rot pose problems for crops, clothing, and technology.

In contrast to Pacific Siberia, West Siberia obtains most of its summer rain as thunderstorms. In the wooded steppe, as much as 150 mm has fallen in a single 24-hour period. Such downpours are extremely infrequent, however, with the overwhelming majority of storms depositing 30 mm or less. Hail also is rarely a problem, happening only once or twice a year in scattered locations. With or without hail, whenever heavy thunderstorms arrive, floods, crop damage, and severe erosion may occur as well.

Snow is far more significant than rain as a constraint to the economic development of Siberia. First, the mere presence of snow is a major determinant of the low temperatures and lengths of winter. It is well known that once snow is on the surface, the ground itself ceases to have much influence on air temperature. The effect of a snow-covered surface on the incidence of insolation has been discussed already: 50 percent or more of the sunlight is reflected. Snow, thus, serves as an insulator between the cold of the air above and the heat from the ground below, the difference between which may be as much as 35 to 40°C. Passing polar continental and arctic air masses are not moderated by the snow cover. The cold, snowy surface encourages radiation inversions and amplifies their intensities. Finally, it has been shown that springtime atmospheric warming is retarded because so much of the solar radiation is expended in fusion and subsequent vaporization. All of which leads to the undesirable harvest-season maximum of rainfall that was just discussed.

In Siberia, snow lies on the ground on average from November to May. The central BAM service area and the Arctic foreland from the Yenisei River to the Chukchi highlands are covered with snow from October to May or June (240 to 280 days). In comparison, along the southern rim of the region, snow may persist for only 160 days (mid-November to mid-April).

Snow duration is more important than snow depth as an environmental constraint. Over most of Siberia, snow depths average 50 cm or less, except in the Middle Yenisei Valley (60 to 80 cm), the Chukchi-Kamchatka uplands (60 to 100 cm), and the Kuznetsk Basin (60 cm) (Figure 6). On a larger scale, isolated mountain ranges and ridges also may bear snow of 100-cm depths.

The shallow Siberian snow cover may be exaggerated when it is blown into drifts. Snowbanks range from a few meters deep in many parts of Siberia to 15 m deep in the arctic and alpine tundra.

With respect to technogenic activities, snow is an obstacle insofar as it affects visibility, mobility, and avalanches. Concerning visibility, usually it must be augmented by the wind (see previous discussion of whiteout). Snowstorms and blizzards occur 25 to 100 days a year in Siberia, generally increasing in number and severity from south (Wind Region III) to north (Wind Region I). As in fog, work normally stops when visibility is reduced to 20 m or winds become excessive (over 12 m/sec).

In winter, mobility is hampered by deep snowbanks and rough, encrusted snow fragments. It is also constrained by the nature of the snow itself. In the southern and western regions of Siberia, the snow is characterized by a high moisture content and densities of 0.25 to 0.45 grams per cm$^3$.[70] At lower temperatures, this snow becomes encrusted, making movement hazardous. While wet, it adheres to the treads of the moving vehicle. The snow that is commonly located north of 58°N is dry, powdery, friable, and non-adhesive (density = 0.8 to .25 g/cm$^3$), which makes for normal traction. However, in regions of very low temperatures (Yakutia and Magadan Oblast), the snow is similar to that of a firn-field, being coarse, granular, near-perennial ice crystals with densities of 0.3 to 0.5 g/cm$^3$. The latter increase the friction of movement and hinder traction.

The accumulation of snow in mountains often leads to conditions which are conducive to avalanche. For instance, in the Udokan Range of the BAM service area, 335 avalanches were recorded in the winter of 1969–70.[71] Udokan avalanches typically are caused by the combination of deep snow (up to 100 cm), numerous snowstorms (up to 100 per winter), and premature thaws in spring.[72] Avalanches, like floods and mudflows, may cause death and destruction in populated areas. Usually, occurring as they do in sparsely populated areas, they interrupt lines of communication and transportation, causing only minor economic loss.

Finally, the spring melting of snow of any depth enhances the volumes and velocities of Siberian rivers. By analyzing the depth of the snow cover, particularly in the mountains, hydrologists can determine the potential for flood or drought and the amount of water that will be available for human needs during the rest of the year. For example, dry years yield drastically lower water levels in the Lena River and its tributaries, reducing their value as transport arteries. They also curtail or even delay the

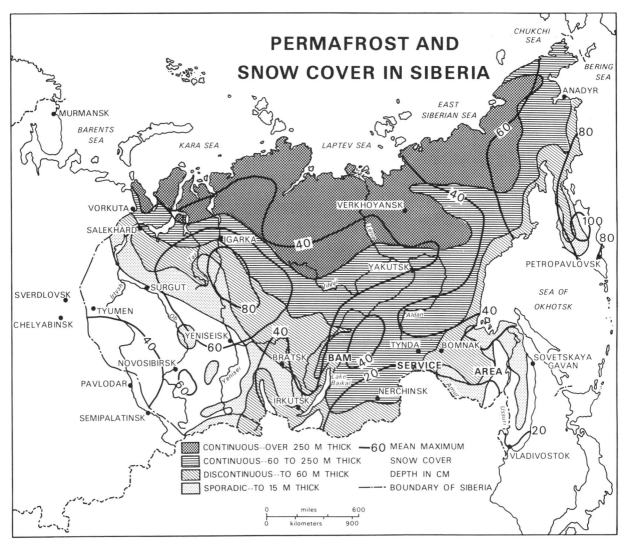

**PERMAFROST AND SNOW COVER IN SIBERIA**

CONTINUOUS--OVER 250 M THICK ── 60 MEAN MAXIMUM
CONTINUOUS--60 TO 250 M THICK      SNOW COVER
DISCONTINUOUS--TO 60 M THICK       DEPTH IN CM
SPORADIC--TO 15 M THICK   ─·─ BOUNDARY OF SIBERIA

Figure 6
SOURCE: Paul E. Lydolph, *Climates of the Soviet Union*, pp. 268, 325.

production of hydroelectric power. In wet years, the water may rise 8 to 13 m, with velocities of up to 4 m per second (8 mph), causing destructive floods. Bad floods were expected in Transbaikalia in the wake of the harsh, snowy winter of 1977–78. In the past, floodwaters have washed out roads and derailed trains in East Siberia where the transportation routes lacked adequate drainage conduits.

It might be said that Russians are connoisseurs of snow, for they have learned to live with it. Snow fences have been in evidence in Siberia for many years. In the developed southern regions, shelter belts and shrubbery have been planted as much to keep the roads clear of snow as to protect plowed fields. Teams of snowplows, graders, and scrapers are supposed to be on call 24 hours a day for road and railroad clearance contingencies. A national avalanche warning and prevention service has been established under the auspices of the State Committee for Hydrometeorology and Environmental Protection. As in the United States, avalanche specialists in the field use artillery barrages to dislodge dangerous snowfields.[73]

Permafrost and Ice

*Causes and Distribution.* Because of subfreezing temperatures induced by insufficient terrestrial radiation coupled with a shallow, poorly insulating layer of snow, moisture within the soil and bedrock of most high-latitude regions exists in a perpetually frozen rather than liquid state. Over a quarter of the earth's land mass, including Antarctica, is underlain by such permanently frozen ground (permafrost). Just under half of the Soviet Union and over two-thirds of Siberia are afflicted with a foundation of permafrost of varying thicknesses and disposition. Deep in the Siberian interior, the permafrost is continuous and is as thick as 1,500 m, although the averages are much less than that (300 to 450 m). Equatorward of 62°N, the deep continuous permafrost zone is ringed by a steadily thinner continuous zone of between 60 to 250 m in thickness. This thin continuous permafrost extends as far south as 50°N, including most of Transbaikalia and some of northern Manchuria. This in turn is surrounded by a narrow band of discontinuous permafrost with thicknesses of up to 60 m which ultimately tapers into mere islands of sporadic permafrost with thicknesses of 15 m or less (Figure 6).

Soviet theorists believe glaciation and permafrost are antagonistic: permafrost, being found in severely continental climates with relatively thin snow cover; glaciation, being associated with maritime polar regions with great potential for deep snow. Their notion is supported well by the fact that the deepest of permafrost is located in Yakutia, the most landlocked of all high-latitude areas. It is here that all the basic prerequisites for permafrost exist in abundance: long periods of low temperatures; light, almost negligible precipitation; thin snow cover; cloudless winter skies (for rapid terrestrial radiation); many calms and temperature inversions (especially in river valleys); short, dry, relatively cool summers (with very cool nights).[74]

*Characteristics.* Permafrost ground may consist of dry rock, sand, or soil. The frozen subsurface moisture serves as a cementing agency, binding rock and soil fragments into an impervious mass. Pure underground ice and unfrozen ground water (taliks) may exist at various levels both within and without the permafrost. But, for the most part, only the surface stratum, the so-called active zone or layer, freezes and thaws seasonally.

The depth of the active zone varies from less than a meter in the high Arctic to roughly five meters in southern Siberia. The zone literally takes on the consistency of butter during summer because the still-frozen permafrost is impermeable to the vadose water. On steep slopes, these thawings may give rise to substantial earthflows. On gradual vegetated slopes, slow-moving (1 to 5 cm per year) frost creep or solifluction lobes may develop. On level surfaces, where there are sufficient moisture-bearing sands and silts, quicksand may be a factor. More likely, swamps or bogs (*mari*) may arise on this kind of relief, especially if the level ground is part of a floodplain.

With the freezing of the active zone between October and March, intense dynamic pressures are created, causing the horizontal movement of soil water and mud. Soil thermometers are broken, fence posts are shifted, and structural foundations crack.

This is called the "annual pulsation," which occurs in association with a collective geomorphic process known as frost action. The latter includes a variety of interrelated weathering and erosional phenomena which shape the Siberian landscape, among which are: frost wedging; frost cracking; and frost heave.

Where exposed bedrock is concerned, frost wedging or shattering is important. It is largely through this mechanism that talus and scree cones, blockfields, and rock streams or glaciers are created in high-latitude and mountainous territories. Moreover, silt is considered to be the finest-grained texture that can be weathered by this process, meaning that Siberian soils are not only infertile because of their high acid content, but they are also coarse.[75] This is a significant constraint with respect to agricultural potentials.

Concerning the disruption of the Siberian landscape, frost cracking is even more important than frost wedging. Frozen ground contracts at a magnitude that is five times greater than that of steel. Thus, even slight frosts may crack the Siberian earth. In the dead of winter in Yakutia, extremely low temperatures may cause the ground to pop like popcorn, literally shattering the earth. After it is established a crack will be filled with summer meltwater, which upon exposure to yearly freezing and thawing steadily grows until an ice wedge is formed. This activity on poorly drained peat bogs frequently leads to the development of temporary frost mounds known as palsas. Where ice wedges are interconnected (ice-wedge polygons), mounded or serrated surfaces may pose formidable obstacle to wheeled vehicles, especially in summer. This necessitates the use of tracked vehicles, which, as we shall learn, damage the tundra and Subarctic forest floors.

Frost heave and thrusting are related to the formation of ice wedges, but not exclusively restricted to that process. Frost heave is actual ground movement induced by the 9 percent volume change which occurs when water converts to ice and to the growth of ice crystals when additional water is drawn from the active zone or water table. It is well known as a major limitation to civil engineering. In Siberia, railroad bridges have been deformed, track has buckled (up to 15 cm), and utility and fence posts have been ejected by frost heave. These events are especially likely on poorly drained permafrost ground.

*Effects on Relief.* Permafrost is intrinsically tied to the Siberian landscape. Any disruption of the relief affects the permafrost and vice versa. The damage can be natural or artificial; the results are essentially the same.

The freezing and thawing of the active layer favor the lateral separation of rock and soil, creating the phenomenon of patterned ground preeminently in the arctic and alpine tundra. This includes polygonal ground, stone rings, and (on slopes) stone stripes. Such patterns are of little consequence to human land use, except as they affect transportation and general mobility.

More significant to ground displacement are pingos, which are permanent ice-cored mounds or hills of 50 to 600 m in diameter and which grow actively from a few centimeters to half a meter per year. One special property of pingos is their potential value as a pure water source, which is curiously scarce in northern realms (see next section). As pingos grow in size, tension cracks are formed on their summits in which pools of potable meltwater collect.

The balance between permafrost and relief is nowhere more delicate than in the case of thermokarst. Whereas, the karst topography of middle and low latitude environments is determined by the chemical reduction of limestone, thermokarst topography is produced by the physical disruption of the permafrost regime, specifically the melting of underground ice. The resultant landforms are similar in both instances: caverns; disappearing streams; sinkholes, sink ponds, and sink lakes; hummocky mounds; and flat-floored valleys. In the thermokarst process, however, the creation of these landforms can occur over a relatively short period of time, often as long as it takes for exposed ice masses to melt.

32    Soviet Resource Development

Thermokarst is produced by downwearing (subsidence) or by the backwearing (undercutting) of a surface water body. The various ways by which this can take place range from the simplest of disruptions (a single passage of a vehicle, wildlife trails) to vegetational changes, stream-channel shifts, and fire. Usually, the disruptions involve the exposure of ice wedges and ice-wedge polygons, which immediately begin to thaw in temperatures above freezing. Removal of vegetation on ice-wedge polygons, either naturally or artifically, leads to the creation of thermokarst mounds between the receding ice wedges. Continued thawing of the ice wedges causes slumping. If the slumping proceeds far enough, the space may be filled by a thaw lake. The presence of the lake accelerates the melting of the permafrost, which simply brings more slumping. Ultimately, a natural balance between landform and permafrost is achieved, at which time an *alas* has formed (Figure 7a). This is a huge flat-floored depression similar to an uvala or polje in a karst landscape. This type of downworn thermokarst is prevalent in the Yakutian Lowland and on parts of the Aldan Upland. In fact, some 60 percent of the hay production of the Yakutian Lowland is raised on alases.[76]

When meandering streams expose frost wedges along their undercut slopes, they are implementing the first stage of backwearing. The weakened ice wedge either shrinks or collapses in the summer sun. Either way, the active layer flows into the stream, either slowly as with solifluction or rapidly as with mudflows. Eventually, large amphitheater-like thermocirques may be created within the valley sides (Figure 7b). This kind of thermokarst development is observed along the Aldan and Yana rivers of Yakutia and along the Taz River in the Lower Ob gas region. Mudflows along the Taz swept away portions of the settlement of Gaz-Sale during a recent flood season. Planners evidently were unaware of the dangers of thermokarst when they approved the town site.[77]

*Effects on Drainage and Water Supply.* A discussion of permafrost as a constraint to the utilization of Siberian water is complicated by the multipurpose nature of the resource. Water is used in Siberia as a means of transport (by boat or barge during summer and when frozen in winter as motor roads), notably as a source of hydropower, and for domestic, industrial, and agricultural purposes.

It is estimated that Siberia contains almost a quarter of the world's surface reserves of freshwater.[78] Lake Baikal alone retains 18 percent, and Siberian streams comprise four-fifths of the Soviet river runoff or 6 percent of the global total. Thus, gross amounts of surface water hardly represent an obstacle to the economic development of the region.

Permafrost inhibits the volumes of available subsurface water. This can be seen clearly in the fact that Siberia maintains only 2 percent of the world's ground water budget. The potential base flow is simply frozen.[79]

Otherwise, small rivers are forced by the permafrost to flow at or near the surface, eroding laterally instead of

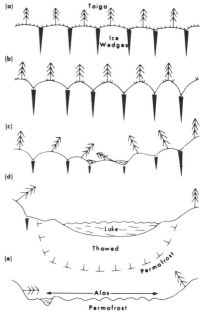

**7a.**    Schematic representation of alas development. (a) Original taiga lowland surface underlain with ice wedges; (b) The first stage after disturbance is the development of thermokarst mounds; (c) Continued thawing and slumping leads to a small central depression; (d) A lake forms in the depression and aids in increasing the size of the alas; (e) The final product is a flat-floored depression with steep sides (alas). Note that permafrost reestablishes itself near the surface of the alas in this final stage.

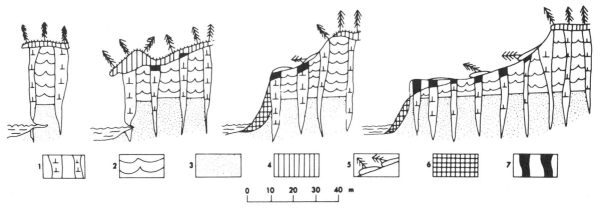

**7b.**    Thermocirque development along a river bank. 1. Ice wedges; 2. Frozen loams; 3. Frozen sand; 4. Active layer; 5. Mud flows; 6. Transported material; 7. Casts of ice wedges.

Figure 7    SOURCE: Larry Price, *The Periglacial Environment, Permafrost, and Man,* pp. 21, 23.

downcutting. Consequently, Siberian valleys are far wider than their stream volume would appear to dictate. Large rivers may cut deeply into the permafrost at flood stage. This lowers the upper surface of the permafrost and may cause extensive gullying along the bluffs, initiating thermokarst processes. The Tynda River in the BAM service area, for example, has many shoreline gullies that are 12 to 15 m wide and 3 m deep. The fact is that most Siberian streams are not well developed because of the permafrost and low amounts of precipitation. As in all Subarctic environments, there is a tendency for the valleys to become filled with the detritus of frost action and mass wasting because the debris cannot be removed effectively by the streams.

Yet, as we have noted above, the rivers are the only reliable source of water; groundwater is rarely available. No wonder the higher population densities of Siberia flank the major rivers and streams. On the smaller rivers and interfluves, water may be obtained only at great expense and effort. The bigger Siberian rivers represent the least costly alternative for water supply.

The main constraint to the use of these rivers is that they flow in the wrong direction—away from the primary population centers—across the permafrost and into frozen seas. In the case of West Siberia, the mouths of the Ob and Yenisei are frozen for fully two months after the spring breakup of their mountain tributaries. The reverse is true in the fall: the freezing of the deltas occurs in early October; the freezing of the headwaters is not complete until late November or early December (Figures 8a and 8b). Thus, West Siberian (and to a lesser degree, Pacific Siberian) rivers have two flood seasons, the stronger in spring, the weaker in fall. The spring breakup is accompanied by ice jams, leading to destruction of river banks, bridge abutments and supports, and shoreline structures. The low-lying concavity of the West Siberian Plain merely encourages extensive flooding, lake formation, and marshification. Flooding is enhanced by permafrost that is increasingly prevalent poleward of 60°N because the soil and vadose water of the active zone is prevented from percolating to the natural water table.

Stagnation of the flood waters in strongly mineralized lakes and swamps serves as a perfect breeding ground for bloodsucking insects, including mosquitoes (70 to 80 percent), midges (18 to 28 percent), horseflies, wood lice, ticks, and gnats.[80] Hatching of these insects begins in May in the Vasyugan Swamps and continues through August. They swarm throughout July. "Emerging from his tent, a person can be covered with mosquitoes in 2 to 3 minutes."[81] In summer, human work is constrained as much by mosquitoes as by the swamps. Massive outbreaks of mosquitoes in Siberia have reduced labor productivity there by 40 to 75 percent.

The stagnant pools, huge slow-moving rivers, and high water tables in general render West Siberia one of the wettest regions on earth. Indeed, four-fifths of the area or almost 2 million km² is considered to be saturated or supersaturated.

But, the abundance and quasi-ubiquity of West Siberian water are no substitute for water quality. Good water

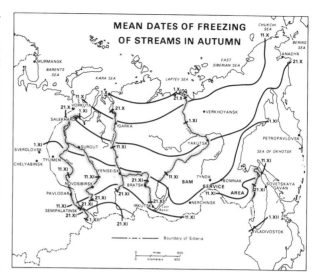

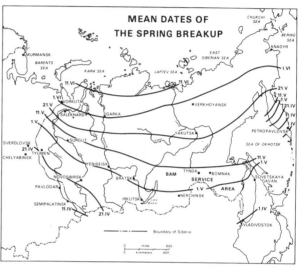

Figure 8
SOURCE: Paul E. Lydolph, *Climates of the Soviet Union*, p. 266.

is that which is oxygen-rich, normally mineralized, and clean. When it is in a liquid state, the surface water of West Siberia tends to be low in oxygen, methane-rich, foul in taste, and brown in color. When ice forms on the lakes and rivers, the content of organic matter, salts, and radioactive substances increases. The longer the ice lasts, the poorer the quality of the water; for oxygen to be absorbed, water must be exposed to the air, and under the ice this is impossible. Fairly frequent cloud cover, especially north of 60°N, is in part responsible for the low levels of dissolved oxygen.

Waters that are poor in oxygen are apparently endemic to West Siberia, and would persist in that state with or without human interference. The reduction of the oxygen levels occurs as a result of the oxidation of organic matter derived from the swamps and the oxidation of iron and manganese compounds. This natural biochemical oxygen demand (BOD) has led to fish kills and eutrophication. In fact, one-hundred years ago, before the Ob was polluted by domestic and industrial wastes, a Russian author wrote:[82]

> Along the entire Lower Ob, the water of winter begins to change color; it has an unpleasant taste and bubbles [from the methane]. Earlier than elsewhere, the water stagnates in Obdorsk [Salekhard] where even the ice yields water with a foul, bitter taste. Therefore, local residents move beyond the ice, several versts away from the village.

Permafrost is more of an environmental constraint in Pacific Siberia than it is in West Siberia, which is closer to the moderating influence of the Atlantic. In Pacific Siberia, surface water tends to be more channelized and therefore less ubiquitous than it is west of the Yenisei. Suslov has noted that there is not enough water to be had year-round in Pacific Siberia because of the eight-month-long winters. This is especially true of settlements that are remote from the major rivers, for smaller streams simply freeze to the bottom.

Though limited, groundwater is available in permafrost regions. Suprapermafrost water is water which stands on the surface of the ground in summer. It presents the illusion of abundance, but it is frozen in winter and rancid in summer. In general, only the very largest of reservoirs of this type of water may be used for water supply. Intrapermafrost water is difficult to locate because it is locked with very few outlets into the permafrost. It is located in the same way that oil and gas are found, with seismic-prospecting instruments. Difficult to locate and generally sporadic, intrapermafrost water is normally too small in volume to satisfy the needs of large settlements. Subpermafrost water is the most dependable source of ground water in permafrost regions, since it never freezes and is kept fresh by the water-tight permafrost roof. It commonly emerges at ground level as springs. Where springs are inadequate, costly, deep wells must be dug, the casings of which are heated where they are in contact with permafrost.

Where neither groundwater nor surface water is available in Siberia, residents have been forced to melt ice or snow to obtain their drinking water. Ingenious devices have been invented in order to cope with the scarcity.[83] But again, these methods are neither sufficient nor efficient enough to sustain large cities.

Interestingly, water presently is more precious than Udokan copper and Molodezhny asbestos to construction workers within the BAM service area. Soviet hydrologists and hydrogeologists have conducted an intensive campaign to locate groundwater stores in and around the new and potential settlements. Subpermafrost water supplies have been discovered in Zvezdny, but in Niya and Magistralny the explorers as yet have not been rewarded. The search is especially difficult in regions of thick crystallized rock or especially broad lenses of permafrost. Known fault lines help to discern the taliks. The presence of icings (see Microscale Physical Limitations) also assists in the search. The city of Tynda is supplied with water from groundwater icings. Finally, near the site of the projected Udokan copper beneficiation plant,

several enormous taliks have been discovered in sandstone aquifers and deposits of unconsolidated rock.[84]

*Effects on Human Activity. 1. Transportation.* Most of Siberia is devoid of roads and railroads at the present time in part because of the lack of demand and in part because of the high costs of construction in severe environments. In comparison with the average expenditures for all-weather surfaced roadways in the developed western USSR, road construction expenses in Siberia are 1.6 to 1.7 times higher.[85] Such motor roads in the Middle Ob swamps cost 0.5 million rubles per kilometer, and on permafrost in the Lower Ob region, they require 1.1 to 1.6 million rubles per kilometer.[86] Winter roads are cheaper alternatives (20 to 50 rubles per km), but by definition they are temporary and reflect similar costs of maintenance.[87]

Railroads are even more expensive, but they are more versatile than other forms of transportation and are particularly advantageous where bulk cargo is concerned. Two major railroad construction projects have been under way in Siberia. Both lie on permafrost. The first is the Surgut-Urengoi railway which links the Middle Ob oil fields with the Lower Ob gas fields. The second is the BAM railroad which will connect Central Siberia with the Pacific. No officially acknowledged expenses have been published for either project, but estimates can be made. Before major permanent roads and railroads were built in the permafrost zone of the Lower Ob in the early 1960s, railroad construction costs per kilometer of a line designed to handle a million tons of freight per annum were estimated to be 160,000 rubles. A similar length of highway was figured at 141,000 rubles, or 8 to 11 times cheaper than the actual construction costs just given. Assuming that the margin of error was the same for railroad expenditures, my estimated cost for the construction of the Surgut-Urengoi railroad is 1.8 million rubles per kilometer. This compares well to the expenses that have been suggested unofficially for the BAM: about a million rubles per kilometer. Including all expenses (track-laying, auxiliary support, and infrastructure), my conservative cost estimates for the entire BAM project run in excess of 11 billion rubles (over 15 billion 1971 dollars).[88]

The quoted expenses do not include subsequent maintenance costs, which on permafrost can be exorbitant. In the 1960s, yearly expenditures on motor road maintenance in the Lower Ob region averaged about 30 percent of the capital investment, compared to 6 percent for railroads. Most of the corduroy roads then built in the Middle Ob oil fields sank into the bogs after their first year in use. On permafrost, "washboarding" was a problem, except where the roads were appropriately insulated. For instance, Siberian oil and gas-field workers have relied on a system of special "floating" roads composed of easily accessible frozen sphagnum subgrade and a surface layer of dry earth that supposedly has kept the peat frozen through summer.

Yet, the road system, even in relatively developed West Siberia, is far from adequate. The controversy over the lack of oil exploration in new areas of the Middle Ob is as much a road problem as it is one of lack of attention. Most of the new sites are 100 to 200 km from the closest advanced support base, and they can be reached only by boat or helicopter. More than 400 km of surfaced roads are designated for the region under the present plan, but the complaint is that the roads will arrive only after a rig has become operational.[89]

Problems of road maintenance on permafrost include: washboarding; subsidence; spring-flood destruction of bridges; slumping and landslides, often burying the road; and, worst of all, icings.[90] Railroads also are plagued by these difficulties.

To avoid tragic consequences in railroad building, an intimate inventory of the permafrost conditions should be carried out; otherwise, the track will be deformed. Not only are there direct costs of repair and maintenance to consider when rails and subgrade become warped, there are also indirect costs to contemplate, such as the expenses involved in the slower delivery of freight as a result of the disruption. In laying track, excavation should be avoided wherever possible, particularly in regions of underground ice. The vegetation should not be removed. In pouring the embankment, it is inadvisable to use local silty sands. The fill pits become quagmires and, on roadbeds built of such materials, the subgrade and ballast shift, the rails buckle, and the palsas arise. Where pilings are required (bridge sites, overpasses, and large culverts), the penetration depth of the supports should be no less than three times the depth of the active zone.[91]

Thus, railroad construction in northern environments must be conducted with the highest regard for permafrost. Initially, the type of permafrost on which the track will be laid is identified. In general, continuous permafrost is more stable than its discontinuous or sporadic forms. The critical factor is the average annual temperature of the ground. When this is −4 to −5°C, the depths of seasonal frost and thaw are in balance. A drop in that temperature brings a strengthening of the permafrost and greater stability of the thermal regime. An increase in the temperature encourages destruction of the permafrost and instability.

Usually, any removal of the overlying vegetation creates instability, subsidence, *mar* (bog) formation, gullying, solifluction, and any number of thermokarst processes. This is especially true when the vegetation being removed is peat moss, which serves as permafrost insulation. Stripping of peat moss in order to lay a railroad bed instigates a rise in ground temperature of 1 to 2°C, enough to cause partial thawing of ice wedges in the continuous zone and total melting of them in discontinuous and sporadic regions.[92]

Particularly damaging in continuous permafrost areas is the accumulation of water adjacent to railway embankments. In well-designed railroad beds, sufficient culverts and overpasses allow free passage of such flood or meltwater, so that it has little time to warm. Otherwise, stagnant water accelerates melting by raising ground temperatures by 3 to 4°C. Thermokarst processes, especially thaw-lake phenomena, begin resulting in differential settlement of the roadbed. The rate of subgrade subsidence in these conditions may be as much as 30 to 50

cm during the first year, followed by a gradual deceleration. In discontinuous permafrost, ground settlement may not cease for ten years.

Great care should be taken in the selection of the materials and design of the railway embankment. These should be suited to not only the type of permafrost but also the ground on which the embankment is being laid. Soviet engineers have found that subgrades composed of large rock fragments (cobbles and larger) raised to a height of 3 m are best for the BAM service area. In general, when the materials are of the same composition as the basement rock, there is a net cooling and the embankment becomes incorporated by the permafrost, effectively damming drainage systems. On earth composed of fine-textured materials, embankments should be lower (between 1.5 and 3 m high) in order to maintain the stability of the permafrost. If the height of the embankment is increased beyond 3 m on this kind of surface, the temperature of the subgrade increases and the permafrost thaws.

In discontinuous and sporadic permafrost areas, some degradation should be expected even with appropriate embankment materials and design. The subsidence accompanying this degradational process can be calculated depending on whether the embankment was poured in winter or summer. The volumes of subgrade materials, which are needed to compensate for the loss engendered by the anticipated subsidence, should be included in the volumes that are required to build a roadbed without subsidence. In the BAM service area, these compensating volumes vary from 1.2 to 4.2 percent of the amounts for the base volumes. Experts calculate that by adding in the subsidence increment before the roadbed begins to settle, some 40 million rubles of subsequent maintenance costs can be saved on the BAM alone.[93]

Where railroads have been built without proper respect for the permafrost in Siberia, the results have been disastrous. The best example of failure is the Salekhard-Nadym railroad, which was under construction on continuous permafrost in the late 1940s and early 1950s, but was then abandoned. It now serves as a model of how not to build on permafrost. Along its entire length, the insulating vegetation was stripped away, disrupting the heat-exchange process. The construction of trestle bridges and the pouring of the embankment caused a redistribution of the snow cover and changed the normal cycle of cryoplanation; certain parts of the embankment thawed more quickly than others, producing a roller-coaster effect. The surface of the permafrost rose into the embankment. This became an impenetrable wall to summer melt-water, creating thaw lakes and expanding the volumes of rancid suprapermafrost ground water. In turn, this led to the formation of thermokarst mounds, subsidence, thermokarst lakes, and further deformation of the roadbed. The embankment was eroded, flooded, and at points broken by frost heave and palsas.[94]

With the discovery and exploitation of natural gas in the Lower Ob region, a segment of the railroad was rehabilitated from Nadym, the gas-development center, to Pangody in the Medvezhye field, and later on to Novy

Urengoi in the Urengoi field. The cost of the renovation was 333,000 rubles per km![95]

In the absence of adequate highways and railroads, Siberians are compelled to rely on river and air transport. Despite the brief shipping season (May-October), shallow rivers, and a virtually constant need for the dredging of shifting shoals and bars, the Siberian fleet is the only practical means of hauling bulk cargoes at this time. The cost of river shipment within the region is one-seventh to one-tenth the cost of trucking and 1/15 to 1/17 the cost of air transport (Table 9). The constraints imposed by the periglacial environments (river icings, floods, and placer deposits) are reduced by correct river forecasting, dams, intensive dredging, and the use of low-draft, heavy-cargo tugs and barges. Today, Siberia's navigable waterways are longer than 75,000 km, and freight turnover is up 320 percent over the output of 1960. Navigation periods and lengths have been extended: with the use of heavy-duty dredging equipment in the Lower Ob region (Nadym River), the Lena River system (Aldan River) and the Amur Basin (especially the Bureya River); by means of atomic ice breakers across the Barents and Kara seas from Murmansk to the West Siberian gas fields, Norilsk, and beyond; and along the shores of Lake Baikal (to help supply the BAM service area together with the Lena and Amur fleets).[96] As indicated earlier, the Lena system is particularly sensitive to drought and, in dry years, navigation on the river is severely hindered.

Despite the high costs, air transport is used to a much higher degree in Siberia than elsewhere in the country because of permafrost and other natural constraints. In addition, shift-work and, in many instances, the sheer need for delivery speed encourage its employment. With or without reliable roads, many small Siberian communities have air strips for regular passenger and mail service. In permafrost-plagued northern-rim regions, geologists, fishermen, and hunters are supplied by ski-planes during winter and by seaplanes that land on lakes and rivers in summer. Soviet heavy-cargo aircraft of the Antonov class (AN-12, AN-26, AN-72) fly up to 700 km/hr and carry up to 45 tons of freight. Where terrain is too rough or too boggy (Yakutia and northeast Siberia, West Siberian swamps, and parts of the BAM service area), heavy-cargo and passenger helicopters of the Mil series (MI-4, MI-6, and MI-8) are utilized. Smaller helicopters are flown for purposes of range management on certain reindeer collectives. The obvious advantage of air transport over other conveyances in Siberia is that it can be used all year.

Otherwise, there is an unusually heavy reliance on tracked vehicles. As has been witnessed in Alaska and Canada, such vehicles in the tundra, even with a single passage, have more or less permanently scarred the landscape. Thus, on part of the Yakutian tundra, where tractors passed only a few times at least a decade ago, the vegetation was damaged, the thermal exchange was disrupted, and thermokarst processes were triggered. The path, which at the time of disruption was no more than four meters wide, today has downworn and expanded by several dozen meters.[97]

In part as a reaction to the disadvantages posed by the tracked vehicle in northern realms, modern and experimental transport alternatives have evolved in the Soviet Union. Snowmobiles have been employed by reindeer herders for at least a decade. There has been talk about using heavy-cargo hovercraft over Siberian swamps and tundra. Supporters of dirigibles periodically call for their use, but they have yet to be introduced. Dirigibles as freight carriers allegedly are four and a half times cheaper than aircraft, making them competitive with motor vehicles, and they have the advantage of year-round service.[98]

*2. Other Construction.* Other types of construction are dependent largely on the efficiency of logistics. Once reliable means of transport are assured, residences, administrative structures, utility requirements and a minimum of infrastructure may be established. Special designs and building sites are required for construction on permafrost.

In the erection of buildings, particular significance must be given to the stability of the foundation. Lacking this understanding, Siberian peasants traditionally built their rough-hewn wooden izbas directly on fine-grained soil. Today, only the second stories of these dwellings are visible at ground level in Yakutsk and other northern cities.

Yakutsk is the headquarters of the Soviet Permafrost Institute, whose research and recommendations for Arctic construction have been used worldwide. Scientists early determined that when the foundation rock is bedrock, sand, or gravel, permafrost can be disregarded. However, such materials ordinarily are not available on river terraces and bluffs, where many Siberian towns and cities are located. On permafrost that is discontinuous and sporadic, if the depth and extent of the frozen substructure are known, it is sometimes practical to remove or thaw the ground.

On continuous permafrost, buildings are set up on pilings. Soviet construction workers pioneered the use of steam drilling in such ground. The holes may be saturated with oil and the pilings greased. The latter then are

TABLE 9
Cost of Haulage in Kopecks
per Ton-Kilometer in Siberia

| Conveyance | Rate (kopecks per ton-km) | |
|---|---|---|
| | 1967[a] | 1978 |
| Motor vehicle | 2.4 | 12.0[b] |
| Railroad | 0.9 | |
| Partial service | — | 5.0[b] |
| Full service | — | 2.6[b] |
| River | 0.24 | 1.2–1.7[c] |
| Air transport | — | 20.4–25.5[c] |
| Oil Pipeline | 0.09–0.12 | — |

[a]"Voprosy promyshlennogo razvitiya rayonov Severa" [Problems of industrial development of regions of the North], *Problemy Severa*, no. 12 (1967): 177; these data were for a one-million-ton shipment over an average of 500 km.
[b]A. Pogrebnoi, et al. "Tynda: Rezervy ispolzuyem" [Tynda: We use the reserves], *Gudok*, 26 June 1978, p. 3; railway and motor vehicle data are for the "Little BAM" service area.
[c]V. Degtyarev, Ye. Zin, and N. Permichev, "Rechnoi transport Sibiri i Dalnego Vostoka" [River transport in Siberia and the Far East], *Rechnoi transport*, no. 3 (1978): 21.

driven into the ground to a depth that is two or three times that of the active zone. The pilings may be wood or metal, but recently in Mirny, Yakutsk, Magadan, and now in the BAM service area, hollow, kerosene-filled steel pipes have been used. The kerosene circulates as a coolant, and the permafrost remains frozen around the pipe at a radius of 12 meters.[99] The deep insertion of pilings (15 meters or more) normally neutralizes problems of frost heave.

Once the pilings are in place, the superstructure is built to heights that are usually lower than the Soviet average. The floors are double- or triple-layered and insulated. In the 1940s and 1950s, this insulation was dry peat or cinders. Today, lighter polymers are becoming available. In some instances, vented subcellars that can be opened in winter and closed in summer are used. Walls and foundations frequently are hollow, which permits the installation of refrigerating pipe, again open in winter and closed in summer. Standing water under these buildings is drained continuously in the warm season. The buildings ordinarily are oriented so that the least possible wall area is exposed to the sun; otherwise, the contiguous permafrost could be melted by surplus radiant heat emanating from the building. North-facing walls are built without windows.

In the past, these recommended procedures often have been ignored by the construction industry. Heavy-brick construction materials and mid-latitude architecture were employed widely in Siberia before 1960. In some Arctic cities only 20 to 30 percent of the buildings were built on stable foundations. This led to severe deformation and damage to the superstructure (Figure 9). Most of the deformation could be traced to the creation of enlarged taliks and quicksand.

Soviet plumbing systems are notoriously bad. Water and sewage pipe, where it exists at all in Siberia, manifestly must be protected or heated. In discontinuous or sporadic permafrost, the pipe may be buried at a depth where the temperature range is slight and minimum temperature is over −2° C. The trench should be appropriately insulated with natural or synthetic materials. In continuous permafrost, the ground simply does not permit pipe burial. Instead, above-ground heated utilidors may be used. In provincial towns and villages, pit privies and individually carried nightsoil buckets are more the rule. The raw sewage is dumped at designated spots along the rivers or into sewerage lagoons. In winter, the effluent simply freezes until the spring thaw. Obviously, modern sewage treatment plants are rare. "River water in the vicinity of almost all cities of the Soviet North is heavily polluted with fecal matter."[100]

Hydropower projects in permafrost areas have been under construction since 1960. Three major reservoirs have been created in the continuous zone; on the Vilyui, the Khantaika and the Kolyma. One more is slated to be filled behind the Kureika dam in the 1980s. Although we can speculate on the damage wrought to the permafrost by reservoir inundation, little factual information is yet available to the public. Representatives of the Yakutsk Permafrost Institute monitor the impact of the Vilyui Reservoir, which has been in existence since the mid

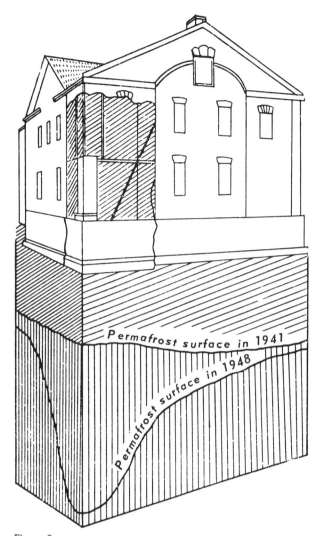

Figure 9
SOURCE: V. V. Kryuchkov, *Kraini Sever: Problemy ratsionalnogo ispolzovaniya prirodnykh resursov* [The extreme North: Problems of rational utilization of natural resources], p. 93.

1960s, and the Kolyma Reservoir is being studied by the Aborigen station. Their studies are to assist dam builders at other Siberian sites.[101] No doubt shallow lagoons along the reservoir edges serve as notorious breeding grounds for bloodsucking insects in summer.

*3. Oil and Gas Operations.* West Siberian oil and gas operations are constrained by permafrost both directly in the Lower Ob gas fields and indirectly in the Middle Ob oil fields, whose floods are in part a response to downstream blockage by permanently frozen ground. Summer inundation in both locations restricts pipeline-laying to the intensely cold winter months. Some of the oil fields can be reached only by boat in the summer. Enormous expanses remain inaccessible.

Permafrost affects oil and gas activities both in exploration and in development. In the initial exploratory phases, seismic reflection and refraction are distorted by the massively frozen ground. After the discovery of the Gubkin gas field in 1965, 21 wells were drilled rapidly over a relatively small area. The operations were insulated improperly and, owing to the melting of the permafrost, a number of rigs collapsed into thermokarst caverns that turned out to be 25 m deep.[102]

Drilling is hampered in all phases. Small ground-fill areas are raised into islets on which drilling platforms are established. From a single isolated platform, dozens of sloping shafts are drilled by means of a method known as 'cluster drilling.' Some cluster-drilling rigs are borne on crane wheels and rails, so that they can be moved easily without dismantling. In isolated instances, wildcat rigs that include a derrick, an in-place drillstring, engines, substructure, and drawworks are mounted in a single package on air cushions and towed by caterpillar tractor over boggy terrain.[103] Otherwise, Soviet rigs are massive structures of up to 184 feet high. They are heavy and cumbersome and require 30 to 90 days for *any* move from one location to another. Modern jack-up rigs are almost unknown in the Soviet Union. Thus, because of protracted drilling-site changes, equipment shortages, and inferior rig quality, West Siberian drilling equipment operates only one day out of three.[104]

Technological quality is covered elsewhere in this volume by Meyerhoff. A brief summary is appropriate here. The Soviet oil and gas industry relies on an outmoded basic exploration tool known as the turbodrill. In turbodrilling, the drill bit is not turned by rotation of the drillstring, as in rotary drilling, but by a downhold turbine, which is driven hydraulically by fluid-injection through the drillstring. It has not been improved significantly since 1950, and despite a government order to switch to modern rotary drilling in 1965, 75 percent of Soviet rigs remain turbodrills. The others are Czechoslovak rotary-type rigs (19 percent) or turbodrills with a rotary table (6 percent) that can be used to penetrate hard strata at depths below which the turbodrill jet alone is least effective.

Because of the emphasis on the turbodrill, drilling productivity is low: 350 m per rig per month for exploratory drilling and 1,500 m per rig per month for development drilling. The average depth of a wildcat well is roughly 3,000 m; a development well—2,300 m. At the latter depths, Soviet tubular steels begin to break down. "During the winter, the drill pipe freezes and shatters like glass [and] at 5,000 m, the drill pipe commonly parts of its own weight."[105] Consequently, drilling times are lengthy. A 3,000-m well cannot be drilled in under 90 days. In the United States, a maximum of 34 days is required for the same depth.

As Soviet drilling operations have gone deeper into the earth and have expanded farther into Siberia, drilling costs have spiraled also. Since 1958, when exploratory drilling averaged 105 rubles per meter, expenses have tripled. Simultaneously, outlays for development drilling have soared from 48 rubles to 96 rubles per meter.[106]

Although lagging in terms of planned requirements, pipelines in the USSR are being laid at the rate of one Alaska pipeline every four to five weeks.[107] In West Siberia, this can be done only in winter. The large-diameter (120 cm, 140 cm) pipe, some of it imported from Western Europe, Japan and Rumania, is delivered to the fields in summer and welded into longer segments. When the weather becomes cold enough to freeze the bogs and rivers, pipeline teams link together sledge-mounted caravans containing equipment, residences, dining rooms, baths, and power units. By means of these self-contained units, the pipe is laid swiftly and relatively cheaply.

Unlike their North American counterparts, Soviet authorities are convinced that oil and gas pipelines in West Siberia should be laid underground, especially in areas vested with deep permafrost. This conclusion may derive from the problems that have arisen with two medium-diameter (70 cm) pipelines that were laid above ground between the Messoyakha gas field and Norilsk. The high winds and radical temperature changes in that region caused numerous breaks along the lines. A third, but improved, above-ground pipeline was being built in the same area. This new gas main lies on supports with rollers that allow greater flexibility in high winds.[108]

The laying of underground pipe on permafrost requires special organization and technology. The mobile caravans are led by timber-felling teams, followed by trench-making equipment. Other groups pad the trenches with insulation. The pipefitters and welders are housed on special platforms between the pipe-support equipment. The pipe is welded together and left behind for pipe-placement teams.

To add to the constraints of permafrost and river crossings, the majority of earth in the swamps and peat bogs is too light and makes for poor ballast. Thus, if the pipe is not properly weighted, it simply erupts to the surface. In the past, Soviet pipe-layers have had to use costly 40-ton reinforced-concrete weights. Recently, an harpoon-anchorage system has been tested successfully. The harpoon device is attached to a crawler-tread-equipped tractor. The anchors—cement-filled steel cylinders—are shot into the solid ground to a maximum depth of three meters, where self-opening blades flare out to help secure the anchorage. A retainer linked to the opposite-facing anchors is looped firmly over the pipe, ensuring its stability. Soviet authorities estimate that 100,000 rubles per km are saved by obviating the heavy concrete, which had to be hauled into these remote regions at great expense.[109]

The impact of the constraints of northern environments on the construction times required for pipe-laying may be illustrated by standard conversion coefficients that have been established by the Soviet planning and construction agencies (Table 10). The coefficients (1.4 and 1.2) are based on unidentified factors of "northernness," presumably low temperatures, long, cold winters, permafrost and the like. For areas exposed to precipitation for more than 120 days per annum, the coefficient is expanded by 20 percent. The number of crossings per 100 km also is considered: from 20 to 40 = 1.1; over 40 = 1.15. Construction times in seismic regions (mainly Transbaikalia) are adjusted according to the potential magnitudes of the earthquake, that is, a quake of 6.0 = 1.1; 6¾ = 1.15; 7.0 = 1.2. In laying pipelines on waterlogged or marshy ground, the conversion factor is modified according to the percentage of the total pipeline length that is actually supersaturated: 3 to 5% = 1.05; 5 to 10% = 1.1; 10 to 15% = 1.15; 15 to 20% = 1.2; 20 to 25% = 1.25.[110] Thus, time frames for pipeline construction

TABLE 10
Conversion Coefficients for Standard Pipeline Construction Times for Siberian
Locations (Standard Construction Time Based on European Russian Conditions = 1.0)

| Region or Place[a] | a)"Northern" Index[a] | b)Precipitation Days[a,b] (120 days a year = 1.0) | c)Crossings Index[a,c] (20–40 = 1.1 over 40 = 1.15) | d)Seismicity Index[a,d] (6.0 = 1.1; 6.75 = 1.15; 7.0 = 1.2) | e)Swampiness Index[a,c] (based on % of pipe length) | Total (a × b × c × d × e) |
|---|---|---|---|---|---|---|
| 1. Norilsk TPC | 1.4 | 1.2 | 1.15 | — | 1.05 | 2.0 |
| 2. South Yakutian TPC | 1.4 | — | 1.1 | 1.15 | 1.05 | 1.9 |
| 3. Buryat ASSR (excludes Ulan-Ude) | 1.2 | — | 1.15 | 1.2 | — | 1.7 |
| 4. Amur Oblast | 1.2 | — | 1.05 | 1.1 | 1.1 | 1.5 |
| 5. Omsk, Novosibirsk, Tomsk, and Irkutsk oblasts and Krasnoyarsk Krai north of Trans-Siberian | 1.2 | 1.2 | 1.1 | — | 1.25 | 2.0 |
| 6. Cities of Tomsk and Bratsk, Maritime Krai (excludes Vladivostok) | 1.2 | 1.2 | 1.1 | — | — | 1.6 |
| 7. Tuva Republic, Khabarovsk Krai (excludes Khabarovsk, Komsomolsk, and Sovetskaya Gavan) | 1.2 | — | 1.1 | — | 1.05 | 1.4 |
| 8. Vasyugan Swamps | 1.2 | 1.2 | 1.15 | — | 1.25 + | 2.1 + |
| 9. Chita Oblast (excludes Chita city) | 1.2 | — | 1.1 | 1.2 | — | 1.6 |

[a]Semenova (n. 110, p. 59–61).
[b]Lydolph (n. 62, p. 302).
[c]Estimated from various maps.
[d]Shabad and Mote (n. 17, pp. 93, 94), [legends translated in *SGRT*, 6, no. 5–6 (May–June 1965)].

in Siberia vary from 140 to 210 percent or more of the average completion times in the more hospitable western regions of the country.

In at least one known instance, the coefficients are too conservative. The 250-km, 70-cm Messoyakha-Norilsk aboveground pipeline required more than two years of construction, whereas an underground pipeline that is twice the diameter and over six times longer between Urengoi and Chelyabinsk was completed in less time in only slightly less severe conditions.

Engineering-Geographic Regionalizations of the USSR and the Macroscale Harshness Index

Under pressure from the government to determine the optimum correlation of technology with this multitude of influential physical factors in the Soviet North, Soviet geographers, beginning in the early 1960s, tackled the difficult task of developing applied engineering-geographic regions. It was evident that temperate-zone machinery and equipment were no match for the extreme environments of Siberia, which deadlined standard steels four to five times more frequently than their mid-latitude counterparts.[111] The solution, of course, was the innovation of so-called northern technology, which could measure up to the challenge. But, before this could be achieved, an understanding of the multifarious macro-

scale physical factors of the different environments of the Soviet North had to be obtained.

Apparently, the first geographer to respond to this need was V. F. Burkhanov, who, in the mid-1960s, developed an engineering-geographic regionalization on the basis of climatic harshness and its effect on machinery.[112] He and his students created a harshness scale that correlated harshness-based ruptures of steel with climatic controls. The key threshold values of the harshness scale were: 4.6, above which structural steel weakens and may rupture; 5.3, above which standard structural steel becomes brittle and is affected by a fifty-fold increase of ruptures; and 7.9, beyond which standard steel ceases to function. On this basis, Burkhanov divided the Soviet North into four engineering-geographic zones, each including several subzones:[113]

Zone I—the Arctic zone of maximum harshness; 10 harshness points; northern designs cost 60% more than standard ones; payoff period is 18 months; northern designs last 350% longer than standard ones.

Zone II—the Subarctic zone of high harshness; 7 harshness points; northern designs cost 45% more than standard ones; payoff period is 12 months; northern designs last 200% longer than standard ones.

Zone III—the northern harsh zone; 5 harshness points; northern modifications of standard equipment raise base costs by 25%; payoff period is 10 months; northern-modified equipment lasts 150% longer than plain standard equipment.

Zone IV—the eastern moderately harsh zone; requires northern modifications only, raising costs by 15%; payoff period is 6 months; increased length of service is 100%.

Burkhanov's subzones were functions of physical and economic conditions, similar to those discussed here (Table 11). His engineering-geographic regionalization based on the harshness of all those factors is illustrated in Figure 10.

Burkhanov's work was complemented by the independent research of Yu. M. Dogayev, a disciple of S. V. Slavin. The Dogayev engineering-geographic framework was formulated in the late 1960s and was related to a complex "conditionally adduced temperature index" and an even more complicated formula for the evaluation of standard motor vehicle performance in various northern regions. In Dogayev's system, the temperature index, which included coefficients of low temperatures and wind chill, ranged from 56 to 144 over all of Siberia. For instance, Norilsk had an index of 112.7; Verkhoyansk, 97.6, and Olekminsk (in the BAM service area) 86.6.[114] Dogayev's engineering-geographic regions and subregions comprised a host of interrelated factors, which are listed in the appendix (Appendices I and II).

There is no clear indication of the practical importance of this work to the introduction of northern designs into

Siberia. In each five-year plan since 1965, there have been renewed cries for equipment of northern specifications, and work is continuing on harshness and its relation to machine breakage, enabling some improvement of earlier research.[115]

In the meantime, northern machinery of Soviet design has come forth in rather impressive quantities. This is especially true with respect to excavators and heavy-duty dump trucks. The Uralmash Plant in Sverdlovsk has produced a lightweight northern-design excavator that bears the world's largest hydraulic shovel.[116] The country's biggest manufacturer of excavators of this type is under construction at Krasnoyarsk.[117] Included in its projected output are both rotary and stand-up excavators. These enormous machines are destined for strip and open-pit mines throughout the whole of Siberia. As reported in the Soviet press, they are intended for "Siberian development into the 21st century." Kamaz and Belorus heavy-duty dump trucks have been tested with success over the severe backwaters of the Kolyma goldfields and on the Mogocha-Chara winter road. The trucks are built with double layered windows, individual heaters for the cab, battery, and gas tank, and cold-resistant tires. Allegedly, the vehicles can withstand temperatures down to −60°C. A factory designated to produce automobiles of this design is said to be under construction in Chita.[118]

In response to the pressing demands of the oil and gas industry, Soviet trench-making and welding equipment have improved. A pipeline-construction concern in Tyumen has been made responsible for the mass production of special tracked trenching machines with mountable

TABLE 11

Geographical Factors Tending to Raise the Costs of Industrial Development in the Northern Regions of the USSR (in percent of the construction costs in the middle-latitude regions)

| Zone | Sector | Natural Geographic Factors | | | | | | | | | | |
|------|--------|---------|------|------|------|--------|-------|--------|--------|--------|-------|-------|
| | | Climate harshness (temperature, wind, humidity) | Snow, blizzards, snow drifting | Duration of polar night | Permafrost | Relief | Seismicity | Swampiness | Avalanches | Water supply | Soil conditions | Total cost increase from natural factors |
| I ARCTIC | Western | 100 | 10 | 3 | 30 | 3 | — | 7 | — | 10 | 7 | 170 |
| | Eastern | 115 | 12 | 3 | 30 | 6 | 4 | 5 | 5 | 15 | 5 | 200 |
| II SUB-ARCTIC | European[b] | 80 | 10 | 2 | — | 5 | 1 | 4 | 3 | 10 | 5 | 120 |
| | Siberian | 85 | 10 | 2 | 18 | 15 | — | 10 | — | 10 | 10 | 160 |
| | Northeast | 00 | 12 | 2 | 30 | 10 | 5 | 3 | 3 | 15 | 5 | 185 |
| III NORTH | European[b] | 40 | 10 | 2 | — | 3 | — | 5 | — | — | — | 60 |
| | Siberian | 50 | 12 | 1 | 15 | 5 | — | 6 | — | 5 | 6 | 100 |
| | Northeast | 50 | 12 | 1 | 15 | 5 | 5 | 3 | 4 | 5 | — | 100 |
| IV EAST | | 30 | 12 | — | — | 5 | 5 | — | 3 | 5 | — | 70 |

[a]Costs are expected to decline because of technical progress, the choice of optimal communication alternatives, and reduction of the delivery time of goods.
[b]Not applicable to this study.
SOURCE: Burkhanov (n. 5, p. 31).

pontoons for summer use. Thus, in a few years pipeline trenches may be dug in West Siberia beyond the winter months. Welding devices, known as North-1 and North-2, have been designed for employment in low temperatures and on large-diameter pipe.[119] The pipeline surfaces themselves now are protected from corrosion by recently innovated polymer shields.

Additionally, owing to the spiraling needs of the West Siberian oil and gas well-drilling sites for electric power—at least a third of the wells are frustrated by shortages of electricity—gas-burning floating power stations of the 'Northern Lights' series have gone on stream beyond the Arctic Circle. According to press reports, these power plants will be used "all over Siberia."[120]

Locomotives of northern specifications and permafrost-refrigerant pipes are found in the BAM service area. The diesel engines, produced at Bryansk and Voroshilovgrad, are reputed to function well in −60°C temperatures.[121] A Tynda pipe-assembly concern has distributed hundreds of kerosene-filled permafrost supports throughout the BAM service area. They are used in bridge abutments and supports, at dam sites, and in building foundations.[122]

Despite this apparently optimistic picture, as was emphasized earlier, the output of northern equipment still lags behind that of standard technology for use in the extreme environments of the USSR. This is particularly true of certain kinds of equipment. In oil and gas production, there is a great demand for seismic-prospecting machinery, data-processing equipment, pipeline valves, orifice fittings, pipeline compressors, casing tongs, modern drill bits, and, of course, rotary drills.[123] Pipe-laying equipment is in relatively short supply; in the past decade, at least one thousand of these machines were provided by the Caterpillar Corporation.[124] Bulldozers of all sizes, coal-agglomeration units, and pulp and paper machinery are needed desperately, especially those capable of resisting low temperatures. Finally, high-quality drills, tunneling devices, and track-laying machinery have not been produced in sufficient amounts domestically.

## Macroscale Physical Limitations: A Summary

As stated in the purpose, this survey is not intended to be exhaustive. Surely, there are other less evident constraints that can be added to the list just reviewed. The given data comprise only the more obvious ones.

With reference to their importance to economic development in general and to production costs in particular, the macroscale constraints may be ranked relatively. Undoubtedly, low temperatures are of paramount significance to Siberian development. To glean this, one needs only to refer to Table 4. The cold is determined directly by low-intensity insolation and related heat deficits and indirectly by the duration of the snow cover, permafrost, cloudiness, and atmospheric humidity. Also important is wind, induced by differential air pressures and enhancing the harshness of the cold by the wind-chill effect. The impact of cold and wind alone is enough to significantly reduce the productivity of labor and machinery. Low visibility, with all its implications for transportation, is influenced strongly by suspended particulates when winds are high or by fog and dense cloud covers when winds are low. The need for energy is greatly increased by the long periods of darkness and cold and, accordingly, costs of all Siberian products, even in a command economy, must be high. Increased energy conversion has a definite impact on air and water pollution, which are exacerbated by cold, low-velocity winds, temperature inversions, and reduced atmospheric turbulence. Costs of the maintenance of human health and equipment naturally are raised by the effects of cold and wind.

Of next importance is permafrost, which is responsible for the instability and impermeability of the Siberian substrata. Their impacts increase the costs of transportation and construction, may lead to extensive structural damage, and lower absolute productivity through flooding, the breeding of bloodsucking insects, and consequent long layoffs of labor and equipment. Permafrost obviously inhibits the availability of ground water—a constraint in and of itself. Indirectly, it encourages surface ice formation, which interrupts the normal exchange of oxygen between the atmosphere and exposed water bodies, leading to low dissolved oxygen levels in Siberian streams and lakes.

Finally, snow in any temperature, depending on its density and depth, tends to be a hindrance to transportation, the durability of structures, and agriculture. Directly, it affects transportation costs, visibility, and may

| Economic Factors | | | Combined Effect | | |
|---|---|---|---|---|---|
| Remoteness of region and poor transport | Poor power supply | Poor social cohesion and labor shortage | Actual cost increase in 1960–64 | Actual cost increase in 1965–66 | Expected cost rise[a] in 1970 |
| 150 | 60 | 80 | 460 | 400 | 300 |
| 180 | 60 | 90 | 530 | 500 | 400 |
| 50 | 30 | 50 | 250 | 200 | 150 |
| 100 | 40 | 60 | 360 | 320 | 250 |
| 150 | 60 | 85 | 480 | 420 | 370 |
| 40 | 20 | 40 | 160 | 120 | 80 |
| 70 | 50 | 50 | 270 | 230 | 200 |
| 50 | 30 | 50 | 230 | 200 | 160 |
| 30 | 10 | 20 | 140 | 130 | 100 |

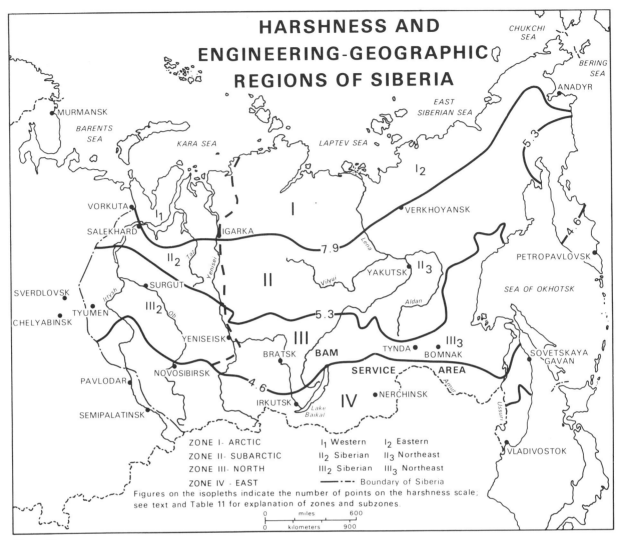

Figure 10

SOURCE: V. F. Burkhanov, "Criteria for Determining an Engineering-Geographic Boundary of the North of the USSR," *Soviet Geography: Review and Translation*, 11, no. 1 (January 1970): 30.

interrupt lines of communication. Indirectly, it induces flood or drought (depending on its presence or absence), undesirable harvest-season rains, and problems of technology and human comfort.

### Microscale Physical Limitations (Natural Hazards)

The phenomena studied so far are more or less ubiquitous to high-latitude environments. They commonly are predictable and expected. They are known quantities.

In comparison, microscale physical limitations are natural phenomena that generally are limited in time and space and occur unpredictably and often unexpectedly. They are not known quantities.

Another difference between the two sets of variables is their relative impact or force. Whereas macroscale physical limitations normally may be contained by specially designed technology, any piece of machinery, no matter how well made, may be damaged or destroyed momentarily by the force of a natural hazard. For this reason,

microscale physical limitations should be viewed as a separate category of constraints.

Four groups of natural hazards are indigenous to Siberia. They are earthquakes and volcanoes; flows, slides, and avalanches; icings; storms and tsunamis. When these categories are viewed collectively, the most hazardous zones of the region turn out to be the Soviet Far East (especially Kamchatka), the BAM service area, and the Arctic coast.

### Earthquakes and Volcanoes

Earthquakes and volcanoes often are the keys to other surface-related natural hazards. Tremors usually instigate flows, slides, and avalanches on steep slopes. Fault lines and geyser vents may serve as outlets for certain kinds of icings. Earthquakes in the ocean basins initiate seismic sea waves or tsunamis. Only catastrophic storms are unaffected by tectonic forces, and even these may be influenced indirectly by volcanic eruptions.

About 20 percent of the USSR is seismically active.[125]

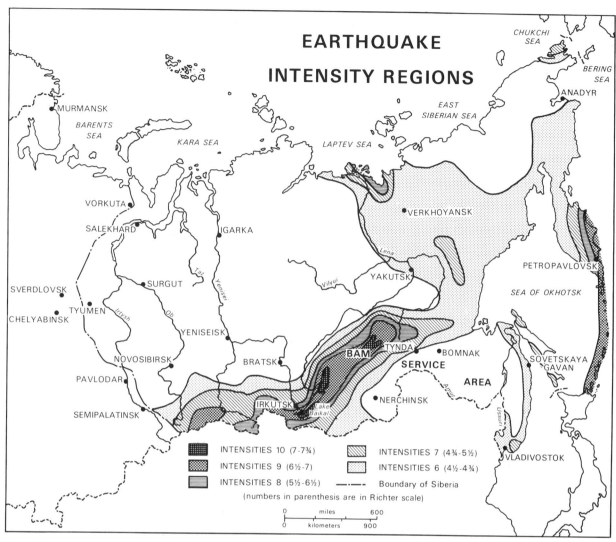

Figure 11
SOURCE: *Fiziko-geografichesky atlas mira* [Physical-geographic atlas of the world], p. 13.

Virtually all of this territory is in Asia. In Siberia, the quakes of greatest magnitude (7.8 to 8.5) tend to concentrate in the subduction zone of the east coast of Kamchatka and the Kuril Islands. Those of greatest intensity (10) occur most frequently in the Mongolian-Baikal rift zone (Figure 11). Here, a new ocean basin, represented by Lake Baikal, is being formed, with rifting of the Far East and East Siberia materializing at a rate of 3 cm per year. As a result, quakes of 7 to 7¾ (Richter) have been experienced in the South Muya, Udokan, Kodar, North Muya, and Delyun-Uran ranges. Since seismographic record-keeping began, some 30 surface earthquakes of 6 or more on the Richter scale have been observed in the BAM service area alone. Events of this magnitude are witnessed in that zone every 15 to 20 years. Within the same region, ground shaking, including all forms of seismic activity, is recorded about 1,500 times per annum. A 200-year surface quake of 7.9 struck the Muya and Chara valleys as recently as 1957. Vertical displacements of 10 to 15 m and horizontal micro-rifts of 20 m have been measured in the aftermath of the worst upheavals.[126]

Concerning their potential impact on human activities, quakes of 6.5 to 7¾ have occurred within the regions designated for the construction of the BAM railway proper, the Udokan copper mine and concentrator (prospective population: over 50,000), and the MOK hydroelectric station.[127] According to Soviet experts, it is not economically feasible to build structures capable of resisting earthquakes of these intensities (9 or more). Ordinarily in the Soviet Union, costs of structures built with earthquake protection exceed average construction costs by 20 percent.

Seismic activity in the northern section of the Mongolian-Baikal rift zone is complicated by the presence of permafrost. Thus, transverse (P) waves are accelerated by a factor of 2 or more in solidly frozen masses versus frostless ground. In these instances, ground flow is enhanced, movement of rock debris is facilitated, the active zone flows more freely, the thermal regime of the permafrost is disrupted, and liquefaction and mudflows occur.[128]

Neocene-Quaternary faults (25 million years to pres-

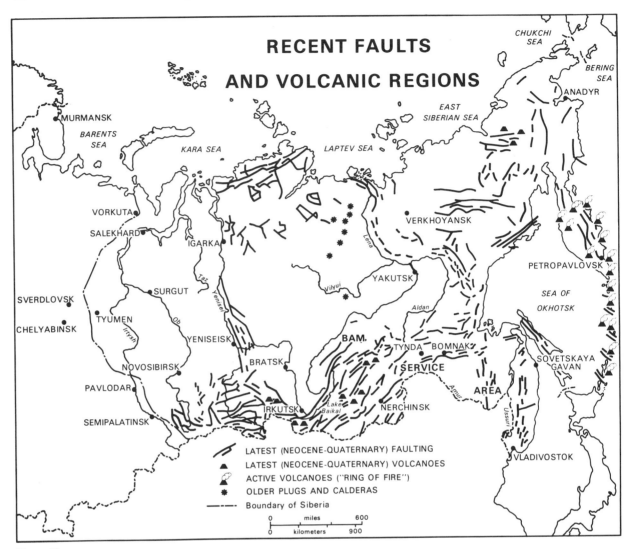

**RECENT FAULTS AND VOLCANIC REGIONS**

LATEST (NEOCENE-QUATERNARY) FAULTING
LATEST (NEOCENE-QUATERNARY) VOLCANOES
ACTIVE VOLCANOES ("RING OF FIRE")
OLDER PLUGS AND CALDERAS
- - - Boundary of Siberia

Figure 12
SOURCE: *Fiziko-geografichesky atlas mira* [Physical-geographic atlas of the world], p. 195.

ent) ring the Aldan and Anabar shields predominantly east of the Yenisei River (Figure 12). There are no recent faults on the West Siberian Lowland. Earthquakes of a magnitude of 4½ or more (intensity of 6) have been recorded in a belt that extends from the Altai Mountains astride Lake Baikal to the Shilka River basin and runs generally to the northeast, including central Yakutia, Kamchatka, and the Kuril Islands. Similar quakes have been registered along the coast of Maritime Krai and on Sakhalin Island (Figure 12). West of the subduction zone in the latter two areas, 90 percent of the epicenters have been calculated to originate at medium and great depths (60 to over 300 km). Elsewhere, they have been detected within 60 km of the surface.[129]

In areas slated for economic development, Soviet earth scientists have been assigned the task of zoning regions for seismic suitability. For example, along the BAM between Kunerma (just west of Lake Baikal) and Tynda, they have determined the civil-engineering requirements for the most hazardous locations. In the vicinity of the North Muya tunnel, investigators have learned that the

emission of helium indicates the likelihood of a fault that is seismically dangerous. Seismicity models have been developed at the workers' settlements of Lopcha and Ust-Nyukzha west of Tynda.[130] Researchers hope that these models will serve as prototypes for seismic planning in other Siberian towns.

Seismicity is a major constraint to the construction of hydroelectric stations. Because of it, hydropower development along the Vitim and Olekma rivers is handicapped.[131] The Zeya Dam is situated tremulously close to recent epicenters of earthquakes that measured 5.8 on the Richter scale. Upstream, at Zeisk, the second largest bridge on the BAM has been built to withstand high seismicity, ice flows, and strong winds. Three-meter casings surround its abutments and supports.[132]

Neocene-Quaternary volcanoes are witnessed in only three regions of Siberia: Kamchatka-Kurils; the Lake Baikal vicinity; and the Lower Amur and Ussuri basins. Older plugs and calderas are found on the Anabar Shield. Active volcanoes are prevalent in Kamchatka and everywhere along the Kuril archipelago because of subduction

Environmental Constraints to the Economic Development of Siberia

melting of the Pacific Plate as it glides beneath the Eurasian Plate (Figure 11). In other areas, Siberian volcanoes are dormant. A dozen or more inactive volcanoes are located near the site of the Udokan copper association. Fifteen recently extinct volcanoes are found upstream in the Vitim River watershed. The fact that they have become dormant only recently is borne out by the absence of permafrost within their craters and by the predominance of mineral springs along their flanks.[133]

Flows, Slides, and Avalanches

Seismic activity in more temperate climates does not necessarily pose serious danger to human works and activities. In periglacial environments like the Soviet North, however, its impact can be significant. Even without earthquakes, life there is subject to persistent instability. Weathering, particularly in mountainous Pacific Siberia, is mainly mechanical as opposed to chemical. Slopes remain steep because of the processes of frost action and backwearing. Permafrost limits the depth of plant roots. Rock spalls and shatters due to ice wedging in relatively shallow cross sections, and loose, angular debris fields readily accumulate at the base of the slopes (talus or scree cones, felsenmeer, rock glaciers, etc.). Ice temporarily serves as a cementing agent, but once it melts, on the steepest slopes rapid mass wasting becomes a strong contingency.

Landslips and landslides are, therefore, quite common in Pacific Siberia, especially during and after earthquakes. Moreover, because any disruption is likely to affect the permafrost, where slopes retain their steepness because of backwearing, landslides, as zones of weakness, tend to breed other landslides. This is not necessarily the case in temperate environments where permafrost and backwearing are the exception rather than the rule. During the 1957 Muya quake, for instance, landslides occurred actively within a 220-km radius of the epicenter (150,000 km$^2$). Rock avalanches were described as literally "leaping" from the mountain faces. As many as two landslides were observed in progress during one recent daylight helicopter reconnaissance of a small portion of the BAM service area.[134]

Debris flows (seli*) are considered the principal natural hazard in the USSR.[135] They are defined as the sudden rapid flow of thousands of cubic meters of loose rock, mud, and water. Hundreds of them have wreaked destruction on life and property in the last 80 years. In Siberia, they are associated with areas of most recent mountain-building and on moraines. They may be induced by running water after torrential rains, by snowmelt in a temporary thaw after a heavy snowstorm, by both of these, or by agitation owing to ground shaking when such debris is near saturation.[136]

The distribution of debris flows in Siberia correlates well with the pattern of earthquake intensity and faulting

(Figures 11–13). The most significantly hazardous zones of flows and slides overlap with areas of greatest earthquake intensity in the south (Cisbaikalia and Transbaikalia). Extreme debris flows in the northeast tend to correspond to regions weakened by snow avalanches (Figures 13–14).

In all instances, where vegetation has been removed by *any* mechanism—mass wasting, fire, animal, or human beings,—the effects of debris flows are heightened. Moreover, by damming streams, the rock, mud, and earth may cause floods in the warm season or icings in the cold season. Because of fire and logging on the shores of Lake Baikal, the primary vegetation has changed dramatically. Mudflows frequently accompany spring and summer downpours around the southern extremity of the lake (1934, 1960, and 1971). Since 1915, serious mudflows have occurred every seven years west of the lake. Throughout the region, bridges, roads, and fields have been destroyed utterly by flowing masses of mud and rock. The 1970 flow eradicated a portion of the Trans-Siberian Railroad in the vicinity of Slyudyanka and Baikalsk. The greatest potential for mudflow is found in the Stanovoi Mountains (Kodar and Udokan ranges), where the BAM is under construction.[137]

In Siberia, debris-flow prevention is carried out chiefly by means of organizational and technical controls. On the lakefront slope of Lake Baikal, logging has been prohibited. In high mountain pastures, range management is supposed to be strictly enforced. Reforestation and afforestation programs have been conducted in some regions. Where debris flows are enhanced by its presence, snow has been melted artifically. On segments of the oft-threatened railroad around the south end of Lake Baikal, slopes require constant shoring up by means of jump dams, trap filters, and directing dams. In a few cases, directed artificial explosions have been set off in order to neutralize pending debris flows.[138]

Obviously, occurring in similar regions and for similar reasons (for instance, both are sensitive to vegetational changes), snow avalanches and debris flows are closely related. But, whereas debris flows occur pre-eminently in spring and summer, snow avalanches are most frequent in late winter and early spring, especially combined with deposition of heavy continuous snowfall and strong winds. They also respond to passing warm fronts that come on the heels of cold-front snowstorms. Contrary to popular belief, avalanches may happen at almost any elevation. For example, they have been observed on Sakhalin Island at altitudes of only 50 to 60 m. A low-altitude avalanche recently severed the railroad near Yuzhno-Sakhalinsk.[139]

Avalanches come in a variety of forms including sluff, channeled, and jumping types, among which the last is the most destructive. Jumping avalanches occur in higher elevations and are distributed widely across Pacific Siberia (Figure 14).

Prevention and control of avalanches are conducted through warning services, artillery bombardment of affected areas, and retainer walls and screens. These measures are undertaken only after careful analyses of landforms, vegetation, soil hydrology, snow mass, snow

---

*Seli usually is translated to mean mudflows. Upon studying the many characteristics of seli, however, they appear to be combinations of mudflows, earthflows, and types of landslides; hence, my translation: debris flow.

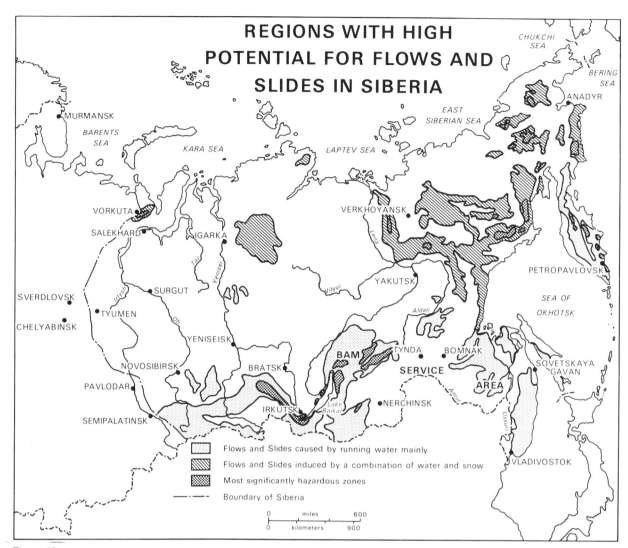

Figure 13
SOURCE: S. M. Fleishman and V. F. Perov, *Seleopasnye rayony Sovetskogo Soyuza* [Mudflow-hazard regions of the Soviet Union], pp. 286, 120, 136a, 154, 162, 167, 172, 189, 196, 212a.

cover, synoptic situations, meteorology, and satellite photography.[140] Avalanche zoning may be used where regions are developing economically, as in the BAM service area.

## Icings

Among the most disruptive of natural hazards in high-latitude environments is the phenomenon of icing. It is also among the most complex in origin (Figure 15). Since water exists as a liquid in all parts of the ecosphere, and ice is the solid form of water, then in polar and subpolar regions, ice also should be ubiquitous. Thus, ice is found in the atmosphere as crystals or snow. It forms from rain, when temperatures of a surface are below freezing (rime). It materializes on rivers, lakes, seas, and from summer meltwater in the cold of winter. It even is present beneath the ground. But, these forms of ice are relatively innocuous. Ice becomes a natural hazard when it bursts forth from the earth or a frozen water body without warning,

or when it is too thin to cross, or when it is unexpectedly too slippery for modes of transportation. These types of ice are called icings.

Among the most common forms of icing in Siberia is groundwater icing. It derives from two sources: spring water via leads in the permafrost and groundwater sources at every level (supra-, intra-, and subpermafrost). Groundwater icings begin with the freezing of the active zone and end with the discharge of groundwater onto the surface in winter. Entire houses have been filled from floor to ceiling by these icings, which have sprung suddenly through the floor from the basement or subcellar. The differences between the temperature of the icing water (0 to 1°C) and that of the air (−40°C) create steam fogs known as "icing boils" in the Soviet Union. As the frozen layers press downward, more groundwater is conducted to the surface, spreading in layers across the landscape. Groundwater icings along the upper Kolyma River basin account for almost 6,000 km² in area and are up to 12 m thick (Appendix II). The thicker the overlying mass of

Figure 14
SOURCE: G. K. Tushinsky, *Lavinoopasnye rayony Sovetskogo Soyuza* [Avalanche-hazardous regions of the Soviet Union], figs. 19–21, 25, 27, 29, 36, 38, and 41.

ice, the faster the groundwater flows to the surface, reaching velocities of over 1,100 liters per second (300 gallons/sec.).[141]

Spring-water icings occur similarly, but usually emit from where a cut is made into a hillside or along a river bank owing to human or natural forces. "The water frequently is under hydrostatic pressure and may flow through much of the winter, causing ice to build up on the road."[142] Spring-water icings are found throughout Siberia on river terraces, along fault lines, or on cliffsides, most prevalently in the northeastern part of the region.

Another kind of icing is river icing, which erupts from streams vertically or laterally as the water body freezes downward toward its bed. These icings are damaging to river crossings and frontage roads.

Though most icings are over a meter thick in Siberia, they may be thin in spots. Nikolai Vereshchagin's theory about many of the deep-frozen mammoths is that they simply fell through thin ice. Modern "mammoth traps" along the Bamovskaya-Berkakit railway ensnared two

mobile cranes in the winter of 1974 in just this manner. "The equipment could not be retrieved for a long time, and only the two metal booms sticking out of the ice indicated the site of the catastrophe."[143]

During the earthquakes, icings may spring forth in massive floods from the subpermafrost zone along dislocated fault lines. The existence of these disruptions indicates the potential benefit of icings as sources of urban water supply. They also can be used as natural refrigeration for perishable items in summer.

Prevention is the best way to deal with icings. Roads and railroads should be oriented away from sites of high icing potential. Road cuts should be avoided as this is a source of spring-water icings. Small icings may be thawed with firepots. At times, blasting and bulldozing may be appropriate. Otherwise, diversions like "sackcloth" dams and "freezing belts" can be employed.[144]

In Siberia, since icings are so prevalent, the only alternative for overcoming the problem would appear to be the design and construction of proper subgrades and

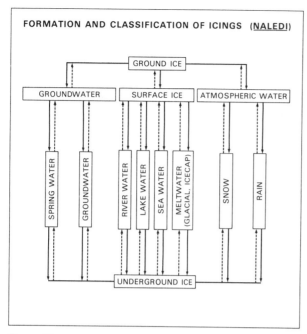

FORMATION AND CLASSIFICATION OF ICINGS (NALEDI)

Figure 15
SOURCE: V. R. Alekseyev, "Naledi Sibiri i Dalnego Vostoka" [Icings of Siberia and the Soviet Far East], in *Sibirsky geografichesky sbornik*, no. 8 (1974), p. 11.

culverts. During the first year of service, the Lena-Zvezdny segment of the BAM suffered from huge icings. The track became engulfed in ice because the anti-icing measures that were utilized were inferior: culvert foundations were not insulated; drainage-ditch blasting turned out to be deeper than necessary. As a result, the culverts shifted and, in some cases, washed out. With the first thaw, the meltwater overflowed the drainage ditches, swamping the track.[145]

This example bodes poorly for the future operation of the BAM, because the Lena-Zvezdny tract represents less than 2 percent (60 km) of the entire route. According to BAM officials, the railroad is afflicted by over 350 active icing zones. The smallest are 1,000 $m^2$, and the largest are over a million $m^2$ with thicknesses of 2.5 to 3m. Moreover, the impact of the icings increases by factors of 2 or 3, when influenced by construction activities.[146]

Storms and Tsunamis

Snowstorms (*meteli*), duststorms (*burany* and *sukhovei*), blizzards (*purgi*), and hurricanes can strike almost anywhere in Siberia at least once a year. Although they adjust work schedules in winds of lower speeds (largely in response to the wind-chill factor), Soviet officials do not consider storms to be hazardous until wind velocities attain gale force (14 to 28 m/sec or 32 to 54 mph). As indicated earlier in this chapter, work usually stops when wind velocities reach 12 m/sec (26 mph).

Snowstorms of varying lengths range from 100 days or more per year along the Arctic coast to 25 days per annum in the steppe. Heavy one-time snowfalls of over 10 cm per occurrence have been recorded most frequently in Kam-

chatka (286 times).[147] The Taimyr Peninsula, the West Siberian steppes, and the Anadyr River basin also have been scenes of especially heavy snowstorms. The number of snowstorms received in the mountains of Pacific Siberia is much higher than in the valleys. In the Udokan Range, for instance, up to 100 days of snowstorms may be experienced, while in the adjacent hollows of the Chara and Muya lowlands, there may be a maximum of five all year. Snowstorms were so heavy in West Siberia during February 1978 that over 10,000 loaded boxcars were snowbound for weeks in marshalling yards.[148] Because such events are more or less expected, roughly 20 percent of the rail lines of the USSR, which are subject to heavy snowfalls, are protected by snow fences. The rest are shielded by shelter belts.

Shelter belts are used also to combat duststorms. The West Siberian steppe is plagued by *burany* in winter and dessicating *sukhovei* in summer. The former is a hurricane-like (28 to 33 m/sec or 64 to 72 mph) windstorm which deflates snow and soil in a blinding pall. *Burany* gusts have been clocked well beyond hurricane velocities (over 33 m/sec or 73 mph). The *sukhovei* is a hot, dry wind which blows easterly or southeasterly out of drought-ridden Kazakhstan between April and October. It brings low relative humidities (under 30%), wind speeds of 3 to 13 m/sec (5 to 30 mph), and high temperatures of 25°C to 40°C. Both *sukhovei* and *burany* usually are choked with particulate matter, the latter most of the time with snow, and may persist for several days. In the Kulunda Steppe, for example, duststorms alone occur 7 to 20 days annually.

*Purgi* or blizzards are the worst kind of Siberian storms because they are accompanied by steep drops in temperature coupled with violent winds and blinding snow. Unlike snowfalls, which seldom cause loss of human life because people ordinarily receive adequate early warnings about their approach, *purgi* may catch laborers, animals, and machinery unawares. Thus, the well-known naturalist on the Soviet Far East, V. K. Arsenyev, once emphasized, "It is positively impossible to go anywhere during a *purga*." According to I. A. Goncharov, the *purga* "is a snow hurricane that obscures earth and sky. You can't take a step forward or backward. If you persist, you're insane: you won't find the road ahead; you won't even recognize where you've been. It's best to stay where you are.[149] Thus, in *purga* country (the Arctic coast, the northeast, and Kamchatka), early-warning systems and appropriate snow-removal equipment are absolute necessities.

Storms with authentic hurricane wind speeds are prone to hit Kamchatka and the Kurils in the fall. During a storm of this type in December 1977, snow-stilted winds raged at 40 m/sec (82 mph). In Petropavlovsk, telephone poles, power lines, and walls were blown down.[150] Only an effective early-warning system enabled the townspeople to escape unharmed. In all instances of damage by storms with winds in excess of gale force (14 m/sec or 32 mph), the Soviet government compensates individuals and communities.

Soviet authorities have operated a "tsunami watch" in the Far East since November 1952, at which time a giant seismic sea wave devastated portions of the northern Kuril Islands.[151] In the past, the seaquake-induced tsunamis have proved hazardous to Kamchatka and Sakhalin as well (Figure 14). Since the 1700s, seven or more of these huge long waves (up to 20 m high in narrow embayments), which move at velocities of over 400 km per hour, have been recorded in the Soviet Far East. The tsunami service is said to be capable of providing an advance warning of 30 to 40 minutes on the approach of one of the waves. However, until now its capabilities have been tested only once (1963).

Microscale Physical Limitations: A Summary

Because of the unpredictable nature of the time and place of their occurrence, the magnitude of the damage that may be induced, and the present sparse settlement patterns throughout Siberia, natural hazards do not lend themselves to easy generalizations in terms of direct costs, work stoppages, and economic development as was the case with the macroscale constraints. Obviously, such effects are radically sporadic with microscale limitations. Earthquakes, for instance, when and where they occur, vary in intensity from tremors which are hardly noticeable (Mercalli I) to major quakes in which damage is total (Mercalli XII). Such extreme variation, where human populations are found, means that activities may proceed as if nothing had happened or may cease for days or months, resulting in exorbitant monetary losses. The same thing may be said of flows, slides, and avalanches. Where these sever lines of communication, they cause direct financial setbacks and economic delays, not to mention the potential loss of human life. But, most of the time they occur harmlessly in remote and undeveloped sectors above timberline. In any case, even without incident, construction times in seismic areas are always protracted because of the special engineering and care required in laying pipe or building roads and structures (Table 10). Icings and major storms are most pertinent to production costs and work stoppages in Siberia. Week-long delays of snowbound or icing-restricted freight trains of as many as 10,000 boxcars must have tremendous economic consequences in a country that is so dependent on the railroad.

With respect to settlement patterns, most natural hazards can be conscientiously avoided. One of the fundamental precepts of socialism is that society, and not the individual, is responsible for human safety. Thus, for the most part, hazard zones in the Soviet Union are well known, and major expenses theoretically can be avoided through proper planning and zoning. This kind of preparation apparently now prevails within the BAM service area, especially in the hazard-prone leg west of the Aldan River, and in Kamchatka.

**Technogenic Hazards
(Human-Induced Environmental Disruption)**

To this point, we have examined the impact of certain physical obstacles to the human use of the earth in Sibe-

ria. Largely, we have discounted man and his influence except as he attempts to tame these physical constraints with his technology. But, of course, there is another aspect to the man-nature relationship. It is the potential disruption that human beings can wreak on the environment either unwittingly or deliberately, during the process of economic development. Is the Soviet regime sensitive to these environmental issues? If so, what measures have been taken in Siberia to ensure that the goals of environmental protection and economic development are in balance?

How delicate is the Siberian environment? It has been established that northern agroclimatic regions have low carrying capacities. What are the implications of this condition for human use of Siberia? Inevitably, exploitation of any landscape leads to some level of disruption. How much of this disruption can the varied environments of Siberia withstand?

Recently, Glazovskaya attempted to answer this question by analyzing the destructive aspects of technogenesis.[152] In essence, she reconfirmed the hypothesis that human-induced disruption has relatively more impact in regions with less biological variety and abundance, i.e., the taiga and tundra, than in areas of great diversity. She then mapped the environmentally sensitive regions of the USSR on the basis of their vested capacity to absorb and neutralize technogenic pollutants (see Appendix III). She determined that of the 26 "technobiogeomes" discerned for Siberia, the overwhelming majority were weak in their ability to absorb particulate matter and solid wastes (because of the cold) and only moderately capacious to process liquid and gaseous pollutants.

Northern environments are unstable and vulnerable to human occupance. Plants and animals are at the limits of their existence. Contrary to what was once thought, the topography is not preserved by the permafrost. Instead, even the slightest disruption leads to ground thawing and gradual destruction of the landscape. Water and air pollution are among the most damaging elements of human activity.

Water Pollution

Researchers have found that the temperature of a water body is of critical importance in determining its capacity to process pollutants. As a river gets colder, oxygen becomes increasingly soluble in water. For example, at 4°C fully saturated water contains 13 ppm oxygen, while at 27°C it contains only 8 ppm.[153] Oxygen-rich streams can oxidize greater quantities of biochemical oxygen demand (BOD). Even if dissolved oxygen levels momentarily fall, a river's capacity for recovery is much higher in wintertime. This happens because the further water is from saturation, the quicker the oxygen diffuses into the river to redress the imbalance. If dissolved oxygen is 4 ppm and saturation is 16 ppm, oxygen will be absorbed by a water body three times faster than if the saturation level is 8 ppm, as it is in summer.

This would imply that rivers and lakes in Siberia are naturally rich in oxygen. However, once the water body becomes iced over, oxygenation no longer takes place. Cloud cover also plays a role in diminishing the efficacy of this process. Instead of being high in oxygen during winter, the frozen Siberian streams and reservoirs reflect the opposite state. Additionally, the number of water-borne decomposers is reduced sharply in cold climates. The result is that wastes are not consumed at all rapidly in water of low temperature. Even though a river may not smell or noticeably change color (if oxygen levels are high, say, before freezing), effluents persist for long periods and, accordingly, for great distances downstream. Thus, in Siberian conditions, water pollutants may remain in rivers for distances that are 8 to 10 times longer than those recorded in temperate climates.[154]

Finally, because of the propensity of Siberian soils and marshes for acidity, water bodies there are naturally non-basic (6.5 pH versus 7.0). Apart from the consequences of pollution then, fish kills may occur simply because of the acid content of the waters.

All of this means that Siberian streams and lakes have a comparatively low self-purification capacity. "In water-logged complexes, the dissolution of oil may take 15 days, and oil may remain in the water for up to 50 years."[155]

During recent five-year plans, Soviet leaders have encouraged campaigns to clean up waterways. Billions of rubles have been allocated to the purpose of establishing up to 10,000 wastewater and sewage treatment plants, some of which have been built or are under construction in Siberia. To indicate the importance of this campaign compared with the one against air pollution, of 671 million rubles that were earmarked for pollution-abatement systems in the Electric Power Ministry during the 10th Five-Year Plan (1976–80), 562 million rubles were designated exclusively for water-pollution control.[156]

According to official reports, the waters of Lake Baikal have improved considerably since the controversies of the 1960s. This has resulted both from legislation and technological improvements. To implement the strict laws that forbid log-rafting on the lake, require constraints on logging in general, and create fishing supervisories, the government has increased the number of pollution-control inspectors around the lake from 5 to 150. An inspector's job is facilitated by the fact that water purification systems have been installed in 70 percent of all the factories in the Baikal drainage basin. Some 125 million rubles have been spent on the Buryat segment of the lake alone, which represents three-fifths of the total shoreline. The much-publicized tertiary treatment program at Baikalsk, from which potable water is alleged to emit, reportedly has been outdistanced in efficiency by the treatment installation at the Selenginsk pulp and paperboard mill.[157] Farther west, the Ust-Ilimsk pulp plant was to have similar controls.

Such examples would tend to indicate that all is well in the abatement of water pollution in Siberia. This is not completely true. Less than half of the sewage-treatment plants projected for the BAM service area in 1977 actually were built. Because of "mislaid" blueprints for the wastewater treatment installation at the site of the new Tomsk petrochemical plant, there is still no water-

pollution control. As was stated earlier, in small towns and villages, the most common sanitary conveyance is a river ice floe during spring breakup.

In another vein, drilling operations in nonpermafrost areas of the Middle Ob oil fields have lowered the water table. This has occurred despite the Soviet practice of utilizing waterlift methods throughout the period of oilfield development versus later secondary and/or tertiary recovery. Though it is not the reason for the forced-draft techniques, the water table in some instances has no doubt remained high, so high, in fact, that 64 to 80 percent of the fluids being extracted at many West Siberian wells is composed of injection water![158]

## Air Pollution

Air pollution is controlled naturally by wind (diffusion through turbulence), vegetation (photosynthesis), precipitation ("rainout"), and, where nitrogen oxides and hydrocarbons are not problems, solar radiation (which kills pathogenic bacteria). Apart from Wind Region I (Figure 5), Siberia is noted for its comparative lack of winds. The brief growing season, chiefly under 160 days, limits plant life to a precious few. Green plants as an oxygen source accordingly are ineffective. Away from West Siberia and the extreme Far East, precipitation is at a premium, even as snow. And solar radiation, obviously scarce in winter, must pass through a far thicker atmosphere to reach most Siberian latitudes than at lower parallels. Because of the near absence of photosynthesis, the oxygen created in these environments is less per unit area than elsewhere. Thus, atmospheric self-purification also must be low, and any air pollution must have significantly greater impact.

Because of the long, cold periods of winter darkness and even the short, cool summer evenings, buildings must be heated and supplied with more electrical output, much of which is produced by the burning of solid fuels. This means that air pollution is higher per unit area in Siberia than in most of European Russia.[159]

In Pacific Siberia, the mountain basins are ventilated poorly. In the Baikal rift zone and beneath the Asiatic High in Yakutia, temperature inversions are extreme and almost incapacitate any kind of atmospheric diffusion.

To make matters worse, the meager vegetation appears to be more sensitive to air pollution than are plant communities in lower latitudes. Nefedova has found that sulfur-dioxide emissions in excess of 50 mg/m³ have disastrous effects on reindeer lichen (*Cladonia*), one of the basic species intrinsic to reindeer grazing lands. She determined that these ranges were the ecosystems that were least likely to withstand toxic gases. These were followed in terms of decreasing vulnerability by moss associations, conifers, and shrubs.[160]

Although coal represents something less than half of all Soviet boiler fuels, its share of use is proportionately higher in Siberia. For the last 20 years, it has been Soviet policy to replace coal with oil and gas in large and medium-size cities. For example, the Kuzbas recently was supplied with associated gas via a pipeline from the

Middle Ob, among the benefits of which is less air pollution. (The Kuzbas traditionally has been among the leading candidates as the most-polluted industrial area in the country.) Outside of West Siberia, the Trans-Siberian tributary area, and the Yakutsk and Norilsk districts, Siberian settlements may have to rely on coal (and hydropower) for years to come. This is especially true of most of the BAM service area, which tends to be deficient in local sources of oil and gas.[161]

Besides shifts to nonpolluting fuels, atmospheric contamination in Siberia is controlled at least in part by engineering. Though the Siberian percentage is unknown, overall Soviet air-pollution control efficiencies were to be raised from 70 to 81 percent between 1976 and 1980. This was to be accomplished by means of the installation of new and rebuilt electrostatic precipitators (97 to 99 percent efficient) and/or wet scrubbers (95 to 97 percent efficient). Power plants that burn low-quality coal from the Kansk-Achinsk Basin were to receive electric filters with rated efficiencies of over 99 percent.[162] Since new power plants are required by law to be equipped with the best-available pollution-control devices, and most Siberian thermal stations are new or under construction, success in preventing further air pollution should be relatively high.

Other Environmental Disruptions

*Vegetation and Wildlife Ecology.* Natural reserves have been present within the boundaries of the USSR since czarist days, and since 1937 the system has expanded by an average of five units per annum.[163] However, of the 107 reserves that existed in the USSR by May 1976, only 18 were in Siberia. Four more, comprising over 3 million hectares (7.5 million acres), were added to the network from the Yakutian Republic in 1978.[164]

The numerical disproportion of European natural areas compared to those in Siberia is counterbalanced to some extent by size. Thus, if Siberian reserves account for under 20 percent of the total number, their combined area is proportionate to the size of the region. (I estimate that the Siberian share of the total area of Soviet reserves is over 55 percent.)

Soviet nature reserves represent true restricted areas, so that the vegetation and wildlife within their territorial limits are relatively safe from human abuses. This is important in the ecological sense, because any disruption of the vegetative cover, particularly in permafrost areas, leads unavoidably to degradation of wildlife habitat. It should be noted that, except for the most recent additions to the system of Siberian reserves, only one is in an area of continuous permafrost and just two more are in regions of discontinuous permafrost. All four of the Yakutian reserves are on continuous permafrost.

Soviet authorities are well aware of the potential impact of economic development on the unstable environments of Siberia. Ostensibly, there are strict regulations on locations and regimes of quarrying and earthwork, forest removal, forest-fire prevention, and on hunting and fishing. In the BAM service area, more than 30 construction enterprises, depending on hundreds of quarries, work deposits of sand, gravel, limestone, and other building materials on a large scale. This is done with high-technology tracked excavators, rock crushers, graders, and bulldozers, which cannot fail to alter the pristine countryside.

Callous disregard for the quality, purpose, and maturity of forests in the path of the railroad has been reported frequently since 1974.[165] The danger is not limited simply to route-clearing operations. Upwards of 70 percent of the commercial species of stone pine, the most valuable of Siberian timber, is found in mountainous areas, serving the special purposes of soil conservation and water regulation. Despite their significance to landscape preservation, these forests reportedly have been zoned for commercial exploitation.[166]

Of even greater concern is the slow growth pattern of virtually all Siberian timber, the fastest-growing of which requires 70 years or more to reach maturity. Even with modern airlifted fire-fighting crews and equipment, wildfires occur regularly in Krasnoyarsk Krai and Irkutsk Oblast, particularly in dry years like 1976. According to Mikhailov, most Siberian forest fires are human-induced, over half by loggers.[167] Whatever the cause, forest fire is disastrous in periglacial environments because of its impact on underground ice and permafrost. The trees, mosses, and lichens that serve as insulators of the subsoil may take decades to return after the occurrence of a single fire.

As humans encroach on the pioneer regions of Siberia, wildlife habitat will disappear accordingly, not only because of the removal of vegetation and an increase of fires but also because of the sheer presence of human beings. This process is complicated by the lack of a coordinated effort to enforce regulations on environmental protection. In the BAM service area, for instance, as of 1980, no single agency was responsible for the overall control of logging, hunting, and fishing activities. According to hunters in the North Baikal ranges, ungulates (mainly, elk and red deer) were abundant in the region until 1974. Now they are gone because of habitat disruption and alleged poaching by railroad construction crews. "Here and there, elk are found in the marshes, but their days are numbered."[168]

The delicacy of the balance is brought into focus by the existence of permafrost (Figure 16.). In temperate climates, natural or technogenic environmental disruption largely ceases with "immediate effects," there being no permafrost. But, in periglacial environments like those of Siberia, because of permafrost, extensive chain reactions may be initiated, so that in time considerable damage can be done. Moreover, in some areas the alteration process can be well-nigh perpetual. To counteract these tendencies in the Lower Ob region, Nefedova has proposed some basic environmental protection measures (Table 12). Buks has identified "landscape-ecological stability regions" throughout the BAM service area, where one-third to one-half of the territory is considered by him to be weakly stable or unstable to human impact and should be exposed to limited development only.[169] On the basis of

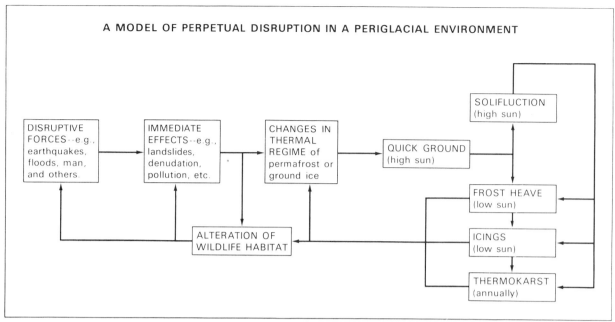

A MODEL OF PERPETUAL DISRUPTION IN A PERIGLACIAL ENVIRONMENT

Figure 16

an impact analysis conducted under the auspices of the Academy of Sciences USSR in 1976, wildlife refuges and national parks were recommended in regions adjacent to the BAM railway. All of these proposals and recommendations await implementation.

*Medical Geography.* Concern for human health and comfort in Siberia is exemplified by the quality of research that has been conducted by medical geographers in the BAM service area. Besides the usual problems associated with residence in a harsh, cold climate (respiratory illnesses and intestinal disorders), ailments common to the region are tick-borne encephalitis and rickettsiosis, rabbit fever, toxoplasmosis, mite fever, conjunctivitis, and endemic goiter. Based on the work of geographers, 34 "comfort zones" have been delineated within the service area. The subregions have been defined by means of indices of human habitability and certain biophysical thresholds. According to these criteria, virtually all of the region has registered low comfort levels or worse, with the central BAM (from Lake Baikal to South Yakutia) reflecting extremely uncomfortable conditions.[170] Ostensibly, similar comfort levels have been observed in the underdeveloped regions of the Northeast and Arctic. Comfort zones, at least in theory, will be utilized as guides for optimum human settlement and land use throughout Siberia.

## Soviet Environmental Protection and Siberian Development

Soviet attitudes toward the environment have gone through three general phases since the 1917 Revolution. They include (1) the Leninist or Formative Phase (1917–24), (2) the Stalinist or Maximum-Growth Phase (1925–60), and (3) the Neo-Leninist or Transitional Phase (1961–

75). More recently, although subject to qualification where specific instances are concerned, a rational-growth policy appears to have been adopted.[171]

### The Leninist Phase

This was a trend that began and ended with Lenin. During this time, particularly between the fall of 1917 and the spring of 1919, there were conscientious attempts, if not by Lenin, then by someone in his administration, to pass meaningful laws protecting the then Russian Federation from environmental abuses, especially in the realms of land use, wildlife, and forest preservation.[172] Although the laws themselves were exemplary,* they set the tone for future legislation without enforcement. The weak, young government, not unlike regimes in underdeveloped countries today, could hardly implement laws related to production, much less laws restricting environmental disruption.

### The Stalinist Phase

For 35 years after Lenin's death, virtually no restraints were placed on the production sector. In fact, between 1925 and 1950 fewer laws concerning environmental protection were passed than were legislated in the first two years of the Leninist phase. No matter; the policy of legislation without enforcement persisted. Most of the legislation throughout the entire period (to 1960) nominally dealt with pollution problems and, after the war, nature transformation. Indeed, Stalin's Plan for the Transformation of Nature and Khrushchev's Virgin Lands Program were quasi-declarations of war on natural

---

*The Decree on Forests passed on 27 May 1918 is probably the one most often cited in Soviet literature.

obstacles. It can be rationalized that this was a logical response by the leadership of a developing country bent on exploitation of resources in the fastest possible manner. All capital, of necessity, went to the production sector and environmental protection was virtually ignored in the rush to fullfill short-run economic plans.

## The Neo-Leninist Phase

Since 1961, greater awareness of the need for environmental protection has emerged in the Soviet Union. The programs of Communist Party congresses in 1961, 1966, and 1971 included passing references to elaboration and implementation of environmental protection measures. The directives of the five-year plans adopted at the 1966 and 1971 congresses called for these efforts in a few short lines. Despite this apparent lack of emphasis, more than 30 major pieces of legislation stressing almost all aspects of environmental protection were approved in the 15 years between 1961 and 1975. By 1970, articles dealing with some facet of conservation, rational resource use, and pollution abatement appeared almost daily in the Soviet press. The fact that these articles were mainly critical of industrial, collective, or, in some cases, individual enforcement remained the rule rather than the exception. However, a distinct change in mood was apparent. Environmental laws were strengthened. More money than ever before was spent on environmental protection. There were public debates and philosophical forums arguing the merits of continued maximum growth versus a rational-growth policy.[173] In short, this was a distinctly transitional period, not unlike that occurring simultaneously in the West, during which the maximum-growth formulas of Stalin and early Khrushchev were de-emphasized, the Leninist quasi-aware approach to nature was lauded, and some hard decisions with regard to industrial polluters were made.

## A Phase of Rational Growth

It was perhaps predictable that the philosophical and economic convolutions of the neo-Leninist phase would lead to important new policy pronouncements on environmental protection during the 25th Party Congress in 1976. Though troubled, the Soviet economy had matured considerably since the Stalinist Phase. In many areas of production, the USSR was clearly competitive with most of the capitalist world. It had made inroads into foreign commerce. It had increased its respectability in the field of diplomacy. And, probably most importantly, in a military sense it had gained parity with the United States. Having achieved all this, Soviet leaders finally could afford to come to grips with environmental problems.

The notion of rational growth was introduced by Kelley in 1976.[174] In contrast to the unrestrained economic growth of developing or frontier societies (maximum growth), rational growth presupposes that an economy grows more slowly, less wastefully, and with proper environmental controls in order to establish a dynamic balance between man and nature. To those familiar with Marxist-Leninist jargon, this sounds like the economy of true socialism, something that still eludes Soviet leadership.

On paper, at least, the 10th Five-Year Plan (1976–80) represented a move in the direction of conscious adoption of a rational-growth policy, including the elevation of environmental protection to the status of an important national goal. For one thing, though probably involuntarily, the Soviet economy was projected to expand at a slower annual rate (4 percent versus 5 percent in the recent past). For another, unprecedentedly, several paragraphs organic to the plan itself were devoted to environmental protection. More state investment than ever before—11 billion rubles—was allocated to this purpose (a figure that did not include outlays by individual factories and plants, which in 1973 exceeded state investment by a factor of four). The Main Administration of the Hydrometeorological Service was upgraded to State Committee for Hydrometeorology and Environmental Protection. And in support of the tenor of the plan, environmental protection was "guaranteed" to Soviet citizens under Articles 18 and 67 of the new constitution.[175] This governmental posture, which is being maintained in the 11th Five-Year Plan (1981–85), is significant when combined with the aforementioned stance of the scientific community; but again, implementation of the targets is even more important, especially in the sensitive environments of the Soviet North and Siberia.

Although they may be more experienced than anyone else in these regions, the Soviet people have proceeded into the Subarctic and Arctic by trial and error. The widespread use of tracked vehicles in the tundra is a good example of poor judgment. The abandoned Salekhard-Nadym railroad is another. Many instances of failure can be listed. However, it is one thing to make mistakes and another thing to profit by them. No less than 70 research institutes are now involved in environmental-impact studies of the BAM service area. Two of them work directly with the construction crews, as the latter blaze the path through the taiga. Apparently firm decisions have been made to ban metallurgical plants (copper smelting and refining; iron and steel) in the inversion-hazardous Chara Lowland (Udokan) and Chulman Basin (South Yakutia). The BAM itself has been reoriented from the vulnerable northwest shore of Lake Baikal with its shifting, desertlike sands, where the railway was to pass originally. Instead, track was laid in mountains near the shore, even though the route is longer and four new tunnels were required by the change.[176] In accordance with the recommendations of the Academy of Sciences, planners have designated Lake Baikal as a place of recreation as opposed to a resource to be exploited. Resort areas and camping sites have been selected and mapped.

Thus, usually ignored in the past, environmental protection is an important part of Soviet decision making in Siberia. If the quality of the impact analyses themselves were not enough, allocations to conservation and rational utilization of resources represent 8 to 10 percent of the total investments in a project as big as the BAM. This eventually will equal over a billion rubles.[177] To see that these and other funds are spent properly, some 24 target programs have been drawn up and 40 academic organiza-

TABLE 12
Basic Environmental Protection Measures in Connection with the Economic
Development of the Northern Part of Western Siberia

| Type of develop-ment | Type of land use | Natural complex | Stability of natural complexes | | Water-logged Unstable |
|---|---|---|---|---|---|
| | | | Relatively well drained | | |
| | | | Limited stability | Unstable | |
| Gas extraction | and trans-portation of oil and gas | Tundra Wooded tundra Northern taiga | Permafrost marine plains with moss tundra; with mossy open larch woodland; with dark needle and birch forest with green mosses | Permafrost marine plains with lichen tundra; with spruce-larch-lichen open wood-land; with spruce-lichen forest | and aquatic complexes |
| Reindeer grazing | Use of grazing lands on sea-sonal basis for domestic and wild reindeer | Tundra Wooded tundra Northern taiga | Permafrost plains with moss tundra; with mossy, open larch woodland with dark-coniferous and birch-forest with green moss | Permafrost plains with lichen tundra; with spruce-larch-lichen open wood-land; with spruce-lichen forest | Bogs |
| Forestry | Commercial and craft use of forests | Middle taiga | Loamy plains with coniferous and broadleaf forests | Sandy and sandy-loamy plains with coniferous and broadleaf forests | Floodplains, bogs |
| Oil extraction | Exploration, development, extraction | Future use: Tundra Wooded tundra Northern taiga Present use: Middle taiga | Glacial and fluvio-glacial loamy plains with haircap-moss and spruce forest | Lacustrine alluvial sandy-loamy and sandy plains Alluvial sandy and sandy-loamy ter-races with Scotch pine, larch and stone pine forest | Meadows, bogs, flood-plains |

SOURCE: V. B. Nefedova (n. 155, pp. 28–30 in *SGRT*).

| Possible consequences of development | Basic environmental protection measures |
|---|---|
| Disruption of permafrost as a result of unsystematic movement of vehicles; Laying of pipelines and driving of support piles without insulation; Fires resulting from pipeline breaks | Provision of permanent roads Laying of pipelines with insulation on support piles Provision of insulation around gas flares |
| Reduction of biota resources as a result of logging at the northern tree limit; Fires resulting from burning off of spilled oil and gas flares; Disruption of wild reindeer migrations; Pollution of reindeer lichen grazing lands by gas-combustion products; Pollution of water-bodies by industrial effluents | Forest conservation Firefighting service Passageways for reindeer through pipeline systems Full utilization of natural gas and associated gas Oil-spill prevention Biological purification of water injected into oil reservoirs Use of air-cooled rather than water-cooled systems in gas-processing plants |
| Thinning and degradation of plant cover Reduction of reindeer lichen lands Deterioration of soils as result of overgrazing | Regulation of domestic reindeer grazing combined with rational grazing of wild reindeer Preservation of reindeer grazing lands in course of oil and gas development |
| Reduction of forest area as a result of fires, insect infestation, overcutting, destruction of undergrowth, poor management of logging areas | Provision of greenbelts where commercial logging is prohibited Coordination of activities between forestry and hunting interests Fire and insect control |
| Possible climate changes as a result of air pollution by combustion products of gas flares and oil spills Oil pollution and accelerated melting of ice in Arctic Ocean Reduction of atmospheric oxygen levels | Collection and utilization of associated gas Quick action in case of oil spills and removal of oil from ice-covered ocean surface Provision of protective forest greenbelts |
| Reduction of clean surface and subsurface water resources as a result of effluent discharges Possible runoff of polluted subsurface waters to Arctic Ocean Flooding of land surface by mineralized subsurface waters | Biological purification of water and water-recycling systems Diking of surface areas subject to flooding by subsurface waters Provision of storage tanks for subsurface waters in case of spills |
| Reduction of biota resources as a result of oil pollution of land and water Deforestation | Prohibition of oil extraction until provision is made for injecting purified water into oil reservoirs Burning off spilled oil at safe distances from forests and populated places |
| Subsidence of land surface and increased water-logging as a result of creation of cavities in depleted oilfields | Reclamation measures and injection of water into depleted reservoirs |

tions are involved in economic development planning under an overall Siberian development program. Their task is not only to supervise the creation of two dozen or more territorial-production complexes in the region, but also to enforce appropriate pollution controls, water use, and construction on permafrost.[178]

Technogenic Hazards: A Summary

At the beginning of this section two questions were asked: (1) Is the Soviet regime sensitive to environmental issues and (2) if so, what measures have been taken in Siberia to ensure that the goals of environmental protection and economic development are in balance? The answers are ambivalent at best. As with the Congress of the United States, the "official" stand on environmental protection among Soviet leaders is unequivocally pro-conservation. This is borne out by published addresses, articles in the Soviet Constitution, and the economic plans themselves. There is an obvious awareness and desire for environmental protection that outwardly compares favorably with attitudes in North America.

Yet, Siberia is in many ways like a developing country. Its vastness and the scope of its untapped raw materials make it a perfect target for unrestricted resource-development policies. In the densely populated, settled western part of the USSR, polluters and plant managers intent on breaking or overlooking conservation laws are now hard-pressed to get away with it, at least in the manner that they once did. But in Siberia, enforcement may be less exacting because of the region's sheer size, remoteness, and sparse population. This is particularly true in the realms of pollution control, forestry, and wildlife management. Investments in pollution-abatement technologies—10 percent or more of the capital investments—except in prominent places like Lake Baikal or the Sayan Dam on the Yenisei still tend to be ancillary to the production targets. The example of spoil banks in the Kolyma goldfields and of a project as large as the Tomsk petrochemical plant are cases in point. Although coal-burning power plants in Siberia are to be equipped with the best-available electrostatic precipitators, Soviet air-pollution control devices reportedly are far inferior to those of Western design and frequently are deadlined. Poaching of wildlife and indiscriminate felling of forests are particularly easy to carry out in Siberia because of its size and comparative lack of surveillance.

In contrast to the environmentalist concern shown by the builders of the Alaska pipeline, there is no similar experience to be witnessed in the annals of West Siberian oil and gas development. Although it may be best for the pipeline now (as a symbol of the lingering Soviet bias for production), pipe burial in the permafrost of West Siberia may lead ultimately to ruptures because of the phenomenon of "thaw halo."* Despite the admonishments of Nefedova and others, Soviet oil and gas field operations in West Siberia are reportedly poor examples of environmental soundness.

Siberian resource development must be based on firm economic grounds. Environmental costs, where possible, undoubtedly are minimized. Already expensive because of their location and the harshness of their physical constraints, Siberian resources theoretically should not be able to bear stringent environmental costs. In the choice between development and conservation, cheaper production schemes should emerge the victor.

In reality, Siberian developers would seem to be meeting this choice selectively. In the swamps of West Siberia, doubtlessly few care about environmental protection. The environment itself, with its rancid water, miasmic air, and insect breeding grounds, is a notorious polluter. But, in the BAM service area, with spectacular gorges, taiga-clad vistas, and comparatively abundant wildlife, economic development proceeds with apparently unusual caution. Despite periodic reports of destructive acts, some of which have been described here, BAM service-area development unfolds on the basis of an ostensibly comprehensive plan that is sensitive to both production and conservation.

## The Siberian Milieu: Territorial-Production Complexes

Siberia obviously is much too big to be developed all at once. Some 30 existing or projected growth centers (territorial-production complexes and lesser nodes) may be identified on the basis of current Soviet literature. These are to serve as springboards for further economic expansion into north and northeastern Siberia (Figure 17). Each unit represents a different stage of development in the Soviet regional planning continuum (see earlier discussion). The Arctic coast and most of northeast Siberia are subregions currently occupied by initial development foci (Stage I). From the Sea of Okhotsk to the northern Urals, including the Lower Ob gas fields and most of the BAM service area, are subregions of pioneer development (Stage II): Bratsk, Ust-Ilimsk, and the Middle Ob oil fields are subregions that are in transition between pioneer status and rear-support functions (Stage III); operating territorial complexes flank the Trans-Siberian Railroad in the south (Stage IV).

The planning units also reflect their own sets of macroscale, microscale, and technogenic constraints to economic development (Table 13 and Figure 18). Among the growth centers with the greatest number of obstacles to production and settlement are the industrial nodes of Khatanga (with 21 constraints), Udokan (with 20), Muya (20), Kotui (20), Igarka (19), Kureika (19), and Yakutsk (19); the territorial complexes of Norilsk (19), Urengoi-Taz (19), Lower Tunguska (18), and North Baikal (17). Among the regions with the fewest number of limitations are the complexes of Tobolsk (9), Komsomolsk (10), Shaim-Konda (10), Aleksandrovskoye-Kargasok (10), Sovetskaya Gavan/Vanino/Kholmsk (10), and Surgut (10). At the moment, no attempt can be made to quantitatively weigh the 21 variables because of their differing qualities, levels of harshness, and degrees of interrelatedness. Nevertheless, Table 13 provides a rough measure of rela-

---

*After one year the ground around a 120-cm pipeline thaws a halo of over 6 m; in 20 years the diameter may expand to 24 m.

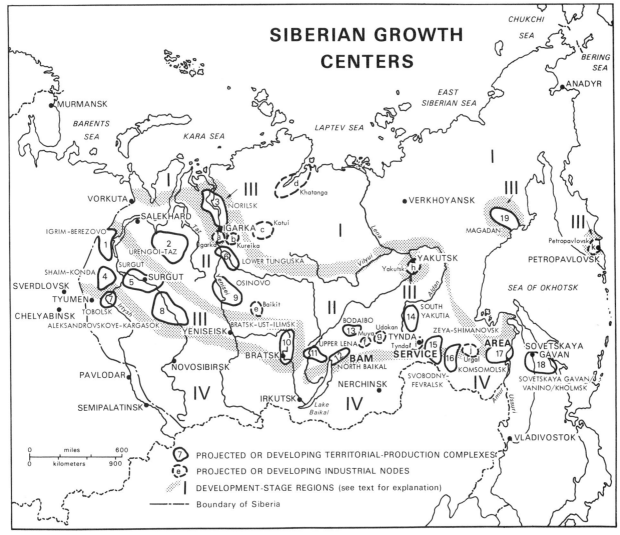

Figure 17
SOURCE: D. V. Belorusov, "Specific Peculiarities of the West Siberian Economic Complex," *Soviet Geography: Review and Translation* 10, no. 6 (June 1969): 274; Victor L. Mote, "Pacific Siberian Growth Centers: A New Soviet Commitment," *Soviet Union* 4, no. 2 (1977): 264–70; V. M. Myakinenkov, "Prospects of the Development of Production and Settlement in the Northern Yenisei Region," *Soviet Geography: Review and Translation* 16, no. 7 (September 1975): 580.

tive environmental difficulty for the leading Siberian growth centers.

**Summary and Conclusions**

Siberian resources will play an increasingly significant role in the world economy for years to come, but they will not come cheaply. Permanent settlement will be difficult, if not impossible, in certain preeminently northern and northeastern areas because of environmental harshness. All but the hardiest of human beings will be discouraged from living in those regions. Indeed, production and settlement there may have to be based on temporary labor pools only (tour-of-duty and work-shift methods).

In this paper, roughly two dozen interrelated environmental constraints have been presented and analyzed on the basis of their physical and economic influence on

Siberian resource development. Siberian resources are abundant, multifarious, and commonly cheap *in situ*. However, the added factors of remoteness and environmental harshness can cause their extraction to be unfeasible economically. Expenses like high labor and transportation costs are obvious enough, but the additional outlays inherent in frequent work stoppages and interruptions in the supply of materials often cannot be foreseen. The Soviet people have experienced for many years the macroscale physical limitations of the subarctic and arctic. They attempt to avoid, restrict, or control natural hazards. They, for the most part, are just as sensitive to the needs of their environments as their North American counterparts and, by law, are supposed to pay the price of environmental protection. This is especially necessary in permafrost regions, where any disruption may persist for decades. Ironically, if Soviet planners implement what is environmentally sound, they simply

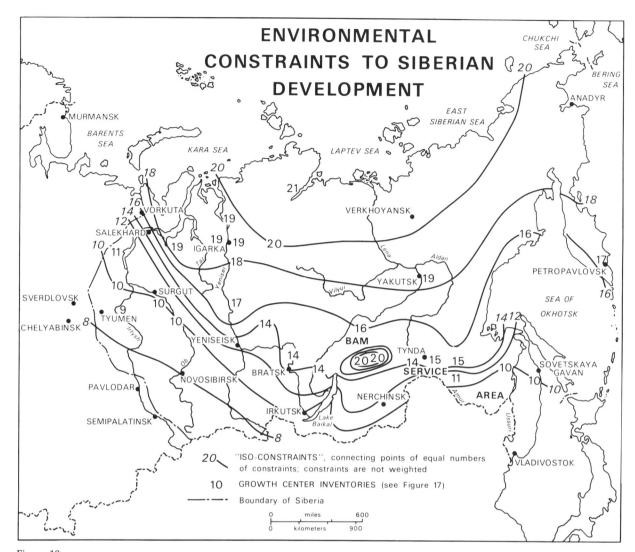

Figure 18
SOURCE: Totals in Table 13.

increase the costs of already expensive raw materials, perhaps rendering them uneconomical on domestic and foreign markets. Therefore, in any economic assessment of the impact of Siberian resources on the world economy, the costs of environmental constraints must be considered carefully, especially if Soviet environmental protection policies are rigidly enforced.

Total costs of Siberian resource development may be determined by the following formula:

$$TC = C_1 + C_{cp} + (C_{ce}) + C_i + R + (S)$$

where $TC$ represents total costs; $C_1$—labor costs; $C_{cp}$—capital production costs (including some measure of depreciation); $C_{ce}$—capital environmental costs, which may include pollution abatement, reclamation, permafrost defenses, and the like; $C_i$—intermediate materials and transportation costs; $R$—costs inherent in unforeseen layoffs and work stoppages caused by macroscale, microscale, and technogenic constraints, that is, costs that are beyond established norms and ordinary rates of depreciation (comparable to risk); and $S$—social costs (not

necessarily all-inclusive). Outlays for $C_{ce}$ and $S$ are in parentheses because, depending on the priority of the raw material that is designated for development and/or the self-purification capacity of the given environment, they conceivably may be ignored by Soviet developers.

Environmental constraints add to the costs of regional development in many, often subtle, ways (Figure 19). Salaries must be high (three to seven times the average wage) to induce even the least-skilled laborers into Siberia. To compensate for the lack of workers, more machinery per capita must be employed. In order to cope with Siberian conditions, the equipment must be nonstandard and thus expensive (15 to 60 percent higher than normal). Likewise, servicing the technology is costly, often over 25 percent of the total value of the unit. Investments in Siberia frequently are not recouped for scores of years; therefore, few benefits accrue over the short run. The sparse population creates a virtually perpetual labor deficit, especially in skilled vocations which means longer construction times and poorer quality work, increasing construction costs by factors of two or

**TABLE 13**
Constraints to the Development of Siberian Growth Centers

| GROWTH CENTERS | Polar Night | COLD (Low Harshness) | COLD (Medium Harshness) | COLD (High Harshness) | COLD (Very High Harshness) | WIND (Low Velocity) | WIND (Medium Velocity) | WIND (High Velocity) | Inversion Hazard | High Humidity | Fog Prevalence | Flood Hazard | Marsh Hazard | Drought Prevalence | Snow Density | Snow Duration | Snow Depth | Seasonal Frost | Sporadic Permafrost | Discontinuous Permafrost | Continuous Permafrost | Seismicity | Flows and Slides | Avalanches | Icings | Storminess | Tsunamis | Air-Pollution Potential | Water-Pollution Potential | SUBTOTALS (● = numerator; ○ = denominator) | TOTALS |
|---|---|---|---|---|---|---|---|---|---|---|---|---|---|---|---|---|---|---|---|---|---|---|---|---|---|---|---|---|---|---|---|
| 1. Igrim-Berezovo | ○ | ● | ● | | | ● | ● | | ● | | | ● | ● | | | ○ | | | ● | ● | | | | | | | | ○ | | 9/2 | 11 |
| 2. Urengoi-Taz | ○ | ● | ● | ● | | ● | ● | | ○ | ● | | ● | ● | | | ● | ○ | ● | ● | ● | | | | | ○ | ○ | | ○ | ○ | 12/7 | 19 |
| 3. Norilsk | ● | ● | ● | ● | | ● | ● | ● | ○ | ● | ○ | | | | | ● | | ● | ● | ● | ● | | | ● | ● | | | ○ | ○ | 15/4 | 19 |
| 4. Shaim-Konda | | ● | | | | | | | ● | | ● | ● | ● | ○ | ● | ○ | | ● | | | | | | | | | | ○ | | 7/3 | 10 |
| 5. Surgut | | ● | | | | ● | ● | | ● | | ● | ● | | | | ○ | | ● | ● | | | | | | | | | ○ | | 8/2 | 10 |
| 6. Lower Tunguska | ○ | ● | ● | ● | | ● | ● | | ○ | ● | | | | ○ | | ● | ● | ● | ● | ● | | | | ○ | ○ | | | ● | ● | 13/5 | 18 |
| 7. Tobolsk | | ● | | | | | ● | | | | ● | ● | ● | ○ | ● | ○ | ● | | | | | | | | | | | | | 7/2 | 9 |
| 8. Aleksandrovskoye-Kargasok | | ● | | | | | ● | | | | ● | ● | ● | | ● | ○ | ○ | ● | | | | | | | | | | ○ | | 7/3 | 10 |
| 9. Osinovo | ○ | ● | ● | | | ● | ● | | ○ | ● | | | | ○ | | ● | ● | ● | ● | ● | | | ○ | ○ | | | | ● | ● | 11/6 | 17 |
| 10. Bratsk–Ust-Ilimsk | | ● | ● | | | ● | ● | | ○ | ● | ● | | | ○ | | ● | | ● | ● | ● | | | | ● | | | | ● | ● | 11/3 | 14 |
| 11. Upper Lena | | ● | ● | | | ● | | | ○ | ● | ● | | | ○ | | ● | | ● | ● | ● | ○ | | | ● | | | | ● | ● | 11/3 | 14 |
| 12. North Baikal | | ● | ● | | | ● | | | ○ | ● | ● | | ○ | | | ● | | ● | ● | ● | ● | | ● | ● | ● | | | ● | ○ | 14/3 | 17 |
| 13. Bodaibo | | ● | ● | ● | | ● | | | ○ | | | | | | | ○ | | ● | ● | ● | ● | ● | ○ | ○ | ○ | ● | | ● | ○ | 10/6 | 16 |
| 14. South Yakutia | | ● | ● | ● | | ● | | | ○ | | | | | | | ● | | ● | ● | ● | ● | ● | | ○ | ● | | | ● | ○ | 12/3 | 15 |
| 15. Zeya-Shimanovsk | | ● | ● | ● | | ● | | | ○ | | | ● | ○ | | | ○ | | ● | ● | ● | | | | | | | | ● | ○ | 10/5 | 15 |
| 16. Svobodny-Fevralsk | | ● | ● | | | ● | | | | | | ● | ○ | | | ○ | | ● | ● | ● | | | | | | | | ● | ○ | 8/3 | 11 |
| 17. Komsomolsk | | ● | ● | | | ● | | | | | | ● | | | ● | ○ | | ● | | | | | | ○ | ○ | | | | ○ | 6/4 | 10 |
| 18. Sovetskaya Gavan/Vanino/Kholmsk | | ● | | | | ● | ● | | | | | | | | ● | ○ | ● | | | | ○ | | ○ | | | | | | | 5/3 | 8 |
| 19. Magadan | ○ | ● | | | | ● | ● | | ● | | | | | | ● | ○ | ○ | ● | ● | ● | | ○ | ● | ● | ● | | | | ○ | 11/5 | 16 |
| a. Igarka | ● | ● | ● | ● | | ● | ● | | ○ | ● | ○ | | ○ | | | ● | | ● | ● | ● | ● | | | | ● | ○ | | ● | ● | 15/4 | 19 |
| b. Kureika | ● | ● | ● | ● | | ● | ● | | ○ | ● | | | ○ | | | ● | | ● | ● | ● | ● | | | ○ | ● | ○ | | ● | ● | 15/4 | 19 |
| c. Kotui | ● | ● | ● | ● | ● | ● | ● | ● | ○ | ● | | | | | | ● | | ● | ● | ● | ● | | ○ | ● | ● | | | ○ | ○ | 16/4 | 20 |
| d. Khatanga | ● | ● | ● | ● | ● | ● | ● | ● | | ● | ● | ● | ● | | | ● | | ● | ● | ● | ● | | | | ● | ● | | ○ | ● | 20/1 | 21 |
| e. Baikit | | ● | | | | ● | | | ○ | ● | ● | | | | | ○ | ● | ● | ● | ● | | | | ○ | ● | | | ● | ○ | 10/4 | 14 |
| f. Muya | | ● | ● | ● | | ● | | | ● | ● | ● | | ○ | ○ | | ● | | ● | ● | ● | ● | ● | ● | ● | ● | | | ● | ○ | 17/3 | 20 |
| g. Udokan | | ● | ● | ● | | ● | | | ● | ● | ● | | ○ | ○ | | ● | | ● | ● | ● | ● | ● | ● | ● | | | | ● | ○ | 17/3 | 20 |
| h. Yakutsk | ○ | ● | ● | ● | ● | ● | | | ● | | ● | | | | ● | ● | ○ | ● | ● | ● | ● | ○ | | | ● | | | ● | ● | 16/3 | 19 |
| i. Tynda | | ● | ● | ● | | ● | | | ○ | | | | | | | ○ | | ● | ● | ● | ● | ○ | | | ● | | | ● | ○ | 10/4 | 14 |
| j. Urgal | | ● | ● | ● | | ● | | | | | | ● | ● | | | ○ | | ● | ● | ● | | | ○ | ● | ● | | | ● | | 12/3 | 15 |
| k. Petropavlovsk | ○ | ● | | | | ● | ● | | | | ● | ● | ○ | | ○ | ● | ○ | ● | ● | | | | ● | ● | ○ | | ● | ● | | ○ | 11/6 | 17 |

☐ **Nil or minor**

⊙ **Minor to major**

● **Major**

SOURCE: Data contained on maps and appendices in the text and footnoted sources.

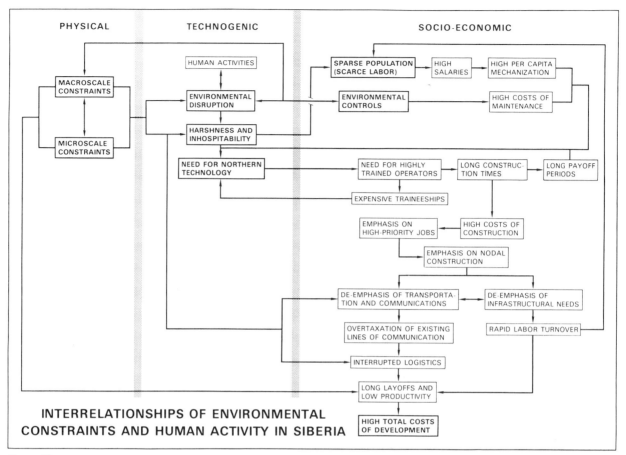

PHYSICAL          TECHNOGENIC          SOCIO-ECONOMIC

INTERRELATIONSHIPS OF ENVIRONMENTAL
CONSTRAINTS AND HUMAN ACTIVITY IN SIBERIA

Figure 19

three. Slow construction translates to greater emphasis on the higher priority jobs and a de-emphasis of infrastructural requirements. The comparative absence of infrastructure and amenities leads to rapid labor turnovers and adds to the expense of training newcomers. Emphasis on nodal construction bodes poorly for long-distance transportation and communications, which overtaxes the few existing lines. This interrupts the flow of supplies and spare parts and results in long, costly layoffs. This pattern of economic development continues even on the latest of Siberian construction projects like the Surgut-Urengoi and BAM railroads.

Hit-or-miss, trial-and-error, the Soviet people expand into their underdeveloped backwaters, albeit at a slow pace. They do so on the basis of steadily improving regional development plans, the latest of which is the program-oriented type. We have noted that these blueprints account not only for production but also for the needs of the environment. Even though this "paper" sensitivity largely remains to be implemented at this time, it appears that more efforts than ever before are taken to ensure that Soviet man and the Siberian environment are considered equally.

This chapter represents an independent analysis of the sundry variables which limit Siberian economic development. More than twenty macroscale, microscale, and technogenic constraints have been examined in some detail. Many of the factors are closely related. Most of

them are sensitive to human intrusion. This is especially true of permafrost. To assimilate these regions rationally, special care and planning must be employed. Today, more concerned for these environments than ever before, Soviet authorities would seem to be on the right track, but appearances should not be accepted at face value. Continued observation, better planning for the future, and a healthy dose of self-criticism are necessary to guarantee that this auspicious beginning results in an exemplary end.

Above all, any estimate of the potential of Siberia must give careful consideration to the environmental constraints that exist in the region. Production costs will be high and, if the environment is to be maintained, development must proceed at a moderate pace and with care. In many cases, the resources of Siberia may not be competitive on world markets until the 21st century.

APPENDIX I
DOGAYEV'S ENGINEERING-GEOGRAPHIC
REGIONS AND SUBREGIONS

A.    Engineering Region I (severest of all zones) (Figure 20)
    1.   temperature index = 101 to 144
    2.   permafrost = continuous and deep

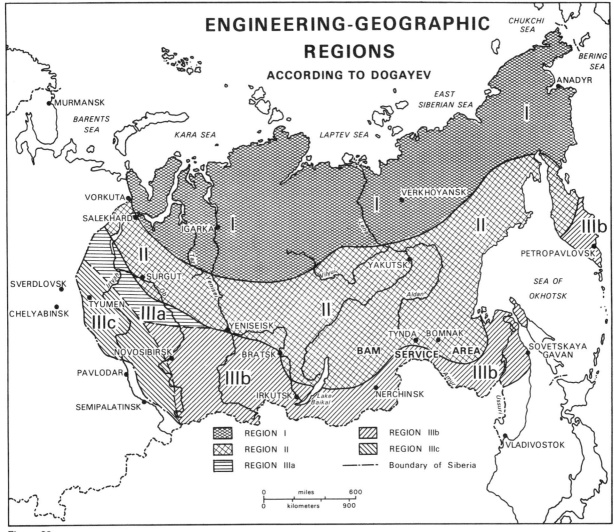

Figure 20
SOURCE: Yu. M. Dogayev, *Ekonomicheskaya effektivnost novoi tekhniki na Severe* [The cost-effectiveness of new technology in the North], p. 49. See Appendix 1 for explanation of characteristics of the regions.

3. relief = dissected thermokarst mounds, pingos, ice cracks and wedges, gullies, thermokarst lakes, and so forth)
4. valley and lowland fogs
5. snow cover duration = 240 to 280 days
6. snowbanks = 13 to 15 m
7. snow density = 0.3 to 0.5 g/cm$^3$
8. polar night = 40 to 90 days
9. summer bogs; active zone = 20 cm
10. almost totally roadless (winter ice and snow-packed roads only)

B. Engineering Needs of Region I
1. special coolant systems
2. special fuel pumps
3. specifically designed low-temperature construction able to resist temperature ranges of +20°C to −60°C
4. special oils and lubricants
5. heavily insulated batteries and electrical systems

6. cold-resistant tires and rubber components
7. heated and insulated equipment cabs
8. cabs should be spacious and situated over the engine in motor transport equipment
9. mining and construction equipment should be wear-resistant, especially to permafrost and rocky ground
10. tracked-amphibian vehicles for use in areas without roads

C. Engineering Region II
1. temperature index = 75 to 100
2. permafrost = continuous to sporadic, but widespread
3. ground = mainly peat
4. snow-friable
5. snow density = .08 to .25 g/cm$^3$
6. relief-frequent ravines and gullies
7. compared to Region I, many winter and dirt roads; a few surfaced roads

D. Engineering Needs of Region II
1. economically advantageous to use specifically designed northern technology
2. excavators should possess wear-resistant blades, buckets, scoops, and so forth
3. tracked vehicles should be used in areas without roads
E. Engineering Region III
1. temperature index = 56 to 76
2. permafrost = sporadic, with main concentrations in Central Siberia
E. 3. relief-flat with gentle passes
4. snow density = .25 to .45 g/cm$^3$
5. roads basically surfaced
F. Engineering Needs of Region III—is basis for sub-regionalization
1. Subregion IIIa—economically advantageous to use specifically designed northern technology
2. Subregion IIIb—use standard technology retrofitted or modified for northern conditions
   a. engine heaters or pre-start pilots
   b. battery and cab heaters.
   c. cold- and frost-resistant components
3. Subregion IIIc—is economically justified to use engine-starting heaters on standard technology
   a. may use semi-tracked vehicles and ski-type conveyances
   b. may use versatile wheeled vehicles
Source: Dogayev (n. 36, pp. 50–52).

---

APPENDIX II
ALEKSEYEV'S ICING REGIONS AND SUBREGIONS

I. Icings on Continuous Permafrost (Figure 21)
I$_3$—Taimyr Peninsula
1. *Spring-water icings* near new fault lines (several km$^2$ and 2 to 5 m thick)
2. *Groundwater icings* near seashore, river terraces, and fjord slopes (thousands of m$^2$ and 1 m thick); develop until end of November
3. *River icings* are common everywhere
   a. freezing of small streams until end of November
   b. freezing of large streams until January or February; Taimyr rivers may produce icings throughout the winter
I$_4$—Anabar-Olenek Region
1. *Spring-water icings* are relatively rare
2. *Groundwater icings* are small in size; are fed by surface water flow issuing from mountain foothills; cease to develop in December
3. *River icings* are generally everywhere; usually found in chains along small and medium-sized streams; on large rivers, icing continues until the spring thaw
I$_5$—Kotui-Vilyui Region
1. *Spring-water icings* are persistent along faults; partly fed by lakes (dozens of km$^2$ and 6 m thick—they may last all year)

2. *Groundwater icings* occur mainly along rock cliffs together with artesian formations (may occur thousands of m$^2$)
3. *River icings* are everywhere (up to 50 to 80 km long; develop throughout the winter)
I$_6$—Upper Kolyma Region. Icing sources are active faults, large rivers, and subsurface water from taliks; within this region icings cover more than 25 km$^3$, with subsurface water sources alone accounting for over 5,700 km$^2$ of area.
1. *Spring-water icings* equal dozens of km$^2$; thickness is up to 12 m; most lie in state all year
2. *Soil-water icings*
   a. rare in Verkhoyansk-Kolyma region
   b. under a dozen thousand m$^2$ of area
   c. thickness is 2 m
   d. found basically along lower slopes of rocky cliffs
3. *River icings* are everywhere, even including the large ones like the Yana, Kolyma, and Indigirka
I$_7$—Chukchi Region
1. *Spring-water icings* equal dozens of km$^2$
2. *Groundwater icings* are most frequent along the Chukchi and Bering seas (fed by subpermafrost water); area equals 1,000 to 100,000 m$^2$; ice thickness is 2 to 3 m
3. *River icings* are everywhere
I$_8$—Yamal-Gydan and
I$_9$—Yenisei-Khatanga regions
1. *Spring-water icings* are mainly in the valleys of small rivers fed from intrapermafrost taliks; area is rarely over .5 km$^2$; some are perennial
2. *Groundwater icings* are found on steep slopes of rivers and seas; are small in size; form until November and December
3. *River icings* are everywhere, often covering the entire valley
I$_{10}$—Central Yakutia
1. *Spring-water icings* are found on right banks of Lena and Aldan valleys (much rarer in central part of region); rarely over one km$^2$; ice thickness of 5 m
2. *Groundwater icings* form on steep slopes and cliff faces
3. *River icings* are everywhere
I$_{11}$—Kolyma Lowland (Northern Coastal) Region
1. *Spring-water icings* are rare
2. *Groundwater icings* are distributed everywhere but they are limited by the shallow thickness of the active zone (.5 to 1 m); they freeze until the end of December
II. Icings of Discontinuous Permafrost
II$_2$—Lena-Tunguska,
II$_3$—Aldan-Uchur,
II$_4$—Transbaikalia, and
II$_5$—Zeya-Bureya regions
1. *Groundwater icings* prevail; are linked to taliks; the icings are associated with fault lines and rifts; relative propensity for icing ranges from .7 to 8%; in thermokarst depressions, where the water table lies below the regional erosion

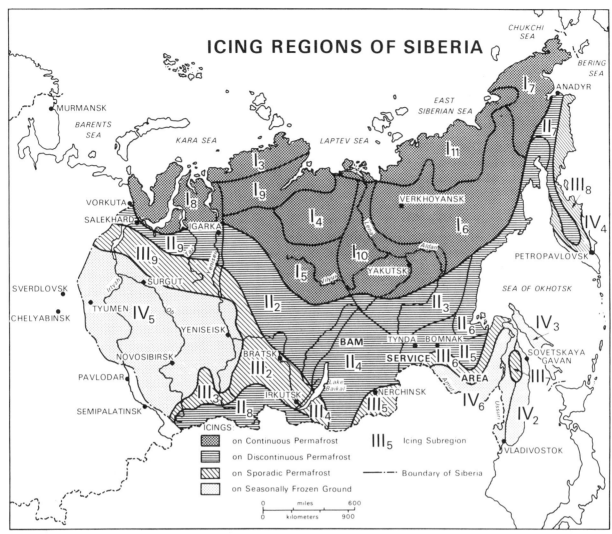

Figure 21
SOURCE: V. R. Alekseyev, "Naledi Sibiri i Dalnego Vostoka" [Icings of Siberia and the Soviet Far East], in *Sibirsky geografichesky sbornik*, no. 8 (1974), p. 23.

level, there are no icings; in comparison to groundwater icings of Region I, the same icings here are larger in size (hundreds of thousands of $m^2$); these are connected to subpermafrost water; take up to 3 to 4 months to develop

2. *River icings* form along all the rivers except in thermokarst areas; in places are 100 to 150 km long

II$_6$—Okhotsk Region. Is distinguished by many icings (icings of all genetic types are represented here)

1. *Groundwater icings* are determined by the great porosity of the permafrost and tectonically fractured rock; formed chiefly along cliffs of river valleys and seashore

2. *Spring-water icings* rarely exceed over 1 to 2 $km^2$

3. *River icings* are found along the entire length of the rivers (relative icing propensity is 1.5 to 2%)

II$_7$—Koryak-Kamchatka Region. Icings are mainly groundwater and river types; found chiefly along faults and river valleys; area is dozens of $km^2$; ice thickness is 8 to 10 m

II$_8$—Sayan-Altai Region. Great icing potential

1. In the Altai, the icings are *glacier-fed*

2. *Spring-water icings* are widespread; areas run up to 10 $km^2$; length along valleys is up to 30 km

3. *River icings* reach 70 km long

4. *Groundwater icings* have limited distribution; found mainly along washes in the mountain slopes and on slopes of the river terraces

II$_9$—Nadym Region. Spring-water icings and groundwater icings are scarce here; are small in area and thickness; the largest of icings form on thermokarst thaw lakes; river icings are on all rivers but are shallow (.5 m)

III. Icings on Sporadic Permafrost

III$_2$—Angara,

III$_3$—Khakasia,

III$_4$—Selenga,

III$_5$—Onon-Argun, and

III$_6$—Amur regions. Small islands of permafrost beneath rivers and waterfalls

1. *Spring-water icings* are 2 to 2.5 m thick and less than 1 km$^2$ in area
2. *Groundwater icings* are linked to subpermafrost taliks, where permafrost lenses exist; generally no more than a tenth of a km$^2$ in area and 1 to 1.5 m thick; cryoplanation of the taliks may cause ice-mounding, causing danger to structures
3. *River icings* are everywhere; icing propensity is up to 3%, but total number of icings is far less than farther north

III$_7$—Sikhote-Alin Region. Rare islands of permafrost along rivers, higher elevations of the mountains, and along fault lines

1. *Spring-water icings* are not large in size; a few hundred m$^2$ in area and 1 m in thickness
2. *River icings* are rare

III$_8$—Kamchatka Region. Like III$_7$ with regard to permafrost

1. *Spring-water icings* are small in size and found along fault lines
2. *Groundwater icings* are less than .1 km$^2$ in area; found along the base of stream terraces, the slopes of mountains, and on the Okhotsk and Bering shores.

IV. Icings on Seasonally Frozen Ground. No permafrost

IV$_2$—Maritime

IV$_3$—Sakhalin, and

IV$_4$—South Kamchatka regions

1. *River and groundwater icings* are rare and usually found on impermeable rock outcrops; area is hundreds of m$^2$
2. *Spring-water icings* are on river terraces

IV$_5$—Ob-Irtysh

IV$_6$—Amur-Ussuri regions

1. *River icings* are small and scattered; usually found in chains about 1 m in thickness
2. *Groundwater icings* are also rare

SOURCE: V. R. Alekseyev, "Naledi Sibiri i Dalnego Vostoka" [Icings of Siberia and the Soviet Far East], in *Sibirsky geografichesky sbornik*, no. 8 (1974), pp. 24–30.

## APPENDIX III
## SELF-PURIFICATION CAPACITIES OF SIBERIAN ENVIRONMENTS ACCORDING TO GLAZOVSKAYA

| Region (Figure 22) | Pollutant[a] | Self-Purification Capacity[b] | Possible Reasons[c] |
|---|---|---|---|
| 1. Tundra | S | VW | Cold |
| | L | M | Cold, Permafrost |
| | G | VI | Strong Winds |
| 2. North Urals | S | VW | Cold |
| | L | I | Swift Streams |
| | G | M | Surface Inversions |
| 3. Lower Ob | S | VW | Cold |
| | L | M | Cold, Slow Streams, Permafrost |
| | G | M | Surface Inversions |
| 4. Byrranga Mts. and North Siberian Lowland | S | VW | Cold |
| | L | M | Cold, Permafrost |
| | G | VI-I | High Winds |
| 5. Putorana Mts. | S | VW | Cold |
| | L | M | Low Precipitation, Cold, Permafrost |
| | G | W-VW | Surface Inversions |
| 6. Central Siberian Lowland | S | VW | Cold |
| | L | M | Cold, Permafrost |
| | G | VW | Asiatic High |
| 7. Verkhoyansk-Chersky Highlands | S | VW | Cold |
| | L | M-I | Swift Streams |
| | G | VW | Asiatic High |
| 8. Lower Yana, Indigirka, and Kolyma | S | VW | Cold |
| | L | M | Cold, Permafrost |
| | G | VW | Inversions |
| 9. Anadyr-Koryak | S | VW | Cold |
| | L | M | Cold, Permafrost |
| | G | W | Low Wind Speeds, Poor Diffusion |
| 10. Upper Middle Ob | S | W | Cold |
| | L | I | Good Precipitation |
| | G | M | Rainout, Level Terrain |
| 11. Lower Middle Ob | S | M | Lower Latitude (Warmer) |
| | L | I | Good Precipitation |
| | G | M | Rainout, Level Terrain |

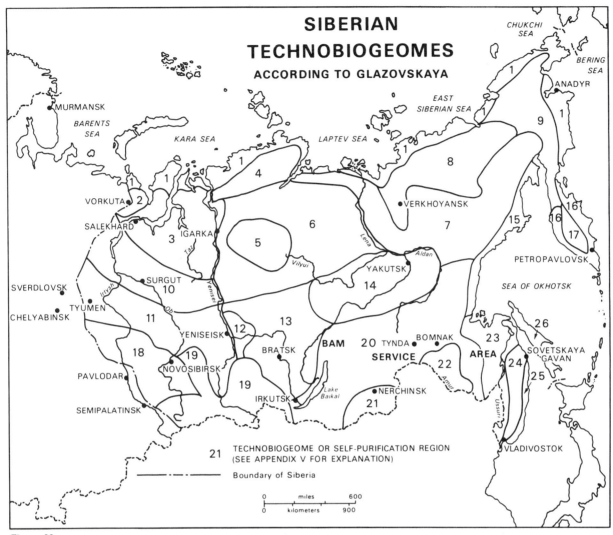

Figure 22
SOURCE: M. A. Glazovskaya, "Current Problems in the Theory and Practice of Landscape Geochemistry," *Soviet Geography: Review and Translation*, 18, no. 6 (June 1977): 372.

## APPENDIX III (*cont.*)

| Region (Figure 22) | Pollutant[a] | Self-Purification Capacity[b] | Possible Reasons[c] |
|---|---|---|---|
| 12. Yenisei Ridge | S | W-M | Lower Latitude |
| | L | M-I | Well Drained |
| | G | M-I | Good Diffusion |
| 13. Lower Central Siberian Plateau | S | W | Cold |
| | L | M | Reasonable Runoff, Low Precipitation, Permafrost |
| | G | VW | Asiatic High |
| 14. South Yakutia | S | W | Cold |
| | L | W | Low Precipitation, Permafrost |
| | G | VW | Asiatic High |
| 15. Okhotsk Coast | S | W | Cold |
| | L | M | Good Runoff, but Permafrost |
| | G | VI | High Winds |
| 16. Kamchatka Coast | S | M | Cold |
| | L | M | Better Precipitation and Runoff |
| | G | VI | High Winds |

APPENDIX III (*cont.*)

| Region (Figure 22) | Pollutant[a] | Self-Purification Capacity[b] | Possible Reasons[c] |
|---|---|---|---|
| 17. Kamchatka Interior | S | W | Cold |
| | L | VI | Good Precipitation and Runoff |
| | G | M | Wind Sheltered |
| 18. West Siberian | S | I | Warm (Bacterial Action) |
| | L | W | Droughty, Poorly Drained |
| | G | I | Open Terrain, Moderate Wind |
| 19. Altai-Sayan | S | W-I | Dependent on Elevation |
| | L | W-WI | Dependent on Elevation |
| | G | VW-I | Dependent on Elevation |
| 20. Baikal-Stanovoi | S | W-M | Cold to Warm |
| | L | M-I | Well Drained Overall but Low Precipitation, Permafrost |
| | G | VW-W | Better Near Coast; Asiatic High, Low Winds, inversions in interior |
| 21. Shilka-Argun | S | I | Warm (Bacterial Action) |
| | L | W | Scarce Precipitation |
| | G | W | Asiatic High, Low Winds, Inversions |
| 22. Zeya-Bureya | S | I | Warm (Bacterial Action) |
| | L | W | Poor Drainage |
| | G | VW | Low Winds |
| 23. Lower Amur-Ussuri Valleys | S | M | Warm (Bacterial Action) |
| | L | M | Reasonable Drainage, Good Precipitation |
| | G | VI | Good Winds, Rainout |
| 24. Sikhote-Alin | S | M-I | Wet Rot |
| | L | M-VI | Good Precipitation, Swift Rivers |
| | G | W-M | Air Drainage, High Humidity, Cloud Cover |
| 25. Maritime Coast | S | I | Wet Rot |
| | L | VI | Good Rain, Good Drainage |
| | G | VI | Good Wind, Rainout |
| 26. Sakhalin | S | M | Moderate (Bacterial Action) |
| | L | VI | Good Precipitation and Drainage |
| | G | VI | High Winds, Rainout |

SOURCE: Glazovskaya (n. 152, p. 372).
[a]S = Solid; L = Liquid; G = Gas
[b]VW = Very Weak; W = Weak; M = Moderate; I = Intensive; VI = Very Intensive
[c]Author's suggestions

## NOTES

1. A. Silin, "For ourselves and our offspring," *Izvestiya* (hereafter *I*), 17 November 1977, p. 2

2. Amilcar Herrera, "The Risks Involved," *Mazingira*, no. 3/4 (1977), pp. 25–26.

3. V. Ya. Vasilenko, "The program-oriented approach to the development of the BAM zone," in *Baikalo-Amurskaya Magistral* (Moscow: Mysl, 1977) (hereafter *BAM–77*), pp. 46–61.

4. N. I. Mikhailov, *Priroda Sibiri* [Nature in Siberia], (Moscow: Mysl, 1976), p. 86, citing the work of Rikhter, Parmuzin, Sochava, and Timofeyev.

5. V. F. Burkhanov, "Criteria for Determining an En-gineering-Geographic Boundary of the North of the USSR," *Soviet Geography: Review and Translation* (hereafter *SGRT*), 11, no. 1 (January 1970): 26–27, citing the work of Breifus, Alisov, Berg, Zubov, Velikanov, and Slavin.

6. "Pacific Siberia" includes Eastern Siberia and the Soviet Far East. An early prediction about the export value of Pacific Siberian resources may be seen in V. A. Krotov, I. I. Borovsky, Yu. F. Mikhailov, and V. P. Shotsky, "The Role of Eastern Siberia in Solving Some of the Economic Problems of the Pacific Basin," *SGRT*, 9, no. 2 (February 1968): 142–44. The original article was written at least six years before the onset of détente.

7. Thomas W. Robinson, "Siberian Development: Implications for the Soviet Union in Asia" (paper presented at the 9th national convention of the American Association for the Advancement of Slavic Studies, Washington 15 October 1977), pp. 3–4; for similar conclusions, see Victor L. Mote, "Pacific Siberian Growth Centers: A New Soviet Commitment," *Soviet Union*, 4, pt. 2 (1977): 256–70.

8. See, for instance, G. A. Agranat, *Novaya tekhnika i osvoyeniye zarubezhnogo Severa* [New technology and the development of the North abroad] (Moscow, 1960) and his *Zarubezhny Sever: Opyt osvoyeniya* [The North abroad: Development experience] (Moscow, 1970); I. P. Gerasi-mov, *Preobrazovaniye prirody i razvitiye geograficheskoi nauki v SSSR* [The transformation of nature and the development of geographic science in the USSR] (Moscow, 1967);

A. E. Probst, *Effektivnost territorialnoi organizatsii pro-izvodstva* [The effectiveness of the territorial organization of production] (Moscow, 1965); V. B. Sochava, *Nekotorye problemy geografii Aziatskoi Rossii* [Some problems of the geography of Asiatic Russia] (Irkutsk, 1968).

9. V. F. Burkhanov, *Tekhnika dlya Severa* [Technology for the North] (Moscow, 1966); Yu. M. Dogayev, "The economic characteristics of the utilization of motor transport in the northeast USSR," *Problemy Severa*, no. 9 (1965).

10. S. V. Slavin, *Promyshlennoye i transportnoye osvoy-eniye Severa SSSR* [Industrial and transport development of the Soviet North] (Moscow, 1961); also *Osvoyeniye Severa* [The development of the North] (Moscow, 1975).

11. Ye. B. Lopatina and O. R. Nazarevsky, *Otsenka prirodnykh uslovii zhizni naseleniya* [An evaluation of the natural conditions of life of the population] (Moscow, 1972).

12. *Stroitelstvo v rayonakh Vostochnoi Sibiri i Krainego Severa* [Construction in regions of Eastern Siberia and the Far North] (Krasnoyarsk, 1963); V. P. Dyachenko and V. G. Venzher, eds.; *Uchet prirodnogo i geograficheskogo faktorov v tsenoobrazovanii* [An assessment of the natural and geographic factors in the determination of price] (Moscow, 1964); S. A. Mekkel, *Materialy ekonomicheskogo analiza ispolzovaniya tekhniki na otkrytykh rabotakh v sever-nykh rayonov* [Materials on the economic analysis of the use of technology for outside work in northern regions] (Novosibirsk, 1964); G. V. Uzhik, *Prochnost i plastichnost metallov pri nizkikh temperaturakh* [Toughness and plastic-ity of steel at low temperatures] (Moscow, 1957).

13. See his articles in *Naledi Sibiri* [Icings of Siberia] (Moscow, 1969). His later work includes bibliographies of almost 300 entries.

14. S. M. Fleishman, *Seli* [Mudflows] (Leningrad, 1970); V. F. Perov, *Otsenka selevoi opasnosti territorii pri izyskaniyakh* [An assessment of the mudflow danger of an area during exploratory prospecting] (Moscow, 1970); G. K. Tushinsky, *Laviny* [Snow avalanches] (Moscow, 1949). These and later works by the same authors include exten-sive bibliographies.

15. V. P. Solonenko, *Ocherki po inzhenernoi geologii Vos-tochnoi Sibiri* [Observations on the engineering geology of Eastern Siberia] (Irkutsk, 1960). Solonenko has been the chief geological consultant for the Baikal-Amur Mainline railway.

16. The work of these persons will be cited elsewhere in this study.

17. This research is cited generously in Theodore Sha-bad and Victor L. Mote, *Gateway to Siberian Resources: The BAM* (Washington and New York: Scripta Halsted, 1977), pp. 106–15.

18. G. A. Agranat and V. Loginov, "On the develop-ment of northern territories," *Kommunist*, no. 2 (1976), pp. 39–48; Leslie Dienes, "Investment Priorities in Soviet Regions," *Annals of the Association of American Geographers*, 62 (September 1972): 437–54.

19. V. M. Myakinenkov, "Prospects of the Develop-ment of Production and Settlement in the Northern Yenisei Region," *SGRT*, 16, no. 7 (September 1975): 578; Robin Knight, "High Cost of Russia's Push for Siberian Oil," *U.S. News and World Report*, 3 April 1978, p. 56.

F. D. Dyakonov, "The BAM as a set of major long-term prospective problems of the national economy," in *BAM-77*, p. 31; V. Dokuchayev et al., "To exploit a little, the main thing is to learn," *Stroitelnaya gazeta*, 24 May 1970, p. 2; G. A. Agranat, "Exploiting and Conserving the Rich Soviet North," *The Geographical Magazine*, July 1976, p. 619.

20. G. A. Agranat, "Rich Soviet North," p. 618 n 19 and V. N. Lazhentsev, "Economic-geographic aspects of the BAM problem," in *BAM-77*, p. 36.

21. Keven Klose, "BAM—A Dream Turns into Real-ity." *The Washington Post*, 2 March 1978, p. A21; country average is about 150 rubles a month. In general, wages increase as one gravitates east and/or north.

22. Agranat and Loginov, "On development," p. 47 n 18.

23. Ye. N. Pertsik, "Problems of regional planning in the BAM zone," in *BAM-77*, p. 191.

24. O. A. Izyumsky, "The natural resources of the BAM zone and their rational utilization," in *BAM-77*, p. 98.

25. K. P. Kosmachev, *Pionernoye osvoyeniye taigi* [Pioneer development of the taiga] (Novosibirsk: Nauka, 1974).

26. Dyakonov, "BAM as a set," p. 32 n 19, and Lazhentsev, "BAM problem," p. 56 n 20; information on the "modular method" is explained in L. I. Brezhnev, "Comrade Brezhnev's Speech," *Gudok* (hereafter *G*), 26 April 1978, p. 2.

27. Vasilenko, "BAM zone," pp. 46–48 n 3.

28. Ibid., p. 56.

29. Larry Price, *The Periglacial Environment, Permafrost, and Man* (Washington: Association of American Ge-ographers, 1972), p. 72. There are several definitions for the word "periglacial." Price used it to refer to environ-ments where frost processes prevail over other forms of weathering. Thus, most of what we have defined as Siberia qualifies as periglacial according to the Price defi-nition. This applies particularly to Pacific Siberia (see Shabad and Mote, *Siberian Resources*, pp. 93–101 n 7).

30. This statistic is based on the maximum limit of one to two per square mile in hunting-and-gathering socie-ties, which are traditional to northern regions. This datum, of course, is subject to change with the introduc-tion of special technologies. John W. Alexander, *Economic Geography* (Englewood Cliffs, N.J.: Prentice-Hall, Inc., 1963), p. 34.

31. Pertsik, "BAM zone," p. 192 n 23.

32. Cloud cover over the majority of Siberia, even in winter, averages six to seven tenths, with the greatest concentrations occurring in summer and fall. Paul E. Lydolph, "Some Characteristics of the Climate of the USSR with a Direct Bearing on Human Activity," *SGRT*, 18, no. 3 (March 1977): 153–55, and S. P. Suslov, *The Physical Geography of Asiatic Russia* (San Francisco: W. H. Freeman, 1961), pp. 14, 34, and 133.

33. V. V. Kryuchkov, *Chutkaya subarktika* [The sensitive Subarctic] (Moscow: Nauka, 1976), p. 7. Albedo of a sur-face is high for low-angle rays on almost any surface. For snow or ice surfaces, albedos are high no matter what the angle (45 to 85%).

34. V. V. Kryuchkov, *Kraini Sever: Problemy ratsional-nogo ispolzovaniya prirodnykh resursov* [The Extreme North: Problems of rational utilization of natural resources] (Moscow: Mysl, 1973), p. 56.

35. U. S. Department of the Army, *Effects of Climate on Combat in European Russia*, Department of the Army Pamphlet No. 20–291 (February 1952), p. 74.

36. Yu. M. Dogayev, *Ekonomicheskaya effektivnost novoi tekhniki na Severe* [The cost-effectiveness of new technology in the North] (Moscow: Nauka, 1969), pp. 33–36.

37. M. A. Czaplicka, *Aboriginal Siberia* (London: Oxford University Press, 1969), pp. 320–321; Paul E. Lydolph, *Geography of the USSR* (New York: John Wiley and Sons, 1977), p. 386.

38. David F. Aberle, "'Arctic Hysteria' and Latah in Mongolia," in *Social Structure and Personality: A Casebook*, ed. by Yehudi Cohen (New York: Holt, Rinehart, and Winston, 1961), pp. 471–75; Seymour Parker, "The Wiitiko Psychosis in the Context of Ojibwa Personality and Culture," *American Anthropologist*, 62, no. 4 (August 1960): 603; Tadeusz Grygier, "Psychiatric Observations in the Arctic," *The British Journal of Psychology*, 39, pt. 2 (December 1948): 90–91; Morton Teichner, "Windigo Psychosis: A Study of a Relationship between Belief and Behavior among the Indians of Northeastern Canada," *Proceedings of the 1960 Annual Spring Meeting of the American Ethnological Society* (Seattle: University of Washington Press, 1960), p. 14. I wish to thank Anthony Colson of the University of Houston's Department of Anthropology for the above references.

39. Kryuchkov, *Kraini Sever*, p. 56 n 34.

40. Dogayev, *Novoi tekhniki*, pp. 38–40 n 36.

41. Originally by Wright Miller, *Russians as People* (New York: Dutton, 1960), p. 22.

42. Zh. A. Zayonchkovskaya and D. M. Zakharina, "Problems of Providing Siberia with Manpower," *SGRT*, 13, no. 10 (December 1972): 681.

43. David K. Willis, "Siberia: Drilling a Frozen Frontier," *The Christian Science Monitor*, 7 February 1978, p. 17.

44. Kryuchkov, *Kraini Sever*, p. 21 n 34.

45. Dogayev, *Novoi tekhniki*, p. 17 n 36.

46. See, among others, "Moscow: Orders for Siberia and the Far East—ahead of schedule with excellent quality," *I*, 16 May 1978, p. 1, and "The Volga: Orders for Siberia and the Far East—ahead of schedule with excellent quality," *I*, 21 May 1978, p. 1.

47. Agranat and Loginov, "On development," p. 48 n 18; V. Kozlov and Ye. Shatokhin, "Steel arteries," *I*, 8 March 1978, p. 2.

48. Klose, "A Dream Turns," p. A21; V. Borisenko, "Soviet-Canadian collaboration," *Vneshnyaya torgovlya* no. 2 (1978), pp. 31–33; V. Myshkov, "V/O Traktoreksport—Caterpillar," *Vneshnyaya torgovlya*, no. 3 (1978), pp. 20–22; L. Petrov, "In the interests of Soviet-Japanese collaboration," *Vneshnyaya torgovlya*, no. 5 (1978), pp. 37–39.

49. A. Koshelev, "Heat for the BAM," *G*, 17 February 1977, p. 2; V. L. Gorovoi and V. M. Shlykov, "Basic Trends in the Development of the Forest Industry along the Baikal-Amur Mainline," *SGRT*, 19, no. 2 (February 1978): 96.

50. Dokuchayev, "To exploit," p. 2 n 19.

51. V. A. Kolyago, "A Classification and Regionalization of the Harsh, Cold Climate of Siberia and the Far East in Relation to Problems of Cold Resistance of Machines," *SGRT*, 11, no. 1 (January 1970): 38–47.

52. John F. Griffiths, *Applied Climatology: An Introduction* (London: Oxford University Press, 1976), p. 8.

53. Suslov, *Asiatic Russia*, p. 130 n 32.

54. L. L. Trube, "On the names of snowstorms," *Geografiya v shkole*, no. 2 (1978), p. 22, [translated in *SGRT*, 9, no. 8 (October 1978): 572–75.]

55. Dogayev, *Novoi tekhniki*, p. 32 n 36.

56. Ibid.

57. Ibid.

58. Ibid., pp. 39, 40, 69.

59. M. Ye. Berlyand, "The Climatological Aspects of Investigation of Atmospheric Contamination with Industrial Wastes," in *Modern Problems of Climatology*, translated by Foreign Technology Division (Wright-Patterson AFB, Ohio: 1967), p. 305; N. F. Nakorenko and F. G. Tokar, *Klimat svobodnoi atmosfery* [Climate of the free atmosphere] (Leningrad, 1959), p. 28.

60. A. I. Karausheva, "Microclimate of the Chara lowland," *Sibirsky geografichesky sbornik*, no. 8 (1974), pp. 163–65; Suslov, *Asiatic Russia*, p. 130 n 32; A. A. Nedeshev, F. F. Bybin, and A. M. Kotelnikov, "The development of the Transbaikal North and the problems of transforming the economy of Chita Oblast in connection with the construction of the Baikal-Amur Mainline," *Sibirsky geografichesky sbornik*, no. 13 (1977), p. 44; the average difference is 5 to 10°C.

61. Lydolph, *Geography of USSR*, p. 402 n 37.

62. Paul E. Lydolph, *Climates of the Soviet Union*, vol. 7 of *World Survey of Climatology*, by H. E. Landsberg, ed., 13 vols. (New York: Elsevier Scientific Publishing Company, 1977), p. 294.

63. Dogayev, *Novoi tekhniki*, p. 33 n 36.

64. Lydolph, *Climates in Soviet Union*, p. 288 n 62.

65. Patrick D. Baird, *The Polar World* (New York: John Wiley, 1964), p. 64 (thanks to Charles Gritzner for this source); Howard J. Critchfield, *General Climatology* (Englewood Cliffs, N.J.: Prentice-Hall, 1974), p. 204.

66. Lydolph, "Characteristics of Climate," p. 153 n 32.

67. Central Intelligence Agency, *USSR Agriculture Atlas* (Washington: CIA, 1974), p. 13.

68. Suslov, *Asiatic Russia*, pp. 14, 131, 133 n 32.

69. S. M. Fleishman and V. F. Perov, *Seleopasnye rayony Sovetskogo Soyuza* [Mudflow-hazard regions of the Soviet Union] (Moscow University, 1976), p. 138.

70. Dogayev, *Novoi tekhniki*, pp. 48–51 n 36.

71. Nedeshev, Bybin, and Kotelnikov, "Development of Transbaikal North," p. 44 n 60.

72. G. K. Tushinsky, *Lavinoopasnye rayony Sovetskogo Soyuza* [Avalanche-hazardous regions of the Soviet Union] (Moscow University, 1970), p. 108.

73. A. Kleva, "BAM: The view from outer space," *I*, 16 May 1978, p. 3; A. Grivtsov, "Test of fortitude," *G*, 4 January 1978, p. 1.

74. Suslov, *Asiatic Russia*, p. 137 n 32.

75. Price, *Periglacial Environment*, p. 26 n 29.

76. Ibid., p. 23.

77. Silin, "For ourselves," p. 2 n 1.

78. T. G. Morozova and D. M. Zakharina, *Novaya geografiya Sibiri* [A new geography of Siberia] (Moscow: Prosveshcheniye, 1972), p. 37; I. P. Gerasimov, D. L. Armand, and K. M. Efron, *Natural Resources of the Soviet Union* (San Francisco: W. H. Freeman, 1971), pp. 14–15.

79. The USSR contains 8%; Siberia's share is 25% of that or 2% of the world total. See M. I. Lvovich, "Water resources," *Bolshaya Sovetskaya entsiklopediya*, 3rd ed., 5: 180–81.

80. V. R. Alekseyev, V. V. Vorobyev, and B. B. Prokhorov, "Problems of interaction between nature, economy, and population in the construction of the Baikal-Amur Mainline," *Doklady Instituta Geografii Sibiri i Dalnego Vostoka*, no. 46 (1975), p. 6; A. Melik-Pashayeva, A. Ivakhnov, and A. Illarionov, "Nature and people: The inimitable world of the taiga," *I*, 20 April 1975, p. 4.

81. Kryuchkov, *Kraini Sever*, pp. 164–66 n 34.

82. Ibid., p. 51.

83. Harley J. Walker, *Man in the Arctic* (Maxwell AFB, Alabama: Arctic, Desert, Tropic Information Center, 1963), pp. 36–59 (thanks to Charles Gritzner).

84. V. Khodi, "In the mainline zone," *P*, 12 December 1976, p. 3; A. Kleva, "In the Udokan Mountains," *I*, 21 June 1978, p. 2; during the summer of 1978, a huge subpermafrost talik was discovered at Udokan. A single aquifer was estimated to produce at a rate that is a thousand times more than the needs of the population.

85. Paul Dibb, *Siberia and the Pacific: A Study of Economic Development and Trade Prospects* (New York: Praeger, 1972), p. 28.

86. Leslie Dienes, "The Soviet Union: An Energy Crunch Ahead?" *Problems of Communism*, 26 (September-October 1977): 48.

87. V. F. Zadorozhny, "An economic-geographical analysis of geological exploration based on a BAM service-area example," *Sibirsky geografichesky sbornik*, no. 13 (1977), p. 114.

88. Shabad and Mote, *Siberian Resources*, p. 67 n 17; Surgut-Urengoi estimates based on information in "Problems of the industrial development of the North," *Problemy Severa*, no. 12 (1967), p. 177. See chapter 7 for a revised estimate.

89. V. Kozlov and Ye. Shatokhin, "Tyumen—the great construction project of the country," *I*, 17 February 1978, p. 2.

90. Price, *Periglacial Environment*, p. 64 n 29.

91. Kryuchkov, *Kraini Sever*, pp. 78–80 n 34.

92. N. A. Mikhaylov and A. K. Pogrebnoy, "Environmental protection in the BAM Zone," *Zheleznodorozhny transport*, no. 11 (1976), pp. 65–67.

93. V. N. Lapkin, "How to deal with subsidence of the foundation of the embankment," *Zheleznodorozhny transport*, no. 11 (1976), pp. 69–70; A. Pushkar, "By order of the BAM," *I*, 8 November 1977, p. 6.

94. Kryuchkov, *Subarktika*, pp. 19–22 n 33.

95. O. Tatevosyan, "The transport factor in setting up territorial production complexes," *G*, 10 March 1978, p. 2.

96. I. Kovrigin, "The Nadym River and its development for navigation," *Rechnoi transport*, no. 1 (1978), pp. 42–44; G. Biryulev and A. Toropov, "Extractive equip-ment operates even in freezing weather," *Rechnoi transport*, no. 2 (1978), p. 43; V. Filkov, "Shipping-channel maintenance in the third year of the five-year plan," *Rechnoi transport*, no. 3 (1978), p. 41; V. Degtyarev, Ye. Zin, and N. Permichev, "River transport in Siberia and the Far East," *Rechnoi transport*, no. 3 (1978), pp. 21–22; A. Lvov, "The Sibir: Heading for the Yenisei," *I*, 13 April 1978, p. 4; A. Lvov, "The ice-navigation experiment is complete," *I*, 14 May 1978, p. 1; V. Zakharko, "The Kara Sea: The ice barrier has been overcome," *I*, 11 February 1978, p. 3.

97. Kryuchkov, *Kraini Sever*, pp. 81–82 n 34; Kryuchkov, *Subarktika*, pp. 21–23 n 33.

98. T. I. Alekseyev, "Dirigibles in the North," *Problemy Severa*, no. 9 (1965), p. 206.

99. V. Bogdanov, "Father Frost in 'Civvies'," *I*, 25 March 1977, p. 4.

100. Kryuchkov, *Kraini Sever*, pp. 52, 92 n 34; Suslov, *Asiatic Russia*, pp. 147–49 n 32.

101. V. Vodolazhsky, "From the Urals to the Pacific," *I*, 4 April 1978, p. 3; Theodore Shabad, "Siberians Studying Reservoir's Impact," *New York Times*, 7 October 1979.

102. Kozlov and Shatokhin, "Tyumen," p. 2 n 89.

103. "Soviet Technology Could Cut Costs," *Oilweek*, 6 February 1978, pp. 12, 14.

104. Knight, "High Cost," p. 56 n 19.

105. Arthur A. Meyerhoff, *Potential for Foreign Participation in the Soviet Union and Chinese Petroleum Industries: A Course Manual* (Boston: International Human Resources Development Corporation, 1978), pp. 79, 83, 87; Eric Morgenthaler, "Kremlin Crunch . . . ," *Wall Street Journal*, 9 January 1978, pp. 1, 14.

106. Meyerhoff, *Potential*, p. 80.

107. Dienes, "Energy Crunch," p. 115 n 86.

108. Larry Auldridge, "Russian Pipelining Boom Will Continue into 80s," *The Oil and Gas Journal*, 10 October 1977, p. 115.

109. Ibid., p. 108 n 108.

110. B. N. Semenova, *Ekonomika stroitelstva magistralnykh truboprovodov* [The economics of building mainline pipelines] (Moscow, 1977), p. 60.

111. S. Vonsovsky, "Steel for Siberia," *I*, 2 September 1977, p. 2.

112. Burkhanov, "Engineering-Geographic Boundary," pp. 24–32 n 5.

113. Ibid., p. 29.

114. Dogayev, *Novoi tekhniki*, p. 38 n 36.

115. Kolyago, "Harsh, Cold Climate," p. 46 n 51; Kolyago proposed to expand his classification and regionalization as of 1968. By 1981, he had not published further work, but Yu. S. Kozhukhov analyzed selected environmental factors in terms of cost increments. See Yu. S. Kozhukhov, "Differentiation of Urban Construction Costs in Light of Environmental Factors," *SGRT*, 21, no. 10 (December 1980): 630–37.

116. S. Savelova, "Now that is a giant!" *I*, 21 February 1978, p. 3.

117. S. Afonin, "The plant that makes the steel giants," *I*, 22 June 1978, p. 3.

118. A. Chetvernikov, "Tested by the North," *I*, 21 February 1978, p. 3: [Photograph and caption] *I*, 21 April

1978, p. 2; Agranat, "Rich Soviet North," p. 620 n 19.

119. V. Kozlov, "The giant complex," *I*, 31 January 1978, p. 3; Kozlov and Shatokhin, "Steel arteries," p. 2 n 47.

120. Yu. Felchukov, "Heat from the Northern Lights," *G*, 18 April 1978, p. 2; V. Kozlov, "A floating power plant," *I*, 17 June 1978, p. 3.

121. A. Borisov, "BAM: The fruits of collaboration," *G*, 29 April 1978, p. 2; V. Safronov, "The locomotive is starting out for tomorrow," *I*, 22 June 1978, p. 3.

122. Bogdanov, "Father Frost," p. 4 n 99.

123. Thanks to all the members of the author's Geography 431 class (Spring 1978) at the University of Houston, with special gratitude for the efforts of Linda Mahr, Godina Ying, Susanne Demchak, Lanny Dumbauld, Donald Liles, and Murray York.

124. Myshkov, "Caterpillar," p. 20 n 48.

125. Zadorozhny, "Geological exploration," p. 104 n 87.

126. Nedeshev, Bybin and Kotilnikov, "Development of Transbaikal North," p. 44 n 60; V. P. Solonenko, "Seismicity of the BAM zone," *Vestnik Akademii Nauk SSSR*, no. 9 (September 1975), pp. 50–59; V. Zhuravlev, "Land-going pilots," *Sotsialisticheskaya industriya*, 17 September 1975, p. 1.

127. Glavnoye Upravleniye Geodezii i Kartografii pri Sovete Ministrov SSSR, *Atlas Zabaikalya* [Atlas of Transbaikalia] (Moscow-Irkutsk, 1967), p. 21; B. Semenov, "Earthquakes are being predicted," *G*, 9 December 1980, p. 4.

128. Solonenko, "Seismicity," pp. 56–58 n 126.

129. Akademiya Nauk SSSR i Glavnoye Upravleniye Geodezii i Kartografii GGK SSSR, *Fiziko-geografichesky atlas mira* [Physical-geographic atlas of the world] (Moscow, 1964), p. 12.

130. A. Gaidai, "Geologists on the BAM route," *G*, 16 June 1978, p. 2; A. Kleva, "What will the helium tell us," *I*, 8 June 1978, p. 3; "Models of Seismicity," *G*, 13 June 1978, p. 1.

131. Izyunsky, "Natural resources," p. 110 n 24.

132. V. Korneyev, "Dependable bridges for the Baikal-Amur Mainline," *I*, 22 April 1978, p. 4.

133. A. Nedeshev, "Siberian Alps," *I*, 4 February 1978, p. 6; L. Shinkarev, "Volcanoes Beyond Baikal," *I*, 17 February 1977, p. 6.

134. Solonenko, "Seismicity," p. 58 n 126.

135. I. P. Gerasimov and T. B. Zvonkova, "Natural Hazards in the Territory of the USSR: Study, Control, and Warning," in *Natural Hazards*, ed. by Gilbert F. White (New York: Oxford University Press, 1974), p. 245.

136. Fleishman and Perov, *Seleopasnye rayony*, p. 134 n 69.

137. Ibid., pp. 147, 149.

138. Gerasimov and Zvonkova, "Natural Hazards," p. 246 n 135; Tolstoi, *Chelovek—preobrazovatel prirody* [Man-transformer of nature] (Moscow: Nedra, 1975), p. 64; N. Davydov, "The tamers of Baikal," *G*, 17 May 1978, p. 4; O. Ognev, "The mudflow is a dangerous foe, but it can be beaten," *I*, 31 January 1978, p. 3.

139. Tushinsky, *Lavinoopasnye rayony*, p. 3 n 72.

140. Kleva, "Outer space," p. 3 n 73; V. Oliyanchuk, "The way is open," *I*, 16 March 1978, p. 1.

141. Suslov, *Asiatic Russia*, pp. 143–45 n 32.

142. Price, *Periglacial Environment*, p. 64 n 29.

143. M. E. Adzhiyev, "Economic-geographic problems of the BAM," *Priroda*, no. 8 (August 1975), p. 7.

144. Price, *Periglacial Environment*, p. 64 n 29.

145. V. Lapkin, "Behind the facade of success," *G*, 21 December 1977, p. 2.

146. S. M. Bolshakov, D. M. Kerkulov, and T. V. Potatuyeva, "Rational anti-icing measures," *Transportnoye stroitelstvo*, no. 9 (1977), p. 6.

147. Gerasimov and Zvonkova, "Natural Hazards," p. 249 n 135.

148. Nedeshev, Bybin and Kotelnikov, "Development of the Transbaikal North," p. 44 n 60; "Raise the rates of ship loading," *G*, 5 March 1978, p. 2.

149. Quoted in Trube, "Snowstorms," p. 23 n 54.

150. V. Kalinichev, "BAM kilometers through the taiga," *I*, 18 May 1977, p. 2.

151. Tolstoi, *Chelovek—preobrazovatel*, pp. 64–65 n 138.

152. M. A. Glazovskaya, "Current Problems in the Theory and Practice of Landscape Geochemistry," *SGRT*, 18, no. 6 (June 1977): 363–73.

153. T. R. Camp, *Water and Its Impurities* (New York: Reingold, 1963), p. 293.

154. T. A. Petrashek, "Urbanization and the problem of environmental protection," *Geografiya v shkole*, no. 4 (July–August 1977), p. 28.

155. V. B. Nefedova, "Research on the state of the environment of northern Western Siberia in connection with economic development and conservation," *Vestnik Moskovskogo Universiteta, seriya geografiya*, no. 5 (1976), p. 37; also see the translation in *SGRT*, 19, no. 1 (January 1978): 25–31.

156. A. M. Nekrasov and M. G. Pervukhin, *Energetika SSSR v 1976–1980 godakh* [Electric power in the USSR in 1976–80] (Moscow: Energetika, 1977), p. 286.

157. David K. Shipler, "Siberian Lake Now a Model of Soviet Pollution Control," *New York Times*, 16 April 1978; A. Kleva, "So that the Selenga might be clean," *I*, 23 June 1978, p. 1.

158. Meyerhoff, *Foreign Participation*, p. 114 n 105; Tolstoi, *Chelovek—preobrazovatel*, p. 26 n 138; V. Kozlov and Ye. Shatokhin, "The giant on the Tom," *I*, 29 April 1978, p. 2.

159. Kryuchkov, *Kraini Sever*, p. 46 n 34; Kryuchkov, *Subarktika*, p. 126 n 33.

160. Nefedova, "State of environment," p. 37 n 155.

161. Ye. I. Yelovoi and V. S. Smetanich, "Electric power supply problems of the BAM zone and some ways to resolve them," in *BAM–77*, p. 142.

162. Nekrasov and Pervukhin, *Energetika SSSR*, p. 273 n 156.

163. Philip R. Pryde, "Recent Trends in Preserved Natural Areas in the USSR," *Environmental Conservation*, 4, no. 3 (Autumn 1977): 173; Philip R. Pryde, "The First Soviet National Park," *National Parks Magazine*, 41, no. 236 (1967): 20–23; Philip R. Pryde, *Conservation in the*

*Soviet Union* (New York: Cambridge University Press, 1972), especially the chapter on *zapovedniki*.

164. A. G. Bannikov, *Po zapovednikam Sovetskogo Soyuza* [Through the nature reserves of the Soviet Union] (Moscow: Mysl, 1974), p. 200a; V. Vodolazhsky, "The taiga will be preserved," *I*, 24 June 1978, p. 3.

165. Melik-Pashayeva, Ivakhnov, and Illarionov, "Nature and people," p. 4 n 80; V. Loshakov, "The BAM and nature management," *Lesnaya promyshlennost*, 11 January 1977, p. 2; F. Shtilmark, "How many stone pines are there along the BAM?" *Literaturnaya gazeta*, no. 36 (3 September 1975), p. 10.

166. G. Polyanskaya et al., "Our forests today and tomorrow," *I*, 5 May 1977, p. 2.

167. Mikhailov, *Priroda Sibiri*, p. 110 n 4.

168. Loshakov, "Nature management," p. 2 n 165.

169. I. I. Buks, "Landscape-ecological characteristics of the BAM Zone and stability of the natural environment," in *BAM-77*, pp. 82–87.

170. V. V. Prokhorov, "Timely problems of medical geography in the BAM Zone," in *BAM-77*, pp. 131–38.

171. Victor L. Mote, "Environmental Protection and the Soviet 10th Five-Year Plan," *Geographical Survey*, 7, nos. 2, 3 (April, July 1978): April—25–27; July—40.

172. Yu. P. Belichenko, "Treat the country's water resources the Lenin way," *Priroda*, no. 12 (1969), pp. 73–76.

173. Donald R. Kelley, "Economic Growth and Environmental Quality in the USSR: Soviet Reaction to *The Limits to Growth*," *Canadian Slavonic Papers*, 18, no. 3 (September 1976): 266–83.

174. Kelley, "Economic Growth," p. 268 n 173; Donald R. Kelley, Kenneth Stunkel, and Richard R. Westcott, *The Economic Superpowers and the Environment* (San Francisco: W. H. Freeman, 1976), pp. 271–72.

175. A. Ryabchikov and Yu. G. Saushkin, "Current problems of environmental research," *Vestnik Moskovskogo Universiteta, seriya geografiya*, 1973, no. 3; "Constitution of the USSR," *Literaturnaya gazeta*, no. 23 (8 June 1977), pp. 2–3.

176. Kalinichev, "BAM kilometers," p. 2 n 150.

177. Silin, "For ourselves," p. 2 n 1.

178. A. Trofimuk, "The 'Siberia' program," *I*, 31 March 1978, p. 2.

# 4

# REGIONAL MANPOWER RESOURCES AND RESOURCE DEVELOPMENT IN THE USSR: 1970–90

ROBERT A. LEWIS
Columbia University

## Introduction

There is a maldistribution of either people or resources in the USSR. Because of past agricultural technologies as related to the natural environment and other historical circumstances, most of the Soviet population lives in the European part of the USSR, whereas most industrial resources are located in Siberia and the Far East. Moreover, the population transition within a developed country does not usually allocate labor according to the needs of the expanding economy. The pattern that normally prevails is relatively low natural increase and growth of the native work force in the more modernized, urbanized and industrialized areas, where job opportunities are usually expanding, and relatively high natural increase and growth of the native work force in the less developed, more rural areas, where additional labor requirements are usually minimal or nonexistent. This imbalance of labor supply and demand is generally equalized by migration. In the USSR, however, where such patterns are intensifying, migration is not always meeting the needs of the economy. Furthermore, in the 1980s the growth of the working-age population will decline sharply relative to previous decades, and the geographic distribution will be less favorable for economic development.

Without a major rise in labor productivity, the availability of labor and its distribution may be a constraint to economic development and, by implication, to resource development in the 1980s. The Soviet Government could expand resource exports to import capital and technology and thus raise labor productivity to alleviate labor shortages.[1] If it decided to do this, it could give resource development high priority, as it has in the case of heavy and

defense industries, and resource development would occur at the expense of other sectors of the economy. Aside from depending on internal productive resources, the Soviet Union could also import labor, but thus far such importations have been minimal and have probably been outweighed by the limited emigration from the USSR.[2] Given the nature of the political system, it would appear to be realistic to consider the USSR as a closed system with respect to overall availability of labor, although this would not exclude the possibility of the temporary utilization of foreign labor on individual projects, as has already occurred.

The purpose of this study is to investigate in a regional perspective the growth of the total, urban and rural populations of working age between 1970 and 1980 and between 1980 and 1990. The study is based mainly on analysis of the age-distribution data of the 1970 census, the last Soviet population count for which such data have been published. The new entrants into the labor force during the decades 1970–1980 and 1980–1990 can be estimated quite accurately since these individuals were already born in 1970; those aged 10–19 in 1970 would by 1980 have become 20–29 and thus constituted the new entrants during that decade; those aged 0–9 in 1970 would become 20–29 in the decade 1980–1990. By using these data and assuming no migration, one can project also the regional distribution of additions to the labor force as well as rural and urban additions.

Future rural-urban and interregional migration, will, of course, affect the regional growth of the working-age population, but is difficult to estimate. Past patterns of migration will be analyzed to appraise the impact of migration on these populations. In view of the importance of the resource base of Siberia and the Far East, special emphasis is given to the growth of the working-age population and labor problems in these regions. The last major source of surplus labor will probably be in the non-Slavic republics, in particular Central Asia. Therefore, the prospect for out-migration from Central Asia is briefly considered. The question as to the degree to which the impending labor shortages will constrain resource development cannot be definitively answered because there is no way to project with any precision future labor needs in the USSR. The intention of this study is to provide a general background as to the regional man-

*The paper includes several tables and maps and summarizes some material from previous publications as cited in the text. Richard H. Rowland of California State College at San Bernardino co-authored these publications and compiled the maps that are being republished, and I gratefully acknowledge his contribution.*

**ECONOMIC REGIONS: 1961**

1. NORTHWEST
2. WEST
3. CENTER
4. VOLGA-VYATKA
5. CENTRAL CHERNOZEM
6. VOLGA
7. BELORUSSIA
8. MOLDAVIA
9. SOUTHWEST
10. SOUTH
11. DONETS-DNIEPER
12. NORTH CAUCUSUS
13. TRANSCAUCUSIA
14. URALS
15. WEST SIBERIA
16. EAST SIBERIA
17. FAR EAST
18. KAZAKHSTAN
19. CENTRAL ASIA

Figure 1

power resources in the period to 1990 to facilitate the evaluation of manpower constraints on resource development. No effort will be made to appraise the quality of the manpower resources in terms of education or training, although these are also important considerations.

## The Population of Working Age

Since a high percentage of the Soviet working-age population is in the work force, this population is a reasonable approximation of manpower resources. The definition of the working-age population is arbitrary. The official Soviet definition includes men aged 16–59 and women aged 16–54. Yet, only about half of the men and women aged 16–19 are in the work force, excluding full-time students, and whether all of the military are reported is unknown.[3] Furthermore, about 44 percent of the women aged 55–59 have remained in the work force,[4] and with intensified labor shortages this percentage may increase. As education levels and skill requirements increase in response to economic necessity, work-force participation in the 16–19 cohort may decrease.

The definition of working-age population used in this study is the population aged 20–59, which is a more conventional definition that more readily permits international comparisons. The chief advantage of this definition over the official Soviet definition is that the standard age cohorts given in the 1970 census can be aggregated and projected on a 10-year basis. Thus, the working-age population for 1970 is the population aged 20–59, the estimate for 1980 is the 1970 population aged 10–49 adjusted for mortality, and the 1990 estimate is the 1970 population aged 0–39 adjusted for mortality. Estimates of new entrants to the work force can be derived by using the 1970 populations aged 20–29, 10–19, and 0–9, adjusted for mortality.[5] Over 90 percent of the men and over 80 percent of the women aged 20–59 were in the work force in 1970.

The regional framework utilized in this study is the 19 major economic regions of 1961, the regions that we have used in other studies to derive territorially comparable data since 1897 (Figure 1).[6] Where appropriate, data have been reordered into the current economic regions. Data have also been aggregated into four quadrants to provide a larger scale of analysis. The four quadrants are Northern European USSR (Northwest, West, Center, Volga-Vyatka, Central Chernozem, Volga, Belorussia and Southwest), the European Steppe (Moldavia, South, Donets-Dnieper and North Caucasus), the Russian East (Urals, West Siberia, East Siberia and Far East), and the non-Slavic South (Transcaucasia, Kazakhstan and Central Asia). The definitions of the urban and rural population are the official Soviet definitions.

## Aggregate Patterns

The outstanding characteristic of the total working-age population in the USSR is the sharp decline in its rate of

TABLE 1

Estimated Population Aged 20–59 and Percentage
Change 1970–90, USSR (based on the 1970 census
and assuming no subsequent migration)

| Year/ Period | Total | Urban | Rural |
|---|---|---|---|
| 1970 | 120,963,719 | 74,343,142 | 46,620,577 |
| 1980 | 142,454,593 | 85,634,959 | 56,819,634 |
| 1990 | 152,557,990 | 86,757,085 | 65,800,905 |
| Percentage Change | | | |
| 1970–80 | 17.8 | 15.2 | 21.9 |
| 1980–90 | 7.1 | 1.3 | 15.8 |
| 1970–90 | 26.1 | 16.7 | 41.1 |
| Average Annual Percentage Change | | | |
| 1970–80 | 1.6 | 1.4 | 2.0 |
| 1980–90 | 0.7 | 0.1 | 1.5 |
| 1970–90 | 1.2 | 0.8 | 1.7 |

SOURCES: Age data are from Tsentralnoye Statisticheskoye Upravleniye
pri Sovete Ministrov SSSR, *Itogi Vsesoyuznoi Perepisi Naseleniya 1970 Goda*
(Moscow: Statistika, 1972), Vol. II, pp. 12–250. Survival rates were derived
from Godfrey Baldwin, *Estimates and Projections of the Population of the
U.S.S.R., by Age and Sex: 1950 to 2000*, U.S. Department of Commerce,
Bureau of Economic Analysis, International Population Reports, Series
P–91, No. 3, March 1973.

growth in the 1980s relative to the 1970s (Table 1). The
increase of 10.1 million between 1980 and 1990 will be 47.0
percent of the increase between 1970 and 1980 and, on an
average annual basis, it will increase 0.7 percent per year
between 1980 and 1990. This should be an important
factor retarding economic development in the 1980s,
without an appreciable rise in labor productivity. If the
Soviet Union plans a 5 percent growth per year of the
gross national product in the 1980s, as it did in the 1976–
80 period, a labor productivity increase of over 4 percent
per year would be required compared to the 1.8 percent
annual increase achieved between 1971 and 1975.[7] Given
current trends related to labor productivity, such as a
declining rate of growth of the capital-labor ratio and
declining rates of investment growth, such an increase in
labor productivity seems doubtful, according to Central
Intelligence Agency analysts.[8] If the official Soviet definition of working-age population is used, this population
will increase from 155.8 to 161.9 million between 1980 and
1990, or 0.4 percent per year.[9]

Changes in the total working-age population reflect
previous natural increase, subsequent mortality, and
higher rate of retirement especially during the 1980s,
because the USSR can be considered a closed system with
insignificant emigration and virtually no immigration.
The urban and rural categories, however, also reflect
internal migration, and it should be realized that the
patterns of urban and rural change presented in Table I
are those that would prevail if there were no rural-urban
migration, which is not a realistic assumption. Nevertheless, these data provide insights into the major component in the change of the working-age population.
Without migration, there would be virtually no change in
urban working-age population between 1980 and 1990,
and therefore virtually all of the change would occur in
rural areas. Consequently, any economic growth in
urban areas not accounted for by increases in labor pro-

ductivity would depend on net rural-urban migration.
The percentage of the total increase in the working-age
population provided by urban areas would also decline,
from 52.5 percent between 1970 and 1980 to 11.1 percent
in the following decade. This is largely the result of a
decline in urban fertility in the last few decades, which is
currently below replacement if the age distribution is not
taken into account.

New entrants to the working-age population are defined as those persons who were aged 20–29 at the end of
each 10-year period. As shown in Table 2, there will be an
absolute decline in the total population aged 20–29 between 1980 and 1990, whereas in the previous decade
there was a substantial increase. A major reason for the
increase of 50.7 percent between 1970 and 1980 is that the
1980 population of that age group, born during the baby-
boom years of 1950–60, was greater than the 1970 cohort,
affected by the sharp decline in fertility during World War
II and fewer births in the years 1940–50. The decline in the
urban 20–29 cohort between 1980 and 1990 from 25.6
million to 21.1 million would, in the absence of migration,
be particularly sharp, by almost 4.5 million, or 1.9 percent
a year. The rural increase would be modest, less than 1
percent a year, even though it will account for all of the
increase. This decline in new entrants accounts for the
declining rate of growth of the working-age population.

## Regional Patterns

Not only will the growth of working-age population decline in the 1980s, but the geographic distribution of that
growth will become less favorable for economic development (Table 3). Regional changes in the total population
aged 20–59 are influenced by previous and future interregional migration as well as natural increase and
retirement. Comparing the 1980–90 decade with the period 1970–80, all four regional quadrants would experience a decline in the percentage change of their total
working-age population, although the decline in the non-
Slavic South would be the least and its percentage growth

TABLE 2

Estimated Population Aged 20–29 and Percentage
Change 1970–90, USSR (based on the 1970 census
and assuming no subsequent migration)

| Year/ Period | Total | Urban | Rural |
|---|---|---|---|
| 1970 | 30,875,621 | 20,731,567 | 10,144,054 |
| 1980 | 46,517,726 | 25,584,833 | 20,932,893 |
| 1990 | 44,085,884 | 21,134,594 | 22,951,290 |
| Percentage Change | | | |
| 1970–80 | 50.7 | 23.4 | 106.4 |
| 1980–90 | −5.2 | −17.4 | 9.6 |
| 1970–90 | 42.8 | 1.9 | 126.3 |
| Average Annual Percentage Change | | | |
| 1970–80 | 4.2 | 2.1 | 7.5 |
| 1980–90 | −0.5 | −1.9 | 0.9 |
| 1970–90 | 1.8 | 0.1 | 4.2 |

SOURCES: See Table 1.

TABLE 3
Estimated Percentage Change in Population Aged 20–59 by Quadrant: USSR
(based on the 1970 census and assuming no subsequent migration)

| Quadrant | Percentage Change | | | Percent of USSR Increase | | Per-centage Point Change |
|---|---|---|---|---|---|---|
| | 1970–80 | 1980–90 | 1970–90 | 1970–80 | 1980–90 | |
| | | | Total | | | |
| Northern European USSR | 12.6 | 0.6 | 13.3 | 33.5 | 4.0 | −29.5 |
| European Steppe | 12.3 | 2.9 | 15.5 | 12.9 | 7.2 | −5.7 |
| Russian East | 22.1 | 5.8 | 29.2 | 23.3 | 16.0 | −7.3 |
| Non-Slavic South | 35.1 | 29.4 | 74.8 | 30.3 | 72.8 | 42.5 |
| | | | Urban | | | |
| Northern European USSR | 11.7 | −2.5 | 9.0 | 36.0 | −84.5 | −120.5 |
| European Steppe | 11.4 | −1.2 | 10.1 | 14.3 | −16.6 | −30.9 |
| Russian East | 19.3 | 2.1 | 21.8 | 26.7 | 34.0 | 7.3 |
| Non-Slavic South | 26.6 | 15.2 | 45.8 | 23.1 | 167.2 | 144.1 |
| | | | Rural | | | |
| Northern European USSR | 14.1 | 5.3 | 20.1 | 30.7 | 15.1 | −15.4 |
| European Steppe | 13.8 | 9.6 | 24.7 | 11.5 | 10.2 | −1.3 |
| Russian East | 28.0 | 13.5 | 45.2 | 19.7 | 13.7 | −6.0 |
| Non-Slavic South | 44.6 | 43.4 | 107.3 | 38.3 | 61.0 | 22.7 |

by far the highest of any quadrant between 1980 and 1990. The increase in the other quadrants in 1980–90 will be slight, and the working-age population of the Northern European USSR will be virtually stationary. With respect to their share of the growth of working-age population, all quadrants would register a relative decline between the two decades, except the non-Slavic South, which will increase its share to almost three-fourths of the total. Thus, without migration, there would be a major regional shift as most of the increase in the working-age population takes place in the non-Slavic South, the least economically developed part of the USSR and the area that has a labor surplus and relatively few industrial resources.

The urban patterns are even more pronounced. Without net urban in-migration, the urban working-age population would decline slightly in the Northern European USSR and the European Steppe between 1980 and 1990 and barely increase in the Russian East, in contrast to moderate growth in the 1970–80 decade. Between 1980 and 1990, the increase in urban working-age population will take place almost entirely in the non-Slavic South, even though its percentage growth will decline compared to the decade 1970–80. There would also be a decline between the two decades in the rate of growth of the rural population of working age in all quadrants, although the decline in the non-Slavic South would be slight. More than 60 percent of the increase in rural working-age population in 1980–90 will take place in the non-Slavic South.

The geographic distribution of the new entrants to the working-age population is important because the young have the highest propensity to migrate, and migration decreases with distance.[10] Thus, new entrants to the work force are generally drawn from local areas, at least when jobs are available. The total population aged 20–29 is projected to decrease between 1980 and 1990 in the Northern European USSR, the European Steppe and the

Russian East by about 5 million, but to increase by 2.6 million in the non-Slavic South. This contrasts with the previous decade, when this population increased in all regional quadrants (Table 4). All of the slight increase of the urban new entrants to the work force (i.e. the age group 20–29) for 1980–90 compared to 1970–80 would also occur in the non-Slavic South, and the decline in the other quadrants is greater than that of total new entrants. In the rural sector, the Northern European USSR and the Russian East would experience a decline in number of new entrants to the labor force in 1980–90 compared with 1970–80. The greatest increase by far in new entrants to the labor force in rural areas will be in the non-Slavic

TABLE 4
Estimated Percentage Change in Population Aged 20–29 by Quadrant: USSR (based on the 1970 census and assuming no subsequent migration)

| Quadrant | Percentage Change | | |
|---|---|---|---|
| | 1970–80 | 1980–90 | 1970–90 |
| | | Total | |
| Northern European USSR | 40.0 | −14.5 | 19.8 |
| European Steppe | 40.8 | −7.8 | 29.7 |
| Russian East | 53.6 | −17.1 | 27.3 |
| Non-Slavic South | 85.8 | 26.6 | 135.1 |
| | | Urban | |
| Northern European USSR | 14.1 | −21.6 | −10.6 |
| European Steppe | 22.3 | −17.8 | 0.6 |
| Russian East | 28.4 | −24.1 | −2.5 |
| Non-Slavic South | 47.4 | 2.7 | 51.4 |
| | | Rural | |
| Northern European USSR | 96.1 | −5.5 | 85.3 |
| European Steppe | 78.6 | 6.2 | 89.6 |
| Russian East | 126.2 | −5.5 | 113.7 |
| Non-Slavic South | 133.6 | 45.4 | 239.6 |

SOURCES: See Table 1.

South, by 3.1 million between 1970 and 1980, and by 2.5 million between 1980 and 1990.

This does not take into consideration migration since 1970 or the migration that will occur in the 1980s. During the 1970s there has been considerable out-migration of the young from rural European areas to urban areas, and it can be expected that it will continue. If 1980 data were available for the population aged 20–29, it would probably show rural declines in all quadrants except the non-Slavic South, and all quadrants would probably be characterized by urban increases. The total population aged 20–29 is also affected by interregional migration, but to a lesser degree than the urban and rural sectors.

The patterns by economic region show the variations within the quadrants (Table 5 and Figure 2). The most urbanized and industrialized economic regions, the Center, Northwest and Donets-Dnieper would have a decline in the working-age population, not counting migration. This is an expected pattern because the transition from high to low birth, death and natural increase rates associated with modernization occur first in the more developed, urbanized areas, where the native work force grows at the slowest rate and labor requirements are usually the greatest. All of the economic regions in the Slavic and Baltic areas show low percentage increase between 1980 and 1990 and would register appreciable declines between the two decades. The component regions of the non-Slavic South would have significant gains, although less than in the previous decade. Central Asia would increase its total working-age population by four million between 1980 and 1990 compared with three million in the previous decade. The increase between 1980

and 1990 in Transcaucasia and Kazakhstan would be 1.6 and 1.7 million, respectively.

With respect to the total new entrants, all regions would experience a decline between the two decades, and, aside from the component regions of the non-Slavic South, only the West would have a gain (Table 5). The remaining regions would register declines, often appreciable. The absolute increase for Central Asia is 2.2 million between 1970 and 1980 and 1.7 million between 1980 and 1990. If one takes into account only the economic regions that would have an increase between 1980 and 1990, Central Asia will account for 66 percent of the increase, Transcaucasia 18 percent, and Kazakhstan 15 percent.

Once again it should be noted that the data for the urban and rural populations of working age are hypothetical because of rural-urban migration, particularly in the Slavic and Baltic areas. Excluding migration, the urban working-age population in all regions would increase between 1970 and 1980, and the percentage increases are often substantial. Eleven regions would have more than a 15 percent increase and only a few below 10 percent (Table 6). In contrast, between 1980 and 1990 only one region, Central Asia, would increase by more than 15 percent (Figure 3) and, with two exceptions, the regions of Northern European USSR and the European Steppe would have declining urban working-age populations. The patterns for the urban new entrants is even more striking. With the exception of the West, all regions would have an increase between 1970 and 1980, but between 1980 and 1990 all but two regions would have declines, often appreciable, and the total of the regions that were increasing would be only 223,345, 81 percent of

TABLE 5
Estimated Percentage Change in Total Population Aged 20–59 and 20–29
by Economic Region (based on the 1970 census and assuming no subsequent migration)

| Region | Percentage Change in Population Aged 20–59 | | | Percentage Change in Population Aged 20–29 | | |
|---|---|---|---|---|---|---|
| | 1970–80 | 1980–90 | 1970–90 | 1970–80 | 1980–90 | 1970–90 |
| Northwest | 12.0 | −1.9 | 9.9 | 24.7 | −20.6 | −0.9 |
| West | 9.0 | 2.5 | 11.7 | 6.4 | 2.9 | 9.5 |
| Center | 9.4 | −4.7 | 4.2 | 32.4 | −23.8 | 0.9 |
| Volga-Vyatka | 18.5 | 3.5 | 22.7 | 76.4 | −19.6 | 41.7 |
| Central Chernozem | 13.6 | 1.0 | 14.7 | 77.0 | −19.5 | 42.4 |
| Volga | 16.7 | 3.8 | 21.1 | 49.0 | −15.7 | 25.6 |
| Belorussia | 18.9 | 6.5 | 26.6 | 53.7 | −5.1 | 45.9 |
| Moldavia | 22.7 | 10.8 | 36.0 | 61.7 | −3.9 | 55.3 |
| Southwest | 10.7 | 2.6 | 13.6 | 34.6 | −2.6 | 31.2 |
| South | 10.2 | 1.1 | 11.5 | 19.4 | −8.1 | 9.7 |
| Donets-Dnieper | 9.3 | −1.1 | 8.2 | 30.7 | −12.9 | 13.9 |
| North Caucasus | 14.9 | 6.9 | 22.9 | 61.2 | −2.9 | 56.6 |
| Transcaucasia | 31.0 | 23.1 | 61.2 | 86.2 | 18.1 | 119.9 |
| Urals | 22.0 | 6.4 | 29.7 | 64.3 | −15.4 | 39.0 |
| West Siberia | 22.5 | 3.5 | 26.8 | 66.1 | −22.9 | 28.1 |
| East Siberia | 24.8 | 8.6 | 35.6 | 49.6 | −13.9 | 28.9 |
| Far East | 17.5 | 4.4 | 22.7 | 9.8 | −16.6 | −8.4 |
| Kazakhstan | 31.1 | 22.2 | 60.2 | 64.8 | 13.9 | 87.8 |
| Central Asia | 41.2 | 38.8 | 96.0 | 102.1 | 39.8 | 182.4 |
| USSR | 17.8 | 7.1 | 26.1 | 50.7 | −5.2 | 42.8 |

SOURCES: See Table 1.

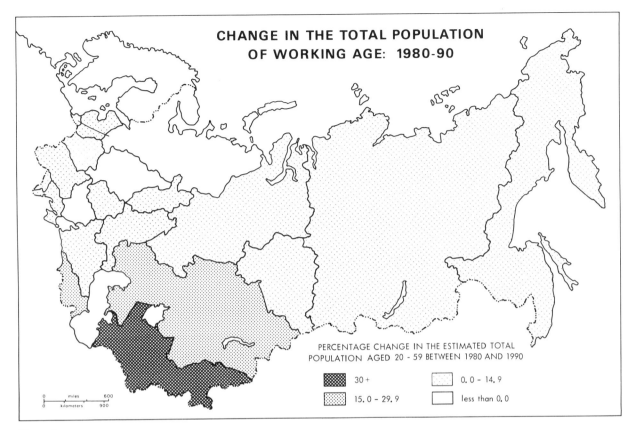

Figure 2

TABLE 6
Estimated Percentage Change in Urban Population Aged 20–59 and 20–29
by Economic Region (based on the 1970 census and assuming no subsequent migration)

| Region | Percentage Change in Population Aged 20–59 | | | Percentage Change in Population Aged 20–29 | | |
|---|---|---|---|---|---|---|
| | 1970–80 | 1980–90 | 1970–90 | 1970–80 | 1980–90 | 1970–90 |
| Northwest | 10.1 | −3.4 | 6.3 | 8.4 | −22.3 | −15.8 |
| West | 9.5 | −1.2 | 8.7 | −8.3 | −5.1 | −12.9 |
| Center | 8.3 | −5.7 | 2.1 | 16.1 | −24.8 | −12.7 |
| Volga-Vyatka | 16.4 | −1.1 | 15.1 | 32.6 | −28.1 | −4.7 |
| Central Chernozem | 14.3 | −2.1 | 11.9 | 29.4 | −27.9 | −6.7 |
| Volga | 15.1 | −0.6 | 14.4 | 21.1 | −25.1 | −9.3 |
| Belorussia | 19.6 | 3.7 | 24.0 | 12.3 | −13.5 | −2.8 |
| Moldavia | 19.5 | 1.9 | 21.8 | 23.9 | −23.2 | −4.8 |
| Southwest | 11.9 | −0.3 | 11.5 | 6.4 | −14.1 | −8.6 |
| South | 9.3 | −2.8 | 6.3 | 2.9 | −18.6 | −16.3 |
| Donets-Dnieper | 11.4 | −1.3 | 9.9 | 22.8 | −17.0 | 1.9 |
| North Caucasus | 11.3 | −0.6 | 10.6 | 33.0 | −17.7 | 9.4 |
| Transcaucasia | 24.2 | 13.2 | 40.5 | 49.5 | 3.3 | 54.3 |
| Urals | 19.5 | 1.7 | 21.5 | 37.0 | −24.7 | 3.2 |
| West Siberia | 19.7 | 0.4 | 20.1 | 35.0 | −28.0 | −2.7 |
| East Siberia | 21.0 | 4.7 | 26.6 | 21.7 | −20.1 | −2.8 |
| Far East | 16.4 | 2.7 | 19.5 | 3.5 | −20.4 | −17.6 |
| Kazakhstan | 25.6 | 10.9 | 39.3 | 35.8 | −7.6 | 25.4 |
| Central Asia | 29.8 | 20.8 | 56.9 | 57.3 | 11.1 | 74.7 |
| USSR | 15.2 | 1.3 | 16.7 | 23.4 | −17.4 | 1.9 |

Sources: See Table 1.

which would be accounted for by Central Asia. If continued expansion of the urban economies is assumed, particularly in European USSR and the Russian East, there will be job opportunities that cannot be met by the declining number of new entrants, the more mobile contingent of the population. This should further stimulate rural out-migration.

Percentage increases in the rural working-age population between 1970 and 1980 would be higher than that of the total and urban in all but five regions, and between 1980 and 1990 in all regions (Table 7 and Figure 4). Only two regions would register an absolute decline. The greatest increases in the second decade would be in the regions of the non-Slavic South. The absolute increase in Central Asia between 1970 and 1980 would be two million, and between 1980 and 1990 over three million. The combined increase of Kazakhstan and Transcaucasia would be about two million in each of the decades. Thus, most of the increase in the rural working-age population would be in the rural sector in the southern tier. Whereas in the 1970–80 period all regions would have an appreciable increase in rural new entrants, the following decade would be characterized by slower growth and declines or only slow growth in the Slavic and Baltic regions, especially those that have experienced heavy rural out-migration. Once again the greatest increases would be in the regions of the non-Slavic South, especially Central Asia, where the absolute increase in each decade would be 1.6 million. Of the regions that had an increase in the

rural working-age population, Central Asia would account for 54 percent of the increase, and the regions of the entire non-Slavic South for 87 percent.

The percentage point change between the two decades reveals regionally the magnitude of the changes that would occur excluding migration (Table 8). Most of the regions of Northern European USSR and the Russian East would have percentage point losses above the USSR average for the total, urban and rural working-age population; the regions of the European Steppe would be close to it, and the regions of the non-Slavic South would be below it. The declines would be the greatest for the urban population and the smallest for the rural. Central Asia would register the only positive change in the rural sector. The patterns of the total, urban and rural new entrants are mixed, with the percentage point change greater than for the total working-age population. The striking pattern for both populations is significant relative decline.

Another important aspect is the relative regional shift of the increase of the total working-age populations in the USSR (Table 9). Between 1970 and 1980, all regions will register positive gains in their share of the increase, and the share of the regions of the non-Slavic South would not be particularly great. Between 1980 and 1990, virtually all regions would have relative declines compared to the previous decade, as reflected in the percentage point figures, except the regions of the non-Slavic South, which would have gains. Whereas the three more urbanized,

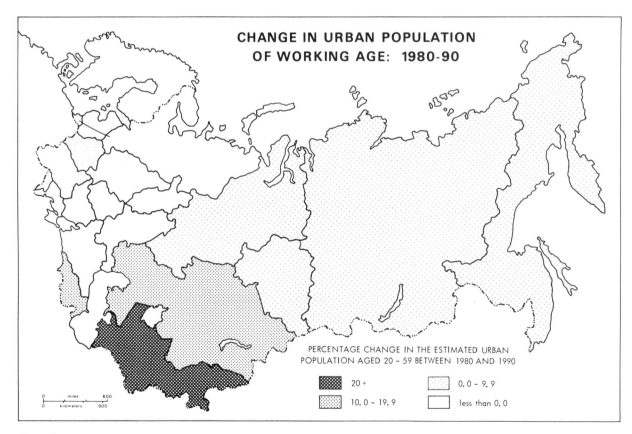

Figure 3

TABLE 7
Estimated Percentage Change in Rural Population Aged 20–59 and 20–29
by Economic Region (based on the 1970 census and assuming no subsequent migration)

| Region | Percentage Change in Population Aged 20–59 | | | Percentage Change in Population Aged 20–29 | | |
|---|---|---|---|---|---|---|
| | 1970–80 | 1980–90 | 1970–90 | 1970–80 | 1980–90 | 1970–90 |
| Northwest | 18.4 | 2.7 | 21.6 | 94.6 | −16.4 | 66.0 |
| West | 8.1 | 8.0 | 16.8 | 37.0 | 13.9 | 56.0 |
| Center | 12.5 | −1.6 | 10.7 | 99.3 | −21.4 | 56.7 |
| Volga-Vyatka | 21.5 | 9.6 | 33.2 | 169.0 | −10.8 | 140.0 |
| Central Chernozem | 13.0 | 3.5 | 16.9 | 134.9 | −13.9 | 102.2 |
| Volga | 19.5 | 11.7 | 33.4 | 121.3 | −2.4 | 115.9 |
| Belorussia | 18.2 | 9.1 | 29.0 | 117.5 | 1.6 | 121.0 |
| Moldavia | 24.4 | 15.6 | 43.8 | 87.5 | 4.8 | 96.4 |
| Southwest | 9.9 | 4.7 | 15.1 | 63.4 | 5.0 | 71.6 |
| South | 11.7 | 6.9 | 19.4 | 50.5 | 5.4 | 58.6 |
| Donets-Dnieper | 3.4 | −0.3 | 3.2 | 61.4 | −0.4 | 60.7 |
| North Caucasus | 19.2 | 15.2 | 37.3 | 99.8 | 10.7 | 121.2 |
| Transcaucasia | 40.2 | 34.9 | 89.2 | 144.7 | 32.5 | 224.3 |
| Urals | 27.3 | 15.7 | 47.4 | 144.1 | −0.2 | 143.7 |
| West Siberia | 28.4 | 9.3 | 40.3 | 156.3 | −15.0 | 117.8 |
| East Siberia | 32.4 | 15.7 | 53.2 | 120.6 | −5.1 | 109.2 |
| Far East | 21.1 | 9.4 | 32.5 | 30.5 | −6.5 | 21.9 |
| Kazakhstan | 38.5 | 35.8 | 88.1 | 108.5 | 35.2 | 181.9 |
| Central Asia | 50.9 | 52.1 | 129.4 | 143.4 | 56.9 | 281.8 |
| USSR | 21.9 | 15.8 | 41.1 | 106.4 | 9.6 | 126.3 |

SOURCES: See Table 1.

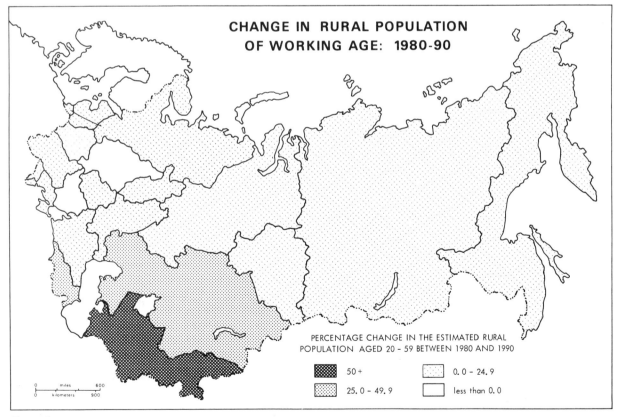

Figure 4

80    Soviet Resource Development

industrialized regions would have declines, Central Asia would account for about 40 percent of the increase, or four million, and the regions of the entire non-Slavic South would account for almost three-fourths of the increase. If just those regions that have an increase are examined, Central Asia accounts for about 37 percent of the total increase and the entire non-Slavic South for

about two-thirds. Of the declining regions, the Center would account for almost three-fourths of the total decline (one million). Thus, without migration, there would be a shift of the total working-age population to the southern non-Slavic tier.

The urban working-age population would experience greater percentage point decline between the two dec-

TABLE 8
Percentage Point Change Between 1970–80 and 1980–90 by Economic Region
(based on the 1970 census and assuming no subsequent migration)

| | Population Aged 20–59 | | | Population Aged 20–29 | | |
|---|---|---|---|---|---|---|
| Region | Total | Urban | Rural | Total | Urban | Rural |
| Northwest | −13.9 | −13.5 | −15.7 | −45.3 | −30.7 | −111.0 |
| West | −6.5 | −10.7 | −0.1 | −3.5 | −3.2 | −23.0 |
| Center | −14.1 | −14.0 | −14.1 | −56.2 | −40.9 | −120.7 |
| Volga-Vyatka | −15.0 | −17.5 | −11.9 | −96.0 | −60.7 | −179.8 |
| Central Chernozem | −12.6 | −16.4 | −9.5 | −96.5 | −57.3 | −148.8 |
| Volga | −12.9 | −15.7 | −7.8 | −64.7 | −46.2 | −123.7 |
| Belorussia | −12.4 | −15.9 | −9.1 | −58.8 | −25.8 | −115.9 |
| Moldavia | −11.9 | −17.6 | −8.8 | −65.6 | −47.1 | −82.7 |
| Southwest | −8.1 | −12.2 | −5.2 | −37.2 | −20.5 | −58.4 |
| South | −9.1 | −12.1 | −4.8 | −27.5 | −21.5 | −45.1 |
| Donets-Dnieper | −10.4 | −12.7 | −3.7 | −43.6 | −39.8 | −61.8 |
| North Caucasus | −8.0 | −11.9 | −4.0 | −64.1 | −50.7 | −89.1 |
| Transcaucasia | −7.9 | −11.0 | −5.3 | −68.1 | −46.2 | −112.2 |
| Urals | −15.6 | −17.8 | −11.6 | −79.7 | −61.7 | −144.3 |
| West Siberia | −19.0 | −19.3 | −19.1 | −89.0 | −63.0 | −171.3 |
| East Siberia | −16.2 | −16.3 | −16.7 | −63.5 | −41.8 | −125.7 |
| Far East | −13.1 | −13.7 | −11.7 | −26.4 | −23.9 | −37.0 |
| Kazakhstan | −8.9 | −14.7 | −2.7 | −50.9 | −43.4 | −73.3 |
| Central Asia | −2.4 | −9.0 | 1.2 | −62.3 | −46.2 | −86.5 |
| USSR | −10.7 | −13.9 | −6.1 | −55.9 | −40.8 | −96.8 |

SOURCES: See Table 1.

TABLE 9
Percent of the USSR Increase of the Population Aged 20–59 by Economic Region
(based on the 1970 census and assuming no subsequent migration)

| | Total | | Percentage Point Change | Urban | | Percentage Point Change | Rural | | Percentage Point Change |
|---|---|---|---|---|---|---|---|---|---|
| Region | 1970–80 | 1980–90 | | 1970–80 | 1980–90 | | 1970–80 | 1980–90 | |
| Northwest | 4.0 | −1.5 | −5.5 | 4.9 | −18.5 | −23.4 | 3.0 | 0.6 | −2.4 |
| West | 1.5 | 1.0 | −0.5 | 1.9 | −1.7 | −3.6 | 1.1 | 1.3 | 0.2 |
| Center | 6.4 | −7.5 | −13.9 | 8.2 | −61.4 | −69.6 | 4.4 | −0.7 | −5.1 |
| Volga-Vyatka | 3.6 | 1.7 | −1.9 | 3.5 | −2.8 | −6.3 | 3.7 | 2.3 | −1.4 |
| Central Chernozem | 2.8 | 0.5 | −2.3 | 2.5 | −4.1 | −6.6 | 3.2 | 1.1 | −2.1 |
| Volga | 5.7 | 3.2 | −2.5 | 6.3 | −3.1 | −9.4 | 4.9 | 4.0 | −0.9 |
| Belorussia | 3.9 | 3.4 | −0.5 | 3.7 | 8.6 | 4.9 | 4.1 | 2.7 | −1.4 |
| Moldavia | 1.8 | 2.3 | 0.5 | 1.1 | 1.3 | 0.2 | 2.7 | 2.4 | −0.3 |
| Southwest | 5.6 | 3.2 | −2.4 | 5.0 | −1.5 | −6.5 | 6.3 | 3.8 | −2.5 |
| South | 1.7 | 0.4 | −1.3 | 1.7 | −5.6 | −7.3 | 1.6 | 1.2 | −0.4 |
| Donets-Dnieper | 4.4 | −1.2 | −5.6 | 7.6 | −9.9 | −17.5 | 0.9 | −0.1 | −1.0 |
| North Caucasus | 5.0 | 5.7 | 0.7 | 3.9 | −2.4 | −6.3 | 6.3 | 6.7 | 0.4 |
| Transcaucasia | 7.7 | 15.9 | 8.2 | 6.6 | 44.7 | 38.1 | 8.9 | 12.3 | 3.4 |
| Urals | 10.4 | 7.8 | −2.6 | 12.0 | 12.7 | 0.7 | 8.7 | 7.2 | −1.5 |
| West Siberia | 5.7 | 2.3 | −3.4 | 6.4 | 1.5 | −4.9 | 5.0 | 2.4 | −2.6 |
| East Siberia | 4.8 | 4.4 | −0.4 | 5.1 | 13.7 | 8.6 | 4.5 | 3.2 | −1.3 |
| Far East | 2.4 | 1.5 | −0.9 | 3.2 | 6.1 | 2.9 | 1.5 | 0.9 | −0.6 |
| Kazakhstan | 8.4 | 16.7 | 8.3 | 7.5 | 40.3 | 32.8 | 9.4 | 13.7 | 4.3 |
| Central Asia | 14.2 | 40.2 | 26.0 | 9.0 | 82.2 | 73.2 | 20.0 | 35.0 | 15.0 |
| USSR | 100.0 | 100.0 | 0.0 | 100.1 | 100.1 | 0.0 | 100.2 | 100.0 | −0.2 |

SOURCES: See Table 1.

TABLE 10
Total Net Migration and Natural Increase by Economic Region: 1959–70

| Region | Population Growth | Natural Increase | Net Migration | Net Migration as Percent of July 1964 Population | Net Migration as Percent of Population Growth | Natural Increase as Percent of July 1964 Population | Percent of Total Natural Increase |
|---|---|---|---|---|---|---|---|
| Northwest | 1,414,842 | 1,152,635 | 262,207 | 2.1 | 18.5 | 9.4 | 3.6 |
| West | 846,748 | 558,100 | 288,648 | 4.5 | 34.1 | 9.2 | 1.7 |
| Center | 1,931,196 | 1,706,536 | 224,660 | 0.9 | 11.6 | 6.7 | 5.3 |
| Volga-Vyatka | 94,779 | 892,838 | −798,059 | −9.6 | −842.0 | 10.8 | 2.8 |
| Central Chernozem | 231,333 | 738,093 | −506,760 | −5.7 | −219.1 | 8.3 | 2.3 |
| Volga | 1,833,004 | 1,576,490 | 256,514 | 1.9 | 14.0 | 11.7 | 4.9 |
| Belorussia | 947,690 | 1,214,300 | −266,610 | −3.1 | −28.1 | 14.3 | 3.8 |
| Moldavia | 684,396 | 609,000 | 75,396 | 2.3 | 11.0 | 18.6 | 1.9 |
| Southwest | 1,694,120 | 2,388,205 | −694,085 | −3.3 | −41.0 | 11.2 | 7.5 |
| South | 1,314,482 | 634,639 | 679,843 | 12.0 | 51.7 | 11.2 | 2.0 |
| Donets-Dnieper | 2,248,869 | 1,786,548 | 462,321 | 2.6 | 20.6 | 10.0 | 5.6 |
| North Caucasus | 2,763,031 | 1,815,814 | 947,217 | 7.1 | 34.3 | 13.6 | 5.7 |
| Transcaucasia | 2,790,502 | 2,777,100 | 13,402 | 0.1 | 0.4 | 25.3 | 8.7 |
| Urals | 1,796,142 | 2,724,978 | −928,836 | −4.6 | −51.7 | 13.6 | 8.5 |
| West Siberia | 543,963 | 1,337,778 | −793,815 | −7.3 | −145.9 | 12.3 | 4.2 |
| East Siberia | 1,167,022 | 1,227,957 | −60,935 | −0.8 | −5.2 | 15.9 | 3.8 |
| Far East | 769,583 | 683,199 | 86,384 | 1.8 | 11.2 | 14.4 | 2.1 |
| Kazakhstan | 3,698,879 | 2,918,600 | 780,279 | 6.6 | 19.6 | 25.0 | 9.1 |
| Central Asia | 6,122,903 | 5,325,900 | 797,003 | 4.8 | 9.9 | 33.3 | 16.6 |
| USSR total | 32,893,484 | 32,068,710 | 824,744 | 3.6 | 2.5 | 14.1 | 100.0 |

SOURCES: Robert A. Lewis and Richard H. Rowland, *Population Redistribution in the USSR: Its Impact on Society, 1897–1977* (New York: Praeger Publishers, 1979), Chapter 2.

ades than the total working-age population, except for the non-Slavic South, where the gains would be greater. Central Asia would account for much of the gain, but, if only the increasing regions are taken into consideration, Central Asia accounts for 39 percent and the entire non-Slavic South for 79 percent of the increase. The Center accounts for 55 percent of the loss of the declining regions. Thus, there also would be a shift of the urban working-age population to the non-Slavic South.

The lowest percentage point decline would occur in the rural sector, although, with the exception of the regions of the non-Slavic South, all regions would experience a decline between the two decades or only a slight percentage point increase. Once again, most of the shift is to the non-Slavic South, and Central Asia alone would have an increase of over three million.

## Migration

To assess the effect of migration on the patterns of change of the working-age population, past regional migration trends will be investigated. Table 10 and Figure 5 present data for the 1959–70 period on net migration estimated as a residual of natural increase and *de facto* census enumerations excluding the military. That there were some 800,000 more in-migrants than out-migrants indicates the approximate nature of these estimates and reflects errors in vital statistics and the census enumerations.[11]

Regional natural increase data for the 1970s are more limited, so the estimates of regional net migration are also

more limited. Because there were no published data on regional natural increase for 1971, it was necessary to estimate it based upon the average for the three other years (Table 11). Because of this and a shorter period, these estimates are even less reliable, but the magnitude of net migration is roughly the same. Of more importance with respect to changes in the working-age population, however, are the regional trends in net migration. It would appear that the contribution of net migration to the total population growth of the regions of the non-Slavic South is minimal. Total net in-migration between 1970 and 1974 in Central Asia is only slight, about 40,000 per year, and the other regions have no net migration. Consequently, most of the redistribution as a result of migration of the total population, and by implication the population of working age, is occurring among the Slavic and Baltic economic regions. Therefore, if these migration trends persist, the estimate of the change in the total working-age population for the regions of the non-Slavic South are realistic, but for the other regions they require some amendment. A general decline between the two periods in natural increase in all regions can be observed in Table 11.

Because both interregional and intraregional migration affects the urban and rural working-age populations, 1970 census data have been reordered to measure the migration that added to or subtracted from the urban and rural populations (Table 12 and Figures 6 and 7). In the 1970 census, migration is defined as the *de jure* population minus the military that moved between settlements in the two years prior to the census. From Table 12, calculations

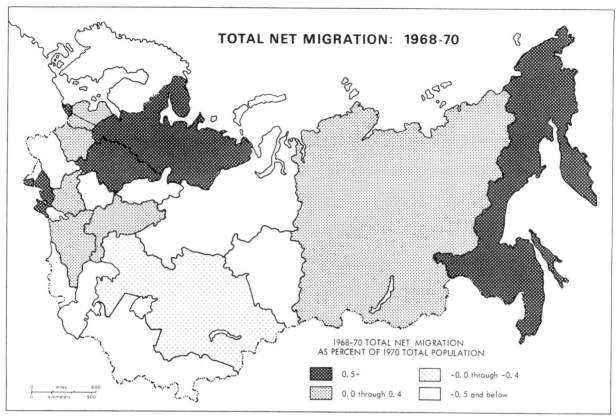

Figure 5

TABLE 11
Regional Net Migration and Natural Increase, 1959–74

| Region | Annual Net Migration | | Annual Natural Increase | |
|---|---|---|---|---|
| | 1959–70 | 1970–74 | 1959–70 | 1970–74 |
| | as Percent of: | | as Percent of: | |
| | July 1964 Population | January 1972 Population | July 1964 Population | January 1972 Population |
| Northwest | 0.2 | 0.4 | 0.9 | 0.5 |
| West | 0.4 | 0.5 | 0.8 | 0.6 |
| Center | 0.1 | 0.2 | 0.6 | 0.3 |
| Volga-Vyatka | −0.9 | −0.7 | 1.0 | 0.5 |
| Central Chernozem | −0.5 | −0.9 | 0.8 | 0.3 |
| Volga | 0.2 | 0.2 | 1.1 | 0.6 |
| Belorussia | −0.3 | −0.1 | 1.3 | 0.8 |
| Moldavia | 0.2 | 0.1 | 1.7 | 1.3 |
| Southwest | −0.3 | −0.1 | 1.0 | 0.7 |
| South | 1.1 | 0.7 | 1.0 | 0.7 |
| Donets-Dnieper | 0.2 | 0.2 | 0.9 | 0.5 |
| North Caucasus | 0.6 | 0.3 | 1.2 | 0.8 |
| Transcaucasia | +0.0 | +0.0 | 2.3 | 1.6 |
| Urals | −0.4 | −0.5 | 1.2 | 0.8 |
| West Siberia | −0.7 | −0.7 | 1.1 | 0.8 |
| East Siberia | −0.1 | −0.0 | 1.4 | 1.1 |
| Far East | 0.2 | 1.0 | 1.3 | 1.1 |
| Kazakhstan | 0.6 | −0.0 | 2.3 | 1.7 |
| Central Asia | 0.4 | 0.2 | 3.0 | 2.7 |

SOURCES: Richard H. Rowland and Robert A. Lewis, "Regional Population Trends in the USSR, 1970–79: Preliminary Results from the 1979 Soviet Census," forthcoming.

TABLE 12
Urban and Rural Migration Rates by Economic Region: 1968–70

| Region | Percent of Urban Population Comprised by: | | | | Percent of Rural Population Comprised by: | | | |
|---|---|---|---|---|---|---|---|---|
| | In-Migrants | Out-Migrants | Net Migrants | Migration Turnover | In-Migrants | Out-Migrants | Net Migrants | Migration Turnover |
| Northwest | 5.1 | 3.1 | 2.0 | 8.2 | 4.9 | 7.0 | −2.1 | 11.9 |
| West | 4.6 | 2.8 | 1.8 | 7.4 | 2.5 | 4.0 | −1.5 | 6.5 |
| Center | 3.9 | 2.0 | 1.9 | 5.9 | 2.9 | 5.5 | −2.6 | 8.4 |
| Volga-Vyatka | 5.7 | 3.4 | 2.3 | 9.1 | 2.0 | 6.3 | −4.3 | 8.3 |
| Central Chernozem | 6.3 | 3.6 | 2.7 | 9.9 | 1.5 | 4.6 | −3.1 | 6.1 |
| Volga | 6.1 | 3.1 | 3.0 | 9.2 | 2.3 | 5.8 | −3.5 | 8.1 |
| Belorussia | 6.4 | 2.7 | 3.7 | 9.1 | 1.4 | 4.2 | −2.8 | 5.6 |
| Moldavia | 7.5 | 3.4 | 4.1 | 10.9 | 0.9 | 3.2 | −2.3 | 4.1 |
| Southwest | 5.4 | 2.5 | 2.9 | 7.9 | 0.8 | 3.6 | −2.8 | 4.4 |
| South | 6.4 | 3.4 | 3.0 | 9.8 | 4.6 | 4.9 | −0.3 | 9.5 |
| Donets-Dnieper | 3.8 | 2.4 | 1.4 | 6.2 | 2.2 | 4.8 | −2.6 | 7.0 |
| North Caucasus | 5.7 | 4.2 | 1.5 | 9.9 | 3.3 | 4.3 | −1.0 | 7.6 |
| Transcaucasia | 1.8 | 1.6 | 0.2 | 3.4 | 0.4 | 1.6 | −1.2 | 2.0 |
| Urals | 5.2 | 4.3 | 0.9 | 9.5 | 3.6 | 7.9 | −4.3 | 11.5 |
| West Siberia | 6.3 | 4.9 | 1.4 | 11.2 | 4.2 | 8.5 | −4.3 | 12.7 |
| East Siberia | 8.1 | 5.4 | 2.7 | 13.5 | 5.1 | 8.6 | −3.5 | 13.7 |
| Far East | 8.1 | 5.8 | 2.3 | 13.9 | 11.3 | 10.2 | 1.1 | 21.5 |
| Kazakhstan | 7.4 | 5.0 | 2.4 | 12.4 | 3.0 | 5.7 | −2.7 | 8.7 |
| Central Asia | 3.9 | 3.6 | 0.3 | 7.5 | 0.7 | 2.0 | −1.3 | 2.7 |
| USSR Total | 5.2 | 3.3 | 1.9 | 8.5 | 2.4 | 4.8 | −2.4 | 7.2 |

SOURCES: Robert A. Lewis and Richard H. Rowland, *Population Redistribution in the USSR: Its Impact on Society, 1897–1977* (New York: Praeger Publishers, 1979), Chapter 2.

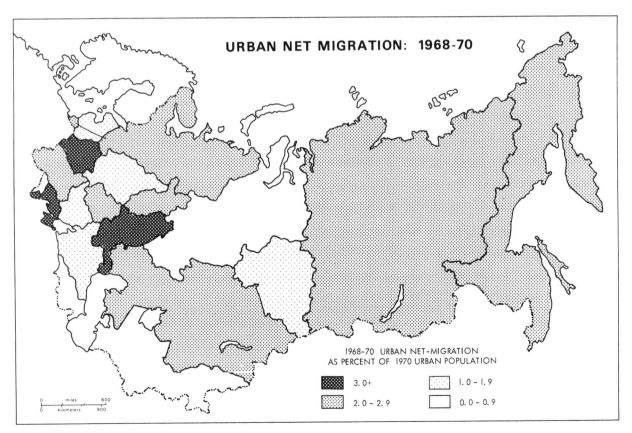

Figure 6

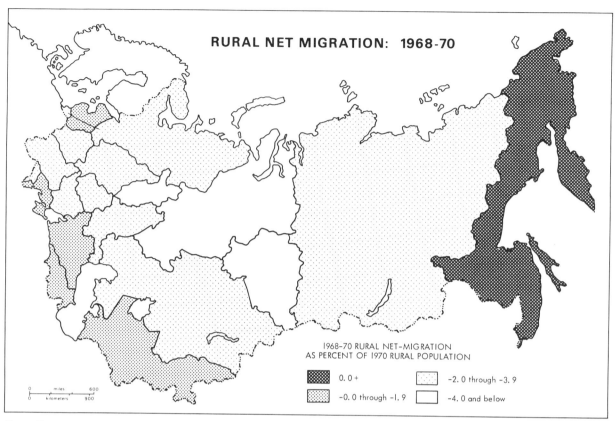

Figure 7

as to the percent of the working-age population comprised by migrants cannot be even crudely estimated. It can be observed, however, that all regions increased their urban population as a result of migration, and all regions, except the Far East where much of the rural population is not functionally rural, registered a decline in their rural population. It is also worth noting with respect to the interpretation of these data that the total number of inmigrants derived from the 1970 census is only about a half of other estimates.[12] Thus, it is obvious that our estimates of the urban and rural working-age populations are more hypothetical than realistic.

This assertion can be further demonstrated by reference to data on the average annual percentage change presented in Table 13. If the 1959–70 and 1970–79 periods are compared, average annual growth rates have declined in all sectors, but the greatest growth in the 1970–79 period was in the urban sector, and 57 percent of this growth was the result of net in-migration from rural areas and reclassification of rural settlements and the remainder was due to natural increase.[13] It can also be observed that the decline in the rural population of the USSR and three of the quadrants has intensified, and only the non-Slavic South experienced an increase between 1970 and 1979, although it was less than during the previous period.

In absolute terms, the combined rural population of Northern European USSR, the European Steppe, and the Russian East declined by 8.6 million between 1959 and

1970 and by 10.3 million between 1970 and 1979. In contrast, the rural population of the non-Slavic South increased by 5.5 million and 3.4 million respectively during these two periods. Although the rural crude birth rate is moderate to high in regions of the non-Slavic South, it is low in the Slavic republics and Estonia and Latvia, slightly above 14 per thousand in the 1969–70 period.[14] In the absence of rural mortality data, if one assumes that the crude death rate was somewhat above 10 per thousand because of an older population due to rural out-migration and that the crude birth rate continued to decline during the 1970s because of out-migration, a natural increase rate of 1 or 2 per thousand might be plausible. Applying a 1.5 per thousand natural increase rate to the mid-point of the 1970–79 period for the three quadrants yields a natural increase of about one million. Currently, there is probably little or no natural increase in these rural areas, so if rural out-migration continues at present rates even a higher rate of rural out-migration and natural decrease can be expected in the near future.

With respect to population redistribution, virtually all of the shift of the total, urban and rural populations during the 1970–79 period was to the non-Slavic South, but on an average annual basis there was a relative decline in the total and urban sectors and a relative increase in the rural population of the non-Slavic South compared to the previous period (Table 13). This trend was probably also fairly representative of the population of working age, in that in 1970 this population comprised 50 percent of the total population, 55 percent of the urban, and 44 percent of the rural, and, as has been pointed out, most migrants are in the working ages.

Regional variations in the average annual percentage change of the total, urban and rural populations for the past two intercensal periods are shown in Table 14 and Figures 8, 9 and 10. All regions had a decline in their rates of change except the Far East for all categories and the rural population of West Siberia. Central Asia and the other regions of the non-Slavic South generally have the highest rates in all categories. Rural depopulation in the Slavic and Baltic regions intensified in that in most instances the rates have declined. Moreover, whereas in the 1959–70 period 12 regions had rural population decline, in the 1970–79 period 15 regions were characterized by decline. It is worthy of note that a 2.5 percent rate of decline yields about a 22 percent decline in 10 years. In the 1980s, rates of decline in these regions may intensify, because, in addition to little or no rural natural increase, most of these regions would experience a significant decline in their urban working-age population, which would indicate the availability of jobs in local urban areas. Most rural migrants in the USSR move to the nearest city. About three-fourths move within their economic region and about a half within their oblast.[15] Clearly, in the last 20 years there has been a significant shift of the population from rural to urban areas in the USSR, particularly in the Slavic and Baltic areas.

## Labor Problems in Siberia and the Far East

The major problem in Soviet resource development is that regions with the most abundant resources, Siberia and the Far East, have acute labor shortages and the greatest labor turnover. Consequently, an attempt will be made to appraise the future availability of labor in Siberia and the Far East. In doing this, data have been ordered into the current economic regions. Tyumen Oblast, a major oil-producing area, was transferred from the Urals to West Siberia, and Yakut ASSR was transferred from East Siberia to the Far East.

Estimates as to the population of working age for Siberia and the Far East in the next decade are tentative because Siberia has been a major area of net out-migration for at least the last two decades and the Far East has been a region of net in-migration. Nevertheless, it is instructive to observe what would happen with respect to the growth of the population of working age if there were no migration, because it provides insights into the size and growth of the native work force and a basis from which rough approximations can be made. Given the sizable base populations, net migration frequently does not greatly affect the native population of working age, which constitutes most of the manpower resources of a region. Table 15 presents absolute data as to the estimated population of working age. It can be observed that almost a half of the total working-age population was

TABLE 13
Average Annual Percentage Change and Redistribution of the
Total, Urban and Rural Populations by Quadrant, 1959–79

| Quadrant | Total | | Urban | | Rural | |
|---|---|---|---|---|---|---|
| | 1959–70 | 1970–79 | 1959–70 | 1970–79 | 1959–70 | 1970–79 |
| | Average Annual Percentage Change | | | | | |
| Northern European USSR | 0.8 | 0.5 | 2.8 | 2.1 | −1.4 | −1.9 |
| European Steppe | 1.6 | 0.8 | 2.7 | 1.7 | 0.3 | −0.7 |
| Russian East | 0.9 | 0.8 | 2.1 | 1.7 | −0.9 | −1.3 |
| Non-Slavic South | 3.0 | 2.0 | 3.9 | 2.7 | 2.2 | 1.5 |
| USSR total | 1.3 | 1.0 | 2.8 | 2.0 | −0.3 | −0.8 |
| | Percentage Distribution | | | | | |
| | 1959 | 1970 | 1979 | 1959 | 1970 | 1979 | 1959 | 1970 | 1979 |
| Northern European USSR | 47.9 | 45.1 | 43.5 | 45.3 | 45.3 | 45.5 | 50.3 | 44.9 | 40.2 |
| European Steppe | 17.4 | 17.9 | 17.8 | 19.0 | 19.0 | 18.3 | 15.9 | 17.0 | 17.0 |
| Russian East | 19.2 | 18.3 | 18.0 | 22.6 | 21.0 | 20.3 | 16.1 | 16.1 | 14.3 |
| Non-Slavic South | 15.6 | 18.7 | 20.7 | 13.2 | 14.7 | 15.9 | 17.7 | 22.1 | 28.5 |
| | Percentage Point Distribution | | | | | |
| | 1959–70 | 1970–79 | 1959–70 | 1970–79 | 1959–70 | 1970–79 |
| Northern European USSR | −2.8 | −1.6 | 0.0 | 0.2 | −5.4 | −4.7 |
| European Steppe | 0.5 | −0.1 | 0.0 | −0.7 | 1.1 | 0.0 |
| Russian East | −0.9 | −0.3 | −1.6 | −0.7 | 0.0 | −1.8 |
| Non-Slavic South | 3.1 | 2.0 | 1.5 | 1.2 | 4.4 | 6.4 |

SOURCES: *Pravda*, 22 April 1979, p. 4, and Tsentralnoye Statisticheskoye Upravleniye, *Itogi Vsesoyuznoi Peripisi Naseleniya 1959 Goda, SSSR* (Moscow: Gosstatizdat, 1962), pp. 20–28.

TABLE 14
Average Annual Percentage Change in the Total, Urban,
and Rural Populations by Economic Region, 1959–79

| Region | Total | | Urban | | Rural | |
|---|---|---|---|---|---|---|
| | 1959–70 | 1970–79 | 1959–70 | 1970–79 | 1959–70 | 1970–79 |
| Northwest | 1.0 | 1.0 | 2.2 | 1.8 | −1.5 | −1.8 |
| West | 1.2 | 0.8 | 2.8 | 2.2 | −0.6 | −1.4 |
| Center | 0.7 | 0.5 | 2.2 | 1.6 | −2.5 | −2.5 |
| Volga-Vyatka | 0.1 | −0.0 | 2.9 | 1.8 | −2.3 | −2.5 |
| Central Chernozem | 0.3 | −0.3 | 3.9 | 2.7 | −1.6 | −2.9 |
| Volga | 1.3 | 0.8 | 3.2 | 2.2 | −1.1 | −1.9 |
| Belorussia | 1.0 | 0.6 | 4.2 | 3.3 | −0.9 | −1.9 |
| Moldavia | 2.0 | 1.2 | 5.1 | 3.5 | 0.8 | −0.2 |
| Southwest | 0.7 | 0.4 | 3.4 | 2.7 | −0.7 | −1.3 |
| South | 2.1 | 1.3 | 3.6 | 2.3 | 0.4 | −0.3 |
| Donets-Dnieper | 1.2 | 0.5 | 2.0 | 1.3 | −0.8 | −1.5 |
| North Caucasus | 1.9 | 0.8 | 3.3 | 2.0 | 0.7 | −0.3 |
| Transcaucasia | 2.3 | 1.5 | 3.3 | 2.4 | 1.4 | 0.5 |
| Urals | 0.9 | 0.4 | 2.0 | 1.6 | −0.8 | −1.7 |
| West Siberia | 0.4 | 0.3 | 2.0 | 1.4 | −1.7 | −1.5 |
| East Siberia | 1.4 | 1.2 | 2.9 | 2.3 | −0.5 | −0.9 |
| Far East | 1.5 | 1.7 | 2.0 | 2.2 | 0.3 | 0.4 |
| Kazakhstan | 3.1 | 1.4 | 4.3 | 2.1 | 1.9 | 0.5 |
| Central Asia | 3.4 | 2.8 | 4.2 | 3.6 | 2.9 | 2.3 |
| USSR Total | 1.3 | 1.0 | 2.8 | 2.0 | −0.3 | −0.8 |

SOURCES: Richard H. Rowland and Robert A. Lewis, "Regional Population Growth and Redistribution in the USSR, 1970–79," *Canadian Studies in Population*, Vol. 9 (1981).

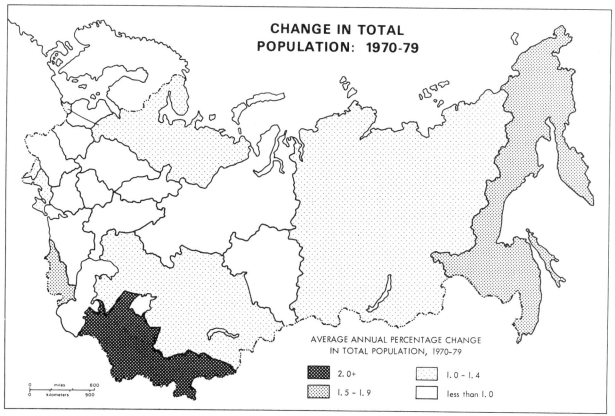

Figure 8

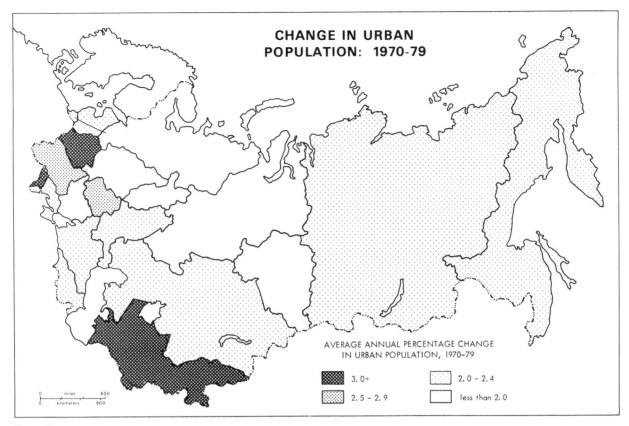

Figure 9

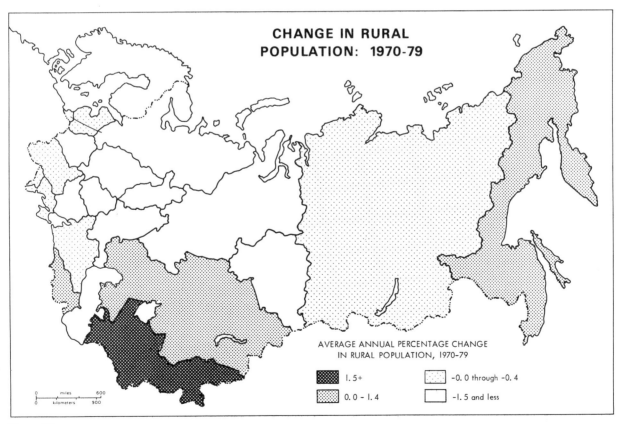

Figure 10

TABLE 15
Estimated Population Aged 20–59 by Economic Region:
Siberia and the Far East (in thousands) (based on
1970 census and assuming no subsequent migration)

| Region | 1970 | 1980 | 1990 |
|---|---|---|---|
| | | Total | |
| Siberia and the Far East | 13,195 | 16,128 | 17,037 |
| West Siberia | 6,172 | 7,571 | 7,885 |
| East Siberia | 3,805 | 4,747 | 5,121 |
| Far East | 3,218 | 3,810 | 4,031 |
| | | Urban | |
| Siberia and the Far East | 8,958 | 10,688 | 10,946 |
| West Siberia | 4,051 | 4,852 | 4,887 |
| East Siberia | 2,519 | 3,053 | 3,186 |
| Far East | 2,388 | 2,783 | 2,873 |
| | | Rural | |
| Siberia and the Far East | 4,237 | 5,441 | 6,091 |
| West Siberia | 2,121 | 2,720 | 2,997 |
| East Siberia | 1,286 | 1,694 | 1,935 |
| Far East | 830 | 1,027 | 1,158 |

SOURCES: See Table 1.

in West Siberia in both 1970 and 1990, and in all regions the urban population is considerably higher than the rural. Because of net out-migration, at least in the early 1970s in Siberia, the total category is probably slightly overstated, and because of net in-migration to the Far East, it is understated. Because of net rural out-migration, the rural category is significantly overstated in all regions, and the urban category is grossly underestimated.

From Table 16 it can be seen that the growth of the total native working-age population would decline greatly between 1980 and 1990 relative to the previous decade in Siberia and the Far East. During the 1970s, when labor shortages were reported throughout the area, there was a considerable increase in the total native population of working age, which must have alleviated labor shortages, but in the 1980s it will be less than a third of that of the 1970s, and the average annual rates would be small and slightly below the USSR average. Thus, if economic development and labor productivity grow at previous rates and net out-migration continues as in the past, labor shortages should intensify. Continued rural out-migration to urban areas in Siberia and the Far East would be necessary to sustain the economic growth of the urban areas, whose working-age population would barely increase without it. Indeed, this is what has happened in the 1970s, because the rural population has declined in Siberia and increased slowly in the Far East, where much of the rural population is not functionally rural (Table 17). In contrast, there has been appreciable urban growth, and the total population increased moderately. Thus, urban labor requirements are being met at the expense of the rural economy, which is also suffering labor shortages.

It is difficult to determine the effect of migration on the working-age population in the 1970s because of a lack of migration data. Estimates for the current economic regions based on the available natural increase data, however, indicate that net out-migration from Siberia has declined and net in-migration to the Far East has increased between 1970 and 1974 relative to the 1959–70 period.[16] Net out-migration from West Siberia during the four-year period was 204,000 and from East Siberia, 45,000. The Far East gained 254,000 as a result of migration. If these estimates are realistic, it would seem that Siberia and the Far East as a whole had no net loss through migration during this period.

On an annual basis, the decline in net out-migration from Siberia appears to be even greater. Between 1961 and 1973, net out-migration from Siberia has been estimated at about one million, 85 percent of which was

TABLE 16
Growth of the Estimated Population Aged 20–59 by Economic Region: Siberia and
the Far East (based on 1970 census and assuming no subsequent migration)

| Region | Total Increase (in thousands) | | Percentage Change | | Average Annual Percentage Change | |
|---|---|---|---|---|---|---|
| | 1970–80 | 1980–90 | 1970–80 | 1980–90 | 1970–80 | 1980–90 |
| | | | Total | | | |
| Siberia and Far East | 2,933 | 909 | 22.2 | 5.6 | 2.0 | 0.6 |
| West Siberia | 1,400 | 313 | 22.7 | 4.1 | 2.1 | 0.4 |
| East Siberia | 942 | 374 | 24.8 | 7.9 | 2.2 | 0.8 |
| Far East | 592 | 222 | 18.4 | 5.8 | 1.7 | 0.6 |
| | | | Urban | | | |
| Siberia and Far East | 1,729 | 259 | 19.3 | 2.4 | 1.8 | 0.2 |
| West Siberia | 800 | 36 | 19.8 | 0.7 | 1.8 | 0.1 |
| East Siberia | 534 | 132 | 21.2 | 4.3 | 2.0 | 0.4 |
| Far East | 395 | 90 | 16.5 | 3.3 | 1.5 | 0.3 |
| | | | Rural | | | |
| Siberia and Far East | 1,204 | 650 | 28.4 | 12.0 | 2.5 | 1.1 |
| West Siberia | 599 | 277 | 28.3 | 10.2 | 2.5 | 1.0 |
| East Siberia | 408 | 241 | 31.7 | 14.3 | 2.8 | 1.4 |
| Far East | 197 | 131 | 23.7 | 12.8 | 2.2 | 1.2 |

SOURCES: See Table 1.

TABLE 17
Population Growth by Economic Region, 1970–79

| Region | Percentage Change | | |
|---|---|---|---|
| | Total | Urban | Rural |
| Siberia and Far East | 10.2 | 20.3 | −7.6 |
| West Siberia | 7.0 | 18.0 | −11.4 |
| East Siberia | 9.3 | 21.5 | −11.4 |
| Far East | 17.9 | 22.9 | 5.4 |
| | Average Annual Percentage Change | | |
| Siberia and Far East | 1.1 | 2.1 | −0.8 |
| West Siberia | 0.8 | 1.9 | −1.3 |
| East Siberia | 1.0 | 2.2 | −1.3 |
| Far East | 1.8 | 2.3 | 0.6 |

Source: *Pravda*, 22 April 1979, p. 4.

attributed to West Siberia. Relative to the 1961–65 period, net out-migration from Siberia increased considerably during the 1966–70 period, but declined significantly in the 1971–73 period. Since 1969, the peak of out-migration, there has been a sharp decline in West Siberia from an estimated 146,000 net out-migrants to 17,000 in 1973, and in East Siberia it fell to an even lower level. Between 1959 and 1973, net out-migration absorbed 50 percent of the natural increase in West Siberia and 11 percent in East Siberia, and rural out-migration intensified resulting in a 15 percent decline of the rural population of Siberia and a 45 percent decline in the rural population aged 20–29. Between 1961 and 1973, the urban population of Siberia grew by about 1.8 million as a result of migration, but the rate of increase due to migration decreased, and the migration turnover increased at least up to 1970. Between 1966 and 1970, intraregional migration accounted for the total growth of the urban population due to migration, because there were more interregional out-migrants than in-migrants. However, the solution to the labor problems does not necessarily lie in attracting more migrants, because each year about 500,000 migrants arrive in Siberian cities from other parts of the country. It has been estimated that if interregional urban out-migration were decreased by 25 percent, in 15 years the urban population of Siberia would increase by two million from this source.[17] If these trends in interregional migration continued in the 1970s, our estimates of the *total* working-age population should be reasonably realistic.

Because there are labor shortages in many parts of the USSR and there are regional differences in the standard of living, one might expect that these differentials in the standard of living would take on particular significance with respect to interregional migration. In fact, V. I. Perevedentsev rightly maintains that the standard of living in labor deficit areas should be higher than in labor surplus areas to attract and maintain labor.[18] Yu. M. Berezkin says that migration is a good barometer for planning agencies as to how well investment is allocated between production and the improvement of the standard of living in a region.[19]

The chief reasons for the out-migration from the labor-deficit eastern regions, in addition to a relatively less

desirable natural environment and its relative isolation, is that real income has been significantly below that of most other regions in the USSR. By 1970, West Siberia and East Siberia still ranked low among the economic regions of the RSFSR.[20] In the past, wages were generally lower, but they became somewhat higher than in the western areas because of wage reforms. Yet, the cost of living is considerably higher than in most other areas of the USSR. It was officially estimated (around 1970?) that the cost of living for a family of four in the eastern regions of the RSFSR was 38 percent above that of the southern part of the USSR and 26 percent above Central Russia. Taking into consideration the necessity to compensate for the less favorable conditions in addition to differences in the cost of living, it has been estimated that wages in Siberia should be 30 to 40 percent higher and in the Far East 50 to 60 percent higher. This would mean that if real wages are not to be below those of European USSR, at a minimum equivalent workers in the east should have wages 20 percent and in many cases 30 to 45 percent above those of the European USSR.[21]

Furthermore, it is acknowledged that housing, social services such as child-care, educational and medical facilities, and the retail trade turnover are relatively inferior and unsatisfactory in Siberia and the Far East. In a migration survey of 18 oblasts and equivalent units in Siberia and the Far East, in 17 of the units the chief reason for migrating was inadequate housing.[22] The relatively low level of real wages probably accounts for the fact that East and West Siberia have the highest rates of labor turnover in industry and construction of the economic regions of the RSFSR.[23]

The net result of these migration processes has been an acute shortage of labor in Siberia and the Far East, which, as has been acknowledged, has been an impediment to economic developments.[24] However, statements as to the extent of these shortages have tended to be vague, leading one to conclude that the extent of the current shortages and of future labor requirements is not known with any precision. It was reported in 1969 that the planned development of the regions east of the Urals would require an additional 500,000 to 600,000 persons of working age.[25] A. Maikov estimated that, between 1971 and 1980, Siberia and the Far East would require several million migrants in the work-force ages.[26] The Institute of Economics and Organization of Industrial Production in Novosibirsk estimated that between 1976 and 1980 planned development in Siberia will require an 18 percent increase in the work force, even though the rate of growth of the native work force will decline significantly.[27] From Table 16, it can be seen that in the whole decade the total native population of working age would increase by only about 23 percent. The projected labor requirements of the BAM alone would seem to strain the available manpower resources of Siberia and the Far East. In his contribution to this project, Victor Mote reports early extravagant predictions that said some 500,000 workers and their relatives would be working on the BAM by 1978, although by 1978 only 80,000 lived along the BAM route and a third of these were soldiers.[28] He further reports that Soviet planners called for at least one million to migrate to the

BAM service area within the next decade.[29] It should be noted that virtually all of the increase in the native total population of working age of East Siberia and the Far East would be located in their southernmost parts in close proximity to the BAM route, and that this increase would be only about a half of the population that was expected to gravitate to the BAM route.

Probably the chief reason for the vague statements as to future labor requirements is that the methods for estimating future labor and population requirements of a region have not been formulated in the USSR.[30] Estimates as to labor requirements are probably made pragmatically and often do not take into consideration varying natural and local conditions. For example, in Neryungri, at the northern end of the branch railroad line from the BAM, the opening of a large open-pit coal mine is requiring 16,000 people, or more than twice as many as was planned, and the cost of production and services is about three times the planned costs.[31]

Furthermore, there are no labor reserves for the labor-deficit urban areas of the eastern regions in the local rural areas, because labor shortages in the agricultural areas have been a problem throughout the eastern regions for more than a decade and between 1966 and 1967 available agricultural labor in West Siberia was only 70 percent of the requirements.[32] In 1971, available labor covered only 86 percent of the requirements in Novosibirsk Oblast, where there had been a considerable improvement in wages, mechanization, housing, and services.[33] The major reasons for the rural out-migration are that wages are significantly higher in the urban areas and the conditions of life better than in the rural areas. Major complaints include the nature and conditions of agricultural labor, inadequate educational facilities, inadequate services, poor housing, a shortage of consumer goods, a lack of recreational facilities, inferior medical facilities, and a relative lack of leisure time.[34] In 1969–70, collective farm wages were two-thirds of industrial wages in the Urals and Siberia.[35] Furthermore, transfer payments per family member of industrial and white-collar workers in the USSR were about twice those of the collective farm population, although agriculture workers supplement their wages with income from their private plots. Currently, rural per capita income in West Siberia is 10 percent below that of the urban areas, although 28 percent of the agricultural income is from the private plots, and housing and services are inferior in the rural areas.[36]

Furthermore, there is no major reserve of labor in Siberia that is not already in the public sector. Although in the past a relatively high percentage of the working-age population was not employed in the public sector, currently only a small percentage of the working-age population of Siberia is to be found in housework and private plots.[37] In 1970, only 4 to 5 percent of the rural working-age population of Siberia was employed in housework and on private plots.[38]

Consequently, considering the declines in the growth of the total native working-age population in the 1980s, these labor shortages will undoubtedly continue and will probably intensify into the future, if current levels of investment are maintained in Siberia and the Far East and labor productivity is not increased. Since the beginning of the Soviet regime investment in Siberia and the Far East has received high priority. In the 1918–28 period it accounted for 14.7 percent of state and cooperative investments, and this level with a few relatively minor deviations has been maintained down to the present, reaching 16.3 percent of the total USSR investment in the 1966–70 period.[39] This has been well above their share of the total population, which was about 10.5 percent of the USSR total in both 1970 and 1979. The 10th Five-Year Plan emphasized the development of the eastern regions of the RSFSR and, considering the abundance of resources in Siberia and the Far East, such an emphasis continues under the current, 11th Five-Year Plan.[40] Thus, it would appear that labor shortages will continue to impede the economic development of Siberia and the Far East.

Although labor problems have been endemic in Siberia and the Far East for at least the last two decades, more recently there has been greater concern about the problem and some concrete measures have been taken. Whether the labor problem will be solved, however, is still in doubt. As to the overall policy of development in the east, it has been maintained that the developmental policy has remained the same since the 1920s, with emphasis on both the independent development of the region and its integration with the total Soviet economy, although economic plans have not always conformed to this policy.[41] Shabad distinguished two major stages in the development of Siberia: the Stalin period when integrated development of Siberia was stressed, and the post-Stalin period when power-intensive industries economizing on the use of labor were developed as a result of labor shortages.[42] There is much empirical evidence to support this contention, and problems related to the relatively lower standard of living and the relatively poorly developed infrastructure further indicate disproportionate development in Siberia and the Far East.

A number of policy recommendations have been made with respect to the future development of Siberia and by implication the Far East. Recent party congresses have called for an improvement of the infrastructure and the standard of living in the east. R. I. Shniper recommends a strengthening of the economic integration of the regions of Eastern USSR, including Central Asia and Kazakhstan, and intensifying the economic ties between Siberia and European USSR to improve the standard of living. It is also widely acknowledged that technology and modernization should be emphasized to raise labor productivity, and labor-intensive industries should not be developed because of labor shortages and the relatively high cost of labor. Furthermore, it has been estimated that in the Siberian North the release of one worker in basic production usually results in the release of three additional auxiliary and service workers, and if family members are included, nine to ten people may be affected.[43] A family of three dependents would seem high, because the average number of children in urban areas of the USSR is closer to two and in the southern areas most women are in the work force.

Probably the most important factor in solving the labor problems of the east has been the increases in wages. In conjunction with wage reforms between 1956 and 1960, a set of regional wage coefficients (percentage additions to wages) and supplements according to length of service was introduced, although they were not applied to all workers or to all industries uniformly, or to all parts of a given region. Most frequently the service industries were not included, and rates for light industry, when included, were below those of heavy industry, which received the major emphasis. As of 1959, the coefficient for Arctic Islands was 2.0, other regions of the Far North, 1.5–1.7; regions equivalent to the Far North, 1.3–1.4; certain regions of the European North, southern regions of East Siberia and the Far East, 1.2; and the Urals, southern West Siberia, Kazakhstan, and Central Asia, 1.15. Not all parts of Kazakhstan and Central Asia were included. Unspecified areas, such as the remaining regions of European USSR and the Transcaucasus had a coefficient of 1.0.[44]

Subsequently, the coefficients were raised and gradually applied to all wage earners outside of agriculture. By about 1972, the coefficient for the Arctic Islands and other regions of the Far North remained unchanged; for regions equivalent to the Far North (including Murmansk Oblast and central regions of Siberia) and regions of the Far East it had been changed to 1.3–1.5, for certain regions of the European North, southern regions of East Siberia and the Far East, 1.2–1.3, for the Urals, southern regions of West Siberia, Kazakhstan and Central Asia, 1.1–1.2.[45] These coefficients have been gradually applied to all workers, and the 10th Five-Year Plan called for extending them to areas not covered. In addition, in the Arctic Islands and in the Far North and roughly equivalent regions, workers receive graduated wage supplements according to length of service based on their base salary excluding the coefficient and additions to salary. The maximum payment usually ranges from 150 to 300 rubles, based on a maximum monthly salary of 300 rubles. There are also other benefits in these areas including additional leave time (12 to 18 days), pregnancy pay, certain additional pension benefits, a guarantee of housing in the former place of residence, and other benefits.[46]

Coefficients and other inducements are used on special construction projects. On the BAM, if a worker signs a contract for three years, he earns a salary of up to 2.5 times the national average and for less than three years 1.25, as well as privileges analogous to the Far North.[47] At Neryungri, at the northern end of the Little BAM, wages are 70 percent above the mean industrial wage.[48]

These wage inducements are particularly important because in the past the contribution of migration organized by the government has not been great. In 1965, it was estimated that not more than 20 percent of the migrants to West Siberia were from this source.[49] Organized migration is directed by the government, generally by means of granting subsidies or certain privileges to migrants, and includes labor recruiting, agricultural resettlement, public appeals, and service after completion of education.[50] The importance of organized migration has declined significantly during the Soviet period. Currently, it accounts for not more than 10 or 12 percent of the total migration, whereas in the 1930s and 1940s it

comprised 30 to 40 percent.[51] It is doubtful that the Soviet government would resort to involuntary migration to solve the labor problems of the east; current proposals center around economic inducements.

Because of the existing and impending labor shortages in Siberia, it would appear that additional workers for resource development will have to come from outside the region. Labor shortages will intensify in European USSR in the 1980s, where the urban working-age population will decline without net urban in-migration, and this may be a major constraint to in-migration to Siberia and the Far East. It is well known, however, that the Soviet government gives priority, in terms of workers and wages, to certain sectors of the economy, such as heavy and defense industries. If the Soviet government were to give priority to resource exports to earn foreign exchange for the importation of technology, and provide more capital to raise labor productivity to solve impending labor problems, it could probably attract the labor to Siberia and the Far East by means of the labor coefficients and other privileges. It is too early to determine whether the existing coefficients will be effective in attracting and retaining labor in the east, but the government could raise these coefficients, as it has on high priority projects, to achieve the necessary labor force. In the absence of a major allocation of investment to the non-Slavic South, this area would appear to be a major source of surplus labor, so the prospect for significant out-migration from this area is worthy of consideration.

## Central Asian Labor Problems

Within a country, as well as internationally, the population transition associated with modernization does not normally allocate labor according to requirements of the economy, because economic development within a country is not uniform. In the Soviet Union, the Slavic and Baltic regions are characterized by low natural increase, and relatively low and declining rate of growth of the native work force and labor shortages, and contain the major regions of economic development. The Turkic and/or Moslem population (hereafter referred to as Turkic-Moslems) and native work force are growing moderately to rapidly, their ethnic areas are relatively less developed, and there are labor surpluses. Migration is the mechanism that equalizes the supply of and demand for labor on a regional basis. Because the non-Slavic South, in particular Central Asia, will be the last major source of labor in the Soviet economy, the central question is whether these indigenous populations, which have been relatively immobile, will migrate in significant numbers to other parts of the USSR in the next decade or so to alleviate impending labor shortages. In addition to the other forces of modernization that lead to the intensified interaction of ethnic groups in multinational developed countries, migration results in heightened ethnic awareness and tensions. The Soviet government could well be faced with a dilemma: if there is significant ethnic out-migration there may be increasing ethnic problems, and if there is little or no out-migration of these ethnic groups, labor shortages will intensify and impede economic development unless there will be a major reallocation of investment funds.

Because we have discussed this problem at length elsewhere, this discussion of the prospects for Central Asian out-migration, and by implication out-migration from other ethnic areas, will be general and brief.[52] We do not contend that this problem can be definitively solved. The intention is to put the problem into a general framework and to investigate briefly the underlying conditions. Our thinking is based conceptually on the hypothesis that there is a considerable universality of demographic process in countries that have undergone significant economic development and modernization. Our working hypothesis is that people throughout the world tend to react in the same manner to the forces that affect their demographic behavior, regardless of political ideology. One cannot claim an absolute universality because theories are inadequately formulated, data are often inadequate, and there are unique features of a society or culture that affect demographic behavior.

In our study of Soviet population, we found a considerable universality of demographic processes in the USSR.[53] With respect to the processes related to population redistribution, migration, urbanization, and rural population change, the expected patterns generally have prevailed. Available data indicate that the expected migration differentials are found in the USSR, in terms of distance, age and education. In response to economic conditions, there is a mass exodus of the young and better educated from rural areas to urban areas, and urbanization is related to investment. Urbanization and urban growth have occurred at an unprecedented rate. The non-European rural population of the southern tier has been relatively immobile, but it is not uncommon for certain areas and ethnic groups within a multinational state to develop and modernize at a slower rate. Ultimately, however, all ethnic groups are integrated into the modern economy because of economic necessity. The chief mechanism is the availability of jobs and wage differentials, although the exact differentials under varying conditions are not known. The world migration literature indicates that people move primarily for jobs and economic improvements, excluding, of course, political migration.

If the Soviet government had an effective population policy, it could not be said that there is a universality of processes, for policy would explain practice. Our work on population policy in the USSR demonstrates that the Soviet government does not have a comprehensive policy. For example, an inferred policy common to most governments is that migration should meet the needs of the economy with respect to labor. Yet, much of the migration in the USSR is economically irrational in that it is from labor-deficit areas to labor-surplus areas. The out-migration from Siberia and from labor-deficit rural areas are notable examples, as well as the immobility of labor in the non-Slavic South. Large cities continue to grow rapidly, despite a policy to the contrary. Clearly, migration in the USSR is not equalizing the supply of labor on a regional basis, and many of the current problems of Soviet society relate to migration. It is also worthy of note that interrepublic and interethnic migration in the USSR is considered ideologically progressive and desirable with respect to the "coming together" of nations and the internationalization of Soviet peoples, as well as being economically rational.[54]

The Turkic-Moslems of Central Asia are experiencing rapid population growth. The total Turkic-Moslem population of Central Asia, excluding Tatars, increased at an average annual rate of 3.4 percent between 1959 and 1970, and if this rate were to continue the population of 15 million in 1970 would roughly double by 1990. Even if there were a decline in fertility, crude birth rates would probably not decline appreciably in the next few decades because 50 percent of the population of the titular nationalities was under age 15 in 1970. Most of this growth would occur in rural areas because in 1970 only 21 percent of the Turkic-Moslem population lived in the urban areas with a population of 15,000 or more. The total population of working age, excluding migration, will almost double between 1970 and 1990 and increase by 7 million, 4 million of which will occur in the 1980–90 period. The rural working-age population will increase by 5 million between 1970 and 1990, 3 million of which will be in the 1980–90 period. New entrants to the total population of working age will almost triple between 1970 and 1990 and increase by 4 million. The estimate for the total working-age population is probably realistic in that net in-migration to the region appears to have declined in the early 1970s, but the estimate for the rural working-age population is overestimated in that rural population growth declined between 1970 and 1979 relative to the 1959–70 period (Table 14), probably indicating increased rural to urban migration and reclassification of rural areas as urban since there is no indication of a significant decline in rural fertility. The total working-age population should be adjusted somewhat with respect to probable participation of women in the work force, owing to the nature of Turkic-Moslem society, although rising levels of education among young women could mitigate this somewhat.

Such rapidly growing population does not necessarily mean that there are population pressures. However, the rural population of Central Asia lives in irrigated oases with limited water and irrigable land, and the irrigated acreage has been expanded slowly, well below the rate of population increase. Between 1959 and 1970, the number of rural inhabitants per sown hectare in Central Asia increased by 25 percent after having remained stable for at least the previous half century. In addition, there has been a drive by the government to mechanize agriculture to produce more cotton and to lower the cost of production. These trends have resulted in labor surpluses and underemployment throughout the rural areas.

Despite reported shortages of skilled labor in the cities, there has been little migration of the indigenous population to local urban centers. In the past, Russians and others have been moving to Central Asian cities, thus impeding the in-migration of the indigenous population. Ethnocentric hiring practices may also account for this situation. Our estimates indicate that even if there were no in-migration into Central Asia, the nonagricultural economy has not expanded rapidly enough to absorb the growing work force, and current investment plans are not directed toward alleviating this situation. If these trends continue, labor surpluses and underemployment in Central Asia will continue to grow and may provide a stimulus for rural out-migration.

Another factor that may promote out-migration is the rise in educational levels among the young; the world over, the young and more educated have the highest propensity to migrate. In 1970, the total Uzbek cohort aged 20–29 had completed 10 or more years of education at the same rate (54 percent) as the ethnic Russian population of the USSR; the rural Uzbek rate was 48 percent. The rates for the other Central Asian titular groups were somewhat lower. Furthermore, there has been a sharp increase in the number of women completing 10 years of schooling. In the rural areas of the Uzbek Republic in 1970, the ratio between the percentages of men and women aged 16–19 completing 10 years of schooling approached parity, which probably accounts for the decline between 1959 and 1970 in the percentage of females aged 16 to 19 who were married. A common pattern in most societies is that high school graduates, regardless of the quality of education, find urban jobs more attractive than rural jobs. Moreover, the characteristics of the young are the most crucial measures of the degree of social and cultural change in a society.

Probably the chief reason for limited rural out-migration in Central Asia has been the relatively high agricultural wages and the low rural-urban wage differential. Although agricultural wage data in the USSR are not abundant and complex because of the various sources of income, it would appear that agricultural wages are considerably higher than the USSR average in Uzbekistan and Turkmenia and slightly lower in Tadzhikistan and Kirghizia. Furthermore, kolkhoz workers in Central Asia work significantly fewer hours. The greatly increased agricultural investment that has occurred in the past decade has dampened the effect of rapidly growing rural population, so that at least by 1970 it appears that economic conditions in the rural areas of Central Asia had not yet begun to deteriorate significantly.

In the Soviet and Western literature on Central Asian migration, the strength of the Turkic-Moslem culture has often been viewed as a major deterrent to migration; it is said that the Moslem peoples of Central Asia are inherently immobile and will not willingly trade the intimacy of their cultural presence for a higher living standard within an alien, urban, non-Moslem environment. The essential question is, if economic conditions deteriorate, will culture be dominant over socioeconomic conditions? It would seem to depend on how bad the economic conditions were. In 1974, there were 600,000 legal Turkish workers in West Germany, 26 percent of which were women, reflecting a drastic change in a society that, before structural changes in its economy, had no migration tradition. Moreover, more than a million applicants for jobs in West Germany were reportedly on a waiting list in Turkey, largely because workers can earn 20 times as much in West Germany than in Turkey.[55] If analogous conditions prevailed in Central Asia relative to other parts of the USSR, there would be Turkic-Moslems all over the USSR, considering that there are no restrictions such as are imposed in international migration. Of course, such wage differentials do not exist in the USSR, and the threshold for out-migration is unknown. In some Russian areas with rural out-migration, migrants have doubled their wages after a few years.

Some writers stress the lack of Russian language proficiency as a barrier to the migration of Central Asians. Between 14 and 19 percent of the population of the titular groups of Central Asia claimed fluency in Russian in 1970, and between 26 and 50 percent in 1979. Comparative research in migration, however, indicates that millions of peoples have migrated despite language differences. Cultural differences can impede migration, depending on economic and socioeconomic conditions, but not stop it. The Russian language competence of the Central Asian Turks is greater than the German language proficiency of the Turks who migrated to West Germany. One does not necessarily need to acculturate before one migrates, as is suggested by the migration history of the United States and, more recently, of Western Europe.

So far there has been no concerted Soviet effort to solve this problem, and inactivity or late or minimal response cannot be ruled out. These alternatives would promote out-migration. Moreover, migration policies in the USSR have not been effective, primarily because the government has not been willing to devote the necessary effort or expense. More recently it has been unwilling to rely upon compulsory mobilization to solve its labor problems, and regional wage incentives appear to be inadequate.

There has been no indication that the Soviet government plans a major reallocation of investment to the southern tier, where most of its labor reserves are. Although labor has generally been the mobile factor of production, the government could invest heavily in Central Asia to utilize the surplus labor. However, Central Asia has the lowest return to capital and combined factor productivity in the USSR, few economies of concentration, scant resources for heavy industry, a remote location from major markets, and a relatively poorly developed infrastructure, particularly transportation. The lack of resources for heavy industry would not rule out investment in labor-intensive agricultural and industry in Central Asia, as the 1981–85 plan calls for. However, a policy of massive investment in Central Asia would be in conflict with the Soviet goal of maximizing the efficiency of the total economy, which at present is not efficient. One might also question whether Soviet planners want to invest heavily for a long period of time in a peripheral, non-Russian, and potentially troublesome area at the expense of the development of the Russian areas where resources are more abundant.

The Soviet Union is a welfare society with considerable equalization of income and transfer payments. Wages could be maintained in rural areas by raising the price paid for cotton and other agricultural products, but this, in effect, would be supporting a large unproductive welfare population on the land and would be costly and in conflict with the goal of cheaper cotton. The maintenance of lower cotton prices would be an impetus for out-migration, and probably the most inexpensive course of action, considering labor requirements elsewhere. However, it should be acknowledged that welfare aspects of the Soviet society could deter migration.

The Soviet government will probably be motivated by economic considerations. Eventually, there will probably be more investment in Central Asia, but it is questionable whether it will be sufficient to absorb the surplus labor. The government may attempt to encourage out-migration because it would be in its economic interest and ideologically desirable. Either by choice or inaction, it could allow the standard of living in rural areas to decline. Measures may be taken to reserve jobs in the local urban centers for the indigenous population, and efforts may be made to facilitate the transition of the rural population to urban areas. For the most part, however, the processes involved will probably be beyond the control of the government, and expected migratory patterns may ultimately prevail.

Other Western writers have maintained that there will be little or no out-migration from Central Asia primarily because of cultural factors, conceivable policies, and other factors specific to the area.[56] We do not deny that there could be conditions specific to Central Asia that may impede migration, at least in the short run, but we can see no particularistic factors in Central Asia that are sufficiently strong and resistant to change related to modernization to counter the strong demographic, economic, and social forces that are intensifying in Central Asia and which elsewhere in the world have generally resulted in substantial out-migration.

The demographic cauldron in Central Asia will be brewing in the 1980s, and there should be considerable surplus labor if current trends in regional economic development persist. At the very least, it would seem reasonable to assume that there will be surplus workers in Central Asia and other ethnic territories that would respond to high wage differentials at specific resource projects for a relatively short period of time. If this is not the case, resource development in Siberia would be very seriously impeded, because job opportunities in other labor-deficit regions should be abundant, which would impede out-migration.

## Summary and Conclusions

With respect to demographic processes in the USSR, there is a major dichotomy between the non-Slavic South and the regions to the north or the European areas of the USSR. The European areas are characterized by low rates of natural increase and population growth, high rates of urbanization and urban growth, high levels of urbanization, high and intensifying rates of rural depopulation, and high rates of mobility. Characteristic features of the non-Slavic South include moderate to high rates of natural increase and population growth, low rates of urbanization but high rates of urban growth, rural population growth, particularly in Central Asia, a pre-

dominantly rural population, and a relatively immobile rural population. Although the non-Slavic South contains only one-fifth of the Soviet population, between 1970 and 1979 it accounted for 44.1 percent of the total population growth, so there has been a redistribution of population to the non-Slavic South, where the percentage of the total population increased from 15.6 to 20.7 between 1959 and 1979.

With respect to the growth of the population of working age between 1980 and 1990, the dichotomy is even more striking. The non-Slavic South will account for 72.8 percent of the growth of the total working-age population or 7.4 million, whereas in the remainder of the USSR it will increase by only 2.7 million. The respective average annual growth rates are 2.6 and 0.2. If the 1970–74 migration pattern of little or no net migration between the non-Slavic South and the remainder of the country persists, these estimates should be fairly reliable. In the absence of migration, 61.0 percent of the increase in the rural population of working age between 1980 and 1990, or 5.5 million, would be accounted for by the non-Slavic South, where it would grow 3.7 percent per year in contrast to 0.8 percent per year elsewhere in the USSR. The urban working-age population of the non-Slavic South would increase by 1.9 million, or 1.4 percent per year, without migration, and would decline by 754,000 in the remainder of the USSR.

The crux of the situation is that not only will the working-age population of the USSR grow slowly, 0.7 percent per year, in the 1980s, but the geographic distribution of this growth will be unfavorable for economic development in that it will be concentrated in the rural areas of the non-Slavic South. There will be a spatial incongruity between the growth of the population of working age and the work force and the availability of resources, particularly those for heavy industry. Aside from northern Kazakhstan, which according to population characteristics (above all ethnic composition) should more appropriately be included in Siberia, resources for heavy industry in the non-Slavic South are not abundant. If the past pattern of high rates of mobility in the northern areas and low rates in the non-Slavic South continues, there should be a tight labor market in the north, where the major areas of economic development are located. The rural exodus in the Slavic and Baltic areas will probably continue at an intensified rate and meet some of the needs of the urban economy, but by the end of the 1980s the rural population should be depleted and undergo natural decrease and acute labor shortages despite the recent emphasis on rural investment to raise agricultural production and retain the rural labor force. The availability of jobs, particularly in the urban centers of the western part of the USSR, could result in less interregional migration, particularly to the east, where resources are abundant, unless appreciable differentials in wages and the standard of living are instituted. In the absence of such differentials, Siberian labor problems should intensify, given the decline in the native working-age population and continued emphasis on economic development.

Some of these labor problems would be alleviated if there were significant out-migration from the labor-surplus areas of the non-Slavic South. If one emphasizes the factors that have universally been associated with out-migration, such as the growth of the working-age population, insufficient investment to accommodate this growth, the mechanization of agriculture, increasing regional and urban-rural wage differentials, rising education levels of the young, deteriorating economic conditions, and the ready availability of jobs elsewhere in the USSR, out-migration could be expected. If one emphasizes cultural and ethnic factors and conceivable policies, a case could be made for little or no out-migration. If the Soviet government decides to maintain agricultural wages and support a large unproductive rural population and to invest heavily in the non-Slavic South, where the return to investment is less, out-migration would probably be minimal. However, other multinational developed countries with roughly similar conditions have experienced a massive redistribution of population, largely because labor is the most mobile factor of production. A country rich in natural resources would not normally direct its incremental investment predominantly to areas that are poorly endowed with resources. That migration is not meeting the needs of the Soviet economy is a problem that must be dealt with sooner or later by Soviet planners.

The essential question is to what degree will resource development be hindered by the impending labor shortages, but this question cannot be definitively answered because it depends on the priority the Soviet government will give to such development. However, it can be stated with some certainty that, unless resource development is given high priority, it will surely be impeded by labor shortages, particularly in Siberia and the Far East. Thus, the regional availability of labor is likely to become a constraint on resource development in the USSR in the 1980s.

## NOTES

1. For a more detailed discussion of this issue, see Victor L. Mote, *Predictions and Realities in the Development of the Soviet Far East*, Discussion Paper No. 3 (May 1978), Association of American Geographers, Project on Soviet Natural Resources in the World Economy, pp. 10–12.

2. Murray Feshbach and Stephen Rapawy, "Soviet Population and Manpower Trends and Policies," U.S. Congress, Joint Economic Committee, *Soviet Economy in a New Perspective* (Washington: U. S. Government Printing Office, 1976), pp. 129–30.

3. For a discussion of this problem and work force participation rates by age and sex, see Stephen Rapawy, *Estimates and Projections of the Labor Force and Civilian Employment in the U.S.S.R. 1950 to 1990*, U. S. Department of Commerce, Bureau of Economic Analysis, Foreign Economic Report No. 10, September 1976, pp. 13–15.

4. Ibid.

5. Survival rates for the various age groups were derived from population projections in Godfrey Baldwin, *Estimates and Projections of the Population of the U.S.S.R., by Age and Sex: 1950 to 2000*, U. S. Department of Commerce,

Bureau of Economic Analysis, International Population Reports, Series P-91, no. 23, March 1973. The survival rates were as follows: The 10–49 cohort, 0.97; the 0–39 cohort, 0.95; the 0–9 cohort, 0.98, and the 10–19 cohort, 0.99. In the absence of rural mortality data, it was assumed that there was no difference between rural, urban, and total mortality.

6. Robert A. Lewis, Richard H. Rowland, and Ralph S. Clem, *Nationality and Population Change in Russia and the USSR* (New York: Praeger, 1976); and Robert A. Lewis and Richard H. Rowland, *Population Redistribution in the USSR: Its Impact on Society, 1897–1977* (New York: Praeger, 1979).

7. Central Intelligence Agency, *USSR: Some Implications of Demographic Trends for Economic Policies*, ER 77-10012, (January 1977), p. 17.

8. Ibid., p. 16.

9. Rapawy, *Estimates and Projections*, p. 4.

10. Lewis and Rowland, *Population Redistribution*, Chapter 2.

11. Ibid., for a more complete description of the procedures.

12. Ibid.

13. *Pravda*, 22 April 1979, p. 4.

14. V. A. Borisov, *Perspektivy rozhdayemosti* [Birth-rate prospects] (Moscow: Statistika, 1976), p. 108.

15. Viktor Perevedentsev, "From countryside to the city," *Nash Sovremennik* no. 11 (1972), p. 104.

16. *Naseleniye SSSR 1973* [Population of USSR 1973] (Moscow: Statistika, 1975), pp. 10–25.

17. Ye. D. Malinin and A. K. Ushakov, *Naseleniye Sibiri* [Population of Siberia] (Moscow: Statistika, 1976), pp. 40–83.

18. D. I. Valentei and I. F. Sorokina, eds., *Naseleniye i trudovye resursy SSSR* [Population and labor resources of USSR] (Moscow: Mysl, 1971), p. 166.

19. M. K. Bandman, ed., *Razvitiye narodnogo khozyaistva Sibiri* [Development of the economy of Siberia] (Novosibirsk: Nauka, 1978), p. 91.

20. Malinin and Ushakov, *Naseleniye*, pp. 89-91; V. I. Perevedentsev, *Migratsiya naseleniya i trudovye problemy Sibiri* [Migration and labor problems in Siberia] (Novosibirsk: Nauka, 1966), pp. 159–74; A. Gladyshev, "Public consumption funds and migration," *Planovoye Khozyaistvo*, no. 10 (1966), pp. 17–22.

21. R. Ivanova, "Development of the eastern regions and their labor supply," *Voprosy Ekonomiki*, no. 10 (1973), p. 44.

22. A. V. Topilin, *Territorialnoye pereraspredeleniye trudovykh resursov v SSSR* [Territorial redistribution of labor resources in the USSR] (Moscow: Ekonomika, 1975), pp. 102–09.

23. Bandman, ed. *Razvitiye*, p. 92.

24. V. G. Kostakov, *Trudovye resursy pyatiletki* [Labor resources in the five-year plan] (Moscow: Izdatelstvo Politicheskoi Literatury, 1976), p. 58; Perevedentsev, *Migratsiya*, p. 51; and B. V. Korniyenko and Ye. D. Malinin, "Migration in West Siberia," *Izvestiya Sibirskogo otdeleniya Akademii Nauk SSSR, seriya obshchestvennykh nauk*, no. 6 (1972), p. 93.

25. G. I. Granik and M. B. Mazanova, *Voprosy razmesh-*

*cheniya proizvoditelnyk sil* [Problems in location of productive forces] (Moscow, 1969), p. 18; as cited in V. A. Shpilyuk, *Mezhrespublikanskaya migratsiya i sblizheniye natsii v SSSR* [Interrepublic migration and ethnic rapprochement in the USSR] (Lvov: Vishcha Shkola, 1975), p. 82.

26. A. Maikov, "Main migration streams and the perfecting of the spatial redistribution of labor resources," in *Narodonaseleniye* (Moscow: Statistika, 1973), pp. 34–35.

27. Malinin and Ushakov, *Naseleniye*, pp. 40–41.

28. Victor L. Mote, *Predictions and Realities*, p. 59.

29. Theodore Shabad and Victor L. Mote, *Gateway to Siberian Resources (The BAM)* (Washington: Scripta, 1977), p. 91.

30. Bandman, ed., *Razvitiye*, p. 90.

31. *New York Times*, 1 April 1979, p. 24.

32. Malinin and Ushakov, *Naseleniye*, p. 78; and V. I. Perevedentsev, *Migratsiya naseleniya*, pp. 52–61.

33. Bandman, ed., *Razvitiye*, pp. 99–101.

34. T. I. Zaslavskaya, ed., *Migratsiya selskogo naseleniya* [Migration of rural population] (Moscow: Mysl, 1970), pp. 150–65; T. I. Zaslavskaya and V. A. Malmyk, eds. *Sovremennaya Sibirskaya derevnya* [The contemporary Siberian countryside], Part II (Novosibirsk: S.O.A.N. SSSR, 1975), pp. 3–105.

35. David E. Powell, "The Rural Exodus," *Problems of Communism* 23 (November-December 1974), p. 8.

36. Bandman, ed., *Razvitiye*, pp. 106–10.

37. Malinin and Ushakov, *Naseleniye*, p. 41.

38. Bandman, ed., *Razvitiye*, p. 100.

39. Shabad and Mote, *Gateway*, p. 5.

40. Kostakov, *Trudovye*, p. 58.

41. Bandman, ed., *Razvitiye*, pp. 36–39.

42. Shabad and Mote, *Gateway*, pp. 1–57.

43. Bandman, ed., *Razvitiye*, pp. 44–56.

44. *Sbornik zakonodatelnykh aktov o trude* [Compendium of labor legislation] (Moscow: Yuridicheskaya Literatura, 1974), pp. 417–19, 650–55, and 889–931; and Y. Manevich, *Problemy obshchestvennogo truda* [Problems of social labor] (Moscow: Ekonomika, 1966), p. 129.

45. Ye. F. Mizhenskaya, *Lichnye potrebnosti pri sotsializme* [Personal needs under socialism] (Moscow: Nauka, 1973), p. 94, as cited in Janet Chapman, "Recent Trends in the Soviet Industrial Wage Structure," Paper presented at the Conference on Problems of Industrial Labor in the USSR, Kennan Institute for Advanced Russian Studies, Washington, 27–29 September, p. 24.

46. *Sbornik zakonodatelnykh aktov*, pp. 891 and 906–20.

47. Shabad and Mote, *Gateway*, p. 92.

48. *New York Times*, 1 April 1979, p. 24.

49. V. I. Perevedentsev, *Sovremennaya migratsiya naseleniya Zapadnoi Sibiri* [Contemporary migration in West Siberia] (Novosibirsk: Zapadno-Sibirskoye Knizhnoye Izdatelstvo, 1965), p. 63.

50. For a more complete discussion of organized migration, see Lewis and Rowland, *Population Redistribution*, Chapter 1.

51. Topilin, *Territorialnoye*, pp. 13–14.

52. Lewis, Rowland, and Clem, *Nationality*, pp. 354–383; and Lewis and Rowland, *Population Redistribution*, Chapter 9. For a more detailed documentation, the reader is referred to these discussions.

53. Ibid.

54. Shpilyuk, *Mezhrespublikanskaya*, pp. 9–40.

55. Nermin Abdan-Unat, "Implications of Migration on Emancipation and Pseudo-Emancipation of Turkish Women," *International Migration Review* 11 (Spring 1977), pp. 31–33; and Kurt M. Mayer, "Intra-European Migration During the Past Twenty Years," *International Migration Review* 9 (Winter 1975), pp. 441–47.

56. Murray Feshbach, "Prospects for Massive Out-Migration from Central Asia During the Next Decade," Foreign Demographic Analysis Division, Bureau of Economic Analysis, U. S. Department of Commerce, February 1977; Jeremy Azrael, *Emergent Nationality Problems in the USSR*, Rand, R-2172-AF (September 1977); Theodore Shabad, "Some Aspects of Central Asian Manpower and Urbanization," *Soviet Geography: Review and Translation*, XX, no. 2 (February 1979); and Michael Rywkin, "Central Asia and Soviet Manpower," *Problems of Communism*, XXVIII, (January-February 1979).

# 5

# THE IMPACT OF RECENT TRENDS
# IN SOVIET FOREIGN TRADE ON
# REGIONAL ECONOMIC DEVELOPMENT
# IN THE USSR

ROBERT N. NORTH
University of British Columbia

## Introduction

This paper examines Soviet development policies from a
viewpoint unlike those adopted elsewhere in the volume.
It does so to close a circle of causes and effects created by
Soviet policies. The AAG project guidelines correctly
state that "a careful analysis of regional development
policies and spatial strategies is essential to a proper
understanding of Soviet natural-resource export potentials and their implications." But the relationship between regional development and exports is circular. The
regional policies and practices that affect export potentials are themselves changing under the influence of new
foreign economic policies, including policies designed to
expand and restructure exports.

This paper, therefore, examines the impact of trends in
Soviet foreign economic relations on regional economic
development. A brief survey of the relevant trends is
followed by a description of their impacts on regional
development to the present, and those planned or confidently expected; an account of the work of Soviet research institutes that are attempting to devise guidelines
for the coordination of foreign trade initiatives and regional policies; and a short discussion of the range of
options from which present regional policies have been
chosen and new choices might be made.

## Trends in Soviet Foreign Economic Relations

In relation to the size of the Soviet economy, the total
amount of foreign trade is not impressive. The world's
second largest economy ranked only eighth in value of
foreign trade in 1980, with less than a third of the American and well under half the West German totals. Twenty

*I wish to acknowledge the help of the Social Sciences and
Humanities Research Council of Canada in financing six
weeks in Moscow in December 1979 and January 1980, and
of Professor N. V. Alisov of Moscow University for many
hours spent answering questions and facilitating my work.*

years previously it had ranked sixth. But the value of
foreign trade has grown rapidly since World War II, and
the rate of growth has increased in each five-year period
since 1960.

Trade is by no means the only manifestation of Soviet
involvement in foreign economic relations. Following the
Soviet categorization we shall review relationships with
other communist, developed capitalist, and developing
countries. Table 1 shows the shares of the groups in
Soviet foreign trade.

"Integration" is the key word in Soviet writings on
current economic relations with the other CMEA countries. Vardomsky and Mironenko identify three types of
integration: specialization in production (*predmetnaya
spetsializatsiya*); the supply of raw and semi-processed
materials; and cooperation in production.[1] The general
pattern of trade, established in the 1950s and 1960s, fits
their first two categories. The Soviet Union supplies Eastern Europe with industrial and energy raw materials and
with heavy machinery and equipment in exchange for
other manufactures. There are exceptions to the pattern,
such as the eastward movement of Polish coal and
Hungarian alumina and the westward movement of
Soviet cameras, watches, and cars, but the principal outcome has been to make industrial growth in Eastern Europe heavily dependent on Soviet oil, iron ore, and other
raw materials. The extraction and transport of these resources have strained Soviet supplies of capital and labor,
so the CMEA partners have been encouraged to help by
extending credits, preferably with long-term payback in
products;[2] by supplying labor;[3] by participating in joint
projects for resource extraction and transport, involving
the provision of capital, labor, and materials;[4] and even
by setting up their own projects on Soviet soil.[5] In other
words there has been a move toward the third type of
integration described above.

The Soviet Union is now pressing its partners to reduce
their dependence by exploiting more of their own resources, of low-quality coal for example, and importing
more from the developing countries.[6] In general the intention is to slow down the rate of growth of Soviet
raw-material exports, or to stabilize them, rather than to
reduce them absolutely. This change in approach can be
accounted for partly by the rise in world energy prices in
the mid-1970s, which made Soviet oil and natural gas

TABLE 1
Soviet Foreign Trade, by Groups of Countries,
1965–81 (percent of total trade)

| Year | Communist countries | Including CMEA members | Developed capitalist countries | Developing countries |
|---|---|---|---|---|
| 1965 | 68.8 | 58.0 | 19.3 | 11.9 |
| 1970 | 65.2 | 55.6 | 21.3 | 13.5 |
| 1975 | 56.3 | 51.8 | 31.3 | 12.4 |
| 1978 | 59.8 | 55.7 | 28.0 | 12.2 |
| 1979 | 56.1 | 51.9 | 32.1 | 11.8 |
| 1980 | 53.7 | 48.7 | 33.6 | 12.7 |
| 1981 | 52.8 | 47.6 | 32.2 | 15.0 |

SOURCE: *Vneshnyaya torgovlya SSSR. Statistichesky sbornik*, relevant years.

outstandingly attractive as exports to hard-currency markets. Also, the rapid rise in domestic and East European demand for energy and other raw materials has begun to strain the Soviet ability to supply, even with foreign help. Of concern are the absolute size of some resources;[7] the speed with which resources can be brought into use, irrespective of their size;[8] and the ability of the transport system to move the volume of traffic likely to be generated in remote regions. A third factor may be more efficient comparative costing of Soviet and developing-country raw-material exports to Eastern Europe than hitherto. A fourth, minor factor may be Soviet irritation at the "leakage" of some Soviet raw-material exports to CMEA countries to the West for hard currency.[9] Finally, the Soviet Union intends to increase the proportion of goods it exports already processed, partly to reduce transport costs but mainly to raise its returns on investment.[10] For several years Soviet writers have been pointing out the high capital requirements, slow returns and low returns of raw-material extraction and processing, in which their country tends to specialize, in comparison with those of the later stages of manufacturing in which their partners specialize.[11] Price changes have reduced the differentials for some raw materials, and the cooperative production arrangements already discussed can help even out the burden, but a shift towards more highly processed and manufactured exports is still considered essential. However, substantial change is not considered feasible in the near future. Indeed, between 1965 and 1979 the share of primary products in Soviet exports grew by about 5 percentage points, while that of machinery fell a little.

In all fields except raw-material supply, and in that field too, insofar as it does not involve keeping pace with the rise in East European demand, the Soviet Union has pursued close integration of the East European economies with its own to a degree and at a pace which its partners have evidently found uncomfortable at times.[12] A swarm of international agencies has been created to coordinate production and trade in metals, manufactures, chemicals and other commodities (though they account for a small proportion of trade so far)[13], to coordinate transport within the CMEA, and to organize measures for industrial standardization, environmental protection and so forth. In manufacturing industry the

Soviet Union has promoted a progression from "interbranch" to "intrabranch" specialization and the setting-up of joint-production facilities. The earlier pattern was of specialization in finished products, while intrabranch specialization involves specialization in the production of parts. It is claimed to minimize imbalances in the internal industrial structure of participating countries.[14]

Overlying all these specific measures has been Soviet advocacy of more closely coordinated general development planning. This has had to be tempered with a cautious regard for national sensitivities among its partners, especially since the Soviet Union accounts for some 70 percent of the population and 75 percent of the industry of the CMEA. In any supranational organization with proportional representation, the Soviet Union could dictate policy. Such organizations have been avoided, but planning has become more closely coordinated during the 1970s, culminating in the adoption of "multi-lateral integrationary measures," covering four broad economic areas up to 1990. The programs are intended respectively to meet the energy, fuel, and raw material needs of CMEA; to raise the level of mechanical engineering; to meet the group's needs for foodstuffs and consumer goods; and to develop CMEA transport facilities.[15]

Earlier Soviet efforts to accelerate integration were not outstandingly successful.[16] In addition to member countries' doubts about the loss of autonomy, they were hampered by the relatively strong attractions of trade with the West. Soviet trade with the developed capitalist countries grew more rapidly than that with its CMEA partners during the 1960s and up to 1974, though the shares of the two groups have fluctuated since then (Table 1).

Innovations in economic relations with the West have been pursued almost as enthusiastically as within the CMEA during the past decade. While stopping short of foreign concessions to exploit Soviet resources, they have included long-term compensatory agreements for raw-material exploitation,[17] licensing arrangements, and joint exploration for natural resources.[18] To a greater extent than in CMEA trade, Soviet exports have been dominated by raw materials, principally oil though including natural gas, a variety of metals and chemical raw materials, and forest products. Soviet writers are urging that the proportion of processed and manufactured exports be raised. Imports have been divided mainly between high technology goods and foodstuffs, including among the former, factories supplied on a turnkey basis, a pattern which seems unlikely to change in the near future. Determined selling of the Lada car in Western markets exemplifies one way in which the imported technology can be used to change the composition of exports. (It has also led to some Western companies refusing to sell their technology.)

Enthusiasm for trade has brought a considerable influx of Western factory equipment, but in assessing its regional impact we should note that it forms a very small share of total installations. In the years 1973 and 1974, for example, the share was 1.3 to 1.5 percent.[19]

The Soviet Union has extended its involvement in Western commerce in one other direction of relevance to this paper, namely by becoming a major participant in the international carrier trade. To this end it has built up its merchant fleet, greatly expanded its ports, and opened the Trans-Siberian container route.

Trade with developing countries has been a small proportion of the whole (Table 1). Of some relevance to this paper are arrangements with neighboring less developed countries, such as Afghanistan and formerly Iran, which affect the border regions of both partners, and in general the tendency to pay more attention to developing countries as potentially cheaper suppliers of raw materials than the Soviet Union, not only to the East European countries, but also to the Soviet Union itself.

The current trends in Soviet foreign economic policy reflect a number of aims and pressures. The desire for imports, especially Western imports, can be considered a major stimulus to the whole complex of policy changes.[20] It is believed that economic growth can be accelerated by importing Western technology and capital, though doubts have been raised about both the criteria for selection of technological imports and the efficiency of the desired multiplier effects.[21] The imports must be paid for, and both the relative availability and the relative salability of Soviet raw materials, compared to the country's manufactures, have compelled payment largely in the former so far. The same applies to payment for wheat imports, though the bulk of foodstuff imports come from developing countries which will take Soviet manufactures at least in part payment.

Economic growth can also be accelerated by expanding markets and achieving economies of scale in more highly specialized factories. Expanding markets by including the CMEA countries and cooperating with them in specialization can bring additional benefits through the pooling of resources. A theme frequently reiterated in Soviet works is the impossibility of any one country, even one with the resources of the Soviet Union, advancing simultaneously in all fields of technology.[22] Cooperation with the East European countries can foster the additional aim of binding their economies more securely together. Such a process is facilitated by the complementarity of the Soviet and major East European economies, though that complementarity needs to be reoriented: in its present form it creates pressures on Soviet raw-material and capital supplies very similar to those created by trade with Western countries.

The combined foreign pressures on raw-material supplies, coupled with rapidly rising domestic demand, have forced raw-material exploitation to shift in one of several directions: to lower-quality or less convenient resources (e.g., in the sense that their exploitation destroys farmland, as in the case of the Kursk Magnetic Anomaly iron ores), still in the more accessible regions; to the more complete utilization of resources (e.g., forests and water resources in European USSR); or to resources in more remote areas. In the last case not only must new infrastructure be created, both locally and for transport to markets, but very often labor turnover becomes a problem, exacerbated by slow growth of the skilled labor force and the ready availability of jobs in most of the more attractive parts of the country. In other words all options

are expensive, so there are obvious incentives to finance raw-material exploitation for export with capital supplied by the receiving countries; to use their labor too where feasible; to obtain high-technology imports on credit—if possible, against payment in products of the new technology—rather than try to expand raw-material exports rapidly enough to pay cash; in the long run, to shift the balance of exports towards manufactures; and to try to increase foreign earnings through such means as participation in the carrier trade and the offering of financial services.

## Types of Impact on Regional Development

The foreign economic policies described above can affect Soviet regional development directly and indirectly.[23] Direct impacts are typified by investments in mines and factories, and in the transport facilities serving them, in order to enable them to export. The allocation of imported factory equipment also constitutes a direct regional impact. One question to investigate is the extent to which such investments and allocations reflect proximity to export markets and suppliers, respectively. Indirect impacts are many and varied. Firstly, transport facilities which are built to serve export markets but can also be used for internal traffic may change the comparative attractiveness of different regions for some industries. In the case of oil and gas pipelines, from which some of the flow can be tapped off for local use, there may be both a direct locational effect and a cost effect. Were it not for the volume requirements of export markets, regions traversed by the pipelines might have been served only by much more expensive rail transport or narrow-diameter pipelines. This cost effect might be regarded as a special case within a more general second category of indirect impacts, namely that the combination of domestic and export demand may make feasible a shift to new technology—a type of threshold effect.

A third category of indirect impacts also constitutes a type of threshold effect. The combination of domestic and export demand may cause shifts in patterns of supply for an industry as a whole. The chemical fertilizer industry provides examples, where new resources are brought into use for the home market, but the reason is that existing production has been allocated to export markets.

Fourthly, regions may be affected differentially by changes in the sectoral structure of the Soviet economy, consequent upon the establishment of foreign trade economic links. For example, decisions on national specialization within the CMEA will bring about changes in the relative requirements for different manufactures in each participating country. Some industries will grow to meet larger-than-national demands, others may disappear or never be set up because domestic demand is met by imports.

Neither direct nor indirect impacts can be analyzed only in terms of investments in or the disappearance of the industry of first concern. Multiplier effects will vary in scale, quality, and nature of spatial impact (e.g., localized or dispersed[24]). For example, a demand for remote resources may bring immigration and necessitate the building of infrastructure—houses, roads, etc. The impact is localized, apart from some of the transport facilities. But housing components and machinery for working the resources may come from factories scattered throughout the country. The same division of impacts holds for new manufacturing industries such as the Kama truck-manufacturing plant or some of the new chemical complexes—though in the latter case, input requirements may have a sharply localized impact elsewhere in the country. But investments in the chemical industry, or in mechanical or electronic engineering, are likely to have a wider range of multiplier effects, especially if they employ imported technology. They may require from their suppliers not only a greater volume of production, but also higher-quality production and the mastery of new technology.

The discussion of multiplier effects illustrates the importance of examining impacts on several spatial scales, which has been emphasized repeatedly by one Soviet writer.[25] In the machine-building industry in particular, export production, direct and indirect, is so scattered that many effects may be distinguishable only on the very local scale.

The preceding paragraphs may suggest that foreign economic ties have an impressively wide range of impacts on Soviet regional development. But it must be remembered that the foreign-linked sector of the Soviet economy comprises a small part of the whole, and that its regional manifestations are affected by many variables generated entirely within the Soviet Union or jointly by domestic and foreign-trade pressures. Particularly difficult to disentangle from the influence of foreign economic links is that of the currently favored strategy of intensification of economic development.[26] The impact of CMEA integration and trade with the West could be identified with much more confidence in any one of the Soviet Union's CMEA partner countries.

Despite these reservations there are a good many recent developments in the Soviet spatial economy which can be explained at least partly in terms of foreign economic policy. They include changing patterns of energy and industrial raw-material exploitation, new projects and additions in manufacturing industry, a relatively small number of agricultural and water-control schemes, and developments in transport. These will be reviewed in turn, and a summary by regions will follow.

## Energy Sources

The cumulative effect of domestic pressures and pressures to export is epitomized by regional developments in the energy industry. The neighboring CMEA countries have a great need for Soviet oil, natural gas, and electricity; the first two items are readily salable in Western Europe and other hard-currency markets; and the growth of domestic demand alone would be sufficient to place considerable pressures on the energy industry. In addition to the growth of total domestic demand for energy, particular pressure has been placed on oil and gas by

rapid changes in the country's energy balance. The two fuels accounted for about 20 and 2.5 percent of production in the mid-1950s, but 45 and 27 percent in 1980. Sources of oil and gas used in the European USSR and farther west are shifting ever farther eastward as the fields west of the Urals peak or decline. New discoveries in north European Russia, Orenburg Oblast, and the Caspian region have only slightly offset the shift. The push into remoter areas requires ever greater capital investment and raises the desirability of obtaining the capital from foreign sources. It also raises the exportability of oil relative to natural gas, since the former moves more cheaply per unit of energy by pipeline, and the attractiveness of resources even farther east, which could be exported to Japan and other Pacific-rim markets. Relatively great exportability of oil, together with the realization that as it becomes scarcer, oil should be used as a chemical feedstock rather than a fuel for power stations, stimulates the substitution of gas for oil in power stations. At the same time pressure on both oil and gas makes other energy sources attractive. Coal has become a preferred fuel for new power stations where it is available close enough to markets. For markets in which coal-based energy cannot be used economically, such as much of the European USSR, the preferred alternative is to build nuclear power stations; another alternative is to use low-grade local fuels such as peat and brown coal. A third possibility is to move the market: Soviet fuel and energy exports are helping to force energy-intensive industries into Siberia, where cheap energy is still available.

Oil and oil products accounted for 75.4 percent of Soviet fuel and energy exports by value in 1981, natural gas for 19 percent, coal and coke for 4 percent, and electricity for 1.6 percent. Together they accounted for 50.1 percent of Soviet exports, compared with 46.8 percent in 1980. The relative importance of production for domestic and foreign markets, and hence the regional impact of exports, varies considerably by commodity.

### Oil and Oil Products

Oil and oil product exports comprise well over a quarter of production and therefore contribute substantially to the general pressure on supplies. The direct regional impact has been to accelerate the eastward shift of extraction. In 1975 most exports originated in the Volga-Ural region, especially the Tatar ASSR and Kuibyshev Oblast, with the Bashkir ASSR some way behind and Perm and Orenburg oblasts just beginning to export. West Siberia, having begun to export in 1971, was increasing its share rapidly.[27] Small contributions came from the North Caucasus, formerly a much more significant exporter, and Belorussia, where a small oilfield opened up for domestic use had been reoriented to exports. Very small amounts originated in the Far East, whence oil moved to Japan, and Kazakhstan. The principal changes since then have been a sharp rise in the share of exports moving from West Siberia and the virtual depletion of Belorussian output.[28]

A second set of regional impacts occurs along the routes leading to export markets. Most Soviet oil is exported unrefined, including nine-tenths of the oil moving to Eastern Europe. Most of that sent to Hungary, East Germany, Poland, and Czechoslovakia moves through the Friendship pipeline, which carries a mix of Volga-Ural, West Siberian and Mangyshlak oil. Belorussian oil is added at Mozyr. Exports to Bulgaria, Cuba, and the Western and developing countries (some 60 percent of gross crude exports) move by pipeline and rail to ports on the Black Sea (Odessa, Reni, Novorossisk and Tuapse), Baltic (Ventspils) and Pacific. Small amounts move to Eastern Europe by rail or via the Danube—in part in order to preserve the characteristics of crudes suited to specific uses, since the Friendship line has the disadvantage of supplying an undiscriminated mix, as indeed do the pipelines serving the ports.[29]

Export activity has brought expansion of the principal ports involved,[30] helped determine the location of major pipelines used also for domestic movements, and led to the building and affected the location of refineries designed to serve both domestic and foreign markets. The refined share of exports has been low, and indeed was declining up to 1975, not by design but because of the country's inability to produce high-quality products in quantity.[31] Nor was it able to produce them conveniently near export markets, a distinct disadvantage since there are few product pipelines. Most refined exports have had to move by rail, at some three times the cost of moving them by pipeline. Depending on the product involved, in the mid-1970s 21 to 52 percent of refined exports originated in the Central Region, 21 to 43 percent in the Volga region, 10 percent in the Urals, and 6 to 8 percent in the Volga-Vyatka region.[32] Current intentions for the oil industry apparently include a shift from crude to refined exports, to the extent of eventually stabilizing or even reducing the former,[33] and a shift of refining for export towards the western frontier regions and ports. Of the regions well located to serve export markets, only the North Caucasus and Transcaucasia were providing a suitably high share of refined exports in the mid-1970s, with 7 to 40 percent and 10 to 45 percent, respectively, depending on the product involved; Belorussia, the Northwest, the South and the Far East were supplying 5 to 11, 3 to 5, 5, and 1 percent, respectively.[34] Even such imprecise figures as these indicate that a spatial shift of the kind envisaged requires considerable investment.

That investment is taking place. Shabad has chronicled the construction of refineries in Belorussia, the Ukraine, and Lithuania from 1963 to the present.[35] One Soviet writer has suggested that the new more northerly pipeline westward from Siberia (Surgut-Polotsk), which was completed in 1981, will herald a more general shift northward of both crude oil flows and refining capacity, mainly because of the shorter distances involved and relative ease of pipeline construction.[36] Whether more in the north or the south, investment in the western regions seems sensible if the Soviet Union is concerned to reduce transport costs for refined products going abroad and to retain the value added in refining, and if there is sufficient world pressure on supplies that it can dictate that its customers take refined products rather than crude. It also has some significance domestically, since in the mid-

1970s the western regions were importing about a million tons of refined products a year from Eastern Europe.[37]

It might seem that such heavy investment primarily to supply export markets constitutes a bet that the country will want to continue exporting on a large scale, which both Western and Soviet specialists have questioned. However, if supplies are cut, presumably the Soviet Union would prefer to reduce crude rather than refined exports if it has the option. Furthermore, Shabad has made a good case for believing the CIA estimates of Soviet potential for oil production to be overpessimistic.[38] To his list of reasons one might add that by Soviet calculations the Soviet Union includes 40 percent of the earth's land surface with oil- and gas-bearing potential. However, as Meyerhoff has pointed out, realization of that potential may depend on the rejection of current drilling technology.[39]

In sum, the pressure to export oil has stimulated economic activity in oil-bearing regions, especially in the east but also (though with little success) in Belorussia, conveniently near the western frontier; in regions with oil-bearing potential, including parts of the Far East being explored with Japanese help; at ports handling export flows; in regions already concerned with refining; and in the western regions where refining capacity is being built up. Future impacts can be expected to comprise more of the same: a stimulus to primary extraction in the east—farther east than home demand alone would require—and a stimulus to processing (and most of the regional multiplier effects, especially as oil use shifts from fuel to the chemical industry), in the west, including areas farther west than home demand alone would require to be developed.

Natural Gas

Soviet natural-gas exports on an appreciable scale began in 1966, when a pipeline with a capacity of a billion cubic meters a year was built from Dashava in the Ukraine to Warsaw. The Dashava district was the only exporter up to 1973, though with the construction of the Brotherhood pipeline its market area expanded to include Czechoslovakia and Austria.[40] After that date it was joined by Shebelinka in the Ukraine and the Timan-Pechora field in North European USSR, and the market area was further extended. The Timan-Pechora field supplied Finland. Now gas is exported to several countries in Eastern and Western Europe, and the supply areas include Central Asia, West Siberia, and Orenburg Oblast.

As in the case of oil, therefore, exports of natural gas have exacerbated the pressure on supplies and have helped force exploitation into regions ever more remote from markets. Although the USSR is exporting a growing percentage of production—some 12 percent in 1980[41]—the pressure is caused mainly by domestic demand. On the other hand, long-term compensatory agreements with both East and West European customers have been particularly important in facilitating the shift to remoter resources. Indeed, the first large-scale long-term compensatory agreements with Western firms were for the supply of gas pipeline in return for gas. Gas is more expensive to transmit over long distances than oil, both because of the lower calorie throughput for a given size of pipe and expenditure on pumping, and because of more exacting technical requirements for the pipelines.[42] Also, the Soviet Union for a long time lacked adequate capacity to produce the large-diameter pipes needed for economical transport over very long distances. Agreements with West European consumers have helped speed the development of deposits in North European USSR and West Siberia, while the main project undertaken with East European help has been the development of the Orenburg field and construction of its pipeline to Eastern Europe.

The Orenburg project has probably had the greatest multiplier effect in a supply region of any natural gas development that can be directly linked to export activity. It stands out because of the direct involvement of foreign customers, the construction of a pipeline specifically (though not entirely) to export the gas and the amount of processing (with recovery of sulfur, helium and natural gas liquids) required before the transport. Nowhere else has so much associated activity been generated in a supply region. Furthermore, no other sizable gas deposit has been developed so specifically for export or is now so closely linked to export markets. Most fields feed into the unified gas grid of European USSR, and there is no constant association of particular fields with particular markets.[43]

Natural-gas exports, like oil exports, could be said to have a regional impact along the routes to markets, insofar as gas is also made available to Soviet users. However, the effect is far less distinguishable than in the case of oil. In the first place, with the exception of the Orenburg pipeline and the Urengoi-Uzhgorod export pipeline now under construction, the routes followed by Soviet pipelines are explainable primarily in terms of domestic, not export, needs. In the second place, most gas pipelines have been routed to serve existing centers of population and industry, rather than creating new ones.[44]

In 1976 natural-gas imports from Iran and Afghanistan were equivalent to 46 percent of exports westward. There were plans to expand imports considerably by the end of the century, partly to compensate for Soviet exports, and to move Iranian gas in transit to Western Europe. These plans are in abeyance insofar as they relate to Iran, the principal supplier. Indeed parts of Transcaucasia, which had become dependent on imported natural gas, have suffered economically (and socially, since the gas was used for domestic heating) from the cessation of flow, a reminder to the Soviet government of the potential problems of foreign economic ties. As a result additional pipeline capacity for supplying domestic gas to Transcaucasia was completed in 1982, and the imports from Iran and Afghanistan have dropped to less than 10 percent of the exports to Europe, East and West.

Although pressure on supplies is forcing gas extraction to shift ever farther from markets, there is clearly more pressure to minimize distance than in the case of oil. Considering also the cost of extraction in northwestern Siberia, export pressure will presumably favor concentration on Orenburg, North European USSR, and Central Asia. Exceptions could arise in the event of liquefied natural gas exports via either Arctic or Pacific ports.

## Coal and Coke

Soviet coal exports rose during the 1950s from 1 million to 12 million tons. About 65 percent of the latter figure went to fuel the growing industries of Eastern Europe. Thereafter exports continued to rise, doubling between 1960 and 1973 and rising another 2 million tons by 1976, but they declined steadily as a percentage of total energy exports.

Almost all exports have come from the Donbas, an increasingly high-cost source. Pechora and the Kama field are possible alternatives in European USSR, but the former is relatively remote and far north (though it does export)[45], and the latter has not yet been opened up. Indeed westward export of Kuzbas coal is considered more of a possibility, despite the distances involved.[46] Eastern Europe is in fact better off in terms of coal reserves per capita than European USSR, and Poland's Upper Silesian basin is a more important supplier to the CMEA countries, including parts of the USSR. Belorussia and the western Ukraine are supplied by rail, and Baltic and northern ports are supplied by sea.[47] Until the decline of Polish coal output associated with the Solidarity crisis, the Soviet Union imported some 10 million tons of coal and coke per annum from Poland, while exporting about 30 million. About 66 percent of the exports by value in 1981 went to the CMEA countries, principally East Germany and Bulgaria (the former by rail, the latter mostly by sea via Zhdanov and the Danube ports), and the rest to a dozen countries, of which the largest customer was Japan.

Since gross exports comprise only about 6 percent of production, and the proportion is unlikely to rise, foreign trade in coal cannot be expected to have a great direct impact on Soviet regional development, at least in European USSR. The principal impact there has probably been to help increase the westward shipments of Siberian coal. Donbas exports in the mid-1970s were approximately equal to the Kuzbas and Karaganda coal moving westward beyond the Urals; in 1980 they were, if they remained at much the same level, equal to about two-thirds of the planned westward movements from Siberia.[48] The only likelihood of a strong direct impact on European USSR would be if coal shortages forced major expansion in the Pechora field or the opening-up of the Kama field, a project occasionally urged by Soviet writers.[49] In the Asiatic part of the country, on the other hand, the export potential of the South Yakutian coalfield has been one of the main stimuli to development of that region and of related port facilities, under a long-term compensatory agreement with Japanese interests.[50]

## Electricity

Soviet exports of electricity have been a small proportion of production, about one percent in the mid-1970s. They have therefore had little impact on the Soviet energy industry as a whole. However, there have been distinguishable regional impacts, which could become more widespread in the future.

Almost all Soviet exports are to Eastern Europe, with Hungary and Bulgaria taking about three-quarters of the total.[51] Until recently most exports originated close to the border: both Moldavia and the Lvov region were exporting about 30 percent of their output in the mid-1970s. Current developments strongly reflect the fall of oil from favor as a power-station fuel. To the extent that the growing demand for electricity in Eastern Europe cannot be met from local low-grade coal-fired, gas-fired, and hydroelectric stations, it is to be met primarily from nuclear power stations built both locally and in the western regions of the USSR. The Soviet stations will of course have local significance too, and the linking of the East European and European USSR grids gives the opportunity to economize on peak capacities by shifting loads between time zones.[52]

Several nuclear power plants are being built in the western USSR[53], and insofar as they will feed into a common grid they could all be said to owe something to the expectation of bigger exports to Eastern Europe. But two in particular will be linked westward: the South Ukrainian power station at Konstantinovka in Nikolayev Oblast and the Khmelnitsky station will both send up to 50 percent of their production to Eastern Europe.[54] A third nuclear station, under construction at Snieckus near Ignalina in Lithuania, would have the same function, and the expansion of conventional power stations in Moldavia and Belorussia is also specifically linked to exports.[55] The construction of power stations for the CMEA as a whole, and of the high-voltage (mainly 750 kv) power lines to integrate the Soviet and East European grids, was given top priority at a CMEA meeting in October 1978.[56]

It has been suggested that in the longer term, electricity transmitted from Kazakhstan (Ekibastuz coal field) and Siberia (the Surgut gas-fired power complex and even the Kansk-Achinsk coal field) could be used in European USSR and free much more European generating capacity to supply Eastern Europe. Such a system would make possible very large transfers between time zones. But at the current state of technology, such an arrangement appears not to be competitive with nuclear or gas-fired stations located in European USSR.[57] More likely, perhaps, is the shift of CMEA's energy-intensive industries east of the Urals through a series of joint projects suggested by Soviet writers.

There have recently been some Soviet expressions of unease with the degree of commitment to nuclear power. They appear to have no official support, but if nuclear power did fall from favor, presumably the main impact of trade in all forms of energy would be to accelerate the Soviet Union's return to dependence primarily on its vast coal reserves.

One other small-scale regional impact of electricity exports can be mentioned. The Gusinoozersk coal-fired power station in the Buryat ASSR has been considerably enlarged in order to export to Mongolia, specifically to Erdenet where the CMEA countries have opened up a copper-molybdenum deposit in a joint project, and to the Baga-Nur brown-coal workings east of Ulan-Bator.

## Extractive and Basic Heavy Industries

Extractive and closely associated industries, such as the chemical, metal and forest-product industries, present a picture broadly similar to that of energy sources. The combination of domestic and East European demand with the desire to export to hard-currency markets has brought pressure on resources and the opening-up of new ones, sometimes remote but surprisingly often still in the European USSR. That part of the country supplies about half of all mined exports.[58] Exploitation has taken place with foreign help, and there is evident determination to shift to more fully-processed exports eventually. Far Eastern resources are being explored and developed with Japanese help for Pacific markets.

### Chemicals

Foreign links in the Soviet chemical industry are of several kinds, with differing regional impacts. We can distinguish the export of chemical raw materials; the import of basic chemicals and of machinery for the chemical industry; arrangements, made with both CMEA and Western partners, to specialize in the production of specific chemicals; as a subdivision of the preceding category, close links between petrochemical plants across the western frontier of the Soviet Union; and finally, projects undertaken by the Soviet Union independently, with the intention of exporting.

In addition to oil and gas which have already been covered, the Soviet Union is able to export several chemical raw materials and basic products. Most are related to the fertilizer industry, and they move principally to Eastern Europe. The regional impacts of current developments reflect a variety of technical responses to problems of supply. Phosphates provide two good examples. In the CMEA, only the Soviet Union and Mongolia have phosphate deposits. Until the 1970s, CMEA supplies came almost entirely from the Soviet Union's high-quality apatite deposits in the Kola Peninsula. Then in 1973 a mine and works, developed jointly with several East European countries, went into operation at Kingisepp, in Leningrad Oblast, producing ammonium phosphate from phosphate rock. Utilization of this deposit reflects in part its location, but also a decline in the much higher-quality reserves of the Kola Peninsula. At the same time production has been expanding, in part to supply export demand, at the Karatau phosphate rock deposit in southern Kazakhstan. Here the low quality and remoteness of the raw material are offset by using it to produce elemental phosphorus, which has a concentration of $P_2O_5$ about six times greater than apatite and is consequently much cheaper to transport. A similar project is envisaged for East Siberia, which has the further advantage of very cheap power, since the production of phosphorus is power-intensive, and another for the Hövsgöl deposit in Mongolia, which could also use Siberian power. In relation to a point made earlier, it should be noted that Eastern Europe already imports phosphates from the developing countries in large quanities, and Soviet writers have been pointing out the possibilities for further expanding this trade, especially with respect to Africa. The Soviet Union itself will begin importing from Morocco during the 1980s, in addition to its imports of superphosphoric acid from the United States, described below.[59]

Analogous to the Kingisepp project is one in the potash industry, at Soligorsk in Belorussia. It has been undertaken with Polish credits and was to supply two-thirds of Polish potash needs by 1980. In this case favorable location appears to some extent to have offset low quality relative to the Solikamsk deposit in the Urals (though there are recurring reports that the low-grade Soligorsk potash meets Soviet domestic needs and it is the Solikamsk product that is exported).[60]

The production of nitrogen fertilizers, the third major group, is based on natural gas. This gives more choice of locations, and nitrogen fertilizer plants have been established near the western frontier, at Grodno in Belorussia, Jonava in Lithuania, and Rovno in the Ukraine. However, export markets were not important in the decision to locate. Hungary and Czechoslovakia do import from the Soviet Union, but this may be temporary, reflecting delay in switching to natural gas as a raw material. In any case, neither imports a large share of its needs. Soviet exports are mainly by sea, to Cuba and a few developing countries, and are a small proportion of production.[61]

The Soviet Union imports both basic chemicals (e.g., soda ash and caustic soda) and machinery and equipment for the chemical industry. The former come largely from Eastern Europe, and three-quarters of the latter from the West. At the height of chemical equipment imports in 1977-79, the chemical industry accounted for 12 to 15 percent of all machinery and equipment imports, the biggest share taken by any industry. Since then, its share has declined, to 5.4 percent in 1981. Much has been purchased as part of long-term compensatory agreements, with payback in products. Even so it is hard to identify any particular impact of either basic chemical or equipment imports at the large regional scale. The equipment has been used not only for new chemical works, but also to reequip scores of existing plants during recent years. Insofar as many of the former and most of the latter are in European USSR, one could say that most of the impact has been there. At the level of the individual town or small region, of course, impacts can be identified.[62] Some of these will be described in the next section, but one example of special locational considerations in deals with the West can be mentioned here. The largest Soviet plant producing Lavsan, a polyester fiber, is located at Mogilev in Belorussia. Other locations would have been preferable economically, but the plant was built with British help and the preferred locations happened to be in regions closed to foreigners.

The Soviet Union has entered into specialization agreements with both CMEA and Western partners. The former have had an impact in the western frontier regions, the latter both at ports and in at least one interior region. All are concerned with petrochemicals.

One of the best-known specialization agreements is that with Hungary for the production of olefins and olefin derivatives. It is also one of the most interesting from the point of view of the decision-making involved. Since 1975 the Hungarian petrochemical plant at Leninvaros, halfway between Budapest and the Soviet border, has been using Soviet oil to produce ethylene and propylene. Surpluses of both are then sent by pipeline and rail respectively to a Soviet chemical works at Kalush on the other side of the Carpathian Mountains. Kalush uses the ethylene to produce polyvinyl chloride, some of which is in turn exported to Hungary.[63] Of interest in the decision-making involved is the fact that before the agreement went into effect, Soviet calculations had shown that it would not be advantageous to engage in olefin chemistry anywhere west of a line running from the Volga region through the North Caucasus to Transcaucasia. Then Hungary purchased a large installation for the production of ethylene. The choice of size took into account considerable economies of scale and the expectation of an "ethylene ring" being set up in Eastern Europe. But Hungary's prospective partners were not ready to set up the ring and Hungary was unable to use all of the ethylene produced. The Soviet Union was therefore approached, and it agreed to the present arrangement despite cost disadvantages. Unfortunately the Hungarians are now able to use all their production, and it may be necessary to supply Kalush from Soviet sources. A pipeline from Novopolotsk is a possibility. (Production was established at Novopolotsk before the present system of working out preferred locations came into use.)[64] The Novopolotsk plant itself constitutes an example of the pull of a frontier-region location in deals with the CMEA countries. Ethylene is produced there in an installation set up with East German help under a compensatory agreement.[65]

The principal specialization agreement with the West is that with Occidental Petroleum. Natural gas from Tyumen Oblast is piped to Togliatti and used in the production of ammonia, which in turn is piped to the new port of Yuzhny, near Odessa.[66] Ammonia is also being fed into the pipeline en route from Gorlovka, and some is being produced at Yuzhny itself. From there it moves by tanker to the United States and Italy. In return, superphosphoric acid from Florida is being shipped to Yuzhny, though the arrangement temporarily ran into trouble with the American authorities after the Soviet intervention in Afghanistan. A similar arrangement has gone into effect at Ventspils on the Baltic, which receives the ammonia from various Soviet sources, not including Togliatti, by tank car.

The decisions behind this arrangement are also of interest as an illustration of where the regional impact of foreign economic links might have been felt. Clearly the main impact will be in the two ports, with their shipping and processing facilities, and in Togliatti. But according to prior calculations by the Ministry of the Chemical Industry, the technically optimal solution would have been to produce the ammonia in Tyumen Oblast, near the source of the raw material, and pipe it to the coast from there. Feasible ports, in addition to those chosen, were Murmansk and Novorossisk. However, it was judged that Tyumen Oblast was fully occupied with building up the oil industry and its infrastructure and that lack of

Soviet experience with ammonia pipelines of such length made it inadvisable to risk building and operating an even longer one. The alternative solution of producing all of the ammonia in a port was rejected because of the length of large-diameter gas pipeline required, so the choice of Togliatti was to some degree a compromise. It was favored by the fact that local construction organizations were just about to complete other major projects and could easily move on to the new one. As for the ports, Novorossisk was rejected because it was being developed as an oil port and the decision was made to keep it specialized, and Murmansk because of the difficult pipeline route. The relative difficulty of building pipelines also decided that Yuzhny rather than Ventspils would be the terminus of the first ammonia pipeline.[67]

One other petrochemical project fits into the final category listed earlier, namely projects undertaken independently by the Soviet Union with foreign trade in mind. That is a synthetic rubber plant at Chaikovsky, near Perm, which will probably be supplied with ethylene by pipeline from Nizhnekamsk.[68] The plant is being built in anticipation of a big rise in the demand for automobile tires in Eastern Europe in the 1980s, though at present there is no great need for imports in the region.[69]

Finally in the chemical industry, current CMEA plans envisage as a general approach to integration the building up of energy-intensive branches (e.g., the production of polyvinyl chloride and methanol) in the USSR, while the East European partners build up less energy-intensive branches. The two sides will attempt to maintain rough parity in value of product and scale of investment.[70] (It may be difficult to do both.) The regional impact in the Soviet Union would presumably be to promote an eastward shift of chemical production.

Ores and Metals

The regional impact of foreign trade in iron ore, iron, and steel has been reviewed thoroughly by Shabad and will only be summarized briefly here.[71] Iron ore ranks with oil as one of the Soviet raw materials most needed in Eastern Europe. In contrast to oil, the Soviet Union has ample iron-ore reserves relatively close to the western frontier, at Krivoi Rog and in the Kursk Magnetic Anomaly. The country exports nearly a fifth of its iron-ore production and covers about 70 percent of the needs of Eastern Europe. In 1981, only some 4 percent of exports, or 1.3 million tons, went outside Eastern Europe.

Krivoi Rog supplies most of the exports, but the Kursk Magnetic Anomaly is being developed and its share of exports is growing. The main regional impact of exports, in fact, has undoubtedly been to accelerate the opening up of the KMA. Ore output from there in 1980 was just about equal to Soviet iron-ore exports. (The impact has been both positive, in the acquisition of major industries, and negative, in the loss of huge acreages of farmland.)

Exports have been mainly from deposits exploited entirely by Soviet efforts so far, but CMEA joint projects are becoming important in ensuring continued growth. They have been particularly directed to enlarging the pelletizing capacity at both Krivoi Rog and the KMA, by a total of 30 million tons for Soviet and East European use together. In addition to these projects, currently under way or completed, the East European countries are interested in working Soviet iron-ore deposits, presumably on a similar basis to the Bulgarian leasing of forest resources in the Komi ASSR. The Soviet government has offered three deposits in European USSR.[72]

Pellets, having a higher iron content, reduce the burden on transport considerably by comparison with direct-shipping ore. Nevertheless, shipments of 40 million tons or more place a strain on the transport system, and the Soviet Union has proposed as a further joint project, the construction of a full-cycle steelworks on the KMA. It would take 10 years to build and produce 10 to 12 million tons of metal per annum. Construction so far has been confined to site preparation. Soviet sources have been referring to the need to convince the CMEA partners that the returns from such investment would be substantially higher than from investing in their own iron and steel industry.[73] In 1978, a "large iron and steel works" was included among the top-priority tasks in CMEA economic cooperation,[74] but recent information suggests that the KMA works will be delayed until after the completion of the Stary Oskol direct-reduction works, referred to below. When the plant is built, it might use Polish coal. This would help even out the extreme imbalance of eastward and westward freight flows across the Soviet western frontier. Westward traffic now predominates in the ratio 10:1 by weight.

Some of the small amount of iron ore exported outside the CMEA bloc comes from Karelia and the Kola Peninsula in northern Russia and is shipped through Murmansk. Considerable expansion under way should make more ore available for export in the 1980s,[75] but it is not primarily directed to that end.

In addition to iron ore, the Soviet Union exports between four and five million tons of pig iron a year to Eastern Europe, approximately the capacity of the largest type of blast furnace currently being built in the country. It also sends ferroalloys, iron and steel scrap, rolled metal, and steel pipes equal to about 1.5 times the weight of the pig iron (exact physical quantities now being secret). Exports to CMEA countries comprise more than half the total exports of these latter items. Available figures for the early and middle 1970s for all metals, among which ferrous metals predominate, show that 61.6 percent by weight of exports to the CMEA originated in the South, 12.8 percent in the Center, 17.3 percent in the Urals, and the remainder largely in West Siberia and Kazakhstan.[76] These shipments represent a small proportion of total Soviet iron and steel output—about 4 percent in the case of pig iron—and cannot be considered to have had a major impact at the large regional scale. There will be discernible regional impact through the building of the new CMEA steelworks, if it goes ahead, insofar as it is intended to replace some of the longer hauls of ferrous metals to Eastern Europe. There is already an impact at a smaller scale in the case of ferroalloys. CMEA joint projects have enlarged the capacities of existing plants at Nikopol in the Ukraine and Yermak near Pavlodar in Kazakhstan. The attraction of the latter location, as of the

Minusinsk Basin in Eastern Siberia where another plant has long been projected, is its cheap power.

Since the Soviet Union is one of the world's major producers of equipment for mining and the steel industry, imports of equipment from outside the CMEA are much less important than in the chemical industry. However, part of the expansion in northern Russia, at the town of Kostomuksha in Karelia, was undertaken with Finnish assistance, and at Stary Oskol, on the KMA, a direct-reduction steel plant has been built with West German help. This could be the forerunner of developments with a major regional impact, since Soviet reserves of coking coal are under pressure, and a technology which eliminates the need for coke is likely to prove attractive if successful. At the same time the process uses a great deal of natural gas and electricity. This might restore some of the attractiveness of the eastern regions for steel production, especially if iron ores being surveyed in southern Yakutia prove suitable.[77] On the other hand, the eastern regions are the ones best supplied with coking coal.

Most other ores and metals have been well reviewed by other writers in this series.[78] The Soviet Union exports copper from the Urals and Kazakhstan, zinc and lead from Kazakhstan and to some extent from the North Caucasus, nickel mainly from Norilsk, and aluminum mostly from Eastern Siberia.[79] In some cases (manganese, chromite) no significant expansion of exports is expected, hence no regional impact. In other cases export potential has been a partial, though rarely the dominant, stimulus to expansion at existing deposits and the opening-up of new ones. An example is the expansion of the copper-nickel complexes in the Kola Peninsula and at Norilsk, with Finnish assistance in the latter case.[80] Export potentials appear to be a major consideration in projects to expand titanium production by opening up a deposit in the Komi ASSR and to develop the Udokan copper deposit near the BAM route, since the Soviet Union already has a surplus of both metals. More complex is the situation regarding aluminum, since the Soviet Union is short of bauxite and has had limited success in using other raw materials (nepheline, alunite), but has ample power, cheap enough to be attractive even in Eastern Siberia when alumina has to be shipped in from Black Sea ports. About 50 percent of Soviet aluminum is now produced from imported alumina or bauxite. The major impacts have been or will be at plants using imported inputs and ports handling them. The former include the Zaporozhye and Volgograd aluminum plants, which use Hungarian and Yugoslav alumina; the Kirovabad alumina plant, using imported bauxite, which supplies the Tursunzade aluminum works in Tadzhikistan; the Nikolayev alumina plant opened in 1980 on the Black Sea coast to use bauxite from Guinea, and the aluminum works being built at Sayanogorsk in southern Siberia which it will supply; and the Yurga abrasives factory in the Kuzbas, which uses imported bauxite. The ports include Nikolayev; Batumi, which ships to Kirovabad; and Berdyansk, which ships to Yurga, all of them on the Black Sea.[81] Clearly the choice of locations reflects a variety of considerations: cheap power from the Sayan and Nurek dams for the Sayanogorsk and Tursunzade aluminum works; the prior existence of works needing inputs, in the

case of Yurga, Volgograd, and Kirovabad—the last-named having had limited success in using local alunite; and the import of bauxites from Guinea, principally, in the case of the Black Sea ports.

Despite the need to import bauxite or alumina, the Soviet aluminum industry does export the finished product. In fact aluminum accounts for over half the country's nonferrous metal exports by weight—529,000 tons in 1974. The main contributors are all in Siberia: Bratsk, Krasnoyarsk, Shelekhov, and Novokuznetsk. Their exports are expected to grow, entirely because of cheap power. All other factors are disadvantageous, though there is a possibility of using bauxites from the lower Angara region. There is also some export from Volgograd in the European USSR to Hungary in exchange for the Hungarian alumina.[82]

Imported machinery and equipment are being used in the aluminum industry, with a particular impact on the Nikolayev alumina and the Sayanogorsk aluminum works. The alumina project was undertaken with French help and the aluminum plant with West German assistance.

## Other Minerals

The Soviet Union exports a fairly wide range of building materials, but not in large quantities relative to production or to total exports. In the mid-1970s they comprised less than one half of one percent of exports. Cement accounted for nearly 60 percent by value, window glass and firebricks about 10 percent each. But even cement exports comprised little more than three percent of production, originating in the European USSR. The border regions—the Baltic republics and southwestern Ukraine in particular—accounted for over half, and the North Caucasus, Volga region, and Central Black Earth region for most of the rest. Export production appears to be very much subsidiary to production for the home market even in these regions, though steps have been taken to incorporate new technology, perhaps partly with an eye to exports. For example, a French process used under licence at Belgorod is producing an improved white cement for decorative purposes. Exports of aluminous cement for use in hydraulic engineering are also considered worth expanding,[83] so there may be more distinguishable regional impact in the future.

The Soviet Union is the world's top producer of asbestos and exports between a fifth and a quarter of output, a little under half of that going to Eastern Europe. Since asbestos is a substantial earner of hard currency, it was to be expected that East European investment would be required if shipments to CMEA countries were to increase. The Yasny asbestos project in Orenburg Oblast is mentioned in virtually every work on CMEA integration.[84] It involves a mine, a mill, water supply arrangements including a reservoir, a 50-kilometer natural gas pipeline, and other infrastructure. The desire to export must also be partly responsible for the opening-up of deposits at Dzhetygara, in northwestern Kazakhstan, and at Ak-Dovurak, in the Tuva ASSR, since domestic needs can be more than met from the Asbest deposit in the north-central Urals, though the relative fiber quality of the various deposits is also important. Construction of the BAM will open up further possibilities for export, from the Molodezhny deposit in the Buryat ASSR.

Forest Products

Forest products comprised 3.3 percent of Soviet exports by value in 1981. Percentages taken by Eastern European CMEA countries, by volume, were roundwood 19, sawn lumber 39, plywood 40, pulp 53, paper 69, and paperboard 59. However, roundwood accounted for over half of all exports to the CMEA countries in the mid-1970s.[85] Quantities of the other items were relatively small, and they were a significant proportion of Soviet production in only two cases, namely pulp (6 percent in 1981), and paper (8.5 percent, though the export share of newsprint was probably over 20 percent).

Forest products exported outside the CMEA were distributed among many Western European and developing countries in 1981, except that Japan took 40 percent and Finland 24 percent of roundwood exports, for sawmilling and pulping respectively.

Forest exploitation has followed the general pattern for extractive and basic heavy industries outlined earlier, though the response to pressures on supply has varied with the particular product. Exports westwards as a whole still originate mainly in the European Northwest, the Volga-Vyatka region, and the Urals, which account for 55, 15 and 13 percent respectively of exports to the CMEA countries.[86] Serious overcutting has occurred, especially near the Finnish frontier, but it is hoped to maintain output in this climatically and locationally most favored area by comprehensive reforestation and fuller use of the resource, to include for example species traditionally ignored. The pressure to export has its most direct impact in Karelia, for the Finnish market, and in the forest hinterlands of the main northern ports which ship to Eastern and Western Europe. Arkhangelsk, strongly specializing in exports, and Leningrad take the largest amounts. Fuller resource use is being promoted by the building of big new multi-product mill complexes, for example at Syktyvkar. One so far unique project related to exports has already been mentioned, namely the Bulgarian enterprise on the upper Mezen River in the Komi ASSR. So far it has been shipping round timber and chips, but it is intended to move on to sawn lumber and other products, partly to cut transport costs. Unlike many of the other forest-product complexes, this one exports by rail.[87]

There has been some shift of export production eastward beyond the Urals, especially in the case of pulp and to a lesser extent sawn lumber exports. Plywood production is also expanding faster than in the European USSR, though the completion of a big new plant at Bratsk still leaves the European USSR with 85 percent of output.[88] Paper production, being more market-oriented, has remained almost entirely in the west (leaving aside Far Eastern production).

The need for ample power and water supplies favors Eastern Siberia for pulp production. There, apart from purely Soviet projects, such as Bratsk and Baikalsk, the Ust-Ilimsk complex has involved all the East European

CMEA countries except Czechoslovakia. The East European contribution to construction is being paid back in pulp at the rate of 205,000 tons per annum for 12 years.[89]

Sawn lumber exports westwards originate as far east as Krasnoyarsk, though in small quantities. Distances involved are very great and a source of complaint for writers on transport—5,575 km to Hungary from Krasnoyarsk. Pulp from Baikalsk covers an even greater distance to the frontier, 6,829 km. Even some roundwood originates as far east as Tyumen Oblast. However, the proportion of total forest-product exports involved in these long-distance movements is small. Of exports to the CMEA countries, only 4.4 percent came from West and 3.7 percent from East Siberia in the mid-1970s. The transport costs involved appear to show why there has been an effort to keep production west of the Urals. To Hungary, the principal importer, the transport costs per ton from Tyumen Oblast are 1.7 times those from Petrozavodsk in the European Northwest, and from points in East Siberia, three times.[90] However, other writers point out that production costs are lower in Siberia and contend that for some products, such as sawn lumber, total delivered costs to the western frontier are cheaper for exports from West (though not East) Siberia.[91] That, of course, would depend on how one assigned costs for the reconstruction of a transport system that could not handle the traffic generated, if that became necessary.

East Siberia also exports eastward, but the main impact of Japanese purchases has been felt relatively near the market, in Khabarovsk Krai and areas to the south. Exploitation for the Japanese market has gone further than for any other primary product. Roundwood forms the great bulk of exports, but the new Amursk forest-products complex is evidence of the intention to shift to higher-value exports.

The forest-products industry has imported machinery and equipment from within and outside the CMEA. A great deal of Western equipment is used in the big new pulpmills, and other branches of the industry have imported from Poland, the specialist in forest-industry equipment among the CMEA nations.[92]

In sum, export activity has affected most regions involved in the forest-products industry. Its influence can be expected to grow in the Far East and remain high in the north of European USSR. How far it will affect Siberian development will depend firstly on the demand for and priority placed on pulp production, and secondly on whether investments in reforestation and reconstruction of the industry in North European USSR are in fact found to be higher per unit of export production (of products other than pulp) than investments in opening up virgin forests in Siberia.

**Manufacturing**

When we turn from energy and industrial raw materials to manufacturing industry, the regional impact of foreign economic policies becomes more difficult to trace. In part, this is because up to the present, despite the building of a number of export-oriented factories and the promise of many more, most exports of manufactured goods have come from existing factories. A factory may apply to become a specialized exporter or to set up an exporting division, and there is some incentive to do so. A successful application signifies recognition of a high-quality product, and an exporting factory may both receive higher payments for its goods from the state and be able to build up foreign-currency credits for the purchase of equipment abroad.[93] But in most cases factories are not specialized: they export in response to individual orders, and their income is no greater than from domestic sales. The orders do not come directly from abroad but from one of the state exporting agencies. If more than one factory can meet the order, the agency normally selects on the basis of quality (this may be a matter of the quality of the product, but it may equally well be a matter of how well the factory can meet packaging requirements for foreign markets); the speed with which the factory can meet the order; and the factory's experience in producing the particular item. (According to some writers, costs are assigned in such a way that the exporting agency may have little interest in minimizing transport costs, so location is relatively unimportant—a point which will be discussed later.) Managers tend to complain that they lack both direct contact with their foreign customers, which would help them match their production to customers' needs, and the assurance of continuity of export business, which would facilitate the retooling often required for efficient export production. For example, Far Eastern lumber mills have complained that in order to meet export assignments, they have been reduced to remilling lumber already cut to Soviet dimensions—a costly procedure. A sawmill achieving 70 percent utilization of its raw material on domestic sales may find that through lack of specialized machinery utilization on exports drops to 20 to 35 percent.[94] Any payments designed to meet extra expenses incurred in exporting may be insufficient to cover such losses. A further problem is that manufactured exports have tended to move to many countries in small quantities. This means that packaging requirements, and probably product specifications, change frequently. In sum, a factory not specializing in exports may find there is little incentive to pursue export business. If it is the only factory in its field, it may be required to export, but in the Soviet Union, growth in industrial output has not been matched by growth in the size of individual factories. Many machine-building works, for example, do or can produce identical goods. This partly results from the policy of building duplicate factories in different parts of the country for strategic purposes.[95] The net result is that exports are a very small percentage of production at thousands of factories, a large percentage at few. In the Soviet Union as a whole, two-thirds of exporting factories export less than five percent of their production.[96]

In such a situation, what is the spatial impact of the government's drive to increase manufactured exports? The general effect has been to strengthen the existing distribution of manufacturing, except that export activity is even more biased towards the western regions than manufacturing as a whole. But the difference is slight. Not only are exports too small a proportion of output at most individual factories to have any influence on their

expansion or continued existence, but also, it is rare for any branch of manufacturing to export more than five to seven percent of its output. In order to detect any appreciable spatial influence, we need to look at certain types of manufacturing in which the Soviet Union has specialized, and at plants built with exports in mind from the outset, particularly at recently-built ones, since it does seem that more attention is now being paid to location.

The strongest component of Soviet manufacturing is machine building. It accounts for over a quarter of the country's gross industrial production and a fifth of all Soviet exports. (It is a salutary reminder of the role of exports in the Soviet economy that the country's entire exports of machinery and equipment amount to 3 percent of production and correspond approximately to the capacity of the machinery factories of one city, Kharkov.[97]) About 74 percent of the exports go to the CMEA, including 65 percent to the European members, and about 16 percent to the developing countries. Prominent categories include metallurgical, mining, and power-generating equipment, equipment for metal working and certain branches of the chemical industry, textile mill equipment, and products of electrical engineering.[98] In certain cases location to facilitate exports has certainly been important. Some of the very heavy machinery and equipment tends to be produced in ports for ease of transport, and some of the factories which cooperate closely with Eastern Europe are near the frontier. The prominence of Leningrad in the production of hydroelectric generating equipment illustrates the first case, and the second is illustrated both by the setting up of a joint Polish, Soviet, and East German factory in Novovolynsk to produce equipment for the electrical industry, and by the cooperation between the Lvov and Hungarian Ikarus bus factories. There are many other cases where similar considerations would seem to be important but have been ignored. One of the main exporters of heavy cranes is in Krasnoyarsk, and of heavy turbines, Kharkov; in 1971 the Khabarovsk machine-tool works sent over 90 percent of its exports to European countries, overland, and the diesel-engine works 85 percent, rather than to Pacific markets or at least by sea from Pacific ports;[99] and the automobile works in Togliatti, which cooperates closely with factories in Eastern Europe, is well away from the frontier. The point is, perhaps, that even in the machine-building industry it is rare for a large share of production to go to export markets. The exception is automobiles. About a quarter of the total production is exported, accounting for nearly a third of the machinery exports to developed capitalist countries.

The principal Soviet regions exporting machinery are the European Center, Belorussia, the Northwest (Leningrad), and the Volga region, followed by the Urals and the Donets-Dnieper region of the Ukraine.[100] Avdeichev and Zaitsev list the main exporting cities and enterprises in various branches of the industry.[101]

Imports of factory equipment and machinery have been particularly significant for the machine-building industry. In the 1971–75 Five-Year Plan period, equipment for 2,000 factories was bought abroad, from CMEA and

Western countries together.[102] The impact, as might be expected, is spatially widespread, but perhaps most affected is the Volga-Urals region, with its automobile and truck plants, chemical works, and the Atommash plant at Volgodonsk, which began operations in 1978 and turned out its first reactor in 1981. One of the reasons for the build-up of industries in the region, apart from its locational advantages, is the presence of large, experienced construction organizations. Since these take several years to establish and are considered relatively immobile, their presence has tended to foster continuity of building and they have become an agglomerative force. The same applies to other regions, for example Eastern Siberia where the organizations were built up for hydroelectric construction. In the case of the Volga region, Togliatti was chosen for an automobile works partly for this reason, over alternative locations in Siberia, the Ukraine, and near Vologda.[103]

In sum, even in the machine-building industry, the main branch of manufacturing and the biggest exporter, the spatial impact of foreign economic ties has been slight. For machine-building and for manufacturing as a whole, we can really only distinguish a general strengthening of the existing distribution, with a small extra bias towards the western regions, certain Baltic and Black Sea ports, and the Volga region. Even spatial biases which seem to reflect locational reasoning (proximity to partner countries or the attractions of a break-of-bulk point) may in fact result from less simple rationales.

## Agriculture and Water Control

Soviet sources usually discuss agriculture as part of the "agro-industrial complex" including industries supplying machinery and chemicals to the farms as well as those processing farm produce.[104] Farm machinery and food industry machinery are the subjects of specialization agreements among the CMEA countries. The Soviet Union is involved more in the former than the latter and is also a significant exporter outside the CMEA.[105] Exports of tractors and farm machinery easily exceed those of the aircraft industry, metal ores and concentrates, or energy equipment, and stand at about 80 percent of the level of truck or car and motorcycle exports. The regional effect in the Soviet Union is felt mainly in the European USSR, which contains most of the factories involved (Minsk, Dnepropetrovsk, Volgograd, Vladimir, Lipetsk, Leningrad, Rostov, Kharkov, etc.), and above all at Minsk. Chemicals have been examined already: the rapid expansion of fertilizer output is in accordance with a plan to meet CMEA needs entirely from within the bloc by 1985.

As far as farm production is concerned, most joint activity has been in breeding, forecasting and similar scientific work, with no particular regional impact. However, there is some crop specialization. The Soviet Union's grain exports to Eastern Europe, formerly quite large and the subject of much discussion by traffic flow analysts, have declined and become intermittent. They have been exceeded by imports on average over the past decade. But the country is still an important source of

vegetable oil, sunflower seeds, and above all cotton for its CMEA partners. The Soviet Union is the world's biggest producer and exporter of cotton. In 1981 it exported 32 percent of its output (or 31 percent net of imports), and covered over three-quarters of the needs of the CMEA countries. Export production is concentrated in Uzbekistan (80 percent) and Azerbaijan (10 percent). It seems surprising that the Soviet Union exports so much of a very capital- and labor-intensive product to countries which in several cases are substantial exporters of cotton cloth. Nevertheless, exports have grown by two-thirds since 1970. They used to cover only about 60 percent of CMEA needs.

The Soviet Union is also the world's biggest producer of sugar. In the 1960s, it began to import Cuban raw sugar and export about half of the refined product, but exports have since declined, probably because of the fall in world prices relative to those paid to Cuba. Imported Cuban sugar now seems to be used to replace or supplement domestic farm production in the regions least suited to growing sugar, and to enable refiners to work for more of the year than they could on the local beet harvest. Thus in the early 1970s Cuban sugar accounted for most of the refinery throughput in Latvia and Lithuania and about half in Belorussia (all supplied via Baltic ports, which handled 40 percent of the imports); two-thirds in Transcaucasia and 20 percent in Kirghizia (via Poti and Batumi), a third in the North Caucasus (via Novorossisk), a half in the Ukraine (via Odessa and Ilyichevsk), with the Black Sea ports together handling over half the imports; and almost all in the Far East.

Partly of relevance to agriculture is the one large-scale joint project for river control being undertaken by the Soviet Union with its CMEA neighbors. Countries involved are Hungary, Rumania, Czechoslovakia, and Yugoslavia outside the bloc. The plan is to control the Tisza River, which is subject to disastrous flooding. Projects include hydroelectric generation, navigation, and irrigation as well as measures purely for flood control—some of which have already been applied. Smaller cooperative schemes are already operating or under construction along the Polish and Rumanian borders.[106]

## Transport

Transport plays several roles in linking foreign trade to regional development. Import-export traffic may place transport under strain, reflected in inability to move the volume of traffic offered or, particularly if export freight is tending to originate farther and farther from markets, in high transport costs. This may lead, first, to the improvement of routes, ports, and frontier transshipment points, and to the building of new ones, i.e., to incremental change in the transport system. Second, it may stimulate qualitative change in the system. Traffic may be switched to new transport modes, and new technologies applied to the old modes. A third response to strain on transport is to modify the traffic flows, to match them more closely to transport capacities. This can mean processing commodities more thoroughly before transport, to eliminate the carriage of wastes; locating traffic-generating activities so as to even out flows in opposite directions; or concentrating flows to achieve economies of scale. All these measures have direct regional impacts. Fourth, the improvements to transport and the new commodity flows may stimulate further regional development. Fifth, transport connects foreign trade and regional development not only through its physical and cost characteristics as they affect responses to the strain of growth in traffic, but also through its tariffs, which are not necessarily related closely to costs. Finally, transport services are themselves a salable commodity, and selling them to foreigners may have a domestic regional impact.

All of the points in the preceding paragraph can be illustrated from recent Soviet experience or the current recommendations of Soviet writers, but it should first be made clear that foreign-trade goods form a very small percentage of Soviet freight—about 2.5 percent in 1960 and 3.6 percent in 1977.[107] However, their impact is distributed unevenly both between and within modes, so that whereas they are of minuscule importance to road transport, they form a substantial element in oil pipeline flows—some 15 percent in 1976; and whereas they comprise about the same percentage of originations by rail and river as they do of all originations, they have placed a heavy strain on a few railway lines. Also, the average length of haul is high, so that foreign-trade goods account for much more than 3.6 percent of ton-kilometers—probably closer to six percent. In 1981 the average haul on the Soviet railways was 936 km, but even some of the best-located raw materials exported to Eastern Europe, the iron ores of Krivoi Rog, are 1,000 km from the frontier. Metal and wood exports in the early 1970s both averaged over 2,000 km to the frontier, while oil and gas moving westward by pipe from West Siberia average well over 4,000 km. Machinery exported westwards from the Far East, and the transit traffic on the Siberian railway (3 million tons in 1975) move over 10,000 km.

Transport improvements which can be unequivocally attributed to foreign trade include work at several ports on the Baltic, Black Sea and Pacific, especially Ventspils, Odessa, Ilyichevsk and Yuzhny, Novorossisk, and Nakhodka-Vostochny, but including also Zhdanov, Riga, Klaipeda, and Leningrad among others.[108] Less completely, but in part linked to export plans are developments at ports along the Volga, serving foreign as well as domestic markets by the use of direct river-sea vessels (about 25 percent of shipments in such vessels were for export in 1976), and the year-round extension of the Northern Sea Route shipping season.[109]

Crossing points on the western frontier, where a change of rail gauge is involved, have also received much attention. About 20 crossing points are used, though the main ones are Chop, near Uzhgorod (for Hungary and Czechoslovakia), and Mostiska, west of Lvov (for Poland).[110] Some of the traffic volumes are very large. Even in 1963, Mostiska and its Polish partners, Medyka and Zurawica near Przemyśl, were handling more traffic than the busiest Polish port, Szczecin.[111] Traffic through Chop in 1980 was expected to be 23 million tons to Hungary alone. However, much of the traffic westward has

been iron ore, and the enormous amount of work formerly required to transfer railcars between gauges has been drastically reduced by continuing Soviet broad-gauge lines to the steel mills which are major customers—Košice in Slovakia, Katowice in Poland, and (a very short link) Galati in Rumania. The lines do not only carry iron ore and coal. About half of all Soviet exports to Czechoslovakia move along the Košice line,[112] and the Katowice line carries sulfur and coal in the return direction.[113] Nevertheless much transshipment and gauge changing is still necessary—a boost to the economies of the frontier regions, which also become potentially attractive for industrial development, processing goods in transit.

The heavy westward rail traffic has also forced the upgrading of Soviet railways in the frontier regions and the construction of new lines, e.g., westward from Krivoi Rog.[114] Another measure to improve the railways' efficiency has been to create a CMEA railcar pool, which is claimed to have steadily lowered the percentage of empty runs.[115] However, probably the main result of pressure on the railways has been to accelerate the building of other forms of transport which are far more efficient for specific purposes—pipelines in particular. Rail transport is more expensive than pipeline transport for oil in ratios ranging from 4:1 to 8:1 over major Soviet routes.[116] The Friendship oil pipeline, the Brotherhood, Orenburg and Urengoi-Uzhgorod gas pipelines and the Togliatti-Yuzhny ammonia pipeline are all primarily intended for export traffic. All, however, also carry internal Soviet traffic and have a present or potential impact on regional development.

In sum, the transport construction associated with foreign trade has focused on certain ports and frontier crossing points and the routes to them. The routes have undergone both incremental and qualitative change. The impact on the Soviet spatial economy is greater than might be deduced from the small proportion of national traffic involved because facilities to carry import-export traffic were relatively neglected for many years. Upgrading has had to be substantial. To what extent the continuing construction in some of the ports reflects their new locational attractiveness, further improved by the new facilities, and to what extent the momentum and inertia of construction organizations, referred to earlier, one cannot tell.

The third response to strain on transport, modification of flows, is at an earlier stage than the modification of the transport system. Examples can be found earlier in this paper of attempts to reduce the waste shipped by rail, e.g., through pelletizing iron ore and reducing round timber shipments. Others include the return to using local fuels such as peat and brown coal for electrical generation and measures to reduce the moisture content of raw materials shipped by rail.[117] The proposed CMEA steelworks in the KMA region would both reduce rail shipments westward, by substituting metal for ore, and help balance flows westward and eastward, if it used Polish coal.

The spatial concentration of production for export to achieve economies in transport is a more tricky problem.[118] Clearly export production in many primary and secondary industries could profitably be much more concentrated than at present, through having a relatively few specialized enterprises engage in exports. But as Alisov points out, in manufacturing industry, with the growth of specialization in the production of components, it is most likely that small, multi-directional flows will develop[119]—presumably needing truck transport.

Finally, the sale of transport services has been an important part of recent Soviet foreign economic policy. Expansion of the merchant marine and the establishment of the Trans-Siberian Container Bridge have been the main elements. Regional impacts have included port development, especially at Nakhodka-Vostochny, and the building of factories to produce flat cars and containers at Abakan and Ilyichevsk.[120]

**Regional Summary**

The difficulty of singling out foreign economic relations from among all the influences on development becomes particularly evident as soon as one attempts to summarize their impact by regions. Consider for example the building of new chemical works in the western USSR. Some of the processes, such as polymer chemistry, are highly water- and power-intensive, and it might be expected that they would be located in the eastern regions, the source also of their raw material. Both water and energy resources are under pressure in the west. Clearly ties with Eastern Europe are one factor favoring western locations, especially in the case of the Kalush plant, linked to Leninvaros. A second factor, however, is the improvement of water conservation through recycling. In the 10th Five-Year Plan the chemical industry was supposed to raise production 63 percent without increasing its use of water, despite the particularly high growth rate of polymer chemistry.[121] A third factor is the previously low level of chemical industry development in the western border regions, stemming perhaps from the time when they were avoided as peripheral and unsafe. In recent years considerable quantities of petroleum products have had to be imported from other Soviet regions or Eastern Europe. In other words there is the attraction of a local market. Fourth, in the case of the Kalush-Leninvaros link, the cross-border ties are not based on the rationale that might appear at first sight, and they may well be only temporary. Finally, the Mogilev chemical fiber plant was also affected by considerations other than CMEA integration. We need to be particularly wary of deducing the importance of foreign-trade-linked locational factors from the relatively rapid growth of economic activity in certain regions.

Soviet writers distinguish three types of impact of exports on a regional economy.[122] First, some export production develops out of existing regional specializations (basic industries). Often the larger market facilitates technological improvements in the industries involved. Much of the export production of machinery and instruments in the Moscow region is of this nature. Second, some export production constitutes the main activity of a region, often at enterprises specially set up for export, such as the

Ust-Ilimsk pulp mill or the Yasny asbestos complex. Third, some export production arises out of existing regional service activities, particularly in the big industrial centers of the country, such as Moscow and Leningrad. The distinction is of some importance, because the second type is clearly the easiest to identify as a regional impact of foreign trade, and the third type has been criticized as a potentially bad impact, since it is likely to bring pressure on resources which a region does not have in surplus, such as water and power supplies.

In examining the regional impact of foreign economic policies, Soviet writers often begin by identifying a macro-region where the great bulk of the impact has been felt. P. M. Alampiyev identified a CMEA "integration region," the eastern boundary of which ran from the middle Ob through northern Kazakhstan to Mangyshlak, or, in another article, from Taz Bay on the Arctic coast through Kurgan to Kara-Bogaz-Gol, in the early 1970s.[123] The boundary would be expected to move gradually eastward. Beyond it, the regional impact reflected enhanced energy, forest-product, and some mineral requirements for markets to the west, plus opportunities in Pacific markets. West of the boundary the impact was much broader. Alampiyev also identified a separate integration region with respect to Mongolia, including parts of southern Siberia from Krasnoyarsk Krai to Chita Oblast. However, for the purposes of this paper a more detailed division of the country will be useful.

The western frontier regions of the Soviet Union—those touching the CMEA countries—have developed rapidly as foreign economic relations have expanded. Consider for example the activity at frontier crossing points, the building and expansion of oil refineries and chemical works, the nuclear power station program, the expansion of engineering (e.g., trucks and tractors in Minsk and buses in Lvov), the more intensive utilization of raw materials and the reorientation to export of some already worked, and the hydro projects along the Tisza tributaries and the Prut. In some cases, as was pointed out above using examples from these regions, the apparent influence of foreign ties does not hold up under close examination, but in other cases there is a clear link. Frontier crossing points have become as busy as major seaports where a change of gauge is involved;[124] the presence of oil and gas trunk pipelines has made petrochemical industries feasible, whatever the reasons for the final choice of location; and location has fostered export activity by the Minsk and Lvov engineering industries, even if it has not been the deciding factor. Yet Soviet writers, except for those directly concerned with transport costs,[125] tend to conclude that where alternative locations exist and bulk raw-material transport is not involved, as in engineering, it really makes little difference whether an exporting factory is in Lvov or the Donbas, or for that matter the middle Volga region. That Minsk exports tractors on a large scale reflects the quality of the product rather than location. What may make a difference is the fact that the western regions include some of the smaller republics, where the stimulation of exports from enterprises under republic control can help build up discretionary funds, including foreign-currency funds. This point is supported by a distinction which Soviet writers make between border regions in the broad sense (*pogranichnye rayony*, e.g., all of Belorussia or Moldavia) and the immediate border oblasts (*prigranichnye rayony*). Whereas extra growth of the *pogranichnye* regional economies can readily be seen, the *prigranichnye* areas often remain little more developed than they were when border locations were basically unattractive.[126] In other words, relative location at this scale is not a major force.

Relative location does become more important when transport costs are a major proportion of delivered costs, of course. The frontier republics' contribution to raw-material exports and the scale of their recent additions to the national stock of utilized natural resources are noteworthy, considering their small share of the nation's natural resources as a whole. The exploration and exploitation of relatively poor resources have stemmed directly from CMEA needs.

The potential for local initiative to promote an impact of foreign economic relations is reflected in writings on *prigranichnaya torgovlya*, i.e., local cross-border trade, often by barter, which is carried out separately from the activities of the centralized trading organizations and represents a small dent in their monopoly. It is carried on across the Finnish border, to some extent across those of Eastern Europe and Central Asia, and in the Far East. In most frontier regions, though not all,[127] there seems to be great enthusiasm for this trade and a belief that it has possibilities which are as yet far from being realized, partly because of several restrictions on the amount of local control. It cannot be said to have had an appreciable impact on regional development so far.[128]

The rapid growth of activities in and around the major Baltic, Black Sea, Arctic, and Far Eastern ports obviously results from the growth of foreign trade. It can be regarded as a more stable, long-term phenomenon than in the case of the western frontier crossing points, though so far it has not been accompanied by population increase on the scale of Brest's. The break of bulk at ports is necessary and permanent, whereas at the frontier crossings there is always the possibility of continuing one or another railway across the border.

When one moves from the border and port regions of European USSR to look at the rest of the area, several distinct regional impacts can be picked out. The first is in regions able to provide raw materials, notably the KMA, Orenburg, Yasny, and the northern forests. The second is in existing major manufacturing centers where exports have boosted production. Leningrad,[129] Moscow, Kharkov, and Zhdanov are leading examples, though the impact is small in relation to the size of the local economies. The third is where new manufacturing and processing industries have been or are being set up with an eye to exports. Here the Volga region stands out, though the location primarily reflects home-market considerations.

For the European USSR as a whole, changes in foreign economic relations have on the one hand increased the pressure on natural resources, but on the other hand stimulated exploration and better resource use. They have modified the transport and traffic geography, changing the pattern of comparative regional advantages

in favor of ports, frontier regions in the broad sense, and the routes to them. In a relatively small way they have favored the regions producing manufactures in which the Soviet Union specializes, primarily machinery and heavy equipment.

For Siberia and northern Kazakhstan the new economic policies can be regarded as one more factor inhibiting the realization of an old dream, "rounded development." Multi-faceted development is certainly taking place in individual territorial-production complexes, such as those based on the Bratsk and Sayan hydroelectric dams, but the overall pattern continues to be one of primary resource extraction and processing, especially energy- and water-intensive processing. The heavy dependence of Soviet exports on energy sources and raw materials is helping to strengthen the specialization orientation of the Siberian economy; CMEA integration makes Siberian locations ever less attractive for manufacturing industries serving the combined markets. However, in this case integration is a much less important factor than the measures being taken to implement the "scientific-technical revolution." Their stress on reconstructing and re-equipping old factories is a far greater force against Siberian development: Siberia probably contains under 5 percent of the old factories on which the program will focus, especially since so many are in light industry.[130]

At present it seems fair to say that most foreign-trade-based developments with a strong multiplier effect are centered in European USSR.[131] This may change to some extent in the future, as distances to markets compel more thorough processing of Siberian resources for export and rising world energy prices strengthen the attractions of cheap Siberian power. On the other hand, advances in long-distance power transmission could reduce those attractions, and the all-year operation of the Northern Sea Route could both reduce the compulsion to process before export and shift the locational advantages of Siberian resources towards those with best access to the Route.

Central Asia plays a highly specialized role in Soviet foreign trade, based on its cotton exports and its contribution to the European gas grid. Its small share of manufactured exports is a reminder of its World War II role, when accessibility westward was similarly important and the region received relatively few evacuated factories. Two factors could bring change: the region's ample labor resources, and its proximity to Afghanistan. (If theocratic rule in Iran were followed by a socialist revolution, or if the present regime turned to the Soviet Union for support against the United States, there could of course be much greater changes.)

The impact of changing external trade policies has been felt most strongly in the Far East. The BAM may have a strategic as well as an economic significance, but the overall impact of foreign trade on the Far East cannot be denied. Long-term compensatory deals with Japan for forest products and coal; joint exploration for oil and gas; port and harbor construction; the container land bridge with its associated shipping lines; one of the most active cross-border trading organizations; North Korean use of leased Soviet forests—these have had a strong impact because of the previously low level of regional development. Further impacts can be expected as the BAM gives access to new resources. Local writers also emphasize change in the character of exports, with more processing of forest products and, they hope, more involvement and development of the local manufacturing sector. The latter already exports machine tools, rice-harvesting combines, marine diesel engines and diesel generators, lifting equipment and many other items—a large share of them westwards, by rail.[132]

In the early 1970s Soviet researchers constructed indices relating regional participation in exports to regional share of national income (Table 2). The main changes since then are probably increases in the shares and indices of West Siberia (oil and gas) and to a smaller extent East Siberia (pulp and aluminum), with corresponding decreases for the North Caucasus and Transcaucasia (oil and gas). As for the future, one would expect to see further gains for West Siberia and large gains, especially in the specialization index, for the Far East. Also, if export production does come to be concentrated much more in special export-oriented complexes, some at least will be located to minimize pressures on local natural resources and therefore, probably, farther for the western frontiers than enterprises which have expanded to meet export requirements. At present the Volga region still looks more attractive for industries with locational options than

TABLE 2
Indices of Regional Specialization in Exports
(Share of Exports ÷ Share of National Income)
and Share of National Industrial Exports, early 1970s

| Region | Index of Export Specialization, c. 1971 | Share of National Industrial Exports, percent (9th Five-Year Plan) |
|---|---|---|
| Central and Northern European USSR | 0.89 | 30 |
| Northwest | 1.33 | |
| Central | 0.78 | |
| Volga-Vyatka | 0.68 | |
| Baltic | 0.80 | |
| Belorussia | 0.86 | |
| South European USSR | 0.93 | 32–34 |
| Ukraine | 0.94 | |
| North Caucasus | 1.24 | |
| Transcaucasia | 1.13 | |
| Moldavia | 0.23 | |
| Central Chernozem | 0.51 | |
| Volga-Urals | 1.39 | 18 |
| Volga | 1.77 | |
| Urals | 1.02 | |
| Siberia | 0.90 ⎫ | |
| West Siberia | 0.74 ⎬ 10–13 | |
| East Siberia | 1.24 | |
| Far East | 0.87 ⎭ | |
| Kazakhstan | 0.91 | 2–3 |
| Central Asia | 1.34 | 5 |

SOURCES: Avdeichev and Zaitsev, ed., *Geografiya proizvoditelnykh sil SSSR: mezhdunarodnoye ekonomicheskoye sotrudnichestvo* (Moscow: Mysl, 1976), pp. 140–79; I. F. Zaitsev in Pavlov, ed., *Regionalnye problemy ekonomicheskoi integratsii SSSR v sisteme stran SEV* (Moscow: Nauka, 1975), pp. 195–96.

anywhere farther east. It appears that several projects in the chemical and machine-building industries were located west of the Urals for infrastructual and labor-supply considerations, and because the eastern regions were considered to be strained to the limit in expanding raw-material exploitation. None of these considerations seems likely to change in the near future. However, for many activities locational options are limited, and these tend to be energy- and resource-located activities, which can less easily avoid shifting eastwards.

### Soviet Research on Foreign Economic Policy and Regional Development

Organizations Involved

Most of the published work on the relationships between foreign economic policy and Soviet regional development has originated in two institutes. The most specifically focused on the topic is a division in the Council for the Study of Productive Forces (SOPS), a research institute under Gosplan. Publications of the division include those by Avdeichev, Zaitsev, Pavlov, and Moskalkov, referred to in this paper. Also concerned with problems of intranational regional development, though more directly with the "international socialist division of labor," is the Institute of Economics of the World Socialist System, an Academy of Sciences institute. Publications by its members, cited in this paper, include those by Bogomolov, the head, Shanina, Gorizontov, Shiryayev, Vais, Kormnov, and Alampiyev.

Among university geography departments, the Moscow University Geography Faculty is represented most strongly by the Department of Economic Geography of Foreign Socialist Countries, formerly headed by Bogomolov. Alisov, the present head, formerly worked on location problems in the Ministry of the Chemical Industry and is still closely associated with location decisions in that field. He has published widely on Soviet regional development in the context of CMEA integration. His colleagues, including Vardomsky, Ilinich, Khudolei, Valev, and the late Professor Mayergoiz, referred to here, touch on Soviet problems but focus mainly on Eastern Europe. (The Department of Economic Geography of the Soviet Union has published little on the topic: its interests seem to have shifted towards social geography.) Outside Moscow considerable interest is shown by the university geographers in the smaller republics, especially those in the west with a high concentration of foreign-trade activities and the potential for cross-border trade. Most of the published work found which uses detailed primary sources emanates from this group. Several examples are to be found in the work edited by Purin, and the older work by Osorgin *et al.*, on the Far East is of the same type.

Other bodies which have published on foreign economic policy and Soviet regional development include the Konyunkturny Institut of the Ministry of Foreign Trade (Savin), and the Moscow branch of the Geographical Society of the USSR (Kibalchich). The latter of course draws together members of many organizations, as in *Territorialnye Struktury Promyshlennosti*, edited by Alisov.

In addition to published works, a great deal of un-published research related to the topic of interest goes on in the branch ministries' scientific research institutes. Also involved, though less directly, are other Gosplan institutes besides SOPS, particularly the Institute of Complex Transport Problems and the Institute of Complex Fuel and Energy Problems, and institutes of the Academy of Sciences other than those already mentioned. They include the Commission for the Study of Productive Forces (the small remnant of what was largely transferred to Gosplan in 1960 as SOPS; its relevant foci include northern development and the water economy), and an institute recently set up to study practical problems of the distribution of economic activity.

The main general lack in the published literature and apparently also in research, to judge from several comments in interviews, is comprehensive study of the relationships between foreign economic links and regional development from the viewpoint of the region. The branch or sectoral-ministry approach predominates very heavily. The models developed by regional economists, like Bandman, Granberg and their colleagues in Novosibirsk, are used in planning new territorial-production complexes like the one focused on the Sayan dam, but there seems to be little concerted research at the national level of the type which would make feasible a regional input into the five-year-plans as strongly based as is the sectoral input through the work of the branch ministries' scientific research and project institutes. The ministries have to consult with regional authorities while formulating their recommendations and the regional authorities can lodge objections—e.g., if they think a chemical works will harm their region. How well based their objections are seems to depend a great deal on their own initiative. Most of the initiative so far has come from the authorities of the smaller republics. Azerbaijan, for example, uses regional input-output models and other tools commonly employed by Western planners in order to assess the impact of new activity in the republic,[133] and the western border republics seem to have been moving in similar directions with a particular emphasis on the impact of foreign policy on their development.

The greatest problem facing such initiatives is data collection. Required information is scattered among dozens of government departments and enterprises, few of which have any interest in making it readily available. What they have readily available even for their own use may not correspond to what a Western researcher would expect to find. A manufacturing enterprise may keep the most detailed information on its suppliers at its fingertips but have practically no knowledge of its customers, though waybills are kept and can be processed to extract such information.

Even if republic and oblast authorities are prepared to take the initiatives required for impact research, most of their regional planning is related to the implementation of plans decided on by Gosplan and the Council of Ministers (or by individual ministries for projects costing below 30 million rubles), rather than to the preparation of plan inputs, on which the ministries spend so much effort. It appears that measures are now under way to strengthen the regional input, in accordance with a July 1979 order by the Council of Ministers designed to promote simultaneous and co-ordinated preparation of plan inputs at the branch and regional levels. The union republics do already receive five-year plan control figures— the guide for preparing suggested plans—as the branch ministries do, so in their case the new measures will require them to strengthen work for which the organization already exists. In the case of RSFSR major economic regions it is likely to involve rebirth of the macroregional economic councils which flourished during Khrushchev's time but were abolished some years ago.

## Research Emphases

Following Avdeichev's approach[134] we shall divide the research foci, of the central institutes in particular, into three groups: national, interregional, and intraregional.

Most of the national-level research is outside the scope of this paper but is essential background to the work at a more restricted spatial scale. It can be summed up as the search for answers to three sets of questions:[135]

I. Given the policy to import foreign technology, what should be imported to ensure the greatest possible desired effects on the national economy, particularly with respect to structural influences (e.g., on the relative development of category A and category B industries) and multiplier effects (e.g., on the raising of technological levels in industries other than those immediately affected)?

II. Given the need to pay for imports, what should be exported to ensure the maximum foreign-currency income coupled with the least deleterious effects on the national economy? In particular, to what extent should export efforts focus on raw materials as opposed to manufactures, and to what extent is it worthwhile encouraging participation by customers in the export effort?

III. Given the policy to pursue CMEA economic integration, on what bases should national specializations be decided? In particular, on what should the Soviet Union seek to specialize, and how can specialization be reconciled with balanced national economic development, however that may be defined?

Research at the interregional level is concerned with achieving the desired "territorial proportions" of the economy and ensuring that import-export activities further those aims or at least do not hamper them.[136] Research into territorial proportions in general focuses on the interregional division of labor (specialization), the allocation of activities to eastern and western regions, the deployment of labor and capital so as to make the best use of immobile natural resources and so forth. In this context the research institutes have tried to work out principles and methods both for locating activities to achieve the maximum monetary effect (e.g., in the case of exporting activities, to pay for imports at minimum cost) and for determining the long-term effects of foreign links on the spatial economy. The effects might be direct (e.g., the constraints imposed by fuel and energy exports or the choice of certain industrial specializations on the long-term regional availability of resources for domestic use and the improvement of spatial efficiency in the economy) or indirect, through an influence on the sectoral structure of the economy (e.g., through the diversion of investment into exporting sectors).

Intraregional research is in part an extension of that at the interregional level: working out how to locate activities most efficiently and determining the impact of foreign links on the regional economy. Work has also focused on methods of improving the regional infrastructure to cope with foreign-linked developments (e.g., the building of very large automobile factories requiring efficient, coordinated delivery of inputs) and on the determination of an optimal mix of regional activities to make the fullest use of available resources, minimize transport costs through the spatial proximity of production-linked activities and so forth. In other words, the intraregional research is closely related to that on territorial-production complexes, and for regions where planning is being carried out in terms of such complexes it involves the specification of the foreign-linked components of the regional models.[137]

Analytical Methods and Criticisms Thereof

It is clear that many of the analytical methods used are experimental. Soviet researchers consider that they are still at an early stage of accumulating experience in a relatively new planning situation, and one in which they face problems (e.g., in the use of price data) which severely limit the utility of foreign methods of analysis.

Several groups of analytical methods can be identified. (Others than those listed are referred to in the literature, but examples have not been found.)

I. Methods for determining what to import and export, at the national level;
II. Methods for describing the foreign-linked component of the existing spatial economy;
III. Methods for determining optimum locations for the production of exports;
IV. Methods for assessing the impact of foreign economic relations on "the general territorial proportions of the national economy and the formation of systems of economic regions;"[138]
V. Methods for describing, forecasting, and planning regional economies, with particular attention to the impact of foreign economic relations.

I. What to import and, especially, export is not always decided on strictly economic grounds. Raw-material exports to Eastern Europe are not at the mercy of price levels in Western markets, and the Soviet Union has prided itself in its willingness to take what developing countries can offer in exchange for its manufactures. But economic calculations are a part of most foreign-trade planning. One set of methods is needed to forecast world trade volumes and prices. Here Soviet researchers have to use two types of models: stochastic for Western trade and programming for CMEA trade.[139] Another set is required to determine prices for intra-CMEA trade, and yet another to calculate the distribution of benefits from that

trade and other CMEA integration measures. Vais implies that little has yet been done in this latter direction at least with respect to the distribution of benefits from labor migration.[140] A fourth set of methods is used to try to indicate the "effectiveness" of exports and imports by calculating the domestic costs of foreign exchange earned through exports and comparing them with the costs which would have been incurred if the goods bought with the foreign exchange, or substitutes for them, had been produced in the Soviet Union. The "indices of import and export effectiveness" are thus conceptually simple, though complications soon arise if attempts are made to take into account, say, the multiplier effects of imports which could not have been produced in the Soviet Union or the opportunity costs of expenditures on export industries. Even without such complications the calculations become difficult in practice. For example, how are costs to be reckoned? None of the various types of domestic prices necessarily reflects costs accurately, and an accurate cost picture for the economy would require millions of calculations. There are many other problems, especially in the determination of meaningful equivalence between nonconvertible currencies, but most have been discussed already in Western sources.[141]

Soviet geographers and regional economists discussing foreign trade have criticized the methods used at the national level on three principal and related grounds: the use of world prices as a basis for CMEA trading prices; the use of average branch costs or prices rather than those of the individual enterprise; and failure to take adequate account of transport costs.[142]

Following an agreement in 1975, intra-CMEA prices are supposed to be based on the average of prices in one of the principal world markets for a given commodity for the previous five years. (In practice there are many exceptions, resulting mainly from concessions made during bilateral trade negotiations between CMEA countries.) The use of world prices serves to reduce the problems of currency conversion referred to above, and the use of five-year average prices is intended to even out cyclic fluctuations. In the case of oil it has also served to cushion the blow of rapid increases in world prices. Once the world prices have been calculated, "cleaned of monopolistic influences," and adjusted, for example, to reflect differences in quality of the goods, transport costs are added in, depending on the geographical position of the socialist countries in relation to the world market chosen and to each other. However, they are not added in for all commodities. They are for bulk goods such as ore, coal, oil, iron and steel, fertilizers, forest products, and grains, but for manufactures they are not considered important enough to add in. Even when they are added in, however, the actual transport expenses of the selling country to its frontier are not taken into account. If the trading countries have a common frontier and goods are being sold FOB frontier, the transport cost component is calculated as half the cost of moving the goods from the base market (the world commodity market chosen for price calculations) to the buyer. If the goods are being sold FOB frontier and there is no common frontier, or if they are being sold FOB port of seller, the transport cost component is calculated as half the difference in cost of delivery from the base market to the buyer's entry point and from the seller's exit point to the buyer's entry point.

The objections to this approach are substantial, if one considers the potential impact on Soviet regional development. Firstly, prices in the world market may be formed under conditions quite different from those relevant to intra-CMEA trade. Secondly, transport costs calculated as described may give irrational results. Actual transport costs to the frontier are usually higher than the transport components in the contract prices. This is especially disadvantageous to exporters of raw materials. For example, in the contract price for Donbas coal delivered at Brest, the transport component is 18 percent. In the actual delivered cost it is 28 percent. Also, it is quite possible for the method to produce higher transport cost components for deliveries to nearby customers than to those far away.

The method described determines the foreign-currency returns from sales to CMEA countries. These returns are then compared to the domestic costs of the sales to produce the index of export effectiveness, so shortcomings of the method may well affect decisions on what to export. CMEA countries seeking to maximize their export-effectiveness indices could be motivated to promote exports from the wrong industries from both their national and the CMEA points of view.[143] As for the calculation of domestic costs, the geographers and regional economists raise a further objection, this time to the common practice for manufacturing industries of basing calculations on average branch costs. Marginal costs at specific enterprises would be more relevant.

Some of these problems affect calculations with respect to exports to hard-currency markets too, but there may be less point in arguing about them. As Shmelev points out, the overriding aim is to obtain hard currency, and "the difficulty of getting competitive goods onto the capitalist markets makes it necessary in a number of cases to resort to subsidizing below-cost or low-profit exports."[144]

II. Methods used to describe the current regional situation with respect to foreign-trade activity all appear to be variations on the location quotient.[145] They compare a region's share of national exports variously with its share of national territory, population, or income:

$$K_q^s = \frac{E_q}{s_q} \ , \ K_q^n = \frac{E_q}{n_q} \ , \ K_q^r = \frac{E_q}{r_q}$$

where $K_q^s$, $K_q^n$ and $K_q^r$ are coefficients of specialization, using as benchmarks territory $(s)$, population $(n)$, and national income $(r)$, $E_q$ is the share of the $q$-th region in Soviet exports, in percent, and $s_q$, $n_q$ and $r_q$ are the region's shares of national territory, population, and income.

Similar indices have been calculated to show the regional concentration of exports to particular CMEA countries, by branches of the machine-building industry.[146] No examples have been found of indices calculated for the regional incidence of imports.

III. Methods for determining optimum locations for foreign-linked activities within the Soviet Union derive in part from those used at the national level. The regional

coefficient of economic effectiveness of exports differs from the national version in that, instead of using national average calculated costs for the particular branch of industry, it employs territorially differentiated costs:[147]

$$X_{ij}^e = \frac{B_e}{Z_e}$$

where $X_{ij}^e$ is the coefficient of export effectiveness of production of a particular branch of industry from the $i$-th region via the $j$-th frontier exit point, $B_e$ is the net foreign exchange receipts from exports (in valuta rubles), and $Z_e$ is the sum of the full calculated production and transport expenses. The coefficient can be modified to take account of export activity undertaken with foreign credits. It has been used in SOPS to calculate relative variations in regional effectiveness of exports for different products. The coefficients are entered in a matrix (export regions x frontier exit points) and divided by the smallest coefficient.[148]

No similar index has been found relating to imports.

The use of such coefficients is considered ideally as an adjunct to programming approaches within global models for the whole economy, but in the absence of such models it becomes a basic approach. The coefficients are presumably most useful when dealing with specialized production for export. If products being exported are identical to those sold on the domestic market, the determination of optimum locations for export production should take domestic flows into account too and attempt to minimize costs for the whole, not just the export component.

When locations for new industries are being chosen, and the industries will not exclusively export, the export effectiveness indices can only be one of many inputs. The comparison of alternative possible locations for new industry normally involves the use of calculated costs (prices having been generally rejected as too unreliable) and the concept of *zamkayushcheye toplivo* (marginal fuel), which in the chemical industry at least has also been extended to other raw materials. The principle involved is that in calculating the best location for a proposed factory, it may not be best to reckon on the cheapest fuel currently available. That fuel might be local natural gas, which might not last the life of the factory or could be put to better use than as fuel. Or if the factory uses it, some other regional activity might have to import a much more expensive fuel. Therefore an attempt is made to calculate costs using those of the cheapest fuel or raw material known to be available in adequate quantities for regional needs—or in some cases, that which it appears should be used for the general good. For example, among possible inputs to a chemical works might be a waste product of another plant, more expensive than alternative inputs but very difficult to get rid of and liable to pollute if dumped. That input might be used as a basis for calculations. Calculations are carried out for 10, 20, 40, etc., years ahead. In other words an attempt is made to take a broader and longer-term view of the situation than is normal in the West. These calculations are used only for deciding location, not for assessing the performance of a factory after construction.

We have already noted objections to the practice of basing natural export-effectiveness indices on average branch costs. A similar situation—and similar objections—arise when an exporting agency, having contracted to export a commodity, needs to identify a supplier. Often there are alternative suppliers. For many industries, enterprise wholesale prices for a given item are standard, irrespective of cost variations between enterprises. There is therefore no reason for the foreign trade organizations to discriminate among suppliers on the basis of production costs. It is also claimed by some writers that the way transport costs are taken into account tends to reduce the foreign trade organizations' interest in the location of suppliers.[149] This is a debated point, however. For some groups of products, bought FOB factory by the trade organizations, an average distance to frontier is calculated, and the trade organizations pay the railway ministry a lump sum for the year on this basis. They claim that this still motivates them to minimize distances.[150] Critics of the system evidently feel that a more specific identification of high transport costs would provide a more powerful motivation.

IV. Methods for assessing the impact of foreign economic relations on the spatial economy as a whole appear not to have been developed very fully as yet. They are expected to be based on models of interbranch balances, designed to optimize interregional and intraregional links,[151] though Alisov warns against methods which tend to suggest that interregional (or long) hauls are bad and intraregional (or short) hauls are good, without full research into other factors.[152]

V. Finally, the foreign-trade role in regional economies seems to have been analyzed qualitatively rather than quantitatively in most of the SOPS work seen. Methodological problems are discussed by SOPS writers and those from the smaller republics,[153] but the main contributions so far, though not with primary reference to foreign trade, seem to have come from the Novosibirsk school of regional economists.

## Potential Impact of Research

Implicit in much of the work reviewed is a strong criticism of present pricing and costing practices as applied to foreign trade. The system used to determine prices for intra-CMEA trade is faulty enough to distort decisions on what to export. Within the Soviet Union prices are not important so long as costs can be calculated accurately, but in many cases they cannot be or have not been. Even when costs are available, they may be used illogically or not at all. Whether these criticisms will have effect is debatable, since the heavily-criticized method used to determine intra-CMEA prices has been in use since 1958 and the Ministry of Foreign Trade seems happy with it.

An explicit recommendation is to concentrate much export production into a relatively few specialized enterprises. Since this coincides with the expressed views of the late Prime Minister Kosygin, further action might be expected along the lines of the partial specialization in exports of the Togliatti automobile works,

the intended similar approach at the Kama truck plant, and the specialization in forest-product exporting at Arkhangelsk.

Beyond general qualitative recommendations of this nature, the impact of institutes like SOPS seems to depend very much on their ability to develop spatial models of the economy at a broad scale, which can be used to evaluate the wider effects of proposals emanating from the branch ministries. Recent publications indicate a movement in this direction. The smaller-regional models of the Novosibirsk regional economists have already been used in the planning of territorial-production complexes in eastern Siberia, though the regional economists have been criticized for excessive faith in the mechanisms of their models, neglect of human dimensions, and lack of a sense of historical process.

## Soviet Government Policies and Options

Changing foreign economic relations affect regional development through chains of choices. From what alternatives has the Soviet government made its choices; how might the regional impact of foreign relations have differed if other choices had been made; and how have the choices made limited future options?

Firstly, some insights into how actual impacts differ from what might have happened with different choices can be gained by comparing the CMEA and the European Economic Community. The CMEA has chosen forms of cooperation and integration which favor forms of regional development very different from those in the EEC. The principal difference is that borders remain relatively closed to the migration of capital and labor. Both do move, but in limited quantities under close national political control. Since the regional allocation of investment within each country also remains under close control, the emergence of a concentrated industrial belt serving the whole of the CMEA, analogous to the London-Rhine-Northern Italy corridor in the EEC, seems unlikely. The CMEA approach is likely to keep international production linkages relatively simple and limited, and to raise the attractiveness of border-region locations which can facilitate international cooperation between factories. It also makes local cross-border trade attractive, since the range of goods available on either side of the border is likely to differ.

Possibilities under the present system have been far from fully exploited. Multinational cooperative projects have become prominent in CMEA integration, but most have been confined to the production of processed materials to be shipped to the participating countries. In the Soviet Union it would be equally reasonable to build joint enterprises to ship to third countries, freeing other production for the participating countries or simply generating profits for them. The freer international movement of capital involved would bring conditions in the CMEA a little closer to those in the EEC.

Secondly, the Soviet Union has made regional investment choices which favor the "pro-Europeans" over the "pro-Siberians." Eastern natural resources have to be brought into use—there are few options in that regard—but there are options as to where to use the resources. The choice of European USSR for most foreign-linked activity other than raw-material extraction and energy- and water-intensive industries is not based only on location to serve a market area extending westwards beyond the national frontier. Other factors include the Siberian labor shortage, the perceived absorptive capacity of Siberian infrastructure, the greater choice of areas open to foreigners in the west, and the trend towards rebuilding and expanding existing enterprises rather than building new ones. Although the trend to European growth seems firmly established at present, some of these factors could in principle change in favor of Siberia. Existing incentives are well able to attract people east of the Urals, and the creation of living conditions adequate to keep them there may be more a matter of improved organization than of substantially increased investment. The shortage of labor may be artificial anyway, judging from recent complaints about the excessive labor-intensity of work and claims that the Soviet northern regions are "grossly over-populated."[154] The choice of the Volga-Urals region for some recently-built engineering and chemical works appears to reflect fairly narrow advantages over Siberian locations. The rejection of a West Siberian location for the Togliatti ammonia works partly because of lack of experience in building a long-distance ammonia pipeline is one example. Perceptions of comparative locational advantage may change if the July 1979 Council of Ministers order does succeed in raising the regional input to five-year plan formulation. It has been a complaint of Far Eastern writers, for example, that the predominance of branch-ministry inputs favors locations for new industry which have good accessibility to the whole national market or to inputs (depending on who pays for transport to market) rather than those which optimize regional economic structure and balance. Optimum solutions from the branch-ministry viewpoint may not be the most efficient for the nation. Unfortunately, it appears that regional planning organizations have a very long way to develop before they can be expected to make an effective contribution.[155]

A third set of choices relates to the calculation of prices for intra-CMEA trade. As we have seen, the methods used do not present a true picture of relative costs. Critics claim that they lead to under-pricing of raw materials and especially of the transport component of the price FOB frontier. This encourages long-distance raw-material movements and western locations for industries using them. Even within the Soviet Union, the price of, say, natural gas delivered to a chemical works or power station in the western USSR does not fully reflect the costs of finding, extracting, and delivering the gas. In other words a different choice of methods for calculating international prices and domestic costs could affect the regional impact of foreign economic relations.

In his paper in this book, Marshall Goldman has discussed a more basic choice: whether or not to trade. The material examined for this paper suggests that the Soviet Union would not have much difficulty retreating from involvement with the West, simply because the degree of involvement is so small relative to total national economic activity. Some industries would suffer by losing access to new technology, but others would gain through the lessening of pressure on natural resources. The regional impact would be felt mainly in and around ports and above all in the Far East. To retreat from CMEA integration would be a different matter. The economic effects on Eastern Europe would be serious, and probably unacceptable to the Soviet Union politically. The economic impact on the Soviet Union would be less serious, indeed the reduced pressure on resources would be beneficial. The regional impact would be felt mainly in and around the western ports and frontier regions.

## NOTES

1. L. B. Vardomsky and N. S. Mironenko, "Some geographic aspects of socialist economic integration in Europe," in *Geograficheskiye issledovaniya v Moskovskom universitete* [Geographic studies at Moscow University], ed. Yu. G. Simonov (Moscow University, 1976), p. 62.

2. Credits provided by Czechoslovakia for iron-ore extraction date back to 1960. Typical of the payback in products approach is the provision of Polish credits for building the Soligorsk potash mines in Belorussia. The complex was due to be providing two-thirds of Polish consumption by 1980. L. A. Avdeichev and I. F. Zaitsev, eds., *Geografiya proizvoditelnykh sil SSSR: mezhdunarodnoye ekonomicheskoye sotrudnichestvo* [Geography of productive forces of the USSR: International economic cooperation] (Moscow: Mysl, 1976), pp. 16, 102.

3. It was estimated in 1975 that there were 50,000 foreign workers in the Soviet Union, of whom 35,000 to 40,000 were Bulgarians. J. L. Kerr, "Gastarbeiter in Eastern Europe," *RAD Background Report/169 (Eastern Europe)*, 4 December 1975. Soviet writers expect continued use to be made of migrant labor. T. A. Vais, *Problemy sotrudnichestva stran SEV v ispolzovanii trudovykh resursov* [Problems of CMEA cooperation in the use of labor resources] (Moscow: Nauka, 1976), pp. 44, 49; S. P. Moskalkov and A. M. Mastepanov in *Regionalnye problemy ekonomicheskoi integratsii SSSR v sisteme stran SEV* [Regional problems of Soviet economic integration in the CMEA system] ed. Yu. M. Pavlov (Moscow: Nauka, 1975), pp. 56–57. Apart from 10,000 to 15,000 Bulgarians in the forest industry (see note 5), most of the foreigners appear to be working in construction.

4. The best-known joint projects included the Ust-Ilimsk pulp mill (six countries), the Yasny asbestos mine (seven countries), the Orenburg gas pipeline (seven countries) and the Vinnitsa-Albertirsa 750 kv power line (six countries). V. A. Shanina, *Transportno-ekonomicheskiye svyazi stran-chlenov SEV* [Transport-economic relations of CMEA countries] (Moscow: Nauka, 1978), pp. 52–53.

5. Such undertakings as the Bulgarian exploitation of forest resources in the Komi ASSR and the similar North Korean project in the Far East are described as "joint projects" by some writers, e.g., P. M. Alampiyev, "Impact of socialist economic integration on the territorial structure of national economies," in *Geograficheskiye*

*aspekty sotsialisticheskoi ekonomicheskoi integratsii* [Geographic problems of socialist economic integration] (Moscow: Nauka, 1976), p. 13 and S. P. Moskalkov, in Pavlov, *Regionalnye problemy*, pp. 154–55. They are joint in the sense that, in the Bulgarian case, for example, the Soviet Union provided funds and transport. But their distinctive feature is that the resources are leased out to the foreign country for exploitation. Vais, *Problemy sotrudnichestva*, p. 46.

6. Moskalkov and Mastepanov, in Pavlov, *Regionalnye problemy*, p. 61 (oil); I. A. Borodkin, N. P. Titov, M. I. Garbar, *Razvitiye integratsii v khimicheskoi promyshlennosti stran SEV* [Development of integration in the chemical industry of the CMEA countries] (Moscow: Ekonomika, 1974), p. 50 (phosphates).

7. Ye.N. Chigilina, "Impact of trade in chemical minerals and basic chemicals on the location of their export centers in the Soviet Union," in *Territorialnye struktury promyshlennosti* [Territorial structures of industry], ed. N. V. Alisov (Moscow Branch, Geographical Society USSR, 1978), p. 38. The main example given is apatite.

8. On the long gestation periods for Soviet extractive-industry projects, see Z. M. Fallenbuchl, "Comecon Integration," *Problems of Communism*, 22, no. 2 (March–April 1973): 35.

9. Moskalkov, in Pavlov, *Regionalnye problemy*, pp. 92–93 (example of metals).

10. L. I. Brezhnev, *Materialy XXV syezda KPSS* [Materials of the 25th party congress], p. 57, refers to the need to insure more thorough processing of raw materials before export, and to substantially increase the share of manufacturing industry in exports. Though A. N. Kosygin, at the 29th session of the CMEA, stated that "the Soviet Union is not only insuring additional deliveries of the principal raw materials on a long-term basis, but undertaking certain changes in the structure of its economy, raising the share of raw-material sectors to take into account the needs of other socialist countries." *Pravda*, 25 June 1975. The Brezhnev version is reiterated by most writers on the subject, e.g., Avdeichev and Zaitsev, *Geografiya proizvoditelnykh sil*, p. 76; Moskalkov and Mastepanov, in Pavlov, *Regionalnye problemy*, pp. 60–61 (both with reference to oil and petroleum products); and Moskalkov in *Geograficheskiye problemy ekonomicheskoi integratsii sotsialisticheskikh stran* [Geographic problems of economic integration in the socialist countries], *Itogi nauki i tekhniki: Teoreticheskiye i obshchiye voprosy geografii*, tom 2, ed. T. V. Galtseva (Moscow: VINITI, 1976), pp. 40 et seq.

11. O. T. Bogomolov, *Teoriya i metodologiya mezhdunarodnogo sotsialisticheskogo razdeleniya truda* [The theory and methodology of the international socialist division of labor] (Moscow: Mysl, 1967), p. 15, stated that the capital needs of raw material export-producing industries in the Soviet Union, per unit growth of production, were 3 to 3.5 times higher than for machinery production for domestic use. To get a ruble worth of export raw materials required 5 to 8 times as much investment as for a ruble of machinery exports. Figures for oil and cotton were higher. O. K. Rybakov, *Ekonomicheskaya effektivnost sotrudnichestva SSSR s sotsialisticheskimi stranami* [The cost-effectiveness of cooperation between the USSR and the

socialist countries] (Moscow: Mysl, 1975), p. 15, states that by comparison with, for example, the production of electrical machinery and equipment, capital expenditures per ruble of growth of output of iron ore are over three times greater, coal almost 1.9 times, and in the coke-chemical industry, over 2.8 times. B. B. Gorizontov, *Sotsialisticheskaya ekonomicheskaya integratsiya i transport* [Socialist economic integration and transport] (Moscow: Nauka, 1975), p. 75, states that Soviet extractive industry accounts for 9 percent of industrial production by value, 16 percent of all industrial workers and 25 percent of all productive capital in industry. Moskalkov, in Galtseva, *Geograficheskiye problemy*, p. 48, compares the chemical industry specializations of the USSR and its European partners and suggests that countries specializing in the production of finished products from imported raw materials are in fact reaping the benefits from the capital investments made in the countries supplying them. A. I. Zubkov, "Territorial aspects of integration in the iron and steel industry," in *Geograficheskiye aspekty*, p. 49, makes the same point with respect to the iron and steel industry, and Vais, *Problemy sotrudnichestva*, p. 43, with respect to fuels and raw materials in general.

12. Bogomolov, *Teoriya i metodologiya*, pp. 19, 24–25, 33–34, refers to early overenthusiasm for integration, the importance of building trust among partners and the need to respect national sovereignty.

13. A variety of references to specific fields suggest about 5 percent of intra-CMEA trade in the mid-1970s.

14. L. A. Avdeichev, in Pavlov, *Regionalnye problemy*, p. 8; Moskalkov, in Galtseva, *Geograficheskiye problemy*, p. 52. Bogomolov, *Teoriya i metodologiya*, pp. 100–01, provides the fullest rationale for intrabranch specialization. N. V. Faddeyev, "CMEA's Role in Strengthening the Community of the Socialist Nations," *Foreign Trade* 1979, no. 1, pp. 6–7, lists areas of specialization on which agreement has been reached so far.

15. Faddeyev, "CMEA's Role," p. 8.

16. Fallenbuchl, "Comecon Integration," p. 29, discusses this.

17. The first were in 1968 with a group of Japanese firms, covering the development of the forest resources of the Soviet Far East. N. P. Shmelev, ed., *Strany SEV v mirokhozyaistvennykh svyazyakh* [The CMEA countries in world trade] (Moscow: Nauka, 1978), p. 173. The first large scale ones, according to Avdeichev and Zaitsev, *Geografiya proizvoditelnykh sil*, p. 17, were for the exchange of pipeline and equipment for Soviet natural gas, concluded with Austrian, Italian, West German and French interests at the end of the 1960s and the beginning of the 1970s. Shmelev lists later agreements of the type.

18. Principally with Japanese firms for exploration for gas in Yakutia and oil and gas on the continental shelf off Sakhalin Island.

19. Shmelev, *Strany SEV*, p. 9.

20. Yu. S. Shiryayev, *Mezhdunarodnoye sotsialisticheskoye razdeleniye truda (Voprosy teorii)* [The international socialist division of labor (Theoretical issues)] (Moscow: Nauka, 1977), p. 48, asserts that import policy is the starting point in any country. Exporting is undertaken to obtain foreign currency.

21. O. Rybakov, "The effectiveness of Soviet participation in socialist economic integration," *Planovoye khozyaistvo* 1979, no. 1, pp. 21–23.

22. For example, I. M. Mayergoiz, "Territorial structure of the economy and some approaches to its investigation in light of socialist economic integration," in *Territorialnaya struktura narodnogo khozyaistva v sotsialisticheskikh stranakh* [Territorial structure of the economy in the socialist countries] ed. V. P. Maksakovsky (Moscow: Nauka, 1976), p. 7.

23. "Direct" and "indirect" impacts are identified by Soviet writers, but their use of the term seems to vary. For example, N. V. Alisov, "Impact of integration processes on the location of industry in the Soviet Union," *Petermanns Geographische Mitteilungen* 1977, no. 3, p. 165, and "Impact of integration processes on the location of productive forces in the Soviet Union," in *Geografiya otraslei rayonov SSSR i zarubezhnykh stran* [Geography of economic activities in regions of the USSR and in foreign countries], ed. O. A. Kibalchich (Moscow: Geographical Sociaty USSR, 1974), p. 42; I. F. Zaitsev, "Conceptual and methodological principles for integrated study of the processes of formation of the republic economy under the impact of foreign trade and socialist integration," in *Ekonomicheskiye svyazi soyuznykh respublik* [Economic relations of the union republics], part 2, ed. V. Purin, (Riga: Latvian University, 1979), p. 54.

24. P. M. Alampiyev, "Impact of socialist integration," p. 8.

25. L. A. Avdeichev, in Pavlov, *Regionalnye problemy*, p. 13; Avdeichev and Zaitsev, *Geografiya proizvoditelnykh sil*, p. 45 et seq.; L. A. Avdeichev, I. F. Zaitsev, S. P. Moskalkov, "Conceptual issues in regional economic study of the integration of the USSR into the CMEA system," in *Problemy teorii i praktiki razmeshcheniya proizvoditelnykh sil SSSR* [Issues in the theory and practice of the location of productive forces in the USSR], ed. N. N. Nekrasov (Moscow: Nauka, 1976), pp. 307–08.

26. N. V. Alisov, "Territorial aspects of the intensification of production in the industry of the Soviet Union," *Vestnik MGU, ser. geogr*, 1977, no. 6, pp. 23–29.

27. On the relative cost-effectiveness of exports from these regions, see Moskalkov and Mastepanov, in Pavlov, *Regionalnye problemy*, pp. 63–67.

28. Moskalkov and Mastepanov, in Pavlov, *Regionalnye problemy*, p. 60; Avdeichev and Zaitsev, *Geografiya proizvoditelnykh sil*, p. 71; Yu. V. Ilinich, "Main geographical aspects of foreign trade in fuels between the USSR and the European member countries of CMEA," in *Territorialnye struktury promyshlennosti* [Territorial structures of the industry] (Moscow: Geographical Society USSR, 1978), p. 31; note from T. Shabad.

29. Ilinich, "Main geographical aspects," p. 31; Avdeichev and Zaitsev, *Geografiya proizvoditelnykh sil*, p. 71; Moskalkov and Mastepanov, in Pavlov, *Regionalnye problemy*, pp. 60–63.

30. Odessa, Novorossisk, and Ventspils.

31. Moskalkov and Mastepanov, in Pavlov, *Regionalnye problemy*, p. 68; Avdeichev and Zaitsev, *Geografiya proizvoditelnykh sil*, p. 69.

32. Avdeichev and Zaitsev, *Geografiya proizvoditelnykh sil*, p. 71.

33. Ibid., p. 76.

34. Ibid., p. 72.

35. Theodore Shabad, "Soviet Regional Policy and CMEA Integration," *Soviet Geography: Review and Translation* (hereafter *SGRT*) 20, no. 4 (April 1979): 235, 257.

36. N. V. Alisov, "Impact of integration processes on the sectoral and territorial structure of the chemical industry of Poland and the Soviet Union," in *Issledovaniye territorialno-khozyaistvennykh struktur sotsialisticheskikh stran v svete kompleksnoi programmy* [Territorial-economic structures of the socialist countries in light of the program of socialist economic integration] ed. I. M. Mayergoiz and V. F. Khudolei (Moscow University, 1978), p. 85.

37. Avdeichev and Zaitsev, *Geografiya proizvoditelnykh sil*, p. 72.

38. Theodore Shabad, *Soviet Raw-Material Exports*, Discussion Paper No. 1 (October 1977), Association of American Geographers, Project on Soviet Natural Resources in the World Economy, pp. 3–4.

39. Shmelev, *Strany SEV*, p. 43; Arthur Meyerhoff, project conference in Washington, D.C., 4 April 1980, and *Soviet Petroleum: History, Technology, Geology, Reserves, Potential and Policy*, Discussion Paper No. 10 (June 1980), Association of American Geographers, Project on Soviet Natural Resources in the World Economy.

40. Avdeichev and Zaitsev, *Geografiya proizvoditelnykh sil*, p. 79.

41. Gas exports were 6.7 percent of production in 1975 and 8.0 percent in 1976. Since then gas-export statistics are no longer published and have had to be estimated.

42. Leslie Dienes, *Soviet Energy Policy and the Hydrocarbons* and *The Regional Dimensions of Soviet Energy Policy (With Emphasis on Consumption and Transport)*, Discussion Papers Nos. 2 and 13 (April 1978 and August 1979), Association of American Geographers, Project on Soviet Natural Resources in the World Economy; Moskalkov and Mastepanov, in Pavlov, *Regionalnye problemy*, p. 72. They give examples to show how rapidly the cost of moving gas rises with distance. Total costs for survey, extraction and movement of gas to the Soviet western frontier are, for Central Asian gas 183 percent and for Tyumen gas 246 percent of the costs for Orenburg gas. For transport alone they are 210 and 260 percent.

43. Ilinich, "Main geographical aspects," p. 33. He has given details of which fields can be linked to which markets.

44. Ibid., pp. 33, 34.

45. V. A. Savin, "Some economic-geographic aspects of the Soviet Union's foreign trade with the socialist countries of Europe," in *Problemy ekonomicheskoi geografii zarubezhnoi sotsialisticheskoi Yevropy* [Problems in the economic geography of socialist Eastern Europe] *Voprosy geografii*, no. 97 (Moscow: Mysl, 1974), p. 58.

46. Avdeichev and Zaitsev, *Geografiya proizvoditelnykh sil*, p. 85.

47. Ilinich, "Main geographical aspects," p. 35.

48. Calculated from Theodore Shabad, "News Notes," *SGRT* 19, no. 4 (April 1978): 285.

49. The lead article in *Pravda*, 21 December 1979, p. 1, called for the faster opening up of coal deposits west of the Urals and the transmission of energy from them to the center of the country. "West" may of course have been a misprint for "East."

50. Theodore Shabad, "News Notes," *SGRT* 19, no. 1 (January 1978): 69.

51. Alisov, "Impact," in *Petermanns*, p. 167.

52. The time zone savings of the Peace grid in the mid-1970s were reckoned at 4 percent, or a generating capacity of 1.7 million kilowatts (Moskalkov, in Pavlov, *Regionalnye problemy*, p. 80). A system spanning a time difference of 8 to 9 hours was reckoned to be able to save 10 percent (Avdeichev and Zaitsev, *Geografiya proizvoditelnykh sil*, p. 86).

53. Theodore Shabad, "News Notes," *SGRT* 18, no. 10 (December 1977): 779; 21, no. 5 (May 1980): 324–26.

54. *Planovoye khozyaistvo* 1978, no. 9, p. 20.

55. Theodore Shabad, "News Notes," *SGRT* 18, no. 4 (April 1977): 273; 19, no. 10 (December 1978): 744.

56. V. Balybin, "The 53rd Meeting of the CMEA Standing Commission for Foreign Trade," *Foreign Trade* 1979, no. 1, p. 10.

57. See resume by Theodore Shabad in *SGRT* 20, no. 3 (March 1979): 203–04, of an article in *Elektricheskiye stantsii* 1978, no. 12.

58. Alisov, "Impact," in *Petermanns*, p. 166.

59. Shabad, "Soviet Regional Policy," pp. 246–47, and "News Notes," *SGRT* 19, no. 7 (September 1978): 500; I. A. Borodkin et al, *Razvitiye integratsii v khimicheskoi promyshlennosti stran SEV* [Development of integration in the chemical industry of the CMEA countries] (Moscow: Ekonomika, 1974), pp. 49–50; V. A. Savin and B. A. Kheifets, "Territorial aspects of CMEA cooperation in the joint development of industrial projects," in *Geograficheskiye aspekty*, pp. 111–13.

60. Avdeichev and Zaitsev, *Geografiya proizvoditelnykh sil*, p. 102; Shabad, "Soviet Regional Policy," p. 247; interview material, Moscow, January 1980; V. Ye. Biryukov, B. S. Kozin, G. D. Kunakhovich. *Ratsionalizatsiya perevozok gruzov* [Freight traffic rationalization] (Moscow: Znaniye, 1982), p. 44.

61. Shabad, "Soviet Regional Policy," p. 247; N. V. Alisov, "Geographical problems of integration in the chemical industry," in *Geograficheskiye aspekty*, p. 74; interview material, Moscow, January 1980.

62. Theodore Shabad, "News Notes," *SGRT* 19, no. 8 (October 1978): 586; 21, no. 10 (December 1980): 676–80, gives several examples.

63. Shabad, "Soviet Regional Policy," p. 248.

64. Interview information, Moscow, January 1980.

65. Avdeichev and Zaitsev, *Geografiya proizvoditelnykh sil*, p. 104.

66. Theodore Shabad, "News Notes," *SGRT* 19, no. 8 (October 1978): 586, and 21, no. 10 (December 1980): 676–78.

67. Interview information, Moscow, January 1980. It may be that Togliatti will eventually supply all the ammonia to Yuzhny under the agreement. Yuzhny could presumably switch to producing methanol, though it is also possible that the pipeline will be continued to Eastern Europe, in which case both Yuzhny and Gorlovka could still feed into it.

68. On ethylene pipelines and Nizhnekamsk, see Theodore Shabad, "News Notes," *SGRT* 18, no. 10 (December 1977): 779.

69. Interview information, Moscow, January 1980.

70. *Planovoye khozyaistvo* 1978, no. 9, p. 22.

71. Shabad, "Soviet Regional Policy," pp. 240–44.

72. *Planovoye khozyaistvo* 1978, no. 9, p. 21.

73. Zubkov, "Iron and steel industry," in *Geograficheskiye aspekty*, pp. 50–51.

74. Balybin, "The 53rd Meeting," p. 10.

75. Theodore Shabad, "News Notes," *SGRT* 10, no. 9 (November 1978): 670.

76. Shanina, *Transportno-ekonomicheskiye svyazi*, p. 131.

77. Shabad, *Soviet Raw-Material Exports*, p. 7.

78. E.g. ibid., pp. 7–10; W. A. D. Jackson, *Soviet Manganese Ores: Output and Export*, Discussion Paper No. 25 (September 1980), Association of American Geographers, Project on Soviet Natural Resources in the World Economy.

79. Avdeichev and Zaitsev, *Geografiya proizvoditelnykh sil*, pp. 98–99.

80. Theodore Shabad, "News Notes," *SGRT* 20, no. 1 (January 1979): 60; 18, no. 2 (February 1977): 138.

81. Theodore Shabad, "News Notes," *SGRT* 20, no. 1 (January 1979): 60; 18, no. 2 (February 1977): 138; 19, no. 10 (December 1978): 742–43; 18, no. 9 (November 1977): 705; 20, no. 4 (April 1979): 268; 21, no. 9 (November 1980): 617; Savin, "Foreign trade," p. 67.

82. Avdeichev and Zaitsev, *Geografiya proizvoditelnykh sil*, pp. 97–98.

83. Moskalkov, in Pavlov, *Regionalnye problemy*, pp. 162 et seq. He also gives details of glass and other building materials exports.

84. Shabad, "Soviet Regional Policy," p. 246; "News Notes," *SGRT* 21, no. 2 (February 1980): 115–16.

85. Shanina, *Transportno-ekonomicheskiye svyazi*, p. 133.

86. Ibid., p. 134.

87. F. I. Gabov, in Galtseva, *Geograficheskiye problemy*, p. 84.

88. Theodore Shabad, "News Notes," *SGRT* 18, no. 5 (May 1977): 350.

89. Moskalkov, in Pavlov, *Regionalnye problemy*, p. 159.

90. Shanina, *Transportno-ekonomicheskiye svyazi*, pp. 133–35.

91. Moskalkov, in Pavlov, *Regionalnye problemy*, pp. 153, 156.

92. Gabov, in Galtseva, *Geograficheskiye problemy*, p. 83.

93. The opportunity to do either of these depends very much on whether the factory is able to exceed planned production, and on the republic in which it is located. Centrally planned export sales bring no extra income above domestic sales, beyond that needed to cover extra costs. Above-plan production can bring bonuses, including the opportunity to use some of the unplanned foreign-currency receipts. Also, foreign-currency income from sales by industries under republic control (light and food industries) can be disposed of by republic authori-

ties. Some of the smaller republics have made good use of this opportunity to acquire funds, sharing them with the factories to encourage production. The RSFSR has not been very active in this field. (Interview information, Moscow, January 1980).

94. A. N. Osorgin et al., *Vneshnetorgovye svyazi Dalnego Vostoka* [Foreign trade of the Soviet Far East] (Khabarovsk, 1973), pp. 99–110.

95. V. A. Savin, "Development of the specialized export-oriented production of machinery and equipment in the western regions of the Soviet Union," Mayergoiz and Khudolei, *Issledovaniye territorialno-khozyaistvennykh struktur*, pp. 138–39.

96. K. O. Kukk, "Some economic problems in the development of export industries in the Estonian SSR," in Purin, *Ekonomicheskiye svyazi*, p. 71.

97. Savin, "Export-oriented production," p. 138; O. Bogomolov, "Economic relations of the USSR with foreign countries," *Planovoye khozyaistvo* 1980, no. 10, p. 85.

98. D. Petrov, "Export of Soviet-Made Industrial Equipment," *Foreign Trade* 1979, no. 1, pp. 13 et seq.

99. Osorgin et al., *Vneshnetorogvye svyazi*, p. 46.

100. Deduced from lists in Avdeichev and Zaitsev, *Geografiya proizvoditelnykh sil*, p. 107, and Shanina, *Transportno-ekonomicheskiye svyazi*, p. 137.

101. Avdeichev and Zaitsev, *Geografiya proizvoditelnykh sil*, pp. 107–11.

102. Ibid., pp. 111–12.

103. Interview information, Moscow, January 1980.

104. Avdeichev, in Galtseva, *Geograficheskiye problemy*, pp. 64–78; Moskalkov, in Pavlov, *Regionalnye problemy*, pp. 172–88; Avdeichev and Zaitsev, *Geografiya proizvoditelnykh sil*, pp. 120–25.

105. Yu. F. Kormnov, ed., *Agrarno-promyshlennaya integratsiya stran SEV* [Agrarian-industrial integration of CMEA countries] (Moscow: Nauka, 1976), pp. 101–02.

106. Galtseva, in Galtseva, *Geograficheskiye problemy*, pp. 98–102; N. V. Alisov and E. B. Valev, "Geographical problems of socialist economic integration," *Vestnik MGU, ser. geogr.*, 1976, no. 3, p. 80.

107. L. B. Vardomsky, "Geographical aspects of the development of international transport connections," in Purin, *Ekonomicheskiye svyazi*, p. 98.

108. Shanina, *Transportno-ekonomicheskiye svyazi*, p. 66.

109. Theodore Shabad, "News Notes," *SGRT* 20, no. 1 (January 1979): 60; 21, no. 1 (January 1980): 48–52.

110. Shanina, *Transportno-ekonomicheskiye svyazi*, p. 61; Gorizontov, *Sotsialisticheskaya integratsiya*, pp. 99–100; Savin, "Foreign trade," p. 65.

111. Gorizontov, *Sotsialisticheskaya integratsiya*, p. 99.

112. Savin, "Foreign trade," p. 65.

113. Shanina, *Transportno-ekonomicheskiye svyazi*, p. 63; *Ekonomicheskaya gazeta* 1980, no. 2, p. 20.

114. Theodore Shabad, "News Notes," *SGRT* 20, no. 2 (February 1979).

115. Gorizontov, *Sotsialisticheskaya integratsiya*, p. 123.

116. Ibid., pp. 78, 103; Shanina, *Transportno-ekonomicheskiye svyazi*, p. 155.

117. Shanina, *Transportno-ekonomicheskiye svyazi*, p. 145.

118. Urged by Shanina, *Transportno-ekonomicheskiye svyazi*, pp. 147–54.

119. N. V. Alisov, "Transport-economic relations of the industry of the USSR under conditions of a full-fledged scientific-technical revolution," in Purin, *Ekonomicheskiye svyazi*, p. 5.

120. Theodore Shabad, "News Notes," *SGRT* 19, no. 1 (January 1978): 67; On a negative impact at Abakan—the diversion of resources from the railcar plant to the container plant—see *Current Digest of the Soviet Press*, 32, no. 50 (14 January 1981): 14–15.

121. Alisov, "Intensification of production," p. 26.

122. Avdeichev and Zaitsev, *Geografiya proizvoditelnykh sil*, p. 133.

123. P. M. Alampiyev, "Geographical aspects of socialist economic integration in Europe," in *Geograficheskiye problemy sotsialisticheskoi ekonomicheskoi integratsii v Yevrope* [Geographical problems of socialist economic integration in Europe] (Moscow: Geographical Society USSR, 1971), pp. 19–40; and "Socialist integration as an economic-geographic problem," *Izv. AN SSSR, ser, geogr.*, 1971, no. 3, pp. 12–19.

124. Most cities in European USSR grew by 25 to 35 percent between 1966 and 1979. Brest, the only crossing point large enough to appear in recent statistics, grew by 95 percent.

125. Especially Shanina, *Transportno-ekonomicheskiye svyazi*, and Gorizontov, *Sotsialisticheskaya integratsiya*.

126. N. V. Alisov and Yu. G. Tsukhanov, "Problems of economic development in Soviet areas bordering on Poland," in Mayergoiz and Khudolei, *Issledovaniye territorialno-khozyaistvennykh struktur*, pp. 122–32; B. A. Giter, "Territorial aspects of the economic relations of the Lithuanian SSR and Poland," in Mayergoiz and Khudolei, *Issledovaniye territorialno-khozyaistvennykh struktur*, pp. 133–37; Yu. V. Shelepov, "Regional aspects of the participation of the Ukrainian SSR in the international division of labor," in Purin, *Ekonomicheskiye svyazi*, pp. 77–79.

127. Interview material, Moscow, January 1980. The particular exception cited was Kaliningrad Oblast. The main reasons cited for lack of interest were the nature of the local economy (lack of tradable items) and inertia or reluctance to depart from established ways, i.e., from relying entirely on domestic trade.

128. Avdeichev and Zaitsev, *Geografiya proizvoditelnykh sil*, p. 132; G. K. Yuzufovich, "Regions in the system of foreign economic relations," in Purin, *Ekonomicheskiye svyazi*, pp. 44–46; V. A. Savin, "Some problems at the present stage of development of foreign trade of the union republics," in Purin, *Ekonomicheskiye svyazi*, p. 49; M. M. Vabar, "Foreign trade as a stimulus of the cost-effectiveness of the economy and as an indicator in the economic mechanism," in Purin, *Ekonomicheskiye svyazi*, pp. 63–65; Osorgin et al., *Vneshnetorgovye svyazi*, passim.

129. A. V. Yakovlev and N. G. Samorodova, "The Leningrad economic region in Soviet foreign trade," in Purin, *Ekonomicheskiye svyazi*, pp. 73–75.

130. N. V. Alisov, "Intensification of production."

131. For an examination of multiplier effects farther east, see R. S. Mathieson, "Urban Growth in Siberia and

the Soviet Far East: Multiplier Effects of Japanese-Supplied Plants," *SGRT* 21, no. 8 (October 1980): 490–500.

132. Osorgin et al., *Vneshnetorgovye svyazi*, passim.

133. Interview material, Moscow, January 1980.

134. In Pavlov, *Regionalnye problemy*, p. 13.

135. Main sources for this section are Avdeichev, in Pavlov, *Regionalnye problemy*, p. 15; Avdeichev and Zaitsev, *Geografiya proizvoditelnykh sil*, p. 10; Moskalkov, in Galtseva, *Geograficheskiye problemy*, pp. 47–48; Bogomolov, *Teoriya i metodologiya*, pp. 14–18.

136. Main sources for this section are Avdeichev and Zaitsev, in Galtseva, *Geograficheskiye problemy*, pp. 20, 143–44; Avdeichev, in Pavlov, *Regionalnye problemy*, pp. 13, 22 et seq., 194; Avdeichev and Zaitsev, *Geografiya proizvoditelnykh sil*, pp. 23, 46.

137. Main sources for this section are Avdeichev and Zaitsev, *Geografiya proizvoditelnykh sil*, p. 131; Avdeichev, in Pavlov, *Regionalnye problemy*, pp. 16, 24, 27; Zaitsev and Moskalkov, in Pavlov, *Regionalnye problemy*, pp. 40, 50; Zaitsev, in Pavlov, *Regionalnye problemy*, pp. 189, 194; Avdeichev and Zaitsev, in Galtseva, *Geograficheskiye problemy*, pp. 21, 136, 144.

138. Avdeichev and Zaitsev, in Galtseva, *Geograficheskiye problemy*, pp. 19–20.

139. Avdeichev, in Pavlov, *Regionalnye problemy*, p. 28.

140. Vais, *Problemy sotrudnichestva*, p. 77.

141. For example, Edward Hewett, *Soviet Primary Product Exports to CMEA and the West*, Discussion Paper No. 9 (May 1979), Association of American Geographers, Project on Soviet Natural Resources in the World Economy; Lawrence Brainard, "Soviet Foreign Trade Planning," in *Soviet Economy in a New Perspective*, U. S. Congress, Joint Economic Committee (Washington, 1976), pp. 695–708, and "CMEA Financial System and Integration," in *East European Integration and East-West Trade*, ed. Paul Marer and J. M. Montias (Bloomington: Indiana University Press, 1980), pp. 121–38. The most useful recent Soviet source on the methods used by Gosplan is S. Zakharov and V. Sulyagin, "Calculating the effectiveness of measures for promoting international cooperation within the automated system of optimal foreign-trade planning," *Planovoye khozyaistvo* 1979, no. 4, pp. 104–13. Comments on the difficulty of using them can be found in Shmelev, *Strany SEV*, pp. 248 et seq.

142. Main sources for this section are Shanina, *Transportno-ekonomicheskiye svyazi*, pp. 167–68, and Shmelev, *Strany SEV*, pp. 248 et seq.

143. The point is developed by Shmelev, *Strany SEV*, pp. 248 et seq.

144. Ibid.

145. Zaitsev, in Pavlov, *Regionalnye problemy*, pp. 194–95; Avdeichev and Zaitsev, *Geografiya proizvoditelnykh sil*, p. 34.

146. I. F. Zaitsev and V. I. Zhilin, in Pavlov, *Regionalnye problemy*, pp. 134–47.

147. Avdeichev, in Pavlov, *Regionalnye problemy*, p. 20.

148. Avdeichev, in Pavlov, *Regionalnye problemy*, pp. 20, 153, where forest product coefficients are shown.

149. Shanina, *Transportno-ekonomicheskiye svyazi*, p. 46; Savin, "Export-oriented production," p. 142.

150. Interview information, Moscow, January 1980.

151. A great deal of this topic can be found in V. P. Yevstigneyev, ed., *Effektivnost i ekonomiko-matematicheskoye modelirovaniye razmeshcheniya proizvoditelnykh sil* [Cost-effectiveness and economic-mathematical modeling of the location of productive forces] (Moscow: Nauka, 1979). This type of work was described in interview as primarily for use within Gosplan, since it is at the Gosplan level that an attempt is made to take overall territorial proportions into account when reconciling the proposals of the various branch ministries and republics.

152. Alisov, "Transport-economic relations," in Purin, *Ekonomicheskiye svyazi*, p. 6.

153. Avdeichev and Zaitsev, in Galtseva, *Geograficheskiye problemy*, p. 19; Purin, *Ekonomicheskiye svyazi*, passim.

154. Conference remarks, Moscow, January 1980.

155. V. Belenki, "What is Hampering the Improvement of Regional Planning?" *Current Digest of the Soviet Press* 32, no. 21 (25 June 1980): 18. Translated from *Pravda*, 27 May 1980, p. 3.

# SOVIET DECISION MAKING IN REGIONAL PLANNING AND ITS POTENTIAL IMPACT ON SIBERIAN RESOURCE EXPORTS

GEORGE A. HUZINEC
Dancer, Fitzgerald and Sample, Inc.
New York City

## Introduction

In structuring the development of any relatively backward region, a number of socioeconomic decisions obviously have to be made at several different geographic scales. Such decision making is supposedly part of the planned Soviet model of economic development and as such should be at least of academic, if not practical interest. Furthermore, at the time of the Soviet takeover, Siberia (unlike European Russia) was relatively underdeveloped and therefore the eastern regions of the country should have proven a fertile testing ground for some of the Soviet ideas on regional economic development.

With these comments in mind and given the theme of this book, the main objective of this chapter will be to evaluate the manner in which Soviet regional development planning has impacted on the USSR's ability (and desire) to engage in international trade. The evaluation will focus on Siberia and will involve three interrelated topics:

1. An interpretation of the relationship of Soviet regional planning to the more all-inclusive national economic planning.
2. A pertinent abstracting of Soviet methods of regional economic planning as they apply to Siberia.
3. An analysis of Soviet views on complex development of regions, especially as these views impact on decisions regarding whether a region's external trade relations should be structured around a national production function or one that is widened to include other nations on a long-term basis.

The connection between Soviet regional development policy and foreign-trade policy will first be shown to be an outgrowth of an autarkic national development strategy. The impact of a relaxation of that autarkic policy is then investigated in light of various constraints stemming from previous regional development policies that focused upon a largely internal production function.

In pursuing this discussion, Soviet methods for the regional planning of economic development are reviewed, both in theory and in practice. This review is enhanced by comparisons to more widely known Western models of regional economic development. In this analysis the relationship between regional planning and industrial location planning is of key importance.

Finally, regional planning's possible impact on Soviet trade policy will be shown to constitute a number of logical conclusions that follow from geographic patterns that have evolved (and are evolving) from Soviet plans for regional economic development. Special emphasis will be placed on Siberian development issues and their relationship to recent external events involving Japan, China, and the United States. In this context, the issue of complex development is investigated as it relates to the East-West controversy that has underlain much of the internal logic of Soviet development plans. The question of whether to provide for relatively full socioeconomic development of the Siberian economy or whether to utilize the region primarily as a supplier of raw materials and energy to the more advanced European portions of the country is shown to be an issue of considerable importance for international trade.

## National Economic Planning and the Role of Regional Planning

Historically, Soviet national economic planning has involved two supposedly complementary planning systems; sectoral (ministerial) planning and regional planning. However, for most of the Soviet period, sectoral planning has dominated. The result of such domination has been that many of the ideas specifically associated with regional planning have remained largely in the realm of theory, or inadequately applied in practice. Nevertheless, all sectoral investment decisions have to be placed in the context of geographic space. Thus spatial decision making has existed de facto, even if such decisions have not been in accord with established locational doctrine. Analysis of the evolving Soviet strategy of economic development provides considerable insight into the manner in which regional development has structured the location of productive activities and therefore impacted upon Soviet foreign-trade needs and possibilities.[1] At the beginning of the Stalinist period of economic development, certain preconditions were instituted so as to "close" the economy. This in essence meant an eventual severance of most economic ties with foreign countries. Along with this went a redistribution of political and economic power and the installment of various institutions (collectivized agriculture, public ownership of enterprises, centralized planning, and so forth).

Under Stalin, the entire system—political and social as well as economic—was pointed toward the single overriding objective of rapid economic growth, especially in the industrial sector, for the purpose of establishing a strong heavy industrial base. Such a policy had the desired advantage of insuring a high degree of military strength. As a result of the Soviet commitment to rapid economic growth, there was an immediate concern for determining the division of national income between consumption and investment. Much of the discussion in the 1920s centered on this vital question. The eventual decision was to maximize investment so that larger stocks would be available for further production in each succeeding period. In essence, the high rate of investment reflected the planner's tendency to discount the future at a very low rate.

With respect to the investment (savings) sources, it is helpful for the present discussion to distinguish between internal and external possibilities. The internal sources were: reduction in consumption, taxation, compulsory lending to the state, inflation, and the absorption of underemployed labor into productive work. External sources were limited in that foreign capital was not readily available except for a period in the 1920s. In addition, the terms of trade had worsened for the USSR as a result of the worldwide depression of the 1930s. This meant that the only possible source of external saving was a reduction in consumption imports.

Faced with the practical problem of mastering the resources for the huge investment in physical capital, the Soviet Union did not simply enforce savings by reducing consumption all around. The government was able to free resources for investment by a consumption squeeze, while at the same time twisting and redirecting consumption in such a way as to combine suppression in some directions with rapid and substantial increases in others, as dictated by the requirements of growth. For example, consumption in housing and clothing was kept low, while health consumption was stimulated.

The investment allocation plan forms the core of the Soviet five-year plans. In regard to investment policy, the USSR, as any economy, must solve four basic problems. The first problem concerns the percentage of national income to be allocated to investment. A very high investment rate was chosen, reflecting one of the basic principles of the Soviet development strategy, namely, to achieve a high rate of capital formation. This principle remains in force today. A second problem concerns the distribution of investment funds by economic sectors. In general, the principles involved here are: priority of the capital-goods industries, import-substitution policy of in-

ternational trade, and heavy investment in human capital.

A third problem involves deciding how capital should be combined with other resources, especially labor. This has traditionally been reflected in the principles of (1) favoring modern, capital-intensive technology in key processes and labor-intensive techniques in auxiliary operations and (2) the utilization of underemployed agricultural labor for capital formation. The technology and capital transfers that are of such key interest today are reflective of the fact that the traditional method of alleviating low levels of technology (substituting labor for capital) is no longer operant. The Soviet economy is unable to sufficiently foster the development of all the necessary innovations required for its economic growth, nor is it able to internally muster adequate funds for the capital-intensive development of Siberia (which is necessitated both by the existing and proposed industrial mix and by the inability to attract permanent workers).

A last problem concerns the choice of locations for investment projects. For most investment projects, the geographic selection involves at least a two-step process in which a regional location is first chosen and then a decision is made on a site within that region. As such, this process tends to involve a complex interaction between both the regional and ministerial planning systems. Figure 1 orders this spatial allocation process within a framework depicting the major decision makers, the relevant location criteria, and the sequencing of macro and micro location decisions. One should note that this schematic model does not cover all situations and that the location criteria are often ignored or only partially employed. As shown in Figure 1, investment allocations are first broken out at a regional level. The determination of this regional distribution plan is mainly controlled by the Politburo, the Council of Ministers, and Gosplan USSR. Institutionally, it is the various ministries that are responsible for the drafting and implementation of plans (including those of location) for the individual economic branches. This is done under the control and evaluation of Gosplan USSR. Gosplan USSR, in turn, responds to the macro guidance outlined by the Politburo. The criteria actually used to determine interregional macro location appear to have been influenced, at least in part, by what are known as location principles and by the tenets of economic regionalization.

The various regional planning bodies do feed into the decision as to regional allocation of investment funds, but interestingly their role has generally been minimal. For the most part, territorial plans at a regional level are usually compiled not by coordinated regional planning but rather by mechanically adding up the targets that have been set for the region by the various sectoral planning agencies.

In summary, as presumably the first step in location planning, distribution plans are compiled for the various branches of industry at a regional level. At this stage, only the locations of the largest enterprises are tied to individual geographic points, the distribution of the majority of enterprises is given only by economic region or union republic. These geographic distribution plans are

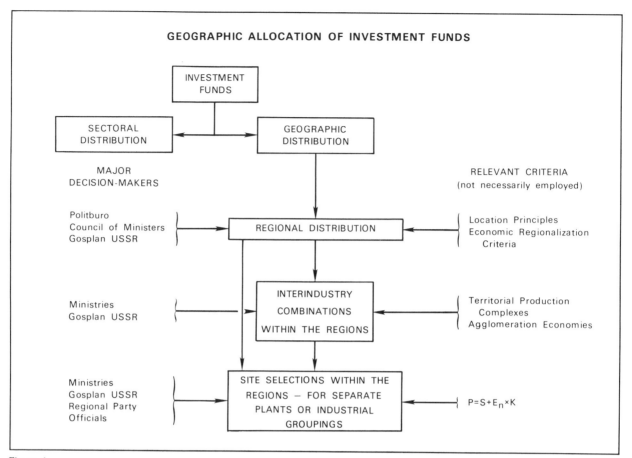

Figure 1

worked out by the individual ministries in consultation with Gosplan USSR. There appears to be relatively little influence from the regional party hierarchy or from the economic region planning bodies because their access to the decision-making process is limited at this level.

Apparently the party plays a differing role depending on whether it is the central leadership or the regional party hierarchy (republic, oblast, and city) that is being analyzed. The role of the central leadership, in addition to providing overall direction, is one of a "referee."[2] It acts to keep the state planning organs, the ministries, and the regional party officials from following their own narrow interests. In this regard, two important institutional ills of Soviet planning need emphasis: departmentalism and localism. These defects result because diseconomies that would be internal to a specific firm in a market economy are externalized in the Soviet system.[3] In the USSR, a ministry or regional unit is concerned only with its specific sector or area. Effects of its decisions on other sectors or areas are external to its concern.

It is at the regional level that these various planning organs and political authorities must decide on an important element of the region's economic structure: regional specialization versus regional self-sufficiency. In theory, economic regionalization criteria provide specifics as to the optimal internal structure for a region. According to these criteria, the regional specialization is to provide the region's identity and in general is to be associated with

the producers goods sector. On the other hand, regional self-sufficiency is supposed to be achieved in the consumers goods industry. This latter point also reflects the Soviet policy of transportation minimization, a policy that tends to focus on consumer industries. In general, consumer goods are viewed as involving shorter, intra-regional movement, whereas producers goods are seen as interregional commodities with longer average hauls. In addition, the ministerial tendency toward giantism, especially prevalent in the producers goods industries, provides impetus to a regional specialization pattern. Institutionally, departmentalism would lead to regional specialization, while regionalism would support tendencies toward regional self-sufficiency.

Once the selection of a regional location has been made, geographic decision making must then be extended to a determination of intraregional location (see Figure 1). At this point arises *possible* consideration of optimal spatial combinations of production within a given region; that is, site selection might take into consideration the project's present and future relations with other productive investments. Therefore, as depicted in Figure 1, it is in the second stage (if completed) that proper interindustry combinations would be attempted for each region. Relevant criteria include the concept of a territorial-production complex as well as an estimation of the agglomeration and external economies to be had by spatial proximity of linked industries. Because regional planning organs are relatively weak, the responsibility for interindustry coordination has fallen mainly on Gosplan USSR. The ministries, also responsible for planning at this stage, tend to have only limited concern for interindustry coordination. Individual ministries tend to follow their narrow economic interests (departmentalism) and therefore have not been a significant force in providing industrial coordination. As a result, proper interindustry coordination within a given region is often not made an explicit part of spatial decision making, or if given consideration, decisions are often difficult to carry out in practice. This second stage is thus often bypassed in decision making. But, interestingly, Siberia has proven somewhat of a testing ground for spatial models like the territorial-production complex, which is discussed in a subsequent section.

The last stage in locational decision making (and the one probably least understood by Western researchers) is the selection of an actual site (or sites) within the economic region for the individual plant or group of plants. The main decision makers remain Gosplan USSR and the ministries; however, the regional party officials also appear to be a significant force, especially the political leaders of the larger cities. The next two sections explore the methods associated with these three stages of locational decision making.

## Soviet Methods of Regional and Site Location Planning[4]

This analysis begins with the observation that much of what has been termed in Soviet and Western literature as "Soviet location theory" is more appropriately defined as belonging in the realm of Soviet regional development thought.[5] More specifically, the three concepts of a "law," a "regularity," and a "principle" become important. The unfortunate aspect related to these three categories is that Western literature has focused on the principles, thereby obscuring some of the more interesting geographic aspects of the two other categories. It is this situation that has contributed to a narrowing of the Western interpretation of what literatures are to be included in any discussion of Soviet location theory. First, consider the oft-quoted principles of the "socialist location of productive forces":

1. Eliminate long hauls (to reduce overall transport costs) by moving the enterprises to their respective raw materials, fuels and markets.
2. Plan the geographical distribution of enterprises so that each region will have specialized industries (utilize available natural resources most efficiently) as well as being economically self-sufficient.
3. Plan an even distribution of production throughout the country so that the labor and natural resources of each region will effectively participate in the national economy.
4. Abolish the contradiction between cities and rural areas that is based on the difference between industrial and agricultural production.
5. Plan the rapid economic and cultural development

of the backward areas (inhabited by non-Russian ethnic groups) up to the level of the leading regions.
6. Strengthen the country's defense potential.

When the Soviet geographic literature on laws and regularities is also reviewed,[6] two major additions can be made to the above guidelines:

7. Develop such progressive forms of socialist organization of production as concentration, specialization, cooperation, and combining (that is, the correct use of economies of scale and interindustry linkages).
8. Combine productive forces spatially in a rational manner in the form of territorial-production complexes, which form the bases of economic regions.

The primary concern will now be to assess the significance of these eight statements for Siberian development, and by extention to note the implications they hold for foreign trade. But first some attention must be given to these locational guidelines so that they are not taken too literally. As is often the case with politically related dogma, the statements are more likely to serve as general guidelines rather than as inflexible rules to be applied in all cases (or even most cases). Perhaps the best example of this is the five-year plan itself. Often the goals set within it are unattainable; however, the important fact is that the plan sets a psychological climate within which subsequent events are nurtured and goals eventually attained (even if not within the time span of a given plan). Although the list of locational guidelines provides a convenient Soviet frame for discussing some of the impact that official locational directives have had on the geographic development of the Soviet economy, it should be kept in mind that some of these locational guidelines were never applied, others were applied only in the past (but are still relevant in that lasting spatial structures resulted), while yet others remain in force today.

The first of the principles ("eliminate long hauls") is reflective both of the huge size of the USSR and of the historical sectoral investment policy that minimized the development of the transport network; in essence, all "unnecessary" hauls were to be eliminated. In several ways this principle becomes vital to understanding some of the present international-trade options facing the Soviet Union. From a transfer cost viewpoint, certain portions of Siberia and the Far East become more amenable to trade with foreign countries than with European Russia and East Europe. Certainly the BAM project increases the access of Siberia to Pacific-rim trading partners. However, at the same time it must be remembered that the BAM is envisaged as playing a domestic, as well as an export, role. Indeed, this situation is reflective of an obvious change in thought as to the feasibility of limiting the average length of haul. Economic and environmental realities dictate that longer hauls are here to stay as the aging industrial heartland of European Russia searches ever farther afield for its necessary domestic raw material and energy supports.

The second principle is also extremely important in that the specialized industries of Siberia are largely in the raw material and energy sectors, both of which are in great demand on world markets. The question for the Soviet

Union then becomes whether the high development and transfer costs of Siberian resources are justified by Soviet and/or international price and demand schedules.

Had the Soviet Union been successful in the application of the third principle, the much argued "East versus West" controversy might not have been spawned. As is well known, the Soviet Union has not been very successful in bringing a complete socioeconomic array of activities to Siberia. The fact that Siberia now appears destined to be mainly a supplier of energy and raw materials is apparently an explicit recognition that an "evenness" in production is not feasible because of environmental and population distribution problems. It is this situation that prompted interest in Siberia's role in future world trade markets. From the Soviet perspective, foreign trade, especially in the Far East, offers an alternative to the long freight movements to European Russia as well as providing a mechanism for obtaining the foreign capital and technology necessary for Siberian development.

The fourth principle, which never received much official support, has little impact on foreign trade possibilities, while the fifth no longer is emphasized (although in the past it was, especially in the context of Central Asia). By contrast, the sixth principle (defense) is much more difficult to interpret. In addition to the economic motivation, Siberian and Far Eastern development has traditionally been viewed as a way of countering Chinese claims to parts of the area. Given United States and Japanese agreements with the Chinese and border skirmishes with Vietnam, serious concerns about China can only have been exacerbated. If foreign trade is a means for accomplishing the economic development of Siberia and thereby militarily strengthening the area, then the Soviet Union would certainly weigh that option seriously. At the same time, Japanese trade agreements with China have seriously undermined Siberian development efforts in that a premise of such growth is that Japan will be an outlet for Siberian products (as well as a supplier of the necessary capital and embodied technology). If China plays the role envisioned for Siberia, then Siberian development is put in economic jeopardy. To a great extent the defense location criterion, often considered irrelevant in the nuclear age, presents itself perhaps as potentially the greatest unknown in this paper. One may ask whether actions taken for reasons of military security (and therefore based on perceptions and beliefs and not necessarily on objective reality) might not give some credibility to renewed thinking about autarkic development (where autarky might allow some trade with friendly countries).

As for the laws and regularities, number seven above refers to industrial economics and is only indirectly relevant to the present concerns. By contrast, the last geographic criterion (number eight) is of considerable significance to Siberia and to the role it might play internationally. Given that Siberia was relatively underdeveloped when the Bolsheviks took power, it has provided a testing ground for "socialist" spatial criteria in that "capitalist" manifestations were not strongly imbedded in the economic landscape. In fact, the territorial-production complex (TPC) is of such potential signifi-

cance that the next section will be devoted to a review of this geographic model of regional development. For now, it suffices to say that this locational model can be important in determining the future internal developments of an area and therefore, by extension, can influence the type and amounts of interaction Siberia will have with outside (domestic and foreign) regions. Indeed, the 10th and 11th five-year plans stress the development of TPCs, especially in the newly developing areas.

Once investments have been allocated to the various regions of the country, some decision must then be made as to a specific area (site) within the region. In the case of such site selection, there is even less likelihood that formal economic analysis will be applied. Noneconomic variables often intervene, such as city size, the strength of the vying political officials, and so forth. However, in those cases where formal analysis does play a role it is profitable to investigate the hypothesis that the Soviet Union uses methodologies similar to those applied in the West. As argued elsewhere,[7] this hypothesis would appear untenable if one consults the official Soviet position. Ever since the Urals-Kuznetsk Combine, Western location theory has been in official disfavor largely because of its supposed emphasis on maximizing profits for the various industries. For the USSR, the dominant criterion is to maximize benefits for the entirety of the country. Especially relevant for Siberia is the position that positive action should be taken on projects that, although not immediately beneficial, would result in long-run growth for the national economy. This view reflects the greater tendency of the state as an entrepreneur, vis-a-vis the private and corporate capitalist, to make investment decision that are aimed at recoupment over a longer time span.

Nevertheless, despite the official tirade against Weberian-related logic, it can be shown that the site selection methodologies applied by Soviet planners lie basically within what has been termed the "least-cost approach" of Western location theory. The emphasis on cost is quite understandable in that Soviet economists most often deal with the cost side, often to the exclusion of various market questions that are normally dealt with in Western models and theories.

In considering costs, the Soviet planners are especially concerned with the two scarce factors in its production function, capital and skilled labor. (Given this, for the ensuing discussion one should keep in mind that it is these two factors that are perhaps most crucial to the development possibilities of Siberia and the Far East.) Ample evidence exists in both the Western and the Soviet literatures as to the importance that has been attached to capital in determining locations for productive activities, whereas the skilled labor factor has manifested itself as a locational constraint in that its availability is highly associated both with the upper end of the Soviet urban hierarchy and with the more socioeconomically advanced or climatically amenable areas of the country.

Given the importance of minimizing costs and of maximizing the effectiveness of capital, how are these goals translated into an operations methodology? Probst talks about net cost (sebestoimost) and capital expenses as being the two practical indices of the productivity of social labor (the criterion of cost-effectiveness).[8] These two items are combined into one formula which, according to Khrushchev,[9] is the basic criterion used to locate plants at all levels. This criterion is represented by the formula:

$$P = S + E_n \cdot K,$$

where:  $P$ = the sum of expenses (*privedenye zatraty*)

$S$ = net cost of the product (*sebestoimost*), including transport delivery to the consumer

$E_n$ = coefficient of effectiveness of the capital inputs

$K$ = capital inputs.

This criterion is obviously concerned only with the cost side of production and therefore the planning goal is to select that variant with the minimum $P$ value. The existence of such locational guidance provides empirical support for the often repeated Western research contention that Soviet site selection methodologies are basically Weberian in origin, at least in the sense of being a least-cost approach within location theory. The existence of this criterion, however, should not lead to the inference that locational decision making within the USSR takes on any uniformity of analysis. Not only can each of the variables associated with the criterion ($S$, $E_n$, $K$) be defined differently depending on the decision maker and the project under review, but the type of traditional economic analysis (e.g., input-output, comparative costing, statistical) in which this criterion is embedded can also vary. It is these "traditional methods of economic analysis" that have recently been augmented by a variety of mathematical programs designed to solve complex spatial allocation problems.

## Complex Development of Economic Regions and the Soviet Concept of a Territorial-Production Complex[10]

The central concept underlying the "complex development" of economic regions is that of a territorial-production complex. According to Kolosovsky, a (territorial) production complex (TPC) is defined as:[11]

An economic (interconditional) combination of enterprises at a single industrial place or in a whole region that produces an economic effect because of a purposeful (planned) selection of enterprises corresponding to the natural and economic conditions of the region, with its transport and economic-geographical position.

Thus, the main characteristics of a territorial-production complex are: industrial linkages, a defined territorial location, planned coordination of the industries, and an "economic effect." Industrial linkages refer to the technological market-supply connections between industries and a defined territory represents the fact that the complex is the geographic location (at differing scales) of the

linked industries. Planning coordination reflects the nature of the Soviet economic system and an "economic effect" refers to the economic (as opposed to the technologic) benefits of grouping linked industries at a given location in geographic space.

To appreciate the relevance that the TPC has to economic regionalization it is necessary to discuss the historical development of Soviet ideas on both regional planning and the internal spatial structure of economic regions. This work began shortly after the Bolshevik Revolution. The research of a number of groups (e.g., Administrative Commission, Kalinin Commission, and Gosplan) resulted in a body of principles that continue to appear in the literature on economic regionalization and the related research on the internal structure of regions.[12] The following are the most pertinent of the major principles of economic regionalization as put forth by Gosplan.[13]

1. Each economic region must have its own strong "territorial-production complex" with a nationwide specialization. In the selection of this complex enter a number of factors: environmental conditions, resource base, population, material and technical bases, existing production and local consumption, and the possibilities of exchange with other regions.

   a. Economic regions represent links in a chain, the totality of which makes up the national economy. An economic region is viewed as a distinctive, insofar as possible economically complete, but not closed part of the country.

   b. The principle of specialization of an economic region is only a part of the "complex development" of the region; regions specialize in those branches that can be developed most fully, the products being exchanged between regions.

   c. "Local" branches of industry grow up in each region to the level at which they (1) guarantee the growth of the major nationwide branches of industry and (2) provide the population of the region with the cheapest (production cost plus transport cost) products and goods.

2. Economic regions are connected with long-term planning and as such are used more as an instrument for long-run changes than as a framework for short-run decisions. This means that the boundaries of the economic region and the territorial organization of the productive forces within it are defined not only by contemporary conditions but also by the prospects of future development.

3. Interregional transport should be reserved for those items of specialization that are produced by the individual regions for the national market.

4. The importance of a regional urban center as an educating force is recognized.

These economic regionalization principles provide some insights into past and future developments in Siberia. Specifically, principles 1 and 3 are of most interest. The first principle refers to the basic employment of the area in that each regional TPC must have a nationwide specialization that provides it with economic ties to other parts of the country. During the autarkic period, Siberian and Far Eastern development was curtailed by artificially restricting its relations with countries of the Pacific Basin. Once exchange is permitted across national boundaries, the hinterland of Siberia (given adequate transportation) is widened, thereby enhancing the development possibilities of the region, especially its eastern portions. Furthermore, combining the logic of principles 1c and 3 means that, under the conditions prevailing in Siberia, the region for the near future must specialize in industries destined for either interregional or international markets. The construction of the BAM is obviously designed to improve the means of transporting the potential specialities out of the region.

A myriad of interpretations as to the distinctions between TPCs and economic regions exist. For Gosplan, an economic region is interpreted as a TPC with a specialization for a national market.[14] Furthermore, at the level of regional TPCs a number of classifications of the involved economic sectors have been proposed.[15] According to SOPS (an agency, under the jurisdiction of Gosplan USSR, that is charged with pre-planning research related to the development and location of productive forces), each territorial complex should have a three-layered structure:

1. The region (TPC) should have a branch or branches in which it specializes for the national market.
2. The region (TPC) should have branches that either supply inputs to the enterprises of specialization or consume some portion of the specialized product(s) (i.e., backward and forward linkages should be developed around the "propulsive" industries of the region).
3. The region (TPC) should utilize local resources (material and human) so as to provide local consumers with goods and services.

Taking regional conditions into consideration, the proper proportional development of these three layers is supposed to ensure the "complex" development of the economy of each economic region. This three-tiered concept of regional economic structure thus involves an intertwining between TPCs and complex development and is thereby helpful in resolving an apparent contradiction of Soviet regionalization criteria: the concurrent call for both regional specialization and regional self-sufficiency can be understood only when the different product spaces being considered are kept distinct. Regional specialization refers to the first layer in the structure (the national market) while regional self-sufficiency is implicit in the third layer (local consumption). Such structural development of regions is an attempt to achieve internal economies associated with economies of scale garnered by the large size of the specialization sectors, as well as external economies associated with the development of backward and forward linkages. Transport savings are also attempted by maximizing "local consumption."

When compared to related concepts in the Western literature, the specialization sectors are envisioned by Soviet authors in a manner similar to the growth-pole and growth-center models. In both models, "lead sectors" are assumed to play a central role in stimulating and transmitting development impulses.[16] The dominant thesis of Perroux is that a growing industry creates external economies for both supplier and user industries and that these industries, along with the propulsive industry, form a "pole of development" that in turn contributes to the growth of the economy. The growth-center model assumes that these developmental impacts are geographically biased via some set of ill-defined "spread effects"; furthermore, the lead firms in the lead sectors are felt to be of crucial significance to the economies of the regions in which they are located. Of course, the relevance of all this lies in the fact that, should the Soviet Union succeed in promoting such forward linkages, the raw materials/energy available for export would be diminished. Instead, finished products would presumably be offered for export (should trade occur). However, at present Soviet finished products suffer from stiff international competition since they are often technologically inferior to Western goods. For now, this scenario remains only a possibility for the somewhat distant future because of the necessary lead time involved in establishing such forward-linked industries.

## Conclusion: Implications for Foreign Trade

Traditionally, Soviet foreign trade has been analyzed within what might be termed a "sectoral" approach wherein the dependent variable, foreign trade, is thought to be explained by some set of independent variables, say $E$. This explanatory set $E$ (e.g., political desires, factor proportions, and so forth) is generally taken as representing point phenomena, that is, any given value within the set of $E$ is considered only as an aggregate for the totality of the Soviet Union. Conversely, this paper has argued implicitly that at least part of these statistics (e.g., sectoral production figures) need to be disaggregated into the various geographic parts that make up the total. In a large country like the Soviet Union, especially when transport is so minimally developed, the need for a regional approach is greatly increased. Within the Soviet context, whether there is autarkic development or a policy of maximizing international trade, the following observations holds: "The volume, direction, and composition of trade between one area and another directly reflect the location of particular types of production and of the markets for such goods. At the same time, the nature of the trading connections between two places helps to determine the kinds of production and consumption that are possible in each."[17] In the case of the Soviet autarkic period, this reciprocal relationship was played out among the various economic regions of the USSR. As a result, the Siberian areas (especially the eastern portions) were severely hindered by their peripheral location, a geographical hindrance exacerbated by minimal transport connections to the economic core in European Russia.

Although the energy/raw material resources of Siberia are now of great interest to world markets, the Soviets must nevertheless contend with the fact that these peripheral areas have been relatively bypassed in socioeconomic and infrastructural development, thus making any Siberian venture a very costly one with only uncertain returns. For most of Soviet history, closed models of productive investment location have been used to help solve geographic problems. Such modeling, of course, was appropriate under conditions of autarkic trade policy, fostered in part by concern about national survival. The decision to locate industry on the basis of a closed model is significant with regard to foreign trade in that such decision making has resulted in a particular location pattern of production and consumption. It is this geographic system that must supply the exports and consume the imports once foreign-trade restrictions are relaxed. Given the vast size of the USSR (and concomitant transfer costs), these previously developed geographic patterns strongly influence the nature, direction, and cost of subsequent Soviet international trade. This is basically the problem facing Siberia, and thus any orientation toward Pacific-rim export markets must necessarily involve long lead times and considerable capital investment.

Given the previous discussion of complex development, one must also raise questions as to the kind of development goals Soviet planners have in mind for Siberia. If the intention is to eventually provide for the comprehensive development of Siberia, then the foreign trade objective might be that of a short-run mechanism whereby the regional specializations of Siberia are exported so as to provide the necessary capital and other infrastructure in the area. This developmental path would eventually lead to a curtailment of raw material/energy export. Alternatively, should the emphasis remain on regional specialization, then different expectations derive. This option appears more likely in that the harshness of Siberia seems to have convinced the Soviet planners of this developmental path (at least for the short run). Indeed, the 11th Five-Year Plan calls for further regional specialization of the economy, especially with regard to the fuels, energy, and industrial raw materials of Siberia. Even this decision does not assure foreign markets of Siberia's riches in that movement can proceed either to international markets or to national (or bloc) markets. Given the proximity of Eastern Siberia and the Far East to the Pacific Basin and given the construction of the BAM, international trade appears to be the option most desired by Soviet policymakers for this portion of their country.

A number of events may affect the evolving substance of these potential foreign-trade movements. The Japanese-Chinese trade agreement, United States-Chinese trade negotiations, and the Vietnamese-Chinese border clashes of 1979 all have had or will have repercussions for the future of Siberian resources. The important question remains as to whether their impact will be largely relegated to the short run or whether they might trigger subsequent events that lead to long-run implications. For example, Japan, as a result of trade agreements with China, is now in a position to extend her resource tentacles into a country where resources are generally more readily accessible than those of the USSR. This action, together with the Vietnamese border clashes can only add fuel to Soviet suspicion of China's trade and power objectives. When to this is added the overall reluctance of

the United States to help finance Siberia's development and American refusal to grant most-favored-nation status to imports from the USSR, Siberia's apparent destiny as an international trader in raw materials and energy is not a certainty.

One might observe that perhaps the important long-term implication of these events is that they raise a question as to whether an autarkic or somewhat modified autarkic policy of development might still be considered a viable long-run option by those in power in the Soviet Union. Granted, there is a compelling short-run argument that the Soviet planners must plunge ahead with putting Siberia on the foreign-trading block. There now exists a great need to overcome some serious technological constraints that are slowing Soviet economic growth. The solution, apart from radically redesigning the system, is to foster a more rapid rate of technological development, especially in the realm of labor-saving innovations.[18] But such research and development has a long gestation period. Therefore, the short-run solution is to import technology-intensive goods and labor-saving machinery and equipment, largely from the West, and to pay for this mainly with exports of raw materials and energy (imports desired by the West). We should therefore expect the Soviet Union to push ahead with this short-run objective, but we should also be aware that other options, which do not include foreign trade may well be made viable by the events of the future—options that the Soviet Union has an historical precedent of taking.

## NOTES

1. In view of the previous comments, this statement obviously refers to location decisions regardless of whether they resulted from regional planning per se or from sectoral investment decisions.

2. See Jerry F. Hough, *The Soviet Prefects: The Local Party Organs in Industrial Decision-Making* (Cambridge, Ma.: Harvard University Press, 1969); and Jeremy Azrael, *Managerial Power and Soviet Politics* (Cambridge, Ma.: Harvard University Press, 1966).

3. See David Dykes, "Industrial Location in the Tadzhik Republic," *Soviet Studies*, 21, no. 4 (1970): 485–506.

4. This section and the following section rely heavily on previous work by the author. Especially relevant are George A. Huzinec, "Some Initial Comparisons of Soviet and Western Regional Development Models," *Soviet Geography: Review and Translation* (hereafter *SGRT*), 17 (1976): 552–65; and G. A. Huzinec, "A Re-examination of Soviet Industrial Location Theory," *The Professional Geographer*, 29, no. 3 (1977): 259–65.

5. See Allan Rodgers, "The Locational Dynamics of Soviet Industry," *Annals of the Association of American Geographers*, 64 (1974): 235: and Huzinec, "Re-examination," pp. 261–62 n 4.

6. For example, consult the listings in Yu. G. Saushkin, I. V. Nikolsky, and V. Korovitsyn, eds., *Ekonomicheskaya geografiya Sovetskogo Soyuza* [Economic geography of the Soviet Union] (Moscow University Press, 1967), p. 124;

A. T. Khrushchev, *Geografiya promyshlennosti SSSR* [Industrial geography of the USSR] (Moscow: Mysl, 1969), pp. 154–55; and Yu. G. Saushkin, *Ekonomicheskaya geografiya: istoriya, teoriya, metody, praktika* [Economic geography: history, theory, method, and practice] (Moscow: Mysl, 1973), pp. 392–97.

7. Huzinec, "Re-examination," pp. 261–62 n 4.

8. A. E. Probst, *Voprosy razmeshcheniya sotsialisticheskoi promyshlennosti* [Problems in the location of socialist industry] (Moscow: Nauka, 1971), p. 127.

9. Khrushchev, *Geografiya promyshlennosti*, p. 159 n 6; also see R. S. Livshits, *Effektivnost kontsentratsii proizvodstva v promyshlennosti* [Cost-effectiveness of industrial concentration] (Moscow: Nauka, 1971), chap. 6.

10. The discussion of this section deals with the conceptual model of a territorial-production complex and the ramifications of that model for foreign trade. No attempt is made to describe individual TPCs; other papers in this book have provided detailed discussion of the relevant existing and proposed Siberian TPCs.

11. T. M. Kalashnikova, *Proizvodstvenno-territorialny kompleks kak slozhnaya territorialnaya sistema* [The production-territorial complex as a complex territorial system] (Moscow University Press, 1970), p. 124; and N. N. Kolosovsky, *Journal of Regional Science*, 3, (1961): 1–25.

12. Yu. G. Saushkin and T. M. Kalashnikova, "Current Problems in the Economic Regionalization of the USSR," *SGRT*, 1 (1960): 50–60.

13. For example, see Saushkin, Nikolsky, and Korovitsyn, *Ekonomicheskaya geografiya*, p. 124 n 6.

14. Khrushchev, *Geografiya promyshlennosti*, pp. 340, 363 n 6; and Ye. P. Maslov, "The Significance and Role of Sectoral-Production Complexes in the Formation and Evolution of Economic Regions," *SGRT*, 11 (1970): 746–54.

15. I. V. Nikolsky, "The Role of Economic Sectors in the Formation of Regional Production Complexes," *SGRT*, 13 (1972): 16–26.

16. William B. Beyers, "On Geographical Properties of Growth-Center Linkage Systems," *Economic Geography*, 50, no. 3 (1974): 203–18.

17. E. Conkling and M. Yeates, *Man's Economic Environment* (New York: McGraw-Hill, 1976), p. 225.

18. S. Rosenfielde, "The Changing Pattern of Soviet Trade," *Current History*, 69, no. 409 (1975): 133–36, 147–48.

# 7

# THE BAIKAL-AMUR MAINLINE
# AND ITS IMPLICATIONS
# FOR THE PACIFIC BASIN

VICTOR L. MOTE
University of Houston

## Introduction

No modern Soviet construction project has attracted so much attention as the Baikal-Amur Mainline (BAM) (Figure 1).[1] If the Soviet press in any way reflects public opinion, then the Soviet people view the railroad as part Pyramid and part Colossus of Rhodes. In length, the BAM is roughly half the Trans-Siberian, built between 1891 and 1904, and twice the size of the Turkestan-Siberian (Turk-Sib) Railway, completed in the 1930s.

Begun initially in the 1940s, the main east-west line of the BAM between Ust-Kut and Komsomolsk (3,145 km) has been under construction since 1974 and originally was scheduled for completion in 1983.[2] Additionally, a 400-km north-south railroad (the Little BAM) has been laid between Bamovskaya (until 1982, Bam) Station on the Trans-Siberian and Neryungri in South Yakutia, crossing the east-west mainline of the BAM at Tynda. Other BAM-related engineering includes double-tracking of the western terminal line between Taishet and Ust-Kut and major improvement of the eastern terminus between Postyshevo (until 1981, Berezovka), Komsomolsk, and Sovetskaya Gavan.[3] Trail-blazing, track-laying, and refinishing operations amount to almost 4,670 km in the sparsely inhabited areas to be served by BAM and Little BAM (BAM service area).

Given environmental constraints (see Chapter 3), the BAM is probably unequaled anywhere in the world as a feat of railway engineering. It traverses or bypasses 22 mountain ranges (seven of them more than 1,500 m above sea level) and 17 rivers with widths of 300 m or more. Around 3,200 major artificial structures must be created or excavated, including 31 km of tunnels (nine altogether, with one over 15 km long); 142 bridges with spans greater than 100 m; and over 230 million $m^3$ of earthwork, three-fourths of which require excavation in solid rock and/or permafrost. Construction of the BAM thus demands one

*This research was facilitated in part by a University of Houston Faculty Development Leave. It was assisted by Lewis Garvey Smith, William Zeis, and Randy Potts, with computer programming by Dinh D. Vu.*

artificial structure per kilometer.[4] Superimpose these necessities on a zone that averages freezing temperatures for over half the year, is plagued with permafrost for two-thirds of its length, suffers earthquakes, slides, and avalanches in its western half, and the prospects for uncomplicated economic development are dim.

The importance of the BAM does not rest with the magnitude of its engineering, but with its potential impact on Soviet domestic development and international strategies. After all, Soviet workers already have no small amount of experience in building railroads in similar, if not harsher, environments of Norilsk, Surgut, and Murmansk. In order to ascertain its contingent impacts, we need to first ask why the BAM is being built, or better yet, why it is being built at this time in history.

There are currently two schools of thought among Western analysts accounting for the upsurge of Soviet interest in the Pacific region: one is military; the other is economic. Alarmists would suggest that the Pacific is a kind of maritime vacuum, what with most of the international sea lanes concentrated in the Atlantic. To them, the ultimate Soviet goal is dominance of the Pacific Basin.

### Military

To some extent, warnings of neo-Mahanism are justified. Since 1965, deployment of Soviet naval forces, in terms of ship-days out of port, has increased from 7,500 to more than 50,000. Simultaneously, the fastest growing activity has occurred in the Pacific and Indian oceans. Since 1972, naval deployment rates in both of these oceans have increased while movement in the Atlantic has declined.

The real problems posed here are: to what extent do military concerns promote economic progress in the BAM area and to what extent do they represent a byproduct of such developments? In a real sense, Soviet Far Eastern naval developments are largely independent of Siberian development questions, just as are the emplacement of air bases and ground division encampments. However, the military contingent in Pacific Siberia is too large to be reckoned independent of the Siberian economy. In 1970, ground troops alone represented 7 to 10 percent of the population of the three border administrative units of the Far East, meaning that one person in 10 to 14 was in

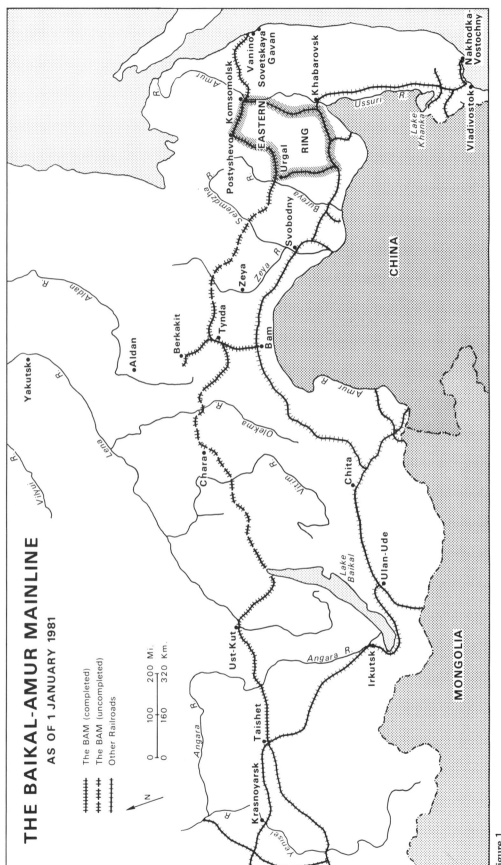

Figure 1

uniform. Adding in the navy, the proportion would be even higher. The ratio for the country as a whole was one in 50 at best. Thus, military forces in the Far East must be considered to have important implications for the regional economy and worthy of study within the auspices of this book (see Chapter 10).

In answer to our first question, Soviet military occupation in several ways directly affects the development of the region. First, it provides a labor force that otherwise might not be available. This is obviously the case in the construction of the BAM east of Tynda (Figure 1), where most of the workers are railroad construction troops. Additionally, troops who are discharged from the service in the area are drawn in increasing numbers to the BAM and related construction projects because of high salaries and other incentives. Whatever the labor turnover is in the Far East—20 to 30 percent per year elsewhere in Siberia—auxiliary labor from the military is proportionately crucial.

Responding to the second question is more difficult, since the real economic growth of the region with respect to the new resource-development programs can be measured only tentatively. It is evident that such projects will not lead to much more permanent settlement than exists already. Moreover, the presence of troops in the region is not determined by regional development itself but by factors external to those events.[5] Even if Soviet authorities are successful in attracting considerably more people to the Far East between now and 1990, it is doubtful that the military contingent there will grow as a byproduct of the larger civilian population.

## Commerce and Access to Raw Materials

Since 1960, the rate of economic growth in the USSR has declined steadily from something over 6 percent to 3 percent and less. Simply stated, economies expand either by increasing the labor force or by raising per capita productivity. In the Soviet Union, all but the least able segments of the labor pool have been depleted, and planned increases in labor productivity have been disappointing. Demographers predict an even more substantial labor shortage in the 1980s and 1990s when, according to best estimates, annual labor force increments will drop to less than one-third of the levels of the 1970s. Moreover, most of these smaller increments will come from the Transcaucasian and Central Asian republics, where levels of productivity tend to be lowest. The need for more labor thus must be offset by an increase of labor productivity. This means that in the absence of more advanced technology, many projected industrial targets, including those in Siberia, may go unfulfilled during present and future five-year plans.

One method of bolstering economic growth is to import machinery and equipment. Technological importation curtails the lead time inherent in domestic innovation, but it is expensive and not without problems of managerial adoption and maintenance.

Siberian resource development is inherently important to the acquisition of needed foreign technology. Soviet planners assert that the resource potential of Siberia is more than sufficient to meet the country's domestic and export requirements for untold decades; that the benefits of export will more than counter the cost of development in the long run.

Unfortunately for Soviet planners, Siberian resources cannot be obtained without the very technology required as imports. The imports may be paid for with hard currency or through credit arrangements for long-term, low-interest loans, but both may be scarcer and harder to obtain in the future, especially in light of Western disapproval of Soviet activities in Africa and the Middle East.

Despite the inherent difficulties of developing a region that is so far removed from the Soviet heartland, authorities apparently have made such a decision. Containerized service over the Trans-Siberian landbridge between Nakhodka and Western Europe soared during the 1970s, and owing to favorable freight-rate structures had garnered 15 percent or more of the container traffic between Europe and Japan by the end of the decade. Nakhodka's new port of Vostochny, often referred to as "the Sea Gates of the BAM," is a modern computerized facility that by 1990 is expected to rival Odessa and Novorossisk for the country's leadership in tonnage moved. Vostochny and another civilian port farther north, at Vanino, are being expanded or renovated rapidly (Figure 2).

## Analysis of Incentives to Eastern Development

What motivations lie behind this expansion? Four possibilities are analyzed here. They are, not necessarily in order of importance: the demand for foreign technology, the need for hard currency, the military requirement, and access to raw materials.

Obviously, each of these criteria is closely related. Defense, especially when the Chinese are viewed with such distrust, is absolutely essential to the protection of the development of Pacific Siberian raw materials and potential commercial exchange. Foreign technology cannot be obtained without hard currency by which required credit and low-interest loans can be justified. Hard currency, for the most part, must be accrued by increasing exports, which in the Soviet case, traditionally means raw materials. These raw materials ever more must be derived from the remote and costly regions of Pacific Siberia. So that these resources may be developed, highly sophisticated machinery, equipment, and expertise are demanded. For instance, Pacific Siberia has been characterized by Dibb and others as among the most poorly equipped territories in the world. What is true here does not necessarily hold for the USSR in aggregate. Thus, a disproportionately large percentage of the technology imported into the Soviet Union is destined for Pacific Siberia and for Western Siberia, particularly because of labor shortages in those areas. Simply put, the flow of imports for raw-material development can be sustained only by increasing the flow of raw-material exports to pay for them, and in the regions of likely raw-material surpluses (Pacific Siberia), where human settlement is most sparse, the process must be protected from real or imagined external intervention.

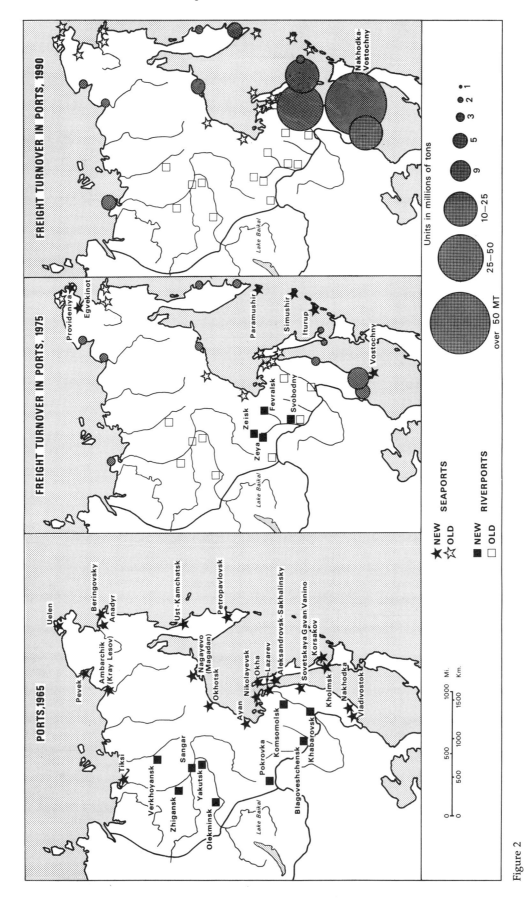

Figure 2

SOURCES: M. I. Galitsky, S. K. Danilov, and A. I. Korneyev, *Ekonomicheskaya geografiya transporta SSSR* [Economic geography of transportation in the USSR] (Moscow: Transport, 1965), p. 74; A. N. Voznesensky et al., eds., *Atlas razvitiya khozyaistva i kultury SSSR* [Atlas of the economy and culture of the USSR] (Moscow, 1967), and numerous other sources. Freight turnover was unavailable for ports where volume is not shown.

Each criterion can be assessed individually from the standpoint of given time periods: 1960 to 1970, 1970 to 1975, 1975 to 1980, and 1980 to 1990. The 1970s are split into five-year increments because of the real shift in the spirit of détente that occurred in the West between the beginning and end of the decade. The relative motivational strengths of the criteria are rated subjectively during each period as weak, moderate, strong, or acute (Figure 3).

## Foreign Technology

Though Soviet authorities have struggled for decades to attract people to major Siberian work projects by means of monetary lures and other unique privileges, they have mostly failed to draw them in satisfactory numbers. Advanced automation and equipment systems have become particularly important in the eastern regions of the country. Therefore, as the need for eastern raw materials has grown, so has the importance of extraction machinery. Since 1960, when the need was weak to moderate, the requirement for improved technology has increased to almost acute levels, and by 1990 is expected to be most severe. This incentive is fundamental to the Soviet policy of détente.

## Hard Currency

Because of the nonconvertibility of the ruble, Soviet leaders have always needed reserves of hard (convertible) currency for commercial dealings with the West. In the 1970s, when they decided to dramatically expand their trade relations with non-socialist countries, the need for exchangeable income reached unprecedented levels (see Chapters 27 and 30). With credit imbalances encouraged by crop failures and possible oil shortages, this requirement should grow more acute in the 1980s.

## Military

Emigres to the West, who reportedly worked for planning agencies responsible for designing the BAM in the 1960s, contend that the needs of the military were the only reasons to be considered in plans at that time. The fact that renewed planning of the BAM rose in almost direct proportion to an increased awareness of a "Chinese threat" only enhances the probability that in the beginning the railroad was a military project. The obvious vulnerability of the Trans-Siberian Mainline needs only to be mentioned for emphasis. And, as the 1979 confrontation between China and Vietnam has indicated, Soviet authorities feel painfully insecure about their Pacific extremity. No doubt this problem will remain sensitive well into the 1980s. For purposes of this analysis, the issue of strength is related to the prospective strict allocation of human resources. Because of the incipient manpower shortage, it would appear to be physically difficult for Soviet military strategists to deploy any further troop strength to their eastern regions without weakening their defenses elsewhere or weakening the overall economy. More sophisticated weaponry and "peace offensives" in the West (and East) would help to maintain the "strong" quality, but by the end of the 1980s, Soviet military presence in Pacific Siberia probably will be less evident proportionally than it was in the early years.

## QUALITATIVE ASSESSMENT OF INCENTIVES FOR PACIFIC DEVELOPMENT

| PERIOD \ INCENTIVE | TECHNOLOGY | HARD CURRENCY | MILITARY | ACCESS TO RAW MATERIALS |
|---|---|---|---|---|
| 1960–70 | Weak–Moderate | Moderate | Acute | Weak– Moderate |
| 1970–75 | Strong | Strong | Strong | Moderate |
| 1975–80 | Strong–Acute | Acute | Strong | Moderate–Strong |
| 1980–90 | Acute | Acute | Strong–Moderate | Strong |

Figure 3

## Raw Materials Access and the BAM

Although the military variable should remain a dominating force in Soviet strategic use of the BAM, outweighing all other factors in times of defensive alert,[6] the requirements for technology, hard currency, and access to raw materials should grow in importance through 1990. Of the three, resource accessibility and development ultimately could become the most important, for in the long run the BAM is slated to obtain a resource-development posture.[7] A clear-cut purpose of the new railroad is the assimilation of virgin raw materials for both domestic and international markets. This purpose has rung clear in the Soviet literature published since the March 1974 an-

nouncement of new BAM construction.[8] The timing of the announcement fell within a year after the Arab oil embargo, and in the early plans for the BAM, West Siberian oil movements eastward toward the Pacific were envisaged as a major traffic component.[9] The subsequent tightness of the Soviet oil supply has probably forced Soviet planners to modify the early projections.

The importance of the BAM project can be explained in large part by depletion or stagnation of resource reserves in the heavily populated European part of the Soviet Union, inducing planners to seek raw materials in resource-rich, but environmentally hostile Siberia.[10] The cost of developing the Siberian potential is almost prohibitive with standard technology, and Soviet planners

TABLE 1
Soviet Role in the World Mineral Supply, 1975
(thousand metric tons unless otherwise specified)

| Symbol | Major commodities | Production[1] | Imports[2] | Exports[2] | Apparent consumption | Share of world production | Rank in world production(%) | Self-sufficiency[3] (%) | Reserves[1] |
|---|---|---|---|---|---|---|---|---|---|
| Al | Aluminum | 1,700 | — | 500 | 1,030 | 12 | 2 | 140 | XX |
| Sb | Antimony, in ore | 8 | 1 | — | 9 | 11 | 4 | 90 | 150 (metal) |
| Asb | Asbestos | 1,900 | — | 600 | 1,300 | 46 | 1 | 150 | 100,000 |
| Ba | Barite | 350 | 330 | — | 680 | 7 | 2 | 50 | 10,000 |
| Al | Bauxite, 26%–52% $Al_2O_3$ | 4,400 | 3,500 | — | 7,900 | 6 | 5 | 60 | 250,000 |
| Cem | Cement[3] | 122,000 | 800 | 3,300 | 119,500 | 17 | 1 | 100 | Large |
| Cr | Chromite | 2,100 | — | 1,200 | 900 | 26 | 1 | 230 | 100,000 (ore) |
| C | Coal:[4] | | | | | | | | |
| | Anthracite[3] | 77,000 | — | 4,500 | 72,500 | 42 | 1 | 110 | 334,000,000[3] |
| | Bituminous[3] | 461,000 | 9,800 | 21,400 | 449,400 | 20 | 1 | 100 | |
| Co | Cobalt, in ore | 2 | — | — | 2 | 5 | 6 | 100 | 100 (metal) |
| Cu | Copper, refined | 770 | 10 | 210 | 570 | 11 | 2 | 130 | 45,000 (metal) |
| Dm | Diamond: | | | | | | | | |
| | Gem (M carats) | 1,900 | — | Large | NA | 18 | 1 | NA | 30,000 |
| | Industr. (M carats) | 7,750 | — | Large | NA | 25 | 2 | NA | 120,000 |
| F | Fluorspar | 480 | 490 | — | 970 | 11 | 2 | 50 | 10,000 |
| Gas | Gas, natural (MM m³) | 289,000 | 12,000 | 19,000 | 282,000 | 21 | 2 | 100 | 25,000,000 |
| Au | Gold (M tr. oz.) | 7,500 | — | 4,350[1] | 3,150 | 19 | 2 | 240 | 200,000 |
| Fe | Iron ore, 55%–63% Fe[3] | 232,800 | — | 43,600 | 189,200 | 27 | 1 | 120 | 111,000,000 (ore)[3] |
| Pb | Lead, refined | 480 | 60 | 100 | 440 | 14 | 1 | 110 | 17,000 (metal) |
| Lig | Lignite[3] | 164,000 | — | — | 164,000 | 19 | 2 | 100 | 190,000,000[3] |
| Mn | Manganese ore[3] | 8,500 | — | 1,400 | 7,100 | 34 | 1 | 120 | 2,600,000 (ore)[3] |
| Ni | Nickel, in ore | 152 | Some | Some | 150 | 19 | 2 | 100 | 6,000 (metal) |
| Oil | Petroleum, crude[3] | 490,800 | 6,500 | 93,100 | 397,700 | 18 | 1 | 120 | 10,000,000 |
| Oil | Petroleum, products | 344,000 | 1,100 | 37,300 | 306,700 | 15 | 2 | 110 | XX |
| P | Phosphate rock[3,5] | 24,100 | 130 | 530 | 23,700 | 22 | 2 | 130 | 5,400,000 (ore)[3] |
| Pt | Platinum-group metals (M tr. oz.) | 2,650 | — | 750[1] | 1,900 | 46 | 1 | 140 | 100,000 |
| K | Potash ($K_2O$)[3] | 7,900 | — | 2,200 | 5,700 | 36 | 1 | 150 | 3,800,000 $K_2O$[3] |
| Steel | Steel, crude[3] | 141,400 | — | — | 141,400 | 22 | 1 | 100 | XX |
| S | Sulfur | 8,200 | 690 | 440 | 8,450 | 16 | 2 | 100 | 500,000 |
| Sn | Tin, in ore | 30 | 10 | — | 40 | 13 | 2 | 80 | 800 (metal) |
| Ti | Titanium | 30 | — | Some | 30 | NA | NA | 100 | 900 (metal) |
| W | Tungsten, in ore | 8 | 4 | — | 12 | 21 | 2 | 70 | 150 (metal) |
| Zn | Zinc, refined | 690 | 45 | 100 | 635 | 12 | 2 | 110 | 22,000 (metal) |

NA—Not available. XX—Not applicable.
[1]Estimated.
[2]Reported in Soviet sources. Trade data taken from *Foreign Trade of the USSR*, Moscow, 1976.
[3]Self-sufficiency is expressed as a ratio of mine production to consumption of primary material.
[4]Run-of-mine coal. The average ash content of coal shipped from mines was 20% and the average calorific value of coal and lignite was little more than 5,000 kilocalories per kilogram (9,000 Btu per pound) in 1975.
[5]Approximately 30% $P_2O_5$.
SOURCE: U. S. Department of Interior, Bureau of Mines, *Mineral Industries of Eastern Europe and the USSR* (Washington: U. S. Government Printing Office, 1978), p. 27.

have found it expedient, since 1972, to buy advanced machinery from the West instead of developing it domestically. The export of raw materials that may be made accessible by the BAM can be considered one way of paying for those machinery imports. In any event, the BAM, by giving access to new raw material sources in Siberia, is expected to enhance further the already strong position of the Soviet Union as a producer of many raw materials (Table 1).

The purpose of this chapter, first, is to analyze the BAM's resource base in detail, defining the raw materials with the greatest potential for export and attraction of hard currency. In light of the cost of BAM construction, the earning power of a particular resource must be considered a key factor in deciding which raw materials should be developed first. It should be added that this problem is one currently being addressed by Soviet planners themselves.[11]

Second, having assumed that resource exportability is an important priority in BAM materials' development, the impact of the railroad on its service area is examined. This includes a study of regional labor and infrastructural requirements as well as environmental and technological constraints.

Finally, considering the total expense of resource development in the BAM service area, the following questions are dealt with:

1. What are the commercial implications of BAM resources, especially for countries of the Pacific Basin?
2. What countries are in the best position to compete with the Soviet Union for those markets?
3. In respect to the many competing variables and forces, what role (or roles), if any, will the BAM and its resources play in the formulation of Soviet strategy in the Far East and the Pacific?

**Improving Transport Access**

Greater interest in foreign trade and higher world prices—whether or not the latter are manipulated or encouraged by Soviet strategists—is not the only factor enhancing the global significance of Soviet raw materials. Whatever their international aims, Soviet officials must improve access to remote resource-development areas at home.

The resource endowment of Siberia is isolated by vast tracts of uninhabited and undeveloped wilderness. Except along its southernmost tier, reliable transportation routes are virtually nonexistent. Siberia's inchoate transport network, even today, is limited mainly to rivers that are frozen for over half the year, cumbersome winter roads, expensive air transport, and the Trans-Siberian Railroad and its feeders. Because of domestic resource requirements and their growing appreciation for the value of exports, Soviet authorities, in the last 15 years, have taken steps to improve accessibility to Siberian raw materials.

First, owing to low-cost capital investment needs and its relative cheapness, river freight transport has increased steadily. The Siberian share of Soviet river traffic has grown and is expected to reach 28 percent by 1985 compared with 26.6 percent in 1980.[12] In some provinces, Tomsk Oblast for example, rivers carry three-quarters of the industrial transport burden. Since 1960, the length of navigable waterways in the Ob-Irtysh basin, serving the West Siberian oil and gas region, has increased by almost a third. Most navigational improvements are the result of intensified dredging of smaller rivers. This is especially true of the watersheds of the lower Ob River and the Soviet Far East, where the proportion of small rivers in river-borne cargoes exceeds 25 percent. Despite problems of direction, silting, and winter icings, on a per-capita basis, Siberian rivers carry 2.5 times as much freight as the average for the country as a whole (Table 2).

Second, motor-vehicle transport and airline services have improved. Trucks of greater capacity and of northern design now negotiate iced-over rivers or utilize winter roads. Faster, heavier aircraft like the Ilyushin series (IL-62 and IL-86) and Antonov class (AN-12, AN-26, and AN-72) are increasingly available. More than 70 percent of all passenger traffic in Pacific Siberia is by air. All rayon centers are connected by regional air service, and villages and towns are linked by mail planes and helicopters.[13]

The most significant transportation developments have occurred in the construction of pipelines and railroads. Because of increased production of oil and gas in West Siberia since 1965, Soviet construction crews have laid, on average, the equivalent of one Alaska pipeline every five or six weeks. The total length of natural gas pipelines has trebled since 1965 from 41,800 kilometers to 132,000 by 1980, with a further increase to 180,000 projected by 1985.[14] Indeed, pipeline transport has grown so swiftly that it now represents 10 percent of all Soviet freight and is expected to double by 1990 (Table 3).

In addition to the significant contribution of pipelines to the economy during the last 15 years, the length and quality of the rail network also continue to expand.[15] In Siberia, the two most important railroad projects are the Surgut-Urengoi railroad in West Siberia (completed in 1982) and the BAM in Pacific Siberia. The former is designed to supply oil and natural gas fields; the latter is slated to develop the complex resource base of northern Transbaikalia, southern Yakutia, and the Amur Basin.

TABLE 2
Siberian River Freight Turnover, 1970 and 1978
(in millions of metric tons)

| River Basin | Turnover | | Percentage | |
|---|---|---|---|---|
| | 1970[a] | 1978[b] | 1970 | 1978 |
| Ob-Irtysh | | 50 | | 43 |
| Other Siberian and Far Eastern Rivers, including the Lena | 74 | 66 | | 57 |
| | | (10) | | (8–9) |
| Totals | 74 | 116 | 100 | 100 |

[a]*Transport i svyaz* [Transport and communications] (Moscow: Statistika, 1972), p. 169. The 1970 Siberian figure represented 20.7 percent of the Soviet total. The 1978 figure was closer to 26 percent. The population of Siberia remains about 10 percent of the Soviet total.
[b]V. Ye. Biryukov, "Strategiya kompleksnogo podkhoda" [The strategy of a complex approach], *Gudok*, 29 August 1978, p. 2.

TABLE 3
Soviet Transport Balance, 1970–90
(percent of freight movement in ton-kilometers)

| Mode of Transport | 1970[a] | 1980[a] | 1990 (Projected)[b] |
|---|---|---|---|
| Railroad | 65 | 56 | 47 |
| Seagoing | 17 | 14 | |
| Inland waterways | 4.5 | 4 | |
| Pipeline (crude oil and products) | 7.4 | 19 | 27 |
| Trucking | 5.8 | 7 | |
| Air | Trace | Trace | |
| Totals | 100 | 100 | |

[a]*Narodnoye khozyaistvo SSSR v 1980* [The economy of the USSR in 1980] (Moscow: Finansy i Statistika, 1981), p. 293.
[b]V. Biryukov, "Arterii ekonomiki" [Arteries of the economy], *Izvestiya*, 19 December 1978, p. 2.

## A BAM Update

The BAM service area (Figure 4) straddles the route of the railroad in a swath 300 to 500 km wide and covering 2 million km², or an area three times as large as France. This includes portions of five major civil divisions of the Russian Republic (RSFSR): Irkutsk Oblast (a linear segment of 290 km); Buryat ASSR (510 km); Chita Oblast (400 km); Amur Oblast (1,600 km, including the Little BAM); Yakut ASSR (150 km of Little BAM); and Khabarovsk Krai (600 km).[16]

Before 1974, this region was populated by 4,000 people outside the city limits of Ust-Kut, Tynda, and Komsomolsk (total population of 265,000). Only 600 of these rural residents lived in the Buryat segment.[17] Since then, over 200,000 people, 35,000 of them in Buryatia, have been drawn to various parts of the service area.[18]

In eight years, the accomplishments of the BAM work-

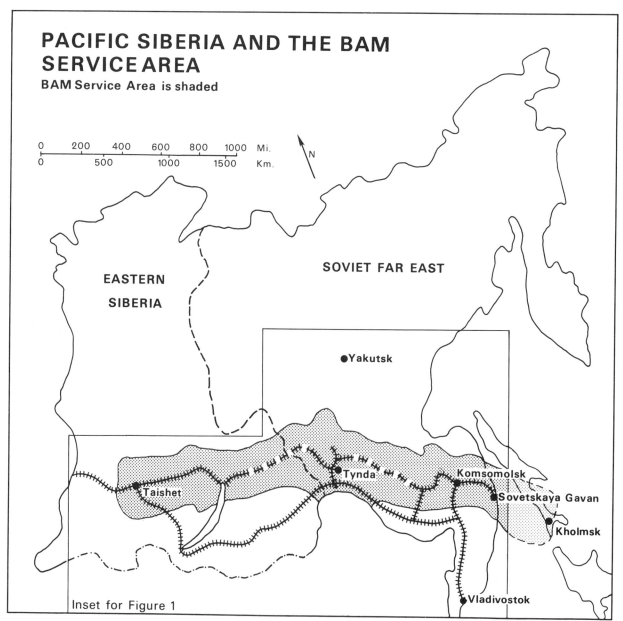

**PACIFIC SIBERIA AND THE BAM SERVICE AREA**

BAM Service Area is shaded

EASTERN SIBERIA

SOVIET FAR EAST

●Yakutsk

●Tynda

Komsomolsk

Taishet

Sovetskaya Gavan

Kholmsk

●Vladivostok

Inset for Figure 1

Figure 4

ers, at least a quarter of whom are army railroad troops, have been impressive. Including the completion of the Little BAM (1978–79; to be extended ultimately to Yakutsk), reconstruction of the Postyshevo-Komsomolsk line (1980) and progress on the second track between Taishet and Ust-Kut, over 2,700 km of rails were laid by Jan. 1, 1981 (Table 4) and some 3,050 km by June 1, 1982, or 65 percent of the total. Dozens of bridges small and large have been built. Two of the nine tunnels (the Dusse-Alin in Khabarovsk Krai and Nagorny on the Little BAM in Yakutia) are open for use, and work has started on others.

Regular rail traffic has begun to flow on some 870 km of track, including the sections from Ust-Kut to Kunerma, Urgal to Komsomolsk, and from Bamovskaya Station to Neryungri were open to freight and passenger traffic. Cargoes over the latter already exceed three million tons per year.[19] Limited traffic, including "temporary service" and railroad-logistics operations, is allowed on other sections. In the North Baikal Range, a temporary bypass is being used pending completion of the Baikal Tunnel. In addition to the earlier Lena and Amur bridges (460 m and 1,500 m, respectively), major crossings over the rivers have been completed, including the second largest BAM bridge, across the northern end of the Zeya Reservoir at Zeisk, in May 1982.

Until 1980, the Soviet press consistently declared that railway construction was ahead of targets despite indications to the contrary.[20] Unofficially, BAM authorities confirmed that the goal of completing the railroad by 1983 was unrealistic. Even given a new completion target of 1985, a record pace of railway construction will be required (Table 5). Originally, work on the nine-year BAM project was to proceed at a rate of roughly 186 km per year or a maximum of 0.5 km per day. Early reports suggested the rates would be much greater.[21] However, even the minimum averages have not been met, except in the cases

TABLE 4
BAM Track Open for at Least Limited Use
(1 January 1981; in kilometers)

| | |
|---|---|
| Taishet—Ust Kut (ultimately 720 km) | 283 (second track only)[a] |
| Ust-Kut—Kichera | 404[b] |
| Tynda—Ust-Nyukzha (west from Tynda) | 337[c] (February 1981) |
| Tynda—Tutaul (east from Tynda) | 200[d] (est.) |
| Urgal—beyond Eterkan (west from Urgal) | 200[d] (est.) |
| Urgal—Postyshevo (east from Urgal) | 303[e] |
| Postyshevo—Komsomolsk | 199 |
| Komsomolsk—Sovetskaya Gavan | 400 |
| Little BAM | 402[f] |
| Total in Use | 2,728 |

[a]Korolkov, "BAM: Crossing new hurdles," *Gudok*, 22 January 1980, p. 1; V. Yermolayev and I. Kazmin, "On the Second Track," *Pravda*, 10 November 1978, p. 2.
[b]I. Korolkov, "The first train is in Kichera," *Gudok*, 26 December 1980, p. 1.
[c]*Izvestiya*, 23 February 1981.
[d]"BAM: railroad and construction project," *Gudok*, 17 September 1980, p. 2; *Stroitelnaya Gazeta*, 7 January 1981.
[e]R. Minasov "The BAM: The rails have arrived in Urkaltu," *Gudok*, 22 June 1979, p. 1.
[f]A. Loginov, "Motherland, take the coal of South Yakutia," *Gudok*, 27 October 1978, p. 1.

of the Little BAM and the Eastern Ring. To finish on time, construction crews must increase their track-laying pace nearly fourfold—an almost impossible task since the highest actual rates appear to be short of the original plan. Work has proceeded especially slowly on the Western BAM and on the Eastern BAM between Tynda and Urgal. Even if the highest rates of track construction are used to estimate the year of completion, the BAM cannot be finished until the mid-1980s. Unofficial statements by Soviet planners suggest a revised target of 1987.[22]

Despite the bottlenecks and construction delays, over 60 new settlements have been built along the BAM route (Figure 5). On the Western BAM, rail-laying crews advancing eastward beyond the north end of Lake Baikal were on the approaches to the Muya Tunnel in late 1982, while workers advancing westward from Tynda had crossed the Olekma River and were approaching the Chara area. On the Eastern BAM, railroad troops moving eastward from Tynda crossed the upper end of the Zeya River reservoir in May 1982, while crews moving northwest from Urgal were approaching Fevralsk on the Selemdzha River by the end of 1982. At the eastern end of the BAM, track improvements on the old logging railroad between Postyshevo (the former Berezovka) and Komsomolsk had been completed on schedule in 1980.[23] As an aid in construction, a total of 3,000 km of temporary roads have been laid within the BAM service area since 1974.[24]

Tunnel construction has posed a particular problem. By the beginning of 1979, in the mountainous region between the north end of Lake Baikal and the Olekma River, only one kilometer of the 27 cumulative kilometers of tunnel had been finished.[25] Six months earlier, just one-tenth of the 6.4-km Baikal Tunnel had been dug after two years of excavation. During that period, workers had fulfilled only 70 percent of their plan.[26] Major difficulties were associated with the hardness of the rock being drilled and blasted, great quantities of subsurface water, and shortages of supplies, particularly explosives. With new rail access from Ust-Kut, the supply situation seemed to improve. Also, by February 1979, BAM workers had excavated a 200-m vertical shaft to the mid-point of the tunnel, enabling blasting to proceed along two additional axes.[27] Since then, tunnel excavation has gone more rapidly to the extent that there was a breakthrough in the main Baikal Tunnel by the opening of the 26th Party Congress in February 1981.[28]

On Lake Baikal, plans called for the construction of four shoreline tunnels, which were required for environmental reasons. Without them, the railroad would have skirted the lake between Severobaikalsk and Nizhneangarsk. Railway construction and subsequent use undoubtedly would have had an impact on the lake's ecology. The four tunnels, with a combined distance of 5.5 km, were designed to pass through the rugged relief several kilometers from the lake shore. As of 1980, work on the shore tunnels was well behind projected targets.[29]

Some 275 km east of Lake Baikal is the site of what will be the world's fourth longest railroad tunnel, the 15.7 km North Muya project. After the announcement of BAM construction in 1974, it took two years to construct access roads to the remote area and two more years for construction workers to build new settlements, Ton-

TABLE 5
Construction of BAM: Theory and Practice (1 January 1981)[a]

| Segment | Distance (km) | Planned Deadline (yr) | Track Laid (km) | Time Laid (yr) | Planned Rate or Rate Needed to Complete the Segment (km/yr) | Actual Rate (km/yr) | Adjusted Date of Completion Remaining Distance/Actual Rate plus 1980 |
|---|---|---|---|---|---|---|---|
| Western BAM, including: | 1,671 | 1985 | 657 | 6.75 | 155.4 | 97.3 | May 1990 |
| Ust-Kut—Kichera[b] | 404 | — | 404 | 6.75 | — | 59.9 | Completed 1980 |
| Kichera—Chilchi area | 1,014 | 1985 | 0 | 0 | 253.5 | 0 | — |
| Chilchi area—Tynda | 253 | — | 253 | 6.75 | — | 37.5 | Completed 1980 |
| Eastern BAM, including: | 1,270 | 1985 | 703 | 6.75 | 118.1 | 104.1 | February 1985 |
| Tynda—Tutaul[c] | 200 (est.) | — | 200 | 6.75 | — | 34.1 | Completed 1980 |
| Tutaul—Eterkan | 537 (est.) | — | 0 | 0 | 126.8 | 0 | — |
| Eterkan—Postyshevo[c] | 503 (est.) | — | 503 | 6.75 | — | 74.5 | Completed 1980 |
| Other segments: Taishet—Ust-Kut[d] (2[d] track) | 720 | 1983 | 220 | 6.33 | 80.0 | 34.8 | June 1987 |
| Postyshevo—Komsomolsk[e] (new track) | 199 | 1980 | 120 | 1.00 | 120.0 | 120.0 | Completed 1980 |
| Komsomolsk—Sovetskaya Gavan[e] (new track) | 400 | 1983 | 0 | 4.00 | 100.0 | 0 | ? |
| Little BAM, including:[f] | 402 | 1979 | 402 | 6.50 | 55.6 | 61.8 | Completed 1979 |
| Bamovskaya—Tynda | 180 | — | 180 | 3.50 | — | 54.0 | Completed 1975 |
| Tynda—Mogot | 80 | — | 80 | 1.75 | — | 45.7 | Completed 1976 |
| Mogot—Yakutia Border | 25 | — | 25 | .25 | — | 100.0 | Completed 1976 |
| Yakutia border—Berkakit | 80 | 1978 | 80 | .92 | — | 86.9 | Completed 1978 |
| Berkakit—Ugolnaya | 37 | 1979 | 37 | .67 | — | 55.2 | Completed 1979 |

[a]"The BAM: railroad and construction project," *Gudok*, 17 September 1980, p. 1; updated from later reports.
[b]I. Korolkov, "The first train in Kichera," *Gudok*, 26 December 1980, p. 1.
[c]"The BAM . . ." [see above], p. 2.
[d]G. Andreyev, "What gladdens and what worries," *Gudok*, 31 August 1978, p. 2.
[e]Yu. Kazmin, Z. Klyuchkov, and G. Petrov, "Long kilometers," *Pravda*, 16 July 1977, p. 2; A. Ishchenko, "They've taken the baton," *Gudok*, 26 December 1980, p. 1.
[f]L. Shinkarev, "The train goes through Yakutia," *Izvestiya*, 30 October 1977, p. 1. The Little BAM was begun during the winter of 1971–72.

nelny at the western portal of the projected tunnel, and Severomuisk at the east portal. Actual excavation work at the west end finally began in 1978, but had to be halted a year later when the workers encountered unexpectedly heavy flooding from an underground stream with high water pressures.[30] It took two years to excavate an auxiliary tunnel designed to divert the water flow before construction could resume in 1981. Because of the delays, the tunnel is not expected to be completed before 1986 at the earliest, although construction of a temporary bypass across the mountains is supposed to make possible some limited traffic before then. Construction of the 28-km electrified double-track bypass route began in 1981 and was to be in operation by 1983.[31]

## Cost of the BAM

Although Soviet authorities were reluctant to announce an overall cost for the BAM and development of its service area, saying the activity was too complex to price, they volunteered various estimates for track-laying alone. For instance, in early 1975, with little practical experience, the cost of building the mainline from Ust-Kut to Komsomolsk was expected to be 6 billion rubles.[32]

This estimate evidently included expenses for crossings, tunnels, and frontage roads, for by 1978, officials in the Urgal area reported that track-laying itself averaged about a million rubles per kilometer. Construction costs in the difficult western BAM sector no doubt were higher. Thus, at 3,145 km of mainline, expenses for the completed BAM track would be 4 to 6 billion rubles. In fact, expenditures on this single project were 40 percent of all capital-construction outlays for railway transportation during the 10th Five-Year Plan (1976–80).[33]

The fragmentary information that has leaked from unnamed service-area planners suggests that total project costs (BAM plus service-area development) may be 13 billion to 27 billion rubles. A broad range indeed!! Based on the cost factors and evidence volunteered in a book by Yuri Sobolev, the upper end of the range is more likely to be the real cost than the lower end (Table 6). In fact, it is quite possible that the BAM investment ultimately will match or surpass the primary development costs of the West Siberian oil and gas fields.[34] By 1977, the latter had reached 30 to 32 billion rubles accumulated in slightly more than 15 years.[35] The "short-range period" for BAM service-area development would represent a timespan similar in length (1974–90).

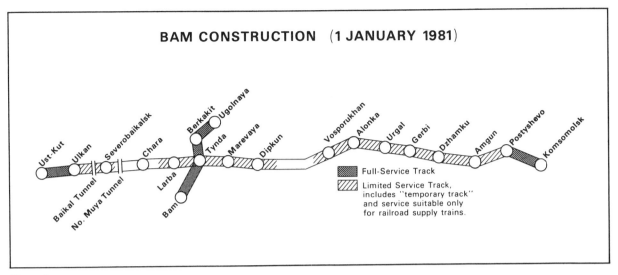

Figure 5
SOURCE: "BAM: Doroga i stroika" [The BAM: Railroad and construction project], *Gudok*, 17 September 1980, p. 1.

## Advantages of the BAM

Although there are alternatives, as Theodore Shabad has stated, "overland transportation is essential" to Siberian resource development.[36] Existing railways cannot meet the needs of the future. Freight flows over the Trans-Siberian, for instance, have expanded 7 to 10 times since 1945; moreover, since 1965, the growth rates of rail shipments in Siberia have outstripped those for the entire country by a factor of three (24 percent versus 7 percent). Lengths of haul have exceeded the national average by more than 100 percent (1,800–2,000 km vs. 936 km). Transport costs are 40 to 400 percent higher than those for the European USSR.[37]

With only one trunk line to serve its needs, Pacific Siberia is particularly deprived of overland connections. Without sufficient all-weather roads, railroad access, and mass-produced experimental vehicles like hovercraft, residents of the region depend more heavily than most on aviation and river transport. However, in the most distant areas, rural folk may see an airplane or helicopter a "few times a year,"[38] and the principal rivers, especially the north-flowing ones like the Lena, often suffer from low water during the brief summer navigation season. Because of shoaling, the Aldan River, the Lena's main right-bank tributary and potentially the most important waterway for the supply of South Yakutia, is navigable for only 10 to 12 days out of the year![39] In some cases, waterborne freight may arrive in a Siberian development site eight months or more after its departure from a shipping head, for example, Osetrovo. Thus, in Yakutia the average share of the total cost of a product that is directly attributable to the expense of transportation is 52 percent.[40]

Inevitably, Soviet planners have opted for the construction of the BAM. Rail transport is relatively swift, hauls a wide variety of freight, performs well in almost any weather, spans vast distances while requiring comparatively less fuel and maintenance than motor transport, and is competitive in comfort with the airplane. Railroads are most efficient for hauling coal, iron ore, wheat, finished steel products, timber, lumber, and most basic commodities; that is, with the addition of oil to the list, precisely the kind of cargo that was originally slated to be hauled by the BAM. Compared to the orientation of the Trans-Siberian, not only is the BAM relatively removed from the China border, but it also results in a net reduction of 240 km between the European USSR and the Pacific ports. It provides access to a broad belt north of the Trans-Siberian and, indirectly, brings an even larger segment of Pacific Siberia closer to the nearest railhead (Figure 6). In so doing, the BAM lessens the freight load on the overburdened Trans-Siberian by 20 million tons.[41]

## Alternatives to the BAM

Originally, the BAM was designed as a specialized oil-tanker railroad. In the wake of the 1973 Arab oil embargo, Soviet planners sought any means of expanding their stock of hard currency through the sale of petroleum at higher world-market prices. The BAM was conceived as helping to serve this purpose by hauling West Siberian oil to consumers in the Pacific Basin, notably Japan. Much earlier, a pipeline had been projected between Irkutsk, Khabarovsk, and Nakhodka,[42] but the project was evidently abandoned in favor of the more versatile BAM. Soviet economic feasibility studies proved that it would be more advisable to build a second railroad specially equipped to haul oil than it would be to rely on the existing railway system and a parallel pipeline. The plan was to move the crude oil via the operational pipeline network from Nizhnevartovsk to Taishet, transship it into volume-efficient eight-axle tankcars, and haul the fuel by super-modern BAM trains to Urgal. From Urgal, a projected pipeline was to funnel the petroleum via Khabarovsk for transmission to Soviet Far-Eastern refineries and port terminals. In this manner, as much as 25 million tons of Tyumen crude oil (fully 70 percent of all BAM shipments) were to be carried annually to the Soviet Far East by 1985 (Figure 7a).[43]

TABLE 6
Estimated Total BAM Service Area Investment
(In billions of rubles)

| Development Project | | Total Cost (italic figures add up to final total) |
|---|---|---|
| BAM railways, tunnels, bridges, earthwork | | 10.600[a] |
| Infrastructure (I), including: | | 1.897[b] |
| Komsomolsk TPC | | .330 |
| Urgal Industrial Node | | .134 |
| Zeya-Svobodny TPC | | .297 |
| Udokan Industrial Node | | .056 |
| Tynda TPC | | .110 |
| South Yakutian TPC | | .200 |
| North Baikal TPC | | .350 |
| Upper Lena TPC | | .104 |
| Rest of Service Area | | .316 |
| Total Industrial and Infrastructural Costs, Based on: | "P-factor" × 1[bc] | 9.610 |
| Komsomolsk | 2.78 × .330 = | .917 |
| Urgal | 5.00 × .134 = | .670 |
| Zeya-Svobodny | 5.00 × .297 = | 1.485 |
| Udokan | — × .056 = | 1.700[d] |
| Tynda | 5.88 × .110 = | .647 |
| South Yakutia | 2.56 × .200 = | .512 |
| North Baikal | 2.27 × .350 = | .794 |
| Upper Lena | 5.26 × .104 = | .547 |
| Rest | 7.39 × .316 = | 2.340 |
| Labor Costs[e] (attraction, salaries, and other labor-support functions) estimated: | | 7.503 |
| Total Investment (sum of italic subtotals) | | 27.713 |

[a]During the 10th and 11th five-year plans, 40 percent of all capital investment in railways has been allocated to the BAM. This probably includes investment in the Little BAM, the Taishet to Ust-Kut second track, and existing railway improvements in the Eastern BAM sector. See *Gudok*, 29 August 1978, p. 2. Capital investments in railroads during the period 1976–80 were expected to be 16 billion rubles.
*Narkhoz SSSR za 60 let* [The economy of the USSR over the last 60 years] (Moscow: Statistika, 1977), p. 437 and *Narkhoz SSSR v 1974 g.* [The economy of the USSR in 1974] (Moscow: Statistika, 1975), p. 525. Total 10th Five-Year Plan BAM investment was therefore 40 percent of 16 billion rubles or 6.4 billion rubles and, if the same patterns persist, 4.2 billion rubles between 1981 and 1983; for a total capital investment in the BAM railway alone of 10.6 billion rubles.
[b]Yu. A. Sobolev, *Zona BAMa* [The BAM Zone] (Moscow: Mysl, 1979), pp. 123, 156, 157, 164, 170, 191, 194, and 199. TPC-development costs represent 80 percent of the service-area investment (p. 208).
[c]The "P-factor" or production factor is the amount by which industrial investments should exceed infrastructural investments (I) expected for a given TPC. The non-TPC factor simply was computed as an average of all the factors (from Sobolev, pp. 207–209).
[d]This figure is quoted in Lawrence V. Brainard, chapter 30 of this book. It is derived from joint-development talks between the Soviet Union and Japan.
[e]An extension of infrastructure category, not included in previous figure. It is based on an allocation of 20,000 rubles per expected migrant (470,000 or more needed by 1990) minus the 1.897 billion rubles computed previously or (470,000 × 20,000 r) − 1.897 br equaling 7.503 billion rubles. The total of 9.4 billion rubles for labor and infrastructure approximates one-third of the total BAM costs, which is almost the same proportion as that allocated to the same purposes in Western Siberia. See chapter 3 and Sobolev, *Zona BAMa*, p. 212 n b above.

Because of the uncertainties associated with West Siberian oil production, doubts about BAM feasibility have been expressed.[44] In the 1970s, around 80 percent of Pacific Siberia's oil and oil products, including exports, arrived by rail. With increased industrial development, demand for petroleum also grew, while local oil production remained unchanged.[45] Volumes of West Siberian petroleum, both for Pacific Siberian domestic and international needs, proponents claimed, simply had to expand. In the early 1970s, few Soviet energy experts foresaw the peaking of petroleum output at Siberia's principal deposit, Samotlor. Although some complained about inadequate exploratory drilling in the Ob Basin, fewer still envisioned a complete absence of additional giant (quasi-Samotlor) oilfield discoveries.[46] Without technological assistance from the West and Japan, critics reasoned, there would be little West Siberian oil left for Pacific domestic needs and virtually none for export to the Pacific Basin by the mid-1980s.

Some antagonists argue that designing the BAM for oil-tanker specialization is self-defeating. Such a specialization, they contend, "will seriously hinder the use of the BAM for the shipment of other freight."[47] With West Siberian oil composing 70 percent of all BAM deliveries, little cargo space is left for service-area resources, whose production the railroad is also slated to promote. Deadheading of the huge eight-axle tank cars (125-ton capacity), reported under construction at Zhdanov,[48] would mean the hauling of 200,000 empty oil cisterns back to West Siberia every year by 1985 (25 million tons divided by 125)!

At least one solution to this problem has been proposed by a Soviet critic. In his view, whatever amount of oil moves from Tyumen to Pacific regions could be carried by the existing pipeline network from Samotlor to the Novorossisk oil port and by tanker through the Suez Canal and the Indian Ocean to Nakhodka-Vostochny (for domestic use), and to Pacific Basin customers.[49] This type of oil shipment would result in a 19 percent savings on transport costs to the Soviet Far East and a 30 percent savings on expenses to Japan (3.6 to 6.2 million rubles per million tons of oil shipped or 90 to 155 million rubles on the 25 million tons that are projected for 1985). Even shipping the fuel around the Cape of Good Hope realizes a saving in comparison to the mixed BAM-pipeline variant. The most important advantage of the sea route, however, is the fact that it frees space for other commodities on the BAM, reduces deadheading, and theoretically permits more rapid regional development of Pacific Siberia (Figure 7b).

## Resources of the BAM Service Area and Its Contiguous Zone[50]

The Soviet Union is well endowed with most of the world's strategic resources. Considering only those reserves of resources recoverable in known areas in accord with prevailing prices and technology, the Soviet Union in 1970 was self-sufficient in 28 of 36 of the world's major industrial raw materials. In comparison, the United

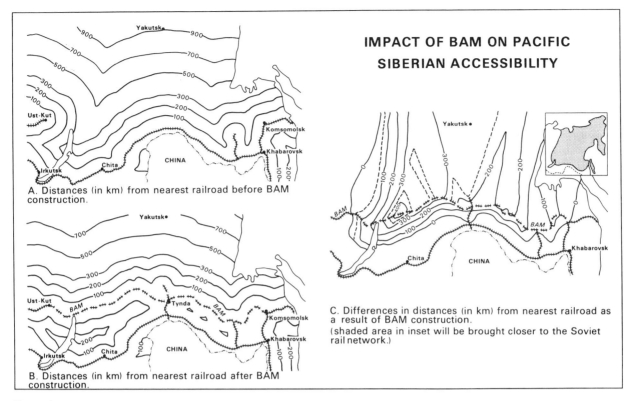

## IMPACT OF BAM ON PACIFIC SIBERIAN ACCESSIBILITY

A. Distances (in km) from nearest railroad before BAM construction.

B. Distances (in km) from nearest railroad after BAM construction.

C. Differences in distances (in km) from nearest railroad as a result of BAM construction.
(shaded area in inset will be brought closer to the Soviet rail network.)

Figure 6
Source: V. I. Poponin, "Changes in Transport Accessibility of East Siberia and the Soviet Far East through Construction of the BAM," *Soviet Geography: Review and Translation*, 19, no. 8 (September 1978): 472–73.

States was self-sufficient in only 13. Because of intensified exploration in geologically promising regions of hypothetical and speculative resources, Soviet recoverable (and conditional) reserves are expected to expand through the end of this century (Figures 8 and 9).

Resource development was of great significance in decision making on the ultimate orientation of the BAM railroad. This has been emphasized by the Minister of Geology, Ye. Kozlovsky: "Frankly speaking, minerals' extraction and processing were basic incentives to BAM construction, *and the largest resource complexes predetermined the selection of the route* (emphases added)."[51]

The resource base of the BAM service area is rich and varied. This is true despite the fact that, by 1975, only 10 to 20 percent of the geologically most-promising areas (Sayan-Stanovoi mountain sequence) had been prospected in any detail.[52] Geological expeditionary work thus has intensified throughout the region. Since 1976, exploration has expanded by 130 percent, so that 20,000 geologists are now out in the field in the BAM zone. Although a few new discoveries have been made, most of the geological work has concentrated on firming up reserves of previously discovered deposits. For instance, geologists' efforts have focused on four main ore complexes: North Baikal; Udokan; South Yakutia; and the vicinity of Komsomolsk. Figure 10 and Table 7 display a current inventory of minerals in the BAM service area and its contiguous zone.

### 1. Asbestos (Ab)

On the Mudirikan River, some 20 to 25 km south of the BAM is the Molodezhny chrysotile asbestos site. Discovered in 1957, the Molodezhny deposit is alleged to be as rich as the Canadian Black Lake and Thetford ore bodies. Although they are far from fully identified, the long fiber resources at Molodezhny are reputed to be larger than the combined total of all other Soviet asbestos deposits.[53] Proved reserves (Soviet *A* plus some *B*) have been established at 18 billion tons of an unusually high grade of long-fiber (12 cm or more) textile-quality ore. An experimental open-cut mine has been in operation at Molodezhny since January 1979. Present plans call for the extraction of 500 tons of the material to determine the appropriate form of processing to be used at the site. A beneficiation plant has been designed for the deposit, where prospecting most recently was conducted between 1960 and 1969. Reports indicate that despite its remoteness, Molodezhny asbestos, which is three times richer than any other Soviet rock fiber, can economically support its own asbestos processing plant along with a mine and concentrator.[54] Exploitation of the Molodezhny deposit, to be reached by a rail spur from Taksimo, will not only eliminate long hauls of asbestos from the Urals to Pacific Siberia but should generate considerable quantities for export to the Pacific Basin.

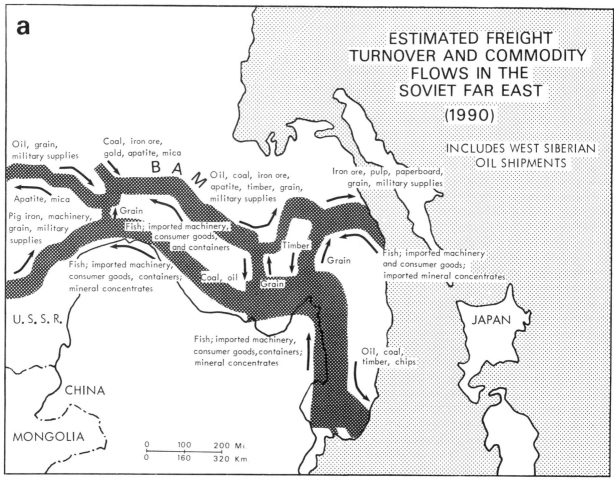

Figure 7a

SOURCE: Victor L. Mote, *Predictions and Realities in the Development of the Soviet Far East*, Discussion Paper No. 3 (May 1978), Association of American Geographers, Project on Soviet Natural Resources in the World Economy.

## 2. Alumina Materials (Aa)

The Soviet Union is a bauxite-deficient territory. In the mid-1970s, the country's aluminum industry relied on domestic low-grade bauxite deposits (37 percent), domestic nonbauxitic materials (24 percent), and alumina-bauxite imports (40 percent).[55] No matter what future exploration brings, it is doubtful that the BAM service area possesses enough alumina-bearing rock to reduce the country's reliance on imports. In fact, the BAM itself may serve as a conduit for even greater imports of bauxite or alumina from Australia and the Pacific Basin.

Two low-grade bauxite deposits of unknown size are proximal to the BAM: on the Goudzhekit River adjacent to the railroad in the North Baikal Range; and on the Marekta River 30 to 40 kilometers farther north. The alumina content of these materials, principally bauxite and nephelitic syenites, is very diverse, ranging from 10 to 75 percent alumina. Most of the ores are considered noncommercial at this time.

Notwithstanding the bauxite deficit, some authorities believe that alumina-bearing resources of the Synnyr

Massif on the border of North Buryatia and Irkutsk Oblast are promising raw materials for Siberian aluminum refineries (Bratsk, Shelekhov, Krasnoyarsk, Sayanogorsk, and Novokuznetsk). The synnyrite rock, which is similar to sillimanite on the Mongolian border, is alleged to be upwards of 57 percent alumina and 13 percent silica. On the whole, the North Baikal association averages only 13 percent alumina, 40 percent silica, 2 percent iron, and 28 percent alkali. Processing of the ore also yields potassium metasilicate (a fertilizer), potash, potassium silicates (dyes, glass, and optics), and cement (in demand locally).

The economic history of Soviet use of exotic nonbauxitic resources like sillimanite and alunite does not augur well for synnyrite; yet, high expectations for the mineral persist among some Siberian geologists.[56] During the winter of 1978, the first ton of synnyrite was extracted from the massif. It evidently was tested for its fertilizer quality at an unidentified chemical plant (probably in the Urals). Thus, in the relatively infertile BAM region, alumina production could be ancillary to fertilizer output where synnyrite is concerned.[57]

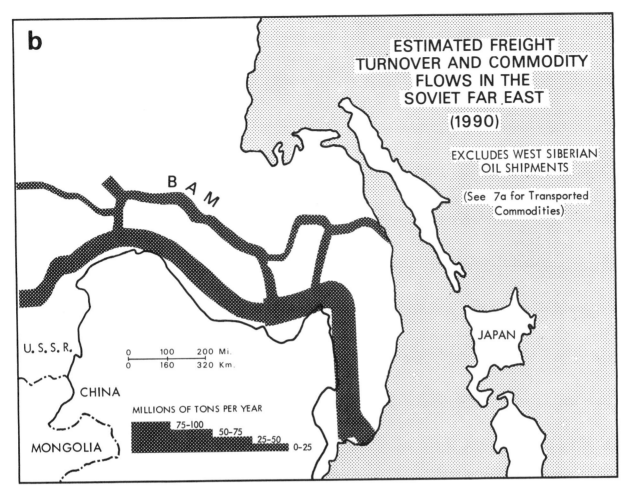

Figure 7b

## 3. Coal (C)

The probable (Soviet: $A + B + C_1$) reserves of coal in the BAM service area and adjacent Maritime Krai exceed 17 billion tons; whereas, the total potential coal resources ($A$ through $D_2$) approximate 68 billion tons. Of the probable reserves, some 12 billion tons are proved in the Neryungri and Urgal districts in the BAM service area, where three-fourths of the fuel is coking variety and strippable. The districts also account for all but 3.5 billion tons of the potential coal resources.[58]

The Neryungri or South Yakutian site is the most promising coal basin in the BAM zone (see Figure 13). Potential resources are estimated at 40 billion tons, comparable in size to the Karaganda Basin. So far, 11 billion tons of coal have been proved in the field, with 500 million tons under development at the Neryungri deposit contiguous to the northern railhead of the Little BAM. Projected annual output from the Neryungri site is 12 to 13 million tons, which can be strip-mined from 20 seams of 10 to 70 meters in thickness, giving this one South Yakutian coal deposit a 40-year lifetime. The Neryungri project is one of only

two BAM activities designated for early development by the 11th Five-Year Plan (1981–85).

Eventually, Japan will receive 5 million tons of Neryungri coking coal every year for 20 years. This export activity was scheduled to start in 1983, but to reach the coking-coal seams, Soviet engineers must remove 240 million m³ of overburden and upper-layer steam coal. This total is more than the aggregate volume of earthwork that is officially designated for the BAM itself (230 million m³)! Because of equipment breakdowns and simple underestimation of the harshness of the Yakutian environment, excavation operations are slow and seriously behind schedule (15 million m³ per annum versus a planned 30 million m³). In other words, unless the work is expedited, the Neryungri coking-coal exports could be delayed for several years beyond the present deadline.[59] In the meantime, the overlying steam coal began to move out of Neryungri over the Little BAM in late 1978 for use in nearby power plants and boilers. This coal traffic was up to 3 million tons by 1982.

In the Bureya Basin is the Urgal coal deposit, with 25 billion tons of potential resources, 2 billion tons of which

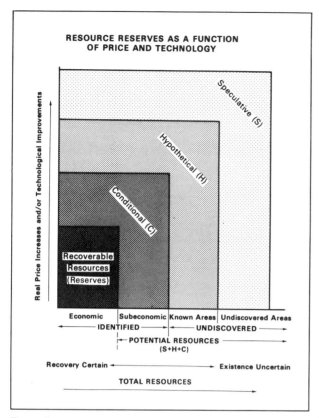

Figure 8

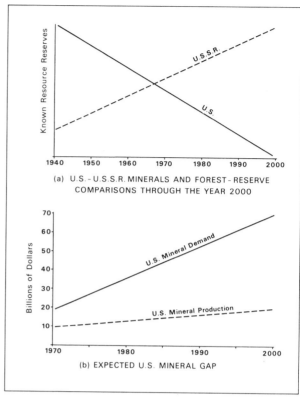

Figure 9
SOURCE: G. Tyler Miller, *Living in the Environment* (New York: Wadsworth, 1975), p. 207.

are classified as possible reserves or reserves in place (Soviet *balansovye*: A + B + C).[60] Although annual output is expected to expand to 5 million tons when the BAM is fully operable, production currently is limited to a single, high-cost, underground mine at Sredni Urgal. Extraction there has been up to 1.2 million tons per year in the recent past, but in 1977 only 500,000 tons was mined.[61] The Urgal mines are now being mechanized and renovated.

Elsewhere in the BAM service area, large deposits of steam coal have been discovered in the Kodar Range near Chara (see Figure 11) and at Nora on a tributary of the Selemdzha River. No data exist on the probable size of these resources.[62]

## 4. Copper (Cu)

Probably the most intensely explored and readily exploitable resource in the BAM service area is the Udokan copper deposit. Discovered in 1948, Udokan is reputed to be the world's largest copper province. The Udokan region, which is 35 km southeast of Chara, is actually an elliptical, northwest-southeast-trending syncline composed of four different deposits, including Udokan, Syulban, Unkur, and Krasnoye. At 12 by 25 kilometers in girth, the entire structure encompasses an area of 300 km² (Figure 11).

The region's copper sandstones, mainly bornite-chalcocites ($Cu_5FeS_4Cu_2S$) and chalcopyrites ($CuFeS_2$), were explored in the 1950s and found to be suitable for open-cut extraction. Potential copper resources were estimated at 1.2 billion tons of 2 percent copper ore.

Udokan is not expected to be developed until after 1985, and even then operations will include only a mine and concentrator. Soviet spokesmen would like to exploit the region jointly with Japanese or American assistance. The first pit is anticipated to yield 20 million tons of copper ore, or 400,000 tons of refinable copper annually. The technology will be of highest quality, including some of the world's largest excavators, Japanese and American bulldozers, 110-ton Belorus dump trucks, and specially designed ore trains, all capable of tolerating temperatures of −60°C. Undoubtedly, a multibillion-ruble investment, the copper at Udokan is so rich and the proposed scale of operations is so grand that the payback period is estimated at only seven years.[63] Proposed sites for smelting and refining of Udokan copper are Abakan, Taishet, Zima, or Nerchinsk.

However, before Udokan can become operational, it requires connections with the outside world. The BAM is the key, but until the railroad arrives (tentatively, in 1983), the site has depended on truck convoys from Mogocha (over 700 km away) during the four winter months alone. Udokan is one of only two priority projects in the BAM service area designated for early development by the 11th Five-Year Plan.

Elsewhere, copper is found in the polymetallic ores of the Chaya deposit north of the BAM, with nickel ores in the Zeya River basin, and in the Namama deposit south of the railroad in Buryatia. The size and richness of these ores are not known.

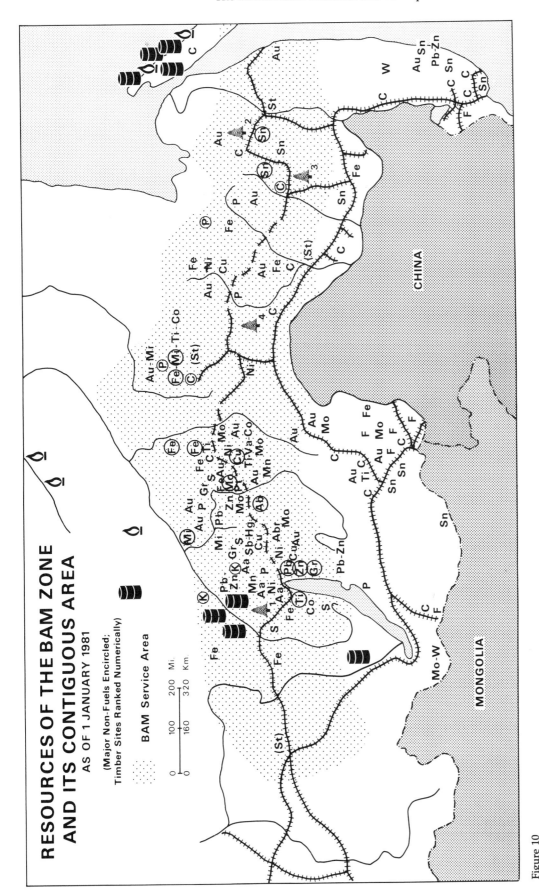

Figure 10

SOURCE: Notes 53–101 of the text.

TABLE 7
Known Minerals within Range of the BAM as of 1979

| | Balance Reserves (Reserves in Place) | | | | |
| | Identified or Proved (A + Some B) | Conditional | | Specu-lative (C_2) | Prognos-ticated Hypo-thetical (D_1 + D_2) |
| Minerals of BAM Service Area and Contiguous Zones | | Probable (Rest of B + Some C_1) | Possible (Rest of C_1) | | |
| --- | --- | --- | --- | --- | --- |
| 1. Asbestos[1] | 24.2 mil T | | | | |
| 2. Alumina Materials | | | | | |
| Goudzhekit[1] | 10–17% Aa in bauxites and nephelitic syenites | | | | |
| Marekta[1] | 20–75% Aa in bauxites and nephelitic syenites | | | | |
| Synnyr Massif[2,3] | 13–57% Aa in "synnyrites" | | | | |
| 3. Coal (c = coking; b = lignite)[4] | | | | | |
| Urgal (c) | | | 2.0 bil T | | 25 bil T |
| South Yakutia (c) | 11 bil T | | | | 40 bil T |
| Tygda (b) | | 466 mil T | | | |
| Raichichinsk (b) | | 318 mil T | | 422 mil T | |
| Artem (b) | | 300 mil T | | | 906 mil T |
| Partizansk (b) | | 300 mil T | | | 1.4 bil T |
| Ussurisk (c) | | 400 mil T | | | |
| Bukachacha (c) | | 39 mil T | | | |
| Chita (b) | | 34 mil T | | | |
| Kharanor (b) | | 1.5 bil T | | | |
| Gusinoozersk (b) | | 530 mil T | | | |
| Sakhalin (b-c) | | 2.0 bil T | | | |
| Luchegorsk (b) | | 721 mil T | | | |
| 4. Copper | | | | | |
| Udokan[5] | | | | | 1.2 bil T of 2% Cu (metal content = 24 mil T) |
| Namama[1] | found in association with As, Sub, Pb, & Zn | | | | |
| Chaya[1] | found in association with Ni & Co | | | | |
| Upper Zeya | associated with Ni | | | | |
| 5. Diamonds[6] | | | | | |
| Yakutia | | | | | |
| Gem | 30 mil C | | | | |
| Industrial | 120 mil C | | | | |
| 6. Gas, Natural[7] | | | | | |
| Vilyui | 857 bil m$^3$ | 1 tril m$^3$ | | | 2.8 tril m$^3$ |
| Irkutsk Amphitheater | | mainly gas condensates | | | 850 bil m$^3$ |
| Sakhalin | 90.7 bil m$^3$ | onshore only | | | |
| 7. Gold[6] | | | | | over 100 mil Tr Oz |
| Aldan | | | | | |
| Kirovsky | | | | | |
| Dambuki | | | | | |
| Solovyevsk | | | | | |
| Polina Osipenko | | | | | |
| V. Darasunsky | | | | | |
| Balei | | | | | |
| Bodaibo District | | | | | |
| Vitim District | | | | | |
| Chara District | | | | | |
| Svobodny-Fevralsk | | | | | |
| Urgal District | | | | | |
| Sovetskaya Gavan District | | | | | |

| Estimated Annual Output (Early to Mid-1970s) | Expected Annual Output (Late-80s or Early 1990s) | Present Annual Exports (Mid-to-Late 1970s) | Expected Annual Exports (Late-80s or Early 1990s) |
|---|---|---|---|
| | 520,000 T | | Large |
| | | | None |
| 1.2 mil T | 5 mil T | | Maybe some |
| | 12–13 mil T | | 5 mil T |
| | | | None |
| 12 mil T | | | None |
| 2.4 mil T | | | None |
| 1.9 mil T | | | None |
| 2.4 mil T | | | ? |
| 1.0 mil T | 1.2 mil T | | ? |
| 2.1 mil T | | | None |
| 1.0 mil T | | | None |
| | 3.0 mil T | | None |
| 5.0 mil T | | | ? |
| 1.5 mil T | 12–14 mil T | | None |
| | 10–20 mil T or .2–.4 mil T Cu | | Much |
| | | | ? |
| | | | ? |
| 1.9 mil C | | Large | Large |
| 7.8 mil C | | Large | Large |
| 520 mil m³ | | | 20.7 bil m³ |
| | | | Some |
| 600 mil m³ | | | 2.4 bil m³ |
| 3–4 mil Tr Oz | | varies: 0–2 mil Tr Oz | Probably Large |

## 5. Diamonds (Shown on Figure 12 as Di)

With the exception of small placer deposits on the Vishera River in the Urals, virtually all Soviet diamonds, both gem quality and industrial, are found in Yakutia (Mirny, Aikhal, and Udachny) along tributaries of the Vilyui River.

Until the discovery of kimberlite pipes in Yakutia, the Soviet Union had no significant resources of industrial diamonds. By 1978, proved reserves of Yakutian industrial stones amounted to 120 million carats, or the second largest reserves in the world after Zaire.[64] Reserves of gem stones were reckoned at 30 million carats. In production since 1957, the Yakutian diamond fields annually yield roughly 8 million carats. Gem diamonds are processed in Leningrad, Sverdlovsk, and Smolensk. A major foreign-exchange earner (300 million rubles in 1974), Soviet stones are marketed in Antwerp through a joint Soviet-Belgian Company.[65] Easily and economically transported as air freight, diamonds undoubtedly will be shipped rarely by rail. The BAM, therefore, should serve as an agent in support of the diamond fields as opposed to an actual means of transport for the mined product.

## 6. Gas

Potentially rich natural gas deposits are on the Vilyui River in Yakutia; on the Middle Botuobuya River in the so-called Irkutsk Amphitheater; and on Sakhalin Island. The Yakutian gas reserves are said to have a potential of at least 2.8 trillion m³ and possibly 13 trillion m³ ($A$ through $D_2$), although only 850 billion to 1 trillion m³ have been reported confirmed by Soviet and foreign field geologists at this time.[66] Like the diamond deposits, the natural gas reservoirs are located outside the BAM service area, but the fuel is expected to play some role in the development of the region, both as a domestically consumed product and as an export. Current output from the Vilyui Basin (at Kysyl-Syr in the Mastakh field) is about 520 million m³ per year, distributed through three pipelines to the city of Yakutsk, some 540 km to the southeast.[67] However, Soviet officials appear to be far more interested in exporting the Vilyui fuel than in keeping it at home.

A trilateral agreement between Soviet, Japanese, and American business representatives for the development of Yakutian natural gas was signed in December 1974, amended in March 1976, and reconfirmed as a memorandum in June 1978. Under the terms of the agreement, a Japanese and American syndicate, the latter composed chiefly of Occidental Petroleum and El Paso Gas, would invest $50 million (1976 dollars) in prospecting and exploratory work. Upon confirmation of a minimum of one trillion m³ of natural gas reserves, reported virtually a reality as of April 1979, the syndicate was to invest at least $5 billion in pipelines, liquefaction plants, and terminals. In return for their shared investments, the Japanese and Americans each would receive some 10 billion m³ of liquefied natural gas (LNG) every year for 25 years, valued in excess of $70 billion.

The question of pipeline routes is still unanswered, although since late 1978 authorities in the USSR evidently

TABLE 7 (*cont.*)

| Minerals of BAM Service Area and Contiguous Zones | Identified or Proved (A + Some B) | Conditional | | Speculative ($C_2$) | Prognosticated Hypothetical ($D_1 + D_2$) |
|---|---|---|---|---|---|
| | | Probable (Rest of B + Some $C_1$) | Possible (Rest of $C_1$) | | |
| **8. Iron Ore[8]** | | | | | |
| Aldan | | | | 600 mil T– 1.5 bil T | 2.2–3.0 bil T |
| Chara-Tokko | | | | | 6–8 bil T |
| Olekma-Amga | | | | | 2–4 bil T |
| Murin[1] | | 30–47% Fe magnetites | | | |
| Tyya[1] | | 36–37% Fe quartzites | | 250–300 mil T | 1.5 bil T |
| Gar | 388 mil T | | | | |
| Kimkan | | 50 mil T | | | |
| Argun | | 500 mil T | | | |
| **9. Lead** | | | | | |
| Kholodnaya | from polymetallic ores of North Baikalia | | | | |
| Ozerny | from polymetallic ores of South Buryatia | | | | |
| Tabor | from polymetallic ores of North Baikalia | | | | |
| Kamenny[1] | Lead-Zinc sulfides | | | | |
| Dalnegorsk | extracted from tin and zinc concentrates | | | | |
| **10. Manganese[10]** | | | | | |
| Oldakit[1] | Vast supplies of Mn-carbonates (5–28% Mn) | | | | |
| Middle Vitim | Shows only | | | | |
| **11. Molybdenum[11]** | | | | | |
| Orekitkan | in Muya Lowland—open pit—large | | | | |
| Katugin | close to Muya Lowland—large | | | | |
| Chara | scattered deposits; probably large | | | | |
| Aldan | trace element in iron ore; small | | | | |
| Shilka-Argun | small | | | | |
| Zakamensk | small | | | | |
| **12. Nickel[12]** | | | | | |
| Tyya-Chaya Districts | Ni associated with Pb – Zn – Cu – Co | | | | |
| Upper Angara District | Scattered large deposits | | | | |
| Udokan-Muya District | Associated with Cu; probably large | | | | |
| Kuvykta-Tynda District | Unknown | | | | |
| Upper Zeya | Associated with Cu | | | | |
| **13. Oil[13]** | | | | | |
| Irkutsk Amphitheater | | | | | |
| Nepa Dome | Presently, site of intense drilling | | | | |
| Markovo | Large, potentially commercial | | | | |
| Syryakha | Large, potentially commercial | | | | |
| North Sakhalin | | | | | |
| Onshore | 10.9 mil T | | | | |
| Offshore | | | | over 100 mil T | 3–5 bil T |
| **14. Phosphates[14]** | | | | | |
| Seligdar | | | | | 3 bil T |
| Uda-Selemdzha | | | | | 500 mil T |
| Buryatia (No. & So.) | | | | | 2.5–3 bil T |
| Zeya River Basin | | | | | ? |
| **15. Pig Iron[15]** | Proposed locations: Chulman, Svobodny, Komsomolsk, or Taishet | | | | |
| **16. Platinum[16]** | | | | | |
| Muya Lowland | Noncommercial deposit | | | | |
| **17. Potash[1,17]** | 18–19% $K_2O$ in Synnyr Massif | | | | over 500 mil T |
| **18. Steel[15]** | Proposed locations: Chulman, Svobodny, Komsomolsk, or Taishet | | | | |
| **19. Sulfur[18]** | | | | | |
| North Buryatia | Sulfides of polymetallics (esp. Pb & Zn) | | | | |
| Iturup | Native sulfur from volcanic extrusions | | | | Large |

| Estimated Annual Output (Early to Mid-1970s) | Expected Annual Output (Late-80s or Early 1990s) | Present Annual Exports (Mid-to-Late 1970s) | Expected Annual Exports (Late-80s or Early 1990s) |
|---|---|---|---|
| | 13–17 mil T | | over 5 mil T |
| | over 3 mil T | | |
| | | | None |
| | | | None |
| | | | None |
| | | | None |
| | | | None |
| | | | None |
| | | | None |
| | will build an agglomeration plant | | |
| small | | | |
| small | | | |
| 2.5 mil T | | | |
| 0.4 mil T | | | 5 mil T (half to Japan) |
| | 30 mil T | | Some |
| | 9 mil T | | Some |
| | | | None |
| | | | Some |
| | 10 mil T | | |
| | | | Some |

have favored a 3,000-km pipeline from the Vilyui fields, running eastward to a point just south of Yakutsk, southward along the Amur-Yakutian motor road to Tynda, eastward along the BAM to Urgal, and southeastward through Khabarovsk to Olga on the coast (Figure 12). American representatives also prefer this route. Earlier Soviet officials argued for a direct, 2,000-km variant between the Vilyui Basin and Magadan, whose port at Nagayevo is kept open by icebreakers. Reluctant originally because of the sea-ice hazard, Japanese authorities reportedly were ready to go along with the Magadan alternative. However, in September 1978, the Soviet side suddenly opted for the longer pipeline: (1) because the gas, mainly destined for export, could be fed to BAM service area development sites through branch pipelines off the meridional trunk and (2) because local electricity demand in the Magadan area would be satisfied by cheap hydropower from the Kolyma Dam, where the first generating unit started up in 1981. Either way, the biggest obstacle rests with financing the multi-billion-dollar project. Without backing from the Export-Import Bank, American companies could hardly invest such sums. Without the Americans, the Japanese could not afford to participate.

A third alternative, once favored by the Japanese, is ostensibly dead. This pipeline would run from the Vilyui fields southeastward across Yakutia to Khabarovsk Krai, under the Tatar Strait to the Okha oil fields on Sakhalin Island, and southward along the length of the island under the La Perouse Strait to Hokkaido.

When and if a pipeline is laid, liquefaction plants would be built at the port terminals, where the fuel would be processed into LNG and exported by tanker to Japan and the Pacific Coast of the United States. The American investment alone would run to $700 million (1978 dollars) for the liquefaction plants and $1.7 billion for a fleet of LNG tankers. Again, the problem lies with financing.

There are related proposals for syndicate assistance in the development of the Middle Botuobuya gas field, whose proved reserves are included in Yakutia's 850 billion $m^3$. In contrast to the proposed Vilyui-Olga pipeline, which is to be 1,400 mm (56 inches) in diameter, the suggested spur to the Middle Botuobuya field is 1,200 mm (48 inches). The entire pipeline distance from the Middle Botuobuya field to Olga is 3,680 km and requires 19 compressor stations with rated capacities of 850,000 to 1,000,000 horsepower each.

Smaller natural gas deposits that are within range of the BAM are situated onshore on Sakhalin (near Okha), and development here may be aided by the BAM as a supply line. Proved reserves amount to only 91 billion $m^3$, but current extraction rates are low.

Officials of the Soviet gas industry have contemplated laying pipelines from Okha to Komsomolsk and from Okha to Hokkaido since the late 1960s, but little has been done to date. The latter pipeline project, described above as an inclusive alternative in the Vilyui deal, was discussed earlier as a joint development activity between Japanese and Soviet concerns. The proposal involved annual shipments of 2.4 billion $m^3$ of Sakhalin natural gas in exchange for Japanese pipeline-development technol-

TABLE 7 (*cont.*)

| Minerals of BAM Service Area and Contiguous Zones | Balance Reserves (Reserves in Place) | | | | |
|---|---|---|---|---|---|
| | Identified or Proved (A + Some B) | Conditional | | | Prognosticated Hypothetical ($D_1 + D_2$) |
| | | Probable (Rest of B + Some $C_1$) | Possible (Rest of $C_1$) | Speculative ($C_2$) | |
| 20. Tin[19] | Probably vast, but USSR is not self-sufficient | | | | |
| Badzhal | Probably huge, but not yet developed (on BAM near Dusse-Alin Tunnel) | | | | |
| Khingan | Worked since 1945; 2 mines and concentrator; new discoveries ⎫ | | | | |
| Solnechny | Largest and cheapest tin operation in USSR; 2 concentrators, many lodes ⎭ | | | | |
| Dalolovo | Near Dalny; lode tin; worked since 1950s | | | | |
| Khrustalny | At Kavalerovo; 2nd largest Soviet output; mines and concentrator ⎫ | | | | |
| Dalnegorsk | Several mines and concentrator; intense prospecting and new discoveries ⎭ | | | | |
| Chita Oblast | Three combines in operation since 1930s; rank last in output | | | | |
| 21. Titanium[1,20] | Soviet Ti is half as cheap as world-market price | | | | |
| North Baikal | Large (17.5 km²) potentially commercial deposit on West Shore of Lake Baikal only 20–30 km south of the BAM; titanomagnetites and ilmenites | | | | |
| Kamenny | Ilmenite-titanomagnetites found with apatite | | | | |
| Chara Lowland | China deposit; associated with Cu, Ni, Co, and Va | | | | |
| Kruchina | Very large (NE of Chita, near Trans-Siberian RR.) | | | | |
| Aldan | Byproduct rutile of iron-ore extraction; small | | | | |
| 22. Tungsten | USSR is not self-sufficient | | | | |
| Vostok | Has increased output, but country will remain dependent | | | | |
| Zakamensk | Mined with molybdenum | | | | |
| 23. Zinc[9,1] | | | | | Probably large |
| Chaya District | | | | | |
| Kamenny R | | | | | |
| Kholodnaya | | | | | |
| Namama District | | | | | |
| Ozerny | | | | | |
| Dalnegorsk | | | | | |
| 24. Other Minerals | | | | | |
| Cobalt | | | | | |
| Chaya[1] | Associated with Ni and Cu | | | | |
| Aldan | Byproduct of iron-mining; Sudbury quality; small | | | | |
| Chara Lowland | China deposit; found with Cu, Ni, Va, and Ti | | | | |
| Mica[22] | | | | | |
| Yanguda R[1] | Muscovite; located by means of remote sensing; details unknown | | | | |
| North Baikalia[1] | Muscovite; commercial quality, but small size | | | | |
| Mama Chuya | Muscovite; producing mines; large in size | | | | |
| Aldan | Phlogopite; producing mines; large in size | | | | |
| Antimony[16] | Associated with Muya Lowland Hg; details unknown | | | | |
| Mercury[16] | Associated with Muya Lowland Sb; details unknown | | | | |
| Vanadium[23] | China deposit; found with Co, Cu, Ni, and Ti | | | | |
| Fluorspar[24] | USSR is deficient | | | | |
| Voznesenka | In Maritime Krai | | | | |
| Kalangui | In Chita Oblast | | | | |
| Graphite[25] | | | | | |
| Ulur[1] | 2.6 mil T (of 30% Gr) | | | | 10 mil T |
| Abrasives[25] | In Buryatia | | | | Large |
| 25. Timber[26] (Roundwood only) | | | | | 15 bil m³ |

NOTE: Table 7 is a largely self-explanatory compilation of data gleaned from Soviet sources. Where quantitative information exists, it has been expressed in Soviet geological categories, which are equated with their closest possible English equivalents. For instance, according to CIA sources, Soviet balance reserves include proved, probable, possible and speculative "reserves in place" (Soviet A through $C_2$), whereas, prognosticated resources ($D_1 + D_2$) are purely hypothetical resources. Where quantitative data are lacking, as with alumina materials, pertinent information on the reserve quality or location is given. In most cases, we can only speculate on relative size.

1. M. L. Alekseyev, ed., *Problemy osvoeniya Severa Buryatskoi ASSR* [Problems of the development of the northern zone of the Buryat ASSR] (Novosibirsk: Nauka, 1978).

2. M. M. Odintsov and A. A. Bukharov, "Mineralnye resursy zony" [Mineral resources of the zone], *Vestnik Akademii Nauk SSSR*, no. 9 (September 1975), p. 47.

3. V. Surkov and V. Botvinnikov, "Baikalo-Amurskaya Magistral: Mineralny kompleks" [The Baikal-Amur Mainline: Mineral complex], *Izvestiya*, 19 August 1976, p. 2.

4. See notes 60–63 in this chapter.

5. See note 65 in this chapter.

| Estimated Annual Output (Early to Mid-1970s) | Expected Annual Output (Late-80s or Early 1990s) | Present Annual Exports (Mid-to-Late 1970s) | Expected Annual Exports (Late-80s or Early 1990s) |
|---|---|---|---|
|  |  |  | None |
| 5.5 th T |  |  |  |
| 4.9 th T |  |  |  |
| 2.6 th T |  |  | Some |
|  |  |  | None |
|  |  |  | Some |
| over 50 th T |  | None | None |
|  |  |  | None |
| 20–25 th T |  | None | None |
| 10–15 th T |  | None | Possible |
|  |  |  | Some |
|  |  |  | Some |
|  |  |  | None |
| over 350 th T |  |  |  |
|  |  |  | Probable |
| 15 mil m³ | 30–35 mil m³ | 8.9 mil m³ | 11–13 mil m³ |

ogy. Both the domestic conduit (between Okha and Komsomolsk), which also was to be built with Japanese assistance, and the export pipeline apparently were tabled as independent projects in the early 1970s, pending more promising finds in the Vilyui Basin.[68]

Finally, in association with oil-drilling operations, dozens of gas-condensate strikes have been made in the Markovo field of the Irkutsk Amphitheater, only 100 km downstream from Ust-Kut, west of the Lena River. No reserve data on this field have been published.

## 7. Gold (Au)

As with diamonds, the development of gold reserves will be facilitated by the BAM. There are just over a dozen gold-placer deposits inside its service area. And with over 100 million troy ounces of potential gold resources and an estimated annual output of 3 to 4 million troy ounces, current horizons for gold in the BAM zone are between 25 and 35 years. Of the total yearly production, up to 2 million troy ounces have been sold to Swiss banks at one time.[69] Gold exports are not expected to be tied so much to the completion of the BAM as they will be to poor Soviet grain harvests and/or commercial strategy. The sale of Soviet gold, usually to pay for imports of grain, is a traditional concern of international speculators because such sales increase Western gold supply and lower prices. In this respect speculators usually hope for a bumper grain harvest in the USSR.

South Yakutia is a leading producer of Soviet gold. With placer deposits almost exhausted, lode-gold output persists around Aldan on the Amur-Yakutian motor road. Elsewhere (Bodaibo, Vitim, Chara, and so forth), placer-gold mining is being conducted or is in prospect.

## 8. Iron Ore (Fe)

Potential resources of iron ore in the BAM service area are estimated at 10 to 15 billion tons, half of which (6 to 8 billion tons) are located in the Chara-Tokko river basins, 350 km west of Neryungri on the border between Yakutia and Chita Oblast.[70] Chara-Tokko iron ore is rich and pure enough to be suitable for direct reduction. It consists of large-grained magnetite quartzite that is low in sulfur, phosphorus, and metallic impurities. The cost of iron-ore mining in this district is alleged to compare favorably with the expenses incurred at other operating sites in the USSR (Table 8).

The Olekma-Amga district, 400 km northwest of Neryungri, bears the second-largest potential resources of iron in the BAM service area. With an estimated 2 to 4 billion tons of iron quartzites, little of the district's ore is geologically established. However, preliminary reports indicate that Olekma-Amga iron may be high in impurities and is probably unsuitable for direct reduction.

Some wildly optimistic predictions about the size and quality of iron ore deposits on the Aldan Upland have been publicized since 1974. Perhaps the optimism has been prompted by the proximity of the ore to Neryungri coking coal. Whatever the reason, previous geological surveys in the region suggest the existence of 2.2 to 3 billion tons of potential resources, including 600 million to 1.5 billion tons in the "identified" category.

The main ore bodies of the Aldan district are 100 km north of Neryungri on both sides of the Amur-Yakutian motor road (Figure 13). The entire region contains 37 different associations and deposits, the largest of which are the Tayezhnoye, Pionerskoye, Sivagli, and Dess magnetite bodies. High in silicates (ranging from 2 to 33 percent), Aldan iron is unsuitable for direct reduction. Its average chemical composition runs from 42 to 59 percent sulfur. Despite its impurities, Aldan ore is expected to be the first iron association to be exploited in the BAM service area, once the BAM goes into operation. Some 13 to 17 million tons of ore are to be extracted from open pits each year. As much as 5 million tons could be exported to the Pacific Basin by 1990.[71] The 11th Five-Year Plan calls for feasibility studies of iron ore development in South Yakutia.

Currently noncommercial deposits of iron ore are located 25 to 30 km north of the Muya Lowland in the Murin River basin and in a dispersed belt of metamorphosed sediments that stretch north from the Tyya River. Both contain magnetites and iron quartzites of 30 to 47 percent iron, and include prognosticated resources in excess of 1.5 billion tons. These sites were discovered recently through the use of aerial photography.

Contiguous to the service area of the BAM are the Gar, Kimkan, and Argun iron deposits, representing a combined total of 938 million tons of probable $(A + B + C_1)$ reserves. Gar iron ore, with proved reserves of 388 million tons, putatively can be beneficiated to concentrates bearing 68 percent iron with the aid of wet magnetic separation. It appears to be suitable for direct reduction.[72] Of the other two sites, the Argun complex would seem to be of better quality, with 500 million tons of 45 percent iron ore in 30 discrete deposits. Although appropriate for open-pit extraction, Argun iron is high in sulfur; an earlier plan for the construction of a 3-million-ton-capacity pig-iron foundry 10 km south of Nerchinsky Zavod apparently has been abandoned.[73]

TABLE 8
Engineering and Economic Parameters of
Iron-Ore Development in the Chara-Tokko District

| Parameter | |
|---|---|
| Production cost of pellets (rubles/ton) | 10–11 |
| Unit investment cost of pellets (rubles/ton)* | 56 |
| Iron content in pellets (percent) | 68 |
| Cost of reduced product (rubles/ton) | 28 |
| Unit investment cost of reduced product (rubles/ton) | 154 |
| Combined ruble cost per ton of reduced product (production cost plus 12 percent of investment cost) | 46.50 |

*Without external investment.
SOURCE: V. S. Sidorova and A. A. Vadyukhin, "New Technology and the Location of the Iron and Steel Industry in the Eastern Portion of the USSR," *Soviet Geography: Review and Translation*, 18, no. 1 (January 1977): 36.

## 9. Lead (Pb)

Potential resources of lead are said to be vast at Kholodnaya and Tabor in the North Baikal region, Ozerny in South Buryatia, and in the Kamenny River basin, a left-bank tributary of the Vitim, 30 km north of the BAM. The North Baikal resources are found along with diverse polymetallic ores. The Kamenny deposits have not been established geologically. Only in an old deposit at Dalnegorsk in Maritime Krai, where lead is processed from tin and zinc concentrates, is the mineral currently produced in any significant amount in all of Siberia.

The Ozerny lead-zinc deposit is actually in the service area of the Trans-Siberian Railroad in the Yeravnoye Lake depression 150 kilometers northwest of Chita. During the 11th Five-Year Plan period (1981–85), a 134-km access railway is to be built to Ozerny from Mogzon on the Trans-Siberian. Construction on the line, which apparently is the first leg of a more than 600-km meridional railroad to Kholodnaya and the BAM, began in the spring

6. U. S. Department of the Interior, Bureau of Mines, *Mineral Industries of Eastern Europe and the USSR* (Washington: U. S. Government Printing Office, 1978), p. 27.
7. See notes 68–70 in this chapter.
8. See notes 72–75 in this chapter.
9. See note 76 in this chapter.
10. See note 77 in this chapter.
11. See note 78 in this chapter.
12. See note 79 in this chapter.
13. See notes 81–83 in this chapter.
14. See notes 84–85 in this chapter.
15. See note 86 in this chapter.
16. Akademiya Nauk SSSR, Sibirskoye otdeleniye, *Atlas Zabaikalya* (Moscow and Irkutsk: GUGK, 1967), p. 28.
17. See note 88 in this chapter.
18. See note 90 in this chapter.
19. See notes 91–92 in this chapter.
20. See note 93 in this chapter.
21. See note 94 in this chapter.
22. See note 95 in this chapter.
23. See note 97 in this chapter.
24. See note 98 in this chapter.
25. See note 99 in this chapter.
26. See notes 100–101 in this chapter.

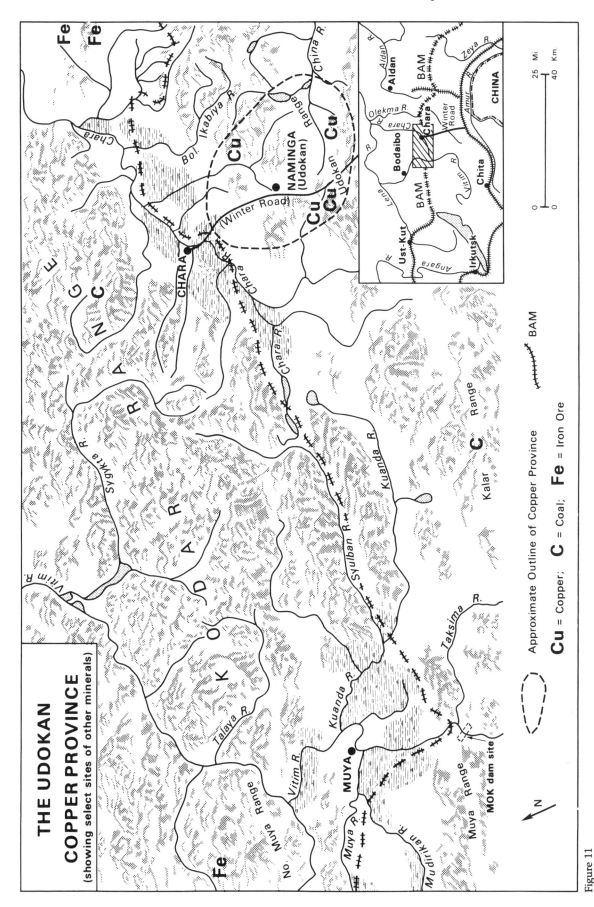

Figure 11

Source: A. I. Karausheva, "Mikroklimat Charskoi kotloviny" [Microclimate of the Chara low-land], *Sibirsky geografichesky sbornik*, no. 8 (1974), p. 146; A. A. Nedeshev, F. F. Bybin, and A. M. Kotelnikov, *BAM: osvoyeniye Zabaikalya* [The BAM and the development of Transbaikalia] (Novosi-birsk: Nauka, 1979), p. 91.

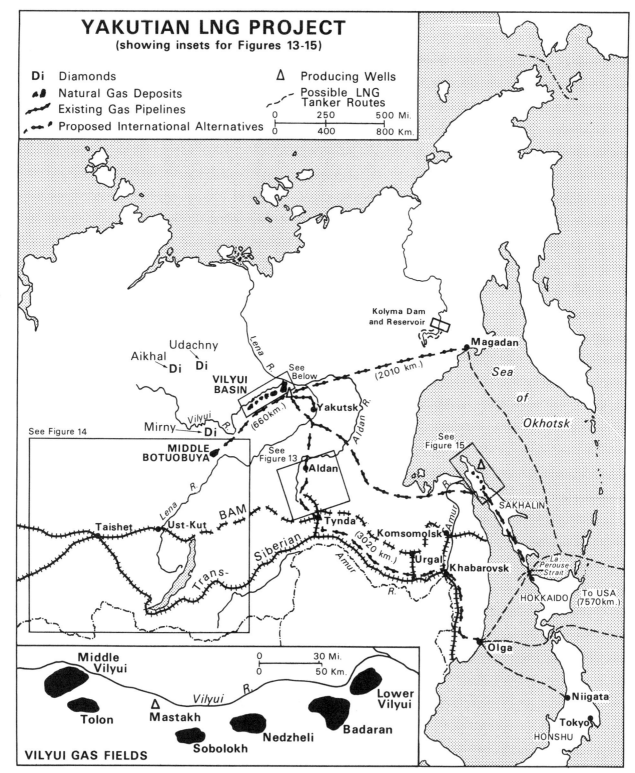

Figure 12

SOURCE: American-Siberian Natural Gas Company, *Yakutia Natural Gas Project* (Houston: El Paso Gas, 1979), Maps 1 and 2; inset is from Arthur Meyerhoff, *Potential for Foreign Participation in the Soviet Union and Chinese Petroleum Industries* (Boston: International Human Resources Development Corporation, 1978), Figure 53.

of 1980. Output from Ozerny and later Kholodnaya should help the USSR to maintain its world leadership in the production of lead and zinc. The country's ore base traditionally has lagged behind smelting capacity in these metals.[74]

## 10. Manganese (Mn)

No large-scale commercial deposits of manganese have been discovered yet in the BAM service area. There are reports of vast supplies of subeconomic manganese carbonates on the Oldakit River 30 km north of the BAM in Buryatia, but the minerals cannot be separated with existing technology. Evidently, manganese indications have also been uncovered in the Middle Vitim region.[75] All of the carbonates consist of metamorphic sediments containing 5 to 18 percent manganese. Some semi-acidic strata possess up to 28 percent manganese. Oldakit is supposed to be comparable in size to deposits at Chiatura and Nikopol. Should processing technologies improve, the Oldakit mineral will be used as a ferroalloy in the BAM zone iron-and-steel industry.

## 11. Molybdenum (Mo)

Molybdenum resources in the BAM service area, particularly flanking the railroad's western segment, are scattered and reputedly large. The biggest site is at Orekitkan in the Muya Lowland region. Here, molybdenum may be open-pit extracted, and an agglomeration plant is planned. Other molybdenum concentrations have been discovered nearby at Katugin and Chara. The mineral is also a trace metal in Aldan iron ore. Small amounts of molybdenum are mined already in the Shilka-Argun basins of Chita Oblast (Vershino-Shakhtaminskiy) and at Zakamensk, south of Lake Baikal. Both of the latter deposits are within the range, but outside the tributary area, of the BAM.[76]

## 12. Nickel (Ni)

Nickel reportedly is found in at least five different locations inside the service area: associated with lead and zinc in the Tyya River district; scattered along the northern bank of the Upper Angara watershed; associated with

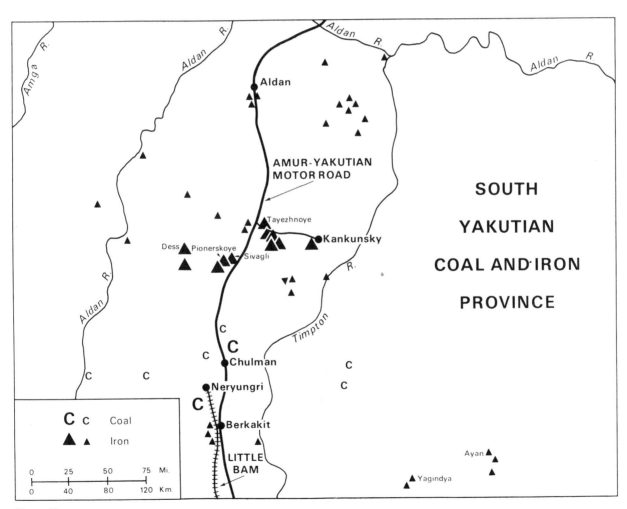

Figure 13
SOURCE: D. P. Serdyuchenko et al., *Zheleznye rudy Yuzhnoi Yakutii* [Iron ores of Southern Yakutia] (Moscow: ANSSSR, 1960), p. 49.

copper in the Zeya River Basin; associated with copper in the Muya-Chara valley district; and along the Getkan River between Kuvykta and Tynda.[77] At the present time no reserve estimates exist.[78]

### 13. Petroleum

Within range of the BAM service area are two broad-based petroleum reservoirs, the Irkutsk Amphitheater and North Sakhalin. The former may consist of more gas than oil. The latter incorporates both onshore and offshore oil deposits.

a. *Irkutsk Amphitheater* (Figure 14). The Irkutsk Amphitheater is an enormous buried anticlinal structure, located northwest of Lake Baikal. It contains three principal drilling sites: Nepa Dome, Markovo, and Syryakha. Although there are severe problems of access, formation porosity and permeability, and development costs, at least one potentially commercial oil strike has been made in each subregion since 1970.

The Nepa Dome is a site of intensive drilling some 450 to 500 km north-northeast of Ust-Kut not far from the border between Yakutia and Irkutsk Oblast. The region is plagued by almost impenetrable taiga and swamp, and logistics are hampered by a short navigation season and lack of winter roads. Consequently, there is a strong tendency to rely on aviation. The costs involved are enormous. For instance, the cost of hauling one ton of freight from Ust-Kut to the Nepa site is 683 rubles by air versus 74 rubles by truck and 31 rubles by mixed water and road. River fleets are of low capacity, with total cargo space for 425 tons, yet a single borehole in the Nepa district requires up to 2,000 tons of materials and equipment. As a result, over 11 million rubles were apportioned to air transport during 1977 and 1978. Another 9 million rubles were earmarked for this purpose in 1979. Plans called for more roads and vehicles in the region. Air freight consisted chiefly of lightweight rigs and equipment. A commercial discovery in the Nepa Dome was reported in 1980 at Voznesenka.[79]

Great potential has been claimed for the Syryakha-

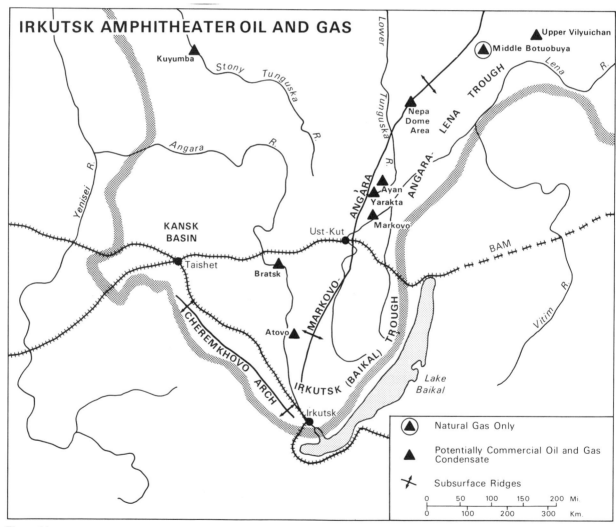

Figure 14

SOURCE: Arthur Meyerhoff, *Potential for Foreign Participation in the Soviet Union and Chinese Petroleum Industries* (Boston: International Human Resources Development Corporation, 1978), Figure 70.

Markovo area, just north of the BAM on the Lena River. The main constraints to the development of these fields are the deep hydrocarbon-bearing formations (over 2,000 m) and the lack of obvious structure. Porosities and permeabilities are poor. Even so, one producing oil well exists in the Parfenovo formation at 2,245 m, and more than 15 gas-condensate strikes have been made.

b. *North Sakhalin Island* (Figure 15). Roughly 11 million tons of proved petroleum reserves remain in the Okha and Sabo fields of North Sakhalin Island. Forming the old delta of the Amur River, the sands and clays of Sakhalin suffer from tension faults induced by subsidence and, as

such, explain the presence of tar and oil muck on the surface of this part of the island. With annual petroleum output running at 3 million tons, the current lifetime of these fields is only 5 to 6 years.[80]

The old delta, including the Odoptu and other deposits, was submerged in the east by the Sea of Okhotsk. In this region during the fall of 1977, a potentially massive oil strike was made. At the time of the discovery, the reserves in place ($A$ through $C_2$) in this single reservoir were estimated at 100 million tons or four times as large as the oil originally in place onshore. Potential resources offshore of Sakhalin have been forecast at up 5 billion tons. As of late 1977, the one offshore test well produced

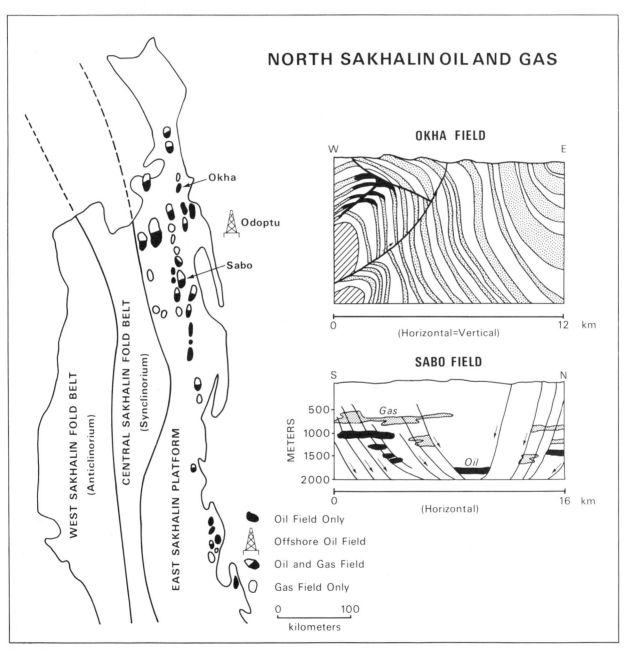

Figure 15
SOURCE: Arthur Meyerhoff, *Potential for Foreign Participation in the Soviet Union and Chinese Petroleum Industries* (Boston: International Human Resources Development Corporation, 1978), Figures 59, 61, and 63.

at a rate of 370,000 tons of oil per year. Under a 1975 joint agreement, the project was managed by the Soviet Oil Ministry with capital investment and technical assistance provided by the Japanese. In return, the Japanese were to receive half of the annual output from the fields.[81]

## 14. Phosphates (P)

Potential resources of phosphates in the BAM service area are estimated to be over 6 billion tons.[82] If true, these resources are larger than the combined total of all other Soviet reserves, including the famous Kola Peninsula and Kara-Tau districts. Probable commercial deposits are located in three general areas: Seligdar in South Yakutia; the Uda-Selemdzha basin; and South Buryatia. New apatite associations have been discovered near Komsomolsk, in North Buryatia, and in the Zeya River basin.

Since 90 percent of Siberian soils are deficient in phosphorus and all current phosphate fertilizer plants are situated in Soviet Europe or Central Asia, the development of a Pacific Siberian industry, theoretically, would be advantageous economically. For instance, transportation costs for a ton of phosphate fertilizer shipped from the Urals to Irkutsk and Khabarovsk are 4.44 and 7.32 rubles, respectively, or two to four times more expensive than it is to ship the same cargo from the Urals to Novosibirsk.

With 3 billion tons of prognosticated phosphorite resources, Seligdar has been suggested as a likely candidate for the construction of a mineral fertilizer plant. Since the early 1970s, there have been plans for a local factory capable of processing 60 million tons of ore per year in South Yakutia. Evidently, sulfuric acid, needed for the production of phosphate fertilizers, could be derived from the byproducts of nonferrous metals smelters using Udokan copper, Kholodnaya lead, and so forth. These smelters are not expected to be located in the service area itself, but nearby on the Trans-Siberian Railway. Otherwise, the thermal-reduction method, requiring much electric power and undoubtedly based on low-cost hydroelectricity or Vilyui natural gas, could be used.

Phosphate ores in the Uda-Selemdzha basin amount to 500 million tons and could serve as raw material for a fertilizer industry in the eastern BAM service area. Their low average $P_2O_5$ content (12 percent) would render them suitable for thermal reduction only. Cheap hydropower from the Zeya Dam and long-range projected structures like the Dagmar and Niman dams could provide the energy source.

Finally, since 1978, the ores of South Buryatia have been given much publicity. Apparently reckoned at 2.5 to 3 billion tons of commercial-quality phosphorites, the deposits are "large enough to meet the requirements of the Soviet chemical industry and Soviet agriculture and to leave a surplus for export.[83] The Oshurkovo deposit, north of Ulan-Ude in the Trans-Siberian zone, evidently can be mined at competitive prices—under 198 rubles per ton versus a marginal cost of 205 rubles per ton for Buryatian ore. Should the fertilizer be processed in the service area, it could be produced from sulfuric acid (Trans-

Siberian smelters) or thermal reduction (Ust-Ilimsk or *Mnogoobeshchayushchaya Kosa* [MOK] hydroelectricity).

## 15. Pig Iron [with (St) on map]

Pig iron production, based on the iron ore of the BAM service area, has been projected at 9 million tons. No final decision has been made with respect to the exact siting of the smelters. Four possible locations have been discussed in the available literature: Chulman, Svobodny, Komsomolsk, or Taishet.[84] The final decision, which may not evolve until the late 1980s, is expected to be influenced by both economic (principally markets) and environmental factors.

## 16. Platinum (Pt)

A single platinum find exists in the Muya Lowland, probably as a placer deposit.[85] No other platinum resources are noted in the literature on the BAM.

## 17. Potash (K)

Reputedly very large potassium resources (over 500 million tons) have been found in the Synnyr Massif of North Buryatia.[86] These are chiefly potassium metasilicates (18 to 19 percent $K_2O$), which yield high quality chlorideless fertilizers. Ostensibly, potash-fertilizer production could develop in concert with alumina reduction from synnyrite.

## 18. Steel [(St)]

Pig iron and steel output from the BAM zone raw materials would originate in the same location (Chulman, Svobodny, Komsomolsk, or Taishet). Crude steel production is projected at 10 million tons per year from a potential integrated plant.[87] The current five-year plan (1981–85) calls for a smaller, 500,000-ton plant producing steel only to be built at Komsomolsk.

## 19. Sulfur (S)

Apparently vast deposits of sulfur compounds and native sulfur exist in the rift zone of North Buryatia. Beyond the range of the BAM on Iturup Island of the Kuril archipelago, native sulfur resources are a product of active vulcanism.[88] The sulfur-bearing ore on Iturup reportedly could support all current sulfur-using industries in the Soviet Far East for the foreseeable future. The raw material has potential in the production of phosphate fertilizers.

## 20. Tin (Sn)

The tin resources of the BAM service area probably are extensive, and they could contribute invaluably to eventual Soviet self-sufficiency in the mineral. Although the USSR is the world's second-largest tin producer (after Malaysia) and its output continues to increase, the country is the fifth largest tin importer. In 1975, the United States Bureau of Mines gave the Soviet Union an 80 percent self-sufficiency rating in tin.[89] Therefore, whatever new tin resources are uncovered in the BAM service area, in the short run, must be applied to the domestic deficit.[90]

Most Soviet tin reserves are located in Pacific Siberia, and a substantial portion is either in, or within range of, the BAM service area. For instance, of a total Soviet production of 25,000 tons of tin in 1975, almost two-thirds of the output originated in Khabarovsk Krai (5,500 tons from two mines), Maritime Krai (4,900 tons from three mines), and Chita Oblast (2,600 tons from two mines).

The largest and most economical tin deposit in the Soviet Union is located in the BAM service area at Solnechny. Along with several lode mines, two tin concentrators are found in the area, which is only 65 km west of Komsomolsk. Linked by motor road with the latter city, a tin smelter is now under construction in Solnechny. Some 100 to 200 km west of Solnechny in the Badzhal Range, just south of the BAM, are the Badzhal tin deposits. Potential resources are reputedly vast, but even with the 1979 completion of the Eastern Ring, tin production at Badzhal is not expected until some time after 1985.

Tin output should expand rapidly with new discoveries in Khabarovsk and Maritime krais. Output in Chita Oblast, however, will probably decline. Depletions there will have to be offset by enhanced production from the BAM service area and Sikhote-Alin mines. Thus, Soviet self-sufficiency in tin will be difficult to attain before 1990. Also, because of the high costs of tin extraction in the USSR, it is doubtful that the Soviet ore will be competitive on international markets before that year, unless it is heavily subsidized (Table 9).

21. Titanium (Ti)

Soviet titanium, in contrast to tin, traditionally is only half as expensive as the current foreign product. Large titanium resources reportedly are located in the North Baikal area along the Kamenny River, and near Kruchina, a rail siding just northeast of Chita on the Trans-Siberian Railway. Other titanium ores are found in association with

TABLE 9
Ratios of Ruble Prices to Dollar Prices for
Selected Soviet Non-Ferrous Metals*

| Metal | 1970 | 1975 |
|---|---|---|
| Magnesium | 0.96 | 0.42 |
| Titanium | 1.07 | 0.51 |
| Gold | 3.47 | 0.68 |
| Zinc | 1.83 | 0.72 |
| Aluminum | 1.04 | 0.75 |
| Nickel | 1.31 | 0.83 |
| Copper | 0.60 | 0.87 |
| Tin | 2.80 | 1.50 |
| Lead | 2.17 | 1.59 |

*Figures do not include transportation costs because they comprise only a small part of the total costs. Ruble/dollar ratios are derived by dividing Soviet wholesale prices by the international price.
SOURCE: U.S., Central Intelligence Agency, *Soviet Tin Industry: Recent Developments and Prospects Through 1980* (Washington: CIA, 1977), p. 4.

copper, nickel, cobalt, and vanadium in the Chara Lowland and as a byproduct of potential iron ore mining (rutile) in the Aldan area.

The Soviet Union is already self-sufficient in titanium ore and metal and is an exporter, without the added benefit of BAM zone discoveries. With new findings in the Timan-Pechora region, the country is in an even better position to export this commodity.[91]

22. Tungsten (W)

No tungsten resources have been discovered inside the BAM service area. However, two tungsten mines are within the range of the new railway. The latest operating Soviet mine and concentrator are located in Maritime Krai about 300 km south of Komsomolsk at Vostok. Under construction since the 1960s, the mine has reached its projected output.[92] An older facility on the Dzhida River at Zakamensk produces tungsten and molybdenum. A new tungsten deposit has been uncovered on the Dzhida, and outputs are expected to increase. The new increments should be welcome to Soviet officials because the country is only 70 percent self-sufficient in tungsten.

23. Zinc (Zn)

Though no reserve data are available, zinc deposits in North Buryatia (Chaya, Kamenny, and Namama districts) are probably large. The metal also is associated with the polymetallic ores of Kholodnaya and the lead of Ozerny.

24. Other Minerals

a. *Cobalt* (Co). No statistics on the BAM service area cobalt reserves exist in the available literature. The metal lies with nickel and copper in the Chaya deposit of North Buryatia. Sudbury-quality cobalt is known to be associated with Aldan iron ore. Elsewhere, in the Chara-Tokko region, the mineral is found together with copper, nickel, vanadium, and titanium.

b. *Mica* (Mi). Although strategic-grade mica evidently is deficient in the USSR, large potential resources of both muscovite (potassium) and phlogopite (magnesium) mica are located within the BAM service area near the confluence of the Mama and Chuya rivers, and on the Aldan Upland, respectively.[93] In recent years, Soviet mica production has been over 50,000 tons per annum, exclusive of 725 tons of high-grade imports. An estimated 20,000 to 25,000 tons of muscovite are produced from the Mama-Chuya mines and 10,000 to 15,000 tons of phlogopite are extracted in the Aldan Region (Kankunsky). The Aldan mines yield 40 to 60 percent raw mica. The commodity is shipped to processing centers which are closer to European markets. Space imagery indicates the existence of muscovite in the Yanguda River region of North Buryatia. Small commercial-quality muscovite deposits are located on the western shore of Lake Baikal.

c. *Antimony* (Sb) and *Mercury* (Hg). Antimony and mercury deposits of unknown potential are found together in the Muya Lowland of the BAM service area. For the time being, because it is one of the few minerals in which the Soviet Union is deficient, BAM antimony is expected to be retained for domestic use. Mercury, on the other hand, is found in excess quantity and may be exported to Pacific-rim countries.[94]

d. *Vanadium* (Va). Within the BAM service area, potential resources of vanadium have been found in association with titaniferous magnetite ores in the Chara-Tokko complex. The raw vanadium ore of the BAM region conceivably can be exported more easily to consumers in the Pacific Basin than to processing centers in the Urals (Nizhni Tagil and Chusovoi).[95] This contingency already is reinforced by the fact that the Soviet Union is an important producer and exporter of vanadium.

e. *Fluorspar* (F). The USSR is only 50 percent self-sufficient in fluorspar. Unfortunately for Soviet planners, no new fluorspar deposits have been discovered in the BAM service area. Interestingly, though, the vast majority of domestic production comes from regions which are contiguous to the tributary area in Maritime Krai (Voznesenka), Chita Oblast (Kalangui and others), and Buryatia. Soviet fluorspar imports derive from Pacific-rim areas also (Mongolia, China, Thailand, and Japan).[96]

f. *Graphite* (Gr) and *Abrasives* (Abr). Considerable volumes of potential resources of graphite and abrasives have been uncovered in North Buryatia.[97] The Ulur graphite deposit, which is 110 km south of the BAM on the eastern shore of Lake Baikal, is reckoned to be the USSR's richest graphite source (30 percent graphite). Identified reserves equal 2.6 million tons and hypothetical resources may amount to 10 million tons at Ulur.

## 25. Timber

Estimated resources of BAM service area timber vary between 1.4 billion $m^3$ of mature timber and 15 billion $m^3$ of exploitable wood of all ages, depending on the width of the belt on either side of the railway. Inclusive of a 400-km swath, total mature timber resources are alleged to be just over 9 billion $m^3$ of roundwood.[98] Current logging operations cut 15 million $m^3$ of timber per year. Once the BAM is fully operational (1985), yields are expected to expand to 30 to 35 million $m^3$, at least a third of which are to be exported.[99]

## The Export Potential of Resources in the Bam Service Area and its Contiguous Zone

A major goal of this book is to determine probable Soviet export potential in selected energy and industrial raw materials to the year 1990. This chapter contributes to that aim by analyzing the export potential of the resources of the BAM service area and its contiguous zone and by assessing the potential impact of those resources on future markets in the Pacific Basin. For this purpose, the Pacific Basin was defined broadly as extending into the Indian Ocean as far west as Iran and as including all of the Americas and the Caribbean (see Figure 16). All of the countries composing the Pacific Basin of this study thus are considered within range of commerce with the BAM service area, whether or not exchange is realized at this time.

The subject commodities included 47 different varieties of the raw materials now known to exist in the BAM service area and its contiguous zone (see Table 7). These commodities consisted of the ores themselves and, where applicable, their potential primary processed forms (unwrought, smelted, and refined variants). In the case of fertilizer materials and other nonmetallics, their crude and manufactured forms also were considered separate categories (Table 10). Using 1973 as a base, data were gathered from *Minerals Yearbook* (Vol 3) and amended or enhanced by statistics found in *Soviet Geography: Review and Translation* and the Soviet foreign trade yearbooks. Growth trends for production, exports, imports, and consumption were calculated on the basis of patterns exhibited by all countries between 1963 and 1975. The long-range trend-line approach was selected in order to eliminate the radical departures which sometimes occur on commodity markets between one year and the next. The ultimate aim of this part of the analysis was to predict the output and consumption of all the given commodities in the Pacific Basin for the years 1980, 1985, and 1990.

For commodities with especially high growth trends (annual rates of 15 percent or more), increments were programmed to fall by 50 percent in each of the designated timeframes (1973–80; 1981–85; 1986–90) until the statistic dipped below 15 percent. This sigmoidal pattern of growth commonly conforms to trends observable in new resource-development projects. For example, Chinese oil production increased by 20 to 25 percent annually through 1975. Earlier, the rates were even higher (more than 50 percent). Recently, output has averaged around 13 percent. Had differential rates not been used in this way, the results of the projection would have been skewed unrealistically in favor of a tiny fraction of categories (easily under one percent of the total array of data).

Finally, since some resource development projects are pending or have gone on stream since 1973, allowances had to be made for new output and/or resource exchanges affected by trade negotiations. For instance, new phosphate deposits that are subeconomic at the present time have been uncovered in the Broken Hill region of Australia, where output could reach 3 million tons by 1990. With Soviet assistance, the Mongolians have opened up a new copper-molybdenum deposit at Erdenet. Imports of crude and processed phosphates of 5 to 10 million and 1 million tons, respectively, have been integrated into the data for the USSR to reflect the results of deals made with Moroccan and American trade representatives since 1973.

Because less-developed countries, like China, and more developed countries, like the United States and the USSR, typically exhibit different patterns of growth,

TABLE 10
Commodities Examined in the Study*

1. Aluminum: Bauxite
2. Aluminum: Alumina (crude and fused)
3. Aluminum Metal (ingots and unwrought)
4. Antimony Ore (metric tons)
5. Chromite
6. Cobalt Ore (metric tons)
7. Cobalt Metal (metric tons)
8. Copper Ore (metal content)
9. Copper, Blister
10. Copper, Refined
11. Diamonds, Gem (thousand carats)
12. Diamonds, Industrial (thousand carats)
13. Gold (metal content, thousand troy ounces)
14. Iron Ore (metal content)
15. Pig Iron (also sponge iron)
16. Crude Steel (also scrap)
17. Lead Ore (metal content)
18. Lead Metal (smelted and refined)
19. Manganese Ore (metal content)
20. Mercury (76-pound flasks)
21. Molybdenum Ore (metric tons)
22. Nickel Ore (metal content)
23. Nickel Metal (smelted and refined)
24. Platinum Group (metal content, thousand troy ounces)
25. Tin Ore (metal content, long tons)
26. Tin Metal (smelted and refined, long tons)
27. Titanium Metal (or equivalent, metric tons)
28. Tungsten Ore (metal content, metric tons)
29. Tungsten Metal (smelted and refined, metric tons)
30. Vanadium (slag and metal, metric tons)
31. Zinc Ore (metal content)
32. Zinc Metal (smelted and refined)
33. Asbestos (chrysotile only)
34. Abrasives (all forms)
35. Fluorspar
36. Graphite
37. Mica (crude and worked)
38. Phosphates, Crude
39. Phosphates, Processed
40. Potash, Crude
41. Potash, Processed
42. Sulfur (elemental: colloidal, non-colloidal, and byproduct)
43. Bituminous Coal
44. Lignite
45. Natural Gas (millions of cubic feet, includes LNG)
46. Oil, Crude (thousands of barrels)
47. Petroleum Products (all forms, thousands of barrels)

*All commodities were collected as thousands of metric tons except where indicated.

two projections—one geometric and the other linear—were computed.[100] The geometric projection, more likely characteristic for all countries except North America (11 and 39), Australia (3), New Zealand (29), Japan (21), and the USSR (1), was calculated by means of the formula for compound interest,

$$p_t = p_o(1 + r)^t,$$

where $p_0$ is production for the year of origin, $r$ represents the annual production increments, $t$ equals the elapsed time in years, and $p_t$ is the production for the end year. The linear projection, usually illustrative of resource development in the more-developed world, was computed by the formula for arithmetic growth,

$$p_t = p_o(1 + tr)$$

The projections were then manipulated to determine whether or not a commodity for a given country would be in surplus or deficit quantities in 1980, 1985, and 1990. The data were then sorted and aggregated by commodity. The results reflected whether a commodity would be in surplus or deficit amounts within the region as a whole. These results theoretically represented the commodity-exchange potential between the USSR and countries of the Pacific Basin. Initially, this was computed without consideration of expected outputs of known resources in the BAM service area. During subsequent computer runs, the known BAM quantities were introduced into the Soviet data for 1985 and held constant through 1990. The year 1985 was selected because it was considered the earliest possible date for any of the new BAM commodities to have any influence on trade. The prospective output of those materials was held constant at maximum annual potential, simply because, realizable or not, that possibility existed. Realistically, production and export of minerals in the BAM zone were bound to come gradually in some cases after 1990, but assignation of projection rates to these developments at this time was considered to be hypothetical at best.

Four data sets were obtained in each operation both with and without the resources of the BAM service area. This included eight computer runs per projection, for a total of 16 printouts, each one exhibiting computations for 1980, 1985, and 1990. The computer was programmed to find:

1. The export capacity of the USSR to the Pacific Basin (*EXPAC*) under circumstances in which the Soviet Union had a commodity surplus ($S_u$) and the Pacific Basin had a commodity deficit ($D_p$), or

$$EXPAC = (S_u/D_p)100.$$

Under *EXPAC* conditions, the USSR ostensibly would have ready-made markets in the Pacific;

2. The export capacity of the USSR and the Pacific Basin to areas outside the Pacific (*EXPOUT*) under circumstances in which both regions had commodity surpluses ($S_u, S_p$), or

$$EXPOUT = S_u + S_p.$$

In these situations, the USSR and the Pacific-rim countries would be competitors for Pacific markets as well as those outside the basin. The Soviet Union's comparative advantage, as shown in Table 11, was calculated as a ratio

$$EXPOUT = (S_u/S_p)100.$$

Thus the *EXPAC* figures should be read as the percent of the total deficit in the Pacific Basin which the Soviet Union could fill with its surpluses. The *EXPOUT* figures should be read as the percent that the Soviet surpluses would add to a projected surplus in the Pacific Basin;

3. The export capacity of the Pacific Basin to the USSR (*IMPAC*) under circumstances in which the Pacific Basin had a commodity surplus ($S_p$) and the USSR had a commodity deficit ($D_u$), or

$$IMPAC = (S_p/D_u)100;$$

TABLE 11
Exportability of Soviet Resources to the Pacific Basin

| | Geometric Projection (G) (In Percent) | | | | | | Linear Projection (L) (In Percent) | | | | | |
| | USSR w/o BAM (USSR 1) | | | USSR w/BAM (USSR 2) | | | USSR w/o BAM (USSR 1) | | | USSR w/ BAM (USSR 2) | | |
| | 1980 | 1985 | 1990 | 1980 | 1985 | 1990 | 1980 | 1985 | 1990 | 1980 | 1985 | 1990 |
|---|---|---|---|---|---|---|---|---|---|---|---|---|
| **I. Ready Market** | | | | | | | | | | | | |
| 3. Aluminum Metal | 11.6 | 9.2 | 8.8 | 11.6 | 9.2 | 8.8 | 11.1 | 8.2 | 7.3 | 11.1 | 8.2 | 7.3 |
| 4. Antimony Ore | 0.1 | 0.4 | 0.3 | 0.1 | 0.4 | 0.3 | 1.6 | 1.0 | 1.0 | 1.6 | 1.6 | 1.0 |
| 5. Chromite | 16.4 | 24.8 | 41.2 | 16.4 | 24.8 | 41.2 | 14.3 | 19.8 | 28.1 | 14.3 | 19.8 | 28.1 |
| 8. Copper Ore | 0.0 | 0.0 | 0.0 | 0.0 | 0.9 | 0.8 | 0.0 | 0.0 | 0.0 | 0.0 | 0.9 | 0.7 |
| 9. Copper, Blister | 0.0 | 0.4 | 0.1 | 0.0 | 0.4 | 0.1 | 0.0 | 0.0 | 0.0 | 0.0 | 0.0 | 0.0 |
| 14. Iron Ore | 0.0 | 2.5 | 0.6 | 0.0 | 3.2 | 0.8 | 0.0 | 0.0 | 0.0 | 0.0 | 0.0 | 0.0 |
| 19. Manganese Ore | 3.0 | 1.6 | 1.0 | 3.0 | 1.6 | 1.0 | 3.8 | 3.0 | 2.5 | 3.8 | 3.0 | 2.5 |
| 24. Platinum | 2.4 | 5.8 | 25.4 | 2.4 | 5.8 | 25.4 | 1.9 | 2.2 | 2.4 | 1.9 | 2.2 | 2.4 |
| 30. Vanadium | 220.0 | 149.1 | 111.6 | 220.0 | 149.1 | 111.6 | 239.0 | 161.1 | 116.5 | 239.0 | 161.0 | 116.5 |
| 33. Asbestos | 4.8 | 6.2 | 7.7 | 4.8 | 9.6 | 10.0 | 4.4 | 5.5 | 6.7 | 4.4 | 9.6 | 9.7 |
| 38. Phosphates, Crude | 4.2 | 1.7 | 0.0 | 4.2 | 1.7 | 0.0 | 3.5 | 1.6 | 0.0 | 3.5 | 1.6 | 0.0 |
| 39. Phosphates, Processed | 1.9 | 0.7 | 0.0 | 1.9 | 40.2 | 17.7 | 3.2 | 2.1 | 0.0 | 3.2 | 126.7 | 76.5 |
| 41. Potash, Processed | 4.7 | 1.7 | 0.9 | 4.7 | 1.7 | 0.9 | 8.8 | 7.4 | 6.1 | 8.8 | 7.4 | 6.1 |
| 43. Bituminous Coal | 0.7 | 0.3 | 0.1 | 0.7 | 0.5 | 0.2 | 1.0 | 0.5 | 0.3 | 1.0 | 0.8 | 0.4 |
| 44. Lignite | 0.0 | 0.0 | 0.0 | 0.0 | 9.1 | 5.6 | 0.0 | 0.0 | 0.0 | 0.0 | 10.5 | 6.5 |
| 45. Natural Gas | 7.7 | 4.5 | 0.0 | 7.7 | 5.9 | 0.0 | 3.5 | 1.7 | 0.0 | 3.5 | 2.9 | 0.0 |
| 46. Petroleum | 3.1 | 2.47 | 1.49 | 3.1 | 2.49 | 1.50 | 2.9 | 2.35 | 1.58 | 2.9 | 2.37 | 1.58 |
| **II. Competitive Market** | | | | | | | | | | | | |
| 9. Copper, Smelted | 172.0 | 0.0 | 0.0 | 172.0 | 0.0 | 0.0 | 40.8 | 42.4 | 49.5 | 40.8 | 42.4 | 49.5 |
| 10. Copper, Refined | 2.6 | 4.2 | 6.4 | 2.6 | 4.2 | 6.4 | 1.8 | 2.5 | 3.5 | 1.8 | 2.5 | 3.5 |
| 14. Iron Ore | 56.3 | 0.0 | 0.0 | 56.3 | 0.0 | 0.0 | 44.6 | 32.8 | 25.4 | 44.6 | 42.3 | 32.2 |
| 15. Pig Iron | 91.6 | 27.9 | 14.1 | 91.6 | 60.5 | 31.5 | 92.4 | 27.3 | 14.1 | 92.4 | 59.4 | 31.7 |
| 16. Crude Steel | 13.7 | 4.2 | 2.8 | 13.7 | 33.5 | 20.3 | 8.3 | 3.7 | 2.9 | 8.3 | 29.9 | 21.1 |
| 18. Lead Metal | 0.0 | 0.0 | 0.0 | 0.0 | 0.0 | 0.0 | 1.8 | 0.0 | 0.0 | 1.8 | 0.0 | 0.0 |
| 32. Zinc Metal | 104.6 | 33.7 | 17.6 | 104.6 | 33.7 | 17.6 | 145.1 | 45.2 | 24.6 | 145.1 | 45.2 | 24.6 |
| 34. Abrasives | 0.1 | 0.0 | 0.0 | 0.1 | 0.0 | 0.0 | 0.1 | 0.0 | 0.0 | 0.1 | 0.0 | 0.0 |
| 36. Graphite | 1.4 | 0.5 | 0.2 | 1.4 | 0.5 | 0.2 | 1.1 | 0.5 | 0.2 | 1.1 | 0.5 | 0.2 |
| 42. Sulfur | 49.1 | 21.8 | 0.0 | 49.1 | 21.8 | 0.0 | 63.4 | 39.9 | 17.6 | 63.4 | 39.9 | 17.6 |

EXPLANATION OF TABLE 11

Table 11 includes a 15-column display of the commodity-exchange potential that should exist between the USSR and the Pacific Basin during the years 1980, 1985, and/or 1990. Its main purpose is to indicate the impact that BAM resources will have on those markets. It is a summary of a data set which was too large to include in this paper.

Two kinds of commodities are exhibited in the table: ready-market commodities and competitive-market commodities. Given a specific year, a ready market for a commodity exists when the USSR possesses a surplus and the Pacific Basin possesses a deficit. A competitive market situation prevails when both the USSR and the Pacific Basin have surpluses.

All numbers in all columns represent percentages. The shares shown in the first twelve columns were computed in the following way.

READY MARKET = Soviet Surplus/Pacific Deficit × 100
COMPETITIVE MARKET = Soviet Surplus/Pacific Surplus × 100

Thus the ready market figures should be read as the percent of the total deficit in the Pacific Basin which the Soviet Union could fill with its surplus. The competitive market figures should be read as the percent that the Soviet surplus would add to a projected surplus in the Pacific Basin. In the latter case, if the percentage is large, say above 40, the Soviet Union could conceivably flood Pacific Basin markets.

Note that the quantities computed for both geometric (G) and linear (L) projections are provided for the sake of comparison. To emphasize the potential impact of the BAM on the markets, the commodity shares of the USSR *without* the BAM (USSR 1) and the USSR *with* the BAM (USSR 2) are displayed simultaneously. By simple subtraction of the percentages (USSR 2 minus USSR 1), we obtain the proportions of the commodity markets which are directly attributable to the BAM service area.

The resultant differences are shown in columns 13 through 15 ("Impact of the BAM"). The differences between the geometric projection data and the linear projection data are found in the numerators and denominators, respectively. For those BAM commodities whose production is not yet available but expected to be great, plus (+) signs have been added. The assumption here, as in all other cases, is that any addition to the Soviet surplus from BAM-service-area resources can only improve the already existing Soviet commodity-exchange potential.

4. The import needs of the USSR and the Pacific Basin from areas outside the Pacific (*IMPOUT*) under circumstances in which both regions had commodity deficits $(D_u, D_p)$, or

$$IMPOUT = D_u + D_p.$$

The object was to determine the commodity-exchange potential between the USSR and the Pacific Basin and, ultimately, the impact of the resources of the BAM service area on that potential. Table 11 provides a convenient summary of the findings.

Interpretation: Soviet Export Possibilities

Soviet resource-development strategies theoretically could have an impact on 25 of the 47 different commodity markets of the Pacific Basin by 1990.[101] Of these markets,

| Impact of BAM (G/L) | | |
| --- | --- | --- |
| USSR 2 − USSR 1 | | |
| 1980 | 1985 | 1990 |
| 0/0 | 0+/0+ | 0+/0+ |
| 0/0 | 0/0 | 0/0 |
| 0/0 | 0/0 | 0/0 |
| 0/0 | .9/.9 | .8/.7 |
| 0/0 | 0+/0+ | 0+/0+ |
| 0/0 | .7/0 | .2/0 |
| 0/0 | 0/0 | 0/0 |
| 0/0 | 0/0 | 0/0 |
| 0/0 | 0/0 | 0/0 |
| 0/0 | 3.4/4.1 | 2.3/2.0 |
| 0/0 | 0+/0+ | 0+/0+ |
| 0/0 | 39.5/124.6 | 17.7/76.5 |
| 0/0 | 0+/0+ | 0+/0+ |
| 0/0 | .2/.3 | .1/.2 |
| 0/0 | 9.1/10.5 | 5.6/6.5 |
| 0/0 | 1.4/1.2 | 0+/0+ |
| 0/0 | .02/.02 | .01/00 |
| 0/0 | 0+/0+ | 0+/0+ |
| 0/0 | 0+/0+ | 0+/0+ |
| 0/0 | 0+/9.5 | 0+/6.8 |
| 0/0 | 32.6/32.1 | 17.4/17.6 |
| 0/0 | 29.3/26.2 | 17.5/18.2 |
| 0/0 | 0/0 | 0/0 |
| 0/0 | 0+/0+ | 0+/0+ |
| 0/0 | 0+/0+ | 0+/0+ |
| 0/0 | 0+/0+ | 0+/0+ |
| 0/0 | 0+/0+ | 0+/0+ |

*Some impact* may be generated by the BAM service area exports of copper (all forms), iron and steel, zinc metal, abrasives, graphite, crude phosphates, sulfur, coking coal, and petroleum. *Some impact* is defined in two ways: (1) a commodity is known to exist in the BAM service area in unknown or moderate amounts, and the Pacific Basin has a slight deficit, or (2) the BAM zone resources are large, but the Pacific Basin is self-sufficient. Exports of crude phosphates and sulfur are classified as only *possible* by 1990 because of expanded demand at home. Accelerated development of the huge BAM zone resources of these commodities could counteract this trend.

Possible impacts apply where the exact size of the BAM resource is totally unknown and/or the impact is dependent on factors other than pure complementarity (e.g., comparative advantage or strategic concerns). They also include the long-distance hauling of much-demanded, non-BAM zone resources like manganese and chromite. According to the former criterion, aluminum is a possible export because of higher energy costs in the Pacific. Soviet authorities not only may import bauxite and alumina from Australia, the Caribbean, and South America for processing in Pacific Siberian refineries, but also, because of the region's low-cost hydroelectricity, the finished Siberian aluminum may be far cheaper than the aluminum produced in the Pacific Basin. The Japanese already are aware of this contingency. "Now that oil prices have soared, to continue aluminum production in Japan would be like trying to grow sugar cane in a cold climate."[103] All energy-intensive products of the Pacific Basin could be so affected.

Finally, of the 25 potential Soviet exports, only four would appear to have a *minor impact* on the Pacific Basin, at least where the BAM is concerned. Antimony, which is almost nonexistent in the BAM service area, should be at or near deficit quantities in the Soviet Union through 1990.[104] Because of steadily increasing domestic consumption, Soviet lead supply continues to be a problem. Even though lead deposits in the BAM service area apparently are numerous, the projection for refined lead indicates that the commodity will not be competitive on Pacific Basin markets after the BAM is completed. Platinum and vanadium resources, thus far, are found in only negligible amounts within the BAM region. Although these minerals are very transportable and could absorb shipment costs from almost anywhere in the country, platinum, like gold and diamonds, is an *opportunity commodity* and vanadium, like cobalt, is strategic.[105] Despite the Pacific Basin's apparent deficit in it, platinum traditionally has not been a major Soviet export to the region. Moreover, neither platinum nor vanadium is expected to be exported by way of the BAM.

## Soviet Export Probabilities in a Temporal Perspective

The preceding interpretation of data suggests a range of options. But, to determine probable outcomes, one must depend on judgments derived from careful evaluation of the literature (Soviet plans, etc.). The following analysis presents the probable outcomes of the efforts of Soviet planners (Table 13).

19 could be affected by activities in the BAM service area. A dozen of the BAM commodities would appear to have ready markets. Seven others eventually could prove to be competitive. Additionally, because of their value and the demand for them in the Pacific Basin, at least two commodities (chromite and manganese) could be hauled over long distances by sea or land from source regions outside of the service area and contiguous zone via the BAM to eastern ports.

The relative impacts of pending BAM zone materials' exports, including principal destinations and competitors, are shown in Table 12. Note that 1985 still is assumed to be the year of earliest possible influence. Commodities with potentials for *major impact* are: asbestos (by virtue of its possible capture of two to four percent of the Pacific Basin market between 1985 and 1990); phosphate fertilizers (18 to 125 percent): lignite (6 to 11 percent); and natural gas (over one percent).[102] *Major impacts* are defined as conditions where the BAM zone resources in a commodity are truly large and an obvious deficit prevails in the Pacific Basin. It should be emphasized that lignite, which is poorly transportable, has but one market, Japan. Moreover, because of stiff competition from Mexico, Southeast Asia, and Canada, natural gas exports from Yakutia to Japan and the United States may be obviated by 1990.

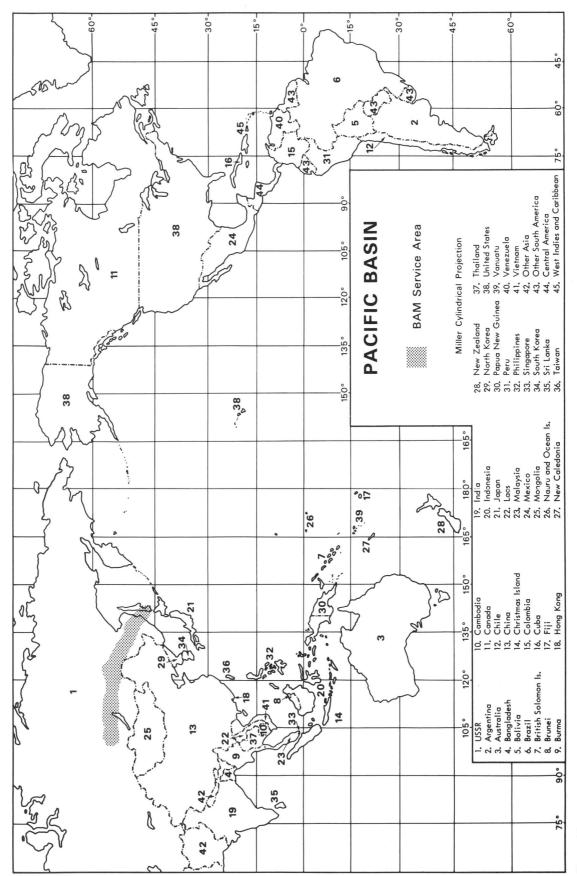

PACIFIC BASIN

BAM Service Area

Miller Cylindrical Projection

1. USSR
2. Argentina
3. Australia
4. Bangladesh
5. Bolivia
6. Brazil
7. British Solomon Is.
8. Brunei
9. Burma

10. Cambodia
11. Canada
12. Chile
13. China
14. Christmas Island
15. Colombia
16. Cuba
17. Fiji
18. Hong Kong

19. India
20. Indonesia
21. Japan
22. Laos
23. Malaysia
24. Mexico
25. Mongolia
26. Nauru and Ocean Is.
27. New Caledonia

28. New Zealand
29. North Korea
30. Papua New Guinea
31. Peru
32. Philippines
33. Singapore
34. South Korea
35. Sri Lanka
36. Taiwan

37. Thailand
38. United States
39. Vanuatu
40. Venezuela
41. Vietnam
42. Other Asia
43. Other South America
44. Central America
45. West Indies and Caribbean

Figure 16

TABLE 12
Impact of Potential BAM Exports[1]

| Mineral | Major 1985 | Major 1990 | Some 1985 | Some 1990 | Possible 1985 | Possible 1990 | Minor | Principal Competition (See Figure 16 for Identity) | Principal Markets (See Figure 16 for Identity) |
|---|---|---|---|---|---|---|---|---|---|
| 3. Aluminum Metal | | | | | * | * | | 3,11,45 | 38,21,6,23,24,36,2 |
| 4. Antimony | | | | | | | * | NA[2] | NA[3] |
| 5. Chromite | | | | | * | * | | 6,19,32 | 21,38,24,36 |
| 8. Copper Ore | | | * | * | | | | 3,12,30,20 | 21,38,13 |
| 9. Copper, Smelted | | | * | * | | | | 38, 31, 12,11 | 6,21,24 |
| 10. Copper, Refined | | | * | * | | | | 38,45,3,21 | 2,34,36 |
| 14. Iron Ore | | | * | * | | | | 3,6,11,40,31,12 | 21,38,34,24 |
| 15. Pig Iron | | | * | * | | | | 3,38 | 34,24,11,2 |
| 16. Crude Steel | | | * | * | | | | 3,21,38 | 36,24,2 |
| 18. Lead, Smelted | | | | | | | * | NA | NA |
| 19. Manganese | | | | | * | * | | 6,39,24,20 | 36,38,34,21,2 |
| 24. Platinum | | | | | | | * | NA | NA |
| 30. Vanadium | | | | | | | * | NA | NA |
| 32. Zinc, Smelted | | | * | * | | | | 11,3,29 | 38,6,40,36,20 |
| 33. Asbestos | * | * | | | | | | 11 | 38,37,34,21,23,20 |
| 34. Abrasives | | | * | * | | | | 11,38 | 45,37,3 |
| 36. Graphite | | | * | * | | | | 24,34,29,13 | 38,36,19 |
| 38. Crude Phosphates | | | * | | | * | | 38,26 | 11,6,21,3,28,34,36 |
| 39. Phosphates, Processed | * | * | | | | | | 38 | 20,6,32,16,12 |
| 41. Potash, Processed | * | * | | | | | | 11(?)[3] | 13,6,19,21,16,34,36 |
| 42. Sulfur | | | * | | | * | | 21,24,11 | 36,13,6,3,2,28,19,20 |
| 43. Bituminous Coal | | | * | * | | | | 19,13,11 | 21,24,4,2,6,34,36,38 |
| 44. Lignite | * | * | | | | | | NA[3] | 21 |
| 45. Natural Gas | * | | | | | * | | 24,21,8 | 21,38 |
| 46. Petroleum | | | * | * | | | | 20,13,24,8,40 | 38,21,34,6,3,19,2,28 |

[1]As calculated:
  Major   = BAM resources are potentially or truly large *and* a clear deficit exists in the Pacific Basin (BAM could supply over one percent).
  Some    = (a) BAM resources exist; Pacific deficit exists (BAM could supply an unknown percentage or up to one percent).
          (b) BAM resources are large; Pacific Basin is self-sufficient.
  Possible = (a) The size of BAM resources is unknown and/or their impact is dependent on factors exclusive of pure complementarity.
          (b) BAM could serve as a conduit for resources originating outside of the Pacific Siberia.
  Minor   = BAM resources are nonexistent, very small, or deficient at home.
[2]Nonapplicable.
[3]No Apparent Competition.

First, with the completion of the Eastern Ring in 1979, some resources found within and outside the BAM zone may be shipped immediately to Pacific markets. Timber from the Komsomolsk and Urgal regions may be transported to Japan. If Soviet officials so choose, aluminum can be exported from the service area and its contiguous zone, when and where spot markets appear in the basin.

When the entire railroad is finished, sometime between 1986 and 1990, commodities most likely to be shipped out of the BAM service area to the Pacific Basin are: coking coal, copper ore, asbestos, iron ore, graphite, abrasives, crude phosphates, and sulfur.[106] Although their low value would militate against longer shipments, minor quantities of lignite could continue to be transported to Japan, as that country shifts from petroleum-based electrical power.[107] Note that all of these resources are crude, unprocessed forms. Because of scarce capital investments and delays of construction in the BAM service area, processing plants and their associated infrastructural requirements are not expected to be operated until after 1990.

Most impact of the BAM service area resource development on markets of the Pacific Basin will occur only after 1990. By that time, the BAM zone phosphate and potash fertilizer plants will have been built, and major influences from their surplus output should be felt. A huge new copper smelter and refinery, based on ores from Udokan, will be in production somewhere in the service area or its contiguous zone, and its products will have some effect on the markets of the Pacific Basin. An integrated iron-and-steel mill, probably fed by South Yakutian iron ore and coking coal, should produce enough for both the Pacific Siberian domestic market and export markets of the Pacific Basin. The zinc deposits of Buryatia, after processing elsewhere, could help to meet the basin's deficit in that metal.

In the post-1990 period, five other raw materials conceivably could be exported from the BAM service area to Pacific buyers. They have been included in the *possible-impact* category because the markets for them are as yet ill-defined. As alleged before, titanium and nickel are strategically valuable and, as with precious metals, would be exported selectively. The Soviet press recently referred to the proposed natural gas pipeline from the Vilyui basin to the Pacific coast as a "bridge to the twenty-first century." Latest estimates indicate that even if the United States and Japan could supply the over $8 billion in investment costs, the joint company could not expect

TABLE 13
A Time-Impact Graph of BAM-Service-Area Resources in the Pacific Basin

| Date*<br>Impact | 1980–85<br>(Via Eastern Ring) | 1986–90 | Post-1990 |
|---|---|---|---|
| Major | Timber | Asbestos | Phosphate Fertilizers<br>Potash Fertilizers |
| Some | | Copper Ore<br>Iron Ore<br>Graphite<br>Abrasives<br>Crude Phosphates[2]<br>Sulfur[2]<br>Bituminous Coal | Copper, smelted and<br>refined; Pig Iron and<br>Crude Steel; Zinc,<br>smelted |
| Possible | Aluminum[1] | | Crude Phosphates<br>Sulfur<br>Natural Gas<br>Titanium[3]<br>Nickel[3] |
| Minor | | Lignite | Antimony<br>Platinum[3]<br>Vanadium[3]<br>Cobalt[3] |

*Except where indicated, the commodities are cumulative from time period to time period.
[1]From Bratsk, Krasnoyarsk and Sayanogorsk aluminum refineries.
[2]1986–90 only.
[3]Strategic minerals; data often withheld and projections are unreliable. The USSR is known to export nickel, fulfilling up to one-fifth of the needs of Japan alone. Soviet titanium sponge, when not withheld from the market to fetch higher prices, has been sold for prices as high as $20 per pound.

to complete the project for at least six years. Soviet intervention in Afghanistan, the fiscal prudence of American banks, and the lack of most-favored-nation status for the Soviet Union would disallow any investment of this size in Soviet projects now or in the near future. The Japanese, in turn, in reaction to the Afghanistan conflict, have canceled indefinitely any new extensions of credits to the USSR. Even if the Soviet Army had stayed out of Afghanistan, Japan would have been unwilling to shoulder the Yakutian deal alone, especially since it is already committed to the Neryungri and Sakhalin projects. Couple these hard pecuniary facts with steadily growing supplies of natural gas from Mexico, Brunei, Indonesia, and Malaysia, and the outlook for Vilyui natural gas would seem to be inauspicious before the year 2000. Finally, the possible impacts of the BAM zone crude phosphates and sulfur are contingent on the magnitude of domestic demand, particulary in Pacific Siberia itself. With the presence of new fertilizer plants in the BAM service area during the 1990s, exports of these commodities, if any, would come as refined products.

In the same decade, because of their scarcity in the BAM zone, shipments of antimony, platinum, vanadium, and cobalt may have minor impacts on the Pacific Basin. The supplies of these minerals could be, and probably will be, supplemented by cargoes from other parts of Siberia (for example, platinum from Norilsk and cobalt from the Tuva Republic).

In sum, the influence of the BAM zone commodities on the Pacific basin should be only slight through 1990. Amounting at the present time to seven percent of total Soviet outgoing shipments, export trade with the Pacific

rim should not change radically once the BAM is completed.[108] If anything, the new railroad could mean an even greater share of imports from Pacific-rim countries; these have already increased from 14 to 16 percent since 1965 because of heavier inflows of capital equipment for regional development.[109] Through 1990, most Soviet exports should continue to focus on Eastern Europe and the Atlantic Basin. This condition should persist not because of an absence of commodity markets in the Pacific but because of the long lead times required for the development and ultimate processing of the BAM resource base.

## Implications for Domestic Development

The BAM service area is, for the most part, a region of pioneer development. This means that its extractable resources are shipped out of its confines for processing.[110] As indicated in the previous analysis, this pattern should persist through 1990. The pioneer-development stage is the second of four basic plateaus that are found along a continuum of Soviet regional planning. Eventually, Soviet authorities hope that the service area will become a functioning economic region composed of 13 or more industrial nodes and territorial-production complexes (TPCs).

### The TPC Concept[111]

A TPC is literally a mechanism for spatial organization which optimizes the use of a given area's human and physical resources for a desired economic effect. The concept is seemingly innocuous enough but for the fact that industries within TPCs are in theory jointly responsible for local investment in production and infrastructure. Such freedom runs counter to centrality and tends to disperse power away from Moscow's ministerial hierarchy. This explains why the idea, which has been in and out of vogue in the USSR since the 1920s, has been so slowly accepted. It has been applied best for planning purposes in pioneer regions of Siberia and the Far North.[112] (There is a compelling economic argument for the creation of TPCs in a pioneer region, to wit, they are alleged to save up to 20 percent of the capital-investment costs.)

According to the prevailing Soviet view, TPCs are nodal regions which, with regular interaction, may lead to the formation of more comprehensive economic regions.[113] TPCs are characterized by a structure of production, comprising both independent and interrelated industries, and territory, incorporating small or large areas as required by the generic regional development projects. In this sense, they are "region-formers," which reflect three levels of organization. Firstly, they contain their own special, *nationally significant* resource or product—the equivalent of an "export" industry. Secondly, they are composed of regionally important auxiliary branches of industry which are supportive of the specialty enterprise. Thirdly, they comprise functions of purely *local significance* ("import" industries).[114] Although the combination of industries among these three categories may vary, industrial inter-connectivity—in both a spatial and nonspatial sense—is of primary importance in the formation of a TPC. This presupposes the development of an adequate electric power base and an efficient transportation network (Figure 17).

### TPCs and the BAM

Since 1974, Soviet officials have applied *sectoral planning* to the BAM service area. Careful analyses have been conducted of individual territorial-resource bases, ecology, current population distribution, local patterns of production and consumption, and potentials for regional interaction. Subregions with apparent priority include South Yakutia, northern Chita Oblast, the middle Vitim Zone, northern Buryatia, and the Far East segment of the BAM in general. At the present time only the largest production enterprises or "lead sectors" have been assigned to specific geographic sites (industrial nodes). Usually, a TPC focuses on a major industrial node (e.g., Neryungri, Udokan, Molodezhny, and others), but subsidiary urban settlements also may be incorporated into its flexible geographic limits. In sectoral planning phases like these, auxiliary enterprises or "secondary sectors" ordinarily are not relegated to specific industrial nodes but to economic regions.

After the BAM is completed, *territorial planning* is to be implemented. It is essentially a reevaluation of the sectoral plan and has as its goal a "rational production structure" based on the "balances" between a TPC's level of development and its allotment of resources. Here, the sectoral plans may be modified to include some industrial

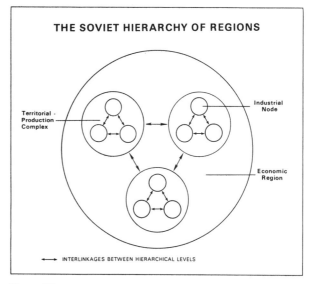

Figure 17
SOURCE: L. I. Vinokurova, "Metodika izucheniya territorialno-proizvodstvennykh kompleksov" [A method for studying territorial-production complexes], *Geografiya v shkole*, no. 3 (May–June 1978), p. 32.

relocation. Thus, one might conclude that sectoral plans are theoretical and territorial plans are pragmatic.

At least half a dozen systems of TPCs have been proposed for the BAM zone by various Soviet authorities.[115] All represent reasonable proposals, but the extent to which they have applications in the planning process remains unclear. For purposes here, the BAM service area is divided into three basic regions: the Western BAM (Baikal-Buryatia); the Central and Little BAM; and the Eastern BAM. These regions, in turn, may be distinguished by a cumulative total of 13 large industrial nodes and TPCs (Table 14).

### Western BAM

The Western BAM incorporates the segment of the railroad that stretches from Taishet in the west to the Olekma River in the east. It comprises both the most advanced regional economies of the BAM service area (Taishet to Ust-Kut) and the most primitive of zones (the Muya-Olekma River interfluve). Within this area, there are six, possibly more, subregions of development that are slated for TPC or industrial nodal class (Figure 18).

1. *Angara TPC.* The industrial nodes of Bratsk (pop. 214,000) and Ust-Ilimsk (pop. 80,000), whose populations have grown fivefold since 1959, have developed on the basis of two huge Angara River hydropower projects, each of which is named for its respective city. The Bratsk Dam is rated at 4.5 million kw of low-cost electric power (0.03 kopecks per kwh). Similar rating and costs are projected for the Ust-Ilimsk Dam, with 3.84 million kw installed by 1981.[116] Both nodes are linked by rail to major routes of communication. Bratsk is actually on the BAM, and Ust-Ilimsk is on a 150-km branch of the mainline. The two cities also are connected by 500-kv transmission

TABLE 14
Domestic Impact of BAM Railway

| Economic Region | TPCs[4] | Resource Categories | | | | | Population[5] (in thousands) | |
|---|---|---|---|---|---|---|---|---|
| | | Main Industrial Nodes | Nationally Significant | Regionally Significant | Locally Significant | Principal Power Source | 1973 | 1990 |
| Western BAM | Angara | Bratsk | Timber | Hydropower | | Bratsk Dam | 200 | 350 |
| | | Ust-Ilimsk | Aluminum[2] | Iron Ore Fresh Water | | Ust-Ilimsk Dam | | |
| | Upper Lena | Ust-Kut Kazachinskoye Magistralny | Timber | Oil Gas Gas Condensates Sulfur Fresh Water Hydropower | | Bratsk Dam Ust-Ilimsk Dam Lena dams[3] Kirenga dams[3] | 40 | 120 |
| | North Baikal | Severobaikalsk | Fresh Water | Potash | Timber | Same as Upper Lena | 6 | 55 |
| | | Nizhneangarsk Kholodnaya | Graphite Recreation areas | Lead Zinc Nickel Titanium Copper Alumina Gold | Manganese Hydropower | MOK Dam Tsipa dams[3] Gusinoozersk | | |
| | Bodaibo (Lena-Vitim) | Bodaibo | Fresh Water | Mica Gold Hydropower | Timber Alumina | Mamakan Dam MOK Dam | 25 | 30 |
| | Middle Vitim (Muya) | Molodezhny Taksimo Vitim | Asbestos Molybdenum | Hydropower Lead Zinc Gold Fresh Water | Timber Manganese | Ust-Ilimsk Dam MOK Dam[3] Tsipa dams[3] Kharanor | 0.5 | 18 |
| | Udokan | Udokan Chara | Copper | Iron Ore Titanium Vanadium Nickel Cobalt Gold | Coal Timber | Ust-Ilimsk Dam MOK Dam Khani Dam[3] Kharanor Neryungri | 2.2 | 60 |
| Central BAM | Tynda | Tynda | | | Timber | Zeya Dam | 3 | 70 |
| | Chulman-Aldan (South Yakutian) | Neryungri Chulman | Coking Coal Phlogopite Mica Phosphorites | Iron Ore Steam Coal Fresh Water Gold | Timber Hydropower | Neryungri Zeya Dam Aldan dams[3] | 70 | 150 |
| | | Aldan Seligdar | | | | | | |
| | Upper Zeya | Zeya Zeisk | Fresh Water | Hydropower Gold Arable Land Lignite | Timber | Zeya Dam Raichikhinsk | 20 | 35 |
| Eastern BAM | Zeya-Selemdzha (Svobodny-Fevralsk) | Svobodny Fevralsk | Phosphates | Iron Ore Hydropower Fresh Water Arable Land Gold | Timber Coal | Zeya Dam Raichikhinsk Bureya Dam Dagmar Dam[3] Lower Bureya Dam[3] | 85 | 140 |
| | Bureya | Chegdomyn Urgal | | Coking Coal Steam Coal Hydropower Timber Fresh Water | Iron Ore | Bureya Dam Lower Bureya Dam[3] Niman Dam[3] Raichikhinsk | 20 | 60 |

TABLE 14 (*cont.*)

| Economic Region | TPCs[4] | Resource Categories | | | | | Population[5] (in thousands) | |
|---|---|---|---|---|---|---|---|---|
| | | Main Industrial Nodes | Nationally Significant | Regionally Significant | Locally Significant | Principal Power Source | 1973 | 1990 |
| | Komsomolsk | Komsomolsk Amursk Solnechny | Timber Tin | Gold | Steam Coal Iron Ore | Bureya Dam Daldykan Dam[3] Raichikhinsk Luchegorsk | 250 | 325 |
| | Sovetskaya Gavan | Sovetskaya Gavan Vanino Kholmsk | Timber Port Facilities | Gold | Steam Coal | Maisky Luchegorsk | 90 | 125 |

[1]Sources in text, footnotes 121–150.
[2]Refined products, based perhaps on imported bauxite and/or alumina (Bratsk only).
[3]Projected only.
[4]Includes industrial-node class also: Urgal, Udokan, and Muya are likely industrial nodes.
[5]Author's estimates with input from Yu. A. Sobolev, *Zona BAMa* [The BAM Zone] (Moscow: Mysl, 1979), p. 212.

lines. Because of their cheap surpluses of electric power, both Bratsk and Ust-Ilimsk are foci for energy-intensive industries. The country's largest aluminum-refining and timber-processing facilities are in operation at Bratsk. Ust-Ilimsk has a major woodpulp mill. For these reasons, timber and aluminum represent the Angara TPC's nationally significant contribution to the economy. Iron ore, hydropower, and freshwater resources enhance the regional economies.

The population of the TPC is expected to increase, albeit at a much slower pace. Part of this growth, from roughly 200,000 in 1973 to 350,000 in 1990, will come as a result of full operations at Ust-Ilimsk and side effects from the completion of the BAM.

2. *Upper Lena TPC.* Since 1974, the population of this zone, which includes the segment of the railroad between Ust-Kut and the Baikal Mountains has grown by over 26,000 people.[117] The foundations of four base settlements have been laid to go along with the previously built nodes of Ust-Kut (pop. 55,000) and Kazachinskoye (pop. 5,000). Towns like Zvezdny, Magistralny, Ulkan and Kunerma, each averaging over 3,000 people, have been constructed from scratch. The settlements are linked by 220-kv transmission lines from Ust-Ilimsk, and television is beamed throughout the region from Ust-Kut.[118] Power-base plans include construction of hydropower facilities on the Lena and Kirenga rivers at yet unknown sites.

Timber represents the Upper Lena's nationally important resource. In fact, the TPC, with its rich stands of Siberian stone pine in the Kirenga River valley, is slated to outproduce all other BAM service area regions in the logging and processing of timber. Regionally significant resources include hydrocarbons, sulfur, fresh water, and hydropower. As a result, petrochemical and other chemical industries are predicted for the area, with the first of these being constructed in Ust-Kut. Otherwise, integrated woodprocessing centers (from sawnwood to wood pulp) are planned for almost every settlement in

the region, with the largest located in Ust-Kut, Kazachinskoye, and Zvezdny. Because of these activities, regional populations are expected to reach 120,000 by 1990.

3. *North Buryatian and Bodaibo TPCs.* During the last five years, impact analyses have been conducted most intensively in the sparsely populated North Buryatian segment of the BAM railway. The outcomes of this work have yielded some excellent case studies which may have applications in other sectors of the service area. Although the Bodaibo TPC is in Irkutsk Oblast, as will be shown, it is in some respects related more closely to North Buryatia than it is to the Upper Lena area, and accordingly it is included in our analyses of the North Baikal and Middle Vitim proto-industrial complexes.

a. *North Buryatia (North Baikal TPC and Middle Vitim Industrial Node)* As indicated, the power base is of utmost importance in the development of any industrial complex. In North Buryatia, electric power consumption will undergo radical changes during the next 10 to 20 years. Preliminary studies show that, in comparison with the period from 1976 to 1982, total demand for electricity in the region will increase 3.5 times in the period from 1982 to 1985 and 14 to 15 times by 1990.[119] In terms of budgeted sectoral requirements, the greatest single consumer in the 1982–85 period will be electric traction for the BAM (Table 15). And, although railway electrification will continue to spiral by 210 percent through 1990, its share of total demand will fall to 35.6 percent owing to the rise of industries in the economic region.

Most of the electrical power in North Buryatia will be supplied by hydroelectric stations. Potential hydropower resources are 15 million kw, over half deriving from the Vitim River and its principal upstream tributary, the Tsipa. Until the completion of the projected MOK Dam (or *Mnogoobeshchayushchaya Kosa*, a term meaning "Promising Spit of Land") sometime during the 1990s (see Figure 11; construction start expected 1985), the region must rely on electricity that is imported via high-voltage lines from Ust-Ilimsk to Ust-Kut and, ultimately, Udokan. The MOK site reflects a rated capacity of 1.5 million kw, or 7.6 billion kwh per year, and, together with the Tsipa Cascade (800,000 kw rated potential), it can supply virtually all of the post-1990 industrial needs of North Buryatia plus those of the Bodaibo TPC and Udokan industrial node.

Meanwhile, supplementing hydropower imports from the Angara TPC, thermal electricity will be brought in over long-distance transmission lines from coal-burning power plants in southern Buryatia (Gusinoozersk, ultimate capacity: 1.2 million kw), Chita Oblast (Kharanor, ultimate capacity: 1.2 million kw), and Yakutia (Neryungri, ultimate capacity: 600,000 kw). Each of these power plants is located 500 to 1000 km from North Buryatia and the nearby Chara Lowland.

Second only in importance to the power base in the formation of TPCs is an effective transport network. At the present time, because of permafrost, marshiness, high drainage densities, and climate severity, all-weather roads are nonexistent in North Buryatia, and those roads which have been built to facilitate movement along the BAM trace are hazardous. For instance, in an average trip by 20 cargo trucks between Severobaikalsk and Ulkan during the winter of 1977–78, six of the vehicles ruined their shocks and three others broke their axles. Average speeds over this road and the one between Severobaikalsk and Kichera were only 20 kph.[120]

In the absence of passable motor roads, summer cargoes must be carried to the Buryatian BAM zone by Lake Baikal lighters (freight capacities of 1,000 tons) and over the Vitim River, whose navigational season of 150 days or less is restricted by icings, floes, rapids, and shoals. Land transport thus occurs in winter only and at a cost that is two or three times higher than the expenses logged in central and southern Buryatia. Even Lake Baikal and Vitim freight rates are costly because of numerous trans-

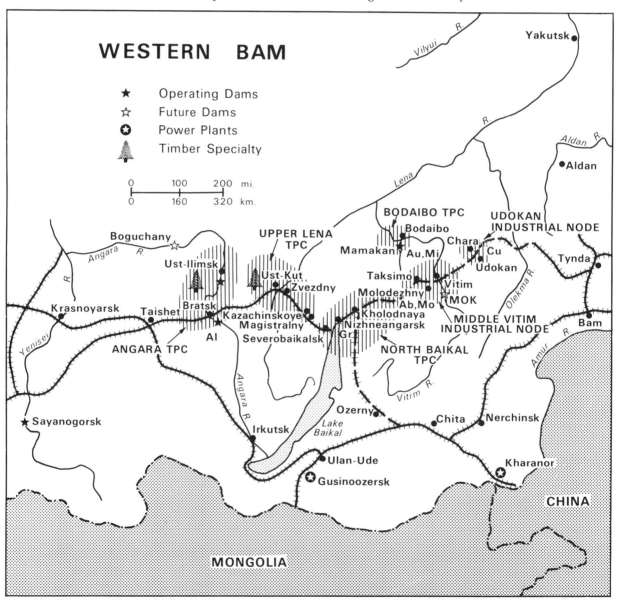

Figure 18

TABLE 15
Predicted Budget for the Consumption
of Electric Power in North Buryatia
from 1982 through 1990 (percent of total)

| Consumer | 1982–85 | 1990 |
|---|---|---|
| Railroad and Other Construction | 26.8 | 5.6 |
| Electric Traction | 69.8 | 35.6 |
| Logging and Wood Processing | 2.0 | 0.7 |
| Agriculture | 1.4 | 0.6 |
| Industry | — | 57.6 |
| Total | 100.0 | 100.1* |

*Figures do not add up to 100 percent because of rounding.
SOURCE: M. L. Alekseyev, *Problemy osvoyeniya Severa Buryatskoi ASSR* [Problems of development of the north of the Buryat ASSR] (Novosibirsk: Nauka, 1978), p. 74.

shipments and a lack of modern loading and off-loading technology. A Baikal lighter hauling 1,000 tons between the southern ports and Severobaikalsk requires five days instead of the 1.5-to-2-day norm. Freight-handling problems account for the three-day delay. Similarly, Vitim River shipments cost 10 to 15 kopecks per ton-kilometer versus a 1.5 kopeck Siberian average.[121] If wharf facilities and freight handling can be improved, it is estimated that lake and river cargoes can be doubled.

Freight volumes are clear indicators of the impact of the BAM on North Buryatia. Cargoes hauled by the Lake Baikal fleet to the northern ports are up 17 times since 1974 (over 150,000 tons). Ninety-five percent of that volume is destined for BAM-related activities and personnel. The rest of the freight includes provisions for the local indigenous population. Similar increases may be expected through 1990. In order to accommodate this expansion, wharves and lake port facilities must be enlarged and mechanized and rivers must be dredged and widened. These improvements at Severobaikalsk alone have cost 50 million rubles.

Because they are relatively cheap to blaze (an average cost of under 50 rubles per km), winter roads will continue to serve the Buryatian BAM service area until the railroad is completed. After that time, they will be converted to permanent highways. For instance, motor roads from Ulan-Ude and Chita are now permanent only as far north as Tazy (in the Barguzin Lowland) and Bagdarin (in Baunt aimak), respectively. Thereafter, winter roads are used to reach Tonnelny at the west end of the North Muya Tunnel, Severomuisk at the east end, and Vitim in the Muya Lowland. These routes, along with unimproved BAM service roads between Severobaikalsk and Vitim, will be reinforced with a hard gravel surface sometime after 1985.

Also in the aftermath of BAM construction (late 1980s), transport construction within and outside the service area will be characterized by "infilling." The first of these efforts will be a 650-km meridional railroad from Mogzon to the Kholodnaya and Ozerny polymetallic deposits, the first link of which is now under construction. The ores will be concentrated at the mineheads and transferred to a chemical-metallurgical plant, tentatively planned at Nerchinsk. Simultaneously, BAM rail spurs will be laid to

the Molodezhny asbestos site and to the MOK Dam. Finally, a permanent motor road will be paved between Taksimo and Mamakan to establish year-round communications with the Bodaibo TPC. Other permanent service roads will be blazed to the Orekitkan molybdenum deposit and the Chaya polymetallic association (lead, zinc, nickel, copper, and cobalt).

Air travel will continue to account for the majority of passenger loadings. BAM development will result in the construction of short take-off and landing strips for medium-sized prop planes at Nizhneangarsk, Ust-Muya, and Taksimo. Full-sized airports will be built in Severobaikalsk, Novy Uoyan, Molodezhny, and in large urban settlements elsewhere.

Prior to 1974, the population of the whole of North Buryatia, including North Baikal and Baunt aimaks, numbered 17,500. Perhaps slightly over one-third of these people lived within the confines of the present day BAM service area and fewer still resided along the route of the railway. Because of BAM development, the population of the Buryatian segment of the railroad is expected to reach 90,000 by 1990.[122] These population increases will place great strain on an already inadequate agricultural base. For example, in 1978, locally raised food supplies could satisfy the demand for only 36 percent of the meat; 25 percent of the milk; 54 percent of the potatoes; 20 to 25 percent of the "fresh" vegetables; 14 percent of the eggs; and 8 percent of the grain.[123] In order to meet the food needs of a population that will be at least five times larger than the 1978 level, grain output will have to increase from 266 tons to 11,600 tons; potato production must rise from 2,292 tons to 11,600 tons, fresh vegetables will have to expand from 565 tons to 11,400 tons; meat production must increase from 919 tons to 6,400 tons; milk yields must grow from 2,857 tons to 41,900 tons; and eggs will have to expand from one million to 27.7 million units.

Estimated costs of raising the agricultural productivity of North Buryatia to its technologically optimum level are roughly 200 million rubles, half of which would go to reclamation of marshes in the Upper Angara, Muya, Kurumkan, and Barguzin lowlands. Under these best of conditions, only the regional consumption of potatoes and fresh vegetables could be satisfied entirely, at least in terms of quantity, whereas 95 percent of the grain, 53 percent of the meat, 41 percent of the milk, and 53 percent of the eggs still would have to be imported.

Housing is inadequate everywhere in the area, even in showplaces like Severobaikalsk, the majority of whose residences in 1978 had no central heating, no sewage, and no water mains. The problem apparently lay with the mismanagement of city funds, which, after four years, had been expended by only 8.3 percent.[124] At the time, one out of five residents in Severobaikalsk lived in a rail car. The city had one grocery, and dry-goods store, and 2 cafeterias for 10,000 people! At Novy Uoyan and Kichera, the situation was similar. The infrastructure at those places, whose populations were both manageable at under 5,000, was only 60 percent of that required.

The nationally significant resources of the North Baikal TPC and Middle Vitim industrial node are fresh water, recreational areas, graphite, asbestos, and molybdenum.

A host of regionally important resources include fertilizer materials, polymetallics, alumina, copper, gold, and hydropower. Timber and manganese are potentially important locally.

Processing of North Buryatian resources is expected to be limited to beneficiation only. Part of the reason for this restriction is environmental. The steep-sided grabens which compose the valleys of the region tend to trap air pollutants. Surface water sources also may be contaminated easily. Thus, most of the cities in the zone are slated to have nonindustrial economic bases: Severobaikalsk (1990 pop. 40,000), administration, tourism, and transportation; Nizhneangarsk (pop. 5,000), transportation, tourism; Kholodnensky (projected population: 10,000 to 15,000), mining and beneficiation of nonferrous metals; Molodezhny (projected population 10,000 to 15,000), asbestos mining and beneficiation: Taksimo, transportation, timber processing, and Vitim, transportation, timber processing.

Curiously, though it may be the single most marketable commodity among potential consumers of the Pacific Basin, Molodezhny asbestos was not specifically highlighted by the 11th Five-Year Plan. Udokan copper and Neryungri coking coal were. BAM geologists were disenchanted enough with the draft plan to send their complaints to Izvestiya.[125]

b. *Bodaibo TPC.* As indicated, eventually (probably after 1990) the Middle Vitim industrial node at Taksimo will be linked by an all-weather road to the old mining district of Bodaibo in northeastern Irkutsk Oblast.[126] The chief industrial node of the latter region is the city of Bodaibo with a population of less than 15,000. Power generation is based on output from a small hydroelectric station at Mamakan (86,000 kw, with a potential ultimate capacity of 450,000 kw). After 1990, this energy bloc should be supplemented by high-voltage imports via transmission lines from the MOK Dam. The region's freshwater stores (Mamakan Reservoir and Vitim River) are considered the Bodaibo TPC's nationally significant resource. Hydropower is of regional importance, as are gold and muscovite mica which have been extracted from the Lena Goldfields and the Mama-Chuya basins, respectively, for a long time. Timber and alumina resources may be of local significance. Although production appears to have peaked, gold and mica resources are alleged to be considerable and may be due for expansion.[127] For the time being, however, the BAM is not anticipated to serve as an impetus to growth in the Bodaibo TPC, since there are higher-priority loci for in-migration closer to the railroad. Until 1990, population increases in the region should occur more as a result of natural increments instead of migration. Total population should reach 30,000 or more by that time.

4. *Udokan Industrial Node.* Like North Buryatia, the Chara Lowland has been the subject of intensive research since the mid-1960s.[128] Energy resources for this developing region include the Kodar steam coal deposits (see Figure 11), real and potential hydroelectricity from the Ust-Ilimsk (by high-voltage line), MOK, and Khani dams, and thermal power that is to be transmitted from Kharanor and Neryungri. Compared to 1973, when the area was occupied by only 2,200 reindeer herders and fur

trappers, energy consumption should increase more than 30-fold by 1990. This should come about as a result of the inflow of upwards of 60,000 new residents and the industrial development associated with the Udokan copper deposit.

Udokan, on the site of the former geologists' settlement of Naminga, will be the focus of the TPC, although the majority of the population will live in Chara (expected 1990 pop. 50,000) on the BAM.[129] Chara will be the site of the copper beneficiation plant, a mechanical-repair shop, a steam electric power plant, construction industries, transportation services, and other activities. A copper smelter will not be built in the node because of persistent temperature inversions and the lack of natural ventilation in the Chara Valley. Rather, it will be built at one of four sites on or near the Trans-Siberian Railroad: Abakan, Taishet, Zima, or Nerchinsk.

Although Nerchinsk suffers from relatively high energy costs and shortages of auxiliary industries, in the opinion of many Soviet planners, it is the most likely location for the new smelter and refinery. The city is situated on a broad stretch of flat land with ample water and a developed agricultural base. The flat land accommodates the need for a 5 to 6 km$^2$ sanitary-protective zone around the plant, and the Nercha River yields coolant-water resources. To enhance supply of the latter, planners suggest construction of a small dam and reservoir.

Along with the metallurgical plant, which will process lead and zinc as well as copper, the prospective Nerchinsk industrial node will support an electric-wire rolling mill and a sulfuric acid batch plant. The wire will serve the purposes of railway and regional electrification projects. The sulfuric acid output will assist in the production of domestic and exportable phosphate fertilizers, the basic raw materials for which eventually may come from the Central BAM service area (Seligdar) and South Buryatia (Oshurkovo). As mentioned, the city, which is near the Trans-Siberian Railway, will be joined to the BAM by 650-km meridional railroad sometime in the 1990s.

Thus, the development of the Udokan region is linked intimately to progress elsewhere. By way of illustration, the area currently is capable of supplying no more than half of its future energy requirement. The balance must be supplied from sources outside of the industrial node. By 1985, Udokan should be linked to Ust-Ilimsk by 220-kv high-tension transmission lines. Future energy supplies will come from the MOK and Khani dams and the Kharanor and Neryungri thermal stations. The Khani Dam is projected for the post-1990 period and will have a designed capacity of 1.2 million kw.

Agriculturally, the Udokan area is in a worse position than North Buryatia. The estimated annual food needs, assuming a population of 50,000, are 7,200 tons of potatoes, 6,600 tons of vegetables, 10,800 tons of whole milk, and 3,400 tons of meat. To indicate the seriousness of the problem, the Udokan TPC supplied a sum-total of 5.9 tons of potatoes in 1973. During the same year, there were only 113 head of cattle, including 45 cows, in the entire region.

In order to accommodate some of the increased demand for agricultural production, BAM officials hope to expand local reindeer herds both for their meat and their hides. Fur trapping and fur farming are slated to be second only to reindeer herding as the most important agriculturally related activities. These functions will be augmented (in a subsidiary way) by the raising of beef and dairy cattle, horses, and, lastly, crops. Indeed, arable land in the Udokan area will be at a high premium, representing far less than the 0.5 percent share of the total land allotment, which is the average for the Western BAM as a whole.[130] For these reasons, over the long run, the Udokan TPC will depend on imports for 75 percent or more of its food needs.

Transportation into and out of the region will continue to be a problem, except by rail. The existing airport at Chara will be improved, and the winter roads between Mogocha and Chara and Chara and Khani will be converted, not without considerable difficulty, to all-weather surfaced roads.

Because the Udokan area is considered by Soviet medical geographers to be a "low-comfort" environment, much of the mining force will be tour-of-duty or work-shift, whose activities in the area will not exceed one or two years all told.[131] Work naturally will focus on the nationally important mining of copper and other nonferrous trace elements at the Udokan mines. Beneficiation and segregation of all the metals will take place at Chara. Iron ores in the Chara-Tokko, Khani, and China fields will be of significance to the BAM service area and its contiguous zone; whereas, the extraction of coal and timber will have local impact. The latter, consisting exclusively of larch, will be processed at small mills in Chara.

Central BAM

The Central BAM represents the railway segment that extends between the Olekma and Selemdzha rivers, including the north-south-trending service area of the Little BAM. Over much of the western half of this region, economic activities are expected to be restricted to railway-support functions and the logging of mature stands of larch. These latter comprise the forests in and around Ust-Nyukzha, Chilchi, and Larba. Because of the noticeable absence of commercial resources, no growth centers have been designed for the Olekma-Tynda segment. TPCs have been suggested or planned for the Tynda, South Yakutian (Chulman-Aldan), and Upper Zeya regions (Figure 19).[132]

1. *Tynda TPC.* As the administrative capital of BAM construction and development, Tynda owes its importance to its location at the crossroads of the main BAM east-west line and the Little BAM.

With a 1973 population of only 3,000, Tynda's numbers are scheduled to swell to 70,000 by 1990. The people drawn to the city will be employed in transportation services (dispatching and locomotive repair), construction (housing and roads), the apparel industry, publishing, logging, and sawmilling. Additionally, a large number of supervisors and bureaucrats will be attracted by Tynda's function as the center of BAM administration.

Energy supplies for Tynda over the next decade will be delivered by high-voltage transmission lines from the Zeya Dam (1.2 million kw) and, eventually, from the Neryungri thermal station. Any vestigial requirements should be satisfied by imports of Neryungri steam coal. This fuel will be consumed by the city's projected thermal-electric central power station which will need 120 tons of steam coal per day.[133]

The over ten-fold increase in population that has occurred at Tynda in only seven years, already has taken its toll on the city's need for infrastructure. Although housing completions are apparently on schedule, residential plumbing and heating are not. Thus, one-third of the initial capital outlays for infrastructure has been invested in temporary housing which eventually must be torn down. As with the Western BAM, Tynda and environs suffer from the absence of a satisfactory local food base. In fact, transport costs for imports of fresh vegetables run up to 8 million rubles per year "and that doesn't include the rate of damage in shipment which is as high as 40 percent for . . . potatoes."[134] To alleviate this problem, hothouses have been planned for Tynda and Mogot. A stockyards-and-slaughterhouse operation is under construction at Taldan, southeast of Tynda on the Trans-Siberian Railroad. Finally, only eight kilometers outside of the city lies several hundred acres of arable land which, according to planners, can be converted to a productive truck farm, yielding potatoes, radishes, and onions, at a cost of under 500,000 rubles per year. This produce theoretically would be sufficient to supply all the vegetable requirements of the entire Central BAM region.

2. *Chulman-Aldan (South Yakutian) TPC.* Along with Udokan and, perhaps, Molodezhny, growth centers in South Yakutia will receive priority in the early-stage development of the BAM service area. With a 1977 population of 90,000, the region should easily reach 150,000 persons by 1990. The bulk of the growth will occur in two industrial nodes: Neryungri (projected year 2000 population: 100,000) and Chulman (projected: 50,000). The phosphate-mining town of Seligdar (projected: 50,000) also will account for some of the increase. Finally, the old mining centers of Aldan and Tommot should experience rebirths, once local iron-ore deposits are exploited.

The energy requirements of the TPC will be satisfied by long-distance electrical transmission from the Zeya Dam and local power production from the Neryungri thermal station, under construction. An older, 20,000 kw coal-buring thermal station will enhance these sources in Chulman. Eventually, most of the electric power will be allocated to resource development projects in the TPC. Coking-coal, phlogopite mica, and phosphorites will be significant nationally, whereas iron ore, steam coal, fresh water, and gold will be more important to the region. Timber (mainly larch) and hydropower (from the Aldan River: 60-65 billion kwh potential output) will be locally significant.

Much of the future success of the TPC is dependent on a comprehensive solution to the controversy surrounding the siting of the above-mentioned integrated iron and steel mill. The arguments themselves have a 20-year history. Traditionally viewed in terms of the comparative advantages of Chulman and Svobodny alone, owing to the advent of new steel-making technology (direct reduc-

## PROJECTED TERRITORIAL PRODUCTION COMPLEXES
## IN THE FAR EAST, POST - 1990

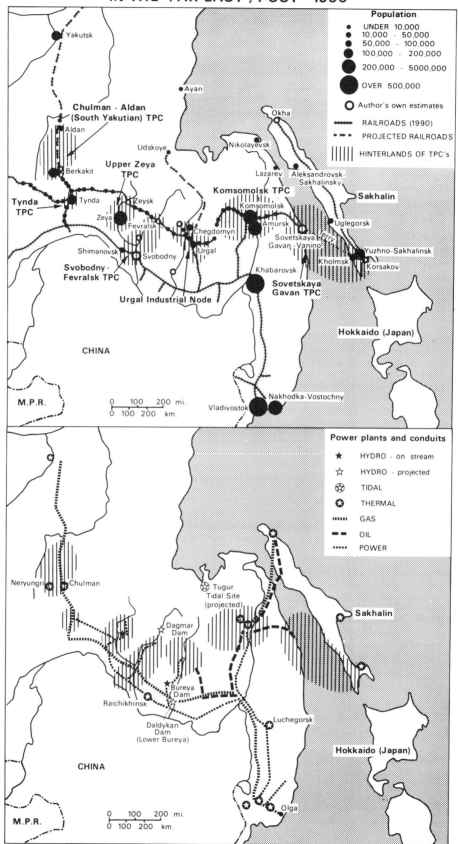

Figure 19

tion), several other BAM service area locations may be competitive. Besides location factors (proximity of coking coal, iron ore, water, and markets) and suitability of technology, criteria still requiring in-depth analysis are construction periods, expected plant lifetime, and metal quality.

Chulman obviously is favored in terms of proximity to raw materials but is disadvantaged with respect to market. Strategically found on the Aldan-Yakutian motor road and linked by the Little BAM, the Chulman site could be developed fairly rapidly and relatively cheaply. Other disadvantages lie with technology (traditional blast-furnace type) and resultant pollution-control costs (up to 40 percent of capital investment); plant lifetime (reduced because of the severity of the South Yakutian environment); and metal quality (impurities in Aldan iron ore). Both full-cycle and partial-cycle processes have been suggested for the Chulman site, with rolled products being shipped to Trans-Siberian metal fabrication centers (Svobodny, Khabarovsk, Komsomolsk, and the like). Some of the output can be exported.

Svobodny possesses the advantages of its location on the Trans-Siberian and its nearness to the Gar iron-ore deposit, which is suitable for direct reduction. It is also favored by proximity to Far Eastern markets, by a well-developed infrastructure, and a more favorable environment. The last two factors combine to reduce construction costs and to increase plant lifetime. Designed to use electric-arc furnaces in the direct-reduction process, the Svobodny site already is supplied with cheap electric power from the Zeya Dam and can be bolstered in the future with output from the Bureya site. The only possible disadvantage at Svobodny might be water shortages during droughts, which undoubtedly would affect Chulman also.

Though off-center with respect to the rest of the service area, Komsomolsk is favored by its proximity to Far Eastern and Pacific markets, by preexisting technologies (the old Amurstal steel mill), construction time, and plant lifetime. Disadvantages are related to distance from suitable energy resources and raw materials. Designed to smelt the limited iron-ore resources of the Little Khingan Range with Urgal coking coal, the Amurstal plant has never produced its own pig iron and, in fact, imports it from the Kuzbas. Under the 11th Five-Year Plan (1981–85), Komsomolsk was chosen as the site for a 500,000-ton electric steel mini-plant using scrap.

Finally, owing to the high quality of its metal and the cheapness of its on-site development, a site chosen somewhere between the Chara-Tokko and Olekma-Amga iron-ore deposits might be economically feasible. As indicated, the Chara-Tokko ores are suitable for direct reduction by means of either hydroelectricity (MOK and/or Khani) or imports of Yakutian natural gas. Militating against this auspicious picture are unfavorable markets, lack of infrastructure, harsh, yet fragile, environments, long construction times, and short plant lifetime.

3. *Upper Zeya TPC.*[135] The power base for this TPC is the Soviet Far East's largest hydroelectric facility at Zeya (1.2 million kw). The dam serves a multiple purpose, controlling formerly hazardous floods, bolstering naviga-

tion, and providing irrigation water for 55,000 additional hectares of arable land and 100,000 hectares of hay and pasture land.[136] The hydropower is transmitted over high-voltage lines to Tynda, South Yakutia, Shimanovsk, Svobodny, and Fevralsk. Also, it is expected to be distributed soon to the BAM railhead at Zeisk, where the Zeya River is spanned by the second longest bridge on the BAM route. Thus, the Zeya Dam is to the Central BAM what the Ust-Ilimsk and Bratsk dams are to the Western BAM, and what the MOK Dam should become for North Buryatia and Udokan. Supplementary blocs of power can come from the Raichikhinsk thermal power plant (270,000 kw) southeast of Svobodny.

Zeya's projected population of 200,000 by the year 2000 is probably unrealistic because of labor constraints and the absence of a rail spur from the Trans-Siberian Railroad, although the city is linked to that line by secondary motor roads. During the last 20 years, the population has swelled from virtually zero to over 18,000 and that pattern should accelerate with the development of the BAM service area. The economic base of the city includes power generation and transmission, apparel industries, food processing, publishing, logging, and woodworking. It is slated to be a center for telecommunications, machine repair, metal fabrication, and machine building.

The one other potential industrial node in the TPC is Zeisk, which is expected to become one of the largest railroad depots on the BAM. It is now noted for gold mining, as a river port and for a major bridge on the BAM.

The only resource of national importance in the Upper Zeya region is fresh water. Of regional significance are hydropower, gold, lignite (at Tynda), and agricultural land. Although the Zeya region is anticipated to be the fourth most important logging zone in the service area, its timber is now used for local purposes only.

Of all the subregions found within the BAM service area, the Upper Zeya and Zeya-Selemdzha (Svobodny-Fevralsk) TPCs are the most promising agricultural bases in the zone. Southern Amur Oblast, for good reason, has been called the "granary of the Far East." It produces fully two-thirds of all crops in the economic region. Thus, as new migrants arrive in the BAM service area, agricultural output must increase on the Zeya and Bureya plains. As an early indicator of the domestic impact of BAM development, since 1976, Zeya-Bureya dairy production has doubled, feed-lot yields have tripled, hog farms have expanded by 76 percent, and fodder crop area is up almost 20 percent. In just two years, meat output has increased 21 percent, milk production is up to 19 percent, and egg yields have increased by 40 percent. Still, if future consumption of these products in the Central and Eastern BAM is to be satisfied, present dairy and fodder production must be quadrupled, simply to keep apace with pre-BAM ratios, which averaged only 40 percent of domestic needs.[137]

Eastern BAM

The Eastern BAM comprises the segment that stretches from the Selemdzha River in the west to southern Sakhalin Island in the east. Within this branch of the BAM service area, there are three TPCs and one industrial node (see Figure 19).

1. *Zeya-Selemdzha (Svobodny-Fevralsk) TPC.* The three major industrial nodes of this TPC are linked neatly by four different types of communication: by railroad and high-voltage lines between Shimanovsk and Svobodny and by waterway, motor road, and high-voltage lines between Svobodny and Fevralsk. Thus, in addition to industrial activities, transport functions must be considered very important to the economic base of the Zeya-Selemdzha TPC.

The principal urban center of the region is Svobodny (pop. 65,000). The city is noted for its iron foundry, automobile parts manufacturing, clothing industry, food processing, and timber transshipment activities. Together with the continency of an iron-and-steel plant, Svobodny is likely to receive a pulp-and-paper mill in the future.

Shimanovsk (pop. 25,000), northwest of Svobodny on the Trans-Siberian, has become the principal supplier of building materials to the BAM service area (reinforced concrete, pre-fab apartment panels, bridge parts, culverts, granites, gravels, and clays). These are shipped by rail to Tynda, where they are dispersed in three directions (north, west and east), and by road and/or river to Fevralsk. The city also processes wood and food, manufactures wearing apparel, and fabricates metal.

Fevralsk (pop. 2,000) is currently no more than a river port and a BAM supply base. Though not expected to grow spectacularly, the town is favored by location with respect to the major resources of the TPC. Nationally significant phosphates are upstream from the settlement in the Uda-Selemdzha Basin, and regionally important iron ore and gold are found in the same area along the Nora River. Nora steam coal and Selemdzha timber stands (larch and pine) are significant locally. Finally, rich reserves of arable land, fresh water, and hydropower enhance the regional resource base.

Should all the alternatives ever be developed, electric power will be in surplus quantity in the Zeya-Selemdzha TPC. In addition to existing blocs of electricity distributed from the Zeya Dam and Raichikhinsk thermal station, the grid will be augmented by inputs from the Bureya Dam, now under construction, and future options from the Dagmar (Selemdzha) and Lower Bureya dams.

2. *Bureya (Urgal) Industrial Node.* The tightly knit Bureya coal-mining district represents a true industrial node. Although the coal is reasonably abundant, it is hardly nationally significant and is consumed principally in the eastern half of the BAM service area. Both the district's steam and coking coals accordingly are important to the region, along with its hydropower, fresh water, timber, and gold. A small nearby deposit of iron ore is only locally significant.

The two largest urban places in the node eventually should coalesce into a single conurbation. Chegdomyn (pop. 18,000) and Urgal (pop. 2,000; expected 1990 pop. 15,000) may house as many as 200,000 people by the turn of the century, although this prediction is very speculative.

Regional hydroelectric resources are abundant. The Bureya Dam is to have an ultimate rated capacity of 2

million kw, larger than the Zeya station. The downstream Lower Bureya site promises to be as large. And the Niman Dam, on an upstream tributary of the Bureya, is also potentially sizeable. The node is now supplied with energy from Chegdomyn coal-burning units and imports of electricity from Raichikhinsk.

In addition to coal mining, which is actually carried out at nearby Sredni Urgal, Chegdomyn is noted for food processing. Urgal currently is a logging center. In the future, these activities are expected to intensify. The region also is slated to produce bricks (from coal residues) and machinery (road-building equipment, wood-processing devices, transportation machinery and repair shop modules). A wood-chip mill is planned for Urgal.

According to early BAM service area projections, Urgal was designed to be a transshipment point for eastward-moving cargoes of West Siberian crude oil. At Urgal, the crude would have been drained from BAM tanker cars and funneled into a new pipeline, through which the oil would have been forwarded to refineries at Khabarovsk, Komsomolsk and Nakhodka-Vostochny. A refinery and oil-storage facility was blueprinted for the Sovetskaya Gavan—Vanino region as well. Because of the serious questions concerning West Siberian oil supply and overall Soviet demand for petroleum, the Urgal transshipment operation would now appear to be in jeopardy.

3. *Komsomolsk TPC.* This TPC centers on the industrial nodes of Komsomolsk (pop. 264,000) and Amursk (pop. 40,000). The tin-mining town of Solnechny (pop. 15,000) represents the only other industrial node in the complex.

Because of developed infrastructure, a relatively hospitable climate, and growing industry, the population of the TPC should increase by at least 50,000 between 1979 and 1990. The energy requirements of these people should be satisfied by two existing power plants (combined rated capacity under 600,000 kw), imports of electricity from Raichikhinsk and Luchegorsk (capacity: 800,000 kw) thermal stations, and future power blocs from the Bureya and Lower Bureya dams.

In addition to steel production and the generation of electrical power not only for itself but also for its hinterland, Komsomolsk is noted for oil refining; chemical and petrochemical industries (based on Sakhalin oil); metal fabrication (cranes, forklifts, diesel motors, and power plant equipment); shipbuilding; logging and woodworking (of Amgun River timber); construction materials; clothing; food processing; and steel. All of these industries should expand because of the influence of the BAM. Also, several new industries are designated for the city, including locomotive repair works, fertilizer and associated chemical industries, and wood-chip processing.

One of the fastest-growing cities in the Soviet Far East, Amursk is known for logging and woodworking (pulp and paper), electrical generation, clothing manufacture, and the quarrying of local building materials. With the advent of the BAM, output at the city's pulp and paper mills, already over 220,000 tons annually, should expand.

Besides high-quality stands of timber, supplied as roundwood for export to Japan, and raw material for domestic plywood, furniture, fiberboard, viscose fiber, cloth, and wood-chemical industries, the minerals of the

TPC are limited to tin, gold, and lignite. Like timber, the tin of the region is nationally significant and the cheapest ore in the country. Tin ore is mined and beneficiated at Gorny and Solnechny. The concentrate is shipped to Novosibirsk and Podolsk for processing. (It recently has been reported that a tin smelter is under construction in the Solnechny-Gorny area.) Gold from Polina Osipenko is the only regionally significant resource in the TPC. Finally, unused low-quality steam coals and iron ores, found west of Komsomolsk, eventually may become important for local consumption.

Due to the impact of the BAM, the food base in the Komsomolsk complex will receive intensive development. According to data issued by the Far East division of the Timber Ministry, "by 1985, land sown to vegetables will quadruple, cattle will triple, and hog populations will double.[138] The fodder crops required for the expanded animal herds will be grown in hothouses near Komsomolsk.

4. *Sovetskaya Gavan TPC.* The principal industrial nodes of this complex are connected by railroad and railroad ferry between the mainland and Sakhalin Island. The cities comprise the mainland urban complex of Sovetskaya Gavan—Vanino (combined pop.: 50,000), Zavety Ilyicha (pop. 15,000), Maisky (pop. 5,000), and the Sakhalin ferry terminal of Kholmsk (pop. 42,000).

Power supplies in the TPC are limited to the coal-burning Maisky thermal power plant, whose generators are to be bolstered soon by gas turbines. Future blocs of electric power eventually may be derived from Luchegorsk.

Both Sakhalin and the mainland have benefited from the railroad-ferry system, which went into operation in the early 1970s. With ice-breaking capabilities, the fleet now contains six diesel-electric ferries, each of which plies the waters of the Tatar Strait twice weekly. By 1982, the fleet was expected to operate ten of these craft.[139] Because of the rapid expansion of the Tatar Strait ferry, and no doubt some influence from the development of the BAM service area, freight turnovers between Vanino and Kholmsk are up 500 percent since 1974 and over 16 percent since 1979.[140]

The growing freight turnover of the ferry fleet has not been accompanied by port transshipment improvements. Vanino, which supplies northeast Siberia as well as Sakhalin, can handle only 190 rail cars per day. During the winter, as many as 900 rail cars await unloading in marshalling yards at Vanino. Consequently, though one-way cruises between Vanino and Kholmsk consume only 32 hours, rail cars may wait five days from the time of their arrival to the time of their departure.

Sovetskaya Gavan is the Soviet Far East's chief submarine port. As such, it serves mainly the interests of the Soviet Navy. Vanino, the civilian port, is noted for logging, wood processing, and clothing manufacture. At nearby Sovetskaya Gavan, military activities are augmented by metal fabrication (associated with ship repairs) and food processing. Food processing also is conducted at Zavety Ilyicha. As BAM development accelerates, the economic bases of the mainland complex should be enhanced by larger port facilities, oil-storage

capacities, and container-docking facilities. New shipyards and fish canneries have been designed for the area.

Early location analyses of the Sovetskaya Gavan—Vanino area indicate that the region may be suitable for oil and natural gas refineries. In the absence of shipments of West Siberian crude, Sakhalin oil, and perhaps gas, might be shipped or piped to the ports for refining. Such contingencies probably are impossible during this century.

Finally, Kholmsk is known for its fishing and marine animals fleet, fish canning and processing, pulp-and-paper manufacture, and building materials base. Possibly the fastest-growing of all Sakhalin cities, Kholmsk should have a population of 70,000 by 1990.

Among the relatively meager resources of this region, only timber can be characterized as nationally important. Beach-sand placer deposits of gold are significant to the region, and presently unmined deposits of steam coal could become important locally as fuel for the Maisky thermal power plant.

## Summary and Conclusions

A primary purpose of this paper was to provide a detailed inventory and analysis of the resources of the BAM service area. Accordingly, roughly 30 different raw materials were examined and enumerated. It was found that these materials varied in quantity and in quality, and some two-thirds of them—20 (including timber) to be exact—could be considered exportable commodities (Tables 11 to 13).

Of the 20 exportable resources, only timber and asbestos possess any high probability of *major impact* before 1990. Simultaneously, *some impact* can be expected from the development of crude reserves of coking coal, copper, iron, graphite, abrasives, phosphates, and sulfur. In the same period, *possible impacts* may accrue from BAM shipments of aluminum. Of minor influence, BAM service area lignite may be transported to Japan, where it may be consumed as boiler fuel. Prior to 1990, all cargoes of BAM service area raw materials, except for timber, should be transported in their crude, unprocessed forms, if at all. As suggested in Table 15, industry and manufacturing in the resource-rich backwaters of North Buryatia and Udokan should not be a factor until after 1990. Because of monetary, technological, and labor constraints, industrial development in the more accessible sectors of the service area (the Central BAM, for example) also may be delayed. (Note, as well, the environmental constraint of 240 million m³ of overburden and steam coal on top of seams of Neryungri coking coal.)

A secondary aim of this research was to make a study of the railroad's impact on its service area. Early, obviously optimistic, population forecasts suggested that the BAM zone could attract anywhere from 1 to 2 million persons by 1990.[141] Recently, a respected BAM service area planner contended that 500,000 laborers would be needed to fulfill the region's industrial goals.[142] Based on the most realistic population projections that could be found for the BAM zone subregions, this study proposed that the population of the service area could grow by as many as 700,000 persons between 1973 and 1990 (Table 13). This calculation included a 17-year increment of 230,000 accumulated via natural increase (at 1.7 percent per year) and an addition of 470,000 by way of in-migration. It was shown that this population would be distributed irregularly within the service area in 13 clusters of industrial nodes and territorial-production complexes. The highest-priority development was revealed to occur in the Angara, Upper Lena, North Baikal, Middle Vitim, Udokan, Tynda, and South Yakutian growth centers, that is, precisely those areas which possess the most valuable raw materials along the BAM.

Convincing 470,000 people to come to the BAM zone by 1990 is not an easy task. Because of the region's environmental harshness—on a par with the Lower Ob and Norilsk[143]—Soviet planners invest up to 20,000 rubles per migrant for wages, infrastructure, services, and other amenities.[144] This means that the total investment for BAM labor support systems between 1973 and 1990 eventually could reach 9.4 billion rubles (470,000 × 20,000 rubles).

Thus, taking data presented above in Table 6, by 1990 the total costs of the BAM development project could approximate 27.7 billion rubles: 10.6 billion rubles (railway capital construction costs); 7.6 billion rubles (industrial capital investment); and 9.4 billion rubles (labor and infrastructure).

An investment of this magnitude cannot be recouped without the addition of considerable benefits from domestic and foreign economies. The resources of the BAM service area do not promise to reap those benefits over the short run (to 1990) because of the delays in BAM construction and constraints on investment. As indicated by the results of our analysis, except for some modest inroads, BAM service area raw materials should not affect the overall stability of Pacific markets, again, *over the short run*. Until 1990, with respect to natural resources, there are simply too many intervening opportunities for Pacific Basin nations (Table 12). Indeed, any impacts derived from BAM service area development are to be realized initially over the medium range (1990–2000) and, chiefly, over the long range (post-2000).

Given the many competing variables and forces, the role of the BAM and its resources in the formulation of Soviet economic strategy in the Far East and the Pacific is expected to be no more than minimal during the next decade. For that period and some time thereafter, the railroad should operate at an apparent loss, at least in terms of immediate opportunity costs. The intangible benefits of regional development (military logistics, new region-formation, geologic establishment of new resources, and so forth), may be sufficient to justify these investments over the medium range. But, until then, the BAM cannot be considered a decisive global factor.

## NOTES

1. "For a Lot of Bucks, BAM!" *Time Magazine*, 20 March 1978, pp. 36–37; Howard Sochurek, "Construction Project of the Century: A New Railroad to Tap Siberian Riches," *Smithsonian*, February 1978, pp. 36–47; Leo Gruliow, "Ivan Working on the Railroad," *The Saturday Evening Post*, November 1975, pp. 66–69, 78–81; Norbert Kuchinke, "The whole country is BAMming," *Der Spiegel*, 8 November 1976, pp. 162–67; and hosts of articles from *The New York Times, Christian Science Monitor, London Times, Sydney Morning Herald*, and so forth.

2. A. I. Alekseyev, "Along the route of the Baikal-Amur Mainline," *Voprosy istorii*, 1976, no. 9, pp. 113–22. The eastern terminus between Pivan, opposite Komsomolsk, and Sovetskaya Gavan (400 km) was laid between 1943 and 1945 (p. 120). The western terminus, linking Taishet with Ust-Kut (720 km), was built between 1947 and 1951 (p. 120), but was not formally inaugurated until 1958. For a history of the BAM, see A. I. Alekseyev, *Khozhdeniye ot Baikala do Amura* [Striding from Lake Baikal to the Amur] (Moscow: Molodaya gvardiya, 1976).

3. The Postyshevo (Berezovka)-Komsomolsk railroad was an old logging road over which even light trains "rocked like ships at sea." Renovation of the segment was completed in 1980. Yu. Kazmin, Z. Klyuchkov, and G. Petrov, "Long kilometers," *Pravda* (hereafter *P*), 16 July 1977, p. 2.

4. Theodore Shabad and Victor L. Mote, *Gateway to Siberian Resources (The BAM)* (New York: Halsted Press, 1977), p. 79; see also Ye. V. Pinneker and B. I. Pisarsky, *Podzemnye vody zony Baikalo-Amurskoi magistrali* [Groundwater in the BAM service area] (Novosibirsk: Nauka, 1977), p. 7, and P. Sobolev, "The BAM through the eyes of an engineer," *Stroitelnaya gazeta*, 8 November 1974, p. 3. New data indicate that the figure originally prescribed for BAM earthwork (230 million m³) was too conservative. Earth-moving operations in the Neryungri coal field alone will entail the removal of 240 million m³, and this is separate from BAM trackwork construction.

5. Thomas W. Robinson, "Siberian Development: Implications for the Soviet Union in Asia" (paper presented at the 9th national convention of the American Association for the Advancement of Slavic Studies, Washington 15 October 1977), p. 11.

6. In 1979, in response to the Chinese invasion of Vietnam, Soviet military activities increased in the Soviet Far East. In August and September 1979, according to witnesses, military maneuvers in Khabarovsk Krai depleted the supplies of diesel fuel to such an extent that train traffic on the Little BAM was curtailed and stripmining at Neryungri ceased even though it should have been the peak of the coal-mining season. There was no fuel for American-made dump trucks.

7. F. V. Dyakonov, "The BAM as a set of major long-term economic problems," in *Baikalo-Amurskaya magistral* (Moscow: Mysl, 1977) (hereafter *BAM-77*), p. 24.

8. L. I. Brezhnev, "L. I. Brezhnev's speech," *Izvestiya* (hereafter *I*), 16 March 1974, p. 2.

9. P. G. Bunich, "The BAM and the economic development of the Soviet Far East," *Planovoye khozyaistvo*, 1975, no. 5, p. 30, subsequently translated in *Soviet Geography: Review and Translation* (hereafter *SGRT*), 16, no. 10 (December 1975): 646; F. Dyakonov, "The Soviet Far East: Problems and prospects," *Ekonomicheskaya gazeta*, 1975, no. 5, p. 13; N. P. Belenki and V. S. Maslennikov, "BAM: Its area of influences and freight flows," *Zheleznodorozhny transport*, 1974, no. 10, p. 46, subsequently translated in *SGRT*, 16, no. 8 (October 1975): 512.

10. For a summary of this, see chapter 3 of this book.

11. Abel Aganbegyan, "Changes That Cause New Problems," *Soviet Life*, December 1978, p. 14. "What should come first? How is maximum efficiency of the projected enterprises to be achieved? On what conditions should people's relations with nature be based? What has to be done so that people could live and work normally in these grim regions?

12. V. Postnikov, "A new stage in technical progress," *Rechnoi transport*, 1978, no. 11, p. 32; P. Trifonov, "On the small rivers of Tomsk Oblast," *Rechnoi transport*, 1978, no. 9, p. 21; O. Strelcheniya, "We're creating a deep-water route in the north," *Rechnoi transport*, 1978, no. 6, p. 40; A. Puzenko, and Ye. Zin, "Development problems of small rivers in the Soviet Far East," *Rechnoi transport*, 1978, no. 10, p. 29.

13. A. Ivashentsov and A. Rozentsvit, *Severnoye Zabaikalye—zapadnaya chast BAMa* [Northern Transbaikalia—the western part of the BAM] (Moscow: Sovetskaya Rossiya, 1977), p. 29; V. Ye. Biryukov, "The strategy of a complex approach," *Gudok* (hereafter *G*), 29 August 1978, p. 2.

14. Theodore Shabad, "News Notes," *SGRT*, 23, no. 4 (April 1982): 286.

15. V. L. Ivanov and B. V. Moskvin, "The development of transportation in the USSR in the 10th Five-Year Plan," *Geografiya v shkole*, 1978, no. 6, p. 9. The plan specified construction of 3,000 km of new track, 2,800 km of second track, 2,500 km of electrified rail line and up to 17,000 km of automatic-blocking and centralized dispatching systems.

16. A detailed description of the physical geography of the BAM and its service area is available in Shabad and Mote, *Siberian Resources*, pp. 68–70, 74–79 n 4. See also B. V. Sochava, V. P. Shotsky and I. I. Buks, "The BAM route and some problems for further study," *Doklady Instituta Geografii Sibiri i Dalnego Vostoka*, 1975, no. 46, pp. 3–12.

17. Gruliow, "Ivan Working," p. 78 n 1; Pinneker and Pisarsky, *Podzemnye vody*, p. 5 n 4.

18. A. Grigorash, "Roadlessness is expensive," 21 January 1979, p. 2. This figure conflicts with a later estimate of 18,000 in R. Minasov, "Quality and tempos," *I*, 15 February 1979, p. 2. The estimates are for the service area only. Recent Soviet data for the Buryat North, including the North Baikal and Baunt aimaks, indicate 17,000 residents in 1973. M. L. Alekseyev et al., *Problemy osvoyeniya severa Buryatskoi ASSR* [Problems of development in the northern zone of Buryat ASSR] (Novosibirsk: Nauka, 1978), p. 7.

19. V. Marikovsky, "Amur Oblast," *G*, 17 October 1978, p. 1. Data indicated that traffic was up to 3.3 million tons per year, and, when the Tynda-Neryungri segment went into service during the fall of 1979, coal cargoes alone were expected to rise from 100,000 tons per annum to over 2 million tons. "The start of the great conveyor," *G*, 1 September 1979, p. 2.

20. L. Brezhnev, "A splendid victory," *I*, 17 November 1978, p. 1, congratulating BAM workers on their achievements through 1978. Numerous other articles cited early completion of the Little BAM and the speedy laying of the "Eastern Ring," which were finished well ahead of schedule. Interviews with Soviet officials indicated that all was not well on other segments (conversation with Allen Whiting, 8 May 1979, Houston).

21. O. A. Kibalchich, "The Baikal-Amur Mainline and the complex economic development of the Soviet Far East," *Geografiya v shkole*, 42, no. 5 (September-October 1975): 8; translated in *SGRT*, 17, no. 6 (June 1976): 387; the rates were expected to be 2.5 times more than those for the building of the Trans-Siberian (0.6 km per day).

22. Interview with Allen Whiting, Houston, 8 May 1979. Dr. Whiting had discussed this issue with BAM construction supervisors in late 1978. In a letter to me, dated 21 September 1979, Theodore Shabad confirmed this report. The 11th Five-Year Plan calls for through traffic by 1985.

23. A. Shirokov, "The program is growing," *G*, 30 January 1980, p. 2; see also a previous issue of *G*, 30 December 1979, p. 1.

24. M. Romanov, "BAM: The project is picking up speed," *G*, 14 February 1980, p. 2.

25. V. Yermolayev, Yu. Kazmin, and A. Starukhin, "Four years later," *P*, 3 July 1978, p. 2., and several more recent reports.

26. R. Minasov, "The BAM: Through the prism of problems," *G*, 23 August 1978, p. 2.

27. Soviet planners hoped that the added dimensions would accelerate construction up to 2 km in 1979. "Into the heart of the Baikal range," *G*, 2 February 1979, p. 1.

28. Romanov, "Picking up speed," p. 2 n 24; this source suggested that the tunnel would be finished in May 1980!

29. V. Kalinichev, "The taiga kilometers of the BAM," *I*, 18 May 1977, p. 2; Yermolayev, Kazmin, and Starukhin, "Four years," p. 2 n 25; and more recent reports.

30. *P*, 5 November 1981; *I*, 30 July 1981; *Ekonomicheskaya gazeta*, 1981, no. 36.

31. *P*, 20 September 1981; *I*, 2 August 1981; *G*, 16 July 1981.

32. Dyakonov, "Soviet Far East," p. 13 n 9.

33. Charles Bremmer, *Reuters News Flash* No. 22 JC6343/4, RNR 623, "Rails 4 Alonka"; V. Ye. Biryukov, "The strategy of a complex approach," *G*, 29 August 1978, p. 2; *Narodnoye khozyaistvo SSSR za 60 let* [The economy of the USSR over the last 60 years] (Moscow: Statistika, 1977), p. 437.

34. V. V. Lazhentsev, "The Economic-Geographical Aspects of the BAM Problem" in *BAM-77*, p. 36.

35. By 1981, this investment had reached 50 million

rubles. I. Nesterov, "The petroleum potential of Tyumen," *G*, 26 December 1980, p. 4.

36. Theodore Shabad, "Soviet Development Policy in Siberia," *Journal of Geography*, 77, no. 7 (December 1978): 280–84.

37. M. E. Adzhiyev, "Economic-geographic problems of the BAM," *Priroda*, 1975, no. 8, p. 4; Dyakonov, "Soviet Far East," p. 13 n 9; Bunich, "BAM and development," p. 29 n 9; Theodore Shabad, "News Notes," *SGRT*, 18, no. 9 (November 1977): 701; A. Sabirov, "Where did the cross-country vehicle get mired?" *I*, 25 March 1979, p. 3.

38. Sabirov, "Cross-country vehicle," p. 3 n 37.

39. V. Goldberg, "Aldan shoals," *Vodny transport*, 10 June 1976, p. 3.

40. Sabirov, "Cross-country vehicle," p. 3 n 37.

41. Dyakonov, "Set of problems," p. 23 n 7.

42. N. P. Nikitin, Ye. D. Prozorov, and B. A. Tutykhin, eds., *Ekonomicheskaya geografiya SSSR* [Economic geography of the USSR] (Moscow: Prosveshcheniye, 1973), pp. 334–35.

43. V. Biryukov, "The Baikal-Amur Mainline: A Major National Construction Project," *SGRT*, 16, no. 4 (April 1975): 225–27; Belenki and Maslennikov, "Area of influence," p. 46 n 9.

44. L. P. Guzhnovsky, "The Siberian contribution to the country's petroleum base," *Ekonomika i organizatsiya promyshlennogo proizvodstva*, 1977, no. 6, pp. 35–43.

45. Excluding Sakhalin and Irkutsk Oblast, there are no oil deposits within reach of the BAM service area.

46. U. S. Central Intelligence Agency, *The International Energy Situation: Outlook to 1985* (Washington: CIA, 1977). Despite criticism, as of early 1981, the CIA's predictions regarding the West Siberian fields were still remarkably on target.

47. Guzhnovsky, "Siberian contributions," p. 41 n 44.

48. Ye. S. Matveyev, "For the BAM, the best of equipment," *G*, 28 September 1978, p. 2.

49. Guzhnovsky, "Siberian contribution," p. 41 n 44.

50. The zone *contiguous* to the BAM service area includes the Trans-Siberian service area east of Taishet, offshore islands, and the Vilyui River basin. The author feels that the new railroad will result not only in direct benefits to its service area as defined earlier, but also in indirect benefits to nearly areas such as those just described. The benefits to those regions would accrue as a consequence of the improved logistics rendered by the BAM. In the inventory that follows, these resources are identified specifically as being located in the contiguous zone.

51. Ye. Kozlovsky, "Raw-material complexes of the BAM," *P*, 15 November 1978, p. 2; for elaboration of the geological prospecting experiences in the Udokan area, see V. F. Zadorozhny, "An economic-geographic analysis of geological prospecting with particular reference to one of the BAM-zone regions," *Sibirsky geografichesky sbornik*, no. 13 (Novosibirsk: Nauka, 1977), pp. 80–125.

52. M. I. Voronin, "The Great Siberian railroad," *Transportnoye stroitelstvo*, 1975, no. 9, pp. 58–62; M. M. Odintsov and A. A. Bukharov, "The mineral resources of the zone," *Vestnik Akademii Naul SSSR*, 1975, no. 9, p. 47.

53. Ivashentsov and Rozentsvit, *Severnoye Zabaikalye*, p. 13. The sum total of Molodezhny asbestos resources is only 160 million tons, the largest deposit in Siberia but the fourth largest in the USSR. However, the mineral can be mined 3 to 3.7 times more cheaply at Molodezhny than at other Soviet domestic sites. Alekseyev, *Problemy osvoyeniya*, p. 31 n 18.

54. A. Kleva, "The asbestos of Transbaikalia," *I*, 1 March 1979, p. 1; P. Shobogorov, "The BAM is spurring on the geologists," *I*, 8 June 1978, p. 2.

55. Theodore Shabad, "Raw Material Problems of the Soviet Aluminum Industry," in *Soviet Economy in a New Perspective* (Washington: Government Printing Office, 1976), p. 661.

56. Odintsov and Bukharov, "Mineral resources," p. 48 n 52; V. Surkov and V. Botvinnikov, "The Baikal-Amur Mainline: The mineral complex," *I*, 19 August 1976, p. 2.

57. A. Kleva, "Rich ore," *I*, 5 January 1978, p. 1; I. Dementyeva et al., "A region striving toward the future," *I*, 19 June 1978, p. 2.

58. V. V. Onikhimovsky, *Geologiya SSSR. Tom XIX* [Geology of the USSR. Volume 19] (Moscow: Nedra, 1976), p. 45; B. I. Andreyev and D. V. Kravchenko, *Kamennougolnye basseiny SSSR* [Coal basins of the USSR] (Moscow: Uchpedgiz, 1958), pp. 170–71; G. I. Chiryayev, "The BAM and Yakutia," *Ekonomicheskaya gazeta*, 1974, no. 32, p. 5; N. V. Melnikov, *Energeticheskiye resursy SSSR* [Energy resources of the USSR] (Moscow: Nauka, 1968), pp. 121–30; A. A. Nedeshev, F. F. Bybin, and A. M. Kotelnikov, "The development of the Transbaikal North and problems of the transformation of the economy of Chita Oblast in connection with the construction of the Baikal-Amur Mainline," *Sibirsky geografichesky sbornik*, 1977, no. 13, p. 71.

59. V. Ryashin, "Neryungri is starting out," *Literaturnaya gazeta*, 1976, no. 11 (17 March), p. 11; A. Kleva, "Taiga treasures," *I*, 1 November 1977, p. 6; the information on the delays at Neryungri is contained in Craig R. Whitney, "In Frigid Siberia, Even U. S. Machines Fail," *New York Times*, 1 April 1979, p. 24.

60. Also called "conditional and speculative resources," Andreyev and Kravchenko, *Basseiny SSSR*, p. 170 n 60; Onikhimovsky, *Geologiya SSSR*, p. 45 n 58.

61. "In the vanguard of competition," *I*, 24 December 1977, p. 1; Melnikov, *Resursy SSSR*, p. 126 n 58; Theodore Shabad, *Basic Industrial Resources of the USSR* (New York: Columbia University Press, 1969), pp. 268–69.

62. In mid-1979, a new deposit of brown coal was discovered near Tygda north of the Amur River. Estimated to contain 466 million tons, the field is touted as one of the richest brown-coal sites in the country. *Soviet Weekly*, 21 July 1979, p. 3. The site is actually in the service area of the Trans-Siberian Railroad, but easily in the BAM's contiguous zone. Soviet geographers often discuss the impact of the BAM upon resources that are located outside of its service area.

63. Yu. G. Melik-Stepanov and L. A. Chirkova, "The nonferrous metallurgy of the USSR during the 10th Five-Year Plan," *Geografiya v shkole*, 1978, no. 5 (September-October), pp. 8–9; "Rich Natural Resources in the Region

of the Baikal-Amur Railway," *Soviet News*, 22 July 1975, p. 253; V. Molchanov, "From Baikal to the Amur," *P*, 25 July 1974, pp. 1, 3; Paul Dibb, *Siberia and the Pacific* (New York: Praeger, 1972), pp. 132, 238; Ivashentsov and Rozentsvit, *Zapadnaya chast*, p. 58 n 13; Nedeshev et al., "Development of Transbaikal North," pp. 71–72 n 58.

64. U. S. Department of Interior, Bureau of Mines, *Mineral Industries of Eastern Europe and the USSR* (Washington: Government Printing Office, 1978), p. 27; U. S. Department of Interior, Bureau of Mines, *Mineral Facts and Problems* (Washington: Government Printing Office, 1975), p. 327. The latter source lists 25 million tons of reserves, but this mistakenly may be for gem stones only.

65. U. S. Department of Interior, Bureau of Mines, *Area Reports: International*, vol 3 of *Minerals Yearbook*, 1974, 3 vols. (Washington: Government Printing Office, 1977), p. 959.

66. Allen Whiting, personal correspondence, 29 March 1979; Arthur A. Meyerhoff, *Potential for Foreign Participation in the Soviet Union and Chinese Petroleum Industries* (Boston: International Human Resources Development Corp., 1978), p. 202; Bunich, "BAM and development," p. 30 n 9. Soviet, Japanese, and American natural gas officials have confirmed that the Yakutian deposits hold one trillion $m^3$ of natural gas. For an analysis of Soviet natural gas potentials, see chapter 15 of this book.

67. Whitney, "Machines Fail," p. 24 n 59; James C. Tanner, "Russia Revives Plan to Tap Gas Deposits with Aid from U. S. and Japanese Banks," *Wall Street Journal*, 19 November 1975, p. 4; Meyerhoff, *Foreign Participation*, figs. 69–77 n 6; see also American-Siberian Natural Gas Company, *Yakutia Gas Project* (Houston: El Paso Gas, 1979).

68. John J. Stephen, "Sakhalin Island: Soviet Outpost in Northeast Asia," *Asian Survey*, 10, no 12 (1970): 1094.

69. U. S. Department of Interior, *Mineral Industries*, p. 27 n 64; U. S. Department of Interior, *Area Reports*, p. 944 n 65.

70. The following information on BAM-zone iron ore is derived from: V. S. Sidorova and A. A. Vadyukhin, "New Technology and the Location of the Iron and Steel Industry in the Eastern Portion of the USSR," *SGRT*, 18, no. 1 (January 1977): 33–38; D. P. Serdyuchenko et al., *Zheleznye rudy Yuzhnoi Yakutii* [Iron ores of South Yakutia] (Moscow: AN SSSR, 1960); Chiryayev, "Yakutia," p. 5 n 58; Bunich, "BAM and development," p. 31 n 9; K. V. Dolgopolov et al., *Zheleznye rudy SSSR* [Iron ores of the USSR] (Moscow: Uchpedgiz, 1963), pp. 11, 139–41; Kleva, "Taiga treasures," p. 6 n 59.

71. Dyakonov, "Set of problems," p. 30 n 7.

72. Sidorova and Vadyukhin, "New Technology," p. 35 n 70.

73. Dolgopolov et al., *Rudy SSSR*, p. 140 n 70. The site is only 10 km from China; I. D. Darzhayev, "On the rails of the BAM,: *G*, 10 February 1979, p. 2.

74. Shobogorov, "Spurring on the geologists," p. 2 n 54; F. Gafurov, "From Baikal to the Amur," *I*, 4 March 1979, p. 2; Darzhayev, "BAM rails," p. 2 n 73; CIA, *Soviet Tin Industry: Recent Developments and Prospects Through*

*1980* (Washington: Central Intelligence Agency, 1977), p. 14; "News Notes," *SGRT*, 21, no. 6 (June 1980): 397–98.

75. Odintsov and Bukharov, "Mineral resources," pp. 47–48 n 52; O. A. Izyumsky, "The natural resources of the BAM zone and their rational utilization," in *BAM-77*, p. 100.

76. Darzhayev, "BAM rails," p. 2 n 73; Serdyuchenko et al, *Yuzhnoi Yakutii*, p. 500 n 70; Izyumsky, "Natural resources," p. 109 n 75; Shabad, *Basic Industrial*, pp. 248–49 n 61.

77. Akademiya Nauk SSSR, Sibirskoye otdeleniye, *Atlas Zabaikalya* (Moscow-Irkutsk: GUGK, 1967), p. 28; Kibalchich, "Soviet Far East," pp. 8–9 n 21; Alekseyev, *Ot Baikala*, p. 64a n 2.

78. One source has referred to northern Buryatia as "the USSR's third major nickel province" after Norilsk and the Kola Peninsula. Alekseyev, *Problemy osvoyeniya*, p. 41 n 18.

79. V. Samsonov, "Irkutsk Oil Drillers Need Lighter Rigs" *Current Digest of the Soviet Press*, 30, no. 43 (22 November 1978): 7; Meyerhoff, *Foreign Participation*, figs. 69–70, 74 n 66; Shabad, "News Notes," *SGRT*, 22, no. 2 (February 1981): 123.

80. Meyerhoff, *Foreign participation*, figs. 59–63, p. 202 n 66; Shabad, "News Notes," *SGRT*, 19, no. 4 (April 1978): 274.

81. A. E. Cullison, "Massive Oil Strike in Sea of Okhotsk," *Houston Chronicle*, 16 November 1977, section 3, p. 24; also see *New York Times*, 13 October 1977, D9; for prognosticated reserves, see Stephen, "Sakhalin Island," pp. 1093–94 n 68.

82. "Big Deposit of Phosphorites Has Been Found in Yakutia," *Soviet News*, 3 June 1975, p. 194; Surkov and Botvinnikov, "Mineral complex," p. 2 n 56; I. Dementyeva et al., "Science—To the Siberian field," *I*. 18 June 1978, pp. 1–2; "Phosphate Deposit," *Soviet News*, 23 January 1979, p. 14.

83. "Phosphate Deposit," p. 14 n 82, quoting a Soviet geologist, Lev Krasny.

84. Whiting, correspondence, footnote 66; Kibalchich, "Soviet Far East," p. 10 n 21; "The Baikal-Amur Mainline," *Rechnoi transport*, 1976, no. 1, p. 55; Izyumsky, "Natural resources," p. 102 n 75.

85. Akademiya Nauk, *Atlas Zabaikalya*, p. 28 n 77.

86. Surkov and Botvinnikov, "Mineral complex," p. 2 n 56; Kozlovsky, *Kompleksy BAMa*, p. 2 n 51.

87. Dyakonov, "Soviet Far East," p. 13 n 9.

88. TASS, "News from everywhere," *I*, 25 November 1977, p. 4.

89. U. S. Department of the Interior, *Mineral Industries*, p. 27 n 64. The remaining information on tin comes from CIA, *Tin Industry*, pp. 1–18 n 74.

90. This would not be the case if Soviet tin could be mined cheaply. Unfortunately, Soviet tin ore is about one-and-a-half times more expensive than the foreign product.

91. Kibalchich, "Soviet Far East," p. 9 n 21; Nedeshev et al., "Development of the Transbaikal North," pp. 72–73 n 58; Serdyuchenko et al., *Yuzhnoi Yakutii*, p. 496 n 70; U. S. Department of Interior, *Mineral Facts*, p. 262 n 64.

92. A. Pushkar, "Maritime Krai's tungsten," 4 May 1978, *I*, p. 2; Shabad, *Basic Industrial*, p. 262–63.

93. Shabad, *Basic Industrial*, pp. 261–62, 279–80 n 61; U. S. Department of Interior, *Area Reports*, p. 962 n 65; U. S. Department of Interior, *Mineral Facts*, p. 684 n 64.

94. Ivashentsov and Rozentsvit, *Zapadnaya chast*, p. 48 n 13; Akademiya Nauk, *Atlas Zabaikalya*, p. 28 n 77; U. S. Department of Interior, *Area Reports*, pp. 942, 955 n 65: U. S. Department of Interior, *Mineral Industries*, p. 27 n 64.

95. Nedeshev et al., "Development of the Transbaikal North," p. 50 n 58.

96. U. S. Department of Interior, *Mineral Industries*, p. 27 n 64; U. S. Department of Interior, *Area Reports*, pp. 942, 955 n 65.

97. Darzhayev, "BAM rails," p. 2 n 73.

98. V. L. Gorovoi and V. M. Shlykov, "Basic trends in the development of the timber industry in the BAM zone," in *BAM-77*, p. 56, in translation in *SGRT*, 19, no. 2 (February 1978): 86.

99. Exports to countries bordering on the Pacific are almost 9 million m³ of roundwood. See *Vneshnyaya torgovlya SSSR v 1979 g* [Foreign trade of the USSR in 1979] (Moscow: Statistika, 1980), p. 69. Brenton Barr expects these exports to reach 11 million to 13 million m³ by 1990.

100. "Less developed" and "more developed" classifications are those used by the Population Reference Bureau. Of the 164 countries in the world with populations over 200,000, only 36 (comprising the Occident and Japan) are considered more developed. Such classifications cannot be applied automatically to the development of individual resources. Whether development proceeds at a geometric or linear rate depends on the characteristics of the commodity being exploited.

101. Note that smelted copper and iron ore appear in EXPOUT in 1980, meaning that the Pacific Basin is self-sufficient then. The two commodities show up in EXPAC during 1985 and 1990, meaning the basin should have a deficit then. The total entries, therefore, total 27, but two of the commodities are listed twice.

102. Lignite is not a major commodity in world trade. Likewise, natural gas, if it ever flows to the Pacific ports, will move by pipeline. The BAM will have influence only in a developmental sense from the standpoint of field and pipeline logistics.

103. Vladimir Savin, "Both Sides Benefit From Compensation Deals," *Soviet News*, 20 March 1979, p. 94.

104. The USSR was only 90 percent self-sufficient in antimony in 1975, but output was growing rapidly (see Table 1).

105. An "opportunity commodity," as it is used here, is an exchangeable resource that is traded or sold according to the whim of the producer. It comprises precious minerals like gold, diamonds, and platinum. As stated earlier, data for vanadium, cobalt, and titanium—all strategic metals—were incomplete and must be considered statistically unreliable. They would appear to be suitable for export to the basin, if only because of their strategic value.

106. Note the absence of oil. Any surplus of West Siberian petroleum between now and 1990 will have to go to Europe. Whatever share enters Pacific Siberia probably will be consumed domestically. Even a Sakhalin surplus is expected to be minimal. See the analysis in Yuan-Ii Wu, *Japan's Search for Oil* (Stanford, Ca.: Hoover Institution Press, 1978), pp. 47–48. Note our quantitative output reflects the same conclusion (see Table 11).

107. Japan's overall strategy is to increase the share of coal, liquefied natural gas, and nuclear power within its energy consumption total by 1990 in order to decrease overall dependence on foreign oil imports. See chapter 9 of this book.

108. The 7 percent estimate comes from Robert N. North, "The Soviet Far East: New Center of Attention in the USSR," *Pacific Affairs*, 51, no. 2 (Summer 1978): 214.

109. Ibid., p. 214.

110. Izyumsky, "Natural resources," p. 98 n 75; also see chapter 3 of this book.

111. The TPC is not unlike, but differs from, the Western concept of "growth center," as defined by Boudeville. See George Huzinec, "Some Initial Comparisons of Soviet and Western Regional Development Models," *SGRT*, 17, no. 8 (October 1976): 552–56; see also chapter 6 of this book.

112. Richard E. Lonsdale, "The Soviet Concept of the Territorial-Production Complex," *Slavic Review*, 24, no. 3 (September 1965): 466–78.

113. L. I. Vinokurova, "A method for studying territorial-production complexes," *Geografiya v shkole*, 1978, no. 3 (May-June), pp. 31–32.

114. Izyumsky, "Natural resources," pp. 99–100 n 75; Huzinec, "Regional Planning," p. 560 n 111.

115. G. Tarasov, "Industrial constellations of Siberia," *I*, 3 December 1976, p. 2; Kibalchich, "Soviet Far East," pp. 6–12 n 21; O. A. Kibalchich, "Production-territorial structure of the BAM service area," *Vestnik Moskovskogo Universiteta, seriya geografiya*, 1975, no. 4 (July–August), pp. 29–35; P. Ya. Baklanov, V. N. Sevostyanov, and I. R. Spektor, "Economic regionalization of the eastern zone of influence of the BAM—conceptualization and method," *Izvestiya Akademii Nauk SSSR, seriya geograficheskaya*, 1978, no. 6, pp. 65–79, translated in *SGRT*, 20, no. 6 (June 1979): 335–53; Yu. A. Burkreyev and Ye. N. Pertsik, "Problems in the general regional planning scheme for the BAM service area," *Opyt razrabotki i realizatsii skhem i proyektov rayonnoi planirovki*, 1976, no. 7, pp. 20–24.

116. The cost of this electricity is over 10 times cheaper than the hydropower produced along the Dnieper Cascade. Sidorova and Vadyukhin, "New Technology," p. 37 n 70.

117. A. Sokolov, "Time introduces amendments," *I*, 5 May 1979, p. 2.

118. "In working operation," *G*, 3 January 1979, p. 2; TASS, "News from everywhere," *I*, 31 December 1977, p. 6.

119. Most of what follows is drawn from information in Alekseyev, *Problemy osvoyeniya*, n 18; for other insights, see Ivashentsov and Rozentsvit, *Zapadnaya chast*, n 13.

120. R. Minasov, "Prism of problems"; L. Lyubimov, "How long must we wait?" *G*, 7 June 1979, p. 2.

121. Alekseyev, *Problemy osvoyeniya*, p. 82 n 18; V. Degtyarev, Ye. Zin, and N. Permichev, "River transport in Siberia and the Far East," *Rechnoi transport*, 1978, no. 3, p. 21.

122. Alekseyev, *Problemy osvoyeniya*, p. 102 n 18.

123. These data are confirmed by A. A. Chernoyarova, "Geographic conditions and characteristics for the creation of the food base in the service area of the west Transbaikal segment of the BAM," *Sibirsky geografichesky sbornik*, 1977, no. 13, p. 186.

124. Only 10 million rubles of 120 million allocated have been spent on the first section of the city. *P*, 13 October 1978, p. 3.

125. R. Minasov, "Prism of problems"; V. Vasilchenko et al., "The advantages are evident," *I*, 30 December 1980, p. 1 on complaints about draft five-year plan.

126. Ironically, Bodaibo, as the center of the Lena goldfields, was the focus of many prerevolutionary, BAM-type railroad proposals. AN SSSR, Komissiya po problemam Severa, *Letopis Severa* [Chronicle of the North], vol 2 (Moscow: Izd. geograficheskoi literatury, 1957), pp.. 197–200.

127. Izyumsky, "Natural resources," p. 100 n 75.

128. Much of the following information is derived from Nedeshev, Bybin, and Kotelnikov, "Development of the Transbaikal North," pp. 50–75 n 58.

129. The long-range projected population of the Udokan mining district is also 50,000. However, these numbers are not expected to be reached until well after 1990.

130. Chernoyarova, "Geographic conditions," p. 187 n 123.

131. V. V. Prokhorov, "Timely problems of medical geography in the BAM zone," in *BAM-77*, p. 137.

132. Much of what follows is derived from Baklanov et al., "Economic regionalization," pp. 65–79 n 115.

133. A. Loginov, "The first coal from Neryungri," *G*, 3 October 1978, p. 1.

134. *Komsomolskaya pravda*, 16 November 1977; A. Loginov, "Will they have their own vegetables on the BAM?" *G*, 11 July 1978, p. 2.

135. Baklanov, Sevostyanov, and Spektor, "Economic regionalization," p. 77 n 115.

136. Ye. I. Yelovoi and V. S. Smetanich, "Problems of energy supply in the BAM zone and some ways to solve them," in *BAM-77*, p. 149.

137. A. Avramenko, "On Amur livestock farms," *I*, 12 May 1978, p. 2 and V. Malafeyev, "The principal reference point," *G*, 30 March 1979, p. 1.

138. G. Podgayev, "The food base of the Krai," *I*, 27 June 1979, p. 2.

139. A. Pushkar, "Reinforcement of the transport line," *I*, 4 April 1979, p. 2 and "A flotilla of ferries," *G*, 30 March 1979, p. 2.

140. "Flotilla of ferries," p. 1 n 139; "Following the example of the Leningraders," *G*, 21 August 1979, p. 1; and S. Karlashov, "How can we speed up the trains?" *G*, 9 January 1979, p. 2.

141. B. Khorev, "Main Movement of Population Is to East of Country," *Soviet News*, 3 June 1975, p. 194 and A. Illarionov and V. Letov, "Portrait of the construction project," *I*, 27 April 1979, p. 2.

142. Ye. N. Pertsik, "Problems of regional planning in the BAM zone," in *BAM-77*, p. 192.

143. See chapter 3 of this book.

144. Nedeshev, Bybin, and Kotelnikov, "Development of the Transbaikal North," p. 54 n 58. This average allocation may have increased recently as a result of a 1 January 1979 resolution to raise Siberian salaries substantially compared with those of European workers. *Soviet News*, 23 January 1979, p. 5. Some say the per capita investment should be increased to 30,000 rubles. Gruliow, "Ivan Working," p. 80 n 1.

# 8

# COMMODITY FLOWS, RESOURCE POTENTIAL AND REGIONAL ECONOMIC DEVELOPMENT: THE EXAMPLE OF THE SOVIET FAR EAST

ALLAN RODGERS
The Pennsylvania State University

This chapter is concerned with regional development policy as it has been reflected in the economic transformation of the Soviet Far East since 1940. That metamorphosis has been and will continue to be mirrored in changing interregional and international commodity flows. Future movements will presumably be a reflection of economic and political change. In the economic sphere, resource development should prove to be a major factor in the future foreign trade of the Soviet Far East. Then too, further development of that region's resources may permit a substitution of local supplies for commodities that hitherto have been imported from Siberia and European Russia.

The central questions then can be phrased as follows: (1) What has been the nature of past interregional and international commodity flows for the Far East and can these movements be explained in the light of Soviet development policy? (2) To what degree may these patterns change over the coming decade and how might such permutations affect trade between the USSR and her Pacific neighbors?

## The Setting

The Soviet Far East, with an area of over six million square kilometers, is the largest economic region of the USSR (Figure 1). It alone accounts for roughly 28 percent of the nation's territory more than double the size of Kazakhstan, the second largest planning region. Yet this huge region because of severe environmental problems and remoteness from the Soviet heartland remains sparsely populated and underdeveloped. Its constituent political divisions, their area and population are demonstrated in Table 1.

The population of the Soviet Far East, as of the 1979 Census, was less than seven million or about 2.6 percent of the total population of the USSR. Its mean density is less than eight per square kilometer. However, this value distorts the actual distribution pattern. Vast areas in the North are virtually uninhabited (with the exception of

Yakutia and the eastern coastal margin). In contrast, the great majority of the population live in settlements along the Trans-Siberian Railroad and its extension to Komsomolsk and Sovetskaya Gavan. The population is highly urbanized with an average of 75 percent compared to a national mean of 62 percent.[1]

The environmental constraints that account for the limited population of this huge area include short and erratic growing seasons, unusually severe and long winters, rough and high terrain, modest and erratic precipitation, permafrost, poor drainage and infertile soils. The severity of each of these deterrents varies significantly within the region, but in the overview, the only truly attractive areas are located in the south and southeast. These include the Zeya and Bureya valleys, the central Amur basin and the Lake Khanka-Ussuri lowlands. However, even in the latter area, which is the most favored subregion, drainage and irrigation are typically required for optimum yields. About 27 million hectares, or 2.5 percent of the area of the Far East, is now classified as "agricultural land" and less than half of this acreage is sown in any one year. The remainder is typically used for the rearing and grazing of cattle. Prospects for the further expansion of the current area under cultivation are minimal at least on a cost-benefit basis. Even given the small population of this region, its limited grain output has over the years necessitated significant imports of grain from Western Siberia, Kazakhstan and abroad.

A discussion of remoteness and the "friction of distance" might focus on the extraordinary distances involved in rail shipment from the west to Far Eastern ports coupled with transshipment to coastal freighters destined for ultimate destinations like Magadan, Petropavlovsk, or Yuzhno-Sakhalinsk. However, these are extreme cases which involve only a fraction of the flows to and from the Far East. More realistically, the focus should be on distances to the Center or to the Urals from the more developed parts of the Far East, such as Khabarovsk. The rail distances to the Urals (Chelyabinsk) and the Center (Moscow) are 6,694 kilometers and 8,505 kilometers respectively. Overcoming these distances clearly involves the expenditure of time and money. Despite limited funds, conflicting sectoral and regional demands and the problems of the Far East cited above, the central authorities have devoted a relatively large share of

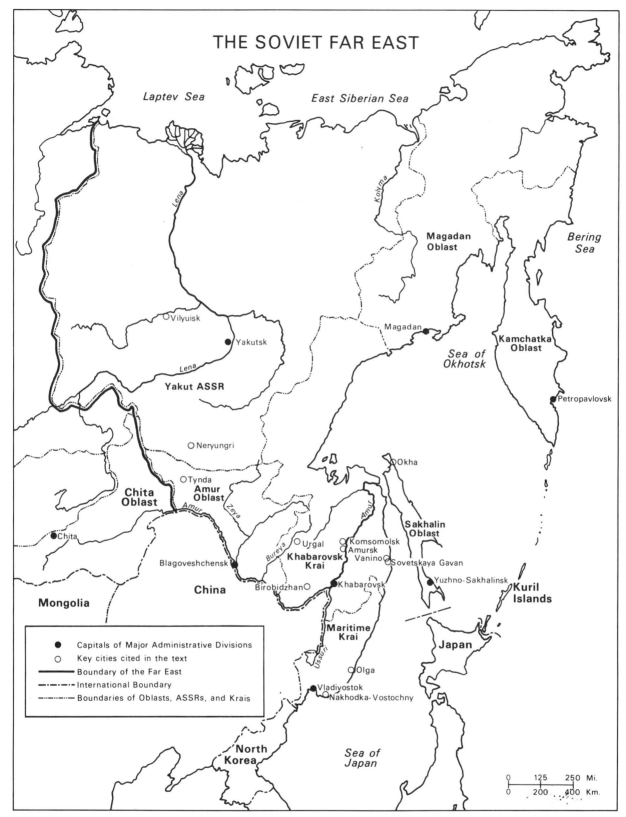

## THE SOVIET FAR EAST

Laptev Sea

East Siberian Sea

Magadan
Oblast

Bering
Sea

OVilyuisk

●Yakutsk

Kamchatka
Oblast

Yakut ASSR

Sea of
Okhotsk

●Petropavlovsk

ONeryungri

OOkha

OTynda
Chita      Amur
Oblast     Oblast

Sakhalin
Oblast

●Chita

OUrgal    O○Komsomolsk
              OAmursk
Blagoveshchensk     Vanino○   ○Sovetskaya Gavan
Khabarovsk
Kr ai
BirobidzhanO   ●Khabarovsk   ●Yuzhno-Sakhalinsk   Kuril
China                                              Islands

Mongolia

Maritime
Kr ai                    Japan

● Capitals of Major Administrative Divisions
○ Key cities cited in the text
──── Boundary of the Far East
─·─·─ International Boundary
─··─··─ Boundaries of Oblasts, ASSRs, and Krais

○Olga

●Vladivostok
○Nakhodka-Vostochny

North
Korea

Sea of
Japan

0    125    250 Mi.
0    200    400 Km.

Figure 1

TABLE 1
The Size and Population of the Major Administrative
Divisions of the Soviet Far East as of 1979*

| Political Units | Area 000 of sq. km. | Population thousands | Population Density per square kilometer |
|---|---|---|---|
| Maritime Krai | 165.9 | 1,978 | 11.9 |
| Khabarovsk Krai | 824.6 | 1,565 | 1.9 |
| Amur Oblast | 363.7 | 938 | 2.6 |
| Kamchatka Oblast | 472.3 | 378 | 0.8 |
| Magadan Oblast | 1,199.3 | 466 | 0.4 |
| Sakhalin Oblast | 87.1 | 655 | 7.5 |
| Yakut ASSR | 3,103.2 | 839 | 0.3 |
| Soviet Far East | 6,215.9 | 6,819 | 1.1 |

*Naseleniye SSSR [Population of the USSR] (Moscow: 1980), pp. 4–11.

capital investment funds to this region, particularly when compared to its share of the nation's population. That priority in the past, at least, reflected the nation's strategic concerns vis-à-vis Japan and, since the sixties, the People's Republic of China. Most recently, especially since 1974, massive investments in the Baikal-Amur Mainline have accelerated economic development in this region.

**Historical Perspective**

Russian explorers first reached the Pacific in 1649. During the two centuries that followed, the Czarist governments, bolstered by treaties imposed upon the Chinese, laid claim to Eastern Siberia and the Far East. However, it was not until the late nineteenth century that settlement, in any meaningful sense, proceeded. Thus by 1860 the estimated Slavic population of the Far East was only about 60,000 (without the Yakutian area). Clearly, if Russia was to retain its territorial sovereignty over that vast region, colonization had to receive high priority. Yet the drive eastward was retarded by the absence of any rail link with European Russia. Nevertheless, state sponsored and subsidized migration grew rapidly in the following decades. Those colonists came mainly by ship via the Suez Canal.

By the time of the 1897 census, the region's population had grown to over 600,000, with one-third of that number in Yakutia. The construction of the Trans-Siberian Railroad, which reached the Amur by 1900 and Vladivostok by 1916, coupled with the building of the Chinese Eastern railway (from Chita across Manchuria to Vladivostok) was a major stimulus for the further economic development of the Far East. These new rail linkages now became the major migration routes to Siberia. Blagoveshchensk, the initial urban nucleus for the Zeya-Bureya lowland was soon surpassed in population size by Khabarovsk and Vladivostok. The Russian defeat in the war with Japan (1905) dealt a major blow to the Czarist state with the loss of suzerainty in Manchuria as well as the ceding of southern Sakhalin to the victor. Yet this humiliating

setback had *positive* economic repercussions for the Far East. It now became apparent to the Russian leaders that their blunders were in part attributable to their failure to develop and strengthen the nation's eastern flank. Without attributing a direct cause and effect relationship, it is noteworthy that the numbers of voluntary migrants, prisoners and exiles increased significantly in the years that followed. By 1913, the population of the region had surpassed 1,500,000.

This brief historical overview will be concluded by summarizing relevant socioeconomic developments in the Soviet Far East during the two decades following the First World War and the Civil War.

The Far East, despite its distance from the western front and the centers of revolutionary activity in European Russia, suffered significant loss of life as a result of war-time mobilization, the Civil War and foreign intervention (particularly by the Japanese). What little industry that had developed in the region, often with foreign assistance and capital, was damaged, destroyed or went into disrepair. By 1926 the date of the first postwar census the population had decreased by 200,000 from 1913 levels. The Japanese had evacuated the Far East and the Russian government, now Soviet, had reassumed sovereignty over the region.

The early twenties was mainly a period of reconstruction for the Far East. By the beginning of the 1st Five-Year Plan (1928–32) industrial production in the region had surpassed 1913 values. However, the absolute level of its output was still minimal. Table 2 demonstrates capital investment by region in the USSR during the prewar plan era. If the population proportion of the Far East (1.1 percent in 1926 and 1.8 in 1939) is compared with the share of capital investment, then the region clearly had received comparatively high priority in capital outlays. Its population nearly doubled to a level of about three million inhabitants by 1939. Nearly half of that number was now classified as urban compared to one-third in 1926. New cities like Komsomolsk had emerged while Khabarovsk had grown fourfold to a level of 207,000, and Vladivostok's population doubled reaching 206,000 by 1939.

TABLE 2
Capital Investment by Region and Plan Period
for the USSR between 1928 and World War II*

| Region | 1928–32 | 1933–37 | 1938– July 1941 |
|---|---|---|---|
| Far East | 4.8 | 5.7 | 7.6 |
| Eastern Siberia | 4.2 | 3.5 | 3.5 |
| Western Siberia | 4.4 | 4.0 | 4.0 |
| Urals | 9.3 | 8.7 | 8.5 |
| Kazakhstan and Central Asia | 8.4 | 7.2 | 7.4 |
| European Russia | 68.9 | 70.9 | 69.0 |
| USSR (percent) | 100.0 | 100.0 | 100.0 |
| Absolute values in comparable monetary terms (millions of rubles) | 6,716 | 15,170 | 15,101 |

*Kapitalnoye stroitelstvo v SSSR [Capital construction in the USSR] (Moscow: Gosstatizdat, 1961), pp. 114–15.

Yet the Far East's industrial structure with its focus on forest products, construction materials, ship building and repair and food processing (mainly fish) remained largely the same as that in the prerevolutionary era (see Table 3).

On the positive side, the machinery industry had progressed from simple repair shops and metal fabrication to modern factory-type production. There had also been a notable growth of nonferrous metallurgy as well as an increase in the mining and processing of precious metals and gems. By 1942 a small nonintegrated steel mill went into operation at Komsomolsk.

More significant was the expansion of linkages westward by the double tracking of the Trans-Siberian Railway (1937) and the installation of sophisticated traffic control equipment. Within the region, connectivity had been strengthened by the completion of the Khabarovsk-Komsomolsk rail line (1940).

The capital investment data, shown in Table 2, for the initial years of the 3rd Five-Year Plan reveal a significant increase in such outlays for the Far East over the preceding years. This absolute and relative growth probably reflects a military build-up in the region in anticipation of war with Japan. In fact, there were several bloody skirmishes with the Japanese along the Manchurian border in 1938.

Table 4 demonstrates inbound and outbound commodity flows for the Far East in 1940. It should be stressed that neither foreign trade (exports-imports for the region itself) nor intraregional freight movements are included in these data.

Given the small population and limited economic development of the region in 1940, the low freight turnover is not unexpected. However, the net deficit of five million tons is a clear indication of the dependence of the Far East on interregional linkages. The additional transport cost burden could only have been defended on political and strategic grounds. Nearly 30 percent of the inbound movements came from European Russia, roughly six to

eight thousand kilometers away. The remainder came mainly from Western and Eastern Siberia. Although it is not anomalous that 54 percent of the outbound movements and 39 percent of the inbound flows terminated or originated in neighboring Eastern Siberia, it is surprising that such a large share of the freight movements were destined for European Russia. Although no statistical breakdown for this period by commodity group has been found, the inbound flows probably consisted mainly of coal, oil, iron and steel, fabricated metals, machinery, durable and nondurable consumer goods, grain and other food products. In contrast, the outbound movements comprised mainly lumber, nonferrous and precious metals and cement.

Finally, a note about Soviet foreign trade. While no data by economic region are available for the prewar period, there are detailed import and export statistics for the USSR as a whole in 1940 by country of origin and destination.[2] These materials show that trade with its neighbors in the Pacific rim was insignificant. By inference, then, the foreign trade of the Soviet Far East was, in turn, negligible.

## Soviet Regional Development Policy

The present author has commented elsewhere on Soviet location criteria.[3] It was argued then that the principles for the spatial allocation of resources in the USSR contain both technical optimization rules and social value concepts. The economic history of the Soviet era, particularly in the past two decades, indicates that their planners face the same dichotomy of choices, growth versus equity, in the regional allocation of resources that confront their counterparts in market-oriented economies. Both options are incorporated into "socialist location principles." However, if there is a conscious regional planning policy in the USSR, it appears to support growth rather than equity. There appear to be two decision-making levels in the Soviet spatial allocation process. Broad judgments as to macro-regional economic development may reflect the equality thesis, strategic concerns, internal bargaining and presumably long-term perspectives of optimum regional economic development. Such determinations may affect allocations to Eastern Siberia, the Far East or the Ukraine, etc. Within each macro-economic region, the locational choice appears to be based increasingly on cost minimization techniques. These methods are used in attempts to optimize the regional distribution of admittedly scarce resources.

### Regional Development and the Far East

Returning to the discussion of the Far East, specific mention of this region in the first two five-year plans was minimal. However, the region received auspicious attention in the 3rd Plan (1938–42). Sonin[4] argued that, in this era, one facet of regional development policy was oriented towards the creation of a balanced first order industrial base in the Far East in order to strengthen the economic and military power of the region. Specifically,

TABLE 3
Employment by Industrial Sector for the
Soviet Far East in 1940*

| Sector | Industrial Employment 000 | Percentages |
|---|---|---|
| Fuel (oil and coal mining) | 30.4 | 10.3 |
| Energy | 15.5 | 5.3 |
| Ferrous and nonferrous metallurgy | 0.1 | — |
| Machinery and metal fabrication | 38.2 | 13.0 |
| Construction materials (especially cement) | 12.2 | 4.1 |
| Forest products (mainly lumber) | 91.0 | 31.0 |
| Light industry | 10.8 | 3.7 |
| Food industry (mainly fish processing) | 92.1 | 31.3 |
| Other | 3.8 | 1.3 |
| Total Employment | 294.1 | 100.0 |

*Compiled from Soviet statistical handbooks and *Dalni Vostok za 40 let Sovetskoi vlasti* [The Far East during 40 years of Soviet Power] (Komsomolsk, 1958).

TABLE 4
Interregional Commodity Flows for the Soviet Far East in 1940*

| Region | Inbound Movements** | | Outbound Movements** | |
|---|---|---|---|---|
| | thousands of tons | percent | thousands of tons | percent |
| European Russia | 1,847 | 28.4 | 465 | 31.2 |
| Urals | 475 | 7.3 | 109 | 7.3 |
| Western Siberia | 1,268 | 19.5 | 57 | 3.8 |
| Eastern Siberia | 2,563 | 39.4 | 805 | 53.9 |
| Kazakhstan and Central Asia | 351 | 5.4 | 57 | 3.8 |
| Far East (total) | 6,504 | 100.0 | 1,493 | 100.0 |

*N. M. Singur, "The role of transportation in the development of the economy of the Far Eastern Economic Region," in T. S. Khachaturov, *Povysheniye effektivnosti transporta v SSSR* [The increase in the effectiveness of transportation in the USSR] (Moscow: Mysl, 1966), p. 32. The absolute values were derived from scattered data found in a variety of Soviet studies of the region. The data do cover *all* carriers.
**Foreign trade is not included in these statistics.

there was to be an expansion of the production of machinery, the forest industries and the production of construction materials. In addition, a steel mill (Amurstal) was to be built at Komsomolsk on the Amur. Strengthening the internal transport network was to receive the highest priority. Fuel production (coal and oil) was to be expanded to serve the new industries and the transport sector.

The population of the Far East reached three million by 1939. Lorimer[5] estimates that in-migration during the 1926–39 period was about 900,000 or nearly two-thirds of the total population growth of the region. What share of these migrants were prisoners and deportees is uncertain, but émigré accounts make it apparent that eastward movement of forced labor was the key element in the increase in population.

World War II for the Soviet Union began in 1941. The German armies ultimately occupied or encircled most of the industrial areas of the USSR. Their belt of maximum advance lay west of the line: Leningrad, Moscow, Stalingrad and the North Caucasus. The Soviets were extraordinarily successful in the evacuation of skilled personnel and strategically important industrial equipment eastward, but that movement was never particularly meaningful for the Far East because of its sheer distance from the front. Nevertheless, modest economic development did proceed. The rail line from Komsomolsk to Sovetskaya Gavan was essentially completed as was the Komsomolsk steel mill which presumably helped to feed the armaments industry. Some indication of the limited pace of economic growth can be gleaned from capital investment data. In percentage terms, the share of the region (7.8 percent) in the total for the USSR was roughly the same as that in the 3rd Five-Year Plan. In contrast, the proportion of the Urals and Western Siberia doubled to 16 and 6 percent respectively.

No firm data exist on wartime migration to the east, but the movement is known to have been highly selective. Kulischer[6] has *estimated* that, in all, the civilian population that moved eastward may have totaled twelve million. However, it was assumed that no significant segment of those that were evacuated were settled in the Far East. Yet the 1959 Census shows a growth of over 1.8

million in the previous two decades. In percentage terms, the population increase was 62 percent compared to a national growth of less than 10 percent. In part, the high percentage change for the Far East is related to the low population numbers in 1939. It also reflects the reoccupation and settlement of southern Sakhalin (termed Karafuto by the Japanese). If the prewar Japanese population of that region is excluded, the number of Russian inhabitants of the island grew from 100,000 in 1939 to 649,000 twenty years later. A study of vital rates for the Far East makes it appear that voluntary migration coupled with forced labor and an expanded military presence help to account for the overall population growth.

Regional Development in the Postwar Era

The population of the Soviet Far East increased more than 40 percent between 1959 and 1979 reaching a level of 6.8 million inhabitants. This percentage compares with a national level of growth, during the same interval, of 26 percent. In contrast, the relative growth rates for the Urals and Western Siberia were only 10 and 15 percent, respectively. Labor turnover in Western Siberia has long been a serious problem with a succession of years with net out-migration. There, urban population growth reflects mainly intraregional rural-urban migration.

Unlike the case of Western Siberia, there has been a small but notable net in-migration to the Far East since 1959. That inflow cannot now be attributed to forced labor! It does reflect, in part, interregional population movements resulting largely from monetary incentives offered by the state. Additionally the absolute increase in the region's population was a result of a higher natural increase than the national average (higher birth rates and lower death rates). However, it should be stressed that despite the growth of the region's population, there is still a severe labor shortage. Clearly, environmental handicaps have repelled potential colonists, while wage and social insurance differentials have not been large enough to counterbalance such perennial problems as inadequate housing, persistent shortages of consumer goods and the insufficiency of social amenities. The limited development of consumer-goods industries is partly

TABLE 5
Capital Investment by Region and Plan Period for the USSR
between 1946 and 1975 (in percentage and per capita index terms)*

| Region | 1946–50 percent | per capita index | 1951–55 percent | per capita index | 1956–60 percent | per capita index | 1961–65 percent | per capita index | 1966–70 percent | per capita index | 1971–75 percent | per capita index |
|---|---|---|---|---|---|---|---|---|---|---|---|---|
| Far East | 4.5 | 208 | 4.8 | 221 | 4.0 | 193 | 4.4 | 214 | 4.6 | 193 | 4.6 | 186 |
| Eastern Siberia | 4.1 | 126 | 4.8 | 144 | 5.1 | 154 | 5.6 | 164 | 4.9 | 159 | 4.6 | 150 |
| Western Siberia | 4.4 | 81 | 5.7 | 105 | 6.0 | 123 | 6.0 | 123 | 6.5 | 127 | 7.2 | 146 |
| Kazakhstan and Central Asia | 7.4 | 71 | 3.7 | 83 | 10.4 | 90 | 12.9 | 106 | 13.6 | 101 | 12.3 | 90 |
| European Russia (including the Urals) | 79.6 | 101 | 76.1 | 97 | 75.0 | 96 | 71.1 | 92 | 70.5 | 99 | 71.0 | 94 |
| USSR | 100.0 | 100 | 100.0 | 100 | 100.0 | 100 | 100.0 | 100 | 100.0 | 100 | 100.0 | 100 |

*Kapitalnoye stroitelstvo and Narkhoz statistical handbooks. Despite territorial administrative regrouping since 1948, the regions listed above are comparable over time. These investment data cover all economic sectors including agriculture and the percentages were derived from absolute value data at comparable price levels.

ascribable to that labor shortage, for such industries are typically labor-intensive.

Table 5 shows capital investment by region and five-year plan period in the postwar era. The relative stability of the percentage values for the Far East has been rather remarkable (ranging from 4.0 to 4.8 percent). While the per capita indices have been roughly double the USSR base level, the relative *decline* in per capita investments in this region and Eastern Siberia contrasts significantly with the rise in Western Siberia. The values for 1971–75 seem to belie the published objectives for that period outlined by Rybakovsky[7] and reported by North.[8] Unfortunately, such data have not been available since 1975. With the ongoing vast investments required for the construction of the BAM (Baikal-Amur Mainline) started in 1974[9] (to be completed by 1985), I assume that both the percentage shares and the per capita indices, particularly for the Far East, and less so for Eastern Siberia, should have risen considerably in the 1976–80 period.

Doubts about the reported high priority of the Far East in Soviet regional planning through 1975 are reinforced by the statistics on the growth, in value terms, of industrial output by region recorded in Table 6. In apprais-

ing these data, it should be emphasized that developing regions, like our study area, commonly have high percentage growth rates simply because of their limited initial industrial base. Yet, in this instance, no such relative advantage is apparent.

Table 7 records shifts over time in the industrial structure of the Far East. Despite the fact that the percentage shares for employment in 1970 and for the value of in-

TABLE 6
Average Annual Growth of the Gross Value
of Industrial Output for Siberia and
the USSR from 1940 to 1975*

| | Regions Average Annual Growth (in percent) | | | |
|---|---|---|---|---|
| Period | Far East | Eastern Siberia | Western Siberia | USSR |
| 1940–50** | 6.3 | 9.8 | 21.4 | 7.3 |
| 1951–55** | 10.8 | 14.6 | 15.8 | 17.0 |
| 1956–60** | 11.4 | 11.8 | 11.6 | 13.0 |
| 1961–65 | 11.8 | 12.2 | 10.0 | 10.0 |
| 1966–70 | 10.0 | 11.6 | 10.2 | 10.2 |
| 1971–75 | 7.8 | 10.2 | 10.4 | 8.6 |

*Various Narkhoz statistical yearbooks particularly those for the RSFSR.
**The Yakut ASSR was included in Eastern Siberia in these years.

TABLE 7
Structural Changes in Employment (1940–60)
and Value of Output (1960–70) by
Industrial Sector for the Soviet Far East

| Sector | Employment* Percent | | Value of Output** Percent | |
|---|---|---|---|---|
| | 1940 | 1960 | 1960 | 1970 |
| Fuels (including mining) | 10.3 | 8.1 | 9.2 | 5.5 |
| Electrical energy | 5.3 | 3.1 | 1.5 | 2.2 |
| Iron and steel | — | 0.7 | 0.8 | 1.0 |
| Nonferrous and precious metals (mining and processing) | ? | ? | 7.6 | 9.2 |
| Metal fabrication and machinery | 13.0 | 24.8 | 16.4 | 20.0 |
| Forest industries | 31.0 | 19.5 | 15.0 | 12.3 |
| Construction materials | 4.1 | 6.4 | 6.5 | 7.1 |
| Chemicals | ? | ? | 0.7 | 1.0 |
| Light industry | 3.7 | 7.1 | 5.1 | 5.6 |
| Food industry (including fishing) | 31.3 | 21.8 | 37.2 | 36.1 |
| Other | 1.3*** | 8.5*** | — | — |
| Total | 100.0 | 100.0 | 100.0 | 100.0 |
| Employment (thousands) | 294.1 | 520.0 | — | — |

*For the source of the 1940 data see Table 3, while the reference for the 1960 employment percentages was A. Korneyev, ed., *Promyshlennost v khozyaistvennom komplekse ekonomicheskikh rayonov SSSR* [Industry in the economic complex of the economic regions of the USSR] (Moscow, 1964), p. 12.
**A. Gladyshev, A. Kulikov and B. Shapalin, *Problemy razvitiya i razmeshcheniya proizvoditelnikh sil Dalnego Vostoka* [Problems of development and distribution of the productive forces of the Far East] (Moscow, 1974), p. 11. Absolute value data in rubles were not available.
***Includes nonferrous and precious metals as well as chemicals.

dustrial production in 1940, by sector, were not available, these statistics still provide a useful data base. These materials, when supplemented by physical output data, demonstrated in Table 8, make it possible to reconstruct the evolution of the extractive industries and manufacturing in the Far East as a basis for an analysis of its interregional commodity flows and its foreign trade.

Despite the reservations noted earlier about the *relative* priority accorded the Far East during the postwar era, it can be estimated that between 1940 and 1970 the numbers employed in the extractive industries, utilities and manufacturing in the region nearly tripled approaching the 800,000 level. Currently, the gross value of its industrial products rose nearly tenfold during the same era (see Table 6). The differences between the relative increases measured in monetary and employment terms in part reflect the value of its rare and precious metals output and, of course, its production of diamonds. Those differences may also be a function of the capital-intensive nature of several of the region's new industries. Finally, the sharp growth in the gross value of its industrial products may conceivably reflect changes in prices over the intervening three decades, although such data are normally adjusted for temporal price permutations.

Turning to the shifts in sector percentages recorded in Table 7 and the absolute production data documented in Table 8, there had clearly been a maturation of the region's industrial structure from 1940 to 1970. Before the war, the percentages of employment by aggregate sector were typically those of a developing region. There were disproportionate numbers employed in the extractive industries and in the initial processing of their products. These activities included mining, forestry and fishing. In fact, the only elements one would expect to appear in the employment structure of a developing region that were missing were the production of textiles, apparel, shoes and other consumer goods. Flour milling, too, was mini-

mally represented. Of course, such activities did exist, but their output supplied only a limited share of the needs of the region. Perhaps the chief positive anomaly was the notable development of a metal fabrication and machinery industries which employed thirteen percent of the industrial work force in 1940. Here shipbuilding and repair coupled with small artisanlike workshops accounted for the largest share of the industrial employment. It can be assumed that the production of equipment for the military establishment was also included in this branch. Thus it appears that by 1940 the more favored parts of Maritime Krai, Khabarovsk Krai and Amur Oblast had in Rostow's[10] terminology achieved "the preconditions for take-off."

Turning to the sectoral data for 1960 and 1970 and the production statistics for 1975, it was noted previously that the postwar era had witnessed a growth and maturation of industry in the Far East. As economic development proceeds in a region, there are typically major structural changes in its industrial fabric. First, there occurs a decline in the *relative* importance of the extractive industries. Clearly, if resources exist, they will continue to be cut, mined or fished, but in this development period these raw materials will typically go through several processing stages so that there result more valuable, more complex and more diverse end products (those high in value added by manufacture). For example, the data in Table 6 show relative declines in the forest and mining industries. Yet at the same time Table 8 documents an absolute growth in physical output. One facet of the changes noted above was the development of paperboard production. There also appears to have been a relative and absolute growth in the production of nonferrous metals (both smelting and refining), and precious minerals like gold and diamonds. New industries include the initial production of steel and chemicals (especially mineral fertilizers). The most striking change,

TABLE 8
Changes in the Production of Mineral and Industrial Products in the
Far East and Shifts in Its Share of Soviet Output from 1940 to 1975*

| Product | Measurement Unit | 1940 | | | 1975 | | |
|---|---|---|---|---|---|---|---|
| | | Amount | Share of USSR (percent) | Per Capita Index | Amount | Share of USSR (percent) | Per Capita Index |
| Coal | millions of metric tons | 7.2 | 4.3 | 269 | 35.0 | 5.0 | 192 |
| Petroleum | millions of metric tons | 0.5 | 1.6 | 100 | 2.4 | 0.5 | 19 |
| Natural gas | billions of cubic meters | 0.0 | 0.0 | 0 | 2.0 | 0.7 | 27 |
| Electrical energy | billions of kilowatt hours | 0.7 | 1.4 | 88 | 23.3 | 2.3 | 88 |
| Timber (cut and hauled) | millions of cubic meters | 8.2 | 6.9 | 431 | 25.9 | 8.3 | 319 |
| Sawn Lumber | millions of cubic meters | 2.5 | 6.4 | 400 | 6.6 | 5.7 | 219 |
| Paperboard | millions of metric tons | 0.0 | 0.0 | 0 | 133.7 | 4.0 | 154 |
| Steel ingots | millions of metric tons | 0.0 | 0.0 | 0 | 1.0 | 0.7 | 27 |
| Cement | millions of metric tons | 0.2 | 4.0 | 250 | 2.7 | 2.2 | 84 |
| Mineral fertilizer | millions of metric tons | 0.0 | 0.0 | 0 | 2.5 | 2.8 | 107 |
| Cotton cloth | billions of square meters | 0.0 | 0.0 | 0 | 14.0 | 0.2 | 8 |
| Shoes | millions of pairs | 0.4 | 0.2 | 12 | 6.0 | 0.9 | 35 |
| Population | millions of inhabitants | 3.1 | 1.6 | | 6.5 | 2.6 | |

*Derived from various *Narkhoz* statistical handbooks and Leslie Dienes and Theodore Shabad, *The Soviet Energy System* (Washington, 1979), various pages.

however, had been in the share and diversity of output in the machinery and metal fabrication industries. I should also add that the regional output of some of the consumer goods, noted above, had also grown, but net deficits still persist.

## Commodity Flows in the Sixties

As is common knowledge in academic circles, the fifties and sixties were extraordinarily fruitful periods for analysis of Soviet regional economic development. In some instances, in the past, more data were available for the USSR than for the United States and Western Europe. In contrast, the past decade has witnessed the implementation of major restrictions on the release of regional economic statistics presumably in response to new legislation concerning "state secrets." These data gaps have clearly hindered this study for no regional traffic data later than those for 1970 have been published, and, in fact, the most recent detailed commodity movements available are those for 1966.

Table 9 demonstrates the sectoral pattern of interregional commodity flows for 1966. Unfortunately, these data are the latest that have been released. Despite the obvious time lag, they are valuable because they are presented in both value and tonnage terms and are relatively comprehensive. However, the statistics for some sectors include foreign trade, while those for other branches do not. The 1966 percentages have been supplemented with absolute tonnage data for 1965 and 1970.

TABLE 9
Volume and Value of Interregional Commodity Movements for the Soviet Far East, by Sector, in 1966**

| Sector** | Tonnage (in percent) | | Value (in percent) | |
|---|---|---|---|---|
| | Inbound | Outbound | Inbound | Outbound |
| Ferrous metallurgy | 11.8 | 19.1 | 4.4 | 4.1 |
| Nonferrous metallurgy | 0.1 | 0.7 | ? | ? |
| Fuels | 47.2 | 38.4 | 8.2 | 7.4 |
| Machinery and metal fabrication | 3.8 | 1.4 | 9.5 | 12.0 |
| Chemicals | 1.4 | 0.0 | 5.3 | 0.6 |
| Forest products | 2.7 | 23.4 | 0.5 | 8.4 |
| Construction materials | 3.0 | 1.1 | 1.4 | 0.9 |
| Ceramics and glass | 0.1 | 0.0 | 0.1 | 0.1 |
| Light industry | 1.0 | 0.3 | 27.6 | 4.1 |
| Food industry | 7.5 | 6.6 | 40.4 | 61.6 |
| Agriculture | 4.1 | 2.0 | 2.6 | 0.8 |
| Other | 17.3 | 7.0 | — | — |
| Total | 100.0 | 100.0 | 100.0 | 100.0 |

*Shniper and Denisova, *Mezhotraslevye svyazi*, p. 79.
**For machinery, chemicals, ceramics and glass, light, and food industry, foreign trade was included; for ferrous and nonferrous metallurgy, forest industries and agriculture, foreign trade was excluded. The authors also indicate that foreign trade for the fuel sector was excluded, but the evidence contradicts that statement and I have proceeded accordingly in my analysis. See *Transport i svyaz* [Transportation and communication] (Moscow, 1972), pp. 68–85.

(Table 10); however, here the sectoral detail is quite restricted. Between 1940 (Table 4) and 1970 the net balance in favor of inbound movements increased nearly fivefold. That growth indirectly reflects the expanding Soviet trade with nations in the Pacific Basin. For example, Shniper and Denisova argue that the net inbound flow of 11 to 12 million tons in 1966 would decrease to one to two millions once export and import movements were included.[11] Exports to Japan, the Soviet Union's chief trading partner in the Pacific, are dominated by sales of bulk commodities like crude oil, coal and forest products. The nation's exports to Japan grew from 166 million rubles in 1965 to 853 million rubles in 1977, and 87 percent of the 1977 exports was accounted for by such bulk products.[12] In contrast to the export pattern, the outbound movements to other regions of the USSR were not low value bulk goods, rather these flows were dominated by foods, particularly fish and comparatively high value, added by manufacture, goods such as fabricated metals and machinery as well as costly wood products. Such commodities command prices high enough to absorb the costs of rail transport over vast distances. The only major bulk goods moving westward from the Far East were probably grain imported from the United States, Canada and Australia, nonferrous and rare metals mined in the northern segments of the Far East and lumber derived from the vast forest resources of the region.

Inbound flows, not destined for export, included petroleum (to supplement the output of the Sakhalin oil fields), coal, chemical fertilizers, scrap and pig iron (to supply the needs of the Amurstal steel works at Komsomolsk), steel products, machinery, foods and consumer goods.

Turning from a commodity-sector approach to a examination of temporal changes in interregional flows, Table 11 is a summary, by macro-regions, of the inbound and outbound movements from and to the Far East from 1950 to 1970. Aside from the absolute growth in tonnage of both the inward and outward streams, there was a rapidly increasing negative balance that has already been attributed mainly to goods ultimately destined for export. However, it is relative and absolute changes, by region, over time that are of concern here.

Note the growth, in percentage terms, of the inward flows from Eastern and Western Siberia (from 39 percent to 70 percent) complemented by a decline in the shares of inbound movements originating in the western regions of the nation. In contrast, while there was a major percentage decline in the outbound flows from the Far East destined for Eastern Siberia, it was offset by marked increases in the outward flows to Kazakhstan, Central Asia and European Russia. It must be emphasized, however, that the decreases in percentage values only reflect *relative* changes; for in absolute terms tonnage increases were registered to and from all of these macro-regions during this two decade interval. Despite these geographical shifts, the length of interregional hauls for the Far East remained, by any standard, enormous. The average distance of the outbound shipments in 1970 was 5,800 kilometers and the value for the inbound flows was 5,200 kilometers. Comparable distances for Eastern Sibe-

TABLE 10
Volume of Interregional Commodity Flows for the Soviet Far East, by Product, in 1965 and 1970*

| | 1965 | | | | 1970 | | | |
| | Inbound | | Outbound | | Inbound | | Outbound | |
| | tons(000) | percent | tons(000) | percent | tons(000) | percent | tons(000) | percent |
|---|---|---|---|---|---|---|---|---|
| Coal | 2,530 | 14.8 | 740 | 10.2 | 3,940 | 13.5 | 240 | 3.2 |
| Oil and oil products | 5,890 | 34.4 | 470 | 6.5 | 10,320 | 35.3 | 110 | 1.5 |
| Ores | 10 | 0.1 | 170 | 2.4 | 100 | 0.3 | 370 | 4.9 |
| Forest products | 470 | 2.7 | 1,150 | 15.9 | 1,720 | 5.9 | 1,780 | 23.5 |
| Cement | 370 | 2.2 | 60 | 0.8 | 640 | 2.2 | — | — |
| Other | 7,839 | 45.8 | 4,640 | 64.2 | 12,550 | 42.8 | 5,080 | 66.9 |
| Total | 17,100 | 100.0 | 7,230 | 100.0 | 29,270 | 100.0 | 7,580 | 100.0 |

*Transport i svyaz, [Transportation and communication] (Moscow, 1972), pp. 68–85. These data exclude foreign trade.

ria, for the same year, were 3,300 and 3,400 kilometers, while the average lengths of outbound and inbound flows for Western Siberia were 2,400 and 2,100 kilometers respectively.[13] The values for the interregional flows for the Far East are *solely* those for rail hauls, while the data for Siberia probably include transport by pipeline as well as minimal interregional movements by road and river.

Table 12 demonstrates the interregional flows for the Far East in 1966. Its utility lies not only in the level of regional detail but in the juxtaposition of tonnage and value data for these economic regions. Unfortunately, no monetary data exist for 1970 or the past decade.

While the contrasts between the tonnage and value data are self-evident, an explanation of the key differences is in order. Note the variance in the tonnage and value percentages for the Center and the Northwest. These mature industrialized regions, dominated by Moscow and Leningrad, produce a wide range of producer and consumer-oriented goods. Essentially, all of their products are high in value per unit of weight. Similarly,

the Far East ships them foods like fish products and relatively costly manufactured goods. Only goods like these can absorb the transportation costs incurred in such long haul movements. In contrast, notice the reduction in the percentages from the Urals and Siberia if you compare their tonnage and value shares.

Interregional freight movements by sector for 1966 were shown in Table 9. An analysis of interregional flows by region and product for 1966 appears in Table 13. Unfortunately, such detailed data are only available for a limited number of commodities: coal, crude oil, iron and steel and forest products.

In the cases of coal and petroleum the patterns are relatively simple. The flows of coal to the Far East totaled roughly two and a half million tons in 1965 (four million tons by 1970). Its sources were Western and Eastern Siberia, and it is my supposition that this was a movement of high calorific-low impurity coking coal ultimately destined for export to Japan. Eastern Siberia was the sole source of inbound shipments of crude petroleum totaling

TABLE 11
The Volume of Interregional Commodity Movements for the
Far East, by Region, from 1950 to 1970*

| | Inbound | | | | Outbound | | | |
| | 1950** | | 1970** | | 1950** | | 1970** | |
| Region | Absolute (thousands of tons) | Percent | Absolute (thousands of tons) | Percent | Absolute (thousands of tons) | Percent | Absolute (thousands of tons) | Percent |
|---|---|---|---|---|---|---|---|---|
| Eastern Siberia | 1,742 | 26.8 | 11,854 | 40.5 | 1,120 | 50.0 | 2,509 | 33.1 |
| Western Siberia | 812 | 12.5 | 8,488 | 29.0 | 304 | 13.6 | 955 | 12.6 |
| Urals | 1,398 | 21.5 | 2,722 | 9.3 | 204 | 9.1 | 758 | 10.0 |
| Kazakhstan and Central Asia | 689 | 10.6 | 1,581 | 5.4 | 103 | 4.6 | 1,213 | 16.0 |
| European Russia | 1,859 | 28.6 | 4,625 | 15.8 | 508 | 22.7 | 2,145 | 28.3 |
| USSR | 6,500 | 100.0 | 29,270 | 100.0 | 2,239 | 100.0 | 7,580 | 100.0 |

*Foreign trade is not included. Tonnage data are my estimates based on index numbers, percentages, and absolute values published in the Soviet press.
**T. S. Khachaturov ed., *Povysheniye effektivnosti transporta v SSSR* [The Increase in the effectiveness of transportation in the USSR] (Moscow, 1966), p. 32.
***Shniper and Denisova, *Mezhotraslevye svyazi*, p. 102.

TABLE 12
Volume and Value of Interregional Commodity
Movements for the Soviet Far East, by Region, in 1966*

| Region | Tonnage (in percent) | | Value (in percent) | |
|---|---|---|---|---|
| | In-bound | Out-bound | In-bound | Out-bound |
| Northwest | 1.2 | 2.7 | 3.6 | 4.8 |
| Central | 3.2 | 7.0 | 20.9 | 15.5 |
| Volga-Vyatka | 1.7 | 2.3 | 3.7 | 2.7 |
| Central Chernozem | 1.3 | 1.2 | 3.2 | 3.3 |
| Volga | 3.8 | 3.6 | 5.3 | 2.2 |
| North Caucasus | 1.8 | 1.3 | 5.0 | 3.1 |
| Urals | 15.3 | 9.1 | 8.3 | 5.4 |
| Western Siberia | 24.7 | 15.3 | 13.1 | 13.0 |
| Eastern Siberia | 39.5 | 32.5 | 23.2 | 21.4 |
| Ukraine | 3.0 | 4.5 | 4.4 | 9.6 |
| Baltic Republics | 0.2 | 1.1 | 0.3 | 1.2 |
| Transcaucasia | 0.6 | 0.6 | 1.5 | 3.2 |
| Central Asia | 1.3 | 4.4 | 3.4 | 5.7 |
| Kazakhstan | 1.8 | 13.8 | 0.9 | 6.6 |
| Belorussia | — | — | — | — |
| Moldavia | 0.2 | 0.1 | 2.2 | 0.2 |
| USSR (percent) | 99.6 | 99.5 | 99.0 | 97.9 |
| tonnage (thousands) | 17,100 | 7,230 | — | — |

*Shniper and Denisova, *Mezhotraslevye svyazi*, p. 102.

nearly six million tons in 1965 (ten million by 1970). This oil was extracted in Western Siberia; it then moved by pipeline to the terminal at Angarsk, near Irkutsk in Eastern Siberia, where it was transferred to tank cars for shipment by rail eastward. Again the immediate terminus was the Far East, but a portion was destined for

Japan. Oil accounted for 40 percent of the exports of the Far East (by weight) in 1966.[14]

With respect to forest products, more was dispatched than received. Of the roughly one million tons that left the Far East in 1966 (almost two million in 1970) over half went to the largely unforested regions of Kazakhstan and Central Asia, and one-third was destined for Western and Eastern Siberia. Shniper notes that one-fifth of the exports of our study region (by weight) were wood products, but the main source was the forest area of the Far East itself.[15] The outbound movements of forest products tended to be pulpwood and fabricated wood products rather than low value roundwood or lumber.

Finally, there are detailed regional data for the flows of iron and steel products. Dibb has estimated the inward flows at one million tons;[16] this value would presumably include pig iron destined for the Amurstal mill and a wide range of steel products (pipe from the Ukraine, beams, bars and rails from the Urals and rails from Western Siberia) designed for producer and consumer markets in the Far East. Yet at the same time about one half million tons of steel products moved westward. Practically every economic region of the USSR was a destination for a share of the steel output of the Far East. Such movements have been described by some Soviet economists as irrational cross hauls.[17] Yet because of scale economies it must be assumed that there would be an excess of certain steel products over local needs. About 10 to 15 percent of the exports of the Far East (in value terms) were steel products destined for markets in the Pacific.

Materials exist on inbound and outbound flows of other commodities for the Far East, but these fragmentary data vary as to their time frame, volume (rarely pub-

TABLE 13
The Volume of Interregional Movements, by Commodity, for 1966 (in percent)*

| Region | Coal | | Petroleum | | Forest Products | | Iron & Steel Products | |
|---|---|---|---|---|---|---|---|---|
| | In-bound | Out-bound | In-bound | Out-bound | In-bound | Out-bound | In-bound | Out-bound |
| Northwest | — | — | — | — | — | 1.6 | 1.7 | 2.2 |
| Central | — | 0.6 | — | — | — | 4.4 | 1.0 | 3.3 |
| Volga-Vyatka | — | — | — | — | — | 1.0 | 0.4 | 2.9 |
| Central Chernozem | — | — | — | — | — | — | 0.9 | 0.2 |
| Volga | — | — | — | — | — | 2.0 | 0.2 | 2.8 |
| North Caucasus | — | — | — | — | — | 0.2 | 0.3 | 3.1 |
| Urals | — | — | — | — | 1.2 | 3.3 | 28.8 | 4.8 |
| Western Siberia | 56.0 | — | — | — | — | 7.7 | 43.4 | 34.9 |
| Eastern Siberia | 44.0 | 99.4 | 100.0 | — | 98.5 | 24.5 | 12.5 | 36.2 |
| Ukraine | — | — | — | — | 0.3 | — | 9.3 | 3.7 |
| Baltic Republics | — | — | — | — | — | 1.6 | — | — |
| Transcaucasia | — | — | — | — | — | — | 1.3 | 1.8 |
| Central Asia | — | — | — | — | — | 5.8 | — | 1.1 |
| Kazakhstan | — | — | — | — | — | 47.9 | 0.2 | 2.3 |
| Belorussia | — | — | — | — | — | — | — | 0.7 |
| Moldavia | — | — | — | — | — | — | — | — |
| USSR (percent) | 100.0 | 100.0 | 100.0 | 100.0 | 100.0 | 100.0 | 100.0 | 100.0 |
| tonnage (thousands)** | 2,530 | 740 | 5,890*** | 470*** | 470 | 1,150 | 1,000 | 500 |

*Shniper and Denisova, *Mezhotraslevye svyazi*, pp. 103–106.
**1965 tonnages while percentages are for 1966; tonnages were from *Transport i svyaz*, 1972, pp. 71–83.
***Tonnage includes oil products, while the percentages are for crude oil alone.

lished) and their degree of regional detail. Thus, they can be used only as crude supplements to the more precise data in Table 13.

Other inbound movements include grain (1.7 million tons in the late sixties) from Western Siberia, Eastern Siberia and Kazakhstan, and sugar from the Ukraine and the Central Chernozem region. Deficit food production in this region requires the inward shipment of potatoes, vegetables, meat and dairy products.[18] Since the manufacture of consumer durable and nondurable goods is minimally important in the Far East, such products as textile fabrics, clothing, shoes and appliances must be purchased elsewhere. Seventy-five percent of these goods are received from European Russia. Local chemical fertilizer production, a relatively new industry in this region, must be supplemented by supplies from the Urals and Western Siberia.

As for the outbound movements not covered in Table 13, the highest value shipment is fish which is processed and shipped to every populous center in the nation. Nonferrous and rare metals rank high in value terms but less so in tonnage. Their destinations are Western Siberia and the Ukraine. Finally, the most complex inbound and outbound flows are those for machinery. Plants in this sector supply only half of the machinery requirements of the region, yet more than half of the output of the machinery sector of the Far East is shipped westward thousands of kilometers. In several instances (depending on the product) two-thirds to three-quarters of the products of establishments in this industrial branch are transported to other regions of the nation including European Russia.[19] Such movements were predictably termed irrational in the Soviet economic and transport literature. Gladyshev argues that the cost of rail transport westward adds about ten percent to the ultimate cost of the product.[20] In constrast, transport costs are estimated by the same author to account for 2.4 percent of the overall cost of machinery for the nation (based on average length of haul). The question of the desirability of regional self-sufficiency will be discussed in the final section of this chapter.

## Economic Development in the Far East After 1970

A discussion of the prospects for changes in commodity flows in and out of the Far East during the coming decade as well as the possibilities for the further development of foreign trade requires an examination of changes in Soviet perspectives of the Far East and shifts, over time, in regional development policy.

The analysis begins with the 1966–70 planning period. Where feasible these materials will be supplemented by data drawn from the 11th Five-Year Plan[21] and the large number of books and articles treating the BAM, particularly the major contribution by Shabad and Mote.[22] The now voluminous literature on Soviet regional policy and practice has also been useful as a basic framework for the analysis.[23] More immediately, over the past decade there has been a burgeoning of Western and Soviet publications on the Far East itself. Of the Western studies,

North's article in *Pacific Affairs*, Dibb's book on *Siberia and the Pacific* and Mote's discussion paper *Predictions and Realities in the Development of the Soviet Far East* dovetail best with the present analysis.[24] The North contribution, though necessarily limited in scope, seems the most provocative. In that paper he argued that in contrast to the sixties when Mieczkowski[25] termed the Far East "a problem region," by the late seventies that area had emerged as a "new center of attention," for Soviet planning and investment.

In light of the present analysis, North may have been overly optimistic about capital investments in the Far East between 1967 and 1975. His positive assessment of economic development during that era was based primarily on a 1967 party and government decree on the Far East (and Chita Oblast).[26] That decree overrode previous commitments to the region stated in the 1966–70 plan, and its mandate was undoubtedly one of the major underlying assumptions of the 1971–75 and the 1976–80 plans. Since this document was amply detailed by North, it will only be summarized here.

The new programs were obviously designed to stimulate and accelerate economic growth, but for the first time, at least with regard to the Far East, there is specific mention of the need to foster the development of linked industries, presumably to take advantage of external economies and avoid "irrational cross hauls." The gross value of industrial output was to increase nearly threefold from 1965 to 1975. Within this sector, products destined for broad national and export markets (in the Pacific Basin) were to receive clear preference. Priority was also given to the lumber and wood-processing industries. Here investments were to be focused on the production of commercial roundwood, wood chips, pulp and paper. Other preferred industries included the extraction and smelting of nonferrous metals, fishing and fish processing. For regional markets, there was to be an expansion of energy output based on local fuel resources, coupled with an increased production of construction materials. Finally, in the industrial sector, the 1967 program called for an increase in the manufacture of consumer goods for local markets. This goal had been reiterated in every postwar plan but never truly fulfilled.

Other initiatives spelled out in this decree or stipulated in the 9th and 10th five-year plans included the long awaited implementation of a "container overland bridge" via the Trans-Siberian Railroad which was designed to compete with maritime services between the Pacific and Western Europe. In this plan and those that followed there has been a continued stress on the need to expand trade relations between the Soviet Union and the nations rimming the Pacific Basin, particularly Japan. In practical terms such interactions meant the exchange of Soviet raw materials and semi-fabricated products for sophisticated technological equipment, especially the kinds of machinery and "know-how" which would further the development of the extractive industries of Siberia. Then too there was a clear recognition of the need to provide larger and more meaningful monetary and other incentives to encourage a further expansion of inward migration to the Far East as well as the retention of its existing labor force.

## The BAM and Little BAM Railroads

The most momentous initiative of the seventies has been the planning and construction of two major rail links: the BAM (scheduled to be completed by the end of 1985) and the so-called Little BAM (in operation as of October 1978). These undertakings may prove to be among the most ambitious and costly ventures in Soviet history. Their potential in terms of regional economic development in the Soviet Far East, interregional commodity flows and trade with the Pacific neighbors of the USSR, will be important, but probably less so than originally envisaged by Soviet planners. These reservations apply solely to economic rationality on a cost-benefit basis. Since these initiatives have been already covered in depth by the excellent contributions written by Shabad and Mote, only a brief review appears appropriate here.[27]

The construction of the new 3,200-kilometer west-east link from Ust-Kut on the upper Lena to Komsomolsk, termed the BAM, was announced by Brezhnev in 1974,[28] and its implementation was a key feature of the 10th (1976–80) Five-Year Plan and will certainly siphon off considerable investment funds from the 11th (1981–85) Plan. This single track line (whose right of way includes ready possibilities for double tracking) runs well over 200 kilometers north of the Trans-Siberian Railroad. Whereas its completion was originally scheduled for 1983, progress to date has been delayed. According to the 11th Five-Year Plan (1981–85) the BAM will not begin regular freight service until the end of 1985. Among associated undertakings will be investments in mining (copper, molybdenum, asbestos, mica and probably apatites), oil refining, forestry, fisheries, logging, wood processing (pulp and paper) and port construction. The Little BAM, whose construction began in 1971–72, is now in operation; it is a northward spur from Bamovskaya Station on the Trans-Sib via Tynda on the BAM to Neryungri in the heart of the South Yakutian coal field.

## Raw-Material and Energy Supplies as Potential Exports from the Soviet Far East

It is apparent from the Soviet literature that it is the view of their leaders, echoed by the nation's planners, that the export of Soviet resources can provide the "hard-currency" earnings to pay for necessary imports of Western technology. Thus it becomes necessary to evaluate the potential for further resource exploration and exploitation in the USSR as well as the relationship between domestic demand and supply (including resource substitution), so that the prospects for exports can be properly assessed. The focus in this chapter is on the export potential of the Soviet Far East. However, the Far East can also be viewed as a type of intervening opportunity, a sort of spatial sponge[29] soaking up potential spatial interaction between the USSR and her trading partners in the Pacific. To the degree then that the Far East becomes less dependent on European Russia, Kazakhstan and the more westerly Siberian regions, there may be an increase in

transit movements. These commodities coupled with materials from the Far East itself would constitute potential exports to the Pacific Basin. Of course, some of the more critical and valuable industrial raw materials such as certain nonferrous metals, rare metals (including gold), gemstones, and industrial diamonds would presumably continue to flow westward. As a preamble to the discussion of the raw-material and energy potential of the Far East, it should be stressed that the analysis will be restricted to those commodities which offer the greatest promise for accelerating exports. Finally, it will consider only those resources that are located within the economic region which is officially designated "the Far East" rather than "Pacific Siberia," "Eastern Siberia" or the "BAM Service Zone—Hinterland" (Figure 2).

### Energy Supplies

Siberia is the largest remaining reserve area of energy supplies in the USSR. While some of its riches such as those of the Kuznetsk Basin were initially tapped on a modest scale as early as 1915, the intensive development of Siberian energy resources is largely a product of the post World War II era.[30] Yet within that vast region remarkably little was known until the fifties about the fuel supplies of the Soviet Far East. Nor, with very limited exceptions, was there actual exploitation of these deposits. This lag in exploration and development is clearly attributable to the availability of more accessible supplies found further west and the extraordinary remoteness and environmental difficulties of most of the study region. Although much still remains to be discovered and explored, some initial judgments can be made about the region's resources.

*Coal.* According to a survey of Soviet coal reserves, the Far East in 1966 possessed roughly 5 percent of the nation's supplies of the major fuel (see Table 14).[31] While known supplies include both bituminous and lignite coals, the great bulk of these resources belong to the latter group which are of low calorific value and high in impurities like ash and sulfur. Thus these lignite deposits are only useful for the generation of steam or electricity with considerable emission problems. Many of the coal deposits of the Far East can be mined by stripping methods thereby reducing extraction costs. However, the largest known reserve areas are plagued by extraordinarily low temperatures for extended periods of the year and by deep permafrost, and these problems far outweigh their shallow depth advantage, as evident in the case of the Neryungri open pit mine in Yakutia.

As was evidenced by the data in Table 14, there are significant reserves in nearly every political subdivision of the Far East, with the largest supplies in the Yakut ASSR. Yet because of physical problems, accessibility and the location of markets, the major production areas are found in the southern part of the region and on Sakhalin Island. These coals are currently used for the manufacture of steam and electricity and to power the steam locomotives that ply the eastern segment of the Trans-Siberian Railroad. Those mines currently under exploita-

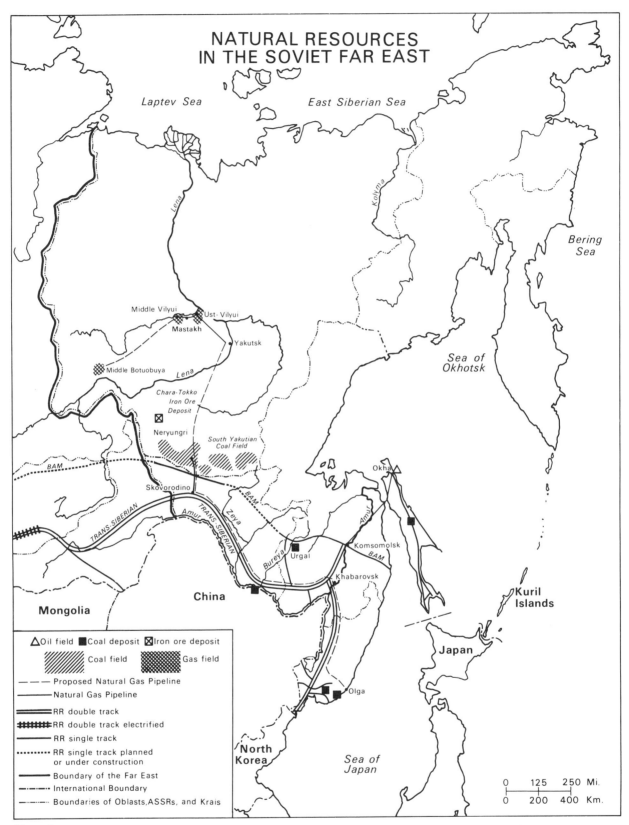

Figure 2

TABLE 14
The Coal Reserves of the Soviet Far East
(millions of tons as of 1966)*

| Region | $A+B+C_1$ | $C_2$ | Total |
|---|---|---|---|
| Amur Oblast | 419 | 3 | 422 |
| Kamchatka Oblast | 67 | 60 | 127 |
| Khabarovsk Krai | 807 | 1,179 | 1,986 |
| Magadan Oblast | 1,068 | 3,259 | 4,327 |
| Maritime Krai | 2,450 | 1,359 | 3,809 |
| Sakhalin Oblast | 2,073 | 1,496 | 3,569 |
| Yakut ASSR | 4,580 | 4,469 | 9,049 |
| Far East | 11,464 | 11,825 | 23,289 |
| USSR** | 237,200 | 235,000 | 472,200 |

*Energeticheskiye resursy SSSR, p. 123. The A, B, $C_1$ reserves indicated here are often termed the "productive categories." Those indicated above are also called balance resources or economically feasible reserves. For a recent analysis of Soviet reserve estimation methods see David Levine, "Oil and Natural Gas Resources of the Soviet Union and Methods of their Estimation," Appendix II, Project Interdependence, U. S. and World Energy Outlook Through 1990, 95th Congress, 1st Session, (November 1977), pp. 821–48.

**Ibid., p. 64. The $C_2$ reserves are termed "prospective" reserves. Soviet agencies appear to rely mainly on the productive category for medium and long range planning purposes.

tion mainly serve the larger urban nodes of the Far East and the smaller centers of extractive industries.

The data in Table 15, which show 1975 coal production by political subdivision, when compared with the reserve statistics demonstrated in Table 14, indicate that the correlation between reserves and output is not strong. The relationship would be even weaker if micro-geographical level reserve and production data were used. The Far East produces about 4 percent of the nation's coal output, which is sufficient for its current needs. Although more than 2.5 million tons of coal were imported to the region from Western and Eastern Siberia in 1966, these coals were apparently then reexported to Japanese markets.

Out of the roughly 35 million tons of coal produced in the region in 1975, less than one-sixth was bituminous coal, and nearly half of this amount was high in undesir-

TABLE 15
Regional Distribution of Coal Production in the
Soviet Far East in 1975* (millions of metric tons)

| Region | Output |
|---|---|
| Amur Oblast | 13.5 |
| Kamchatka Oblast | negligible |
| Khabarovsk Krai | 1.5 |
| Magadan Oblast | 2.2 |
| Maritime Krai | 10.1 |
| Sakhalin Oblast | 5.0 |
| Yakut ASSR | 2.0 |
| Far East | 34.3 |
| USSR | 701.0 |

*L. Dienes and T. Shabad, The Soviet Energy System, (Washington, 1979), p. 111. These values include both bituminous and lignite coals.

able impurities. About 90 percent of the region's coal output was strip-mined. The regional pattern was relatively simple. Roughly 35 percent of 13.5 million tons came from the southeastern segment of Amur Oblast or the Bureya Basin. All of this area's production was lignite and the dominant field was that at Raichikhinsk located near the Trans-Siberian. A secondary mining center is being developed at Svobodny. Second in order of output is a group of small lignite deposits located in the southern segment of Maritime Krai not far from Vladivostok and Ussurisk. These include: Partizansk, Artem and Tavrichanskoye. All told their production was only 10 million tons. The remaining notable mining center is the bituminous coal field at Urgal located in Khabarovsk Krai where a north-south line leading from the Trans-Siberian joins the BAM. These coals can be of coking quality when mixed with higher grade coals from the Kuzbas or Yakutia; their output in 1975 was 1.5 million tons. Finally, there is a series of fields in central and southern Sakhalin that produced about five million tons in 1975. These deposits contain both bituminous and lignite coals. In terms of export potential, none of the fields noted above offer any real prospect.

As for the coal deposits of the Yakut ASSR, the data presented in Table 14 suggest that its productive reserves $(A,B,C_1)$ are the largest in the Far East. It possesses an estimated 40 percent of those overall supplies. More than half of these reserves lie in the Lena basin, but these are lignite or brown coals of minimal immediate or even future utility. The South Yakutian deposits are, in contrast, the largest reserves of quality coals in the overall region, and it is these resources that are one of the key elements that stimulated the planning of the Territorial-production complex (TPC) that is being implemented in southern Yakutia.[32]

Interest in the South Yakutian field, as reflected in significant outlays for mineral exploration, is a product of only the last three decades. It began when Soviet planners realized that this region contained what are believed to be the only large coal deposits suitable for the production of metallurgical coke located east of Lake Baikal.[33] The bulk of the coals in this vast region, as they discovered, were either lignited or subbituminous varieties.

Within the South Yakutian field, it is the Chulman and Neryungri deposits that have received the greatest attention. Their reserves, as of 1966, are detailed in Table 16. Production was first confined to the Chulman area, where small amounts of coal were mined for electricity generation. Since the mid-seventies, attention has shifted to the Neryungri area. That shift reflects mainly the physical contrasts between the two deposits. The Chulman field, though well endowed with regard to the size and quality of its coals, is far more complicated geologically and far more difficult to exploit. These deposits are relatively deep, with one report citing depths of 300 to 600 meters. Thus the extraction of these coals requires the construction of expensive shafts and tunnels that would have to be excavated in permanently frozen ground. In addition, the coal seams are comparatively thin (ranging from 1 to 4 meters) and structurally complex. In contrast,

TABLE 16
Coal Reserves of the South Yakutian Basin*
(millions of metric tons as of 1966)

| Field | A | B | $C_1$ | $ABC_1$ | $C_2$ | Total |
|---|---|---|---|---|---|---|
| Neryungri | 183.7 | 220.7 | 122.8 | 527.2 | 138.8 | 666.0 |
| Chulman | 40.9 | 123.4 | 368.2 | 532.5 | 128.5 | 661.0 |
| Other explored areas | 16.3 | 29.4 | 943.9 | 989.6 | 3,103.9 | 4,093.5 |
| Total | 240.9 | 373.5 | 1,434.9 | 2,049.3 | 3,371.2 | 5,420.5 |

*Energeticheskiye resursy SSSR, p. 123. The A and B categories have been termed "industrial reserves" by D. Shimkin, Minerals, a Key to Soviet Power (Cambridge, 1953), pp.19–20.

the Neryungri deposit, particularly its Moshchny seam, have a shallower overburden (60 to at most 150 meters), average 25 meters in thickness, and can readily be mined by stripping. Its coals are low in sulfur content (0.2 to 0.5 percent) and have only traces of phosphorus, another undesirable impurity. A major problem, but one common to most coking and noncoking coals, is the share of ash in the raw coal. At Neryungri that share averages from 18 to 20 percent. As a result its coals require washing and cleaning which then reduces the ash to an acceptable level of about 9 percent, but cleaning will obviously raise the cost and reduce the size of its final product (suitable for the production of coke). Such a coal cleaning plant is to be completed during the 11th Plan.[34] Perhaps a more serious problem is the presence of a thick oxidized layer in the overburden. Thus, as Dienes has reported,[35] 30 million tons of this material must be removed before the shipment of coking coal can be under way. Though the oxidized coals can be used for steam and power generation, there is currently a surplus of such coals in Yakutia. Russians are working on methods of using these coals in a coke-oven mix.[36] However, their apparently successful pilot-plant tests can be meaningful only if they implement long discussed plans for the construction of a Far Eastern integrated steel mill using South Yakutian iron ores. This possibility, of course, has no direct relevance for the export question.

The beginnings of mining at Neryungri can be traced to the signing of an economic agreement with Japan in 1974. The accord called for the export of coking coal to Japan beginning in 1979 for an ultimate total of about 104 million tons over 20 years, including 5 million tons a year from Neryungri starting in 1983. In turn the Japanese were to extend a loan of $450 million for the Neryungri project (later increased by $90 million). This money was to be used for the purchase of coal excavators, dump trucks, cranes and consumer goods. The BAM and the Little BAM were, as noted earlier, linked to the plan as transport outlets for Yakutian coals. While plans called for an ultimate raw coal capacity of 13 million tons at Neryungri, the product of its cleaning plant, now under construction, would be only 9 million tons of coking coal concentrate. Soviet sources indicate that only 5 million tons of cleaned coking coal will be shipped each year from Neryungri to Japan starting in 1983.[37] Of course, depending on that country's demands this level could conceiv-

ably be raised, but the current world glut of steel makes such an increase unlikely at least for the near future. The development of new markets in the Pacific Basin also appears to offer little promise during that time horizon. In contrast, the growth of domestic demand, particularly in the Far East, for Yakutian coking coals would appear to offer the greatest potential. This, of course, would necessarily be tied to the construction of a much discussed but never implemented 9 million ton integrated steel mill in that region.[38]

Difficulties do not exist solely on the demand side. Production problems are far more severe than originally anticipated. Aside from the presumably underestimated troubles of coping with the oxidized layer mentioned previously, mining, labor, housing and other costs have escalated. However, given the fact that the Soviet press and the New York Times have reported in ample detail on these problems, I need only summarize them here.[39]

The estimated cost of the Neryungri project was 936 million rubles, or about 1.5 billion dollars at the current rate of exchange; this sum was designed to cover the cost of building the mine (including its equipment), the cleaning plant and the town of Neryungri. As of January 1979, that cost had risen to over 3 billion rubles and presumably even more as of the moment. That threefold increase in costs is attributable to additional mining costs incurred in removing the overburden and the oxidized steam coals and the difficulties of mining when temperatures drop to less than 62 degrees below zero Centigrade. As a result, according to Craig R. Whitney of the Times, the teeth of the huge 35 ton American-designed excavators have become brittle and broken.[40] The original plan had called for a total of 5,000 workers; whereas by 1979 there were already 13,000. All told, there were 16,000 workers in 1979, including those involved in services. One gets the impression that there are few if any families there. Regional wage increments make labor costs 70 percent higher than those in Moscow (an average of 270 rubles per month). This differential, which is intended to offset the difficulties of living in this hardship region, clearly helps to explain the higher than anticipated cost of the project. Food and consumer goods are expensive and in short supply, while housing is crude and apparently inadequate. Given the problems that have arisen in the development of the Neryungri deposit, it is apparent that the 1983 target for the first shipments of coking coals cannot conceivably be met. However, the mine's steam coal output is rising and most of its product will be consumed in a 600,000 kw thermo-electric plant to be completed during the current plan. The remainder will be shipped south via the Little BAM. In sum, the shipment of Yakutian coking coals to Japan may be delayed by as much as two years. There is ample coal for decades to come, but its cost will be far higher than envisaged, and the question of additional domestic and foreign markets remains to be resolved. And finally, it has been argued that Chinese coking coals offer severe competition to Yakutian coals for any increased Soviet sales to the Japanese steel industry. This argument cannot be readily refuted because clearly the cost of mining in Hebei Province as well as in southern Manchuria is far less than that in Yakutia and transportation costs to Japan would be much lower because these fields are located on or near the coast of North China. However, such coals are less suitable for coking than those from Neryungri. Not only are they higher in such troublesome and difficult to extract impurities as sulfur and phosphorus, but their physical structure is inferior for coking requirements to that of the Yakutian coals. Thus the disadvantage of Chinese coals may offset the mining and transportation cost advantages noted above. However, for the moment, the question is still moot because of the glut in new or expanded markets for Japanese steel products.

*Petroleum and Natural Gas.* As indicated earlier, the sole center of oil production in the Soviet Far East thus far is Sakhalin Island. Yet as oil production stabilizes and eventually declines in Western Siberia, the Soviets will presumably attempt to tap potential resources further east. Exploration in that vast region has barely begun. However, aside from reported preliminary surveys in the Yakut ASSR, development of oil deposits in the interior seems less likely than prospects in its coastal regions. This preference, of course, is related to the relative costs involved in oil extraction and transportation of the crude produce to markets. Aside from the Sakhalin continental shelf project, to be discussed shortly, there is a growing interest in potential developments in the shallower areas of the Sea of Japan and the Arctic coast.

The onshore Sakhalin fields were one of the first regions of oil production developed under the Soviets. Operations, through the vehicle of a Japanese concession, began in the twenties around Okha located near the northeastern coast. That region continues to be the main center of production, although additional fields have been opened nearby. The island's output moves via two pipelines across the narrow strait to refineries located on the mainland at Komsomolsk and Khabarovsk. By 1980, output was three million tons, or less than one percent of the Soviet total. Over time with the growth and gradual maturation of the economy of the Far East, its demand for petroleum and petroleum products has soared. As a result, according to Dienes, Sakhalin's oil output now accounts for only 20 percent of the region's oil requirements.[41] The remainder must be imported, via the Trans-Siberian, from the Angarsk refinery in eastern Siberia. Eventually, this oil will move to the Far East via the BAM.

As for offshore drilling, as part of an agreement signed in 1975, the Japanese agreed to lend the Soviets 152 million dollars for the project, and would apparently get half of its production. The plan is scheduled to last ten years and is designed to finance the exploration of the continental shelf off the northeastern coast near Okha.[42] Exploration is also under way off the southwest coast. Initial drilling, in cooperation with the Gulf Oil Corporation, began in August of 1977.[43] The potential size of the oil pool has not been reported, nor has there been any indication when or if commercial operations will get under way. There is apparently hope that gas too may be found here. There is no indication that the Sakhalin offshore fields will become a major center of production compara-

ble ultimately to developments in the North Sea. One indication of the general skepticism about the size of possible oil discoveries was the abandonment of plans to build a pipeline to Hokkaido, the northernmost Japanese island.[44] At best, new discoveries and production in the Sakhalin area may reduce current product hauls from Angarsk. This shift, then, would make possible some increase in possible exports of petroleum and petroleum products from Western Siberia to Japan. Note should be taken in this context of Chinese oil exports to Japan and the degree to which they may affect potential Soviet exports to Japan. Available information is spotty. It appears that Chinese oil is inferior to the rival Soviet product because of its higher sulfur content, but the Japanese are apparently planning to adapt several of their refineries with the technology to treat such inputs. Then too, crude petroleum that is high in sulfur like Gulf Coast oil can be used for the production of residual fuel oils. However, such products obviously cannot, without special treatment, serve those markets that require the lighter fractions. Although the Japanese, on technical grounds, prefer Soviet oil, they are also acutely aware of current and impending production difficulties. They are, however, also eager on political, economic and perhaps cultural grounds to bolster Sino-Japanese ties. Thus their reactions to the Sino-Soviet competition for Japanese markets must necessarily be mixed.

While Soviet petroleum production has stabilized and conceivably will decline in the coming years, the prospects for increases in natural gas output are much brighter.[45] In fact, the USSR has pressed in recent years for loans and contracts with private Western firms and state agencies that would call for the export of gas, in natural liquefied form (LNG), to markets in the U.S., Japan and Western Europe. The two most notable natural gas projects are the so-called "North Star" or Urengoi scheme, now apparently shelved mainly because of legal impediments enacted in the United States, and the Yakutian venture in the Far East which, though troubled, may still be viable and is of concern to us here.[46]

Yakutia has long been viewed by Soviet geologists as a major gas reservoir for the future. Their overall estimate according to Dienes and Shabad is a reserve of 13 trillion cubic meters, or about one-fifth of the potential natural gas reserves in the USSR as of 1965.[47] That long-term perspective is now slowly becoming a reality as the USSR attempts to develop its Siberian resources destined, in part, for hard-currency markets in the West. The first firmly based discoveries in this region were made in the mid-fifties near the junction of the Vilyui and Lena rivers about 400 kilometers northwest of Yakutsk. Gas from the Tas-Tumus field began to be piped to that regional capital in 1968 where it was used for local consumption principally in a small thermo-electric facility. With the decline of output in that field in the early seventies, production shifted to the Mastakh deposit located 190 kilometers to the west. This new oil center is called Kysyl-Syr, and by 1975 its output was about 500 million cubic meters. As a result of further exploration and after considerable negotiation, an agreement for the sale of natural gas was finally signed in 1976 between the Soviet Union, the

United States and Japan. It called for the purchase by Japan and the U.S. of 10 billion cubic meters each annually for a period of 25 years. This accord was to activate once further exploration assured a "proven" reserve of at least one trillion cubic meters. In turn, the USSR was to receive a loan for the first phase of the operation of 50 million dollars. That credit was to be defrayed equally by the U.S. and Japan. According to Whitney and Edmonds some 850 billion cubic meters had been confirmed by the spring of 1979,[48] suggesting that the necessary reserve level would be reached.

More critical is the second phase of this multi-stage operation. It now calls for the building of a large diameter pipeline for a distance of 3,500 kilometers to Olga, a deepwater, ice-free port located in the southern part of Maritime Krai, about 320 kilometers northeast of Vladivostok. Presumably the pipe would be provided by Japan, for the Soviet capacity for the production of this key material is inadequate. Pipe for other oil and gas lines is already commonly purchased in the West. The U.S. is unlikely to be a supplier because of the restrictions first imposed by the Trade Act of 1974 and its amendments[49] and then reinforced by the constraints. The Japanese are reported to be reluctant to proceed without American participation but they, of course, may still go ahead.

The final phase of the Yakutian project would be the construction of facilities at Olga for the liquefication and storage of LNG, the building of reconversion plants and storage facilities in Japan and perhaps eventually on the west coast of the United States coupled with the construction of a number of LNG carriers to service the flow between the Soviet Far East and the various markets. If the U.S. were to reconsider its stand on Soviet trade, it appears that El Paso and Occidental Petroleum would be the participating firms. The former is already heavily involved in a similar but much smaller exchange with Algeria. That agreement may be foundering because of Algeria's demand for a major increase in price for its gas so that it would be comparable with the price currently charged for petroleum by the OPEC trade bloc.[50]

Early estimates, made in 1974, indicated that the ultimate investment in the overall project, *excluding* facilities on the west coast of the U.S. would be $8.5 billion.[51] Presumably these calculations were far outdated by inflation in the ensuing years. Nevertheless, the central non-political question for both the U.S. and Japan is the long-run economic viability of the project. In simple terms the question is, would the cost of the delivered natural gas be competitive with that of petroleum delivered to the same markets by the end of this decade (the earliest projected date for possible completion of the overall plan). An additional and not unimportant question would be the reaction of Japanese and American authorities to the creation of terminal facilities for this highly flammable material in their ports.

As to the current status of the project in the USSR, the Russians, according to Whitney,[52] appeared confident that they would reach the reserve target specified in the 1976 agreement. Thirteen hundred workers were then engaged in the drilling operations at Kysyl-Syr despite winter temperatures that were even below those cited earlier at Neryungri. The project's planners were already designing the pipeline route which would have to pass through hundreds of kilometers of territory where permafrost is the rule and earthquakes are not uncommon. They apparently understood the political and economic realities of the tripartite agreement, but they claim that barring foreign participation they will proceed on their own, though at an understandably slower pace. From this observer's vantage point, it is difficult to rationalize their purported optimism, for it appears inconceivable that markets in the Soviet Far East could absorb more than a fraction of the previously planned natural gas output of Yakutia. Then too, the sharp competition for scarce investment funds would not augur well for the project's future. Yet even given these obstacles, with the unquestioned pressure on Soviet energy supplies by the late eighties, the future delivery of Yakutian gas to markets in eastern and western Siberia is not unthinkable.

## Forest Resources

If there is one category of materials which has been and presumably will continue to be a major export from the Far East, it is unquestionably forest products. What does appear to be in question, however, is not *whether* such exports will continue, but what will be the volume, character and value of that trade. There has been considerable debate among Western specialists as to the level of Soviet forest reserves and the potential cut of its timber supplies. To summarize Sutton's view,[53] "contrary to popular belief the USSR appears not to possess a vast underutilized forest resource of high quality. By area and volume the potentially exploitable forests of the USSR are comparable to the combined resources of Canada and the USA. The total increment is comparable to that of the USA alone." Others like North and Solecki are more sanguine: "After fuels, forest products offer one of the best long term potentials for foreign earnings, if the country's share of world resources is compared to expected world demand."[54] These authors hedge this conclusion by adding a rather obvious caution; that is the growth of Soviet forest-product exports will require heavy capital investment in that sector. In fact, it is certainly true that this industry has not received significant priority in resource allocation during the Soviet era. Barr, in his provocative discussion paper written for the AAG Project, supports North and Solecki's conclusions.[55] These and other Western contributions coupled with the Soviet literature[56] make it amply clear that the Far East's share of the timber production of the USSR should increase markedly over the coming decade. There is likely to be a notable expansion of the proportion of fabricated goods, other than roundwood, in the future forest-product output of the region.

By far the largest share of the Soviet Union's forest area is located in the 'taiga' or the northern coniferous forest region stretching from Karelia in the west to the Pacific. All told, northern European Russia, the Urals, Siberia and the Far East accounted for about 90 percent of the actual timber growing stock of the USSR in 1973.[57] Of these regions, only the European North and the Urals are readily accessible to the main markets of the nation. Even if one adds Western Siberia, their share was only one-fourth of the total forest resources. Not only are there great regional disparities in the volume of growing stock, but there are also significant geographical variations in the composition (species), maturity and quality of the Soviet forest stands.

As might be expected, much of the forested area of the West has been overcut or replaced by farmland. That which remains is in many instances immature or lower quality second growth. It does, however, because of relative location and climate offer the best prospects for replanting and rejuvenation under proper forest management. In contrast, the "eastern" stands are typically over-mature; which though not necessarily a handicap does, as Braden has noted, reflect lost past economic opportunities.[58] More important, the dominant tree in many areas is the larch, a problem species. In addition, the quality of a large share of the Siberian forests is low as reflected in narrow trunk diameters and low densities. Then too, in many instances these stands are inaccessible to existing rail transport. Those that are within such reach are still far from the forest deficient areas west of the Urals; yet, as we shall see, the relative accessibility of the Far Eastern forests to Pacific ports may be an offsetting advantage.

Several measures can be used to assess the significance of Far Eastern forests. The Far East in 1973 accounted for roughly one-third of the forested area of the USSR.[59] This compares with the estimate cited earlier of 28 percent of the nation's area. However, the former value does in this instance inflate the importance of the forested area of the region because of regional variations in timber volume. In terms of the actual growing stock of 21 billion cubic meters, the share drops to 27 percent, which is more consistent with the areal comparison. Yet even this value fails to take into account the environmental difficulties under which the forest grows in the Far East. Another measure is the so-called mean annual increment. This value, which was reported as 230 million cubic meters, was only 22 percent of the total for the USSR. However, even this gross measure may, in fact, exaggerate the economic importance of the forest resources of the Far East for the reasons cited above.

A subregional evaluation has to rely, in part, on rather dated Soviet forest-reserve statistics for 1961. While there are data for 1973 for the region as a whole and for total forest resources by subregion, no detailed forest-reserve materials for that year exist on an oblast, krai, or ASSR basis.[60] However, the data presented in Table 17, which compares total forest resources by subregion for the Far East in 1961 and 1973, suggest that the differences were, in fact, minimal. The use of the older data can thus be justified.

In terms of actual growing stock more than half of the timber resources of the overall region are found in what Barr and others have termed the "Siberian North," or Kamchatka and Magadan oblasts plus the Yakut ASSR. Yet this area, is likely to play an extremely modest role in the future timber production of the Far East. Other than accessibility and environmental problems, which are of course critical, the growth of timber output in the Siberian

TABLE 17
Comparison of the Total Forest Resources
of the Far East in 1961* and 1973*

| Region | 1961 millions of m³ | Percent | 1973 millions of m³ | Percent |
|---|---|---|---|---|
| Maritime Krai | 1,440 | 6.8 | 1,800 | 8.5 |
| Khabarovsk Krai | 4,804 | 22.7 | 4,900 | 22.7 |
| Amur Oblast | 2,196 | 10.4 | 2,100 | 9.8 |
| Kamchatka Oblast | 741 | 3.5 | 600 | 2.7 |
| Magadan Oblast | 833 | 3.9 | 900 | 4.1 |
| Sakhalin Oblast | 526 | 2.5 | 600 | 3.0 |
| Yakut ASSR | 10,619 | 50.2 | 10,500 | 49.2 |
| Soviet Far East | 21,159 | 100.0 | 21,400 | 100.0 |

*Lesnoi fond RSFSR [Forest reserves of the RSFSR] (Moscow, 1962), pp. 346–59, 503–21. Group III *total* reserve data only. Both columns cover "Actual Growing Stock."

**Gladyshev, *Problemy Dalnego Vostoka*, p. 35. I suspect that these data cover all three categories of forest resources (Groups I, II and III). Group III is the major commercial forest.

North is also dependent on the demand for its product. Here the question of species becomes important for at least 85 percent of the trees in this northern region are the Siberian larch variety. The broad categories (rather than the specific tree types) are demonstrated in Table 18. It should also be noted that only in Maritime Krai is the larch of minor significance. There are two key negative characteristics of this tree. First, there is the density of the wood, for it will not readily float. Where water transport is feasible the larch logs require special towing equipment for the movement to road and rail junctions or directly to processing centers. Second, while the technology for the effective use of this tree is slowly developing, its wood is not easily amenable for pulping. Its chips tend to clog the pulp machinery because of their high resin content. Thus Japan, the Far East's leading customer has set strict limits on the share of larch that it will purchase.[61]

Maritime Krai in the extreme south and, to a lesser degree, Sakhalin are not plagued by the dominance of this species in their stands. However, in these areas the forests contain large admixtures of deciduous hardwoods which are fine for railroad ties, pit props, poles, furniture, etc., but cannot readily be used for pulping. Soviet loggers, like others, typically prefer the coniferous species and ignore such hardwoods as oak, ash, and linden. Their neglect of the birch stands is more understandable.

*Timber Supply.* In terms of timber extraction, the Far East stands out more for its potential than its actual removals. Table 19 compares the cutting area and the use of that area, by region, for the heavily forested areas of the USSR and the overcut and poorly forested regions of the nation. Note that the conifers were more heavily used than the overall timber area. For some regions, the use percentage was clearly greater than the allowable cut, yet it is these areas that, because of their environmental advantages, offer the greatest potential for rejuvenation. Yet, in contrast, the values for Western Siberia, Eastern Siberia and the Far East are quite low. The southern portion of the Far East had a particularly low percentage. It is this relation-

TABLE 18
Exploitable Forest Resources in the Soviet Far East, by Region and Species, in 1961*

| Region | Species** (millions of m³) | | | | | Total | |
| | Conifers | Including Larch | Other | Deciduous Hardwoods | Deciduous Softwoods | Amount | Percent |
|---|---|---|---|---|---|---|---|
| Maritime Krai | 620.7 | 37.2 | 583.5 | 151.4 | 829.8 | 1,601.0 | 16.6 |
| Khabarovsk Krai | 2,353.3 | 1,144.3 | 1,209.0 | 101.5 | 149.2 | 2,604.0 | 27.1 |
| Amur Oblast | 609.4 | 561.5 | 47.9 | 10.0 | 93.8 | 713.2 | 7.4 |
| Kamchatka Oblast | 80.8 | 56.6 | 24.2 | 94.7 | 19.1 | 194.6 | 2.0 |
| Magadan Oblast | 437.4 | 437.4 | — | — | 14.1 | 451.5 | 4.7 |
| Sakhalin Oblast | 321.1 | 83.3 | 237.8 | 34.0 | 7.0 | 362.1 | 3.8 |
| Yakut ASSR | 3,677.8 | 3,177.4 | 500.4 | — | 16.8 | 3,694.6 | 38.4 |
| Soviet Far East | 8,100.5 | 5,497.7 | 2,602.8 | 391.6 | 1,129.8 | 9,621.0 | 100.0 |
| Percent | 84.2 | 57.1 | 27.1 | 4.1 | 11.7 | 100.0 | |

*Lesnoi fond RSFSR [Forest reserves of the RSFSR] (Moscow, 1962), pp. 556–69, Group III commercial resources only. Growing Stock.
**Excludes "other" category which accounted for 364 million m³.

ship which clearly fosters the current optimism about the future of forest extraction in the Far East. Yet, such gross data must necessarily be viewed with caution for they fail to give proper weight to such problems as production costs (including wages), accessibility and transport costs, environmental constraints, forest characteristics and demand (both foreign and domestic). Table 20 is an attempt to reconstruct the use percentages, demonstrated in the previous table, at the subregional scale. No data were available for the "allowable cut," so it was necessary to use statistics for the mean annual increment by oblast, krai, and ASSR for 1961. The results for the southern segment of the Far East are certainly in accord with those shown in Table 19. The remarkably low percentages for the Siberian North were to be expected, as were the

relatively higher values for the political divisions fronting on the Pacific. Accessibility clearly accounts for most of the geographical variation in use within the "South." The highest values, as expected, were recorded for Maritime Krai and Sakhalin.

*Forest Industries.* Before World War II and the return of southern Sakhalin (Karafuto) to Soviet control, the forest industries of the Far East were rather poorly developed. Over half of the region's production, as was true for the USSR as a whole, was still used to meet local fuel requirements. Exports of forest products from the Far East were minimal, particularly as opposed to those from northwestern European Russia.

By 1965, with the return of the important lumbering

TABLE 19
The Use of the Cutting Area, by Region, in the USSR as of 1973*

| Region | All Trees | | Conifers | |
| | Cutting Area millions of m³ | Use*** percent | Cutting Area millions of m³ | Use*** percent |
|---|---|---|---|---|
| Heavily Forested Areas | | | | |
| Urals | 61.6 | 84 | 33.2 | 115 |
| West Siberia | 94.1 | 28 | 48.8 | 40 |
| East Siberia | 159.7 | 39 | 115.6 | 38 |
| Southern Far East** | 102.3 | 32 | 84.2 | 37 |
| European Russia | 114.3 | 91 | 82.4 | 108 |
| Poorly Forested or Overcut Areas | | | | |
| Northwest | 11.6 | 74 | 4.6 | 96 |
| Baltic | 4.4 | 98 | 2.3 | 100 |
| Belorussia | 5.0 | 101 | 2.3 | 104 |
| Center | 30.8 | 87 | 8.8 | 133 |
| Volga | 7.8 | 90 | 1.3 | 92 |
| Ukraine | 5.7 | 98 | 2.5 | 100 |
| Caucasus | 4.0 | 90 | 0.5 | 80 |
| Urals and West Siberia | 16.1 | 63 | 4.6 | 93 |
| Kazakhstan and Central Asia | 3.3 | 54 | 1.0 | 55 |
| USSR | 620.3 | 57 | 392.9 | 68 |

*V. Glotov, Razmeshcheniye lesopromyshlennogo proizvodstva [Location of forest industries] (Moscow, 1977), p. 21.
**In Glotov's Table 21 this region is termed the "Far East" but the cutting area is clearly that of the *southern* part of that region excluding Yakutia, Kamchatka, and Magadan.
***Forest removals as a proportion of the "allowable cut."

TABLE 20
The Relationship between the Mean Annual Timber
Increment in 1961 and the Actual Timber Cut
in 1973, by Region, in the Soviet Far East*

| Region | (1) Mean Annual Timber Increment 1961 000 of m³ | (2) Timber Cut 1973 000 of m³ | (2 ÷ 1) Percent |
|---|---|---|---|
| Maritime Krai | 15,300 | 6,100 | 39.9 |
| Khabarovsk Krai | 45,900 | 13,800 | 30.1 |
| Amur Oblast | 24,800 | 3,800 | 15.3 |
| Sakhalin Oblast | 6,500 | 3,800 | 58.5 |
| Southern Far East | 92,500 | 27,500 | 29.7 |
| Kamchatka Oblast | 5,400 | 800 | 14.8 |
| Magadan Oblast | 4,800 | 500 | 10.4 |
| Yakut ASSR** | 91,400 | 3,000 | 3.6 |
| Northern Far East | 101,600 | 4,300 | 4.2 |
| Far East | 194,100 | 31,800 | 16.4 |

*F. Dukanov, V. Pokshishevsky and A. Khomentovsky, *Dalni Vostok* [The Far East] (Moscow, 1966), p. 149.
**Lesnoi fond RSFSR* [Forest reserves of the RSFSR] (Moscow, 1962), p. 584.

areas of southern Sakhalin and the accelerated economic growth of the overall region, commercial roundwood output in the Far East had doubled to a level of nearly 17 million cubic meters. A decade later, that product had swelled to 26 million cubic meters for a growth of 55 percent. This relative growth was greater than that for all other economic regions of the USSR. During this period too, with the shift of the region's household fuel consumption to coal, the proportion of the timber used for

firewood declined to 22 percent. Thus far, more of the cut was available for direct commercial use or for further processing. Despite these positive assessments, given the wealth of the Far East's forest resources, its share of the nation's commercial roundwood output in 1975 was still only 8 percent, a value that was hardly commensurate with its potential.

Moving to the subregional scale, Table 21 depicts the production of forest products, by political subdivision, in 1975. In roundwood, Khabarovsk Krai clearly dominated production with nearly half of the Far East's output. In fact, its rate of growth between 1965 and 1975 was double that of its region. In contrast, only 8 percent of the commercial timber output of the Far East was cut in the "Siberian North." Despite new endeavors in that difficult area, the South continues to be the leading timber extraction region of the Far East. What then is the future, viewed from a geographical perspective, of roundwood production in the overall region?

To properly assess such prospects, it is necessary to return to some of the themes that were discussed briefly in the preceding sections. The problem of accessibility clearly is an overriding issue. It should be recalled that the Far East has long been served by the Trans-Siberian Railroad, a double-tracked rail line (with its short branches), and by a scattering of highways. To these must be added the Amur River and its tributaries, most of them only usable for limited portions of the year. This restricted transport network is, of course, concentrated in the southern and southeastern margins of the Far East. To it must be added the Little BAM and ultimately the BAM mainline itself. Soviet planners believe that among the major commodities that will move along the BAM will be roundwood, sawn lumber and, at some future date, fabricated wood products, particularly pulp and paperboard. Dyakonov, in 1975, predicted that *ultimately* there would be 10 lumber-industry enterprises in the BAM zone (in-

TABLE 21
Forest Product Production in the Soviet Far East in 1975

| Region | Product | | | | |
|---|---|---|---|---|---|
| | Commercial Roundwood millions of meters³ | Commercial Sawn Lumber millions of meters³ | Plywood millions of meters³ | Paper 000 of tons | Paperboard*** 000 of tons |
| Maritime Krai | 4.9 | 1.7 | 30.2 | — | — |
| Khabarovsk Krai | 12.3 | 2.4 | 16.5 | 9.0 | 42.9 |
| Amur Oblast | 3.0 | 0.8 | — | 4.3 | — |
| Kamchatka Oblast | 0.5 | 0.2 | — | — | — |
| Magadan Oblast | 0.3 | 0.2 | — | — | — |
| Sakhalin Oblast | 3.6 | 0.7 | — | 215.7 | 90.8 |
| Yakut ASSR | 1.3 | 0.6 | — | — | — |
| Soviet Far East* | 25.9 | 6.6 | 46.7 | 229.0 | 133.7 |
| USSR** | 312.9 | 116.2 | 2,196.0 | 5,215.0 | 3,368.0 |
| Soviet Far East as percent of USSR | 8.3 | 5.7 | 2.1 | 4.4 | 4.0 |

*Narkhoz RSFSR v 1975* (Moscow, 1976), pp. 86–96.
**Narkhoz SSSR za 60 Let* (Moscow, 1977), pp. 232–38.
***The plant in Khabarovsk Krai is located in the Jewish Autonomous Oblast. By 1976 the Amursk forest products plant, which previously had only produced wood chips and pulp, inaugurated a new paperboard mill with a capacity of 139,000 tons per year (*Soviet Geography: Review and Translation*, 17, no. 9, (1976): 648).

cluding four in the Far East) producing from five to six million cubic meters of wood per year.[62] This volume would presumably be in addition to the existing round-wood output of that zone. In contrast, Gorovoi and Shlykov have argued that "in the forseeable future" the entire BAM zone would produce 30 to 35 million cubic meters of wood, two-thirds of which should originate in the Far East.[63] If this plan were fulfilled, the overall BAM zone would produce about 10 percent of the current timber output of the USSR. Their projections appear overly optimistic. A growth of this dimension would require truly significant increases in capital investment in an industry that has hitherto been badly neglected. To date, there is no evidence of investments of this magnitude in the Far Eastern forest industry, other than those under way at Amursk, located south of Komsomolsk. They may yet materialize once this new rail line is finally completed. However, such an allocation of scarce resources would not appear to be justified by any currently anticipated growth in domestic demand, and an expansion of foreign markets for the larch product of the BAM hinterland is unlikely without a significant breakthrough in pulping technology. Nor can such investments be defended in the light of the excessively high costs that are prevalent in this area because of zonal wage increments and high transport costs to shipping centers.[64] Labor supply continues to be a problem, although the use of North Korean workers, currently employed further south, may prove to be one solution.[65] What then of the future of timber extraction in the Far East? The likelihood, which appears to be supported by Barr,[66] is that significant growth of round-wood production will take place in the region, but the BAM zone will not account for the bulk of that increase. Most of the increment should come from an intensification of production in the older lumbering areas of the "South" and by penetration of the virgin forest outward from the previously established logging centers. Expansion of timber extraction in the BAM hinterland is likely to be more modest than previously predicted. Much of the increase in the Far Eastern segment of that zone will focus on the Komsomolsk district of Khabarovsk Krai, a region that is hardly representative of the true taiga region. The Little BAM may also witness the growth of new logging sites; however, that zone replicates many of the problems common to the service area of the BAM itself, so that its development, too, will be modest.

As for the production of forest products other than roundwood in the Far East, the current and potential role of these goods in interregional flows and exports is relevant to the themes of this paper.

Table 21 shows the difference between the share of the Far East in the Soviet output of roundwood and that of sawn lumber. While the Far East's timber cut grew appreciably from 1965 to 1975 (59%), the product of its sawmills stagnated. The lag in capacity of this basic activity may be understandable in the light of the failure of the Soviets to find Pacific markets for the sawn lumber output of the region. Only 4 percent of its product was exported in 1972.[67] As a result, the Far East's surplus must be shipped, at high transport costs, thousands of kilometers to markets in Siberia, Kazakhstan and Central Asia (see Table 13). These regions might better be served at lower cost from less remote sawmilling centers. However, the deciduous hardwoods of Maritime Krai produce some of the highest quality lumber in the nation, and it is apparently this commodity that finds a ready market further west.

Statistics on the production of paper and cardboard, by region, in 1975 are also depicted in Table 21. Here the dominance of Sakhalin is evident reflecting the inheritance of mills built by the Japanese before the war. On the mainland, the only significant area of production was located at Birakan in Khabarovsk Krai. Were more recent data available, they would exhibit a striking change; for in 1976 the first stage of a paperboard plant was inaugurated at Amursk with a capacity of 139,000 tons. That would make it the largest in the Far East. This integrated wood complex which produces roundwood, sawn lumber, etc., produced 160,000 tons of pulp in 1975. The second stage of the paperboard plant has a planned capacity of 278,000 tons.[68] As Shabad has already noted the Soviets have focused paper-making facilities in European Russia and paperboard plants in Siberia. By 1975 Siberia produced 23 percent of the latter product and only 7 percent of the nation's output of paper. The Soviets have failed to develop markets for paper and paperboard in Japan or elsewhere in the Pacific, and the rapidly increasing output of Siberian mills is still destined for domestic markets.

*Forest Product Exports.* The Soviet Union exported $2.3 billion worth of forest products in 1977 or about 5 percent of the value of exports in that year.[69] Of that total, about one billion dollars was the value of sales to hard-currency countries.[70] Japan was the USSR's chief customer accounting, in dollar terms, for half of the exports of timber products to the entire hard-currency bloc. The data cited in Table 22 make it apparent that the Far East was the chief supplier.

Soviet exports of timber to Japan can be traced back to the fifties, and over time these grew to a level of five million cubic meters in 1967.[71] However, these sales were not part of a development program either for the Far East or Siberia, as a whole. With the signing of the "First Far East Forest Resource Development Project" in 1968, the nature of Soviet-Japanese trade relations began to shift. Sales were regularized, and the Japanese made their first formal commitment to participate in Siberian resource development. Edmonds has effectively treated these agreements in his discussion paper.[72] In capsule form, the agreements called for low interest-deferred payment loans for the purchase of lumbering and transport machinery as well as chipping and pulping equipment. In turn, the Soviets sold roundwood, pulpwood, wood chips and sawn lumber to Japan, but semi-processed roundwood dominated the shipments. The USSR currently provides 28 percent of Japan's imports of this crude material and only a minor share of the pulp needs. Despite Soviet attempts to urge the Japanese to purchase a larger share of semi-fabricated and even fabricated wood products, the available statistics show no shift in past trade patterns.[73] Sales of Far Eastern forest products to Japan will probably increase in the coming decade as the

TABLE 22
Forest Product Exports of the Soviet Far East, by Region, in 1972*

| | Product | | | | | | | |
|---|---|---|---|---|---|---|---|---|
| Region | Round-wood 000 of meters$^3$ | Percent of Soviet Exports | Sawn Lumber 000 of meters$^3$ | Percent of Soviet Exports | Cellulose 000 of tons | Percent of Soviet Exports | Paper and Paperboard 000 of tons | Percent of Soviet Exports |
| Maritime Krai | 1,494 | 8.8 | 112 | 1.4 | — | — | — | — |
| Khabarovsk Krai | 4,834 | 27.2 | 104 | 1.3 | 11.0 | 2.2 | — | — |
| Amur Oblast | 849 | 5.4 | — | — | — | — | — | — |
| Kamchatka Oblast | 62 | 0.6 | — | — | — | — | — | — |
| Sakhalin Oblast | 497 | 3.6 | 48 | 0.6 | 46.1 | 9.2 | 35.8 | 4.6 |
| Soviet Far East | 7,736 | 45.6 | 264 | 3.3 | 57.1 | 11.4 | 35.8 | 4.6 |

*Percentages derived from M. Kanevsky and G. Shaytanov (editors), *Lesnoi eksport SSSR* [Forest exports of the USSR] (Moscow, 1975), pp. 110–12. Absolute data derived from those percentages coupled with production data from Soviet statistical handbooks. These values check remarkably well with those in *Vneshnyaya torgovlya SSSR za 1972 god* (Moscow, 1973).

Japanese diversify their sources of supply. However, Soviet dreams of a structural change in those exports are unlikely to materialize. As noted earlier, expanded paperboard output will continue to be destined for domestic markets.

## The Foreign Trade of the Soviet Far East

The question of Soviet trade with the 'Pacific-rim' countries has been thoroughly explored in other chapters prepared for this volume.[74] However, none have focused directly on the question of the present and prospective trade of the Soviet Far East with respect to the recurrent theme of resource development.

Table 23 provides an abbreviated summary, in value terms, of Soviet foreign trade data with nations in the Pacific for 1968 and 1978. Note the striking relative and absolute growth in both imports and exports during that era.

The U.S., Canadian and Australian data for 1978 are dominated by the exports of food and feed grains to the USSR. It can be assumed that, depending on the vagaries of climate, such flows should fluctuate drastically from year to year and that only a relatively small share of those flows would move via the Far East to Soviet markets. Similarly, the exports of high value machinery from the U.S. to the USSR probably moved chiefly via the Atlantic. Only a very small fraction of those goods moved to Far Eastern markets.

Japan was clearly the Soviet Union's leading trade partner in the Pacific and those flows were channelled via the Far East. Most of the exchange consisted of transit movements such as West Siberian petroleum, Kuznetsk coal and Central Asian cotton. In turn, machinery, steel products, chemicals and consumer goods flowed west via the Trans-Siberian. With the implementation, since the late sixties, of joint Soviet-Japanese ventures for the economic development of the Far East, it can be assumed that an important portion of the machinery imports in 1978 were destined for the Far East. The only resource that

apparently moved in significant volume from the Far East to Japan was roundwood.

The trade patterns of the remaining nations in the list are more complex and difficult to decipher. It is apparent that the USSR acts as the developed nation serving less developed trading partners. This is particularly true of Mongolia, North Korea, Vietnam and China. The Far East would appear to play no major role in these exchanges other than as a funnel for transit movements.

What, then, are the prospects for growth and structural change in Far Eastern trade during the coming decade. Here the answer must be conjectural; for even the Soviets hesitate to project such flows, except in broad outline. Most probably, the Far East will play a significantly expanded role in the production and export of such basic raw materials as coal, timber and possibly natural gas. It is also conceivable that there will be significant exports of nonferrous and rare metals.

In the case of coal, there appears to be no question that output in southern Yakutia can be expanded beyond previously projected levels. Additional cleaning plants, over and above those currently under construction, can be built to process this additional product. The chief problem will be a delay in shipments, for the technical reasons outlined earlier. Since the Soviets can set prices for exports at market levels, they can presumably meet expected competition from Australia, South Africa, China and possibly the United States. The actual volume of sales will depend less on the growth of production at Neryungri than on the willingness of the Japanese to become more dependent on Soviet supplies than present commitments portend.

With regard to timber, as already discussed, there is still ample opportunity to expand the current output of the Far East. Forest cutting in the BAM service area may not expand at the pace envisaged by Soviet planners, but growth of timber production both there and in the South will, nevertheless, proceed. Sales of forest products will continue to be confined to Japanese markets. Here, as in the case of coal, the Soviets will face continued competition. In this instance, their main rivals are the United

TABLE 23
Soviet Trade With Countries in the Pacific Basin in 1968 and 1978 (in millions of rubles)*

| | Exports | | | Imports | | |
|---|---|---|---|---|---|---|
| Countries | 1968 | 1978 | Main Products** (1978) | 1968 | 1978 | Main Products** (1978) |
| Vietnam | 143.3 | 305.5 | MPTG | 16.1 | 152.3 | GXM |
| China | 53.4 | 163.8 | M | 33.0 | 174.9 | GTX |
| North Korea | 155.0 | 176.5 | MPCG | 108.8 | 201.6 | IG |
| Malaysia | 0.1 | 4.2 | | 90.4 | 121.1 | P |
| Japan | 352.1 | 736.1 | PFCT | 166.5 | 1,583.7 | MChIT |
| Mongolia | 174.5 | 596.1 | MP | 47.8 | 147.0 | OTM |
| Canada | 17.6 | 28.7 | | 113.6 | 358.9 | GM |
| U.S. | 38.6 | 253.1 | PCh | 50.9 | 1,599.3 | MG |
| Australia | 1.0 | 4.6 | | 35.9 | 274.8 | TG |
| Total | 935.6 | 2,268.6 | | 663.0 | 4,613.6 | |
| All Soviet Exports | 9,570.9 | 35,667.8 | | 8,469.0 | 34,556.6 | |
| Percent | 9.8 | 6.4 | | 7.8 | 13.4 | |

*From *Vneshnyaya torgovlya za 1968g.* and *Vneshnyaya torgovlya v 1978g.* This table is patterned after North's compilation in 1978, but uses different years and different symbols for historical comparisons. Countries with less than 50 million rubles of trade in 1978 with the USSR are omitted. Mongolia is added because of its proximity to the Soviet Far East.
**Symbols: C—Coal; Ch—chemicals; F—forest products; G—grain, flour and other foods; I—iron and steel products; L—livestock and meat; M—machinery; O—ores; P—petroleum; T—cotton, wool and other textile fibres; and X—clothing.

States and Canada. However, with increasing pressure on the forest resources of Anglo-America, that competition may be somewhat less potent in the coming decade. Far Eastern exports can thus be expected to grow at a comparatively rapid pace. However, there are no signs that the Japanese will shift the character of their purchases. There is no evidence that they will buy greater amounts of sawn lumber, paperboard, etc. that the Soviets will be eager to sell as their production capacity expands. Forest product exports from the Far East will continue to be dominated by sales of semi-processed roundwood.

As noted previously, the prospects for large scale production of natural gas in Yakutia appear excellent. Even the construction difficulties of building the 3,500-kilometer pipeline to Olga can eventually be surmounted. However, the political obstacles in the United States remain the overriding issue, for they will also affect Japanese participation in the project. If American objections to the financing of this undertaking can be overcome, then the exports of Yakutian LNG to Japan and the U.S. may become a reality. The time horizon of 1990 that has been envisaged may be premature for the completion of the entire project, even in the best of circumstances. There is, of course, still the question whether, given all of the costs outlined earlier, LNG delivered to the West Coast of the United States will be truly competitive with the cost of alternative fuels. The future export of natural gas to the U.S. and Japan is thus a possibility but in no sense a certainty.

## Conclusions

At the outset, some central questions were raised in the introduction to this chapter. What will be the nature of economic growth in the Far East in the coming decade,

and how will such developments affect that region's domestic and foreign interchanges?

No attempt was made here to explore prospective changes in all sectors of the Far Eastern economy by 1990. However, a review of the Soviet and American literature has provided some perspective on these questions. It is apparent that the eighties will be a period of accelerated economic development in the Far East. That rapid advancement will partly be a product of the completion of the BAM and developments in its hinterland. However, that growth will also be a function of the drive to develop the region's resources to serve both local needs and foreign demand. Only secondarily, will its resource development be designed to supply the broader national market. Thus, with the possible expansion of Sakhalin oil production resulting from offshore wells, the need for oil from Western Siberia may well be eliminated. Gas from Yakutia, too, will ultimately help to 'drive' Far Eastern development. Sawnwood and paperboard production will not only fulfill increasing local requirements, but also provide a surplus for markets in the western reaches of the country.

There has long been talk of the possibilities for building an integrated steel plant in the Far East. That possibility now has come closer to fruition with the development of the Neryungri coking coal deposits. Major deposits of iron ore have been identified in the Chara-Tokko district of the Aldan region (near the border between the Yakut ASSR and Chita Oblast). These ores are essentially free of undesirable impurities and amenable to pelletization; thus, the building of such a nine million ton plant becomes even more feasible.[75] In the meantime, the 11th Plan calls for the building of a mini-steel plant without pig iron production. When this venture is completed, the imports of steel products from the Ukraine, the Urals and Siberia may cease.

The maturation of industrial development should

bring with it the growth of many industries which cannot profit from local scale economies. Heretofore, transportation costs on the inbound movements of machinery, fabricated metals, chemical products like fertilizers and plastics, and consumer goods have been a growing burden. While it would be senseless to argue that the Far East should become self-sufficient in the production of this range of manufactured goods; the necessity to import so large a share of its needs may be counterproductive from a regional perspective. The initial plans to create a series of integrated territorial-production complexes in the Far East, similar to the one already approved for Southern Yakutia, may be an augury of future development trends.

It was argued earlier that the Far East can be viewed as an intervening opportunity soaking up potential spatial interaction between the USSR and its trading partners in the Pacific. As that region becomes less dependent, in the next decade, upon European Russia, Kazakhstan and the Siberian region to her west, a process that is already under way, there will clearly be an expansion of transit movements. These additional commodities would, of course, be exported mainly to Japan and the Communist nations of East Asia. A move toward greater regional self-sufficiency may also be deemed by the Politburo to be a strategic necessity in the light of their increasing strategic concerns about changes on the Chinese political scene and the continuing belligerence of pronouncements by their new leaders. The building of the BAM is often cited as a reflection of the worries of the Soviets![76]

Finally, the thoughts of one Soviet scholar on Far Eastern economic development are worth repeating here. The late Professor Mayergoiz, in 1974, noted that because of the vast distances separating the Far East from the economic core of the USSR, the economy of the region needed to be oriented increasingly to the Pacific.

In the long run, we may have to revise the traditional concept that industrialization in the Soviet Union necessarily advances from west to east . . . A more reasonable point of view is to look to the opening up of the Siberian interior not only from the European side, but from both sides of the country, thus giving play to the impact of the development of the Soviet Pacific coast.[77]

## NOTES

1. *Naseleniye SSSR* [Population of the USSR] (Moscow, 1980), pp. 4–11.

2. *Vneshnyaya torgovlya SSSR, statistichesky sbornik 1918–66* [Foreign trade of the USSR; statistical handbook 1918–66] (Moscow, 1967), various pages.

3. Allan Rodgers, "The Locational Dynamics of Soviet Industry," *Annals, Association of American Geographers*, 46, (June 1974): 226–41.

4. M. Sonin, "Resettlement of Population during the Third Five-Year Plan," *American Quarterly on the Soviet Union*, (November 1940): p. 47.

5. F. Lorimer, *The Population of the Soviet Union* (Geneva, 1946), p. 170.

6. E. Kulischer, *The Displacement of Population in Europe* (Montreal: International Labor Office, 1957).

7. L. Rybakovsky, *Vosproizvodstvo trudovykh resursov Dalnego Vostoka* [Reproduction of labor resources in the Far East] (Moscow, 1969), p. 124.

8. Robert North, "The Soviet Far East: New Centre of Attention in the USSR," *Pacific Affairs*, 51, (1978): 195–215.

9. See Theodore Shabad and Victor L. Mote, *Gateway to Siberian Resources (The BAM)* (Washington, 1977), p. 189.

10. W. W. Rostow, *The Stages of Economic Growth* (Cambridge, 1960).

11. R. Shniper and L. Denisova, *Mezhotraslevye svyazi i narodnokhozyaistennye proportsii Vostochnoi Sibiri i Dalnego Vostoka* [Intersectoral relations and economic proportions in East Siberia and the Far East] (Novosibirsk, 1974), p. 77.

12. *Vneshnyaya torgovlya SSSR za 1977 god* [Foreign trade of USSR in 1977] (Moscow, 1978).

13. Shniper and Denisova, *Mezhotraslevye svyazi*, p. 80.

14. Ibid., p. 107.

15. Ibid., p. 104–05.

16. Paul Dibb, *Siberia and the Pacific* (New York, 1972), p. 64.

17. S. Mikhailov and L. Turkevich, "On specialization and disproportions in the economy of the Far East," *Planovoye khozyaistvo*, 1964, no. 8, pp. 16–24.

18. Rybakovsky, *Vosproizdvodstvo*, p. 66.

19. A. Gladyshev, A. Kulikov, and B. Shapalin, *Problemy razvitiya i razmeshcheniya proizvoditelnikh sil Dalnego Vostoka* [Problems of development and location of productive forces in the Far East] (Moscow, 1974), p. 88.

20. Gladyshev et al., *Problemy Dalnego Vostoka*, p. 39.

21. *Pravda*, 5 March 1981.

22. Shabad and Mote, *Gateway*

23. Theodore Shabad, "Some Geographic Aspects of the New Soviet Five-Year Plan," *Soviet Geography: Review and Translation* (hereafter SGRT), 19, no. 3 (March 1978): 202–04; Robert Jensen, "Soviet Regional Development Policy and the Tenth Five-Year Plan," *SGRT*, 19, no. 3 (March 1978): 196–201; Leslie Dienes, "Investment Priorities in Soviet Regions," *Annals, Association of American Geographers*, 64 (1972): 437–54; and the excellent contributions in V. Bandera and Z. Melnyk, eds., *The Soviet Economy in Regional Perspective* (New York, 1973).

24. North, "Soviet Far East"; Dibb, *Siberia and Pacific*, and Victor L. Mote, *Predictions and Realities in the Development of the Soviet Far East*, Discussion Paper No. 3 (May 1978), Association of American Geographers, Project on Soviet Natural Resources in the World Economy.

25. Z. Mieczkowski, "The Soviet Far East: Problem Region of the USSR," *Pacific Affairs*, 41 (1968): 214–29.

26. Rybakovsky, *Vosproizdvodstvo*, pp. 120–23 and N. Nikolayev and I. Singur, *Perspektivy razvitiya ekonomiki Dalnego Vostoka* [Prospects of development of the economy of the Far East] (Khabarovsk, 1968), pp. 47–48.

27. Shabad and Mote, *Gateway*; Mote, *Predictions and Realities*, and Theodore Shabad, "The BAM, Product of the Century," *Soviet Economy in a Time of Change*, vol. 1, Joint Economic Committee, (Washington, 1979), pp. 164–76.

28. L. Brezhnev, "Comrade Brezhnev's Speech," *Pravda*, 16 March 1974.

29. The notion of a spatial sponge and spatial interaction is usually credited to the late Edward Ullman.

30. For obvious reasons, given my concern with exports, hydroelectric power will not be discussed here.

31. *Energeticheskiye resursy SSSR: Toplivno-energeticheskiye resursy* [Energy resources of USSR: Fuel-energy resources] (Moscow, 1968) pp. 64, 123.

32. A. Gladyshev et al., *Novye territorialnye kompleksy SSSR* [New territorial complexes of the USSR] (Moscow, 1977), pp. 163–90.

33. N. Shabarova and A. Tyzhnova, eds., *Zapasy uglei i goryuchikh slantsev SSSR* [Coal and oil shale reserves of the USSR] (Moscow, 1958), pp. 134–37; and S. Dvorin, M. Rabinovich and A. Turkin, "Fuel base of the iron and steel industry," in I. Bardin, ed., *Problemy razvitiya chernoi metallurgii v rayonakh vostochneye Ozera Baikal* [Problems of development of the iron and steel industry in regions east of Lake Baikal] (Moscow, 1960), pp. 55–75.

34. *Pravda*, 5 March 1981.

35. Leslie Dienes, *The Regional Dimensions in Soviet Energy Policy*, Discussion Paper No. 13 (August 1979), Association of American Geographers, Project on Soviet Natural Resources in the World Economy, p. 62.

36. V. Frishberg et al., "Rational exploitation of South Yakutian grade SS coals," *Koks i khimiya*, no. 8 (1977), pp. 3–6.

37. I. Ya. Fatkulin et al., "Development of Siberia and the Far East: Utilization of coals from the South Yakutian and Bureya fields in carbonization blends," *Koks i khimiya*, no. 1 (1979), pp. 4–7.

38. *Ekonomicheskaya gazeta*, 1975, no. 5, p. 13.

39. *Sotsialisticheskaya industriya* 21 January 1979, p. 2 and C. Whitney "In Frigid Siberia Even U.S. Machines Fail," *New York Times*, 1 April 1979, p. 24.

40. Whitney, "Frigid Siberia," p. 24.

41. Leslie Dienes and Theodore Shabad, *The Soviet Energy System: Resource Use and Policies* (Washington, 1979), p. 61.

42. Richard Edmonds, *Siberian Resource Development and the Japanese Economy: The Japanese Perspective*, Discussion Paper No. 12 (August 1979), Association of American Geographers, Project on Soviet Natural Resources in the World Economy, p. 11.

43. Ibid.

44. Ibid., p. 35.

45. *Allocation of Resources in the Soviet Union and China, 1979*, Joint Economic Committee of the Congress, 96th Congress, First Session, 26 June and 9 July 1979, (Washington, 1980), various pages, and Jonathan Stern, *Soviet Gas in the World Economy* (Washington, 1979), various pages.

46. Stern, *Soviet Gas*, pp. 37–38.

47. Dienes and Shabad, *Soviet Energy System*, p. 93. The details reported here were drawn mainly from this study whose data were derived from Soviet sources.

48. Whitney, "Frigid Siberia," and Edmonds, *Japanese Economy*, p. 11.

49. Stern, *Soviet Gas*, pp. 38–39.

50. *New York Times*, 15 July 1980, pp. D1, D5.

51. Stern, *Soviet Gas*, p. 38.

52. Whitney, "Frigid Siberia," p. 24.

53. W. R. J. Sutton, "The Forest Resources of the USSR: Their Exploitation and Their Potential," *Commonwealth Forestry Review*, 54, no. 2 (1975): 110–38. Among its other scholarly merits, this paper is unquestionably the best review of both the Soviet and Western literature in the forest field. However, it was of only restricted value for this paper because of the absence of regional detail in its analysis.

54. R. North and J. Solecki, "The Soviet Forest Products Industry: Its Present and Potential Exports," *Canadian Slavonic Papers*, 19, no. 3, (1977): 281–311.

55. Brenton Barr, *Domestic and International Implications of Regional Change in the Soviet Timber and Wood Processing Industries, 1970–90*, Discussion Paper No. 4, (June 1978), Association of American Geographers, Project on Soviet Natural Resources in the World Economy.

56. V. Belousova, *Optimalnoye planirovaniye razvitiya i razmeshcheniya otraslei lesnoi promyshlennosti* [Optimal planning of the development and location of forest industry sectors] (Novosibirsk, 1969); V. Belousova and N. Salatova, "Ways of enhancing the cost-effectiveness of forest industries and the use of forest resources in Siberia," in *Priroda lesov i povysheniye ikh produktivnosti* [The nature of forests and enhancement of productivity] (Novosibirsk, 1973), pp. 243–58; V. Glotov, *Razmeshcheniye lesopromyshlennogo proizvodstva* [Location of forest industries] (Moscow, 1977); V. Gorovoi and G. Privalovskaya, *Geografiya lesnoi promyshlennosti SSSR* [Geography of forest industry of the USSR] (Moscow, 1966); I. Holland, "Comparative Advantage and Potentials for World Trade in Wood Products," *Forest Products Journal*, vol. 27, no. 10 (1977), pp. 55–58; M. Kanevsky and G. Shaitanov, eds., *Lesnoi eksport SSSR* [Timber exports of USSR] (Moscow, 1975); A. Tsymek, *Lesoekonomicheskiye rayony SSSR* [Forest economic regions of the USSR] (Moscow, 1975); *European Timber Trends and Prospects 1950 to 2000*, vol. 29 (Supp. no. 3) Timber Bulletin for Europe, F. A. O. (Food and Agriculture Organization); United Nations, 1976.

57. Barr, *Regional Change in Timber Industry*, p. 21.

58. Kathleen Braden, *The Role of Imported Technology in the Export Potential of Soviet Forest Products*, Discussion Paper No. 16 (November 1979), Association of American Geographers, Project on Soviet Natural Resources in the World Economy.

59. Barr, *Regional Change in Timber Industry*, p. 21.

60. Forest censuses were apparently taken in 1966 and 1973. Barr, *Regional Change in Timber Industry*, various pages.

61. Braden, *Role of Technology*, p. 23.

62. F. Dyakonov, "The Far East: Problems and Prospects," J. P. R. S. Translation 64236, 4 March 1975, from *Ekonomicheskaya gazeta*, 1975, no. 5, p. 13.

63. V. Gorovoi and V. Shlykov, "Basic Trends in the Development of the Forest Industry Along the Baikal-Amur Mainline," *SGRT*, 19, no. 2 (February 1978): 88.

64. Braden, *Role of Technology*, p. 16, translated from Glotov (1977): 177. Glotov cites significant differences in production costs. In the case of logging, for example, Amur Oblast and Khabarovsk Krai were credited with an

index number of 133 compared to a base level of 100 for Sverdlovsk Oblast. Other values were 114 for Chita Oblast and the Buryat ASSR, 119 for Tyumen Oblast and 137 for Arkhangelsk Oblast. For a discussion of regional wage increments and overall production costs in the forest industries see: Dibb, *Siberia and Pacific*, p. 110, while a map of general salary increments by zone in Eastern Siberia and the Far East, as of 1968, can be found in North, "Soviet Far East," p. 199.

65. Barr, *Regional Change in Timber Industry*, p. 173.

66. Barr, *Regional Change in Timber Industry*, p. 17, demonstrates projected timber output, by region, for the USSR in 1990.

67. Kanevsky and Shaitanov, *Lesnoi eksport*, pp. 110–12.

68. *SGRT*, 17, no. 9 (November 1976): 648.

69. National Foreign Assessment Center, *Handbook of Economic Statistics 1979*, (Washington, 1979), p. 100.

70. Marshall Goldman, *The Changing Role of Raw-Material Exports and Soviet Foreign Trade*, Discussion Paper No. 8 (June 1979), Association of American Geographers, Project on Soviet Natural Resources in the World Economy.

71. *Vneshnyaya torgovlya SSSR za 1968 god* [Foreign trade of USSR in 1968] (Moscow, 1969).

72. Edmonds, *Japanese Economy*, pp. 8–13.

73. Roundwood accounted for 82 percent of the Soviet exports of forest products, in value terms, to Japan in 1977. *Vneshnyaya torgovlya SSSR v 1977 g.* [Foreign trade of USSR in 1977] (Moscow, 1968), p. 241.

74. Mote, *Predictions and Realities*; Edmonds, *Japanese Economy*; Goldman, *Changing Role, Raw-Material Exports*; Lawrence Brainard, *Foreign Economic Constraints on Soviet Raw-Material Development in the 1980s*, Discussion Paper No. 19 (June 1980), Association of American Geographers, Project on Soviet Natural Resources in the World Economy; and Robert North, *The Impact of Recent Trends in Soviet Foreign Trade on Regional Economic Development in the USSR*, Discussion Paper No. 21 (June 1980), Association of American Geographers, Project on Soviet Natural Resources in the World Economy. Many other papers as well, in this series, have treated exports as part of their product analyses.

75. V. Kozlov and V. Pavlov, "The iron ore base for an iron and steel industry in Southern Yakutia," *Gorny zhurnal*, no. 11, (1974); and V. Sidorova and A. Vadyukhin, "New Technology and the Location of the Iron and Steel Industry in the Eastern Portion of the USSR," *Izvestiya Akademiya Nauk SSR, seriya geograficheskaya*, 1975, no. 6, pp. 47–52, as translated in *SGRT*.

76. Allen Whiting, *Siberian Development and East Asia: The Strategic Dimension*, Discussion Paper No. 20 (May 1980), Association of American Geographers, Project on Soviet Natural Resources in the World Economy, pp. 5–12.

77. I. Mayergoiz, "The Unique Economic-Geographic Situation of the Soviet Far East and Some Problems in Using It Over the Long Term," *SGRT*, 15, no. 4 (1974), pp. 428, 434.

# 9

# SIBERIAN RESOURCE DEVELOPMENT AND THE JAPANESE ECONOMY: THE JAPANESE PERSPECTIVE

RICHARD LOUIS EDMONDS
The University of Hong Kong

## Introduction

Russian and Japanese contact began with territorial conflict in the 18th century. Territorial conflict continues, but the Soviet Union and Japan now find themselves drawn together in a symbiotic relationship. Post-World War II Japan, stripped of its resource-rich possessions—Karafuto (southern Sakhalin), Korea, Manchukuo (Manchuria), and Taiwan—now faces a future of growing energy dependence. In order to fulfill growing long-range energy needs Japan has embarked on a policy of cooperation and participation in foreign resource development. The Soviet Union, resource-rich by comparison, lacks capital and in some respects technology for resource development, particularly in the eastern half of its territory. This chapter attempts to uncover the Japanese attitude toward Siberian development by examining the aspirations of Japanese politicians, businessmen, and scholars with regard to Soviet resources.

To comprehend the future of Siberian resources in the Japanese economy, it is necessary to review the development of Soviet-Japanese trade relations since 1945 with a focus on Siberia and to review Japan's dependence on raw-material imports which could be supplied by Siberia. With this in mind one can begin to examine special issues and the perspective of various groups in Japan toward Siberian resources. Special issues which must be assessed include the northern islands political issues, the 1979 Soviet incursion into Afghanistan, and the future of Sino-Japanese trade, each of which influences the Japanese perspective of Siberian resources as well as regional interests in Siberian trade within Japan.

Analysis of the Japanese perspective is based on personal interviews with knowledgeable individuals and a review of relevant Japanese literature. The persons having the greatest impact on Japanese policy are those who work for semi-public foundations. These individuals represent a blending of government, business, and to a lesser extent, academic interests. This paper is based on the work produced by these few individuals and government reports. Often the Japanese literature does not contain footnotes, but it appears the Japanese rely heavily on Soviet and American data and have not been able to do much field work in Siberia.

## Review of Japanese-Soviet Trade Since 1945

Basic data on postwar Japanese-Soviet trade indicate the first major trade increase coincided with the restoration of diplomatic relations in October 1956 (Table 1). After 1957, the total volume grew annually until 1976. Despite a 9.3 percent increase in Soviet imports to Japan, a 14.1 percent decrease in Japanese exports resulted in a reduction of the total amount of trade in 1977.[1] In 1978 exports bounced back with a 29.4 percent increase, while stockpiling of resources in Japan slowed the increase in imports to 1.4 percent.[2] In 1979 exports decreased 1.6 percent due to a slowdown in the shipment of equipment for Siberian development while imports rose 32.5 percent cutting Japan's 1978 favorable balance of trade in half.[3] In 1980, however, overall trade rose 12.9% with imports to Japan reduced by 2.7% and exports nearly doubling in value from 1979.

Postwar Soviet-Japanese trade can be divided into three periods: General Headquarters supervised trade, private-level nonagreement, and government-level agreement trade. Siberian resource development emerges in the government-level agreement period.

### Supervised Trade 1946–49

During this early postwar period when trade was supervised by the General Headquarters of the Allied Occupation Forces, Japan exported wooden boats, steam engines, freight cars, fishing nets, rope and other materials to the Soviet Union. Imports included coal, coking coal, santonin, and so forth. Such trade was conducted on an open account basis in coordination with the Soviet representatives in the General Headquarters and came to a close when the open accounts were transferred to the Nippon Bank at the end of 1949.

### Private-Level Nonagreement Trade 1950–57

These were by far the most difficult years, reflecting the Cold War era in which there were neither commercial treaties, nor trade or payment agreements between Japan

TABLE 1
Soviet-Japanese Trade, 1946–79 (1000s of U.S. dollars)

| Period | Year | Japanese Exports | | Imports to Japan | | Total Volume | |
|---|---|---|---|---|---|---|---|
| General | 1946 | 24 | | 0 | | 24 | |
| Headquarters | 1947 | 140 | | 2,004 | | 2,144 | |
| supervised | 1948 | 4,385 | | 2,670 | | 7,055 | |
| trade | 1949 | 7,360 | | 1,933 | | 9,292 | |
| | 1950 | 723 | | 738 | | 1,461 | |
| | 1951 | 0 | | 28 | | 28 | |
| Private- | 1952 | 150 | | 459 | | 609 | |
| level | 1953 | 7 | | 2,101 | | 2,108 | |
| nonagreement | 1954 | 39 | | 2,249 | | 2,288 | |
| trade | 1955 | 2,710 | | 3,070 | | 5,780 | |
| | 1956 | 760 | | 2,860 | | 3,620 | |
| | (19 October 1956 restoration of Soviet-Japanese relations) | | | | | | |
| | 1957 | 9,294 | (100) | 12,324 | (100) | 21,618 | (100) |
| | (6 December 1957 Treaty of Commerce & Trade Payment Agreement) | | | | | | |
| | 1958 | 18,100 | (195) | 22,150 | (180) | 40,250 | (186) |
| | 1959 | 23,026 | (248) | 39,490 | (320) | 62,516 | (289) |
| Government- | (1960–62 Trade Payment Agreement signed) | | | | | | |
| level | 1960 | 59,976 | (645) | 87,025 | (706) | 147,001 | (680) |
| agreement | 1961 | 65,380 | (703) | 145,409 | (1,180) | 210,789 | (975) |
| trade | 1962 | 149,390 | (1,607) | 147,309 | (1,195) | 296,699 | (1,372) |
| | (1963–65 Trade Payment Agreement signed) | | | | | | |
| | 1963 | 158,136 | (1,701) | 161,940 | (1,314) | 320,076 | (1,481) |
| | 1964 | 181,810 | (1,956) | 226,729 | (1,840) | 408,539 | (1,890) |
| | 1965 | 168,358 | (1,811) | 240,198 | (1,949) | 408,556 | (1,890) |
| | (1966–70 Trade Payment Agreement signed) | | | | | | |
| | 1966 | 214,022 | (2,308) | 300,361 | (2,437) | 514,383 | (2,379) |
| | 1967 | 157,688 | (1,697) | 453,918 | (3,683) | 611,606 | (2,829) |
| | 1968 | 179,018 | (1,926) | 463,512 | (3,761) | 642,530 | (2,972) |
| | 1969 | 268,247 | (2,886) | 461,563 | (3,745) | 729,810 | (3,376) |
| | 1970 | 340,932 | (3,668) | 481,038 | (3,903) | 821,970 | (3,802) |
| | (1971–75 Trade Payment Agreement signed) | | | | | | |
| | 1971 | 377,267 | (4,059) | 495,880 | (4,024) | 873,147 | (4,039) |
| | 1972 | 504,179 | (5,425) | 593,906 | (4,819) | 1,098,085 | (5,079) |
| | 1973 | 484,210 | (5,210) | 1,077,701 | (8,745) | 1,561,911 | (7,225) |
| | 1974 | 1,095,642 | (11,789) | 1,418,143 | (11,507) | 2,513,785 | (11,628) |
| | 1975 | 1,626,200 | (17,497) | 1,169,618 | (9,491) | 2,795,818 | (12,933) |
| | (1976–80 Trade Payment Agreement signed) | | | | | | |
| | 1976 | 2,251,894 | (24,230) | 1,167,441 | (9,473) | 3,419,335 | (15,817) |
| | 1977 | 1,933,877 | (20,808) | 1,421,875 | (11,537) | 3,355,752 | (15,523) |
| | 1978 | 2,502,195 | (26,923) | 1,441,723 | (11,698) | 3,943,918 | (18,244) |
| | 1979 | 2,461,464 | (26,484) | 1,910,681 | (15,504) | 4,372,145 | (20,225) |
| January–October | 1980 | 2,188,085 | | 1,491,730 | | 3,679,815 | |

NOTE: Numbers in parentheses are indices of trade change with 1957 equal to 100.
SOURCE: Soren Too Boeki Kai, "Nisso Boeki Tokei," *Soren Too Boeki Chosa Geppo* no. 2 (1980), p. 27. January–October 1980 figure also supplied by Soren Too Boeki Kai (Japan Association for Trade with Soviet Union and Socialist Countries of Europe).

and the Soviet Union. The Korean War ushered in controls on the export of strategic goods to Comecon countries. In June 1954, various Soviet trade organizations and Japanese companies reached a provisional agreement for an $80 million trade exchange over the remainder of 1954 and 1955. After an actual agreement was reached and the specified period came to a close, only one-eighth of the amount of trade indicated in the provisional agreement materialized. This caused a great amount of despair, especially in the Japanese shipbuilding industry, which came to doubt Soviet credibility.[4]

In October 1956, Japan and USSR restored diplomatic relations. This led to the signing of the Soviet-Japanese Treaty of Commerce and the Soviet-Japanese Trade Payment Agreement in December 1957, the most important events in the history of post-1945 Soviet-Japanese trade relations. The level of trade in 1957, six times that in 1956, demonstrated the utility of these documents. The Soviet-Japanese Treaty of Commerce has remained in effect, being renewed automatically every five years, while the Soviet-Japanese Trade Payment Agreement also has been renewed, at differing time intervals (Table 1).

Government-Level Agreement Trade Since 1958

Since 1958, trade has persisted under the following four forms: public corporation (or general) trade, cooperative trade, coastal trade, and Siberian development-project trade (a special form of public corporation trade).[5]

*Public corporation trade.* Conducted between Japanese companies on the one hand and over fifty Soviet regional, industrial or product-related public corporations under the Ministry of Foreign Trade on the other, this form of trade has occupied the largest portion since 1958. In some ways both coastal trade and the Siberian development projects are variants of public corporation trade but will be discussed separately.

*Cooperative trade.* Cooperative trade is carried on between various cooperatives or small to middle-sized corporations in Japan and the Soviet Cooperative Trade Corporation (*Soyuzkoopvneshtorg*) in the foreign trade section of the Soviet Cooperative Central Union (*Tsentrosoyuz*). The major commodity imported by Japan through cooperative trade has been timber, but various agricultural goods also have been purchased. Japan has exported manufactured textiles and sundry goods. The contracts are renewed yearly and the levels of imports and exports have been settled by barter agreements or letters of credit.

*Coastal trade.* This form of trade has been conducted on a barter-exchange arrangement between various Japanese companies or prefectural (*ken*) level trade cooperatives and the Soviet Far East Trade Office (*Dalintorg*) established in Nakhodka in 1965. Coastal trade, which will be discussed in detail later, has grown but not as fast as the Japanese had hoped. Cooperative and coastal trade together make up only about four percent of Soviet-Japanese trade.

*Siberian development-project trade.* With the announcement that the Soviet Union was going to allocate over 50 percent of it capital investment to the eastern regions (Central Asia, Kazakhstan, the Urals, Siberia, and the Far East) under the 6th Five-Year Plan (1956–60), Japanese government and business leaders became optimistic about Japan's future role in Siberia. However, in 1959, the Soviet government replaced this plan with a Seven-Year Plan (1959–65) in which just over 40 percent of total investment was devoted to the eastern regions (20 percent to Siberia and the Far East). The Seven-Year Plan was not fulfilled as many of the goals were later reduced or included in the 8th Five-Year Plan (1966–70).

In any event, Japanese interest in Siberia greatly increased during the early 1960s. In 1966 this interest culminated in the formation of the Soviet-Japanese collaborative projects in Siberia and the Soviet Far East. The enterprises formed at these conferences have become the key elements of Siberian development-project trade. The Soviets have previously engaged in similar product-sharing trade with Italy and other Western European nations.[6] The basic plan has been for Japan to supply facilities, machinery, and other material in return for a guaranteed portion of the exploited resources. These projects, which promise steady resource supplies from a new source plus new markets have seemed ideal to the Japanese. The sharp rise in trade during the early 1970s reflects the impact of these projects, which became possible due to a relaxing of Japan's bank loan position, and also indicates the optimism which the Japanese felt toward Soviet trade at that time. The total investment under the first seven projects listed below amounts to nearly $1.5 billion.[7]

(1) The first Far East forest resource development project. On 29 July 1968 an agreement was signed marking the beginning of Soviet-Japanese collaboration in the development of Siberia. Under this project $133 million in construction machinery, vehicles, and work vessels for lumbering and transport, were exported from Japan with a five-year deferred payment (20 percent downpayment at 5.8 percent interest). In return, Japan received 7.6 million cubic meters of timber and pulp at a constant price from 1969 to 1973, and 320 thousand cubic meters of sawn lumber between 1971 and 1973.

(2) The Vostochny harbor construction project. An agreement for this project was signed on 18 December 1970. In order to improve transport facilities between the USSR and Japan, a new port on Wrangel Bay, 18 kilometers east of Nakhodka, was built. Japan was responsible for a coal pier and a comprehensive freight loading facility. Part of the capital, the equivalent of $80 million in machinery and material, was exported with a seven-year deferred payment (12 percent down at 6 percent interest). This is the only project which did not include guaranteed imports of raw materials to Japan. By the end of 1975, 97 percent of the Japanese exports had been delivered. The Soviets looked with favor on this kind of project.

(3) Pulp and wood-chip development project. The agreement for this project was signed on 6 December 1971. Japan exported the equivalent of $45 million in chip and pulp facilities, machinery, and special ships equipped to haul chips with a six-year deferred payment (12 percent downpayment at 6 percent interest, not including ships) plus $5 million (cash base) of consumer goods for local needs. In return, a total of 8 million cubic meters of chip timber and 4.7 million cubic meters of pulp timber were to be imported between 1972 and 1981. Japan, however, imported 2.8 million cubic meters of chip timber and 2.8 million cubic meters of pulp timber by 1978, only 62 percent of the chip and 86 percent of the pulp deliveries expected.

This project had initial problems since the flow of goods was reduced by slow Soviet delivery and an unwillingness of the Japanese to accept pulp and chips when they were ready to be delivered because market conditions were poor in Japan. It was doubtful that the stipulated amounts of chip timber and pulp would be delivered by 1981. The Japanese, however, expressed interest in a second project to begin in 1982.

(4) The South Yakutian coking coal project. With the signing of this agreement of 3 June 1974, Japanese and Soviet collaboration entered the field of energy resource development. The scale of this project also facilitated a change in credit arrangements from supplier's credit to bank loans. To develop the South Yakutian coal field (Neryungri) and to improve facilities at the Kuznetsk coal field, the Export-Import Bank of Japan and commerical banks are furnishing yen loans equivalent to $390 million for development machinery plus $60 million for consumer goods allotted to local needs. As a result, facilities for coal extraction, freight vehicles, crane parts, tools,

cable and consumer goods are being exported to the USSR. The bank loan was being furnished over eight years from 1975 to 1982 and was to be repaid from 1983 to 1990 at an interest rate of 6.375 (the local consumer goods loan was at 7.25 percent). Due to a rise in prices, Japan later agreed to an additional $90 million loan.

In return, Japan was to receive coking coal imports totaling 104.4 million metric tons between 1979 and 1998. Neryungri coal will not begin to arrive until 1983 or later. The quality of this coal is said to be inferior to Australian coking coal but the equivalent of U.S. coal and can be used with no problem. The basic concern of the Japanese with this project is transportation and consequently, stability of supply. With the Little BAM railway, completed in October 1978, and new port facilities at Vostochny, transportation problems could disappear if jam-ups do not occur. Another concern is the possibility of production problems at Neryungri, which could seriously affect Japan's coal imports.[8] Soviet intervention in Afghanistan put a stop to negotiations on this project in the spring of 1980, but by September of that year the Japanese government approved bank credits to keep it going.

(5) The second Far East forest resource development project. The agreement for this project, which can be considered a continuation of the 1968 project, was signed on 30 July 1974 with the loan agreement following on 23 October of the same year. The Export-Import Bank of Japan and commercial banks loaned $435 million for timber exploitation facilities, $65 million for boats, and $50 million for local costs. In return, Japan received 7 million cubic meters of timber and sawn lumber between 1975 and 1979.[9] The value of this timber was adjusted annually. The basic contract for a third Far East forest resource development project was signed in March 1981.

(6) The Yakutian natural gas exploration project. When exploration confirmed at least one trillion cubic meters, the United States and Japan were to begin contract negotiations for each to receive 10 billion cubic meters of natural gas (7.5 million metric tons of liquefied natural gas) annually for 25 years. On 11 December 1974, the agreement was officially signed, but due to some changes in the loan arrangements, the loan agreement was not signed until 31 March 1976. A $50 million bank loan was made, half by the Export-Import Bank of Japan and half by the Bank of America, to support the exploration effort. As of March 1979, the export of American and Japanese exploration equipment was complete and 850 billion cubic meters of gas reserves were confirmed.[10] This project will include construction of a pipeline, from the gas sites to Olga, over 3,000 kilometers long and requiring 3 million metric tons of pipe.[11] Japan's concern that the Americans would discontinue participation at some point during the second phase was in part realized in August 1980 when the El Paso Corporation proposed that this project be slowed because of the Afghanistan incursion. There is now little chance that Yakutian natural gas will be imported to Japan anytime soon.

(7) The Sakhalin continental shelf oil and natural gas exploration and development project. The agreement was signed on 28 January 1975, and the loan agreement was concluded on 1 July of the same year. The purpose of this project is to discover oil and natural gas on the continental shelf both northeast and southwest of Sakhalin Island. The initial credit from the Japanese side amounted to $152.5 million over a five-year period, most of it going for the purchase and lease of exploration equipment and the rest for facilities such as computers and local costs. A $70 million supplementary loan was agreed to in 1979.

The initial exploration period was to extend from 1976 to 1982, drilling having begun in August 1977. Japan was to receive 50 percent of the new oil production plus an agreed upon amount of the new gas discoveries at a discount during the period the loan and interest were being repaid and for 10 years after repayment. Ice forces the Soviets to restrict their operations to the period from 1 July to 15 October (107 days) in the northeast and from 15 March to 30 November (261 days) in the southwest.[12] The American corporation, Gulf Oil, has become Japan's partner in this project. In spite of America's attempt to impose economic restrictions on the USSR after Afghanistan, this project will probably continue uninterrupted with actual development beginning in 1983. The Soviets plan for delivery of 5.1 billion cubic meters of gas to begin in 1985 and to continue for a 20 year period.[13]

(8) The third Far East forest resource development project. The basic contract was approved in March 1981. The amount of timber to be imported between 1981 and 1986 should amount to about two-thirds of that delivered under the second project, thereby reducing wood imports to less than 60 percent of 1975–79 levels. The Export-Import Bank of Japan plans to deliver a one billion dollar loan.

Many projects have failed to materialize such as the Far East iron ore development project suggested in 1959, the Udokan copper mining development project, and the Tyumen oil development project both suggested at the initial Soviet-Japanese Economic Committee meeting in Tokyo during December 1966. The Far East paper and pulp project, first suggested by Prime Minister Kosygin to Prime Minister Tanaka in October 1973, and the expansion of the Vostochny port facilities are under discussion. There is a slight possibility that by 1990 a Far East steel plant project and the Molodezhny asbestos development project could materialize along with some sort of railroad construction project. The Japanese were also expected to supply pipe to a new natural gas pipeline linking the Urengoi field in Western Siberia with West Germany and other West European countries.[14] The Soviet Union has also informally proposed the establishment of a nuclear power station in Sakhalin which the Japanese are not enthusiastic about, power compensation for nuclear power plant equipment, and the refurbishment of Japanese paper and pulp plants built in Karafuto (now southern Sakhalin).

Postwar Soviet-Japanese trade has remained at the low level of 2 to 4 percent of both countries' total foreign trade. Since 1958 most of this trade has been conducted through public corporations. The Siberian portion has been transacted mainly in the form of projects although a small part has been conducted as coastal trade. The Siberian trade has resulted in manufactured goods from Japan being sent on credit in exchange for Soviet timber products and coking coal. The Soviets have also agreed to exchange natural gas.

## Japan's Traditional Dependence on Raw-Material Imports and Siberia

Resource-deficient Japan must rely on raw-material imports to support its economy. The Japanese strategy is to buy critical imports from as wide a range of countries as possible in order to avoid dependence on any particular country. Experts are reluctant to give any maximum percentages. For certain items, such as whale meat and palladium, the share of imports from the USSR has run as high as 60 to 70 percent. Data on past purchases, however, suggest that the Japanese generally try to limit dependence on the USSR to less than 20 percent. Yet, if necessary, the Japanese will buy whatever they have to from whomever they have to. Still it is useful to examine the traditional share of each commodity purchased from the USSR and other countries by Japan to evaluate their potential dependence on Soviet imports to 1990.

### Wood Products

Japan currently imports nearly 70 percent of the timber it uses and it does not seem likely that the proportion or quantity will increase much in the near future. Wood products, imported under various forms of trade, accounted for 38.3 percent of Soviet exports to Japan in 1979. Soviet exports, in turn, represented 16.1 percent of Japan's 1979 wood imports. The United States share was 28 percent while Malaysian and Indonesian imports each accounted for about 20 percent.[15]

Pulp imports are dominated by Canada (1979, 43.6 percent) and the United States (1979, 25.2 percent). Since Japan only has to import about 10 to 11 percent of the pulp it uses there is no major concern about having to find new sources. The Japanese would probably prefer to import more pulp from New Zealand (1979, 12.5 percent) and Oceania, Latin America, and Europe rather than from Siberia.

By 1990 imports of wood products are likely to remain unchanged or be reduced slightly depending on Japan's needs, the amount finally stipulated in the third Far East forest resource development project, and the ability to purchase from other sources.

### Food Imports

Soviet food products constitute a very small share of Japan's total food imports. The quantity of seafood imported has been rising more rapidly than meat in recent years. Future increases in food imports from the Soviet Union could occur if prices were low, but it is not likely that the Soviet Union will become a major supplier given transportation constraints and the availability of alternative suppliers.

### Energy

Japanese interest in Siberian resources centers on energy. Past increases in energy consumption plus predictions by the Japanese government that total energy consumption in Japan may double between 1975 and 1985 and triple between 1975 and 2000, unless government and private enterprise enact an accelerated energy saving policy, clearly suggest that Japan will have to import increasing amounts of coal, petroleum, liquefied natural gas, liquefied petroleum gas, and uranium to meet energy needs (Table 2 and Figure 1).[16] The overall Japanese strategy is to increase the share of coal, liquefied natural gas, and nuclear power in the domestic energy balance to 17.6, 9, and 10.9 percent respectively by 1990 in order to reduce dependence on foreign oil.

*Coal.* The Japanese do not feel there will be a major coal import crisis since coal is a plentiful fuel, available from a larger number of countries than oil. Moreover, past consumption increases in Japan were modest compared with petroleum products (Tables 3 and 4). Japanese domestic coal, about 23 percent of the coal consumed in Japan during 1979, exists in relatively larger quantities than domestic oil (0.2 percent of the oil consumed in Japan during fiscal year 1979).[17] However, any major increase in coal consumption will have to be met by foreign imports since it is virtually impossible to increase domestic production.

During the 1970s Soviet coal accounted for 4 to 6 percent of Japanese imports and it is expected that by 1990 the USSR share will not exceed 7 percent. Japan has signed long-term contracts with Australia and Canada, and imports from South Africa and China are on the increase. Future coal suppliers may include Indonesia, Mozambique, Botswana, New Zealand, Venezuela, Colombia and other countries.[18] Imports from the Soviet Union, however, should begin to increase in the 1980s when deliveries guaranteed under the South Yakutian coking coal project begin to arrive.

*Oil.* More than any other single event, the oil shock of the early 1970s prompted Japan to reconsider Siberia as a supplier of natural resources. Japan sees the noncommunist world's oil supply peaking between 1980 and 2000.[19] The peak, most likely between 1985 and 1995, could come sooner or later, depending on the pricing policies of the exporting nations.

Beginning with the energy shock in 1973, imports of crude oil to Japan decreased until 1975, and had not reached 1973 levels by 1979 (Table 4). Traditionally Siberia has played almost no role in the Japanese market. Since the Soviet Union is the world's largest oil producer, exports to Japan could increase but every indication in the Japanese literature as well as conversations with Japanese experts point to a continued low level.[20] In the past, one Japanese oil company received oil directly from Iraq which the Soviets were to obtain in trade for military weapons. In return Japan sent machinery to the USSR.[21] The only hope for an increase of USSR oil exports to Japan hinges on the Sakhalin continental shelf oil and natural gas project. Small quantities of marine diesel oil and other special petroleum products may continue to be imported and shipments of Middle East oil may be received as in the Iraqi example, but chances of major Soviet oil shipments by 1990 are small.

TABLE 2
Japan's Energy Supply (Percentages)

| Fiscal Year | Total (10 billion kcal) | Imported | Hydro-electric energy | Nuclear energy | Domestic coal | Imported coal |
|---|---|---|---|---|---|---|
| 1955 | 56,011 | 24.0 | 21.2 | — | 44.8 | 4.4 |
| 1960 | 93,749 | 44.2 | 15.3 | — | 34.4 | 7.1 |
| 1965 | 165,614 | 66.2 | 11.3 | 0.0 | 19.1 | 8.2 |
| 1970 | 310,468 | 83.5 | 6.3 | 0.4 | 8.1 | 12.6 |
| 1975 | 365,719 | 88.0 | 5.8 | 1.7 | 3.3 | 13.1 |
| 1976 | 384,087 | 88.0 | 5.6 | 2.2 | 3.2 | 12.2 |
| 1977 | 384,456 | 88.8 | 4.8 | 2.0 | 3.3 | 11.6 |
| 1978 | 385,236 | 87.3 | 4.7 | 3.8 | 3.3 | 10.5 |
| 1979 | 408,738 | 87.0 | 5.1 | 4.2 | 2.9 | 11.1 |

| Fiscal Year | Domestic Petroleum | Imported Petroleum | Imported Petroleum Products | Imported Liquefied Petroleum Gas | Natural Gas | Imported Liquefied Natural Gas |
|---|---|---|---|---|---|---|
| 1955 | 0.6 | 15.6 | 4.0 | — | 0.4 | — |
| 1960 | 0.6 | 33.0 | 4.1 | — | 1.0 | — |
| 1965 | 0.4 | 49.7 | 7.9 | 0.4 | 1.2 | — |
| 1970 | 0.3 | 62.0 | 7.4 | 1.1 | 0.9 | 0.4 |
| 1975 | 0.2 | 67.3 | 3.8 | 1.9 | 0.7 | 1.8 |
| 1976 | 0.2 | 67.1 | 4.5 | 2.1 | 0.7 | 2.1 |
| 1977 | 0.2 | 67.1 | 4.9 | 2.3 | 0.8 | 2.9 |
| 1978 | 0.1 | 65.1 | 5.1 | 2.6 | 0.7 | 4.0 |
| 1979 | 0.1 | 63.0 | 5.2 | 2.8 | 0.6 | 4.9 |

SOURCE: Bureau of Statistics, Office of the Prime Minister, *Statistical Handbook of Japan 1978* (Tokyo: Japan Statistical Association, 1978), p. 42; and *Statistical Handbook of Japan 1981*, p. 44.

*Gas.* The Japanese prefer liquefied natural gas to other forms of energy since it is a clean-burning, low-polluting fuel. Recently pollution concerns have been on the increase in Japan. Between 1960 and 1965, dependence on natural gas imports was nil but by 1970 it has risen to 34.8 percent and by 1978 to 82.6 percent.[22] In 1977 Japan consumed 51.9 percent of the world's liquefied natural gas imports. These imports have come from Alaska (since 1969), Brunei (1972), Abu Dhabi (1977), and Indonesia (1977) (Table 5). The Japanese have recently established a contract with Australia to begin delivery of 6.5 million metric tons of liquefied natural gas in 1985.[23] By 1990 Soviet natural gas will probably be imported. If methanol made from liquefied natural gas can be used as an auto fuel by 1990, significant amounts of natural gas processed into methanol may also be imported from the USSR.[24]

Liquefied petroleum gas from Saudi Arabia, Kuwait, Australia, and the United Arab Emirates accounted for 94.8 percent of Japan's 1979 imports (Table 6). The Japanese will try not to increase the use of petroleum-based gases but instead shift to coal-based gases sometime after 1990. Liquefied natural gas, liquefied petroleum gas, and coal gas, however, could all be processed from Siberian resources and the Japanese government is interested in expanding their supply of these fuels. The success of the Yakutian natural gas exploration project along with the Sakhalin continental shelf project should bring the Soviets into the Japanese gas market as an important supplier.

Minerals

*Iron Ore.* Iron ore imports from the Soviet Union have stagnated (Table 7). Any hope for a major Soviet role disappeared with the shelving of the Far East iron ore project. The Japanese do not see their steel output increasing greatly by 1990. Japan has purchased most of its iron ore under long-term contracts and will most likely buy Soviet iron ore in the same fashion.

*Copper Ore.* Japan currently imports almost no copper ore from the Soviet Union. Major exporters to Japan include the Philippines, Canada, and Papua New Guinea (Table 8). In 1978, some of Japan's imported copper was completely developed by Japan (11 percent), most was obtained from Japanese-financed mines (51 percent), and the rest was purchased on the market (38 percent).[25] Although foreign imports are increasing, without the Udokan project, there is little hope for a major Soviet role in the Japanese market by 1990. Since July 1976, Japan has been importing copper through a national metal ore stockpiling enterprise to insure a stable supply.

*Asbestos.* In 1979, 9.8 percent of Japan's imported asbestos came from the USSR.[26] Major suppliers also included Canada (43.1 percent), South Africa (35.7 percent), and the United States (4.8 percent). Other suppliers have included Australia, Italy, China, South Korea, and India. Japan desires to purchase more asbestos but there is

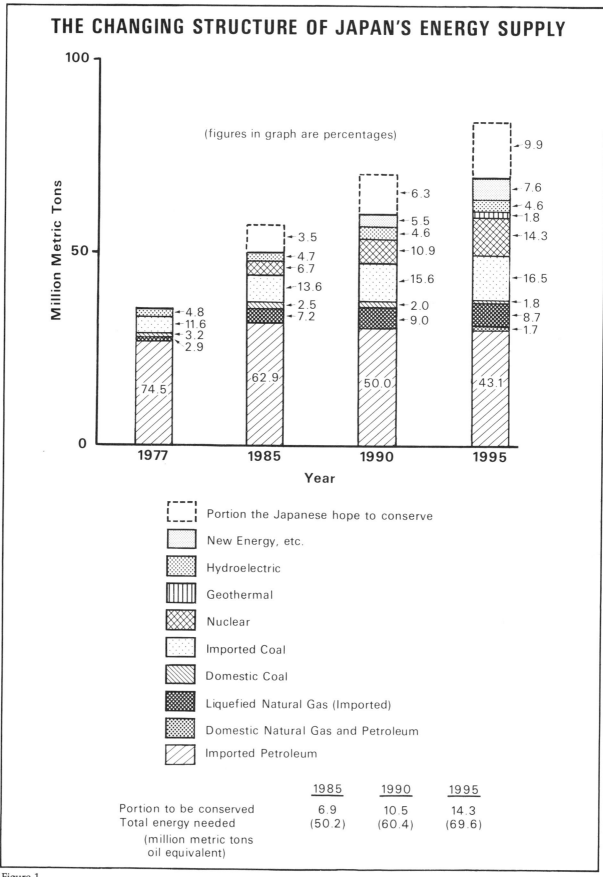

THE CHANGING STRUCTURE OF JAPAN'S ENERGY SUPPLY

(figures in graph are percentages)

Legend:
- Portion the Japanese hope to conserve
- New Energy, etc.
- Hydroelectric
- Geothermal
- Nuclear
- Imported Coal
- Domestic Coal
- Liquefied Natural Gas (Imported)
- Domestic Natural Gas and Petroleum
- Imported Petroleum

|  | 1985 | 1990 | 1995 |
|---|---|---|---|
| Portion to be conserved | 6.9 | 10.5 | 14.3 |
| Total energy needed | (50.2) | (60.4) | (69.6) |
| (million metric tons oil equivalent) | | | |

Figure 1
SOURCE: Tsusho Sangyo Sho, *Tsusho Hakusho (Soron)* (Tokyo: Okura Sho, 1980), p. 253.

TABLE 3
Percentage of Japanese Coal Imports by Country[a]

| Year | Total[b] | USSR | Australia | United States | Canada | South Africa | P.R. China | Poland | Vietnam[c] | West Germany | New Zealand |
|------|----------|------|-----------|---------------|--------|--------------|------------|--------|------------|--------------|-------------|
| 1970 | 50,172 | 5.7 | 32.8 | 50.3 | 6.9 | 0.6 | 0.5 | 1.8 | 0.6 | — | — |
| 1971 | 46,923 | 5.2 | 41.8 | 39.4 | 14.4 | 0.5 | 0.7 | 2.4 | 0.9 | — | — |
| 1972 | 49,278 | 5.1 | 41.6 | 33.6 | 15.8 | 0.2 | 0.5 | 2.5 | 0.1 | — | — |
| 1973 | 56,854 | 4.8 | 43.8 | 29.1 | 18.3 | 0.4 | 0.5 | 2.1 | 0.3 | — | — |
| 1974 | 64,151 | 5.2 | 35.7 | 39.6 | 15.1 | 0.2 | 0.6 | 1.9 | 1.0 | 0.1 | — |
| 1975 | 62,107 | 5.1 | 37.0 | 36.1 | 17.3 | 0.2 | 0.7 | 1.7 | — | 0.5 | — |
| 1976 | 60,759 | 5.4 | 43.3 | 28.7 | 17.1 | 1.4 | 0.5 | 1.6 | — | 0.6 | 0.02 |
| 1977 | 60,841 | 5.1 | 43.5 | 24.9 | 17.8 | 4.1 | 0.8 | 1.3 | 1.5 | 0.6 | 0.1 |
| 1978 | 52,177 | 4.8 | 48.3 | 17.0 | 21.0 | 4.8 | 1.5 | 1.1 | 0.8 | 0.6 | 0.02 |
| 1979 | 58,554 | 4.0 | 46.2 | 23.1 | 18.0 | 4.1 | 2.4 | 0.9 | — | 0.6 | — |
| 1980 | 68,228 | 3.1 | 43.1 | 28.7 | 16.0 | 4.8 | 3.0 | 0.6 | 0.5 | — | 0.1 |

[a]The statistics in this table were calculated on the basis of statistics found in the source listed below and differ somewhat from those found in the *Nippon Kogyo Nenkan* [Japan Industrial Annual] (Tokyo: Nippon Kogyo Shinbunsha, various years).
[b]In thousand metric tons.
[c]Before unification, North Vietnam only.
SOURCE: Tsusho Sangyo Sho, *Tsusho Hakusho (Kakuron)* (Tokyo: Okura Sho), 1973, p. 286; 1976, pp. 329–30; 1978, pp. 263–64; 1979, p. 220; 1980, p. 138; 1981, p. 138.

concern about health hazards, primarily cancer. Nonetheless there is a good chance that more Soviet asbestos will be imported by 1990.[27]

*Manganese.* Japan imports 95 percent of the manganese it needs, mostly for the steel industry. South Africa, Australia, and India provided 81.3 percent of the 1979 imports while the Soviet Union's 1978 share was 1.2 percent. Although supplies of manganese seem to be abundant, they are concentrated in a relatively small number of countries. Japan does not need to press for increased Soviet manganese imports and it appears doubtful that imports will increase by 1990.

*Chrome.* The Soviet Union supplied 3.7 percent of Japan's chrome in 1978. South Africa, India, the Philippines, and Iran supplied larger quantities.[28] The unstable political situations in Iran and South Africa could force the Japanese to look elsewhere for chrome if they are denied

those supplies. The Japanese feel the Soviet Union will not be interested in selling more chrome to Japan. However, if the Soviets make a reasonable sale offer the Japanese will probably accept.

*Others.* The Soviet Union supplied Japan with 9.5 percent of its aluminum and aluminum alloy imports, over 27 percent of its platinum, over 74 percent of its palladium imports and about 15 percent of the nickel and nickel alloys imported in 1979.

**Political Problems**

The Northern Territories Issue

Since World War II, the horizon of Soviet-Japanese economic cooperation has been clouded by the lack of a peace treaty, the most important obstacle being the so-

TABLE 4
Percentage of Japanese Oil Imports by Country[a]

| Year | Total[b] | USSR | Saudi Arabia | Indonesia | United Arab Emirates | Iran | Kuwait | Oman | Brunei | Iraq | P.R. China | Qatar | Malaysia | Venezuela | Libya | Algeria | Australia |
|------|----------|------|--------------|-----------|----------------------|------|--------|------|--------|------|------------|-------|----------|-----------|-------|---------|-----------|
| 1970 | 197,108 | 0.29 | 14.7 | 13.2 | — | 43.4 | 8.7 | 3.0 | 0.002 | — | — | — | 0.1 | 0.3 | 0.2 | — | — |
| 1971 | 222,492 | 0.22 | 16.9 | 11.8 | — | 43.1 | 9.4 | 2.5 | 1.0 | 0.1 | — | — | 0.1 | 0.2 | 0.2 | — | 0.1 |
| 1972 | 249,193 | 0.17 | 22.5 | 12.9 | 5.7 | 38.6 | 11.5 | 3.3 | 2.2 | 0.1 | — | 0.1 | 0.1 | 0.2 | 0.1 | — | 0.1 |
| 1973 | 289,698 | 0.47 | 23.5 | 14.3 | 9.2 | 33.6 | 8.9 | 2.7 | 3.4 | 0.04 | 0.4 | 0.05 | 0.2 | 0.2 | 0.4 | — | 0.1 |
| 1974 | 278,393 | 0.09 | 27.2 | 14.0 | 11.1 | 25.5 | 10.0 | 2.0 | 3.2 | 0.8 | 1.6 | 0.1 | 0.3 | 0.2 | 1.5 | 0.1 | 0.1 |
| 1975 | 263,373 | 0.03 | 29.8 | 11.4 | 9.0 | 25.3 | 9.2 | 2.7 | 3.2 | 2.0 | 3.5 | 0.1 | 0.6 | 0.1 | 1.3 | 0.1 | 0.03 |
| 1976 | 267,754 | 0.03 | 34.1 | 12.0 | 11.5 | 20.2 | 7.4 | 3.2 | 3.4 | 2.8 | 2.6 | 0.03 | 1.0 | 0.1 | 0.9 | 0.03 | 0.05 |
| 1977 | 278,017 | 0.03 | 33.8 | 13.6 | 11.4 | 17.0 | 8.3 | 3.7 | 3.4 | 3.1 | 2.8 | 0.8 | 1.5 | 0.1 | 0.4 | 0.1 | 0.06 |
| 1978 | 270,650 | 0.02 | 32.9 | 12.9 | 10.1 | 17.3 | 8.6 | 3.8 | 3.2 | 3.3 | 3.2 | 2.3 | 2.0 | 0.1 | 0.06 | 0.1 | 0.08 |
| 1979 | 281,203 | — | 34.5 | 14.4 | 10.2 | 9.7 | 9.6 | 3.9 | 3.4 | 5.4 | 3.0 | 2.9 | 2.4 | 0.2 | 0.1 | 0.1 | — |
| 1980 | 254,447 | 0.04 | 35.3 | 14.3 | 13.6 | 6.6 | 4.0 | — | 3.1 | 7.8 | 3.6 | 3.0 | 2.2 | 0.9 | 0.5 | 0.6 | — |

[a]Minor suppliers include Angola, Brazil, Egypt, Mexico, Nigeria, Singapore, and the United States.
[b]In thousand kiloliters.
SOURCE: Tsusho Sangyo Sho, *Tsusho Hakusho (Kakuron)* (Tokyo: Okura Sho), 1973, p. 287; 1975, p. 237; 1976, p. 330; 1978, p. 264; 1979, p. 221; 1980, p. 139; 1981, p. 140.

TABLE 5
Percentage of Japanese Liquefied
Natural Gas Imports by Country[a]

| Year | Total[b] | Indonesia | Brunei | United Arab Emirates | United States |
|------|--------|-----------|--------|----------------------|---------------|
| 1972 | 952    | —         | 3.5    | —                    | 96.5          |
| 1973 | 1,947  | —         | 52.1   | —                    | 47.9          |
| 1974 | 3,394  | —         | 73.3   | —                    | 26.7          |
| 1975 | 4,560  | —         | 77.1   | —                    | 22.9          |
| 1976 | 5,792  | —         | 83.5   | —                    | 16.5          |
| 1977 | 7,260  | 6.7       | 74.3   | 5.3                  | 13.7          |
| 1978 | 11,173 | 33.3      | 47.1   | 11.3                 | 8.3           |
| 1979 | 13,806 | 44.7      | 39.2   | 9.0                  | 7.1           |
| 1980 | 16,841 | 50.5      | 32.9   | 11.4                 | 5.1           |

[a]The 1977 and 1980 percentages do not add up to 100 percent because of rounding.
[b]In thousand metric tons.
SOURCE: Tsusho Sangyo Sho, *Tsusho Hakusho (Kakuron)*, (Tokyo: Okura Sho), 1975, p. 238; 1978, p. 266; 1980, p. 141; 1981, p. 141.

called northern territories issue. Prior to World War II, southern Sakhalin, the entire Kuril Island chain, plus Shikotan and the Habomai Islands were all Japanese possessions (Figure 2). The Soviet occupation of these territories, especially Shikotan, the Habomais, and what the Japanese government now calls the "South Kurils," namely Etorofu (Iturup) and Kunashiri (Kunashir), has raised the anger and opposition of the Japanese people.[29]

*The Japanese position.* Although the Soviets claim that Russians first discovered and developed the Kurils, the Japanese officially contend that the indigenous Ainu inhabitants were Japanese. The Ainu dwelled in Hokkaido, the Kurils, and the southern part of Sakhalin prior to settlement and exploration by Japanese and Russians. The Japanese note that the Matsumai Clan, located in southern Hokkaido, had contact with the Kuril area in the early 17th century, whereas the first Russian explorers did not appear in the Kurils until 1711.[30]

TABLE 6
Percentage of Japanese Liquefied Petroleum Gas Imports by Country[a]

| Year | Total[b] | Saudi Arabia | Kuwait | Australia | United Arab Emirates | Indonesia | Canada | Iran | Qatar | South Korea | Venezuela | United States |
|------|--------|--------------|--------|-----------|----------------------|-----------|--------|------|-------|-------------|-----------|---------------|
| 1970 | 2,683  | 35.9 | 38.4 | 4.6  | —   | —   | 9.9 | 9.6  | —   | —    | 0.1  | 1.5 |
| 1971 | 3,310  | 29.6 | 34.8 | 13.5 | —   | —   | 5.9 | 15.2 | —   | —    | 0.9  | —   |
| 1972 | 4,265  | 23.5 | 29.2 | 16.5 | —   | —   | 6.5 | 15.2 | —   | —    | 6.7  | 1.1 |
| 1973 | 5,089  | 31.8 | 25.5 | 19.2 | —   | —   | 4.6 | 15.3 | —   | —    | —    | —   |
| 1974 | 5,643  | 43.6 | 20.4 | 17.0 | —   | —   | 4.1 | 13.7 | —   | 0.5  | —    | —   |
| 1975 | 5,683  | 46.3 | 13.1 | 19.9 | —   | —   | 4.1 | 12.7 | 1.6 | 0.5  | —    | —   |
| 1976 | 6,410  | 52.3 | 12.7 | 17.0 | —   | —   | 3.9 | 10.9 | 2.4 | 0.6  | —    | —   |
| 1977 | 7,258  | 52.1 | 14.6 | 16.8 | 0.4 | —   | 3.3 | 10.3 | 0.9 | 0.9  | 0.4  | —   |
| 1978 | 8,065  | 54.1 | 12.1 | 19.5 | 4.0 | —   | 2.7 | 6.5  | —   | —    | 0.0  | —   |
| 1979 | 9,419  | 55.1 | 19.5 | 14.9 | 5.3 | —   | 2.6 | 1.6  | —   | —    | 0.5  | —   |
| 1980 | 9,670  | 54.1 | 18.4 | 12.1 | 7.3 | 2.8 | 2.2 | 0.7  | —   | 0.03 | 0.2  | —   |

[a]Minor suppliers include the United Kingdom, Netherlands, Italy, Algeria, Libya, and the People's Republic of China.
[b]In thousand metric tons.
SOURCE: Tsusho Sangyo Sho, *Tsusho Hakusho (Kakuron)*, (Tokyo: Okura Sho), 1973, p. 288; 1975, p. 238; 1977, p. 273; 1978, p. 266; 1980, p. 141; 1981, p. 141.

TABLE 7
Percentage of Japanese Iron Ore Imports by Country[a]

| Year | Total[b] | USSR | Australia | Brazil | India | South Africa | Chile | Canada | Philippines |
|------|----------|------|-----------|--------|-------|--------------|-------|--------|-------------|
| 1972 | 111,519,562 | 1.0 | 43.3 | 8.4  | 16.0 | 2.1 | 6.0 | 1.9 | 2.2 |
| 1973 | 134,723,787 | 1.0 | 47.7 | 9.5  | 14.2 | 2.3 | 6.3 | 2.5 | 1.7 |
| 1974 | 141,950,832 | 0.7 | 47.8 | 13.7 | 12.2 | 1.6 | 6.0 | 3.2 | 1.1 |
| 1975 | 131,752,783 | 0.9 | 48.0 | 17.8 | 12.8 | 1.3 | 6.1 | 3.0 | 1.1 |
| 1976 | 133,758,450 | 0.8 | 47.9 | 19.0 | 13.2 | 1.8 | 5.7 | 4.2 | 0.7 |
| 1977 | 132,614,147 | 0.7 | 47.6 | 17.9 | 13.5 | 4.2 | 5.1 | 2.7 | 1.5 |
| 1978 | 114,690,930 | 0.9 | 45.9 | 18.1 | 12.5 | 5.1 | 5.3 | 2.2 | 3.2 |
| 1979 | 130,276,000 | 0.5 | 42.4 | 20.1 | 13.1 | 5.5 | 5.1 | 3.6 | 3.1 |
| 1980 | 133,721,000 | 0.1 | 44.9 | 21.3 | 12.3 | 4.7 | 5.3 | 2.6 | 3.0 |

[a]Other suppliers include Angola, Indonesia, North Korea, Liberia, Sierra Leone, and the United States.
[b]In metric tons.
SOURCE: Tsusho Sangyo Sho, *Tsusho Hakusho (Kakuron)*, (Tokyo: Okura Sho), 1975, p. 211; 1976, pp. 304–305; 1978, p. 237; 1980, p. 124; 1981, pp. 124–25.

The Treaty of Shimoda (February 1855) defined the border between Russia and Japan as lying between the islands of Etorofu and Urup (Japanese *Uruppu*) while Sakhalin remained divided between the two states. In May of 1875 the Treaty of St. Petersburg modified the above arrangement: Japan renounced its rights to Sakhalin and acquired the whole Kuril chain. The Japanese also stress that the Treaty of St. Petersburg did not mention Etorofu and Kunashiri as part of the Kurils, indicating that these islands had already been recognized as Japanese territory.[31]

Another change in the Russian-Japanese boundary occurred during the Treaty of Portsmouth in September 1905, at the termination of the Russo-Japanese War, when Japan received the portion of Sakhalin south of the 50th parallel which was called Karafuto. According to the Japanese, the Soviet government conceded in 1924 that the Japanese torpedo-boat attack on the Russian fleet at Port Arthur (Luda) starting the 1905 war was, politically speaking, an act caused by the agressive policy of the Czarist Government.[32]

In the Japanese view, the unilateral occupation of Karafuto, the Kurils, Kunashiri, Etorofu, Shikotan, and the Habomai Islands by the USSR at the end of World War II was not completely within the accords agreed to by Japan or by the other Allied governments. The Yalta Agreement of February 1945 between Churchill, Roosevelt, and Stalin stated that if the Soviets joined the war against Japan, they would receive, among other concessions, Karafuto and the Kurils. The Soviet Union had to break its neutrality treaty with Japan, however, to attack. Furthermore, the Yalta Agreement, which was kept secret from Japan until the war's end, is not considered binding by the Japanese since they were not consulted and it was never included in any peace treaty. Nevertheless, on 2 February 1946 the Soviet Union annexed Karafuto and the Kurils.

In 1951, Japan signed the San Francisco Peace Treaty by which it renounced all claim to the Kuril Islands and Karafuto. The Soviet Union did not sign this treaty. Moreover, the treaty did not specify to whom these possessions should be transferred. And finally there remains the problem whether Etorofu and Kunashiri were part of the Kurils.

| New Zealand | Peru | Swaziland | Mauritania |
|---|---|---|---|
| 1.0 | 6.2 | 2.0 | — |
| 1.5 | 4.5 | 1.2 | — |
| 1.7 | 4.2 | 1.4 | — |
| 1.9 | 2.1 | 1.3 | — |
| 1.7 | 1.8 | 1.1 | — |
| 1.9 | 2.2 | 0.8 | — |
| 2.9 | 2.3 | 0.7 | 0.4 |
| 2.7 | 2.3 | 0.7 | 0.5 |
| 2.2 | 1.9 | 0.4 | 0.7 |

*The Soviet position.* Briefly, the Soviet position is based on two premises, might makes right and the Yalta Agreement, which stated that Karafuto and the Kurils would be given to the Soviet Union provided they entered the war against the Japanese Empire. Since Japan lost, the Soviets feel that it was the right of the Allies to determine what territories should be transferred to what state.[33] Although the Soviet action as regards Shikotan and the Habomais as well as Etorofu and Kunashiri was unilateral, it was not clear whether Shikotan and the Habomais were part of the Kurils. The Soviets contend that Etorofu and Kunashiri are part of the Kurils. Indeed, the Soviet Ambassador to Japan said that there was no territorial issue between the Soviet Union and Japan.[34] These islands are now Soviet territory.

Yalta, the Potsdam Proclamation, and the San Francisco Peace Treaty clearly state that Karafuto and the Kurils would be given up by Japan.[35] Therefore, in the Soviet view, Japan has no right to claim any of these territories.

*Siberian Resource Development.* Although many Japanese feel that the Soviet Union has no right to any of Japan's former northern territory, since Japan renounced her claim to Karafuto and the Kurils, the government is in no position to demand their return. In 1956 the Soviet government offered to return Shikotan and the Habomai group. Therefore these islands could possibly be returned if a peace treaty were signed. Every political group within Japan, however, demands Etorofu and Kunashiri as well. The Japanese have given up hope for the return of Karafuto but many continue to demand return of all the Kurils.

So far this territorial problem has not stopped Japan and the Soviet Union from establishing diplomatic relations and joining in various Siberian development projects. The territorial dispute, however, has caused widespread distrust of the Soviet Union in Japan and indirectly facilitated trade contact with China which recognizes Japan's claim to Etorofu and Kunashiri. The Japanese say that trade relations are a corporation matter while the northern territories issue is a political matter. Academicians and politicians raise the northern territories issue with the Soviet Union but Japanese businessmen avoid it. If a company raises this issue in trade negotiations with the USSR, the Soviets give the contract to another Japanese company.[36] Some Japanese have urged the government to put off this issue for a long time.[37] Yet as long as the issue remains it will have a negative psychological impact on Soviet-Japanese relations. Nonetheless, it will not prevent Japanese resource dependence from increasing above the current level.

Fishing Negotiations

Tied closely to the northern territories issue is the problem connected with the 200 nautical mile economic sea zone. The latter has put a strain on the Japanese fishing industry, further complicated Soviet-Japanese relations, and forced Japan to negotiate for fishing rights from the USSR. On 1 March 1977 both the USSR and the United

States enforced a 200 nautical mile economic zone. Since then both countries have forced Japan to negotiate for fishing rights. The Soviet Union proclaimed a law to protect its sea resources within 200 miles on 10 December 1976. The line was disclosed on 24 February 1977 and included the northern territories claimed by Japan. Japan declared its own 200 nautical mile limit on 1 July 1977.[38]

During the April 1978 fishing talks, which reduced Japan's catch in the Soviet zone by 30 percent, it was decided that annual meetings would be held to reach more permanent agreements. The first meeting opened on 20 March 1979 in Moscow. Three committees were formed and seven cooperative projects were discussed.[39] The Japanese contended that the supplies of fish in the

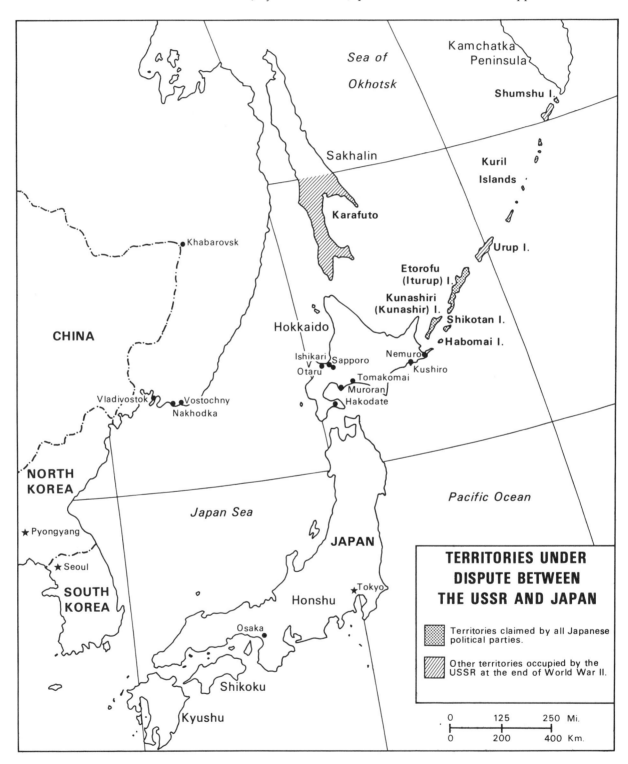

Figure 2
SOURCE: *Japan's Northern Territories* (Tokyo: Northern Territories Issue Association, 1974).

northern seas had increased while the Soviets maintained that they were still at a low level and fishing must be restricted. As a result, the Japanese were just barely able to persuade the Soviets to maintain the same northern sea catch levels as in 1978 by agreeing to teach the Soviets advanced fishing technology. In April 1980, preliminary meetings were as difficult as in the past. Shrimp and crab joint-fishing contracts, however, were reapproved at nearly the 1979 levels indicating that joint fishing ventures may be the path of the future.[40]

The average Japanese feels the Soviets have put tremendous pressure on the Japanese fishing industry but experts confide that the Soviets have not been very strict in enforcing the regulated catches. One Japanese friend mentioned that in the past several years the prices of salmon and trout have gone up but the quantities he sees in the department stores are still about the same. This of course could be due to the high cost. Even if the amount of fish caught has not been reduced greatly in practice, Japan cannot expect any increase in the amount of fish it is allowed to catch within the USSR's 200 nautical mile economic sea zone by 1990.

## The Afghanistan Incursion

The December 1979 Soviet incursion into Afghanistan worsened Japanese-Soviet relations. Soviet attempts in the following year to improve relations were not received warmly in Tokyo. Like the northern territories issue, the Japanese want to keep the Afghanistan problem in the political sphere. Economic restrictions however, are enacted "keisu-bai-keisu".[41] In this case-by-case atmosphere, the South Yakutian coking coal project, the third Far East forest resource project, and the Sakhalin continental shelf project should continue without any problem.[42] The Yakutian gas project has slowed down, at the request of the Americans.

In July 1980, the Japanese Foreign Ministry was discouraging contact between Soviet officials and the Japanese Sakhalin Oil Development Aid Corporation.[43] Yet visits by Soviets continue, since various people are "exempted" from restrictions which have been placed on Japanese-Soviet contact after the incursion.[44] The Japanese are following the examples of West Germany and the United States in their relations with the Soviet Union. It is too early to assess the role this issue will play in Japanese-Soviet Siberian trade. The Soviet Union has delayed the 1980 fishing negotiations because of Japan's restrictions on contact.[45] The Japanese feeling is one of frustration. They will do the minimum required to please the United States and shall try to maintain all current Siberian projects. No new projects are likely until the Afghanistan problem recedes.

## The Japanese View of Soviet Resources

### The Japanese Regional Perspective

Trade between Japan and the Soviet Union is usually considered in terms of Siberia and the Soviet Far East on the one hand and Japan on the other. Even though Japan's population outnumbers that of Siberia, physical area leads one to consider Japan as a whole in relations with the Soviet Union. However, some Japanese have tried to view Siberian resource development as a catalyst for regional development in sparsely populated and relatively nonindustrial parts of Japan. Aspirations for Soviet-related regional development have generally focused on the Japan Sea side rather than the highly industrialized Pacific coastline.[46] Nearest to the Soviet Union, the possibility of economic advantage for Hokkaido has also been studied.[47]

*Japan Sea coast trade.* Although the Japan Sea coast benefitted from the first ten years of postwar Soviet-Japanese trade (1957–67), the establishment of consulates in Sapporo and Nakhodka in 1967 can be construed as the beginning of an intensification of relations between Siberia and the Soviet Far East on the one hand and the Japan Sea coast and Hokkaido on the other. Coastal trade, which officially began in 1965, stimulated interest along the Japan Sea coast. The idea for the coastal trade was suggested by the Soviets and widely accepted by the ken or prefectures located on the Japan Sea which set up cooperative trading groups. The Soviet Union sees coastal trade as exchange between the Soviet Far East, Irkutsk, the Yakut ASSR, the Buryat ASSR, other eastern Siberian regions, and Japan. The Soviets have engaged in regional trade between Leningrad and Finland (1960, later expanded to include Norway) as well as between Baku and Turkey and Iran (1964). The establishment of the Soviet Far East Trade Office (Dalintorg) in Nakhodka began the Soviet's third experience in regional trade. Dalintorg has also become responsible for trade with North Korea.

By 1970, in spite of the fact that coastal trade had grown 20-fold since 1963, it still made up only 2 percent of the total trade between the USSR and Japan. Problems in coastal trade from the Japanese point of view have been (1) a lack of desirable import items from the Soviet Far East coupled with barter arrangement trading, (2) the small population of the Soviet Far East which limits the market for Japanese goods, (3) the obstruction of various Soviet marine edible imports which are desired in the various Japan Sea coast ken by the Hokkaido fishing industry, (4) the lack of a guarantee by the Soviet government (Dalintorg) to return goods for Japanese exports, and (5) the high price of Soviet imports.

The regional interest in Japanese-Soviet trade can be seen in the map of administrative units which participated in the coastal trade fairs in Khabarovsk during 1966 and 1970 (Figure 3). By 1970 participation beyond the Japan Sea coast is evident.[48] The Japan Sea *ken* and *fu* (prefectures) have formed an Alliance for Promotion of the Japan Sea Coastal Region (Nippon Kai Engan Chitai Shinko Renmei) with one of its functions being promotion of Soviet Far Eastern and Japan Sea trade (Figure 4).

*Hokkaido.* Like the Japan Sea coastline of Honshu, Hokkaido has held high hopes for an increase in Japanese-Soviet trade. This hope was encouraged by the choice of

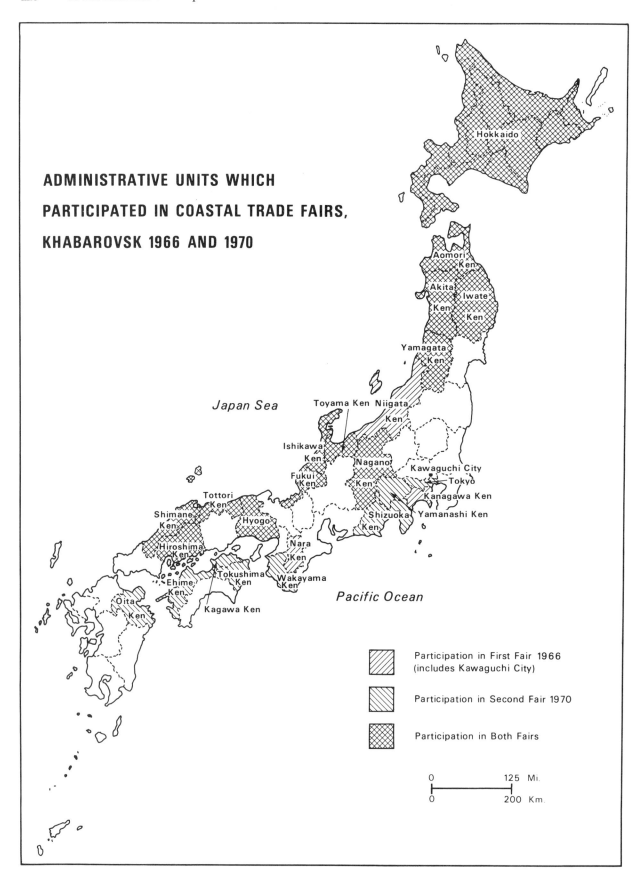

Figure 3
SOURCE: Kitabayashi Yoshiro, "Taigan boeki no genjo to mondaiten," *Chiri*, 8 (1973): 47.

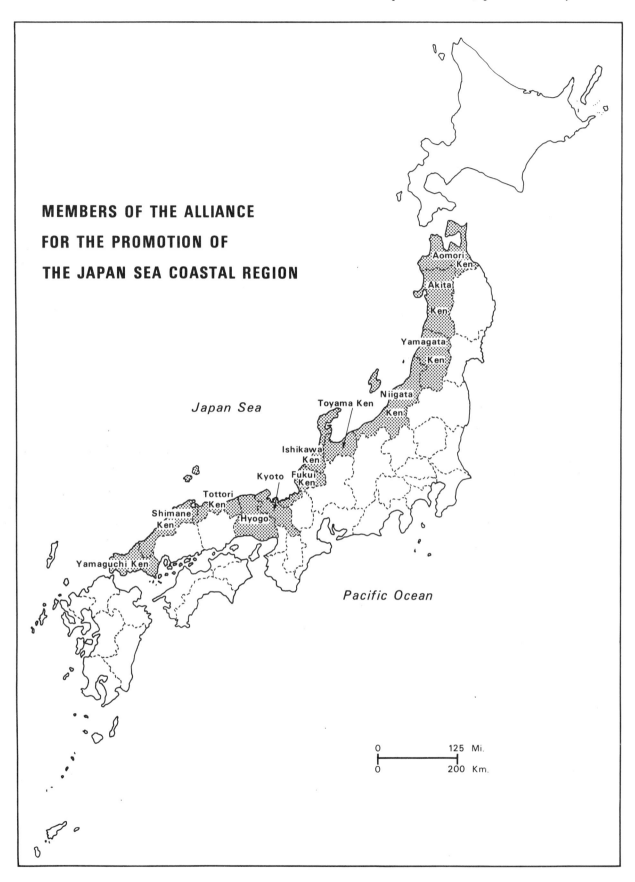

MEMBERS OF THE ALLIANCE
FOR THE PROMOTION OF
THE JAPAN SEA COASTAL REGION

Figure 4
SOURCE: Kitabayashi Yoshiro, ''Taigan boeki no genjo to mondaiten,'' *Chiri*, 8 (1973).

Sapporo for the USSR's first consulate general in preference to a Kansai or Japan Sea coast city.[49] However, between 1967 and 1971 while receiving 7 to 10 percent of Japan's imports from the USSR, goods from Hokkaido composed only 1 or 2 percent of the export trade. A report published in 1973 stressed that Hokkaido should not rely on the coastal trade agreement alone (half of the island faces the Japan Sea), but must become deeply involved in projects and other forms of trade with the Soviet Union.[50] Products already produced in Hokkaido which could be exported under the coastal agreements include apples, onions, and potatoes. The 1973 report also placed hopes on the Sakhalin continental shelf project with its proposed pipeline to Hokkaido. However, the Hokkaido pipeline idea is now almost defunct. The research team also stressed the need to reestablish scheduled shipping between Otaru, Hakodate, and other Hokkaido ports and the Soviet Far East. The Tyumen oil project, it was hoped, would make use of the rapidly developing port facilities at Tomakomai. It was also hoped that Yakutian natural gas would be shipped to Japan via the Hokkaido pipeline. It now appears none of these hopes will be realized, at least not by 1990.

In order for Hokkaido to increase its share of Soviet trade it must change its industrial structure. It must move away from producing its own food goods, lumbering products and fishing into processing these and other goods for export. The report also stressed that Hokkaido's cooler climate should provide the proper environment for the development of cold resistant products which could be used in Siberia. Industry could be developed around Tomakomai, Kushiro, Muroran, Hakodate, Otaru, and the new Ishikari port. In June 1980, I visited the Ishikari port construction site. Progress had been very slow, no railroad had been planned, and the highway from Sapporo was still incomplete, to say nothing of the fact that no major industrial plants had been erected. With the nearby port of Otaru in a slump and relations between the Soviet Union and Japan on the ebb, it is obvious why the Ishikari port is proceeding at a snail's pace. One possibility of major Soviet resource impact on Hokkaido by 1990 would be the direct importation of electric power from Sakhalin.[51]

*Regional overview.* Interest in Soviet trade has been strong along the Japan Sea coast and in the north. Regional studies shed light on what the Japanese feel are their disadvantages in trading with the Soviet Union. In order for the Japan Sea coast and Hokkaido to deal with the USSR two modifications in the local economies are stressed: reorganization and adaptation.

The Soviets, operating under a system of state-controlled industry, appear very organized to the Japanese. Regional organizations are deemed a necessity in order to deal with the Soviets on an equal footing. Also, the Japanese feel they must adjust their regional economies to fit Soviet needs. So far goods bound for the Soviet Union are being produced primarily in the Kanto (Tokyo-Yokohama) and Kansai (Osaka-Kobe-Kyoto) regions. For the Japan Sea side of Honshu and northern Japan to benefit from their geographical advantages they will have to change their economies from agriculture and fishing to industry. For the immediate future the dreams of these two regions for an increased share in Siberian trade have subsided with the realization that Siberia's needs are being fulfilled by industrial goods they do not produce and the feeling that Soviet-Japanese trade is not going to expand in the near future.

### The Chinese Alternative

In 1981 Japan was more optimistic about trade with China than with the Soviet Union. In the media and elsewhere cultural affinity and war guilt towards China contrast starkly with the unknown culture, northern territorial problems, and aggressive foreign policy which affect Japan's image of the Soviet Union.[52] However, culture and politics are not business, and discussions with knowledgeable Japanese suggest that Japan will make raw-material purchases in accord with economic factors. Furthermore, experts do not see Chinese and Soviet raw-material imports as entirely competitive. Oil, coal, and iron ore are the major exportable resources now known to be found in both countries although the Japanese hope that future exploration in China will uncover other sizable mineral deposits. The Japanese are currently most interested in importing oil and coal.

It appears that the USSR will not be willing to sell oil to Japan in significant quantities by 1990. Japanese oil companies are not enthusiastic about purchasing Chinese oil because of refining problems caused by its high sulphur content. However, Japan is building refineries capable of processing Chinese crude and, after a small beginning in 1973, by 1975 crude made up almost half the total Chinese import figure.[53] In 1979 oil imports from China increased 32.7 percent over 1978. Without sizable Soviet oil imports, there will be less competition for Chinese oil imports and more willingness to build refineries capable of processing it.

As stated previously, coal imports must be increased and Japan will probably be willing to buy as much as China and the USSR are willing to sell, especially since the country is trying to minimize reliance on nuclear energy due to the 1979 Three Mile Island incident. In that year Chinese coal imports increased 87.8 percent over 1978. New coal imports from China will probably be used in the Kyushu region while Soviet coal will be used primarily in northern Japan. In any event, it is likely that the level of coal imports from China will increase more rapidly than from the Soviet Union.

Transport costs give Kyushu and Shikoku an advantage over Hokkaido and the Tohoku region should the China trade increase and vice versa if the Soviet trade increases. However, trade decisions are made in Tokyo and will be decided on the basis of market and political conditions.

The Baoshan steel works construction project began under the auspices of Japanese enterprises in December 1978 with the first furnace to be completed in 1982. An agreement was reached on 30 April 1980 for a 50 billion yen government loan to cover costs on various projects started in 1979. Projects now under way include the Shijiusuo Port construction, Yanzhou-Shijiusuo Railroad, Beijing (Peking)-Qinhuangdao Railroad expansion, Guangzhou (Canton)-Hengyang Railroad expansion, Qinhuangdao Port expansion, and Wuciangxi Hydroelectric construction projects as well as the Beijing Nippo-Chinese Friendship Memorial Hospital project.[54]

Although the Japanese may prefer to buy Chinese raw materials they also know that Siberia is a richer alternative.

### The Perspective of Various Groups in Japan Toward Siberian Resources

The overall attitude of the Japanese toward Soviet resource trade is pessimistic or ambivalent. Most individuals are aware that Soviet trade has failed to develop as the Japan of the late 1960s and early 1970s hoped it would.[55] Representative of this feeling is the often heard comment that Siberian trade used to receive a lot of coverage in the papers but now it is no longer a popular topic. There is also concern about energy problems and their bearing on Japan's relations with the Soviet Union. That Japan is not making better preparations for the day when it may have to rely on the USSR for greater amounts of energy is a frustration to some experts. The Japanese still hope to forestall that day by purchasing energy resources from a wide range of nations thus keeping dependence on the Soviet Union to a minimum.

It is often said that government and business in Japan are inseparable. My research leads to the same conclusion. With respect to the Siberian resource question, the view of government and business seems identical. The government may worry more about overdependence on Soviet resources, but if the Soviets will sell resources needed by Japan, both business and government will lend their support.[56]

This government-business group views the future bargaining position of Japan as becoming weaker and is pessimistic about the overall future of Japanese-Soviet natural-resource trade. No one predicts any major increases in Siberian imports or overall Japanese-Soviet trade by 1990. Natural gas may begin to arrive but not in the quantities originally hoped for.

Scholars have little to say on the subject of Siberian resources and suggestions put forward by this group have little impact on Japanese policy. In Japan there is only one Slavic Studies Center, at Hokkaido University, with a staff of six, only one of whom is working on the problems discussed in this paper. The number of Japanese scholars working on Soviet-Japanese economic relations probably does not number more than a dozen. Most of the academic work has been based on Soviet and American data and research.

In 1976 at a meeting of the Japan Association for Trade with the Soviet Union and Socialist Countries of Europe (Soren Too Boeki Kai), the organization in Japan which has done the most research on Soviet resources, the following ideas for future Japanese-Soviet projects were suggested:[57]

1. A third Far East forest resource development project.

2. Yeniseisk paper pulp project (continuation).

3. An agricultural improvement project (exchange of primary energy imports for aid in Siberian and Far Eastern vegetable production).

4. Jointly managed enterprises in the vicinity of the Pacific Ocean region (e.g., marine product processing).

5. Harbor development projects (such as expansion of Vostochny harbor).

6. Steel plant, refinery, and petrochemical plant construction.

7. Collaboration projects in cold weather resistant technology.

8. Electric power development and importation projects.

9. Comprehensive timber exploitation projects.

10. Nonferrous metal development projects.

11. Mutual research on comprehensive projects including civil construction.

12. Marine product processing plant construction projects.

This list reflects what the Japanese feel is feasible in the way of future Siberian natural-resource imports. The paucity of projects connected with direct resource extraction is notable. Timber, nonferrous metals, and marine products represent the only Siberian resource projects deemed feasible. Of the listed projects, only the third Far East forest resource project stands a good chance of being signed and completed by 1990.

At the 1977 meeting of the Soviet-Japanese Economic Committee no new projects were suggested, indicating the beginning of a slow down in the pace of Siberian resource delivery.[58] Many of the projects now in progress will begin delivery in the 1980s but the overall attitude about future projects is pessimistic. The literature expresses a desire for more first-hand investigation of Siberian resource sites by Japanese. The Japanese are also concerned that the USSR has not signed a long range economic accord with Japan as the Soviets have done with several West European countries and Canada.[59] This makes the Japanese feel they are in a weak competitive position. The Japanese literature also consistently points out that all the past projects have been suggested by the Soviets, indicating that Japan should take more initiative in negotiations.[60]

The third Far East forest project, a paper and pulp plant modernization and construction project and the Vostochny Port Container and Coal Loading expansion project were seriously discussed at the 8th Soviet-Japanese Economic Committee meeting held during September 1979 in Moscow.[61] The paper and pulp project may be slowed down because the Japanese want both chips and pulp in compensation while the Soviets want to give only pulp plus paper. The Japanese responded more favorably to the modernization of paper pulp plants in Sakhalin than to construction of new plants in the Far East. The Vostochny project was delayed because the Soviets wanted three base container terminals constructed while the Japanese preferred to construct one and then talk about the other two.

Long range project possibilities discussed included Far East steel plant construction, Udokan copper and the

Molodezhny asbestos project. The Soviets would like to
start these projects during the 1986–90 Five-Year Plan.
Japanese participation is most likely in the steel plant and
least likely in the asbestos project. Also, they would like
the participation of a West European state.

The Japanese see Siberia as an important supplier of
resources but feel that it will be difficult to obtain them.
This concern takes precedence over the worry of overdependence of the Soviet Union. All Japanese view the
USSR as a better source of raw materials than China.
Resource projects with China are a new topic in Japan and
as such there is more enthusiasm. The worsening of
Soviet-Japanese relations in 1980 due to the Afghanistan
incursion improves this Chinese alternative. Yet Japanese in government and business feel that China will
not be able to supply either the quality or quantity of
resources that are available in Siberia.

Frustration, pessimism, and a feeling of inadequacy
characterize the Japanese attitude toward Siberian resources. Siberian raw materials are needed but dependence on the Soviets is thought to be undesirable. Resources are being imported but not in the quantities desired by the Japanese. Finally, government and business
as well as regional leaders feel unprepared to bargain
equally with the Soviets and compete with other nations
for Soviet resources. Despite such pessimism, the quantity of Siberian natural resources imported by Japan is
likely to increase gradually during the 1980s.

## NOTES

1. Tsusho Sangyo Sho, *Tsusho Hakusho (Kakuron)*, 1978
[White paper on international trade] (Tokyo: Okura Sho,
1978), p. 817.

2. Ibid., 1979, p. 677.

3. Ibid., 1980, p. 230.

4. Fukamizu Akemi, "The development of postwar
Soviet-Japanese trade," *Bunka to gengo*, 12 (1978): 54.

5. Fukamizu, "Postwar trade," pp. 59–67; Ogawa
Kazuo, *Shiberia kaihatsu to Nippon* [Siberian development
and Japan] (Tokyo: Jiji Tsushin Sha, 1974), pp. 196–230;
Ogawa Kazuo, *NisSo boeki no jitsujo to kadai* [The facts and
problems of Japanese-Soviet trade] (Tokyo: Kyoikusha,
1979), pp. 9–51; Soren Too Boeki Kai [Japan Association
for Trade with the Soviet Union and Socialist Countries
of Europe] *NisSo boeki yoran 1978 nen* [A handbook of
Japanese-Soviet trade 1978] (Tokyo: Soren Too Boeki Kai,
1978), pp. 387–450; Kitabayashi Yoshiro, "Present status
and problems of trade between the east and west coasts of
the Japan Sea," *Chiri*, 8, no. 5 (1973): 43–44 mentions a
fifth type of trade, technical exchange trade, whereby
technology is sold between the two states.

6. Yamamoto Satoshi, *Shiberia kaihatsu* [Siberian de-
velopment] (Tokyo: Kodan Sha, 1973), p. 176.

7. Fukamizu, "Postwar trade," p. 64.

8. Correspondence from Victor L. Mote, 12 April 1979;
indicates that increased loadings may cause traffic jam-
ups at or near terminals on the BAM and at Nakhodka-
Vostochny. For a discussion of production problems at
Neryungri see *New York Times*, 1 April 1979, p. 24.

9. *Nippon Keizai Shinbun*, 22 December 1980, p. 1.

10. Ibid., 19 August, 1980, p. 4. *Asahi Shinbun*, 15
March 1979, p. 6 gives a 825 billion cubic meter figure. The
*Asahi Shinbun* article quoted a Soviet geological technician
who says the one trillion cubic meter mark should be
reached by 1980 or 1981.

11. Soren Too Boeki Kai [Japan Association for Trade
with the Soviet Union and Socialist Countries of Europe],
*Soren tennen gasu kaihatsu mondai* [Problems of Soviet natural gas development] (Tokyo: Soren Too Boeki Kai, 1979),
pp. 78–80.

12. Dates are from correspondence with Allen S. Whiting, 23 April 1979. Whiting says his source was Matsu-
zawa Akira of the Japan Petroleum Development
Corporation.

13. *Nippon Keizai Shinbun*, 17 September 1980, p. 9.

14. *Yomiuri Shinbun*, 9 September 1980, p. 1.

15. Tsusho Sangyo Sho, *Tsusho Hakusho*, 1980, p. 133.

16. Statistics Bureau, Prime Minister's Office, *Statisti-
cal Handbook of Japan 1980* (Tokyo: Japan Statistical Association, 1980), pp. 42–45; Shigen Enerugii Cho, ed., *Wagakuni enerugii mondai no choki tenbo* [The future outlook for
Japan's energy problem] (Tokyo: Tsusho Sangyo Chosa
Kai, 1977), pp. 9, 12. The nuclear waste leak at Three Mile
Island, Pennsylvania in the spring of 1979 alarmed the
Japanese since their nuclear power plants use the same
American equipment. Japanese experts feel that public
opinion will oppose the construction of new nuclear en-
ergy plants.

17. Tsusho Sangyo Sho, *Tsusho Hakusho*, 1980, pp.
100–102.

18. According to the *Asahi Shinbun*, 8 March 1979, p. 7,
Japan and Australia have signed a new two year coal and
iron ore contract with the amount of coal to be delivered,
approximately 23 million metric tons a year.

19. Shigen Enerugii Cho, *Wagakuni enerugii mondai*, p.
128.

20. Ibid., pp. 102–104.

21. Conversations with Ogawa Kazuo and a Keidanren source, May 1979.

22. Kuroiwa Toshiro, ed., *Nippon Shigen dokuhon* [A
Japan natural resource reader] (Tokyo: Toyo Keizai
Shinpo Sha, 1975), p. 125; Tsusho Sangyo Sho, *Tsusho
Hakusho (Soron)*, 1980, p. 239.

23. *Asahi Shinbun*, 16 March 1979, p. 12.

24. Conversations with a Keidanren source, May 1979.

25. Tsusho Sangyo Sho, *Tsusho Hakusho*, 1979, p. 195.

26. Ibid., 1980, p. 134.

27. Conversations with Ogawa Kazuo and a Keidanren source, May 1979.

28. Tsusho Sangyo Sho, *Tsusho Hakusho*, 1979, p. 199.

29. The term northern territories (*hoppo ryodo*) is vague.
The Japanese do not seem to known what it means in
geographical terms. As Nakano Miyoko, *Henkyo no Fukei*
[The Frontier View] (Sapporo: Hokkaido Daigaku Tosho
Kanko Kai, 1979), p. 39 points out, the Liberal Democratic
Party says that the South Kurils, Shikotan, and the Habo-
mais have always been Japanese territory, the Socialist
Party says the government should have never agreed to
the San Francisco Peace Treaty which says that the Kurils
include the South Kurils, the Komeito says the South

Kurils must be returned immediately, the Democratic Socialist Party demands the whole Kuril chain and the Communist Party says that Japan should get Shikotan and the Habomai group back first. Individuals offer an even wider range of viewpoints. For a complete discussion of the northern territories problem see John J. Stephan, *The Kuril Islands Russo-Japanese Frontier in the Pacific* (Oxford, UK: Clarendon Press, 1974), pp. 197–236.

30. Northern Territories Issue Association, *Japan's Northern Territories* (Tokyo: Northern Territories Issue Association, 1974), pp. 12–16.

31. Ibid.

32. Ibid., p. 23. From the League of Nations Journal, May 1924.

33. Young C. Kim, *Japanese Soviet Relations: Interaction of Politics, Economics and National Security* (Beverly Hills, CA: Sage Publications, 1974), p. 66 feels that the Soviet Union has underestimated Japan's sensitivity to the northern territorial issue and overestimated its desire for access to Soviet resources.

34. Speech delivered by the Soviet Ambassador to Japan, Dmitri S. Polyansky, at Hokkaido University, Sapporo, 2 February 1979.

35. The Potsdam Proclamation was made by China, the United Kingdom, and the United States of America, although the Soviet Union supported this document after declaring war on Japan. The USSR refused to sign the San Francisco Peace Treaty, since it did not recognize Soviet sovereignty in southern Sakhalin (Karafuto) and the Kurils.

36. Conversation with Fukamizu Akemi, 30 March 1979.

37. Kurashige Hirasawa, "Japan's Emerging Foreign Policy," *Foreign Affairs*, (October 1975): 165. See also *Japan Echo*, 3 (1976): 42–46.

38. Hokkaido Shinbun Sha, ed., *Hokkaido nenkan, Showa 54 nen han* [Hokkaido yearbook, 1979 edition] (Sapporo: Hokkaido Shinbun Sha, 1979), pp. 254–55.

39. *Hokkaido Shinbun*, 31 March 1979, p. 1. The Japanese are also involved in fishing negotiations with Australia and New Zealand.

40. *Nippon Keizai Shinbun*, 5 April 1980, p. 6; 13 April 1980, p. 3; 23 May 1980, p. 8.

41. Ibid., 15 July 1980, p. 1.

42. Ibid., evening ed., 3 September 1980, p. 9.

43. Ibid., 22 July 1980, p. 2.

44. Ibid., 14 July 1980, p. 2.

45. Ibid., 18 March 1980, p. 4.

46. Kitabayashi, "Present status," pp. 42–49.

47. Hoppoken Chosa Kai, ed., *Hokkaido to Shiberia Kyokuto Chiiki to no keizai koryu ni kan suru chosa hokoku sho* [An investigative report relating to economic exchange between Hokkaido and the Siberia-Far East Region] (Sapporo: Hoppoken Chosa Kai, 1973).

48. Kitabayashi, "Present Status," p. 47 raises the example of Gifu Ken, which did not participate in either trade fair, but reached its own agreement to export pottery in exchange for lumbering materials after the American pottery market was crushed due to changes in the yen-dollar exchange rate.

49. Yamamoto, *Shiberia kaihatsu*, p. 182 says this choice reflected the USSR's interest in Hokkaido and the possibility of the construction of a pipeline from Sakhalin to Sapporo.

50. Hoppoken Chosa Kai, *Hokkaido to Shiberia*, pp. 254–55.

51. Conversation with a Keidanren source, May 1979.

52. A book by Shimizu Hayao, *Nipponjin wa naze Soren ga kirai ka* [Why do the Japanese hate the Soviet Union?] (Tokyo: Yamanote Shobo, 1979) attempts to explore the Japanese feelings of ill will.

53. *Hokkaido Shinbun*, 24 March 1979, p. 4 carried an article indicating that Hokkaido is interested in building facilities to refine Chinese crude oil. Tsusho Sangyo Sho, "The unfolding of a comprehensive energy policy," *Sekiyu Shiryo Geppo*, 9 (1980): 40, shows that the government is looking to Mexico and China as alternatives to Middle East oil, not the USSR.

54. Interview of Okaki Makoto, Vice President Shin Nippon Seitetsu, "Is the construction of the Baoshan steel plant on schedule?" *Ekonomisuto* 21 October 1980, pp. 40–43; "Concerning yen loans to China," *NicChu Keizai Kyokai Kaiho*, 7 (1980): 55–58.

55. Ogawa Kazuo, *Tozai keizai kankei—Nippon no taio to sentaku* [East-West relations—Japan's responses and options] (Tokyo: Jiji Tsushin Sha, 1977), pp. 296–97 sees Japanese exports to the USSR growing but Soviet imports to Japan will have trouble due to Japan's market conditions. This statement contrasts with the 1979 trade statistics (Table 1). Of the five major imports of the 1960s: coal, oil, iron ore, pig iron, and timber, only timber continued to increase in the 1970s. Cotton and nonferrous metals came to take their place. Ogawa sees this as a bad trend for Japan as it tries to secure Siberian resources in the future. He also stresses the importance of project trade.

56. Kim, *Japanese-Soviet Relations*, p. 75 cites an example of government-business cooperation when in 1972, Prime Minister Tanaka Kakuei and a Foreign Ministry official urged business leaders to proceed with project agreements regardless of the progress made on the northern territories problem.

57. Ogawa, *NisSo boeki*, pp. 144–46; Ogawa, *Tozai keizai kankei*, pp. 303–304; Soren Too Boeki Kai, *NisSo boeki yoran*, p. 449.

58. Ogawa, *Tozai keizai kankei*, pp. 292–93, 304 notes that the MIG incident of autumn 1976 was responsible for cooling Soviet-Japanese relations and slowing down the signing of trade agreements.

59. Ogawa, *NisSo boeki*, pp. 157–58. Ogawa, *Tozai keizai kankei*, p. 302 indicates that Japan's refusal to give the USSR general loans and her insistance on tied loans has hurt her competitive position.

60. For example Soren Too Boeki Kai, *NisSo boeki yoran*, pp. 447–48.

61. *NisSo-SoNichi keizai iinkai dai 8 kai godo kaigi kokokusho* [Report of the eighth Soviet-Japanese Economic Committee joint meeting] (September, 1979).

# 10

# SIBERIAN DEVELOPMENT AND EAST ASIA: THE STRATEGIC DIMENSION

ALLEN S. WHITING
University of Arizona

## Introduction

Over most of the past 100 years, a triangle of tension has characterized the relationship among Russia, China and Japan. A simple chronology of conflict illustrates why a heritage of mutual mistrust dominates present-day relations in East Asia:

| | |
|---|---|
| 1894–95: | Sino-Japanese War |
| 1904–05: | Russo-Japanese War |
| 1918–25: | Japanese intervention in Siberia and Sakhalin |
| 1929: | Russo-Chinese conflict over Chinese Eastern Railroad |
| 1931: | Japanese seizure of Manchuria |
| 1938–39: | Soviet-Japanese border clashes |
| 1937–45: | Sino-Japanese War |
| 1945: | Soviet-Japanese War |
| 1969: | Sino-Soviet border clashes |

This history is readily recalled by policymakers as well as the public media. It provides a political dimension to the economic development of East and Far East Siberia which must be assessed if we are to appreciate its full implications for the region. Central to our inquiry is what impact such development will have on Soviet military capabilities. We will attempt to see this from the subjective vantage points of Moscow, Peking, and Tokyo as well as through a more objective analysis. To calculate change, however, we must first examine present force dispositions on land and sea, after which we can estimate the effect of Siberian development on precombat and combat capability.

*This essay draws on my larger work,* Siberian Development and East Asia: Threat or Promise? *(Stanford: Stanford University Press, 1981), made possible by grants from the Rockefeller Foundation, the Ford Foundation, and the East-West Center's Resource Systems Institute. Additional assistance was provided by the Center for Chinese Studies, University of Michigan. The Soviet Academy of Sciences was host to visits to various institutes in Novosibirsk (Akademgorodok), Irkutsk, Yakutsk, and Khabarovsk. None of these organizations are responsible for the views expressed herein.*

In addition to the conventional focus on military power, strategic analysis must consider economic relations for their relevance in confrontation or conflict situations. As foreign countries become involved in Siberian development, economic leverage may accrue to one side or the other. Where large amounts of capital and technology are exchanged for energy resources, as between Japan and the USSR, strategic considerations can play a role in the calculations of policymakers, if not in reality.

Before proceeding further, it is necessary to delineate more precisely that portion of Siberian development which actually or potentially pertains to East Asia. West Siberia's resources supply the European portion of the Soviet Union together with East and West Europe. While it is possible that Tyumen oil will eventually flow eastward to Japan, the amount is not likely to be very great. Similarly Krasnoyarsk Krai is oriented almost wholly westward through the Yenisei hydroelectric projects, the Kansk-Achinsk industrial complex, and the Norilsk mines.

Therefore our study will be limited to that area which is primarily oriented toward the Pacific Basin in general and toward China and Japan in particular, whether through the input of capital and technology and the output of resources or through factors, real and perceived, that relate to Soviet strategic policy and posture in Asia. We shall designate this area East Asian Siberia (EAS), including therein the Yakut and Buryat autonomus republics, Khabarovsk and Maritime krais, and Irkutsk, Chita, Amur, Sakhalin, Magadan, and Kamchatka oblasts.[1] The inner boundary of EAS may be compared to an economic watershed dividing Siberia north to south according to the flow of resources to the east or west. Although EAS does not conform to Soviet terminology for the so-called planning regions of East and Far East Siberia, it does coincide with Soviet administrative divisions. This facilitates the analysis of official data on such phenomena as demographic trends and industrial development.

## Soviet Military Capabilities in East Asia

Before we can estimate what difference, if any, future Siberian development may make in Soviet precombat and warfighting capability, we must first ascertain Moscow's military effectiveness in the region based on past and present development. According to Central Intelligence Agency estimates, in 1978 from 675,000 to 750,000 military personnel were assigned to missions directed against China.[2] These totals included all three service and missile units. As of 1980, 43 divisions, roughly one-fourth of the Soviet Army, faced China.[3] Twenty were arranged in the Far East, mostly in Maritime Krai and eight stood along the Trans-Siberian Railroad between the Amur's eastern bend and Lake Baikal for a total of 28 divisions in EAS.[4] Together with 10,000 medium tanks and 75,000 KGB border guards, this offered an impressive array of power, compounded by a formidable battery of nuclear missiles targeted against China.

This situation was far removed from the heyday of "monolithic unity" in the Sino-Soviet alliance. During the 1950s, Moscow provided Peking with an entire jet air force, laid the foundations for a coastal navy and submarine capability, and modernized its army with tanks and artillery.[5] A short-lived but relatively generous nuclear assistance program equipped China's scientists with the essential training and technology to produce atomic weapons.

This cooperation ended in 1960 when Sino-Soviet differences prompted Nikita Khrushchev to withdraw all economic and technical aid. But despite the ensuing polemics, the relationship did not appear threatening to Moscow until 1964. That year two events occurred to arouse Soviet anxiety. In July, Mao reportedly declared to a visiting Japanese Socialist party delegation, "A hundred years ago they [the Russians] incorporated the territory to the east of Lake Baikal, including Khabarovsk, Vladivostok, and the Kamchatka Peninsula. Those accounts are difficult to settle and we have not settled these accounts with them."[6] Supporting the Japanese demand that Moscow return the Kuril Islands to Japan, Mao's remarks suggested that China would demand more than 1.5 million square kilometers (600,000 square miles) of Siberia and Central Asia which the Manchu rulers ceded to Czarist Russia. Following an upsurge in incidents along the 7,500 kilometer (4,650 mile) border—more than 4,000 allegedly occurred in 1963—his threat carried ominous implications.[7]

Then on 16 October 1964, China detonated its first atomic bomb. Shortly thereafter Premier Zhou Enlai flew to Moscow for discussions following Khrushchev's ouster. However, no reconciliation resulted. In February 1965, Prime Minister Aleksei N. Kosygin visited Peking but his meeting with Mao proved equally fruitless.

These developments apparently prompted the decision to strengthen Soviet military defenses against China. Between 1965 and 1969, the ground forces in Siberia and Central Asia more than doubled, from 15 to nearly 35 divisions.[8] New airfields, including several in Mongolia, together with medium range missiles encircling northeast China, extended Soviet striking power against key population and industrial centers.

Speaking on the 50th anniversary of the Bolshevik Revolution in November 1967, Leonid I. Brezhnev, the Soviet leader, warned that any attempt at surprise attack against the USSR "wherever it may come from—the north or the south, the west or the east—will encounter the all-

conquering might of our glorious armed forces."[9] His blunt words depicted China as a greater threat than had previously occurred at so authoritative a level.

The paroxysm of xenophobic violence unleashed by the Red Guards at the height of Mao's Cultural Revolution in 1967 gave just cause for concern. Division at the highest policy levels in Peking and disruption throughout China's urban centers coincided with violent demonstrations in foreign capitals.[10] Sacking of the British Embassy together with bombings in Hong Kong and violence at the nearby border put that colony's fate in serious doubt. With near anarchy sweeping Chinese cities, the possible spillover effects on the Sino-Soviet frontier could not have been ignored in Moscow. Special concern for the safety of the Trans-Siberian Railroad would arise from its proximity to the Chinese border along the Ussuri River.

In March 1969 this concern was heightened by the first major armed clash between Soviet and Chinese troops which occurred at the island of Damansky (Chenpao) in the Ussuri River. The preponderance of indirect evidence suggests to most observers that the Chinese side initiated the incident.[11] By Peking's own account, Moscow had previously warned that further encroachments on the disputed island would be met with force and the Chinese Army prepared for this contingency with concealed deployments.[12] Tension increased that spring and summer with a successful Soviet retaliation at Damansky and further fighting elsewhere, including the Xinjiang border. Meanwhile statements in Moscow focused on China as a direct threat to the USSR.[13]

In addition to this chain of events from 1964 to 1969 which heightened Soviet defensive concerns, offensive motivations may have entered into Moscow's calculus by this point. At a minimum level, the show of force and threat of war could have aimed at dictating a border settlement on Soviet terms. As a maximum goal, Moscow may have seriously contemplated a "surgical strike" which would destroy China's burgeoning nuclear production facilities without engaging in an all-out war. But regardless of whatever offensive gains may have been weighed in 1969, the timing, context, and nature of the military buildup seems to have been basically prompted by defensive preoccupations.

Moscow's concentration of ground and missile units opposite northeast China is readily understandable. The Trans-Siberian Railroad provides the only lateral route around this 2,400 kilometer (1,500 mile) frontier and terminates at the major naval base of Vladivostok. In its final north-south run, the line comes within 2.5 kilometers (1.5 miles) of the border above Lazo, along the Ussuri River.[14] From Dormidontovka to Lesozavodsk, a distance of 280 kilometers (174 miles), much of the track lies less than 16 kilometers (10 miles) from Chinese territory. Moreover the adjacent terrain is largely broad flatland with no natural defense points other than the river itself. The longer east-west run which parallels the border from Khabarovsk to Mogocha is less vulnerable to ground attack. Its nearest approaches to China are approximately 15 kilometers away (9.3 miles) and occur at only two points.[15] The remainder is generally twice this distance or more with the broad Amur River providing a natural barrier.

Interdiction of the Trans-Siberian would cut the one overland supply route to Vladivostok, interrupting the main source of petroleum from West Siberia. The next alternate link with the European sector of the USSR is the long sea line to Leningrad and ports on the Black Sea. But this 16,000 kilometer (10,000 mile) route transits the Suez Canal and is not reliable in wartime. This would leave the even longer route around the Cape of Good Hope as the only supply line. Under the circumstances, the strengthening of Soviet military defenses in the area, especially given the Cultural Revolution, reflected prudence, not paranoia.

Viewed objectively the military situation is not the nightmare sometimes conjured up by journalistic visions of massive Chinese armies overrunning empty Siberian territory. In contrast with the Soviet side of the border, no lateral railroad traverses northeast China's frontier region. Instead eight spur lines terminate at widely separate intervals across this extensive border.[16] The thin road network traverses heavily forested mountains and swampy lowlands. This inhospitable terrain also inhibits settlement. While Heilongjiang Province has a total population of more than 31 million, the actual density in most of the frontier area is less than one person per square kilometer (2.5 per square mile).[17] By comparison the Soviet territory adjacent to the Amur is much more settled and developed in the lowlands and foothills, thanks to the Trans-Siberian Railroad.

But this objective view is not shared by all sectors of Soviet society where the crude image of one billion Chinese confronting sparsely populated Siberia arouses widespread apprehension. This Sinophobia is rooted in historical accounts of the Mongol invasion which has come to be linked with the perceived Chinese threat in a common "yellow peril" mythology. Thus in March 1969, following the clash at Damansky Island, the poet Yevgeny Yevtushenko exploited this linkage in lurid imagery, referring to "the Chinese God-khan" and more specifically, "Vladimir and Kiev," who "see in the smoking twilight the new Batu khans, bombs rattling in their quivers."[18] His allusion to these classic cases of Mongol pillage struck home. Conversations with academicians, other than China specialists, echo the Sinophobia encountered more casually in hotel and taxi.[19] A curious exception occurs in contacts with residents of Khabarovsk and Vladivostok, suggesting that the fear may increase together with the distance from China, being most evident in Moscow.[20]

Whatever the shadings of public opinion, Soviet military planners apparently hold a more rational and relaxed view of the Chinese threat. After the initial bolstering of their capability to defend East Asian Siberia, the pace of deployments slowed. Some divisions are combat ready but nearly half are at one-third strength or less and some remain in skeletal formation.[21] More advanced weaponry comes only after its delivery to Warsaw Pact armies. A qualitative upgrading of weapons has improved firepower without expanding the size of forces but the over-

all disposition of strength is more suggestive of precautionary moves than of preparations for actual combat.

Nevertheless the high command in Moscow has long been sensitive to the logistical weaknesses of the Trans-Siberian Railroad. This undoubtedly won its support for the construction of the Baikal-Amur Mainline (BAM) as a second route, further removed from the Chinese border. Aside from the aforementioned danger of hostile interdiction, the Trans-Siberian poses problems of a more mundane nature. It is vulnerable to flooding, on one occasion requiring a prolonged airlift in order to bridge separate areas with necessary supplies.[22] Moreover it has bent under the steadily growing freight associated with an expanding civilian economy, heightened military traffic, and the increased use of overland transshipment from the Pacific coast to Europe. This has resulted in a 50 percent expansion in the freight load every five years, making bottlenecks and breakdowns more frequent and more difficult to cope with.[23] We will examine BAM's prospects in the next section, but it deserves mention at this point because its emergence as a major project resulted in part from developments in the late 1960s.

By comparison with land deployments, Soviet naval activity in the Pacific is less susceptible to analysis of its implications for northeast Asia. Large naval units, because of their mobility, possess far more flexibility of mission as well as movement in and out of the area. The analytical problem is exemplified by the fact that the Soviet Pacific Fleet is also responsible for the Indian Ocean. Thus in 1977 it spent 5,800 ship-days in the Pacific and 6,200 in the Indian Ocean.[24] Combat ships showed an even greater disparity, with a typical day in 1976 registering two major Soviet vessels in the Pacific as against seven in Indian Ocean waters. Multiple missions preclude an accurate calculation of how much force would be available in Northeast Asia or the West Pacific at any future time.

In addition, protecting the long sea lanes of communication between the European part of the USSR and the Soviet Far East is a joint responsibility of the Atlantic and Pacific fleets. The submarine base at Petropavlovsk is serviced by sea in the absence of a land line to the Kamchatka Peninsula. Yet it is difficult to distinguish this local mission from the larger one in terms of specific ship assignments.

Vietnam became another responsibility during the American mining and bombing of Hanoi and Haiphong in 1972 when the first major Soviet naval contingent positioned itself in the South China Sea.[25] This activity expanded significantly in 1979 when China invaded Vietnam. Yet so long as Hanoi does not grant the full use of Cam Ranh Bay as a permanent base, Vladivostok must serve this function.

Finally and most important, there is the strategic mission of the Soviet Pacific fleet as part of the global confrontation with the United States. Defensively it must protect the homeland against U.S. aircraft carriers and nuclear submarines with ballistic missiles. Offensively its own ballistic missile submarines are targeted against the U.S. These activities are based in the main ports of Vladivostok, Sovetskaya Gavan, and Petropavlovsk, with ancillary facilities at Nakhodka and Magadan.[26] However all those forces earmarked for defensive or offensive strategic engagement with the United States fall outside of our purview which focuses upon the consequences of EAS development for East Asia.

The relationship of the Pacific fleet to global considerations as viewed from Moscow is revealed by the degree to which the general expansion of the Soviet navy is proportionately reflected in an increased Pacific presence. Table 1 illustrates this phenomenon, the numbers in parentheses indicating the Pacific share of the overall navy.[27] These figures show the relative consistency of allocations to the Pacific fleet, except for the submarine increase which is largely more ballistic missile boats to strengthen the strategic capability against targets in the U.S. As a further indication of its status, the Pacific fleet is the last to enjoy newer and better equipment. For example, it did not receive any Kara class cruisers until 1979, although they had appeared in other fleets in 1972.[28]

The global dimension of the fleet's responsibility was dramatically demonstrated in April 1975 during the worldwide Soviet naval exercise Vesna (Okean II). Four task forces ranged widely in the Pacific. One grouped 400 kilometers (250 miles) east of Shanghai and moved on station south of Taiwan. Another covered the North Pacific. A third was positioned 480 kilometers (300 miles) east of Japan. The fourth remained near the Tsushima Strait.[29] Their varied activity included anti-submarine warfare, amphibious ship exercises, convoying in the Philippine Sea, and sea lane interdiction east of Japan. This was an impressive display of power compared with what would have been possible a decade previous. It attracted understandable attention and comment, all adverse, in both Peking and Tokyo, coming as the final collapse of South Vietnam appeared to symbolize the decline of American power in the West Pacific. Yet it was largely geared to missions outside the immediate area under review. Moreover it was carried out in a military vacuum, no enemy being in active confrontation.

Narrowing the focus to northeast Asia, an authoritative naval analyst concludes, "As it has always been for the Soviet Pacific fleet, the primary mission must be to secure the regional waters that wash Soviet Siberia, particularly the Sea of Japan. The numerous small combatants assigned to the Pacific fleet would be good for little else."[30] This addresses the problem of access to the Pacific. Three potential choke-points confront Soviet naval commanders. The southern route via the East China Sea transits the Tsushima Strait between South Korea and Japan. The most direct passage to the Pacific passes through the the Tsugaru Strait between the Japanese islands of Honshu and Hokkaido. Further north the La Perouse Strait between Sakhalin and Hokkaido links the Sea of Japan with the Sea of Okhotsk from which the Pacific can be reached through the Kuril islands. The only alternative to these vulnerable points of passage is the very narrow and shallow Tatar Strait between Sakhalin and the Siberian mainland. From here ships must cross the Sea of Okhotsk, a distance of 1,280 kilometers (800 miles) which is blocked with ice for up to six months a year.[31]

Except for the Tsushima Strait where swift currents impede their use, mines can block movement from the Sea of Japan. Ships could deploy to blue water before a pending crisis escalated into conflict but they would still need to return for refuelling, resupply, and repair. This explains why nearly one-fifth of the fleet consists of minesweepers. Should the choke-points be closed, the long route to Vladivostok via the Tatar Strait could be abandoned in favor of Petropavlovsk which lies on the Pacific. However it lacks the facilities of mainland ports and is itself vulnerable to mining.

A further complication lies in the importance of merchant shipping to supply the Soviet Far East. Enemy submarines could exact a heavy toll along the lengthy route across the Indian Ocean, the East China Sea, and the West Pacific. A revealing statement by Admiral Sergei Gorshkov stressed the limited effectiveness of Allied anti-submarine warfare (ASW) efforts in World War II, warning, "If ASW forces which were so numerous and technically up to date (for that time), possessing a vast superiority, turned out to be capable of only partially limiting the operations of diesel submarines, then what must this superiority be today to counter nuclear-power submarines, whose combat capabilities cannot be compared with the capabilities of World War II era submarines."[32]

TABLE 1
Soviet Pacific Fleet Combat Force Levels (as percent of total Soviet fleet strength)

|  | 1968 | 1973 | 1978 | 1980 |
|---|---|---|---|---|
| Submarines[a] | 100 (27%) | 101 (30%) | 113 (32%) | 110 (30%) |
| Major surface combatants[b] | 58 (29%) | 58 (27%) | 67 (29%) | 85 (30%) |
| Minor surface combatants | NA | 135 (22%) | 113 (22%) | |
| Amphibious ships[c] | NA | 18 (25%) | 18 (22%) | |
| Mine warfare craft | NA | NA | 110 (25%) | |

NA = Not Available.
[a]Includes ballistic missile, cruise missile and attack boats.
[b]Includes cruisers, destroyers and frigates.
[c]Includes medium and tank landing ships only.
SOURCES: Totals reflect a reconciling of data from a variety of unclassified American, British, West German, and Japanese sources. Totals for 1978 are almost exclusively from the United States Defense Intelligence Agency, *Unclassified Communist Naval Orders of Battle* (DDB–1200–124–78; Washington, 1978), pp. 1–4. 1980 data are from John M. Collins, *U.S.-Soviet Military Balance* (New York: McGraw Hill, 1980), p. 250.

Within the confines of this essay, we cannot explore the many variants of war-fighting scenarios to test the hypothetical capabilities of the Soviet Pacific fleet. The task is highly complex and it is not directly relevant to our inquiry. But despite the ambiguities which constrain our ability to infer intent from deployment, the defensive concerns of Soviet naval planners in the Pacific are readily apparent and an important factor in determining deployments. So far as supporting offensive operations on land are concerned, the sea force in hand consists of 18 amphibious ships and two naval infantry regiments totalling 4,000 troops.[33] In itself, this poses no threat to Hokkaido, despite the relatively narrow jump from Sakhalin. Of course additional forces could be deployed from the nearby islands of Kunashiri, Etorofu, and Shikotan where upwards of 10–12,000 troops were stationed by 1980.[34]

In the absence of actual hostilities, the Soviet fleet plays an important political role in projecting an image of power which is heightened in Japan by media attention. This traditional use of a navy to "show the flag" is manifest in the recurrent passage of Soviet ships near Japan's territorial waters. The attendant press publicity arouses public anxiety and political pressure for some response.

In 1967 Moscow began to increase its activity in the Sea of Japan, in the course of which one of its destroyers sideswiped its American counterpart during a joint U.S.-South Korean exercise. In 1968 sixteen Soviet ships gathered between the North Korean coast and an American task force which had concentrated in the Sea of Japan after Pyongyang's seizure of the intelligence ship *Pueblo*. In 1969 another large contingent sailed there in seeming response to a U.S. naval force after the North Korean shootdown of an EC-121 aircraft. However, the Soviet ships actually attempted to help locate the aircraft and crew. After a five year lull, in 1974, the carrier *Midway* together with several destroyers and two landing ships engaged in amphibious exercises near South Korea. This triggered monitoring flights by nearly forty Soviet aircraft in three days.[35]

The heightened visibility of Moscow's fleet contrasts with the reduced profile of Washington's naval presence in the West Pacific. The number of ships assigned to the U.S. Seventh Fleet declined precipitously during the decade 1969–79 when the gradual winding down of the Vietnam war led to mothballing or reassignment elsewhere, as shown in the following figures.:

U.S. Naval Presence in the Pacific

U.S. Seventh Fleet Strength[36]
1969: 225
1970: 145
1971:  95
1978:  50

U.S. Naval Shipdays in the Pacific[37]
1965: 54,200
1972: 47,300
1974: 34,800
1977: 20,818

In simple aggregate numbers, as of 1978 the Soviet Pacific Fleet totaled 500 ships to the U.S. 50, displacing 762,000 tons to the U.S. 503,000 tons, with an average age of nine years compared with fifteen.[38] However it registered only 5,800 shipdays compared with the U.S. 20,818.

The key comparisons depend on whether a war is global or regional. The data shown in Table 2 for 1978 highlights this important analytical distinction.

If the U.S. West Pacific force is compared with that of the USSR the combat ship ratio of 21 to 67 could present Japan with a precarious situation. This prospect is accentuated by the 1 to 16 disparity in attack submarines. The Soviet upgrading of ships adds still another dimension, with four Kresta cruisers and five Krivak destroyers entering the Pacific fleet and more on the way.[39] As shown during the Afghanistan crisis in 1980, the U.S. Seventh Fleet may be drawn upon for service elsewhere, in that case losing its only aircraft carrier.[40] This leaves little reassurance for Japan's dependence on sea supply for food, raw materials, and energy resources.

However in a war confined to East Asia, the combined West and East Pacific fleets give the U.S. a clear preponderance of power over the USSR, except in submarines. They could also be reinforced by detachments from other units if necessary. In the Vietnam War, the three American carriers then assigned to the Seventh Fleet grew to six by 1972. Against the present two carriers, or six if the total Pacific complement is counted, Moscow has only the *Minsk*. The *Kiev*, its only other carrier, would have to be moved from the Mediterranean Sea, a long and vulnerable journey.

As further reassurance, it should be noted that simple statistics do not reveal performance comparability. A considerably greater American capacity for the replenishment of fuel, ammunition, and other supplies at sea provides U.S. ships with longer operational periods than is true for the Soviet fleet.[41] Combined with a more efficient maintenance capability, the shorter time in port permits a smaller number of American vessels to register many more ship-days than a larger Soviet fleet. Better detection and data-processing systems also enhance the American ASW capability compared with that of the Soviet Union, particularly given the less adequate shielding of sound in Soviet submarines. In short, the American technological lead in research and development of new electronic sys-

TABLE 2

U.S.-Soviet Naval Balance: East Asia and Pacific

| Naval Ships | United States | | | USSR |
|---|---|---|---|---|
| | West Pacific | East Pacific | Total | |
| Surface Combatants | | | | |
| Carriers | 2 | 4 | 6 | 0 |
| Cruisers | 4 | 12 | 16 | 9 |
| Destroyers | 8 | 24 | 32 | 28 |
| Frigates | 7 | 26 | 33 | 30 |
| Total | 21 | 66 | 87 | 67 |
| Submarines | | | | |
| Strategic | 10 | 0 | 10 | 30 |
| Attack | 5 | 28 | 33 | 80 |
| Total | 15 | 28 | 43 | 110 |

Source: John M. Collins, "The Military Balance Between Superpowers in the Far East: A Study in Constraints," *Asian Perspective*, Fall 1978, vol. II, no. 2, 158.

tems and weaponry can be counted upon to provide a significant qualitative advantage that will continue to offset most of the quantitative shortfall in the U.S. naval position when measured against that of the USSR. The overall situation is likely to become increasingly favorable as the expansion in U.S. shipbuilding appropriations undertaken in the early 1970s produces a greater number of new ships.[42]

In the meantime, however, public perceptions do not turn on a sophisticated analysis of combat capabilities, missions, and technology. Instead they tend to rest on a simplistic juxtaposition of aggregate numbers and hypothetical "worst case" scenarios. This tendency is reinforced by the parochial interest of military bureaucracies to enlarge their budgetary allocation by emphasizing another country's apparent strength. Thus the 1977 Japanese White Paper on Defense declared that the "buildup of the Soviet Navy cannot be simply ignored since it has ramifications for the region. In particular the advance of the Soviet Navy into the open sea has further heightened the relevant countries' concerns for their security, especially Japan, which is positioned close to the straits through which the Soviet Navy passes for its access into the oceans."[43] This does not reflect a consensus of governmental opinion as will be seen when we focus on the Japanese factor. But it is worth noting at this point as illustrating the peacetime implications of Soviet naval activity.

## Siberian Development: What Difference?

At the outset we defined our problem in terms of what difference in military capability is likely to ensue from Siberian development. In this regard the best point of departure is the Baikal-Amur Mainline (BAM) as the most strategically important project currently underway.

Down to the present, the Trans-Siberian Railroad has proven adequate for the basic military need. Although the Czarist navy met defeat in 1904–05, approximately 250,000 troops succeeded in forcing Tokyo to seek American mediation.[44] At the time, this was an impressive force to support so far from European Russia against an enemy so proximately located. In 1938 at Changkufeng (Lake Khasan) on the Manchurian-Soviet border and again in 1939 at Nomonhan (Khalkhin-Gol) on the Manchurian-Mongolian border, the Red Army inflicted heavy casualties in division-size engagements with local Japanese units.[45] Japanese intelligence claimed the Soviet forces grew from 20 divisions in 1937 to 30 divisions in 1939, or from 370,000 to 570,000 troops.[46] Although the celebrated commander, Marshal G. K. Zhukov, acknowledged logistical problems in his memoir, he singled out the Transbaikal Military District for special commendation.[47]

Perhaps the most remarkable logistical feat was the massive movement of men and material from the European front, after defeating Nazi Germany, to East Asian Siberia in order to attack Japan within three months as agreed at Yalta. According to an authoritative Soviet history, in May 1945 no more than 40 divisions defended the Far East region, equipped with obsolete tanks.[48] By

August this force had grown to "eleven field, one tank, three air, and three air-defense armies . . . with over 1,500,000 officers and men, more than 26,000 guns and mortars, and more than 5,500 tanks and self-propelled guns."[49] This entailed deployments from Europe to Asia of between 9,000 and 12,000 kilometers (5,580 and 7,440 miles), as well as inter-front and inner-front regroupings of up to 1,500 kilometers (930 miles) between Blagoveshchensk and Maritime Krai. The main body of troops actually came from beyond the Soviet frontier in Europe. Altogether some 136,000 railroad cars were involved; during June-July, between 22 and 30 trains per day ran east of Lake Baikal.

The more recent military expansion opposite China in 1965–76 pales by comparison both in terms of the much smaller deployment and the longer time involved. Nonetheless the doubling of armed strength in Siberia from 1965 to 1969 proved the Trans-Siberian's capacity to meet a sudden military demand as determined in Moscow.

This impressive record notwithstanding, Soviet defense officials were undoubtedly concerned over the Trans-Siberian's vulnerability to disruption by human and natural causes. Already in the mid-1930s, the first step was taken toward building a second railroad to cross the region, with a spur line running north to Komsomolsk from Volochayevka, west of Khabarovsk.[50] During World War II, this line was extended east to Sovetskaya Gavan, providing a second railhead on the Sea of Japan at Vanino. This opened an alternate route if needed to replace the Trans-Siberian section which ran along the Manchurian border between Khabarovsk and Vladivostok.

After the war, further work halted because of the greater priority given to rebuilding the devastated portions of the Soviet Union. Then in the late 1960s, a coincidence of factors revived Moscow's interest in BAM. We have already seen how the perceived threat from China grew in importance from 1964 to 1969. In addition, the completed reconstruction of wartorn areas gradually freed more funds for less developed regions, among which Siberia had long held a special attraction for economic planners. This attraction was strengthened by postwar surveys and studies which showed a wide range of natural resources to be available for exploitation if access and technology could become available. Finally, the decision to involve foreign governments and companies in Siberian development provided the possibility of gaining the necessary capital as well as technology to undertake the difficult venture.

BAM promised to serve these various needs and in 1974 the massive project was officially launched amid nationwide fanfare. In strategic terms, BAM offers more than adequate assurance against interdiction by ground attack. Its closest point to the Chinese border is almost 200 kilometers (125 miles) away. Much of BAM lies between 250 and 270 kilometers (155 and 170 miles) distant with the remainder even further removed.[51] Moreover while the Trans-Siberian frequently parallels the Amur and Ussuri rivers on fairly flat ground, BAM is separated from China almost everywhere by mountainous terrain.

Thus should the north-south line to Vladivostok be cut, BAM could still supply the main naval base through Vanino and Sovetskaya Gavan.

However the more likely threat of attack by aircraft or missiles is not so drastically reduced. Allowing for the necessity to site Chinese bases well behind the border, the consequent distance of 500 kilometers (310 miles) to BAM offers no decisive advantage for its defense. In addition, the 3,145 kilometers (1,965 miles) of single track between Ust-Kut and Komsomolsk offers numerous potential chokepoints. Approximately 3,700 bridges and culverts will span bogs and rivers, many of which swell with water from thawing snow and summer rains.[52] More than 140 of the bridges exceed 90 meters (300 feet) in length. Three are 1,365 meters (4,500 feet) 490 meters (1,620 feet) and 412 meters (1,375 feet) long.[53] These offer attractive targets for airborne attack. Less vulnerable but more disabling if damaged are BAM's tunnels which total 24 kilometers (15 miles), including one of 14.4 kilometers (9 miles) and another of 6.4 kilometers (4 miles).[54]

Most of the line passes over permafrost which is unevenly distributed in location and thickness.[55] Here the track must be elevated on a berm of wood or gravel to a height of two meters or more (six feet plus) to guard against the effects of heat and thaw on surface ground.[56] Bridge pilings frequently must be individually designed for depth and stress to allow for the varied subsoil conditions.[57] These factors complicate the maintenance of BAM in wartime. The situation is worsened by the weak infrastructure of service roads, warehouses, and repair stations to speed the restoration of traffic following an attack.

An additional vulnerability lies in the plan to electrify the western portion of BAM so as to exploit the large surplus of cheap hydropower and to minimize pollution. Because of the permafrost, lines and installations will be above ground, increasing their exposure to attack and the cost of protective shelters. The destruction of power lines and stations would paralyze movement until diesel equipment could arrive or the damage be repaired.

Beyond these specific wartime hazards, a host of natural phenomena makes BAM a high risk railroad with uncertain reliability.[58] East of Lake Baikal it traverses on one of the most seismic areas of the USSR. Nearly 30 earthquakes of six points or greater on the Richter scale have been recorded in the BAM service area, occurring on an average of one every 15 to 20 years. The effects are worsened by permafrost which heightens the acceleration of transverse waves by a factor of two or more, resulting in greater ground flow, rock debris movements, liquefaction and mudflows. The concentration of tunnels in the seismic area poses special problems in their alignment and reinforcement.[59]

Landslides and mudflows occur with particular frequency in the central BAM area. Avalanches pose an additional hazard. Icing is a major problem in hundreds of places along the route, with active zones ranging from one thousand to over a million cubic meters. Cumulatively these phenomena pose a threat of interrupted service that could cut freight shipments for weeks at a time, depending upon the origin, severity, location, and timing of the event.

North-south links between BAM and the Trans-Siberian provide alternate routes to bypass afflicted portions but these are few in number and widely separated. As already noted, service roads and storage points for emergency equipment will be inadequate for many years because of the slowness in developing ancillary facilities, especially in the most hazard prone section west of Aldan. Soviet engineers and planners are fully apprised of these problems and have made every effort to anticipate them. Nevertheless the supply of human, fiscal, and technological resources is extremely limited by comparison with the magnitude of the task.

Taking these various factors into consideration, BAM would appear to have greater military value in a precombat situation than in actual war. It provides a major logistical addition for strengthening Soviet forces throughout the area compared with sole reliance on the Trans-Siberian. This facilitates the stockpiling of essential supplies, such as ammunition and petroleum, to sustain prolonged fighting on land and sea. It also provides access to additional territory for the stationing and dispersal of military personnel and installations.

These advantages enhance Moscow's ability to prepare for war in East Asia. Once war begins, however, BAM's liabilities may outweigh its assets. Much depends on the specific circumstances, of course. It can make a considerable difference whether the war is of short or long duration, whether it is fought with conventional or nuclear weapons, and whether the enemy can target with sufficient accuracy and damage to keep BAM inoperative. Yet regardless of the scenario, the reliability and vulnerability of BAM in conditions of modern warfare remain open to question.

It may be this uncertain prospect which prompted a high Soviet official to remark privately, "Don't overstate BAM's military importance. In the next war, it won't be a question of moving lots of troops over long distances. In the first hours, missiles will be flying and many people will be killed—on both sides."[60] It is impossible to know the degree to which this view is shared by military strategists. A major portion of the labor for BAM's construction was provided by railroad engineering divisions from the Soviet Army.[61] It is doubtful that so costly a project, consuming nearly one percent of the annual USSR investment budget, could be undertaken against military opposition.[62]

Yet BAM does not appear to enjoy the priority in funding and staffing of a project that is primarily seen as having strategic importance. The initial goal of completion by 1982–83 seems unlikely to be achieved. Soviet officials informally suggest 1985 as the earliest year to begin test runs over the entire line, with perhaps another two years before BAM can be fully operational.[63] This stretched out schedule involves more than a decade of investment before the returns can begin to be realized. It implies that BAM's limitations have been realistically assessed by Soviet strategists and that they do not envisage the line as improving their Far East capability sufficiently to justify a more accelerated effort.

Whether this same perception prevails in Peking, or will at the time of BAM's completion, is difficult to determine. In 1974, Peking protested privately to Tokyo over Moscow's proposal for a joint Soviet-Japanese project to transport Tyumen oil from West Siberia to the Pacific by a combined pipeline and rail route.[64] The Chinese stressed the strengthening of Soviet military capability that would result, thereby furthering Japanese unwillingness to undertake the project which had already risen in cost and declined in promised deliveries compared with the initial proposal.[65] Subsequently, however, the Chinese made no serious effort to dissuade Japanese and American firms from providing engineering equipment for BAM.[66] This suggests that the pipeline aroused greater concern than did the railroad.[67]

For its part, Tokyo shows no sign of giving BAM the strategic significance that was attributed to the Trans-Siberian Railroad at the end of the last century. Although the competition between Russia and Japan for spheres of influence in Korea and Manchuria was the basic cause of conflict in 1904–05, the war's timing was to a large part determined by apprehension that completion of the transcontinental line would give St. Petersburg a decisive advantage.

No such alarm over BAM appears to concern Tokyo officials.[68] On the contrary, the railroad is viewed as facilitating the exploitation of Siberian resources, particularly timber and coal to meet Japan's needs. No Japan Export-Import Bank loans are involved but the close consultation between business and government on such matters makes it certain that official approval underlies the involvement of Japanese firms in BAM's construction. This would not be the case were the railroad seen as increasing the Soviet threat.

To sum up, the strategic significance of BAM is highly variable, depending upon whether it is assessed in a precombat or combat context and whether the point of assessment is Moscow, Peking, or Tokyo. It clearly enhances the Soviet ability to strengthen its forces in the region. It also offers defense in depth against a ground invasion that might threaten the Trans-Siberian Railroad. Whether these attributes heighten or lessen the likelihood of tension and conflict, however, will depend on specific situations.

For example, if Soviet military planners are more relaxed about the consequences of incidents, escalation, or surprise attack cutting the Trans-Siberian because of BAM's fallback capacity, they might be less likely to unleash a preemptive attack in a Sino-Soviet crisis. On the other hand, if Chinese military planners anticipate another massive expansion of Soviet forces as a consequence of BAM's completion, they might press more vigorously for countervailing measures that would heighten a local arms race.

On balance, it appears that BAM's strategic significance for East Asia is worth noting but without exaggeration or undue emphasis. Certainly of much greater interest to Japan and the United States is the strengthening of Moscow's maritime presence in the Pacific. In this regard the most relevant Siberian development project is the new port of Vostochny at Nakhodka. By 1990, Vostochny will be able to handle 40 million tons of cargo a year.[69] This will facilitate many more Soviet merchant vessels serving the area. Together with BAM, they can significantly augment the logistical flow to meet military needs.

In addition these ships can perform multiple tasks of intelligence collection and the clandestine transport of weaponry.[70] During conflict their preplanned conversion to military support roles offers a valuable auxiliary fleet for the Soviet navy. Vostochny also can relieve congestion at military bases for refueling and repair, depending on the nature of hostilities in the area.

Beyond these direct contributions to military capability, indirect improvements can emerge through an expanding economic infrastructure. This might provide an enlarged population base and labor force, an improved transportation network, a modern metallurgical industry, and the general upgrading of locally manfactured products. Such developments could reduce dependence on distant sources of supplies and spare parts.

None of these factors are significant in themselves. Taken together, however, they contribute to the efficiency and effectiveness of a fighting force that is held in place against a remote future contingency. To this extent, the overall development of East Asian Siberia could eventually change the human environment within which the armed services, particularly the army, function.

But this will be slow in coming. The prospects for a rapid expansion of population centers are slim. In 1979 concentrations of more than a half million existed in only three cities: Vladivostok (550,000), Irkutsk (550,000), and Khabarovsk (528,000). Seven additional cities exceeded 100,000 each.[71]

Urban growth rates are not impressive, although some interesting exceptions exist. During 1970–79, the two fastest growing cities were Yakutsk (41 percent) and Bratsk (38 percent). Curiously, the first was in one of the coldest areas as was Magadan (33 percent). The remainder registered increases ranging from 25 percent down to 15 percent over nine years. This growth was only in part a function of movement from outside the region. Much of it was generated by high birth rates resulting from the large proportion of younger persons and local migration from countryside to city.[72]

The constraints on growth are serious and will remain so. The BAM zone produces only one-third of its present food requirement.[73] The severity and vagaries of local climatic conditions, the effects of permafrost, and the scarcity of arable land combine to preclude the region from becoming self-sufficient in agriculture. The resultant, long distance hauling from more fruitful areas of the USSR raises prices and reduces variety. The cost of living is further increased by the greater expense for construction, maintenance, heating and clothing necessitated by the harsh environment.

These circumstances inhibit migration into the BAM zone. They also induce planners to cluster support services such as hospitals, schools, cultural activity, and entertainment in existing population centers. However the continued growth of a few very large cities could pose a risk in wartime. Enemy missiles need hit only Vladivostok, Khabarovsk, and Irkutsk to endanger 14 percent of the population and a much larger proportion of the industry in East Asian Siberia. All three targets lie within easy range of possible launching sites in northeast China. Vladivostok and Khabarovsk are also within reach of sea-based attack from the east.

The effect on Soviet strategists' thinking is problematic. The vulnerability of those nodal points in the region's economy places a premium on preempting a perceived threat of attack. However this defensive concern should be alleviated to the extent that population and industry can be more widely distributed, as is envisaged in the next decade. Soviet economic analysis suggests that cities of approximately 100,000 persons are optimal for this region, being large enough to justify the necessary services without requiring an excessive network of transportation, supply lines, and sewage disposal facilities.[74] In addition to reducing the problem of defense, the proliferation of new cities would improve the support environment for military units scattered throughout the area.

Economic development will also improve transportation throughout the region. This should enhance military logistics in terms of mobility and reliability. In addition to BAM's lateral route, its northward extension network of roads will penetrate previously inaccessible areas for the exploitation of local resources. Maintenance will improve as the necessary manpower and equipment become available. River use may increase with more icebreakers and dredging.

A modern metallurgical industry would also be helpful from a military point of view. The only existing steel works, at Komsomolsk, are inadequate for more than local requirements of low alloy steel.[75] Large deposits of iron ore located near good coking coal offer an attractive base in south Yakutia. It seems likely that a major metallurgical complex will eventually be built in the region to meet the growing local need and to exploit local resources. This will enhance self-sufficiency but it may not meet it completely. Moreover all of the prospective sites lie within range of Chinese missiles. Reliance on a single point of production could invite a crippling attack. Thus as in other respects, a precombat increase in capability may be offset by wartime vulnerability.

In sum, Siberian development offers only a limited increase in the Soviet strategic military capability beyond that which already exists in the area. Its greatest contribution is in strengthening of the region's logistical and support capacity before hostilities begin. Once a war starts, however, the defensive liabilities appear to outweigh the offensive advantages.

## Economic Leverage and Strategic Implications

Economic leverage on an importing country is a familiar phenomenon in East Asia. Prior to World War II, the United States embargoed strategic goods to Japan, initially scrap iron and subsequently oil, to dissuade Tokyo from further aggression. Beginning in 1950 Washington imposed a total embargo on American trade with the People's Republic of China and a strategic embargo on selected items traded by its allies with Peking. Although the total embargo was lifted in connection with President Nixon's trip to China in 1972, the strategic embargo remained through controls exercised by NATO and Japan well after the "normalization" of relations in 1979.

Siberian development offers Japan access to energy resources—coal, gas, and oil—as well as less critical items such as timber, asbestos, and copper which play an important role in the economy. To what extent might dependence on the Soviet Union for such commodities present a risk in terms of Moscow's ability to manipulate supply for political purposes in peacetime or military ends in war?

As a rule of thumb, Japanese officials indicate a willingness to rely on Soviet supplies for up to a fifth or so of the total importation of particular items but not to go much beyond that limit.[76] For example, in 1976, the USSR provided 27.4 percent of Japan's imported steam coal.[77] In 1977, 23.9 percent of its imported asbestos and approximately 20 percent of its imported nickel came from the Soviet Union.[78]

According to one official estimate, if the Yakutian natural gas project comes to fruition, the USSR could supply nearly 20 percent of Japan's total LNG consumption by 1990. However LNG might contribute only 7.7 percent of the overall energy need.[79] Therefore the potential Soviet leverage, while perhaps pinpointed for certain sectors of the economy, would be minimal for the country as a whole.

Similarly South Yakutian coking coal is anticipated to meet 7 to 10 percent of Japanese consumption by 1985–90. With 40 percent coming from Australia, 25 percent from the U.S., and 15 percent from Canada, the Soviet portion will be relatively small. Steam coal is anticipated to provide only 4 percent of the total energy requirement in 1990, thereby permitting a somewhat greater share of this import to the Soviet Union. Sakhalin oil will comprise only 1 percent of total petroleum imports, a wholly expendable amount which can be supplied elsewhere.

The combined impact of all four commodities suddenly being cut off by Moscow would cause short-term dislocation in selected areas and industries. However, there would be no long-term impact, assuming that other suppliers could increase their deliveries. Japan's various trading partners in the Pacific Basin appear more than capable of filling whatever gap would arise from a Soviet embargo on energy exports after perhaps a brief interval necessary to increase production and reorient transportation. This fact is so obvious as presumably to deter Moscow from any such threat, much less action.

Timber is a less critical item but looms somewhat larger, with 28.4 percent of Japan's 1977 imports coming from the USSR. This compares with 63.7 percent from the United States.[80] Moreover the higher grade softwoods are North American while their hardwood counterparts originate in Southeast Asia. Thus as with other items, the Soviet supply is useful but not essential to the economy.

Conversely, the degree to which any such embargo or attempted leverage would hurt the Soviet economy varies from one commodity to another and from one point in time to another. Where the export is in repayment for already acquired capital and technology, Moscow has the advantage. But where it earns foreign exchange needed to pay other bills, such as for grain imports, the embargo would inflict a cost on the Soviet economy. Furthermore in the case of natural gas, Japan will provide the only foreign market other than the

U.S. There is not likely to be sufficient domestic demand to take up the slack in distribution of output. This in turn would reduce the return on Moscow's original investment. These calculations reveal the symbiotic relationship which both countries enjoy in Siberia's development.

Soviet involvement in the world economy raises risks on other fronts if Moscow were to apply economic pressure against Tokyo. Reneging on energy exports as payment for acquired technology in Sakhalin and Yakutia would jeopardize the Soviet ability to acquire oil and gas equipment elsewhere. This could paralyze its effort to expand off-shore oil production, a vital need in the 1990s.[81] In addition, Washington could support Tokyo with a retaliatory embargo against grain sales to Moscow. This would hit hard, given the chronic vulnerability of Soviet agriculture to bad climate and the continuing inability to raise output.[82] In short, the backlash effects of singling out Japan for economic leverage could be severely damaging.

Economics aside, it is difficult to define a plausible situation whereby Moscow might be tempted to apply such pressure. It would be wholly inadequate for a major goal, such as forcing Tokyo to renounce the American alliance or to exclude American bases. It would probably boomerang as an effort to reduce Japanese defense expenditures or to brake a growing Peking-Tokyo entente. It certainly would not silence public opinion on such issues as the northern territories and fishing incidents. Finally, once such leverage were attempted, no further Japanese cooperation in Siberian development could ever be anticipated, without which much of the program would have little hope of realization in this century.

## Japanese Views

As is clear from our analysis, Japan is a key country for determining the implications as well as the future of East Asian Siberia's development. Whether as the source of capital, technology, and markets or as the potential target of Soviet economic, political, and military pressure, Japan is far more sensitive to future developments in this region than either China or the United States.

Japanese views are particularly well-informed where they are derived from direct experience. More than a decade of involvement with EAS project negotiations and billions of dollars in loans and investment provide an excellent basis for judgment. This is reflected in the private admission of one Soviet official that the best research and data for the Yakutian natural gas project was generated by Japanese and not Soviet analysts.

Yet emotion and politics continue to introduce a strong negative bias into Japanese perceptions of the USSR. This historical heritage is a bitter one, including as it does the Soviet attack in August 1945 only four months after Moscow informed Tokyo it would not renew the Neutrality Pact in 1946, the subsequent detention of more than 100,000 prisoners of war in labor camps until the early 1950s, the loss of Sakhalin and the Kuril Islands, and the occupation of the so-called "northern territories" near Hokkaido. These islands—the Habomais, Shikotan, Etorofu, and Kunashiri—not only represent an irredentist issue but also provided access to profitable fishing areas. Japanese domestic politics has so embroiled this issue as to prevent conclusion of a peace treaty with the USSR. The perennial negotiations over fishing agreements took a particularly difficult turn in 1977 when Moscow proved especially obdurate. While subsequent interactions proceeded more smoothly, the issue continues to obstruct good relations. Last but not least, Japanese media attention to Soviet ground forces in the "northern territories," together with repeated Soviet air and naval penetration of Japanese territorial space, keeps alive the image of a potential threat.

As a result, there is no single "Japanese view" of Siberian development. The various prognoses are diverse and contradictory, depending on whether they are inferred from gross public opinion polls, special interest lobbying, official statements, or private interviews. They are also subject to change over time as a function of Soviet behavior, Chinese attitudes, and shifts in the U.S.-USSR power balance, both regional and global. Finally they tend to be relatively short-term in focus whereas the true significance of Siberian development lies in its long-term implications, whether in resource access or military strength.

With these caveats in mind, we can summarize briefly the main Japanese views of the 1970s. It was not a time of serious concern or alarm over Soviet behavior. For example, a *Jiji* press survey in 1962 showed the Soviet Union to be "disliked" by nearly half the respondents but ten years later this group had shrunk to less than a third.[83] A *Sankei Shimbun* poll of March 1975 corroborated this change with the percentage of those in the "dislike" column being highest among persons over sixty years of age but lowest amount those under forty.[84] These surveys reveal a dilution of anti-Soviet feeling with the passage of time since World War II.

However a decrease in attitudes does not necessarily lead to an increase in positive affect. Thus, in the *Jiji* polls those who "like" the Soviet Union were so few as to be virtually unmeasurable throughout this period.[85] Similarly the *Sankei* survey found only two percent to be positively disposed toward the USSR.[86]

Such polls are little more than popularity contests. At best they measure surface attitudes which may be acted upon by governments, national or foreign. More significant is the perception of threat posed by other countries. Here public opinion is surprisingly relaxed when placed against the past history of Soviet-Japanese relations and the present disparity of power between the two proximate neighbors. Thus in 1971 less than half the respondents could be specific when asked "at present from what country is an attack possible?"[87] Among those who do specify the source of threat, the largest number consistently single out the Soviet Union.[88] However in 1970 this comprised only 13 percent.[89]

Public attitudes often respond to media stimuli. These in turn may result from actual events involving Soviet behavior or official statements that represent bureaucratic interests. In this regard a Japan Defense Agency official noted that by 1978–79 it was no longer difficult to persuade newspapers to publish photographs and stories concerning Soviet air and ship violations of Japan's territorial sovereignty. In fact, he remarked somewhat jocularly, the press sometimes provided better photos than did the government.[90]

This increased press attention to Soviet military developments reflects perceived changes in the superpower balance in the West Pacific. In March 1979, *Yomiuri* devoted a full page to an imminent visit by the director of the Japan Defense Agency, Yamashita, to Washington, headlined "To Search For Response to Soviet Far East Forces."[91] After a detailed analysis of the added capability of the carrier *Minsk* and the *Backfire* bomber being deployed to the area, *Yomiuri* quoted unidentified defense agency sources as fearing that "if the U.S. Seventh Fleet's actions can be controlled, it (*Backfire*) may impede the U.S. aircraft carrier groups' advance into areas around Japan." The writer included a statistical comparison of the American and Soviet naval forces in the Far East based on defense agency estimates which showed Soviet superiority in all categories except naval aircraft.

Another stimulus to heightened press coverage of Soviet activity came with the expansion of Moscow's military forces in the "northern territories." In January 1979 the Japan Defense Agency confirmed the presence of one brigade of 5,000 troops on Kunashiri and Etorofu, together with three airfields, several dozen tanks, and ten cannon of a 20-kilometer range. While this was well below the pre-1960 deployment of a division and a brigade, it was considerably more than the 2,000 border guards stationed there in the interim.[92] Although much publicity attended the report and the subsequent foreign ministry protest, most press comment speculated on the probable role of the two islands in protecting the Sea of Okhotsk as a sanctuary for submarines with ballistic missiles targeted against the United States.[93] Only *Nihon Keizai* called for more vigorous defense preparations against a possible Soviet threat to Japan.[94]

Within the government bureaucratic interests differed on how to handle the matter. The Foreign Ministry limited itself to an oral protest which simply stressed the territorial issue of the islands' ownership, avoiding any implication of a perceived threat in the buildup.[95] Foreign Minister Sonoda tactfully suggested that "it will not be wise to fan anti-Soviet sentiments and the Japanese-Soviet confrontation unnecessarily."[96] Military spokesmen, however, sought to exploit the situation for a more favorable reception in the Diet budget hearings which were under way. In March press reports claimed that the four divisions in Hokkaido were being reorganized with more armored strength and artillery.

The Soviet deployment acquired greater potential significance during 1979 as it expanded to nearly 12,000 troops and included Shikotan Island in its operations.[97] Military officials released American intelligence to this effect in September, coincidental with the opening of semi-annual Soviet-Japanese talks in Moscow on Siberian development. While the press responded with considerable publicity and some commentary of concern, the foreign office spokesman echoed the earlier line by noting,

"It is premature to express any final judgment about this situation."[98] Meanwhile in New York, Sonoda and Gromyko held their annual tete-a-tete at the opening U.N. General Assembly with routine pledges to improve relations.

In contrast with the media attention given the Soviet buildup, military officers sounded no alarm. The air force commander on Hokkaido specifically noted that the *Backfire* bombers based in the Irkutsk region "appear to be directed toward China" with none being seen over the Sea of Japan or the Pacific Ocean by late 1979.[99] Earlier a ground commander on Hokkaido had acknowledged marked improvements in Soviet military capabilities, including the more rapid deployment of new weaponry to Far East forces compared with the past delay of three to four years after deployments to the European theater.[100] But he saw this as part of an overall change in strategic doctrine and not narrowly aimed at Japan. He dismissed foreign press accounts of alleged Japanese concern reflected in the suggestion that the Sea of Japan be called "Sea of the Soviet Union." On the contrary, he declared, "The U.S. Seventh Fleet together with the narrow straits for exiting to the Pacific leave Soviet forces severely handicapped, so that I'd rather have my problems than theirs."

The contradiction in view is highlighted by comparing the specific Siberian projects based on Japanese cooperation with the "worst case" projections of possible Soviet threat elaborated by Japanese specialists on military strategy. On the one hand there is the port of Vostochny, one of the largest in the entire USSR, also an 80,000 ton drydock, and the exploration for Sakhalin's off-shore oil, all made possible by Japanese capital and technology. On the other hand there are ritualistic briefings on Soviet air and naval expansion which point toward a capability to isolate Japan from its overseas economic lifelines. One official warns against the possibility of an eventual bridge or tunnel linking Sakhalin with the Siberian mainland to facilitate a massive buildup for an invasion of Hokkaido. The opposing views arise specifically with respect to the drydock. A responsible civilian authority said, "They told us it would be for merchant ships and we know they have ships this large. Therefore we had to trust their word or we would have appeared hostile." However, a military official self-critically remarked, "We Japanese often make our own situation worse."[101]

Takuya Kubo, Director General of the National Defense Council in 1976–78 after previously serving as Vice Minister of Defense, addressed the contradiction by noting, "There are two aspects to security: negative and positive. Negative security is military strength against attack. Positive security is economic cooperation to reduce perceptions of hostility which arouse tension and threat. We must pursue both aspects. We cannot have one without the other."[102] He admitted that this dual approach is not without "a certain degree of danger, risk, and cost" but "to avoid the risk and reduce the cost, we should go ahead on such projects as Yakutia gas if United States' cooperation is possible." According to Kubo, the danger of Moscow's reneging on repayment through mineral exports is reduced if Washington is a partner with Tokyo. The risk of Siberian development strengthening Soviet military power in East Asia is small relative to other factors which contribute to that power.

Kubo asserted that there are also risks in non-participation which must be weighed against those of cooperation. For example, if Soviet energy resources are not made available because of insufficient foreign credits and technology, a shortage could develop in the next ten years which might prompt Moscow to increase its pressure on the Middle East and the Persian Gulf. Alternatively Moscow might reduce its energy exports to East and West Europe. Either move would destabilize the international situation.

Kubo's call for a policy of "balanced diplomacy" rather than one of "equi-distance" was prompted by the China factor. He argued that there could never be "equality" in Japan's handling of China and the Soviet Union. Japan and China have a long history of contact between the two peoples and the two economies. Russia's historic orientation was toward Europe and no close contact has ever existed with Japan. Therefore "we cannot have the same relationship with both countries." But if America joins with Japan in Siberian development, this would reassure the Chinese. Kubo cautioned, "The Chinese should not have the power of veto . . . We have concluded the treaty with China against Soviet opposition and we should cooperate with the Soviet Union despite Chinese opposition."[103]

Wholly opposed to this view is Shinsaku Hogen, former ambassador to Moscow and former Vice Minister of Foreign Affairs. A 40-year specialist on the USSR, Hogen commands respect among an influential if limited circle of older, more conservative figures. He firmly believes that the past record of Russian behavior predicts more perfidy and pressure on Japan. "Russia is by nature expansionist," he warns, "They really want Hokkaido."[104] He argues strongly against any economic cooperation, particularly in Siberia, as simply strengthening the future threat to Japan.

But despite Hogen's claim that "the foreign office people agree with me," there is little support for his unalloyed anti-Soviet position at the ministry. One Soviet specialist there differentiated Japan's role from that of the United States by noting that Washington confronts Moscow globally and therefore must react to daily developments everywhere. However Tokyo should be "a stabilizer in the region." Whereas other countries have the responsibility of coping with the USSR strategically whenever necessary, whether in Africa, the Middle East, or Europe, Japan's long-term relationship is economic, not strategic and centers around East Asia, not the other regions.[105]

Another official put it in broader terms, "I think it is in the interest of the Free World to encourage the development in the Soviet Union of all energy resources—coal, oil, and natural gas. This will give Moscow foreign-currency reserves, it will enlarge trade relations, and it will increase the exchange of personnel and information. In short, it will increase interdependence. Moreover we must remember that there is no guarantee the Soviet Union will always remain open to such interdependence

and that it will remain willing to share Siberian resources. If we do not cooperate now, it may become resource nationalistic and keep everything at home."[106]

His closing remarks reflected the ambivalence of Japanese attitudes toward the USSR. The sense of opportunity as transient increases the willingness to take limited risks now so as to keep open the possibility of greater gains later. Yakutia may have oil, in addition to natural gas. A refusal to cooperate may foreclose this prospect indefinitely, not only because of a possible change in Soviet policy but also because of inadequate Soviet technical and capital resources to explore and develop the area in the absence of foreign participation.

The well known close relationship between business and government is manifest in the similarity of views expressed in Japanese firms engaged in Siberian development compared with those we have cited from past and present officials. A major business figure was typical in his remark of early July 1978, "If we get a treaty with China, we will need closer relations with the Soviet Union." He noted, with obvious gratification, that U.S.-USSR relations were very sensitive to such questions as human rights and arms control negotiations but Japan had no such problems and therefore should take the lead in economic cooperation.

While Japanese bankers and entrepreneurs are basically interested in a profitable undertaking, they also express concern over how to reduce international tensions, especially in northeast Asia. In this regard they justify their investment in Siberian development as a contribution to better relations both because of its immediate effect on Soviet perceptions and because of its indirectly balancing off the much larger investment in China's economic development. In this regard it is worth noting that the firm involved in Sakhalin oil exploration subsequently won the Bo Hai Gulf concession while Komatsu's participation in the construction of BAM did not preclude its winning a sizeable engineering contract in China.

To summarize, there is no clear consensus in Japan concerning the Soviet Union beyond the generally unfavorable comparison of its desirability as a neighbor compared with China. The issues which serve as irritants in the relationship, mainly the "northern territories" and fishing, are more serious obstacles than exist in Sino-Japanese relations but in themselves do not block cooperation in Siberia. The proximity of Soviet ground, air, and naval forces arouses media attention and public opinion while serving to justify small increases in the modest Japanese defense forces. Yet this does not yet appear to worry those responsible for Japan's security nor has it constrained Japanese participation in port construction or oil exploration, both of which have clear military implications.

Within the government, the Ministry of Foreign Affairs is the strongest advocate for "balanced diplomacy" and the muting of anti-Soviet positions as compared with the Japanese Defense Agency whose interests, understandably, prompt it to highlight Moscow's military activity. Yet privately JDA officials neither voice alarm over Soviet intentions nor express opposition to Siberian development except for the drydock project. Instead, they are concerned over the psychological impact on Japanese policy of a waxing Soviet military presence coincidental with a waning American military presence. As one official put it, "The United States is heard but not seen while the Soviet Union is seen but not heard."[107]

## China and the United States

It is impossible to isolate Siberian development from the overall context of Sino-Soviet and Soviet-American relations to any degree comparable with our analysis of Soviet-Japanese relations. Nor, as we have indicated, does it loom as large in the perspective of either country as for Japan, either in terms of its attraction or its threat. East Asian Siberia has the greatest concentration of ground forces directed against China and serves as the base for the Soviet Pacific Fleet targeted against the United States, but this is a long-standing situation, wholly independent of future development. Moreover as our earlier analysis showed, except for BAM's pre-combat logistical service, there is little for either China or the United States to worry about should Siberian development proceed as planned.

However China and the United States deserve at least brief consideration because of their ability, whether separately or together, to obstruct Siberian development. In 1974–75 Peking's protests contributed to Tokyo's refusal to facilitate the construction of a pipeline-railroad network for shipping oil from West to East Siberia. Although China subsequently muted whatever concern it may have felt over other projects, the renewal of pressure on Japan to desist from further cooperation would complicate matters considerably. The thickening of ties between the two countries provides Peking with multiple channels for subtle measures of persuasion or coercion aimed at reducing, if not eliminating altogether, Tokyo's participation in Moscow's programs.

Washington's role is already one of obstructing Japanese participation to the extent it is dependent on an American partnership, as in the case of Yakutian natural gas. So long as U.S. Export-Import Bank loans are limited to $40 million for Soviet energy projects with a total ceiling of $300 million for the entire USSR, there is little likelihood that the Yakutian gas proposal will be realized. Even should Bank of America, as the leading financial interest, succeed in raising sufficient funds among other American and European institutions, the higher interest rate would almost certainly be unacceptable to Moscow. Furthermore the seesaw U.S.-Soviet relationship with its swing from summitry to confrontation in the 1970s inhibits any major industrial commitments that lack governmental guarantees against the risk of interruption because of political tension.

As a final point, the "parallel strategic interests" professed between Peking and Washington, most pointedly during Secretary of Defense Brown's visit to China in early 1980 after the invasion of Afghanistan, align the two countries against the Soviet Union so as to reinforce their separate positions outlined above. This tacit alliance can act as further constraint against Siberian development through its impact on Japanese policy. Indeed, the dramatic deterioration in U.S.-Soviet relations at the beginning of this decade could ultimately reverse the slow but steady strengthening of Soviet-Japanese economic relations evident in the latter half of the 1970s.

## Conclusion

Thus in the final analysis, it is not the facts or realities of Siberian development that are likely to determine its course and the role of other countries therein as much as the perceptions and politics of all the governments concerned, whether in Moscow, Tokyo, Peking, or Washington. Nor can these perceptions and politics be projected with confidence, dependent as they are on unforeseeable events in various portions of the world. The instability of governments and the volatility of relations between nations in Asia, the Middle East, and Africa, combine to provide an unstable context for contention between the two superpowers, with China an acrimonious bystander and Japan a helpless but committed observer.

Absent this context, however, Siberian development offers positive prospects for economic cooperation with all three countries. East Asian Siberia and northeast China traditionally had a complementary relationship, with food flowing northward in exchange for natural resources.[108] This relationship could revive if politics permitted. China's timber shortage is acute as is the Soviet labor shortage. In the mid-1950s Nikita Khrushchev proposed and Mao Zedong agreed that 200,000 Chinese workers would work in Siberian forests.[109] China's copper prospects are dim compared with Udokan, believed to be among the largest deposits in the USSR. The Amur River, long a point of confrontation, could be of mutual benefit. In the late 1950s it was dubbed "river of friendship" by a joint Sino-Soviet survey which recommended a cooperative approach to harnessing the Amur for flood control, irrigation, and power generation.[110]

For the United States, the direct benefits of Siberian development are relatively few and largely peripheral to the American economy, particularly compared with more reliable and ready sources elsewhere. Yet two indirect considerations deserve mention. Japan, as the most important American ally in Asia, is more secure the more that it can diversify its dependence on overseas sources of vital raw materials. This is especially true for energy resources where the dominant role of Middle East oil is a point of major vulnerability. To the extent this need can be met through Siberian development, Japan's benefit is of interest to the United States as well. Moreover, if *inter alia*, multi-lateral cooperation in Siberian development can reduce tension in the area as argued by some, this advances an American interest together with that of Japan.

Viewed in a larger context, Siberian development could relieve the Soviet Union of eventual resource shortages. This in turn would lessen the need to seek those resources elsewhere, as might ultimately become the case with oil. Theoretically there is no resource problem that cannot be met by human ingenuity, whether through reducing consumption, increasing recovery with recycling, devising alternative products, and expanding extraction at higher cost or with more advanced technology.[111] But these are long-run solutions that entail effort, cost, and risk whch may be rejected in favor of seeking to expand one's share of the extant world supply through monetary or politico-military means. This can be destabilizing and disruptive, especially when an economy as large as the Soviet Union is involved.

Therefore if politics permit, the development of East Asian Siberia can serve the mutual interests of China, Japan, and the United States albeit in different proportions and in different ways. But whether or not this indeed comes about, the strategic implications of East Asian Siberia's development do not loom so large as in themselves to preclude the participation of other countries, much less compel them to work against it.

## NOTES

1. This differs from the term Pacific Siberia, which encompasses East and Far East Siberia, including Krasnoyarsk Krai. See Paul Dibb, *Siberia and the Pacific* (New York; Praeger, 1972). It does, however, coincide with the proposal of Yu. G. Saushkin and T. M. Kalashnikova, "Basic Economic Regions of the USSR," translated from *Voprosy geografii*, no. 47 (1959) in George J. Demko and Roland J. Fuchs, eds. and translators, *Geographical Perspectives in the Soviet Union: A Selection of Readings* (Columbus: Ohio State University, 1974).

2. *Allocation of Resources in the Soviet Union and China—1978*; Hearings Before the Subcommittee on Priorities and Economy in Government of the Joint Economic Committee, Congress of the United States, 95th Congress, 2nd session, (Washington, 1978) Part 4: Soviet Union, p. 88.

3. John M. Collins, *U.S.-Soviet Military Balance, Concepts and Capabilities, 1960–80* (New York: McGraw-Hill, 1980), p. 355.

4. Ibid.

5. Raymond Garthoff, "Sino-Soviet Military Relations, 1945–66," in Raymond Garthoff, ed., *Sino-Soviet Military Relations* (New York: Praeger, 1966), pp. 84–88.

6. Mao Zedong, "Speech to Japanese visitors, 10 July 1964," in *Mao Zedong Suxiang Wan Sui* [Long Live Mao Zedong Thought] (Taiwan: Nationalist Government, 1974) 1969 ed., pp. 540–41. For a similar version see Dennis J. Doolin, *Territorial Claims in the Sino-Soviet Conflict: Documents and Analysis* (Stanford: Hoover Institute, 1965), p. 44. The English version was translated from *Sekai Shuho*, 11 August 1964, in turn based on the original Chinese. No authorized transcript was issued by Peking.

7. Morris Rothenberg, *Whither China: The View from the Kremlin* (Miami: University of Miami, 1977), pp. 89–90.

8. Based on the author's access to official U. S. data at the time. For a lower but incorrect estimate, see *Strategic Survey*, 1969 (London Institute of Strategic Studies, 1970); much higher figures were reported by Harrison Salisbury, *New York Times*, 24 May 1969 and 31 August 1969.

9. Rothenberg, *Whither China*, p. 91.

10. Edward E. Rice, *Mao's Way* (Berkeley: University of California, 1972), ch. 22, pp. 358–81.

11. The most careful reconstruction of the incident and examination of alternative hypotheses is Thomas W. Robinson, "The Sino-Soviet Border Dispute, Background, Development, and the March 1969 Clashes," *American Political Science Review*, December 1972, no. 4, pp. 1175–1202.

12. Neville Maxwell, "The Chinese Account of the 1969 Fighting at Chenpao," *The China Quarterly*, October/December 1973, no. 56, pp. 730–39.

13. Rothenberg, *Whither China*, pp. 91–92.

14. Data from U. S. Army Map Service. 1:250,000. (L-542, Sheet NL 53-7, *Hu-lin China*). (Washington: Defense Mapping Agency, 1955). The particular point of proximity to China is at Ebergard. At Lazo the distance is five kilometers (3.1 miles); see L-542, Sheet NL 53-4, *Pao-ch'ing, China*.

15. *The World Atlas* (Moscow, 1967), p. 44 shows the Trans-Siberian east-west route on this alignment; a slightly greater distance from China is depicted on *Baikalo-Amurskya Zheleznodorozhnaya Magistral*, scale 1 centimeter to 25 kilometers, published by the Main Administration of Geodesy and Cartography, Council on Ministers USSR (Moscow, 1977). Both maps correspond to the Army Map Service measurements for the north-south line to Vladivostok.

16. *The Times Atlas of China* (New York: Quadrangle/New York Times, 1973), p. 29.

17. Ibid., pp. 17, 22.

18. Yevgeny Yevtushenko, "On the Red Russian Snow," *Literaturnaya gazeta*, 19 March 1969, in *Current Digest of the Soviet Press* (hereafter *CDSP*), vol. 21, no. 15, 30 April 1969.

19. The author visited the USSR in 1972, 1975, and 1978, on the latter two occasions traversing Siberia between Novosibirsk and Khabarovsk in addition to consulting in Moscow with academic specialists.

20. In addition to personal conversations, a similar observation may be found in Victor Louis, *The Coming Decline of the Chinese Empire* (New York: Times Books, 1979), pp. 175–76.

21. Collins, *Military Balance*, p. 355.

22. Interview with informed Soviet official, September 1978.

23. Interview with Academician A. G. Aganbegyan, 27 September 1978.

24. A "ship-day" registers the presence of a single naval vessel, regardless of size or function, in a designated area. Thus, Soviet Far East naval movement to and from the Indian Ocean is counted in the Pacific Ocean en route as well as in its ultimate destination on arrival. Data supplied by Barry M. Blechman, *Guide to Far Eastern Navies* (Annapolis: Naval Institute Proceedings, 1978).

25. Ibid., pp. 44–45.

26. Ibid., p. 40.

27. Donald C. Daniel, "The Soviet Navy in the Pacific," *Asia Pacific Commentary*, Summer 1979, p. 69.

28. Collins, *Military Balance*, p. 250.

29. Blechman, *Far Eastern Navies*, p. 45.

30. Ibid., pp. 46–47.

31. Paul E. Lydolph, *Geography of the USSR*, 3rd ed., (New York: Wiley and Sons, 1977), p. 439.

32. Admiral Sergei Gorshkov, "Navies in war and peace," *Morskoi sbornik*, no. 11, 1972, p. 26, translation supplied by Donald C. Daniel.

33. Collins, *Military Balance*, p. 355.

34. *New York Times*, 28 September 1979.

35. Blechman, *Far Eastern Navies*, pp. 43–45.

36. Ibid., pp. 16–17.

37. Ibid., p. 9.

38. Ibid., p. 52.

39. John M. Collins, "The Military Balance Between Superpowers in the Far East: A Study in Constraints," *Asian Perspective*, 2, no. 2 (Fall 1978): p. 160.

40. *New York Times*, 20 January 1980.

41. Blechman, *Far Eastern Navies*, pp. 15–16.

42. Ibid., p. 62.

43. Defense Agency, *Defense of Japan, 1977 (White Paper)*, pp. 24–25.

44. David Walder, *The Short Victorious War* (New York: Harper and Row, 1973), p. 80.

45. Alvin D. Coox, *The Anatomy of a Small War: The Soviet-Japanese Struggle for Changkufeng-Khasan, 1938* (Westport, Connecticut: Greenwood Press, 1977), p. 285; Hata Ikuhiko, "The Japanese-Soviet Confrontation, 1935–1939" in James W. Morley, ed., *Deterrent Diplomacy: Japan, Germany, and the USSR, 1935–40* (New York: Columbia, 1976), pp. 131 ff.

46. Morley, *Deterrent Diplomacy*, p. 131.

47. G. K. Zhukov, *The Memoirs of Marshal Zhukov* (New York: Delacorte, 1971), ch. 7.

48. M. V. Zakharov, ed., *Finale: A Retrospective Review of Imperialist Japan's Defeat in 1945*, translated by David Skvirsky (Moscow: Progress Publishers, 1972), p. 69.

49. Zakharov, *Japan's Defeat*, p. 74.

50. Theodore Shabad and Victor L. Mote, *Gateway to Siberian Resources (The BAM)* (Washington: Scripta, 1977), pp. 74–79.

51. See note 14.

52. Shabad and Mote, *Gateway*, p. 79.

53. Ibid., pp. 74–76.

54. Ibid., p. 74.

55. Ye. V. Pinneker and B. I. Pikarsky, *Podzemnye vody zony Baikalo-Amurskoi Magistrali* [Subsurface waters in the BAM zone] (Novosibirsk: Nauka, 1977). Longitudinal graphs chart the subsoil conditions throughout the BAM zone.

56. Shabad and Mote, *Gateway*, p. 103.

57. Interviews at Permafrost Institute, USSR Academy of Sciences, Yakutsk, October 1978.

58. Victor L. Mote, *Environmental Constraints to the Economic Development of Siberia*, vol. 2, Discussion Paper No. 6 (December 1978), Association of American Geographers, Project on Soviet Natural Resources in the World Economy. This and the following paragraph draw heavily on Mote's excellent synthesis of Soviet and Western literature illuminating the complex interaction of human and natural hazards which confront BAM.

59. See note 62.

60. Interview with Soviet official, 17 September 1978.

61. Mote, *Environmental Constraints*, pp. 64–69; his citations therein were amplified upon in subsequent correspondence.

62. The estimate of BAM's cost as a proportion of total investment was offered by Aganbegyan in an interview, 27 September 1978.

63. Interviews of September-October 1978; the 1981–85 Five-Year Plan projects through traffic by 1985.

64. Gerald L. Curtis, "The Tyumen Oil Development Project and Japanese Foreign Policy Decision-Making," in Robert A. Scalapino, ed., *The Foreign Policy of Japan* (Berkeley: University of California, 1977), pp. 147–73.

65. The cost rose from $1 billion to $3.3 billion and proposed delivery dropped from an estimated 25 to 40 million tons annually down to 25 million tons maximum.

66. In the fall of 1979, press reports claimed that Komatsu, a major engineering firm involved with BAM, was negotiating the first Japanese joint venture project in China; Foreign Broadcast Information Service, (hereafter FBIS), People's Republic of China, 16 October 1979.

67. Alternatively changes in leadership following the death of Mao Zedong and purging of the radical faction dubbed the "Gang of Four" may have led to a change of posture toward Japan.

68. Interviews in July and October 1978, also March 1979.

69. For an eyewitness account of Nakhodka–Vostochny, see Stephen Uhalley, Jr., *The Soviet Far East: Growing Participation in the Pacific* Field Staff Report, vol. 24, no. 1 (New York: American Universities Field Staff, September 1977).

70. For specific examples in the Angolan and Ethiopian campaigns, see Robert F. Ellsworth, "Trends in International Maritime Transport," International Symposium On The Sea (ISS), mimeo, (Tokyo: *Yomiuri Shimbun*, 1978), p. 11.

71. *Izvestiya*, 22 April 1979.

72. V. V. Vorobyev, *Naseleniye Vostochnoi Sibiri* [Population of East Siberia] (Novosibirsk: Nauka, 1977).

73. Interview with Aganbegyan, 28 September 1978.

74. Ibid.

75. Violet Conolly, *Siberia Today and Tomorrow* (New York: Taplinger, 1976), p. 97.

76. Interviews in July and October 1978, also March 1979.

77. Official study, Ministry of Foreign Affairs, Tokyo, June 1978 (mimeo).

78. Richard L. Edmonds, *Siberian Resources Development and the Japanese Economy: The Japanese Perspective*, Discussion Paper No. 12 (August 1979), Association of American Geographers, Project on Soviet Natural Resources in the World Economy, pp. 24–25.

79. See note 78 above. Subsequent reports indicate this may rise to 10 percent.

80. Edmonds, *Japanese Economy*, p. 13.

81. John P. Hardt, Ronda A. Bresnick, and David Levine, "Soviet Oil and Gas in the Global Perspective," *Project Interdependence: U. S. and World Energy Outlook Through 1990; A Report by the Congressional Research Service, Library of Congress* (Washington, 1977), pp. 798–801.

82. *USSR: Long-Term Outlook for Grain Imports* (Washington: Central Intelligence Agency, January 1979), ER79-10057.

83. Akio Watanabe, "Japanese Public Opinion and Foreign Affairs, 1964–1973," in Robert A. Scalapino, *The Foreign Policy of Modern Japan* (Berkeley: University of California, 1977), p. 125.

84. Gupta, Bhabani Sen, *Soviet-Asian Relations in the 1970s and Beyond* (New York: Praeger, 1976), p. 314.

85. Watanabe, "Public Opinion," p. 125.

86. Gupta, *Soviet-Asian Relations*, p. 314.

87. Watanabe, "Public Opinion," p. 116.

88. Ibid., p. 118.

89. Gupta, *Soviet-Asian Relations*, p. 113.

90. Makato Momoi, Professor of the National Defense College, Tokyo and an official of the National Defense Agency, public lecture at Asilomar, California, 5 May 1979.

91. *Yomiuri*, 11 March 1979, in *Daily Summary of the Japanese Press* (hereafter *DSJP*), American Embassy, Tokyo, 15 March 1979.

92. *Asahi*, 30 January 1979, *DSJP*, 2 February 1979.

93. *Asahi*, 8 February 1979, in *DSJP*, 14 February 1979, and *Yomiuri*, 15 February 1979 in *DSJP*, 23 February 1979.

94. *Nihon Keizai*, 5 February 1979, in *DSJP*, 10–13 February 1979.

95. *Mainichi*, 5 February 1979, in *DSJP*, 7 February 1979.

96. *Nihon Keizai*, 5 February 1979, in *DSJP*, 7 February 1979.

97. *New York Times*, 28 September 1979.

98. *Asian Wall Street Journal*, 29 September 1979.

99. *Reuters*, London, 16 October 1979, in FBIS, People's Republic of China, 17 October 1979.

100. Interview of 21 July 1978.

101. Interviews of 20 October 1978.

102. Interview of 7 July 1978.

103. For a succinct, albeit elliptical, summary of his views see Takuya Kubo, "Security in Northeast Asia," in Richard H. Soloman, ed., *Asian Security in the 1980s: Problems and Policies for a Time of Transition* (Santa Monica: Rand Corporation), R-2492-ISA, November 1979, p. 105.

104. Interview of 26 July 1978.

105. Interview of 24 July 1978.

106. Interview of 9 July 1978.

107. Interview of 25 October 1978.

108. M. I. Sladkovsky, *Istoriya torgogo-ekonomicheskikh otnoshenii SSSR s Kitayem, 1917–24* [History of Soviet commercial-economic relations with China, 1917–24] (Moscow: Nauka, 1977), pp. 173–74 gives data for 1947–49.

109. Nikita Khrushchev, *Khrushchev Remembers: The Last Testament*, translated and edited by Strobe Talbott (Boston: Little, Brown, 1974), pp. 249–50.

110. Sergei Klopov, *Amur—reka druzhbi* [Amur—a river of friendship] (Khabarovsk, 1959); also O. B. Borisov and B. T. Koloskov, *Soviet-Chinese Relations, 1945–70*, Vladimir Petrov, ed. (Bloomington: Indiana University, 1975), p. 327.

111. John E. Tilton, *The Future of Nonfuel Minerals* (Washington: Brookings, 1977).

# III

SOVIET ENERGY AND INDUSTRIAL
RAW MATERIALS: POLICY,
PROBLEMS AND POTENTIAL

# 11

# THE SOVIET POTENTIAL IN NATURAL RESOURCES: AN OVERVIEW

THEODORE SHABAD
Soviet Geography

Having examined the regional dimension of Soviet resource development, we will now proceed to discuss the Soviet potential in specific resources and primary industrial products in relation to the world economy. The discussion will draw on, or refer to, subsequent chapters devoted to detailed analysis of particular energy goods and industrial raw materials. But it is also designed in large part to fill in the gaps for commodities that, for various reasons, have not received individual attention in separate chapters.

As will become readily apparent, the treatment of most of the commodities under discussion is hampered by a poor data base and by limited information about the Soviet Union's long-term development plans. When the project was first conceived in the mid-1970s, the Soviet Union was still publishing detailed information on the distribution of production and foreign trade of fossil fuels and some industrial raw materials, notably the ferrous metals, although statistical data on nonferrous and precious metals had traditionally been restricted. Moreover, work was reported under way in Soviet planning agencies on a 15-year plan extending to 1990, and this long-range projection was expected to be published, providing clues to Soviet intentions in resource development. However, Soviet planners evidently found it difficult to project economic goals over such a long period and reluctant to commit themselves to particular targets through publication. As the years passed and the target year 1990 drew closer, the projections ceased to be a "15 year" program and became known simply as a forecast "for the period to 1990." The expectations were that at least some of the truncated projections would be made public in 1980–81 as part of the 11th Five-Year Plan guidelines, which were known officially as the "Basic Directions of Economic and Social Development of the USSR for 1981–85 and the Period to 1990." However, when the draft guidelines were made public in December 1980 and approved in February 1981 at the 26th Party Congress, they were found to contain no specific projections to 1990 beyond some generalized policy directions for the decade

of the 1980s. Moreover, the final version of the 11th Five-Year Plan (1981–85), when approved by the Supreme Soviet USSR in November 1981, dropped all references to the longer-range forecast.

The absence of information on future intentions was aggravated by a sharp reduction in current statistical data that began in the mid-1970s. A useful regional table that had long appeared in Soviet statistical yearbooks breaking down the large RSFSR into three major components—European Russia, Urals and Siberia—was last published with data for 1973. Systematic information for the production of the fossil fuels, pig iron and crude steel by republics was last published for 1976, although some data continued to be published for the two principal industrial republics, the RSFSR and the Ukraine. In 1981, the coal and steel production figures even for these two republics became secret and no longer appeared in current statistical reports. Through an odd bureaucratic twist, the third-ranking coal-producing republic, Kazakhstan, resumed publication of coal output statistics in 1980.

The reduction of data on the regional distribution of key fuels and primary products was matched by restrictions on the publication of foreign trade information. Soviet export and import statistics had been fairly complete except for listings of such highly secret items as gold, diamonds, platinum-group metals and some other metals such as nickel. However, detailed data on physical trade volumes in such energy goods as coal, oil, natural gas, iron and steel products and various metals last appeared in foreign trade yearbooks for 1975 or 1976, with subsequent information limited to value or, as for particular nonferrous metals, eliminated altogether.

In the absence of systematic statistical publication since the mid-1970s, diligent scanning of Soviet newspapers and trade journals continued to turn up fugitive data that could be assembled into more or less cohesive patterns of distribution for the principal fossil fuels and some ores and metals, but the information base became undeniably less complete. The discussion of particular commodities that follows should be judged in that light. Moreover, in the absence of published long-term development goals, the listings of projects with a potential bearing on exports and the world economy do not pretend to be complete. It includes information gathered from scattered Soviet sources on resource sites that are already reported under development or are likely to come into play over the next decade or so.

The following discussion begins with the crucial energy goods, which are present in the USSR in reserves that are undoubtedly of huge magnitude though not necessarily always easy of access and development, and have been by far the most important earners of foreign exchange in trade with the Western industrial countries. The energy section is followed by one on wood and wood products, traditionally one of the largest product groups in Soviet exports. Then the analysis shifts to the potential prospects for metals and metallic ores and nonmetallic minerals, and it concludes with a brief survey of basic chemicals, which are assuming increasing significance in Soviet exports insofar as they are related either to hydrocarbons production, as in the case of petrochemicals, or to other minerals used in the chemical industry.

## Energy

The Soviet Union's potential in the production and export of energy goods has been related in large measure to questions of energy policy, involving mainly the priorities being attached to the development of particular energy sources. Chapter 12, on Soviet energy policy by Leslie Dienes, in effect sets the stage for the subsequent discussion. Coal was king among Soviet energy sources until the 1950s, when the hydrocarbons era began with emphasis initially on oil and later on natural gas. In the early 1950s, coal represented some 65 percent of Soviet fuel production (in heat value) and the hydrocarbons 20 percent. Within a quarter of a century, by 1980, the production of coal, though doubled in tonnage, represented only 25.4 percent of total fuels output because of the rapid rise of the hydrocarbons, with oil accounting for 45.3 percent and gas for 27.1 percent. In effect the relationship between coal and hydrocarbons had been reversed compared with the earlier period. The growing value of oil and gas in the 1970s as well as the prospect of resource limitations in oil prompted reconsideration of the all-out emphasis on hydrocarbons and renewed interest in coal. But the revival of coal was proposed at a time when older producing basins yielding high-ranking coals in the developed western regions of the USSR began to peak and incremental production had to be sought in lower-ranking subbituminous and lignite resources of the more remote eastern regions. Development of new coal resources starting in the middle 1970s was unable to keep up with depletion of older producing areas, and for the first time in Soviet peacetime history, a downward trend in coal production tonnage began in the late 1970s after a peak had been reached in 1978. The decline appeared to be arrested in 1982.

The long-term objective in the USSR is still to shift increasingly to the use of coal as an energy source, certainly for the generation of electric power, but because of the long lead times evidently needed for the revival of coal, the priority over the near term at least has shifted to the development of natural gas, discovered in vast re-

serves astride the Arctic Circle in West Siberia. Natural gas is being called upon to replace or supplement oil in some applications such as power generation and petrochemicals and as an earner of foreign exchange, particularly through deliveries to Western Europe. With oil production leveling off and its future uncertain, the Soviet Union is expected to maintain high-earning oil exports to the maximum extent possible both by seeking interfuel substitution, within the limitations discussed by Leslie Dienes in Chapter 12, and by fostering a program of oil conservation and savings in domestic consumption. The extent of success in carrying out these policies remains to be seen. Much will depend on the Soviet Union's ability to restrict incremental domestic demand for energy, and the problems of estimating such demand are discussed in Chapter 13 by Judith Thornton.

### Coal

Among the fossil fuels, coal appears to have the poorest prospects of making a contribution to the world economy, at least over the next few decades. Although coal is an abundant resource in the Soviet Union—350 years left at current output volumes[1]—the industry began running into development problems in the mid-1970s as mining capacity in older, more accessible locations, mainly underground mines producing a high-quality coal, started to become depleted, and the development of new deposits, mainly strip mines in eastern regions producing lower-quality coals, did not keep up with capacity losses elsewhere.

As a result, total coal production began to slip after having reached a mine output of 724 million metric tons in 1978, and the decline continued through 1981, recovering only in 1982 (Table 1). The deterioration of Soviet coal production was particularly pronounced in underground mines, which yield most of the high-grade steam coals and coking coals suitable for the export market. After having reached a peak of 480 million tons in 1976, underground mine output declined precipitously to 428 million tons by 1981. Judging from the 11th Five-Year Plan (1981–85), Soviet planners hope to arrest the decline in underground mine production, setting a 1985 goal of 460 million tons. But coal production plans have been underfulfilled by wide margins in recent years, and fulfillment of the 1985 goal is problematical, especially in light of current trends. Most of the emphasis has been on developing strip-mine capacity, and the surface deposits, by and large, yield lower-ranking coals not suitable for export.

Most of the decline in underground mine production has resulted from deteriorating performance of the Donets Basin, the leading producer, which dropped in output from 224 million tons in 1976 to some 198 million in 1981. The decline, stemming mainly from the depletion of accessible seams and delays in completing deeper mines, has had serious consequences for the Soviet coal industry. The Donets Basin is well situated in the southern European USSR relative to the principal markets and it has produced virtually all the Soviet anthracite, some 40

TABLE 1
Soviet Coal Production (million metric tons of mine output)

|  | 1975 | 1976 | 1977 | 1978 | 1979 | 1980 | 1981 | 1982 est. | 1985 Plan |
|---|---|---|---|---|---|---|---|---|---|
| USSR total | 701 | 712 | 722 | 724 | 719 | 716 | 704 | 721 | 775 |
| Hard coal | 538 | 548 | 555 | 557 | 554 | 553 | — | — | — |
| Lignite | 164 | 164 | 167 | 167 | 165 | 163 | — | — | — |
| Underground | 476 | 480 | 478 | 470 | 460 | 445 | 428 | — | 460 |
| Strip-mined | 226 | 232 | 244 | 254 | 259 | 271 | 276 | — | 315 |
| Donets Basin | 222 | 224 | 222 | 216 | 210 | 204 | 198 | — | 210 |
| Kuznetsk Basin | 139 | 142 | 145 | 148 | 148 | 144 | — | — | 157 |
| Karaganda Basin | 46 | 47 | 48 | 47 | 47 | 49 | 48 | — | 50 |
| Pechora Basin | 24 | 26 | 27 | 27 | 29 | 28 | 28 | — | 28 |
| Ekibastuz | 46 | 46 | 50 | 56 | 59 | 67 | 68 | — | 84 |
| Kansk-Achinsk | 28 | 29 | 32 | 32 | 34 | 35 | 36 | — | 48 |

SOURCE: *Soviet Geography: Review and Translation,* April issues for various years.

percent of the valuable coking coal, needed by the iron and steel industry, and more than half of the better-grade bituminous steam coals, used by thermal power stations.

Of the three other major basins producing coking coal and good steam coal, the Kuznetsk Basin of southern Siberia has not been expanding its production despite ample resources, and output appears to have leveled off at just under 150 million tons. Because of the decline of the Donets Basin, the Kuznetsk Basin has been meeting an increasing share of the demand in the European USSR for coking coal and steam coal, placing a serious burden on the rail system. The large shipments of Kuzbas coal westward beyond the Urals, now running around 35 million tons or more, have greatly added to the average length of haul of coal, which represents 20 percent of the rail car loadings in the Soviet Union. The average length of coal hauls soared from 695 km in 1975 to 819 km in 1980, or by 18 percent; it had been virtually constant in the preceding five-year period. In the two other basins producing bituminous coals, Karaganda in central Kazakhstan and Pechora in northern European Russia, output has also leveled off, at just under 50 million and under 30 million tons, respectively.

The Soviet Union's emphasis, in seeking to compensate for the decline or stagnation of production in the underground mines of the high-grade bituminous coal basins, has been on strip-mine development of inferior coals in the resource-rich eastern regions of the country. The focus thus far has been on the subbituminous coal of the Ekibastuz Basin of northeast Kazakhstan, which has shown the highest growth rates among the major coal basins, and in 1981 yielded close to 70 million tons. Despite a high ash content, Ekibastuz coal has been delivered to power stations as far west as the Urals, but the shipments have strained the rail system to capacity, and future increments in coal output are to be burned in mineside power stations for long-distance transmission of electricity to western consumers over extra high voltage lines. A similar coal-by-wire approach is to be used for the even lower-ranking lignite of the Kansk-Achinsk Basin of southern Siberia, where production now runs around 35 million tons.

While the development of these low-ranking coals is expected to help resolve the need for more coal-based electricity generation in the Soviet Union for domestic needs, it does not contribute directly to the Soviet export position. The only foreseeable project that is likely to generate high-grade coking and steam coals for export is the South Yakutian Basin at Neryungri, where the excavation of a strip mine has been under way since 1975. Japan is helping to finance the development of the mine, and is to be paid in product, at the rate of 5 million tons of coking coal a year starting in 1983. The Neryungri mine was reached by a railroad in 1978 and has been shipping some 3 million tons of steam coal a year as work continues on excavation to reach the deeper coking coal seam. When the first stage of the project is completed in 1983 or thereafter, Neryungri is to yield 13 million tons of bituminous coal, including 4 million tons of steam coal and 9 million tons of crude coking coal, to be upgraded in a local washery to 5 million tons of concentrate for export to Japan.

In anticipation of growing coal exports to the Pacific Basin, the Soviet Union built a large coal-loading terminal in the 1970s at the new port of Nakhodka-Vostochny, east of Vladivostok. The port, built in part with Japanese aid, began operations in 1973 with a sawtimber loading terminal, and is designed to become ultimately the Soviet Union's largest bulk-handling seaport. The coal terminal, a 380-meter-long pier capable of accommodating 100,000-ton coal carriers, opened in 1978 with a first-stage capacity of 5 million to 6 million tons of coal, but was found to be defective and was out of commission for several months in early 1980 for repairs. Its coal-handling capacity is to be expanded to 10 million tons during the second stage of construction in the 11th Five-Year Plan (1981–85).

Pending the generation of additional coal exports from the South Yakutian Basin to Japan, coal has been playing a minor role as an export commodity group. Coal exports were last reported in physical units in 1976. Starting in 1977, they have been included in a product group called "solid fuels," which is reported in value terms only and also includes coke exports (coke was last listed in physical terms in 1975). The overall share of solid fuels in the total value of exports has been declining since 1975, when it reached a peak of 4.2 percent, to 2.0 percent in 1981. Judging by the physical structure of solid-fuels exports when last reported in the mid-1970s and the trend in export value, the principal customers for Soviet coal are Bulgaria, East Germany and Czechoslovakia among the Comecon countries, and Japan among the capitalist industrial countries. Soviet coke has been going mainly to East Germany, Rumania and Hungary, in Eastern Europe, and to Finland among the capitalist countries (Table 2).

The Soviet Union has also been importing coal from Poland. These shipments, averaging 9.5 million tons (one-fourth of Polish exports) and supplying areas near the western border of the Soviet Union adjoining Poland, ceased to be reported in Soviet trade statistics starting in

TABLE 2
Soviet Exports of Solid Fuels

|  | 1975 | 1976 | 1977 | 1980 | 1981 |
|---|---|---|---|---|---|
| Total export value (million rubles) | 1,006 | 1,021 | 1,046 | 1,101 | 1,149 |
| Percent of Soviet exports | 4.2 | 3.6 | 3.1 | 2.2 | 2.0 |
| Coal exports |  |  |  |  |  |
| Million rubles | 799 | 808 | — | — | — |
| Thousand metric tons | 26,143 | 26,896 | — | — | — |
| Coke exports |  |  |  |  |  |
| Million rubles | 208 | 207 | — | — | — |
| Thousand metric tons | 4,208 | — | — | — | — |
| Bulgaria (total value) | 164 | 167 | 172 | 222 | 289 |
| Coal—Million rubles | 153 | 155 | — | — | — |
| Thousand tons | 6,006 | 6,083 | — | — | — |
| Coke—Million rubles | 12 | 12 | — | — | — |
| Thousand tons | 282 | — | — | — | — |
| East Germany (total value) | 175 | 176 | 177 | 156 | 165 |
| Coal—Million rubles | 123 | 124 | — | — | — |
| Thousand tons | 3,964 | 3,837 | — | — | — |
| Coke—Million rubles | 52 | 52 | — | — | — |
| Thousand tons | 1,076 | — | — | — | — |
| Czechoslovakia (total value) | 82 | 81 | 86 | 90 | 119 |
| Coal—Million rubles | 79 | 80 | — | — | — |
| Thousand tons | 2,820 | 2,892 | — | — | — |
| Coke—Million rubles | 3 | 1 | — | — | — |
| Thousand tons | 67 | — | — | — | — |
| Rumania (total value) | 66 | 68 | 84 | 77 | 76 |
| Coal—Million rubles | 22 | 22 | — | — | — |
| Thousand tons | 635 | 664 | — | — | — |
| Coke—Million rubles | 44 | 45 | — | — | — |
| Thousand tons | 999 | — | — | — | — |
| Hungary (total value) | 46 | 46 | 55 | 57 | 66 |
| Coal—Million rubles | 12 | 12 | — | — | — |
| Thousand tons | 382 | 368 | — | — | — |
| Coke—Million rubles | 33 | 35 | — | — | — |
| Thousand tons | 741 | — | — | — | — |
| Yugoslavia (total value) | 54 | 66 | 61 | 71 | 86 |
| Coal—Million rubles | 54 | 66 | — | — | — |
| Thousand tons | 1,441 | 1,873 | — | — | — |
| Finland (total value) | 54 | 56 | 61 | 93 | 112 |
| Coal—Million rubles | 12 | 12 | — | — | — |
| Thousand tons | 486 | 528 | — | — | — |
| Coke—Million rubles | 42 | 43 | — | — | — |
| Thousand tons | 608 | — | — | — | — |
| Japan (total value) | 109 | 112 | 105 | 70 | 57 |
| Coal—Million rubles | 109 | 112 | — | — | — |
| Thousand tons | 3,303 | 3,224 | — | — | — |
| Italy (total value) | 50 | 45 | 40 | 41 | 6 |
| Coal—Million rubles | 50 | 45 | — | — | — |
| Thousand tons | 1,230 | 1,260 | — | — | — |
| France (total value) | 50 | 43 | 31 | 37 | 31 |
| Coal—Million rubles | 50 | 43 | — | — | — |
| Thousand tons | 1,719 | 1,554 | — | — | — |

SOURCE: *Vneshnyaya torgovlya SSSR* [Foreign trade of the USSR], statistical yearbook, various years.

1977. The Polish economic crisis and the slump in Silesian coal production have also affected these shipments to the Soviet Union. They were reported down to 6.2 million tons in 1980 (or two-thirds of the normal volume), and an even lower delivery target of 5.5 million tons in 1981 was not being met.[2]

In light of the tightness of Soviet domestic coal supplies and the trend toward greater production of lower-ranking, strip-mined coals for mine-side electric power generation and coal-by-wire transmission, it is unlikely that Soviet exports of coal will increase significantly over the near term, with the exception of the South Yakutian development for export to Japan starting around 1983. The flow of Neryungri coking coal from the Yakutian basin, at the rate of 5 million tons a year, would make Japan one of the principal markets for Soviet coking coal. In 1975–76, Japan imported 12 to 13 percent of Soviet coal exports, making it the largest user after Bulgaria and East Germany. Soviet trade statistics indicate a decline in coal exports to Japan in 1980–81 (to one-half the 1975–76 level by value) (Table 2), but this trend is expected to be reversed once the deliveries of Yakutian coal begin.

## Oil

Crude oil and refined products have traditionally been a major export of the Soviet Union, but the rise in world prices beginning in 1973–74 has propelled this product group to the largest Soviet export by far. In 1972, before the start of the upward movement in prices, crude oil and refined products accounted for 13 percent of Soviet exports by value (with crude oil representing two-thirds and refined products one-third). By 1976, the last year for which the two categories were distinguished in total Soviet trade data, they accounted for 27.4 percent of exports (in the same 2-to-1 ratio). And in 1981, crude oil and refined products represented 37.8 percent of Soviet exports by value, and 56 percent of Soviet exports to hard-currency countries (see also Table 1 in Chapter 27).

Soviet oil export volumes in relation to domestic production have been obscured since 1976, the last year for which Soviet trade statistics reported tonnage of oil exports by countries (these were combined tonnages for crude and refined products; separate tonnages for crude and refined products by countries were last reported in 1967). However, it has been possible to reconstruct tonnage data for Soviet oil export volumes on the basis of partner country data.[3] These reconstructions suggest that the Soviet Union, the world's largest oil producer since 1974, has been exporting over one-quarter of its oil output through the 1970s, a period of rapid growth of production as the vast West Siberian fields were coming on line (Table 3).

However, 1980 marked a turning point from the period of high rates of increase of oil output to a period of stagnation or even gradual decline. Older fields in the Soviet Union, especially the Volga-Urals region, have started a downward trend as reserves approach depletion, and the oil industry has been hard pressed to compensate for the decline in older fields by developing new fields in remote and environmentally hostile regions like West Siberia. The basic problems that the Soviet Union faces over the long term in bringing technology to bear on the geological potential in oil resources are discussed by A. A. Meyerhoff in Chapter 14.

The rapid development of oil production in the 1970s was made possible by high rates of growth in West Siberia, where the exploitation of the single giant field of Samotlor near Nizhnevartovsk yielded annual increments that not only compensated for declines in older fields but insured steady increases of overall oil output in the Soviet Union. By 1980, however, Samotlor had reached its designed production level of 150 million tons a year (one-half of West Siberian production). Further production increases were beginning to be slowed by the need for opening up a large number of smaller fields scattered through the roadless, swampy forest terrain that makes West Siberian oil development so difficult.

TABLE 3
Soviet Exports of Crude Oil and Refined Products

|  | 1976 | 1977 | 1978 | 1979 | 1980 | 1981 | 1985 Plan |
|---|---|---|---|---|---|---|---|
| Total crude and refined exports (million metric tons) | 149 | 157 | 165 | 164 | (161) | — | (145) |
| Percent of USSR crude output | 29 | 29 | 29 | 28 | (27) | — | (23) |
| Crude oil (million metric tons) | 111 | — | — | — | 119 | — | 97 |
| Refined products (million metric tons) | 38 | — | — | — | (42) | — | (48) |
| Total crude and refined exports (billion rubles) | 7.7 | 9.4 | 10.1 | 14.5 | 18.1 | 21.6 | — |
| Percent of USSR exports by value | 27 | 28 | 28 | 34 | 36 | 38 | — |
| Crude oil (billion rubles) | 5.1 | — | — | — | — | — | — |
| Refined products (billion rubles) | 2.6 | — | — | — | — | — | — |
| Eastern Europe (million tons)[a] | 69 | 71 | 75 | 78 | 80 | — | (80) |
| Western Europe (million tons)[b] | 47 | 54 | 56 | 54 | (51) | — | (40) |
| Others (million tons) | 33 | 32 | 34 | 32 | (30) | — | (25) |

[a]Eastern Europe excluding Yugoslavia.
[b]Western Europe including Finland.
SOURCES: Export tonnage for 1976 from *Vneshnyaya torgovlya SSSR v 1976 g.* [Foreign trade of the USSR in 1976], statistical yearbook. Other years from C.I.A., *International Energy Statistical Review* (ER IESR 81–008) 25 August 1981. Value figures from *Vneshnyaya torgovlya SSSR*, various years. 1980 and 1985 planned tonnages are author's estimates, except total crude oil exports, which are taken from Table 5.

This slowdown in West Siberian development comes at a time when the depletion of older producing fields is accelerating.

Soviet planners have shown awareness of the problem by envisaging less than a 1 percent increase of oil production a year during the 11th Five-Year Plan (1981–85); during the preceding five-year period, oil production in the USSR rose by an average of 4.2 percent annually, from 491 million tons in 1975 to 603 million in 1980. The projected output goal for 1985 is 630 million tons (Table 4).

The Russians' ability to maintain oil production levels above 600 million tons a year will hinge on their success in being able to retard the downward trend in the declining producing areas. In the previous five-year plan (1976–80), Soviet planners were apparently able to project the trend with remarkable accuracy in the Volga-Urals, where the small Udmurt Autonomous Republic has been the only area with rising production. Actual Volga-Urals output seems to have been within a million tons or so of the five-year projection (Table 4). But other areas approaching depletion declined more rapidly than predicted, accounting to a large extent for the failure to reach the projected 1980 output goal of 640 million tons.

In the present five-year plan, the planners project an output increase of nearly 100 million metric tons in four expanding production areas: West Siberia, which alone accounts for three-fourths of the projected increment; Komi ASSR in northern European Russia, where the development of the Usinsk field has spurred some growth; Kazakhstan, where the development of the Buzachi Peninsula on the Caspian Sea has reversed a downward trend; and the Udmurt ASSR. The projected reduction in the declining areas is about 70 million tons. The challenge for the Soviet oil industry in the first half of the 1980s will be to adhere as closely as possible to the planned depletion of these older producing areas and, in any event, to keep the loss of output in those areas from exceeding the increment, planned at nearly 100 million tons, in the expanding producing districts.

The key to success will be the ability of the industry to develop the many small- to medium-size fields in West Siberia fast enough to compensate for the expected declines in older fields. The rate of development rather than the availability of reserves appears to be the crucial factor. Although Soviet oil reserves are not being published, a speech by Leonid I. Brezhnev in late 1981 suggested that West Siberian oil reserves were adequate for projected development. Speaking at a meeting of the Communist Party's Central Committee in November 1981, he disclosed that Soviet planners had reviewed oil and gas reserve data for West Siberia and that they showed "once again that nature did not do us out of our fair share."

"The resources at the nation's disposal," Brezhnev said in the context of West Siberian oil and gas potential, "allow us to face the future with confidence."[4]

The maintenance of Soviet oil production at the highest possible level would appear to be crucial because of the importance of oil in exports, and particularly in hard-currency earnings, enabling the Soviet Union to purchase badly needed grain as well as advanced technology from the West. Much will also depend on the Soviet Union's ability to constrain domestic consumption through various conservation measures and interfuel substitution, issues with which Leslie Dienes deals in detail in Chapter 12. A projection of the Soviet oil production and oil-use budget based on published figures for the 11th Five-Year Plan (1981–85) suggests that Soviet planners hope to keep the rise in domestic consumption of refined products to some 10 percent over the five-year period (Table 5). This may well seem like an unrealistic goal if one considers that domestic consumption rose by 20 percent over the previous five-year period 1976–80.

Even with such a stringent constraint on domestic consumption increments, Soviet planners project a decline in overall exports of crude oil and refined products by 1985, with a drop of some 20 percent in crude oil exports being compensated in part by continued growth of refined products exports. The projected decline in crude oil exports derives mainly from the fact that the rate of expansion of refinery capacity—some 10 percent over the period 1981–85 (Table 5)—will be considerably higher than the projected 4 percent increase in crude oil production. A number of new refineries that were not completed as planned during the 1970s are scheduled to come on stream in the period of the new five-year plan; they are

TABLE 4
Soviet Oil Production (million metric tons)

|  | 1975 | 1980 Plan* | 1980 Actual | 1981 | 1982 est. | 1985 Plan |
|---|---|---|---|---|---|---|
| USSR | 491 | 640 | 603 | 609 | (613) | 630 |
| Expanding producing areas | 187 | 375 | 360 | 383 | — | 457 |
| West Siberia | 148 | 315 | 313 | 334 | (354) | 395 |
| Komi ASSR | 11 | 25 | 20 | 21 | — | 25 |
| Kazakhstan | 24 | 27 | 19 | 19 | — | 25 |
| Udmurt ASSR (Volga-Urals) | 3.7 | 8 | 8 | 9 | — | 12 |
| Declining producing areas | 304 | 265 | 243 | 226 | — | 173 |
| Volga-Urals (exc. Udmurt) | 222 | 184 | 183 | 167 | — | 123 |
| Others | 82 | 81 | 60 | 59 | — | 50 |

*Original five-year plan goal for 1980.
Source: *Soviet Geography: Review and Translation*, April issues for various years.

TABLE 5
Estimate of Soviet Oil Budget[a] (million metric tons)

|  | 1965 | 1970 | 1975 | 1980 | 1985 Plan |
|---|---|---|---|---|---|
| 1. Crude oil production | 243 | 353 | 491 | 603 | 630 |
| 2. Net crude oil exports | 43 | 63 | 87 | 119 | 97 |
| 3. Apparent refinery throughput | 200 | 290 | 404 | 484 | 533 |
| 4. Net products exports | 19 | 28 | 36 | (42) | (48) |
| 5. Apparent domestic consumption | 181 | 262 | 368 | (442) | (485) |
| 6. Total net exports | 62 | 91 | 123 | (161) | (145) |

[a]Field and refinery losses are ignored. Field losses may be running around 3 percent of output (see Robert W. Campbell, *Trends in the Soviet Oil and Gas Industry* (Baltimore: The Johns Hopkins University Press, 1976), p. 44, note under Table 14). Refinery losses were officially given as 1.51 percent in 1975 and 1.25 percent in 1980, with a further reduction to 1.1 percent of refinery throughput planned for 1985 (*Ekonomicheskaya gazeta*, 1981, no. 46, p. 2).
Sources: 1965, 1970, 1975—Leslie Dienes and Theodore Shabad, *The Soviet Energy System* (New York: John Wiley, 1979), p. 66, Table 16. 1980 and 1985 Plan—Crude oil production from *Soviet Geography: Review and Translation*, 23, no. 4 (April 1982); apparent refinery throughput from official index series in *Ekonomicheskaya gazeta*, 1981, no. 46, p. 1 (1970 = 100; 1975 = 139; 1980 = 167; 1985 Plan = 184); net crude oil export by subtraction; net products export estimated; apparent domestic consumption by subtraction; total net exports by addition of crude oil and refined products exports.

Achinsk in southern Siberia, Chimkent in southwest Kazakhstan, and Neftezavodsk in eastern Turkmenia.

The increased refinery capacity, combined with the virtually stagnant level of crude oil production, is expected to reduce the exportable surplus of crude oil by some 20 million tons, from around 120 million in 1980 to around 100 million by 1985. Since the Soviet Union has committed itself to maintaining a stable level of supplies to its East European allies, at least through 1985, the decline of crude oil exports is expected to affect mainly the West European market. Western Europe had been taking 20 to 25 million tons of crude oil in the second half of the 1970s (not counting Finland, which is not a hard-currency paying country). Over the longer term, it may well be that the Soviet Union will reduce its exports to Eastern Europe in an effort to maintain adequate amounts of crude oil exports to Western Europe. Soviet exports of refined oil products, in contrast to crude oil, have been marketed mainly in Western Europe, which has been taking more than half of the products exports in the 1970s. The expansion of domestic refinery capacity in the Soviet Union is likely to continue to generate products exports at least at the 1980 level, provided domestic consumption increases can be kept within bounds. These higher-priced products exports are expected to compensate to some extent for a decline in crude oil exports to Western Europe, where West Germany, France, Italy, the Netherlands and Belgium have been the principal buyers. Finally, any decline in hard-currency earnings from oil exports may also be balanced to some extent by increases in natural gas exports as shall be seen below.

Natural Gas

In contrast to coal and oil, natural gas has been a late starter among Soviet exports of fossil fuels, but it offers the best prospects for growth over the long term. These prospects and the potential role of Soviet gas in the world economy are discussed in detail by Jonathan P. Stern in Chapter 15. Unlike oil reserves, which are a state secret in the Soviet Union, gas reserves are being made public, and as of the end of 1980, they were 34 trillion cubic meters in the explored reserve categories ($A + B + C_1$), including 27 trillion in West Siberia alone. Virtually all the increments

in Soviet reserves have been recorded in West Siberia over the last decade, as explored reserves in the region rose from 9 trillion cubic meters in 1970 to 17 trillion in 1975 and 27 trillion in 1980.[5] While West Siberia's oil reserves are scattered among a large number of small- and medium-size fields, the region's gas reserves are concentrated in five supergiant fields with reserves in the trillions of cubic meters each; the largest of these fields, Urengoi, contains 7.4 trillion. The principal constraints on development of these fields are their far northern location—they are astride the Arctic Circle, several hundred miles north of the oil fields—and the need for laying large-diameter pipeline systems over thousands of miles to deliver the gas to markets in the European USSR and in Eastern and Western Europe. The implications of the remote location of the Soviet Union's vast gas resources, which have caused the mean distance of pipeline transmission to be tripled over the last 20 years (from 366 miles in 1960 to 1,150 miles in 1980), are discussed by Leslie Dienes in Chapter 16.

During the 11th Five-Year Plan (1981–85), natural gas continues to receive priority in development, at least as an interim measure, as the production of oil is leveling off and the Soviet Union's vast, but low-grade coal reserves are being gradually opened up as a major future energy source, especially in electric power generation. Despite the remote location of Soviet gas and the tremendous investment required in pipeline construction, the development of gas reserves is facilitated by their concentration in supergiant fields. In the current five-year plan, for example, the single Urengoi field is planned to account for virtually the entire incremental increase of some 200 billion cubic meters of gas (Table 6). After having been tentatively set within the range of 600 billion to 640 billion cubic meters early in 1981, the five-year plan goal for 1985 was fixed at 630 billion in the final version of the five-year plan, a projected increase of 195 billion cubic meters over the 1980 level.

Except for a small increase in the Central Asian republic of Turkmenia, the entire increment is to be achieved through the development of the Urengoi field, where production is planned to rise fivefold over the 1980 level of 50 billion cubic meters. This emphasis on a single field appears to have been adopted early in 1981. Until that

TABLE 6
Soviet Production of Natural Gas (billion cubic meters)

| | 1970 | 1975 | 1980 | 1981 | 1982 est. | 1985 Plan |
|---|---|---|---|---|---|---|
| USSR | 198 | 289 | 435 | 465 | (500) | 630 |
| West Siberia | 9.3 | 36 | 156 | 190 | (230) | 360 |
| Urengoi | — | — | 50 | 81 | — | 250 |
| Medvezhye | — | 30 | 71 | 71 | — | 71 |
| Vyngapur | — | — | 16 | 16 | — | 16 |
| Oilfield gas | 0.1 | 2.2 | 12 | 14 | — | 20 |
| Orenburg | — | 20 | 48 | 49 | — | 48 |
| Central Asia | 46 | 90 | 110 | 109 | — | 120 |
| Turkmenia | 13 | 52 | 70 | 70 | — | 82 |
| Uzbekistan | 32 | 37 | 39 | 39 | — | 37 |
| Others | 143 | 143 | 121 | 116 | — | 102 |

SOURCE: *Soviet Geography: Review and Translation*, 23, no. 4 (April 1982).

time, Soviet planners proposed to proceed simultaneously with the further development of Urengoi and with opening up a new gas field, Yamburg, on the Taz Peninsula, some 250 km north of Urengoi. The Yamburg field was earmarked as the point of origin of a new gas-export pipeline to Western Europe, and the new pipe-for-gas project being negotiated with the West Europeans was generally referrd to as the Yamburg project (some sources used the name Yamal, for the Yamal Peninsula, which was actually not involved).

However, in August 1981, it was disclosed that the development of the Yamburg field would be delayed, and that the entire effort during the new five-year plan would be focused on Urengoi, which would also supply the projected additional gas exports.[6] The Soviet decision to concentrate its development effort exclusively on Urengoi was evidently based on a desire to focus scarce construction resources on a single objective instead of scattering them among two huge fields under the harsh environmental conditions of the Arctic tundra. Another consideration was undoubtedly the magnitude of the explored reserves at Urengoi. Since its discovery in 1966, reserves have been continuously upgraded as a result of detailed exploration, and were confirmed in July 1979 at 7.4 trillion cubic meters, including 6.2 trillion in the readily accessible Cenomanian stage (Upper Cretaceous) at 4,000 feet and 1.2 trillion in the deeper Valanginian (Lower Cretaceous) stage with a high content of natural gas liquids. Development drilling at Urengoi began in 1974, and the field yielded its first gas in 1978. After having reached a production level of 50 billion cubic meters in 1980, it became the Soviet Union's largest gas producer in 1981, having passed the output level of the Medvezhye field, West Siberia's first supergiant, some 130 km west of the Urengoi field. The development of the Urengoi field has given rise to the gas workers town of Novy Urengoi. It was reached in 1982 by a railroad from Surgut; the rail line, under construction since 1976, had reached Tikhaya Station, the site of the projected new town of Tikhy near the old trading post of Urengoi, in late 1980. Work was also under way on a 500 kv power

transmission line from the Surgut electric station to improve the power supply in the isolated gas-development area astride the Arctic Circle.

After the development of the Urengoi field is completed and it reaches its designed capacity of some 250 billion cubic meters of gas a year around 1985, the Soviet gas development strategy calls for exploitation of the Yamburg field, to the north of Urengoi, on the Taz Peninsula. Yamburg appears to have the second largest reserves among the West Siberian supergiants, with 3.4 trillion cubic meters (explored $B + C_1$ reserves) in the more accessible dry gas-bearing Cenomanian strata at depths of 3,400 to 3,900 feet, and 0.7 trillion cubic meters $(C_1)$ in the deeper Neocomian gas condensate horizons at 8,200 to 10,000 feet.[7] Other supergiants are not likely to be developed before the 1990s. They include the Zapolyarnoye field, east of Urengoi, with some 1.9 trillion cubic meters $(B + C_1)$ in the higher Cenomanian gas-bearing strata and 0.6 trillion $(C_1)$ in the lower gas condensate reservoirs. Finally, there are the two huge fields on the Yamal Peninsula—the supergiant Bovanenko field, with 2.2 trillion cubic meters $(C_1)$, and the Kharasavei field, which is also expected to achieve supergiant status (over 1 trillion cubic meters) with 0.86 trillion cubic meters $(B + C_1)$ identified by the beginning of 1980.[8]

Aside from the difficulties of developing these huge gas fields under the harsh conditions of an Arctic tundra environment, the crucial problem will be to install the thousands of miles of large-diameter pipelines that would transmit the gas to markets in the European USSR and in Eastern and Western Europe. There appear to be physical transport limitations to the amount of pipe that can be delivered and laid in the remote West Siberian region; in the 9th Five-Year Plan (1971–75), some 19,400 miles of gas pipelines were installed, expanding the transmission system in the USSR to 61,400 miles, and in the 10th Five-Year Plan (1976–80), 20,600 miles were installed, bringing the system up to 82,000 miles. In the present five-year plan, there has been some evidence of high-level disagreement on the potential pipeline construction program. The original directives, approved in early 1981, envisaged the highly ambitious target of 30,000 miles of new pipeline, which would bring the length of the gas transmission network to some 112,000 miles by 1985. After reassessment of the pipeline program in the course of 1981, the five-year plan construction goal was revised down to 24,000 miles, or a 1985 system of 106,000 miles.[9] Soviet planners hope to speed deliveries to West Siberia by shipping some of the pipe by sea directly from a West German loading terminal in Hamburg. The new route, tested in 1979 and 1980, calls for delivery of the pipe by freighter to the Ob River Gulf off Novy Port and transshipment to barges that take the pipe up West Siberian rivers to heads of navigation for second transshipment to overland trailer trucks. The traditional route by rail and river from the south will also continue to be used.

Close to half of the pipeline construction envisaged in the five-year plan 1981–85 involves six large-diameter (56-inch) transmission mains from Urengoi, including the

2,800-mile export pipeline to Uzhgorod on the Czechoslovak border. These six pipelines would supplement four out of Urengoi already in place in 1980 and are to help accommodate the projected Urengoi output of 250 billion cubic meters by the mid-1980s at the rate of 30 billion cubic meters or more per 56-inch line using pressures of 75 atmospheres.

Gas pipelines out of West Siberia have been following three basic corridors across the Urals: (a) a northern route through Ukhta, Gryazovets and Torzhok; (b) a central route through the Perm area; and (c) a southern route through Surgut and Chelyabinsk. Along the northern corridor, the so-called Northern Lights route, a fourth string being installed in 1980–81 raised the transmission capacity to 90 billion cubic meters a year. Most of the new pipeline construction contemplated for the first half of the 1980s is to follow the central corridor, where improved transport access in the settled regions west of the Urals is expected to speed construction. The central corridor will accommodate two transmission mains to Yelets, a pipeline hub in central Russia; one each to Petrovsk, near Saratov, and Novopskov, in the eastern Ukraine, and the export pipeline to Uzhgorod. The new pipelines are to raise the throughput of gas along the central route from 39 billion cubic meters in 1980 to 118 billion in 1985.[10] No further expansion is contemplated for the time being on the southern route, through Surgut, Tyumen and Chelyabinsk, where a two-string transmission system, installed in 1978–80, handles about 60 billion cubic meters of Urengoi gas.

The huge capital cost of these pipelines—each line costs 2.5 billion to 3 billion rubles and requires 2.5 million tons of high-quality steel pipe—will call for more efficient transmission technology in the late 1980s and in the 1990s as West Siberian gas output rises to some 550 to 600 billion cubic meters by 1990.[11] The proposed improvements, as discussed in greater detail by Leslie Dienes in Chapter 16, include higher pressures, up to 100 and 120 atmospheres, and the chilling of gas to enhance the transmission capacity of pipelines. The Russians are planning to use a new generation of multilayer steel pipe to withstand the proposed higher pressures. The first stage of a mill producing the new pipe was completed at Vyksa, near Gorky, in late 1981; its initial capacity is 250,000 tons, rising ultimately to 1 million tons. According to Soviet calculations, a 56-inch pipeline transmitting chilled gas at pressures of 120 atmospheres will be able to carry two to three times as much gas as the present 56-inch lines operating at 75 atmospheres with nonchilled gas.[12]

The focus on West Siberian gas development has overshadowed three significant natural gas prospects elsewhere in the Soviet Union, involving supergiant fields discovered in the late 1970s and slated for development in coming years. The Karachaganak field, on the northern edge of the North Caspian hydrocarbon basin, just south of the town of Ilek, is envisaged as a reserve field for the Orenburg gas-processing complex. The Astrakhan field, on the southwest margin of the North Caspian basin, is planned to give rise to a separate gas-processing complex, similar to Orenburg in yielding gas condensate and

byproduct sulfur.[13] And in Central Asia, the discovery of the Sovetabad field (initially called Dauletabad-Donmez) near the Iranian and Afghan borders is expected to preserve the position of Turkmenia through the 1980s as the second most important gas-producing region of the USSR, after West Siberia.[14]

The emphasis on the overland pipeline transmission of Urengoi gas also appears to have overtaken two export-oriented liquefied natural gas projects that were much in the news in the 1970s. One was an LNG project for the East Coast of the United States and possibly for Western Europe, initially proposed by an American consortium headed by Tenneco Inc. and to be based on Urengoi reserves. The other involved the development of natural gas reserves yet to be proved in Yakutia and was of interest both to an American consortium headed by El Paso Company, for use on the West Coast of the United States, and a Japanese consortium headed by Tokyo Gas. The Urengoi-based LNG project appears to have been shelved by the Soviet Union in view of its own development of Urengoi reserves and the adoption of a strategy of building up a system of large-diameter pipelines for the overland transmission of gas to Western Europe. The Yakutia LNG project, after an initial protocol of intent was signed in 1973, led in late 1974 to an agreement on exploration, which required the proving of 1 trillion cubic meters to support 20 billion cubic meters of exports a year over a 25-year period. This resource base was reported to have been virtually confirmed by the end of the 1970s, with the reserves divided between the Vilyui Basin of central Yakutia and the Middle Botuobuya field to the southwest. However, United States interest in importing LNG from the Soviet Union appears to have waned, and Japan seems reluctant to proceed with a project of such magnitude without American participation.

As a result, attention on the future of Soviet gas exports is now focused squarely on West Siberian resources and their impact on Europe. As Jonathan P. Stern discusses in detail in Chapter 15, Soviet natural gas potential is expected to play an increasingly important role in supplies to Western Europe in the 1980s and 1990s. The new export pipeline from Urengoi, with a designed capacity close to 40 billion cubic meters,[15] would raise gas deliveries to Western Europe from some 25 billion cubic meters in 1980 to 65 billion in the middle to late 1980s. Further expansion is likely as West Siberian development proceeds and additional West European export projects are negotiated. The largest West European user of Soviet natural gas is West Germany, whose imports would double from some 11 billion cubic meters in 1980 to 22 billion, followed by Italy and France. It is estimated that these three countries may derive one-third to one-half of their gas imports from Soviet sources by the 1990s.[16]

Although Soviet hard-currency income from natural gas imports is still far below income from the export of crude oil and refined products, gas sales to the principal West European countries have accounted for a growing share of earnings from hydrocarbon exports, and the trend is likely to continue in the 1980s as gas exports increase and exports of crude oil, in particular, decline

TABLE 7
Soviet Hydrocarbon Exports to Selected West European Countries (million rubles)

| | 1975 | 1976 | 1977 | 1978 | 1979 | 1980 | 1981 |
|---|---|---|---|---|---|---|---|
| West Germany | 531 | 667 | 829 | 961 | 1,533 | 2,333 | 2,896 |
| Oil | 475 | 577 | 683 | 641 | 1,147 | 1,604 | 1,707 |
| Gas | 55 | 90 | 147 | 320 | 386 | 728 | 1,189 |
| Italy | 431 | 836 | 842 | 904 | 1,000 | 1,721 | 2,193 |
| Oil | 392 | 783 | 744 | 736 | 742 | 1,209 | 1,390 |
| Gas | 38 | 52 | 97 | 169 | 258 | 512 | 803 |
| France | 200 | 406 | 458 | 521 | 1,069 | 1,855 | 2,084 |
| Oil | 193 | 372 | 391 | 428 | 959 | 1,557 | 1,612 |
| Gas[a] | 7 | 33 | 67 | 93 | 110 | 298 | 472 |
| Austria | 135 | 193 | 254 | 277 | 338 | 455 | 745 |
| Oil | 78 | 99 | 148 | 130 | 176 | 239 | 364 |
| Gas | 57 | 93 | 106 | 147 | 162 | 216 | 381 |
| Total (four countries) | 1,297 | 2,102 | 2,383 | 2,663 | 3,940 | 6,364 | 7,918 |
| Oil | 1,138 | 1,832 | 1,966 | 1,934 | 3,023 | 4,609 | 5,073 |
| Gas | 158 | 269 | 416 | 729 | 916 | 1,755 | 2,845 |

[a]French imports include some liquefied gas, averaging 8 million rubles a year.
SOURCE: *Vneshnyaya torgovlya SSSR*, statistical yearbooks, various years.

(Table 7). The table shows the rapid increase in the value of natural gas exports to the four hard-currency paying gas customers in Western Europe—West Germany, Italy, France and Austria—after 1975, with the share of gas in total earnings from hydrocarbon sales to these four countries rising from 12 percent in 1975 to 36 percent in 1981. In Austria, the smallest of the four countries, natural gas has represented close to one-half of the Soviet sales of hydrocarbons. In West Germany, the principal customer, the share of gas rose from 10 percent in 1975 to 41 percent in 1981.

Electric Power

Aside from furnishing fossil fuels, the Soviet Union has been developing a potential for delivering electric power abroad. The member countries of the Soviet bloc's economic alliance, the Council for Mutual Economic Assistance (CMEA), were quick to realize the benefits that can be derived from interconnections among national power systems, and electricity was the first sector of the bloc economies in which cooperation was developed. Interties between the Soviet Union and its East European allies were particularly useful because of a two-hour time difference at the western border of the Soviet Union. Aside from the usual benefits of system interconnections, such as enhanced reliability, the diversity in the occurrence of peak loads made it possible to supply additional electricity as needed and to effect savings in standby capacity. A coordinated Soviet bloc system of electric power interconnections, known as the Mir (Peace) electricity grid, has been in existence since 1962, when the Lvov power system of the western Ukraine began delivering electricity to Czechoslovakia, Hungary and Rumania. In 1972 a direct intertie was completed between Soviet Moldavia and Bulgaria. However limitations in transmission capacity of the interties (up to 400 kilovolts) kept net Soviet electricity deliveries to a maximum of 12 billion kilowatt-hours a year through 1978.

A new stage in Soviet power exports began in 1979 with the completion of the first of a proposed system of 750 kv interties to be based on a series of large nuclear steam-electric stations that will supply a substantial portion of their output to the East European countries. The first 750 kv interconnection, between Vinnitsa in the Ukraine and Albertirsa in Hungary, had the effect of virtually doubling deliveries to Hungary, the largest importer, from over 4 billion KWH in 1978 to 7.5 billion in 1980 (Table 8). The Ukraine's first nuclear power station, the Chernobyl plant at Pripyat, was connected to the Hungarian intertie in 1980. The Chernobyl station, where the third 1,000 MW reactor went on line in late 1981 (the first two started up in 1977 and 1978), was originally projected for a capacity of 4,000 MW. However, further expansion is now projected for the second half of the 1980s.[17]

Similar 750 kv interties are planned for two other 4,000 MW nuclear stations under construction in the Ukraine. The Khmelnitsky station near Slavuta is scheduled to start its first 1,000 MW reactor in 1984 and is to be connected by a 750 kv intertie with the Polish power system at Rzeszow. With electricity deliveries over that line planned to begin in 1985, the Khmelnitsky station will ultimately export 12 billion KWH, or half of its projected power output, with the exported share to be divided among Poland, Czechoslovakia and Hungary.[18] The South Ukrainian station at Konstantinovka (Nikolayev Oblast) is to deliver electricity over a 750 kv line to Rumania under an accord signed in July 1981. The 4,000 MW nuclear station, where the first reactor started up in 1982, is part of a power generating complex that will ultimately include a 400-MW hydroelectric plant and a 1,700 MW pumped storage station, for a total capacity of 6,100 MW.[19]

With the expansion of the Rovno nuclear station at Kuznetsovsk, designed for a capacity of 4,880 MW by 1990, and the construction of the Ignalina station at Snieckus in Lithuania, planned for 6,000 MW, about 25,000 MW of nuclear generating capacity may be arrayed

TABLE 8
Soviet Electricity Exports (billion KWH)

| | 1965 | 1970 | 1973 | 1975 | 1978 | 1979 | 1980 | 1981 |
|---|---|---|---|---|---|---|---|---|
| USSR total | 1.52 | 5.3 | 9.9 | 11.27 | 12.09 | 15.41 | 19.90 | 20.19 |
| Eastern Europe | | | | | | | | |
| Hungary | 1.05 | 2.93 | 4.18 | 4.24 | 4.41 | 6.00 | 7.50 | 8.00 |
| Bulgaria | — | 0.20 | 2.96 | 4.01 | 4.50 | 4.50 | 4.50 | 4.50 |
| Czechoslovakia | 0.19 | 1.23 | 0.99 | 1.12 | 1.24 | 1.60 | 2.20 | 2.20 |
| East Germany[b] | — | — | — | — | — | — | 1.80 | 1.80 |
| Poland | 0.16 | 0.33 | 0.30 | 0.36 | 0.31 | 0.36 | 0.33 | 0.30 |
| Rumania | 0.03 | 0.003 | 0.013 | 0.04 | 0.005 | 0.05 | 0.14 | 0.28 |
| Others | | | | | | | | |
| Finland[a] | 0.05 | 0.40 | 0.45 | (0.5) | (0.5) | (0.7) | 2.33 | 1.73 |
| Norway | — | 0.002 | 0.05 | 0.013 | 0.05 | 0.07 | 0.05 | 0.03 |
| Unallocated[b] | 0.04 | 0.2 | 0.9 | (0.9) | (1.0) | (2.1) | 1.05 | 1.35 |

[a]Electric power exports to Finland were reported only by value in the second half of the 1970s. Physical units were again reported for 1980 after exports tripled over the 1979 level with completion of a higher-capacity transmission line.

[b]The unallocated portion through 1979 includes exports to East Germany, which were reported separately for the first time for 1980. The unallocated portion starting in 1979 also reflects the start of power transmission to Mongolia over a 220 kv line supplying electricity from the Gusinoozersk station in the Buryat ASSR to the Erdenet copper-molybdenum mining center, which began operations at the end of 1978.

SOURCE: *Vneshnyaya torgovlya*, statistical yearbook, various years.

within transmission distance of Eastern Europe by the end of the decade. The 11th Five-Year Plan (1981–85) provided that virtually all new generating capacity in the European part of the USSR, which is short on fossil fuel supplies, be in nuclear electric stations, and the generation of nuclear power in the Soviet Union, virtually all of it in the European part, is planned to rise from 73 billion KWH in 1980 (5.6 percent of all power generation) to 220 billion in 1985 (14 percent of the projected total). If nuclear power generation is taken as part of the European USSR alone (including the Urals), its share is planned to rise from 7.8 percent in 1980 to 20 percent in 1985 (Table 9).

## Wood and Wood Products

Wood and wood products have been traditionally one of the largest product groups exported by the Soviet Union, and are examined in two chapters in the present study. Brenton M. Barr, in Chapter 17, evaluates the ability of the Soviet Union's timber resources to meet demand in domestic and world markets. Contrary to the findings of

TABLE 9
Soviet Electricity Production and the Nuclear Share
(billion KWH)

| | 1975 | 1980 | 1985 Plan |
|---|---|---|---|
| USSR total | 1,039 | 1,295 | 1,555 |
| Asian part | 285 | 355 | 460 |
| Siberia | 185 | 230 | 278 |
| Kazakhstan | 53 | 62 | 98 |
| Central Asia | 47 | 63 | 84 |
| European part | 754 | 940 | 1,095 |
| Nuclear | 20 | 73 | 220 |
| Percent nuclear in USSR total | 1.9 | 5.6 | 14 |
| Percent nuclear in European USSR | 2.7 | 7.8 | 20 |

SOURCE: *Soviet Geography: Review and Translation*, April 1982.

some other analysts of the Soviet forest industries, Barr concludes that the Soviet forest-resource potential is sufficient to satisfy domestic requirements and a large share of foreign demand provided that technological improvements in the comprehensive use of roundwood continue to be made in the USSR. One of the distinctive aspects of the Soviet forest industries has been an emphasis on roundwood production and a lag in the output of processed wood products such as woodpulp, plywood, paper and paperboard, fiberboard and particleboard. Kathleen E. Braden, in Chapter 18, examines the prospect of technological change in the Soviet forest products industry and its potential impact on Soviet exports. Western forest technology has been a traditional input in the Soviet production process, but the author cautions that it cannot be regarded as a panacea for the problems in the Soviet forest industries. Foreign technology, in her view, may help improve the quality of Soviet wood exports and upgrade the product mix of exports, which continue to be heavily weighted toward roundwood and sawnwood. But she concludes that the export potential presented by the Soviet forest resource must be realized mainly through appropriate investment decisions by Soviet planners.

That the forest product industries continue to be a low-priority sector of the Soviet economy despite their evident export potential is suggested by the material on the 11th Five-Year Plan (1981–85) made public in late 1981. Nikolai K. Baibakov, the chief Soviet economic planner, in presenting the new economic program to the Supreme Soviet USSR, disclosed no detailed production goals in the forest industry sector, in contrast to energy goods, chemicals and other priority sectors. He said, without statistical documentation, that the five-year plan called for "the provision of new technology in the forest products industries, improved use of existing capacities and upgrading of the product mix to meet growing demand of the economy and the population."[20] At a session of the Supreme Soviet of the RSFSR, the chief planner,

Nikolai I. Maslennikov, in presenting the five-year plan for the republic, merely said that "further development" is planned in the forest product industries.[21] The RSFSR is by far the most important producer of wood and wood products in the Soviet Union, accounting for 92 percent of the roundwood, 82 percent of the sawnwood, 95 percent of the woodpulp, 84 percent of the paper and 74 percent of the paperboard.

Judging from performance during the 10th Five-Year Plan (1976–80) and the guidelines for the 11th plan period published in late 1980, the emphasis in the forest industries will continue to be more on improving the product mix than on expansion of logging and sawmill activity. In the second half of the 1970s, both of these sectors declined by some 13 to 14 percent from the peak levels achieved in the earlier years of the decade. The outlook is for continuing slow decline of these basic forest operations. Among processed wood products, high growth rates over the five-year period 1981–85 are planned for particleboard (50 percent) and fiberboard (25 percent) as well as woodpulp (25 percent), all of which were the principal growth industries in the forest products sector in the 1970s. The five-year plan guidelines also envisaged production increases of 30 to 40 percent for paperboard and 18 to 20 percent for paper. Both of these industries peaked in 1978 and then declined to 1980, evidently because of underutilized capacity, with gains of only 1 to 2 percent during the 10th Five-Year Plan period.

Despite the long proclaimed desire to improve the product mix in the forest industries, especially for export, the situation showed little improvement during the 1970s. Roundwood, including sawtimber, pulpwood, pitprops and similar items, represented 34 percent of total wood and processed products exports by value in 1970, dipping slightly to 31 percent by 1980. Since most of the roundwood is being exported outside the Soviet trading bloc, it represented an even larger share (35 percent) of forest product exports to the hard-currency countries. Japan alone has been taking 75 percent or more of all the sawtimber and one-sixth to one-fifth of the pulpwood exported by the Soviet Union, mainly as a result of a series of long-term accords. Finland has been the destination of some 35 percent of the Soviet pulpwood exports. The market is more diversified for Soviet sawnwood, with the West taking 45 percent of Soviet exports in 1980. On the other hand, the Soviet bloc has been the principal

market for Soviet exports of paper, half of which is newsprint, and of paperboard.

The importance of roundwood in Soviet exports of forest products becomes even more marked when net trade is considered (Table 10). The table shows that the Soviet Union has been exporting some 5 percent of its roundwood harvest and 7 percent of its sawnwood production, with negligible imports (mainly tropical hardwood logs from West Africa and sawn hardwoods from Rumania). But the Soviet Union has been a major importer of high-grade products such as paper and paperboard, mainly from Finland, and in 1980, imports of paper in fact exceeded exports as receipts from Finland surged by some 60 percent over the 1979 level.

Only in woodpulp does the Soviet Union appear to have gradually improved its export position, mainly because of the favorable production conditions provided by the availability of forest resources, electric power and water in East Siberia. The development of the huge woodpulp mill at Bratsk, which went on stream in 1967, has been reflected in exports. While net exports of major wood products held steady or even declined in the 1970s, net exports of pulp rose by 3.7 times, from 161,000 metric tons in 1970 to 599,000 in 1980. The trend has been particularly striking in exports of sulfate pulp to Western Europe since the Bratsk mill reached its designed capacity of 1 million tons in 1975 (Table 11). Sulfate (or kraft) pulp, the type produced by the new Siberian mills, accounts for a growing percentage of world pulp produced because its process creates fewer pollution problems and yields pulp of greater strength than the other major pulping process, the sulfite method. The surge in Soviet pulp exports that began in the mid-1970s is expected to be sustained in the 1980s by the completion of another large Siberian producer, the Ust-Ilimsk pulp mill, which is situated downstream from Bratsk on the Angara River. The Ust-Ilimsk mill, which started up the first of two 250,000-ton stages in 1980 (the second was added the following year), was built mainly with assistance from the East European countries, which are to be paid back with 40 percent of the mill's output over a period of 12 years. But the mill is also expected to enhance the Soviet Union's export position relative to the hard-currency countries of Western Europe. Over the longer term, Soviet success in exporting wood products would seem to depend on further compensation arrangements aimed at developing Siberian

TABLE 10
Soviet Output and Trade of Selected Forest Products

|  | 1970 | | | 1975 | | | 1980 | | |
|---|---|---|---|---|---|---|---|---|---|
|  | Output | Exports | Imports | Output | Exports | Imports | Output | Exports | Imports |
| Commercial roundwood (million cubic meters) | 299 | 15.3 | 0.09 | 313 | 16.9 | 0.29 | 278 | 13.9 | 0.26 |
| Sawnwood (million cubic meters) | 116 | 8.0 | 0.29 | 116 | 7.8 | 0.32 | 98 | 7.0 | 0.36 |
| Woodpulp (thousand metric tons) | 5,110 | 448 | 287 | 6,815 | 515 | 244 | 7,123 | 820 | 221 |
| Paper (thousand metric tons) | 4,185 | 475 | 417 | 5,215 | 617 | 485 | 5,288 | 647 | 691 |
| Paperboard (thousand metric tons) | 2,516 | 247 | 63 | 3,368 | 308 | 89 | 3,445 | 372 | 214 |
| Plywood (thousand cubic meters) | 2,045 | 281 | 56 | 2,196 | 303 | 47 | 2,022 | 314 | 52 |

SOURCES: Production figures from *Narodnoye khozyaistvo SSSR* [The economy of the USSR], statistical yearbook, various years; trade figures from *Vneshnyaya torgovlya SSSR*, various years.

TABLE 11
Soviet Sulfate Pulp Exports to Western Europe (thousand metric tons)

|  | 1970 | 1975 | 1976 | 1977 | 1978 | 1979 | 1980 | 1981 |
|---|---|---|---|---|---|---|---|---|
| Total USSR exports | 448 | 515 | 632 | 680 | 776 | 681 | 821 | 844 |
| Sulfite pulp | 299 | 239 | 240 | 206 | 202 | 175 | 199 | 168 |
| Sulfate pulp | 149 | 276 | 392 | 474 | 574 | 506 | 622 | 676 |
| Percent to West Europe | 10 | 7 | 18 | 26 | 37 | 31 | 27 | 33 |
| Austria | — | — | — | 8.2 | 26.9 | 17.6 | 26.0 | 32.0 |
| Britain | 2.2 | 2.6 | 5.6 | 9.3 | 11.7 | 6.2 | 5.5 | 16.3 |
| France | 5.5 | 4.5 | 22.9 | 32.2 | 60.6 | 44.4 | 49.3 | 79.9 |
| Italy | — | 8.5 | 20.4 | 16.8 | 27.4 | 24.2 | 33.5 | 31.3 |
| Netherlands | — | — | — | 13.4 | 19.4 | 19.6 | 10.4 | 15.5 |
| West Germany | 7.5 | 4.0 | 21.5 | 44.7 | 64.9 | 43.3 | 41.5 | 49.2 |

Source: *Vneshnyaya torgovlya SSSR*, statistical yearbook, various years.

resources. There have long been discussions between the Soviet Union and foreign companies regarding the development of a new wood products complex at Lesosibirsk, on the Yenisei River. There have also been suggestions that the Baikal-Amur Mainline may open up Far Eastern forest areas for newsprint production for the Pacific market, mainly Japan, provided technological and quality-control problems can be resolved.

## Metals and Metallic Ores

A discussion of the Soviet potential in metallic ores, concentrates and metals is hampered by uneven statistical coverage and the gradual restriction of data since the middle 1970s. The information is most complete for the ores of ferrous metals—iron, manganese and chromium—which have been traditional Soviet exports, but with the possible exception of chromium have been increasingly restricted to the Soviet-bloc market. As the world's leading iron and steel producer, the Soviet Union would seem to have a potential for significant exports of iron and steel products, but the large size of the domestic market and considerations of product quality and assortment have limited the impact of that industry to the countries of the Soviet bloc. The significance of the Soviet trade in iron and steel products, moreover, has been obscured by data limitations; iron and steel exports and imports were last reported in tons in 1976 and, with the exception of scrap exports, have since then been stated only in value terms. The information is most limited for nonferrous metals, for which domestic production data have been traditionally secret and the limited foreign trade information (covering mainly base metals and aluminum) was last reported in 1975. As it happens, the nonferrous category is the most significant among the metals as an earner of foreign exchange, especially in such traditional export items as platinum and platinum-group metals, aluminum, copper and nickel. Finally, there is the elusive issue of the role of Soviet gold production, variously estimated at one-third to one-fourth of world output and used mainly to pay for hard-currency deficits in the Soviet balance of trade.

Ferrous Ores and Metals

*Iron Ore.* As shown in detail in Chapter 19 by Tony Misko and Craig ZumBrunnen, conditions for Soviet iron-ore development have deteriorated in recent years and these problems have been reflected in the foreign trade posture. Although the Soviet Union has long been the world's leading iron-ore producer, having surpassed the United States in the later 1950s, the Soviet industry has not been able to develop a major export market outside the Soviet bloc. The demands of the Soviet iron and steel sector, also the world leader in volume of production, and of the iron and steel industries of the East European countries, notably Poland and Czechoslovakia, have been such as to leave little surplus for other destinations. The Soviet iron-ore industry, moreover, like the iron and steel sector as a whole, began to stagnate in the middle 1970s. Unlike many Soviet natural resources, iron-ore reserves are not handicapped by being located in remote northern and eastern regions. Most of the explored reserves are found in the accessible European part of the USSR, notably in the Krivoi Rog basin of the Ukraine and in the Central Russian region known as the Kursk Magnetic Anomaly (so called because of the impact of large ore bodies on compass needles). The main problem in sustaining production has been the gradual depletion of high-grade, direct-shipping ores and the need for costly development and enrichment of lower-grade ores. In 1960, it took 142 million tons of crude iron ore to produce 106 million tons of material usable in the iron and steel industry, or a ratio of 1.34 to 1. In 1980, with a vast increase in the mining of lower-grade ores, it took 498 million tons of crude ore to yield 244.7 million tons of usable ore, or a ratio of 2.04 to 1.[22]

The Soviet export position in iron ore has also been constrained by the fact that the mines of the Kursk Magnetic Anomaly, favorably situated with respect to European ore markets, have been obliged to ship a large part of their output (as much as 14 million tons in 1980, or a third of KMA's production) eastward to the iron and steel industry of the Urals. The Urals mills, accounting for some 29 percent of Soviet steel production, have been suffering from a shortage of local ore supplies. Soviet planners hope that the development of the Kachar ore deposit of northwest Kazakhstan, where a huge pit is being excavated, will improve the ore supply for the Urals industry and reduce the need for eastward ore hauls from the Kursk Magnetic Anomaly. By making available more KMA ore for other uses, the Kachar project may improve the Soviet Union's iron-ore export position toward the end of the 1980s. The first stage of the Kachar operation, where difficult stripping of waterlogged overburden has been under way since 1975, is long overdue; under the 11th Five-Year Plan it is now scheduled to start up in 1985, but further delays are likely. Kachar is designed to produce ultimately 21 million tons of crude ore, to be converted to 11 million tons of pellets, the preferred modern form of blast-furnace charge, with a first stage capacity of 5 million tons of crude ore.

Aside from the crucial Kachar project, the Soviet Union's export position may be enhanced by the completion of another major iron-ore development, the Kostomuksha mine and concentrator, which are being built with Finnish participation in Karelia near the Finnish border. The first stage, put in operation in 1982, is to produce 8 million tons of crude ore for conversion to 3 million tons of pellets, of which 1.2 million would be shipped to the Finnish iron and steel plant at Raahe, 180 miles to the west. The ultimate designed capacity of the Kostomuksha operation is 24 million tons of crude ore and 9 million tons of pellets.

Pending expansion of the Soviet iron-ore base in the middle to late 1980s, the supply situation is expected to continue tight and the export position is likely to remain constrained, with virtually all ore exports moving to Eastern European iron and steel mills (as much as 97 percent of Soviet ore exports in 1980). The structure of these ore exports to Eastern Europe has been upgraded since the mid-1970s as the Soviet Union began to supply pellets from pelletizer plants in whose construction the East European steel producers participated on a product payback basis. Under an agreement signed in 1974, the East Europeans agreed to help develop pellet plants at Komsomolsk and the North Krivoi Rog mines in the Ukraine and the Zheleznogorsk and Lebedi (Gubkin) mines in the Kursk Magnetic Anomaly, with a view to raising iron-ore deliveries to Eastern Europe from 38 million tons in 1975 to 48 million in 1980.[23] As it turned out, the Soviet Union missed that objective by 2.6 million tons and, in order to meet its East European commitments, had to virtually eliminate the non-bloc portion of its iron-ore exports (in 1975, some 5.6 million tons, or 13 percent of exports, were still moving to hard-currency countries). The increasing flow of iron ore and pellets to East Europe has required rail-transport improvements. The completion in 1978 of a 93-mile link between Dolinskaya and Pomoshnaya in the Ukraine shortened the rail haul to the East European steel mills from the Krivoi Rog Basin, and the following year a direct ore-transport line opened between the Kursk Magnetic Anomaly and the new Katowice iron and steel plant in Poland.[24]

In 1981, the Soviet Union exported 9.2 million tons of iron pellets, representing some 18 percent of Soviet pellet production, and 34.2 million tons of other iron-ore mate-

rials (direct-shipping ores and concentrates), or 18 percent of the marketable ore other than pellets (Table 12). Pellet exports began in 1976, with 2.4 million tons going to Rumania, and rose through the second half of the 1970s. At the same time other types of ore materials declined. The trend is expected to continue through the 1980s as the higher-value pellets replace nonpelletized iron-ore materials.

Over the longer term, there may be prospects for the development of an iron-ore export base in East Siberia, where reserves in the newly explored Chara-Tokko district have been estimated at 5 billion tons.[25] The geological exploration settlement of Torgo was founded on the site in 1977. However, development will have to await the completion of the Baikal-Amur Mainline in the middle 1980s and the construction of a branch railroad running some 100 miles north to the ore deposit from the BAM's Khani River segment.

*Manganese.* One of the traditional mineral exports of the Soviet Union, manganese no longer holds the foreign markets that it once occupied before the growing East European iron and steel industry as well as the Soviet domestic steel production began to make increasing demands on a deteriorating resource base. The outlook is for no significant change in the situation as Soviet manganese production will be used mainly to meet the needs of Soviet bloc steel industries. Virtually all Soviet manganese, as shown in Chapter 21 by W.A. Douglas Jackson, is being mined in two areas: the Chiatura Basin of the Georgian Republic, in Transcaucasia, which contributes over a quarter of Soviet output, and in the Nikopol Basin of the Ukraine, with more than 70 percent of national production. A change in the Soviet resource base occurred in the 1960s, when the high-grade Georgian ore began to become depleted and beneficiation plants were not yet ready to take up the slack by processing lower-grade ores. Soviet production came to rely increasingly on the larger, but lower-grade Ukrainian deposits. By 1980, with the completion of concentrators, Georgia had virtually recovered its earlier output level of some 3 mil-

TABLE 12
Soviet Exports of Iron Ore and Pellets
(million metric tons)

| | 1970 | 1975 | 1980 | 1981 | 1985 Plan |
|---|---|---|---|---|---|
| USSR usable ore output | 197.3 | 235.0 | 244.7 | 242 | 262 |
| Pellets | 10.6 | 27.1 | 50.9 | — | 68 |
| Others[a] | 186.7 | 207.9 | 193.8 | — | 194 |
| USSR usable ore exports | 36.1 | 43.6 | 46.9 | 43.4 | — |
| Pellets | — | — | 8.8 | 9.2 | — |
| Others | 36.1 | 43.6 | 38.1 | 34.2 | — |
| Exports to East Europe | 31.7 | 38.0 | 45.4 | (42) | — |
| Other destinations | 4.4 | 5.6 | 1.5 | (1) | — |

[a]Nonpellet output ignores any losses in pellet manufacture.
SOURCES: Total usable ore production from *Narodnoye khozyaistvo SSSR v 1980 g.* [The economy of the USSR in 1980], statistical yearbook (Moscow: Finansy i Statistika, 1981), p. 159; Pellet production: *Gorny zhurnal,* 1975, no. 1 (1970 output); 1977, no. 3 (1975 output); 1981, no. 5 (1980 output). Exports from *Vneshnyaya torgovlya SSSR,* statistical yearbook, various years. 1985 plan from *Gorny zhurnal,* 1982, no. 3.

TABLE 13
Soviet Manganese Production and Exports (thousand metric tons)

|  | 1965 | 1970 | 1975 | 1980 | 1981 | 1985 Plan |
|---|---|---|---|---|---|---|
| USSR production |  |  |  |  |  |  |
| Marketed ore | 7,576 | 6,841 | 8,459 | 9,750 | 9,400 | 10,100 |
| Metal content | 2,485 | 2,446 | 2,951 | 3,040 | — | — |
| Average grade (percent) | 32.8 | 35.8 | 34.9 | 31.2 | — | — |
| USSR ore exports | 1,020 | (1,228)[a] | 1,411 | 1,255 | 1,194 | — |
| Percent of output | 13.5 | (18) | 17 | 13 | 13 | — |
| to East Europe | 561 | 773 | 1,130 | 1,147 | 1,112 | — |
| other destinations | 459 | (455) | 281 | 108 | 82 | — |

[a]Total export for 1970 was published in a rounded figure of 1.2 million tons, meaning at most 1,250,000 tons; identified country destinations add up to 1,228,000.
SOURCE: *Narodnoye khozyaistvo SSSR v 1980 g.*, p. 159; *Vneshnyaya torgovlya SSSR*, various years; *Gorny zhurnal*, 1982, no. 1 and no. 3.

lion tons, but the exhaustion of rich ores brought about a general decline in metal content of the marketed material in the 1970s, especially in the second half. The average manganese content of Soviet marketable ore dropped from 34.9 percent in 1975 to some 31 percent by the end of the decade (Table 13). The decline in ore grades has been a worldwide phenomenon. As the table shows, Soviet exports have gradually become restricted to the East European steel producing countries. Their share of Soviet exports rose from 55 percent in 1965 to some 65 percent in 1970 and 93 percent in 1981. Although the USSR remains the world's largest producer, domestic demand and the needs of its East European allies are soaking up virtually all of the output, and world demand is now being met by such countries as South Africa (the second world producer), Gabon, Brazil, Australia and India.

*Chromium.* Soviet exports of chromium, another traditional mineral commodity being supplied to the world market, appear to be affected by an intricate interplay of demand in the world's steel industries, domestic consumption, the Soviet need for hard currency, technological change and the Soviet Union's deteriorating resource base. Virtually all Soviet chromite, as W.A. Douglas Jackson discusses in detail in Chapter 22, originates in a single mining district, the Khromtau area of northwest Kazakhstan. After rapid growth of output until the early 1970s in easily accessible surface mining operations, incremental production began to slow as the Soviet industry faced the need to develop deeper ore bodies through the time-consuming and costly construction of shaft mines. Delays in the completion of the new shaft mines kept production substantially below the 1980 goal of 4.2 million tons originally envisaged in the 10th Five-Year Plan.[26] The first deep mine, the Molodezhnaya, finally yielded its first product in 1981, and is to have an ultimate capacity of 2 million tons of ore.[27] Construction of the second deep mine, the Tsentralnaya, is continuing.

Despite the continuation of high production levels, Soviet chromite exports declined sharply at the end of the 1970s. The share of exports going outside the Soviet bloc had been holding fairly steady until the mid-1970s, when 75 percent of Soviet chromite exports were still going to hard-currency countries, notably the United States, West

Germany, Sweden, France and Japan. But chromite exports continued to decline in the second half of the decade, and the Western share dipped to 44 percent of the sharply reduced total exports in 1981 (Table 14). The decline of exports in light of high production levels has been variously attributed to a soft market because of stagnation in the Western steel industry, increased Soviet chromium consumption in a drive to upgrade steel quality, reduced Soviet needs for hard currency in view of the high prices obtained for sales of oil and gold, and technological change in chromium technology. Demand for Soviet chromite in the world market had been traditionally high because of the high grade of the Soviet material, meeting the minimum standard of 46 percent chromic oxide ($Cr_2O_3$) for metallurgical use. However, technological advances during the 1970s, notably the so-called argon-oxygen decarburization process, have made possible the use of lower-grade (and lower-cost) material in the manufacture of stainless steel. The technological change has favored South Africa, long the world's second-ranking producer after the USSR. As a result of the expanding market for what used to be considered chemical-grade chromite, South African chromite production more than doubled during the 1970s to reach the Soviet Union's production level in excess of 3 million tons.

The shift to increasing deep-mined production in the Khromtau district, though raising mining costs, is ex-

TABLE 14
Soviet Chromite Production and Exports
(thousand metric tons)

|  | 1965 | 1970 | 1975 | 1980 | 1981 | 1985 Plan |
|---|---|---|---|---|---|---|
| USSR production | 2,500 | 3,000 | 3,400 | 3,400 | 3,300 | 3,800 |
| USSR exports | 748 | 1,148 | 1,171 | 567 | 567 | — |
| Percent of output | 30 | 38 | 34 | 17 | 17 | — |
| to East Europe | 123 | 203 | 297 | 307 | 317 | — |
| other destinations | 625 | 945 | 874 | 260 | 250 | — |

SOURCE: Central Intelligence Agency, *Handbook of Economic Statistics, 1980* (ER 80–10452, October 1980), p. 139, with adjustments based on Soviet sources; *Vneshnyaya torgovlya SSSR*, various years; *Gorny zhurnal*, 1982, no. 1 and no. 3.

pected to assure continued high output levels in the USSR once the two huge shaft mines reach their designed capacity. The Soviet Union's ability to recover the market share it once had is expected to depend on demand by the Western steel industries and adjustments to the new technological situation, which has reduced the automatic advantage enjoyed by the Soviet Union because of its abundant supply of high-grade material.

*Iron and Steel Products.* Although the Soviet Union has the world's largest iron and steel industry in terms of physical volume of pig iron and crude steel, it has not derived much trade benefit from it because of the vast needs of the Soviet domestic market and a traditional lag in quality and product assortment. Exports and imports have been roughly balanced over the long term, with exports predominating in some years and imports in others. However, Soviet exports of iron and steel products go mainly to the Soviet bloc and to developing countries while imports are generally high-quality products from the Western industrial countries. Nearly two-thirds of iron and steel exports in 1981 consisted of rolled products, for which East Germany was by far the largest customer (40 percent of the total). Other major export items are pig iron and steel scrap, also moving mainly to the East European countries. On the import side, large-diameter steel pipe for gas transmission mains and other high-quality rolled steel products predominate, originating mainly in West Germany and Japan.

Over the long term, there may be prospects in strengthening the Soviet export position in ferroalloys, which is bolstered both by the presence of alloy metals (manganese, chromium) and the availability of low-cost electricity sources for this power-intensive industry. The East European steel producers have already joined with the Soviet Union in developing additional ferroalloy capacity for export. A 1974 agreement of the Soviet-bloc countries called for expansion of ferroalloy capacity at Nikopol, in the Ukrainian manganese district, and at the new ferroalloys center of Yermak in northeast Kazakhstan. The Yermak plant, using cheap electricity from the local lignite-fired 2.4 million kw power station, started operations in 1968 and is to have a capacity of 1 million tons of ferrosilicon when completed by 1985. The Soviet bloc accord had the effect of shifting a larger share of Soviet ferroalloys exports to Eastern Europe, whose market share rose from 55 percent in 1975 to 83 percent in 1981, with Rumania (the largest importer), Poland and East Germany substantially raising their imports of Soviet ferroalloys in the late 1970s. There have been suggestions that a major ferroalloys capacity for the Western market might also be developed on a compensatory basis (payback in kind for Western equipment) on the basis of the Sayan hydropower complex in southern Siberia.

### Nonferrous metals

While ferrous ores and metals from the USSR are being exported mainly to Eastern Europe, the nonferrous metals group ranks high as an earner of foreign exchange for the Soviet Union in hard-currency countries. By far the most important export by value is the platinum metals group (including palladium and rhodium), followed by nickel; others are aluminum, titanium, copper and lesser known materials like rare-earth metals. These exports have fluctuated over the years, depending on a combination of changing demand conditions, prices and Soviet foreign exchange needs. Platinum-group metals, in particular, have been used by the USSR traditionally as a residual financing mechanism, much the way in which gold appears to be used to adjust balance-of-payment deficits. The resource position of the Soviet Union in all these nonferrous metals appears to be strong, and they are expected to continue to play a significant role among primary-product exports.

*Platinum-Group Metals and Nickel.* These two associated commodity groups, which are discussed in detail by Russell B. Adams in Chapter 23, are apparently being given particularly high priority in development with an eye to their export potential. Most of the Soviet production originates in the Norilsk district of northern Siberia, which also contributes associated copper, cobalt, gold, silver and lesser coproducts like tellurium and selenium.

The development of the Norilsk resource base, bolstered notably by the discovery of large additional reserves in the nearby Talnakh area, has given rise to one of the world's largest mining centers north of the Arctic Circle, with a population of some 200,000. The value attached to the minerals output of the Norilsk complex, notably the platinum-group metals, can be judged from the fact that some of the deepest shaft mines in the Soviet Union are being developed to extract the ore. With a view to providing a year-round transport outlet from Norilsk, which lacks overland connections, the Soviet Union has developed an Arctic shipping route to Murmansk that is being kept open during the long northern winter by a fleet of nuclear and conventional icebreakers.

The production capacity of the Norilsk complex continues to be expanded, and is thus likely to enhance the Soviet Union's export position. A new smelter, known as Nadezhda, was inaugurated in 1981[28] and the new Taimyr mine, the fourth and largest underground operation in the Talnakh area, was scheduled to yield its first ore in 1982 after eight years of excavation. It will be tapping a huge ore body through six shafts at a depth of 5,000 feet.

The USSR publishes neither production nor foreign trade statistics for platinum-group metals and nickel. Western estimates place the Soviet Union in first place for overall platinum-group metals, mainly on the strength of its dominance in palladium; in platinum proper it ranks second after South Africa, the other major world producer. Foreign trade data, reconstructed on the basis of the statistics of partner countries, suggest that the United States and Japan are by far the principal markets for Soviet exports of platinum-group metals. In nickel, the USSR is believed to have come close to the level of Canada, long the world leader in mine output, as a result of the expansion program at Norilsk. Since the Soviet Union refines all its nickel at home and Canada exports some of its intermediate product for refining elsewhere, the USSR has established itself since the mid-1970s as the world leader in the production of refined nickel. Nickel exports, as reconstructed from partner statistics, move mainly to the United States, West Germany, Japan and France.

*Titanium.* The discovery and development of important ancient stream deposits of titanium minerals (ilmenite and rutile) have propelled the Soviet Union into first place among producers of titanium metal, a crucial material for aerospace applications. The mineral deposits, situated in the western Ukraine around Irshansk and in the eastern Ukraine at Volnogorsk, support three major metal reduction plants: at Zaporozhye in the Ukraine; Berezniki in the Urals; and Ust-Kamenogorsk in eastern Kazakhstan. Total metal production was estimated in 1980 at some 45,000 tons, double the United States level.[29] The Soviet Union has also built up a substantial capacity for the production of titanium dioxide pigment, the principal use of titanium, but is exceeded in pigment manufacture by the leading Western industrial countries. Except for the Soviet Union, which relies entirely on domestic mineral output, the major titanium consuming countries all import at least part of the raw materials, which originate chiefly in Australia, Norway and Canada. The United States, whch also mines ilmenite, consumes all of its mineral production.

The Soviet titanium industry has been generating exports of titanium metal and scrap, mainly to the United States. In the late 1970s, titanium ranked third among metal imports from the USSR, after the platinum group and nickel. During the period 1974–79, American imports of titanium sponge metal totaled 17,000 tons (16 percent of U.S. consumption), and the Soviet Union contributed 34 percent of the imports (the principal supplier was Japan, with 57 percent).[30]

*Aluminum.* This metal occupies an unusual position in the Soviet foreign trade structure because its production is based partly on imported raw materials. Because of the availability of low-cost hydroelectric power, a key locational factor for the power-intensive aluminum reduction industry, and a shortage of high-grade domestic bauxite resources, the Soviet Union has developed the world's second largest aluminum industry (after the United States) by relying to a large extent on bauxite imports, mainly from Guinea. A calculation of the raw-material balance of the Soviet aluminum industry in 1975 indicated that as much as 45 percent of aluminum reduction, estimated at a total of more than 2 million metric tons, was derived from imported raw materials, divided about equally between bauxite, the ore, and alumina, the intermediate product.[31] Since then, the startup of a new seaboard alumina plant at Nikolayev on the Black Sea has bolstered domestic alumina capacity and shifted the import structure toward a larger proportion of bauxite and less alumina while generally maintaining the 45 percent dependency on imported aluminum-bearing materials.

There have long been recommendations within the Soviet Union for greater use of a domestic aluminum-bearing ore known as nepheline, which now accounts for roughly 20 percent of Soviet alumina production. Nepheline is being mined in large quantities in the Kola Peninsula of northern Russia as a coproduct of the phosphatic ore known as apatite, but most of the nepheline is being discarded in tailings. Advocates of greater nepheline use in the Soviet aluminum industry contend that it could provide as much as 45 to 50 percent of Soviet alumina production, thus eliminating the need for bauxite imports.[32] However, aluminum industry planners continue to prefer to import high-grade bauxite rather than cope with the complex nepheline technology, which requires large limestone inputs and yields soda and cement as coproducts.

In 1975, the last year in which the Soviet Union disclosed its aluminum exports, they amounted to 500,000 tons, or some 25 percent of production. Aluminum represented half of the tonnage of nonferrous metals exports and one-third of the value. More than 70 percent of Soviet aluminum exports moved to Eastern Europe; the principal buyer among the capitalist industrial countries was Japan. Over the long term, aluminum is likely to remain a major Soviet export as the continuing buildup of hydroelectric capacity on the Angara and Yenisei rivers of southern Siberia is used to expand aluminum reduction capacity. The startup of the long delayed Sayan reduction plant at Sayanogorsk, now planned for the mid-1980s, will furher enhance the Soviet aluminum potential as part of the plant's projected 500,000-ton output is exported as payback for Western European plant equipment. Looking beyond the Sayan project, one can envisage further development of Soviet aluminum potential on the basis of bauxite imports from countries other than Guinea, say, from Australia. Such bauxite might be converted into alumina at a Pacific seaboard plant, and the alumina might be shipped to the reduction plants of the Angara-Yenisei region for transformation into aluminum metal for reexport to Japan and other Western markets. In general, the growing hydroelectric capacity in southern Siberia would seem to give the Soviet Union an important asset as a purveyor of aluminum metal to world markets in view of the energy-intensive nature of the industry and the worldwide rise in energy costs.

*Copper.* Soviet exports of copper, when last reported in 1975, amounted to 200,000 tons, or 15 percent of estimated production. In contrast to the two other major base metals—lead and zinc—in which domestic production and consumption are more closely balanced, the Soviet copper industry has provided a surplus for export. Moreover, while lead and zinc exports serve mainly to meet the needs of the East European countries, copper has been shipped in larger amounts to the Western industrial countries, although with significant fluctuations. The principal buyers have been West Germany, the Netherlands and Britain. Over the long term, there are prospects for more substantial Soviet copper supplies entering the world market once the large Udokan copper reserves in East Siberia are developed. This project will have to await completion of the Baikal-Amur Mainline in the mid-1980s and probably arrangements with foreign partners of a compensation deal involving payback in product. In the meantime, feasibility studies relating to Udokan development have been the subject of a number of planning conferences in the Soviet Union.[33] Until the Udokan project materializes, copper exports will probably not be much more significant than they have been in the recent past, relying largely on the present production capacity in Kazakhstan, the Urals and Uzbekistan.

A discussion of Soviet metal exports would not be complete without a mention of gold, which is used by the Soviet Union mainly as a device for settling balance-of-payment deficits. Much of the secrecy that surrounds nonferrous metals production and trade in general is compounded in the case of gold, and Western estimates range widely. In Chapter 24, Michael Kaser derives a set of estimates based on a detailed field-by-field survey of the Soviet gold-mining industry, which is generally believed to rank second to that of South Africa. As Kaser shows, Soviet gold production, after having long been confined to Siberia, notably the Kolyma district in the northeast, shifted in the 1970s in part to newly discovered lode deposits in the Central Asian republic of Uzbekistan and to Armenia in Transcaucasia while byproduct gold contributed by the copper and lead-zinc industries also played an increasingly important role.

### Nonmetallics

Nonmetallics, which as a group have been one of the largest earners of foreign exchange for the Soviet Union, consist mainly of apatite concentrate, a phosphatic fertilizer raw material, and asbestos, on both of which some data are being made public by the Soviet Union, and diamonds, which like gold and platinum-group metals are couched in utter secrecy. The exports of nonmetallics other than diamonds were last reported in Soviet foreign trade statistics for 1975, and in the process of shifting to a new method of statistical reporting the official data also indirectly revealed the ruble value of diamond exports for that year. With total Soviet exports in 1975 running at 24 billion rubles, the lower-value nonmetallics (mainly apatite concentrate and asbestos) totaled 361 million rubles and diamonds 275 million for a total of 636 million. In 1980, the total value of nonmetallics (including diamonds) was 701 million rubles out of total Soviet exports of 50 billion rubles (Table 15).

### Apatite

As Table 15 shows, apatite concentrate is a high-value export, which in 1975 was worth almost as much as exports of diamonds. Until detailed foreign-trade reporting ceased in 1975, apatite concentrate exports were running about 6 million tons a year, or 38 percent of the Soviet Union's production of 15.3 million tons in 1975. Apatite, which is considered by the Russians to be one of their most distinctive natural resources, occurs in the Khibiny Mountains of the Kola Peninsula of northern European Russia in combination with nepheline, the aluminum-bearing ore mentioned in the discussion of aluminum. Natural apatite ore contains about 16 to 17 percent $P_2O_5$, the phosphorus pentoxide nutrient, and is upgraded in the concentrate to 39.4 percent $P_2O_5$, making it a valuable

TABLE 15
Value of Soviet Exports of Nonmetallics
(millions of rubles)

| Soviet commodity class | 1970 | 1975 | 1980 |
|---|---|---|---|
| 25 Nonmetallic total | — | 636 | 701 |
| 250 Nonmetallic minerals | 148 | 361 | — |
| 25001 Asbestos | 47 | 100 | — |
| 25006 Sulfur | 14 | 15 | — |
| 25010 Graphite | 1.7 | — | — |
| 25011 Cryolite | 1.0 | — | — |
| 25012 Apatite ore | 0.3 | — | — |
| 25013 Apatite concentrate | 83 | 243 | — |
| — Diamonds | — | 275 | — |

SOURCES: *Vneshnyaya torgovlya SSSR,* various years. For 1975, the all-inclusive commodity class (25) was reported in the 1976 yearbook, the more restrictive class (250) was reported in the 1975 yearbook, and the difference is presumed to represent diamonds. Before 1970, apatite concentrate was reported as part of the chemical fertilizer category, with the commodity class number 34001.

raw material for the manufacture of phosphatic fertilizers. The Soviet Union's apatite, aside from representing a significant mineral export commodity, also furnishes the raw material for some 75 percent of the domestic production of phosphatic fertilizer.

In view of the value of Kola apatite, Soviet planners have decided to husband reserves by slowing the rate of development. Apatite output, after having surged from 7.6 million tons in 1965 to 15.3 million in 1975, or an average annual growth of 0.77 million tons, has slowed down. The increment in production was kept to 2 million tons in the second half of the 1970s, and the same increment is planned for the period 1981–85, or an average annual growth of 0.4 million tons. Instead the Soviet Union has sought to develop the more abundant, though lower-grade phosphate resources of the Karatau district of southern Kazakhstan and has turned increasingly to imports of phosphatic raw materials. Under a barter arrangement of ammonia, urea and potash (see below in the discussion of chemical exports) for phosphatic materials with Occidental Petroleum Corporation, the Soviet Union began importing superphosphoric acid from Florida in late 1978.

The flow was interrupted in February 1980 by a United State's embargo following the Soviet military intervention in Afghanistan, but the embargo imposed by President Jimmy Carter was lifted in 1981 by the Reagan Administration. In face of the American embargo, which reduced Soviet imports of Florida superphosphoric acid in 1980 to one-sixth of the 1979 level, the Soviet Union turned to Morocco for phosphoric acid. Morocco, which has been furnishing superphosphate to the Soviet Union since 1978 in exchange for ammonia and urea, is expected to become an increasingly important phosphate source for the Soviet Union in the 1980s from a mine being developed with Soviet assistance.

### Asbestos

A traditional export of the Soviet Union, asbestos represented only one-half of the export value of apatite concentrate when last reported in Soviet foreign trade statistics in 1975. Physical exports of 613,000 tons in that year represented about 30 percent of an estimated Soviet producton of 2 million tons (all fiber grades, including shorts and refuse). Soviet asbestos output has been traditionally concentrated at Asbest in the central Urals, which remains the nation's principal producing district. With the development of additional mines at Dzhetygara (600,000 tons capacity) in northwest Kazakhstan, starting in 1965, and at Ak-Dovurak (250,000 tons capacity) in the Tuva Autonomous Republic, starting in 1964, the Soviet Union surpassed Canada and moved into first place among world producers. Soviet production was further enhanced with the development of the Kiyembay deposit at Yasny in the southern Urals. The first stage of this project, developed with East European assistance on a compensatory basis, came on stream in late 1979 and the second stage in late 1980, with a combined designed capacity of 500,000 tons. In 1975, about two-fifths of Soviet asbestos exports moved to Eastern Europe, and the joint development of the new mine at Yasny is expected to provide for the incremental needs of the Soviet Union's allies. In trade with the West, asbestos remains a steady export, going mainly to Western Europe (France, West Germany, Italy) and Japan.

Although the Soviet Union accounts for about half of the world production of asbestos, its domestic needs are such that the Soviet product represents only one-quarter of the asbestos entering world trade, and, if the Soviet-bloc trade is excluded, one-tenth of supplies to the Western industrial countries. Canada remains by far the main exporter, with two-thirds of supplies outside the Soviet bloc, and South Africa, with superior varieties, supplies about 15 percent.[34]

The Soviet position in asbestos quality is expected to improve as soon as the completion of the Baikal-Amur Mainline makes possible the start of development of the long-fiber deposit of Molodezhny near Taksimo in the Buryat Autonomous Republic. The Russians have approached the Japanese for possible participation in the development of the Molodezhny deposit. If Japan were to make a compensation deal with the Soviet Union, Sibe-

rian asbestos would probably enlarge the Soviet share in the Japanese market now dominated by imports from Canada and South Africa. In any event, with continued growth of production capacity in the Soviet Union and more limited prospects for expansion elsewhere, the Soviet Union's position as the leading world producer will probably go unchallenged for years to come, and despite the large domestic demand, the Russians may even be able to enlarge their share of the world market, especially if new resource developments bring superior asbestos qualities into play.

Diamonds

Soviet diamond sales, which represent the third largest earner of foreign exchange for the Soviet Union (after crude oil and refined products, and natural gas), consist mainly of rough stones marketed through the London-based DeBeers organization, a monopoly that produces, purchases and markets the output of both gem and industrial diamonds from producing countries, including the USSR. Since DeBeers is the principal outlet for Soviet diamond exports, some 70 to 80 percent of these exports figure in trade with Britain. Other importers of Soviet diamonds are Belgium, the Netherlands, West Germany, Japan and the United States. Very little data is available on Soviet diamond production and trade.

According to estimates of the United States Bureau of Mines, based on indirect indications, the Soviet Union accounted in 1978 for some 45 percent of world production of industrial diamond stones (not suitable for gems), ahead of South Africa (22 percent), Botswana (13 percent) and Zaire (6 percent) (Table 16).[35] Total world production of stones was estimated at 16.9 million carats (3,380 kilograms). In addition to stone-sized diamonds, used for tool and die and drilling applications, natural diamond also occurs in the form of finer materials (bort, grit, powders) for use in grinding wheels, impregnated bits and tools, abrasives, etc. The Bureau of Mines estimated 1978 world production of this finer material at 11.6 million carats, of which about 83 percent was contributed by Zaire. In overall natural diamond production, Zaire thus

TABLE 16
Soviet Position among Industrial Diamond Producers (1978) (million metric carats; 5,000 carats = 1 kg)

|  | Natural Diamond | | | Synthetic Fines (4) | Total Fines (5) | Overall Total (1+4) or (2+5) |
|  | Total (1) | Stones (2) | Fines (3) |  |  |  |
|---|---|---|---|---|---|---|
| World | 28.5 | 16.9 | 11.6 | 79.4 | 91.0 | 107.9 |
| USSR | (8) | 7.6 | — | (22) | 22.8 | 30.4 |
| United States | — | — | — | 28.7 | 28.7 | 28.7 |
| South Africa | (4) | 3.6 | — | (6) | 10.4 | 14.0 |
| Zaire | 10.7 | 1.1 | 9.6 | — | 9.6 | 10.7 |
| Ireland | — | — | — | 10.0 | 10.0 | 10.0 |
| Japan | — | — | — | 3.7 | 3.7 | 3.7 |
| Sweden | — | — | — | 3.0 | 3.0 | 3.0 |
| Botswana | 2.4 | 2.13 | 0.24 | — | 0.24 | 2.4 |
| Ghana | (1) | 1.0 | — | — | — | (1) |

SOURCE: Constructed from data in U.S. Bureau of Mines, *Mineral Facts and Problems*, 1980 edition. Industrial Diamond chapter.

ranked first, with 10.7 million carats in 1978, followed by the USSR with about 8 million and South Africa with 4 million. Finally there is also synthetic diamond production, which yields only fine material, estimated at 79.4 million carats in 1978. The principal producers are the United States, the USSR, Ireland, South Africa, Japan and Sweden.

Although some diamond placer deposits had been worked for a century on the western slopes of the Ural Mountains, in the basin of the Vishera River, the Soviet Union did not emerge on the world scene as a major diamond producer until the discovery of diamond-bearing kimberlite pipes in western Yakutia in 1954–55. Since then three pipes have been commercially developed and have become the basis for the important diamond exports. The first mill went into operation in 1957 at the Mir (Peace) pipe, giving rise to the workers settlement of Mirny, which was raised to the higher urban status of city under Yakut ASSR jurisdiction in 1959. In 1966–67, the much larger No. 3 mill, a structure the height of an 11-story building, began operations as the power of the nearby Vilyui hydroelectric station with an installed capacity of 312 MW came on line. Mirny has become the Soviet Union's principal diamond-mining center, with a population of 30,000 to 35,000 in 1980.

The two other diamond centers are some 400 km to the north astride the Arctic Circle and, because of problems of access, were developed after Mirny. Aikhal was made a workers settlement in 1962, but large-scale operations probably had to await the arrival of a power-transmission line from the Vilyui hydro station in 1969. The other diamond center, based on the Udachny pipe, 60 km northeast of Aikhal, apparently gave rise to a more important operation than Aikhal. The first mill, No. 11, began operations in 1968 at the settlement of Novy, which was then renamed Udachny and raised to the urban status of workers settlement. The No. 11 mill was reported in 1974 to have been converted from seasonal to year-round operation. A much larger facility, No. 12 mill, similar in size to the No. 3 mill at Mirny, began operations in 1976 at the subsidiary settlement of Nadezhny, just west of Udachny.[36] The Udachny cluster, which also includes the settlement of Polyarny, west of Nadezhny, sits right on the Arctic Circle and is not accessible overland except by winter road. The harsh conditions under which the diamond industry operates in the Soviet Union is suggested by the fact that some work sites in the Udachny area entitle workers to a regional salary coefficient of 2, or double the basic salary, which is the maximum increment paid in harsh environments.

Sulfur

The Soviet Union is also a major producer of sulfur, ranking fourth in 1975 after the United States, Canada and Poland, but because of a large domestic consumption has not been a significant exporter. The exports shown until 1975, when trade secrecy was imposed (Table 15), were roughly balanced by imports from Poland. The exports went mainly to Czechoslovakia, Cuba and Hungary.

The sources of elemental sulfur in the Soviet Union have undergone two major shifts in recent decades. Until the late 1950s, most of the sulfur (70 to 80 percent) was derived from pyrite deposits in the Ural Mountains, with only 10 percent obtained by underground mining in small deposits mainly in Central Asia.

The first major shift took place in 1959 with the start of open-pit mining in newly discovered shallow native sulfur deposits at Rozdol in the Carpathian foothills of the Ukraine. The share of native sulfur was further increased when the Frasch process of melting deeper-lying sulfur underground through steam injection began to be introduced at Yavorov, another West Ukrainian deposit, and at Gaurdak, in southeast Turkmenia. By 1965, native sulfur represented 75 percent of Soviet production of elemental sulfur, with the pyrite share down to 19 percent. (Pyrite continued, however, to be the main source of sulfuric acid in the Soviet Union.)

The second shift in the production of elemental sulfur began in the 1970s with the development of sulfur-bearing natural gas (sour gas) reserves, which in 1975 accounted for 13 percent of the Soviet Union's proven gas reserves. With the start of production of the Orenburg sulfur-recovery plant in 1974 and the smaller recovery operation at Mubarek in Central Asia (which started in the early 1970s), 15.2 percent of the elemental sulfur in 1975 was recovered from natural gas (Table 17). In that year, Soviet production of elemental sulfur was 3.27 million tons, of which 497,000 tons was recovered at natural gas plants—403,000 tons at Orenburg and 94,000 at Mubarek.[37] By the end of 1981, Orenburg was producing at its designed capacity of 1 million tons of recovered sulfur a year, and Mubarek had expanded to a capacity of 450,000 tons.[38] This suggested an overall production level of about 4.5 million tons of elemental sulfur, with one-third coming from natural gas plants.

The development of the sour-gas reserves is expected to strengthen the Soviet Union's sulfur position and, in view of economic problems in Poland, turn the balanced sulfur trade into net Soviet exports. These are likely to continue to go mainly to member countries of Comecon, as in the past.

Chemicals

Basic chemicals are briefly considered here because they have been among the most rapidly growing export categories, based in part on the development of the petrochemical industry under a variety of compensation deals with Western countries. The surge in chemical exports began in the late 1970s and is expected to continue through the 1980s as product payback from compensation arrangements comes increasingly into play (Table 18). In 1979, product payback represented about 38 percent of chemical exports to Western countries.

The most prominent new foreign-exchange earner among the chemicals is ammonia. Large-volume compensation shipments of ammonia began in 1978, and in 1981 ammonia exports represented 33 percent of all chemical exports by value (285 million rubles out of 867

TABLE 17
Soviet Foreign Trade and Production of Sulfur (1975)
(thousand metric tons)

| | |
|---|---|
| Soviet imports | 690 |
| Soviet exports | 441 |
| Domestic production | 3,270 |
| Native sulfur | 2,300 |
| Recovered sulfur | 970 |
| Natural gas | 497 |
| Crude oil | 200 |
| Coal | 40 |
| Pyrites | 230 |

SOURCES: Trade figures from *Vneshnyaya torgovlya SSSR v 1975 godu*, pp. 26, 40. Production from *Gorny zhurnal*, 1977, no. 11.

million), with some 20 percent of the ammonia going to the United States. This represented the implementation of the barter agreement with Occidental Petroleum Corporation, involving the exchange of United States phosphoric acid for Soviet shipments of ammonia, urea and potash. Using its abundant gas resources, the Soviet Union has built up the world's largest ammonia manufacturing industry, which in 1980 produced 16.7 million tons, double the 1970 level. Although ammonia plants are widely dispersed, a high concentration has been established at Togliatti, on the Volga river, with a designed capacity of 2.7 million tons. As part of the arrangement with Occidental, the Soviet Union has built a special-purpose Black Sea chemical port named Yuzhny, east of Odessa, and has linked the Togliatti ammonia center with the Black Sea terminal by a 2,400-mile pipeline with an annual capacity of 2.5 million tons of ammonia. The Yuzhny port, with an ultimate ammonia handling capacity of 4 million tons, opened in 1978, and the pipeline

TABLE 18
Value of Soviet Chemical Exports (millions of rubles)

| | 1970 | 1975 | 1978 | 1979 | 1980 | 1981 |
|---|---|---|---|---|---|---|
| Total | 165 | 276 | 391 | 579 | 727 | 867 |
| Western countries | 35 | 83 | 142 | 295 | 360 | 384 |
| Product payback | — | 6.3 | — | 112 | — | — |
| Others | 130 | 193 | 249 | 284 | 367 | 483 |
| West Germany | 6 | 19 | 48 | 107 | 104 | 118 |
| United States | 0.6 | 3.0 | 23 | 38 | 74 | 61 |
| Italy | 3.1 | 8.9 | 8.3 | 35 | 47 | 53 |
| Netherlands | 4.7 | 7.6 | 18 | 32 | 43 | 48 |
| Product groups | | | | | | |
| Alkalis | 12 | 28 | 53 | 104 | 213 | 311 |
| Ammonia[a] | 4.5 | 7.9 | 41 | 87 | 189 | 285 |
| Salts | 25 | 44 | 51 | 54 | 58 | 61 |
| Petrochemicals | 19 | 41 | 35 | 66 | 54 | 43 |
| Plastics | 36 | 52 | 81 | 107 | 138 | 148 |
| Resins | 14 | 23 | 44 | 55 | 78 | 93 |
| Alcohols | 15 | 27 | 30 | 37 | 40 | 47 |
| Methanol | 11 | 11 | 19 | 24 | 28 | 32 |
| Wood chemicals | 5.6 | 6.5 | 9.3 | 7.7 | 7.3 | 8.6 |
| Phosphorus | 4.1 | 18 | 25 | 39 | 42 | 44 |

[a]In 1970, ammonia was transferred from the chemical salts category to the alkali category in Soviet trade statistics. Product-group totals in the table have been adjusted.
SOURCE: *Vneshnyaya torgovlya SSSR*, various years. Product payback under compensation deals from *Soviet Geography: Review and Translation* 21, no. 10, (December 1980): 676–80.

went into full operation in 1981. A smaller ammonia export terminal, with a handling capacity of 1 million tons, has been built at the Baltic Sea port of Ventspils in Latvia and is being supplied by rail. Closely associated with the production and export of ammonia are those of urea, a concentrated nitrogenous fertilizer derived from ammonia. The Soviet Union has built up the world's largest urea capacity, and in 1981 exported 2.2 million tons, some 35 to 40 percent of Soviet production.

Another broad chemical product category in which the USSR has been able to build up an export position, using plants purchased in the West, is that of synthetic resins and plastics. These products are based on aromatics, olefins and other primary petrochemicals derived either from oil refinery gases or from natural gas liquids. The products include polyethylene, polypropylene, polystyrene, polyvinyl chloride and acrylonitrile, the raw material for acrylic fibers.

Polyethylene production more than doubled during the 1970s, to 623,000 tons in 1980, and was scheduled to double again during the 11th Five-Year Plan (1981–85) to 1.2 million tons by 1985. In 1979, compensation payback shipments alone were 62,000 tons, or 11 percent of 1979 production.[39] Exports originated at Novopolotsk (Belorussia) and Severodonetsk (Ukraine), on the basis of oil refinery gases, and at Kazan (Tatar ASSR) and Budennovsk (North Caucasus; opened in 1980), on the basis of natural gas liquids.

Polyvinyl chloride, which also more than doubled during the 1970s, from 160,000 tons in 1970 to some 400,000 tons in 1980, is scheduled to be increased by about 60 percent during the 11th Five-Year Plan, or to 640,000 tons. Exports of polyvinyl chloride and of its monomer, vinyl chloride, originated mainly at Kalush in the western Ukraine during the 1970s. In the present decade they are to be supplemented by exports from the long-delayed Zima chemical complex at Sayansk in Eastern Siberia. In 1980, the Soviet Union accounted for roughly one-tenth of the world's export of vinyl chloride.[40]

Polystyrene production tripled during the 1970s, from 82,000 tons in 1970 to some 250,000 tons in 1980, mainly through the development of capacity at Gorlovka in the Ukraine, which also accounted for the exports. In the 11th Five-Year Plan, production in the USSR is scheduled to more than double, to some 575,000 tons, mainly because of the addition (in 1981) of two 100,000-ton plants, at Shevchenko (Kazakhstan) and Omsk (West Siberia). Part of the additional production will figure in Soviet exports product payback.

Acrylonitrile exports are from a plant that was built with Italian aid at Saratov and came on stream in 1978.[41] The 150,000-ton Saratov plant raised estimated Soviet capacity from 75,000 tons to 225,000 tons, and part of the output is being exported in the form of payback.

A major export-oriented chemical project is the Tomsk petrochemical complex of West Siberia, based on natural gas liquids from the region's oil fields. The first production unit at Tomsk, a 100,000-ton polypropylene plant, went into operation in 1981; the total Soviet production of this polyolefin, which resembles polyethylene, was some 35,000 to 40,000 tons before the opening of the Tomsk unit. The next stage of the complex was one of the world's largest methanol plants, with an annual capacity of 750,000 tons, which was to go on stream in 1982 and raise Soviet production from 1.8 million tons to 2.6 million. Even before the addition of the Tomsk capacity, the Soviet Union exported a quarter of a million tons of methanol, mainly from Severodonetsk, accounting for 17 percent of world methanol trade. The Tomsk unit and a second methanol plant, at Gubakha in the Urals, are expected to result in a surge of methanol exports in the 1980s, with 400,000 tons a year alone being shipped as product payback. To accommodate this flow of methanol, a special-purpose export terminal was under construction in the early 1980s at Ventspils on the Baltic Sea.

The Soviet Union was also expected to enter the world chemical market in the early 1980s with exports of another basic chemical building block, xylene, recovered at oil refineries at Ufa and Omsk. The commercially most important form of xylene, the para-xylene, is used in the manufacture of polyester fibers and films. Another form, the ortho-xylene, which will also be exported by the USSR, is used to make phthalic anhydride, which is used in alkyd resins, certain polyester resins and in polyvinyl chloride resins. In the second half of the 1970s, the Soviet Union had started exports of phthalic anhydride and dimethyl terephthalate, the intermediate products based on the xylenes, and the completion of the plants at Omsk and Ufa was to add the basic feedstocks to the Soviet exports.

Strong export positions have also been established in carbon black and in phosphorus. The Soviet Union used to be an importer of carbon black, but its dependency on foreign supplies ceased in 1963, and since then it has developed into a major exporter, accounting for some 20 percent of the world carbon black trade. The production of carbon black, which is a key ingredient in rubber manufacture, rose from 300,000 tons in 1960 to 691,000 tons in 1970,[42] and current production is estimated around 900,000 tons, of which some 100,000 tons are being exported, mainly to Eastern Europe. The surge of carbon black production in the 1960s was accompanied by a shift to a modern technology, from the old channel black de-

rived from natural gas to furnace black using liquid oil-refinery residues.

The Soviet Union's position in the production of elemental phosphorus developed in the late 1960s and early 1970s on the basis of the phosphate deposits of the Karatau district in southern Kazakhstan. This phosphate, as opposed to the higher-grade apatite concentrate of the Kola Peninsula, has too low a phosphorus content to be suitable for the usual wet process, in which phosphoric acid is produced by reacting phosphate rock with sulfuric acid. The Karatau phosphate is treated by the electric furnace reduction method to yield elemental phosphorus for shipment to phosphatic fertilizer plants around the Soviet Union. Significant exports began in 1967 with the opening of the first of three phosphorus plants in southern Kazakhstan, at Chimkent. Both production and exports jumped in 1974 and again in 1979 with the startup of two additional phosphorus plants at Dzhambul. In 1980, Kazakhstan produced some 85 percent of the Soviet Union's elemental phosphorus, or about 300,000 tons out of 350,000 tons. The 1985 plan for Kazakhstan has been set at 520,000 tons on the basis of full utilization of the 220,000-ton capacity of the second Dzhambul plant.[43] Exports in 1980 were 46,000 tons, or some 13 percent of Soviet production, with further growth likely during the 1980s. The phosphorus exports go mainly to Eastern Europe, with lesser amounts to Japan and West Germany.

Among the fertilizers, in addition to the increasingly important urea, the Soviet Union has traditionally been a major exporter of potash, ranking first among world producers, ahead of Canada, East Germany, West Germany and the United States. After a sharp increase in the 1960s and the first half of the 1970s, both production and exports of potash have held fairly steady since 1975, at an output level of 20 million tons (41.6 percent $K_2O$) and an export level of 6 million tons, or 30 percent of production. Soviet potash mining was originally limited to the Berezniki-Solikamsk district in the Urals, but since the early 1960s a major new potash deposit, at Soligorsk in Belorussia, has been developed, and now surpasses Urals production (Table 19). Part of the Belorussian capacity was developed with Polish assistance, and Poland has

TABLE 19
Soviet Production and Exports of Potash (thousand metric tons; 41.6 percent $K_2O$ content)

|  | 1960 | 1965 | 1970 | 1975 | 1980 | 1981 | 1985 Plan |
|---|---|---|---|---|---|---|---|
| USSR production | 2,606 | 5,691 | 9,824 | 19,097 | 19,385 | — | 27,000 |
| Urals | 2,258 | 3,444 | 3,995 | 9,588 | (8,456) | — | 12,000 |
| Belorussia | — | 1,602 | 4,786 | 8,317 | (10,100) | — | 13,600 |
| Ukraine | 348 | 630 | 959 | 1,096 | (811) | — | — |
| Others | — | 15 | 84 | 96 | (100) | — | — |
| USSR exports | 629 | 826 | 3,147 | 5,986 | 6,605 | 5,245 | — |
| Percent of production | 24 | 15 | 32 | 31 | 34 | — | — |
| To the West | 482 | 416 | 823 | 1,615 | 1,551 | 793 | — |
| Percent of exports | 77 | 50 | 26 | 27 | 24 | 15 | — |

SOURCES: *Narodnoye khozyaistvo SSSR v 1980g.* [The economy of the USSR in 1980] (Moscow: Finansy i Statistika, 1981), p. 161; *Narodnoye khozyaistvo RSFSR v 1980 g.* [The economy of the RSFSR in 1980] (Moscow: Finansy i Statistika, 1981), p. 72; *Narodne gospodarstvo Ukrainskoi RSR u 1980 rotsi* [The economy of the Ukrainian SSR in 1980] (Kiev: Tekhnika, 1981), p. 98; *Narodnoye khozyaistvo Belorusskoi SSR, 1981* [The economy of the Belorussian SSR, 1981] (Minsk: Belarus, 1981), p. 56; *Vneshnyaya torgovlya SSSR*, various years.

been compensated with annual shipments of 2.5 million tons a year, or 30 percent of Belorussian production.

Although the share of potash exports going to the Western countries has declined over the years, as much as one-fourth was still being shipped to hard-currency countries, with Japan, Belgium, Italy and Britain being the principal Western customers. In terms of total value, potash exports ranked among the top three chemical-related exports, with ammonia and urea. The Western share in Soviet potash exports is likely to increase somewhat during the 1980s as part of the barter deal with Occidental Petroleum Corporation, in which phosphoric acid from Florida is being exchanged for ammonia, urea and potash from the Soviet Union. The expected increase in shipments was foreshadowed by the expansion of potash-handling facilities at the export harbor of Ventspils on the Baltic Sea. A new terminal that started up in February 1981 raised the potash shipping capacity of the port from 800,000 tons to near 2 million a year.[44] The incremental exports are expected to come from Belorussia, where a fourth mining complex at Soligorsk began production in 1979. At full capacity, it is expected to raise Belorussian potash production to some 14 million tons.

The outlook for the Urals is more problematical. Although mining capacity in the Berezniki-Solikamsk district was raised to 12 million tons by the mid-1970s with the opening of the Berezniki complex in 1974–75, production has remained far below capacity. Soviet commentaries have attributed the problem to transport bottlenecks because of an overburdened railroad serving the mining district. The situation was particularly serious in 1979, when Urals potash output declined by one-third below the previous year's level, to 6.2 million from 9.7 million tons. The problem was especially acute in the first quarter of 1979, when only a fraction of normal Urals potash output was delivered. Production improved somewhat in 1980, when 8.5 million tons was mined, but this was still far below the theoretical capacity of 12 million tons. In the meantime, excavation has been under way on two more mining complexes, Berezniki No. 4 and the Novo-Solikamsk (New Solikamsk) mine, with the latter yielding its first potash in 1983. It remains unclear how the additional potash is to be moved if the previously developed mining capacity could not be fully utilized. There has been pressure on the potash industry to move more of its product by water on the Kama River during the icefree shipping season. But the traditional aversion of Soviet shippers to make greater use of waterways has not been overcome. Only some 200,000 tons of potash a year is being transported by water, and the potential waterway traffic out of the Urals potash mines has been estimated at 2.5 million to 3 million tons.[45] This represents roughly the theoretical mining capacity that could not be moved by rail, even before the continuing expansion of the Urals potash operations.

Finally, note should be made under chemical exports of Soviet uranium enrichment services, which figure prominently in foreign trade with Western European countries, especially with West Germany and France. Starting in 1974, when the Soviet Union began to make part of its enrichment capacity available to Western electric utilities,

West German utilities, in particular, have been sending uranium purchased from uranium-producing countries to the Soviet Union for enrichment. Soviet-enriched uranium has even figured in trade with the United States. In 1980, uranium originating in Canada and enriched in the Soviet Union was then transferred directly to the United States for fabrication into nuclear fuel elements before finally reaching the ultimate consumer, a nuclear electric station in West Germany. Although the enriched uranium was destined for reexport in fabricated form, it appeared in United States trade statistics in 1980 as an import from the Soviet Union worth $43.8 million, or 10 percent of the total value of United States imports from the Soviet Union in that year.[46]

## NOTES

1. The reserve categories $A + B + C_1$, which are used for long-term planning, are 255 billion tons; 1980 coal production was 716 million metric tons, and 1981 output 706 million.

2. *Ekonomicheskaya gazeta*, 1981, no. 42.

3. For a reconstruction of Soviet oil export data in physical units on the basis of partner country statistics, see the series *International Energy Statistical Review*, a monthly publication of the Central Intelligence Agency; also J.B. Hannigan and C.H. McMillan, "The Soviet Union and Western Trade in Oil and Gas." (Paper read at a conference on the Soviet Impact on Commodity Markets, Montreal, 8–9 October 1981.)

4. *Pravda*, 17 November 1981.

5. Gas reserves for 1970 and 1975 from Leslie Dienes and Theodore Shabad, *The Soviet Energy System* (New York: Halstead Press, 1979), p. 69, Table 17, and for 1980 from *Izvestiya*, 11 November 1981.

6. Theodore Shabad, "Siberian Gas Field Delayed by Soviet," *New York Times*, 20 August 1981, p. 17.

7. S.A. Orudzhev, *Goluboye zoloto Zapadnoi Sibiri* [The blue gold of West Siberia] (Moscow: Nedra, 1981), pp. 34, 36.

8. Ibid., p. 37.

9. The preliminary gas pipeline plan appeared in *Ekonomicheskaya gazeta*, 1981, no. 13; the revised plan in *Ekonomicheskaya gazeta*, 1981, no. 43. However, the Soviet economic planning chief, Nikolai K. Baibakov, in announcing the final version of the 11th Five-Year Plan (1981–85) preserved the 48,000-km of new gas pipeline construction.

10. Yu. A. Zakharov, *Tekhnika odinnadtsatoi pyatiletki* [Technology in the 11th five-year plan] (Moscow: Znaniye, 1981), p. 20.

11. Yu. Bokserman, "The steel channels of gas streams," *Izvestiya*, 11 November 1981.

12. Ibid., *Pravda*, 15 June 1981.

13. Theodore Shabad, "News Notes," *Soviet Geography: Review and Translation* (Hereafter, *SGRT*) 22, no. 7 (September 1981): 456–58.

14. Shabad, "News Notes," *SGRT*, 22, no. 8 (October 1981): 541–43.

15. L.A. Kostandov, "USSR-FRG.—Mutually ben-

eficial collaboration," *Ekonomicheskaya gazeta*, 1981, no. 46, p. 9.

16. U.S. Congress, Office of Technology Assessment, *Technology and Soviet Energy Availability*, 97th Cong., 1st sess., 1981, p. 378.

17. *Ekonomicheskaya gazeta*, 1978, no. 7, spoke of expanding the Chernobyl nuclear station at Pripyat to a capacity of 10,000 to 12,000 MW. *Pravda Ukrainy*, 13 February 1981, said a fifth 1,000 MW unit was planned for 1975. *Sovetskaya Litva*, 22 December 1981, said the ultimate capacity was now planned for 6,000 MW.

18. For background on the Khmelnitsky nuclear station, see Shabad, "News Notes," *SGRT*, 23, no 1 (January 1982).

19. *Voprosy ekonomiki*, 1981, no. 9, p. 112.

20. *Pravda*, 18 November 1981.

21. *Sovetskaya Rossiya*, 12 February 1981.

22. *Razvedka i okhrana nedr*, 1981, no. 7.

23. Shabad, "Soviet Regional Policy and CMEA Integration," *SGRT*, 20, no. 4 (April 1979): 242.

24. Ibid.

25. V.S. Sidorova and V.A. Vadyukhin, "New technology and the location of an iron and steel industry in the eastern portion of the USSR," *SGRT*, 18, no. 1 (January 1977): 33–38; Shabad, "News Notes," *SGRT*, 18, no. 8 (October 1977): 609; *Sovetskaya Rossiya*, 10 June 1981.

26. *Razvedka i okhrana nedr*, 1976, no. 5, p. 2.

27. *Gorny zhurnal*, 1981, no. 6, pp. 12–13; *Kazakhstanskaya pravda*, 17 May 1981.

28. Shabad, "News Notes," *SGRT*, 22, no. 10 (December 1981): 692–93.

29. Central Intelligence Agency, *Handbook of Economic Statistics, 1980* p. 152; for a background discussion of the Soviet titanium industry, see Theodore Shabad, *Basic Industrial Resources of the USSR* (New York: Columbia University Press, 1969), p. 64.

30. U.S. Bureau of Mines, *Mineral Facts and Problems*. Titanium chapter, 1980 edition.

31. Theodore Shabad, "Raw Material Problems of the Soviet Aluminum Industry," *Resources Policy*, December 1976, pp. 222–34.

32. *Osobennosti i problemy razmeshcheniya proizvoditelnykh sil SSSR v period razvitogo sotsializma* [Peculiarities and problems of development of productive forces in the USSR in the period of developed socialism] (Moscow: Nauka, 1980), pp. 49–50.

33. V.F. Zadorozhny, "Problems of development of the Udokan copper deposit," *SGRT*, 22, no. 5 (May 1981): 325–30.

34. For a detailed analysis of the role of Soviet asbestos in world markets, see Petr Hanel (University of Sherbrooke, Canada), "Soviet Impact on International Trade in Asbestos" (Paper delivered at conference on the Soviet Impact on Commodity Markets, Montreal, 8–9 October 1981).

35. U.S. Bureau of Mines, *Mineral Facts and Problems*. Diamond chapter, 1980 edition.

36. *Stroitelnaya gazeta*, 12 November 1978; *Sovetskaya Rossiya*, 23 June 1976; *Sotsialisticheskaya industriya*, 11 June 1974; *Pravda*, 13 July 1968.

37. *Gorny zhurnal*, 1977, no. 11; *Ekonomika gazovoi promyshlennosti*, 1979, no. 10; *Gazovaya promyshlennost*, 1977, no. 11.

38. For information on sulfur recovery in the Orenburg gas field, see *Pravda*, 11 October 1981; for Mubarek, *Sotsialisticheskaya industriya*, 28 November 1981.

39. Shabad, "News Notes," *SGRT*, 21, no. 10 (December 1980): 676–80, provides details on Soviet chemical exports on a product payback basis.

40. *Vneshnyaya torgovlya*, 1981, no. 10, p. 15.

41. Shabad, "News Notes," *SGRT* 19, no. 10 (December 1978): 741.

42. V.M. Bushuyev, *Khimicheskaya industriya v svete reshenii XXIV syezda KPSS* [The chemical industry in light of decisions at the 24th party congress] (Moscow: Khimiya, 1974), p. 82.

43. *Kazakhstanskaya pravda*, 4 December 1981.

44. *Sotsialisticheskaya industriya*, 5 November 1980; *Sovetskaya Latviya*, 7 February 1981.

45. *Izvestiya*, 28 March 1981; *Sotsialisticheskaya industriya*, 29 May 1976; 16 June 1981.

46. *New York Times*, 17 August 1981.

# SOVIET ENERGY POLICY
# AND THE FOSSIL FUELS

LESLIE DIENES
University of Kansas

## Introduction

Economic development involves the enhancement and use of natural resources through human skills and technology. The very unequal distribution and cost of the earth's resources (natural and human), combined with dramatic innovations in transportation and business organization, mean that such a process increasingly takes place in a global context. Since World War II, international trade has become a prime engine of economic development. The inputs of production today are assembled and joined across five continents. Historically, the increasing complexity and maturation of economies have led invariably to a declining share of natural resources in the production of current income. Yet this has failed to diminish the importance of the resource sector. Indeed, the exhaustion of a whole range of domestic energy and other raw materials (or at least those accessible at current prices and technology) in Western industrial nations and the mounting dependence of these nations on foreign and distant sources of supplies can only underscore the increasing significance of these inputs. At the same time, the abrupt price changes a few years ago halted, if not reversed, the decline in the share of the resource sector in the world economy.

Today we are witnessing a growing concern over the adequacy and cost of natural resources for the world's future population. With the absence of supplies or serious depletion at home (at least for accessible, conventional sources) and overdependence on a relatively few foreign countries now able to control output schedules, the Western world is seeking new resource frontiers. Without such new frontiers, demand for several key commodities may start to outrun supplies in the not-too-distant future, leading to fierce competition, price spirals and excessive strain on the fabric of world economy. Energy supplies, particularly hydrocarbons, seem most clearly to be so affected, but other commodities also may not be immune.

Together with the oceans and Antarctica, the USSR (specifically Siberia) appears as the greatest resource frontier today, whose riches exist on a truly massive scale and are able to make a global impact. Unlike the oceans and Antarctica, Siberia is already explored to an appreciable degree, some of its resources are being exploited and its potential has been better assessed. Despite its harsh environment, it appears more accessible through present technology than the two other frontiers mentioned. However, unlike these others, Siberia is part of sovereign realm of one of the two superpowers of the day, whose ideology, political organization and aspirations are alien to, and on several fundamental issues irreconcilable with, those of Western societies. The issue of Western (and Japanese) assistance to develop the Siberian resource frontier, therefore, involves economic as well as strategic and political assessment and judgment on the part of both the Soviet and non-Soviet governments. Moscow's commitment to whole-hearted, full-scale participation in world trade is still uncertain.[1] Yet Soviet dependence on the remote eastern regions is growing so rapidly that the accelerated development of these resources has become vital to the Soviet economy itself. At the same time, a looming manpower shortage, sluggish productivity gains and persistent agricultural woes seem to have convinced Soviet leaders of the urgency of more rapid technological advancement. The role of Western technology in this process is inextricably linked with the accelerated development of the Siberian resource frontier. Soviet ability to pay for technological imports and Western needs for energy and other raw materials combine to thrust the resources of the Asian USSR onto center stage in any such collaboration.

The following analysis deals with Soviet energy policy planning as it applies to the main fossil fuels. The author investigates the development of energy intensity and needs of the Soviet economy, demands for fuel in the aggregate and in specific technological uses, the growing conflict between domestic and export requirements and the prospect of substitution to free oil for hard-currency export. Finally, and very briefly, Soviet energy modeling to optimize energy supplies is described and prospects for expanding output of the three major fuels are analyzed. The author concludes on a pessimistic note. He is convinced that in the forthcoming decade Soviet planners will be unable to restrict domestic energy consumption in general, and petroleum consumption in particular, without drastically slowing an already sluggish economic growth. Nor will they be able to effect really significant substitution and alter the fuel mix to free more than marginal quantities of oil. And lastly, despite vast potential resources and, in the case of gas and coal, explored reserves as well, the output of the three major fuels cannot be expanded at a pace sufficient to make the USSR more than a *very minor* factor in world energy exports. Indeed, outside the ruble area, even that position must be regarded as precarious. Gas exports beyond the CMEA will be considerable, though not decisive, but *at best* only a fraction of present oil export beyond the Soviet bloc can be preserved on a tonnage basis. Since the poor performance of the coal industry is almost certain to continue, a substantial drop in petroleum production would inevitably lead to a stagnant aggregate energy supply, with increments in gas and nuclear power at most compensating for supply losses by the oil industry. The potential impact of Soviet hydrocarbon resources is not denied, but the shadow that falls between idea and reality may be very long.

### Energy Intensiveness and the Growth of Soviet Energy Demand

Long-run correlations between economic development and the growth of aggregate energy use have been high. Over shorter periods such a systematic relationship is harder to detect. The general experience has been that in the period of early industrialization, when countries build up their basic industrial infrastructure and capital stock, the growth rate of energy consumption surges ahead of the growth rate for national income and the energy intensiveness of the economy rises. In the later stages of development, the opposite situation tends to prevail, and energy intensiveness declines. This means a greater economic punch from a unit of energy input and, other things being equal, is a sign of increased efficiency. The perception of energy-GNP relationships may be critical for public policy. It is obviously crucial in command economies for the drawing up of long-range plans since the mobilization of energy resources provides a most vital underpinning of a country's economic and military strength.

The beginning of the Soviet industrialization drive was associated with extremely high annual increases in aggregate energy consumption. Soviet leaders pressed to the utmost the development of heavy, capital-intensive and power-oriented industries as the basis of their economic strategy at the expense of other sectors and, as in most other aspects, the Soviet industrialization drive was unique in its energy intensity. Indeed, a fall in the average rate of growth set in soon afterward to be interrupted by another upsurge in the years of war preparation. Following reconstruction from World War II, the rate of increase in gross energy consumption continued to drop until the 1970s in each subsequent five years. Although this trend was interrupted in the first half of the 1970s and in the original targets of the 10th Five-Year Plan (1976–80), the mounting troubles in the Soviet energy sector, the sharp deceleration of economic growth, combined with export needs, soon reestablished the decline in the rate of energy consumption (Table 1). But what does this decline show? Does it show greater effectiveness in energy use or has the latter merely followed the trend for GNP? What is the degree of flexibility Soviet leaders are likely to have in the future concerning the highly con-

TABLE 1
Average Annual Growth Rates of Soviet Energy Consumption and National Income (Percent per Annum)

| Periods | Gross Energy Consumption | Delivered Energy | Net Energy Consumption | National Income | |
|---|---|---|---|---|---|
| | | | | Soviet Data (national income utilized) | Western Estimates |
| 1929–40 | 13.9 | — | — | — | — |
| 1929–32 | 17.2 | — | — | — | 5.3 |
| 1933–40 | 12.3 | — | — | — | — |
| 1933–37 | 7.3 | — | — | — | — |
| 1938–40 | 21.2 | — | — | — | — |
| 1951–60 | 7.4 | 6.4 | 7.6 | 10.2 | 5.9 |
| 1961–65 | 5.8 | 5.9 | 8.7 | 5.9 | 4.9 |
| 1966–70 | 4.6 | 4.9 | 6.4 | 7.0 | 5.3 |
| 1971–75 | 4.8 | 4.0 | 5.2 | 5.1 | 3.7 |
| 1976–78 | 4.3 | n.d. | n.d. | 4.2 | 3.7 |

SOURCES: Column 1: Prewar growth rates computed from data on apparent consumption as given in Robert Campbell, *The Economics of Soviet Oil and Gas* (Baltimore: Johns Hopkins, 1968), p. 4. Postwar rates from *Narodnoye khozyaistvo SSSR*. Various issues. Tables on fuel-energy balance. Nuclear power added according to the heat rates of utility stations of corresponding year. Nuclear electricity output from A. A. Nekrasov and M. G. Pervukhin, eds., *Energetika SSSR v 1976–1980 godakh* (Moscow: Energiya, 1977), p. 11 and *Elektricheskiye stantsii*, 1980, no. 4, p. 7.
    Column 2: R. Campbell, "Energy in the USSR to the Year 2000," Paper prepared for the *Conference on the Soviet Economy towards the Year 2000*, 23–25 October 1980, Airlee House, Virginia.
    Column 3: A. A. Beschinsky and Yu. M. Kogan, *Ekonomicheskiye problemy elektrifikatsii* (Moscow: Energiya, 1976), p. 208 and A. A. Makarov and A. G. Vigdorchik, *Toplivno-energetichesky kompleks* (Moscow: Nauka, 1979), p. 81.
    Column 4: *Narodnoye khozyaistvo SSSR*. Various issues.
    Column 5: Herbert Block, "Soviet Economic Performance in a Global Context," in U. S. Congress, Joint Economic Committee, *Soviet Economy in a Time of Change* (Washington: Government Printing Office, 1979), p. 136.

troversial relationship between energy consumption and economic growth?

If the Soviet definition of national income and its growth rates are accepted, the energy intensiveness of the Soviet economy (i.e., gross energy input per ruble of national income) declined significantly during the 1950s and 1960s, but stabilized during the 1970s, with remarkably small year-to-year oscillation (Table 2). Using the lower Western estimates for the growth of Soviet GNP, however, we find a small rise in energy intensiveness as measured by gross energy input through the 1950s and a gradual return to the 1950 level in the subsequent two decades. Though the energy intensiveness of the economy in the past decade shows more viability when Western GNP estimates are applied, some stabilization is, again, observable during the last few years (Table 2, column 3).

Looking at changes in energy-GNP ratios based on aggregate energy input alone may be misleading. At least as important is the development of net (useful) energy consumption[2] relative to national income and of gross consumption weighted by productivity coefficients for energy sources in principal uses.[3] As Table 2 makes clear, *net* energy use, i.e., energy turned into useful work or incorporated into products, remained remarkably constant per ruble of national income throughout the last thirty years. With Western calculations for Soviet GNP in dollars, *net* energy input per unit of GNP increased substantially (Table 2, columns 2 and 4). Recent Soviet research attests to the fact that sectoral changes had virtually no influence on *net* energy use per unit of national income and there was little, if any, systemic shift toward a less energy-demanding economic structure. Within industry, the impact resulting from some shift toward the lighter, less energy-intensive engineering branches was compensated by the opposite effect of the rapid development of the chemical industry and of the declining quality and accessibility of mineral resources. Minor reduction in the *net* energy intensity of the domestic-municipal economy was counteracted by the adverse trend in agriculture and, to some extent, transportation.[4] Soviet experts contend that the remarkable stability of relationship between

TABLE 2
Energy Intensiveness of the Soviet Economy

| | Energy/GNP Ratio Based on Official Soviet Data | | Energy/GNP Ratio Based on Western Estimates of Soviet GNP in U. S. Dollars | |
| --- | --- | --- | --- | --- |
| Year | Gross Energy Input kg of SF*/ruble of utilized national income** | Net Energy Input kg of SF*/ruble of utilized national income** | Gross Energy Input kg of SF*/$1 of GNP*** | Net Energy Input kg of SF*/$1 of GNP*** |
| 1950 | 6.08 (7.34)[a] | 1.69 (204)[a] | 1.72 | 0.48 |
| 1955 | 5.76[b] | 1.65 | 1.86 | 0.54 |
| 1960 | 4.70 | 1.60 | 1.94 | 0.60 |
| 1962 | — | — | 1.91 | 0.63 ca. |
| 1965 | 4.53 | 1.65 | 1.94 | 0.67 |
| 1968 | — | — | 1.88 | 0.68 ca. |
| 1970 | 4.08 | 1.63 | 1.69 | 0.68 |
| 1972 | 4.08 | — | 1.80 | 0.73 ca. |
| 1974 | 4.06 | — | 1.78 | 0.71 ca. |
| 1975 | 4.05 | 1.64 | 1.81 | 0.73 ca. |
| 1976 | 4.09 | 1.62 | 1.74 | 0.74 ca. |
| 1977 | 4.02 | 1.68 | 1.74 | 0.74 ca. |
| 1978 | 4.07 | 1.71 | 1.77 | 0.77 ca. |

[a]The figure in parenthesis is after Beschinsky and Kogan (1976), p. 200; the others are after the *Narodnoye khozyaistvo SSSR* series. After 1950, the two series are virtually identical, but no explanation is given in Beschinsky for the discrepancy for that year.

[b]No official data are available for consumption in 1955. The figure is based on apparent consumption, computed as production minus *net* export on an even calorific basis.

*1 kg of Standard Fuel = 7,000 kilocalories; roughly equivalent to the heat content of 1 kilogram of very good hard coal.

**Soviet concept: the value of net *tangible* material output. Excludes "non-productive" services and capital consumption allowances.

***Western definition: The value of all final goods and services. Computed in 1975 U. S. dollars.

NOTE: The amount of energy input per ruble of national income (Soviet concept) is much larger than the amount of energy input per U. S. dollars of national income. The reason is found not merely in the exclusion of services and capital consumption allowances from the Soviet definition of national income, but, still more, in the different price weights. The Soviet GNP (the denominator) value in rubles is roughly 60 percent of the one computed in dollars. A detailed ruble calculation, however, could not be made by Western analysts for many years because of the lack of a comprehensive price list since 1955. But for the purpose of discussion here, what matters is not the absolute values of energy intensity but their change through time. The 1975 ratios are somewhat anomalous, since the denominator (GNP) was drastically depressed because of the poor harvest.

SOURCES: National income utilized in rubles for two benchmark years (1950 and 1971) taken from A. A. Beschinsky and Yu. M. Kogan, *Ekonomicheskiye problemy elektrifikatsii* (Moscow: Energiya, 1976), p. 208. Indices of growth for intervening years and gross energy consumption without nuclear power are taken from various issues of *Narodnoye khozyaistvo SSSR*. Nuclear power production from A. A. Nekrasov and M. G. Pervukhin, *Energetika SSSR v 1976–1980 godakh* (Moscow: Energiya, 1977), p. 11 and *Elektricheskiye stantsii*, 1980, no. 4, p. 7. Nuclear energy added to official total of gross energy consumption by the heat rate of utility stations of corresponding years as given in *Narodnoye khozyaistvo SSSR*.

Net energy use for 1950 is from Beschinsky and Kogan (1976), p. 208; for subsequent five-year intervals until 1976 inclusive from A. A. Makarov and A. G. Vigdorchik, *Toplivno-energeticheskiy kompleks* (Moscow: Nauka, 1979), p. 81. For intervening years, marked in column 4 by ca. (circa), it was estimated from coefficients computed from data for these five-year intervals.

Western estimates of Soviet GNP in 1975 U. S. dollars are taken from Herbert Block, "Soviet Economic Power Growth," in U. S. Congress, Joint Economic Committee, *Soviet Economy in a New Perspective* (Washington, 1976), p. 246. Growth rate from 1975 to 1978 from Herbert Block, "Soviet Economic Performance in a Global Context," in U. S. Congress, Joint Economic Committee, *Soviet Economy in a Time of Change* (Washington, 1979), p. 136.

*net* energy use and national income will be maintained well into the future (Table 3).

The drop in aggregate energy consumption per unit of national income could be explained by the rapid shift to hydrocarbons and the especially swift substitution of these efficient fuels in certain sectors or functions (railway haulage, chemical industry) with particularly large energy savings and/or economic effect. Electrification was an equally significant factor. As in other countries, it greatly enhanced the flexibility and efficiency of factory and, later, agricultural operations. Meanwhile, the share of conversion losses implicit in increased electrification was kept within bounds by improvements in the heat rate and the growth of cogeneration. The thermodynamic efficiency of the Soviet energy system as a whole increased greatly between 1955 and 1975, total energy waste being reduced from 72 percent to 56 to 58 percent. Improved heat capture diminished the share of losses occuring after delivery to final consuming apparatus, but these still account for about three-fifths of all energy squandered.[5]

If past experience suggests no decrease in *net* energy use per ruble of national income, *aggregate* energy requirement (i.e., the demand for raw fuels, hydro and nuclear electricity) per unit of GNP can continue to decline only if one or both of the following take place: (a) structural shifts in the economy toward less energy and material intensive sectors and branches with high value added; (b) improved utilization efficiency, namely the ratio of gross to net consumption in specific applications. Soviet experts do not expect the former, but do expect the latter to continue, albeit at a significantly reduced pace.[6]

In my view, inexorable secular trends may largely counterbalance such improvements. Further electrification must now be pursued with heat rates that, in the best plants today, are approaching thermodynamic limits, while the substitution of hydrocarbons for less efficient solid fuels has basically come to an end (indeed, over the long term, some degree of reverse substitution is envisaged, especially in power generation). In addition, the quality and/or accessibility of both fossil fuel and metallic resources continue to decline at an accelerated rate, requiring massive material and energy inputs and still

more to forestall unacceptable environmental damage. Largely as a consequence of worsening accessibility, the energy industries have become large direct consumers of their own output and consume still more fuel and power indirectly through their mounting material demands. Self-use, with internal losses, amounts to 11 to 12 percent of gross domestic availability and has been rising since 1970 after a period of relative decline.[7] Direct and indirect consumption of their own output by the producers of primary energy probably approximates one-third of all domestic supply.[8]

Since further technological improvements in energy efficiency for the remainder of this century will be slower than during the last two decades, compensations for the worsening trends above must come mostly from vigorous and organized conservation measures that are now receiving great emphasis. In the Soviet Union, however, energy consumption has stronger structural, institutional, and geographic ties with the sinews of the economy, with high priority sectors, than in most Western countries. Municipal and household use in the USSR accounts for less than one-sixth of all stationary energy demand; taxis, leisure related transport and the private car increase the amount only slightly. Moreover, in 1975, half of all residential consumption was still accounted for by unsorted coal, lignite, peat, and wood burned in fireplaces and stoves, much of it cut by the population itself.[9] Conservation of heat furnished to households via cogeneration is difficult because of the inflexibility imposed on electric plants by the combined heat and power regime,[10] by the frequency of poorly designed housing units and the absence of metering devices on the premises.[11]

In individual years such as 1970 and 1977, Soviet planners successfully curtailed the rise of energy demand, in large part by restricting oil consumption in favor of export.[12] Yet opportunities to do this regularly without depressing industrial growth are limited. Indeed, throughout the 1976–80 plan, a number of heavy fuel-energy industries showed abnormally low growth rates and even absolute declines in the last two years.[13] The causes of poor performance are many and complex, but a tightening supply of energy for them must be a significant contributing factor. Given the present structure of the Soviet economy and the incremental energy demand imposed by worsening resource conditions west of the Urals and the accelerated development of Siberia, continued planned curtailment in the rise of gross energy input will substantially retard the expansion of the Soviet economy.

TABLE 3
Energy Intensiveness of National Economy by Final Uses (Kcal/1000 rubles of national income)

| Indicator | 1955 | 1965 | 1975 | Projection |
|---|---|---|---|---|
| National economy | 11.7 | 11.65 | 11.7 | 11.4–11.6 |
| Industry | 6.3 | 6.25 | 6.2 | 6.0– 6.1 |
| Transport | 0.6 | 0.8 | 1.0 | 1.2– 1.25 |
| Agriculture | 0.45 | 0.6 | 0.7 | 0.9– 0.95 |
| Services and households | | | | |
| – per unit of national income | 3.75 | 3.5 | 3.3 | 3.0 |
| – per capita | 1.75 | 3.95 | 4.65 | 5.8– 5.9 |

SOURCE: L. A. Melentyev et al., "The Relationship between Economic Growth and Energy Development," in *11th World Energy Conference*, 8–12 September 1980. Munich. *Preprint*, vol. 4A, p. 554.

**Soviet Energy Strategy—The Recent Past**

Since the latter 1950s, Soviet energy strategy has followed the world trend and begun an accelerated development and utilization of oil and gas resources. Between 1960 and 1980, 92 percent of all *increment* in aggregate fuel production on a calorific basis was accounted for by these two fuels.[14] Without this structural shift, it would have been economically and physically impossible to achieve the 3.7-fold growth in calorific output. Had the share of oil and gas remained constant over these years, such a growth would have required an increment of more than 1,900 million physical tons in coal production, some 70 percent of it from underground mines, and a capacity expansion of perhaps 2,600 million tons.[15] Because even large, modern underground coal mines have production capacities of only 4 to 8 million tons per annum and take a decade to construct, such an expansion appears beyond the realm of the possible even today. In addition, the upsurge of oil and, later, gas output generated huge benefits to the USSR through international trade, enabling it to finance a large share of its Western imports with energy exports. Aided by the huge price rise of 1973, petroleum and natural gas now provide over one half of Soviet hard-currency earnings from trade.[16] Until about 1970, the structural shift in the fuel mix also led to a decline in the average production cost and, still more, in the delivery cost of fuel (between 1955 and the late 1960s the mean production cost of 7 million kilocalories fell from over ten rubles to around seven)[17] and yielded large economies through more efficient heat capture, locomotive power, reduced handling charges and far greater flexibility in chemical synthesis.

With petroleum output rising vigorously until the later 1970s, Soviet leaders were spared the difficult decisions about priority allocation between exports and domestic needs. The dampening of growth in domestic oil consumption in favor of exports involved relatively small quantities. It could be effected by drawing down on stocks, by some substitution of natural gas and by relatively easy conservation measures. Between 1973 and 1978, Soviet oil production was growing annually by 25 million to 29 million tons, increments never reached before, while gas output was again accelerating after several years of declining increments.[18] Soviet leaders could thus augment oil and gas exports to both the CMEA and hard-currency markets. In the four years from January 1975 to January 1979, oil exports to countries beyond the bloc grew much faster than to CMEA states and, thanks to the new world prices, pushed hard-currency earnings to a record high. However, oil deliveries to the CMEA also increased by perhaps 20 million tons only 12 to 13 million less than increments in sales beyond the bloc,[19] despite the much lower prices paid to the Soviets by communist states.

We cannot confidently forecast Soviet priorities between exports and internal demand once petroleum output peaks or declines. Three Western observers not long ago voiced somewhat contrary opinions,[20] and I venture to say that Soviet planners themselves had no answer to this question. The regular and quite rapid decline in the *increment* of petroleum production since 1975 and the large absolute drops in output in all but three of the Soviet petroleum provinces suggest that this choice may soon have to be faced.[21] I hold the view that, if Soviet petroleum flow indeed peaks, only a part of oil exports could be preserved. In particular, most, though perhaps not all, hard-currency sales will be eliminated. In the more controversial case of a substantial drop in oil production, predicted by the CIA, the economic and possible political consequences throughout the bloc are likely to be so profound that speculations become pointless.

## Energy Policy Issues for the Future

It is clear that Soviet energy development has entered a new phase. The large economic gains accruing from the rapid rise of cheap oil and gas in the fuel mix cannot be repeated; in addition, exports and domestic needs have come into clear conflict. Since the latter sixties, the production and delivered costs of both petroleum and natural gas have been rising steeply, apparently faster than those for coal, and incremental capital requirements per ton of new capacity have multiplied.[22] And while the gap between the cost of solid fuels and that of hydrocarbons may remain substantial in many regions of the USSR, the drastic rise in the export value of petroleum has largely eliminated the economic rationale of further increasing the share of oil (if not gas) in the domestic fuel mix. Finally, the mounting anxiety felt by Western leaders over the adequacy of future petroleum supplies has made a deep impression on Moscow. The proven, as opposed to potential, reserves of oil in the USSR also appear unsatisfactory and prospects for this pivotal energy source seem far more worrisome than for other fuels.

The three major policy issues facing Soviet energy planners over the next dozen years or more, therefore, concern:

(a) Substitution possibilities among domestic fuel-energy sources and feasible modifications in the proportions of sectoral demand patterns;

(b) Possible modifications in the proportions of geographic demand patterns. Such modifications could result in savings of scarce resources and may be fairly significant if supplies tighten. Administrative measures restricting demand may affect regional consumption directly (and not just through the sectoral pattern), particularly outside high priority industries;

(c) Expansion of domestic supplies at the requisite mix to match demand over an area larger than North and Central America combined, with a population of 265 million today and some 285 million by 1990.

These issues are obviously interrelated. They are also intertwined with the structure and spatial dimension of the economy as a whole, of which the energy sector forms only a part. Policy problem (b) is treated in chapter 16 of this volume and space will permit only a brief analysis of the two other points.

### Substitution Possibilities: Coal for Hydrocarbons

At whatever rate and in whatever precise mix Soviet planners may be able to expand their energy base, a problem summarized later, the desire to economize on petroleum resources can serve as a starting point of this analysis of policy issues. Speculation about substitution policies is meaningless without some knowledge of the functional breakdown of fuel consumption, i.e., the technological uses to which energy is applied. In recent years enough information has been released to permit such an analysis and to project it forward on the basis of Soviet plans and various assumed rates of aggregate consumption growth. Technological uses that by their very nature are tied to hydrocarbons as well as industrial and household furnaces constructed to burn oil and gas (see subtotals A and B in Table 4) demanded about 509 million standard tons of petroleum products and natural gas in 1976. A mixture of trends, achievements, and projections for different uses suggests 655 million standard tons for these completely and virtually nonsubstitutable categories for 1980. In both years, large field, pipeline and distribution losses are included in the breakdown. By

TABLE 4
Functional Breakdown of Oil and Gas Use
(1976 and 1980) (million tons of standard
fuel; 1 ton = 7 million kilocalories)

| Use categories | 1976 Natural gas | 1976 Oil | 1980 Natural gas and oil |
|---|---|---|---|
| Mobile uses | — | 195[a] | 220* |
| Liquefied gases | 5.3[b] | 7[b] | 16[c] |
| Field use and losses | 3.1 | 20[d] | 32* |
| Gas pipelines—fuel | 18.0[c] | — | 43[c] |
| Gas pipelines—losses | 6.6[c] | — | 43[c] |
| Gas processing plants—fuel and losses | 3.6 | — | 6* |
| Petroleum refining—fuel and losses | 2.5[e] | 29[e] | 38[c] |
| Blast furnaces | 10.1 | 0.5[f] | 15[g] |
| Open-hearth furnaces | 6.8 | 3.5[f] | 11[g] |
| Chemical raw materials, industrial lubricants, bitumen (hydrocarbons other than liquid gases) | 22.2 | 45[h] | 85* |
| Household furnaces and stoves | 15.8 | negl. | 24* |
| Subtotal (A) | 94.0 | 300 | 490 |
| Steel pipes | 1.8 | — | — |
| Rolled steel | 6.4 | — | — |
| Furnaces in nonferrous metallurgy | 2.8 | — | — |
| Cement kilns | 12.4 | — | — |
| Furnaces and ovens for glass, ceramics, other construction and refractory materials | 12.2 | — | — |
| Forges and related devices for shaping metals | 8.3 | — | — |
| Other applications | 11[i] | — | — |
| Subtotal (B) | 55.0 | 60* | 165* |
| Subtotal A + B | 149.0 | 360 | 655 |
| Electric Power Ministry and industrial power stations | 111.3 | 136[j] | 315[j] |
| Industrial boilers | 49.1 | — | — |
| Municipal boilers | 33.0 | | |
| Small boilers and isolated power stations | 10.1[i] | 45* | 105* |
| Total power station and boiler use (subtotal C) | 203.5 | 181 | 425 |
| Net addition to stock and storage and to fill new pipelines | 15.5[k] | 1[l]* | 40* |
| Apparent consumption (production minus net export) | 368.0 | 542 | 1,115* |

NOTES AND SOURCES: Except where otherwise noted, all 1976 figures for natural gas are from an authoritative study in *Gazovaya promyshlennost*, 1978, no. 6, pp. 12 and 29. Figures noted with letters are a mixture of Soviet and Western data and the author's calculations derived from a variety of sources as explained below.

*Denotes estimates by the author that appear reasonable but cannot be supported by solid evidence.

Apparent consumption for 1976 is factual, converted to standard ton equivalents from physical tonnage given in *Narodnoye khozyaistvo SSSR za 60 let*, p. 205 and *Vneshnyaya torgovlya SSSR v 1976 g.*, pp. 26 and 38.

[a]Estimated by assigning all gasoline and most kerosene to mobile uses. Fuel oil and diesel fuel were assigned according to their percentages in the transport sector and, for diesel fuel, also in the agricultural, construction

contrast, power stations and industrial and municipal boilers consumed 385 million standard tons of hydrocarbons in 1976 and were slated to burn about 425 million tons by 1980 according to the plan (Table 4).

Not only must hydrocarbon demand by blast furnaces and open-hearth furnaces be considered nonsubstitutable, but in other industries, too, furnaces fired by gas or petroleum could be converted to coal only with difficulty over a long time period. With some caveat for the small share of household furnaces, this category of demand, together with mobile and petrochemical uses, must be regarded as having priority claim on hydrocarbon resources in the sense that no alternatives are in sight. Whatever Soviet perceptions may be about the adequacy of hydrocarbon resources or about oil and gas as hard-currency earners, Soviet writers show no indication that a relative expansion of coal use in the above categories of demand is viewed as a rational course. Fuel use by industrial furnaces, however, is expected to increase more slowly in the future than energy consumption as a whole, reducing the share of these sectors in aggregate demand. Soviet scholars also project a slightly slower rate of

and other sectors. The output of refinery products for 1975 is available from R. W. Campbell, *Soviet Fuel and Energy Balances* (Santa Monica, Ca.: RAND Corporation, Research Report R–2257, 1978), Appendix. The consumption breakdown by sectors is given in *Vestnik statistiki*, 1978, no. 1, p. 9.

[b]Total for 1975 given in *Energetika SSSR v 1976–1980 godakh* (Moscow: Energiya, 1977), p. 149, was adjusted upward and broken down between oil and gas according to Campbell, *Soviet Balances*, Appendix.

[c]For 1976, *Ekonomika gazovoi promyshlennosti*, 1977, no. 11, p. 27; for 1980, *Energetika SSSR*. (1977), pp. 149 and 151.

[d]Field and transport losses are conservatively estimated to be about 3 percent. V. V. Arenbrister, *Tekhniko-ekonomichesky analiz poter nefti i nefteproduktov* (Moscow: Khimiya, 1975), pp. 18–19, gives 5 percent for total losses (in addition to internal fuel use in the various operations) from fields through supply depots of refined products. Of this 5 percent, less than one-third, or 1.5 percent, was lost during the refinery operation.

[e]Total for 1975 is given by *Energetika SSSR* (1977), pp. 149 and 151. It was adjusted upward slightly and the consumption of natural gas separated out according to Campbell, *Soviet Balances*, Appendix.

[f]Consumption of oil in blast and open-hearth furnaces projected from 1972 and 1974 data as given in *Ekonomika chernoi metallurgii*, no. 5 (Moscow: Metallurgiya, 1976), pp. 91–93, and N. I. Perlov et al., *Tekhnichesky progress i toplivno-energopotreblenie v chernoi metallurgii* (Moscow: Metallurgiya, 1975), p. 131.

[g]Natural gas consumption projected from 1970, 1975 and 1977 volumes as given in *Gazovaya promyshlennost*, 1978, no. 6, p. 12. Growth in oil consumption is given in *Energetika* (Prague), 1977, no. 9, p. 445.

[h]Natural gas is said to provide 44 percent of all raw material for chemical synthesis. Most of the rest originates from petroleum. *Ekonomika gazovoi promyshlennosti*, 1977, no. 11, pp. 30–31 and G. F. Borisovich and M. G. Vasilyev, *Nauchno-tekhnichesky progress i ekonomika khimicheskoi promyshlennosti* (Moscow: Khimiya, 1977), p. 29. Heavy, nonfuel refinery products from Campbell, *Soviet Balances*, Appendix.

[i]The categories "other branches of industry" and "other branches of the economy" given in *Gazovaya promyshlennost*, 1978, no. 6, p. 29, were divided between furnace-type application and boiler use as in the table. This conforms to data about gas consumption by all types of electric stations everywhere. *Energetika SSSR* (1977), p. 111.

[j]*Energetika SSSR* (1977), p. 151.

[k]Residual for the columns. Data unavailable, but this figure is reasonable, since net additions to storage have been increasing from 1.7 million tons of SF equivalent in 1973 to over 6.8 million tons of SF equivalent in 1975. The 1976–80 plan called for rapid growth of storage. Data from S. A. Orudzhev, *Gazovaya promyshlennost po puti progressa* (Moscow: Nedra, 1976), p. 71.

[l]According to *Narodnoye khozyaistvo SSSR za 60 let*, p. 83, stocks of all fuels declined during 1976 evidently in response to the export drive. Since the latter concerned only hydrocarbons, and primarily petroleum, it is reasonable to assume that petroleum stocks were drawn down somewhat. On the other hand, 2,000 km of new oil pipelines had to be filled up in 1976.

growth for gross energy use by mobile units, despite the accelerated development of Siberia with the attendant rise of transport and construction activities. The household and municipal economy is a small consumer of hydrocarbons, primarily pipeline gas and liquefied petroleum gases. Detached furnaces, fired individually for space and water heating, account for 70 to 75 percent of all energy use in this sector. Because of their inefficiency and enormous manpower requirement (estimated to reach 400 million labor days in 1976[23]), Soviet planners intend to expand the role of central heating, pipeline and bottled gas in this sector. It is also fair to assume that coal, but in small measure also hydrocarbons, will gradually supplant at least a part of the large volume of firewood and self-produced fuel, reportedly still amounting to 25 million standard tons (1 ton = 7 million kilocalories) in 1975.[24]

Given these Soviet claims and plans and the projections shown in Table 3, one could estimate hydrocarbon needs *other than electric stations, industrial and municipal boilers* to grow from 509 million standard tons in 1976 and about 655 million standard tons in 1980 (Table 4) to somewhere between 720 million and 800 million tons by 1985, depending on the rate at which aggregate energy consumption is going to rise.

While substantial, the expected 1980 hydrocarbon requirements in these specialized uses were less than half of the 1980 oil and gas output. Nor will they be likely to exceed 55 percent of hydrocarbon output even in the second half of the 1980s as long as Soviet oil production does not decline below 500 million tons per year (10 million b/d). There are no real strains, therefore, on hydrocarbon supplies from mobile, furnace, and chemical uses—areas of demand where oil products and gas yield the highest economic value. Nor do they compromise continued exports of crude oil and products at close to the present level or stand in the way of a surge of gas exports. A serious strain is building up, however, in the boiler fuel area, where hydrocarbons show the lowest opportunity costs and where their replacement by alternative, and from a technological point of view perfectly feasible, sources has a strong economic argument. Here export

opportunities come into clear conflict with a domestically suboptimal use.

In the USSR, both petroleum and natural gas provide much larger shares of the fuel supply to electric stations than in the United States. The 10th Five-Year Plan (1976–80) called for a stabilization in the relative proportions of both hydrocarbons in the generation of electric power, with a corresponding marginal increase in the share of coal (Table 5). These constant proportions actually implied large absolute increments (more than 20 million natural tons of oil and some 24 billion cubic meters of natural gas),[25] though these increases, it seems, were not fully needed because of the delay in bringing new generating capacity on line.[26] Yet, it is clear that, even with diminishing shares in the contribution of these quality fuels to power generation after 1980, their absolute growth in electric station use cannot be arrested before mid-decade. Altogether, 31 *new* oil and gas fired power plants were to be started during 1976–80, most of them to be completed only in the present decade,[27] though some of these may have been scrapped, since oil supplies failed to expand as planned.

Oil and gas requirements by power stations will develop differently in the European and Asian parts of the country. The expected Soviet demand by thermal electric plants must therefore be aggregated from regional projections reflecting the dissimilar needs of these areas. A close examination shows that in East Siberia, the Far East, and most of Kazakhstan, hydrocarbons will have to cover no more than a few percent of total power station demand, chiefly to meet peaking needs and the requirement of diesel units in remote areas. In both West Siberia and the Urals, however, natural gas and, to a smaller extent, petroleum will have to comprise 30 to 33 percent of all fuel consumption for the generation of electricity.[28] (The accelerated development of the Siberian gas fields inevitably increases the share of hydrocarbons as power-station fuels in West Siberia, while in the Urals the coal transported from the Kuznetsk Basin and Ekibastuz is needed more and more to replace output from exhausted local deposits and will be able to make only a partial contribution to incremental demand.)[29] When these per-

TABLE 5
Soviet and U. S. Fuel Structures in Thermal Electric Stations (in Percent of Total)

| Fuels | Soviet Fuel Structure | | | | | U. S. Fuel Structure | | | |
|---|---|---|---|---|---|---|---|---|---|
| | 1960 | 1965 | 1970 | 1975 | 1980 (Forecast) | 1960 | 1970 | 1975 | 1979 |
| Natural gas | 12.3 | 25.6 | 26.0 | 25.7 | 25.1 | 26.0 | 30.0 | 20.8 | 19.6 |
| Liquid fuels | 7.5 | 12.8 | 22.5 | 28.8 | 28.0 | 7.6 | 14.7 | 20.0 | 19.3 |
| Coal | 70.9 | 54.6 | 46.1 | 41.3 | 42.5 | 66.4 | 55.4 | 59.3 | 61.1 |
| Peat | 7.0 | 4.5 | 3.1 | 2.0 | 2.6 | 0.0 | 0.0 | 0.0 | 0.0 |
| Shale | 1.0 | 1.5 | 1.7 | 1.7 | 1.4 | 0.0 | 0.0 | 0.0 | 0.0 |
| Others | 1.3 | 1.0 | 0.6 | 0.5 | 0.4 | negligible | negligible | negligible | negligible |
| Total | 100.0 | 100.0 | 100.0 | 100.0 | 100.0 | 100.0 | 100.0 | 100.0 | 100.0 |

NOTE: U. S. percentages given for all stations, including nuclear and hydro. Percentages recomputed to include conventional thermal stations only. Totals may not add up to 100.0 percent because of rounding.
SOURCES: For Soviet Union, *Energetika SSSR v 1976–1980 godakh* (Moscow: Energiya, 1977), p. 151. For U. S., *Statistical Abstract of the United States, 1976*, p. 553; U. S. Department of Energy, *Monthly Energy Review*, October 1980 (Washington: DOE/EIA–0035/80/10), p. 23.

centage requirements are combined with a 5 percent yearly growth rate of power demand in the Asian USSR and allowance is made for the output of hydroelectric plants under construction and preparation, the conclusion emerges that the Urals and the Asian regions must retain over 50 million standard tons equivalent of their gas and oil resources for power stations each year by the early and middle 1980s.[30] Given the historical relationship of fuel demand between electric stations and other boilers, the generation of electricity, steam, and hot water for all purposes is likely to require 60 to 70 million tons of standard fuel in the form of gas and oil products even in the east.[31]

West of the Urals, the demand for gas and oil in boiler uses will be vastly greater. Western boiler fuel demand reached about 430 million standard tons in 1978.[32] With a 3.0 to 3.5 percent yearly growth, it would range between 530 million and 550 million tons by 1985 and exceed 600 million tons even with nuclear power satisfying nearly all the increment in baseload power generation after mid-decade.[33] In contrast to these demands, the provinces west of the Urals can dispose of no more than 190 million standard tons of solid fuels annually for noncoking purposes, even including centrally furnished firewood and the shipment of coal from the Asian USSR.[34] And roughly a third of these solid fuels have to be assigned to the household economy and to minor furnace uses in industry, leaving only 120 million tons for the production of steam and electricity under boilers.[35] A huge gap thus exists in the European USSR between aggregate boiler demand and the quantities of solid fuels available. This gap, which, according to the above figures, approximated 310 million standard tons in 1978, will widen by roughly 100 million tons during the 1980s. It can stabilize only toward the end of that decade with the implementa-

tion of the ambitious nuclear program, a significant increase in coal transport and/or electricity transmission from beyond the Urals.[36]

It is gas and oil that must close the gap between boiler fuel requirements west of the Urals and solid fuels available for that purpose. In addition, as shown above, they must also provide appreciable quantities (60 million to 70 million standard tons in 1980) for electricity, steam, and hot water even in the Asian regions and the Urals. All these add up to almost 400 million standard tons of hydrocarbons for the boiler market throughout the USSR. During the 1980s, Soviet planners should be able to restrain demand for gas and oil in coal-rich Siberia, Kazakhstan and perhaps also in the Urals, but not in the European provinces, where coal production is likely to stagnate through much of the decade. It is also certain that the burgeoning population of underdeveloped Central Asia will increase demand for the boiler use of natural gas, in which this region is richly endowed, since other fuels to produce steam and electricity are in short supply.[37]

Data concerning fuel consumption under boilers of all kinds are scanty, but those pertaining to electric stations, the most important users, are satisfactory. Tables 5 and 6 show the changes in the fuel mix of thermal power plants both nationally and regionally through the 1970s to 1980. Both petroleum and natural gas generate larger shares of thermal electricity in the USSR than in the United States. In the cis-Volga regions, with a little over half of all energy demand, but in Central Asia and the Far East as well, even the *share* of petroleum used in power plants has been increasing, while in West Siberia, the relative contribution of natural gas has grown substantially.

There is little that the Soviet leadership can do about the situation until and unless Siberian lignites or the

TABLE 6
Fuel Structure of Soviet Electric Stations in Major Economic Regions in 1970–80
(Percent of Total)[a]

| Regions | 1970 | | | | 1975 | | | |
|---|---|---|---|---|---|---|---|---|
| | Petroleum Products | Natural Gas | Solid Fuels | Total | Petroleum Products | Natural Gas | Solid Fuels | Total |
| Cis-Volga USSR and European North of which: | 20.5 | 26.7 | 52.8 | 100 | 35.0 | 17.0 | 48.0 | 100 |
| Ukraine and Moldavia | 7.9 | 34.7 | 57.4 | 100 | n.d. | n.d. | n.d. | — |
| Belorussia | 20.5 | 16.0 | 63.5 | 100 | n.d. | n.d. | n.d. | — |
| Baltic Republics | 28.5 | 14.5 | 57.0 | 100 | n.d. | n.d. | n.d. | — |
| Transcaucasia | 72.4 | 25.0 | 12.6 | 100 | 42.8 | 55.7 | 1.5 | 100 |
| Volga Region | 59.4 | 23.2 | 17.4 | 100 | 55.6 | 34.9 | 9.5 | 100 |
| Urals | 11.2 | 28.5 | 60.3 | 100 | 16.4 | 28.6 | 55.0 | 100 |
| Kazakhstan | 12.1 | 11.5 | 76.4 | 100 } | 14.0 | 37.9 | 48.1 | 100 |
| Central Asia | 16.0 | 61.8 | 22.2 | 100 } | | | | |
| West Siberia | 11.4 | 1.1 | 84.5 | 100 | 10.7 | 8.1 | 81.2 | 100 |
| East Siberia | 0.7 | 0.0 | 99.3 | 100 | 1.0 | 0.0 | 99.0 | 100 |
| Far East | 8.7 | 1.8 | 89.5 | 100 | 8.4 | 2.6 | 89.0 | 100 |
| USSR | 23.5 | 23.8 | 52.7 | 100 | 29.5 | 22 | 48.5 | 100 |

SOURCES: *Energetika SSSR v 1981-1985 godakh* (Moscow: Energoizdat, 1981), p. 232; *Energetika SSSR v 1976-1980 godakh* (Moscow: Energiya, 1977), p. 153; *Energetika SSSR v 1971-1975 godakh* (Moscow: Energiya, 1972), pp. 172–73.
[a]Refers only to electric stations under the jurisdiction of the Electric Power Ministry. These stations generate 94 percent of all electric power in the USSR.
[b]1980 forecast.

electricity generated from them can reach the Volga River in large quantities and nuclear plants can take over most of the entire base load and not just the increment. The ambitious nuclear power program cannot be accelerated greatly. It is also a moot question whether an economically acceptable solution can be found for the transport problem of Siberian lignites and whether the Soviet leadership is willing to make the effort needed for the venture. The modernization of the rural and small town household sector may be delayed (though this, too, will cost the economy dearly) and the state supply of energy to the rural sector may not be expanded, but present levels surely cannot be reduced. At any rate, this sector is not a major consumer of gas and still less of oil and could not release very much. What is certain is that the requirement for hydrocarbons in boiler uses will continue to be determined by the size of the shortage of solid fuels west of the Urals and by the rate at which Siberian and Kazakhstan coal fields can expand production and supply consumers in the European provinces.

Declines in coal production in recent years and increasingly obvious problems in the Soviet coal industry support my long-standing skepticism concerning its ability to expand production sufficiently to permit stabilization of oil and gas consumption in the power station and other boiler markets. Even with a vigorous growth of nuclear capacity and strict conservation measures, such expansion would have to approximate, if not exceed, the rate for energy consumption as a whole. Even a 3 percent annual increase translates into an *increment* of 250 million to 255 million physical tons between 1980 and 1990; a 4 percent annual increase means an *increment* of 345 million to 350 million tons over a decade for an industry that expanded by less than 20 million tons during the last five

years.[38] Such a growth would presuppose a manifold jump in investment level and an impossible speed of mine construction. All except a small fraction of these increments would have to originate from deposits east of the Urals, one half or more from the vast but distant field of Kansk-Achinsk, which produces a cheap but troublesome lignite not yet transportable to distant markets.

Substitution: Gas versus Oil

In stationary processes substitution between the two hydrocarbons encounters no technological problems. In both boiler and furnace uses the required changes in equipment are simple and cheap. Many, perhaps even most plants are also designed to burn both fuels, since inadequate storage capacity for natural gas results in significant seasonal oscillation of supply. However, the impending exhaustion of most gas fields west of the Urals, making them available for seasonal storage, will mitigate this difficulty in the future. The long-distance pipeline transmission of crude oil costs less than one-fifth that of natural gas.[39] In addition, at present prices, crude oil exports to the West still earn appreciably more hard currency than gas exports. If such price relationships were to continue, economic logic would work against a surge of gas deliveries for the foreign market beyond the existing long-term contracts (mostly barter deals for large-diameter pipe) and for the growing use of gas to replace oil at home.[40]

On the other hand, Soviet scholars concede that, even with the availability of exhausted reservoirs, the need to multiply gas storage capacity (by 10 to 15 times) and expand the distribution network is a serious brake on the planned substitution of gas for oil.[41] One must also note that without the restructuring of the present refinery mix, with gasoline, diesel fuel and kerosene comprising hardly more than half of Soviet refinery output,[42] natural gas would free for export the less valuable heavy fractions, those most abundant on the world market and which also must be moved to ports or border points by rail, being too viscous for pipeline transport. Such a change in the refinery mix toward a larger share of light products has long been advocated, but the expansion of secondary refinery capacity to achieve that purpose has been slow.

Nor is the wide price difference between oil and gas on the Western export market likely to continue much longer. In addition, the increasingly apparent difficulties in the Soviet petroleum industry and rising West European interest in Soviet gas both point to a rapid expansion in the importance of that commodity in Soviet foreign commerce. Most experts now believe that gas will become the leading hard-currency earner by the mid-1980s, replacing oil in that role. According to one source, Soviet gas exports to Western Europe in 1980 reached 40 percent of Soviet oil exports in calorific content, with gas deliveries reaching 24.1 billion cubic meters compared with 50 million tons for oil.[43] Eastern Europe, too, is evidently accepting increases in gas deliveries in place of most or all the increments in petroleum supply beyond the present decade. Therefore, given the uncertainties

| 1980 | | | |
|---|---|---|---|
| Petroleum Products | Natural Gas | Solid Fuels | Total |
| 36.1[b] | 16.0[b] | 47.9[b] | 100 |
| n.d. | n.d. | n.d. | — |
| n.d. | n.d. | n.d. | — |
| n.d. | n.d. | n.d. | — |
| 43.0[b] | 54.0[b] | 3.0[b] | 100 |
| 62.7 | 30.2 | 7.1 | 100 |
| 11 | 36.1 | 52.9 | 100 |
| 17.4 | 35.6 | 47 | 100 |
| 11.2 | 28 | 60.8 | 100 |
| 2.7 | 0.0 | 97.3 | 100 |
| 15.9 | 4.4 | 79.7 | 100 |
| 35.7 | 24.2 | 40.1 | 100 |

concerning future levels of oil production and the structural difficulties of substitution between the two hydrocarbons, the surge in gas exports appears understandable and may even be *economically* rational, provided export prices for the two fuels approach each other on a calorific basis.[44] Natural gas is also being exported indirectly, being converted first into ammonia to obtain a higher value per quantity. Indirect exports via methanol are also planned on a large scale. The USSR may well have a greater comparative advantage this way than in the direct sale of gas, especially if Western equipment, paid by the chemicals produced, is installed.[45]

Notwithstanding the structural impediments noted above, some replacement of fuel oil with natural gas evidently has taken place in the domestic economy, a process that is likely to continue, even if fitfully, in the future.[46] The geographic dimension, however, strongly influences the proportions between the two hydrocarbons. Since natural gas is more expensive to transport than crude oil (which today is refined in all major provinces), the chief gas producing regions and those consumers relatively close to the principal Asian sources of supply received the largest quantities and highest shares of this fuel as early as 1975. In addition, for political and environmental reasons, the Moscow area has long enjoyed preferential allocation of this clean, high quality energy source.[47] The locational advantage of the Ural and Volga regions with respect to the Siberian gas fields should favor a greatly increased role for gas in these provinces and also in the entire northern half of the Russian plain.

Because transport and distribution account for most of the cost of gas and because the final distribution network is still skeletal, significant oil-by-gas displacement should be expected only in concentrated bulk uses. Planners will find such a switch for scattered, smaller consumers more costly and in many cases physically impossible. Many industrial and smaller municipal boilers may find it difficult to change to gas from fuel oil, while in power stations, cement plants, and large industrial furnaces the substitution of gas presents less of a problem.[48] As a corollary, this suggests that hard coal could be a more economical substitute for oil in dispersed uses than in concentrated ones. The market comprised by industrial boilers (many of which are small and scattered) and smaller power stations will be shared by all three of the major fuels, though one of the latter may dominate in certain geographic regions. In big thermal power plants, a determined effort could reduce the proportion and, eventually, the absolute amount of petroleum products.

While gas-for-oil substitution is expected to be substantial, it will not resolve the conflict between export opportunities (or, in the case of Eastern Europe, obligations) for petroleum and the relentless growth of domestic requirements. Given the inability of coal to stabilize, let alone augment its share in the energy mix over the forthcoming decade, and its inability to cover more than a portion of the underboiler market west of the Urals, oil exports beyond the CMEA can be preserved only in case of a *simultaneous* increase of both oil and gas output (with at least a modest growth rate, say 1 percent per annum,

for oil and a vigorous growth rate for gas). Information released about the forecasting and energy modeling work under way in the USSR indicates that Soviet planners are aware of the decisive, if not supreme, role of oil and gas through the remainder of this century. Indeed, the latest projections by energy specialists make clear that no reduction in the *relative* contribution of hydrocarbons can begin before the 1990s, while the absolute amount required would need to increase beyond the year 2000.[49]

### Soviet Energy Modeling and the Expansion of Domestic Supplies

The Soviet leadership exercises far greater control over energy demand than is possible in an economy of the market type. Thus the difficulties stemming from consumer response, from income, and price elasticities with respect to various energy forms barely arise. Soviet energy modeling consists primarily of various scenarios matching specified, discrete levels of aggregate demand with difficult combinations of supplies in a linear programming framework. The objective function is to minimize the total cost of meeting the desired gross demand, which in more advanced, recent models may include the requisite capacity expansion by the supplying industries. Such models are applied both to the main energy-producing branches individually (and even to separate coal fields and petroleum provinces) and to the energy sector as a whole.

Types of use (i.e., the equipment categories treated briefly above) will continue to influence the solution and objective function such models yield. However, the controlling variable, with the most crucial impact on feasible choices and total costs, is the geographic one. This variable now plays its role in a more straightforward and blunt fashion than during the 1960s and even the early 1970s, when easily accessible resources in the European USSR generated a tremendous, though regionally sharply varying, set of economic rents (from 2 to 6 times that of the production costs of hydrocarbons).[50] With the exhaustion of most of these well located resources, this issue has faded from importance. In the European core area, which contains most of the Soviet population and economic output, it is no longer possible to speak of energy-rich and energy-poor regions. Even the Ukraine has become a massive *net* importer of fuel from provinces farther east.[51]

Under these circumstances, breaking down predicted demand regionally *within* the three-fifths of the Soviet energy market west of the Urals has lost most of its importance. It has little impact on the feasible choices, costs, and inputs of various energy scenarios. Incremental supplies of fuel and increasingly also Soviet exports must originate from remote provinces of the Asian USSR, whose environmental extremes, distances, and lack of infrastructure make projections of output and delivery costs uncertain and tentative. Aggregate future costs in the Soviet energy economy as a whole will be influenced by the speed and expense of Siberian development and fuel transport to such an extent that the minor consequences on total energy costs resulting from demand variations *within* the European regions will be almost entirely submerged. By contrast, the growth of fuel demand in the cis-Ural territories *as a whole* versus that in the eastern regions will become even more decisive for Soviet energy policy.

In all scenarios described in Soviet works, the least-cost path calls for a rapid expansion of Siberian oil and gas output but also of surface coal and lignites east of the Urals and nuclear power west of the Volga. *Direct* investment for incremental output in standard tons (7 million kilocalories) is said to be lowest for lignites from the Kansk-Achinsk Basin (and by implication also for Ekibastuz coal). Energy increments from Siberian oil allegedly need somewhat greater investment, and increments from Siberian gas about twice as much. In addition to direct investment, such increases require large capacity expansion by the supplying industries, with the volume depending on specific conditions and varying with the speed of exploitation. Again, for nearly all industrial inputs such indirect effects will be greater for natural gas than for oil or for surface coals east of the Urals. The major interindustry inputs for the hydrocarbons are and will continue to be steel pipe and other metal products; those for eastern lignites and coal, equipment and machinery for production, transport and enrichment (the last not yet solved for Kansk-Achinsk lignite) as well as electric power.[52]

Beside the uncertainties concerning Soviet petroleum resources (proved reserves as opposed to the probable and potential categories) and the feasible pace of expansion in the uncommonly harsh environments of northern Siberia, the huge interindustry demands put serious constraints on the optimal plans, particularly with respect to gas. Even with relatively minor drops in production at older gas fields, such plans call for an increment of 100 billion cubic meters of West Siberian gas every two to three years, and its delivery to market. This, in turn, would require the following increases in annual production capacity by 1990 to service the West Siberian gas industry alone: 32 million tons of rolled steel (almost one-third of present capacity), 300,000 tons of nonferrous metals and close to 25 million tons of cement (one-fifth of present capacity).[53] As in the past, the Russians are understandably counting on imports to ease these constraints, and some of their optimization efforts attempt to model the import effect. A recent study, for example, suggests about half a billion rubles of total saving for every two million tons of imported, large-diameter pipe.[54] Imports of compressor stations may be even more crucial, but I have seen no work trying to quantify their impact on alternative energy paths.

Soviet planners are evidently aware that the attainment of the optimum levels of hydrocarbon output called for by their models may be problematic. They incorporate more pessimistic output and cost constraints for oil and gas (as well as nuclear power) in subsequent iterations to arrive at second and third-best solutions. The latter, as a rule, result in a greater role for coal, particularly Siberian lignites.[55] Such second-best solutions assume that investment resources between the hydrocarbon and coal variants are reasonably transferable and that an economic-

ally acceptable resolution to the difficult enrichment and transport problem for self-igniting Siberian lignites is imminent. These are far from certain and, indeed, unlikely, at least within the required time frame, and going from an optimal to a second-best alternative probably will not be feasible within the next decade. The latest Soviet forecasts show a clear appreciation of this problem. They anticipate that a further marginal reduction in the *share* of coal is inevitable until the end of the century and expect nuclear power to shoulder no more than a tenth of aggregate energy supply even two decades hence.[56]

## Energy Resources and the Growth of Supplies

Compared to other industrial powers, the USSR is in an enviable position concerning the magnitude and range of its energy resources. In both total and individual energy sources, the Soviet Union is endowed with greater potential than any Western nation. With the probable exception of Canada, this holds true even on a per capita basis. However, when the proved reserves and transportability of specific fuels and the accessibility of the waterpower potential are considered, this situation is somewhat altered. At present rates of exploitation, proved coal resources would last hundreds of years and proved plus indicated reserves of gas for some 60 to 70 years, depending on the recovery ratio.[57] On the other hand, proved reserves of oil, the most versatile and transportable fuel, appear far less satisfactory. Despite the absence of official data, Soviet sources reveal that new discoveries have long failed to keep up with the continued growth of production. The reserve-to-production ratio has been deteriorating for about two decades,[58] and, at the present high level of output only about 10 years or less of fully proved, recoverable reserves may be at the disposal of Soviet energy planners.[59] Together with the more tenuous indicated category, petroleum reserves are undoubtedly larger, perhaps double those of proved reserves alone. However, in contrast to gas, for which most of the indicated reserves are expected to be promoted to the proved, recoverable category, only a portion of indicated oil reserves can be firmed up and considered recoverable.[60]

In projecting Soviet energy supplies, one must look not merely at the size of resources, but also at location, transportability, cost to consumers, and the technological lead time that controls their exploitation and delivery. On a calorific basis, total fuel production in the European USSR is declining and will continue to do so through most of the decade.[61] All growth in aggregate demand in the European regions must be covered by a westward flow of resources from distant Asian provinces, primarily Siberia, where a harsh environment, sparse population, and lack of infrastructure hamper development and transport.

### Petroleum

On an even calorific basis, petroleum is the largest contributor to the Soviet fuels balance, accounting for 45 percent of all fossil fuels production in 1980 and about 38 percent of consumption. During 1974, the USSR became the leading producer in the world and its output of crude oil and condensates reached 609 million tons in 1981.[62] Despite this prominence, the prospects for petroleum appear more worrisome than for other primary energy sources. Growth rates have slowed drastically from over 10 percent in the early 1960s to 6.8 percent on the average in the first half of the 1970s to only 2 to 3 percent in the last two years of the 10th Five-Year Plan (1976–80) just ended. More importantly, the annual increments peaked in 1975 at under 32 million tons and declined drastically since, to 4 million tons in 1981.[63] All signs indicate that further growth in production cannot be sustained and, as the CIA predicted, downturn in the 1980s is possible. The 11th Five-Year Plan (1981–85) looks to annual growth rates of 1 percent, but oil production plans have not been fulfilled in recent years.

The problems besetting the Soviet oil industry have been well documented. To maximize current output, the Russians overemphasized development at the expense of prospecting and exploratory drilling, which was less in recent years (at least until 1978) than in the mid-1960s.[64] Rash, at times even reckless, production methods inflicted serious damage to oil fields. By Soviet admission, this resulted in a loss of oil ultimately recoverable and a drastic decline in the flow rate of oil wells in several provinces, above all Tyumen Oblast.[65] New production capacity, which needed merely to offset depletion in old fields, has multiplied and by 1979 exceeded three-fourths of all new capacity comissioned.[66] Despite prodigious costs in terms of material and manpower (with twice as many workers and roughly the same number of rigs as in the United States), the Soviet Oil Ministry in recent years has managed to drill only about one-fifth as much meterage as American companies.[67] Rig productivity, i.e. meters per rig, has improved slowly; in exploratory drilling it failed to improve at all, and in the crucial West Siberian province it has declined since 1975.[68] The turbodrill, developed by Soviet engineers, accounts for over 70 percent of all rigs. It has merits in shallow depth, but is useless below 3,000 meters, where most future discoveries are expected.[69] Geophysical work and technology remain inadequate and, by Soviet admission, continue to grow more slowly than prospecting and exploratory activities as a whole. All these drastically reduce the effectiveness of exploration, forcing the Russians to concentrate almost exclusively on anticlinal traps and miss reservoirs of more complex and elusive types, and make penetration to deeper strata costly and slow.[70]

For over a decade now, the success of the Soviet oil industry has been critically dependent on the performance of the West Siberian petroleum province, located almost entirely in Tyumen Oblast. This will remain true during the forthcoming years as well. West Siberia, which is now producing 55 percent of all Soviet oil, accounted for *all* the increment in output and also had to compensate for the decline experienced by most other provinces. Since the downturn elsewhere is accelerating, Soviet dependence on the Tyumen fields will intensify. In contrast to the 1970s, when a few large fields supplied all

the gain (with supergiant Samotlor alone responsible for more than half the increment), growth in the future must come from many more smaller pools, scattered in the vast swampy forest of West Siberia and thus more difficult to tap. A score of large fields producing today have already peaked, with several entering the declining phase. Soviet sources show that both the drilling program and the rate at which new fields are developed have fallen behind goals.[71]

Since no major additional petroleum province has been developed, Soviet leaders have to depend on new finds in West Siberia. A vast increase in prospecting and exploratory activities in the province has been ordered; yet the 1979 plan for exploratory drilling remained 30 percent unfulfilled.[72] In addition to the original crews, dozens of prospecting and drilling teams have been flown in from other oil regions and investment in housing, roads, and other infrastructure has risen sharply. West Siberia's potential is unquestionably great and the basin is only half explored. In the more accessible areas, however, the obvious structural traps in shallower depths have already been tested. The search will have to concentrate on more elusive stratigraphic traps and/or strata in the depth range of 2.5 to 5 km, below the range of the turbodrill.[73] Looking further down the road, Soviet oilmen must also develop new petroleum provinces: in East Siberia, the Arctic shelves or the superdeep folds of geosynclines along the southern periphery of the USSR. This is not likely to happen before the late 1980s or even later. It will be slower without large-scale imports of Western technology, but the level of such imports will depend on Soviet hard-currency earnings, competing needs and political factors, all of which are subject to uncertainties.

## Natural Gas

Natural gas in 1980 contributed 27 percent of Soviet fuels production and almost as much of consumption[74] and these shares should continue to increase for at least a dozen years. After a long period of immaturity and below-plan performance (though still with more than respectable growth rates), the industry has become the most vigorous sector of the Soviet energy system, with annual increments ranging from 25 to 35 billion cubic meters since 1974.[75] In 1981, the USSR produced 465 billion cubic meters, or about 80 percent as much as the United States, and it should surpass the declining American output before the mid-1980s.[76] In contrast to the uncertainties surrounding other energy resources, natural gas represents a solid, central pillar of long-term energy policy on which Soviet leaders intend to capitalize.

Unlike the petroleum industry, the gas industry is not hampered by any reserve bottleneck and, as mentioned above, explored resources are sufficient to guarantee expansion well into the next century. The problems of Soviet gas are due almost entirely to geography and the difficulties of transport, aggravated of course by systemic ills peculiar to Soviet planning and by shortcomings of domestic technology. Seventy percent of all gas reserves are located in Siberia (more than three-fifths in the northern half of Tyumen Oblast alone in a few supergiant fields) and 13 to 14 percent in the deserts of Central Asia.[77] Soviet gas producers, therefore, have had to and must still overcome tremendous obstacles to field development in harsh environments and bridge distances of up to 1,800 miles with very large-diameter pipelines capable of transporting large quantities of gas.

Most deposits west of the Urals are now in decline and even the Central Asian reservoirs have peaked. At the same time, backwardness in Soviet seismic and deep drilling technology makes further large discoveries in more accessible areas improbable over the next decade. Northwest Siberia represents the sole reliable source of major increments in gas production. Difficulties in field development and especially transport to make this resource available in the necessary quantities are and will continue to remain severe. The Russians are installing what amounts to the world's biggest large-diameter trunkline system from a single gas province, composed of three giant subsystems, all with pipes of 48 and 56 inches in diameter. About four-fifths of the Soviet gas industry's fixed capital is in the pipeline network, which now receives 65 to 70 percent of all investment earmarked for that industry each year.[78]

As Soviet modeling work on the energy system has shown, the interindustry demand for rolled steel, nonferrous metals, compressors, cement, etc. for the West Siberian gas industry is placing immense strain on the Soviet economy. A leading Soviet expert on the gas industry has stated that 30,000 kilometers and 20 million metric tons of top-grade, large-diameter pipe, requiring 22 to 25 billion rubles of capital investment would be needed to transport an additional 300 billion cubic meters per year into the European USSR. The official conceded that "it is virtually impossible for us to allocate such large amounts to the gas industry."[79] Pipeline quality and long delays in the installation of compressor stations are also chronic problems. Many breaks, noted in the Soviet press, occur even at low pressures, raising questions about Soviet ability to proceed with intended pipeline operations at pressures higher than those employed on the best Western lines. In addition, less than half of the compressor stations are generally installed at the time the gas pipelines are completed, resulting in underused capacity for several years.[80] In fact, only heavy reliance on Western technology made the recent rapid growth of gas output possible. Through most of the 1970s over 60 percent of all long distance gas pipelines laid and a similar share of compressor stations were apparently made in foreign mills.[81] Such imports will ease somewhat the transport bottleneck in the future as well, but at the cost of mortgaging a large part of gas output and most exports for several years in exchange for equipment and pipe already received.

A deeper understanding of these constraints is leading to greater caution among gas industry officials of Tyumen Oblast, the linchpin in the Soviet gas drive. In an unusually frank interview, a former chief of the Tyumen gas industry and then secretary of the oblast's party committee, revealed the spirited struggle waged against Gosplan's attempt to force the industry prematurely to fields yet farther north (150 to 300 miles beyond the Arctic

Circle) because it was technologically unprepared for pipeline and field construction on the ice-saturated permafrost.[82] Meanwhile, Soviet researchers were studying and experimenting with new transport technology: with multilayer pipe to withstand higher pressures, the cooling and refrigeration of gas and even liquefaction in pipelines to increase throughput capacity. While eventual breakthroughs may be forthcoming, none of these technologies are likely to be widely employed before the late 1980s.[83] With production increases coming from the world's largest reservoirs, Soviet gas production will continue to grow by large increments, never so far achieved anywhere in the world. But gas alone cannot fully compensate for the poor performance of other fuel industries and solve the deepening energy problem.

Coal and Lignite

Since 1950, the production of coal (including lignite) has been growing more slowly than oil and gas production, with the annual rate of expansion falling to 2.05 percent in the 1960s and to 1.5 percent when measured in heat content. In the first half of the 1970s, the growth of production picked up slightly, only to slow drastically in the second half, with a rate of increase averaging 0.5 percent (slow growth between 1975 and 1978 and an absolute decline from 1978 to 1981).[84] This retardation was experienced despite the proclamation of a new fuel policy that reemphasized the importance of coal, with higher planned rates than in any of the previous three five-year plans. The USSR has long been the leading coal producer by tonnage; this adds up to a lower heat content than output in the United States, where more bituminous coal is produced and output has been faster than in the USSR. The poor performance of the Soviet coal industry and the problems besetting it cast doubt on hopes concerning the relative resurgence of coal at least for a dozen years. A 1976 Soviet source that forecast a growth rate in the coal industry's fixed capital until 1985 substantially below that experienced during the 1960s and early 1970s appears to have been accurate.[85] The CIA calculates that three-quarters of gross annual commissioning simply offsets mine depletion. In two important basins (Moscow and Karaganda) depletion during 1976–80 equaled new commissioning.[86]

Soviet coal reserves are vast, adequate for hundreds of years. Faster growth is hindered by geological conditions, location and transport constraints, increasing capital needs and labor problems and, to a lesser extent than in the United States, by environmental considerations. In the European USSR demand far exceeds supply and power stations alone could use more coal than available. However, output is in decline and is likely to remain stagnant throughout the 1980s because of difficult geological conditions and inadequate reserves of new manpower. East of the Urals, where the geological situation is more favorable and much of the coal can be produced by open-pit method (thus largely obviating the labor shortage), the local market is restricted. The great distances from the fuel short regions of the European USSR, combined with already overburdened railways and the poor transportability of much of the eastern coals, restrict the quantities that can be hauled westward to and across the Urals. This is now conceded by responsible Soviet scholars. Their latest projections indicate that not even by the year 2000 can such coals transported to the European provinces compensate for the declining share of this fuel in the energy balance of those regions.[87]

The Donets Basin, which has been producing for some 130 years, has the most favorable location of all major basins with respect to markets and is endowed with fairly large reserves of high grade coal. However, the depletion of the upper coal beds and rapidly increasing depth, thin and discontinuous seams, fairly high sulfur and ash content, all make the further growth of output difficult and costly. Worked-out mines have been closing at an accelerated rate: to replace those exhausted, a 30 percent increase in output over the longer term requires a roughly threefold expansion in capacity.[88] In addition, by the early seventies nearly half the mines were operating at or below 2,000 feet, and a growing number below 3,000 feet. About half of all the longwalls are on seams less than 28 inches thick and almost 15 percent of all coal is mined from seams of less than 20 inches.[89] Under these circumstances, it is not surprising that the recruitment of young workers is increasingly difficult, that only a quarter of the miners are in the 20 to 35 age group and labor turnover is a serious problem.[90] Conditions in the smaller coal fields of the European USSR are more or less similar and, at any rate, they are capable of only limited contribution. Only the Pechora Basin, also difficult geologically and most of it beyond the Arctic Circle, is capable of more sustained expansion, albeit at a high cost.

The most economic coal resources (and those capable of the greatest expansion) are all found east of the Urals, with the Kuznetsk Basin and the Kansk-Achinsk Basin in Siberia and Ekibastuz in northeast Kazakhstan the most important. Most of these deposits easily lend themselves to strip mining, and the two latter areas can produce energy at a cost lower than all oil fields and virtually all natural gas reservoirs in the country.[91] Most of the cheap surface coals of Siberia and Kazakhstan, however, are of too poor quality to serve for anything but boiler fuel, mainly in power stations[92] and are transportable for only short distances. Kansk-Achinsk lignite suffers from variable chemical composition, coking problems and, worst of all, self-combustion during transportation beyond short distances. Its wide-ranging ash-melting points pose problems even in local power stations, which suffer from reduced efficiency and wasted capacity.[93] The better located Ekibastuz Basin has become the third largest coal producer in the USSR, with 67 million tons in 1980 but it, too, faces problems. This coal is abrasive on boilers and its high ash content prevents its haulage beyond the western slope of the Urals. Though as much as half of the basin's output feeds power stations in the Urals, Soviet planners project virtually all increments to be consumed within Kazakhstan, mainly in gigantic mine-mouth electric stations. The success of these plans however, will be predicated on the construction of extra high-tension power lines, including an 800-mile, 1,150 kv AC line to the Urals region.[94]

Of all eastern coals, only Kuzbas coal can be moved west of the Volga, doubling its cost by the time it reaches Moscow, but the quantities available for the European provinces can only make a small dent in their huge and growing energy deficit. In recent years much research has focused on the enrichment and briqueting of Siberian (primarily Kansk-Achinsk) lignites and on the economics of coal-slurry pipelines to permit large-scale transportation westward, at least to the Urals, a move that would also free more Kuzbas coal for the European USSR. Soviet scholars, however, are divided on how to attack the problem, on what proportions of these eastern coals produced should be targeted for long distance shipment and what form that should take.[95] A pilot plant of 1.2 million ton capacity to process Kansk-Achinsk coal is reported under construction, with a large-scale complex projected for the second half of the 1980s.[96] Similarly, the first intermediate-size slurry pipeline (250 km and 4.3 million ton capacity) merely for technical evaluation and data gathering is projected only for 1984. The bigger lines (40 to 60 million tons per year) over distances of 2,000 to 3,000 km are in the preplanning stage, with the necessary equipment entirely lacking.[97]

The rapid eastward shift in coal production, combined with the deteriorating quality of the coals mined, is intensifying the burden on the railways. Fuels have long comprised about one-third of all freight turnover (measured in ton-kilometers) on railroads, and coal and coke alone for half that share. From 1970 to the end of 1978, freight turnover for coal rose more than twice as fast as the output of this fuel and the average length of haul, relatively stable during the 1960s and early seventies, has also begun to increase noticeably.[98] The mounting demand for eastern coal in the European USSR and the full development of the South Yakutian coal basin under long term export contract with Japan can only accentuate these trends.

To further exacerbate Soviet energy policy, the growth of Soviet coal transport (which, as noted, is faster than the expansion in coal output) is concentrated almost exclusively on a few lines, which are already choked to capacity. Outside the Donbas area, where the increasing washing and treatment of coal has augmented short hauls, the transport of coal in the European provinces is holding steady. Here, the railway net is relatively dense, alternate routes to consuming centers exist and the railroads seem able to cope with the growing freight. In the east, by contrast, the already overburdened three or four leading lines must accommodate more than 90 percent of all growth in coal freight turnover (in ton-kilometers). Further increases in westward shipments will have to funnel through two of these railways.[99]

## Aggregate Energy Supplies: Implication

Fossil fuels in the Soviet Union account for 96 percent of aggregate energy consumption and will continue to define both the gross volume and the rate of increase of total energy supply for the rest of this century. According to the latest Soviet projections, their share should be some nine-tenths of the total even by the year 2000.[100] We may ignore peat, shale, and wood, which now contribute less than 2 percent and will diminish further in importance. The previous sections have shown that Soviet planners cannot count on solid fuels to substitute widely for hydrocarbons and cannot effect a rapid acceleration of coal output. Coal production increased by only 18 million tons, or 2.5 percent, through the entire 1976–80 plan period and fell 89 million tons short of the original five-year plan goal for 1980.[101] Growth rates may pick up slightly during the present decade, but a great upsurge is simply unfeasible. The burden on hydrocarbons cannot be relieved. The Soviet oil industry, however, is plainly in trouble. Its future will determine the growth rate for Soviet energy consumption as a whole, prospects for hard-currency earnings and, to a large degree, even the nature of CMEA relations and the primary trade orientation of East Europe. The pressure on natural gas will also intensify, but geographical and technological constraints will prevent the gas industry from fully making up for the shortfalls in the other fuels.

Table 7 shows that with a 0.9 percent annual increase in petroleum production through the 1980s, the USSR could continue to achieve a roughly 3 percent yearly rise in domestic fuel consumption, maintain close to present levels of oil shipments to Eastern Europe and remain a small net petroleum exporter beyond the CMEA. In part, however, such a satisfactory rise in energy use would be the result of worse than expected performance during the 10th Five-Year Plan, which depressed the 1980 base. With rising prices and a doubling of gas shipments to Western Europe, hydrocarbon exports could still earn as much convertible currency in the latter part of the 1980s as today, even if oil sales to such markets drop to 10 to 12 million tons. However, since import prices are also certain to increase by perhaps two-thirds as fast as those for oil and gas, the USSR would still lose some half of its exchange value from hydrocarbon sales to the developed world. With the peaking, let alone decline, of petroleum output, oil deliveries beyond the CMEA will have to be eliminated in the second half of the 1980s or shipments to Eastern Europe drastically cut. This would appear unavoidable since it would seem unlikely that Soviet leaders could operate and develop the economy with aggregate fuel demand expanding by less than 2 percent per annum. If oil production suffers an absolute decline, some of the exports to Eastern Europe would have to cease and the Soviet bloc would have difficulties weathering that shock on top of the Soviet hard-currency loss.

It was shown earlier that energy-GNP elasticities are unlikely to fall significantly in the next dozen years. Labor and capital shortages and systemic ills, however, should further retard Soviet economic growth even without an energy pinch, and slower GNP growth should also mean a more sluggish rise in energy demand. Moscow planners could and will be able to live with an economic expansion of only 2.5 to 3 percent. As in the past, they can tighten their nation's collective belt. However, the political and psychological consequences of economic growth much below that rate may be profound. A concurrent pinch of labor, energy and other material and capital resources,

together with the slow rise of labor productivity and the perennially unpredictable weather, would herald a new era in Soviet economic planning. In Gregory Grossman's words, "the tension between goulash communism and Gulag communism may again come into sharper focus."[102]

---

## NOTES

1. Marshall I. Goldman, "Autarchy or Integration—the USSR and the World Economy," in U. S. Congress, Joint Economic Committee, *Soviet Economy in New Perspective* (Washington: Government Printing Office, 1976), pp. 81–96.

2. Net consumption here refers to that portion of gross consumption which is turned into useful work and incorporated into products. The difference between gross consumption, i.e. the use of raw fuels, hydro and nuclear electricity, and net consumption comprises total energy losses. Some of these losses occur during production, processing, transport and conversion into electricity and steam, that is before and during delivery to final consuming apparatus. The rest of the losses occur after such delivery in consuming equipments and engines. The first category of waste may be computed with reasonable accuracy, at least in developed countries. The wide variety, dispersion and age of consuming apparatus tends to frustrate any such attempt concerning waste of the second category. Figures for the latter are evidently derived from rough engineering estimates concerning the average thermodynamic efficiency of the main categories of engines and equipment installed throughout the economy.

3. Such an exercise, based on rather tentative Soviet productivity estimates, was made in Leslie Dienes, *Soviet Energy Policy and the Hydrocarbons*, Discussion Paper No. 2 (April 1978), Association of American Geographers, Project on Soviet Natural Resources in the World Economy. It will not be reproduced here. However, the results support the conclusion derived from the development of net (useful) energy consumption quite consistently.

4. *Teploenergetika*, 1979, no. 2, pp. 2–3; A. A. Makarov and A. G. Vigdorchik, *Toplivno-energeticheskiy kompleks* [The fuels and energy complex] (Moscow: Nauka, 1979), pp. 86–90 and L. A. Melentyev et. al., "The Relationship Between Economic Growth and Energy Development," in *11th World Energy Conference, Preprints*. Division 4: Energy, Society and the Environment (Munich, September 1980) pp. 553–54.

5. Makarov and Vigdorchik, *Toplivno-energeticheskiy kompleks*, pp. 128–29; A. A. Beschinsky and Yu. M. Kogan, *Ekonomicheskiye problemy elektrifikatsii* [Economic problems of electrification] (Moscow: Energiya, 1976), pp. 413–15 and Robert Campbell, *Soviet Energy Balances* (Santa Monica, Ca.: Rand Corporation, Research Report R-2257-DOE, December 1978), p. 8. Campbell's energy balances estimate only losses occuring before energy is delivered to final consuming apparatus. Quite legitimately, but unlike the Soviet sources cited, this author includes oil well gases flared among energy losses. Mak-

arov and Vigdorchik estimate that 63.6 percent of all losses occur in final consuming apparatus. Including oil well gas flared as waste before that final stage would slightly lower the share occurring in consumer equipment.

6. Makarov and Vigdorchik, *Toplivno-energetichesky kompleks*, p. 129; Beshinsky and Kogan, *Ekonomicheskiye problemy elektrifikatsii*, pp. 23–24 and A. Makarov and L. A. Melentyev, "The future structure of the fuels and energy balance of the USSR and its principal zones" (Paper presented to a joint U. S.-Soviet seminar, 1979).

7. Campbell, *Soviet Energy Balances*, p. 8 and Campbell, "Energy in the USSR to the Year 2000" (Paper prepared for the Conference on the Soviet Economy toward the Year 2000. 23–25 October 1980, Airlie House, Virginia).

8. To my knowledge, the only serious attempt to compute total (direct and indirect) self-consumption of energy by the energy industries was made recently for Britain. This share was concluded to be more than 30 percent. In view of the greater geographic and transport burdens in the USSR, the Soviet self-consumption share can be assumed to be greater. P. F. Chapman et al., "The Energy Cost of Fuels," *Energy Policy*, September 1974, pp. 233–44.

9. R. S. Ryps, *Ekonomicheskiye problemy raspredeleniya gaza* [Economic problems of gas distribution] (Leningrad: Nedra, 1978), p. 20.

10. For a detailed examination of these problems see Leslie Dienes, "Energy Conservation in the USSR," in John P. Hardt ed., *Energy in Soviet Policy*. Congressional Research Service. Prepared for the Subcommittee on International Economics, Joint Economic Committee (Washington: Government Printing Office, June 1981), pp. 101–118.

11. Ibid.

12. *Narodnoye khozyaistvo SSSR v 1980 godu* [The economy of the USSR in 1979], p. 53 and *Narodnoye khozyaistvo SSSR v 1970 godu*, p. 63.

13. See tables on yearly plan fulfillments in early January issues of *Ekonomicheskaya gazeta* or major Soviet dailies in last few years.

14. *Narodnoye khozyaistvo SSSR v 1980 godu*, p. 156.

TABLE 7
Projection of Soviet Fuel Balance with Different Scenarios for Petroleum Output 1985 and 1990

| | Petroleum | | | | | | Natural Gas | |
| | 1985 Plan and Same Rate of Growth until 1990 | | Stationary Output | | Substantial Decline | | 1985 Plan | |
| Fuel Balance | mill. tons | mill. tons of SF | mill. tons | mill. tons of SF | mill. tons | mill. tons of SF | bill. m³ | mill. tons of SF |
|---|---|---|---|---|---|---|---|---|
| **1980** | | | | | | | | |
| Output | 603 | — | — | — | — | — | 435 | — |
| Net Export | 150 | — | — | — | — | — | 52 | — |
| Apparent Consumption | 453 | 648 | — | — | — | — | 383 | 454 |
| **1985** | | | | | | | | |
| Output | 630 | — | 603 | — | 500 | — | 620 | — |
| Net Export | 125 | — | 100 | — | 80 | — | 70 | — |
| Apparent Consumption | 505 | 722 | 503 | 719 | 420 | 601 | 550 | 652 |
| **1990** | | | | | | | | |
| Output | 666 | — | 603 | — | 520 | — | 780 | — |
| Net Export | 100 | — | 80 | — | 80 | — | 80 | — |
| Apparent Consumption | 566 | 809 | 523 | 748 | 440 | 629 | 700 | 830 |

Total Fossil Fuel Consumption (million tons of SF)

| Year | With Planned Growth of Petroleum Output | With Stationary Petroleum Output |
|---|---|---|
| 1980 | 1,624 | 1,624 |
| 1985 | 1,913 | 1,910 |
| 1990 | 2,194 | 2,133 |
| *Average Yearly Growth Rate of Fossil Fuel Consumption* | | |
| 1980–85 | 3.3 percent | 3.3 percent |
| 1985–90 | 2.8 percent | 1.3 percent |

SOURCES AND NOTES: 1980 output for the three major fuels are official data from Shabad, "News Notes," *Soviet Geography: Review and Translation* 22, no. 4 (April 1981): 272–82. 1980 net export figures are estimates after Robert Campbell, "Energy in the USSR to the Year 2000," (Paper presented for the *Conference on the Soviet Economy Toward the Year 2000*, 23–25 October 1980, Airlee House, Virginia) and from 1979 petroleum exports as given in *The Oil and Gas Journal*, 28 July 1980. 1985 projections for petroleum (in first scenario) and for natural gas represent roughly the mid-points of the official plan, given as a range in *Ekonomicheskaya gazeta*, 1980, no. 49, p. 6. The planned range for coal, however, was rejected as unrealistic, given the recent performance of the coal industry.

15. Increments, share and average calorific content of coal from ibid., pp. 144–45. For depletion rate and new capacity see CIA, *USSR: Coal Industry. Problems and Prospects*. ER 80-10154, March 1980, p. 15.

16. A. J. Lenz and H. Kravalis, "Soviet—EE Hard Currency Export Capabilities," Office of East-West Policy and Planning, Bureau of East-West Trade, Department of Commerce, 11 October 1977. In 1979, the contribution of oil and gas to hard-currency earnings from trade may have reached two-thirds of the total. See Jan Vanous, "East European and Soviet Fuel Trade, 1970–1985," in U. S. Congress, Joint Economic Committee, *East European Assessment*. Part 2 (Washington: Government Printing Office 1981); *The Oil and Gas Journal*, 28 July 1980.

17. Leslie Dienes, "Geographical Problems of Allocation in the Soviet Fuel Supply," *Energy Policy*, June 1973, p. 4.

18. *Narodnoye khozyaistvo SSSR*. Various issues.

19. In 1976, the USSR (in violation of specific provisions of the 1975 Helsinki agreement) ceased publishing data on the quantities of fuel traded. For a detailed study of price and quantity relationships of hydrocarbon exports to the different market, see Vanous, "East European and Soviet Fuel Trade."

20. Robert E. Ebel writes, "What must give, then, must be the volume of oil available for exports to non-Communist buyers, which in the past have been defined as a residual, and will continue to be in the future," *The Oil and Gas Journal, Special Supplement: Petroleum/2000*, August 1977, p. 505.

John P. Hardt avers, "Soviet needs and planned commitments require it to be a modest exporter of oil and natural gas to hard-currency Western nations and to East Europe throughout the period of the seventies and eighties," in "Soviet Oil and Gas in the Global Perspective," in U. S. Congress, *Project Interdependence: U. S. and World Energy Outlook Through 1990*. Report printed at the request of John D. Dingell, Henry M. Jackson and Ernest F. Hollings by the Congressional Research Service, Library of Congress (Washington: Government Printing Office, 1977), p. 787.

Marshal Goldman also expects the USSR to persist under foreign trade pressure to export oil for hard currency by continuing to restrict domestic oil consumption. *Wall Street Journal*, 27 February 1978, p. 6. Neither of the last two scholars projects a plateau, let alone a drop in Soviet petroleum output.

21. *Narodnoye khozyaistvo SSSR v 1980 godu*, p. 156, and Theodore Shabad, "News Notes," *Soviet Geography: Review and Translation* (hereafter *SGRT*), 23, no. 4 (April 1982): pp. 277–83. Indeed, the expected tonnage decline of petroleum exports to noncommunist states reportedly began in 1979. *The Oil and Gas Journal* estimated that sales to the latter group of countries fell from 1,325,000 barrels a day in 1977 and 1978 to about 1,000,000 b/d in 1979. Deliveries to Communist nations probably rose slightly. Despite somewhat reduced volumes of exports to the West, sharply higher prices far outweighed lower quantities and raised earnings to record highs. *The Oil and Gas Journal*, 28 July 1980, pp. 128–30.

22. During 1966–70, total capital investment in the oil industry averaged 2.2 billion rubles per year; by 1978 the figure was 5.27 billion and now it is believed to be close to 7 billion, a 3.2-fold growth in a decade. Meanwhile output increased by only 1.7 times since 1970. Soviet specialists expect the required investment for an incremental ton of oil to rise more than 10 times in the next two decades compared to the previous two; for gas, they expect a 4 to 5-fold rise. Makarov and Melentyev, "Future structure," and *The Oil and Gas Journal*, 8 September 1980, p. 29.

23. *Ekonomicheskaya gazeta*, 1977, no. 48, p. 13.

24. Ryps, *Ekonomicheskiye problemy*, p. 20.

25. Computed from *Energetika SSSR v 1976–1980 godakh* [The Electric power industry of the USSR in 1976–80] (Moscow: Energiya, 1977), pp. 149–51.

26. Theodore Shabad, "News Notes," *SGRT*, 22, no. 4 (April 1981): pp. 282–87.

27. Theodore Shabad, "News Notes," *SGRT*, 17, no. 10 (December 1976): p. 717.

28. See Tables 5 and 6 for the share of various fuels in thermal electric stations.

29. *Elektricheskiye stantsii*, 1977, no. 2, p. 6.

| Coal | | Peat, Shale and Firewood |
|---|---|---|
| mill. tons | mill. tons of SF | mill. tons of SF |
| 716 | — | 48 |
| 12 | — | — |
| 704 | 474 | 48 |
| 740 | — | 50 |
| 10 | — | — |
| 730 | 489 | 50 |
| 765 | — | — |
| 10 | — | — |
| 755 | 505 | 50 |

| With Substantial Decline of Petroleum Output | | |
|---|---|---|
| 1,624 | | |
| 1,792 | | |
| 2,014 | | |
| 2.0 percent | | |
| 2.4 percent | | |

30. No nuclear stations are operating or are planned for these regions, excepting a small one in the remote northeast and a secret military plant identified by the Russians as "Siberian," but believed to be in the Urals near Troitsk. Therefore, the difference between total power production and hydroelectric output must come from conventional thermal plants both today and in the foreseeable future. The 1975, 1976, and planned 1980 production figures of electric power for all republics, Siberia, and the European USSR were given in *SGRT*, 18, no. 4 (April 1977): pp. 271–77. Hydroelectric capacity and output potential through 1980 in the different regions was given by *Energetika SSSR v 1976–1980 godakh*, p. 129.

31. Total boiler fuel consumption given in *Narodnoye khozyaistvo SSSR v 1980 godu*, p. 53 and earlier issues of same table. Since 1975 the statistics in this category include compressed air, but the latter comprises only a few percent of the total.

32. Ibid., for data referring to USSR as a whole. For regional consumption figures of boiler and furnace fuels see chapter 16, Tables 4–6 in this volume. Shares for boiler fuels alone are believed to be very similar.

33. The 73 billion kwh of nuclear electricity produced in 1980 (nearly all of it west of the Volga, *Ekonomicheskaya gazeta*, 1981, no. 12) saved 23 million tons of standard fuel. Assuming that nuclear capacity during the 1980s grows 4-fold, from 13 to 50 million kw, then perhaps 100 million tons of standard fuel could be saved by atomic stations by the year 1990.

34. If these plans are realized on time, by the mid-1980s about 250 million standard tons of solid fuels annually will be available for regions west of the Urals for noncoking purposes in place of the present 190 million. These amounts include both local production and coal shipped and transmitted indirectly via electricity from Soviet Asia. Theodore Shabad, "News Notes," *SGRT*, 23, no. 4 (April 1982): pp. 287–90 for regional coal production, and *Narodnoye khozyaistvo SSSR v 1980 godu*, p. 156 for minor solid fuels in recent years. Physical tons converted to calorific equivalents.

Rail loading of eastern coal destined for regions west of the Urals was expected to rise from 31.3 million natural tons in 1975 to 45.7 million in 1980 (or from 27 million tons standard fuel to 39 million). *SGRT*, 17, no. 9 (November 1977): p. 701. Much of this had to be coking coal, since the expansion of an integrated iron and steel industry in European Russia was proceeding largely on the basis of Kuzbas coal.

After repeated delays, the construction of the Ekibastuz-Tambov 1,500 kv DC line, 1,500 miles, was reported to have started in 1980. But priority has now shifted to an 800-mile, 1,150 kv AC line from Ekibastuz to the Urals. At any rate, the 35 billion to 40 billion KWH of power to be ultimately transmitted over either line would be equivalent to the shipment of 11 million to 13 million tons of standard fuel, at the heat rates of thermal stations.

35. According to Ryps, *Ekonomicheskiye problemy*, p. 20, 111 million standard tons of state-supplied solid fuels were used by the household-municipal sector in 1975 in stoves and small boilers. If household consumption fol-lows population distribution, 60 percent of solid fuels supplied to households must have been used west of the Volga.

36. See note 33.

37. For further development of this idea see chapter 16 in this volume.

38. The average heat content of Soviet coals in 1978 reached only 4,711 kilocalories per metric ton (i.e., 0.673 tons of standard fuel per physical ton). With the increasing role of the Ekibastuz Basin and Siberian lignites, the average heat content will deteriorate further in the future.

39. A crude oil pipeline can transport more than 5 times as much heating value as a gas pipeline of the same diameter and the latter is subject to more stringent quality requirements. In addition, gas pipelines of over one meter diameter must be equipped with expensive cooling devices all along the way since the ground alone cannot provide the necessary temperature difference for the gas to expand, and thus move, between compressor stations.

40. Robert Ebel, "Soviet Oil Looks to the West," *The Oil and Gas Journal, Special Supplement: Petroleum 2000*, August 1977, p. 508.

41. *Teploenergetika*, 1979, no. 2, p. 5, and Makarov and Vigdorchik, *Toplivno-energetichesky kompleks*, pp. 168–69.

42. Makarov and Vigdorchik, "Future structure," U. S.-Soviet seminar, 1979 and A. S. Arkhipenko and V. I. Nazarov, *Ekonomicheskaya effektivnost geologorazvedochnykh rabot na neft i gaz v zapadnosibirskoi nizmennosti* [Cost-effectiveness of geological exploration for oil and gas in the West Siberian plain] (Leningrad, 1973), p. 55.

43. *Wall Street Journal*, 25 June 1980, p. 21. Negotiations for another giant pipeline, designed to carry 40 billion m³ of gas to Western Europe from the Urengoi field, have since been concluded.

44. In 1979 prices, a cubic meter of gas sold to Western Europe in 1980 would have earned 35 to 40 rubles ($53 to $60) at the official exchange rate. This would have been equivalent to a little less than $10 per barrel on a calorific equivalent. Thus, if gas prices in 1980 rose by 50 to 60 percent, natural gas would have earned 70 to 75 percent as much per calorie as crude oil, whose average price in 1980 was $20.40 per barrel. *Vneshnyaya torgovlya SSSR v 1979 godu* [Foreign trade of the USSR in 1979] (Moscow: Statistika, 1980), p. 61, and U. S. Department of Energy *Monthly Energy Review*, January 1980 (Washington: Government Printing Office), p. 80.

45. The first large-scale export of this kind, the ammonia-phosphate deal of Occidental Petroleum Corporation was briefly interrupted by the United States in 1980–81 in retalitation for the military intervention in Afghanistan.

46. S. A. Orudzhev, *Gazovaya promyshlennost po puti progressa* [The gas industry on the road of progress] (Moscow: Nedra, 1976), p. 59 and V. I. Manayev, "Bashkir ASSR: Its production complex today and in the future," *Ekonomika i organizatsiya promyshlennogo proizvodstva*, 1977, no. 2, pp. 46–67. Brezhnev himself called for the further substitution of gas for fuel oil in presenting the annual 1980 plan. *Ekonomicheskaya gazeta*, 1979, no. 49, p. 4. It is also strongly advocated by such respected energy specialists as Styrikovich, Melentyev, and Vigdor-

chik. The latter two contend that, in the longer term, one-half to three-fourths of fuel oil being consumed can and should be substituted by natural gas. M. A. Styrikovich, "The world energy situation," *Ekonomika i organizatsiya promyshlennogo proizvodstva*, November 1979, no. 11, p. 87, and Makarov and Vigdorchik, "Future structure," U. S.-Soviet seminar, 1979.

47. See chapter 16, Tables 4–6 and Figures 1–2 in this volume.

48. Substitution of gas in industrial furnaces, kilns and ovens is especially attractive because it produces greater economic savings than substitution under boilers. In addition, fuel demand by furnace-type uses in industry is, on the whole, subject to less seasonal oscillation than demand by boilers, an important consideration for gas use, given the difficulties and cost of seasonal storage. Ye. N. Ilyina and L. D. Utkina, *Ekonomicheskaya effektivnost ispolzovaniya prirodnogo gaza* [Cost-effectiveness of gas use] (Moscow: Nedra, 1978), Chapter 3, pp. 39–101; and Ye. N. Ilyina and L. D. Utkina, "The unevenness of gas consumption," *Ekonomika gazovoi promyshlennosti*, 1978, no. 9, pp. 8–15.

49. M. A. Styrikovich and S. Ya. Chernyavsky, "The development and role of nuclear energy in the future electric power balance of the world and its major regions" (Paper delivered at U. S.-Soviet seminar under energy agreement, 1979), Tables 5 and 6; Makarov and Melentyev, "Future structure," U. S.-Soviet seminar, 1979, Figures 4 and 5, and Makarov and Vigdorchik, *Toplivno-energetichesky kompleks*, pp. 196–201.

50. See Dienes, "Issues in Soviet Energy Policy," *Soviet Studies*, July 1971, and Dienes, "Geographical Problems." Since that time, production costs in the older fields multiplied by several times and they have now almost completely exhausted their reserves. A. D. Brents et al., *Ekonomika gazodobyvayushchei promyshlennosti* [Economics of the gas industry] (Moscow: Nedra, 1975), pp. 49–51, and R. D. Margulov, Ye. K. Selikhova and I. Ya. Furman, *Razvitiye gazovoi promyshlennosti i analiz tekhniko-ekonomicheskikh pokazatelei* [Development of the gas industry and an analysis of technical-economic indicators] (Moscow: VNIIE, 1976), pp. 23, 25.

51. Leslie Dienes, "Minerals and Energy," chapter 7 in I. S. Koropeckiy ed., *The Ukraine within the USSR. An Economic Balance Sheet* (New York: Praeger, 1977), pp. 155–89, and Theodore Shabad, "News Notes," *SGRT* 23, no. 4 (April 1982), pp. 277–90 for declining fuel output in the Ukraine.

52. Makarov and Vigdorchik, *Toplivno-energetichesky kompleks*, pp. 28–64, 130–95; Akademiya nauk SSSR, Sibirskoye otdeleniye i Sibirsky energetichesky institut, *Voprosy vliyaniya razvitiya energetiki na drugiye otrasli narodnogo khozyaistva* [The impact of energy development on other sectors of the economy] (Irkutsk, 1975), and earlier, less comprehensive sources.

53. V. Z. Tkachenko, "Methods for investigating materials linkages between the fuels and energy complex and other economic sectors" (Dissertation, Academy of Sciences USSR, Siberian Division and Siberian Energy Institute, Irkutsk, 1975).

54. Akademiya nauk SSSR, *Voprosy vliyaniya*, pp. 68–84, especially p. 79.

55. Makarov and Vigdorchik, *Toplivno-energetichesky kompleks*, pp. 152–94.

56. See sources in note 49.

57. Explored (proved plus probable, or $A + B + C_1$) reserves in 1976 were said to reach 28 trillion $m^3$ (990 trillion cubic feet) by a Soviet source. *Geologiya, bureniye i razrabotka gazovykh mestorozhdenii*, 1977, no. 4, p. 3. Meyerhoff in a recent paper cites a lower figure, 850 trillion cubic feet, which still amounts to 34 percent of the world's total. He believes potential reserves in the USSR to be 2.5 times as much, or 48 percent of the total for the globe. Arthur Meyerhoff, "Proved and Ultimate Reserves of Natural Gas and Natural Gas Liquids in the World," in 10th World Petroleum Congress, Bucharest, 1979, *Proceedings*, vol. 2, pp. 307–11.

The recovery rate of gas is higher than that of oil, varying in the USSR from 80 to 90 percent of older explored reserves. However, since the West Siberian fields have low reservoir pressure, recovery rates at these deposits may be appreciably lower. This is conceded by Soviet authorities, including the Minister of the Gas Industry. *Gazovaya promyshlennost*, 1975, no. 8, p. 4 and 1976, no. 11, p. 6 and *Pravda*, 26 February 1977, p. 2.

58. At the 9th World Petroleum Congress, the then Soviet Minister of the Oil Industry, Shashin, declared: "From 1961 through 1974, the Soviet Union produced 31 billion barrels of oil and condensate, which is somewhat more than the oil and condensate discovered during this period." Ninth World Petroleum Congress, Tokyo, 1975, *Proceedings*, vol. 2. Summary. For other sources, see N. Melnikov and V. Shelest, "The Fuels and energy complex of the USSR," *Planovoye khozyaistvo*, 1975, no. 2, p. 11; M. V. Feigin, *Neftyanya resursy: metodika ikh issledovaniya i otsenki* [Oil resources: methods of investigation and estimation] (Moscow: Nauka, 1974), p. 27; NATO Directorate of Economic Affairs, *Exploitation of Siberia's Natural Resources* (Brussels, 1974), pp. 76, 110–11 and *Sotsialisticheskaya industriya*, 1 July 1980, p. 2. The last source concedes that in the crucial West Siberian region the relationship between production and reserve growth is even worse than in the rest of the Soviet Union.

59. For two exhaustive studies of Soviet oil and gas reserves, see David Levin, "Oil and Natural Gas Resources of the Soviet Union and Methods of Their Estimation," in U. S. Congress *Project Independence: U. S. and World Energy Outlook Through 1990*, Congressional Research Service, Library of Congress (Washington: Government Printing Service, 1977), pp. 821–48, and A. A. Meyerhoff, "PetroStudies Reports: 1978–1980," *Review of Sino-Soviet Oil* (Geneva: Petroconsultants), vol. 16, no. 1 (1981). On the basis of authoritative Soviet articles, mistranslated and misinterpreted by PetroStudies, Meyerhoff shows that the USSR "has less than 43.5 billion barrels of proved reserves, probably about 35 billion," i.e., reserves comparable to the American Petroleum Institute's corresponding category. Among a wide range of Soviet scientific work, Meyerhoff carefully analyzes the article by G. P. Ovanesov and M. V. Feigin, "On the issue

of confirming the oil reserve categories $C_1$ and $C_2$," in *Geologiya nefti i gaza*, 1975, no. 8, pp. 7–14, an important study. Meyerhoff shows that contrary to PetroStudies' claim, only 62.1 percent × 52.1 percent (i.e. 32.4 percent) of the initial $C_1$ volume of reserves was ultimately transferred to the B category. Only $A + B$ reserves can be considered *proved* by API definition.

60. Between 1959 and 1972, as much as 37.9 percent of the initially assumed $C_1$ reserves had to be written off and 62.1 percent could be confirmed as such reserves. This ratio remained virtually constant during the period. Outside West Siberia, 45.3 percent of the $C_1$ reserves had to be written off during 1966–72. In addition, even placement into the B category does not necessarily guarantee recoverability. Ovanesov and Feigin, "Confirming oil reserve categories," especially pp. 9–11.

61. Theodore Shabad, "News Notes," *SGRT*, 23, no. 4 (April 1982): pp. 277–90. Physical units converted to calorific equivalent.

62. Ibid., pp. 277–83. The consumption estimate implies a net oil and refinery product export of 150 million tons and a net gas export of 52 billion cubic meters and *net* coal export of 10 million tons.

63. *Narodnoye khozyaistvo SSSR*. Various issues, and Shabad, "News Notes," *SGRT*, 23, no. 4 (April 1982): pp. 277–83.

64. *The Oil and Gas Journal*, 10 October 1977, p. 73, and 6 February 1977, p. 36 gives data until 1978. During 1978–79, exploratory drilling in West Siberia grew by 50 percent but only by diverting drilling crews to the region from other petroleum provinces. Since West Siberia accounted for about a fifth of total Soviet exploratory meterage in the mid-1970s, it is unlikely that drilling for the rest of the country would have increased at all. V. Filanovsky, "The West Siberian oil and gas complex: results and prospects," *Planovoye khozyaistvo*, 1980, no. 5, p. 21.

65. For damage to oil fields see *Neftyanoye khozyaistvo*, 1976, no. 10, pp. 27–29; 1976, no. 4, pp. 51–54; 1976, no. 3 pp. 24–25; 1977, no. 7, pp. 5–7; 1977, no. 6, pp. 30–33; 1977, no. 4, p. 9; *Problemy geologii nefti*, 1976, no. 8, pp. 130–36; and *Sotsialsticheskaya industriya*, 20 November 1969, p. 2. The decline in the flow rate of oil fields is shown in A. P. Krylov, "Rates of exploitation of oil field," *Ekonomika i organizatsiya promyshlennogo proizvodstva*, 1980, no. 1, especially pp. 68–69; Filanovsky, "West Siberian oil and gas complex," p. 23. In West Siberia, Filanovsky's table shows declines from 162 tons per day in 1975 to 71.1 tons per day in 1980. Another source expects flow rates to drop to 38 tons by the mid-1980s. *Sotsialisticheskaya industriya*, 21 May 1980, p. 1.

66. *World Oil*, 15 August 1979, p. 165.

67. U. S., CIA, *Prospects for Soviet Oil Production. A Supplementary Analysis* ER-77-10425, June 1977, p. 2 and A. Meyerhoff, "Soviet Petroleum," chapter 14 in this volume.

68. Filanovsky, "West Siberian oil and gas complex," p. 21.

69. Meyerhoff, "Soviet Petroleum," chapter 14 in this volume.

70. *Pravda*, 28 February 1978, p. 2; 10 August 1977, p. 2; 24 August 1977, p. 2; and V. V. Fedynsky, "Exploration geophysics in the USSR on the 60th anniversary of the October Revolution," *Vestnik Moskovskogo Universiteta, geologiya*, 1977, no. 4, pp. 123–24.

71. According to a deputy chairman of Gosplan USSR, exploratory drilling in West Siberia was to increase from 4.9 million meters in the 1976–80 plan to 12.5 million during the following five years. *Sotsialisticheskaya industriya*, 21 May 1980, p. 1. This seems unrealistic. In 1979, the Tyumen Geology Trust, which accounts for nine-tenths of all such drilling in West Siberia, completed only 763,000 meters compared with the planned 1,086,000, a 70 percent plan fulfillment. The Ministry of the Petroleum Industry almost completely disassociated itself from prospecting in the region. It reserves its resources for production drilling and accounts for only a tenth of exploratory drilling in West Siberia. Filanovsky, "West Siberian oil and gas complex," p. 21 and *Sotsialisticheskaya industriya*, 1 July 1980, p. 2.

72. Filanovsky, "West Siberian oil and gas complex," p. 21.

73. Meyerhoff, chapter 14 in this volume.

74. The consumption estimate implies a *net* oil export of 150 million tons, *net* gas export of 52 billion cubic meters and *net* coal export of 10 million tons.

75. *Narodnoye khozyaistvo SSSR*. Various issues.

76. Shabad, "News Notes," *SGRT*, 23, no. 4 (April 1982): pp. 283–87.

77. Orudzhev, *Gazovaya promyshlennost*, p. 12; Yu. Bokserman, "Ways of enhancing the cost-effectiveness of fuel transport," *Planovoye khozyaistvo*, 1975, no. 2, p. 21. Half of all Soviet reserves are found in six supergiant fields, of which four are in northwest Siberia, one in Central Asia and one in Orenburg Oblast of the European USSR. An additional supergiant field is shaping up on the Yamal Peninsula of northwest Siberia. The Urengoi field in West Siberia alone concentrates one-fifth of all explored reserves and is by far the largest gas field in the world discovered to date.

78. *Gazovaya promyshlennost*. 1978, no. 11, p. 2.

79. Yu. Bokserman, "On new, progressive forms of transport," *Planvoye khozyaistvo*, 1977, no. 4, p. 5.

80. *The Oil and Gas Journal*, 2 April 1979, p. 42 and *Gazovaya promyshlennost*, 1977, no. 4, p. 5.

81. Dienes, chapter 16 n 94 in this volume and *Business Week*, 17 October 1977, p. 52.

82. For more detail see Dienes, chapter 16, in this volume.

83. Ibid., and S. S. Ushakov and T. M. Borisenko, *Ekonomika transporta topliva i energii* [Economics of fuel and energy transport] (Moscow: Energiya, 1980), p. 96–101.

84. *Narodnoye khozyaistvo SSSR*. Various issues and Shabad, "News Notes," *SGRT*, 23, no. 4 (April 1982): pp. 287–90.

85. N. I. Nikolayev and A. A. Kosar, *Effektivnost kapitalnykh vlozhenii v ugolnoi promyshlennosti Kuzbassa* [Cost effectiveness of investment in the coal industry of the Kuzbas] (Kemerovo: Politekhnichesky Institut Kuzbassa, 1976), p. 48.

86. U. S., CIA, *USSR: Coal Industry. Problems and Prospects*. ER 80-10154, March 1980, p. 3.

87. See sources in note 49.

88. Makarov and Vigdorchik, *Toplivno-energetichesky kompleks*, p. 147.

89. *Ugol*, 1979, no. 6, p. 51 and F. N. Sukhopara and V. I. Udod, *Problemy razvitiya i razmeshcheniya proizvoditelnykh sil Donetsko-Pridneprovskogo rayona* [Problems in the development and location of productive forces in the Donets-Dnieper Region] (Moscow: Mysl, 1976), pp. 49–54, 95–99; *Izvestiya*, 25 January 1974.

90. R. Z. Kosukhin, "Contemporary problems of socio-economic development of a mining enterprise," in *Ekonomicheskiye parametry gornykh predpriyatiy budushchego* [Economic parameters of future mines] (Moscow, 1976), p. 187.

91. Ye. N. Ilyina and D. Utkina, "Methodological problems of creating an information system on the cost-effectiveness of gas use," *Ekonomika gazovoi promyshlennosti*, 1975, no. 8, p. 23.

92. In the early 1970s, 94 percent of Ekibastuz coal and 65 percent of Kansk-Achinsk coal was used by the Ministry of Electric Power Industry. Much of the rest was also apparently used for power generation in plants not under the ministry. I. L. Yakubovich et al., *Pryamye svyazi po postavkam uglya i slantsa* [Direct linkages in coal and oil shale deliveries] (Moscow: Nedra, 1974), p. 36. Data for Ekibastuz coal also show that virtually all of it is burned for electricity generation. Shabad, "News Notes," *SGRT*, 21, no. 3 (March 1980): p. 190.

93. *Sotsialisticheskaya industriya*, 19 November 1977, p. 2.

94. Shabad, "News Notes," *SGRT*, 21, no. 3 (March 1980): pp. 187–90 and A. A. Troitsky, "Main directions of development of the electric power industry under the future fuels balance," *Elektricheskiye stantsii*, 1978, no. 12, pp. 11–14, also in *Planovoye khozyaistvo*, 1979, no. 2, pp. 18–25; G. A. Illarionov and I. A. Odinokov, "The role of the Ekibastuz fuels and power project in the development of Soviet electric power," *Elektricheskiye stantsii*, 1979, no. 10, pp. 8–11. See also note 34.

95. Leslie Dienes and Theodore Shabad, *The Soviet Energy System: Resource Use and Policies* (Winston and Sons, distributed by J. Wiley, New York, 1979), p. 271.

96. P. S. Neporozhny and Z. F. Chukhanov, "Comparative analysis of traditional and complex processing methods for deriving liquid fuels from coal" (Paper presented at U. S.-Soviet seminar under energy agreement, 1979).

97. Ye. Olofinsky, "Development of progressive forms of transport for coal and ore concentrates," *Planovoye khozyaistvo*, 1980, no. 8, pp. 91–92.

98. *Narodnoye khozyaistvo SSSR v. 1980 godu*, pp. 157, 295–96. Average distance equals freight turnover in ton-km divided by car loadings in tons. See also *SGRT*, 23, no. 4 (April 1982): p. 291.

99. For calculations and more detail see chapter 16 in this volume.

100. Styrikovich and Chernyavsky, "Nuclear energy in the future."

101. Shabad, "News Notes," *SGRT*, 22, no. 4 (April 1981): p. 279.

102. *The Daily Telegraph* (London), November 1977.

# 13

# ESTIMATING DEMAND FOR ENERGY IN THE CENTRALLY PLANNED ECONOMIES

JUDITH THORNTON
University of Washington

## Introduction

Projections of Soviet potential to export energy products are based on underlying projections of Soviet production and domestic consumption. While the prospects for Soviet production have been considered in many sources, such as Campbell and Dienes,[1] estimates of Soviet and East European consumption deserve further study. One of the most useful methodologies for analyzing energy consumption is the estimating of demand elasticities for energy inputs, i.e., the estimation of measures that reflect how the consumption of each energy product changes in response to changes in other variables such as relative prices and the level of income.[2]

This study reports estimates of price and income elasticities of demand for energy inputs for the Soviet Union, six countries of Eastern Europe, and China. These estimates provide evidence as to whether the centrally planned economies do respond to changes in relative international prices by substituting one input for another. They give us some basis for judging the extent of the error introduced into projections of energy use in the centrally planned economies by the assumption that consumption changes on a one-to-one basis with output or income.

Most Western forecasts of Soviet and East European energy consumption ignore the possibility of price sensitivity in demand for energy inputs. There are historical reasons for such an approach. The nonresponsiveness of planners and managers to price changes of all sorts is part of the folk-wisdom about the centrally planned economies. Indeed, the isolation of domestic economies from world markets, the absence of internal market-clearing prices, and the quantitative allocation of many products by the planners all decrease the information available for price-sensitive input choices.

At the same time, the lack of markets with clearing prices does not make the centrally planned economies immune to the effects of world price changes. The four-fold increase in world oil prices that occurred in 1973 offered the Soviet Union a substantial incentive to shift their petroleum from domestic uses to hard-currency markets. It also raised the cost to them of providing Eastern Europe with petroleum at prices below world prices. The Soviets responded by raising bloc export prices toward world levels, thereby confronting the countries of Eastern Europe with larger oil import bills.

Few Western projections of Soviet energy use attribute any flexibility to Soviet planners. Sawyer forecasts consumption with simple extrapolation of past trends.[3] Jack, Lee, and Lent apply fixed coefficients of energy use per unit of gross output to projections of the growth of output, making energy use move on a one-to-one basis with output.[4] Daniel Kazmer has constructed more detailed estimates of energy consumption. He applies fixed input-output coefficients of energy use to each of the main energy-using sectors of the economy. Thus, forecasts of output imply forecasts of energy "requirements."[5] In Kazmer's framework, reduced energy use occurs either through slower growth of output or through a shift away from energy-using sectors. After a careful regional analysis of individual energy products, Dienes, too, projects the parallel change of energy use and GNP. He writes:[6]

It was shown above that for the past two decades there was no evidence of any decline in the *true* energy intensiveness of the Soviet economy. Net energy consumption rose slightly faster than national income as officially reported and much faster when national income is estimated according to Western concepts. The rate of improvement in heat capture and conversion efficiency has slowed drastically with only marginal gains expected through the next 15 years or so. At the same time, worsening resource conditions and the colossal efforts to develop remote Siberia are increasing energy requirements. It is extremely unlikely, therefore, that Soviet energy consumption can grow appreciably slower than GNP for any sustained period and may even grow faster. The rise in energy consumption will basically depend on projections for GNP and on the rate of economic growth Soviet leaders push for and will find politically acceptable.

*I profited from the comments of Robert Halvorsen and from the research assistance of Ross Finke.*

By contrast, the implication of this study is that, to the extent that the centrally planned economies do show responsiveness to changes in world prices, the growth of consumption of individual energy products and of all energy products as a group may diverge from the rate of growth of total output.

Although there are no recent studies of price elasticities of demand for energy products in Eastern Europe, a substantial study of eight East European countries and the Soviet Union by J.G. Polach provides estimates of income elasticities for total energy.[7] Polach's elasticity estimates, measured as the ratio for the percentage increase in energy consumption to percentage increase in net material product, show wide variation across countries. The income elasticity coefficients for selected periods from 1950 to 1967 presented in Table 1 range from 1.480 for Albania to .332 for East Germany.

Kelly uses linear regression analysis to compare Soviet GNP with Soviet energy consumption for two periods, 1950 to 1966 and 1967 to 1975.[8] He argues that his results show a reduction in energy intensity since the 1967 price reform. As his analysis did not extend to other inputs or the rate of technical progress, the case for energy savings since 1967 is still unclear. But he is one of the few economists to search for indirect evidence of price-related substitution responses on the part of central planners.

Western studies of energy demand find price to be an important factor in explaining rates of consumption. In a survey of recent Western estimates, Lester Taylor concludes:[9]

The evidence strikes me as nearly overwhelming that the price of energy is an important determinant of the amount of energy that is consumed and the form in which it is consumed. Indeed, I am not aware of any study of energy demand that I consider to be credible in terms of specification and the way that price (or prices) is defined that does not

yield an own-price elasticity of some magnitude and statistical importance. Energy consumption is not simply a matter of income and lifestyle.

Virtually all recent studies of energy demand in the West find the own-price and income elasticities of demand for all energy to be inelastic, i.e., the percentage change in consumption is less than the percentage change in price or income. Further, magnitude of the response is larger in the long run than in the short run.[10] For individual energy products, Halvorsen provides estimates of long-run price elasticities of demand for electric energy, fuel oil, natural gas, and coal, based on a sample of U.S. manufacturing industries. He finds the own-price elasticities to be $-0.92$ for electric energy, $-2.82$ for fuel oil, $-1.47$ for natural gas, and $-1.52$ for coal—all except electricity highly elastic.[11] Other Western studies summarized by Taylor yield similar results. For electricity, own-price elasticity estimates are about $-0.2$ in the short run, rising to $-0.7$ to $-0.9$ in the long run; for natural gas, they are $-0.15$ in the short run to $-1.0$ or more in the long run; for coal, $-0.4$ in the short run, rising to $-0.7$ to $-0.9$ in the long run.

In a recent paper, Robert Halvorsen and the author compared the responses of eight market and eight centrally planned economies to the quadrupling of the world price of crude oil in 1973.[12] We found that income-adjusted consumption of crude oil fell in all of the market economies and in several of the centrally planned economies. However, in three centrally planned economies—the Soviet Union, China, and Poland—income-adjusted consumption continued to rise. Domestic production of crude oil was predicted to increase, but instead decreased relative to trends in the Soviet Union, the United States, and Canada. It appeared to us that the actual responses to an exogenous shock such as the increase in the world price of crude oil did not depend in a systematic way on the type of economic system. But

TABLE 1
Eastern Europe and USSR: Elasticity Coefficients* for Energy Use
In Relation to Net Material Product and Industrial Product in Selected Periods

| | Net Material Product | | | | Industrial Product | | | |
|---|---|---|---|---|---|---|---|---|
| | 1960/ 1950 | 1967/ 1950 | 1967/ 1960 | 1967/ 1965 | 1960/ 1950 | 1967/ 1950 | 1967/ 1960 | 1967/ 1965 |
| | (1) | (2) | (3) | (4) | (5) | (6) | (7) | (8) |
| Albania | 1.388 | 1.480 | 1.276 | 2.000 | 0.384 | 0.427 | 0.974 | 1.462 |
| Bulgaria | .733 | .951 | 1.403 | .809 | .439 | .445 | .777 | .630 |
| Czechoslovakia | .607 | .618 | .813 | −.150 | .357 | .336 | .521 | −.200 |
| East Germany | .349 | .332 | .484 | −.200 | .302 | .240 | .294 | −.154 |
| Hungary | 1.338 | 1.065 | .705 | −.062 | .617 | .476 | .463 | −.062 |
| Poland | .694 | .569 | .528 | .429 | .315 | .255 | .384 | .400 |
| Rumania | .667 | .616 | .720 | .889 | .467 | .331 | .415 | .593 |
| Yugoslavia | 1.408 | .908 | .385 | .375 | .852 | .536 | .291 | .750 |
| Soviet Union | .612 | .628 | .847 | .800 | .495 | .449 | .625 | .600 |

*An elasticity coefficient is defined as
$(\Delta E/E)/(\Delta Q/Q)$,
where E is energy consumption and Q is aggregate product (net material or industrial).
SOURCE: Polach, "Energy in Eastern Europe."

responses did seem to be affected by the existence of a significant domestic fuel industry.

In this study, I bring information on prices to bear to investigate further whether the centrally planned economies show the same kind of price-responsiveness that we see in the West and to ask what sorts of differences emerge among countries. To the extent that the centrally planned economies do respond to changes in world prices, our forecasts of future behavior need to take that into account.

I first discuss the way in which the rise in the world price of oil would be expected to affect the consumption of energy products directly through prices and indirectly through income variables. Then I survey the actual responses of eight centrally planned economies for the period 1960 (or 1955) until 1976. Although the time since 1973 is too brief to allow for a full adjustment to changes in world oil prices, estimates of the responses of these countries to changes in relative prices over the full period provide useful evidence as to whether these countries make appropriate cost-minimizing adjustments and whether we can expect such adjustments in the future.

### Predicted Responses

To the extent that the centrally planned economies are responsive to changes in relative world prices, we can describe the adjustments that they would be predicted to make over time in response to a change such as the rise in the world price of oil. This price rise would be predicted to cause both movements along and shifts in the demand and supply curves of related commodities in those economies. While predictions of the total response can only be captured in a general equilibrium model, we can account for some of the shift effects on the demand side by estimating income elasticities. Estimates of price elasticities with respect to world prices are used to estimate demand substitution responses.

Consider an oil-importing country that takes the world price of crude oil as given. The effects of an increase in the price of oil on the production, consumption, and net imports of oil are illustrated in Figure 1. (We assume that government policy does not prevent markets from clearing after the increase in price.) Given the original domestic supply curve, $DS_0$, domestic demand curve, $DD_0$, and world price of crude oil, $WP_0$, the quantity of domestic production would be $DP_0$, and the quantity consumed would be $DC_0$. Net imports would equal the difference $DC_0 - DP_0$. Assuming for the moment that there were no shifts in domestic demand and supply curves, an increase in the world price of crude oil to $WP_1$ would result in an increase in domestic production to $DP_1$, a decrease in domestic consumption to $DC_1$, and a decrease in net imports to $DC_1 - DP_1$.

The assumption above that the rise in the world price of crude oil would not shift the demand curve is implausible, because the higher world price of crude would affect national income. The direction of the effect on quantity consumed would depend on both the sign of the elasticity of crude-oil consumption with respect to national income

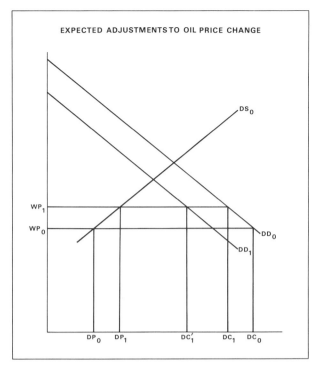

Figure 1

and the sign of the change in national income. The increase in the world price of crude could cause national income to either increase or decrease. For example, if oil imports were small (large) relative to exports of a competing energy good, an oil-importing country would benefit (suffer) from the higher price of oil. As drawn in Figure 1—representing a large importer whose national income declines following the price increase to $WP_1$—the reduction in the demand curve to $DD_1$ further reduces domestic consumption to $DC_1'$ and net imports to $DC_1' - DP_1$.

The analysis of a non-cartel exporting country is symmetric with that of an oil-importing country. Net imports, which would be negative for an oil-exporter, would be expected to decrease; that is, oil exports would be expected to increase. If the price increase were large, some countries that had been net importers could become net exporters (China is such a case in our study).

In summary, if the governments of the centrally planned economies responded by (in effect) letting domestic markets clear, an increase in the world price of crude oil should increase domestic production, decrease domestic consumption, and decrease net imports of crude compared with the previous values. Evaluated at world prices, the profitability of domestic crude oil production would be substantially higher. The short-run balance-of-payments effects would be expected to be positive for the net exporter and negative for the net importer, unless the oil importer were exporting a competing energy good.

While the effects of an increase in the world price of crude oil would extend to virtually all goods, we shall limit our analysis to selected energy goods, which would be most directly affected. Because coal and electricity are substitutes for crude oil,[13] their demand curves should increase (i.e., shift upward). Since crude oil is a direct input into the production of electric power and an indirect input into the production of coal, the supply curves of electricity and coal would also be expected to decrease (i.e., shift upward). As a result of the shifts in both demand and supply, the market-clearing prices of electricity and coal would be higher. For coal, the shift in the supply curve would be small relative to the shift in the demand curve, so both production and consumption of coal would be likely to increase. For electricity, production and consumption could either increase or decrease. If the shift in the supply curve dominated, the quantities of electricity produced and consumed would decrease.

The demand curve for natural gas, which is a substitute for crude oil, would increase. Because natural gas is produced jointly with crude oil to a considerable extent, the expansion of domestic oil output could cause an increase in the supply curve of natural gas. Therefore, the direction of the effect of an increase in crude-oil price on the market-clearing price and quantity of natural gas could be either positive or negative. If production techniques in the extraction of crude oil and natural gas were relatively fixed in the short run, we would expect the quantity of natural gas produced and consumed to rise.

The above analysis of responses to an increase in the world price of crude oil assumes that the increase is viewed as a one-time shift to a new equilibrium price. If the increase in price were viewed instead as the beginning of a process of continually rising real crude oil prices, the analysis would be complicated in a number of ways. The responses of production from existing reserves and of exploration for new reserves would be affected by perceptions of the time path of oil prices. For example, output might fall in the short run despite the higher price if producers withheld production in anticipation of still higher prices in the future. However, the assumption of one-time shifts in crude-oil prices more accurately describes the situation facing the centrally planned economies in 1974–78 and 1979–81 than the assumption of continual increases. Therefore, the more straightforward analysis of their responses to higher oil prices presented above is adequate to our purposes.

In the centrally planned economies, the level and structure of domestic prices is partially insulated from world prices. Foreign trade prices in Comecon also may diverge from world levels. Since the Soviet Union and Eastern Europe trade crude oil under long-term agreements, the initial adjustment in the level of bloc crude-oil prices to the increased Western price occurred with a lag of more than a year before a new price-adjustment formula was developed. In the absence of market-driven domestic price changes, producers and consumers of energy lack a price incentive to adjust to the changed situation. The cost to the planners of measuring and directing the appropriate adjustments may be considerable; yet they clearly have an incentive to make such adjustments.

Measurement of the responses of the centrally planned economies to the rise in the world price of oil provides evidence, then, of the extent to which the planned economies are able to adjust to changes in the economic environment even in the absence of domestic market-clearing prices.

## Patterns of Energy Use

Patterns of energy use in the centrally planned economies differ from patterns in the West. In the United States in 1975, natural gas made up about one-third of total energy use, oil about 44 percent, and coal 7 percent. In the Soviet Union, coal contributed 30 percent, oil 43 percent and natural gas 21 percent in the same year.[14] In Eastern Europe, coal contributed 69 percent, oil 17 percent, and natural gas 12 percent to total energy use in 1970; in Poland and East Germany, the two largest economies, over 80 percent of the energy used came from coal.[15]

While almost one-third of United States fuel use in 1975 went to the provision of refined oil products for final demand, only 7 percent of Soviet energy was directed to the same use. Industry, mining and construction accounted for over half of energy consumption in Eastern Europe, with 60 to 70 percent of net energy going to these uses in East Germany, Poland and Czechoslovakia.[16]

Table 2 shows that rates of increase in the consumption of crude oil declined after the 1973 price increase in all the Communist countries studied here except Rumania

TABLE 2
Average Annual Increase in Consumption of Major Energy Forms, 1965–73 and 1973–76 (percentages)

| Country | (1) 1965–1973 | (2) 1973–1976 | (3) 1965–1973 | (4) 1973–1976 | (5) 1965–1973 | (6) 1973–1976 | (7) 1965–1973 | (8) 1973–1976 |
|---|---|---|---|---|---|---|---|---|
| | Crude Oil | | Coal | | Natural Gas | | Electricity | |
| USSR | 7.3 | 5.9 | 1.5 | 2.0 | 8.3 | 8.4 | 7.6 | 6.7 |
| Bulgaria | 19.1 | 3.0 | 2.1 | 1.2 | — | — | 11.9 | 7.4 |
| Czechoslovakia | 10.9 | 5.8 | 1.2 | 2.0 | 14.9 | 16.9 | 7.4 | 4.9 |
| East Germany | 15.3 | 4.0 | −0.5 | 0.5 | 6.2 | 22.5 | 4.8 | 4.6 |
| Hungary | 9.4 | 7.0 | −2.3 | −2.0 | 17.0 | 14.2 | 7.7 | 8.4 |
| Poland | 15.8 | 10.5 | 3.7 | 4.8 | 18.0 | 9.7 | 9.7 | 8.0 |
| Rumania | 4.7 | 8.6 | 9.3 | 9.1 | 6.5 | 7.2 | 12.5 | 9.5 |
| China | 22.4 | 10.0 | 7.0 | 5.5 | 15.3 | 10.0 | 11.6 | 6.2 |

SOURCE: Tables used for calculation are available from the author upon request.

(which is a major exporter of refined oil products).[17] The pattern of changes in the use of coal, natural gas, and electricity is mixed, reflecting such differential factors as availability, price, and long-run policies. Table 3 further shows that these countries were not able, for the most part, to adjust to the higher prices of oil and other energy goods by expanding domestic production.

## Estimation Procedures

Data on energy production and trade are available for the planned economies for the period 1960–76 and for selected years in the 1950s. Sources used are listed in the footnotes. Series on apparent consumption may be calculated from production and net imports. Price series show the most serious defects. Domestic price indices are aggregate and, for the most part, constant. Unit values of energy products in foreign trade are available for Eastern Europe for selected years in Campbell and Haberstroh.[18] In addition, I am indebted to Edward Hewett for his estimates of unit values for Soviet imports and exports of energy products (see chapter 28 in this volume).

We are interested in measuring whether consumption of energy products by the centrally planned economies responded to changing world prices. To the extent that the centrally planned economies adjusted rates of energy use in response to changes in relative energy prices, simple extrapolations of energy demand will be too high.

A direct measure of the response is the elasticity of demand with respect to income and prices for each energy product in each country. The elasticities of demand are estimated for each country by estimating equations of the form:

$$(1) \quad \ln C_t^i = a + b_1 \ln Y_t + b_2 \ln P_t^i + b_3 \ln P_t^o + u,$$

where superscript $i$ refers to the individual energy products (oil, coal, natural gas, and electric power); subscript $t$ refers to the year; $C$ is domestic consumption of an energy product; $Y$ is GNP; $P^i$ is the own price of the product; $P^o$ is the prices of other energy products (an index except where sufficient observations for separate products are

available); and $u$ is the error term. The coefficient $b_1$ is the estimated income-elasticity of demand (where GNP is a proxy for national income); $b_2$ is the estimated own-price elasticity of demand; and $b_3$ is the estimated cross-price elasticity of demand with respect to the other energy prices.

Estimates are made for the period 1955–76, with some variation in the sample period depending on the availability of price and quantity data. Soviet series are estimated for 1950–76. Because an earlier study by Thornton and Halvorsen[19] suggested that the planned economies responded more slowly than the market economies to the energy crisis, I also calculated estimates of the elasticities in which both price variables were lagged by one year for comparison:

$$(1') \quad \ln C_t^i = a + b_1 \ln Y_t + b_2 \ln P_{t-1}^i + b_3 \ln P_{t-1}^o + u.$$

Demand elasticities in per capita terms were also estimated, yielding similar coefficients and slightly lower levels of significance. The equations were estimated using the Cochrane-Orcutt procedure to correct for serial correlation in the error terms, as well as by ordinary least squares. As expected, the Cochrane-Orcutt results were superior and are reported here.

## Responses of the Centrally Planned Economies

Actual and predicted responses are examined for eight centrally planned economies—the Soviet Union, Bulgaria, Czechoslovakia, East Germany, Hungary, Poland, Rumania, and China for the period 1955–76 (1950–76 for the Soviet Union). Most of the countries examined were net importers of crude oil during all of the period studied. The Soviet Union was a net exporter for the entire period, and a large exporter for most of the recent years. China was a net importer until 1973, but became a net exporter after 1973. Rumania, which imported crude oil, was a net exporter of petroleum products. (The underlying data on production, consumption, and trade in energy products are summarized in a set of tables available from the author upon request.)

TABLE 3
Average Annual Increase in Production of Major Energy Forms, 1965–73 and 1973–76 (percentages)

| Country | Crude Oil 1965–1973 | Crude Oil 1973–1976 | Coal 1965–1973 | Coal 1973–1976 | Natural Gas 1965–1973 | Natural Gas 1973–1976 | Electricity 1965–1973 | Electricity 1973–1976 |
|---|---|---|---|---|---|---|---|---|
| USSR | 7.2 | 6.5 | 1.5 | 2.1 | 8.0 | 10.7 | 7.7 | 6.7 |
| Bulgaria | — | — | 0.9 | −1.6 | — | — | 10.0 | 10.8 |
| Czechoslovakia | — | — | 1.1 | 2.6 | −1.6 | −0.9 | 6.7 | 5.5 |
| East Germany | — | — | −3.0 | 0.1 | 4.4 | 3.3 | 4.6 | 5.0 |
| Hungary | — | — | −2.0 | −2.0 | 18.6 | 8.2 | 5.9 | 11.6 |
| Poland | — | — | 4.1 | 3.7 | 17.8 | 7.4 | 9.9 | 7.3 |
| Rumania | 2.1 | −0.2 | 11.7 | 2.7 | 6.4 | 6.9 | 13.3 | 7.6 |
| China | 22.4 | 15.3 | 7.0 | 5.5 | 15.3 | 10.0 | 11.6 | 6.2 |

SOURCE: Calculated from appendix tables (available from the author upon request).

Crude Oil

In the 1960s, consumption of crude oil increased more rapidly than GNP in most of the East European countries as they shifted from coal to oil. As seen in Table 2, crude oil consumption continued to grow, but more slowly than GNP in most cases, after 1973. In Bulgaria consumption of crude stopped growing altogether after 1974, although imports of petroleum products continued to climb.

In the results presented in Table 4, estimated elasticities of demand for crude oil are greater than 1.0 for all countries except Rumania. Most of the countries were making major efforts to shift away from a coal-based economy during this period.

Estimated own-price elasticities of crude oil demand are negative (as predicted) and significant at the 95 percent level in four of the eight cases. The estimates for Bulgaria, Czechoslovakia, and China are not significant, suggesting little own-price responsiveness in these two countries. The significant but positive estimated elasticity for Rumania may be partly explained by the large derived demand for crude oil to refine into products for reexport; however, this interpretation requires further research.

Own-price elasticities for crude oil are roughly unitelastic for East Germany ($-1.0$) and Poland ($-0.9$), and inelastic for the USSR and Hungary. Price elasticities for oil are slightly larger in absolute sign than for other fuels; this may correspond to the finding in Western demand studies of relatively large price elasticities for industrial demand for fuel oil, e.g., an elasticity of $-1.3$ for Canadian industry estimated by Fuss, Hyndman, and Waverman, and of $-2.8$ for United States manufacturing, estimated by Halvorsen.[20]

Significant estimates of cross-elasticities with respect to

a price index of other energy inputs have the expected positive signs in the case of Hungary. The estimates are not significant for Bulgaria, Czechoslovakia, Poland, and Rumania. For the Soviet Union and East Germany, there were sufficiently long price series to estimate separate cross-elasticities of crude-oil demand for natural gas and coal. In both cases, the estimated coal cross-elasticity is significant and positive as predicted; contrary to hypothesis, however, the gas cross-elasticity is significant and negative. An important extension of the results presented here will be the estimation of separate cross-elasticities for individual energy inputs as more detailed price series are developed. For example, when the Soviet demand equation was estimated with the index of other prices, the coefficients were insignificant. As shown here, with individual input prices the coefficients are significant.

In the case of Hungary, the demand equation on current prices yielded insignificant results, but coefficients are significant for the equation with a one-year price lag. One interpretation would be an extra delay in administrative responses to changes in Hungary, although this interpretation would be at odds with received doctrine about the comparative flexibility in central planning among the East European countries. For the other countries, estimates with a one-year price lag were similar to estimates with simultaneous variables, but individual coefficients were larger and levels of significance were lower.

Coal

All of the centrally planned economies are coal producers, and for the period studied all produced the major

TABLE 4
Crude Oil Consumption: Estimated Equations[1]

| | Income | Own Price | Other Price | Price of Nat. Gas | Price of Coal | $R^2$ | S.E. | D.W. |
|---|---|---|---|---|---|---|---|---|
| USSR | 1.821[a] (0.073) | −0.226[a] (0.091) | — | −0.122[a] (0.067) | 0.319[a] (0.130) | .996 | .052 | 1.35 |
| Bulgaria | 5.401[a] (0.845) | −3.497 (2.556) | 2.392 (2.355) | — | — | .934 | .503 | 1.94 |
| Czechoslovakia | 1.512[a] (0.730) | −0.385 (0.453) | 0.402 (0.471) | — | — | .984 | .092 | 2.30 |
| East Germany | 5.427 (0.256) | −1.024[a] (0.285) | — | −0.230[a] (0.107) | 0.710[a] (0.311) | .996 | .076 | 1.64 |
| Hungary: Lagged Prices | 2.212[a] (0.343) | −0.240[a] (0.107) | 0.196[a] (0.086) | — | — | .993 | .048 | 1.68 |
| Poland | 3.092[a] (0.553) | −0.934[a] (0.385) | 0.552 (0.572) | — | — | .977 | .178 | 2.12 |
| Rumania | 0.521[a] (0.081) | 0.122[a] (0.039) | 0.061 (0.047) | — | — | .983 | .031 | 1.66 |
| China | 1.653[a] (0.408) | 0.297 (0.181) | — | — | −0.112 (0.161) | .970 | .178 | 1.20 |

[1]Coefficients are designated *a* if they are significant at the 95 percent level and *b* if significant at the 90 percent level. Note: standard errors in parentheses; $R^2$ = coefficient of determination (proportion of total variation explained), here *not* adjusted for degrees of freedom; S.E. = standard error of estimates; D.W. = Durbin-Watson statistic, a measure of serial correlation of the residuals (null hypothesis: D.W. = 2.00; values less than 2.00 indicate positive serial correlation, greater than 2.00 negative serial correlation).

share of coal used in domestic consumption. Two—the Soviet Union and Poland—exported large amounts of coal. With the exception of Rumania, coal output grew more slowly than national income in all of these countries and continued to grow more slowly than national income after the rise in the price of oil.

The empirical results are poorer for coal than those for crude oil. One possible reason is that the unit price data for coal products reflect varying mixes of hard and soft coal as well as varying levels of quality. The quantity data themselves are heterogeneous; some series are available in standard fuel equivalents and others in physical units of possibly variable quality. For a number of countries, coal consumption and production are the same or almost the same, so the estimates are subject to simultaneity bias.

The consumption data (see Table 2) do show some price sensitivity in the demand for coal, but the size of the response is small. Only in the Soviet Union, Czechoslovakia, and East Germany did both production and consumption of coal grow more rapidly after 1973 than before.

As shown in Table 5, the demand for coal in most of the centrally planned economies studied is both income and price inelastic, and the absolute values of the elasticities are lower than those found in Western studies. The income elasticities are less than 1.0 for all countries except Rumania and China; for the Soviet Union and Hungary, the income-elasticity estimates are only 0.2 and 0.1 respectively. Own-price elasticities have the expected signs and are significant at the 90 percent level or better in four cases; moreover, the four coefficients are all similar in magnitude: $-0.29$ for Bulgaria (lagged prices), $-0.25$ for East Germany, $-0.37$ for Hungary, and $-0.30$ for China (lagged prices). These estimates are only slightly lower than the average short-run elasticity for coal of $-0.4$ that Taylor finds in Western studies.[21] Cross-price elasticities have the expected signs and are significant at the 90

percent level or better in four cases, which show similar low values or 0.23 or less. The significant coefficients with the opposite sign to that predicted—Czechoslovakia for both own- and cross-price elasticities, and Hungary for the cross-price elasticity—are cause for further research.

Natural Gas

For the period studied, natural gas contributed a small but rapidly growing share to energy consumption in all the centrally planned economies except for the Soviet Union, which consumed and exported a substantial quantity of natural gas. The estimated income elasticities of demand for natural gas presented in Table 6 are significant and greater than 1.0 in all cases except China and Bulgaria (with the coefficient for the latter being not significant). In contrast, income elasticities for industrial demand for natural gas are usually less than 1.0 in Western studies, although Houthakker and Taylor have estimated the long-run income elasticity of residential demand to be 3.11 when the quantity demanded is a function of a lagged structure of previous prices.[22]

Own-price and cross-price elasticities are significant in only half the cases, and signs often differ from those predicted. East Germany is the only country in which both the price elasticities and the rates of increase in consumption (see Table 2) indicated a clear attempt to substitute natural gas for oil after 1973. The Soviet Union also shows a slight tendency to shift consumption toward natural gas and away from oil. Stern foresees a strengthening of this trend as long as the price advantage for exporting oil over natural gas persists.[23]

Electricity

Over the period studied, production and consumption of electric power grew rapidly, more rapidly than national income in most of the countries. As shown in Table 7,

TABLE 5
Coal Consumption: Estimated Equations[1]

| | Income | Own Price | Other Price | $R^2$ | S.E. | D.W. |
|---|---|---|---|---|---|---|
| USSR | 0.225[a] (0.026) | $-0.015$ (0.039) | 0.061[a] (0.029) | .984 | .014 | 1.94 |
| Bulgaria: Lagged Prices | 0.592[a] (0.139) | $-0.286$[a] (0.097) | 0.121[a] (0.053) | .990 | .043 | 2.44 |
| Czechoslovakia | 0.225 (0.177) | 0.086[a] (0.046) | $-0.060$ (0.040) | .952 | .027 | 1.88 |
| East Germany | 0.411[a] (0.114) | $-0.245$[b] (0.146) | 0.227[b] (0.137) | .861 | .032 | 1.25 |
| Hungary | 0.116 (0.200) | $-0.367$[a] (0.178) | $-0.208$[a] (0.056) | .915 | .035 | 1.90 |
| Poland | 0.839[a] (0.073) | $-0.054$ (0.046) | 0.021 (0.049) | .980 | .039 | 1.31 |
| Rumania | 1.449[a] (0.150) | 0.047 (0.089) | 0.044 (0.097) | .981 | .070 | 1.72 |
| China: Lagged Prices | 1.372[a] (0.210) | $-0.300$[a] (0.137) | 0.217[a] (0.123) | .921 | .116 | 1.16 |

[1]See note to Table 4.

significant estimates of income elasticities are well in excess of 1.0 for five countries, less than 1.0 for Rumania (and not significant for Poland and China). In Western studies, industrial and commercial income elasticities of demand for electricity tend to be a little below 1.0 in the short run and well above 1.0 in the long run. Significant own-price elasticities of demand for electricity are negative and inelastic in three cases, positive in two. (There were no price series for electricity in China.) Own-price elasticities of demand for electricity in Western studies also tend to be less than 1.0.

The predicted cross-elasticity of demand for electricity,

which both competes with and uses other energy sources, would be positive if demand effects dominate and negative if the supply effect of fuel cost dominate. The measured signs are negative and significant for the Soviet Union, Bulgaria, Czechoslovakia, and East Germany. They are positive and significant for Hungary, Poland, and China. A decline in the rate of growth of electricity production after 1973 for most of the countries was consistent with the rising cost of fuel supply. Demand coefficients for Hungary were insignificant when simultaneous prices were used but were significant, with the predicted signs, when prices were lagged one year.

TABLE 6
Natural Gas Consumption: Estimated Equations[1]

| | Income | Own Price | Other Price | Price of Oil | Price of Coal | $R^2$ | S.E. | D.W. |
|---|---|---|---|---|---|---|---|---|
| USSR: Lagged Prices | 1.067[a] (0.163) | −0.030[a] (0.014) | 0.025 (0.032) | — — | — — | .998 | .025 | 1.87 |
| Bulgaria | 0.481 (0.998) | 1.417[a] (0.617) | −3.535[a] (0.620) | — — | — — | .840 | .481 | 2.00 |
| Czechoslovakia | 1.239[a] (0.673) | 0.151 (0.267) | 0.366 (0.277) | — — | — — | .916 | .175 | 0.675 |
| East Germany | 1.507[a] (0.149) | −0.169[a] (0.049) | 1.265[a] (0.246) | — — | — — | .965 | .039 | 2.09 |
| Hungary | 3.998[a] (0.567) | 0.549[a] (0.279) | −0.405 (0.319) | — — | — — | .973 | .208 | 1.90 |
| Poland | 3.212[a] (0.373) | 0.243 (0.173) | −0.498[a] (0.195) | — — | — — | .987 | .124 | 1.29 |
| Rumania | 1.301[a] (0.111) | 0.097 (0.073) | −0.160[a] (0.069) | — — | — — | .985 | .056 | 1.47 |
| China | 0.888[a] (0.445) | — — | — — | 0.132 (0.193) | −0.153 (0.204) | .987 | .192 | 2.29 |

[1]See note to Table 4.

TABLE 7
Electricity Consumption: Estimated Equations[1]

| | Income | Own Price | Other Price | Price of Oil | Price of Coal | $R^2$ | S.E. | D.W. |
|---|---|---|---|---|---|---|---|---|
| USSR | 1.875[a] (0.046) | −0.355[a] (0.127) | −0.063[a] (0.027) | — — | — — | .997 | .033 | 2.06 |
| Bulgaria | 2.390[a] (0.048) | 0.394[a] (0.173) | −0.204[a] (0.057) | — — | — — | .997 | .056 | 1.23 |
| Czechoslovakia | 2.397[a] (0.111) | −0.210 (0.156) | −0.110[a] (0.043) | — — | — — | .993 | .036 | 1.48 |
| East Germany | 1.859[a] (0.067) | −0.281[a] (0.110) | −0.103[a] (0.034) | — — | — — | .993 | .030 | 1.47 |
| Hungary: Lagged Prices | 2.385[a] (0.262) | −0.506[a] (0.183) | 0.288[a] (0.084) | — — | — — | .983 | .068 | 1.91 |
| Poland | 0.329 (0.213) | 0.305[a] (0.127) | 0.173[a] (0.054) | — — | — — | .998 | .029 | 1.82 |
| Rumania | 0.872[a] (0.265) | 0.094 (0.160) | 0.031 (0.049) | — — | — — | .998 | .038 | 1.38 |
| China | 0.485 (0.333) | — — | — — | 0.047 (0.144) | 0.497[b] (0.260) | .963 | .139 | 1.23 |

[1]See notes to Table 4.

## Conclusions

Almost without exception, the demand for crude oil in the centrally planned economies shows strong evidence of responsiveness to changes in the world price of oil. Rates of growth of oil consumption, which had been higher than growth of national income in most countries, fell off substantially after the price rise in 1973. Estimated own-price elasticities are negative and significant for the Soviet Union, Bulgaria, East Germany, Hungary, and Poland; only for Rumania, which reexports petroleum products, was the own-price elasticity significantly positive.

While the direct response of oil consumption to oil price is clear, the evidence for substitution to other fuels is mixed and shows relatively small responses during the time period studied. Consumption of coal and natural gas did not show substantially faster rates of increase after the rise in oil prices. The cross-price elasticity of demand for coal was significant and positive in half the cases, but in only one case for natural gas. Growth rates of consumption and production of electric power declined slightly in most of the planned economies, as did rates of growth of national income.

Regarding the speed with which adjustment occurred, estimation on simultaneous variables yielded estimates with higher significance levels than estimates on lagged variables in most cases. For Hungary, estimates with lagged price variables gave a better fit for consumption of crude oil and electric power. For Soviet demand for natural gas, lagged price variables also worked better.

Based on the results presented here, I think that the next step (pending construction of better individual price series) would be the estimation of the parameters of energy use, including substitution and price elasticities for individual energy inputs, using an explicit production function (probably the translog). The data base would allow estimation of intercountry coefficients as well as single-country time-series coefficients such as those presented here.

For all their weaknesses, the results presented above provide enough evidence that the centrally planned economies do respond to changing world terms of trade in energy products to cast doubt on forecasts that are based on fixed energy-to-GNP ratios. Demand equations for energy inputs estimated for the centrally planned economies do not appear to differ qualitatively from similar estimates for other countries. With some expansion of the data base for these countries, we should be able to improve our estimates of the values of individual coefficients.

## NOTES

1. Robert W. Campbell, *Trends in the Soviet Oil and Gas Industry* (Baltimore: Johns Hopkins University Press, 1976); Leslie Dienes, "Soviet Energy Policy and the Fossil Fuels," chapter 12 in this volume.

2. Formally, an elasticity is a ratio of two percentage changes. Thus, a price elasticity of demand is the percentage rate by which quantity demanded changes divided by a given percentage change in price; for example, for energy, the price elasticity of demand is (approximately) $(\Delta E/E)/(\Delta P/P)$, where $E$ is the quantity of energy demanded, $P$ is price, and $\Delta$ denotes a change in the value of a variable. Similarly, the income elasticity of energy demand is $(\Delta E/E)/(\Delta Y/Y)$, where $Y$ is income. Elasticities measure the change in one variable (e.g., the quantity of energy demanded) when another variable (e.g., price or income) varies, *relative* to initial values of the variables: recombining terms, the price elasticity of energy demand is $(\Delta E/\Delta P) \cdot (P/E)$, where $P$ and $E$ are the initial values from which the changes are measured; similarly, the income elasticity of energy demand is $(\Delta E/\Delta Y) \cdot (Y/E)$, where $Y$ and $E$ are pre-change values of the variables. Elasticities of demand with respect to a good's own price, so-called own-price elasticities, are hypothesized to be algebraically negative, because an *increase* in price typically causes a *decrease* in quantity demanded, and vice versa. Income elasticities of demand are usually positive in sign. Demand elasticities with respect to prices of other goods, so-called cross-price elasticities, that are substitutes are hypothesized to be positive, and of other goods that are complements, negative.

3. Herbert L. Sawyer, *The Soviet Energy Sector: Problems and Prospects*, Harvard Russian Research Center Paper, January 1978.

4. Emily Jack, Richard Lee, and Harold Lent, "Outlook for Soviet Energy," in U.S. Congress, Joint Economic Committee, *Soviet Economy in a New Perspective*, 94th Cong., 2nd sess., 1976, pp. 460–78.

5. Daniel Kazmer, "A Comparison of Fossil Fuel Use in the U.S. and the U.S.S.R.," in Joint Economic Committee, *New Perspective*, pp. 500–34.

6. Dienes, "Soviet Energy Policy."

7. J. G. Polach, "The Development of Energy in Eastern Europe," in U.S. Congress, Joint Economic Committee, *Economic Developments in Countries of Eastern Europe*, 91st Cong., 2nd sess., 1970, pp. 348–433.

8. William Kelly, "Effects of the Soviet Price Reform of 1967 on Energy Consumption," *Slavic Studies* 30 (1978): 394–402.

9. Lester Taylor, "The Demand for Energy: A Survey of Price and Income Elasticities," in William Nordhaus, ed., *International Studies of the Demand for Energy* (Amsterdam: North-Holland, 1977), p. 37.

10. For example, Ernst R. Berndt and David O. Wood, "Technology, Prices and the Derived Demand for Energy," *Review of Economics and Statistics* 57 (1975): 259–68; James M. Griffin and Paul R. Gregory, "An Intercountry Translog Model of Energy Substitution Responses," *American Economic Review* 66 (1976): 845–57; and Robert Halvorsen, *Econometric Models of U.S. Energy Demand* (New York: Lexington Books, 1978).

11. Halvorsen, *U.S. Energy Demand*.

12. Robert Halvorsen and Judith Thornton, "Comparative Responses to the Energy Crisis in Different Economic Systems: An Extensive Analysis," *Journal of Comparative Economics* 2 (1978): 187–209.

13. Strictly speaking, coal and electric power are substitutes for refined oil products, not crude oil. As the

manufacture of those products is virtually the sole use made of crude oil, however, we use the simpler term, crude oil.

14. Kazmer, "Comparison of Fossil Fuel Use."

15. John Haberstroh, "Eastern Europe: Growing Energy Problems," in the U.S. Congress, Joint Economic Committee, *East European Economies Post-Helsinki*, 95th Cong., 1st sess., 1977, p. 380.

16. Leslie Dienes, "Energy Prospects for Eastern Europe," *Energy Policy* 4 (1976): 119–29.

17. This fact, together with its historic position as an oil producer and (until 1979) a non-importer of Soviet oil, makes Rumania a special case. Thus, I exclude Rumania in subsequent discussions of "East European" responses to increases in oil prices. The results for Rumania are, however, reported and interpreted as appropriate.

18. Campbell, *Trends in Soviet Oil and Gas*; Haberstroh, "Eastern Europe"; see also Polach, "Energy in Eastern Europe."

19. Halvorsen and Thornton, "Comparative Responses to the Energy Crisis."

20. M. Fuss, R. Hyndman, and L. Waverman, "Residential, Commercial, and Industrial Demand for Energy in Canada: Projections to 1985 with Three Alternative Models," in Nordhaus, *International Studies*; and Halvorsen, *U.S. Energy Demand*.

21. Taylor, "Demand for Energy."

22. H. S. Houthakker and L. D. Taylor, *Consumer Demand in the United States* (Cambridge, Ma.: Harvard University Press, 1970).

23. Jonathan Stern, "Soviet Natural Gas in the World Economy," chapter 15 in this volume.

# 14

# SOVIET PETROLEUM: HISTORY, TECHNOLOGY, GEOLOGY, RESERVES, POTENTIAL AND POLICY

ARTHUR A. MEYERHOFF
Meyerhoff and Cox, Inc.
Tulsa, Oklahoma

## Introduction

The petroleum industry of the USSR was developed in virtual isolation from that of Western and other non-Communist countries. This independent development of the USSR's petroleum industry resulted in part from the deliberate isolation imposed by the Communist regime, beginning in 1917, and in part from Russia's traditional history of isolation, which dates back to the Czars.

Numerous sources were used for this compilation, some published and others unpublished. Although nearly all published sources are cited in the text, some of them were more important than others because (1) they are available in the English language and (2) they themselves represent compilations of materials from a large number of sources. The most important compilations include those by Clarkson, Campbell, Shabad, Meyerhoff, Owen, Dienes and Shabad.[1] Unpublished data came almost entirely from the following organizations: Ministry of Geology USSR; Ministry of Oil Industry USSR; Ministry of Gas Industry USSR; and the All-Union Geological Research Institute USSR. Much information and numerous conclusions were derived from conversations with individuals within the three Soviet ministries listed above.

I thank Edgar W. Owen for his invaluable help in reviewing this manuscript, and the appropriate ministries of the Soviet Government for letting me use data and interpretations that otherwise would not have been available. In addition, I thank R. W. Campbell, Leslie Dienes, Robert G. Jensen, Theodore Shabad, and Arthur W. Wright for constructive criticisms which improved the manuscript. Full responsibility for the statements made here is my own.

## History

### Pre-1917

The knowledge and exploitation by the ancients of the oil springs in the Caspian-Caucasus region of southern Russia (Figure 1), and the worship of the "eternal fires" of Baku, are well known.[2] From antiquity to the mid-19th Century, the Caspian-Caucasus was one of the best-known oil regions in the world, and exploitation by collection from springs and shallow pits (later from hand-dug wells) was noted in the earliest historical records. A considerable commerce was carried on in the area, providing oil for cooking, lighting, and medicinal purposes.

By 1737, 52 hand-dug wells were productive on the site of the present giant Balakhany field at Baku, and in 1829 Alexander von Humboldt counted 82 such wells. Production in 1830 was reported as the equivalent of 30,000 barrels and 28,000 barrels in 1843.

The Czarist government anticipated the modern petroleum industry when it drilled a well for oil at what is now the giant Bibi-Eibat field in 1871. Bibi-Eibat, close to the city of Baku, overlies an anticline intruded by a clay diapir, an ancient mud volcano. Production here, as in the other Baku fields, is from the middle Pliocene productive series.

Robert and Ludwig Nobel deserve the credit for bringing the Czarist petroleum industry to world prominence. Despite many difficulties, the Nobel interests drilled more than 500 wells over a period of 50 years, employed as many as 12,000 men in the oil business, and produced about 150 million barrels of petroleum, greatly augmenting the fortune that has been the continuing source of the famous Nobel Prizes.

The Rothschilds founded the Société Caspienne et de la Mer Noire in 1892 and worked for a time with the Nobel companies. Initially they were marketeers, but later purchased important producing leases. They and the Nobels built small tank steamships to transport refined products across the Caspian Sea for transfer to the barges of the Volga River. These barges were towed up the river to various railheads, whence the products were distributed to many parts of western Russia, Germany, and the Austro-Hungarian Empire. The Rothschilds were largely instrumental in the construction of a railroad from Baku on the Caspian to Batumi on the Black Sea and a later pipeline which was built part way in 1901 and finished in 1905. These rail and pipeline facilities were the main routes by which Russian petroleum products reached Western Europe. Distillate was shipped to England, France, and Belgium for purification. A few shipments were made to the United States; the purpose was political, to show what Russia was capable of doing.

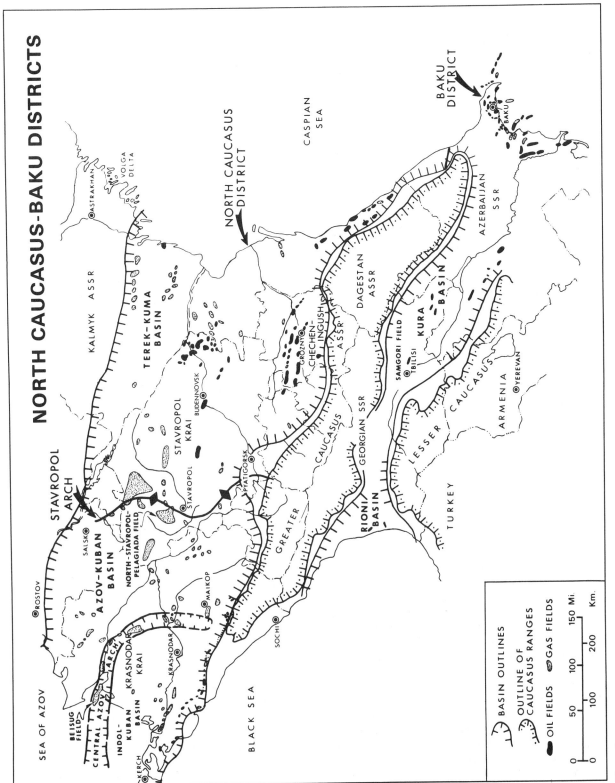

Figure 1

British capital entered the Baku and Grozny oil fields in 1893; English oil men and geologists had an active role from then until the Bolshevik Revolution. Numerous Russian firms besides the Nobel interests operated in the Baku area, where the practice of leasing small tracts admitted many producers.

Russian production in 1891 was 34.6 million barrels. Russia became the largest oil-producing country in 1898, a position which it held until 1902 (USSR production surpassed that of the United States once again in 1974). The peak production year was 1901, when 85.2 million barrels were produced—slightly more than 50 percent of the world's output. All but approximately 4 million barrels of the 1901 total came from the giant Bibi-Eibat and Balakhany-Sabunchi-Ramana fields of the Baku district in Azerbaijan. Most of the remainder was from Grozny in the present Chechen-Ingush ASSR. Cumulative production from 1821 through 1910 was 1.3 billion barrels from European Russia, and 3.1 million barrels from its Asian territories.

Russian production declined after 1901. In 1913, it was down to 62.8 million barrels. Although there was an increase during World War I, it was not enough. The overall downward trend continued through 1920 when only 25.4 million barrels were produced. Reasons for the decline were numerous: the government's leasing system was not conducive to either exploration or orderly development; open flow and waste of gas aggravated depletion of the producing reservoirs; the drilling methods were incapable of exploiting deeper zones on productive and prospective structures; and, hostility between the Tatar and Armenian populations, who supplied most of the workers in the Baku and North Caucasus fields, caused disruptive work stoppages, strikes, and near-civil war. Several discovered fields were remote from consuming centers and lacked transport facilities. Finally, there came the chaos of World War I and the Bolshevik Revolution.

Russia's cumulative production through 1917 was 1,952,000,000 barrels, but its enormous resources had barely been tapped. The two fields that had supplied the bulk of the oil were thus far the world's greatest: Balakhany-Sabunchi-Ramana and Bibi-Eibat, which have estimated ultimate recoveries of 2,400 and 2,000 billion barrels, respectively.[3] The nearby Binagadi and Surakhany fields also were of major importance. Next in rank to the Baku area was the western part of the North Caucasus basin (Figure 1), where Starogrozny (Old Grozny) with 650 million barrels of recoverable oil, and Oktyabrskoye, with 520 million, had proved highly productive. Voznesenka had been discovered in 1915, the first sector in the Malgobek-Voznesenka-Aliyurt complex which contained about 3 billion barrels. Maikop had been disappointing, although it held more than 3 trillion cubic feet of gas reserves and 74 million barrels of liquids. The southern provinces of Asiatic Russia were very promising but had not been intensively exploited. The ancient field at Cheleken Island, at the eastern side of the Caspian Sea, produced about 6 million barrels between 1900 and 1920, a mere token of its ultimate 640 million barrels. Old fields in the Fergana Basin, near the Chinese border, had sup-

plied about 4 million barrels to the populated region around Tashkent and Samarkand. Salt domes in the Emba Basin at the northern end of the Caspian Sea proved productive in 1912 and yielded almost 10 million barrels by 1920, but were more promising than rewarding.

The Russian petroleum industry was in strong hands and seemed on the verge of an era of more orderly progress when World War I erupted. With the end of World War I, the progress and direction of the oil industry were changed drastically.

## 1917–World War II

The Czarist Empire ended in 1917, and a revolutionary government was set up in Moscow. The Caspian-Caucasus oil region endured a period of turmoil during the Civil War until the Communists seized control in 1920. They confiscated all private properties and shipped enough oil from them to threaten European markets with cheap refined products, but never compensated the former owners. As Lenin gained supreme authority, he realized that nationalization had gone too far too fast, and in 1921 he announced a New Economic Policy of admitting foreign investment.[4]

Thus the state officially adopted a foreign-investments policy which was radically different from that originally envisioned. The new policy was to encourage the investment in the Soviet Union of foreign capital which had bolstered Russian industry before World War I. Various foreign companies conducted long and complex negotiations with the government, most of which proved inconclusive. Negotiations between Western corporations and the Communists finally collapsed in 1927, and Stalin announced the 1st Five-Year Plan.

The plan ended the vacillation regarding petroleum policy. To accomplish its goals, the state assumed full responsibility for central planning—determining the place, time, method, and the amount of production, drilling methods, types and capacities of refineries, and modes of transport.

The specially privileged role that geologists enjoy in the Soviet planned economy began to be evident after 1927 as petroleum geology truly came into its own. Oil production surpassed the former 1901 peak in 1928 largely by benefit of the resumption of drilling in 1924 that had developed extensions and deeper sandstone pays in the Baku fields. In 1929 seismic-refraction methods were applied in the Grozny area of the North Caucasus. Emphasis on oil prospecting was in the North Caucasus region and the salt-dome area of the Emba Basin (Figures 1 and 2).

Soviet geologists made sound technical progress under favorable administrative auspices, most notably under the petroleum geologist Ivan Gubkin. Under Gubkin's guidance, the most consequential discovery during the 1st Five-Year Plan was in the virgin basin of the Volga-Urals, a region destined for greatness (Figure 2). On 14 May 1929, at Chusovskiye Gorodki, Perm Oblast, oil was found in Artinskian (Permian) limestone at a depth of 332 meters. The discovery was entirely serendipitous, in-

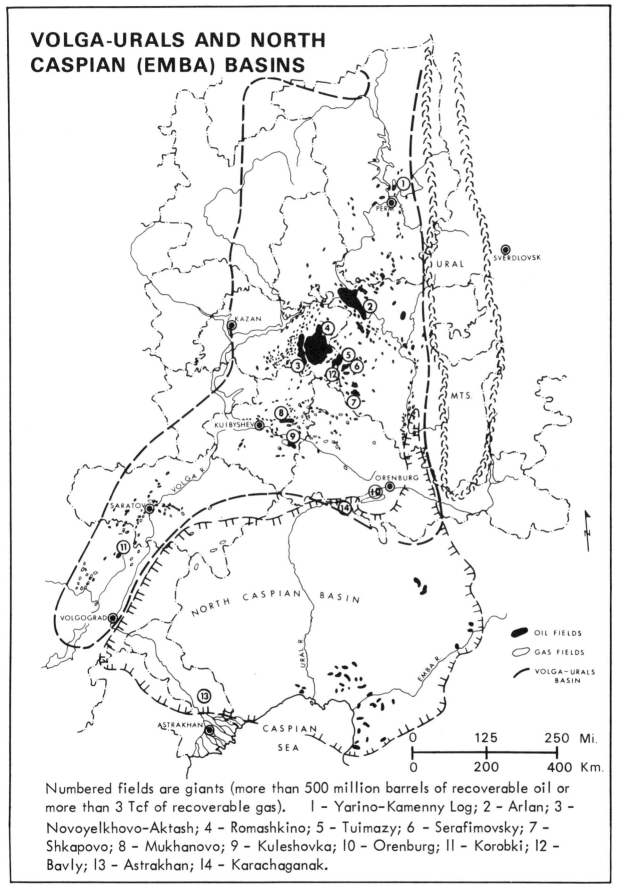

**VOLGA-URALS AND NORTH CASPIAN (EMBA) BASINS**

Numbered fields are giants (more than 500 million barrels of recoverable oil or more than 3 Tcf of recoverable gas).    1 - Yarino-Kamenny Log; 2 - Arlan; 3 - Novoyelkhovo-Aktash; 4 - Romashkino; 5 - Tuimazy; 6 - Serafimovsky; 7 - Shkapovo; 8 - Mukhanovo; 9 - Kuleshovka; 10 - Orenburg; 11 - Korobki; 12 - Bavly; 13 - Astrakhan; 14 - Karachaganak.

Figure 2

asmuch as the purpose of the drilling had been to explore a potential deposit of potassium salts. However, the well produced only for a short time and the location was abandoned. Oil output amounted to 156.2 million barrels in the last year of the plan, but most of it came, as in the past, from the Caspian-Caucasus region.

Although the oil industry grew substantially during the 2nd Five-Year Plan, growth was not consistent. Operations had improved materially; the old hand-bailing oil-producing practice had come to a halt; the traditional Soviet percussion drilling method had been abandoned in favor of rotary tools; large quantities of equipment had been imported; and expanded refineries provided more in-depth processing. Oil production increased to 263.2 million barrels in 1938. However, most of it still came from the Baku-Caucasus region, where exploratory drilling was concentrated. Gubkin had advocated that the Soviet government should explore for oil in new areas, and that the Soviet Union would not be secure until it had a strong petroleum industry in many areas of the country, particularly in the interior where foreign armies could not reach, and near population centers where oil transportation would not be so expensive. Thus, Gubkin "bent every effort toward the development of the region between the Volga and the Urals."[5] He was particularly interested to test the thick Devonian sandstones which overlie metamorphic and igneous basement.

In 1941, two years after Gubkin's death, the decision was made to drill a deep Devonian test at Tuimazy (Figure 2). However, the well was suspended before the Devonian was reached because, as explained by Trofimuk ". . . of a shortage of bits, the difficulty of drilling a deep well, and because of the urgency of using the well to add output from shallower formations to help meet urgent war needs."[6] Moreover, available rigs had to be used to expand other Volga-Urals fields.

Both the Czarist and the Soviet authorities had concentrated almost all of their exploration and production efforts on oil. Natural gas generally was ignored. Production came mainly from the Baku district, although gas was also produced from Starogrozny, Maikop, and the Emba fields (northern Caspian). Large quantities of natural gas are at Maikop. Much of the gas of the other North Caucasus-Baku fields is associated gas.

Gas was discovered also in the Timan-Pechora basin of the northern Soviet Union during the 1920s. However, there was no local market, and the gas was capped (Figure 3). It was not until the 1950s that a major gas industry bloomed in the Soviet Union—beginning in the Dnieper-Donets graben of the Ukraine (Figure 4).

War Years, 1941–45

World War II terminated the 3rd Five-Year Plan before it was completed, and the nation refocused its objectives and concentrated on the necessities of war. One of the many reasons for the German attack on the Soviet Union was the Germans' urgent need for the Caucasus-Baku oil. The attack of the German armies resulted in the Soviet destruction and German capture of several oil fields in the Maikop region. The advance did not quite extend to the

Grozny fields, but the Soviet forces closed them and prepared to destroy them. The USSR's overall production fell sharply—more than 35 percent between 1940 and 1945; Baku production fell considerably, and in 1945, the Soviet Union produced only 140.8 million barrels of oil. Much of the petroleum supplied for the war effort came from the Allies, for even the normal routes of transportation in the Caucasus were seriously disrupted by the German onslaught. In 1943 the Tuimazy project to drill to the Devonian was resumed. In 1944, oil was discovered in Late Devonian sandstone ($D_1$) of Frasnian age. However, the Devonian prospects were not pursued further until several years later and other Soviet developments during this period were minor. Thus, at the end of World War II, oil accounted for only 15 percent of the USSR's energy mix, a decrease of 3.7 percent from 1940. Gas rose only slightly to 2.3 percent.[7]

Postwar Progress

After World War II, major discoveries were made in several parts of the Volga-Urals region (Figure 2), in the North Caucasus basin (Figure 5), and in other parts of the Soviet Union. In 1953, the first discovery was made in the West Siberian basin (Figure 6). This was Berezovo, a gas field. Disappointment at finding gas instead of oil delayed further exploration in West Siberia, but nevertheless led to the ultimate exploitation of this huge region, which finally became known as the Third Baku.

During 1947, oil-reserve figures were placed under the official State Secrets Act, and have not been released since that period. Gas-reserve figures, however, have been released because at first no commercial importance was attached to gas. Even today, as the value of gas is being realized in the Soviet Union, oil-reserve figures remain secret whereas those of gas are publicized.

Achievements during the 4th, 5th, and 6th five-year plans were impressive. Oil production of 825.6 million barrels in 1958 was more than five times greater than that of 1946. More significant was the ascendancy of the new producing regions so that the nation was no longer utterly dependent on the Caspian-Caucasus region for its petroleum. By 1958, the Baku and North Caucasus districts accounted for only 23 percent of Soviet production. Exploration, however, was far ahead of development.

The period of the Seven-Year Plan (1959–65) was also notable for accomplishments. Oil production was 949 million barrels in 1959 and 1.77 billion barrels in 1965. It passed that of Venezuela in 1962 for second place in the world, behind the United States. In 1974, Soviet oil production became the largest of any nation in the world.

Gas production increased from 1,580 billion cubic feet in 1960 to 15,000 billion cubic feet in 1980. Trunk lines were laid from remote oil and gas fields to oil industrial centers and new industries in underdeveloped areas. During the first two years of the Seven-Year Plan, 8,000 km of gas transmission lines were completed—more than the total length which existed previously. Other major gas trunks were finished in succeeding years.

During the 1966–70 period, annual production increased consistently to 2.58 billion barrels of oil and 7,060

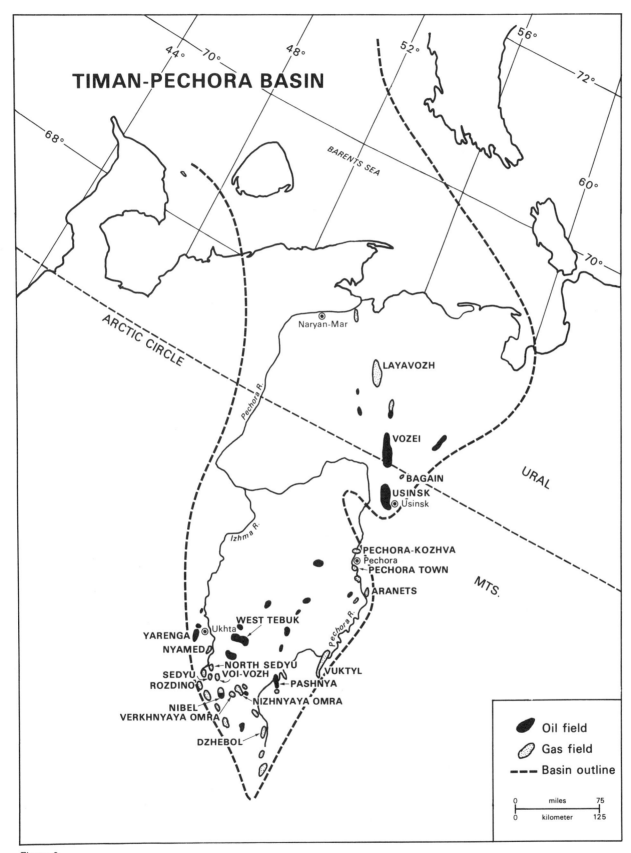

**TIMAN-PECHORA BASIN**

Figure 3

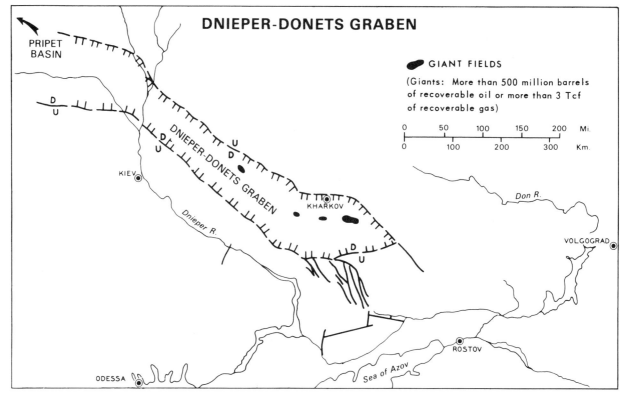

Figure 4

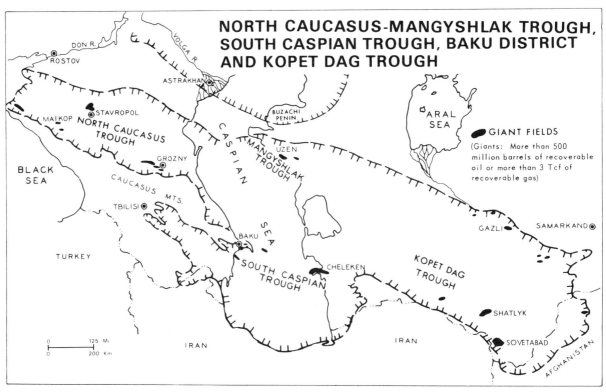

Figure 5

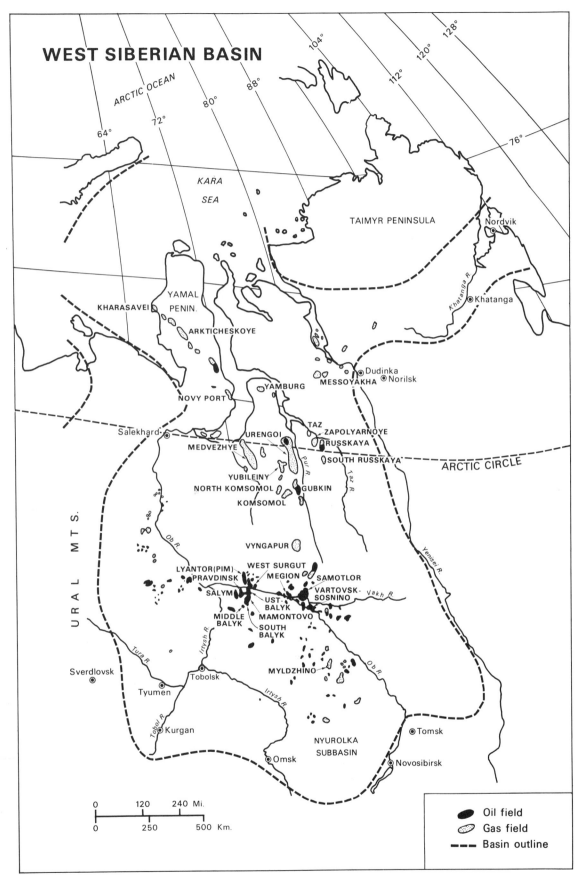

WEST SIBERIAN BASIN

ARCTIC OCEAN

64° 72° 80° 88° 104° 112° 120° 128°

76°

KARA
SEA

TAIMYR PENINSULA

Nordvik

YAMAL
PENIN.

KHARASAVEI

ARKTICHESKOYE

Khatanga

KHatanga R.

NOVY PORT

YAMBURG

MESSOYAKHA

Dudinka
Norilsk

Salekhard

URENGOI

TAZ

ZAPOLYARNOYE

MEDVEZHYE

RUSSKAYA

SOUTH RUSSKAYA

ARCTIC CIRCLE

YUBILEINY

Pur R.

NORTH KOMSOMOL

GUBKIN

KOMSOMOL

Taz R.

URAL MTS.

Ob R.

VYNGAPUR

Yenisei R.

LYANTOR(PIM)

WEST SURGUT

PRAVDINSK

MEGION

SAMOTLOR

SALYM

VARTOVSK-
SOSNINO

UST-
BALYK

Vakh R.

MIDDLE
BALYK

MAMONTOVO

SOUTH
BALYK

Tura R.

Irtysh R.

Ob R.

MYLDZHINO

Sverdlovsk

Tyumen

Tobolsk

Irtysh R.

Tobol R.

Kurgan

NYUROLKA
SUBBASIN

Tomsk

Omsk

Novosibirsk

0    120    240 Mi.

0    250    500 Km.

Oil field
Gas field
Basin outline

Figure 6

TABLE 1
Percentage of Reserves by Geologic Age
(Reserve Categories) $A + B + C_1$

| Age | 1 January 1966 | | 1 January 1970 | |
|---|---|---|---|---|
| | Oil | Gas | Oil | Gas |
| Paleozoic | 61.0 | 21.8 | 37.0 | 10.0 |
| Mesozoic | 24.2 | 58.5 | 50.0 | 80.0 |
| Cenozoic | 14.8 | 19.7 | 13.0 | 10.0 |

billion cubic feet of gas. Geographic spread of productive areas continued as dominance of the Volga-Urals declined. This geographic shift is reflected in the changed proportions of reserves attributed to rocks of the various geological ages (Table 1); the Mesozoic reservoirs of Asia gained at the expense of the European Paleozoic.

Exploration utilized all available methods of areal-geologic, surface-structural and geomorphic, airborne-magnetic and gravimetric, and land and marine seismic surveying. Electrical and geochemical prospecting and hydrogeologic studies received more emphasis than in most Western countries. Many stratigraphic, parametric, and structural wells were drilled, partly cored, logged by several methods, and subjected to various laboratory analyses. The general procedure, which differed from region to region, was summarized by Eremenko et al.[8] (see Figure 7).

Fifteen giant gas fields and one giant oil field were discovered in the West Siberian basin during the period 1966–70, including the giant Samotlor; in other parts of the Soviet Union, nine giant gas fields were discovered, but no giant oil fields.

Continued successful development demonstrated the vast West Siberian basin to be potentially the most important hydrocarbon region in the USSR and in the Btu value, probably the second largest single hydrocarbon basin in the world after the Middle East. Oil reserves are mostly in the southern and central parts, and especially in the middle reaches of the Ob Valley. The northern half is almost exclusively gas-bearing. Urengoi, the world's largest gas field with proved, probable, and potential reserves greater than 210 trillion cubic feet—more than the total gas reserves remaining in 16,200 fields in the U.S.—was discovered in 1966 (Figure 6). This field is 210 km long and 18 to 45 km wide. Other new gas fields looked small, but only in the shadow of Urengoi. Gas discoveries were made at far-out locations in the Yamal Peninsula, also beyond the Arctic Circle, and on the Yenisei River where the northern-most pipeline in the world was built to the nickel-platinum center of Norilsk.

The Vilyui basin near the Lena River in eastern Siberia developed into a major gas district where eight fields (including two giants) were discovered in Jurassic, Triassic, and Permian sandstones (Figure 8). Several large gas discoveries were made in the Kopet Dag foredeep of Central Asia (Figure 5) and at least one giant discovery was made in the Dnieper-Donets graben (Figure 4).

The first Soviet well drilled from a mobile self-elevating platform, the *Apsheron*, was completed in the Caspian Sea in 1966. An earlier (1962) mobile platform had collapsed and sunk. Marine operations formerly had been on dirt-filled poles, piling stockades, and steel trestles. In 1970, the tenth offshore field was discovered in the Caspian Sea. For the first time, the bulk of the oil from the Baku district was coming from the sea, and engineers were routinely designing and constructing permanent platforms for directional drilling programs and the inevitable water-injection wells. Recent trends indicate that production from this region may be increased as development moves outward into increasingly deeper water.

By 1969, oil production in the Volga-Urals was beginning to level off, and many fields were yielding alarming percentages of water; the situation was saved temporarily

| Steps | Stages | Purposes and Tasks of Operations | Types and Methods of Operations | Categories of Reserves |
|---|---|---|---|---|
| Exploration | Regional operations | Evaluation of oil and gas potential | Regional geophysics; stratigraphic, parametric, structural drilling | $D_2$, $D_1$ |
| | Preparation of areas for exploration drilling | Revealing of prospective areas, and preparing them for exploration drilling | Detailed geophysics, structural, and parametric drilling | $D_1$, $C_2$ |
| | Exploration for oil and gas fields | Discovery of oil and gas fields, and their preliminary evaluation | Exploration drilling, geophysical investigations in welling (logging) | $C_2$, $C_1$ |
| Extension and Development | Development of oil and gas fields | Preparation of fields for production | Offset drilling, production tests | $C_1$, $B$ |

SOURCE: Eremenko, et al. (1972).

Figure 7
Stages of Exploration and Exploitation in the Development of USSR Basin Reserves.

by the mass purchase of 1,200 U.S.-built submersible pumps and the construction of 11,000 Soviet submersible pumps.

Soviet exploration and production continued to increase steadily through the 1970–80 period. Oil production, by 1980, had passed the 4.38 billion barrel-a-year mark (12.06 million barrels per day) and gas production surpassed 15 trillion cubic feet per year (41 billion cubic feet per day). Although more than 11 giant gas fields were discovered in the West Siberian basin, only one new giant oil field was discovered, Fedorovsk in West Siberia. For the first time since the early 1920s, the Soviet Union openly turned to foreign private and national oil companies for help in developing the country's resources. Oil production was showing increasing signs of leveling off, something which could not be permitted if national industrial growth and oil exports for hard currencies were to continue. At present, Japanese interests are drilling offshore from Sakhalin Island in the Pacific, but discoveries there, contrary to press reports, are small. The success of Sakhalin, however, may lead to more cooperative ventures with foreign concerns. One project, still awaiting Soviet drilling results, is the Vilyui basin (East Siberian)

gas project, which is to be implemented by several Japanese and U.S. concerns.

As a consequence of the Soviet realization that oil production was about to peak—probably between 1979 and 1982—an unpublished report stating this was circulated in the Council of Ministers during 1974. A CIA report published in April 1977 predicted that the peak would come at the latest by 1982. Soviet sources officially denied that Soviet production would peak, but privately admitted that the Soviet Union, during the 1980s, will have to reduce exports to the West, Cuba, and Eastern Europe. Soviet sources also predict that, unless a drastic change in technology takes place or unless giant fields are found in the West Siberian basin, the Soviet Union may have to purchase oil abroad. If the Soviet Union is forced to turn to OPEC countries for oil imports in the 1980s, the Soviet Union would be competing with many foreign countries, most notably the United States and Japan, for this oil. Because OPEC oil production in some countries is beginning to decline, it is quite possible that these nations will not be able to supply the Soviet Union, in addition to the United States and Japan. This could have serious consequences in world economics and politics.

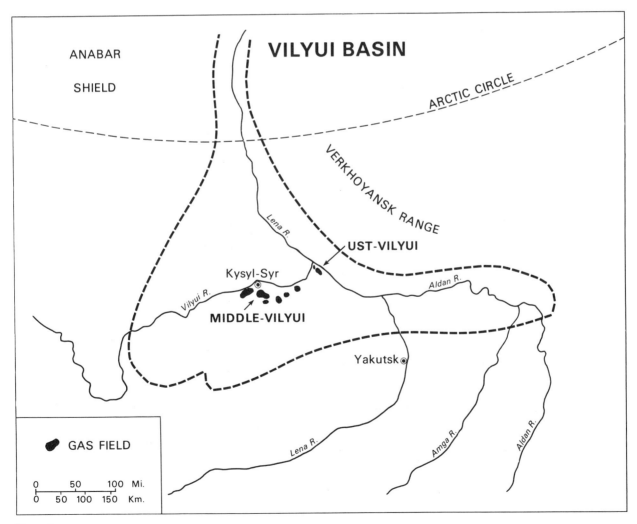

Figure 8

The Soviet Union still has an enormous oil and gas potential, not only onshore, but also offshore, particularly in the Arctic regions. The problem is that Soviet technology has not changed significantly since the 1950s, and, therefore, it is impossible for the Soviet Union to drill development wells at a rate commensurate with its petroleum demands. The old turbodrill system still is used; seismic methods are antiquated; common depth point (CDP) techniques are primitive; and the quality of steel used for drilling is so poor that rigs continue to break down systematically below depths of about 2,300 to 3,000 meters. Because the average exploratory hole is deeper than 3,000 meters, this means simply that Soviet technology is unable to keep abreast of the needs of the country.

The continuing failure of Soviet technology and the rapidly depleting reserves in known fields at shallow depths (less than 3,000 m) make it very unlikely that the Soviet Union will be able to solve its problems in time to avert an imports program during the 1980s. Because oil production will be falling off, and because hard-currency requirements will increase, the 1980s promise to be an extremely interesting decade in the development of the world's economy. Perhaps some recent Soviet purchases of rigs and other drilling technology from the U.S., Canada, India, and Finland for use in the Caspian and Barents seas indicate a shift in Soviet policy and Soviet attitudes, and may herald the beginning of a new trend in the USSR—at least in the field of petroleum technology.

## Soviet Petroleum Technology in Exploration and Production

Equipment manufacture and supply comprise a major area in which the Soviets are facing great difficulties—both presently and in the future. Equipment technology and equipment supply are severe problems in almost all Soviet civilian industry, but nowhere more so than in the critical petroleum industry, without which most other industries will not function. Soviet equipment is deficient at every level, from the most simple exploration tool to downstream items of pipelining, refining, and marketing operations. A discussion of Soviet equipment problems is presented here, because it is essential to the understanding of future Soviet petroleum-resource development. One of the first in-depth discussions of Soviet equipment deficiencies was by Campbell.[9] Although his experiences are summarized here, I have relied equally on the report by Hovey and my own on-the-ground experiences since 1970, from Moldavia to Sakhalin, and from Nordvik to Afghanistan.[10]

Many of the problems of deficient equipment technology and supply have been discussed in the Soviet press—particularly by members of Gosplan and the Central Committee, and more recently by even L. I. Brezhnev himself. Articles about inferior equipment and lack of spare parts appear repeatedly in such Soviet journals as *Sotsialisticheskaya industriya, Ekonomicheskaya gazeta, Ekonomika neftyanoi promyshlennosti, Planovoye khozyaistvo,* and many others. Yet little seems to get done, mainly because of the unwieldy bureaucracy. As one official once said to me, "You can be certain that, if the Soviet Union has ever invented anything on its own and perfected it beyond belief, it is bureaucracy." Classic articles outlining these deficiencies in Soviet equipment and supply are numerous.[11] English-language summaries of the problems have been written by Campbell, Hovey, Owen, Meyerhoff, and the CIA.[12] The bare-bones basics, as they affect exploration, production and, to a certain extent, pipelining, are summarized below.

### Geologic Exploration

Geologic and paleontologic methods used in the Soviet Union are not greatly different from those used elsewhere. In general, the Soviet geologists and paleontologists are better trained than their Western or Japanese counterparts, especially in the realm of theory and in the area of advanced degrees. Because funds for application of theory are limited, the Soviet scientist and engineer do not fare as well as their non-Soviet counterparts. Consequently, the ability of Soviet petroleum people to apply knowledge is restricted and people experienced in modern (i.e., Western) techniques are very few in number.

### Seismic Work

*Seismic-Refraction Studies.* Seismic-refraction methods are employed to study the gross structure of basins, and are used to delineate basin margins, deep faults at the earth's crust, and sedimentary layers by the refraction of wave energy generated by explosions at the surface. The quality of Soviet seismic-refraction work has been good for many years. The equipment is bulky and difficult to transport, but the quality of data and of interpretation is, in general, very good. The principal problem with Soviet seismic work is the quality of the reflection-seismic equipment.

*Seismic-Reflection Studies.* Seismic-reflection work is based on the principle that wave energy produced by surface explosions and other surface energy sources reflects from each different rock type in the subsurface. Seismic-reflection methods are used for small-scale mapping for drillable structures. Thus reflection work is used for detailed exploration, in contrast to refraction work which is employed for broad reconnaissance studies. Reflection-seismograph crews in the USSR still use 690 m cables with up to 24 traces per cable. The cables are several inches in diameter, are extremely bulky, and very difficult to handle. They are similar to field seismic cables used in Western countries in the 1930s and early 1940s. The separate cables to each trace are taped together every few centimeters. Each cable has 12 recording "stations" or traces, in contrast to Western equipment which has 24 to 96 traces. At each trace are 5 to 12 recorders or geophones, in contrast to hundreds of recorders on Western cables. The Soviet geophones are large and bulky, each weighing up to two kg apiece, versus a few ounces apiece in the West. Recording equipment is poor, and depth penetration rarely exceeds 1,500 to 3,000 m. In contrast, in the West, depth penetration of 5,000 to 10,000 m is commonplace.

Lack of penetration has been a serious handicap in the USSR, where the average exploratory well depth now is approximately 3,000 m or more. Deep structure is difficult or impossible to map, and wildcat wells commonly are drilled on the basis of shallow structural interpretations. Nevertheless, the seismic equipment available is far superior to the corehole drilling techniques used widely until the early 1960s. Prior to 1965, many structures were identified on the basis of 300-m-deep structural drillholes. Because cores from these holes could not be oriented, structures interpreted to be anticlines commonly turned out to be synclines, and the dry-hole ratio was phenomenal. In areas covered by thick sections of carbonate rocks, seismic-wave penetration rarely exceeds more than a few hundred meters. As a result, Soviet drilling success in regions with thick carbonate-rock sections is abnormally low.

CDP (common depth point or "stacking") work has only recently been introduced into the USSR. Two-fold stacking techniques were used for the first time on a large scale in 1972–73 (versus 24-fold to 50-fold stacking techniques in the West). Despite the introduction of this rudimentary stacking technique, the ability to obtain data deeper in the sedimentary section was not greatly enhanced. Turn-around time from the field recording crews to the data-processing centers and back commonly exceeds 90 days (versus 24 hours or less in most of the West). There has been little improvement since 1973, except in the rare cases where Western equipment has been purchased and tested. Digital field computer units (for interpreting and displaying seismic lines) were not introduced until 1969, and these are still few in number and are very elementary in design. Computers used at the data centers also are far behind Western computers. The Minsk models in general use compare with U.S. designs of the 1959–65 era, and thus are hopelessly outdated.

A few more advanced (12-fold) CDP units have been introduced since 1974, but these are extremely few in number. Methods of record display have advanced little beyond the variable-area and variable-density types of displays used in the West during the 1950s and early 1960s. Lack of well-integrated velocity mapping has led to some very poor—in fact wholly erroneous—structural interpretations.

Marine seismic-reflection studies have been conducted since the late 1950s, but most of the equipment is single-channel (single-fold), sparker-type equipment (based on Japanese design) with very shallow penetration capability, usually about 1,500 m, but in some cases, 2,000 and 3,000 m. Although a few multichannel (CDP) seismic surveys with foreign vessels were done in Soviet waters before 1978, they generally were unreported. GECO (Norway), for Petrobaltic, a USSR-Polish-East German consortium, did a multi-channel seismic survey during 1978, but the Soviets complained about the price. Regardless, some lines were shot and provided the best quality reflection-seismic data ever obtained in Soviet territory up to early 1978.

In 1977, the Soviet Union negotiated the purchase through GECO (Norway) of a modern seismic-research vessel with 48-fold CDP equipment. The ship began service in the Barents Sea during 1978. Purchase of this ship was, effectively, a quantum leap forward in Soviet seismic capability. Unfortunately, several dozen such ships will be needed before effective and large-scale seismic-exploration programs can be conducted in the huge Soviet offshore areas. Data-processing equipment, not available in the USSR, also will be needed in sizable amounts. The Soviets still cannot handle the new GECO-type data with existing data-processing computers.

Despite the lack of CDP seismic equipment, the amount of single-channel equipment has increased greatly during the last few years, largely as a result of purchases from Japan and some Western countries. Soviet research vessels now are doing old-fashioned single-channel surveys in almost all Soviet waters. Much of this type of exploration, however, is for academic use and is not exclusively for the Soviet petroleum industry. Moreover, the poor results are inadequate for the petroleum industry.

Drilling and Production

*General.* The USSR drilling industry traditionally has relied on the turbodrill as its basic exploratory and development drilling tool. Approximately 74 percent of all Soviet rigs are turbodrills, as opposed to 89 percent in 1965. The remaining 26 percent consists of rotary-type rigs, turbodrills with a rotary table that can be used to penetrate hard strata at great depth, and electric drills.[13] The turbodrill has been the Soviet Union's greatest cross to bear, because of its general ineffectiveness below depths of about 2,300 to 3,000 m. In 1974, the Soviet petroleum industry drilled 3,800 wells, and in 1975, 4,300 wells.[14] In 1977, 6,000 wells were to have been drilled.[15] This compares with 46,479 wells in the United States during 1977. Yet the number of rigs available in both countries is nearly the same—2,300 in the USSR and 3,100 in the U.S. (These statistics illustrate the relative efficiencies of the rotary and the turbodrill.) Also, by way of contrast, there are 26,200 oil and gas fields in the United States and Canada, versus 2,500 fields in the Soviet Union. This last statistic gives some measure of the relative maturity of drilling in these two areas.[16]

*Steel Quality.* Major problems of the Soviet petroleum industry are (1) the low quality of steel used, (2) the short supply of steel, and (3) the lack of diversity of manufactured steel products. Drilling masts are made of tubular steel. Most steel goods do not meet minimum Western requirements for quality and construction standards. The result is that drilling equipment generally begins to break down at depths below 2,300 m.[17] Because the average depth of an exploratory well is about 3,000 m and because development wells now have average depths greater than 2,300 m, serious problems in drilling have arisen throughout the USSR. Drill pipe is too weak to withstand the torque for rotary drilling. All pipe has numerous flaws and imperfections. During the winter the drill pipe freezes and shatters like glass, so that the pipe must be heated from its own weight. Heaving shale, key-slotting, and crooked holes are extremely destructive to USSR drill pipe. The USSR turbodrill is very susceptible to crooked-hole drilling, as Canadian drillers have found only too well.[18] Hole deviations from the vertical *commonly* exceed 55 degrees, a characteristic which clearly violates most property-owner and lease laws in non-Soviet countries.

It is of some interest to note that the poor quality of USSR steel in the petroleum sector was the direct result of the USSR's decision to use turbodrills rather than rotary drills and the resulting inability to manufacture large volumes of high-alloy steels. The turbodrill was selected as the USSR's main drilling tool, because there is no weight placed on the bit. Therefore low-alloy steels could be used, and high-quality steels could be allocated to the military and certain heavy industries. The results of this policy adopted many decades ago are being felt severely now.

*Turbodrills.* One of the most serious problems related to steel quality is the design and construction of the turbodrill. At present, 74 percent of all Soviet rigs are turbodrills, a technology developed between 1924 and 1948. This technology has not made significant forward strides since 1950. In 1965, the industry was instructed to convert to predominately rotary drilling, but failed to do so except to construct some combination turbodrill and rotary rigs. Only since 1973 has some progress been made, and this has been brought about with technical help from Eastern Europe, particularly East Germany. Finland and France also helped the USSR to develop more rotary drills.

One reason for this failure is the quota system used in the five-year plans. Each segment of industry competes for rubles with which to operate. Every ruble diverted to R & D (research and development) is one less ruble which can be used to meet production quotas. As a result, production quotas, as established by Gosplan, come first and R & D is ignored.

Another reason for the failure to convert to the rotary drill is the lack of sufficient good alloy metals, as noted above. However, some research is being conducted on ways and means to improve turbodrill efficiency in deep drilling. One program has been to develop methods of increasing mud flows with lower rpms (200 to 300 rpm versus the currently used 700 to 900 rpm) and to develop antifriction bearings to replace the currently used rubber-metallic bearings. Another program has been to increase the rpms to 1,200. None of the experimentation has been very successful, because the new models are not adaptable for jet bits. As a result, the steel industry continues to produce turbodrill models which are obsolete. To compound matters, a method for producing precise turbine castings still has not been perfected.[19]

One "breakthrough" has helped considerably. This is the technique of "double barrel" cluster drilling. All wells are clustered on one platform, as at Samotlor. Two wells are drilled simultaneously with the same rig and drill pipe. This rig is mounted on rails so that it can run drill pipe into the second well during round trips to change bits in the first well. A second mud pump is now standard, in case the first pump breaks down. The Soviet

drillers like to run the two pumps in tandem. This makes it possible to jet the hole and beat the meterage quota. However, jetting in this manner makes the borehole very irregular in diameter and leads to poor cement jobs and numerous cave-ins.

Because of the failure of drilling equipment to withstand the stresses and strains below depths of about 2,300 m, drilling costs below that depth rise astronomically. At 2,500 m, the average cost per meter is about $220; at 4,000 m, the cost is $800 per meter. At 6,000 m, the turbodrill cost can reach $9,000 per meter. The principal reason for the astronomical cost rise with increasing depth is related to the great amount of time involved. Modern wells in the Western world now can be drilled to 3,000 m in 34 days; no Soviet rig can drill this amount in less than 90 days, except under exceptional conditions, and usually they require 12 to 14 months to drill to 3,000 m. A 5,000-m hole in the Soviet Union commonly consumes up to five years; two holes drilled below 7,000 m took more than 14 years each to drill.[20] A well drilled more recently in Moldavia to below 7,000 m took only five years and 11 months; however this well could have been drilled in the West in 12 to 18 months. The current world depth record is held by the Soviet Union (more than 10,000 m), but this well has been drilling for more than eight years and an East German rotary rig was used below 8,000 m.

Thus, drilling-time problems are not being faced, and they continue to plague Soviet industry because of the huge expenses that are incurred. During the first quarter of 1979, the average well in West Siberia was drilled at a rate of only 71 feet (22 m) per day, versus 328 feet (100 m) in the West in similar types of rock.

*Moving to New Locations.* Most Soviet turbodrills are massive structures up to 58 m high which require 22 to 33 days to move to adjacent locations, and 90 days or more to move to distant (10 km +) locations, versus 1 to 10 days in the West. (In addition, the average time for *testing* a well, for example, in West Siberia was 51 days during the first quarter of 1979, versus 2 to 20 days in the West.) Jackknife (portable) rigs are just appearing in the USSR. There has been a strong appeal from the Ministry of Oil Industry to acquire more such rigs.[21] The amounts of time lost in rig-up and rig-down plus testing while on location are unbelievable—nearly 2½ months per well per location in West Siberia.

*Other Lost-Time Causes.* An actual record from the Chechen-Ingush ASSR, north of the Caucasus Mountains, showed that, during the drilling of one 6,000-m hole, 1,411 man-days were lost because of breakdowns and lack of spare parts. Campbell implied that large man-day losses are typical in many areas;[22] they are. In one Vilyui basin location, more than 1,300 man-days were lost in a 4,800-m hole from breakdowns, and more than 1,500 man-days were lost because of illnesses. Some of the "illnesses" turned out to be wife and girlfriend problems, which were partly solved by importing lady social workers into gas-field camps at remote locations. I was working in eastern Siberia during the winter of 1973–74 when this "solution" was applied successfully for the first time in that region.

The seriousness of the breakdown problems can be appreciated if one considers the fact that, of 16 wells programmed for 5,000-m depths (to have been completed in 1975) in the North Caucasus, only three made it; the other 13 wells were lost and abandoned.

*Mud Programs.* All rotary and turbodrill equipment requires lubrication for effective penetration of rock formations by the drilling bit. However, it is essential to use muds (or water or air) which will not react with the underground rock formations in such a way that the formations will be damaged and oil or gas zones overlooked. Moreover, some rock formations are under "abnormal" (higher than normal) pressure, so that specially weighted (scientifically planned) muds must be used to prevent blowouts. Yet scientifically planned muds are almost unknown in the Soviet Union. When a location is staked, crews are sent out to find a local clay pit. This clay, regardless of composition, is mixed with water, some additives, and used to drill the hole, thus causing severe formation damage in subsurface strata. Mud weights are not calculated because abnormal pressures rarely are encountered in the USSR, except in the Caspian and North Caucasus areas. Moreover, the same mud is used over and over again—commonly in 3 to 6 or more holes. Use of the same mud in more than one borehole makes it difficult or impossible to use electric-logging tools, because oil in a mud used in a preceding hole may register as an oil show in a second hole which does not contain oil. Reused muds are also contaminated severely by rock formations penetrated at other locations and the true rock formations cannot be identified.

Moreover, because of the great length of time consumed in deep drilling, the strata in the borehole are washed constantly by fluids. This causes extreme damage from the muds, and invasion problems (invasion by drilling fluids into potentially productive strata) render log interpretations almost useless. In areas of relatively shallow drilling, log interpretations still are quite good, because invasion is not too serious. In areas of deep drilling, log interpretation is a nightmare. As a result, formation evaluation in some areas is not possible. After porous formations become clogged with clay particles from improperly prepared drilling mud, they cannot be tested. As a result, the USSR has begun to use formation testers while drilling the wells. The formation testers generally can detect oil or gas shows while a hole is being drilled. Thus, the formation can be tested later with more conventional drill-stem-test tools. All testing is done after each hole is drilled. Casing is set and the hole is tested on the way out of the hole, contrary to Western practice (where most formations are tested while drilling the hole). Unfortunately, even the formation-tester method cannot be used everywhere, because there are not enough to go around.[23] In addition, the practice of setting casing and testing while coming out of the hole is extremely costly and wasteful, because the casing is set in

cement and cannot be jarred loose—especially in the USSR where the casing is of such poor quality. This results in large losses of costly steel. The method of testing while "going in," as in the normal practice in Western countries, is not feasible in the Soviet Union because of the extreme formation damage caused by jetting the bits as the bits work down the hole.

*Reservoir Stimulation and Completion.* The USSR still has not developed efficient hydrafrac and acid-treatment techniques, processes designed to open up pore spaces in "tight" formations and increase production. The procedures presently followed are akin to those used in the U.S. in the early 1930s.

*Logging.* Soviet electrical and other mechanical logs, like everything else in the USSR petroleum industry, are 20 to 30 years behind the Western and Japanese petroleum industry. Some of the logs are good, particularly the sonic (sound-wave) logs, but the rest are poor at best. During logging, only one log can be run at a time, a practice that uses up enormous amounts of rig time, which could be spent more profitably in drilling (in the West, up to three or more logs could be run simultaneously). As noted in a preceding paragraph, the value of the logs is questionable because of the extreme formation damage caused by improper muds and deep formation invasion.

Log recording also is a nightmare. The quality of the stylus which records the various curves is so bad that the curves must be traced onto graph paper as soon as possible after logging. The result is that up to seven or eight different log curves are drafted manually on a single piece of paper with different line patterns, one on top of the other. Any review of the Soviet literature on logging or any reading of field studies will demonstrate the primitive logging quality. It is surprising that logging techniques are so poor in the Soviet Union, when one considers the historical fact that logging was accepted on a massive scale in the Soviet Union (because of an arrangement with the Schlumberger Company) well before it was accepted in any other country and, at one time (1930–38), log-correlation techniques developed by Soviet scientists were among the best in the world.

*Bits.* It is commonplace to see piles of used drilling bits around Soviet rigs. Some are badly worn and others are almost as good as new. The reason for this is that bits are used only for specified drilling intervals according to depth, and not according to the hardness of the rock being drilled. In the turbodrill system, the weight of the drill string is not placed on the bit. As a result, there is no means of determining whether a bit is wearing rapidly or not at all. For this reasons, bits are used only for specified amounts of vertical penetration. The method is a wasteful one, and is compounded by other factors. For example, between 4,000 and 5,000 m, average penetration per bit is between 5 and 6 m and consumes between 4 and 5 hours. Round-trip time to replace each bit above 3,000 m averages 25 to 30 hours, or 2 to 4 times as long as in the West. Round-trip times at depths below 5,000 m rise almost exponentially, consuming 19 days or more per well, versus 24 hours in the West. Such waste is even more puzzling, because there is a serious bit shortage in the USSR.[24]

*Multiple Completions.* Until about 1965, multiple-completion equipment (equipment which makes it possible to produce up to three zones in each well) was not available in the Soviet Union. Even today it is scarce. At the Samotlor field in West Siberia, separate holes are drilled to each productive zone. It is not at all uncommon to observe from 3 to 5 "christmas trees" at each drillsite, each representing a separate hole drilled at the same location to a separate reservoir. In the West, dual, and even triple, completions in each borehole are commonplace. Thus the Soviets must drill an average of 2 to 3 wells per location for each well drilled in the West.

*Blowout Preventors.* The Soviet drilling industry has used blowout preventors on only a very limited scale, because blowouts occur only in a few areas, such as the North Caucasus, the Kopet Dag foredeep, the Caspian, and North Sakhalin (Figure 1). In 1969, there were only 16 to 18 blowout preventors in the entire country, although this number has increased substantially in recent years. The number available still is inadequate and serious offshore accidents will one day take place because of Soviet inattention to these devices.

*Downhole Submersible Pumps.* Downhole pumps (which are needed to pump water out more rapidly to the surface, thus speeding oil production) are becoming fairly common, as a result of the importation of U.S.-built BJ and Reda pumps (more than 1,200 by 1976), and the manufacture of similar pumps in the Soviet Union (more than 11,000 by 1975). U.S. submersible pumps, with servicing, are designated for a life—before rebuilding—of about 500 days. Soviet pumps are designed for about 120 days. Because of the failure to control bottomhole conditions, hole fluids, and similar phenomena (paraffin, sand entering the hole, etc.), U.S. pumps last about 90 to 120 days in the USSR and Soviet pumps last about 30 to 45 days. The Soviets cannot produce the pumps quickly enough, and were about 1,200 short in West Siberia alone during 1977.[25] To date, the Soviets have not permitted foreigners to service their own pumps used in the USSR. As a result, numerous foreign-built submersible pumps lie around wellsites, or in machine shops, unrepaired.

*Pumping Jacks.* The Soviet petroleum industry normally waterfloods an oil field from the time it first is put on production. Soviet engineers claim that the reason for this practice is that it is a more efficient recovery method. Moreover, the giant Volga-Urals fields discovered in the 1940s and 1950s had little or no natural water drive. USSR engineers and geologists once claimed that artificial waterlift, if used from the earliest history of a field, would guarantee a 40 to 47 percent initial recovery of oil. Now that they have experience in basins other than Baku and the Volga-Urals (where the sandstones are rather clean and easy to produce), they are finding that their claims are not true—especially in West Siberia, where some

fields appear to have only 22 to 26 percent primary recovery and only up to 33 percent recovery with artificial waterlift.

Analysis of the Soviet manufacturing sector shows that until a few years ago they did not manufacture many pumping jacks (the oilfield pumps which typically dot the ground of most Western oil fields)—and have not done so on a large scale until the last decade. The reason is a lack of raw materials and technology for building them. Now that downhole or submersible pumps are in such great demand, the Soviets have had to develop the capacity for manufacturing pumping jacks for surface pumps to move the fluids forced upward by the submersible pumps. Therefore, the true reason for using waterlift from the beginning of an oil field's history was the inability to manufacture significant numbers of pumping jacks.

*Other Equipment Problems.* There are literally hundreds of additional problems with equipment in the USSR petroleum industry. The perpetual shortage and the very poor quality of all materials are problems that have plagued the Soviet Union since the beginning of its petroleum history. A few items in great demand, but almost impossible to obtain—items without which whole oil and gas fields have remained shut in—include oil/gas/water separators (heater-treaters and gunbarrels), compressors, pipe for casing, drill pipe, pipeline pipe, tubing, pipe joints for pipelines, drill collars, automated control systems (in a country which has a desperate labor shortage), in-depth refining capacity, the capacity for producing many types of petrochemicals, etc. One example of a disaster which resulted directly from shortages is the very large number of leaks that have taken place along new pipelines, because of the lack of pipe joints. Along at least two lines, ice dams had to be constructed (182 leaks along the Ust-Balyk-Nizhnevartovsk line in West Siberia in 1976) to catch the oil. Much of the oil ran into rivers, and drained into swamps and into the Arctic Ocean. However, some was recovered by the construction of ice dams. The oil in the resulting pools was collected each day in barrels hauled by trucks and jeeps on "winter roads" (frozen tracks).

*Well Spacing and Injection Wells.* The general practice of drilling Soviet fields is to drill them on a regular spacing pattern, for purposes of conservation. In some of the Caspian fields, spacing has been on the order of 20 hectares (50 acres). Many of the Volga-Urals fields were drilled on a spacing of 48 hectares. Most of the West Siberian fields are being drilled on a 100-hectare spacing. Two types of patterned water-injection systems are used.

In elongate, sharply folded anticlines, rows of water-injection wells (line-injection method) are drilled at right angles to and parallel with anticlinal trend at intervals supposedly determined by reservoir properties and well performances. In large, gently domed, equidimensional structures, contour drilling is used. The production-well pattern parallels the structural contours, and the injection wells are drilled in rows, parallel with the production wells. At Romashkino field (the largest field on Figure 2), for example, there are three to five rows of production wells separated by single rows of water-injection wells. The number of rows is determined by the size of the unit being produced and injected, and by the reservoir properties within each unit. Each unit is termed a separate "production pool," although the only barrier separating one production pool from the next is a row of injection wells.

*Stages of Production.* Next, the field is organized into operational units. This is deemed especially necessary in large fields so that the water can be injected uniformly within the field for maximum recovery efficiency. The production of an oilfield in the USSR is carried out in four general stages:[26]

(1) During the first stage, oil production rises and the only water produced is near the oil-water contact and adjacent to the lines of injection wells. At the end of this stage, the maximum rate of oil production has been attained.

(2) Stage two involves maintenance of a high rate of production, stable output, increased water flooding, drilling of production wells at intermediate locations where required (infill drilling), and placing some wells on pump. About 40 to 60 percent of the recoverable oil should be produced by the end of this stage.

(3) Stage three is marked by a significant production decline, rapidly increasing waterfloods, and reduction in the number of producing wells. A large amount of additional infill drilling is conducted, and existing production is stimulated by various modifications and corrective procedures. About 80 to 90 percent of the recoverable oil will have been produced by the end of this stage. Water production averages about 80 percent of the daily output.

(4) The fourth, or terminal stage, is characterized by low oil production, slowly decreasing yields per well, and high water output. Forced fluid production is used where feasible to fulfill production goals.

It is clear from the fact that massive waterfloods are used that tertiary recovery methods (waterflooding is a secondary recovery method) will be difficult to apply in many Soviet fields. Because of the extensive waterflooding, the number of tertiary processes available are few.

*Method of Waterflooding.* Ideally, water should be injected beneath an oil column at a pressure great enough to push the lighter oil before it, but not at too high a pressure, which could cause the water to break through the overlying oil and bypass it. In the ideal case each well must be monitored separately with due consideration for the fact that porosity and permeability differ in each reservoir from one part of an oil field to the next. Unfortunately, Soviet engineers paid no attention to changes in reservoir quality from one well to the next; moreover, they injected water at dangerously high pressures which caused large-scale water break-throughs, or bypassing—and therefore loss of oil—in many fields. Many geologists, beginning with Mirchink, took the engineers to task for their practices which were designed for meeting production quotas, and not for conservation.

Mirchink noted that "the problem at present is not to exploit oil fields on a less dense net than earlier but to

determine that density of distribution of wells which is compatible with the physical-geological and natural conditions of the pools, the technology of recovery of oil, and also practical and economic factors. Unfortunately, there are many opposing points of view here."[27] Mirchink also emphasized the advantage of well spacing suited to the reservoir conditions of particular pools and compatible with existing technology and economic factors. He was especially critical of one group who argued categorically for wide spacing (i.e., large distances) between wells, even in fields of nonuniform strata. Mirchink cited data by Bashkir geologists which showed oil losses of 13 to 17 percent with spacing of 30 hectares per well, even at Tuimazy and Shkapovo in the Volga-Urals basin, where Devonian reservoirs had favorable physical parameters (Figure 2). In Arlan, where oil-bearing strata are lenticular and the oil is highly viscous, a spacing of 48 hectares left many wells circumvented by the waterflood and resulted in oil losses exceeding 30 percent (Figure 2) (more than 200 million barrels).

The flooding practices also were subjected to disagreement between the specialists of engineering groups and other investigators. The former advocated maximum buildup of pressure differential between the injection front and the zone of withdrawal. Mirchink agreed with their opponents, who presented data which indicated that such extreme pressure differentials would cause excessive advance of water through the more permeable layers with premature flooding, coning, and loss of much oil by bypassing.[28]

Mirchink's criticism pertains to most of the larger fields in the Volga-Urals basin, and pertains today to the Central Ob fields of West Siberia, including Samotlor. In the Volga-Urals, the potential for damage was the greatest in the Romashkino field which contained reserves of 14 billion barrels, of which about 90 percent is in the Devonian (Figure 2). The area of oil saturation in this pool is enormous—760,000 acres. The pay zone is about 90 m thick and more than half is underlain by water.[29]

The producing zone ($D_1$) is composed of two members, the lower of which has good reservoir characteristics, and the upper of which has an extremely varied lithology and low permeability. Mirchink noted the extremely different movements of water and oil in different parts of these members during production.

As an additional complication, the underlying $D_2$ zone is water-bearing but is hydrodynamically connected with $D_1$. In one of the 11 sectors of the Romashkino field, water flowed from both $D_2$ and $D_1$ during the early period of development until artificial injection was begun in $D_1$ in mid-1955. Then the flow reversed. It was estimated that more than three million barrels of oil escaped into the $D_2$ water sandstone from 1955 through mid-1958 in one sector alone.

This was not the only unsatisfactory effect of the injection program. Reservoir inhomogeneity caused many wells and productive areas to be completely bypassed by the injected water. The number of idle and intermittently producing wells ranged from 3 to 54 percent in various parts of the Romashkino field on 1 January 1962, and amounted to 20 percent of the wells in the field as a whole by 1964.[30] Although this situation now has been corrected partly by infill drilling, the great oil losses during the 1950s continue to cause huge production problems, because so much water must be produced with the oil. This requires the use of larger than normal pumps and excessive numbers of submersible pumps.

Mirchink attributed these difficulties to "inadequate evaluation or even downright ignoring of the complexity of the geology" by the engineers who planned the development of the field.[31] All of the bad effects of poor practices in waterflooding are evident—channeling, coning, bypassing, and sequestering of oil—at least 150 to 200 million barrels are beyond recovery in Romashkino. However, these practices were in some degree forced on the engineers where it was required to meet high production quotas at low cost from a thick net of wells. This practice of forced production continues even today. Water production now exceeds 74 percent of all fluids produced in the Volga-Urals fields.[32]

*Associated Gas.* Because gas dissolved in oil (associated gas) provides a natural means of pushing oil out of a reservoir, it is now illegal to flare gas in the Soviet Union, except under special circumstances. However, recycling of gas reservoirs, until the 1970s, was an almost unknown practice in the Soviet Union, and still is not as widespread a practice as it should be. Where gas markets are not available, gas commonly is still flared, because compressors for recycling are not available. In fact, the amount of flaring in the West Siberian basin was enormous until the installation of gas collecting plants in the 1970s, as could be seen both on the ground and from aircraft at night. Nighttime satellite pictures of flares in the Central Ob district in West Siberia were particularly spectacular. The whole history of gas waste in the Soviet Union is one of the great tragedies of our times.[33]

A particularly good example was in the Uzen field, on the Mangyshlak Peninsula, Kazakh SSR, in the eastern Caspian region (Figure 5). Press reports describe almost incredible ineptitude in the development of the Uzen field. Uzen, with estimated reserves of 3.6 billion barrels, was discovered in 1961, and began production in 1964. A pipeline was completed to Kuibyshev on the Volga River in 1970. The field went on stream at a rate of 96,000 barrels per day. According to *Kazakhstanskaya pravda*, (30 May 1968), "The Uzen wells produced 13,000 tons daily of high-quality, paraffin-base crude and 6,000,000 tons of oil have been sent to refineries in less than four years since production began at the fields.

"It is a disappointment that the field management and the Kazakhstanneft Trust at times break the mandatory production rules established for the overall plan of field production.

"The Mangyshlak oil is found to be saturated with gas—a plus factor, because gas increases the mobility of the oil and supplements the natural formation pressure. Intelligent utilization of the primary mechanical force within the framework of an orderly production plan could extend considerably the flowing of the wells.

". . . However, the field was produced for almost three years without such pressure maintenance. Cold water injection into the production reservoirs began only recently in one of the three main pools."

An obscure article which appeared in *Sotsialisticheskaya industriya* (20 November 1969, p. 2) is a tale of such astounding folly that even the most hardened bureaucrat in the Soviet Union should have been appalled. This article reveals that, after production began, the planners ordered all of the associated gas to be flared, without taking into account the fact that the Uzen oil has a very high paraffin content—about 29 percent. Water pumps were installed early in the field's development. A pipeline was built to bring cold Caspian Sea water across 150 km of desert to the Uzen field. The cold water was injected into the reservoirs, which had been prepared early in the development of the field. Inevitably, the paraffin congealed. The result was chaos. Of the 210 field wells, at least 90 ceased to flow, and the production in the others declined sharply. Production declined to a few thousand barrels per day.

Within the field, only 10 of the 210 wells were duly completed. Formation pressure and oil and gas production were not being measured in the 200 wells that were producing. Associated gas was not being reinjected for pressure maintenance, but was being flared—700,000,000 cubic feet per month. At the end of February 1968, 93 wells were shut in because they were not connected to a line or the lift pressure was too low. Electric-power connections to keep the wells flowing were not yet installed in many parts of the field.

*Well-Sampling Techniques and Reserve Calculations.* In rotary drilling, good sample "cuttings" (pieces of rock cut by the drilling bit) can be recovered, if desired, in almost all rock formation. Formation damage is minimal, and 3-m or longer cores of nearly undamaged rock can be taken at any depth in a well. In contrast, turbodrills destroy rock formations because of excessive jetting and formation damage by fluids. Cuttings are of poor quality and commonly are confused with the rock particles present in clays minded locally for use as drilling muds. Fluid invasion of the rock formations makes the taking of cores very difficult. The cores, even if recovered intact, generally are flushed by water and mud which is jetted through the drill string. As a result, the original formation fluids are destroyed and the volume and type of original formation waters cannot be determined accurately. Moreover, the original types of clays in potential reservoirs are removed or chemically altered. The result is that the volumes of clays and water originally present in oil and gas reserves cannot be calculated accurately, and therefore, computations of oil and gas reserves are uniformly too high—up to 40 percent and averaging 25 percent.

*General Problems.* Despite the tremendous waste of gas and other questionable production practices, water flooding under pressures higher than adjacent reservoir pressures, well spacing without regard to lateral changes in porosity and permeability, and multiple holes at the same location to each reservoir, Soviet production managed to rise at a very impressive rate. Even with the enormous number of inefficient practices, the Tuimazy field with

123,000 acres originally was produced from about 1,000 wells, compared with 25,000 that were drilled in the East Texas field (which is only half again as large as Tuimazy). However, several rounds of infill drilling (about 3,000 additional wells) were later conducted at Tuimazy to recover bypassed oil. Infill drilling is now standard practice in all old Soviet fields.

To develop optimal producing conditions, Soviet technology has a long path to travel. The share of flowing wells in total output has fallen from 64.4 percent in 1965 to 40 percent in 1973 and to 35 percent in 1977. Increasing numbers of wells are being placed on pumps and other enhanced-production techniques, which will raise production costs. Because the standard pumping jack is inappropriate for Soviet waterflood operations, as the injected water-production levels reach those of the oil, it becomes necessary to extract very large volumes of liquid if considerable amounts of oil are to be recovered. This can be done only with larger jacks and increasing numbers of submersible pumps. Wells so equipped now account for more than a third of all oil output. The expense is enormous. However, the Soviets continue to explore for and develop fields today as in the past, and no major changes are readily visible. As a result, the USSR petroleum industry is compounding its problems for the future.

Although there has been considerable depletion in oil output per well, the average well productivity for the USSR as a whole actually has risen because of the West Siberian basin discoveries. However, there are indications that production at the Samotlor field is peaking at close to 3 million barrels per day. At the same time, output in the big fields of the Volga-Urals basin began to decline in the middle 1970s. There is considerable official concern about the adequacy of reserves, the drilling activity, and the necessity for secondary and tertiary recovery. The rate of increase of Soviet oil production began to decline in the late 1970s and may peak in the early 1980s. The introduction of submersible BJ and Reda pumps should delay this peaking by two or three years at the very least;[34] the development of the giant Fedorovsk field west of Samotlor in West Siberia will provide little additional relief. In addition, there are many small fields in the West Siberian basin which still have not been put on stream. However, the Soviet oil industry, by and large, has been sustained in part by intensifying production from existing fields, and in part by drilling infill production wells. This practice both accelerates the depletion of existing fields and hinders the growth of new reserves, because the drilling of exploratory wells is being curtailed as the drilling of exploitation (development) wells is being increased. This situation is getting worse rather rapidly as more infill drilling is done and the problem of drilling more exploratory wells, the sine qua non of petroleum-industry survival, is not being faced.

Depletion of oil in the old areas has brought about a significant shift in the regional distribution of production. The Volga-Urals region dropped from 71 percent of national production in 1965 to 32 percent in 1980. Azerbaijan's Baku output was only 4 percent of the total output in 1972, and has declined since, as have the North Caucasus and the Ukraine. The major source of new output, as is well known, is the West Siberian basin. This output increased to 52 percent of the Soviet total by 1980, a greater growth rate than ever planned. The reason for the greater output is that the wells are consistently being overproduced, with the resultant problems of water coning and bypassing. Thus, many West Siberian fields will be prematurely produced and thereby destroyed in part instead of being produced at a sensible and economic rate. Reservoir damage is large.[35] Production costs are about 8.37 rubles per ton of oil, although—surprisingly—West Siberian oil is being found at a cost of about 3.50 rubles per ton. However, one should keep in mind that it is very difficult to equate Soviet costs with those in the West. The true costs, measured in Western currencies, could be considerably more because many factors that enter into the cost of finding oil are not recorded in Soviet accounting procedures.

## Exploration Procedures and Methods

In 1946, total exploration costs in the Soviet Union were 54.6 million rubles. The total cost of exploration in the Soviet Union is now approaching 2 billion rubles a year. However, as noted in previous sections, more effort is being given to exploitation-production and less to exploration.

### Stages of Exploration

Exploration generally is conducted in two stages (Figure 7). Stage 1 is the "search" stage and includes geological, geophysical, and geochemical surveys, together with stratigraphic core drilling. Stage 1 consists of two phases. The first involves studies to determine the principal structural patterns, geologic history, and stratigraphic sequence of whole or part of the prospective province. Predictions of prognosticated reserves ($D_1$ and $D_2$ on Figure 7) are permitted. Phase 2 is a more detailed examination of the most promising parts of a basin for selection and preparation of areas for further exploration. Estimates of $C_2$ reserves (or $C_1$ reserves, if a well is drilled) may be made. On Figure 7, these two phases correspond respectively to the phase of "regional operations" and the phase of "preparation of areas for exploration drilling."

Stage 2 is what the Soviets call "true exploration," and also consists of two phases. Phase 1 of this stage is preparation "by seismograph and/or core drilling" of structures for detailed exploration. This is the "exploration for oil and gas fields" of Figure 7. The aim of this phase is to ascertain by drilling the presence or absence of commercial oil or gas accumulations. Generally it discloses $C_1$ reserves, and may disclose some $C_2$ reserves. (Reserve classifications are discussed in a subsequent section.) In some cases, this phase can lead to the discovery of $B$ reserves. During this phase, a plan for exploratory drilling is made. Well locations are selected, and the order of drilling the wells is determined. Objective depths are estimated. Several wells may be drilled.

During the second phase of "true exploration," if a

commercial discovery was made during the first, the pool is delineated and its reservoir characteristics are determined (on Figure 7, this is "development of oil and gas fields"). The pool may or may not be drilled up at this stage. Commonly the complete drilling of the pool, or pools, is deferred to a later phase of this stage of exploration.

Sufficient wells are drilled, cored, and logged so that all possible reservoir parameters may be established—thickness, area, porosity, permeability, temperature, pressure, production tests, and identification of gas-oil, gas-water, and oil-water contacts. The purpose of this elaborate procedure is to establish an estimate of reserves for official certification by the GKZ (State Commission for the Certification of Reserves) planners, and to formulate a plan for development drilling. No well can be exploited (produced) until the GKZ certifies the initial reserves estimate, determines that the reserve estimates are accurate, and that they are economic. If the reserve estimates are accurate and economic, the GKZ then approves the plan for development.[36]

## Regional Exploration

A tremendous advantage enjoyed by a monolithic government, where no competition is permitted or present, is the ability to explore a basin "at leisure." All available groups and tools for exploration purposes are brought to bear on the basin, and it is explored systematically from the first phase of stage 1 to the last phase of stage 2.

The vast extent of the Soviet Union, the formidable nature of much of the terrain, and the state of the indigenous geophysical art have dictated a somewhat different procedure of regional exploration than is used elsewhere in the world. Unusual emphasis is placed on mapping the basement surface and delineating major fault systems. In those aspects of geophysics that are used for large-scale regional studies (in contrast to local prospecting), the USSR is well ahead of the rest of the world, if only because of the sheer size and scale of the nation. The Soviets bring to bear such techniques as electrical resistivity surveys, telluric (natural electrical currents) surveys, magnetic surveys, (aerial and ground), gravity surveys, refraction-seismic studies (in the Russian language, translated DSS—Deep Seismic Sounding), reflection-seismic lines as needed, and geologic field mapping. The Soviets are well ahead in techniques of electrical resistivity surveys, telluric surveys, and they are on a par with Western countries in magnetics, gravity, and refraction-seismic techniques. One of the most impressive features of the Soviet magnetic exploration is their extremely thorough coverage of large basins. Most of the Soviet Union has been covered by surveys having flight-line spacings of 2 to 10 km. Electrical and seismic-refraction surveys are utilized almost as much as magnetic surveys. Less use is made of gravity. Seismic-reflection work has limited application in regional work.

Refraction lines as long as 1,100 km are shot during the early stage of exploring a new basin, and shot-point distances as great as 100 km have been used to map the basement and to obtain data of intrabasement dis-

continuities. Deep refraction work (DSS) began in 1949. This method was used with tremendous success in the Dnieper-Donets graben (Figure 4) for outlining the margins of this huge depression and for determining the depth to, and thickness of, the Devonian salt. Preoccupation with the basement and basement faults is a partial result of prospecting for other minerals, and may have been stimulated also by the continued belief of many Soviet geologists in the inorganic hypothesis for the origin of oil.

Electrical prospecting in the Soviet Union began in 1928 and has been used more extensively than in Western countries.[37] It has been employed effectively in basement studies and also for mapping sedimentary interfaces with large resistivity contrasts. Schlumberger considered it especially important in the North Caucasus basin and in the Carpathian trough, where thick shale sections exist. Induced and natural electrical methods were used in the Dnieper-Donets graben for detecting faults. Magneto-telluric and natural electric-current methods were used in the Irkutsk amphitheater of south central Siberia to map the structures in which the Proterozoic and Early Cambrian oil and gas fields of that region were found. In 1966, there were not less than 20 telluric, 30 magneto-telluric, 50 resistivity, and 100 transient resistivity (dipole) crews in the field, in addition to 500 additional crews of these types engaged in prospecting for metallic deposits.

Deep stratigraphic (in Russian, the words are "key" [opornaya] and "parametric") tests are important parts of the regional studies and in some cases such tests are drilled in rather close networks. If feasible, they are drilled to basement and in some places to considerable depths within the basement rocks. Basement rocks are cored so that age determinations can be made of the basement. Detailed basement maps are very common in the overall Soviet exploration program.

Thus the various electrical methods are used to determine the depth and the configuration of basins, to determine the location of major faults, and to find contrasts in the composition of the basement. The Soviets have found these methods to be extremely useful in locating horsts, grabens, major strike-slip and dip-slip faults, and to find conductive layers such as salt and salt-water-bearing formations. Magnetic, gravity, and refraction methods are used for the same purposes. Where used together, they become extremely effective tools.

Of all the tools used in regional surveys, the reflection-seismic methods are the worst. The reasons were given in a preceding section. The geologic field work which is done in conjunction with the geophysical studies is of extremely high caliber and is very good in enabling Soviet scientists to predict the thicknesses of sections, and to obtain some ideas of the various lithologic changes which may be expected in large basins covered by younger rocks.

## Detailed Exploration Methods

Detailed exploration methods are outlined here with some care, because Western and Japanese exploration groups generally are unaware of Soviet regulations for exploration promulgated by the GKZ. These were published in English for the first time by Meyerhoff.[38] They provide some indication of Soviet attitudes toward exploration and exploitation of oil and gas.

The limited effectiveness of Soviet reflection seismology has handicapped the detailed mapping of prospective areas. Only about half of the seismic recording trucks use magnetic tape, and data processing is cumbersome. Only recently (as noted in preceding sections) has CDP technology been employed, and this is primitive. Vibroseis-type methods have been utilized only in the last five years and these were done only on a very small scale. (Vibroseis reflection work involves striking the ground with heavy weights to generate a wave-energy source; other seismic techniques employ an explosive source, such as dynamite.)

The reflection-seismic tools rarely penetrate below 3,000 m, and generally penetrate to only 1,000 to 2,000 m. Consequently, the mapping of deep structures is extremely difficult. Until very recently, it has been impossible to map reflections below salt deposits (because salt absorbs energy) which blanket many parts of the USSR. Even today, subsalt exploration techniques are primitive. In addition, it has been very difficult to detect low-relief structures, to identify multiple reflections, and to adapt the seismic method to search for stratigraphic traps.

Recourse to core-hole drilling for identifying drillable structures was unavoidable during much of the history of exploration in the Soviet Union. This was especially true in regions where adverse surface conditions exaggerated the seismic problem. One of these adverse conditions has been the thickness of the permafrost layer (up to 1,500 m; in 1976, a 2,200 m permafrost zone was drilled in a well in the Kolyma Valley) in many of the Arctic regions of the Soviet Union. The core-drill method itself had no serious limitation. Until 1965, most core-drilling rigs could not reach much below 300 m and, to the present, there has been no method perfected in the Soviet Union for orienting cores.[39] Consequently, anticlines and synclines have, in many cases, been confused with predictable results. Most modern core rigs in the USSR now drill to 1,000 m.

Another problem with the core-drill method for mapping subsurface structure is that, where angular unconformities are present in the subsurface, shallow structure maps will not necessarily reflect the presence of deeper unconformities. A common feature found on many aerial photographs within the Soviet Union is the presence of long lines of core holes, some as long as several hundred kilometers. However, this expensive method of exploration has been downgraded considerably in recent years as better seismic techniques have been employed.

The drilling of "key wells" is one of the first steps taken during the detailed exploration of a basin. "Key wells" are wells located in critical, and unknown, parts of a given sedimentary basin. As Seregin pointed out, key wells are drilled in accordance with the State Plan for each basin.[40] Key wells are drilled with complete (or at the very least, extensive) coring, supplemented by all types of well logging, obligatory casing, cementing, and testing of all

potentially productive zones. Key wells are projected to reach the basement or drill to a technically possible depth (normally 4,500 m), regardless of the great expenditure in both time and money. The location for each well is selected separately on the basis of analysis of available geological and geophysical data.

The cores which are taken are processed in laboratories. On the basis of data obtained from the analyses of cores, studies of water samples, studies of oil and gas recovered, mud logging, electric logging, and reservoir tests, a composite report is presented on all of the research done. This report concludes, in addition to the actual data from the well, succinct conclusions on the geologic patterns ("regularities") and petroleum potential of the part of the basin that was drilled. If the basement is penetrated in key wells, it is dated by paleontologic methods (if the rocks are fossiliferous), or by radiometric methods (if the rocks are metamorphosed or of igneous origin).

On the basis of the results of the drilling of key wells, areas within the basin are selected for more detailed study. These areas are then drilled with "parametric wells." The purpose of these wells is to obtain detailed geologic information of certain intervals within the sedimentary sequence, the physical parameters of the intervals of interest, studies of facies changes, and detailed geological correlations of marker beds found in the key wells. Correlations of these marker beds are established with seismic and paleontologic data which may be available. Structural maps are constructed on the basis of the data from key and parametric wells, and from the seismology. It is usual to drill parametric wells along already existing geophysical profiles—magnetic, electrical, or seismological.

The amount of coring done in parametric wells depends on the geologic objectives. Cores are taken principally from the zones which are expected to be productive. They also are taken from market zones and from unexplored parts of the sedimentary sequence. This is particularly true in basins such as West Siberia, where most of the subsurface section is not exposed anywhere at the surface. If possible, each potentially productive zone is tested with a formation tester during the course of drilling. Just as in the drilling of key wells, cores, drill cuttings, water, and oil and gas samples are obtained from parametric wells and are carefully studied. A scientific report is prepared for each parametric well.

Once the parametric drilling of areas of interest has been completed, structural core holes are drilled. Core-hole drilling was particularly important in areas with thick Quaternary cover. Core drilling of specific structures, however, now has been almost completely abandoned in favor of reflection-seismic techniques.

The entire process of detailed exploration, preliminary detailed seismic investigation and the actual drilling of structures, takes approximately 5 to 10 years. The length of time obviously depends on the size of the basin being studied and the complexity of its geologic patterns. Such investigations are routinely incorporated in the various five-year plans, as well as in annual revisions of the five-year plans. Thus the plans which are worked out for every large region incorporate the anticipated results of detailed exploration, the objectives to be drilled for petroleum, the depth to which the studies are to be carried out, the sequence and nature of the various types of investigations and investigatory tools, the technical implementation and funds required, the list of reports that will be submitted on completion of work, and a tentative schedule for the work to be done. At the beginning of each five-year plan, the nature of each investigation must be outlined—whether it is to be of a reconnaissance, semi-detailed, or detailed nature. The results obtained from each of these regional investigations are summed up in final reports prepared by the field and resource organizations assigned to the program, under the supervision of regional supervisory councils. The final report on the research work consists of text supplemented by proper illustrations. According to required plans, the text must incorporate, in addition to the usual geological chapters, sections dealing with the comparative petroleum potentials of different parts of the basins, an estimation of the prognosticated ($D$) reserves, and a program for further search and exploration. All illustrations accompanying the report must include maps showing the petroleum potential of each stratigraphic unit in the entire sedimentary sequence. The compilation of these maps—the most important documents of the report—must indicate qualitatively the petroleum prospects of each area.

Recently the USSR geology groups have begun to plot maps of prognosticated reserves based on the qualitative and quantitative data obtained from detailed exploration. In addition, maps showing the prognosticated distribution of oil and gas reserves in the various basins must be included.

## Summary of Soviet Geologic Approaches

Although theoretical training of Soviet geologists, geophysicists, and petroleum engineers is better than in other countries, in the practical application of science, particularly in the mineral-extraction industries, the non-Soviet scientist is well ahead of his USSR counterpart, largely because of the superior quality of the support equipment available. Because geology is not the speciality of those who may read this report, my observations on geologic expertise are limited to a few of the most important aspects of the petroleum-geology field so that at least a general appreciation of the "state of the art" may be gained. Geophysical techniques are not discussed, because this topic has been covered. In addition, petroleum-engineering expertise has been reviewed in a general way. Therefore, this section deals mainly with geologic expertise, together with some comments on Soviet geochemical methods.

*"Regularities."* There exists in the Soviet Union an almost fanatic preoccupation with the search for the laws or regularities of nature. Just as Marxist-Leninist theory teaches that the ideal world is one with a single socio-political system, so the same theory teaches that each natural phenomenon or feature of the earth must have a logical, immutable, and recognizable regularity or pattern (*zakonomernost*). The laws of nature, therefore, must

be predictable, and it is the obligation of the earth scientist to discover these laws so that accurate prediction (and therefore accurate exploration results) is possible. The Soviet oil and gas literature, like other Soviet literature, is replete with articles entitled "The regularities of . . .". This same literature is also filled with pep talks to the earth scientist, and with articles which regale each and every exploration or exploitation organization (trust) that has failed to find its quotas of oil and gas, with accusations of its inability to find nature's "regularities," as they apply to the area where failure has occurred. (For classic examples, see any annual collection of articles from *Geologiya nefti i gaza.*) Thus, each prospective petroleum area, district, or basin, must have its own set of "regularities"—such as: (a) the pattern of oil and gas distribution within the basin; (b) the pattern of structural and stratigraphic traps in which oil and gas may be found; (c) the pattern of rock types (sandstone, siltstone, shale, limestone, dolomite, etc.) toward which exploration must be directed; (d) the pattern of sedimentation which, in turn, predicts the pattern of rock-type distribution; (e) the geochemical pattern which determines potential oil and gas recovery; and (f) any other pattern pertaining to petroleum exploration.

The resulting plethora of literature ranges from very high-quality articles with genuinely innovative concepts of well-conceived syntheses of new data, to absolute masterpieces of double-talk, vagueness, and double-thinking. The Soviet petroleum-geology literature, in this respect, is not too much different from that of other countries. (Publish or perish policies in the Soviet Union embrace both the academic and applied-science sectors.) The principal difference in Soviet petroleum-geology literature is that there is at least 100 percent or more of it than in all of the other countries in the world.

*Petroleum-Bearing or Prospective Basins.* A distinct dichotomy exists in the literature on Soviet basins. The academic people "copy-cat" Western and Japanese literature; on the other hand the petroleum geologists use a classification of petroleum-prospective basins which is much more practical than that used outside of the Soviet Union. A basin is described in terms of the petroleum prospectivity or potential, and rarely in terms of its inferred manner of origin, as is so common in Western countries. Thus, the USSR geologist shows a refreshing practicality in his writing.

*Classification of Traps for Petroleum.* The non-Soviet classification of potential oil and gas traps is subdivided into 3 or 4 types. The USSR geologists recognize that petroleum traps are of at least 18 types. This fact has enabled the Soviet petroleum industry to explore for more specific targets than is possible in most noncommunist countries. Unfortunately, as a result of inadequate tools for geophysical and geological exploration of the subsurface, the advantages of USSR trap classifications are dissipated and, in areas of deep drilling, almost lost.

*Theories of Oil and Gas Distribution.* Such theories—and hypotheses—are on a par with those of any other country, except in areas where mobile subsurface waters have produced lateral hydrodynamic gradients. In this arena, the Soviets have constructed far more detailed basin models than their Western and Japanese counterparts.

*Direct Detection Methods (Including Geochemical Methods).* No country has developed such methods (including the much-touted Western "bright spot" method). The Soviet Union, which has spent more effort in the research for direct-detection techniques, is no exception.

*Geochemical Analysis.* Soviet studies of rock geochemistry, especially with regard to petroleum source beds, generally have been superior to those in the West. Only during the past five years has the West begun to overtake the USSR in all exploration techniques of geochemistry.

*Petroleum Objectives.* It long has been a cliche outside of the USSR that Precambrian rocks cannot possibly be either sources or host rocks (reservoirs) of petroleum. The USSR, 30 years before Japan and the West, developed detailed paleontologic zonation in upper Precambrian rocks (2,000 to 570 million years old), and found both rich source beds and reservoirs. With the sole exception of a small Precambrian field in Australia, the USSR and China are the only countries which never accepted the unfounded Western dogma that life on the earth began in Cambrian time. As a result, the USSR has found some major (including two giant) oil and gas fields in Precambrian rocks.

*Sedimentary Models of Prospective Basins.* USSR geologists have had good success in discovering ancient sedimentary analogues of modern marine and deltaic sedimentation patterns. However, they lag in the study of specific sedimentary structures within sandstone bodies. In addition, their studies of current carbonate environments are far behind those of the noncommunist countries, largely because carbonate reservoirs are not abundant in the USSR and because there is no modern carbonate deposition in the high-latitude areas of the USSR. Therefore, Soviet sedimentologists have had almost no areas in which to study modern carbonate basins, except in Cuba—and even there, not until 1961, when carbonate-basin studies were already far advanced in the West and Japan.

Finally, Soviet geologists—like their Western and Japanese counterparts—failed while they were active in China to develop continental-basin models. China, unlike most countries of the world, produces a disproportionately large amount of oil from continental (nonmarine) basins (94 percent of China's oil). As a consequence, only China has developed to any reliable degree sedimentary models of ancient nonmarine basins.

*Conclusions.* Soviet earth scientists, in general, have developed brilliant theories or hypotheses for the exploration and exploitation of oil and gas fields. Unfortunately, their lack of modern technology makes it impossible to employ most of these theories and hypotheses to their advantage. Moreover, the preoccupation with nature's regularities has partly blinded them to the fact that there

are no pat rules of order in nature, and that many problems have to be tackled through experience, and with a high level of technology that simply is not available in the USSR.

**Soviet System of Reserve Categories**

Methods of establishing and categorizing petroleum reserves in the USSR have been formalized for many years in a standard "Instructions Booklet" published by the Oil and Gas Department of the GKZ (State Commission for the Certification of Reserves), Council of Ministers USSR.[41] The methods utilized do not differ greatly from those employed in noncommunist countries, but these methods are spelled out in great detail, a phenomenon which is not observed in most non-Soviet organizations. Moreover, the categories of reserves used in the USSR differ in significant ways from those used in the noncommunist countries. An understanding of the categories is essential to foreigners wishing to read Soviet literature on reserves.

The quantitative determination of a field's reserves is the responsibility of the GKZ. Reserve calculations for each field are carried out by several teams of geologists, geophysicists, log analysts, geochemists, engineers, economists, and other persons knowledgeable in the petroleum industry. Oil reserves are not published, because they are governed by the State Secrets Act of 1947; gas reserves are published because they were not considered to be important in the early history of the USSR, and therefore are not governed by the State Secrets Act. Moreover, the standards for determining oil reserves are much more strict than those for determining gas reserves.

Government policy until 1966 was to maintain a reserves-to-production ratio of not less than 16:1 for reserve categories $A + B + C_1$, preferably 20:1. As demand for petroleum increased and therefore as production increased, this ratio was permitted to fall during the period 1967–70 to 12:1, and now the ratio is even lower; it appears to be as low as 8:1 or 6:1. This fact is causing much official concern, because the rate of increase in demand is far ahead of the rate of discovery and the certification of new reserves. Some measure of the concern felt in official quarters is reflected in the fact that a public statement was made by the then Minister of Oil Industry, V. D. Shashin, at the Ninth World Petroleum Congress, Tokyo, 1975, where he declared that Soviet production during the preceding 14 years (1961–74) had exceeded the volume of discovered new reserves ($A + B$ categories) during the same period of time. This means simply that the volume of newly proved reserves during the period 1961–74 was less than 30.8 billion barrels, which was the volume of production during that period.

Contradictions—some apparent, as in the example given, and some real—are commonplace in the speculative literature on the petroleum resources of the Soviet Union.[42] Most of these contradictions would be eliminated if the Soviet State Secrets Act of 1947 were abolished. Others would be eliminated if the Soviet reserve categories were more widely understood by organizations working outside of the communist countries. Therefore, the purposes of this section are to describe the various reserve categories and to list the basic requirements for each category.

## Classification of Pools and Fields

The GKZ instructions state that "all explored and developed reserves of oil, natural gas, condensate, and also of accompanying components contained therein, which serve as a raw-material base or as sources of supply for operating plants, or plants under construction, or plants in the planning stage, are subject to mandatory verification and certification by the State Commission of Mineral Reserves, Council of Ministers USSR."[43] Oil and gas reserves, after verification and certification, are classified as (1) commercially proved, or (2) not as yet commercially proved. The classification as "commercial" or "noncommercial" is related to the size of the field, the reservoir properties, the composition of the hydrocarbons, and the distance of the accumulation(s) from a pipeline, railroad, or commercial market.

Reserves are computed first as "in-place" reserves ("geological reserves" is the Russian technical term used for in-place reserves). The reservoir properties, as well as the properties of the hydrocarbons themselves, are studied to establish a "recovery coefficient."[44] Two overall types of accumulation are recognized: (1) simple and (2) complex. In the first type, the reservoir properties are uniform, the chemical composition of the hydrocarbon poses no major economic problem in recovery and refining, and the trap is simple (i.e., offset and development wells can be drilled according to a normal, fixed spacing pattern). In complex fields, at least one fundamental characteristic of the field requires abnormal expense in development. This may include erratic reservoir characteristics within the area of accumulation, unfavorable chemical and physical properties of the hydrocarbons, a complex trap (e.g., numerous faults, complex fracture systems, etc.), or two or more of these complicating factors.

Generally speaking, Soviet industry recognizes three types of reservoir accumulations: (1) oil (oil reservoirs with some volume of dissolved gas); (2) oil and gas (where reservoirs contain oil with dissolved gas *and* a free gas cap, or where gas pools have oil rings); and (3) gas (generally those reservoirs containing mainly free gas, with or without condensate). In recent years, the USSR has begun to use more Western terms, such as "gas-condensate fields."

Three thickness values are used to describe reservoirs: (1) overall or total bed thickness (the total thickness of an oil- and/or gas-bearing zone, including all beds of permeable and impermeable reservoir and non-reservoir rocks in the zone); (2) effective thickness (the sum of the thickness of hydrocarbon-saturated reservoir rock, whether permeable or impermeable; this term is not equivalent to the Western term "effective thickness;" only very recently (ca. 1975) has the term been used sporadically in the Western sense); and (3) the producible oil- or gas-saturated thickness (net effective pay of Western terminology).

The number of fields (including about 400 fields which presently are noncommercial) discovered in the USSR is about 2,600—in contrast to 26,000 in the United States and Canada and about 3,000 in the rest of the world. This small number is a measure of the immaturity of petroleum exploration. The implication is clear: the U.S. industry has reached "old age," whereas that in the USSR is at the stage of "early maturity."

## Classification of Wells

Types of wells are the following: (1) key wells (designed to sample the stratigraphy of a basin which has never been drilled); (2) parametric wells ("stratigraphic tests" of Western terminology designed to establish the lithologic, chemical, physical, and other parameters of the stratigraphic section); (3) exploration wells; these are divisible into: (a) "search" wells (i.e., Western-style exploratory or wildcat wells); and (b) confirmation, stepout, and other wells drilled to establish the full reserve potential of a field; both types are "exploration wells" in the Russian language; (4) exploitation wells: these are production wells drilled to *infill* the exploration-well grid (i.e., they are wells designed to "drill up" the field); (5) piezometric wells to establish pressure differentials across hydrocarbon pools and across different fault blocks or closures on a single structure; these can be wells drilled deliberately for this purpose, or can be other categories of wells utilized in part for this purpose; and (6) injection wells.

## Reserves Classification

*General.* Oil and gas are classified as $A$, $B$, $C_1$, $C_2$, and "prognosticated;" the prognosticated category includes the old $D_1$ and $D_2$ categories of the pre-1971 instructions. $A$ is the highest category of reserves, and prognosticated is the lowest category of reserves.

Before 1971 it was not permitted to commence production of a field, either simple or complex, until most reserves had been certified in the $B$ category by the GKZ. $B$ reserves are proved reserves; therefore the pre-1971 instructions effectively required that a field, including all or nearly all of its separate pools, be fully developed before production could commence. Such a practice obviously led to abnormal delays between the time of field discovery and the time when a field could be put on stream.

Because of these delays and the resulting drop in the reserves-to-production ratio, a new set of instructions was prepared and published in 1971. Permission was granted in the new instructions to commence commercial production of an oil field: (1) if seismic data indicate the size of the trap to be of probable commercial size (commercial size is defined in terms of accessibility of pipelines, other transport, and market availability); and (2) if, in the case of a simple trap, 30 percent of the reserves are in the $B$ category, if the structure is in a remote region, or if 20 percent are in the $B$ category, if the structure is in a developed region. Thus, for the first time, a large percentage of the reserves is permitted to be in the $C_1$ category. In the case of a complex trap, production is permitted if the reserves are only in the $C_1$ category. The stated reason for this difference between the treatment of simple and complex traps is the high cost of development work in complex traps.

For gas fields, commercial production is permitted if: (1) seismic data indicate that the trap is of probable commercial size; and (2) in the case of simple traps, 50 percent of the reserves are in $B$ plus $C_1$ categories. In the case of complex traps, production is permitted if all gas reserves are categorized as $C_1$. Thus, this change in the instructions permitted production to commence much earlier than under the pre-1971 instructions and reduced the delay time between discovery and production.

*Category A.* "These are reserves in a pool or accumulation (or in a part of it) which are explored and studied in such detail that the following information is known: (1) a complete definition of the form and size of the accumulation; (2) the effective oil- or gas-saturation capacity; (3) the nature of the changes in reservoir properties; (4) the degree of oil and gas saturation in the reservoirs; (5) the qualitative and quantitative composition of oil, gas, and the accompanying components; and (6) other parameters.

"In addition, the fundamental features of the accumulation, on which the program for its production depends, also must be known (i.e., the pool performance, productivity of wells, pressure, permeability of reservoir beds, hydro- and piezoconductivity, and other specific features). Reserves of category $A$ are re-calculated during the process of producing each pool."[45]

*Category B.* "These are reserves in an accumulation (or a part of it), the oil and gas content of which was established on the basis of obtaining commercial flows of oil or combustible gas with various choke sizes, and favorable logging data, as well as studies of core samples. The following information is known: (1) the shape and size of the pool; (2) the effective oil- and gas-saturation capacity; (3) the nature of the changes in reservoir properties; (4) the degree of oil and gas saturation of the reserves; and (5) other parameters.

"Some fundamental specific features that would govern the program of pool development were studied approximately, but sufficiently for planning the production of the pool; these include compositions of oil, combustible gas, and accompanying components under reservoir and surface conditions. For oil pools, drill-stem tests were made in each well. In gas accumulations, either the absence of an oil ring was established or, if one was present, the commercial value of the oil ring was determined."[46]

*Discussion of A and B Calculations.* The preceding quotations from the GKZ instructions show that: (1) $A$ and $B$ category reserves would be proved reserves by Western standards; and (2) the difference between $A$ and $B$ categories is that $A$ reserves are now being produced (i.e., there is a production history for each pool), whereas $B$ reserves are not yet in production. As a field is produced, $A$ category reserves are repeatedly recalculated.

Exploration experience and statistics show that rarely are Soviet $A$ plus $B$ reserve calculations more than 75 percent accurate. Continued development drilling and production necessitate a 25 percent writedown over a four-year period before commercial production begins. This fact is rarely mentioned in the Soviet press or technical publications. Thus, almost all $A$ plus $B$ reserve estimates by the GKZ should be regarded as about 25 percent too high. (I personally have plotted preproduction reserve estimates versus actual production; the 25 percent figure is a good average, although the range is about 0 to 40 percent.)

There are several reasons for this overestimation of reserves, of which three are the most important: (1) the necessity to meet quotas (and, therefore, excessive damage to the reservoirs caused by overproduction); (2) the poor production practices described in a preceding section; and (3) failure to make accurate measurements of interstitial clays, clay-absorptive properties, and formation-water saturation in advance of production.

*Category $C_1$.* "These are reserves of pools or accumulations in which the oil or gas content was established on the basis of commercial drill-stem tests of individual wells (some wells can be tested with formation testers), or on the basis of favorable logging data on several other (nearby) wells. $C_1$ reserves also include probable pools in separate fault blocks adjacent to areas with reserves of higher categories."[47] These higher categories must be $A$ and/or $B$.

*Category $C_2$.* "These are reserves of oil and combustible gas, the existence of which is deemed possible on the basis of favorable geological and geophysical data extrapolated to unexplored (undrilled) structures, structural fault blocks, and potential reservoir beds. Also included are reserves in new structures within the areas of oil- and gas-bearing regions delineated by verified geological and geophysical studies."[48]

*Discussion of $C_1$ and $C_2$ Categories.* Unlike $A$ and $B$ reserves, $C$ category reserves include only a very small volume of proved reserves, and these are in the first division of $C_1$ reserves. Most of the $C$ category reserves are potential reserves, and some, particularly in the second division of $C_2$ category reserves, are speculative.

Unlike the pre-1971 instructions, the 1971 instructions divide both the $C_1$ and $C_2$ categories into two divisions. The first division of $C_1$ includes reserves estimated on the basis of drill-stem test data and reserves estimated on the basis of favorable logging data. However, favorable logging data from a particular well are not by themselves sufficient to permit assignment to the $C_1$ reserve category. The logging data are considered to be reliable *only* if the equivalent zone in an adjacent well has been tested with favorable results and if the log characteristics from the untested zone are the same as those from the zone which was tested favorably in the adjacent well.

The second division of $C_1$ reserves include potential reserves from an untested structure, fault block, or other trap which lies between two tested structures or traps having category $A$ and/or $B$ reserves. Such reserves were classified as $C_2$ in the pre-1971 instructions. The structure or trap has been delineated geophysically and/or geologically.

The first division of $C_2$ reserves includes mainly extrapolated reserves (potential and speculative). Extrapolation is from nearby (not necessarily adjacent, but preferably so) structures, structural fault blocks, and other traps within the same basin—traps which are known to contain commercial volumes of oil and/or gas nearby. The structure or trap has been delineated geophysically and/or geologically.

The second division of $C_2$ reserves is mainly a speculative category for structures, structural fault blocks, and other traps in a known oil- and gas-bearing basin. Such structures commonly are removed some distance from structures having commercial oil and/or gas accumulations. $C_2$ category reserves cannot be assigned to such structures or traps unless the structure or trap has been delineated geologically and/or geophysically.

Most Soviet reserve estimates include both divisions of $C_1$, in addition to computations of $A$ and $B$ reserves. In the evaluation of the worth of published Soviet reserve calculations (almost all of which are gas), it is essential to know what percentages of the estimates are in the two divisions of $C_1$ and in the two divisions of $C_2$. Many Soviet claims of reserves include figures based largely on $C_2$ extrapolations, and therefore are unreliable.

*Prognosticated Reserves.* Prognosticated reserves (the $D_1$ and $D_2$ categories of the pre-1971 instructions) are speculative reserves and must be viewed with skepticism and great caution. According to the instructions, prognosticated reserves are estimated on the basis of general geologic studies and have to be approved by the Ministry of Geology USSR, jointly with the Ministries of Oil Industry and Gas Industry.[49] An example of prognosticated reserves is a basin containing marine sedimentary rocks, potential reservoir rocks, and favorable structures, none of which have been explored geophysically, geologically, or by drilling. For example, estimates for the entire offshore area of the Soviet Arctic shelf fall within the category of prognosticated reserves.

*Reserves Predicament.* Soviet officials in September 1979 discussed with me the existing reserves estimates being used in the Soviet Union. These officials did not suggest to me that their remarks should be treated confidentially. The most important statement made, during a four-hour review of oil reserves (gas was discussed only very briefly), was that production performance in West Siberia had been so disappointing that official reserves estimates are (1) far too optimistic and (2) the downgrading of West Siberian reserves was leading to a complete reexamination of country-wide reserves estimates. The officials at this meeting were extremely discouraged and pessimistic.

## Geology of USSR Basins

Figure 9 shows the locations of all productive and prospective basins in the USSR. The basins are discussed generally from west to east. Details of the Arctic basins were given by Meyerhoff.[50]

### Baltic Syneclise

Twelve oil fields have been discovered in sandstone and siltstone beds of the Middle Cambrian. Noncommercial flows of oil have been recovered from carbonate banks of Ordovician and Silurian ages. The sequence of Middle Cambrian-Silurian objective formations, with an average thickness of approximately 1,000 m, is overlain unconformably by Devonian sandstone, siltstone, shale, and some carbonate. Toward the south-southwest, there is a gradual onlap by Permian through Cretaceous strata.

All drilling to date has been onshore. The offshore part of the basin has not been drilled. On the Swedish side of the Baltic Sea, minor Ordovician carbonate production has been found in three places on Gotland Island. In the last few years, a joint USSR-Polish-East German governmental consortium—Petrobaltic—has been formed to explore the offshore part of the Baltic syneclise. The first offshore drilling equipment was purchased from The Netherlands in 1979 and commenced drilling offshore on the Polish coast in July 1980.

The total section in the Baltic syneclise ranges in thickness from 1,850 to 2,500 m. Traps are partly stratigraphic and partly structural. Estimates of proved and probable reserves range up to 200 million barrels (Table 2). There is good reason to expect additional discoveries, both onshore and offshore, because the area is approximately 100,000 square km, and only 268 exploratory wells had been drilled as of 1 January 1975.[51]

### Dnieper-Donets Graben

This large graben system is close to Kiev in the Ukraine (Figures 4, 9). The area is a major gas-producing province with several giant fields (the giant fields are shown on Figure 4). The basin is an elongate graben, approximately 900 km long and more than 100 km wide at its widest point. However, during 1978 a deep (5,000 m) Devonian oil discovery was reported from this graben. Devonian oil resources have been predicted for many years, and this region ultimately may be a major Devonian oil province. However, the great drilling depths make the region impossible to develop economically with present Soviet technology, although such depths would be routine drilling in the West.

The average thickness of the section within the graben is about 6,000 m, but ranges from about 3,000 m to more than 10,000 m. The section consists of Devonian (including salt), overlain unconformably by Carboniferous and Permian. A thin veneer, up to 2,000 m thick, of Triassic, Jurassic, Cretaceous, and Cenozoic overlies the Paleozoic section. Strata older than the Middle Devonian are unknown.

There are numerous salt uplifts and anticlines, with some salt piercement or diapir structures. Most of the salt structures are circular or ovate, with a complex system of faults above them. By the end of 1974 the region had produced more than 19 trillion cubic feet of gas and 971 million barrels of oil.[52] Estimated reserves are about 31

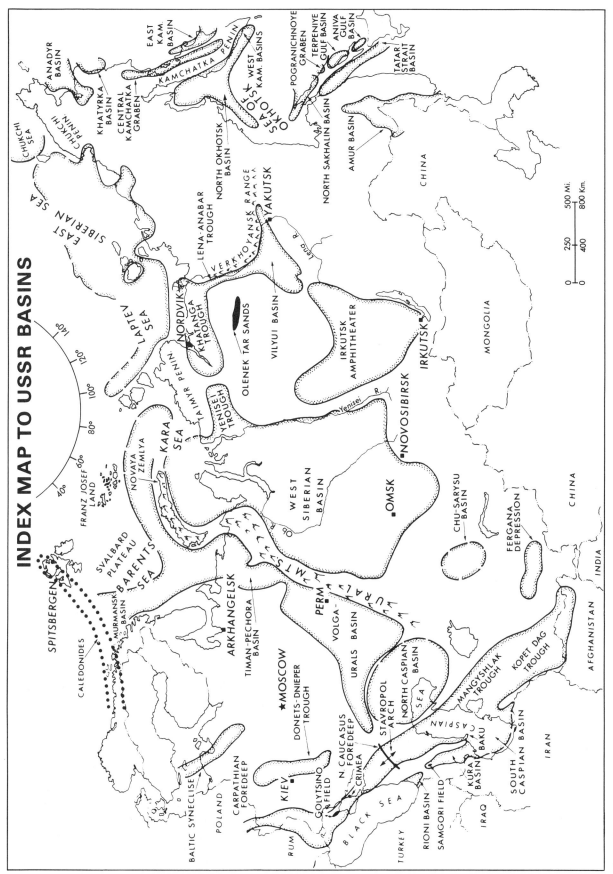

# INDEX MAP TO USSR BASINS

ANADYR BASIN

CHUKCHI SEA

CHUKCHI PENIN.

EAST KAM. BASIN

KHATYRKA BASIN

CENTRAL KAMCHATKA GRABEN

KAMCHATKA PENIN.

WEST KAM. BASINS

SEA OF OKHOTSK

NORTH OKHOTSK BASIN

POGRANICHNOYE GRABEN

TERPENIYE GULF BASIN

ANIVA GULF BASIN

TATAR STRAIT BASIN

NORTH SAKHALIN BASIN

AMUR BASIN

CHINA

EAST SIBERIAN SEA

LENA-ANABAR TROUGH

VERKHOYANSK RANGE

YAKUTSK

Lena R.

LAPTEV SEA

NORDVIK

KHATANGA TROUGH

OLENEK TAR SANDS

VILYUI BASIN

IRKUTSK AMPHITHEATER

IRKUTSK

MONGOLIA

TAIMYR PENIN.

YENISEI TROUGH

KARA SEA

NOVAYA ZEMLYA

Yenisei R.

WEST SIBERIAN BASIN

NOVOSIBIRSK

OMSK

CHU-SARYSU BASIN

FERGANA DEPRESSION

CHINA

INDIA

500 Mi.
800 Km.
250
400
0
0

FRANZ JOSEF LAND

SVALBARD PLATEAU

BARENTS SEA

MURMANSK BASIN

SPITSBERGEN

CALEDONIDES

ARKHANGELSK

TIMAN-PECHORA BASIN

MOSCOW

URAL MTS.

PERM

VOLGA-URALS BASIN

NORTH CASPIAN BASIN

STAVROPOL ARCH

CASPIAN SEA

MANGYSHLAK TROUGH

KOPET DAG TROUGH

AFGHANISTAN

IRAN

BALTIC SYNECLISE

POLAND

CARPATHIAN FOREDEEP

DONETS-DNIEPER TROUGH

KIEV

GOLYTSINO FIELD

N. CAUCASUS FOREDEEP

CRIMEA

BLACK SEA

TURKEY

RUM.

RIONI BASIN

SAMGORI FIELD

KURA BASIN

BAKU

SOUTH CASPIAN BASIN

IRAQ

Figure 9

TABLE 2
Petroleum Resources of the USSR: Produced, Proved, Probable, and Predicted (through 1974)[1]

| Basin | Produced Oil and Condensate (million barrels) | Produced Gas (billion cubic feet) | Proved, Probable and Predicted Oil and Condensate (million barrels) | Proved, Probable and Predicted Gas (billion cubic feet) |
|---|---|---|---|---|
| Baltic syneclise (basin) | 5 | — | 200 | 1,000 |
| Dnieper-Donets graben | 971 | 19,000 | 1,029 | 31,000 |
| Carpathian foredeep | 584 | 8,200 | 426 | 4,800 |
| Black Sea-Crimea (Sivash trough) | <1 | 193 | 10 | 1,307 |
| North Caucasus-Mangyshlak trough | 4,750 | 18,700 | 7,000 | 35,000 |
| Baku-Cheleken district | 7,960 | 2,700 | 7,960 | 2,700 |
| Kopet Dag trough | — | 18,400 | — | 100,000 |
| Volga-Urals basin | 27,000[2] | 7,100[2] | 20,000 | 200,000 |
| Timan-Pechora (onshore) basin | 285[2] | 2,740[2] | 8,000 | 100,000 |
| Timan-Pechora (offshore) basin | — | — | 16,000 | 100,000 |
| North Caspian depression | 482 | 1,500 | 10,000 | 100,000 |
| Fergana depression | 365 | 175 | 500 | 300 |
| West Siberian basin | 6,070[2] | 19,200[2] | 194,000 | 1,880,000 |
| Vilyui syneclise (basin) | — | 30 | 1,000 | 100,000 |
| North Sakhalin basin | 400 | 356 | 80 | 3,200 |
| Irkutsk amphitheater | — | — | 100 | 200 |
| Natural gas—lost and/or unrecorded[3] | — | 35,000 | — | — |
| Subtotals | 48,873 | 133,294 | 282,305 | 2,659,507 |
| Offshore (except Timan-Pechora and existing Caspian fields) | — | — | 158,822 | 357,699 |
| Totals | 48,873 | 133,294 | 441,127 | 3,016,507 |

[1]Through 1974 (from Dikenshtein et al., 1977), unless otherwise noted. Proved and Probable are API definitions. These = $A + B + C_1$. Predicted = Potential and/or Speculative = part of $C_1$, all of $C_2$ plus prognosticated ($D$).
[2]Production through 1977 (from various Soviet trade journals) is given for the Timan-Pechora, Volga-Urals, and West Siberian basins.
[3]Estimated.

trillion cubic feet of gas and 1,029 million barrels of oil (Table 2). These estimates do not include potentially large Devonian oil reserves.

Most of the production consists of gas from the Carboniferous. Minor production of oil comes also from the Carboniferous. Some production comes from the Lower Permian, and minor production comes from the Upper Permian, Triassic, and Jurassic. Most of this production is from sandstone reservoirs, but some of it is from carbonate reservoirs. The largest gas reserves are in the Lower Carboniferous. In recent years, increasing amounts of oil production have been discovered in the Devonian and Carboniferous of the northwestern third of the basin. A total of 81 fields have been discovered in the basin, six of them of giant size (Figure 4). Through 1974, 2,023 exploratory wells had been drilled.[53]

Carpathian Foredeep

The Carpathian foredeep is a continuation of the Carpathian trough of southern Poland and possibly of Rumania. It is connected to the North Caucasus foredeep via the Crimea in the northern part of the Black Sea. The exact nature of the intersection between the North Caucasus foredeep and the Carpathian foredeep is unknown (Figure 9).

The area contains 41 oil and gas fields, within an area of 20,800 square km. Oil has been produced in the region since 1860, and the largest field, Dolina, once the property of Poland, was discovered in 1920. It was ceded to the Soviet Union after World War II.[54]

The area is strongly faulted and folded with many thrust faults directed from southwest to northeast. In some areas, as many as six or seven overthrust nappes are present, and production is obtained from numerous sandstone and carbonate reservoirs ranging in age from Late Cretaceous through the Miocene. Production is present in older rocks, the oldest being in Devonian fault slivers. A few wells produce from Jurassic beds. Total production through 1975 was 584 million barrels and 8.2 trillion cubic feet.[55] The reserves are largely depleted, although drilling for small traps is continuing. Estimated reserves remaining are about 426 million barrels and 4.8 trillion cubic feet (Table 2).

Black Sea and Crimea

This region, the western extension of the North Caucasus foredeep, is relatively little explored, because most of it is offshore in the northern shelf area of the Black Sea (Sivash trough, Figure 10). The major onshore area is Crimea, where 21 oil and gas fields have been discovered on- and offshore. The onshore fields are very small, and produce from rocks of Early Cretaceous through Miocene ages. The first field was discovered in 1959. Total area is 38,000 square km.

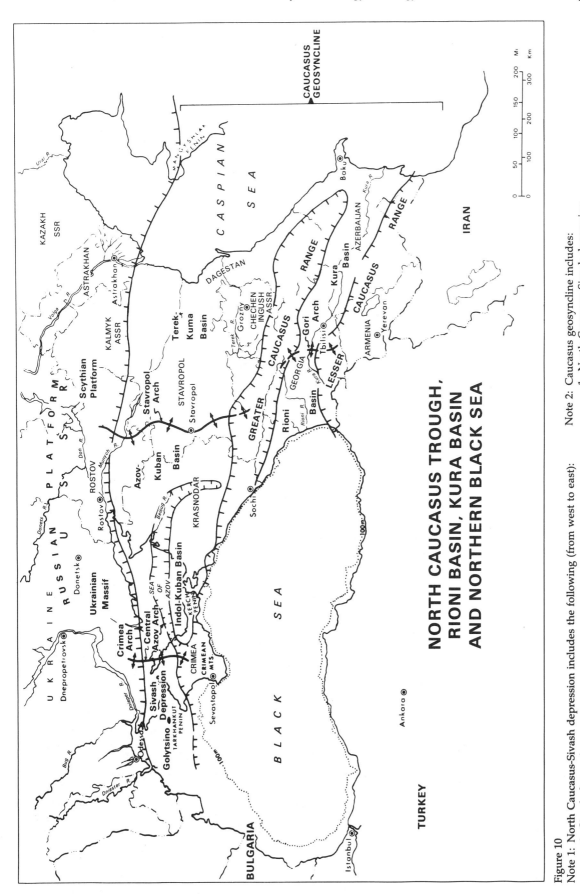

**NORTH CAUCASUS TROUGH, RIONI BASIN, KURA BASIN AND NORTHERN BLACK SEA**

Figure 10

Note 1: North Caucasus-Sivash depression includes the following (from west to east):
1. Sivash depression
2. Crimea arch
3. Azov-Kuban basin
4. Stavropol arch
5. Terek-Kuma basin

Note 2: Caucasus geosyncline includes:
1. North Caucasus-Sivash depression
2. Crimean Mountains
3. Indol-Kuban basin
4. Great Caucasus Range
5. Rioni-Kura basin
6. Lesser Caucasus Range

Note 3: Ukrainian massif and Scythian platform are southern extensions of the Russian platform.

Structure is very complex on Crimea, but less complex within the Sivash trough. The overall tectonic setting is shown on Figure 10, together with the probable relations between Crimea and the various sedimentary troughs of the North Caucasus-Sivash system. The first offshore (1975) discovery, Golytsino field, is shown. This may be a giant gas field in Eocene and Oligocene sandstones. The true size of the field will not be known for several years because drilling is done very slowly from fixed platforms.

Through 1974, Crimea had produced 193 billion cubic feet of gas and a small amount of oil. Proved reserves are nil; possibly 6 to 7 trillion cubic feet is in offshore structures found to date. However, the potential is very large.

## North Caucasus–Mangyshlak

This trough extends from the eastern end of the Sivash trough, north of the Crimea Peninsula, to the south side of the Mangyshlak Peninsula, east of the Caspian Sea; it includes the entire North Caucasus trough (Figures 1, 5, 9, 10). It is the oldest of the explored basins in the USSR, where an 1866 discovery was made by an American drilling contractor.[56] Therefore, the fact that there are only 150 oil and gas fields in this huge region is a great anomaly in the history of Soviet petroleum development. A statistical analysis, using other basins in the world of comparable size, indicates that there should be about 2,000 fields.

The answer to the puzzle probably lies partly in the complex geologic conditions of the region. This huge trough is characterized by numerous lateral rock-facies changes, which produced numerous stratigraphic traps, for which Soviet seismic technology has no means of exploring. Second, the region is one of abnormally high temperature gradients, high subsurface pressures, and heaving shales, with which Soviet drilling and logging techniques cannot cope. Finally, much of the new production (gas) is in fractured Cretaceous carbonates with which Soviet engineers have no experience. The result is extremely costly drilling and a very low success ratio, making it difficult to obtain drilling funds, and exploration of the region, therefore, has been minimal.

According to Dikenshtein, this structural province does not include the old Baku district of the central Caspian Sea, or the Kopet Dag trough east of the Caspian.[57] The total area of the North Caucasus-Mangyshlak trough system is 530,000 square km. In the North Caucasus part, there are 140 oil and gas fields; in the Mangyshlak part, there are 10 oil and gas fields. Total production through 1974 was 4.75 billion barrels and 18.7 trillion cubic feet, of which 3.2 billion barrels and 17.9 trillion cubic feet came from the North Caucasus trough. Remaining reserves in the two regions are estimated to be 7 billion barrels of oil and 35 trillion cubic feet of gas (Table 2). These are conservative figures.

The general tectonic scheme of the area is shown on Figure 10. The North Caucasus trough is divided into two parts by the Stavropol arch. The western part is the Azov-Kuban basin; the eastern part includes the Terek-Kuma basin on the western side of the Caspian Sea and the Mangyshlak trough on the eastern side of the Caspian Sea.

Early production in the area was from shallow Pliocene, Miocene, and Oligocene sandstone beds. Most of this production was oil. Subsequently, major gas deposits, as well as some oil, were found in deeper Eocene-Oligocene sandstones, Cretaceous carbonates, Jurassic marine carbonates and sandstones, and some Triassic sandstones. Giant gas reserves have been found in the Cretaceous (fractured carbonates), largely since 1955. Although production in this region has been declining (except in the Mangyshlak trough), the region contains many still-untested structures (too deep to map with Soviet seismographs) and numerous stratigraphic traps. In the Mangyshlak area is the Uzen field, where a disaster occurred during the 1960s because of failure to take into account the high-paraffin content of the oil.[58] Numerous giant oil and gas fields are present, including the North Stavropol-Pelagiada field (Figure 1). The district also includes the famous Maikop and Starogrozny fields, discovered in 1909 and 1893 respectively.

The basin is an asymmetric one, with the Caucasus geosyncline on the south. This geosyncline has been thrust northward repeatedly onto the Ukrainian and Scythian massifs which form the southern part of the Russian platform. Very sharp folds characterize the southern part of the North Caucasus trough, and more gentle folds and basement-type arches characterize the northern part of the trough. The total thickness of the section in the North Caucasus area ranges from approximately three km at the northern margin of the trough to more than 12 km in the Caucasus foothills.

In the Mangyshlak trough area on the east, the Mangyshlak uplift was thrust southward into the trough, so that this part of the North Caucasus-Mangyshlak trough complex is rather sharply folded. In both areas, major unconformities separate the Triassic from the Jurassic, and the Middle Jurassic from the Upper Jurassic and younger rocks. Locally, an unconformity separates the Upper Jurassic from the Lower Cretaceous.

There are excellent possibilities for finding large reserves beneath the northern part of the Caspian Sea between the Mangyshlak trough and the North Caucasus trough. Possible reserves in this offshore area have not been taken into account in the reserve estimates presented here. They are included in the offshore figures given in Table 2.

## Rioni and South Caspian Basins

These basins are in a trough between the Greater Caucasus and the Lesser Caucasus Ranges (Figures 1, 10). The region is extremely complex structurally and stratigraphically. Only tiny amounts of production have been discovered in the Rioni basin adjacent to the Black Sea, and in the Kura basin on the east, between Tbilisi and the Caspian Sea. A potentially important oil field was found 17 km east of Tbilisi in 1973; this is the Samgori field. Production in this 17-km long anticline is from the middle Eocene marine conglomerate. The few small fields southeast of Tbilisi have produced miniscule amounts of oil and gas. The total number of fields in the Rioni and Kura basins is only 15.

## Baku-Cheleken Districts

This subdivision includes the Baku producing district and the Cheleken district on the opposite side of the Caspian Sea (Figures 1, 5, 9). Many giant oil fields have been found in this area.

By the end of 1974, the Baku and Cheleken districts had produced 7.96 billion barrels of oil and 2.7 trillion cubic feet of gas. Of this amount, 1.53 billion barrels came from offshore and 1.55 billion barrels came from the Cheleken district on the eastern side of the Caspian Sea.[59]

All production is from a monotonous series of loosely consolidated sandstone, siltstone, and shale of the Pliocene productive series. Production has been from the same beds on both sides of and in the Caspian Sea. Numerous undrilled anticlines remain offshore, and gradually are being drilled. Progress in drilling offshore is being hampered by the fact that only five mobile drilling platforms are available for use in the area. Only three of these are capable of drilling in water sufficiently deep for developing the central part of the Caspian Sea. However, none of the available offshore rigs is capable of drilling the full sequence of potentially productive section—a minimum of 7,000 m. A probable total of 12,000 m of Tertiary underlies the Apsheron Peninsula at Baku. More than 3,000 m of Jurassic and Cretaceous is believed to underlie the Cenozoic.

The total area of the district, including the Kura basin (but excluding the Rioni basin), is 200,000 square km. Potential reserves in the area are at least the same as the volumes of oil and gas already produced (Table 2).

## Kopet Dag Trough

This region includes the entire area east of the Mangyshlak trough and the Cheleken district, east of the Caspian Sea, and extending to the Afghanistan border. It includes the Amu Darya oil and gas producing region in the east, adjacent to Afghanistan, and the Surkhan-Vakhsh district just north of Afghanistan and adjacent to the Amu Darya region on the northeast. The Surkhan-Vakhsh district includes 16 oil and gas fields in an extremely complex overthrust belt. Production is from Paleogene, Cretaceous, and Upper Jurassic sandstones and limestones. The Surkhan-Vakhsh district is 70,000 square km.

The Amu Darya area, with 360,000 square km in central and eastern Turkmenia and western Uzbekistan, is underlain by 1,000 to 16,000 m of sedmentary rocks, with 16,000 m close to the Kopet Dag on the south and 1 to 6 km beneath the Ust-Urt platform on the north. This is a gas-bearing region, with many major and giant fields. Production is from Late Jurassic carbonates associated with salt, and from Early Cretaceous sandstone reservoirs. Some production in the northern platform area is from Upper Cretaceous. At least 85 fields, almost all of them gas, have been discovered in the Amu Darya district of the Kopet Dag trough. Production trends extend southeastward into Afghanistan and northwestward toward the Mangyshlak trough and Cheleken district (Figure 5).

Production from the Surkhan-Vakhsh district totaled only 36 billion cubic feet through 1974; production from the Amu Darya district totaled 18.1 trillion cubic feet through 1974. A conservative estimate of remaining gas reserves (mainly in the Amu Darya district) is 100 Tcf (Table 1). Numerous giant fields have been found in the area, and probably many more remain to be discovered.

## Volga-Urals Basin

The basin, as interpreted here (Figures 2, 9), specifically excludes the Emba salt basin (North Caspian basin of Figure 9, or the Caspian basin of Dikenshtein).[60] This is the second great oil-producing region of the Soviet Union, the so-called "Second Baku." Numerous giant fields have been discovered here, as located on Figure 2 by number: (1) Yarino-Kamenny Log, (2) Arlan, (3) Novoyelkhovo-Aktash, (4) Romashkino—the second largest field in the Soviet Union, (5) Tuimazy, (6) Serafimovsky, (7) Shkapovo, (8) Mukhanovo, (9) Kuleshovka, (10) Orenburg, (11) Korobki, and (12) Bavly.

Romashkino alone had in-place reserves in the Devonian of 13 billion barrels.[61] Orenburg, a Permian gas field had original reserves of 105 Tcf. Tuimazy, at Oktyabrsky, was the original discovery field for the giant Devonian production in the Volga-Urals basin (discovered in 1944). Romashkino, at Almetyevsk, was the second of the giant Devonian fields to be discovered (in 1948).

The total ultimate recoverable reserves from these 12 giants is 29 billion barrels, 55 percent from the Lower Carboniferous and 45 percent from the Devonian; the corresponding figure for gas is 188 Tcf mainly from the Permian. The oil has a high sulfur content (slightly more than 3 percent), is high in asphaltines, and low in paraffin. There are more than 595 fields in the basin. The thickness of the section ranges from 1,800 m in the central part of the basin, to 4,000 m along the eastern edge of the basin, and 6,000 m in the border region between the North Caspian basin and the Volga-Urals basin. The area is essentially a platform region, along the eastern margin of the Russian platform. Thrust sheets exist along the western flank of the Urals which borders the eastern side of the basin. Numerous thrust faults have been discovered during recent drilling along the Urals flank.

Through 1977, 27 billion barrels had been produced from the basin, 57 percent of it from the Carboniferous. A total of 7.14 Tcf of gas had been produced, mostly from the Permian. The central and northern parts of the basin are mainly oil-productive; the southern part of the basin has most of the gas fields.

The total area of the basin is 700,000 square km. The deep southern part of the basin still is almost unexplored below the upper part of the Paleozoic. There are numerous small structures in the central and northern parts of the basin which never have been drilled. There also exists a good potential to find additional oil and gas along the Urals foothills. Maksimov wrote that more than 2,000 structures had been delineated by 1968.[62] Of these 595 were commercial fields, 305 were noncommercial or dry, and 1,100 were considered to be too complex or too small to warrant drilling. Estimated oil still to be produced and discovered in the basin is 20 billion barrels. The estimated volume of gas still to be discovered is 200 Tcf (Table 2).

## Timan-Pechora Basin-Barents Sea

The Timan-Pechora basin (Figures 3, 9) has an onshore prospective area of 200,000 to 250,000 square km and an offshore prospective area of 800,000 square km.[63] No offshore drilling has been conducted except on Kolguyev Island (two dry holes) and in Franz Josef Land (also two dry holes). Just 70 oil and gas fields have been discovered, some of them giants. The total thickness of section ranges from 11 km close to the Urals to about 1 km in the Timan Range which borders the southwestern flank of the basin. The oldest known rocks in the basin are an Ordovician carbonate-sandstone-shale sequence on top of Pre-cambrian granite. This is overlain unconformably by a Silurian carbonate section which, locally, is productive. Most of the production comes from the Devonian, which is unconformable on the Silurian, and from the Carboniferous and Permian above. There are two giant gas fields in the area: Vuktyl (Figure 3), which produces from an Early Permian-Carboniferous carbonate sequence below a Permian anhydrite; and Layavozh, not in production, with Permian and Late Carboniferous carbonates beneath an evaporite seal. The reserves of Vuktyl field alone are 17.5 Tcf. However, most of the production in the basin is oil from the Devonian which in this basin is in a deltaic facies, similar to the deltaic sandstone facies of the Volga-Urals basin. The Volga-Urals basin connects with the Timan-Pechora basin at latitude 62°.

An enormous amount of exploration and development remains to be done in the basin. This is true in the onshore region, but is even more true of the offshore region which contains numerous elongate anticlines similar to the Vuktyl field (Figure 3) which parallel the northern extensions of the Urals. Westward from Novaya Zemlya (Figure 9), the Timan-Pechora basin beneath the Barents Shelf extends across a broad foreland toward the Svalbard platform. There is a considerable development of prospective Devonian reefs along the western side of the basin.

Two giant oil fields, Usa and Vozei, are present in the east-central part of the basin, and a third large field discovery appears to have been made near Makarikha. All of the fields in this part of the basin lie on northwest-southeast-trending arches which extend from the Ural Mountains front to the Barents Shelf. These trends continue well offshore. Usa produces oil from Late Carboniferous-Early Permian carbonates and from Devonian, and Carboniferous sandstones. Vozei also produces from Devonian, Carboniferous, and Early Permian sandstones and carbonates. Usa has recoverable reserves of 3 billion barrels; Vozei appears to have about 500 million barrels, although this figure may increase as more wells are drilled.

In the offshore region, where the Timan-Pechora basin foreland approaches the Svalbard platform, Triassic rocks crop out on the shelf floor. The presence of Triassic on several submarine highs suggests that large structures are present. Seismic data indicate that up to 12 km of section is present in the Novaya Zemlya region and that about 2 km is present next to the Svalbard platform.

Through 1977, this basin had produced 285 million barrels of oil and 2,740 billion cubic feet of gas—most of it since 1972. Proved plus probable oil reserves are not less than 4 billion barrels and gas reserves not less than 24 trillion cubic feet. Proved plus probable plus potential onshore reserves are not less than 8 billion barrels and 100 Tcf; offshore potential is estimated to be much more than this—16 billion barrels of oil and 100 Tcf of gas (Table 2). Offshore, west of Novaya Zemlya, production also can be expected from the Triassic, Jurassic, and possibly from the Cretaceous.

## North Caspian (Emba) Basin

This basin (Figures 2, 9) is a southern continuation of the Volga-Urals basin. It embraces an area of 500,000 square km, including the northern part of the Caspian Sea and the Buzachi Peninsula, where a major heavy-oil discovery was made in 1974 in Cretaceous and Jurassic sandstones between 300 and 500 m; this is the Karazhanbas field. In 1975, the giant Astrakhan (initially called Shiryayev) gas-condensate field was found just north of Astrakhan (no. 13 on Figure 2). Most of the basin is underlain by thick Permian salt deposits which have formed numerous domes and diapirs in the basin. The Astrakhan field will be producing from Lower Permian and Carboniferous beds beneath the salt.

The thickness of the section to the base of the Permian salt is estimated to range from 1,500 m on the north to approximately 8,500 m in the basin center. Postulated Paleozoic beneath the salt may extend to a Proterozoic basement at depths ranging from 5,000 to 11,000 m. Production in the area is mainly oil, and the age of the productive reservoirs range from Late Permian through Early Cretaceous. At the northern rim of the basin, Carboniferous carbonates are productive as in the newly discovered (1979) giant Karachaganak field, southwest of Orenburg (no. 14 on Figure 2). Soviet geologists hope to find a thick productive Devonian (and possibly older) Paleozoic sequence within the basin.

The basin has not been developed because of the great depths of drilling and the numerous salt domes around which only small fields have been found. Because no large fields were found early in the basin's exploration history, attempts to develop it have been desultory. Only about 50 fields have been found in the area. During the period 1911–74, a total of 482 million barrels of oil was produced from the region. Gas reserves have been calculated officially at 1.5 Tcf. Estimated future potential is not less than 10 billion barrels and 100 Tcf of gas (Table 2). Most of this probably will be found in small deposits, or in large reservoirs (Devonian) at great depth beneath the salt. To find fields beneath the salt, much more advanced seismic and drilling technology will be required.

## Aral Sea Area

During the last few years, exploration has begun north of the Kopet Dag trough and east of the North Caspian basin, in the vicinity of the Aral Sea (Figure 9). This area is northwest of the newly discovered Chu-Sarysu basin. Eight small fields have been found in this area; however, none has been produced. Oil is present in the Middle and Upper Jurassic, and gas is present in the Paleogene. The Paleogene reserves are in sandstone and siltstone of the upper Eocene; the oil reserves are in Callovian (Upper Jurassic) sandstone, as well as in sandstones of the Middle Jurassic. The known reserves are small. Depth to the base of the Permian (which possibly is at the top of the Precambrian) ranges from 5,000 to 11,000 m.

The area has been largely unexplored because it is the site of large-scale Soviet rocket tests, missile ranges, military stockpiling, and space launches. As a result, the region has been off limits to Soviet citizens, including the petroleum industry. The area is believed to have some potential, mainly because of its very large size (about 100,000 square km).

## Chu-Sarysu Basin

This area (Figure 9) contains four small gas fields discovered since 1973. Basement is 2,000 to 8,5000 m below the surface and consists of Middle Devonian and older volcanic rocks. Late Devonian and Early Carboniferous limestone and sandstone reservoirs are present at depths of 2,000 to 4,000 m. Reserves are not known, because sufficient drilling has not been done. There is some potential to the Permian, but as yet there is no production history. The area, 150,000 km in size, appears to be entirely a gas province on the basis of the four discoveries to date.

## Fergana Depression

The Fergana depression (Figure 9), with an area of 38,000 square km, contains 37 small oil and gas fields. These fields are enclosed in a small intermontane basin among the great ranges of Central Asia, one of the most beautiful places on earth for forest and mountain scenery. Noncommercial production was started in 1880, and commercial production in 1885. Since 1885, 360 million barrels of oil and 175 billion cubic feet of gas have been produced from sandstones of Early-Middle Jurassic and Cretaceous ages, from limestone of Cretaceous age, from limestone of Paleogene age, and from sandstone and conglomerate of Miocene age. Future potential is probably less than 0.5 billion barrels of oil and less than 300 Bcf of gas (Table 2).

## West Siberian Basin

This basin (Figure 6) has a prospective area of 1,750,000 square km onshore, and an area of 350,000 square km offshore in the Kara Sea. Depth to basement is 3 to 6 km. By 1980, this basin—the "Third Baku" of the USSR—was producing 52 percent of the country's 12 million barrels per day. Its importance will continue to grow.

Toward the northeast, the basin deepens into the Yenisei-Khatanga trough. Although deepening into the Kara Sea is not proved, recent geophysical work suggests that basement does deepen appreciably beneath the Kara Sea. In the Yenisei-Khatanga trough, basement reaches depths of 6,000 m. There are now about 250 discovered oil

and gas fields in the West Siberian basin (Figure 6); however, about 80 of these are not commercial. In addition, 174 dry structures had been drilled by 1 January 1975.[64]

The entire basin began to form in Middle Jurassic time and sank rather uniformly across a vast area of 2,100,000 square km. The Jurassic sediments at the base are mainly nonmarine, with thick coal measures, but grade upward into more marine beds near the top. (These coal measures, though at uneconomic depths, are the largest on earth.) The best-developed marine facies within the Jurassic is along the western or Urals margin of the basin, where productive reefs are present along the eastern flank of the Urals. Jurassic deltaic, paralic, and nonmarine beds predominate toward the east and southeast, and locally contain coal gas (e.g., Myldzhino, Figure 6). In the southern part of the basin, the Jurassic overlies marine carbonates of Carboniferous and Devonian ages which are productive in seven fields. The reserves in the Paleozoic fields are small, not exceeding 30 million barrels of recoverable oil in each. As more exploration is done, it is possible that Paleozoic reserves will be found to be greater. The area of Paleozoic production is called the Nyurolka subbasin (Figure 6).

The Jurassic grades upward into a complex of nonmarine Cretaceous in the south, a deltaic to marine complex in the south-central and eastern parts, and a more marine complex in the northern and western parts of the basin. The age of this huge Cretaceous deltaic complex ranges from Neocomian at the base (one of the most prolific productive zones in the basin) to early Turonian at the top. The most productive zones of the entire West Siberian basin include all substages of Neocomian, and the Cenomanian. However, the Aptian and Albian are productive in many places, and Campanian rocks are productive locally in the northeast. A Turonian marine shale seal covers almost the entire basin and serves as a seal or cap rock for nearly all of the oil and gas fields. The Turonian is succeeded by an increasingly continental sequence (marine on the west and continental on the east) which includes the remainder of the Cretaceous and the lower part of the Tertiary. The sea retreated toward the west and the north of the basin, the last vestiges disappearing in Tertiary time.

The entire basin has been subdivided into several oil and gas provinces. Along the western side of the basin (the eastern flank of the Urals) are a large number of small fields, including the original discovery fields of Berezovo (gas in 1953) and Trekhozero (oil in 1960). These fields are generally of small size, and the largest of them, with about 2.8 Tcf of recoverable reserves, is Punga. Like many of the small fields along the eastern flanks of the Urals, the Punga field produces from Callovian-Kimmeridgian (Upper Jurassic) limestone banks and forereef talus surrounding basement highs.

In the Central Ob district (Figure 6) are several north-south-trending arches that extend nearly to the Arctic coast. The western of these is the Surgut arch on which such giant fields as Mamontovo, Ust-Balyk, Surgut, and Fedorovsk are located. Fedorovsk may be the Soviet Union's third largest oil field. About 200 to 250 km east of the Surgut arch is the Nizhnevartovsk arch. The Soviet Union's largest field, Samotlor, is on this arch, as are other giant fields, including Megion and Vartovsk-Sosnino.

Many of the fields shown on Figure 6 have large reserves, although most are small (5 to 25 million barrels) to intermediate (26 to 99 million barrels) fields. The Punga gas field has about 2.8 Tcf of gas in the Late Jurassic. The Pravdinsk field has about 1.5 billion barrels of recoverable oil.[65] Mamontovo has nearly 3.0 billion barrels of recoverable reserves, and Ust-Balyk may have the same amount. If so, the combined Mamontovo and Ust-Balyk fields have approximately 6 billion barrels of recoverable oil. The Surgut field has nearly 2 billion barrels. Fedorovsk has an estimated 7 billion barrels. On the east, the Megion field has a recoverable reserve of about 885 million barrels, and the Vartovsk-Sosnino field has a recoverable reserve of about 4.2 billion barrels. The Samotlor field—the largest oil field of the USSR, with an original recoverable reserve of 14.6 to 15.1 billion barrels—may produce somewhat more than 15.1 billion barrels, despite the downgrading by Clarke.[66] The field accounts for one-fourth of the USSR's annual production (Figure 13).

In the northern part of the West Siberian basin is the Cenomanian and Neocomian gas district. Only a few oil deposits have been found, the largest being a heavy-oil deposit at Russkaya (in the Neocomian; Figure 6). Among the gas fields shown on Figure 6, Novy Port has 5.1 Tcf of recoverable reserves, Gubkin has 12.3 Tcf, Komsomol has a minimum reserve of 16.0 Tcf,[67] North Komsomol has a reserve of 7.0 Tcf, Taz has a reserve of 3.0 Tcf, and Messoyakha field, which supplies gas to the mining center of Norilsk, had an original reserve of 14.0 Tcf.

The world's largest gas field is Urengoi with 210 Tcf, equivalent to the total gas reserves of all gas fields in the lower 48 United States. The field went on stream during 1978, although it was discovered in 1966. Numerous deep wells now have been drilled in the field, and 7 to 10 pre-Cenomanian reservoirs are known to the base of Neocomian. However, none of the lower reservoirs contains nearly as large a volume of gas as the Cenomanian reservoir. The Cenomanian gas is coal gas; the Neocomian gas is of marine origin. In 1978, a gas-condensate reservoir was discovered in the northern part of the field below 3,500 m.

Proved plus probable oil reserves of the West Siberian basin are estimated by most to be no greater than 20 billion barrels. However, there is good evidence from Soviet sources to indicate that the proved plus probable, plus some $C_1$ reserves, are closer to 30 billion barrels, and the proved plus probable (plus some $C_1$) gas reserves are not less than 759 Tcf. The ultimate recoverable hydrocarbons from the West Siberian basin are not less than 194 billion barrels and 1,880 Tcf (including the offshore). As of mid-1980, the West Siberian basin had produced nearly 12 billion barrels of oil and condensate and 28 Tcf of gas.

## Vilyui Basin

Figure 9 shows the general location of the Vilyui basin (with an area of 380,000 square km) and Figure 8 shows the location of the eight gas fields in the basin. The principal reserves are in the Triassic and Late Permian, with smaller reserves in the Jurassic. All of the reservoirs are

sandstones, and were deposited to a marginal-marine to paralic environment. Deeper drilling has revealed the presence at depth (4,500 m plus) of very large volumes of Permian gas. To date 9.66 Tcf of gas is proved, and 6.74 Tcf of gas is probable or potential ($C_1$), a total of 16.4 Tcf. (Some sources place the reserve at 22.1 Tcf, but 5.7 Tcf of this is $C_2$. The 28 Tcf claimed by the Soviets to be proved includes gas from both the Vilyui basin and the Irkutsk amphitheater.) The ultimate potential of the basin is not less than 100 Tcf (Table 2). However, very deep drilling will have to be done to find such large reserves. Established reserves at present are at depths ranging from 1,000 m to a little more than 3,500 m. Wells currently are being drilled to 4,500 to 5,000 m in the Permian. Total Lower Cretaceous through Permian thickness in the basin ranges from less than 1,000 m on the west to more than 11,000 m on the east, at the base of the Verkhoyansk Range. The Ust-Vilyui field, which originally supplied gas to Yakutsk, now is depleted, and the Middle Vilyui field is being produced and supplies gas to that city (Figure 8).

In 1972, a group of American and Japanese companies, with which I am involved, was formed to help the USSR develop the Vilyui basin—the so-called Yakutian gas project. In a 1974 agreement with the Soviet Union, the foreign concerns were to build a pipeline to Olga, northeast of Vladivostok, and an LNG facility at Olga, together with a modern port. The project was to commence when the Soviets have proved reserves of 35 Tcf or more, and half of the production was to go to the USSR and the remainder was to be divided between the U.S. and Japan. However, it will be several more years before the required amount of reserves have been proved. Moreover, some political problems have arisen which may make completion of the project impossible, at least for U.S. participation.

## Lena-Anabar Trough

The location of this trough is shown on Figure 9. Little is known of the geology. There are Permian salt domes around Nordvik, along the Arctic coast, and the Triassic and Permian sandstones around and above the salt domes produce small amounts of very heavy oil for local use. It will take quite a bit of drilling to determine the full extent and potential of this trough, which has an area of nearly 200,000 square km. A basement ridge separates the Lena-Anabar trough from the Laptev Sea basin.

## Laptev Sea Basin

Nothing at all is known about this basin (Figure 9). It is separated from the onshore area by a basement ridge, and from the East Siberian Sea basin by a chain of islands. It probably will be many years before this area is explored. Total area is 414,000 square km.

## East Siberian Sea Basin

Nothing is known about the geology of this basin (Figure 9) except that there are fairly extensive Cretaceous outcrops onshore. The basin, with an area of 968,000 square km, may be a continuation of the geology of Alaska. This seems likely, because Wrangel Island, which separates the East Siberian Sea basin from the Chukchi Sea, is a continuation of the geology of northern Alaska.

## Chukchi Sea Basin

The Chukchi Sea basin is not shown on Figure 9, but is offshore, east of Wrangel Island (east of 128° E longitude). The area is 357,000 square km. The geology on Wrangel Island exposes formations ranging in age from Mississippian or older to Mesozoic. The limestone of Mississippian age on Wrangel Island resembles closely the productive Lisburne Group limestones of northern Alaska and the Prudhoe Bay area. One deep test well drilled onshore, in the Kolyma River valley, was drilled to a depth greater than 2,600 m during the winter of 1976–77. Details of the well have not been released, except that the well found the thickest permafrost layer in the world, finally drilling through it at a depth of 2,320 m.

## Amur Basin

The Amur basin lies along the Chinese frontier (Figure 9). It is underlain by continental Cretaceous and Jurassic rocks. No marine facies are known to be present. Drilling depths are in the range of 1,000 to 3,000 m. It is believed that the sediments are too immature to provide more than a small amount of gas, possibly derived from coal in the

Jurassic rocks. Other small intermontane basins are present in the region, especially on the Zeya and Bureya Rivers, but their potential is small.[68]

## North Sakhalin Basin

The North Sakhalin basin—with a combined off- and onshore area of 24,000 square km—contains 50 oil and gas fields which produce from deltaic sandstones of the upper Miocene (95 percent of all production) and sandstones of the lower Pliocene (5 percent of all production). The locations of the fields are shown on Figure 11. They are in strongly uplifted and faulted anticline. (Uplift and faulting took place during the Pleistocene.) Almost all are asymmetrical toward the east.

The amount of sandstone in this section increases markedly toward the west, and shows the deltaic nature of the sediments plus the presence of a western source. During Miocene and Pliocene times, this basin was the delta of the present Amur River. Because of the high percentage of sandstone and lack of shale source and seal in the westernmost folds, very few fields in the western part of the basin are productive. Eastward, the amount of organic shale increases; in addition, the sizes of the fields, the amount of oil or gas preserved in each, and the structure improve, so that the best fields are in the east. Only two fields, however, had original reserves greater than 100 million barrels each, and the total remaining reserves of Sakhalin are less than 80 million barrels. There are

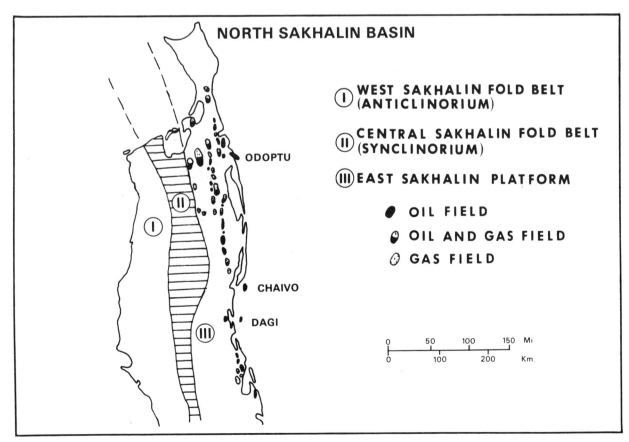

Figure 11

approximately 3.2 Tcf of gas reserves (Table 2). A total of 402 million barrels of oil has been produced in the area plus 238 Bcf of gas.

During the summer of 1977, a joint Japanese-Soviet group began to develop the offshore section of Odoptu field; this field is partly onshore but mainly offshore. Before 1977, several slant holes had been drilled and were productive from the late Miocene. The first offshore rig, while drilling in August 1977, encountered at least four zones in the Miocene which produced, during drill-stem tests, more than 2,000 barrels of oil per day. The field was hailed as possibly "the largest oil field found in eastern Asia," a statement which is patently untrue, inasmuch as Daqing in northeastern China has proved reserves greater than 8 billion barrels. The seismic data indicate that Odoptu probably is not much greater than Okha, the largest field on the island (originally 175,000,000 barrels or less).[69] Since the first successful well was drilled in 1977, eight more successful wells have been drilled, including the discovery wells for two more fields—Chaivo and Dagi Marine (Figure 11). Chaivo is mainly gas and condensate. Flows are promising. The first offshore production is planned for 1984 or 1985, but many problems associated with icebergs must be solved first.

The drilling of offshore Sakhalin is vital both to the USSR and Japan, but especially for the USSR which has no other energy resources on the Pacific coast. Most oil energy used must be transported by rail from West Siberia. Two small oil pipelines now extend from the North Sakhalin basin to the industrial areas of the mainland of the Soviet Far East. However, this oil will not last for many more years, and the strain on the Trans-Siberian Railway, because of the huge volumes of transported oil to the industrial centers of the Soviet Far East, makes it imperative that the Soviets find more oil in the Pacific coastal region.

To solve this energy problem and to build a large industrial base in the Soviet Far East, the Soviet Union is looking urgently for partners to help develop its potential petroleum resources in various areas. Most of the effort is being concentrated around Sakhalin Island.

## Pogranichnoye Graben

The location of the Pogranichnoye graben (1,050 square km) is shown on Figure 9. It is a small extension of the North Sakhalin basin. One commercial field was discovered there in 1971, and there is a possibility that two or three more fields may be discovered onshore. However, the greatest potential for this extension of the North Sakhalin basin is offshore. Several structures remain to be drilled.

## Terpeniye Gulf Basin

This basin (13,500 square km) is largely offshore, and has been explored thoroughly onshore. The only shows are of gas in a mud volcano in Late Cretaceous shale. Offshore drilling, in the opinion of the Soviet geologists, looks promising, but the graben system which goes through the Terpeniye Gulf is complicated by multiple faults and probably will yield only small fields, even offshore.

## Aniva Gulf Basin

Several small structures (seven anticlines) have been located in the onshore part of this basin (4,200 square km). The basin extends into eastern Hokkaido, where drilling commenced during 1978. In the Soviet part of the basin, one gas field in Miocene sandstone has been found. Plans were announced during 1980 to develop the field—East Lugovskoye. A second discovery appears to have been made, but a third anticline, with gas shows, was not commercial. The other anticlines remain to be tested adequately. The gas which has been discovered will be piped to the capital city at the south end of the island, Yuzhno-Sakhalinsk. The potential of the basin seems to be fairly good for small fields, particularly offshore, and the structure is less complicated than that of the Terpeniye Gulf basin.

## Tatar Strait Basin

This basin (Figure 9; 20,000 square km) occupies most of the Tatar Strait and extends onshore in different places along the western coast of central and southern Sakhalin. Numerous oil and gas seeps have been found in Eocene coastal-deltaic sediments in this area, and there are many coal beds in this section. The Oligocene appears to be moderately favorable, but the reservoir quality of the sandstones in the Eocene and Oligocene is extremely poor. The Miocene is largely volcanogenic, has no source materials, and no reservoirs. A large structure drilled on an offshore island off southwestern Sakhalin revealed the presence, beneath an upper Miocene tuffaceous sandstone sequence (with no seals), of a thick sequence of andesite lava flows in what is probably the lower or middle Miocene. In fact, there is a chain of submarine and partly emergent topographic highs offshore along the western coast of southern Sakhalin. The gamnetic data indicate that these are extinct volcanos. They are directly on strike with a long chain of Pliocene and Miocene (now extinct) volcanos in western Hokkaido and offshore from western Hokkaido. Soviet geologists are trying to get foreign companies to drill the Tatar Strait on the basis of numerous oil shows there. However, all of the structures that they have mapped appear to be volcanic plugs or volcanic piles, and the results from the five dry holes drilled offshore by the USSR and Japan support this statement. The potential of this area, in my opinion, is nearly zero.

## West Kamchatka Basins

The West Kamchatka basins (108,000 square km) include numerous anticlinal structures.[70] However, within the two basins present along the western shelf region of Kamchatka, the folds are strongly deformed and faulted, and many of them are overturned toward the west, even to the coastline. One small gas discovery was made during 1973 in the southwestern part of the peninsula in sandstones of Late Cretaceous age. This entire area of western Kamchatka is a foreland for the geosyncline farther east. However, even this relatively stable foreland has been strongly deformed. Although many structures remain to be drilled, all of those (with the one exception of the Late Cretaceous discovery) have been dry, or have had only minor shows with small flows (a few thousand cubic feet a day) of gas.

## North Okhotsk Basin

This extensive basin (45,000 square km) along the northern shelf area of the Sea of Okhotsk (Figure 9) is an east-west-striking feature with low-relief anticlinal structures. It has been very poorly mapped, and only two or three structures are known. There is perpetual ice flow in this area and it is difficult to shoot seismic lines. The sediment-source area includes zones of ancient granitic rocks which could have provided clean quartz sandstones through the basin. It is the most attractive prospect of all the basins around the Sea of Okhotsk, with the exception of the North Sakhalin basin.

## East Kamchatka Basin

This basin, shown on Figure 9 (28,000 square km), has numerous oil shows and seeps. Several small producing wells have been drilled, wells which produce from a Miocene sandstone at rates of from a few liters to a few barrels a day. Approximately 28 shallow holes have been drilled. Oil also occurs in the caldera of Uzon Volcano which is adjacent to the basin. This oil is brought up along the central conduit of the volcano to the surface from Miocene sandstones at depth. Between 1941 and 1957, 88 structural core holes (450 to 500 m) and five deeper wells (1,400 to 2,790 m) were drilled. Between 1957 and 1967, three anticlines were drilled, and the small flows mentioned above were found in impervious volcanic sandstones of the Miocene. The area has no big potential because so many of the potential reservoirs are of volcanic origin.

## Central Kamchatka Graben

The Central Kamchatka graben (Central Kamchatka-Olyutorka trough = 75,000 square km), shown on Figure 9, is the site of many gas seeps, presumably from the Miocene. The basin has not been explored extensively, because it contains thick nonporous graywacke sequences interbedded with tuffaceous beds and some lava flows. More than 11,000 m of section is present.

## Khatyrka Basin

The Khatyrka basin, shown on Figure 9, contains numerous anticlinal structures, oil and gas seeps, and shale or clay diapirs in an area onshore of 4,000 square km. Two wells have been drilled; one, drilled in 1970, was a small discovery in Oligocene sandstone. The seeps are from Oligocene sandstones, as well as from some Eocene and Miocene sandstones. This basin is a continuation of the

Navarin basin offshore which extends across the international boundary within the Bering Sea into the United States. Its potential probably is not great onshore, but could be large offshore.

## Anadyr Basin

The Anadyr basin, with a surface area onshore of more than 30,000 square km and an equivalent area offshore, probably extends eastward into the St. Lawrence basin, United States. It has been explored extensively onshore. More than 29 key wells, parametric wells, and exploratory wells have been drilled. The location of the basin is shown on Figure 9.

In 1972, two discoveries were made in the basin, but both proved to be noncommercial. Both wells found gas in the upper Miocene. Both wells tested between 7 million and 10 million cubic feet of dry (99 percent methane) gas per day.[71] On extended drill-stem tests, both wells went to water. A third structure (Tumanskaya) also found noncommercial hydrocarbons. Oil shows have been found in the Oligocene and Eocene.

The best reservoir properties were found in the Miocene. All older beds appear to be too tuffaceous to produce commercial quantities of oil or gas. However, seaward the sandstones show cleaner properties, particularly in the Miocene. When exploration begins offshore, it is very possible that commercial reserves of Miocene (and possibly older) gas will be found.

## Irkutsk Amphitheater and Proterozoic Hydrocarbons

The location of the Irkutsk amphitheater is shown on Figure 9, and a general map of the amphitheater is shown on Figure 12. The amphitheater, or basin, occupies a U-shaped southern extension of the Siberian platform on the southern margin of the Angara shield. The total area is 2,827,000 square km, and is the world's largest continental platform overlain by almost undisturbed Proterozoic and Early Cambrian marine sedimentary rocks; the prospective area is not less than 1,737,000 square km.

The basin is most unusual, because it was the site of deposition of 500 to 10,000 + m of marine Proterozoic (late Precambrian) terrigenous clastic sediments with indigenous Proterozoic oil and gas. Proterozoic oil and gas are almost unknown elsewhere in the world. Most of the reserves found to date are gas.[72] Twenty-two discoveries have been made, of which 13 are noncommercial. Five are good fields—ranging in size from medium-sized to giant.[73] The two fields at the northeastern end of the Irkutsk amphitheater have proved and probable Proterozoic and Lower Cambrian reserves of 16.45 trillion cubic feet. The first field discovered in this huge basin was Markovo (1962), with 26 million barrels of oil and condensate, and 0.6 Tcf of gas, more than 65 percent of it in the Proterozoic. Chemical and radiometric studies of the Proterozoic gas and condensate prove that they originated from Proterozoic marine algae which flourished between 588 and 925 million years ago. The only other Proterozoic fields in the world are Mereenie in the Amadeus basin of central Australia; Renqiu, just north of

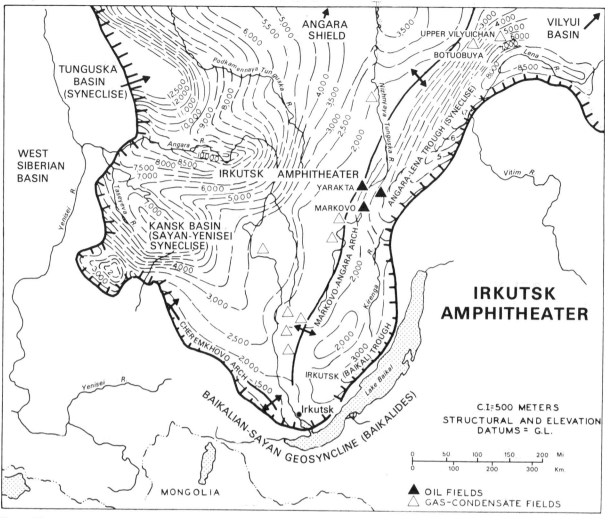

Figure 12
Structural contour map—top of metamorphosed basement (isopach map of post metamorphic proterozoic and early paleozoic rocks). Modified from Provodnikov, 1965.

Tianjin, and Weiyuan, Sichuan, both in China. Ultimate recovery from Proterozoic and Cambrian strata of the Irkutsk amphitheater will be about 100 million barrels of oil and condensate, and 200 Tcf of gas (Table 2).

## Future of the Soviet Petroleum Industry

Production, Reserves, and Resources

As of 31 December 1980, the Soviet Union had produced about 63 billion barrels of oil and 187 Tcf of gas (the figure for oil includes some condensate; the figure for gas includes an estimated 35 Tcf that has been flared, blown, or otherwise unrecorded). The remaining quantities of oil and gas—proved plus probable plus predicted (predicted = potential)—include a minimum of 82 billion barrels of oil and 763 Tcf of gas, exclusive of the West Siberian basin (Table 2). The West Siberian basin should contain not less than 194 billion barrels of additional oil and condensate, plus 1,880 Tcf of additional gas. This is a total of 335 billion

barrels of oil and 2,793 Tcf of gas to be found in the onshore areas of the Soviet Union. (The figure for liquids includes 54 billion barrels of natural gas liquids.)[74] These figures are considered excessive by many. However, ultimate recovery estimates made by the Ministry of Geology, the Ministry of Oil Industry, and the Ministry of Gas Industry, in conjunction with my work, suggest that these figures are reasonable. The CIA estimated that, of the oil remaining to be produced and/or found, only 35 to 40 billion barrels is proved (A + B categories).[75] The Oil and Gas Journal estimates that not less than 61 billion barrels of proved plus probable remains. A more recent study shows that proved reserves of oil and condensate do not exceed 43.5 billion barrels.[76]

In earlier predictions, I wrote that the Soviet Union ultimately would produce not less than 592 billion barrels of oil and condensate, and not less than 3,850 Tcf of gas, including the offshore.[77] More recent calculations indicate that these estimates are too high, inasmuch as the offshore would have to contain recoverable volumes of 261 billion barrels of oil (44 percent of the anticipated recoverable oil onshore) and 1,057 Tcf of gas.[78] Recalculation suggests that ultimate offshore recoverable (excluding the Barents Shelf and the proved fields of the offshore Caspian and Black seas) is closer to 155 billion barrels of oil and condensate and 358 Tcf of gas. (The figures given in the text differ from those in Table 2, because Table 2 is complete only through 1974 in 12 of the 15 basins, and through 1977 in three basins.)

There are some authors, such as Lvov, who estimate that the ultimate recovery—particularly gas—will be much greater than these figures.[79] Privately, some Soviet geologists at the ministerial-administrative level believe that oil totals will be less than predicted here, but the gas totals will be greater. If the Kara Sea geology (the offshore continuation of the West Siberian basin) is a continuation of the onshore geology, ultimate gas recovery may well approach the 3,850 Tcf figure predicted earlier.[80] I also agree that the figure of 490 billion barrels of oil and condensate may be high, but it is realistic on the basis of present geologic knowledge.

The *prospective* sedimentary-basin area of the Soviet Union is greater than the total area of either the United States or Canada. Conservatively, more than 900 undrilled surface and seismic structures remain in the Kopet Dag trough and the West Siberian basin alone. Only a few hundred wells have been drilled below 4,000 m, in areas where the section is known to have an average thickness greater than 5,000 m or more. The deep (greater than 4,000 m) prospective zones cover an area of not less than 1,000,000 square km. Almost all of the offshore Caspian Sea, as well as the onshore part of the North Caspian basin, is unexplored; the deep areas of the North Caucasus trough are unexplored except in a few scattered places; the northern part of the Black Sea shelf area is almost totally unexplored; the Kopet Dag basin is less than half explored; the West Siberian basin is less than half explored; the Vilyui basin is less than a fifth explored; the Timan-Pechora basin (onshore) is less than half explored, its offshore extension in the Barents Sea and the Arctic shelf area east of the Urals are both totally unexplored. In addition, the basin areas around the Aral Sea and the Chu-Sarysu basin are mostly unexplored.

The problem, therefore, as stated earlier, is not a lack of resources; it is a lack of technology to develop the deeper zones and the offshore areas, plus a lack of equipment and technology to explore even the shallow areas at a pace sufficient to keep up with growing production needs. This conclusion leads to a discussion of what has been called "the Soviet energy crisis" and a review of the different viewpoints which have been published concerning it.

The Soviet Energy Crisis

The Soviet economy, now in the 11th Five-Year Plan, clearly is experiencing difficulties in the energy sector. At first glance, these difficulties would appear to be no more serious than those encountered in other industries, such as agriculture, steel, and cement, except that all other industries also depend on the energy sector to sustain

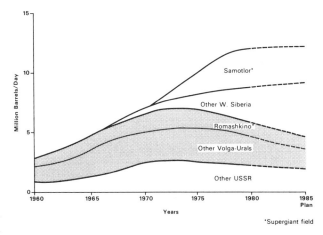

Figure 13

them. Consequently, the health of the Soviet oil and gas industries, which supply 72 percent of the USSR's fuel mix, is vital for the nation's survival. If the industry is experiencing difficulties, the effects will not be limited to the Soviet Union. I review briefly some of the problems which have been discussed in the Soviet literature, by Western observers, and with me by Soviet officials during my nine years as a consultant with the Ministry of Oil Industry.

First, it is instructive to see what actually is happening in the Soviet oil and gas industry. Figures 13 through 21 provide an overview of the industry, particularly the oil industry. Figure 13 shows USSR oil production from 1960 through 1980. It is plain from the figure that production is declining almost everywhere except in West Siberia. The great importance of the Samotlor field is clear, as is that of Romashkino. (Samotlor, the country's largest field, at Nizhnevartovsk, is in West Siberia; Romashkino is at Almetyevsk in the Volga-Urals basin.) Figure 14 shows

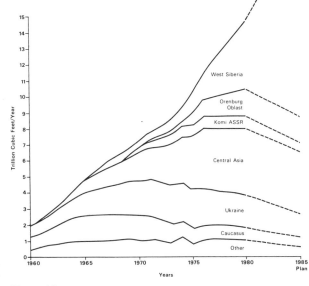

Figure 14

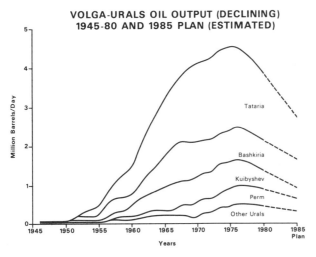

Figure 15

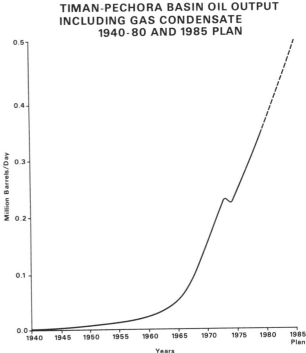

Figure 17

gas output in the USSR from 1960 to 1980, and indicates that most areas are growing or holding even. Only a few areas show decline.

Figure 15 shows oil output by district within the Volga-Urals basin, the principal producing area of the Soviet Union until 1977. Figure 16 shows the remaining areas of oil-production decline—the Ukraine, North Caucasus, Kazakhstan, Turkmenia, Belorussia, and Azerbaijan. The only bright spots on the horizon are shown on Figures 17 and 18 which indicate production in areas of oil-production increase—the Timan-Pechora basin (Komi ASSR), Sakhalin, Georgia and parts of Central Asia. The four areas together produced only 470,000 barrels per day in 1980, so that their contribution to the USSR's overall production is not sufficient to reverse the declines outside of West Siberia.

Figures 19 and 20 only make the picture more dismal. The two figures show the finding rates (barrels of oil found per foot drilled) outside of and within West Siberia. Figure 21, which shows the average new well flows in West Siberia, also presents the Soviet government's official forecast through 1990 for new well flows in West Siberia. The data on Figure 21 only make the future out-

look more discouraging. In fact, all of the curves on Figures 13 through 21 were compiled from Soviet sources as well as Shabad's "News Notes" in *Soviet Geography*.[81] Thus the Soviets not only are well aware of their problem, but are doing little to disguise it.

The initial guidelines for the 10th Five-Year Plan required an increase of crude-oil and condensate production from 3.584 billion barrels (491 million metric tons = mmt) in 1975 to 4.526–4.672 billion barrels (620 to 640 mmt) by 1980. Natural gas production was to increase from 10.1 Tcf (389 million m³ = mm³) in 1975 to 14.0–15.2 Tcf (400 to 435 mm³) by 1980. The final five-year plan published in late 1976 stated that the 1980 goals should conform to the higher limit of the initial range (4.672 billion barrels and 15.2 Tcf). Press reports during 1977

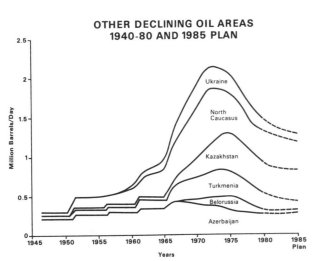

Figure 16

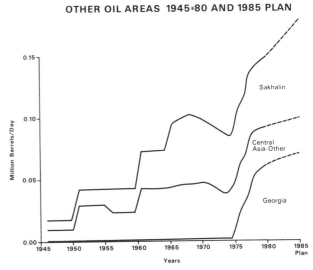

Figure 18

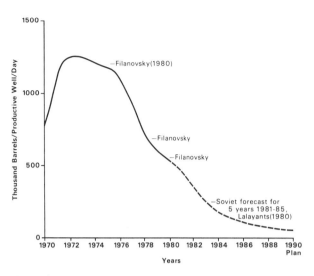

**FINDING RATE OF OIL PER FOOT DRILLED OUTSIDE WEST SIBERIA**

Figure 19

**OIL DISCOVERY RATE AND PROJECTION FOR WEST SIBERIA**

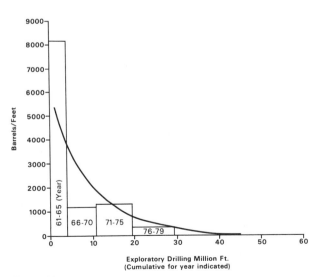

Figure 20

**WEST SIBERIA- NEW WELL FLOWS 1970-1980-1990**

Figure 21

said that oil- and gas-production costs were rising steadily, partly for unavoidable reasons and partly because of "bad management." There have been repeated published complaints about (1) the waste in all types of energy and (2) the increasing proportions of oil and gas that must be piped rapidly, at higher costs, from West Siberia and Central Asia. Moreover, apparently, as the result of a reluctance to publicize production declines, most oil and gas producing republics of the USSR ceased the publication of production statistics in 1977.[82]

In 1977, crude-oil and condensate production increased above that of 1976 by only 190 million barrels (5 percent) to 10.92 million barrels per day, or 29.2 million barrels below target for the year; production during 1978 reached 11.42 million barrels per day, or 4.168 billion

barrels, which also is 29.2 million below the year's target; 1979 production was only 11.72 million barrels per day, or 4.28 billion barrels, or 51 million below target; 1980 production was 12.06 million barrels per day, or 4.4 billion barrels, also below target. (For various summaries of the problems and suggested remedies, read Graifer, Arzhanov, and others.)[83] It is clear that the original goals were not met. In contrast, the gas industry has been doing nicely, with the 1977, 1978, 1979, and 1980 goals being exceeded by 6 to 8 percent.[84] The increasing oil shortfall which became apparent during the early 1970s, became the topic of five well-known CIA reports[85] that have caused considerable world controversy, increasing debates among rival observers in the West, and sizable profits to at least one European consulting firm which adopted a position diametrically opposed to that of the CIA. A little publicized fact is that the Soviet Embassy staffs in both Washington and New York were formally briefed by the CIA before the 1977 report was published. The debates that have continued ever since in the West already were debates in the Soviet Union during the 1960s.[86] They are the topics of continuing debates and heated discussions in the USSR within the Politburo, the Council of Ministers, the Central Committee, and Gosplan, especially where West Siberia is involved.[87] The USSR is facing a severe crisis, as regular reading of the Soviet press and literature establishes beyond any doubt, and which Neporozhny stressed at an October 1979 symposium in Moscow (see Figures 15, 16, 19, 20, 21).[88] This crisis was emphasized most dramatically by the unprecedented visit of Leonid I. Brezhnev himself to the West Siberian fields during April 1978 and by his December 1979 speech, in which he outlined the "belt-tightening" measures required to conserve energy. At the same time, the administrative structure and the administration heads of the West Siberian area were thoroughly reshuffled. Brezhnev's comments were given the greatest possible publicity within the USSR (and are unprecedented in the sense that they were directed at the inefficiency of the USSR's most important industry). Today Soviet journals are replete with articles which suggest remedies for West Siberia's lagging production, including proposals to import 2 to 3 million workers and up to 60,000 engineers into Tyumen Oblast, as well as other vital logistical needs to the West Siberian basin.[89]

Because it is clear from Soviet publications that there is indeed an energy crisis, it might seem unnecessary to review the arguments in great detail. However, because of the general ignorance outside of the Soviet Union of the extent of the crisis and of the debates, the salient facts are worth reviewing.

The CIA Reports

The principal theses of the CIA reports follow:[90]

(1) USSR proved reserves generally are the same as those of the United States—possibly somewhat more—in the 30 to 40 billion barrels range. (This figure may be too low, but proved plus probable reserves for the USSR almost certainly are no higher than 43.5 billion barrels.)

(2) Soviet oil production might peak as early as 1978 at 11 to 12 million barrels of oil and condensate per day. Peaking would be no later than about 1982. (In 1980, production was 12.06 million barrels and rising at a rate of a little over one percent per year.)

(3) There is little chance that new oil discoveries (of which there has been only one since Samotlor in 1965: i.e., Fedorovsk) will be found in time to increase appreciably the reserves-to-production ratio.

(4) Abundant resources remain to be discovered in the Arctic, eastern Siberia, and offshore, but it will take at least 8 to 10 years to find and develop these for exploitation.

(5) The production from oil fields, particularly the Volga-Urals basin, will decline.

(6) The giant Samotlor oil field of the West Siberian basin was to reach peak production about 1980 and hold that peak for no more than four years. Production at Samotlor during 1980 was close to 3 million barrels per day. The Nizhnevartovsk oilfield administration, which includes Samotlor and lesser adjacent fields produced 4.05 million barrels a day in 1980, or two-thirds of West Siberian output.

(7) Because of the predicted production decline, the USSR was expected to compete for OPEC oil by the mid-1980s. A large volume of imports was seen by the CIA as a potential irritant in international relations that might lead to direct confrontation between Japan and the West, on the one hand, and the Soviet Union, on the other, competing for OPEC oil. (Subsequently, the CIA revised its estimate, saying that large Soviet oil imports by the mid-1980s were unlikely.)

(8) The principal reason for the Soviet failure to maintain or even increase its reserves-to-production ratio is its backward technology, for which there is little hope of significant improvement for several years—too late to help the existing crisis.

These conclusions are supported by some and contested by others. Even though imports of some Western

technology (e.g., BJ and Reda submersible pumping units) have pushed the Soviet Union's production peaking to 1983–85, these imports still are not sufficient to stem indefinitely the rising tide of Soviet production problems.

To illustrate the divergent Western opinions on the topic of Soviet oil production, I have selected those by Jermol and Magnusson, Park, and Segal for their diversity of viewpoints concerning the Soviet production problems.[91] The validity of their conclusions, as well as those of the CIA and myself, are understood best in the context of what has been published in the Soviet press and literature. The next three sections, therefore, summarize some pertinent Soviet literature and press statements.

Summary of Soviet Publications

Many Soviet publications have stressed the technical problems facing the Soviet petroleum industry—in drilling, oil-production and pumping equipment, pipeline construction, and the development of remote oil and gas fields, particularly in the West Siberian basin.[92] Until recently, most Soviet experts regarded the West Siberian basin's petroleum potential as vast, although underexplored and underdeveloped. Future industry development, however, was expected to be hindered by growing infrastructure problems as operations moved outward from present production centers.[93] During 1977, Kontorovich and Yerofeyev—along with other leading Soviet geologists—reappraised West Siberia's future petroleum potential, as well as other highly prospective areas, through 1990.[94] They concluded that the outlook had changed markedly for the worse. They concluded further that the future discovery of new oil and gas fields would be more complicated than in the past. In October 1979, Pyotr Neporozhny, the Minister of Power and Electrification, published four "scenarios" of the Soviet power mix for the years 1990 and 2000.[95] The contents of these scenarios should end the debate over Soviet energy problems once and for all.

During late 1977 and early 1978, high-level Soviet officials focused attention on the need to conserve all types of resources, especially energy. In December 1977, Brezhnev raised the issue before a Central Committee meeting. The theme which he presented has been reiterated in numerous speeches and press articles, and was illustrated dramatically by his April 1978 visit to the West Siberian fields in Tyumen Oblast. The key points of Brezhnev's conservation program are:[96]

(1) In all phases of industry, no element is more important than that of fuel and energy.

(2) Oil and gas, most of it from Tyumen, will continue to play a decisive role in the supply of fuel and energy to the country.

(3) The groundwork has been laid for the development of West Siberia's production. The next step, finding new resources there, must be carried on "with all urgency."

(4) Coal will have an important place in the present and the future of the USSR's energy balance. (Actually the coal industry has not been performing well in recent years. Gross mine output reached a record of 724 million

tons in 1978, and then began a slow decline, to 711 million in 1981.) Hydropower and nuclear power developments are to "proceed at an exceptionally rapid pace."

Before Brezhnev's speech, one could infer from Soviet literature that the resources of Tyumen were infinite. After the speech, a decided air of uncertainty entered all writings about Tyumen. Predictions that Tyumen's annual production would rise eventually to 3.65 billion barrels (500 million tons) of oil and 17.5 Tcf (500 Bcm) of gas became "goals to be desired," and the prediction that Tyumen ultimately would produce not less than 150 billion barrels of oil were toned down. However, in early 1981, Farman K. Salmanov, the chief of the Tyumen Geological Administration, again affirmed that Tyumen Oblast had the potential of reaching a 1990 production of 450 to 500 million tons of oil and 1,000 billion cubic meters of gas.[97]

Kontorovich and his colleagues reviewed the entire history of the development of Tyumen Oblast, and noted that the obvious structural traps had been found and tested.[98] They noted further than almost all production from Tyumen currently is from structural traps. They then discussed in detail the different criteria for identifying future structural traps, and the criteria and tools necessary to identify and discover stratigraphic traps. Of the 250 oil and gas fields found in Tyumen and Tomsk, almost all are structural. Only 170 are commercial; 80 are noncommercial; 174 dry structures had been drilled. Kontorovich proposed a deliberate search for obscure and difficult-to-find traps. However, the problems of finding such traps involve the development and use of highly sophisticated technology which is not available in the Soviet Union. Therefore, present efforts are being placed on increasing production from known fields, and on beginning production from discovered, but undeveloped fields. There are a fair number of the latter, but, with the exception of Fedorovsk, they are small in contrast to the huge fields which have been exploited to date.

*Sotsialisticheskaya industriya* (12 April 1978, p. 1) reported: "General Secretary L. I. Brezhnev reemphasized the need to increase oil and gas production in Tyumen during his April visit. Nearly all of the two dozen fields which are being produced, including Samotlor, have reached their planned levels of production. This means that, to ensure growth, the country must develop new fields. This task is complicated by the fact that each new field is 20 to 30 kilometers from existing population centers and production bases. The construction of roads and the supply of power are behind schedule." Both road and pipeline construction and the number of meters drilled during the 10th Five-Year Plan would have had to be triple the figures of the 9th Plan if Tyumen was to meet the plan of 2.3 billion barrels of oil and condensate from West Siberia during 1980. The 1980 plan was just barely met, with 2.28 billion barrels (312 million metric tons).

In August 1977, *Pravda* spelled out the need to accelerate petroleum development in Tyumen.[99] The article (by I. I. Nesterov) noted first that only a part of the potential oil and gas reserves had been found. New discoveries were to be expected along the middle Ob River and in the northern part of the oblast. However, Nesterov carefully qualified his statements about potential reserves by underscoring the need to *intensify* the search.

Nesterov went on to point out that a new and more complex phase of petroleum exploration was commencing along the Ob River and that all simple structural-type fields had been located and mapped. This conclusion, considering the huge size of the basin, is questionable and may be based on the poor seismic technology employed. In any case, he wrote that several prominent geologists agreed that now was the time to search for nonstructural traps in the oblast. The article went on to state that Tyumen geologists had failed to meet the plan for new oil and condensate reserves in 1976 for the first time in 15 years. Nesterov cited two reasons for the failure of the Tyumen Geological Administration: (1) "The poor quality of Soviet geophysical equipment" and (2) the failure of drilling crews to meet their drilling quotas "for quite some period of time." *Pravda* then observed that "He who drills little will find little."

As discussed elsewhere in this paper, the greater depth at which future fields will be found is at the root of the Soviet problem. Future discovery depths will be from 2,500 to 6,000 m, below the range of the Soviet seismographs and well below the economic range of the turbodrill (especially from 3,000 to 6,000 m).

In October 1977, a Deputy Oil Minister, N. S. Yerofeyev, and coauthors stressed the need for much scientific and technical improvement in geophysics and in drilling, if the goals of the 25th Party Congress were to be carried out.[100] Four areas in which improved drilling methods are needed were stressed:

1. Better drilling fluids to cope with anomalous high-pressure formations;
2. More advanced deep-drilling methods and technology for operation at depths of 5,000 m or more;
3. Construction of light-weight and highly mobile drilling units (like U.S. jackknife rigs) for more rapid moves from one drilling location to the next—with special emphasis on quality for severe operating conditions;
4. Improved technology for identifying and testing potential producing strata in the course of drilling operations.

Four areas for improvement in geophysical-exploration techniques were also listed:

1. New seismic methods for locating and mapping deep structures below salt beds (in the European USSR) and for finding subtle or deep structural traps;
2. New seismic methods for locating stratigraphic traps in sedimentary rock complexes at great depths;
3. New geophysical (and computerized) methods for predicting cross-section views of the earth from seismic records and well logs;
4. Better well-logging techniques to evaluate potentially productive formations, their physical and chemical parameters, and related phenomena, particularly in deep carbonate (limestone and dolomite) rocks.

Yerofeyev and his colleagues concluded that achievement of the planned increases in national production of oil and gas would be impossible if there were no improvement in geological/geophysical exploratory work, both in old and in new producing areas. The research and development branches of the petroleum industry are to play a decisive role in developing these new techniques (no mention was made of foreign imports). The authors wrote that "most of the equipment and technology needs were identified *at least a decade ago* and *all remain unfulfilled today*" (italics added).[101]

In 1974, the Soviet Union's daily production exceeded that of the United States for the first time since 1902, as output reached 9.82 million barrels per day. Thus huge production was made possible by (1) the discovery of deeper fields in West Siberia, and (2) the completion of several major pipelines to fields previously developed but not produced. Except for the shallow Cenomanian gas deposits of the northern part of the West Siberian basin, most of the new fields of West Siberia are at a depth of 1.6 to 2.4 km, deeper than the Volga-Urals fields (1.1 to 2.0 km). New discoveries, therefore, will be well below 2.0 km and most will be in the 3.2 to 5.5 km range, which is below the economic depth limits of the turbodrill.

Basin et al. outlined six additional types of hydrocarbon entrapment for which no scientific-technical solutions were available.[102] By 1980, Soviet geologists were no closer to solutions of the problems outlined by Basin et al. than they were in 1977 or, for that matter, in 1967. It takes rubles and manpower for research and development, and if people and funds are not allotted for this specific purpose, the research and development will not be done. It is one of the great contradictions of the USSR's modern economic history that no one in the Soviet Government will make this vital decision.

Many outside observers have pointed out repeatedly that the USSR petroleum industry has not attempted to develop numerous discoveries reported from the Volga-Urals and West Siberian basin.[103] (The implication is that development of these discoveries will solve the crisis.) What these observers apparently do not understand is that the undeveloped Volga-Urals discoveries are, for reasons outlined by Maksimov et al., uneconomic by *any* standard;[104] and that the West Siberian deposits are small and at almost economically prohibitive distances from existing pipelines and other support facilities. They can be developed economically only if large new fields are found close to them, or if they lie along a logical pipeline route which will be constructed at some future date. The only other way to develop them is to make a decision to do it, regardless of cost.

A fact which underscores the point that the undeveloped discoveries in the Volga-Urals and other basins are uneconomic by any standard is the intensified exploration which has taken place since 1976 for small fields, especially in the Volga-Urals. Several significant, but small, discoveries have been made and are being brought into production rapidly. In addition, the North Caspian basin has been the site of giant gas-condensate discoveries (Astrakhan on the southwest rim and Karachaganak on the northern rim—Figure 2), so that this basin will be explored more intensively. Moreover, a

large part of the eastern margin of the Volga-Urals basin is an "overthrust belt," similar to that in the Rocky Mountain states of the U.S. Exploration of this Urals overthrust belt has intensified; the major technological problems which are being encountered are (1) failure of seismic equipment to penetrate below the thrust sheets; (2) lack of deep-drilling equipment which can reach subthrust rocks economically; and (3) lack of equipment for high-pressure subsurface conditions (i.e., rotary drills, muds and mud programs for high-pressure formations, blowout preventors, etc.).

The severity of the Soviet energy crisis was brought forcefully to the attention of USSR and foreign observers in early 1980, in an article by one of the USSR's most respected industry spokesmen. Academician Aleksandr P. Krylov, chairman of the Academy of Sciences' Research Council on Oilfield Development, wrote that, if present Soviet practices of drilling infill wells rather than increasing numbers of exploration wells continues, "production in our country will reach a maximum in a relatively short time, after which it will start to fall.[105] Although he himself won the Lenin Prize for introducing waterflood methods in the Romashkino field, he stressed that there was no way for the USSR to avert a production decline unless the entire approach toward exploration and exploitation, including waterflood methods, was altered drastically and at once. (Academician Krylov died May 1981 at the age of 76.)

As a consequence of the deteriorating conditions within the petroleum industry, Melentyev and Makarov wrote of the need to (1) stabilize oil production, (2) promptly increase gas production, and (3) ultimately increase coal production so that the fuel balance (now 72 percent oil and gas, 25 percent coal, 3 percent other sources) will begin to reverse.[106] Contrary to prospects in the mid-1970s, when planners were looking to coal to replace oil under boilers, the strategy has now changed in favor of gas, with coal expected to play a greater role only toward the end of the 1980s and beyond.

### West Siberia's Needs

The following is a brief condensation of articles in *Pravda, Planovoye khozyaistvo* and *Neftyanoye khozyaistvo*.[107] These are articles by high Soviet officials and their spokesmen. The most interesting is that by Arzhanov in *Neftyanoye khozyaistvo*, largely because it is detailed and explicit in its condemnation of existing practices, the equipment in use, and future needs if West Siberia is to "save" the USSR's production goals. Perhaps the most illuminating part of the articles is that the Soviet spokesmen, imbued with a "five-year plan mentality" (i.e., the inability, through decades of training, to see more than 5 to 10 years ahead at a time), limited their remarks to the solution of their problems through 1980, the last five-year plan. Almost no one considered the long-range solutions, or the question: "After 1980, what?"

On 26 January 1978, an expanded collegium of Soviet petroleum-industry officials was called into session to adopt new 1978 goals that would comply with the revised national economic plan adopted at the December 1977 session of the Central Committee. The chief of the main Tyumen Oil and Gas Trust, F. G. Arzhanov, obviously inspired by Brezhnev's speech, announced the new tasks for the Tyumen administration. He summarized 1977's achievements, including the production of 1.54 billion barrels (211.2 million mt) of oil and condensate; the drilling of 1,485 wells on production, all exceeding the original 1977 plan. The remainder of Arzhanov's report dwelt on 1977 shortfalls and the effects of such shortfalls on 1978 and later plans. The shortfalls included the failure to meet the goal of finding new reserves to exceed the volume of oil produced; the breakdown of rigs; the shortage of rigs; the reequipping of oil-flowing wells with pumps; and the lack of roads, housing, and electricity. Only 3,135 wells were equipped with submersible downhole pumps during 1977, versus the plan to place pumps in 4,542 wells.

During 1978, the Tyumen administration was to produce 1.794 billion barrels (245.7 mmt) and to drill 5.1 million meters in new wells. However, actual production was projected at 1.779 billion barrels (243.7 mmt) because the 33 percent increase in meterage was not met (3.8 to 5.1 million meters). At an average depth of 2,587 m per well, at least 1,972 new wells would have to be drilled in 1978 (this goal was not met). The wells brought into production during 1978 would have to produce 176 million barrels (24.1 mmt), averaging 321 barrels per day per well (44 mt per day). Output from the existing (pre-1978) wells was set at 1.618 billion barrels (221.6 mmt), averaging about 766 barrels per day (105 mt per day). Arzhanov hedged by noting that this plan could be met only if depletion of the older producing capacity did not exceed 1.5 percent for the year (depletion for 1977 was 2.5 percent and production of these same wells obviously would *increase* the percentage of depletion, not decrease it).

Drillers were presented with the problem of drilling 1.3 million additional meters. In addition, Arzhanov stated that it would be necessary during 1978 and 1979 to develop smaller and more remote discoveries. Also, the related infrastructure would have to be dealt with—the construction of roads, housing, electricity, etc. In addition to 10 new fields brought into production during 1977–78, 13 others would have to be put on stream by 1980. Of the 8 new fields to be brought on stream during 1978, only 4 would have completed access roads during 1978 and just 7 would have electricity to power the diesel-electric drilling rigs. Skilled workers were too few to complete the infrastructure construction, and more would have to be brought from other regions of the country that were also labor poor (2 to 3 million workers, according to Fainburg, would have to be shifted to West Siberia).[108] In addition, drillers would have to drill 3.8 million meters in new wells at the small fields during 1979; and 6.0 million additional meters at these fields during 1979; and 6.0 million additional meters at these fields during 1980. (These figures excluded drilling targets in the huge Tyumen gas fields.) If these goals were accomplished, the 1980 West Siberian goal of 2.3 billion barrels (315 mt) could be met. This drilling would have to be accompanied by the completion of 820 km of hard-surface roads, 1,170 km of electric power lines, and

3,590,000 sq m of new housing. (The goals through 1979 were not met.)

An additional 445 new drilling rigs, with support equipment (servicing trucks, helicopters, etc.) also would be required. However, 1977 rig deliveries fell below those of 1976. Moreover, the number of producing wells in 1980, to meet the meterage and production quotas, would have to be more than two times the 1977 active rig count, and the number of pumping units (downhole submersible pumps) would have to be 3.5 times greater than during 1977. All of this activity would result in more breakdowns and would therefore require more maintenance, which meant additional machinery and mechanics. Arzhanov concluded that the main Tyumen Oil and Gas Trust would have to consider the question of adopting "more supplementary measures" in order to reach the 1980 goal of 2.3 billion barrels.

Drilling plans have fallen behind because of rig and drilling-crew shortages. The number of development wells required is far behind schedule. Additions to reserves have fallen short of goals for three years.[109] Moreover, Samotlor, Ust-Balyk, and Mamontovo, the largest productive fields, are at peak production, or reached peak production during 1979, and Fedorovsk is barely coming on stream. Even with Fedorovsk's production, production levels will increase only slightly, because it will reach its peak as Samotlor begins to decline.

Therefore, the problem is not only one of technology, but also of trained manpower. Fainburg's plan to bring in 2 to 3 million additional workers is drastic, and would be only a temporary solution.[110] Regardless, the new people brought in would have to be trained, and people-power is not a substitute for adequate technology and related logistic support.

Brezhnev's Speech and the Neporozhny Report

On 15 December 1979, TASS reported a Brezhnev speech that seemed to support the CIA studies. Brezhnev noted the fact that oil-production goals were not being met and that, as a result, the Soviet people would have to "consolidate their wills" to conserve energy. Brezhnev noted that oil-production goals had not been met for some time, and that strong conservation measures would have to be taken. These included the installation of more fast breeder reactors and new nuclear power plants; a rapid expansion of the coal industry; increases in the use of hydroelectric power; conversion where possible to gas energy and an increase in gas production; and the use of oil and gas "with foresight." "Belt tightening" was to be strict in the civilian sector.

Brezhnev's speech was foreshadowed by an interesting paper delivered in October 1979 by Pyotr Neporozhny, Minister of Power and Electrification, to the joint Soviet-British Symposium on Power Engineering.[111] He wrote that the emphasis on oil and gas was to be changed; the oil and gas "happy period is over, and the power industry of the world is now entering its new and possibly most difficult period of development."[112] He also said that, "We think that with rational expenditure of energy resources it would be possible to secure a decreasing ratio of energy use to gross national output."[113] He noted further that electricity and nuclear power will increase substantially in future USSR planning. He then published four different "scenarios" for the future Soviet energy mixes—each based on a different set of conditions. The results of each set of conditions are reproduced here as Table 3 (the assumptions are not important here, because the end results are similar). It should be clear from Table 3 that the Soviet government plans to deemphasize the use of oil and condensate, and to give a larger role to gas—and possibly to coal—until nuclear energy and hydropower are built up.

### The 1978 PetroStudies Report

In September 1978, M. M. Jermol and L. A. Magnusson of the PetroStudies consulting company in Malmö, Sweden, published a report taking issue with the CIA predictions.[114] PetroStudies contended that the Soviet Union was consistently *under*producing each of its fields and that the lack of development of several hundred fields in the Soviet Union was part of an official policy to conserve oil and gas for the future. In November 1979, PetroStudies published an even stronger document.[115] Because these reports have been circulated widely in Western and Japanese companies and government circles, especially among economic planning groups, much confusion has resulted. For this reason, I review the reports in some detail.

On the basis of their assumption, Jermol and Magnusson concluded that "*total Soviet imports to the West may triple by 1985* in comparison with 1977, reaching a volume of 185 million metric tons (3.7 million barrels daily); the bulk of this oil would go to Western Europe where the *Russians may capture nearly one-fourth of the 1985 market* for crude oil and refined products, compared with a share of 9.7 percent in 1977" (italics by Jermol and Magnusson).[116] Moreover, this goal was not to be attained by the discovery of new reserves or the modernization of technology, but by a change in the economic criteria that the authors said were being used to determine oil-field production.

The PetroStudies authors further asserted that the CIA had made misleading statements about water cuts in Soviet fields (a contention that was correct in only one instance—Samotlor), that the CIA had confused the Samotlor field with the Romashkino field in the Volga-Urals basin (which was not true), and that the Soviets routinely produce oil and gas fields at minimum capacity rather than at maximum capacity. Here the PetroStudies authors suggested a lack of knowledge of the Soviet literature and, at least as important, of first-hand field observations; they also appear to have mistranslated some of the literature that they used.

The PetroStudies conclusion that Soviet fields were being produced at minimum capacity was based on published studies of the All-Union Oil Research Institute in Moscow, whose personnel developed a mathematical formula for ideal production rates for oil wells. This idealized formula was wrongly assumed by Jermol and Magnusson to be the formula used in actual Soviet practice. Since the assumption was the basis for the remainder of their report, their final conclusions were largely erroneous. Several examples follow.

Although the PetroStudies authors were correct in criticizing the CIA for applying a 47 percent water cut to the Samotlor field as a whole (only marginal or edge wells actually produced 47 percent water), Jermol and Magnusson were wrong in condemning the CIA reports in their entirety with regard to the discussion of water cuts. In 1979, water cuts rose to more than 15 percent in the field as a whole, according to several published articles[117] and it increased to 52 percent during 1977. It is still rising. The average water cut for the West Siberian basin was 15.8 percent in 1976, a figure that has since risen to 23 percent or more in the older large fields.

The West Siberian fields were not developed according to a preset formula for minimizing costs. Moreover, they were developed at different rates than the Volga-Urals fields. The PetroStudies authors cited the work of I. D. Karyagin as their authority for the statement that the West Siberian fields were developed slowly on the model of the Volga-Urals fields.[118] In actual fact, Karyagin wrote that the Volga-Urals model was not acceptable for West

TABLE 3
Four Schemes for the Future Energy Mix in the USSR (in percent)

| Case | Year | Oil and Condensate | Gas | Coal | Nuclear | Hydro | Other |
|---|---|---|---|---|---|---|---|
| Case 1 | 1975 | 43 | 21 | 30 | nil(0.06) | 1 | 5 |
| | 1990 | 36–37 | 27–26 | 27–28 | 4–5 | 2 | 3 |
| | 2000 | 28–30 | 28–27 | 28–31 | 11–13 | 2 | 2 |
| Case 2 | 1975 | 43 | 21 | 30 | nil(0.06) | 1 | 5 |
| | 1990 | 34–35 | 26–27 | 28–29 | 5–6 | 2 | 2 |
| | 2000 | 25–27 | 26–29 | 31–33 | 13–15 | 3 | 2 |
| Case 3 | 1975 | 43 | 21 | 30 | nil(0.06) | 1 | 5 |
| | 1990 | 33–35 | 31–33 | 25–27 | 6–7 | 1.5–2.0 | 2–3 |
| | 2000 | 25–30 | 25–30 | 26–29 | 8–10 | 4–5 | 2–3 |
| Case 4 | 1975 | 43 | 21 | 30 | nil(0.06) | 1 | 5 |
| | 1990 | 33–35 | 31–33 | 25–27 | 6–7 | 1.5–2.0 | 4–5 |
| | 2000 | 25–30 | 25–30 | 27.5–33 | 8–10 | 2–3 | 2–3 |

SOURCE: Neporozhny (1979).

Siberian development, because faster development rates were needed. An analysis in *Ekonomika neftyanoi promyshlennosti* showed that the West Siberian fields were developed twice as fast as the Volga-Urals fields, at greater expense, and with higher water cuts.[119] Another article in *Ekonomika neftyanoi promyshlennosti* made it clear that the producing fields of West Siberia were approaching their levels of maximum production (through maximum pumping of oil and maximum water injection).[120] The article stated further that 7 large to giant fields had reached their peak output. The article noted that 3 fields of the 7 never reached their planned level; that 2 reached the planned level but declined after one year; and that only 2 exceeded the planned production level.

Jermol and Magnusson appear to have ignored a large literature on overproduction and wasteful production practices, starting with the article by M. F. Mirchink (this article was discussed in a preceding section).[121]

The PetroStudies report cited M. M. Umansky, who had noted that only half of the discovered fields in the European USSR had been opened to development.[122] However, there were good reasons why these fields had not been opened for development—poor porosity, low permeability, tiny reserves, heavy oil, high sulfur or $CO_2$ content, reasons explained in the classic book by Maksimov et al.[123] Yet the PetroStudies report stated of the shut-in fields: "The Soviets thus have a substantial volume of passive oil reserves right at the doorstep, so to say, of the local refineries located in areas with well-developed infrastructure."[124]

The authors paid little attention to the fact that (a) infill drilling has begun at Samotlor (infill drilling begins when the first net of wells begins to show production declines); (b) there have been three full rounds of infill drilling at most of the Volga-Urals fields (Romashkino had a fourth set drilled); and (c) it was the introduction of submersible downhole pumps (11,000 of Soviet manufacture; more than 1,200 of United States manufacture) that enabled the Volga-Urals production level to maintain a peak level for three years beyond the decline originally predicted by Soviet planners. (United States pumps last 4 to 5 times longer than Soviet-built pumps.) There is a substantial literature on all of these subjects, as well as on the shortcomings of Soviet-built technology.

Jermol and Magnusson wrote: "Samotlor's annual withdrawal rates have been very low, despite the high absolute levels of output. By April 1978, the field's cumulative output was 500 million tons, or only 16.7 percent of the recoverable reserves."[125] Projection of the 16.7-percent figure means that the recoverable reserve is 22 billion barrels, a figure that is at least 40 percent too high. V. D. Shashin, the late Soviet Minister of Oil Industry, announced in 1969, in a widely publicized statement, that ultimate recovery from the field would be about 14.6 billion barrels;[126] Clarke et al. speculated that ultimate recovery might be as high as 11 billion barrels.[127] Present performance suggests that Samotlor will produce at least 15.5 billion barrels. The in-place reserves at Samotlor are known to be 27 billion barrels; Jermol and Magnusson's statement, therefore, implies about an 80 percent recovery factor (30 to 43 percent recovery rates are more normal; in fact, anything higher than 56 percent is almost unknown for an oil field).

## The 1979 PetroStudies Report

The 1979 report, titled *Soviet Proved Oil Reserves, 1946–80* stated that proved oil reserves in the USSR were 153 billion barrels and that these were the largest proved reserves of any nation on earth.[128] The 153-billion-barrel figure hinges on (1) the authors' interpretation of a quotation from Nesterov et al.[129] and (2) the authors' interpretation of the Soviet $C_1$ reserve category. Following is a review of these assumptions.

Nesterov et al. wrote the following: "Within the Jurassic, Neocomian, and Aptian-Albian-Cenomanian deposits that are in the region studied in West Siberia, the average rates of deposition were 20,000, 76,000, and 174,000 cubic kilometers per 1,000,000 years. These volumes are roughly proportional to the volumes of explored reserves that are present."[130]

Since only the explored reserves for gas are known, the PetroStudies authors converted the gas into oil-equivalent-gas volumes and calculated the volume of oil from the volumes and distribution of gas. Because almost all gas is in the Aptian-Albian-Cenomanian and almost all oil is in the Neocomian, they could use the Vasilyev and Zhabrev figures for gas reserves and the Dikenshtein et al. figures for percentages of hydrocarbons in rocks of each age in each basin to derive figures for volumes of oil.[131] Jermol and Magnusson thus arrived at a figure of 46 to 48 billion barrels of proved reserves of oil in the Cretaceous of West Siberia.

The authors defined explored reserves according to the Soviet definition as including reserves categories $A + B + C_1$[132] As explained by Meyerhoff, $A + B$ is proved by American Petroleum Institute standards.[133] $C_1$ reserves, however, include four types of reserves, *only one of which can be proved by API definition*. The one type of $C_1$ reserve that may, in some cases, be proved is the discovery well for a possible new field. For example, the discovery well is drilled. Several zones of possible oil and/or gas-bearing rocks are penetrated. Each zone is tested. Each zone yields possible commercial amounts of hydrocarbons. However, there is only the one well on the structure. *The field is not yet proved to be commercial.* Therefore, the hydrocarbons in the tested zones are classified as $C_1$. However, because the drilling fluids used in the wells were not programmed, serious mud invasion of possible productive zones presumably took place. As a consequence, the only way in which the presence of oil and/or gas can be detected is by use of a formation tester as the well is being drilled. The electric logs, which are run much later, in many cases will not detect possible oil- and gas-bearing zones. It is common to detect the hydrocarbons on the basis of the formation tester which is used while the hole is being drilled. A full test of the zone is not made. Hydrocarbon-bearing zones thus detected are assigned to $C_1$. This is the reason why Eremenko and Maksimov equated *a small percentage* (usually less than 10) of $C_1$ reserves to the API proved category.[134] The Eremenko and Maksimov article, which is the official Soviet article on how to equate American and Soviet reserve categories, is not cited in the PetroStudies report.) Technically the reserves found in a discovery well are not proved because commerciality of the structure is not established on the basis of a single well. Therefore, even this type of $C_1$ reserve does not truly belong to the proved category.

The three other types of $C_1$ reserves, which constitute more than 90 percent of all *confirmed* $C_1$, are shown schematically in Figure 22.

In the first type an exploratory well is drilled through five productive zones (Figure 22A). Each zone is tested and proved to be commercial. These reserves ultimately are classified as $B$ reserves, once the structure itself is shown to contain sufficient reserves for economic exploitation. A second well is drilled as an offset to the first. Logs show that all five zones are present, and they look promising. However, for some reason, only two zones are tested. They prove to be commercial, and may be classified as $B$ reserves. The three other zones are not tested. They are *assumed* to be commercial, but because they were not actually tested, they are given $C_1$ status. This is similar to one type of probable reserve in United States terminology.

In the second type a structure is drilled and several zones are found to be commercial. All stepout wells are commercial (Figure 22B). The areas between the discovery well and the stepout wells are still undrilled, but they

## THREE TYPES OF $C_1$ RESOURCES

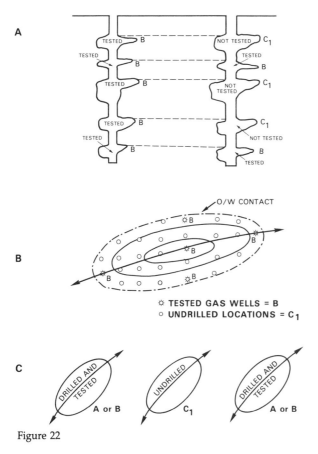

☼ TESTED GAS WELLS = B
○ UNDRILLED LOCATIONS = $C_1$

Figure 22

are *assumed* to be productive and commercial. These undrilled locations also are $C_1$, another type of probable reserve in American terminology.

In the third type two structures are drilled and are commercial. A third structure lies *between* the first two structures (Figure 22C). It is undrilled. It is *assumed* that this third structure will be like the first two. These also are $C_1$ reserves, similar to one type of potential reserves in United States terminology.

With such a diversity in the $C_1$ category, some $C_1$ reserves cannot even be considered reserves, but resources. The total percentage of $C_1$ reserves within $A + B + C_1$ must be known before they can be included in the proved category. Jermol and Magnusson, through an apparent mistranslation of a paper by Ovanesov and Feigin[135] assigned 70 percent of all $C_1$ reserves to the API proved category, and thus arrived at the figure of 153 billion barrels of proved oil and condensate reserves.

According to the PetroStudies authors, Ovanesov and Feigin showed that, of the $C_1$ reserves delineated in the 1959–72 period, 62.1 percent was raised to the $B$ (proved) category. Because the largest percentage of $C_1$ reserves elevated to the $B$ category was in West Siberia (79.2 percent), the PetroStudies authors selected 70 percent as a more realistic figure, and then assumed that $0.7C_1$ is the volume of $C_1$ equivalent to proved. This approach ignored the fact that (1) 62.1 percent was a national *weighted* average and (2) the last three types of $C_1$ discussed above were not proved, by API's own definition of proved.

Ovanesov and Feigin reported that, of the reserves discovered during the period 1959–72, 37.9 percent had to be written off and only 62.1 percent was valid. They also wrote that the percentage of $C_1$ in the sum $A + B + C_1$ rose from 32.6 percent to 52.1 percent during that period. Thus the *rate of increase* in proved reserves ($A + B$) slowed by about 40 percent during the 14-year period, even though the actual volume of $A + B$ increased slightly. Therefore, truly recoverable (explored) $A + B + C_1$ reserves are $A + B + (0.621 \times .521 = 0.324)C_1$, of which, by API definition, only $A + B$ actually is *proved*. The $0.324C_1$ is equivalent to "very probable," and part of the remaining $C_1$ is somewhere in the very low end of the spectrum embraced by the word "probable." Because a large volume of $C_1$ reserves actually is in *undrilled structures*, one cannot use either the word "proved" or "probable" in connection with them and at least half of the $C_1$ reserves are in the "potential" category of American terminology.

Having assumed that 70 percent of $C_1$ reserves is proved, the PetroStudies authors suggested that the USSR equivalent of proved reserves (in United States terminology) was $A + B + 0.7C_1$.[136] The authors then used an oil-to-gas conversion figure that Nesterov et al. wrote was about 5,000 cubic feet of gas = 1 barrel of oil.[137] The internationally used ratio is actually 6,000 standard cubic feet = 1 barrel. The PetroStudies authors used gas reserves as of 1 January 1974, for their calculation, because the Vasilyev and Zhabrev book provides the gas figures for this date, and the Dikenshtein et al. book bases its conclusions on the data for 1974.[138] I have used the identical figures in the following computation, but come up with a lower number than the 46 to 48 billion barrels derived by Jermol and Magnusson.

In 1974, when the Nesterov et al. book was written, recoverable $A + B + C_1$ gas reserves in the West Siberian basin were 493.5 trillion cubic feet, of which 466 trillion was in the Aptian-Albian-Cenomanian.[139] Most of the oil is in the Neocomian; some is in the Jurassic. If we used the conversion of 6,000 standard cubic feet = 1 barrel of oil and the sedimentary volume ratio of 76:174 for the Neocomian to Aptian-Cenomanian,[140] then:

$$\frac{76}{174} = \frac{x}{466 \text{ trillion cubic feet}} = \frac{x}{77.6 \text{ billion barrels}};$$

then,

$x = 33.9$ billion barrels of recoverable oil in the Neocomian.

Of this amount, 14.6 billion barrels of recoverable oil was in the Samotlor field, according to Shashin.[141] This leaves about 20.3 billion barrels outside of Samotlor. The problem is that the 20.3 billion barrels is not a known figure; it is a derived and therefore an assumed figure. Whatever the figure, it includes $A + B + C_1$. And if it is correct, the problem boils down to this: how much of the 20.3 billion is $C_1$?

This question cannot be answered without additional information. One means of obtaining an approximate figure is to compute reserves for each field on the basis of published reservoir data. Because Samotlor had produced only a small part of its reserve by 1974 and because the giant fields of Ust-Balyk, Pravdinsk, Mamontovo, West Surgut, Megion, and Sosnino-Vartovsk were just peaking, a rough calculation can be made on the basis of the Halbouty et al. published reserves figures.[142] $C_1$ reserves were not included for reasons given in preceding paragraphs.

Calculations based on the Halbouty et al figures show that the proved $(A + B)$ reserve in West Siberia on 1 January 1974 was 18 billion barrels. Since that time, 10 billion barrels have been produced and at least 8 billion barrels have been discovered and proved. Thus, remaining $A + B$ reserves in the West Siberian basin are 16 billion barrels.

A study of each field on the basis of reservoir data from the Ministry of Geology leads to a similar result—a range of 14 to 20 billion barrels, including the heavy oil at Russ-kaya (where 3 billion barrels of in-place oil is present, only 400 million of which is recoverable).

Jermol and Magnusson also suggest that annual reserves growth (in PetroStudies parlance, $A + B + 0.7C_1$), averaged 700 million metric tons (5.1 billion barrels) during the 1961–66 period; about 1,100 million metric tons (7.5 billion barrels) in the 1974–76 period; and were projected at 1,570 million metric tons (11.5 billion barrels) per year during the 1976–80 period.[143]

This would mean that the USSR has been discovering—and continues to discover—far more oil each year than is produced, and, at least during the last few years, at an accelerating rate. No large, fully industrialized country on earth ever has done this.

Oil Minister Shashin, in a widely publicized speech in 1975 at the 9th World Petroleum Congress in Tokyo, stated that Soviet oil and condensate production was slightly less than 31 billion barrels during the period 1961–74, and that this production *exceeded* the volume of reserves discovered during the same time period.

Furthermore, according to Arzhanov, 1.6 billion barrels of oil and condensate was produced from West Siberia in 1977, mainly in Tyumen Oblast.[144] Arzhanov stated that this was more than the volume of new oil discovered.

*Additional Assumptions*—When the PetroStudies authors arrived at a figure of 46 to 48 billion barrels proved for the Cretaceous of the West Siberian basin, they made undocumented assumptions for calculating the Cretaceous reserves of the remainder of the Soviet Union. The figure derived is 1.9 to 3.3 billion barrels, for a total of 48 to 51 billion barrels of proved Cretaceous oil for the whole country. One may then use the Dikenshtein et al. percentages to derive a figure for total reserves of the USSR.[145] According to Dikenshtein et al., 41.39 percent of the USSR's oil reserves are in the Cretaceous. Therefore, by extrapolation, about 117 to 124 billion barrels of proved oil is in the USSR.

In contrast, if one uses my own figure of 33 billion barrels for the West Siberian basin and uses the figure of Ovanesov and Feigin of 50 to 55 percent for the unproved $C_1$,[146] then the amount of proved $(A + B)$ oil in the West Siberian basin is in the order of 16 billion barrels. If I then accept the PetroStudies report's *lower* estimate (1.9 billion barrels) for the remaining proved Cretaceous oil in the country, proved Cretaceous oil reserves are 18 billion barrels. Use of Dikenshtein's percentage leads to a proved reserve of 43.5 billion barrels for the entire country.

Since 1979, PetroStudies has issued other reports that have raised questions in the world oil industry. On 5 December 1980, for example, a dispatch of The Associated Press datelined Paris stated that PetroStudies had reported a discovery in the West Siberian basin of 619 billion metric tons of oil, referring to this unusual find as the Bazhenov Formation. The figure, cited by I. I. Nefedov in the geological journal *Sovetskaya geologiya*, actually refers to the volume of dispersed bituminoids contained in the Bazhenov Formation, a layer of marine clays with dispersed organic matter that underlies the entire West Siberian basin.[147] The technology for recovering oil from this unconventional source does not exist.

Park's View

Park also downgraded the CIA predictions, but admitted that the CIA was correct in its assessment of Soviet technological problems.[148] He made a serious error in drawing a direct parallel between the causes of the USSR's technological delays and the causes of the delays in putting Alaska's North Slope oil on stream.[149] In Alaska, the principal reasons for delay were related to environmental and political factors, and only peripherally to technology problems. (Imagine, for a moment, a Soviet environmental-lobby group attempting to delay oil production in West

Siberia!) Park wrote, "In short, the [CIA] report identified a series of genuine technical problems besetting the Soviet oil industry and assumed that none will be solved. It also ignored the substantial adjustments that Soviet planners have made in the energy balance to allow for the oil industry's problems."

Park erroneously assumed that the USSR had made a substantial adjustment in the nation's fuel mix, an assumption which is negated by Brezhnev's statements during his April 1978 visit to West Siberia and by his December 1979 statements repeated by TASS. The validity of Park's assumption is negated even further by the excellent and well-documented analysis by Dienes, by the facts cited by Segal, as well as by my own work in the USSR.[150] Park also assumed that recent large increases in Soviet gas production meant that gas is being used on a much greater scale, not only in new plants but also in old plants being converted to gas use. The fact is that the conversion to gas-consuming from oil-consuming plants is proceeding far behind schedule. (The USSR cannot produce rapidly enough the necessary equipment for conversion.)

Park even cited, but ignored the implications of, fuel-production and fuel consumption projections by the Polish analyst, S. Albinowski, and by the Hungarian analyst, I. Dobozi, apparently on the ground that the dates which they gave for the impending Soviet energy crisis were in error by a few years.[151] Both analysts predicted an oil-supply crisis not only in the Soviet Union by 1980, but also in Eastern Europe. Dobozi predicted an annual deficit in the USSR during 1980 of 3.06 to 3.46 million barrels per day (153 to 173 mmt), only three years earlier than the CIA prediction. The fact that both Albinowski and Dobozi were wrong in predicting the date of the crisis has little to do with their principal points, largely ignored by Park. Both authors, for mainly the correct reasons, saw clearly a Soviet oil deficit looming on the horizon. The very fact that their predictions and analyses were published speaks worlds. (It is only fair to mention that both Albinowski and Dobozi were wrong in their gas projections; however, gas had been ignored in the Soviet Union through most of its history, and there was little reason to be able to foresee the abrupt policy change regarding gas.)

Park went further: "Western estimates of Soviet energy consumption made in the early to mid-seventies tended to the view that the rate of growth in consumption, especially of oil and gas, would be greater than the rate of growth in production, and that this would result in a decline in exports. The actual trends ran counter to expectation . . . There has been a substantial degree of substitution of oil and gas . . . The major effect, however, has been a lower level of total energy demand than anticipated, due to the declining growth rate of the economy as a whole."[152] Park is wrong about the conversion to other forms of energy, as Dienes showed clearly, and as Soviet officials have discussed with me on many occasions.[153] However, Park otherwise is right, at least through 1976, the latest year for which he published statistics. After 1976, as Segal has pointed out, things went from bad to worse,[154] and they continued to deteriorate through 1980. The situation may be viewed as even critical, when one

considers the USSR's immediate and urgent need for substantial amounts of hard currencies to repay its international debts, and to provide funds for foreign imports. The renewed start of construction during 1974 of the Baikal-Amur Mainline (BAM) undoubtedly was influenced in part by the country's growing problems with petroleum. Completion of this new trans-Siberian rail link in the mid-1980s may make available additional mineral and timber supplies for barter (for oil and other goods) and for payment of Soviet debts.[155]

Park, on the basis of the data which he considered (a very good analysis but one which omitted too many components of the overall picture), concluded that, "There is comparatively little technical difficulty in producing the desired 1980 level from existing operations, though it must be admitted that this could only be achieved at a cost considerably higher than estimated for the 10th Plan, and with severe long-term loss."[156] He admitted that, "if new reserves are not discovered during the 10th Plan, the point at which Soviet energy planners are faced with the problem of optimizing the energy balance to an oil production level that has reached its peak, may come in the late eighties. Nonetheless, available Soviet material gives no indication that planners and energy analysts foresee this eventuality, in spite of their acknowledgement of the problems faced by the industry."[157] In support of his view that the USSR will meet its 1980 plan with "comparatively little technical difficulty," Park—without understanding the geologic and logistics conditions—perpetuated the idea that only 25 out of 150 commercial West Siberian fields were on stream by 1978.[158] (The implication, again, is that West Siberia is producing at a reduced potential.) He stated that this "fact" was overlooked by the CIA; this statement is incorrect, because he had read only two of the five CIA reports.[159] He made the further error of stating that imported Western technology would be utilized best in the USSR offshore.[160] He clearly did not understand the facts (1) that only 60 percent of the prospective onshore basins are explored; (2) that only 50 percent of the explored basins have been drilled to 2.5 km; (3) that less than 75 percent of these are explored to 3.2 km; and (4) that less than 95 percent are truly explored below 3.2 km. Nor did he understand that this lack of exploration onshore was due to the impossible Soviet technology problems, despite his admission that such problems exist. It is a great pity that the meeting in June 1977, at which the CIA presented to the Soviets a survey of Soviet problems, was not more widely attended. Park, among many, would have been awakened rather rudely.[161] Although one cannot detract from the scholarliness of, and wealth of data in, Park's book, his lack of knowledge of geology and his lack of a true appreciation of Soviet technology needs are reflected in its inadequate conclusions.

## Segal's Observations

Segal recognized the potential accuracy of the CIA forecasts, and analyzed subsequent (post-1976) Soviet publications in this light.[162] In 1978, Segal wrote that, "All the evidence currently available . . . tends to justify the CIA's conclusion."[163] Only one error was made by Segal; he accepted A. A. Trofimuk's evaluation of the oil potential of Eastern Siberia, and of the Soviet Far East.[164] Segal wrote that "it is proven that East Siberia has more oil than West Siberia ever had. The same applies to the shelf area and offshore; the trouble is lack of investment, inadequate infrastructure, particularly in East Siberia, and the nonavailability of the latest Western technology." Trofimuk, whose views of the petroleum potential of the eastern Soviet Union long have been unduly optimistic, has greatly overestimated the potential of the Vilyui basin, the Irkutsk amphitheater, and other areas of Eastern Siberia and the Far East (see Table 2, and the section on "Geology of USSR Basins"), as has Lvov.[165] Segal concluded that, "The overall picture does lend support to the CIA's contention that the USSR may soon become a competitor for OPEC oil."[166] If the USSR's recent moves in Iraq, Afghanistan, and Iran prove nothing, they at least suggest that the Soviet Union's interest in these countries is something more than its love for its own brand of socialism.[167] These moves can be interpreted in different ways, but the most likely explanation is that the USSR is taking active steps to insure its oil supplies through the 1980s and 1990s. Segal wrote further: "The argument which has been raging amongst analysts and commentators of Soviet oil developments over the past two years as to whether or not the Soviet oil industry is running out of reserves seems, on the basis of the latest Soviet evidence, to be moving conclusively in favor of those who argue that the USSR is heading towards an oil crisis."[168] After presenting detailed evidence from Soviet publications, he concluded that "the short term outlook for Soviet oil is not a rosy one and the CIA must surely have been right to argue that this must have foreign policy consequences."[169]

Internal Conversations with Officials of the USSR Ministries of Geology, Oil Industry, and Gas Industry

Between January 1972 and October 1979, I had private conversations with various Soviet officials, conversations which provide a perspective on the nation's petroleum reserves and resources which, in point of fact and attitude, differ substantially and in many ways from material published in Soviet journals and books. The following conversations (taped with permission) were held without any suggestions that they should be treated confidentially. In fact, in September 1979, while visiting these officials, I specifically asked permission to use two quotations in this paper. Permission was granted with the provisos that no names, specific dates (other than years), or meeting places be given. I received the clear impression that the various officials concerned wanted the statements repeated in the West. I realize that none can be verified, as would be the case in the course of normal research. However, they seem to me to be of such importance that they should be included with this report. One conversation took place in 1974.

The present $A + B$ reserves of the USSR will be depleted not later than 1977, and all existing $A + B + C_1$ reserves will be gone by 1980. Our discovery rate is falling far below the rate of production be-

cause of (1) lack of money, (2) constant shifts in money allocations among different ministerial groups and projects, (3) terrible drilling equipment (3 to 4 years to drill 3.5 to 5.40-km wells), and (4) terrible seismic equipment (maximum penetration is 1,000 to 3,000 m). Our present instructions are for production to reach 550 mt (4 billion barrels) by the end of 1975, a clearly impossible target; the thought is absolutely unrealistic. By 1980, unless we can purchase equipment abroad, production will begin to decline. In actual fact, I have submitted a memorandum to my colleagues in which I show that, without immediate foreign equipment imports, our production will reach its peak in the period 1979–82, and that it will decline thereafter, despite our huge potential.

You cannot imagine or conceive of the problems which we face. It is commonplace for us to begin a two-year project here, a one-year project there, or a three-year program somewhere else, only to have it cancelled in the middle because another trust or institute managed, through personal influence, to divert our project's funds to one of its own. This is a daily occurrence in my country, and can be countered only by doing the same thing, accompanied by constant vigilance and political infighting.

Moreover, as things stand now, our system has no foreign exchange, or at least, not enough. Therefore, we cannot purchase equipment such as downhole pumps. Our own equipment is a national disaster wreaked upon us by the party's bureaucracy and its stubborn adherence to Lenin's doctrine of self-sufficiency for each Soviet republic and for the nation as a whole. It is as though we were permitted to use U.S.A. equipment that first had been bombed by the Nazis and then stripped of all spare parts. What spare parts we order for a project seldom reach us, because they are diverted to some other organization before we see them. So we lose endless time waiting for the parts that never arrive.

Our drilling-mud programs are not programs at all, because there is no program. We send out our drilling crews at each well location to find a local clay pit, to which we add some water and possibly other things. Then we take so long to drill wells. The mud is little more than watery mud or clay, not designed for the real geologic conditions which we encounter in the well bore. Thus, with our slow drilling, we cause enormously deep mud invasion into potentially productive formations. As a result, our well logs cannot evaluate the formations. Therefore, many potentially productive zones give dry tests. Sometimes, after we have plugged one of these dry tests, we return out of curiosity to open it again, and we find the well gushing oil or gas. We have missed many potential discoveries in this way.

In fact, almost all of our equipment here is 20 to 30 years out of date by your standards. You went to our Exposition grounds at Moscow, and you saw the Hall of Petroleum Industry. The equipment which you saw there is not used in the field. Some of it is prototype equipment that is untested; sometimes we exhibit our only example of new equipment, and have not produced it for field use. Even when it is field tested, we may take it to the exhibit hall to show it to the people.

Our economic system also is a disaster. We now charge seven kopeks per liter of gasoline. But for bottled mineral water, we pay 20 kopeks per liter! The Central Committee will not raise the price of gasoline now, because (1) a black market for gasoline will spring up everywhere, and (2) the collectives, which receive 40 percent of all gasoline receipts, will demand the same percentage or more of any new price, say 44 to 66 kopeks per liter. The collective farms are so inefficient that any new monies obtained through higher gasoline prices will either be wasted, or they will feather more nests, but they will not further farm efficiency. Another result would be that the economy would suffer inflation, which already is affecting my country.

Either Minister ***** or ***** has proposed during the past few years at least seven different plans for raising the price of gasoline by 100 to 200 percent. Minister ***** has just now presented a scheme to raise gasoline prices by 50 percent. If this latest scheme had been accepted, the collectives would receive the same amount received now, and we would get the increase. This would give us some of the much-needed capital to do more drilling. However the Politburo and the Central Committee say that these proposals are out, because the farmers will not tolerate our getting more money, while they get the same amount and, at the same time, have to pay more for fuel for their tractors. So, with our present system of management, we shall fall short of our 1975 goals. Moreover, our 1976–80 goals will have to be revised downward substantially, and no later than 1982 our production will begin to decline.

Finally, in my last proposal to the Committee, I requested that we not sell any more liquids (condensate and oil) abroad, only dry gas, because we shall need these liquids for the country's future. Unless we stop this export of oil and condensate, our own needs will not be met by the 1980s, our economy will collapse, and my country will face a disaster not less important than in 1942.

Subsequently, the 1975 goal was reduced to 496 mmt (3.62 billion barrels), but still fell short (491 mmt = 3.58 billion barrels). Gasoline prices were more than doubled on 1 March 1978, with agriculture still getting 40 percent of the receipts. The 1976–80 oil production goals, first planned in 1974–75, were revised drastically downward. The original target plans (more than 550 mmt for 1976 alone) never were published. BJ, Reda, and Soviet-built downhole submersible pumps were introduced on a large scale, with the result that this same group of geologists and planners does not anticipate a production decline before 1985 to 1986. These same people characterized the CIA reports as "most realistic," but denounced them in public.

In 1979, the following conversation was recorded:

The present situation in our country is a serious one, because the May 1978 production and the May 1979 production figures for the whole country were almost exactly the same. This shows that our earlier (1974) prediction was very accurate. We have brought the Fedorovsk field into production, and find that it is a giant field, but it will only offset the declines in the production of West Surgut, Pravdinsk, and Mamontovo. These last-named fields are declining rapidly and have very large water cuts. Perhaps more serious, we honestly do not know what our oil and condensate reserves are. The Minister has instructed us to reevaluate every field in the country so that we can arrive at a more nearly correct figure than we have at any time in the past. If you must know the truth, your own reserve calculations for our fields have been as good as—and in some cases better than—our own. Others made by you, however, turned out to be far too optimistic.

In a reference to the PetroStudies report of September 1978, the following statement was made:

We do not understand where those people come from or why they print what they do. Who, in fact, are they? They are not petroleum people; this is clear. Their statements are utterly unrealistic. It is almost as though some organization had connived with them to publish such rubbish, because it is very embarassing to our administrators.

## Conclusions

There is no question but that the Soviet Union is facing an energy crisis. However, unlike the energy problems of the West and Japan, caused mainly by a lack of indigenous petroleum resources, the Soviet difficulties are the product of a backward technology that is 15 to 35 years behind that of Japan and the West. The resource potential of the Soviet Union remains huge.

Of all the non-Communist sources, only the Central Intelligence Agency foresaw the Soviet energy problem and made reasonably sound predictions regarding it. The predictions that Soviet oil production would peak below 12 million barrels a day have proved to be wrong, but not seriously so. The Soviet Union is now producing at the rate of 12.15 million barrels a day, and the rate of growth has decreased to about 1 percent a year. As a result of the evident slowdown in the growth rate, the Soviet Union has revised its production estimates downward for the 1980s, predicting a production of 12.4 to 12.9 million barrels a day by the end of the current five-year plan in 1985, or almost the same output level that had been projected originally for the end of the last five-year plan ending in 1980.

The CIA's estimates regarding Soviet gas production have also been generally correct, although somewhat pessimistic.

If the USSR continues to supply Eastern Europe with

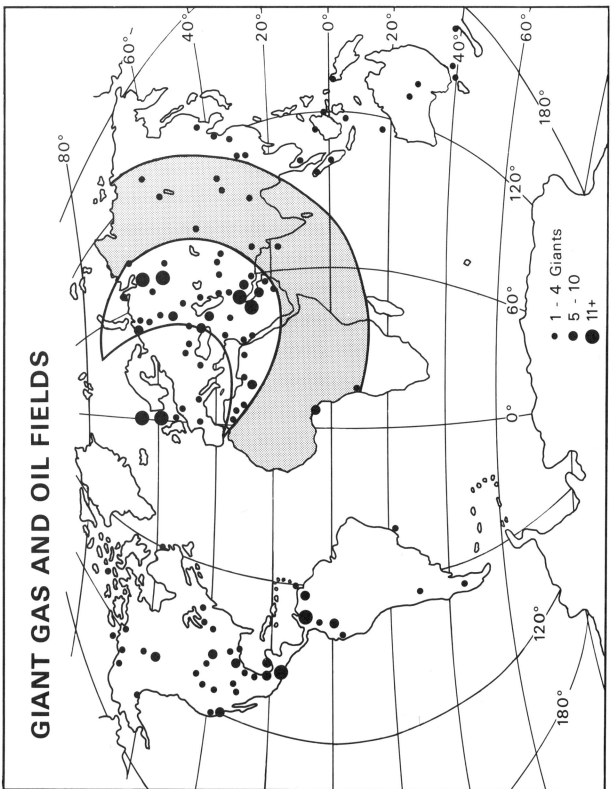

**GIANT GAS AND OIL FIELDS**

1 - 4 Giants
5 - 10
11+

Figure 23

oil and if oil exports to the West are to continue to be a major source of hard-currency earnings (in 1979, oil exports to the West accounted for 54 percent of such earnings), internal oil consumption will have to be curtailed and oil substitutes will have to be introduced rapidly. The substitution of coal for oil appears to have run into problems because of stagnation in the Soviet coal industry, and Soviet planners appear to be looking to natural gas as a partial substitute for oil in the fuel mix of electric thermal stations before more coal becomes available later in the 1980s. Nuclear energy is also being counted on as an increasingly important source of electric power, especially in the European USSR, where fossil fuel scources are being depleted.

Continued oil exports to Eastern Europe, which the Soviet Union has pledged to maintain at the level of 1.6 million barrels a day through the first half of the 1980s, would appear to be essential if the Soviet Union does not want to risk losing an important source of political leverage among its East European allies. Moreover, a decline in hard-currency earnings through lower oil exports to the West would erode Soviet ability to pay for Western technology imports in the volume needed to insure the Soviet Union's progress. A sharp reduction or loss of oil exports for hard currency would be a severe economic blow to the USSR.

Natural gas, aside from beginning to play an increasingly important role in the domestic fuel mix, is not expected to be a major substitute for oil as a means of earning hard currency, at least not for many years. Even if natural gas prices rise to the point of being equivalent to oil prices, much of the gas being piped to Western Europe is in repayment for the large-diameter pipe in which the gas is flowing and which has been obtained from Western Europe by barter.

Although natural gas and coal are available in the Soviet Union in abundant resources and an intensive program of nuclear power development is being pressed, the substitution of these sources of energy for oil has been lagging. The Soviet Union may therefore be hard-pressed to curtail domestic oil consumption over the near term and the possibility that it may become a net oil importer by the late 1980s cannot be totally ruled out, with the potential political frictions that such a development may entail.

Even if the USSR purchases more modern petroleum technology abroad, it may take about 14 to 18 years to modernize its industry; if the Soviet Union tries to modernize without foreign technology, it may take more than 18 years before the oil industry again starts to show significant growth. But modernization, with or without foreign help, appears to be the key to a renewed upsurge of oil production. In theory, the USSR, with completely modern equipment, could maintain its position as a major producer of oil, possibly yielding up to 20 million barrels a day. Much of the future growth would be from smaller structures in already productive basins, at greater depths in productive basins, in little explored basins on shore and in wholly unexplored basins off shore.

Three scenarioa may be advanced for Soviet approaches for dealing with the energy crisis of the 1980s.

The first, and most likely, alternative is to continue to "muddle through" both through continued purchases of foreign oil technology and retooling of domestic technology and by efforts to constrain domestic consumption and make the necessary amounts of oil available for export to Eastern and Western Europe. Such a course of action may eventually lead to Soviet self-sufficiency in advanced technology, a prime goal of the Soviet leadership. Second, the Soviet Union may open its doors and invite Western and Japanese help in the development of its resources. Such an approach is less likely, both because it would require a measure of foreign participation in the Soviet economy that Moscow has been reluctant to grant in the past and because it would presume a return to the détente of the early 1970s, which has not been apparent since the Soviet military intervention in Afghanistan in late 1979. Finally, there is the much debated possibility that the Soviet Union, confronted with a serious oil shortage and an inability to muster the vast amounts of hard currency needed for large imports, will seek to gain greater access to the oil of the Persian Gulf.

Thus, Soviet actions in the energy field are a vital part of its foreign policy. Figure 23 shows two crescent-shaped areas in the Eastern Hemisphere. The inner crescent, extending through North Africa, the Middle East, and the central USSR, contains 74 percent of the world proved oil and gas reserves; the second crescent, which includes southern and central Africa, Afghanistan, and the Kazakhstan and Yakutia mineral belts, contains 61 percent of the world's other proved minerals, with the exception of coal. Soviet and Cuban activities abroad during recent years have been mainly in these two crescents. It would be well for us if we do not forget this fact.

## NOTES

1. J. D. Clarkson, *A History of Russia* (New York: Random House, 1961); R. W. Campbell, *The Economics of Soviet Oil and Gas* (Baltimore, Md.: Johns Hopkins University Press, 1968); R. W. Campbell, *Trends in the Soviet Oil and Gas Industry* (Baltimore, Md.: Johns Hopkins University Press, 1976); Theodore Shabad, *Basic Industrial Resources of the USSR* (New York: Columbia University Press, 1969); Arthur A. Meyerhoff, "Geopolitical Implications of Russian and Chinese Petroleum," in *Exploration and Economics of the Petroleum Industry* vol. 11, Southwestern Legal Foundation Proc., Dallas (New York: Matthew Bender and Co., 1973), pp. 79–127; Arthur A. Meyerhoff, "Requirements for GKZ Certification of Reserves Categories," Petroconsultants, *Review of Sino-Soviet Oil*, vol. 10, no. 12 (1975): 1–19; Arthur A. Meyerhoff, "The Soviet System of Reserve Categories," Petroconsultants, *Review of Sino-Soviet Oil*, vol. 10, no. 11 (1975): 1–14; Arthur A. Meyerhoff, "Equipment Problems in the Soviet Petroleum Industry," Petroconsultants, *Review of Sino-Soviet Oil* vol. 11, no. 1 (1976): 1–8; Arthur A. Meyerhoff, "Comparison of National and Private Petroleum Company Exploration Techniques, Philosophy, and Success," *Canadian Soc. Petrol. Geol. Bull.* vol. 24, no.

2 (1976): 282–304; Arthur A. Meyerhoff, *Communist goals, Soviet minerals policy and the CIA reports* (Geneva: Business International S.A. (April 1978); E. E. Owen, *Trek of the Oil Finders: A History of Exploration for Petroleum*, American Association Petroleum Geol. Mem. 6, 1975; and Leslie Dienes and Theodore Shabad, *The Soviet Energy System* (New York: John Wiley, 1979).

2. Owen, *Oil Finders.*

3. M. T. Halbouty, A. A. Meyerhoff, R. E. King, R. H. Dott, Sr., H. D. Klemme, and T. Shabad, *World's Giant Oil and Gas Fields, Geologic Factors Affecting their Formation, and Basin Classification*, American Association Petrol. Geol. Mem: 14, 1970.

4. Clarkson, *History of Russia.*

5. A. Safanov, "Ivan Mikhailovitch Gubkin," *Amer. Assoc. Petrol. Geol Bull.* vol. 23, no. 8 (1939): 1283.

6. A. A. Trofimuk, *Uralo-Povolzhye—novaya neftyanaya baza SSSR* [Volga-Urals, a new oil base for the USSR] (Moscow: Nedra, 1957), p. 91.

7. Shabad, *Industrial Resources*, p. 6.

8. N. A. Eremenko, G. P. Ovanesov and V. V. Semenovich, "Status of Oil Prospecting in the USSR in 1971," *Amer. Assoc. Petrol. Geol. Bull.* vol. 56, no. 8 (1972): 1711–22.

9. Campbell, *Soviet Oil and Gas.*

10. R. D. Hovey, "Status of Soviet Geophysical Exploratory Methods," Standard Oil Co. Calif. Unpub. ms.

11. V. D. Shashin, "Enhancing the cost-effectiveness of oil production is the main objective of the industry," *Ekonomika neftyanoi promyshlennosti*, 1975, no. 7, pp. 3–11; V. I. Graifer, S. M. Levin, and L. A. Kolosova, "An important direction of economic work in the industry," *Neftyanoye khozyaistvo*, 1977, no. 7, pp. 5–8; A. E. Kontorovich, V. S. Surkov, I. I. Nesterov, A. A. Trofimuk, F. K. Salmanov, and Yu. G. Ervye, "Basic stages and results of prospecting in the West Siberian oil and gas province," *Geol. nefti i gaza*, 1977, no. 11, pp. 21–25; N. S. Yerofeyev, A. A. Aksenov, A. G. Aleksin, and V. F. Mazanov, "Oil and gas exploration tasks in light of the decisions of the 25th party congress," *Geol. nefti i gaza*, 1977, no. 10, pp. 12–16; "The complex development of productive forces in West Siberia at the center of attention of scholars and practical workers," *Planovoye khozyaistvo*, 1978, no. 9, pp. 97–114. This article was by the Central Committee; "Basic problems of complex development in West Siberia," *Voprosy ekonomiki*, 1978, no. 8, pp. 15–37. This article was by the Central Committee: Central Committee CPSU, "From an expanded session of the Oil Ministry collegium," *Neftyanoye khozyaistvo*, 1978, no. 5, pp. 3–15; Z. I. Fainburg, in "The complex development of productive forces in West Siberia at the center of attention of scholars and practical workers," *Planovoye khozyaistvo*, 1978, no. 9, pp. 97–114; and A. M. Shaparov, in "Basic problems of complex development in West Siberia," *Voprosy ekonomiki*, 1978, no. 8, pp. 15–37.

12. Campbell, *Soviet Oil and Gas*; Campbell, *Soviet Oil and Gas Industry*; Hovey, "Exploratory Methods"; Owen, *Oil Finders*; Meyerhoff, "Equipment Problems": Meyerhoff, "Petroleum Company Exploration Techniques"; Arthur A. Meyerhoff, "Proved and Ultimate Reserves of Natural Gas and Natural Gas Liquids in the World," 10th World Petroleum Cong., Bucharest, 1979, Proc., vol. 2, p. 303–311; Central Intelligence Agency, *Prospects for Soviet Oil Production*, ER 77–10270 (April 1977); and Central Intelligence Agency, *Prospects for Soviet Oil Production: A Supplemental Analysis*, ER-10425 (July 1977).

13. Rotary (gasoline and electric powered) drills penetrate subsurface rock formations by placing the full weight of the drill pipe on a rock-cutting tool (the bit) at the bottom of the hole. The drill pipe and bit are rotated on the rock to drill the well. Turbodrills, in contrast, jet water and mud ahead of the bit. The rock formation is softened by fluids and the bit cuts more easily through the softened rocks. No weight is placed on the drill pipe or bit, and only the bit turns. The drill pipe therefore does not rotate. Because of this, very low-quality steel can be used in turbodrills. The weakness of the turbodrill (in addition to the low-quality steel) is that jetting of fluids ahead of the bit is effective only to depths of 2,300 m. Those interested in the turbodrill are referred to Campbell's (1968) excellent summary of the qualities of the turbodrill.

14. Shashin, "Enhancing the cost-effectiveness."

15. Yerofeyev et al., "Oil and gas exploration."

16. Halbouty et al., *Oil and Gas Fields*; D. A. Holmgren, J. D. Moody, and H. H. Emmerich, "The Structural Settings for Giant Oil and Gas Fields," 9th World Petroleum Cong., Tokyo, 1975, Proc. vol. 2, p. 45–54; and Arthur A. Meyerhoff, "Significance of Giant Petroleum Fields in the World's Economy," *Am. Scientist*, vol. 64, (September-October 1976): 536–41.

17. Campbell, *Soviet Oil and Gas.*

18. A. S. Murray and J. R. Tilbe, "Canadian Report Results of Drilling Exchange with Soviets," *Oil and Gas Journal*, vol. 77, no. 17 (1979): 51–60.

19. Owen, *Oil Finders*, p. 1402.

20. Owen, *Oil Finders.*

21. Yerofeyev et al., "Oil and gas exploration."

22. Campbell, *Soviet Oil and Gas.*

23. Yerofeyev et al., "Oil and gas exploration."

24. Ibid.

25. F. G. Arzhanov, in Central Committee CPSU, "From an expanded session of the Oil Ministry collegium," *Neftyanoye khozyaistvo*, 1978, no. 5, pp. 3–5.

26. S. A. Orudzhev, "Main tasks in perfecting the exploitation of oil fields in their late stages of production," *Neftyanoye khozyaistvo*, 1969, no. 2, pp. 1–5.

27. M. F. Mirchink, "Status of theory and practice of working oil fields," *Geol. nefti i gaza* (1964) (Eng. trans. in *Petroleum Geol.*, McLean, Va., vol. 8, no. 6, 1969, pp. 307–06), p. 313.

28. Ibid., p. 314.

29. Ibid., p. 309.

30. Ibid., pp. 309–10.

31. Ibid., p. 310.

32. V. P. Maksimov, *Ekspluatatsiya neftyanykh mestorozhdenii v oslozhnennykh usloviyakh* [Oil field exploitation under complex conditions] (Moscow: Nedra, 1976).

33. Dienes and Shabad, *Soviet Energy System*, pp. 94–97.

34. Central Intelligence Agency, *Soviet Oil Production*

(April); Central Intelligence Agency, *The International Energy Situation: Outlook to 1985*, ER 77–10240 U (April 1977).

35. Ibid.; J. W. Clarke, O. W. Girard, Jr., J. Peterson, and J. Rachlin, *Petroleum Geology of the West Siberian Basin and a Detailed Description of the Samotlor Field*, U.S. Geol. Survey Open-file Rept. 77–871, 1977.

36. GKZ (State Commission on Reserves), *Instruktsiya po primeneniyu klassifikatsii zapasov k mestorozhdeniyam nefti i goryuchikh gazov* [Instructions for applying the reserve classifications to oil and gas fields] (Moscow: Gosudarstvennaya komissiya po zapasam poleznykh iskopayemykh pri Sovete Ministrov SSSR, 1971).

37. V. D. Shashin, *Neftedobyvayushchaya promyshlennost SSSR 1917–1967* [The Oil industry of the USSR 1917–67] (Moscow: Nedra, 1968).

38. GKZ, *Instruktsiya*; Meyerhoff, "Requirements for GKZ Certification."

39. Campbell, *Soviet Oil and Gas*, p. 72.

40. A. M. Seregin, "Regional investigation for petroleum," in S. N. Battacharya and V. V. Sastri, eds., *Selected Lectures on Petroleum Exploration*, vol. 1: Dehra Dun (India), Inst. Petroleum Explor., Oil and Nat. Gas Comm., 1969, pp. 37–49.

41. GKZ, *Instruktsiya*.

42. Meyerhoff, "Requirements for GKZ Certification."

43. GKZ, *Instruktsiya*.

44. Meyerhoff, "Soviet System."

45. GKZ, *Instruktsiya*, p. 20.

46. Ibid.

47. Ibid., pp. 20–21.

48. Ibid., p. 21.

49. Ibid.

50. Arthur A. Meyerhoff, "Petroleum Basins of the Soviet Arctic," *Geol. Magazine*, vol. 17, no. 2 (1980): 101–86 (issued in 1979 as Cambridge University Arctic Shelf Programme Rept. 112–113).

51. G. Kh. Dikenshtein et al., *Neftegazonosnye provintsii SSSR* [Oil and gas bearing provinces of the USSR] (Moscow: Nedra, 1977), p. 96.

52. Ibid., p. 78.

53. Ibid., p. 79.

54. Clarkson, *History of Russia*.

55. Dikenshtein et al., *Neftegazonosnye provintsii*, p. 261.

56. Owen, *Oil Finders*.

57. Dikenshtein et al., *Neftegazonosnye provintsii*, pp. 190–91.

58. Owen, *Oil Finders*, pp. 1406–07.

59. Dikenshtein et al., *Neftegazonosnye provintsii*, p. 230.

60. Ibid., p. 260.

61. Halbouty et al., *Oil and Gas Fields*.

62. S. P. Maksimov, et al., *Geologiya neftyanykh i gazovykh mestorozhdenii Volgo-Uralskoi neftegazonosnoi provintsii* [Geology of oil and gas fields in the Volga-Urals oil and gas province] (Moscow: Nedra, 1970).

63. Meyerhoff, "Petroleum Basins."

64. Kontorovich et al., "Basic Stages."

65. Halbouty et al., *Oil and Gas Fields*; Arthur A. Meyerhoff, I. A. Mamantov, and Theodore Shabad, "Russian Arctic Boasts Big Potential," *Oil and Gas Journal*, vol. 69, no. 43 (1971): 122, 124–26.

66. Clarke et al., *Petroleum Geology*.

67. V. G. Vasilyev and I. P. Zhabrev, *Gazovye i gazokondensatnye mestorozhdeniya* [Gas and gas condensate fields] (Moscow: Nedra, 1975), p. 189.

68. Arthur A. Meyerhoff, *Oil and Gas Potential of the Far East* (Beaconsfield, England: Scientific Press, 1981), originally prepared as a Cambridge University Arctic Shelf Programme Report, 1980.

69. Ibid.

70. A. A. Trofimuk, ed., *Neftegazonosnye basseiny Dalnego Vostoka SSSR* [Oil and gas basins of the Soviet Far East] (Moscow: Nedra, 1971).

71. Arthur A. Meyerhoff, "Russians Look Hard at the Anadyr Basin," *Oil and Gas Journal*, vol. 70, no. 43 (1972): 124, 129; vol. 70, no. 44 (1972): 84, 89.

72. Arthur A. Meyerhoff, "Stratigraphy of Late Proterozoic (Riphean and Vendian) through Early Silurian productive Section, Irkutsk Amphitheater, Eastern Siberia," Petroconsultants, *Review of Sino-Soviet Oil*, vol. 10, no. 6 (1975): 1–13.

73. Arthur A. Meyerhoff, *Geology and Petroleum Fields in Proterozoic and Lower Cambrian Strata, Lena-Tunguska Petroleum Province, Eastern Siberia, USSR*, Am. Assoc. Petrol. Geol. Mem: 30, 1980 (issued in 1979 as Cambridge University Arctic Shelf Programme Rept. 150).

74. Arthur A. Meyerhoff, "Proved and Ultimate Reserves of Natural Gas and Natural Gas Liquids in the World," 10th World Petroleum Cong., Bucharest, 1979, Proc., vol. 2, pp. 303–311.

75. Central Intelligence Agency, *Soviet Oil Production* (April); Central Intelligence Agency, *International Energy*.

76. Arthur A. Meyerhoff, "PetroStudies Reports: 1978–1980," Petroconsultants, *Review of Sino-Soviet Oil*, vol. 16, no. 1 (1981): 1–20.

77. Meyerhoff, "Geopolitical Implications."

78. Meyerhoff, "Proved and Ultimate Reserves"; Meyerhoff, "Petroleum Basins"; and Meyerhoff, "PetroStudies Reports."

79. M. S. Lvov, *Resursy prirodnogo gaza* [Natural gas resources] (Moscow: Nedra, 1969).

80. Meyerhoff, "Geopolitical Implications."

81. V. G. Vasilyev, *Gazovye mestorozhdeniya SSSR. Spravochnik* [Gas fields of the USSR, a handbook] (Moscow: Nedra, 1968); V. G. Vasilyev, ed., *Geologiya nefti. Spravochnik* [Oil geology, a handbook], tom 2, kniga 1: Oil fields of the USSR. (Moscow: Nedra, 1968); Vasilyev and Zhabrev, *Mestorozhdeniya*; Dikenshtein et al., *Neftegazonosnye provintsii*; L. P. Guzhnovsky, *Ekonomika razrabotki neftyanykh mestorozhdenii* [Economics of oil field development] (Moscow: Nedra, 1977); V. I. Muravlenko and V. I. Kremneva, *Sibirskaya neft* [Siberian oil] (Moscow: Nedra, 1977); V. Filanovsky, "The West Siberian oil and gas complex; results and prospects," *Planovoye khozyaistvo*, 1980, no. 3, pp. 19–26; A. Lalayants, "The oil and gas complex: today and tomorrow," *Sotsialisticheskaya industriya*, 21 May 1980, p. 2; and Theodore Shabad, "News Notes," *Soviet Geography: Review and Translation*, various years.

82. Theodore Shabad, "News Notes," *Soviet Geography: Review and Translation* 22, no. 4 (April 1981): 272.

83. Graifer et al., "Important direction"; "Productive forces in West Siberia"; "Complex development in West

Siberia"; and Arzhanov, in Central Committee CPSU, pp. 3–5.

84. Central Intelligence Agency, *USSR: Development of the Gas Industry.* Rept. ER 78–10393 (July 1978); G. Segal, "Reassessing the Soviet OIl Outlook" *Petroleum Rev.* (April 1978), pp. 51–53; and G. Segal, "CIA's Dire Forecast for USSR Oil Looks Accurate as Output Slumps," *Petroleum Rev.* (January 1979), pp. 17–18.

85. Central Intelligence Agency, *Soviet Oil Production* (April); Central Intelligence Agency, *International Energy*; Central Intelligence Agency, *Soviet Oil Production* (July); Central Intelligence Agency, *Soviet Economic Problems and Prospects*, Rept. ER 77–10436 U (July 1977); Central Intelligence Agency, *The Soviet Economy in 1976–77 and Outlook for 1978* Rept. ER 78–10512 (August 1978).

86. For example, Mirchink, "Working oil fields"; M. M. Brenner, "On the ratio of oil production to reserves." *Geol. nefti i gaza*, 1966, no. 12, pp. 46–51; M. M. Brenner, *Ekonomika neftyanoi i gazovoi promyshlennosti SSSR* [Economics of the oil and gas industry of the USSR] (Moscow: Nedra, 1968); M. M. Brenner, "On proportions in the oil industry and ways of determining them," *Geol. nefti i gaza*, 1968, no. 11, pp. 48–53; M. V. Dobrovolsky and F. F. Dunayev, *Osnovnye voprosy ekonomiki poiskovykh i razvedochnykh rabot na neft i gaz* [Basic issues in the economics of oil and gas prospecting and exploration] Syktyvkar: Izd. Komi ASSR, 1966; M. Mkrtchyan, "Standardizing rent payments in extractive industry," *Planovoye khozyaistvo*, 1966, no. 10, pp. 50–60; M. F. Mirchink and M. V. Feigin, Estimation of present oil reserves in the higher categories," *Geol. nefti i gaza*, 1967, no. 11, pp. 34–389; F. F. Dunayev, et al., *Problema opredeleniya ratsionalnykh sootnoshenii mezhdu dobychei nefti i zapasami* [The Problem of determining rational oil production and reserve ratios], VNIIONG (Research Inst. Economics of Oil and Gas), 1968; Ye. Galperson, D. Dunayev, R. Mingareyev, N. Timofeyev, and N. Titkov, "Review of the book by M. M. Brenner, *Ekonomika neftyanoi promyshlennosti*," *Neftyanoye khozyaistvo*, 1970, no. 1, pp. 65–68.

87. Shashin, "Enhancing the cost-effectiveness"; Kontorovich et al., "Basic stages': Yerofeyev et al., "Oil and gas exploration'" Arzhanov, in Central Committee CPSU, pp. 305; Fainburg, in "Productive forces in West Siberia," p. 110; Shaparov, in "Complex development in West Siberia," p. 32; and P. Neporozhny, "Prospects for the development of Soviet and world power engineering during the period when capital investments of the coming decade will give results," Preprint for Soviet-English Symposium of Power Engineering Problems, Moscow, October 1979.

88. Neporozhny, "Soviet and world power engineering."

89. Fainburg, in "Productive forces in West Siberia," p. 110; and Shaparov, in "Complex development in West Siberia," p. 32.

90. Central Intelligence Agency, *Soviet Oil Production* (April); Central Intelligence Agency, *International Energy*; Central Intelligence Agency, *Soviet Oil Production* (July); Central Intelligence Agency, *Problems and Prospects*; and Central Intelligence Agency, *Soviet Economy.*

91. M. M. Jermol and L. A. Magnusson, *Soviet Preparations for Major Boost of Oil Exports.* Malmö, Sweden:

PetroStudies Rept. GOP-782, 1978; M. M. Jermol and L. A. Magnusson, *Soviet Proved Oil Reserves, 1946–1980.* Malmö, Sweden: PetroStudies Rept., 1979; D. Park, *Oil and Gas in Comecon Countries.* (London: Kogan Page, 1978); Segal, "Soviet Oil Outlook"; and Segal, "CIA's Dire Forecast."

92. Graifer et al., "Important direction"; Kontorovich et al., "Basic stages"; Yerofeyev et al., "Oil and gas exploration"; "Productive forces in West Siberia"; "Complex development in West Siberia"; Central Committee CPSU, "Oil Ministry Symposium."

93. Fainburg, in "Productive forces in West Siberia," p. 110; and Shaparov, in "Complex development in West Siberia," p. 32.

94. Kontorovich et al., "Basic stages"; and Yerofeyev et al., "Oil and gas exploration."

95. Neporozhny, "Soviet and world power engineering."

96. *Pravda*, 18 December 1977, p. 2.

97. *Pravda*, 13 February 1981.

98. Kontorovich et al., "Basic stages."

99. *Pravda*, 11 August 1977, p. 2.

100. Yerofeyev et al., "Oil and gas exploration."

101. Ibid.

102. Ya. N. Basin, Ye. V. Karus, L. G. Petrosyan, V. Yu. Zaichenko, and F. K. Salmanov, "Enhancing the effectiveness of geophysical investigations in Tyumen Oblast wells," *Geol. nefti i gaza*, 1977, no. 9, pp. 55–58.

103. Jermol and Magnusson, *Soviet Preparations*; Jermol and Magnusson, *Oil Reserves*; and Park, *Oil and Gas.*

104. Maksimov et al., *Mestorozhdeniya.*

105. A. P. Krylov, "On the rates of oilfield development," *EKO*, 1980, no. 1, pp. 65–74.

106. L. Melentyev and Ya. Makarov, "Long-term development of the fuels and energy complex," *Planovoye khozyaistvo*, 1980, no. 4, p. 91.

107. *Pravda*, 5 June 1978, p. 2 and 10 June 1978, p. 2; *Planovoye khozyaistvo*, 1978, no. 5, pp. 73–81; and *Neftyanoye khozyaistvo*, 1978, no. 5, pp. 3–5.

108. Fainburg, in "Productive forces in West Siberia."

109. Arzhanov, in Central Committee CPSU, pp. 3–5; Segal, "Soviet Oil Outlook"; and Segal, "CIA's Dire Forecast."

110. Fainburg, in "Productive forces in West Siberia."

111. Neporozhny, "Soviet and world power engineering."

112. Ibid., p. 1.

113. Ibid., p. 2.

114. Jermol and Magnusson, *Soviet Preparations.*

115. Jermol and Magnusson, *Oil Reserves.*

116. Jermol and Magnusson, *Soviet Preparations*, p. 48.

117. For example, see Maksimov, *Ekspluatatsiya neftyanykh mestorozhdenii.*

118. Jermol and Magnusson, *Soviet Preparations*, p. 16.

119. *Ekonomika neftyanoi promyshlennosti*, 1978, no. 2, pp. 17–20.

120. *Ekonomika neftyanoi promyshlennosti*, 1978, no. 7, p. 17.

121. Mirchink, "Working oil fields."

122. Jermol and Magnusson, *Soviet Preparations*, p. 26.

123. Maksimov et al., *Mestorozhdeniya.*

124. Jermol and Magnusson, *Soviet Preparations*, p. 26.

125. Ibid., p. 15.

126. Shashin, in Halbouty et al., *Oil and Gas Fields*.

127. Clarke et al., *Petroleum Geology*.

128. Jermol and Magnusson, *Oil Reserves*.

129. I. I. Nesterov, V. V. Poteryayeva, and F. K. Salmanov, *Zakonomernosti raspredeleniya krupnykh mestorozhdenii nefti i gaza v zemnoi kore* [Patterns of distribution of giant oil and gas fields in the earth's crust] (Moscow: Nedra, 1975), p. 73.

130. Ibid.

131. Vasilyev and Zhabrev, *Mestorozhdeniya*; Dikenshtein et al., *Neftegazonosnye provintsii*.

132. Jermol and Magnusson, *Oil Reserves*, pp. 27–30.

133. Meyerhoff, "Requirements for GKZ Certification"; Meyerhoff, "Soviet System"; and GKZ, *Instruktsiya*.

134. N. A. Eremenko and S. P. Maksimov, eds., *Perspektivnye neftegazonosnye provintsii Soyedinennykh Shtatov Ameriki* [Perspective oil and gas bearing provinces of the United States of America] (Moscow: Nedra, 1974).

135. G. P. Ovanesov and M. V. Feigin, "Questions on the confirmability of oil categories $C_1$ and $C_2$," *Geol. nefti i gaza*, 1975, no. 8, pp. 7–14.

136. Jermol and Magnusson, *Oil Reserves*, pp. 28–29.

137. Nesterov et al., *Zakonomernosti raspredeleniya*.

138. Vasilyev and Zhabrev, *Mestorozhdeniya*; Dikenshtein et al., *Neftegazonosnye provintsii*.

139. Vasilyev and Zhabrev, *Mestorozhdeniya*.

140. Nesterov et al., *Zakonomernosti raspredeleniya*, p. 73.

141. Owen, *Oil Finders*.

142. Halbouty et al., *Oil and Gas Fields*.

143. Jermol and Magnusson, *Oil Reserves*, Table 8, p. 106.

144. Arzhanov, in Central Committee CPSU, pp. 3–5.

145. Dikenshtein et al., *Neftegazonosnye provintsii*, Table 3.

146. Ovanesov and Feigin, "Confirmability of oil categories."

147. *Sovetskaya geologiya*, 1980, no. 4.

148. Park, *Oil and Gas*.

149. Ibid., p. 133.

150. Leslie Dienes, "Soviet Energy Policy and the Fossil Fuels," chapter 12 in this volume; Segal, "Soviet Oil Outlook"; Segal, "CIA's Dire Forecast."

151. S. Albinowski, in *Politika*, 24 September 1966 (Eng. trans. in R. E. Ebel, *Communist Trade in Oil and Gas*. New York: Praeger, 1970, pp. 249–54); I. Dobozi, "Energy carriers in the CMEA economies," *Valosag*, 1973, no. 1, pp. 18–27.

152. Park, *Oil and Gas*, p. 181.

153. Dienes, "Soviet Energy Policy."

154. Segal, "Soviet Oil Outlook"; Segal, "CIA's Dire Forecast."

155. Theodore Shabad and Victor L. Mote, *Gateway to Siberian Resources (The BAM)* (New York: John Wiley and Sons, Halsted Press Book), 1977.

156. Park, *Oil and Gas*, p. 215.

157. Ibid., p. 216.

158. Ibid., p. 220.

159. Park had read the CIA reports *Soviet Oil Production* (April) and *International Energy*, but not three subsequent reports—*Soviet Oil Production* (July), *Problems and prospects*, and *Soviet Economy*.

160. Park, *Oil and Gas*, p. 221.

161. Central Intelligence Agency, *Soviet Oil Production* (July).

162. Segal, "Soviet Oil Outlook"; Segal, "CIA's Dire Forecast."

163. Segal, "Soviet Oil Outlook," p. 51.

164. Ibid.

165. Trofimuk, *Neftegazonosnye basseiny*; Lvov, *Resursy prirodnogo gaza*.

166. Segal, "Soviet Oil Outlook," p. 53.

167. For production of the Soviet moves in the Middle East see Meyerhoff, "Geopolitical Implications"; Arthur A. Meyerhoff, "Communist Goals, Soviet Minerals Policy, and the CIA Reports, Pt. I: Historical Background, Motivations, and Present-day Policies," Petroconsultants, *Review of Sino-Soviet Oil*, vol. 12, no. 12 (1977): 1–21; Arthur A. Meyerhoff, "Communist goals, Soviet Minerals Policy, and the CIA Reports, Pt. II: Implications, Outlook and Conclusions," Petroconsultants, *Review of Sino-Soviet Oil*, vol. 13, no. 1 (1978): 1–14; and Meyerhoff, *Communist Goals* (April 1978).

168. Segal, "CIA's Dire Forecast," p. 17.

169. Ibid., p. 18.

# 15

# SOVIET NATURAL GAS IN THE WORLD ECONOMY

JONATHAN P. STERN
Conant & Associates, Ltd.

## Introduction

In the past, the Western literature on the Soviet energy situation has concentrated primarily on the production and export potential of Soviet oil. This emphasis was understandable in view of the paramount position of oil in the energy balances of Western industrialized countries and the importance that the Soviets themselves have attached to oil exports to the West. However, an estimated one-third of the world's natural gas reserves are also located on Soviet territory. The country has, in a relatively short time, become a major gas producer and exporter, and there is reason to expect significant expansion of both these functions in the future.

Despite the incredible wealth of resources, however, the problems of developing the Siberian regions, in which the major deposits are concentrated, are formidable, as are the distances between these regions and centers of consumption. Much remains to be accomplished in the development of equipment and technology of the gas industry and particular attention focuses on long-distance pipeline transportation, which holds the key to how much gas can be produced over the next decade. The first part of this paper[1] suggests production parameters for the Soviet gas industry in the light of the problems that it faces in the 1980s.

The second part of the paper attempts to assess Soviet gas trade as a partial response to some of these problems and suggests a rationale for each of the Soviet gas trades. The different trading partners of the USSR provide a means by which some of the problems of the gas industry can be offset, notably locational problems, lack of advanced equipment and technology, lack of investment, scarce manpower, etc.

The third section analyzes the demand for Soviet gas in Western markets in the light of competing supplies and other factors that may influence such trade, notably political relations of importing countries with the Soviet Union. Having analyzed the situation from the viewpoint of the world economy, it is necessary to take into account the demand from other Comecon countries, notably those in Eastern Europe, to which the Soviet Union has definite commitments. In conclusion, the paper offers an estimate of Soviet natural gas exports to the world economy in 1990, fully recognizing that, in its conduct of energy policy within the Comecon region, there are a number of options open to the USSR, of which the export of natural gas to the West is only one.

## Soviet Natural Gas to 1990

Reserves: Estimates and Distribution

On a subject that lacks accurate data, there is little argument about the proposition not only that the Soviet Union possesses proven gas reserves of immense proportions, but that additional sizable discoveries can be expected in the future. In discussions of Soviet fuel reserves, much attention is devoted to the fact that Russian classifications are not comparable to those used in the West.[2] This need not detain us here, since unlike the situation in the Soviet oil industry, the reserve position is not a factor that will retard the development of Soviet natural gas over the next decade. As of 1 January 1980, the USSR was reckoned to possess 30.6 trillion cubic meters (Tcm) of gas, or 41.4 percent of world proven reserves. The country with the next largest resource base was Iran with 14.5 percent of world reserves; the entire gas reserves of North America were estimated at no more than 11 percent of the world's total.[3]

For ultimately recoverable reserves, the figures become more tenuous. In January 1971, the potential resource base was estimated by a Soviet source to be 150.2 Tcm, comprising 124.7 Tcm onshore and 25.5 Tcm offshore (in the one million square miles of promising petroliferous coastal shelf of waters no deeper than 200 meters).[4] Since that estimate, further large finds have been made, especially offshore in the Arctic seas.[5] These figures do not include gas hydrates (also referred to as "solid gas") which exist in the northern latitudes where a combination of low temperature and high pressure gives rise to crystalline ice structures containing a high proportion of gas.[6]

Table 1 shows the regional distribution and development of Soviet gas reserves from 1951 to 1976. (The detailed distribution of Soviet gas reserves, last published in 1974, is mapped in Figure 1.) The table has been de-

TABLE 1
Soviet Natural Gas Reserves $(A + B + C_1)$ Distribution (billion cubic meters, beginning of year)

| | 1951 | 1960 | 1971 | 1974 | 1976 |
|---|---|---|---|---|---|
| USSR[i] | 173.0 | 2,202.4 | 15,750.1 | 22,413.6 | 25,800 |
| European USSR and Urals: | 167.5 | 1,554.4 | 3,026.2 | 4,221.4 | 4,200 |
| Komi | 20.8 | 18.1 | 405.6 | 367.1 | |
| Bashkir | 0 | 23.1 | 54.5 | 58.2 | |
| Perm | 0 | 0 | 40.8 | 61.5 | |
| Kuibyshev | 3.1 | 4.6 | 4.1 | 3.4 | |
| Orenburg | 4.3 | 16.9 | 1,124.9 | 2,108.0 | |
| Saratov | 21.3 | 66.9 | 59.4 | 62.2 | |
| Volgograd | 6.4 | 141.6 | 85.7 | 77.3 | |
| Astrakhan and Kalmyk | 0 | 11.6 | 20.4 | 16.4 | |
| Rostov | 0 | 0 | 8.9 | 9.3 | |
| Krasnodar | 0 | 359.4 | 89.7 | 256.0 | |
| Stavropol | 26.8 | 249.6 | 198.6 | 171.3 | |
| Dagestan | 0.5 | 0.1 | 35.0 | 31.2 | |
| Chechen-Ingush | 4.9 | 2.0 | 8.3 | 8.2 | |
| Ukraine | 70.3 | 544.8 | 810.0 | 868.7 | |
| Azerbaijan | 9.1 | 115.7 | 80.3 | 122.6 | |
| East of Urals: | 5.5 | 627.2 | 12,506.9 | 18,026.1 | 21,600 |
| Tyumen* | 0 | 50.2 | 9,252.3 | 13,749.5 ⎫ | |
| Tomsk and Novosibirsk* | 0 | 0 | 231.2 | 256.3 ⎪ | |
| Krasnoyarsk | 0 | 0 | 149.8 | 302.9 ⎪ | 18,200 |
| Irkutsk | 0 | 0 | 12.9 | 12.9 ⎬ | |
| Yakutia | 0 | 0 | 259.5 | 316.2 ⎪ | |
| Sakhalin | 1.1 | 7.4 | 57.5 | 68.2 ⎭ | |
| Tadzhikistan | 0 | 3.4 | 31.7 | 29.0 ⎫ | |
| Kirghizia | 0 | 7.7 | 15.6 | 15.3 ⎪ | |
| Kazakhstan | 0 | 1.2 | 177.3 | 167.6 ⎬ | 3,400 |
| Uzbekistan | 4.4 | 544.2 | 796.8 | 949.6 ⎪ | |
| Turkmenistan | 0 | 13.1 | 1,522.3 | 2,158.6 ⎭ | |

*Tyumen plus Tomsk and Novosibirsk make up the energy-producing region of Western Siberia.
[i]Totals do not necessarily add.
SOURCES: *USSR: Development of the Gas Industry*. Central Intelligence Agency ER 78–10393, July 1978, adapted from Table J–11, p. 68. 1976 figures from Dienes and Shabad, *The Soviet Energy System* (New York: Wiley, 1979), Table 17, p. 69.

liberately presented with the division of the country into two 'halves,' with the vast majority of the population and industry being found in the European USSR and Urals but, in the 1970s, the fuels reserves increasingly located east of the Urals. Two phases stand out in the development of the reserve base: in the 1950s there was the rapid discovery of reserves in the western part of the country and also in Central Asia; in the 1960s and 1970s there was the phenomenal expansion of reserves, mainly in the eastern part of the country, but especially in West Siberia. By the mid-1970s, 80 percent of the reserve base was situated in the eastern regions and if more recent figures were available, they would certainly show a continuation of this trend, accompanied by a decline in the reserve position of the European zone.

It is difficult to appreciate the magnitude of the Soviet reserve position, but a comparative example may prove helpful. The largest natural gas field in Western Europe is at Groningen in the Netherlands, where reserves of 2.2 Tcm were uncovered. The newest American deposit at Prudhoe Bay in Alaska is thought to contain 0.7 Tcm. In West Siberia, the Urengoi field has proven reserves of 6 Tcm and 3 Tcm of possible reserves. In the same area, there are five other fields with reserves well over 1 Tcm, with the figures being constantly uprated. These figures clearly demonstrate that the reserve position of natural

gas in the USSR is adequate to meet considerably increased production totals. As has been the case in the past, any failure to produce the gas at the required rate must be attributable to other factors relating to the location rather than the size of the resource base.

Production

The geographical imbalance in the reserve position is starting to be reflected in the regional production totals (Table 2). The major characteristic of the production situation in the 1970s as compared to the previous decade was the shift in location from the European fields of the North Caucasus and Ukraine, first to Central Asia and then increasingly to West Siberia. This has taken place as a result of depletion of reserves at the European deposits, where fuel has become correspondingly difficult and expensive to extract. Nevertheless, the locational advantages of these fields with respect to market has meant that great attempts have been made to keep them in maximum production for the longest possible time.

As attention now focuses on West Siberia, it should not be forgotten that, until 1976, the Ukraine remained the single most important producing region in the country. Totals then began to fall since many of the smaller deposits have become uneconomic, largely on account of

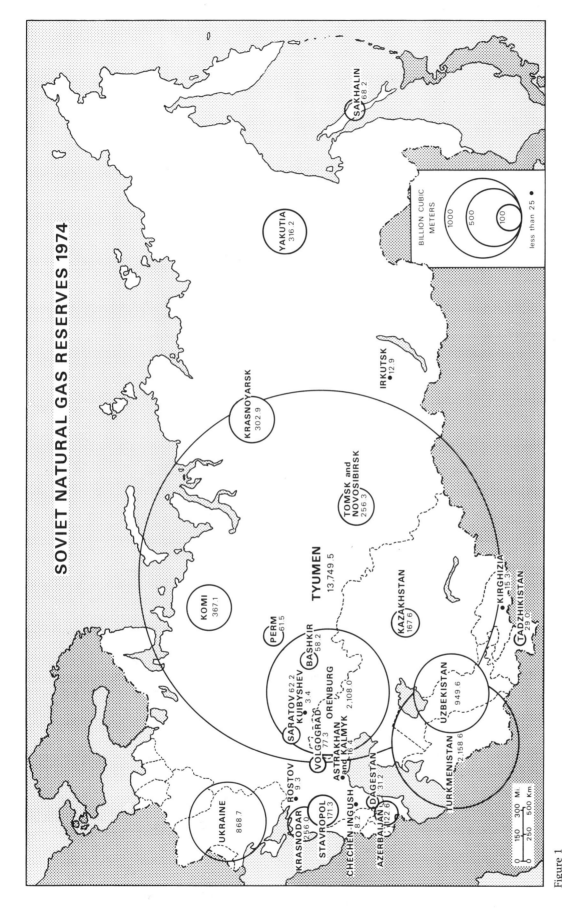

Figure 1
SOURCE: Data from Table 1.

TABLE 2
Soviet Gas Production by Region (billion cubic meters)

| | 1960 | 1970 | 1975 | 1980 | 1981 | 1985 Plan |
|---|---|---|---|---|---|---|
| European USSR and Urals: | 44.5 | 138.9 | 155 | 160 | 155 | 140 |
| Ukraine | 14 | 61 | 68.7 | 52 | 49 | (40) |
| Azerbaijan | 6 | 6 | 9.9 | 14.5 | 15 | (13) |
| North Caucasus | 14 | 47 | 23 | 14 | — | (5) |
| Orenburg | 1 | 1 | 19.6 | 48 | 48 | (48) |
| Komi ASSR | 0 | 7 | 18.5 | 17.5 | — | (17) |
| East of Urals: | 0.8 | 59.0 | 134 | 275 | 310 | 490 |
| West Siberia | 0 | 9 | 35.7 | 156 | 190 | 357 |
| Kazakhstan | 0 | 2 | 5.2 | 5 | 5 | 7.9 |
| Uzbekistan | 0 | 32 | 37.2 | 39 | 39 | 37 |
| Turkmenistan | 0 | 13 | 51.8 | 70.3 | 70 | 82 |
| USSR Total | 45.3 | 198 | 289 | 435 | 465 | 630 |

SOURCES: Margulov, Selikhova and Furman, *Razvitiye gazovoi promyshlennosti i analiz tekhniko-ekonomicheskikh pokazatelei* [Development of the gas industry and analysis of technical-economic indicators], Ministerstvo Gazovoi Promyshlennosti, Moscow, 1976, Tables 3 and 31, pp. 6 and 41.

Theodore Shabad, "News Notes" in *Soviet Geography: Review and Translation*, various issues, especially April 1982.

Leslie Dienes and Theodore Shabad, *The Soviet Energy System* (New York: Wiley, 1979), Table 18, pp. 70–71.

the depths at which work must be carried out.[7] Throughout the 1960s, the Ukraine and North Caucasus bore the brunt of the burden of production, although by the end of the decade, Central Asia had also become an important producing region. The 1970s saw Central Asian production rise dramatically with the deposits at Uzbekistan (particularly the Gazli field) and Turkmenistan (Shatlyk, Achak, Naip), accounting for nearly one-third of total Soviet production. West Siberian production rose from practically nothing at the beginning of the 1970s to about 190 Bcm in 1981. This rapid development of a remote region must be considered a remarkable achievement that has been overshadowed by the even more remarkable expansion of oil production in West Siberia. As two Western chroniclers of Siberian development note, "The development of West Siberian natural gas resources has been lagging behind the development of oil, partly because the Central Asian gas fields also provide a substantial source of gas for the Soviet economy, but also because of the more remote location of the gas fields near the Arctic Circle."[8]

In addition to these major trends, a few words should be said about the Orenburg deposit. Apart from the Vuktyl field in Komi ASSR (which, on account of its northerly latitude, presents Siberian-type characteristics), the Orenburg gas deposit is the only sizable accumulation to have been developed in the 1970s in a part of the country relatively proximate to markets and where the climatic conditions are relatively temperate. Production totals have reached a capacity level of 48 billion cubic meters (Bcm) a year and much of the gas is being exported to Eastern (and Western) Europe via the Orenburg pipeline (of which more will be said below).

*The Growth of Gas Production.* In terms of total production, the gas industry can be considered to have made a com-

paratively slow start in its contribution to the Soviet energy economy. There was a lack of appreciation of the relative efficiency of gas utilization and hence lack of interest in promoting exploration. One Western authority notes: "The main reason for the late development of gas is that the Russians were simply unaware during the whole of the prewar period of their potential riches. It was not wrong policy but ignorance."[9]

By the end of the 1950s, annual percentage increases were startling (nearly 60 percent for 1958) but actual volumes remained small, with production totaling only 44 Bcm in 1960.[10] The first years of the 1960s witnessed annual volume increases of around 16 Bcm, or 23 percent, which fell to 14 Bcm (9.2 percent) in the latter part of the decade. Over the 9th Five-Year Plan (1971–75) the average annual percentage increase declined further to 7.9 percent although volume increases rose to 18.3 Bcm per year (Table 3).

Table 4 shows the composition of Soviet gas production, from which it can be seen that the vast majority of the gas utilized is natural gas. Gas extracted from coal and shale (which is not included in these statistics) is quantitatively unimportant, accounting for only 1.5–2.0 Bcm per year.[11] Associated gas (also known as oilwell or casinghead gas) is extracted together with oil by the oil industry, which also collects some natural gas not associated with oil fields. Oil Ministry and Gas Ministry production is

TABLE 3
Soviet Gas Production, Planned and Actual and Annual Percentage Increases 1960–80 (billion cubic meters)

| | Plan | | | Annual Percentage |
|---|---|---|---|---|
| | Original | Revised | Actual | Increase |
| 1960 | 60 | 53 | 45.3 | 28.0 |
| 1961 | — | 60.1 | 59.0 | 30.2 |
| 1962 | — | 70.5 | 73.5 | 24.6 |
| 1963 | — | 91.6 | 89.8 | 22.2   1961–65 |
| 1964 | — | — | 108.6 | 20.9   23.1% |
| 1965 | 150 | 129.4 | 127.7 | 17.6 |
| 1966 | 142 | 148 | 143.0 | 12.0 |
| 1967 | 158.3 | 160 | 157.4 | 10.1 |
| 1968 | 170.3 | 171.3 | 169.1 | 7.4   1966–70 |
| 1969 | 191.1 | 184.0 | 181.1 | 7.1   9.2% |
| 1970 | 225–240 | 198 | 197.9 | 9.3 |
| 1971 | 211 | 211 | 212.4 | 7.3 |
| 1972 | 229 | — | 221.4 | 4.2 |
| 1973 | 250 | 238 | 236.3 | 6.7   1971–75 |
| 1974 | 280 | 257 | 260.6 | 10.3   7.9% |
| 1975 | 320 | 285.2 | 289.3 | 11.0 |
| 1976 | — | 313 | 321.0 | 11.0 |
| 1977 | — | 342 | 346.0 | 7.8 |
| 1978 | — | 370 | 372.2 | 7.6   1976–80 |
| 1979 | — | 404 | 406.6 | 9.2   8.5% |
| 1980 | 435 | 435 | 435 | 7.0 |
| 1981 | — | 458 | 465 | 6.9 |
| 1982 | — | 492 | (500) | (7.5) |
| 1985 | 600–640 | 630 | — | 7 (plan) |

SOURCES: J. L. Russell, *Energy as a Factor in Soviet Foreign Policy*, (Saxon House/Lexington Books, 1976), Tables 1.4 and 1.5, pp. 20–21.

Theodore Shabad, "News Notes," *Soviet Geography: Review and Translation*, various issues.

TABLE 4
Soviet Natural and Associated Gas Production 1950–70
(billion cubic meters)

| | Total | Natural | Associated* |
|---|---|---|---|
| 1951–55 | 36.1 | 23.5 | 12.6 |
| 1956–60 | 138.3 | 111.7 | 26.6 |
| 1961 | 59.0 | 50.4 | 8.6 |
| 1962 | 73.5 | 63.5 | 10.0 |
| 1963 | 89.8 | 77.7 | 12.1 |
| 1964 | 108.6 | 94.4 | 14.2 |
| 1965 | 127.7 | 111.2 | 16.5 |
| 1961–65 | 458.6 | 397.2 | 61.4 |
| 1966 | 143.0 | 125.2 | 17.8 |
| 1967 | 157.4 | 138.6 | 18.8 |
| 1968 | 169.1 | 149.5 | 19.6 |
| 1969 | 181.1 | 159.5 | 21.6 |
| 1970 | 197.9 | 174.9 | 23.0 |
| 1966–70 | 848.5 | 747.7 | 100.8 |
| 1971 | 212.4 | 187.4 | 25.0 |
| 1972 | 221.4 | 195.6 | 25.8 |
| 1973 | 236.3 | 209.8 | 26.5 |
| 1974 | 260.6 | 233.0 | 27.6 |
| 1975 | 289.3 | 260.7 | 28.6 |
| 1971–75 | 1,220.0 | 1,086.5 | 133.5 |
| 1976 | 321.0 | 290.4 | 30.6 |
| 1977 | 346.0 | 314.5 | 31.5 |
| 1978 | 372.2 | 338.4 | 33.8 |
| 1979 | 406.6 | — | — |
| 1980 | 435.2 | 405 | 30 |
| 1981 | 465 | 433 | 31.7 |

*These figures refer only to associated gas that is utilized.
SOURCES: Brents, Gandkin, and Urinson, *Ekonomika gazodobyvayushchei promyshlennosti* [Economics of the gas industry], Moscow, 1975, p. 34.
Leslie Dienes and Theodore Shabad, *Soviet Energy System*, Table 22, p. 96.

totaled to arrive at the overall gas production figure. In the early 1950s, associated gas was important, amounting to more than one-third of the total production. By 1960, the share of this gas was 18 percent and more recently it has fallen to less than 10 percent.

Relative to plan targets, the performance of the industry in the 1960–75 period was extremely poor. As shown in Table 3, hardly a single original plan was met after 1960.[12] Nor has it been a case of near misses: the 1965 plan stipulated 150 Bcm with an actual achievement of 128 Bcm; the 1970 plan target was 225–240 Bcm, but the industry managed only 198 Bcm. In the 1971–75 period, the shortfall was less striking, but production remained consistently below target. The industry made a bad start in that period from which it never recovered, despite good results in the last two years. The goal of 320 Bcm for 1975 necessitated a sustained 10 percent rate of growth. Over the first three years, increases in production averaged only 6 percent. Although 1974 and 1975 were to bring increases of 10.3 and 11.0 percent respectively, the effects of such a bad start could not be overcome and the 1975 total reached only 289.3 Bcm.

*The 10th Five-Year Plan (1976–80).* The result that the gas industry has achieved since 1975 can only be called re-

markable, especially when contrasted with the record cited above. The plan targets were fulfilled each year.

There are a number of reasons for the improvement in the industry's performance but three factors are of particular salience. First, the industry appears to have been more successful in halting depletion in the western part of the country than many Western analysts had expected. Although the North Caucasus has suffered a decline, the Ukraine has held fairly steady, although it can now be expected to decline at an increasing rate. Second, the Tyumen region of Western Siberia, where formidable technical and infrastructural problems were encountered at the outset of operations, began to come on stream rapidly. Third, and possibly most important, one gets the feeling that unrealistic plan targets made the performance of the industry in the 1960s and early 1970s seem somewhat worse than it actually was, given the range and complexity of the problems that were being encountered during that period.

In general terms it is probably correct to say that the industry has been the victim of a long series of obstacles: it has suffered from an inadequate volume of capital investment for the construction of an infrastructural base; poor management and organization of the functions of the industry; inadequate technology; poor support from other industries (particularly the construction industry) with regard to the provision of key materials; competition with other sectors (particularly the oil industry) for financial and infrastructural resources.

Taking these factors into account, together with the additional problems regarding the regions into which the industry is moving, one tends to arrive at the conclusion that performance has been quite acceptable and that planners have made achievements seem disappointing by unrealistically bullish forecasts. It is certainly true that the other energy industries faced the same kind of problems and managed to cope with them more successfully. The gas industry was particularly unfortunate, however, in experiencing all these difficulties at such an early stage in its development when it was accorded the status of a major energy-producing industry and expected to perform as such without sufficient priority status in either capital investment or materials.

Although by no means all (or indeed any) of these problems had been completely overcome by the start of the 10th Five-Year Plan, one could discern a number of favorable trends that began to indicate that the industry could look forward to a period of enhanced growth.

First, a proven resource base of considerable proportions had been established with a number of extremely large fields in Western Siberia. While not ideally located in relation to centers of consumption, these fields are relatively close to each other and this should facilitate bringing them into production once the basic infrastructure has been laid down.

Second, a more realistic approach has been adopted to the problems of the industry and a greater effort to solve these in some systematic fashion has been evident. The reform of the administration was the first positive step in this direction.[13] There was also official recognition that many of the technical problems facing the industry resulted from a lack of equipment that could not be domestically produced; a policy of importing pipeline and compressor stations was instituted.

Third, some of the technical problems of the industry show signs of being resolved. The Soviets are overcoming their inability to handle large diameter pipe that had hampered progress in the construction of the pipeline network for a number of years. The same is true in the areas of compressor station and gas treatment technology where the Soviets have made great effort to master the efficient utilization of the units they import from the West.

In this connection, it is interesting to note the presence of Soviet observers at natural gas installations in West Germany (as part of the repayment package for Soviet gas exports). Also, the Japanese have specifically agreed to train Soviet crews as part of the Sakhalin offshore venture.[14] Such cooperation has resulted in a more technically proficient, higher caliber labor force, in comparison to the 1960s.

Overall, perhaps the best analysis of the situation in the mid-1970s comes from a Soviet source who notes that the development of the industry can be divided into two periods, the years before 1972, "characterized by the adoption of assignments that were overstated in comparison to resources and unreliable . . . The second period since 1972 is still taking shape, but one can say that it has been characterized chiefly by more realistic plans, achieved at the expense of reduced development rates."[15] Overall, the 10th Five-Year Plan must be regarded as an extremely satisfactory period for the industry. The 1980 production goal was originally given in terms of a range 400–435 billion cubic meters, which represented a projected average annual increase of 6.7–8.5 percent over the five years and reflected the 7.9 percent achieved over the previous five years. In the West, the plan was met with understandable skepticism and an authoritative source stated that "the present plan appears as optimistic as those of the recent past and production in 1980 is unlikely to exceed 390 Bcm."[16]

The industry in fact met the 1980 target of 435 Bcm. Rather more important than this, however, is the fact that over the first four years of the period, the industry delivered 19.2 Bcm above plan and this should be the primary measure of its success rather than the more often quoted final-year result.

*The Decade of the 1980s.* A long-range Soviet projection that would have provided a Soviet estimate for gas production in 1990 had been expected but has not appeared. In the absence of such a document, we have little to guide us in terms of Soviet estimates of production, save some earlier prediction of 1990 production suggesting a total of 900–920 Bcm.[17] Given a 1980 production of 435 Bcm, this estimate would indicate an increase of 7.8 percent per year throughout the decade. Considering the expanding size of the base of the industry, this growth must be seen as unrealistically high. Volume increases probably provide a better yardstick for feasible targets than percentages, and for the industry to be able to more than double its production within the decade would be a most remarkable feat.

As far as Soviet forecasts are concerned, the drastic overestimation of plan targets in the 1960–75 period, followed by underestimation of the capability of the industry in the 10th Five-Year Plan, suggests that the planners have no very clear idea of how much gas can be produced by 1990. Given that the planners have the best available information at their disposal, this gives an idea of just how much guesswork is involved in any figures that are put forward here. Nevertheless, on the basis of the judgment that the industry is entering a period of sustained growth, it is not unlikely that volume increases in production will rise by 5 Bcm annually from the current 30–35 Bcm (Table 3) to 35–40 Bcm per year. Working from a production figure of 435 Bcm for 1980, this would imply a 1990 production total of 800–850 Bcm. The official Soviet plan for 1985 of 630 Bcm would appear to be in line with such a forecast.[18]

In terms of regional production trends in the 1980s, it is no exaggeration to say that the industry will stand or fall by its performance in the Tyumen region of Western Siberia, more specifically in the Urengoi field, where production is scheduled to quintuple from some 50 billion cubic meters in 1980 to 250 billion in 1985. Later in the decade, development is expected to get under way at Yamburg and Zapolyarnoye and possibly Bovanenko and Kharasavei on the Yamal Peninsula.[19]

Despite these incredible riches, the enormity of the task that faces the Soviet gas industry, if it is to reach the production levels that have been suggested here, should not be underestimated. In the 1980s, the industry will have to deal with many of the same problems as in the past, but on an ever-increasing scale. Its ability to improve on past performance in dealing with these problems will determine whether our forecasts are proved correct.

Problems in the Natural Gas Industry

The two basic obstacles facing the development of the Soviet natural gas industry (and indeed all the Soviet energy industries) are the nature of the climate and terrain in which important deposits are located; and the distance of those deposits from the major centers of consumption. In addition, as the centers of consumption move progressively farther east and north, these two trends will intensify; hence, in the future, the Soviets can expect to face these problems on an increasing scale.

The success of the industry in the 1980s will depend on its capacity to cope with these two factors more successfully than it has managed hitherto. Any improvement will therefore have to assume at least two major elements: a greatly expanded transportation network, and the acquisition (and correct utilization) of the relevant equipment and technology to deal with the conditions found in the areas into which the industry is moving.

*The Transportation Network.* The history of the gas pipeline network goes back to before World War II when Lvov was supplied with gas from the Dashava field through a 200 mm diameter pipeline. In 1946, the first "long-distance" pipeline, 788 km long, began to deliver gas from Saratov to Moscow.[20] From these small beginnings, the network has expanded tremendously in terms of length, throughput and diameter of pipe. More than 25 percent of the network consists of pipe greater than 1,020 mm in diameter and the use of 1,420 mm pipe increased from 3.6 percent of the network in 1975 to 11 percent in 1980.[21] The structure of the natural gas pipeline network is shown in Figure 2.

Over the past decade, efforts in the pipeline sector have been directed toward the creation of a unified pipeline network by constructing links between the major pipelines. These endeavors are based on the argument that a united system of pipelines and storage reservoirs would be more secure, as it would guarantee alternative supplies to the most vital areas and allow a reduction in stocks at various fields. It would also make possible, with the aid of computers and greater automation, an elaboration of optimum patterns for individual supply systems, as well as for the network as a whole. It was envisaged that the third and fourth strings of the Central Asia-Central Russia trunkline would serve as a backbone to the proposed network.[22]

In view of the regional trends of the industry, it is evident that the distance over which an average cubic meter of gas has to be transported is constantly growing. Table 5 shows the growth in the average length of haul rising from 589 km in 1960 to 1,851 in 1980.[23]

Furthermore, the additional lengths of pipeline are being constructed under increasingly harsh conditions and on difficult terrain. It is not surprising, therefore, that the economic indicators of transportation worsened considerably in the first half of the 1970s, with return on capital falling by 40 percent and costs per thousand cubic meters transported rising by more than 30 percent.[24]

In order to cope with both the larger volumes of gas and the longer distances, the total length of the system increased by a factor of five in the 15 years since 1960, measuring nearly 100,000 kilometers in 1975 and 132,000 km in 1980. In the 11th Five-Year Plan, 40,000–50,000 km is to be added, including 26,000 km of 1,400 mm pipe, to reach a network length of 170,000–180,000 km.[25]

Given the magnitude of the transportation problem, it is not surprising that an immense amount of Soviet indigenous technological effort is being devoted to new methods of transportation. In the mid-1970s, this effort had come to center on the development of liquefied natural gas (LNG) technology. Normally LNG technology refers to transportation (for export) of liquid gas in tankers, such as for the Yakutia and North Star projects (see below). In addition to the export possibilities, however, there is increasing awareness that LNG technology has applicability for the solution of the transport problem within the country.[26]

In the early 1970s there was talk of producing pipe of 2,500 mm diameter but this never got beyond a prototype, apparently due to difficulties in technology and extremely high cost. There now exists a technology that can use liquefaction and increased pressurization to transport a vastly increased quantity of gas (three to five times as much) through the same diameter pipeline. Use of this method would reduce transport costs by 20 to 25 percent and thus obviously be an extremely attractive prospect for the Soviets, given the necessity of expediting long-distance transport of increasingly large quantities of gas.[27] This venture is an extremely ambitious attempt by the Soviets to develop a technology that has not yet been either fully tested or commercially proven in the West.[28] There were reports that a test laboratory had been set up in Komi ASSR, where a closed ring of pipeline with two reservoirs and a gas liquefaction plant were being built on the Northern Lights pipeline.[29]

The most recent reports suggest that the gas may not actually be transported in liquid form but chilled to a temperature of zero to −10°C. Such an experimental system is being set up for the pipeline running between the Urengoi deposit and the town of Nadym, a distance of 150 miles.[30] In fact, research is under way to adjust all the variables in the transportation system: the temperature of the gas; the pressure in the pipeline; the number of compressor stations in the line.[31]

One big problem in this effort will be the development of metallurgical processes required to produce steel pipe of sufficiently high quality to withstand the high-pressure, low-temperature transmission. Inadequate domestic production of pipe has in the past led to large-scale imports of Western pipe. Poor quality of Soviet pipe has been responsible for large-scale pipe rupture on main trunkline routes. In order to increase the strength of the pipe and lessen the chance of rupture, the Soviets are now developing multilayer pipe that is twisted when drawn from sheet metal in the mill so that it is spiral in cross section. Two plants are slated to begin producing multilayer pipe in the near future, but such is the customary delay in Soviet pipe construction that it would be surprising to see large-scale results of this effort before the early 1980s.[32]

Although these developments are still at an early stage, it is interesting that the late Minister of the Gas Industry, S. A. Orudzhev, called them the most pressing problems facing the industry in the current period. The reason why it is worth devoting some detailed discussion to them is that, if the Soviets could really make a breakthrough in gas transportation, it could make a great deal of difference to the volume of gas that could be produced in the near to medium term and go some way toward offsetting the locational imbalance.

In addition to improving the pipeline network, however, the gas industry also needs to devote more resources to building and installing compressor stations to pump gas through the pipelines at the correct rate, thus insuring efficient utilization. The 1960s saw a very slow building program materialize for these vital installations and, although performance in the 1970s has been better (with 30 stations per year being completed during the 9th Five-Year Plan), there is still underutilization of some major pipelines.[33] Overall, it seems possible that the transportation system in 1975 was underutilized by as much as one-third as a result of inadequate provision of compressor stations.[34]

*Equipment and Technology.* Nearly three-quarters of the drilling in the Soviet energy industries is still performed by turbodrill, a method that is extremely inefficient at depths below 3,000 meters. Insufficient investment has

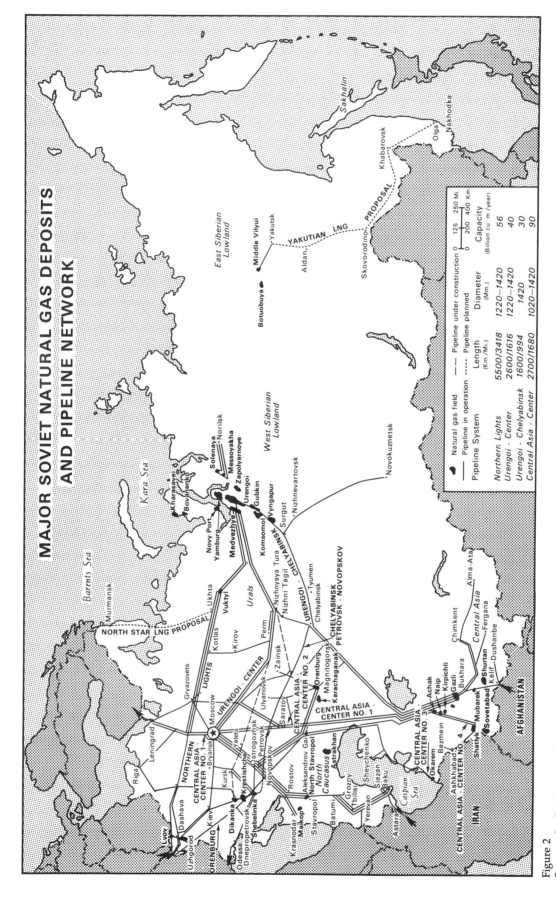

Figure 2
SOURCE: Leslie Dienes and Theodore Shabad, *The Soviet Energy System* (New York: Wiley, 1979),
Figure 5, pp. *72–73*; CIA, *USSR: Development of the Gas Industry ER 78-10393 (July 1978)* p. 88.

TABLE 5
Development of the Soviet Gas Trunkline System

| | Total Length of System (1,000 km) | Average Length of Haul (km) | Commercial Gas Transported by Trunkline (billion cubic meters) |
|---|---|---|---|
| 1960 | 21.0 | 589 | 32.8 |
| 1961 | 25.3 | 601 | 41.9 |
| 1962 | 28.5 | 611 | 53.6 |
| 1963 | 33.0 | 616 | 68.6 |
| 1964 | 37.1 | 644 | 87.7 |
| 1965 | 41.8 | 656 | 112.1 |
| 1966 | 47.4 | 678 | 128.8 |
| 1967 | 52.6 | 744 | 143.3 |
| 1968 | 56.1 | 864 | 155.1 |
| 1969 | 63.2 | 909 | 166.0 |
| 1970 | 67.5 | 917 | 181.5 |
| 1971 | 71.5 | 964 | 209.8 |
| 1972 | 77.7 | 1,004 | 219.9 |
| 1973 | 83.5 | 1,051 | 231.1 |
| 1974 | 92.1 | 1,154 | 245.7 |
| 1975 | 98.8 | 1,237 | 279.4 |
| 1976 | 103.1 | 1,341 | 309.5 |
| 1977 | 110.4 | (1,456) | 334.6 |
| 1978 | 117.6 | — | 351.1 |
| 1979 | 124 | — | 378 |
| 1980 | 132 | 1,851 | 401 |
| 1985 Plan | 170–180 | — | — |

SOURCE: *Narodnoye khozyaistvo SSSR* for respective years, for length of system and transported gas. Length of haul series from J. L. Russell, *Energy as a Factor in Soviet Foreign Policy* (Lexington: Saxon House, 1976), p. 67; 1967 length of haul from: S. S. Ushakov and T. M. Borisenko, *Ekonomika transporta topliva i energii* [Economics of fuel and energy transport] (Moscow: Energiya, 1970), p. 66; 1980 length of haul from *Problemy razvitiya transporta SSSR* [Problems in the development of transportation in the USSR] (Moscow: Transport, 1981), p. 161.

been devoted to the introduction of new drilling techniques although the average hole depth, particularly in the older regions, is increasing rapidly. Continued reliance on the turbodrill will have serious implications since average hole depth increased from 1,900 meters in 1970 to 2,100 meters in 1975 and was to rise to 2,700 meters by 1980.[35]

Soviet wells cannot be commercially drilled much deeper than 4,500–5,000 meters. There are well publicized "super-deep" wells that are extremely expensive and take a great deal of time to complete. Depths greater than 3,500 meters are termed "deep drilling" in the industry literature.[36] Complications often set in at around 2,500 meters, when the equipment begins to break down often, in the case of rotary drilling, because Soviet drill pipe cannot withstand the torque generated by this method.

There are many other equipment and technical problems relating to the drilling process: shortage of high-yield casing pipe, shortage of drilling muds, poor-quality drill bits; the whole question of drilling in a permafrost, often hundreds of feet thick, still has to be satisfactorily resolved.

A general problem resulting from these shortcomings in equipment and technology is the volume of fuel wastage throughout the industry. This problem has received particular attention of late, as the necessity for maximum

utilization and fuel savings throughout CMEA has assumed the character of a major campaign. One of the most glaring examples of waste in the natural gas industry is the volume of associated gas that is flared each year for lack of collecting and processing facilities.[37] For example, in addition to the 28.6 Bcm of associated gas utilized in 1975, 19 Bcm was flared.[38] This wastage was reduced somewhat in the second half of the 1970s as more gas-processing capacity came on stream in West Siberia. The industry can ill afford to throw away billions of cubic meters of gas per year, but the infrastructure for collecting, transporting and storing the gas simply was not available, short of diverting resources from other oil and gas projects. If more associated gas is to be utilized, then the pipe, processing plant and compressors will have to come from somewhere. As indicated above, all these items are in short supply throughout the energy industries.

*Labor and Infrastructure.* The Soviet economy is labor-deficient and the energy sector is no exception. Apart from a generalized shortage of labor in the energy industries, the conditions in the new areas require workers to operate at high levels of skill. Planners are trying to reduce high turnover rates in order to build up a core of skilled labor in the outlying areas where yearly turnover can amount to as much as 90 percent of the labor force. The primary reason for worker dissatisfaction is poor housing. In a survey conducted in Tyumen Oblast, nearly half the workers gave inadequate housing conditions as their reason for leaving.[39] Material incentives in the form of higher wages, better leave conditions, early retirement, high pensions, etc., do not seem to outweigh the considerable physical hardships sustained by the worker and his family.[40]

Labor-related problems have received substantial attention from the authorities, as a large part of future production increases are dependent on growth in labor productivity. The 1976–80 plans called for a 32 percent increase in labor productivity, compared with 8 percent in the previous five years.[41] To realize such goals, planners must systematically construct, especially in the Siberian regions, a social infrastructure with a range of amenities. Prefabricated housing units have been neither technically perfected nor adopted by the workers as acceptable long-term accommodation, and a program of permanent housing construction was being pressed in the early 1980s. Clearly these matters will be a key area of concern in the years ahead.

Investment in infrastructure requires a large proportion of the total investment in the industry, especially in Siberia, where transportation combined with socio-cultural facilities amounted to more than half the expenditure at the Medvezhye deposit.[42] Each length of road and rail laid in these regions costs two to three times its equivalent in the west of the country and frequently neither of these modes of transport is possible, necessitating materials being flown in or the development of other forms of transport (dirigibles, hovercraft, etc.) that require further expenditure.

There is no doubt that in the decade 1965–75 the gas

372   Soviet Energy and Industrial Raw Materials

industry "failed to meet production goals largely because of the inability to coordinate field development with construction and efficient operation of pipelines and gas treatment plants."[43] The industry was also battling with the conditions encountered in the new areas and the costs associated with overcoming these handicaps. Despite the fact that many problems are being coped with more successfully and that costs of infrastructure in Siberia may begin to level off somewhat as the basic installations and transportation lines are completed, there is no way to get around the fact that rates of return are declining in the industry; i.e. that increases in production require more than proportional inputs of capital (see Table 6).

The Soviets have explicitly recognized this problem. "When these indices are compared at five-year intervals from 1960 onward, it is found that all indices achieved their best level in 1965—between 1965 and 1970, return on capital fell 41 percent in extraction and by 23 percent in transportation, while the unit cost of extraction and transportation rose 10 and 21 percent respectively; for 1975, return on capital will decline by 27 percent in extraction and by 40 percent in main line transport and the corresponding unit costs will rise by 17 and 31 percent. There is no question but that this tendency for basic indices to fall will persist for some time."[44] Thus while natural gas may remain a cheaper fuel for the Soviet Union to produce in comparison to oil and coal, costs of extraction are rising rapidly in terms of extraction and transportation per cubic meter and in terms of declining returns on capital investments.[45]

This section has attempted to demonstrate the fact that the problems of the industry stem from the location of gas reserves with respect to markets, which places enormous stress on the transportation network and the technological problems that arise partly in transportation and partly in coping with a rapidly developing industry in harsh climatic and terrestrial conditions. We have tried to point to some Soviet indigenous efforts to combat these problems, but the other way in which the industry has come to terms with its difficulties is through foreign trade.

## Soviet Foreign Trade in Natural Gas

Somewhat anomalously, the country with one-third of the world's gas reserve was a net gas importer in the early 1970s. Imports of gas commenced in the late 1960s with small volumes from Afghanistan which were supplemented by deliveries from Iran which began in 1970 (see Table 7). Both import arrangements were part of larger Soviet trade deals with the two countries: natural gas from Iran formed partial repayment for the construction of a 1,000 km pipeline (IGAT 1) that conveyed gas to the Soviet border (and to Iranian consumers along its route) and for a Soviet-built steel plant. The gas imported from Afghanistan represents payment for supplies of mechanical equipment, technical aid and other commodities. All the imported gas—11.8 Bcm in 1976—was used in the southern republics.

The USSR has exported small quantities of gas to Poland since World War II. In 1967, exports were extended to include Czechoslovakia and in 1970, a further extension of deliveries included the first trade with a West European country, Austria. In 1974, the circle of countries

TABLE 6
Economic Data from Selected Gas Production Corporations

| Production Corporation | | Gas Production (billion cm[1]) | Share of USSR Production (percent) | Total Gas Wells | Active Wells | Mid-Year Value of Capital Stock (million rubles) | Return on Capital (ruble/ruble) | Average Cost of Extraction (rubles/1,000 cm) |
|---|---|---|---|---|---|---|---|---|
| Ukraine | 1970 | 55.0 | 28 | 1,142 | 960 | 308.0 | 1.08 | .48 |
| | 1975 | 58.5 | 20 | 1,438 | 1,257 | 515.8 | .70 | 1.07 |
| Turkmen | 1970 | 11.8 | 6 | 84 | 55 | 34.0 | 2.09 | .35 |
| | 1975 | 47.0 | 16 | 299 | 260 | 269.2 | 1.05 | .73 |
| Uzbek | 1970 | 31.5 | 16 | 393 | 276 | 97.0 | 2.04 | .23 |
| | 1975 | 36.6 | 13 | 533 | 412 | 219.4 | 1.00 | 1.08 |
| Tyumen | 1970 | 9.2 | 5 | 84 | 53 | 84.7 | .65 | .95 |
| | 1975 | 33.5 | 12 | 181 | 153 | 407.0 | .51 | 1.46 |
| Orenburg | 1970 | .8 | 0 | 20 | 6 | 8.1 | .64 | 1.29 |
| | 1975 | 18.3 | 6 | 174 | 136 | 192.4 | .59 | 1.59 |
| Kuban (Krasnodar) | 1970 | 22.5 | 11 | 580 | 426 | 179.3 | .79 | .91 |
| | 1975 | 5.8 | 2 | 818 | 578 | 201.5 | .18 | 5.47 |
| Komi | 1970 | 6.2 | 3 | 33 | 22 | 34.6 | 1.25 | 1.17 |
| | 1975 | 17.8 | 6 | 102 | 78 | 283.5 | .41 | 1.70 |
| Stavropol | 1970 | 15.7 | 8 | 757 | 574 | 83.4 | 1.14 | .44 |
| | 1975 | 10.5 | 4 | 1,089 | 935 | 139.8 | .46 | 1.54 |

[1]The actual gas production total for a region may exceed that for the gas corporation itself because associated gas is contributed by oil production corporations. Derived from Margulov, Selikhova and Furman, *Razvitiye gazovoi promyshlennosti i analiz tekhniko-ekonomicheskikh pokazatelei* [Development of the gas industry and analysis of technical-economic indicators], Ministerstvo Gazovoi Promyshlennosti, Moscow, 1976, Tables 22 through 29, pp. 20–30, 32–34, 38.

TABLE 7
Soviet Natural Gas Trade 1970–80
(billion cubic meters)

| | 1970 | 1973 | 1974 | 1975 | 1976 | 1980[ii] |
|---|---|---|---|---|---|---|
| **Imports** | | | | | | |
| Iran | 1.0 | 8.7 | 9.1 | 9.6 | 9.3 | 1.0 |
| Afghanistan | 2.6 | 2.7 | 2.8 | 2.9 | 2.5 | 2.5 |
| Total[i] | 3.6 | 11.4 | 11.9 | 12.4 | 11.8 | 3.5 |
| **Exports** | | | | | | |
| Poland | 1.0 | 1.7 | 2.1 | 2.5 | 2.5 | 5.9 |
| Czechoslovakia | 1.4 | 2.4 | 3.2 | 2.7 | 4.3 | 7.3 |
| Bulgaria | — | — | 0.3 | 1.2 | 2.2 | 4.6 |
| East Germany | — | — | 2.9 | 3.3 | 3.4 | 5.7 |
| Hungary | — | — | — | 0.6 | 1.0 | 3.5 |
| Rumania | — | — | — | — | — | 1.0 |
| Yugoslavia | — | — | — | — | — | 2.0 |
| Austria | 1.0 | 1.6 | 2.1 | 1.9 | 2.8 | 2.9 |
| West Germany | — | — | 2.2 | 3.1 | 4.0 | 10.7 |
| Italy | — | — | 0.8 | 2.3 | 3.7 | 7.0 |
| France | — | — | — | — | 1.0 | 4.0 |
| Finland | — | — | 0.4 | 0.7 | 0.8 | 1.0 |
| Total[i] | 3.3 | 5.7 | 14.0 | 19.3 | 25.8 | 55.6 |
| Net Exports | −0.3 | −5.7 | 2.1 | 6.9 | 14.0 | 52 |

[i]Totals may not add due to rounding.
[ii]Western estimates; official Soviet gas trade figures in physical units ceased to be published in 1977.
SOURCE: *Vneshnyaya torgovlya SSSR* for respective years.

was widened again to include Bulgaria, East Germany, West Germany and Italy. Finland also began to receive small amounts of gas through a pipeline from Leningrad.

This large jump in exports to Western Europe, which for the first time made the USSR a gas exporter of substantial proportions, was made possible by the construction of a pipeline network through Eastern Europe. At the eastern end the network is known as the Bratstvo (Brotherhood) pipeline and a more recent addition is known as the Transit pipeline, but it is convenient to think of the two as forming a network throughout Europe as shown in Figure 3.

From Uzhgorod, on the Soviet-Czechoslovak border, the main transmission system runs through Czechoslovakia to Bratislava, where one branch heads north to East Germany and the other branch continues west into Austria and farther southwest into Italy. The northern branch continues into East Germany to the south of Berlin, but another line divides from it before it reaches the East German border and proceeds west via Prague to West Germany.

Two other lines make up this growing network. One runs from the south of Uzhgorod to Budapest and enabled Hungary to receive its first gas from the USSR in 1975 (although the country had been importing small quantities from Rumania for some years). The other line runs from the Ukraine via Odessa and transits Rumania and Bulgaria where it terminates at Sofia. Rumania took no gas from this line originally, but received its first Soviet gas via this route as payment for its contribution to the Orenburg pipeline. In addition, the West German extension of the network was further extended to France.[46]

Soviet Gas Exports in the 1980s

*The Orenburg ("Soyuz") Pipeline.*[47] The main increment of Soviet gas exports to Eastern Europe in the early 1980s is coming from the Orenburg pipeline, the agreement for which was signed in June 1974 at the 24th Comecon Conference at Sofia. Shortly thereafter, the member countries commenced the construction of a 2,750-km pipeline from the Orenburg field to Uzhgorod, in order to tie in the existing pipeline network. Everything about this project was on a large scale, including the technical problems involved in dealing with the "sour" (high-sulfur) gas at the deposit, for which a vast processing plant of formidable technical complexity has been set up.[48] The pipeline is 1,420 mm diameter pipe with 22 compressor stations of 25,000 kw units. Many Western contractors were involved in the project, with much of the pipe coming from West Germany and Japan; France was foremost in the construction of the processing plant; American and Italian companies supplied the compressor stations for the line. The total cost of the project has been estimated at more than two billion rubles.

The project represented a showpiece of Comecon cooperation in energy, since the original blueprint called for each of the countries to take an equal share in the financing and construction of the line. However, due to the general inexperience of East European crews in handling such large diameter pipe, this experiment had to be partly abandoned and Soviet crews took over the majority of the laying and welding functions.[49] Thus the East Europeans were required to deliver more equipment and credits to the USSR as compensation.

The pipeline was completed in late 1978,[50] although not all of the 22 planned compressor stations had yet been installed. At full capacity, the Orenburg pipeline was designed to carry 28 billion cubic meters of gas a year, out of a total Orenburg gas production level of around 48 Bcm, reached in 1979. About 40 percent of the designed throughput, or 11.2 Bcm, was to be in payment for East European contributions to the project, with 2.8 Bcm each going to Czechoslovakia, East Germany, Hungary, and Poland. The Bulgarian share of 2.8 Bcm and the Rumanian share of 1.5 Bcm were to move over a separate pipeline already in place to those more southerly countries (see Figure 3).

As a general trend, the Orenburg project is interesting in terms of future Soviet-East European cooperation. The shortage of manpower in the Soviet energy sector has been mentioned as an important unresolved problem and it seemed possible that part of the payment for future deliveries of fuel to Eastern Europe might be the participation of workers from those countries in energy projects on Soviet soil. This arrangement had already been tried prior to Orenburg when Polish workers built a stretch of oil pipeline in return for oil deliveries.

In any event, the experiment does not seem to have worked particularly well, partly on account of the attitudes of some of the East Europeans toward such exercises in fraternal cooperation. Friction is known to have developed between different nationalities in the labor force on account of wage differentials. Any future cooper-

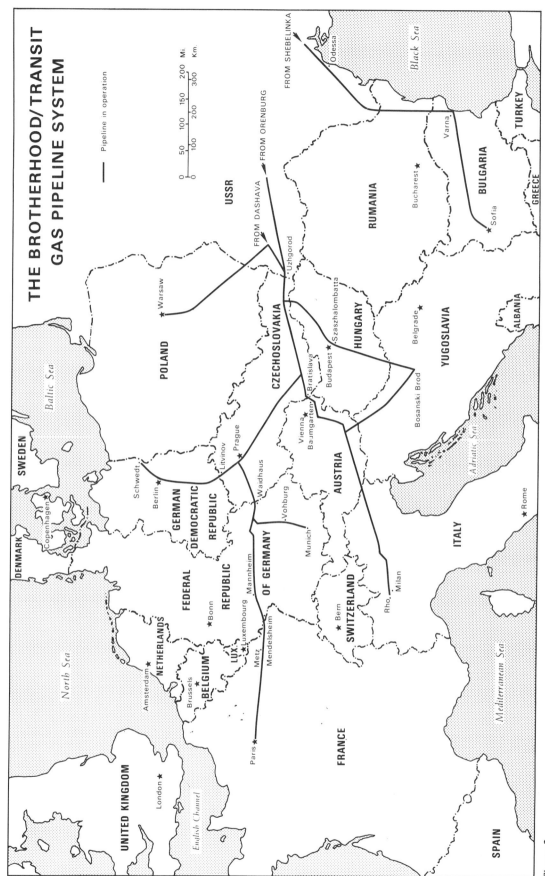

THE BROTHERHOOD/TRANSIT
GAS PIPELINE SYSTEM

Figure 3

ation of this kind should obviously insure that East European labor possesses the necessary skills for the job, otherwise their presence seems of marginal use. It may well be, however, that these countries will prefer to make good their debt in other terms, as many of them face labor shortages themselves and can ill afford to send workers abroad.

The arrangement by which Yugoslavia was to receive Soviet natural gas would seem to be an adjunct to the Orenburg project. One part of the contract concerned an agreement between Yugoslavia and Hungary by which Hungary arranged for the transit of 1.65 Bcm of Soviet gas to be delivered to Serbia, Voivodina and Bosnia-Herzegovina. In addition, 1.35 Bcm would be delivered to Slovenia and Croatia via the Czechoslovak-Austrian pipeline. The agreements, which were signed in late 1976 and early 1977, therefore provided for a total of 3 Bcm of Soviet gas to be delivered to Yugoslavia which, by 1980, was to constitute 50 percent of total gas consumption in that country.[51]

*The Trilateral "Switch" Deal (IGAT 2).* The major increment in Soviet gas exports to Western Europe over the next decade was to have been accomplished via the Trilateral Switch arrangement between the two partners and Iran. The basic agreement, signed in Teheran on 30 November 1975, provided for a switch of exports by which gas would be piped into the Soviet Union from Iran and an equivalent volume, minus certain transit fees, would be delivered to the West European border from Komi and Tyumen[52] via the Bratstvo-Transit system. A 1,440-km pipeline was planned from the Kangan fields in southern Iran to the Soviet border at Astara at a cost of $2.4 billion.[53] The capacity of the line would have been approximately 25 Bcm,[54] of which 10.9 Bcm was to be delivered to Western Europe;[55] 2 Bcm to be retained by the Soviets as a transit fee, to run the compressor stations and to allow for natural wastage; 3.4 Bcm to be delivered to Czechoslovakia starting in 1983 (under a supplementary agreement concluded in late 1976); and the residual 8.7 Bcm to be retained by Iran for domestic consumption plus the fuel needed to run the compressor stations.[56]

The West European countries were to receive their share in the following proportions: West Germany, 5.5 Bcm; France, 3.6 Bcm; Austria, 1.8 Bcm.[57] The West European countries were to reportedly meet 80 percent of the cost of the gas in supplies of equipment and the remaining 20 percent in cash. This agreement was to have commenced in 1981 (reaching full capacity in 1983) and continue for 20 years thereafter.

The period since the Iranian revolution of late 1978 has witnessed considerable changes in Iran's economic strategy, particularly with respect to natural gas. Sabotage to the IGAT 1 pipeline halted the flow of gas to the Soviet Union at an early stage in the revolution. Although supplies resumed in mid-1979, they never regained former levels (partly due to reduced oil production and partly to further sabotage to the pipeline) and ceased entirely in March 1980, as a result of the Soviet refusal to pay the new Iranian price amounting to five times the existing rate. The IGAT 2 project was an early casualty of Iran post-revolution cutback of industrial projects. While about half the pipeline had been constructed, the leadership announced that the gas would be utilized domestically; since then, nothing more has been heard.[58]

*The New Siberia-Western Europe Export Pipeline.* With the disappearance of Iran as a possible source of gas for Western Europe, the Soviet Union has fallen back on its own resources to provide the increment in exports to Western Europe in the 1980s. In early 1980, it was announced, mainly on West German initiative, that there were plans for a new pipeline that would carry up to 40 Bcm of Siberian gas to six West European countries commencing in 1984, at a total project cost of $9–11 billion.[59] By the end of 1982, the gas utilities of two countries had signed supply contracts—West Germany for 10.5 Bcm with an additional 0.7 Bcm for West Berlin, and France for 8 Bcm. Interest had also been expressed by Italy, Austria, Belgium, the Netherlands and other countries.[60] The West European decision to proceed with an expansion of Soviet gas deliveries through the new pipeline led to friction with the United States, which under the Reagan Administration opposed construction of the pipeline. American opposition appeared to be based both on a desire to deprive the Soviet Union of the additional foreign exchange earnings from gas sales and on a desire to retaliate for Soviet support for the imposition of martial law in Poland in late 1981. Despite an American embargo (later lifted), work proceeded on the new pipeline, which appears to have been conceived originally as an alternative to the aborted North Star project.

*The Urengoi (North Star) Project.*[61] In this venture, for which discussions commenced in 1972, gas from the Urengoi field (in Western Siberia) was to be piped to Pechenga (about 100 miles west of Murmansk) on the Kola Peninsula, liquefied, and shipped to the east coast of the United States. Preliminary estimates of the total cost of the project were in the region of $6.7 billion, of which $1.5 billion were for the LNG liquefaction facilities in the USSR, $2.2 billion for the LNG tankers and $0.4 billion for the U.S. regasification facility.[62] A feasibility study was prepared by an American consortium of Tenneco, Texas Eastern Transmission, and Brown and Root. The contract was scheduled to run for 25 years, with gas deliveries of 20 Bcm per year to the U.S., commencing in 1980. The whole venture was to have been financed by the U.S. Export-Import Bank and a consortium of private banks.[63]

*The Yakutian Gas Project.* In November 1974, an agreement to export LNG from the Yakutia deposits in Eastern Siberia was approved in principle between the Soviet Union and Japanese and American companies (El Paso Co. and Occidental Petroleum Corp.), commercial banks and Export-Import banks. The gas would be piped 1,800 miles to the port of Olga on the east coast of the Soviet Union, liquefied and shipped to the U.S. west coast and Japan.[64] In return, the U.S. and Japan would supply technology, equipment and credits for the gas to be proved up during a two year exploration phase. Meanwhile, discussions would proceed to the next phase, in which a liquefaction plant and loading facilities for the LNG carriers would be designed and constructed at Olga and the pipeline would be laid to carry the gas to the coast.

Preliminary (1974) estimates indicated that the total cost of the project would be around $4 billion and that the Soviets would require an additional $2 billion for the purchase of equipment, pipe, and other supplies for the operation. The cost of the American LNG tanker fleet would be around $1.5 billion and a further $1 billion would be needed for the Japanese LNG fleet and regasification plant.[65] The agreement would yield 10 Bcm per year for each of the foreign partners over a 25 year period.[66]

Both the LNG projects received a major setback with the enactment of the Trade Act of 1974, which contained the Jackson-Vanik and Stevenson Amendments. The Jackson-Vanik Amendment, concerned with the rights of Soviet citizens (in fact, mainly Jews) to emigrate, stated that "No nonmarket economy shall be eligible to receive Most-Favored-Nation treatment or credits while it (a) denies its citizens the right or opportunity to emigrate, or (b) imposes more than a nominal tax on emigration."[67] The Stevenson Amendment focused particularly on the question of Soviet energy resource developments: "No loan or financial guarantee which exceeds $60 million shall be finally approved and no loan which exceeds $25 million for the export of goods and services involving research, exploration or production of fossil fuel resources in the USSR shall be finally approved unless in each case the bank has submitted to Congress a detailed statement describing and explaining the transaction at least 25 days prior to the date of final approval."[68]

These two amendments were enacted into law on 3 and 4 January 1975, and one week later Secretary of State Kissinger announced that the USSR had made it clear that "it does not intend to accept a trade status that is discriminatory and subject to political conditions, and accordingly, that it will not put into force the 1972 Trade Agreement."[69]

This sequence of events effectively ruled out further discussion of the two projects since both required the extension of credits, way above what the legislation would permit. Since that time, however, there have been a number of developments. In 1976, the North Star project was recast with partial European involvement whereby the gas would be delivered to the U.S. and France in the proportions 15.5 Bcm to 5 Bcm.[70] However, this arrangement never seemed particularly promising and it was no great surprise to find that it had been shelved in favor of an all-European pipeline project (described above) on a much increased scale.

As far as the Yakutia project was concerned, without U.S. participation, the Japanese reviewed their commitment and, for over a year, the project foundered. In March 1976 it was announced that financing for the exploration phase had been arranged with U.S. commercial bank credits and a combination of Japanese commercial and Export-Import bank credits to cover a $50 million loan equally divided between the two countries.[71]

Regular meetings have been held between the partners since the commencement of the exploration phase, but there has been no firm announcement of plans for commencement of the production and export phases. Part of the problem has been proving up sufficient reserves. The original target for the deposit was 1.3 Tcm of reserves but this was subsequently scaled down to 1.0 Tcm and even this reduced target has created problems because of the nature of the deposit, which consists of two separate fields rather than one large accumulation. Soviet claims that the target for reserves would be met by the end of 1980 were refuted by one Western authority who had personal experience of the project, ". . . (the Soviets) claim they have 0.77 Tcm (of reserves) but this is absolutely false. They have 0.57 Tcm over a six year period and at that rate it will take many more years. As a result the deal will collapse on that basis alone."[72]

The other possibility of Soviet LNG exports concerns the joint Soviet-Japanese exploration currently under way off the coast of Sakhalin Island in the Soviet Far East. The Sakhalin agreement concerns primarily oil and does not provide for the exploitation of natural gas, but one may assume the development of any such deposits on the same basis as oil, with the Japanese taking a half share in any production.[73] It is entirely possible that Sakhalin gas could be arriving at Japanese ports before any deliveries from Yakutia. At the present time, neither looks very likely.

## The Rationale Behind Soviet Natural Gas Trade

Looking at the current and probable natural gas trading partners of the USSR, one can discern a rationale behind each of the trading agreements that is perhaps not immediately obvious and relates to some of the problems that have been identified above.

*Eastern Europe.* Soviet gas exports to Eastern Europe can be properly explained only in the context of the overall relationships among Comecon countries. While there is little doubt that Eastern Europe is an economic, and particularly an energy, liability to the USSR, economic considerations are greatly outweighed by political and strategic considerations.[74] In the context of Comecon energy supplies, it is clear that the slowdown in growth of Soviet oil production coupled with the continuous expansion of oil exports to the West, has made for a tight situation with respect to oil supplies throughout the bloc, but particularly in Eastern Europe. Whether or not one foresees a future need for major imports of oil from outside the bloc, the need to diversify into other fuels is pressing and it is for this reason one can expect the USSR to substitute increasing quantities of gas for oil in its fuel exports to Eastern Europe.

*Iran and Afghanistan.* Importation of natural gas may seem something of a contradiction in terms for a country that possesses the largest gas reserves in the world. However, these imports have been important to the gas-supply logistics system in the USSR. A glance at the map shows that these imports enter the country in the southwest corner, which is the region that is hardest for the Soviets to supply from their own trunkline system. These imports therefore offset an important locational and transportation problem for the planners.

The severance of Iranian supplies caused by the revolution led to many towns in the southern republics of the USSR suffering severe power losses for a considerable part of the severe winter of 1978–79. These events highlighted the Soviet vulnerability in this region. Although some power stations could be switched to fuel oil and the flow of some gas pipelines reversed to provide fuel for major cities, hardship was suffered in Armenia and Azerbaijan and some inconvenience in Georgia.[75]

With virtually no gas flowing from Iran and gas supplies from Afghanistan threatened by the internal security situation in the country, the Soviets can no longer use this logistic device. Even if trade with Iran is restored at some future date (which is by no means impossible given the advantages of the arrangement for both sides), the Soviets would find it necessary to institute contingency plans to safeguard against the possibility of a similar occurrence. Accordingly, the Soviet Union announced in early 1981 that a large-diameter pipeline would be built in the 1980s from the main Soviet transmission network at Novopskov south through Rostov and Mozdok to Azerbaijan, to insure a stable supply for the Transcaucasian republics from gas sources within the Soviet Union. The new transmission system is planned to carry 9 Bcm to Transcaucasia by 1985 and 15 Bcm by 1990.[76]

The collapse of the Trilateral agreement could have put the Soviets in severe contractual difficulty with West European customers. The agreement was reached with each company and country negotiating separately, i.e., Soyuzgazexport agreed on terms with the National Iranian Gas Company and with each of the West European gas companies on price and quantity. Each operated in this way to safeguard its own interests, so that if any part of the contract should fall through, the other portions would go ahead as planned. On this basis, a refusal by the Iranians to supply gas would not have released the Soviets from their commitments to Western Europe.

What appears to have happened is that the West European countries did not wish to precipitate a confrontation with the Soviet Union by pressing this aspect of the agreement. In addition, the West European Trilateral partners can now expect these obligations to be fulfilled, albeit at a later date, by the more recent 40 Bcm Siberian export contract. Finally, the Soviets must be hoping that the agreement with Iran can be successfully renegotiated, as much for political as economic reasons. Depending on the political alignments which result from the Iran-Iraq war, there is no reason why this should not occur. As far as Afghanistan is concerned, Soviet political involvement in that country will mean the continuation of economic projects, of which natural gas has been the most successful. While exports from Afghanistan may even increase slightly in the next ten years, their impact will remain minor in terms of the overall Soviet gas balance, but logistically important in the south of the country.

*Western Europe.* If asked to give the major rationale for Soviet gas exports to Western Europe, it would be natural to put earnings of hard currency before everything else. This would be correct, with the qualification that all gas sent to Western Europe is bartered for reciprocal deliveries of large-diameter steel pipe and compressor stations from West European countries. Thus the USSR has used West European trade to take care of at least part of its technology and equipment problems in the industry.

Despite the widespread impression that the United States is the major supplier of energy technology and equipment to the USSR, it appears to be Western Europe and Japan that fulfill this role. During 1972–76, Soviet orders of Western oil and gas equipment technology totaled $3.1 billion, of which the U.S. share was $550 million. These figures do not include $4.1 billion of large-diameter pipe imported over the same period from non-American sources (see Table 8). Thus the American contribution to Western exports of energy technology to the USSR amounted to $550 million out of $7.1 billion.[77]

The contribution of Western equipment and technology has been a crucial factor in the improved performance of the gas industry in the 1970s and will doubtless play an important part in the 1980s as the Soviets continue in this arrangement. The degree of reciprocity in the arrangements should go some way towards allaying the fears of Western analysts who feel that the Soviet aim of such trade is to make Western Europe dependent on Soviet gas to the point where substantial political concessions could be extracted by the threat of severance of this source of fuel. In fact, volumes will not be great enough (at least in the 1980s) to make such a threat credible, but it should be remembered that the sudden severance of pipe and compressor station deliveries by Western partners would cause the Soviet gas industry serious inconvenience.[78]

*The United States and Japan.* The rationale behind Soviet gas trade with the U.S. and Japan tended to depend on the way in which commercial relations were viewed as a factor in superpower détente. Whereas most commentators saw the Soviet rationale behind the LNG deals

TABLE 8

Main Suppliers of Steel Pipe to the USSR 1973–81
(thousand tons)

| | 1973 | 1976 | 1976 | 1981 |
| | (thousands metric tons) | | (millions of rubles) | |
|---|---|---|---|---|
| Japan | 150.4 | 577.7 | 240.9 | 640.2 |
| West Germany | 720.3 | 875.3 | 300.7 | 327.3 |
| Italy | 322.9 | 584.6 | 205.3 | 201.4 |
| France | 236.4 | 186.3 | 110.3 | 88.3 |
| Rumania | 138.5 | 210.2 | 84.6 | 78.5 |
| Sweden | 23.9 | 7.9 | 5.5 | 17.3 |
| Belgium | 31.5 | 9.8 | 5.0 | — |
| Others | 403.8 | 534.0 | 167.9 | 222.6 |
| Total | 2,027.7 | 2,985.4 | 1,120.2 | 1,575.6 |

SOURCE: *Vneshnyaya torgovlya SSSR,* for respective years. Data in physical units were last published for 1976; since then pipe imports are being published by the Soviet Union only in value terms.

as acquisitions of technology and hard currency, I would suggest that these were not the primary objectives. Rather, the primary objective was to offset adverse locational and transportation factors.

The major reason that the Soviets lost interest in the North Star project is that once the Urengoi deposit commenced production, in 1978, gas from that deposit could be produced and utilized domestically, or exported to European countries with a higher return than the LNG venture would have yielded. Conversely, the reason why Moscow is still keenly interested in the Yakutia project is that, in the absence of an export deal, utilization of East Siberian gas on a large scale is still a decade away.

The acquisition of liquefaction technology could be important to the Soviet Union (although this is not the same as the LNG transport technology mentioned above, many of the processes are related), but in the absence of an export market, the Soviets have no use for liquefaction plants and cryogenic tankers.

### Soviet Natural Gas in the World Economy

Thus far we have considered the problems and prospects for Soviet natural gas production and outlined current and potential export markets for the fuel. It remains to consider the constraints on Soviet natural gas exports from the demand side, i.e. in the light of world demand and competing sources of supply; and, more importantly, from the supply side, in the light of general Comecon energy problems and the options open to Soviet planners.

World Demand and Competing Supply Sources

*Western Europe.* The discussion of current and potential foreign trade has established that Soviet exports of natural gas outside Comecon will be overwhelmingly concentrated in Western Europe. The question therefore arises as to whether Western Europe will be requiring additional volumes of gas in the 1980s and the extent to which other West European gas import options are available and more attractive than Soviet gas imports.

Although numerical estimates show considerable differences, a variety of studies suggest that the countries of Western Europe are planning to increase their imports of gas significantly in the coming decade.[79] Furthermore, incremental imports will increasingly come from countries outside the region. In 1980, around 40 percent of Western Europe's gas imports came from the Netherlands, which supplies West Germany, France, Italy, Belgium, and Switzerland. The forecasts of indigenous gas production in continental Europe over the next decade give cause for concern. Almost everywhere, production increases are declining and in many countries absolute totals are falling. Especially important is the fact that the Netherlands, for so long the major gas supplier to the Continent is experiencing falling production and is becoming a competitor for gas on world markets.[80]

The only bright spots on the West European gas map would seem to be Britain, where North Sea production is still increasing, and Italy, where production is increasing slowly. As far as exports are concerned however, the real hope lies with Norway where reserves are adequate to greatly increase production but internal political decisions have imposed a limit on oil and gas production of 90 million tons of oil equivalent (for both fuels combined). If this limit remains in force, then Norwegian gas export potential will only increase sufficient to counteract the fall in exports from the Netherlands over the next decade.[81]

Thus the North Sea is unlikely to provide increments of continental West European gas consumption by the mid-1980s. Britain will retain almost all of its gas for domestic consumption; Dutch production will be declining and the Netherlands is not renewing export contracts as they expire; and the Norwegians must be persuaded to a change of exploration and production policy before any large volumes can be seen from that source.

Apart from indigenous sources of gas, Western Europe has recently gained an alternative pipeline source other than the USSR (and Iran). A breakthrough in under-sea pipeline technology has allowed a project to be signed that will enable Algeria to export gas to a number of European countries via a pipeline across Tunisia and Sicily to the Italian mainland.[82] Work commenced in 1977 and the first gas was to be delivered at the beginning of 1982. In addition to pipeline sources, LNG deliveries have been in operation for some years from Algeria and Libya and there is a possibility of future deliveries from Nigeria. Algeria is in fact the West Europeans' major alternative to the USSR for imported gas supplies. In addition to the trans-Mediterranean pipeline, there are also plans to build another pipeline across the sea to Spain.[83]

In the winter of 1978, two things happened that made Soviet gas appear less attractive to Western Europe and made Algerian gas easier to obtain. The Iranian revolution cast a doubt over security of supplies from that source and virtually ruled out the possibility of any future deals over and above the Trilateral project. The second event was the veto, after three years of consideration, by the United States Department of Energy of two major LNG projects that would have brought 20 Bcm of Algerian gas to the United States.[84] The Algerian government had announced that, in the event of a U.S. veto, there were ready markets in Western Europe. Almost immediately after the U.S. decision, the Algerian oil and gas company, Sonatrach, signed contracts with West Germany, the Netherlands, Sweden, and Italy, with further possibilities of supplying France, Spain, Austria, and Yugoslavia.[85]

Since that time however, Algerian supplies have become less attractive to West European customers with the Algerians instituting a stoppage in LNG deliveries to France and the U.S. for a six month period in 1980 when those two countries refused to pay massively increased prices.[86] In the wake of this action, the USSR has once again begun to seem a more favorable prospect for secure gas supplies. In addition, the Soviets do have one factor in their favor that will insure that they command at least part of any increase in Western European imports. The trade in steel pipe that accompanies Soviet natural gas imports is beneficial to West European economies. The steel industries in the West European countries had been experiencing a severe depression in the 1970s that has led to contraction in capacity and unemployment. In these circumstances, the competition among countries for Soviet contracts and the pressure on governments to conclude further deals is considerable.

In conclusion, Soviet natural gas is already important in Western Europe and this trade is likely to expand in the 1980s, particularly with the countries of Northern Europe and Finland, for which Algerian gas is a more costly alternative.

*Japan.* Japan's almost total lack of indigenous natural resources and extremely high dependence on Middle East oil have led the country to vigorously seek diversification into different types and sources of fuel. The USSR would be well placed geographically to take advantage of these initiatives, but commercial relations are overshadowed by a legacy of enmity in which the territorial dispute over ownership of some islands in the Kuril Island chain, annexed by the Soviet Union after World War II, has been an important factor hindering the development of a large scale commercial relationship.[87]

There is no doubt that Japan could profitably use imports of Soviet gas, but it is unclear where the USSR would figure as a priority in the list of current and future gas suppliers that Japan has already lined up. The country already imports LNG from Brunei, Alaska, Abu Dhabi and Indonesia; plans are in progress for further contracts with Sarawak and Australia. China has also been mentioned as a possible source of gas for Japan.[88]

Whether Japan does eventually import gas from the USSR depends very much on whether sufficient momentum has been built up to carry the Yakutia project through and, fundamentally, on the action of Japan's partner in the venture, the United States.

*The United States.* There are enormous problems in attempting to comment on U.S. policy toward LNG imports from the Soviet Union. The United States has yet to evolve a coherent policy toward natural gas imports in general and the desirability of these imports when contrasted with the different varieties of domestically-produced gas.[89] The Carter Administration and Energy Secretary James R. Schlesinger, in particular, gained a reputation for being against LNG imports on principle. The lengthy and complex regulatory procedures that may keep trade partners waiting for years with no guarantee of success have made the United States a less attractive market in the eyes of possible suppliers.

The position of the Carter Administration on LNG imports was that, as supplementary fuel sources, they ranked behind domestic and Alaskan gas production and pipeline imports from Canada and Mexico. There was then a differentiation between short-haul LNG imports (Trinidad, Colombia, Ecuador), which rank before synthetic natural gas, with long-haul LNG imports (Algeria, Indonesia, Iran), including the Soviet Union, bringing up the rear.[90] In addition, it was not sufficient to point to the general energy deficiency of the United States as a

rationale for LNG imports; such imports will be approved only when end users can prove "overriding regional need."[91]

When these factors are added to the political and legislative difficulties of entering into an LNG project with the Soviet Union, it becomes obvious that a great deal of policy would have to be changed to bring Soviet gas to the United States. It does not seem out of place to note that it will not be sufficient for Soviet natural gas imports simply to be tolerated by Congress and the Administration. If this trade is to take place, there will have to be individuals and groups who want to see it happen enough to actively push for the necessary executive and legislative approval.

The overall point to be remembered about Soviet natural gas trade with the U.S. (and to a lesser extent Japan) is that it was conceived in the early 1970s at a time when cooperation between the Superpowers, particularly in commercial fields, was considered desirable. By the end of 1982, with the Soviet intervention in Afghanistan, the imposition of martial law in Poland, and the generally poor political relations between the Superpowers, such trade was no longer possible even if it were to have proved economically feasible which, in truth, never looked very likely.

## Comecon Energy Problems and the Options for Soviet Energy Planners

Any judgment on the volumes of Soviet natural gas that will be available in the world economy fundamentally involves larger considerations of Soviet and Comecon energy availabilities and the options open to Soviet planners as they make their energy policy over the next decade. Here we can present only what seem to be the major problems and choices involved in the decision to increase natural gas exports in the world economy.

Possibly the most important factor affecting Soviet natural gas exports will be the performance of the Soviet oil industry. The whole question of Soviet oil production was brought into sharp focus by the publication of two reports by the Central Intelligence Agency stating that the Soviet Union would be compelled to enter the international oil market with an import requirement of 173 to 225 million tons per year by 1985.[92] According to the CIA, Soviet oil production was to peak, possibly as early as 1978 and certainly not later than the early 1980s.[93]

Thus far, it seems fair to say that the Soviet oil industry does not appear to be experiencing problems that would lead to a downturn in production as early as the agency suggests nor that the country would be forced to import oil on a large scale. Nevertheless, the oil industry has certainly performed less well in the 10th Five-Year Plan than in the previous quinquennium. Production in 1980 was 603 million tons and the five-year plan targets show that increases in production will average barely 1 percent per annum during 1981–85 reaching 630 million tons by the end of that period, roughly what had been expected in the previous quinquennium.[94]

In general terms, the CIA view of oil production trends is being borne out. It does appear that oil production increases are slowing and that there are indeed problems with finding new reserves and stemming the problems of water encroachment at major deposits. It appears, however, that these trends are not occurring as rapidly and will not affect oil production levels as quickly as the CIA reports suggested. More importantly, there is as yet no suggestion that the USSR will become an oil importer of major proportions, although East European countries are seeking oil on the world market, having been informed by Moscow that they cannot expect to rely on the Soviet Union for the totality of their requirements.[95]

On current trends, this writer sees a Comecon oil import requirement around 50 million tons of oil by the mid-1980s. These imports would consist of East European purchases on the world market, or (less likely), Soviet purchases on East European account. The important point is that such imports would not be required for the Soviet Union itself and, even if purchased by the latter, would represent the commitment of Moscow to its East European neighbors. Thus it is more correct to refer to a possible Comecon oil deficit in the 1980s rather than a Soviet oil deficit.

Nevertheless, the prediction of a tight oil supply situation throughout the bloc will have important consequences for other fuels. It will test the degree of substitution of oil for other fuels (gas and coal primarily) that is possible in the Comecon economies.[96] Such substitution will also take place in Soviet exports to Eastern Europe, where gas is likely to gain greatly at the expense of scarce oil.

World market prices will also have a bearing on this situation since they will determine the relative profitability to the USSR of exporting oil as against gas to the West. In the past, gas exports have earned only one-third to one-half as much as oil exports on a heat-content basis. However, by the end of 1980, price parity with crude oil appeared to have been accepted by most West European gas importers. Algeria has attempted (unsuccessfully) to impose even higher prices on its European customers. Overall, the time appears not far away when it will be as profitable for the Soviets to export gas as oil, in terms of the volume of hard currency received per btu of oil or gas.[97] Nevertheless, until that time does arrive, the most profitable Soviet energy export policy—the maintenance and expansion of oil exports to the West—is also the least likely prospect, given the slowdown in Soviet oil production and rising rates of consumption throughout the bloc. It may prove that by the mid-1980s, Soviet oil exports may not be available to countries outside Comecon.

## Summary

Tables 9 and 10 show a possible Soviet natural gas balance and exports to the world economy in 1990. They have been constructed with a view to the overall shape of the situation rather than strict arithmetical accuracy which would belie the many uncertainties involved in such a prediction.

Soviet domestic comsumption has been set at around 6 percent per annum in line with the gradual decline in the rate of growth in gas consumption over the previous 15 years.[98] East European consumption, and hence Soviet

TABLE 9
A Possible Soviet Gas Balance for 1990
(billion cubic meters)

| | |
|---|---|
| Production | 800–850 |
| Consumption | 660–710 |
| Exports: | |
| Eastern Europe | 95 |
| Western Europe | 65 |
| | 160 |
| Imports: | |
| Iran | 10 |
| Afghanistan | 10 |
| | 20 |

gas exports to Eastern Europe, have been estimated to rise slightly faster, at 7–8 percent per annum, recognizing the rate of natural increase and adding some substitution effects in anticipation of growing oil supply difficulties.

Given these levels of production and consumption in the USSR and Eastern Europe, plus the contracted levels of exports to Western Europe and the new 40 Bcm pipeline from Urengoi, it seems that there is a gap of around 20 to 30 Bcm which will need to be filled. Without doubt, the Soviets will be hoping for a small increase in gas deliveries from Afghanistan and, at least, the reestablishment of the IGAT 1 project with Iran. If these two import sources can be reestablished on a secure basis, then there seems no reason why the USSR should not be able to meet its other commitments. In the event that the link with Iran remains permanently broken, the gas may have to be found from Soviet domestic consumption rather than East European supplies.

Western Europe will therefore be importing around 65 Bcm of Soviet gas in 1990 of which one-third will go to West Germany. While all West European countries will be seeking to diversify their sources of imported gas over the next decade, West Germany, France, Italy, Austria, and Finland will probably opt more strongly for Soviet gas (over the North African alternative) as the cheapest fuel source.

TABLE 10
Estimated Soviet Natural Gas Exports to the World Economy in 1990 (billion cubic meters)

| | Contracted | Additional Amounts Under Consideration | 1990 Estimate |
|---|---|---|---|
| West Germany | 10.0 | 11.2 | 21–22 |
| Italy | 7.0 | 7–11 | 14 |
| France | 4.0 | 8 | 12 |
| Austria | 2.8 | 3–5 | 6 |
| Belgium | — | 5–6 | 5 |
| Netherlands | — | 3 | 3 |
| Sweden, Spain, Switzerland | — | 2–5 | 2 |
| Finland | 1.4 | — | 1.4 |
| | 25.2 | 40–50 | 65 |

## Conclusions

By 1990, natural gas will have equaled and possibly over-taken oil in the Soviet fuels production balance; it will also have become more significant in the fuel balances of other Comecon countries in Eastern Europe.[99] Some time prior to this, probably around 1984, the USSR will surpass the United States in gas production and thus become the world's largest producer of both major hydrocarbons. It is for these reasons, irrespective of its role in the world economy, that the Soviet Union's natural gas will command considerable attention over the next decade.

The single most important factor that will determine the future availability of Soviet natural gas relates to the means of overcoming the locational problems facing the industry. These problems relate, first, to coping successfully with the Siberian environment, in which the major new deposits are located, in terms of developing correct exploration and production techniques, acquiring new types of equipment and technology, putting in a transportation and social infrastructure, etc.; and, second, the massive requirements of the pipeline network that is needed to bring the gas thousands of miles to centers of consumption. A failure to cope adequately with these problems hampered progress in the 1960s and early 1970s, but there are indications that the industry is experiencing greater success in the late 1970s, and the 1990 production total projected here reflects the belief that this trend will continue through the next decade.

One of the ways in which the Soviets have attempted to come to terms with the problems of the gas industry is through foreign trade. Natural gas exports of Western Europe have been a critical factor in enabling the industry to purchase the equipment and technology vital for its progress.[100] These exchanges are likely to expand in the 1980s, particularly with West Germany, France, Italy, Austria, and Finland. By contrast, the two liquefied natural gas proposals were, from the Soviet side, aimed mainly at opening up new locations for gas production, although an added attraction was certainly the United States and Japanese technology and credits that would have accompanied them.

A critical distinction should be made, however. For the Soviet energy industries in general, and natural gas in particular, it is Western Europe and Japan that have been and will continue to be the most important sources of equipment and technology, whereas United States concerns are likely to play a smaller role in this connection. Liquefied natural gas trade with the United States now seems out of the question, while trade with Japan (itself heavily dependent on United States participation), though not impossible, seems a rather long-term project.

The Iranian revolution of 1979 has come as a great blow to the planners who were counting on Iranian gas imports to offset the locational problem of transporting gas to the southern republics of the USSR and hoping to phase in further deliveries as production in the western part of the Soviet Union declines further in the 1980s. The cancellation of Iranian deliveries and the growing energy deficit in the southwest of the Soviet Union are forcing alterations to pipeline routes and thus partly nullify the logistic advantages that had been enjoyed from this arrangement, as well as the potential revenues to be gained from the role of middleman between Iran and Western Europe. While Iranian gas exports to the USSR may recommence in the 1980s, the likely lack of political stability in Iran will prevent the Soviets from incorporating Iranian energy supplies into their economy in the way in which they once hoped would be possible.

The bulk of Soviet natural gas exports in 1990 will find a market in Eastern Europe. Natural gas is likely to play an important part in substituting for oil supplies to prevent the necessity of large imports of oil by the Comecon countries, particularly in the event that Soviet oil production levels off. Given the continued relative profitability, in hard-currency terms, of exporting oil as against gas, it is likely that the Soviets will prolong their oil exports to the West for the maximum possible time. But the likely move to crude oil parity of natural gas export prices will mean that the USSR will have greater freedom in its choice of fuels to export for hard currency and this may be significant at a time of stringency in oil supplies throughout the CMEA.

In any event, the country's reserves and production potential are such that there is likely to be a substantial increase in gas exports to the Western world in the 1980s. These exports will be overwhelmingly concentrated in Western Europe and probably limited to five countries, in comparison with the diverse destinations of Soviet oil exports. With the North Sea states using almost all their gas for domestic consumption, North African supplies will be the most important competition for Soviet gas in Western Europe. However, to judge by current trends, West European countries will be grasping for any available source of energy in the 1980s and it is more likely to be Soviet availability rather than competing supplies that limit Soviet-West European gas trade in the 1980s.

In the last analysis, it is the Comecon energy supply situation that will determine the quantities of Soviet gas reaching the world economy in the 1980s. Where such trade does take place, the USSR will require continued aid, in the form of credits and/or equipment and technology, to open up incremental sources of supply. By the end of the 1980s, it is likely that the USSR will be exporting rather less energy to the world economy than at present. It also seems likely, however, that natural gas will be the predominant fuel in any such trade.

---

## NOTES

1. Much of this paper is drawn from research sponsored by the Rockefeller Foundation for the author's book: *Soviet Natural Gas Development to 1990: The Implications for the CMEA and the West* (Lexington, Ma.: Lexington Books, D. C. Heath and Co., 1980). The perspective of this paper, however, differs from the author's larger study.

2. For a full discussion on comparability of Soviet and Western reserve terminology, see David E. Levine, "Oil and Natural Gas Resources of the Soviet Union and Methods of their Estimation," in U.S. Congress, Senate,

Committee on Energy and Natural Resources, *Project Interdependence: U.S. and World Energy Outlook Through 1990*, 95th Congress, 1st sess., 1977, pp. 820–48. Throughout this paper, "proven" refers to Soviet reserves in categories $A + B + C_1$; "ultimately recoverable" refers to categories $A$ through $D_2$.

3. Jeffrey Segal, "Natural Gas: Rapid Growth in Output Expected," *Petroleum Economist* (August 1980), pp. 336–37. This is the highest estimate for the USSR; the CIA suggested a figure of 28 Tcm in 1978.

4. A. D. Brents, V. I. Gandkin, G. S. Urinson, *Ekonomika gazodobyvayushchei promyshlennosti* [Economics of the gas industry] (Moscow, 1975), p. 25.

5. *Offshore Magazine*, (April 1976) pp. 62–67. Also see Joseph P. Riva, Jr., "Soviet Offshore Oil and Gas," in U.S. Congress, Senate, Committee on Commerce, *Soviet Oceans Development*, 94th Congress, 2nd sess., 1976, pp. 479–500.

6. "Soviets Mull Counting Gas Hydrates in Fuel Reserves," *Oil and Gas Journal* (hereafter *OGJ*), 23 October 1978, p. 63.

7. R. D. Margulov, E. K. Selikhova, I. Ya. Furman, *Razvitiye gazovoi promyshlennosti i analiz tekhniko-ekonomicheskikh pokazatelei* [Development of the gas industry and analysis of technical-economic indicators] (Moscow, 1976), pp. 31–32.

8. Theodore Shabad and Victor L. Mote, *Gateway to Siberian Resources (The BAM)* (New York: Halsted, 1977), p. 53. See also pp. 41–45 for a discussion of natural gas development in Siberia.

9. R. W. Campbell, *The Economics of Soviet Oil and Gas* (Baltimore: Johns Hopkins University Press, 1968), p. 13.

10. Brents et al., *Ekonomika gazodobyvayushchei promyshlennosti*, p. 34.

11. *Narodnoye khozyaistvo SSSR v 1970 g.* (Moscow, 1971), p. 186.

12. "Original" five-year plan schedules should be distinguished from the subsequently "revised" annual versions, which are issued by the planners at a later date to minimize poor performance.

13. For a full account of the structure of the Soviet gas industry, a statement of the reforms and a summary of their achievements, see J. L. Russell, *Energy as a Factor in Soviet Foreign Policy* (Lexington: Saxon House, 1976), pp. 224–26; Alice G. Gorlin, "Industrial Reorganization—the Associations," in U.S. Congress, Joint Economic Committee, *Soviet Economy in a New Perspective*, 94th Congress, 2nd sess., 1976, pp. 174–76. S. Orudzhev, "Scientific and technical progress and the improvement of management—the basis of the accelerated development of the gas industry," *Planovoye khozyaistvo*, 1975, no. 1, pp. 22–30.

14. *Petroleum Economist*, May 1977, pp. 191–92.

15. V. A. Smirnov, "Defining Progress in the Gas Industry," *Current Digest of the Soviet Press*, 28, no. 1, 7–10.

16. Emily E. Jack, J. Richard Lee, Harold H. Lent, "Outlook for Soviet Energy," in *Soviet Economy in a New Perspective*, pp. 460–78.

17. *Soviet Long Range Energy Forecasts*, CIA A(ER) 75–81, September 1975, p. 8.

18. Theodore Shabad, "News Notes," *Soviet Geography*, April 1982, p. 284.

19. For details of the giant gas fields in Western Siberia, see *USSR: Development of the Gas Industry*, CIA (ER) 78–10393, (July 1978) Table C3, p. 45.

20. I. F. Elliott, The Soviet Energy Balance (New York: Praeger, 1974), p. 15.

21. Margulov et al., *Razvitiye gazovoi promyshlennosti*, Table 8, p. 13; "Soviets Press Line Work to Boost Gas Production," *OGJ*, 2 April 1979, pp. 39–43; *Problemy razvitiya transporta SSSR* (Moscow: Transport, 1981), p. 160.

22. *Soviet Gas to 1985*, Economist Intelligence Unit Special, QER no. 24, (August 1975), p. 17.

23. *Problemy razvitiya transporta*, p. 161.

24. Smirnov, "Defining Progress in the Gas Industry."

25. There has been some inconsistency in Soviet statements on pipeline plans. *Ekonomicheskaya gazeta*, 1981, no. 13 and no. 43; *Gazovaya promyshlennost*, 1981, no. 4 and no. 11; Shabad, "News Notes," *Soviet Geography*, April 1982, p. 286.

26. Smirnov, "Defining Progress in the Gas Industry," and O. M. Ivantsov, "The Promise of Liquefied Natural Gas," *Current Digest of the Soviet Press*, 27, no. 1, 11–13.

27. *BBC Summary of World Broadcasts* SU/W874/A/6 16 April 1976, Tass in English, 2 April 1976.

28. J. M. Stuchly and G. Walker, "LNG Long Distance Pipelines—A Technology Assessment," *OGJ*, 16 April 1979, pp. 59–63.

29. *BBC Summary of World Broadcasts* SU/W906/11, Moscow in Turkish, 4 November 1976. The same source reveals that a liquefaction plant is being built at Sala in Czechoslovakia to operate with gas supplied from the USSR.

30. "Soviets Prodding Pipeline Research," *OGJ*, 31 July 1978, pp. 104–05.

31. "Soviets Study Ways to Increase Gas Transmission Capacity," *OGJ*, 20 November 1978, pp. 131–34.

32. Ibid.

33. Russell, *Energy in Soviet Foreign Policy*, p. 64.

34. Soviet officials admit to 15 to 20 percent underutilization. *OGJ*, 20 June 1977, pp. 38–39.

35. CIA, *Development of the Gas Industry*, Table 10, p. 9.

36. Campbell, *Trends in the Soviet Oil and Gas Industry*, pp. 14–25.

37. Overall, the USSR has a much higher utilization ratio than some countries, notably the Middle East oil producers, but Soviet coefficients of utilization do not approach those of the United States.

38. Leslie Dienes and Theodore Shabad, *The Soviet Energy System* (New York: Wiley, 1979), Table 22, p. 96.

39. *Neftyanik*, 1970, no. 11, pp. 2–3.

40. For example, Keith Bush, in *The Exploitation of Siberia's Natural Resources*, NATO Directorate of Economic Affairs, NATO, 1974.

41. *OGJ*, 20 June 1977, pp. 38–39.

42. Margulov et al., *Razvitiye gazovoi promyshlennosti*, p. 21.

43. Jack et al., "Outlook for Soviet Energy."

44. Smirnov, "Defining Progress in the Gas Industry."

45. "High Costs Plague Russian Arctic Gas," *OGJ*, 20 June 1977, pp. 38–39.

46. Although Soviet trade statistics reported France as receiving gas from the USSR since 1976, no actual deliveries were made until 1980. Before that time, a logistical

agreement existed whereby the USSR exported more gas to Italy and an equivalent volume of Dutch gas was transferred to France on Italian account.

47. Material for this section is drawn from Harry Trend, "The Orenburg Gas Project," Radio Free Europe RAD Background Report/165 (Eastern Europe), 2 December 1975; Russell, *Energy in Soviet Foreign Policy*, pp. 229–31; Zbynek Zeman and Jan Zoubek, *Comecon Oil and Gas within the Overall Energy Context* (London: Financial Times, 1977), pp. 82–83.

48. W. L. Shierman, "World's Largest Processing Complex Handles Orenburg Gas," *OGJ*, 2 May 1977, pp. 243–46.

49. Most of the pipelaying was done by Soviet crews, the other countries performing secondary building work. Rumania was not assigned a section of the line, but helped in the construction of part of the main gas processing plant. J. B. Hannigan, *The Orenburg Natural Gas Pipeline Project and Fuels-Energy Balances in Eastern Europe* (Research Report 13. East-West Commercial Relations Series, Institute of Soviet and East European Studies, Carleton University, Ottawa, July 1980).

50. Viktor Petrenko, "Gas pipeline Soyuz is in operation," *Ekonomicheskoye sotrudnichestvo stran-chlenov SEV*, 1979, no. 1, pp. 88–92.

51. *BBC Summary of World Broadcasts*, Tanjug in English, 8 December 1976, and 8 April 1977.

52. Some gas from Orenburg was also involved.

53. Middle East Economic Digest (hereafter *MEED*), 17 July 1976.

54. The minor variances in volumes to be delivered which were cited in the various account of this project stemmed from the different temperatures at which each country measures the gas.

55. West Germany (Ruhrgas), France (Gaz de France), Austria (OMV).

56. *MEED*, 19 November 1976.

57. *MEED*, 5 December 1975.

58. Fereidun Fesheraki, "Iran's Energy Picture After the Revolution," *Middle East Economic Survey* (Supplement), 22, no. 46 (3 September 1979).

59. Rober Boyes and David Satter, "Deutsche Bank Visit to Moscow stirs East-West Tension," *Financial Times*, 8 February 1980.

60. Joseph Fitchett, "U.S. Worried by Proposed Europe-Russia Gas Deal," *International Herald Tribune*, 2 December 1980.

61. Full details of the project can be found in Joseph T. Kosnik, *Natural Gas Imports from the Soviet Union, Financing the North Star Joint Venture Project* (New York: Praeger, 1975).

62. Ibid., Table 4.3, p. 50.

63. Russell, *Energy in Soviet Foreign policy*, pp. 172–75; Zeman and Zoubek, *Comecon Oil and Gas*, p. 102.

64. Several routes were discussed for the pipeline. The original proposal cited Nakhodka as the Soviet terminal but later plans featured Olga, which has a deep bay and is thus more suitable for big tankers. Using Olga, the pipeline would be closer to 2,200 miles in length.

65. Russell, *Energy in Soviet Foreign Policy*, pp. 160–61.

66. Zeman and Zoubek, *Comecon Oil and Gas*, p. 103; note that if the cost of transporting the gas to the U.S.

proved too high, the U.S. group would have the option of selling the gas to Japan.

67. *U.S. Statutes at Large*, vol. 88, part 2, 2056–62.

68. Ibid., pp. 2333–37.

69. Secretary of State Press Conference, *PR 12–46*, 14 January 1975.

70. *OGJ*, 10 May 1976, p. 120.

71. Jack Brougher, "USSR Foreign Trade: A Greater Role for Trade With the West," in *Soviet Economy in a New Perspective*, pp. 677–94.

72. Comment by Arthur Meyerhoff in: Robert G. Jensen, ed., *Conference on Soviet Natural Resources in the World Economy*, Discussion Paper No. 24 (October 1980), Association of American Geographers, Project on Soviet Natural Resources in the World Economy, p. 91.

73. B. A. Rahmer, "Offshore Problems and Prospects," *Petroleum Economist* (May 1977), pp. 191-92.

74. See for example, Paul Marer, "Has Eastern Europe Become a Liability to the Soviet Union? The Economic Aspect," in Charles Gati, ed., *The International Politics of Eastern Europe* (New York: Praeger, 1976), pp. 59–80.

75. Craig B. Whitney, "Iran's Gas Cutoff Disrupts Soviet Border Republics," *New York Times*, 24 January 1979, p. 1; "Russians Seen Hurt by Iranian Oil Strike," *International Herald Tribune*, 16 December 1978.

76. *Kommunist* (Yerevan), 24 January 1981; *Zarya Vostoka* (Tbilisi), 25 January 1981.

77. *Prospects for Soviet Oil Production: A Supplemental Analysis*, ER 77–10425, CIA, (July 1977), p. 28. For an interpretation which suggests that the U.S. contribution has become more important than that of Western Europe and Japan, see Mark E. Miller, "The Role of Western Technology in Soviet Strategy," *Orbis*, 22 (1978): 539–68.

78. These points are discussed at length in Stern, *Soviet Natural Gas to 1990*, especially chapter 10.

79. For instance Peter R. Odell, *The West European Energy Economy* (Leiden: H. E. Stenfert Kroese B. V., 1976), Table 2, p. 38; G. F. Ray and G. M. Walsh, "The European Energy Outlook to 1985," *National Institute Economic Review*, no. 86 (November 1978), pp. 65–73.

80. B. A. Rahmer, "Natural Gas Across Frontiers," *Petroleum Economist* (December 1980), pp. 518–19.

81. Martin Quinlan, "Norway: Year of Decision over North Sea," *Petroleum Economist* (November 1980), pp. 476–78.

82. "World Watches as Med Pipelines are Laid," *The Middle East*, (January 1978), pp. 70–73; G. Bonfiglioni, "Trans-Med Pipeline will Stretch Offshore Laying Technology," *OGJ*, 5 September 1978, pp. 108–15.

83. Martin Quinlan, "Bold Plan to Pipe Algerian Gas," *Petroleum Economist* (May 1977), pp. 189–90.

84. U.S. Department of Energy, Economic Regulatory Administration, *ERA Docket No. 77–010–LNG*, Opinion no. 3, 18 December 1978; and *ERA Docket No. 77–006–LNG*, Opinion no. 4, 21 December 1978.

85. Margaret Greenhalgh, "Gas Deals May Still be Saved if the U.S. Changes its Mind in Time," *MEED*, 19 January 1979, p. 7; M. Belguedj, "The Marketing of Algerian Gas," *Petroleum Economist*, (December 1978), pp. 515–19.

86. "Algeria: Gas Export Policy Gets Big Rethink," *Petroleum Economist* (August 1980), p. 347.

87. John J. Stephan, "The Kuril Islands: Japan Versus Russia," *Pacific Community* (April 1976), pp. 311–30.

88. Edward K Faridany, *LNG Review 1977*, Energy Economics Research Ltd. 1977, pp. 22–23.

89. U.S. Congress, House, Committee on Interstate and Foreign Commerce, *Supplemental Natural Gas Source: Factors and Policy Issues* (June 1978).

90. "DOE Sees Short Haul LNG as Contributor to Meeting Increased Demand," *Inside DOE*, 2 April 1979, p. 12.

91. "Industry Reading Recent ERA Decisions as DOE Policy 'by Proxy' on LNG Imports," *Inside DOE*, 1 January 1979, p. 4.

92. *Prospects for Soviet Oil Production* ER 77–10270, (April 1977); and *Supplemental Analysis*, ER 77–10425, (July 1977).

93. *Prospects for Soviet Oil Production*, p. 9.

94. *Pravda*, 2 December 1980, p. 2.

95. For a good account of the East European situation see John M. Kramer, "Between Scylla and Charbydis: the Politics of Eastern Europe's Energy Problem," *Orbis* (Winter 1979), pp. 929–50.

96. Leslie Dienes, *Soviet Energy Policy and the Hydrocarbons* and Robert G. Jensen, ed., *Soviet Energy Policy and the Hydrocarbons: Comments and a Rejoinder*, Discussion Papers No. 2 and 7 (April 1978 and February 1979), Association of American Geographers, Project on Soviet Natural Resources in the World Economy, contain interesting insights into this complex subject.

97. Nordine Ait Laoussine, "Oil-Gas Price Parity: Suggestions for a Transitional Compromise" *Middle East Economic Survey*, 24, no. 2 (27 October 1980): 1–4.

98. Assumptions underlying these projections are elaborated in Stern, *Soviet Natural Gas to 1990*, chapter 3.

99. Jack et al., "Outlook for Soviet Energy."

100. Up until 1980, these purchases made the gas industry a hard currency deficit sector. The industry should go into an impressive surplus position in the early 1980s.

# 16

# THE REGIONAL DIMENSIONS OF SOVIET ENERGY POLICY

LESLIE DIENES
University of Kansas

## Introduction

Geographic space, as the locus of production factors and the matrix for the placement of economic activities, is an explicit variable in economic growth. In the USSR, the elements of geography and their legacy through time have played and continue to play a particularly influential, if not decisive, role. The immense size, extremely uneven and mismatched distribution of population and natural resources are coupled with a territorially defined multinational structure. These factors, combined with the ideological as well as strategic concerns and commitments of the Soviet leadership, result in a manifest involvement with regional issues.

Decisions concerning the fuel-energy sector are closely intertwined with questions involving the spatial dimensions of the Soviet economy as a whole. The striking geographic disparities in resource endowment and energy demand have momentous consequences for investment strategy, transport development and regional economic policy. For many years now, energy production and transport have received some 30 percent of all *productive* investment in industry[1] (i.e. not counting that for supporting infrastructure) and close to a half of all such investment in outlays for energy utilization equipment at the consumer end are included.[2] Altogether, directly energy-related expenditures are certain to exceed a fifth of all investment in the national economy.[3] The energy industries also claim a large and rapidly growing share of the country's transport inputs. Even without natural gas, and thus considering only tonnage freight, mineral fuels represented two-fifths of all Soviet *internal* freight turnover in 1980, up from one-third in 1960.[4] With natural gas added at the corresponding calorific and weight equivalent of hard coal, the share of mineral fuels approaches one-half.[5]

Chapter 12 in this volume examines the crucial issues of Soviet energy policy planning on the national level, with particular emphasis on the hydrocarbons.[6] Relevant developments in Soviet energy demand were investigated both in the aggregate and in specific technological uses.

The severe technical and geographical constraints both on fuel substitution (to free oil) and on the rate of expansion of the three major fuels were analyzed in detail. The regional dimensions of the USSR, however, were dealt with only insofar as they played an explicit controlling role on the growth and level of national demand, the availability of supplies and substitution among primary sources.

This paper specifically focuses on the areal dimensions of Soviet energy policy: on regional fuel consumption, mixes and flows and the relationship of energy strategy and regional development. Energy is used not in an abstract, spaceless world but in concrete geographic space and with specific technological applications. Especially in the USSR, the great bulk of it is consumed by locationally concentrated, highly capital intensive facilities with a host of specific regional linkages. The regional proportions of *aggregate* energy consumption, therefore, are subject to pronounced inertia; huge efforts and long lead times are required to modify them considerably. The regional energy mixes, i.e. the shares of different energy sources in each areal unit, however, are more prone to change, since in each case, these shares apply only to a fraction of the national total. Be that as it may, the worsening spatial discordance between production and consumption and the immense transport burden this imposes on the economy highlight the importance of the regional dimension. Even modest developments in regional consumption patterns and energy flows should have more than negligible economic effect. At any rate, given the geography of the USSR, Soviet planners are confronted with the problems of regional energy growth, consumption mixes and flows at every step in their attempt to formulate a more or less comprehensive energy policy.

## Regional Developments in Aggregate Fuel Consumption and Energy Intensity

In the USSR, with its strongly centralized system of resource allocation, planners' control over the distribution of energy is applied with particular force. Given the vertical, ministerial structure of planning, the most conspicuous priorities are sectoral: the continued emphasis on heavy, capital goods, industries is the core of development strategy. In the allocation of energy, industry overwhelmingly dominates. Including electric stations, this sector took 60 percent of all aggregate domestic energy input in the mid-1970s and virtually the same share when power stations were regarded merely as energy transforming agents, with their output redistributed. In the U.S., industry and electric plants consumed only half of aggregate energy and, with electricity redistributed, industry used only 35 percent.[7]

Such sectoral priorities, however, find an immediate geographic expression since heavy industries, the most intensive users, are spatially concentrated. Regional per capita variations in energy demand, particularly in stationary uses, tend to follow the distribution of heavy industry and thus show pronounced areal differences. The Spearman rank correlation coefficient between per capita consumption of all boiler and furnace fuels, virtually synonymous with stationary energy demand, and the per capita value of industrial fixed assets over the 18 major economic regions plus Moldavia indicates a close relationship for the years 1965 and 1970 ($R_s$ = 0.93 and 0.92).[8] Variations in per capita consumption among these areal units ranged from 33 percent to 220 percent of the

Soviet average in 1965 and from 38 percent to 220 percent in 1970. With a finer regional mesh, such differences, of course, would be much greater (Table 1).

Not surprisingly, the Donets-Dnieper and Urals regions, the two iron and steel bastions of the country, are the leading per capita fuel consumers followed by Siberia and the Volga (with ferrous and nonferrous metal smelting, cellulose, etc. dominating in the former, petroleum refining and petrochemicals in the latter). The Northwest, where iron and steel and pulp and paper industries are, again, important is also high on the list. All non-Russian provinces, with the exception of the Eastern Ukraine (Donets-Dnieper) rank well below the Soviet mean. The poorly industrialized but agriculturally significant regions (North Caucasus, Southwest, South, Belorussia, Central Asia, Moldavia) and some coastal provinces, particularly the Far East, show appreciably higher shares in total fuel consumption than in boiler and furnace fuel demand. This speaks of the relatively greater importance of mobile users, requiring tractor and fleet fuel, in their consumption mix than in that of the country as a whole. The comparatively low per capita fuel demand in the Central Russian and Baltic regions is not due to industrial backwardness, but to the great emphasis on

TABLE 1
Regional Fuel Consumption in the USSR (1965 and 1970)

| | All Fuels | | Boiler and Furnace Fuels | | | | | |
| | percent | Index of per capita demand (USSR = 100) | In million tons of standard fuel | | percent | | Index of per capita demand (USSR = 100) | |
| Region | 1965 | 1965 | 1965 | 1970 | 1965 | 1970 | 1965 | 1970 |
|---|---|---|---|---|---|---|---|---|
| Group 1 | | | | | | | | |
| Northwest | 6.1 | 121 | 42 | 50 | 5.95 | 5.53 | 118 | 110 |
| Central Russia | 10.5 | 91 | 74 | 96 | 10.48 | 10.62 | 91 | 93 |
| Donets-Dnieper | 14.8 | 176 | 131 | 140 | 18.55 | 15.49 | 221 | 187 |
| Urals | 12.7 | 194 | 100 | 121 | 14.16 | 13.38 | 216 | 215 |
| Group 2 | | | | | | | | |
| Volga-Vyatka | 2.7 | 76 | 19 | 23 | 2.69 | 2.54 | 75 | 74 |
| Central Chernozem | 2.9 | 84 | 21 | 26 | 2.97 | 2.88 | 86 | 88 |
| Volga | 8.4 | 110 | 59 | 78 | 8.36 | 8.63 | 110 | 114 |
| North Caucasus | 4.3 | 74 | 27 | 36 | 3.82 | 3.98 | 66 | 67 |
| Southwest | 4.3 | 49 | 24 | 40 | 3.40 | 4.42 | 39 | 52 |
| South | 1.6 | 63 | 7 | 15 | 1.00 | 1.66 | 40 | 63 |
| Baltic | 2.7 | 87 | 18 | 23 | 2.55 | 2.54 | 82 | 81 |
| Belorussia | 2.3 | 62 | 15 | 21 | 2.12 | 2.32 | 57 | 62 |
| Moldavia | 0.6 | 41 | 4 | 6 | 0.57 | 0.66 | 39 | 45 |
| Transcaucasia | 3.0 | 61 | 22 | 30 | 3.12 | 3.32 | 63 | 65 |
| Group 3 | | | | | | | | |
| West Siberia | 7.0 | 134 | 49 | 65 | 6.94 | 7.19 | 132 | 145 |
| East Siberia | 5.3 | 169 | 30 | 39 | 4.25 | 4.31 | 136 | 140 |
| Far East | 3.4 | 142 | 20 | 24 | 2.83 | 2.66 | 118 | 110 |
| Group 4 | | | | | | | | |
| Kazakhstan | 3.0 | 57 | 26 | 42 | 3.68 | 4.65 | 70 | 87 |
| Central Asia | 4.4 | 58 | 18 | 29 | 2.55 | 3.21 | 33 | 38 |
| USSR | 100.0 | 100 | 706 | 904 | 100.00 | 100.00 | 100 | 100 |

SOURCE: Leslie Dienes and Theodore Shabad, *The Soviet Energy System* (Washington: Winston and Sons. Distributed by John Wiley, 1979), p. 24.

precision and light manufacturing in their economic structure.

It is worthy of note that the first four regions in Table 1, which represent the traditional pre-World War II (indeed, pre-Revolutionary) concentration of industry, still accounted for some 45 percent of all boiler and furnace fuel consumption at the beginning of the 1970s. Despite the still noticeable concentration, however, the spread of manufacturing from these old, established centers is gradually affecting other provinces as well, both in the European and in the Asian parts of the country. As Table 1 shows, two-thirds of the regions outside Group 1 improved their share in boiler and furnace fuel consumption during the second half of the 1960s. Nearly all bettered their per capita position, even the Moslem area of Central Asia, where burgeoning population growth makes per capita improvements difficult to achieve.

In line with the growth of mechanization and Soviet emphasis on producer goods, the energy intensiveness of industry increased rapidly, though not spectacularly, since the start of the five-year plans in nearly all regions. On the average, fuel consumption per industrial worker in the USSR doubled between 1928 and 1965 and rose 2.4 times by 1970 (Table 2). Such achievement appears more impressive when placed against the 7.3-fold and 8.4-fold increase in industrial employment between those respective dates.[9] Equally important, regional differences have been substantially reduced. The coefficient of variation among the prewar (1928) areal units decreased from 0.40 at the onset of the five-year plans to 0.29 by 1970. During the second half of the 1960s alone (and within a somewhat more extensive regional set), the coefficient of variations declined from 0.32 to 0.31 (Table 3).

It is also noteworthy that the data imply only a minor shift in the relative fuel intensiveness of Soviet industry from the European to the Asian USSR. While fuel consumption per industrial worker from 1928 through 1965 and 1970 did increase somewhat faster east of the Urals, than west, the difference in the respective growth rates is surprisingly small. The industry of the Urals region experienced slower growth in energy intensity as measured by fuel use per worker than either the Asian or the European territory taken as a whole. Surprisingly, the Urals area comprised one of the two most energy-intensive industrial clusters as early as 1928. The high priority accorded to this region through much of the Soviet era led to a broadening of its manufacturing base and a less sharply dominant energy intensive profile. In two other regions (North Caucasus and Transcaucasia), the narrow, fuel-intensive industrial structure in 1928 was associated mainly with petroleum production and refining. The exhaustion of reserves and the geographic shift in primary resource-processing activities resulted in slow growth of fuel consumption per industrial worker and a drastic decline in *relative* energy intensity in these provinces (Table 2).

The data also show that, *relative to the Soviet mean*, fuel use in Siberia remained constant until 1965 and only a minimum *relative* gain was registered during the second half of the 1960s (Table 2). The comparative position of the Far East actually declined and by 1970 its fuel con-

sumption per industrial worker was no better than average. It is true that the index, which excludes hydroelectricity, understates somewhat the growth of energy use and its relative intensity reached by Siberian industry in 1970 because of the extensive waterpower development during the previous decade. This, however, does not apply to the Far East, where the expansion of hydroelectric capacity lagged behind the rate experienced by the country as a whole.[10] At any rate, until the close of the 1960s, the increase in the comparative energy intensiveness of industry in the eastern regions of the Russian Republic can be described only as modest. More vigorous growth in fuel demand per industrial worker was recorded in Central Asia and Kazakhstan, admittedly from a low base which made faster rates easier to achieve. Until 1965, data are given for the two regions combined; for the second half of the sixties the available evidence shows little change in the energy intensity of industry in Central Asia but a rapid rise in that for the industry of Kazakhstan (Tables 2 and 3).

There are signs that the growth of energy consumption by Siberian industry sharply accelerated in the 1970s. With the construction of the Baikal-Amur Mainline under way, the relative drop in the position of the Far East should also be reversed. Unfortunately, post-1970 data on regional fuel-energy consumption are lacking. They can be approximated for 1975, but only for the economy of the trans-Ural territories of the RSFSR as a whole. Aggregate fuel demand in Siberia and the Far East in 1975 reached 200–210 million tons of standard fuel, about a 35 percent rise in 5 years (5.6 per annum) as compared to a 27 percent increase (4.9 percent per annum) in aggregate fuel demand in the country as a whole.[11] The utilization of waterpower potential in Siberia was also more rapid than the Soviet average and increased faster than west of the Urals (nearly twice as fast or as much as 2.6 times in the five-year period 1971–75, depending on the method employed).[12] In addition, production, hence consumption, of hydroelectricity in Siberia tends to be far more stable than in the European USSR or in Central Asia, with years of low water regimes being less common. In the first half of the seventies, as in the previous five years, the output of hydroelectricity in Siberia rose substantially despite some annual fluctuation. It declined in the other provinces, resulting in a stagnation of hydropower produced in the USSR in the first half of the 1970s.[13]

Despite some legitimate Western doubts about the cost-effectiveness of the BAM and some of the vast resource projects initiated in the eastern half of the Asian USSR, it appears that Soviet leaders are determined to develop a new raw-material production base in Pacific Siberia. Because of the virgin resources of the vast area between the Yenisei and the seaboard, "the Soviet Union may maintain self-sufficiency in virtually every strategic mineral, well into the next century." The country may thus "be vested with strong bargaining power" vis-a-vis the resource poor industrial West in forth-coming years after these projects mature.[14] Whether such a vast commitment to the distant eastern half of the Asian USSR is a recognition of "manifest destiny" or an example of supreme economic folly remains to be seen. The thrust is real, seems to be for the long term and should acquire a momentum of its own. The ideal of complex and multi-faceted regional development appears to have been abandoned and Siberia assigned the role of the resource supplying and exporting hinterland in a "core-periphery" relationship with the European heart.[15] But the large amount of new construction, a specialization on resource production with certain primary industries, and a capital intensive, labor-saving strategy of development can only increase the energy intensity of the Siberian economy relative to the rest of the country.

This also means, however, that in view of the tightening supplies of energy and the high probability of a serious crunch, fuel-energy demand by the Asian and European parts of the country will be competitive as much as complementary. It will certainly be competitive in the way funds are allocated for projects and this rivalry will affect the long term growth of energy supplies themselves. The cis-Urals provinces (exclusive of the Urals region itself) accounted for 77 percent of Soviet national income in 1968 according to the Marxist definition of the term.[16] With services added, their share probably exceeded 80 percent.[17] In industry alone, these same provinces generate over three-fourths of all value added today, and the European USSR is destined to remain the economic heart of the country well into the next century.[18] Thus it is hardly possible to project a much lower growth rate in energy demand for the cis-Ural territory than for

the Soviet Union as a whole, despite a serious attempt to concentrate energy intensive activities in the eastern regions. This means that the probable supply crunch almost certainly will affect the significantly higher growth rates of energy consumption and, consequently, the ambitious development plans envisaged for Siberia and Kazakhstan by the Soviet leadership. A retardation in the development of these areas, however, will endanger the expansion of energy and raw material supplies in the longer run because in the forthcoming decades Soviet dependence for resources on the Asian USSR can only intensify.

At the very least, regional and institutional rivalries concerning the development priorities of eastern energy sources should continue and may increase. The BAM and other giant projects east of the Urals notwithstanding, the growing strain on Soviet investment resources, combined with the drastic slowdown in the expansion of the labor force, is enhancing the locational inertia of Soviet industry as a whole. The number of new enterprises put on stream annually has declined sharply, from about a thousand in the 1960s to some 400 in 1970 and 250 in 1976.[19] The share of investment going to greenfield sites as opposed to the reconstruction and modernization of existing plants decreased from almost one-half of the total at the end of the fifties and 42 percent even in 1970 to 28 percent by 1980.[20] All these trends are bolstering those forces that want to strengthen the economic role of the

TABLE 2

Fuel Consumption per Industrial Worker in Soviet Regions (1928, 1965, and 1970) (within 13 areal units)
(In million tons of standard fuel (SF) and relative to Soviet average)

| | 1928 | | | 1965 | | |
|---|---|---|---|---|---|---|
| Regions | In million tons of SF | Relative to Soviet average USSR = 100 | Index of Growth 1928 = 100 | In million tons of SF | Relative to Soviet average USSR = 100 | Index of Growth 1928 = 100 |
| Northwest and Central Russia | 7.5 | 66 | 100 | 14.5* | 66 | 193 |
| Volga-Vyatka and Central Chernozem | 6.4 | 57 | 100 | 13.0* | 59 | 203 |
| Baltic | — | — | — | 14.5 | 66 | — |
| Belorussia | 8.6 | 76 | 100 | 14.7 | 67 | 171 |
| Ukraine | 17.8 | 158 | 100 | 25.1 | 115 | 141 |
| Moldavia | — | — | — | 13.5 | 62 | — |
| North Caucasus | 18.2 | 161 | 100 | 17.3 | 79 | 95 |
| Transcaucasia | 21.1 | 187 | 100 | 23.4 | 107 | 111 |
| Volga | 9.4 | 83 | 100 | 30.0 | 137 | 319 |
| Urals | 21.2 | 188 | 100 | 33.7 | 154 | 159 |
| West Siberia and East Siberia | 14.0 | 124 | 100 | 27.2* | 124 | 194 |
| Far East | 15.2 | 135 | 100 | 26.2 | 120 | 172 |
| Kazakhstan and Central Asia | 8.2 | 73 | 100 | 20.1* | 92 | 245 |
| European USSR (without Urals) | 10.6 | 94 | 100 | 19.5 | 89 | 184 |
| Urals | 21.2 | 188 | 100 | 33.7 | 154 | 159 |
| Asian USSR | 12.4 | 110 | 100 | 24.6 | 112 | 198 |
| USSR | 11.3 | 100 | 100 | 21.9 | 100 | 194 |

SOURCE: A. Ye. Probst and Ya. A. Mazanova, eds., *Razvitiye i razmeshcheniye toplivnoi promyshlennosti* [Development and location of the fuels industry] (Moscow: Nedra, 1975), p. 38.
*For 1965 and 1970, the source gives data separately for the two regions combined. The weighted average was computed to make the figures comparable to 1928. Industrial employment to calculate the weighted average for Kazakhstan and Central Asia was taken from *Nar. khoz. SSSR v 1965 godu*, pp. 562–63; *Nar. khoz. v 1970 godu*, pp. 514–15. For the three combined regions of the RSFSR, industrial employment can be estimated from population-employment ratios for 1965 as given in A. I. Vedishchev, "Commensuration of economic development levels in the economic regions of the USSR," in AN SSSR and Gosplan SSSR, SOPS, *Ekonomicheskiye problemy razmeshcheniya proizvoditelnykh sil SSSR* [Economic problems in the location of productive forces of the USSR] (Moscow: Nauka, 1969), p. 63.

The Regional Dimensions of Soviet Energy Policy 389

European provinces and to subordinate the development of Siberia and the Far East to the needs of the economic core.[21]

The advocates of this market oriented strategy press for priority exploitation of locationally mobile, transportable energy sources, those which can fuel cities and farms in the European USSR or can be exported. These are, of course, mostly hydrocarbons, though relatively well located hard coal deposits (Ekibastuz, Neryungri) also fall into this category. Giant heat and power complexes based on Siberian lignites and waterpower and associated industrial agglomerations are clearly not in this class. The scale of development of these so far nontransportable energy potentials and the size and complexity of the Siberian market to be created for them continue to be highly controversial. A recently expressed strongly pro-European view holds that efforts to shift the economic center of gravity toward the East, to diversify economic activity there beyond a narrow range of power-intensive but highly automated industries (aluminum, magnesium, titanium, cellulose and acetate fibers), would run counter to the needs of a modern economy and to the principal socioeconomic goals of the Soviet Union.[22] Though no longer advocating full-scale, multifaceted development, the opposite Siberian strategy still favors accelerated expansion of a broad range of heavy industries in the southern belt of Siberia: not only the fuel, electro-metallurgical and wood processing branches, but also iron and steel production, heavy machinery, basic chemicals and virtually the whole line of petrochemical synthesis.[23]

## Changes in the Regional Fuel Mix (1965–75)

Available data, through arduous and time-consuming effort, made it possible to produce estimates of the changing Soviet fuel mix in regional detail (Table 4, 5, and 6). The data cover boiler and furnace fuel consumption, which closely approximates stationary fuel demand, from 1965 to 1975 at five-year intervals. In all three years, accuracy is judged to be fairly high for natural gas and reasonable for solid fuels, while in the first two periods at least each separate regional total is also from a reliable source. On the other hand, information about regional consumption of liquid fuels is nearly impossible to find. It must be derived essentially as a set of residuals and matched with available data on the national level.

Since the virtual elimination of steam traction from the railways during the 1960s, solid fuels have been almost entirely restricted to boiler and furnace uses, and within this category mainly to power stations and coking plants.[24] Although such fuels under boilers suffer a lesser economic and technological disadvantage compared with hydrocarbons than in other installations, while metallurgical coal remains indispensable for coking, the decline of the share of coal, peat, shale and wood in boiler and furnace uses proved to be just as rapid as in the energy balance as a whole. Between 1965 and 1975, their share in such uses decreased from 65 percent to 47 percent. The biggest drop was registered in the Urals region and the European USSR, particularly the cis-Volga provinces of the Russian Republic, Belorussia and the Baltic (Tables 4 and 6). In the Urals, the contribution of solid fuels dropped from 72 percent in 1965 to 41 percent ten years later. In the Russian Plain and the Baltic-Belorussian areas combined, it declined from 63 percent to 40 percent. The Volga region, the North Caucasus, Transcaucasia, and the Ukraine experienced less dramatic change, the first three because of the already dominant position of hydrocarbons in the fuel mix, the last because of the continued importance of coal. Though less overwhelmingly than before, coal remains dominant also in all economic regions east of the Urals, except in Central Asia with its substantial gas and oil reserves and lack of other fuel resources.

It is also instructive to note that between 1970 and 1975 the growth in the relative contribution of hydrocarbons at the expense of solid fuels in stationary uses proceeded almost as swiftly as during the previous five years. The rapid *relative* decline of coal, peat and shale (as of firewood) continued despite the mounting pressure on oil and gas and an increasing concern for their prudent use. Moreover, the share of solid fuels declined in every economic region save the Baltic, where an upsurge in shale production to fire two huge power stations took place during the first half of the seventies[25] (Tables 5 and 6).

In Kazakhstan, Siberia and the Far East, coal is both abundant and clearly the cheapest fuel.[26] The rising con-

| | 1970 | | |
|---|---|---|---|
| | In million tons of SF | Relative to Soviet average USSR = 100 | Index of Growth 1928 = 100 |
| | 18.7* | 68 | 249 |
| | 19.1* | 70 | 298 |
| | 18.0 | 66 | — |
| | 17.3 | 63 | 201 |
| | 34.3 | 126 | 193 |
| | 16.6 | 61 | — |
| | 20.6 | 76 | 113 |
| | 27.0 | 99 | 128 |
| | 28.1 | 103 | 299 |
| | 44.3 | 162 | 209 |
| | 34.5* | 126 | 246 |
| | 27.8 | 102 | 183 |
| | 28.7* | 105 | 350 |
| | 24.2 | 89 | 228 |
| | 44.3 | 162 | 209 |
| | 31.4 | 115 | 253 |
| | 27.3 | 100 | 242 |

sumption and share of hydrocarbons between 1965 and 1975 were not the result of tight supplies and high costs but of technological considerations, such as peaking needs by electric stations and specific furnace requirements, for which low-grade coals are unsuited. Heightened environmental concern, too, may have had some influences and the difficulty of furnishing small, dispersed consumers with coal and lignite also must have played some part in the growth of fuel oil demand east of the Urals.

All of the above factors clearly contributed to the sharply diminished role of solid fuels in boiler and furnace uses in the European USSR as well. Indeed, because of greater fluctuation in electric power demand, higher urban densities and the importance of cogeneration in space heating, the need for clean and/or flexible fuels, such as gas and oil, seems to have been even more significant than in Soviet Asia. Yet the strongest and, for the future, most influential reason behind the steep decline in the contribution of coal, peat and shale lies in the inability of Soviet planners to expand the production of solid fuels at more than a fraction of the rate of aggregate energy demand. Geological, labor and capital constraints on increasing coal production in the European USSR are particularly severe. In these parts, such constraints will limit the growth of solid fuel output during the forthcoming decade to barely over one percent per annum. Thus, even with growing shipment of Kuznetsk and Ekibastuz coal from beyond the Urals, the share of solid fuels in the European USSR must continue to decline (particularly in regions west of the Volga) and the strain on hydrocarbons will intensify still further.[27]

The changing geography of hydrocarbon supplies and the greater transport constraint on gas compared to oil have also affected developments in the consumption mixes of Soviet regions between 1965 and 1975. They are likely to do so in the future as well. This relationship deserves a brief look both for its own sake, as an empirical example of the problem of spatial optimization, and because of the nexus between energy and other resource flows and regional policy. In the huge, multi-ethnic state of the USSR, with large regional differences in the level of development and per capita economic growth, this linkage cannot be ignored.

Both in the Soviet Union and in the cis-Ural provinces taken as a whole, the *rate* of increase in the contribution of oil and gas to boiler and furnace fuel consumption slowed appreciably in the second half of the 1965–75 period. Surging export needs, particularly for petroleum, and a squeeze on supplies from accessible, mature fields took their toll, even though hydrocarbons continued to experience a large absolute growth in demand and raise their share in the fuel balance. On the national scale, the relative importance of gas versus oil to the *increase* of boiler and furnace fuel consumption also remained similar throughout the ten years 1965–75. Gas contributed 53 percent to the total hydrocarbon increment by heat value during 1965–70 and 51 percent during 1970–75 (Tables

TABLE 3
Fuel Consumption per Industrial Worker in Soviet Regions (1965 and 1970) (within 17 areal units)
(In million tons of standard fuel (SF) and relative to Soviet average)

| | 1965 | | | 1970 | | |
|---|---|---|---|---|---|---|
| Regions | In million tons of SF | Relative to Soviet average USSR = 100 | Index of Growth 1965 = 100 | In million tons of SF | Relative to Soviet average USSR = 100 | Index of Growth 1965 = 100 |
| Northwest | 17.5 | 80 | 100 | 24.4 | 89 | 139 |
| Central Russia | 13.1 | 60 | 100 | 16.1 | 59 | 123 |
| Volga-Vyatka | 13.0 | 59 | 100 | 16.2 | 59 | 125 |
| Central Chernozem | 13.0 | 59 | 100 | 24.1 | 88 | 185 |
| Baltic | 14.5 | 66 | 100 | 18.0 | 66 | 124 |
| Belorussia | 14.7 | 67 | 100 | 17.3 | 63 | 118 |
| Ukraine | 25.1 | 115 | 100 | 34.3 | 126 | 137 |
| Moldavia | 13.5 | 62 | 100 | 16.6 | 61 | 123 |
| North Caucasus | 17.3 | 79 | 100 | 20.6 | 75 | 119 |
| Transcaucasia | 23.4 | 107 | 100 | 27.0 | 99 | 115 |
| Volga | 30.0 | 137 | 100 | 28.1 | 103 | 94 |
| Urals | 33.7 | 154 | 100 | 44.3 | 162 | 131 |
| West Siberia | 27.6 | 126 | 100 | 33.3 | 122 | 121 |
| East Siberia | 26.5 | 121 | 100 | 36.7 | 134 | 138 |
| Far East | 26.2 | 120 | 100 | 27.8 | 102 | 106 |
| Kazakhstan | 23.0 | 105 | 100 | 34.6 | 127 | 150 |
| Central Asia | 17.4 | 79 | 100 | 22.5 | 82 | 129 |
| European USSR (without Urals) | 19.5 | 89 | 100 | 24.2 | 89 | 124 |
| Urals | 33.7 | 154 | 100 | 44.3 | 162 | 131 |
| Asian USSR | 24.6 | 112 | 100 | 31.4 | 115 | 128 |
| USSR | 21.9 | 100 | 100 | 27.3 | 100 | 125 |

SOURCE: A. Ye. Probst and Ya. A. Mazanova, eds., *Razvitiye i razmeshcheniye toplivnoi promyshlennosti* [Development and location of the fuels industry] (Moscow: Nedra, 1975), p. 38.

4–6). An examination of the regional mixes, however, reveals important changes in the relationship of the two fuels.

All through the 1960s, the penetration of natural gas into the boiler and furnace market was rapid over the entire European USSR and also in Central Asia. (Regional data for the contribution of gas, though not of other fuels, are available for the early sixties as well.)[28] By 1970, however, the absolute growth of gas consumption slowed appreciably. Throughout the cis-Volga provinces, which still contain some three-fifths of all Soviet population and industry, the share of gas in the fuel balance stabilized between 1970 and 1975 and actually declined in certain regions (Tables 5 and 6). Supplies in Transcaucasia doubled, with a surge in the share of gas, but entirely on account of Iranian imports.[29] North of the Caucasus and the Black Sea, however, it was not natural gas but liquid fuels which contributed most dramatically to the increase of hydrocarbon consumption in stationary uses. The proportion of refinery products in the first half of the seventies rose sharply in every region west of the Volga, except Moldavia.

The slowdown in the rise of gas consumption and the consequent surge in the demand for liquid fuels by most

European provinces was the result of the peaking, even decline, of production from mature reservoirs and the delays experienced in delivering large quantities of natural gas from the remote West Siberian fields to market in the European USSR areas. Western petroleum deposits were similarly peaking. However, the intensive development of the Tyumen oil fields (also in the forbidding West Siberian swamps but better located than the gas) and the greater transportability of crude oil enabled Soviet planners to throw this resource into the breach.

The difficulties and delays involved in tapping the vast gas reserves of West Siberia were instrumental in the overworking and premature peaking of hydrocarbon reservoirs in several established provinces. They also accounted for much of the injudicious haste and rash production practices applied to Siberian and Kazakhstan oil fields, with consequent loss of large quantities of petroleum.[30] Finally the tremendous transport bottleneck for Siberian gas heightened regional competition for the remaining reserves in mature provinces and affected interregional flows during the 1970s. It is probable that such effects will persist at least through much of the eighties. Relative to demand, Siberian gas will continue to experience severe transport difficulties (see below). In addition,

TABLE 4
Boiler and Furnace Fuel Consumption by Economic Regions (1965)
(Million tons of standard fuel (SF) and percentages)

| Regions | All Fuels | | Solid Fuels* | | Natural Gas** | | Liquid Products*** | |
|---|---|---|---|---|---|---|---|---|
| | Million tons of SF | Percent | Million tons of SF | Percent | Million tons of SF | Percent | Million tons of SF | Percent |
| Northwest | 42 | 100 | 29 | 69.0 | 7 ( 7.6) | 16.7 | 6 | 14.3 |
| Central Russia | 74 | 100 | 41 | 55.4 | 23.5 ( 26.4) | 31.8 | 9.5 | 12.8 |
| Volga-Vyatka | 19 | 100 | 12.5 | 65.8 | 4 ( 4.4) | 21.1 | 2.5 | 13.1 |
| Central Chernozem | 21 | 100 | 13.5 | 64.3 | 3.0 ( 3.2) | 14.3 | 4.5 | 21.4 |
| Baltic | 18 | 100 | 12.5 | 69.4 | 2.0 ( 2.6)**** | 11.1 | 3.5 | 19.4 |
| Belorussia | 15 | 100 | 10 | 83.3 | 2.5 ( 2.6) | 13.9 | 2.5 | 13.9 |
| Moldavia | 4 | 100 | 2.5 | 62.5 | — — | — | 1.5 | 37.5 |
| Ukraine | 162 | 100 | 115.5 | 71.3 | 38.5 ( 40.7) | 23.8 | 8 | 4.9 |
| North Caucasus | 27 | 100 | 10.5 | 38.9 | 12.5 ( 13.1) | 46.3 | 4 | 14.8 |
| Transcaucasia | 22 | 100 | 3.5 | 15.9 | 9 ( 9.0) | 40.9 | 9.5 | 43.2 |
| Volga | 59 | 100 | 14.5 | 24.6 | 20 ( 21.0) | 33.9 | 24.5 | 41.5 |
| Urals | 100 | 100 | 72 | 72.0 | 12 ( 12.0) | 12.0 | 16 | 16.0 |
| West Siberia | 49 | 100 | 44.5 | 90.8 | — — | — | 4.5 | 9.2 |
| East Siberia | 30 | 100 | 29 | 96.7 | — — | — | 1 | 3.3 |
| Far East | 20 | 100 | 18 | 90.0 | 0.5 ( 0.7) | 2.5 | 1.5 | 7.5 |
| Kazakhstan | 26 | 100 | 23.5 | 90.4 | 0.5 ( 0.7) | 1.9 | 2 | 7.7 |
| Central Asia | 18 | 100 | 8 | 44.5 | 6 ( 6.9) | 33.3 | 4 | 22.2 |
| USSR | 706 | 100 | 460 | 65.2 | 141 (150.9) | 20.0 | 105 | 14.8 |

*Coal, coke, peat, shale and state supplied firewood. Also include by-product gases at coke ovens and blast furnaces which are overwhelmingly attributable to coal.

**Figures in brackets refer to gross consumption, i.e. including losses and gas used by compressor stations on gas pipelines. Figures to the left of brackets apparently refer to actual consumption, i.e. excluding losses and compressor use. They have been adjusted to 0.5 or the whole million to avoid the impression of spurious accuracy.

***Includes still gas in refinery operations. Liquefied gases may also be included, but their contribution in 1965 was still very small.

****Apparently includes shale gas.

NOTE: Columns 1 and 4 (gas in brackets) from Vsesoyuzny institut nauchnoi i tekhnicheskoi informatsii [All-Union Institute of Scientific and Technical Information] *Razrabotka neftyanykh i gazovykh mestorozhdenii* [Development of oil and gas fields] vol. 4 (Moscow, 1972), pp. 44–45. The breakdown among the major fuels for each region computed according to percentages supplied in A. Ye. Probst, ed., *Razvitiye toplivnoi bazy rayonov SSSR* [Development of the fuel base in regions of the USSR] (Moscow: Nedra, 1968), pp. 62–322, *passim.* The Probst tables for boiler and furnace fuels exclude coke, but percentages for the latter are given in adjoining columns referring to aggregate fuel consumption. The data for boiler and furnace fuel uses, therefore, could be adjusted accordingly. Similar percentages for the major fuels are also given by economic regions in M. Kh. Gankin et al., eds., *Perevozki gruzov* [Freight hauls] (Moscow: Transport, 1972), p. 78. The total for solid fuels, natural gas and liquid products each accord closely to the stationary uses of these fuels in 1965 as can be rearranged from Robert Campbell, *Soviet Energy Balances* (Santa Monica, Ca.: Rand Corporation Research Report, R-2257, 1978).

large amounts of Soviet gas are mortgaged for Western pipes and compressors already delivered, at a time when the oil industry has reached a virtual plateau in production and could easily face a downturn in its volume of output. This effect of competing regional pressures on remaining hydrocarbons in mature provinces and consequent changes in the interregional flow of gas, the cleanest, most effective and in most cases cheapest fuel, is treated below.

Through most of the 1960s, the primary interregional flow of gas took place between the European South (Ukraine and the North Caucasus) and the Baltic, Belorussian and European Russian provinces to the north, with Moscow being the chief recipient (smaller shipments of this fuel from the Volga to the Moscow-Gorky region were less important). A second major interregional flow connected Central Asia with the Urals and by the beginning of the seventies with the Moscow area as well. During the 1965–70 period, some 30 percent of all gas produced in the European South was piped out, mostly northward to Russian and the Baltic urban centers but increasingly by the end of the decade for export as well.[31] Four-fifths of all gas consumed between the Baltic

Sea and the Volga River originated in the North Caucasus and the Ukraine in 1965 and over half even in 1970 while most Soviet exports also flowed from these regions.[32] Similarly, each year since 1964 saw more than 75 percent of Central Asia's natural gas output piped out to the Urals and later also to the European USSR and in a number of years this share easily topped 80 percent.[33]

Such large scale outshipment of a scarce, prime fuel from well populated and, in the case of much of the South, industrialized areas was by and large an example of spatial optimization. Apart from the iron and steel industry of the South, where gas replaced expensive, scarce coke, savings through the greater applications of natural gas have tended to be largest north of the Ukraine, in the Moscow, Baltic and Northwest regions of the Soviet Union. The difference between the delivered cost of gas and that of alternative solid fuels was clearly greatest in those gas-consuming regions; consequently, fuel costs for the Soviet spatial system taken as a whole were improved by such outshipments.[34] Because of the lower cost of coal in the Urals, the economic benefit from the heavy export of Central Asian gas to the Urals at the expense of Uzbekistan consumers is less clear. Higher

TABLE 5
Boiler and Furnace Fuel Consumption by Economic Regions (1970) (Million tons of SF)

| Regions | Total* | Percent | Solid Fuels** | Percent | Natural Gas*** | Percent | Liquid Products (including LPG****) | Percent |
|---|---|---|---|---|---|---|---|---|
| Northwest | 50 | 100 | 29 | 58.0 | 10.5 | 21.0 | 10.5 | 21.0 |
| Central Russia | 96 | 100 | 40 | 41.6 | 39 | 41.6 | 17 | 17.7 |
| Volga-Vyatka | 23 | 100 | 11 | 47.8 | 6 | 26.1 | 6 | 26.1 |
| Central Chernozem | 26 | 100 | 13 | 50.0 | 5.5 | 21.2 | 7.5 | 28.8 |
| Baltic | 23 | 100 | 12 | 52.2 | 4 | 17.4 | 7 | 30.4 |
| Belorussia | 21 | 100 | 9 | 42.8 | 3.5 | 16.7 | 8.5 | 40.5 |
| Moldavia | 6 | 100 | 4 | 66.7 | 0.5 | 8.3 | 1.5 | 25.0 |
| Ukraine | 195 | 100 | 125 | 64.1 | 55 | 28.2 | 15 | 7.7 |
| North Caucasus | 36 | 100 | 12 | 33.3 | 18 | 50.0 | 6 | 16.7 |
| Transcaucasia | 30 | 100 | 4 | 13.3 | 10 | 33.3 | 16 | 53.4 |
| Volga | 78 | 100 | 16 | 20.5 | 27 | 34.6 | 35 | 44.9 |
| Urals | 121 | 100 | 63 | 52.1 | 33 | 27.3 | 25 | 20.6 |
| West Siberia | 65 | 100 | 53 | 81.5 | 0.5 | 0.8 | 11.5 | 17.7 |
| East Siberia | 39 | 100 | 35 | 89.7 | 1 | 2.6 | 3 | 7.7 |
| Far East | 24 | 100 | 19 | 79.1 | 1 | 4.2 | 4 | 16.7 |
| Kazakhstan | 42 | 100 | 33 | 78.6 | 3.5 | 8.3 | 5.5 | 13.1 |
| Central Asia | 29 | 100 | 7 | 24.1 | 14 | 48.3 | 8 | 27.6 |
| USSR | 904 | 100 | 485 | 53.6 | 232 | 25.7 | 187 | 20.7 |

*The total figures and thus apparently the regional figures as well, clearly include coke oven gases but not blast furnace gases. The quantity of coke oven gases utilized in 1970 reached 18 million tons of SF. A. M. Nekrasov and M. G. Pervukhin, *Energetika SSSR v 1976–1980 godakh* [Electric power of the USSR in 1976–80] (Moscow: Energiya, 1977), p. 149.

**Coal, coke, peat, shale and state supplied firewood. Apparently also include coke oven gases, as they are attributable entirely to coal.

***Gross consumption, i.e. includes losses and gas used by compressor stations on gas pipelines. They have been adjusted to 0.5 or the whole million to avoid impression of spurious accuracy.

****The contribution of liquefied gases to boiler and furnace fuel consumption was 7.6 million tons of SF in 1970. Nekrasov and Pervukhin, *Energetika SSSR*, p. 149.

NOTE: Columns 1 and 3 from Vsesoyuzny institut, *Razrabotka neftyanykh i gazovykh mestorozhdenii*, pp. 44–45.

The regional breakdown of coal consumption, assumed to be on a calorific basis, and of shale and peat consumption is given by V. A. Shelest, *Regionalnye energoekonomicheskie problemy SSSR* [Regional power-economic problems of the USSR] (Moscow: Nauka, 1975), p. 212. With the help of 1965 data, these regional figures have been adjusted to include the estimated consumption of firewood. (See Probst, ed., *Razvitiye toplivnoi bazy rayonov SSSR*, in 1965 table for regional consumption of boiler and furnace fuels.) Coal consumption also includes that of coking coal and, apparently, coke oven gas recovered during the process of coke production. The regional consumption of liquid products was estimated as residuals.

The independently given or derived regional estimates for boiler and furnace fuels as a whole, solid fuels and liquid products in their respective columns all sum up to within 0.5 to 1 percent of the Soviet totals given for them in Nekrasov and Pervukhin, *Energetika SSSR*, p. 149. The regional gas consumption figures likewise add up to within 0.6 percent of total apparent consumption, i.e. production minus net export.

labor productivity in the Urals and the presence of high priority industries may be the economic and certainly the strategic rationale for such a resource transfer.

The 1970s witnessed a striking change in the interregional flow of natural gas west of the Urals, suggesting a response by planners to the energy requirement of producing provinces in the later stages of resource exploitation. Since equity consideration about resource flows cannot be ignored in the case of union republics, one may ask whether similar developments in the future may be in store regarding the huge volume of gas piped out of Central Asia. (Figures 1 through 3 reflect the chang-

ing and probable future distribution of natural gas consumption in the Soviet Union.)

The large-scale export of gas from the European South, combined with heavy outshipment of coal (a traditionally important activity) and until the mid-sixties also of some oil,[35] hastened the shrinking of hydrocarbon reserves in the area. It has contributed significantly to a rapidly growing energy deficit which has overtaken this formerly well-endowed province. And without doubt, it has strengthened the Ukrainians' claims on their remaining gas reserves and those of the neighboring North Caucasus, while reducing interregional coal exports as well.

TABLE 6
Boiler and Furnace Fuel Consumption by Economic Regions (1975) (Million tons of SF)

| Region | Total* | Percent | Solid Fuels** | Percent | Natural Gas*** | Percent | Liquid Products (including LPG****) | Percent |
|---|---|---|---|---|---|---|---|---|
| Northwest | 64 | 100 | 28 | 43.8 | 16 | 25.0 | 20 | 31.2 |
| Central Russia | 122 | 100 | 42 | 34.4 | 46 | 37.7 | 34 | 27.9 |
| Volga-Vyatka | 29 | 100 | 11 | 37.9 | 6 | 20.7 | 12 | 41.4 |
| Central Chernozem | 35 | 100 | 14 | 40.0 | 7 | 20.0 | 14 | 40.0 |
| Baltic | 29 | 100 | 15 | 51.7 | 5 | 17.3 | 9 | 31.0 |
| Belorussia | 27 | 100 | 7 | 25.9 | 5 | 18.5 | 15 | 55.6 |
| Moldavia | 7 | 100 | 5 | 71.4 | 2 | 28.5 | 0.5 | 0.5 |
| Ukraine | 248 | 100 | 148 | 59.7 | 70 | 28.2 | 30 | 12.1 |
| North Caucasus | 46 | 100 | 15 | 32.6 | 21.5 | 46.7 | 9.5 | 20.6 |
| Transcaucasia | 38 | 100 | 6 | 15.8 | 20 | 52.6 | 12 | 31.6 |
| Volga | 100 | 100 | 19 | 19.0 | 43.5 | 43.5 | 37.5 | 37.5 |
| Urals | 154 | 100 | 63 | 40.9 | 46 | 29.9 | 45 | 29.2 |
| West Siberia | 85 | 100 | 65 | 76.5 | 3.5 | 4.1 | 16.5 | 19.4 |
| East Siberia | 51 | 100 | 44 | 86.3 | 3 | 5.9 | 4 | 7.8 |
| Far East | 31 | 100 | 22 | 71.0 | 1.5 | 4.8 | 7.5 | 24.2 |
| Kazakhstan | 55 | 100 | 38 | 69.1 | 12 | 21.8 | 5 | 9.1 |
| Central Asia | 37 | 100 | 8 | 21.6 | 21 | 56.8 | 8 | 21.6 |
| USSR | 1,558* | 100 | 550 | 47.5 | 329.0 | 28.4 | 279.5 | 24.1 |

*Total includes both coke oven and blast furnace gases, i.e. 19.8 million and 25.9 million tons of SF respectively. The coverage, therefore, is slightly broader than for 1970. Total boiler and furnace fuel consumption given in Nekrasov and Pervukhin, *Energetika SSSR*, p. 149, is 20 million standard tons larger than here. About 11.5 million tons of the discrepancy comes from the authors' figure for aggregate consumption of natural gas, a figure which is that much larger than production minus net export and must, therefore, be in error. (Net addition to storage exceeded withdrawal and could not explain the discrepancy.) The other 8.5 million standard tons of difference is represented by losses of natural gas which are not included in the column for that fuel. This figure is confirmed in UN Economic Commission for Europe, *Annual Bulletin of Gas Statistics for Europe*, 1975, vol. 21, pp. 54–57.

**Coal, coke, peat, shale and state supplied firewood. Also include by-product bases at coke ovens and blast furnaces, which are overwhelmingly attributable to coal.

***Includes gas used by compressor stations on gas pipelines, but excludes straight losses which amounted to 8.5 to 9 million tons of SF in 1975. The coverage, therefore, is slightly smaller than in the 1970 table.

****The contribution of liquefied gases to boiler and furnace fuel consumption in 1975 reached 11.1 million tons of SF. Nekrasov and Pervukhin, *Energetika SSSR*, p. 149.

The USSR total of 1,158 million tons of SF (see note above) was distributed regionally according to data for the 1970 breakdown, with adjustments made for regions where fuel consumption is known to have grown appreciably faster or slower than the national average.

Consumption of natural gas for most areal units is taken from R. S. Margulov et al., *Razvitiye gazovoi promyshlennosti* [Development of the gas industry] (Moscow: VNITZGAZPROM, 1976), p. 8, supplemented for three regions by data from P. Ye. Semenov and V. F. Kosov, *Problemy razvitiya i razmeshcheniya proizvoditelnykh sil Kazakhstana* [Problems in the development and location of productive forces in Kazakhstan] (Moscow: Mysl, 1974), p. 67 and A. A. Adamesku and Akinshin, *Problemy razvitiya i razmeshcheniya proizvoditelnykh sil Volgo-Vyatskogo rayona* [Problems in the development and location of productive forces in the Volga-Vyatka region] (Moscow: Mysl, 1974), p. 91 and Theodore Shabad, "News Notes," *Polar Geography*, January–March 1977, p. 90. For Central Asia gas, consumption was figured as production plus import minus export to other regions. From *Nar. khoz. SSSR v 1975 g.*, p. 241; *Vneshnyaya torgovlya SSSR v 1975 g.*, p. 98, and utilization of pipeline capacity as given in Margulov et al., p. 46. The figures on consumption throughout the table have been adjusted to the nearest half or whole million. Consumption of solid fuels is essentially estimates from coal consumption, supplemented by data for regions where other solid fuels are important. Regional coal shipments are given in Table 9. Another monograph showing percentages of total shipment served as an independent check. M. M. Guren, *Tseny na ugol i khozyaistvenny razchet* [Coal prices and economic accounting] (Moscow: Nedra, 1977), p. 141. Also, Semenov and Kosov, *Problemy Kazakhstana*, p. 67; Adameshu and Akinshin, *Problemy Volgo-Vyatskogo rayona*, p. 92; M. Ya. Gokhberg and N. A. Solovyev, *Problemy razvitiya i razmeshcheniya proizvoditelnykh sil Tsentralnogo rayona* [Problems in the development and location of productive forces in the Central region] (Moscow: Mysl, 1975), and Theodore Shabad, "News Notes," *Soviet Geography: Review and Translation* 19, no. 6 (June 1978): p. 430.

Regional consumption of liquid products is estimated as a residue, supplemented by data from monographs cited in the previous paragraph. The separately derived columns from both solid fuels and liquid products add up to well within one-half percent of the Soviet totals for these fuels, as given in Nekrasov and Pervukhin, *Energetika SSSR*, p. 149. The regional figures for gas also sum up to production minus net export minus the 8.5 million standard tons for losses. (See note for natural gas above.)

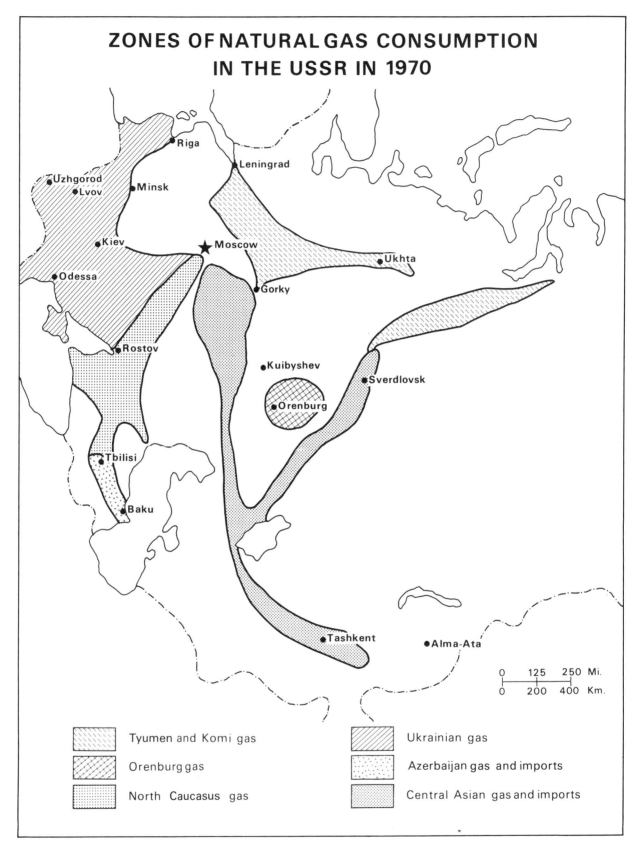

ZONES OF NATURAL GAS CONSUMPTION
IN THE USSR IN 1970

Tyumen and Komi gas

Orenburg gas

North Caucasus gas

Ukrainian gas

Azerbaijan gas and imports

Central Asian gas and imports

Figure 1
SOURCE: I. Ya. Furman, *Ekonomika magistralnogo transporta gaza* [Economics of gas trunk transmission] (Moscow: Nedra, 1978), p. 38.

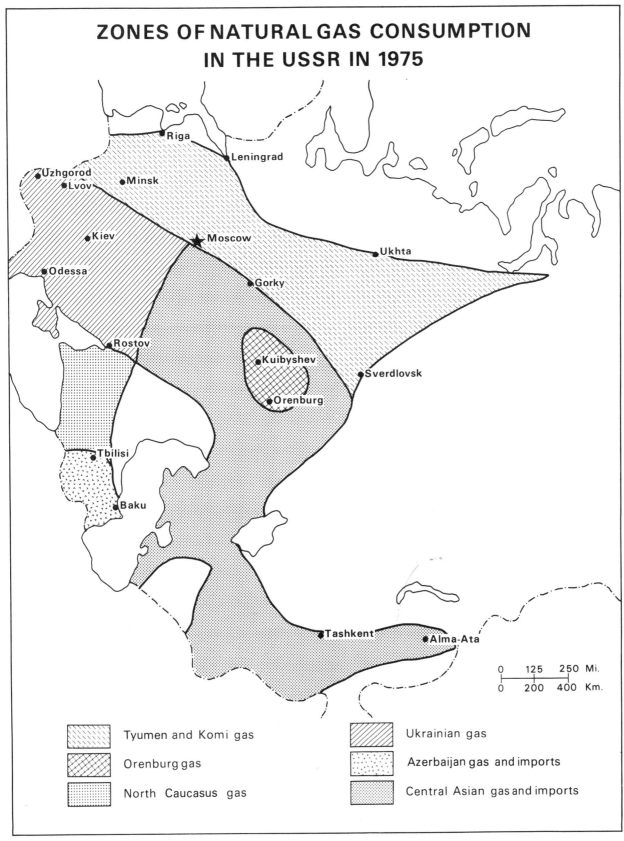

## ZONES OF NATURAL GAS CONSUMPTION IN THE USSR IN 1975

Riga

Leningrad

Uzhgorod
Lvov
Minsk

Kiev

Moscow

Ukhta

Odessa

Gorky

Rostov

Kuibyshev

Sverdlovsk

Orenburg

Tbilisi

Baku

Tashkent
Alma-Ata

0    125    250 Mi.

0    200    400 Km.

Tyumen and Komi gas          Ukrainian gas

Orenburg gas                 Azerbaijan gas and imports

North Caucasus gas           Central Asian gas and imports

Figure 2
SOURCE: Furman, *Ekonomika magistralnogo transporta gaza*, p. 39.

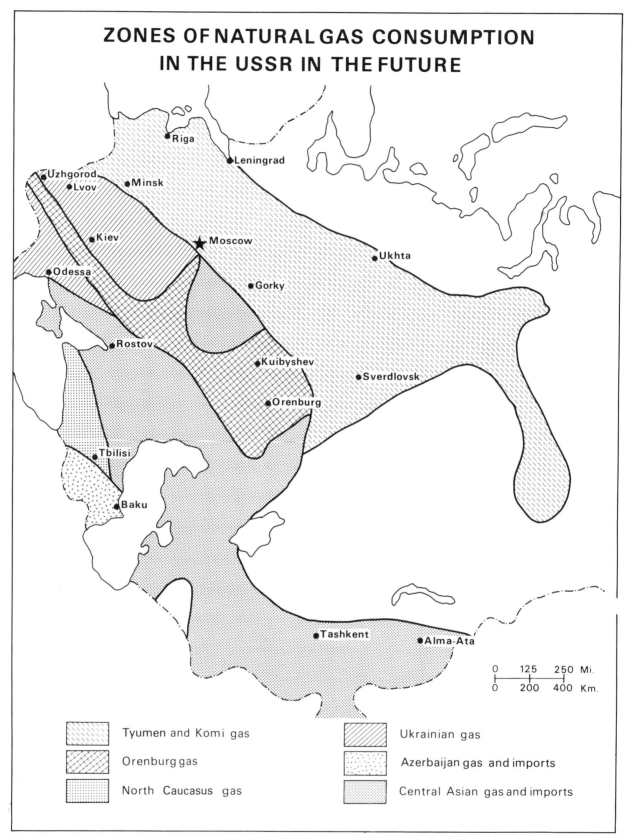

**ZONES OF NATURAL GAS CONSUMPTION
IN THE USSR IN THE FUTURE**

Tyumen and Komi gas

Orenburg gas

North Caucasus gas

Ukrainian gas

Azerbaijan gas and imports

Central Asian gas and imports

Figure 3
SOURCE: Furman, *Ekonomika magistralnogo transporta gaza*, p. 40.

With reserve-production ratios for hydrocarbons declining noticeably throughout the 1960s and the coal industry beset with grave difficulties,[36] the outflow of gas from the European South began to decrease rapidly after 1970. Outshipment was reduced from 30 billion cubic meters to less than 15 billion by mid-decade and at most to a couple of billion cubic meters in recent years[37] (Figures 1 and 2).

Political motives, the balancing of ethnic and regional interests may have been the principal cause behind that swift change. The economic benefit for the Ukraine from such a rapid decline in interregional export has been immediate and clear; for the whole system of Soviet regions, however, it is much less obvious and may have been nonexistent at least until recently. The delays in delivering Siberian gas to the Moscow-Baltic areas (the first 42-inch pipeline but with only some of the needed compressor stations was completed only in 1975)[38] meant that Ukrainian and North Caucasus gas continued to enjoy a high opportunity cost value in nearly every province west of the Volga. While costs have increased sharply, gas from these deposits remained the cheapest fuel through the 1970s over most of the Russian Plain, since it could be delivered by long-amortized pipelines. Its replacement cost by more expensive fuels has risen everywhere but in roughly equal fashion.[39] Though gas output in the South as a whole peaked in the early part of this decade (in the Ukraine alone only at mid-decade), modest new discoveries enabled the South to hold reserve-production ratios to about a dozen years at the 1975 rate of withdrawal.[40]

Although Central Asia is a much less industrialized region than the Ukraine or the whole of the European South and has less influence in the leadership hierarchy, it is at least possible that in the future political and economic pressures will lead to similar reduction in the vast quantities of gas piped out from the Moslem republics to the RSFSR. With capacities of 20 billion and 68 billion cubic meters respectively, the Central Asia-Urals and Central Asia-Central Russia transmission systems transmit 76 to 78 percent of all gas produced in the five Moslem republics. Turkmenia, the largest producer, exports over 95 percent of its output.[41] Most of the gas flows to the Urals and the Moscow area but increasingly also to the European South and for export to Eastern and Western Europe.[42]

Given the burgeoning population, cultural and linguistic barriers to migration and the huge cohort of young people entering the labor force, one may question whether such rates of withdrawal of an immensely valuable, depletable resource can continue through the eighties. Since 1960, the rate of industrial growth in Central Asia has fallen behind the Soviet average—ahead during 1970–75 but lagging beind in the sixties and barely matching the national rate since 1975.[43] At the same time, population increase eroded the region's per capita position, and the participation of indigenous ethnic groups in the industrial economy remains low.[44] Recent studies published in Central Asia do indeed show a deep concern about the slow rate of modernization of the area's energy economy and the skeletal development of gas and oil pipelines *within* these republics, when such vast quanti-

ties of their hydrocarbons are shipped out. Both here and in neighboring Kazakhstan economic modernization is believed to require a sharp rise in the distribution and consumption of natural gas which may well be unattainable at the present level of export.[45]

## The Transport Burden: Recent Developments and Prospects

In all their variety and complexity, transport and transfer operations may be viewed as a matrix of means (modes) and purposes which have social, political as well as economic functions. The more technologically advanced and specialized the mode, the more restrictive the type of movement and the purpose of the transfer.[46] Energy on a large scale is increasingly moved by highly specialized modes. Over land for great distances it is transferred by unit trains, pipelines, transmission lines, which sacrifice flexibility for sharp reduction in unit cost. Such modes have high fixed cost components and depend on high load factors to operate efficiently. As a consequence, they tend to reach full capacity soon after completion, with further expansion in throughput possible only by new construction, in large, discrete lumps at given time intervals.

Transport in Soviet economic strategy has long functioned as the handmaiden of industry, rather than an agent that precedes and stimulates development. "Industrial and military strength has thus been built, using in part the resource that might otherwise have gone into expansion of transport capacity." With respect to the energy sector, this strategy of "industrial strength through transport strigency"[47] applies most clearly to railroads and roads, multifunction media, which can serve as well as facilitate resource development. Pipelines and high-voltage power lines for bulk transmission* are too specialized carriers to act as successful development agents even in market economies, except during their construction phase through a larger multiplier effect.

By all evidence, Soviet planners' traditional view of transport as a service provided grudgingly and only when and to the degree absolutely necessary continues to hold today. The Baikal-Amur Mainline may be the only partial exception, but in its case the strategic-military role seems as strong as the economic one. Even in pioneer areas of resource exploitation, transport facilities are provided primarily and sometimes exclusively for the product, when exploitation is ready to begin or has been underway for a number of years. Roads and railways, even communication lines, remain primitive or entirely nonexistent throughout the preparation and developmental phase.[48] Several recent sources support the frustrated judgment of F. G. Arzhanov, chief of the Tyumen Oil and Gas Administration, that West Siberian oil-

---

*Transmission lines of lower voltages, whose function is not to transfer energy in great bulk but to supply power for working tools, do not fall into this category. They are part of the general infrastructure, a minimum level of which is essential for development under any economic strategy.

men habitually arrive to develop new deposits in the mud, swimming through marsh, and leave the nearly depleted fields with ease on freshly completed hard surface roads.[49] The party secretary of Tyumen Province declared in equally strong language: "To build fast, one must be able to transport rapidly. And we must haul as if by oxen."[50]

Clearly, Soviet failure to alter traditional transport policy for the development of fuel reserves is not the result of ignorance or needless obstinacy. The tremendous benefits that the prior establishment of even a sparse, crude, but year-round network could mean for the Siberian oil and gas industries in terms of both current production and reserve additions (and thus future prospects) seem obvious to all. Yet every sign points to a continuation of past and present policy. Transport facilities will be provided to the minimum degree essential for the exploitation and delivery of specific energy products to market. The preparation and development of Siberian fuel reserves will proceed overwhelmingly as before: in the southernmost belt with the still more intensive use of the *existing* network; in the middle and northern zone with primitive and slow improvised haulage, and an essential role for air cargo and without any permanent overland facilities until exploitation is well under way. A railroad branch running north from the Trans-Siberian Railway did not reach Surgut in the Middle Ob oil fields until these fields yielded 29 percent of Soviet oil; by the time the railroad reached the Urengoi area in 1980, the West Siberian gas fields were contributing 33 percent of Soviet gas. The coking coal resources of southern Yakutia, tapped by the Little BAM and destined for export, are the only partial exception (with the railway preceding full scale development) for at least a decade. Sheer distances, the uncommonly harsh environment and the speed with which the Russians are pursuing the exploitation of Siberian energy and, particularly, hydrocarbon resources at a time of growing labor and capital shortages will continue to impose a nearly insuperable transport burden on the economy. Even with a policy of utmost stringency, the pace of Siberian energy development will require new construction, especially of pipelines, and further increase

loads on existing railways to a degree faced by very few nations at any time of their history.

### The Railroads and the Burden of Fuel Transport

Fuels have long comprised about one-third of all freight turnover on Soviet railways, representing 32 percent of all ton-kilometers in 1980.[51] As in other countries, coal is the most important commodity hauled, but Soviet railroads are also burdened by heavy freight in refined oil products, a situation unique among industrialized states. Coal and coke accounted for 58 percent of all freight turnover by the fuel group in 1980 (coal alone 52), and oil refinery products for 42 percent[52] (Tables 7 and 8). The construction of product pipelines in the USSR has been lagging badly even in regions of bulk transport, river and coastal shipments remain very small while the vestigial road network and a shortage of road tankers hold truck haulage to a minimum. In 1975–76, a mere 8 percent of the tonnage transported by oil pipelines consisted of products and over 87 percent of all products were moved by rail.[53]

In the 1980s, demand for rail transport will rise substantially for coal, and probably also for refined products, if the Soviet economy is to cover its energy needs. While it is clear that Soviet planners grossly underestimated the difficulties involved in accelerating coal production and achieving significant substitution for hydrocarbons, official policy does appear committed to a relatively greater role for coal in the future. Such a role will inevitably demand more transportation, which should maintain and probably even increase the share of coal in total freight turnover. Nor is there much chance to shift oil products off the railways. The Soviet economy is already strained to expand its pipeline network for gas and crude oil at sufficient pace. Excessive optimism has been evident in pipeline construction planning in recent years.

The rapid eastward shift of coal production, combined with the deteriorating quality of the coal, is intensifying the burden on the railways. In 1965, 351 million tons of coal, 61 percent of the Soviet total, was mined in the European provinces, including the Urals. Taking into

TABLE 7
Domestic Freight Turnover by Types of Transport Including Gas Pipelines* (In billion metric ton-km)

| Year | Total | Railroads | Rivers | Domestic Seas** | Trucks | Oil Pipelines (for crude and products) | Gas Pipelines* | Air |
|---|---|---|---|---|---|---|---|---|
| 1960 | 1,811.7 | 1,504.3 | 99.6 | 38.5 | 98.5 | 51.2 | 19.0 | 0.6 |
| 1965 | 2,511.5 | 1,950.2 | 133.9 | 52.1 | 143.1 | 146.7 | 84.2 | 1.3 |
| 1970 | 3,435.7 | 2,494.7 | 174.0 | 65.6 | 220.8 | 281.7 | 197.0 | 1.9 |
| 1975 | 4,932.9 | 3,236.5 | 221.7 | 73.6 | 338.0 | 665.9 | 394.6 | 2.6 |
| 1980 | 6,274.6 | 3,439.9 | 244.9 | (84.8) | 432.3 | 1,196.8 | (872.8) | 3.09 |
| 1985 Plan | 7,732 | 3,880 | 292 | (92) | 524 | 1,380 | 1,560 | 3.7 |

*Freight turnover for gas pipelines added according to the heat equivalent of gas transported in standard tons (7 million kilocalories), i.e. the calorific content of one metric ton of good hard coal. Furman, *Ekonomika transporta gaza*, p. 14.
**Estimated by subtracting the percentage share of foreign trade (90 percent) from total seaborne freight. H. Hunter, "The Soviet Transport Sector," in U.S. Congress, *New Directions in the Soviet Economy*, p. 576, and I. V. Nikolsky et al., *Geografiya vodnogo transporta SSSR* [Geography of water transport in the USSR] (Moscow: Transport, 1975), p. 79.
Sources: *Narodnoye khozyaistvo SSSR v 1980 godu*, p. 293, and Furman, *Ekonomika transporta gaza*, p. 14. 1985 plan from *Ekonomicheskaya gazeta*, 1982, no. 16, and V. Ye. Biryukov, *Transport v odinnadtsatoi pyatiletke* (Moscow: Znaniye, 1981), p. 13.

TABLE 8
Freight Turnover of Fuels by Rail, River, Oil and Gas Pipelines* (In billion metric ton-km)

| Year | Total Fuels | Railroads | | Rivers | | Oil Pipelines | Gas Pipelines |
|------|-------------|-----------|---|--------|---|---------------|---------------|
| | | Coal and Coke | Oil and Oil Products | Coal and Coke | Oil and Oil Products | Oil and Oil Products | Natural Gas |
| 1960 | 632.7 | 333.9 | 205.4 | 4.7** | 18.5 | 51.2 | 19.0 |
| 1970 | 1,327.2 | 448.1 | 353.9 | 7.4** | 39.1 | 281.7 | 197.0 |
| 1975 | 2,125.0 | 527.4 | 481.4 | 9.7** | 46.0*** | 665.9 | 394.6 |
| 1980 | 3,217.8 | 628.8 | 460.8 | 9.9** | 48.7*** | 1,196.8 | 872.8 |

*See corresponding note to Table 7.

**Estimated as total freight for coal and coke in million tons multiplied by the average distance of haul for all dry freight, except rafted timber, in 1960, 1970, and 1973. From *Transport i svyaz SSSR* [Transport and communications in the USSR] (Moscow: Transport, 1975), p. 70.

***Estimated as total freight for crude oil and refined products in million tons multiplied by the average distance of river haul for these products in 1973. *Nar. khoz. SSSR v 1977 g.*, p. 315 and Nikolsky et al., *Geografiya vodnogo transporta SSSR*, p. 70.

Sources: For railroads and oil pipelines *Narodnoye khozyaistvo SSSR v 1980 godu*, pp. 295 and 305, and *v 1970 godu*, p. 431. For oil and oil products on rivers in 1960 and 1970, *Transport i svyaz SSSR* (Moscow, 1972), pp. 170–71. For gas pipelines see Table 7 above.

account net exports, the European USSR could satisfy all but some 30 million tons of its consumption from its own resources and most of this net deficit was coking coal shipped to the Urals from Soviet Asia.[54] Since the mid-1960s, however, production in the European USSR has stagnated and ten years later the region accounted for only one-half of Soviet output, a share which is even lower today.[55] Concurrently, the volume of coal shipped to the west of the Urals from Siberia and Kazakhstan rose sharply, reaching 96 million tons in 1975. The 1980 plan called for 120 million tons to be so shipped,[56] but it is unlikely that this goal was reached.

At the same time, the deteriorating quality of solid fuels has led to rising transport input per unit of heat value, which has been only partly counterbalanced by beneficiation. The average ash content of run-of-the-mine coals increased from 20.1 percent in 1960 to 23 percent in the mid-seventies.[57] In the Ukraine, where, in 1975, 72 percent of the coal was treated, the ash content of the fuel sent to processing works reached almost 32 percent of the mined mass.[58] In the Urals, power plants working on untreated Ekibastuz coal routinely receive shipments with ash content of 45 to 47 percent, and even in the Ukraine, power stations sometimes have to cope with fuel which is 40 percent ash and 18 percent moisture.[59] The growing importance of beneficiation results in significant savings of transport input measured in ton-kilometers because some 50 million tons of ballast is removed.[60] However, the price is a rapid rise in relatively short-haul freight to and from enrichment plants, which are seldom located in the immediate vicinity of the mines. In the Donets Basin, for example, which supplies well over half of Soviet coal sent to processing plants (though only 30 percent of all coal produced), two-thirds of all hauls to such plants are over 50 kilometers, resulting in a sharp rise in transport despite a slight reduction in the volume of shipment to consumers.[61] Indeed, as Table 9 shows, the haulage of coal on the Donetsk railroad from 1970 to 1975 increased almost at the national rate, and the absolute growth of tonnage exceeded that on all the other railways except those of Kazakhstan.

The situation is likely to deteriorate during the 1980s. The huge energy deficit which has engulfed the whole European USSR is bound to intensify with the approaching depletion of oil and gas fields in the area.[62] Already the region consumes twice as much energy in calorific terms as it is able to produce and the gap is widening rapidly since gross fuel output is in decline.[63] In the past decade the growing shortage of fuel in the country's economic heart was compensated mostly by the intensive development of West Siberian oil and Central Asian gas reserves and the transfer of their resources to the European USSR. In five short years, from 1970 to 1975, the transport of oil from Soviet Asia to the Urals and westward increased by 98 million tons and that of gas *by* almost 60 billion cubic meters (a total of 136 to 147 million tons of oil equivalent), all but a small fraction of that growth being West Siberian oil and Turkmen gas.[64] By now, however, expansion in Central Asia has virtually come to an end and increments of oil from West Siberia are one percent a year. Moreover, a growing portion of these eastern resources must be devoted to offset the decrease in hydrocarbon output west of the Urals. It is questionable whether Soviet oil production can remain stable through the 1980s.[65] Further growth in energy consumption in the European USSR, therefore, must be covered primarily by nuclear power and by the transport of large quantities of West Siberian and Kazakhstan coal and of West Siberian gas.

Developments in freight turnover for coal in recent decades already show the shape of things to come. The increase in freight hauls for that fuel, practically identical with the growth rate of production through the fifties, began to overtake the latter in subsequent years by a widening margin. From 1970 to 1980, freight turnover for coal rose almost three times as fast as output (respectively by 41 percent and by 15 percent). The average length of haul, relatively stable during the sixties and early seventies, has also been increasing appreciably in recent years.[66] The mounting demand for eastern coal in the European USSR and the full development of the South Yakutian coal basin under a long-term export contract with Japan will intensify both of these trends.

Because of the long hauls, the Yakutian project will raise total freight turnover by the fuel group but will not greatly burden the railroads, whose carrying capacity in the Far East should be strongly expanded by the BAM.

TABLE 9
Transport of Coal on Various Soviet Railroads (In million tons)

| Railroads | 1970 | 1972 | 1973 | 1975 | Absolute change | Index (1970 = 100)* |
|---|---|---|---|---|---|---|
| Donetsk | 201.8 | 211.0 | 218.2 | 228.7 | + 26.9 | 113.3 |
| North Caucasus | 21.1 | 22.0 | 19.9 | 19.9 | − 1.2 | 94.3 |
| Southeast (Ukraine) | 8.9 | 9.1 | 11.9 | 12.3 | + 3.4 | 138.1 |
| Moscow | 24.9 | 25.1 | 23.6 | 24.1 | − 0.8 | 96.7 |
| October (Moscow-Leningrad) | 0.66 | 0.7 | 0.7 | 0.92 | + 0.26 | 139.6 |
| West Siberia | 110.1 | 118.3 | 123.6 | 135.8 | + 25.6 | 123.3 |
| Northern (Komi-Leningrad) | 20.6 | 21.4 | 21.4 | 22.3 | + 1.7 | 108.1 |
| Sverdlovsk | 24.6 | 20.7 | 18.0 | 15.7 | − 8.9 | 63.8 |
| Southern Urals | 16.6 | 16.1 | 15.9 | 14.5 | − 2.1 | 87.2 |
| Kuibyshev | 4.1 | 4.5 | 4.1 | 4.4 | + 0.3 | 107.3 |
| East Siberia | 35.8 | 40.6 | 41.5 | 45.9 | + 10.1 | 128.2 |
| Transbaikalia | 16.6 | 19.4 | 20.2 | 22.3 | + 5.6 | 134.0 |
| Far East | 10.0 | 10.4 | 10.3 | 10.4 | + 0.3 | 103.3 |
| Lvov | 11.8 | 13.8 | 14.0 | 13.9 | + 2.1 | 117.9 |
| Odessa-Kishinev | 3.5 | 3.7 | 3.8 | 4.1 | + 0.6 | 118.5 |
| Dnieper | 3.0 | 4.6 | 5.9 | 6.3 | + 3.3 | 211.1 |
| Southwest | 0.5 | 0.5 | 0.5 | 0.6 | + 0.1 | 125.1 |
| Kazakhstan | 57.1 | 68.0 | 75.3 | 86.5 | + 29.4 | 151.5 |
| Transcaucasia | 3.3 | 3.2 | 3.1 | 3.1 | − 0.2 | 93.5 |
| Central Asia | 6.3 | 6.1 | 6.2 | 6.9 | + 0.4 | 109.4 |
| TOTAL | 581.4 | 619.0 | 638.4 | 678.7 | + 97.3 | 116.7 |

*Index based on unrounded numbers.
SOURCE: Adapted from Dubinsky, *Analiz raboty*.

The mining operation is to reach 13 million tons by 1983, and more likely later, but some of that coal will be burned locally and annual commitments to Japan will average only 5 million tons.[67] By contrast, coal shipments from Siberia and Kazakhstan to the European USSR are even now on an altogether larger scale and would have to be greatly increased if an enhanced role for coal in the USSR is to be achieved. The rail lines leading to the Urals from the east are already among the most overburdened in the country and the share of coal in total shipment on these lines is much higher than the average for the country as a whole.[68]

Over the past 15 years, virtually all increases in westward coal hauls originated in the Kuznetsk and Ekibastuz basins and this pattern will continue. Table 10 permits an assessment of the change in transport burden from 1970 to 1975 resulting from developments in coal transport. It can be estimated with reasonable confidence that Kuznetsk coal was responsible for about one-half and Ekibastuz coal for over 40 percent of the 73.4 billion tonkilometers of *increase* in official freight turnover for coal during that period. Most of the remaining 8 to 9 percent of that increment was accounted for by East Siberian coals.[69] With the slow growth and, more recently, stagnation, of production in the Donets Basin, the supply area of Donets coal contracted significantly, resulting in a reduction of freight turnover associated with long hauls. Through the first half of the 1970s, freight turnover of this fuel declined *by* at least 12 billion ton-kilometers, and only some 30 million tons of that coal was shipped over distances of 1,000 kilometers or more compared with 43 to 45

million in the early sixties.[70] Yet, rail loading within the Donbas area has continued to increase because more and more coal is sent to beneficiation plants before shipment to consumers (Table 9).

Further exacerbating Soviet energy policy, the growth in Soviet coal transport (which itself is much faster than the expansion in output) is concentrated almost exclusively on a few lines, those of the Donbas, northern Kazakhstan and the southernmost strip of Siberia between the Urals and Chita (Table 9). Outside of the Donbas area, the transport of coal is holding steady in the European provinces, where the railway net is denser, there are often alternative routes to major consuming centers and railroads are better able to cope with the growing freight flows. By contrast, the four groups of lines where nearly all growth in coal hauls is concentrated are already choked to capacity. Further increases in westward shipments will have to funnel through two of these four railways.

As in the days of the Ural-Kuznetsk Combine, these rail lines are again becoming a severe transport bottleneck and unquestionably so for any energy strategy that attempts to reemphasize solid fuels. But, in contrast to the thirties and the sixties, it is doubtful whether this bottleneck can again be opened by relatively cheap technological innovations as in the two earlier periods. In my view at least, large expansion in coal carrying capacity can be achieved only by a major construction effort in new and, for best results, specialized railway lines or in the alternative mode of slurry pipelines. Indeed, a recent article by a staff member of Gosplan USSR concedes that inadequate transport capacity is limiting the greater use of Ekibastuz coal and the otherwise highly cost-effective Kuznetsk coal in the electric stations of the Urals.[71]

The ambitious production targets for the Ekibastuz Basin and its satellite at Maikuben are, therefore, predicated on Soviet plans for the erection of extra high voltage transmission lines and gigantic, 4,000 MW on-site power stations in this semi-arid area.[72] While the first generating units of the mineside Ekibastuz stations have now gone into operation and construction is finally under way on the 1,150 KV AC line to the Urals and the 1,500 KV DC line to Central Russia, the effectiveness of these long heralded energy bridges seems in doubt. The realization of yet more gigantic transmission projects from East Siberia is even more questionable.[73] I expect these coal-by-wire energy trunklines to become as much a bottleneck for the full scale exploitation of cheap but low quality eastern coals as the railroads have become.

Transport is destined to be an especially crucial determining factor for the success of the long planned Kansk-Achinsk lignite and power complex, on which the fortunes of the Soviet coal industry for the rest of the century will primarily rest. Although Gosplan has promulgated plans for an eventual yearly output of 300 million tons from this vast lignite field, the use and transport of these heavily caking and self-igniting fuels, with highly variable physical and chemical properties and combustion characteristics, still remain unsolved.[74] Soviet scholars are divided on how to attack the problem, what portion of the basin's production should be targeted for long distance shipment and what form that should take. Without processing of the lignite, long-distance, large-scale movement by rail is unfeasible. What seems clear is that transport costs alone would comprise almost half of all *direct* capital costs for making this fuel available outside Central Siberia, where its market will continue to be limited, and processing and transport costs combined would equal about nine-tenths of the total.[75] A few years ago, one scholar, known for his sanguine views, advanced the questionable opinion that the yearly transport of 100 to 120 million tons of enriched lignite might be possible without a new railway line, though still with heavy capital investment. Larger amounts would require the construction of a specialized super-trunkline.[76] A more recent study, produced in Siberia, says such a new 3,000 to 3,200 kilometer long single track line, restricted entirely to solid fuels, could transport only 80 to 85 million tons of extra coal.[77] And the Gosplan research cited above arrives at the unequivocal conclusion that the long-distance rail shipment of Kansk-Achinsk (as well as of Ekibastuz) coal is irrational, but so are plans to transmit electricity from them over distances of 1,500 to 2,000 miles.[78] Pending resolution of the transport problem for Kansk-Achinsk lignite, the 11th Five-Year Plan has announced plans for the construction of the first giant strip mine and mineside power station by the middle 1980s.

The Pipeline Bottleneck

Pipeline transport represents the most dramatic growth in Soviet freight movement in the last two decades. If natural gas piped over long distance lines is counted at its calorific equivalent in standard tons, the transport work by pipelines rose 30-fold in less than 20 years. It reached 33 percent of all domestic freight turnover in 1980 compared with less than 4 percent in 1960 (Table 7). And it accounted for 64 percent of all internal movement (in ton-kilometers) by the fuel group (Table 8). In view of the late development of the Soviet gas industry, the length of the gas pipelines did not surpass the length of those for crude oil and refined products until 1960. Today, however, gas lines exceed the length of crude pipelines by 2.3 times and are almost double the length of crude and product pipelines combined.[79]

Despite the very rapid growth of the Soviet gas transmission network, an expansion even more vigorous than experienced by the oil transport system, the pipeline bottleneck applies mainly to gas. Crude oil suffers from few transport difficulties, though some temporary worsening of the situation is likely as average size and accessibility of new fields decrease during the eighties. The rudimentary development of product pipelines *is* and will continue to be a serious problem, aggravating the burden of the railways. Freight hauls of refinery products, however, are dispersed on many lines, lessening the chance of severe tie-ups. By contrast, natural gas transport overland is dependent exclusively on pipelines. In addition, gas trunklines can deliver less than a fifth of the calories carried by crude oil pipelines of the same diameter, and steel pipes for gas lines are subject to more stringent quality requirements than those which transport oil. It is instructive that despite the much greater dimensions of the Soviet gas pipelines network (almost twice the extent of oil pipelines, with two-fifths of its length comprised of pipes 40 inches or more compared with one-fifth for oil pipelines),[80] the final result of their operation in distance times calories delivered is little more than a fourth of that produced by the operation of the oil pipeline system.[81] About 75 percent of the gas industry's fixed capital is in the pipeline network, which in the 1971–75 period consumed 8 billion rubles, or almost half of all investment in the gas industry.[82] The corresponding total for the oil extraction industry came to less than 4 billion, which represents a 19 percent share of total investment.[83]

Since the gas industry now depends on the huge fields of northwest Siberia for all its increment (and increasingly also to compensate for declining output elsewhere), the expansion of the multistring pipeline bridges from northern Tyumen Oblast to major consuming centers is the key to the growth of Soviet gas output. In Chapter 12, I dealt briefly with the constraints the tremendous interindustry demand for rolled steel, nonferrous metals, compressors, cement, etc., from the West Siberian gas industry is placing on the economy. Planned increments of 100 billion cubic meters from West Siberia every 2 to 3 years require 20 to 30 percent capacity expansion in some supplying industries during the next decade.[84] Yuri I. Bokserman, one of the foremost experts on the gas industry, has stated that 30,000 kilometers and 20 million metric tons of top grade, large diameter pipes, requiring 22 to 25 billion rubles of capital investment would be

TABLE 10
Regional Matrix of Coal Shipment 1970 and 1975* (In million natural tons)

| | Supplying Basins | | | | | | | | | |
| | Total | | Donets Basin | | Kuznetsk Basin | | Ekibastuz | | Karaganda | |
| Consuming Regions | 1970 | 1975 | 1970 | 1975 | 1970 | 1975 | 1970 | 1975 | 1970 | 1975 |
|---|---|---|---|---|---|---|---|---|---|---|
| Northwest | 29.5 | 28.4 | 3.8 | 1.0 | 6.5 | 7.8 | — | — | — | — |
| of which: Leningrad and Leningrad Oblast | 6.1 | 5.9 | 2.6 | 0.6 | 3.3 | 4.2 | — | — | — | — |
| Central Region | 47.0 | 51.3 | 10.7 | 5.0 | 4.3 | 11.4 | — | — | — | — |
| of which: Moscow | 2.8 | 3.6 | 1.9 | 1.4 | 0.9 | 2.3 | — | — | — | — |
| Tula Oblast | 21.3 | 21.7 | 1.8 | 0.2 | 0.3 | 2.3 | — | — | — | — |
| Central Chernozem | 13.7 | 14.6 | 8.5 | 7.5 | 1.9 | 3.4 | — | — | — | 0.4 |
| Belorussia | 6.5 | 3.1 | 5.0 | 1.8 | — | — | — | — | — | — |
| Baltic** | 10.0 | 11.0 | 4.5 | 3.0 | — | — | — | — | — | — |
| Volga | 17.4 | 14.9 | 4.1 | 2.9 | 5.9 | 3.9 | — | — | 3.3 | 3.6 |
| Volga-Vyatka** | 7.5 | 6.0 | 3.5 | 2.0 | 3.0 | 3.0 | — | — | — | — |
| North Caucasus | 13.2 | 14.9 | 13.0 | 14.8 | — | — | — | — | — | — |
| Ukraine | 144.5 | 165.5 | 127.0 | 139.1 | — | 1.7 | — | — | — | 2.1 |
| of which: Donets-Dnieper | 110.0 | 130.0 | 110.0 | 125.0 | — | 1.7 | — | — | — | 2.1 |
| Southwest and South | 34.5 | 35.5 | 17.0 | 14.0 | — | — | — | — | — | — |
| Moldavia | 4.5 | 5.6 | 4.1 | 5.2 | — | — | — | — | — | — |
| Transcaucasia | 3.6 | 3.2 | 1.8 | 1.6 | — | — | — | — | — | — |
| Urals | 81.9 | 80.1 | 0.2 | 0.1 | 21.7 | 20.9 | 10.4 | 23.6 | 9.8 | 9.5 |
| Kazakhstan | 42.3 | 55.0 | — | — | 9.2 | 10.1 | 11.0 | 19.3 | 20.9 | 24.4 |
| West Siberia | 60.7 | 75.4 | — | — | 51.8 | 62.8 | 1.5 | 2.9 | — | — |
| East Siberia | 46.5 | 57.9 | — | — | 0.4 | 0.2 | — | — | — | — |
| Far East | 30.6 | 36.0 | — | — | — | — | — | — | — | — |
| Central Asia | 10.2 | 13.1 | — | — | 0.4 | 0.6 | — | — | 1.9 | 3.0 |
| TOTAL | 569.6 | 636.0 | 186.2 | 184.0 | 105.1 | 125.8 | 22.9 | 45.8 | 35.9 | 43.0 |
| Net Export from Ukraine | 13.9*** | 12.8 | 11.5*** | 11.6*** | — | — | — | — | — | — |
| Net Export from Kuzbas | 3.4*** | 3.5 | — | — | 3.4 | 3.5 | — | — | — | — |
| Total Shipment, Ministry Data | 591.5 | 657.8 | 197.9 | 197.8 | 108.5 | 129.1 | — | — | — | — |
| Total Shipment as Sums of Rows | 585.9 | 652.3 | 197.7 | 195.6 | 108.5 | 129.3 | — | — | — | — |
| Statistical Discrepancy | +4.6 | +5.5 | +0.2 | +2.2 | 0.0 | −0.2 | — | — | — | — |

| | Supplying Basins | | | | | | | | | |
| | Lvov and Dnieper Basins | | Bashkir and Ural Basins | | Georgian SSR | | East Siberia | | Far East | |
| Consuming Regions | 1970 | 1975 | 1970 | 1975 | 1970 | 1975 | 1970 | 1975 | 1970 | 1975 |
|---|---|---|---|---|---|---|---|---|---|---|
| Northwest | — | — | — | — | — | — | — | — | — | — |
| of which: Leningrad and Leningrad Oblast | — | — | — | — | — | — | — | — | — | — |
| Central Region | — | — | — | 1.0 | — | — | — | — | — | — |
| of which: Moscow | — | — | — | — | — | — | — | — | — | — |
| Tula Oblast | — | — | — | — | — | — | — | — | — | — |
| Central Chernozem | — | — | — | — | — | — | — | — | — | — |
| Belorussia | 1.5 | 1.3 | — | — | — | — | — | — | — | — |
| Baltic** | 2.0 | 3.2 | — | — | — | — | — | — | — | — |
| Volga | — | — | 4.1 | 4.5 | — | — | — | — | — | — |
| Volga-Vyatka** | — | — | 1.0 | 1.0 | — | — | — | — | — | — |
| North Caucasus | — | — | — | — | — | — | — | — | — | — |
| Ukraine | 13.5 | 16.8 | — | — | — | — | — | — | — | — |
| of which: Donets-Dnieper | — | — | — | — | — | — | — | — | — | — |
| Southwest and South | 13.5 | 16.8 | — | — | — | — | — | — | — | — |
| Moldavia | 0.5 | — | — | — | — | — | — | — | — | — |
| Transcaucasia | — | — | — | — | 1.8 | 1.6 | — | — | — | — |
| Urals | — | — | 39.8 | 26.0 | — | — | — | — | — | — |
| Kazakhstan | — | — | — | — | — | — | — | — | — | — |
| West Siberia | — | — | — | — | — | — | 7.3 | 9.7 | — | — |
| East Siberia | — | — | — | — | — | — | 46.1 | 57.7 | — | — |
| Far East | — | — | — | — | — | — | 0.2 | 1.6 | 30.4 | 34.4 |
| Central Asia | — | — | — | — | — | — | — | — | — | — |
| TOTAL | 17.5 | 21.3 | 44.9 | 32.5 | 1.8 | 1.6 | 53.6 | 69.0 | 30.4 | 34.4 |

| Supplying Basins | | | |
| Pechora Basin | | Moscow Basin | |
| 1970 | 1975 | 1970 | 1975 |
|---|---|---|---|
| 19.2 | 19.6 | — | — |
| n.d. | n.d. | — | — |
| 0.5 | 3.0 | 31.5 | 30.8 |
| — | — | — | — |
| — | — | 19.0 | 19.0 |
| — | — | 3.3 | 3.2 |
| 0.5 | — | — | — |
| — | — | — | — |
| — | — | — | — |
| — | 0.8 | — | — |
| — | 0.8 | — | — |
| — | — | — | — |
| — | — | — | — |
| — | — | — | — |
| — | — | — | — |
| — | — | — | — |
| — | — | — | — |
| — | — | — | — |
| — | — | — | — |
| 20.2 | 23.4 | 34.8 | 34.0 |
| — | — | — | — |
| — | — | — | — |
| — | — | — | — |
| — | — | — | — |
| — | — | — | — |

| Supplying Basins | | | |
| Central Asia and Minor Basins of Kazakhstan | | Polish† Import | |
| 1970 | 1975 | 1970 | 1975 |
|---|---|---|---|
| — | — | — | — |
| — | — | — | — |
| — | — | — | — |
| — | — | — | — |
| — | — | — | — |
| — | — | — | — |
| — | — | 3.0 | 4.8 |
| — | — | — | — |
| — | — | — | — |
| — | — | 4.0 | 5.0 |
| — | — | — | — |
| — | — | 4.0 | 5.0 |
| — | — | — | — |
| 1.2 | 1.2 | — | — |
| — | — | — | — |
| — | — | — | — |
| 8.0 | 9.6 | — | — |
| 9.2 | 10.8 | 7.2† | 9.8† |

needed to transport an additional 300 billion cubic meters per year into the European USSR. The official concedes that "it is virtually impossible for us to allocate such large amounts to the gas industry."[85] Pipeline quality and long delays in the installation of compressor stations are also chronic problems. Many breaks, noted in the Soviet press of late, occur at pressure as low as 20 to 50 atmospheres, when modern, large capacity lines operate at 75 atmospheres and Soviet plans call for still higher pressures.[86] The main Tyumen Oil and Gas Administration was, in fact, forced to establish an entire factory for the repair of defective pipes.[87] As to compressor stations, an article in the main gas industry journal has said: "It should become a practice to put on stream at least 50 percent of all compressor stations at the time the gas pipelines are completed."[88]

The excessive optimism that characterized pipeline construction plans in recent years is giving way to greater apprehension over the magnitude of the transport requirement. Of the 35,800 kilometers of planned expansion in the gas trunkline network for 1976–80, only about 31,000 was completed.[89] The Russians seem capable of laying 10,000 to 12,000 kilometers per year of gas and oil pipelines, including lines for refinery products, and it is unlikely that they will be able to go much beyond the upper end of that range in the next five years. As before, most of the work will be on gas transport. However, the expansion of that network is bound to fluctuate somewhat from year to year, not only because of physical obstacles and economic problems but also because of variations in the proportion between gas and oil pipelines in the annual plans.

Yuri Bokserman, the authority on gas, has for some years been calling for the rapid development of multilayer pipes, able to withstand pressures of up to 120 atmospheres. This would nearly double throughput capacity, thus permitting a 22 to 23 percent reduction in metal outlays per cubic meter carried, while providing savings in capital investment and operating cost as well.[90] According to U.S. steel and pipeline experts, Western companies are uninterested in that technology, which goes against the trend toward further improvement in steel quality and see no advantage in it for themselves. For the USSR, where special steel is in short supply and tensile strength a perpetual problem, the development of multilayer pipes made of low-alloy conventional steel may, indeed, be a rational course. The first factory with a one million ton/year ultimate capacity went into opera-

Footnotes to Table 10

*Excludes direct losses at the mines and in the coal preparation plants of the Ministry of the Coal Industry. Losses in the preparation plants of other ministries, such as the Ministry of Iron and Steel, and most self consumption by the Ministry of the Coal Industry are *not* excluded.

**These two regions are omitted from the major source used. Coal shipments were estimated by the author, partly guided by a 1969 Soviet flow chart in *Perevozki gruzov*, p. 88 and scattered evidence.

***Exports to Japan and North Korea, the only two Asian countries receiving Soviet coal, are known to have originated from the Kuzbas. Other exports are assumed to have come from the Ukraine. The breakdown between the two Ukrainian basins is an estimate.

†Imported Polish coal is known to be used in the Southwest region and the Baltic, with small quantities in Belorussia. The breakdown is arbitrary.

SOURCE: Adapted from Dubinsky, *Analiz raboty*.

tion at Vyksa in 1982.[91] Still, this is not a technology which is likely to be in extensive use soon, even if the Soviet system were adept at rapid dissemination of innovations. By Bokserman's own admission, complementary new techniques of electric welding and steel fitting and still higher capacity compressors would have be be mastered for its large scale use.[92]

The impressive, though still barely adequate, expansion of the Soviet pipeline system in recent years has been facilitated by heavy reliance on Western technology. From 1970 through 1976, after which data on foreign trade became restricted, the USSR imported over 45 percent of its total large-diameter steel pipe requirements. Since most of these imports are known to have gone to the gas industry, one may estimate that some 60 to 65 percent of all gas pipelines laid during the better part of that decade were made in foreign mills.[93] Two hundred, i.e. again two-thirds, of all compressor stations to be installed during the 1976-80 plan were also to be imported, and this proportion remained probably unchanged by the serious underfulfillment of this goal, with only 208 compressor stations put on line.[94] The apparently unrealistic goals of the 11th Five-Year Plan of 1981-85 (50,000 km of gas trunklines and 360 compressor stations with a 25 million KW overall capacity compared with 30,000 km and 208 compressor stations with less than 15 million KW overall capacity achieved in the previous five-year plan)[95] would require roughly a doubling of annual deliveries of foreign-made 40- to 56-inch pipe compared to the mid-1970s,[96] and a huge increase in the import of compressors.

Clearly, the Soviets were able to ease the gas transport bottleneck through trade, but at the expense of mortgaging a substantial part of their gas output for supplies already imported. For example, payments for the 9 million tons of pipe bought in the seven-year period 1970-76 plus 28 compressor stations ordered for two giant trunklines, required almost all the earnings from gas exports to Western Europe, amounting to 90 billion cubic meters or slightly more, during the 10th Five-Year Plan (1976-80).[97] Prices for the currently still undervalued Soviet gas in Western Europe are likely to rise sharply in the 1980s, but so will the prices of Soviet imports, though perhaps not quite to the same degree. And, in all likelihood, the sale of gas in the 1980s would not only have to provide the bulk of any increment in Soviet hard-currency exports, but probably have to compensate for some decline in hard-currency oil trade.

A deeper understanding of all these constraints is leading to greater caution among gas industry officials and functionaries of Tyumen Oblast, the linchpin in the Soviet gas drive. In an unusually frank interview, Ye. G. Altunin, former chief of the Tyumen Gas Industry Corporation and later secretary of the Oblast Party Committee reveals the spirited struggle waged by the Tyumen Gas Corporation against Gosplan's attempt to force the industry prematurely to the Yamburg and Kharasavei fields yet farther north. Besides problems of still greater remoteness, the gas industry was said to be technologically unprepared for pipelines and field construction on the ice-saturated permafrost north of Urengoi on the Taz and Yamal Peninsulas.[98] Altunin believes that an

*average* annual output of 300 billion cubic meters until 1990 is a reasonable expectation. It would be attainable from deposits already reached and those realistically accessible in that decade (the three supergiants of Medvezhye, Urengoi and Zapolyarnoye and three additional nearby fields of modest size).[99] Altunin's figure implies a cumulative production of about 3 trillion cubic meters over the period 1979-90 and may be approximated most reasonably with annual increments of around 31 billion cubic meters. Output would then rise from 112 billion in 1979[100] to 470 billion cubic meters in 1990.[101]

## Summary and Conclusion

This paper explicitly focused attention on the regional dimension of Soviet energy policy in recent years, stressing issues and trends important for the future. It analyzed changes in the geographic patterns of fuel consumption both in the aggregate and with respect to detailed regional energy mixes and consequent supply flows. It also examined the enormous and growing transport burden placed on the country by the energy industries at a time of rapid spatial shift in supplies and relative inertia in demand.

Economic development has been accompanied not only by a rapid growth of energy use but also by a significant geographic diffusion in energy consumption, a substantial reduction in regional disparities of demand and levels of energy intensity. Nevertheless, these disparities are still very large both per capita and per industrial employee. More interestingly, the paper showed that until the 1970s, Soviet industry experienced very little areal shift in relative fuel intensiveness between the European and Asiatic USSR, the relative gain of Siberia being particularly small. That shift seems to have accelerated in the present decade with the vast construction projects initiated east of the Urals both for the domestic economy and export. However, that acceleration has occurred at a time of sharply tightening supplies of energy and raw materials as well as labor and capital resources which have also enhanced the locational inertia of Soviet manufacturing as a whole. Thus despite the theoretical complementarity among the country's major parts, the competitive pressure for energy, investment and human resources among the chief area divisions, both directly but still more within the sectoral-ministerial framework, continue to exert strong influence and may even be on the rise.

The study produced detailed estimates of the changing fuel mixes of the 17 economic regions (covering the entire area of the USSR) since the mid-1960s. Important developments in the contribution and very different roles of the major fuels in contrasting areas of the country were examined. The paper put into focus the upsurge of natural gas consumption in regions of the European USSR (as well as Central Asia) during the sixties, its *relative* stabilization west of the Urals in the first half of the seventies, accompanied by a dramatic rise in oil consumption. On the demand side at least, it is these huge increases not only in the quantities used but even in the relative contribution of liquid products in all but four of the 17 regions and nearly everywhere in the European provinces (at a time of growing concern for oil reserves, mounting East European needs and vastly improved export opportunities) that lie at the heart of the impending Soviet energy crunch. Despite the belated surge of gas shipments from remote Siberian fields and the accelerated nuclear program, the gap between energy supplies and demand has continued to widen since the mid-seventies in all regions west of the Urals. This has increased the pressure on the now flattening curve of petroleum resources available to Soviet planners.

Recent spatial developments in fuel supplies, combined with the evolution of regional fuel mixes, involved and resulted in radical changes in the geography of energy flows. They have also been accompanied by an escalating transport burden, requiring large current inputs and vast capital resources and playing a significant role in the poor performance and still poorer prospects of the Soviet economy. In a territorially organized multinational state, openly committed to balanced regional development, equity considerations about the direction, duration and scale of resource flows seldom can be ignored very long no matter how cynical or autocratic the leadership. Aside from crude oil shipments from the Volga area, the huge interregional transport of natural gas (as well as coal) from the European South to the great urban centers of the Russian Plain formed the geographic pivot of the Soviet energy system in the 1960s. The even larger and more distant transfer of Central Asian gas to the RSFSR represents one of the most crucial "energy bridges" on Soviet soil during the seventies. The paper has shown, however, that rapid withdrawal and depletion, combined with mounting local needs, resulted in a drastic reduction of outshipment from the South, strengthening Ukrainian claims on the remaining reserves of the region. The conscious political balancing of ethnic-regional demands, of course, cannot be proved. Nevertheless, as given regional reserves of hydrocarbons are depleted, the energy needs of "exporting" republics (provinces) do seem to acquire greater weight in Soviet plans. Similar reductions of gas exports from Central Asia before the end of the eighties cannot be ruled out.

The study demonstrated that in the development and exploitation of remote fuel reserves today, Soviet planners continue their traditional transport policy. Transport and communication services are provided only when and to the degree absolutely necessary. Facilities are built chiefly and often exclusively to ship the product when exploitation has begun: they remain primitive or nonexistent throughout the preparation and development phase. This has led to waste, slowed the growth of reserves and contributed greatly to the energy problems that loom ahead. Soviet planners, however, should not be unfairly blamed. Even with a policy of utmost stringency, the transport burden has grown sharply in recent years, taxing the economy to an even larger extent. Matters are destined to get worse in the 1980s and, as in the 1930s, transport is becoming one of the key bottlenecks to growth. Unlike in earlier periods, however, relatively simple, cheap solutions today are not in sight.

The fuel industries contribute the lion's share to that transport burden. Conversely, prospects in the energy sector are tied extremely closely to the efficiency and performance of the transport system. In the USSR, the energy industries account for nearly one-half of all internal freight turnover when natural gas is counted at an appropriate calorific and weight equivalent. The analysis showed that, among fossil fuels in the USSR today, coal and natural gas produce the greatest strain on the transport system—coal on the existing railways, gas on resources required for new pipelines and compressors. In the case of coal, more than two-thirds of all shipments are concentrated on three sets of railway lines and in the first half of the seventies two of these (both east of the Urals) were responsible for 90 percent of all ton-kilometers increase in coal freight turnover.

The long-term prospects of both fuels will depend on the speed new facilities can be provided for their delivery from production sites to distant consuming centers. For coal, virtually all growth in interregional freight in the future will have to funnel through those same lines which carried most of the increase in the seventies and which now are choked to capacity. For natural gas, the staggering interindustry requirements for steel, equipment, etc. and construction problems have pushed the 1980 pipeline targets well beyond reach. These difficulties caused the Soviets to mortgage their entire 1976–80 gas exports for pipes and construction *already* received and caused grave concern among knowledgeable gas industry officials of the USSR. All signs indicate that in the years ahead the speed of new transport construction will not match that required by the economy for coal or gas. The transport bottleneck will thus play a key role in the coming energy crunch.

## NOTES

1. *Narodnoye khozyaistvo SSSR v 1980 godu* (Moscow: Statistika, 1981), p. 338 (hereafter *Nar. khoz. SSSR*).

2. N. Fitelman, "Current problems in the development of the fuels and energy complex," *Ekonomicheskiye nauki*, 1976, no. 4, p. 32 and Ye. A. Nitskevich, "Problems of perfecting the fuels and energy balance of industry," *Promyshlennaya energetika*, 1976, no. 8, pp. 30–31.

3. *Productive* investment received by the energy industries, thus not counting investment by consuming enterprises, reached 10 percent of all investment in the national economy in 1979 and 9.8 percent in 1970. *Nar. khoz. SSSR v 1980 godu*, pp. 337–38. In the new energy producing areas, which today account for all the increment and much of aggregate output, capital outlays on infrastructural development have escalated. At the supergiant Medvezhye gas field of Tyumen Oblast, for example, investment in roads, housing, service and other facilities comprise more than half of all outlays as compared to 15 to 16 percent at such better located deposits as North Stavropol and Gazli. U.S. CIA, *USSR: Development of the Gas Industry*, ER 78-10393 (July 1978), pp. 41–42 and 46. A similar situation is certain to exist in the petroleum industry and, to a lesser extent, in other branches as well.

4. Freight turnover (ton-km) by the different fuels is shown for the railroads, rivers and pipelines in Table 8. For domestic sea hauls and roads, data are available only

for total freight but not for fuels. For fuels, the importance of these two transport modes is known to be even smaller than for total freight.

5. This actually understates the contribution of natural gas pipelines, since the average heat content of coal hauled is substantially less than 7 million kcal/ton.

6. Chapter 12 is a revised version of Leslie Dienes, *Soviet Energy Policy and the Hydrocarbons*, Discussion Paper No. 2 (April 1978), Association of American Geographers, Project on Soviet Natural Resources in the World Economy.

7. Robert Campbell, *Soviet Energy Balances*, Research Report R-2257 (Santa Monica, Ca.: Rand Corporation, 1978), Tables 7 and 8, pp. 16 and 22.

8. Leslie Dienes and Theodore Shabad, *The Soviet Energy System: Resource Use and Policies* (Washington: Winston and Sons, 1979. Distributor John Wiley), pp. 24–30.

9. *Nar. khoz. SSSR v 1960 godu*, p. 636, and *Nar. khoz. SSSR 1922–1972*, p. 346.

10. In 1970, less than seven percent of the 4.5 million KW capacity of the Far East was comprised of hydro stations, represented essentially by the Vilyui station of 308,000 KW which took nine years (from 1960 to 1969) to be put on line. V. A. Rylsky et al., *Elektricheskaya baza ekonomicheskikh rayonov SSSR* [The electric base of economic regions in the USSR] (Moscow: Nauka, 1974), p. 194 and Dienes and Shabad, *Soviet Energy System*, pp. 132 and 138.

11. Aggregate fuel production in the Asian USSR and total westward flow out of the area are available for 1975 in calorific equivalent (standard tons) from an authoritative source. Subtracting a further 6 million standard tons of oil and coal exports to a few Asian states leaves 345 million standard tons, which should approximate apparent consumption in the Asian USSR in 1975. A. M. Nekrasov and M. G. Pervukhin, eds., *Energetika SSSR v. 1976–1980 godakh* [Electric power of the USSR in 1976–80] [Moscow: Energiya, 1977), pp. 148–49 and *Vneshnyaya torgovlya SSSR v 1975 godu* [Foreign trade of the USSR in 1975] (Moscow: Statistika,1976), p. 68. Assuming that the combined share of Kazakhstan and Central Asia grew only slightly since 1970, the trans-Ural provinces of the RSFSR consumed 200 to 210 million tons standard in 1975. See Dienes and Shabad, *Soviet Energy System*, footnote 8, p. 24.

12. Nekrasov and Pervukhin, *Energetika SSSR*, p. 129.

13. Ibid, pp. 125–27.

14. Victor Mote in Theodore Shabad and Victor Mote, *Gateway to Siberian Resources (The BAM)* (Washington: Scripta Publishing Co., 1977. Distributor Wiley), p. 105.

15. Robert Jensen, "Soviet Regional Development Policy and the 10th Five-Year Plan," *Soviet Geography: Review and Translation* (hereafter *SGRT*), 19, no. 3 (March 1978): 199.

16. L. N. Telepko, *Urovni ekonomicheskogo razvitiya rayonov SSSR* [Economic development levels in regions of the USSR] (Moscow: Ekonomika, 1971), p. 92.

17. While in the USSR as a whole, 24.3 percent of all workers were in the non-productive, i.e. service, sphere during 1974, in Siberia the corresponding percentage was 23.7 percent. In the Central Asian republics, this sphere is also lower, reaching 23.3 percent in Uzbekistan for the

same year. Akademiya nauk SSSR Sibirskoye otdeleniye, *Razvitiye narodnogo khozyaistva Sibiri* [ Development of the Siberian economy] (Novosibirsk: Nauka, 1978), p. 126 and *Nar. Khoz. Uzbekskoi SSR v 1975 godu* [Economy of the Uzbek SSR in 1975] (Tashkent: Uzbekistan, 1976), p. 284. In addition, the productivity of service personnel, at least in the scientific, cultural and educational fields, is most probably lower east of the Urals.

18. Leslie Dienes, "Investment Priorities in Soviet Regions," Association of American Geographers, *Annals*, September 1972, pp. 442–43.

19. N. V. Alisov, "Spatial Aspects of the New Soviet Strategy of Intensification of Industrial Production," *SGRT*, 20, no. 1 (January 1979): 4.

20. *Nar. khoz. SSSR*, various issues.

21. See *inter alia* Alisov, "Soviet Intensification," and the still more forceful statement of the late A. A. Mints, which has the tone of a policy paper. A. A. Mints, "A Predictive Hypothesis of Economic Development in the European Part of the USSR," *SGRT*, 17, no. 1 (January 1976): 1–28.

22. Mints, "Predictive Hypothesis," pp. 24–26. Also Alisov, "Soviet Intensification," p. 6.

23. For some recent views on this topic see, *inter alia* N. N. Nekrasov, "The general development strategy and life," *Ekonomika i organizatsiya promyshlennogo proizvodstva*, 1979, no. 4, pp. 53–54 and 58–60. M. B. Mazanova, *Territorialnye proportsii narodnogo khozyaistva SSSR* [Spatial proportions of the Soviet Economy] (Moscow: Nauka, 1974), especially chapter 6; M. B. Mazanova, "The Role of Eastern Regions in the Economy of the USSR," *SGRT*, 13, no. 10 (December 1972): 655–71, and V. V. Kistanov and A. S. Epshtein, "Problems of Optimal Location of an Industrial Complex," *SGRT*, 13, no. 3 (March 1972): 141–52. See also the very informative chapter by Vsevolod Holubnychy, "Spatial Efficiency in the Soviet Economy," in V. N. Bandera and Z. L. Melnyk, ed., *The Soviet Economy in Regional Perspective* (New York: Praeger, 1973), pp. 1–44.

24. In 1975, all types of boilers (for electricity, steam and hot water), coking and coke-chemical plants consumed 77.3 percent of all coal shipped. About 1.5 percent went to the railroads and a quarter of the remaining 21.2 percent was burned directly in household furnaces and stoves. V. Voropayeva and S. Litvak, "On the fuels and energy balance of the USSR," *Vestnik statistiki*, 1978, no. 1, Tables 3 and 5, pp. 8–9, and Campbell, *Soviet Energy Balances*, pp. 93–94. Seventy-five percent of all shale and 64 percent of all peat were used under boilers. Voropayeva and Litvak, Table 3.

25. Dienes and Shabad, *Soviet Energy System*, pp. 125–26.

26. Ibid., pp. 232–33.

27. Ibid., pp. 104–21, 226–28, and 250–51.

28. A. Ye. Probst and Ya. A. Mazanova, eds., *Razvitiye i razmeshcheniye toplivnoi promyshlennosti* [Development and location of the fuel industry] (Moscow: Nedra, 1975).

29. Of a total consumption of 16.7 billion cubic meters in 1975, Transcaucasia produced less than 9.9 billion. This means that 6.8 billion cubic meters of the 9.56 billion imported from Iran was consumed in Azerbaijan, Armenia and Georgia. Iranian export of gas in 1970 was still

under a billion cubic meters. R. D. Margulov et al., *Razvitiye gazovoi promyshlennosti i analiz tekhniko-ekonomicheskikh pokazatelei* [Development of the gas industry and analysis of technical-economic indicators] (Moscow: Ministerstvo Gazovoi Promyshlennosti, 1976), p. 8; *Nar. khoz. SSSR v 1975 godu*, p. 241; *Vneshnyaya torgovlya SSSR za 1971 god*, p. 101, and *v 1975 godu*, p. 98.

30. See several Soviet sources quoted in Chapter 9, footnote 37 and in Dienes and Shabad, *Soviet Energy System*, p. 260. The almost incredible mismanagement of the development of the Uzen field (Mangyshlak Peninsula, Kazakhstan) and the irreparable damage inflicted on this huge reservoir are discussed by Arthur A. Meyerhoff in Chapter 14.

31. Dienes and Shabad, *Soviet Energy System*, pp. 70–71; Margulov et al., *Razvitiye gazovoi promyshlennosti*, pp. 41–42 and 44–45 and V. N. Kalchenko, *Gazova promyslovist i tekhnichny progres* [The gas industry and technical progress: in Ukrainian] (Kiev: Naukova Dumka, 1972), pp. 98–100.

32. See Tables 4 and 5 and citations to Margulov and Kalchenko in note 31.

33. Dienes and Shabad, *Soviet Energy System*, pp. 70–71 and 80–84 and CIA, *Gas Industry*, pp. 59–60.

34. Leslie Dienes, "Geographical Problems of Allocation in the Soviet Fuel Supply," *Energy Policy*, (June 1973) pp. 6–13.

35. A. N. Markova, "Development of interregional linkages in refined oil products," *Voprosy geografii*, 1965, no. 65, pp. 65–66.

36. Kalchenko, *Gazova promyslovist*, pp. 72–75 and 95; M. Tikhonov and S. Polevoi, "Some issues in the rational use of Ukrainian fuel resources," *Ekonomika Sovetskoi Ukrainy*, 1974, no. 8, p. 8; CIA, *Gas Industry* (July 1978), p. 31–34 and Dienes and Shabad, *Soviet Energy System*, pp. 51, 53 and 107–112. A recent Soviet source reveals that during 1966–70 reserve additions did not materialize for 14 billion cubic meters of gas output, one quarter of the Ukrainian total. Apparently, this quantity had to be produced by drawing down existing reserves at a faster than planned rate. In I. Maksimov and Z. P. Tsimdina, eds., *Optimizatsiya i razmeshcheniye neftegazovoi promyshlennosti* [Optimization and location of the oil and gas industry] (Novosibirsk: Nauka, 1977), p. 58.

37. Margulov et al., *Razvitiye gazovoi promyshlennosti*, pp. 42 and 44–45 and I. Ya. Furman, *Ekonomika magistralnogo transporta gaza* [Economics of the gas trunk transmission] (Moscow: Nedra, 1978), pp. 38–40 and 76–77.

38. *Izvestiya*, 26 October 1974, pp. 1–2 and Theodore Shabad, "News Notes," *SGRT*, 16, no. 2 (February 1975): p. 121.

39. Marginal costs of natural gas, fuel oil and sorted coal have been ranging between 22 and 26 rubles per 7 million kilocalories throughout the cis-Volga area south of 60° Lat. where half of the Soviet people live. In the Volga valley and the North Caucasus, marginal costs are 2 to 3 rubles lower. A. A. Beschinsky and Yu. M. Kogan, *Ekonomicheskiye problemy elektrifikatsii* [Economic problems of electrification] (Moscow: Energiya, 1976), p. 95.

40. Akademiya nauk SSSR, *Izvestiya Sibirskogo otdeleniya, Seriya obshchestvennykh nauk*, 1978, no. 6, pp. 50–54. However, the recent imposition of secrecy on regional

reserves and output data suggests that since the mid-seventies reserve additions in mature provinces have not materialized and production is declining faster than anticipated.

41. Dienes and Shabad, *Soviet Energy System*, pp. 70–71, 80, 82 and 84.

42. Margulov et al., *Razvitiye gazovoi promyshlennosti*, p. 42 and Furman, *Ekonomika transporta gaza*, pp. 39–41.

43. *Nar. khoz. SSSR v 1969 godu*, p. 149; *Nar. khoz. SSSR v 1975 godu*, p. 203; "Overall Industrial Plan Results for the Union Republics in 1978," *Radio Liberty Research*, 26 January 1979 and Ann Sheehy, "Industrial Growth Lags in Turkmenistan," *Radio Liberty Research*, 3 January 1978.

44. In Uzbekistan, the most advanced and by far the most populous of all the Central Asian republics, *less than one-third* of the labor force in light industry consisted of Uzbeks at mid-decade. Large textile mills in Tashkent, Fergana, Ashkhabad and Dushanbe employed the indigenous ethnic groups for only 9 percent to 16 percent of their total labor force. In more skill demanding branches, the participation of native groups must surely be lower still. Ye. A. Afanasyevsky, *Legkaya promyshlennost: ekonomicheskiye problemy razmeschcheniya* (Light industry: economic problems of location] (Moscow: Mysl, 1976), p. 216.

45. See for example, P. K. Savchenko and A. R. Khodzhayev, *Toplivno-energeticchesky kompleks Sredneaziatskogo ekonomicheskogo rayona* [The fuels and energy complex of the Central Asian economic region] (Tashkent: Uzbekistan, 1974), especially pp. 176–77; Sh. Chokin, *Energetika i vodnoye khozaistvo Kazakhstana* [Electric power and water management in Kazakhstan] (Alma-Ata: Kazakhstan, 1975). p. 77; K. M. Kim, *Sovershenstvovaniye struktury toplivno-energeticheskogo balansa Srednei Azii* [Perfecting the structure of the fuels and energy balance in Central Asia] (Tashkent: FAN, 1973), pp. 197, 198, and 208–09.

46. Edgar M. Hoover, *An Introduction to Regional Economics*, Second ed. (New York: Alfred A. Knopf, 1975), p. 38.

47. Holland Hunter, "The Soviet Transport Sector," in U.S. Congress, Joint Economic Committee, *New Directions in the Soviet Economy*, 89th Cong., 2nd sess., 1966, p. 571.

48. In 1978, Urengoi-Surgut-Chelyabinsk gas pipeline was under construction at full speed. But not a single one of the 53 radio relay towers were ready and radio communication was lacking along the entire length. The 570 km Nadym-Punga section of the West Siberian transmission system, where four parallel trunklines are in operation, still had no hard surface road. From mid-April to mid-December, servicing and repair can be done only by helicopters and ruptures take 8 to 10 days to fix. Ye. G. Altunin, "A strategy must be chosen today," *Ekonomika i organizatsiya promyshlennogo proizvodstva*, 1979, no. 2, p. 22.

49. F. G. Arzhanov, "Around the drilling site," *Ekonomika i organizatsiya promyshlennogo proizvodstva*, 1979, no. 2, pp. 26–27. Altunin, "Strategy," p. 21 expresses a similar sentiment.

50. Altunin, "Strategy," p. 20.

51. *Nar. khoz. SSSR v 1980 godu*, p. 295.

52. Ibid.

53. Theodore Shabad, "News Notes," *SGRT*, 18, no. 9 (November 1977): 702 and *Pravda*, 29 March 1978, p. 2.

54. Shipment to consumers, including export, in the European USSR (including the Urals) amounted to 376 million tons; *net* export from the European USSR reached 14.2 million tons. Of the 351 million tons produced, about 20 million, two-thirds of the Soviet total, was lost in the coal washing plants of the Ministry of the Coal Industry and during mining operations. *Perevozki gruzov*, pp. 84–86; *Vneshnyaya torgovlya SSSR za 1966 god*, pp. 72 and 187, and Campbell, *Soviet Energy Balances*, p. 75.

55. Dienes and Shabad, *Soviet Energy System*, pp. 110–111.

56. Ibid., p. 28.

57. G. Ya. Burshtein and S. V. Arabyan, *Ekonomika obogashcheniya uglei* [Economics of coal beneficiation] (Moscow: Nedra, 1974), p. 18.

58. *Ugol Ukrainy*, 1976, no. 2, p. 6; and P. K. Dubinsky, *Analiz raboty zheleznodorozhnogo transporta ugolnoi promyshlennosti v devyatoi pyatiletke* [Analysis of coal transport by rail in the 9th Five-Year Plan] (Moscow: Ministry of Coal Industry, TsNIEIugol, 1977), pp. 14–15.

59. *Pravda*, 1 March 1979, p. 3 and *Sotsialisticheskaya industriya*, 23 March 1977, p. 2.

60. Dubinsky, *Analiz raboty*, p. 15.

61. Ibid., pp. 13–15.

62. About 70 percent of the original proved oil reserves of Tatar ASSR and more of the Bashkir ASSR have already been produced. All but two or three of the Soviet petroleum provinces have entered the phase of absolute decline. In the European USSR, the situation with respect to natural gas is similar. *Izvestiya*, 21 January 1979, p. 1. *Sovetskaya Tatariya*, 7 November 1976, p. 3, and 27 November 1976, p. 2; Richard Nehring, *Giant Oil Fields and World Oil Resources*, R-2284 (Santa Monica, Ca.: Rand Corporation, June 1978), pp. 129–31; *Oil and Gas Journal*, 4 June 1979, p. 65; Dienes and Shabad, *Soviet Energy System*, pp. 51–56, and CIA, *Gas Industry*, pp. 6–10, 12–14 and 31–34.

63. Production converted to calorific equivalent for physical units. Dienes and Shabad, *Soviet Energy System*, pp. 46–47, 70–71, 110–111, 125–27. Heat content of coal from different basins given in A. Ye. Probst et al., *Sravnitelnye tekhniko-ekonomicheskiye pokazateli po dobyche i transporte topliva* [Comparative technical-economic indicators for the extraction and transportation of fuels] (Moscow: Nauka, 1964), p. 37. According to plan not less than 75 percent of all fuel consumption in 1980 was to be accounted for by the European USSR and that share was evidently exceeded. Nekrasov, "General development strategy," p. 50, and *Nar. khoz. SSSR v 1980 godu*, p. 53.

64. Nekrasov and Pervukhin, *Energetika SSSR*, p. 148.

65. The output set by the 11th Five-Year Plan for 1985 is 630 million tons of crude oil compared with 603 million in 1980, but oil production goals have not been fulfilled in recent years.

66. *Nar. khoz. SSSR v 1980 godu*, pp. 157 and 295–96; *Nar. khoz. SSSR v 1969 godu*, pp. 445–46, and Theodore Shabad, "News Notes," *SGRT*, 18, no. 9 (November 1977): 701, and *SGRT*, 23, no. 4 (April 1982): 291.

67. *Moscow Narodny Bank, Press Bulletin*, 20 August 1975, p. 3 and Dienes and Shabad, *Soviet Energy System*, p.

115. Staggering technical, labor and construction problems, however, beset the project and planned capacity is unlikely to be reached by 1983. The coking coal lies under a thick oxidized layer of steam coal which must be removed before the coking coal can be reached. This means that up to 30 million tons of ordinary but expensive steam coal, which Siberia has in abundance, must be extracted *before* the shipment of coking coal from the complex can begin. *Sotsialisticheskaya industriya*, 21 January 1979, p. 2. The article also catalogues the unexpected labor and construction troubles and states that the builders have found themselves "in the situation of the runner who is told near the finish line that the distance has been increased severalfold."

68. In 1970, coal comprised almost 35 percent of all rail freight *tonnage* in the country's eastern zone (West Siberia, East Siberia, Far East, Kazakhstan, Central Asia) but only 16.4 percent in the western zone (European USSR, including the Urals) and 21.2 percent in the USSR as a whole. Through the first half of the 1970s, 60 to 65 percent of all the coal carried in the eastern zone was hauled on two main lines leading from the Kuznetsk, Ekibastuz, and Karaganda coal fields to the Urals. If the chief distribution lines in the Urals are included, these railroads transported three-fourths of all coal in the eastern zone. Because other bulk freight was more evenly distributed, the share of coal in total tonnage must have been much higher still on these few lines than in the eastern zone as a whole. Dubinsky, *Analiz raboty*, p. 48 and Nikolsky et al. *Geografiya vodnogo transporta SSSR* [Geography of water transport in the USSR] (Moscow: Transport, 1975), pp., 53–58.

69. Table 10 (see text) shows the detailed regional breakdown of coal shipment for 1970 and 1975. By taking the railway distance between the relevant coalfields and the rough geographic or principal urban centers of economic regions, the total freight turnover for coal in ton-kilometers can be estimated for the two dates with reasonable accuracy. Rail distances taken from *Spravochnik po tarifam zheleznodorozhnogo transporta* [Railroad freight rates manual] (Moscow: Transzheldorizdat, 1955), pp. 306–25 and *Zheleznye dorogi SSSR. Napravleniya i stantsii* (Moscow: GUGK, 1969).

70. *Spravochnik; Zheleznye dorogi SSSR*, and A. M. Belikov, *Ekonomika obogashcheniya i ispolzovaniya uglya* [Economics of coal beneficiation and use] (Moscow, 1963), pp. 24–25.

71. A. A. Troitsky, "Basic trends of electric power development in light of the future fuels balance," *Elektricheskiye stantsii*, 1978, no. 12, pp. 13–14. A somewhat longer version of the article is also published in Gosplan's own journal, *Planovoye khozyaistvo*, 1979, no. 2, pp. 18–25. The Minister of Railroads USSR stated recently that, in 1977, more than 40 percent of the *total* increase in the volume of rail freight turnover was accounted for by the West and East Siberian, Virgin Lands, Sverdlovsk and Southern Ural Railroads. Several lines have now reached the limit of their carrying capacity. *Pravda*, 29 March 1978, p. 2.

72. Plans initially envisaged 115 million tons by 1985 and as much as 170 million by 1990; Dienes and Shabad, *Soviet Energy System*, p. 116, but the 11th Five-Year Plan

reduced the 1985 goal to 84 million tons; Shabad, "News Notes," *SGRT*, 23, no. 4 (April 1982): 288.

73. Troitsky, "Basic trends," pp. 13–14.

74. Dienes and Shabad, *Soviet Energy System*, pp. 117–19 and 251; *Pravda*, 25 August 1978, p. 5, and 22 March 1979, p. 2. A fascinating report documents the fact that even the present level of output exceeds demand for Kansk-Achinsk lignites by 2.5 to 3 million tons, since power stations are not equipped to burn this troublesome fuel. Every year, thousands of railway cars remain unloaded, tying up rolling stock. Meanwhile, the Ministry of Coal Industry receives credit for 2.5 to 3 million tons of unused and unusable coal toward fulfillment of its plan. *Sotsialisticheskaya industriya*, 19 May 1979.

75. G. A. Andreyev et al., *Osobennosti vneshnikh proizvoditelnykh svyazei energetiki na drugiye otrasli narodnogo khozyaistva* [Characteristics of foreign production linkages of electric power on other sections of the economy] (Irkutsk, 1975), pp. 30–31.

76. V. A. Shelest, *Regionalnye energoekonomicheskiye problemy SSSR* [Regional power-economic problems in the USSR] (Moscow: Nauka, 1975), pp. 268–69.

77. Akademiya nauk SSSR, Siberskoye otdeleniye, *Toplivno-energetichesky kompleks Sibiri* [The fuels and energy complex of Siberia], V. Ye. Popov. ed. (Novosibirsk: Nauka, 1978), p. 206–07. Such heavy use, however, would require the replacement of rails in less than a decade, which puts the whole project still more in doubt.

78. Troitsky, "Basic trends," pp. 13–14.

79. *Nar. khoz. SSSR v 1965 godu*, pp. 490–91; *Nar. khoz. SSSR v 1980 godu*, p. 305 and V. G. Dubinsky, *Ekonomika razvitiya i razmeshcheniya nefteprovodnogo transporta v SSSR* [Economics of development and location of oil pipeline transport in the USSR] (Moscow: Nedra, 1977), p. 13.

80. Dienes and Shabad, *Soviet Energy System*, pp. 63 and 83.

81. Furman, *Ekonomika transporta gaza*, p. 14.

82. Ibid., pp. 3 and 5.

83. P. S. Sapozhnikov and G. D. Sokolov, *Ekonomika i organizatsiya stroitelstva v neftyanoi i gazovoi promyshlennosti* [Economics and organization of construction in the oil and gas industry] (Moscow: Nedra, 1976), pp. 8 and 10, and *Nar. khoz. SSSR v 1980 godu*, p. 338.

84. Dienes, Chapter 12 of this volume. Same information in Dienes and Shabad, *Soviet Energy System*, pp. 240–41.

85. Yu. Bokserman, "On new, progressive transport modes," *Planovoye khozyaistvo*, 1978, no. 11, p. 19.

86. *Oil and Gas Journal*, 2 April 1979, p. 42.

87. Arzhanov, "Drilling site," p. 30.

88. *Gazovaya promyshlennost*, 1977, no. 4, p. 5.

89. *Ekonomicheskaya gazeta*, 1977, no. 6, p. 2; 1981, no. 13, p. 2; *Oil and Gas Journal*, 2 April 1979, p. 41.

90. Bokserman, "Progressive transport modes," p. 21 and Yu. Bokserman, "Ways of enhancing the effectiveness of fuel transport," *Planovoye khozyaistvo*, 1977, no. 10, pp. 97–98.

91. *Oil and Gas Journal*, 2 April 1979, pp. 40–41; *Izvestiya*, 12 December 1976, p. 2; Shabad, "News Notes," *SGRT*, 23, no. 2 (February 1982): 120–21.

92. Bokserman, "Progressive transport modes," p. 21 and *Oil and Gas Journal*, 2 April 1979, p. 41.

93. From 1970 through 1976, almost 9 million tons of large-diameter pipe, valued at $4.3 billion, was imported. Domestic production during the 7 years totaled 101.7 million tons, 18 to 19 percent of which (ca. 19 million tons) was of large diameter. *Oil and Gas Journal*, 10 October 1977, p. 110; *Nar. khoz. SSSR v 1975 godu*, p. 246; *Nar. khoz. SSSR v 1976 godu*, p. 209 and Theodore Shabad, "News Notes," *SGRT*, 18, no. 3 (March 1977): 215.

There appears to be a significant discrepancy between the total amount of pipe available (from domestic production and import) and the length of pipelines laid. This suggests long delays between the time pipe is delivered and installed and a large percentage of defective pipe in domestic production. R. Campbell, *Soviet Energy Technologies* (Bloomington: Indiana University Press, 1980), pp. 210–12. However, Campbell's estimate of 350 tons per km of pipe as an average weight for pipe over 40 inches may be too low (see note 96 below) and something like 450 to 500 tons per km may be more realistic. At any rate Campbell also suggests that a very large share, perhaps two-thirds or more, of the increment in large-diameter gas pipelines during the 1970s has been accounted for by imports (Ibid., p. 209).

94. *Business Week*, 17 October 1977, p. 52; *Gazovaya promyshlennost*, 1976, no. 11, p. 2. and *Ekonomicheskaya gazeta*, 1981, no. 13, p. 2.

95. *Ekonomicheskaya gazeta*, 1981, no. 13, p. 2.

96. Citing Soviet sources, Campbell states that most Soviet pipe 1,020 mm (40 inches) and above has a wall thickness of 11 to 12 mm. The weight of 40-inch pipe is given as 299 tons/km, 48-inch pipe is 358 tons/km, and 56-inch 446 tons/km (Campbell, *Soviet Energy Technologies*, p. 210). These, however, must refer to some theoretical desideratum, since Soviet and Polish sources give the total weight of the 56-inch diameter Orenburg pipeline as 1.7 and over 2 million tons, respectively, the Polish source specifically stating that 10 meters weigh 7.5 tons. The Nadym-Ukhta-Torzhok line, also of 56-inch diameter, weighs 6.49 tons per 10 meters, with the average wall thickness of both lines being 16 to 18 mm. J. B. Hannigan, *The Orenburg Natural Gas Project and Fuel-Energy Balances in East Europe* (Ottawa: Carleton University, Institute of Soviet and East European Studies, 1980), p. 35 and *Ekonomika gazovoi promyshlennosti*, 1976, no. 2, pp. 22–23. By implication, the weight of present 48-inch pipe should reach or exceed 500 tons/km. Pipe of 48-inch and 56-inch diameter accounts for 30 percent of the total Soviet gas pipeline network (*Gazovaya promyshlennost*, 1981, no. 3, p. 2) and for most of the new lines from Siberia.

The 11th (1981–85) Five-Year Plan calls for up to 50,000 km of gas trunklines, one third consisting of 56-inch pipe, (*Ekonomicheskaya gazeta*, 1981, no. 13, p. 2 and *Planovoye khozyaistvo*, 1981, no. 4, p. 50) and nearly 12,000 km of oil product pipelines (*Pravda*, 28 February 1981, pp. 3–4), though only part of these would require large-diameter pipe, which are variously given in Soviet sources as those above 478 or 426 mm (Campbell, *Soviet Energy Technologies*, p. 211). Adding 4,000 to 5,000 km of crude oil pipeline brings the total for large-diameter lines planned close to 60,000 km. About a fourth of all Soviet pipe production, 18.2 million tons in 1980, is of large diameter, with some 3 million tons being of 40-inch (1,020-mm) diameter or more. Soviet imports of large-diameter welded pipe of all sizes, not all of which was 40 inches and over, increased from about 1 million tons in the beginning of the 1970s to 1.7 million in 1975, after which data in tonnage were no longer available (*Nar. khoz. SSSR v 1980 g.*, p. 158, and Campbell, *Soviet Energy Technologies*, p. 211). Since 1970 nearly all gas trunklines laid were over 40-inch diameter, most of them being 48 inches and over (Dienes and Shabad, *Soviet Energy System*, p. 83 and *Gazovaya promyshlennost*, 1981, no. 3, p. 2), one may confidently assume that some 55,000 km out of the ca. 60,000 km large diameter gas, oil and product pipelines would again be over 40 inches. Assuming 470 to 500 tons per km of such pipe (*supra*) and that 6 to 7 percent of domestically produced pipe is defective or substandard, domestic production would, at best, provide for 30,000 km of trunklines. The remaining 25,000 km would require the annual importation of 2.4 million tons of 40- to 56-inch pipe.

97.  The cost of these purchases came to $5.5 billion. *Oil and Gas Journal*, 10 October 1977, p. 110, and 20 December 1976, p. 23. In 1977, the weighted average price of 1,000 cubic meters of Soviet gas was about $36 on the hardcurrency market. *Vneshnyaya torgovlya SSSR v 1977 godu*, p. 61, and *Gas Wärme International*, 3 February 1978. While this price was still below that of oil in calorific equivalent it was certain to go up.

98.  Altunin, "Strategy," pp. 17–18.

99.  Altunin, "Strategy," p. 17. The more accessible English translation of that article in *Current Digest of the Soviet Press*, 13 June 1979, p. 4, which speaks of a 300 billion cubic meter production level *in 1990*, is in error.

100.  Theodore Shabad, "News Notes," *SGRT*, 21, no. 4 (April 1980): 245.

101.  The formula for the sum of an arithmetic progression for $t$ years, $S_t = \frac{t}{2}(2a + (t-1)d)$ gives a constant annual increment $d$ of 31.3 billion cubic meters until 1990 and an output of a little over 470 billion cubic meters in that year, where $a$ is output in the initial year. The 1978 increase was already 24 billion cubic meters and the plan called for 31 billion in 1979 and 1980 (*SGRT*, 20, no. 4 (April 1979): 258.

The constant annual increment computed above may be regarded as the average slope, which (by the fundamental law of calculus) is the same as the average rate of change for *any* curve. A roughly linear relationship between time and output approximating that average slope is virtually certain. Given expected improvements in pipeline transport, increments toward the end of the eighties are unlikely to be much lower than average, even with anticipated shortages of pipe and equipment. Nor can they be much higher, else the cumulative total given by Altunin (see text) would have to be greatly exceeded or a very erratic production curve would have to be assumed. With a nonlinear relationship of the simplest kind between time and output, a parabola (output $= a + bt \pm ct^2$), where $a$ is the intercept and $b$ and $c$ are coefficients), larger than average slopes in early years would have to be compensated for by lower than average ones in later years for the area under the curve, representing cumulative production, to remain unchanged.

With relatively constant increments around 31 billion cubic meters, the annual *percentage rates of growth* will, of course, decline drastically, from over 30 percent today to about 7 percent a decade hence.

# 17

# REGIONAL DILEMMAS AND INTERNATIONAL PROSPECTS IN THE SOVIET TIMBER INDUSTRY

BRENTON M. BARR
University of Calgary

## Introduction

### Objectives and Order of Analysis

This paper evaluates the spatial relationship between the regional availability of Soviet industrial roundwood (timber) and the regional and international location of timber consumption. The paper determines the influence of foreign and domestic demand for industrial roundwood (or its equivalent) in 1990 on the regional supply of Soviet timber, estimates demand by each type of consumer for roundwood in eighty-seven Soviet regions, derives optimal roundwood flows to satisfy regional timber demand, and assesses optimal regional "costs" and "prices" associated with the location of domestic timber supply and demand. Satisfaction of these objectives enables statements to be made concerning the ability of the USSR to sell significant quantities of timber on the international market by 1990, and to satisfy domestic and international demand for timber from specific regions. Analysis in this paper rests on the belief that the prospect of massive Soviet participation in world timber markets can be fully evaluated only within the context of those regions currently affecting timber production and possessing significant potential for influencing its future development.

   The timber and wood-processing industries are analyzed for 1970, 1975, and 1990; this analysis represents an appropriate sequel to previous work by the author on

The author gratefully acknowledges the support provided for this research by the directors of the Association of American Geographers project on Soviet Natural Resources in the World Economy, and by the Killam Awards Committee of The University of Calgary. The author is indebted to the following colleagues for their helpful suggestions and encouragement: Dr. Neil C. Field, Dr. Robert N. North, Dr. Kathleen Braden, and Dr. Len Hills.

   Some of the materials in this chapter appeared in an earlier discussion of Soviet timber by the author in Arctic, 32, no. 4 (1979): 308–328, and are included here by permission.

these industries for the years 1956, 1960, and 1964.[1] The year 1970, representing the beginning of a decade in which the Soviet Union participated heavily in international markets, symbolizes the structure of the Soviet wood-processing and timber industries in the years prior to détente, the much-publicized expansion of commercial relations in the 1970s between the USSR and the Industrial West. The year 1975 represents the latest year for which comprehensive data were available for this study, the final year of the 9th Five-Year Plan, and a benchmark year for evaluating the prospects and performance of the unpublished, but much publicized, long-range plan running to 1990. The year 1990 is the final year of a period in which the Soviet Union is expected to fulfill a comprehensive set of economic objectives which have attendant geographical implications for regional development and international commodity sales. Although a draft of the long-range plan was rejected by Gosplan in 1977, its basic propositions were retained in the working document now described as the "General Outline for the Location of Productive Forces in the USSR for the Period Ending 1990."[2] The year 1990 is retained in this study for consistency with other chapters and is deemed to represent the final year of a period in the intermediate-term future for which a scenario of regional resource extraction and consumption can be acceptably derived now. A scenario for 1990 of regional distribution of the timber and wood-processing industries, and the spatial flows of roundwood between surplus and deficit regions is intended to represent the geography of these industries which will occur if Soviet planners and administrators continue acting in a manner consistent with their performance during the period 1960–75. The downturn in Soviet timber and wood-processing in the late 1970s may reduce the importance of forest exports in the 1980s but reflects planning and investment priorities, not the physical ability of Soviet regional forests to sustain harvesting through 1990.

   The present discussion focuses on the relationship between the forest resource and timber production and export as it has evolved throughout most of the post World War II period, and asks, what could the Soviet timber industry ceterus paribus achieve in 1990? The study recognizes, however, that economic and planning constraints beyond its scope such as investment and operational shortcomings in the timber and wood-processing industries, the recent growth in petroleum export as a major source of foreign exchange, and a host of technological and managerial problems in high priority Soviet industries may lead the USSR to neglect further large scale capital investment in reforestation and wood-processing in the next decade, a prospect indeed reflected in the lackluster proposals for this industry in the 11th Five-Year Plan.

The scenario for 1990 is not an econometric forecast; it is offered as a statement of what may occur in the Soviet timber and wood-processing industries, and the significance these industries may have for other industrial nations of the world and other sectors of the Soviet economy. The scenario will be deemed to have utility if it elicits criticism and modifications in the prognostications of related research on the USSR, and if it clarifies the impact on the performance of the Soviet timber and wood-processing industries of such factors as the physical quality and regional location of the resource, the levels of domestic demand and importance of foreign trade, the costs of transporting timber to market, the economics of timber harvesting and processing, and the size of capital investments in forestry and processing relative to other sectors of the Soviet economy.

The paper is divided into six major sections. Section one assesses the relevant literature, describes the methodology and related assumptions of the paper, and discusses the data employed to analyze the Soviet timber and wood-processing industries. The second section describes Soviet timber reserves. The characteristics of Soviet timber consumption—policies, practices, and the structure of domestic demand—are discussed in section three. Section four evaluates the spatial concurrence of timber supply and demand in 1990 by drawing particular attention to regional levels of timber harvest and growth, optimal patterns for shipping timber to domestic consumers, policies governing timber export, and the expected impact of Soviet timber on world markets. A broad discussion of problems and options in the timber and wood-processing industries occurs in section five. The study concludes in section six with a statement of the possible significance of the timber and wood-processing industries for Soviet regional resource development and international economic relations in 1990, and with a review of those topics receiving cursory treatment in the present analysis which require further elaboration and investigation.

Related Literature

Analyses of Soviet forest, timber, and wood-processing industries currently include four groups, one Soviet and three Western. The works of Soviet analysts are issued in official publications such as monographs, special reports, chapters in books, articles in magazines, journals, and newspapers to provide a broad coverage of the basic characteristics of the entire Soviet forest industry. These sources rarely offer complete analyses of problems and are notoriously lacking in hard empirical data. On the other hand, when gleaned for information, they offer a

relatively fertile basis for understanding problems, issues, and trends in the major subfields of Soviet forestry. They permit the Western observer to speculate on the likely outcome of such aggregate matters as regional investment decisions, resource utilization policies, industrial development planning, locational priorities, and foreign trade objectives. Soviet sources underlie and support all of the topics covered in the present paper, for example, although the method of analysis and arrangement of data in this study differ noticeably from those in Soviet reports.[3]

Soviet publications related to economics and the economic geography of forest, timber, and wood-processing industries are mainly intended for internal consumption by different members of Soviet society. These materials provide a major means for the dissemination of information within the channels of myriad Soviet economic and industrial administrations. The sources more or less represent general accounts or reports of common problems and broad issues; the nature of the publications suggests that those who need omitted data probably can obtain them in the course of their jobs. Published sources thus are long on description and are relatively weak in analysis.

Few studies are specifically related to geography and those which do emphasize regional variation generally rely on a typology of regional units consisting of the fourteen non-Russian republics and the ten major economic regions of the RSFSR. Soviet publications thus offer on the one hand a plethora of observations, projections and general comments, and on the other hand, force the non-Soviet observer to piece together data from many diverse sources, including statistical handbooks. Both data and problems must be rearranged to accommodate geographical conditions in the USSR and the conceptual framework of western economic-geographical thought and patterns of analysis.

For the past two decades, western research on the Soviet Union and its forest industry has relied heavily on numerous annual and occasional Soviet statistical handbooks (discussed below under "data") in addition to fugitive information contained in diverse publications. In the 1980s, however, many of the tables of economic data are being omitted or their information is not published for the regional subdivisions of the USSR. Regional figures on the production of chemical pulp, plywood, particleboard, fiberboard, and matches, for example, common in the 1960s, are now unavailable in the statistical handbooks. The task of obtaining the type of regional data for the eighty-seven regions used in this study has become increasingly onerous and may soon become so great as to preclude the micro-regional analysis presented in this paper.

Western analyses of Soviet forest industries comprise publications and reports based on scrutiny of numerous Soviet sources. One group contains research synthesizing disparate aspects of Soviet forestry into conceptual modes intellectually comparable to those of Western disciplines in order to serve the needs of their constituent societies for understanding topics of current concern such as the Soviet potential for exporting timber and other natural resources. Previous studies by the author,[4] for example, emphasize the spatial variation in timber and wood-processing and the general problem of the efficient allocation of regional surpluses to deficit areas within the USSR. Sutton[5] and North and Solecki[6] review the general operational economic and investment characteristics of timber supply, industrial production, and trade, and from numerous published evaluations of specific aspects of the forestry industry seek a consensus estimation of the USSR's ability to achieve significant increases in foreign sales of wood and wood products. Sutton concludes that "the optimism of many overseas commentators on the size of the USSR forest resource and its ability to boost future world supplies is not supported by a detailed analysis of the resource or the current plans for its utilization."[7] North and Solecki suggest that the Soviet Union has the potential to increase supplies of timber to domestic and international consumers and that "forest products offer one of the best long-term potentials for foreign earnings" but caution prophetically that many competing economic and policy considerations mean that "substantial growth in the Soviet Union's forest product exports to western countries seems, at the very least, unlikely in the foreseeable future."[8]

These studies by Sutton, North and Solecki are comprehensive general reviews of the implications of past Soviet performance for the development of timber and wood-product export in the future. They present many of the key observations, arguments, and opinions of those Soviet analysts closest to the forest industry and probably are as accurate in their assessments as any overview of such a large geographical problem could be from a distant vantage point. These studies offer a valuable background to the empirical analysis presented in the present paper and obviate the need for a similar comprehensive overview of the Soviet forest industry here. Empirical evidence presented in the present paper, however, strongly supports the contention that the Soviet Union has the physical or resource capacity to achieve significant increases in the production of timber and wood products by 1990 if the annual increment of production in each industry is similar to that achieved between 1964 and 1975. Furthermore, the expected 1990 harvest of industrial roundwood and household fuelwood is only 86 percent of the "most realistic" estimate of the USSR's annual allowable cut reported in Sutton.[9] The expected 1990 harvest, however, represents a still smaller proportion (72.4 percent) of the USSR's allowable annual cut estimated by the Canadian forester, J. H. Holowacz, but rejected by Sutton.[10]

Although the cost of the incremental supplies of roundwood from developing regions is likely to be higher than roundwood cut in existing regions of activity, Soviet ability to develop peripheral areas efficiently on the basis of new technology cannot be precluded or dismissed without thorough analysis (analyzed by Kathleen Braden).[11] Soviet plans for railway construction alone seem to indicate that sufficient new timber supplies will be accessible via combined water and rail transport to support the scenario of wood processing for 1990 presented in this chapter. Thus, although the forecasts of future wood shortages by other investigators appear intuitively correct for some unspecified future date, careful assessment of the incremental supply and demand in the timber and wood-processing industry since 1964 leaves little doubt that the Soviet Union will be able to play a significant role on international markets throughout the rest of the twentieth century *if it continues to expand its forest industries in the same modest manner as that recorded for 1964–75.*

Because of the general need to seek data in many obscure or diverse Soviet publications, the academic group of forestry analysts is relatively small compared to the groups represented by private corporations and government agencies which have the resources and contacts to monitor the daily developments of the forest industry. Studies compiled in private corporations and agencies reflect the need by Western manufacturers and suppliers of forest related equipment to assess the potential market for their commodities within the USSR. Prediction of Soviet demand is also necessary if suppliers are to integrate their promotional campaigns with Soviet decision-making and planning periods. Private forecasting agencies also provide an important service to the USSR's competitors in world markets. Reports of this type, however, are not widely available at their time of issue because of the high fees which must be charged to customers to recoup the high cost of compilation. The reports, for example, by Dirosab[12] in Sweden and Jaakko Pöyry Consulting Oy[13] in Finland demonstrate the ability of some Western groups to monitor developments in the Soviet forest industry and to prepare careful predictions of future development in selected aspects of Soviet forestry of interest to Western producers.

Reports in Western trade journals and publications of government departments and agencies of the United Nations are more accessible than those of private corporations and cover many facets of the Soviet timber and wood-processing industries. These reports also frequently relate to other sectors and areas of concern which impinge upon the economic geography of timber and wood-processing. Trade journals such as *World Wood* and *Pulp and Paper International* contain news items related to specific Soviet capital investments in different sectors of the forest industry plus annual reports or reviews by Soviet and western forest analysts. Reports in such journals are useful capsule summaries but suffer from the confines of short time horizons and the general preoccupation of their readers with facts of immediate rather than long-term significance.

Publications by government agencies, however, frequently accord ample space to penetrating analyses of the Soviet economy and aspects of regional economic development. Seldom the main focus of these reports, the forest industry receives adequate attention as an earner of foreign exchange, a consumer of Western technology, a resource propellent to regional growth, and the *raison d'être* for the continuation of settlement throughout different regions of the taiga.

Few agencies of individual Western governments, however, appear truly comfortable with Soviet forestry. Perhaps this industry lacks the glamor or apparent sophistication of aluminum, chemicals, or fossil fuels in the eyes of government analysts who, despite forest products' role as the second most important earner of foreign exchange for the Soviet Union (after oil), allow their colleagues in the Economic Commission for Europe (ECE) and the Food and Agriculture Organization (FAO) to assume prime responsibility for analysis of Soviet forestry. The United Nations review, "European Timber Trends and Prospects, 1950–2000"[14] fills an important need in the present study by estimating the potential demand for forest products in Europe for the rest of this century and the possible role which North America and the USSR might play in satisfying future world and European timber demands because "they increasingly affect the supply of forest products to Europe."[15] If the predictions of demand in Europe and Japan, the major foreign destinations of Soviet timber, are accepted as valid, then the possible role accorded to Soviet timber supply can be integrated with the present study's estimates of the regional values of Soviet timber available for international sale by 1990.

All four categories of reports on the Soviet timber and wood-processing industries discussed above are rich in the apparent quantity and quality of information they contain. Like all secondary sources, however, they generally contain predigested information on selected topics. Most of these topics do not pay great attention to spatial variations in the forest industry although subjects not of direct economic significance such as those related to regional biological attributes of different timber species receive close attention in Soviet reports at least. None of the categories contains up-to-date economic-geographical analyses of Soviet timber and wood-processing industries. Comprehensive forecasts or scenarios of possible future regional characteristics of these industries are also absent from the existing literature. The present study, therefore, acknowledges the important role which non-spatial factual, analytical, and even speculative presentations of the existing literature play in complementing the present spatial analysis of the Soviet timber and wood-processing industries.

## Data

Problems related to Soviet forest statistics discussed previously by the author[16] have not abated in the interim. Furthermore, occasional statistical handbooks of the 1960s specifically related to Soviet industry have never been included among the publications of official data in the 1970s. Despite the greater general volume of Soviet literature now associated with the forest industry, the availability of "hard" data has declined and the relevant forestry sections of the two most important annual general statistical handbooks, *Narodnoye khozyaistvo SSSR* and *Narodnoye khozyaistvo RSFSR*, have diminished in size. These two publications, however, remain the most important sources of information on the physical volume of regional production by the timber and wood-processing industries.

The handbook *Narodnoye khozyaistvo SSSR v 1979 godu*[17] contains figures for the production of timber, lumber, and paper by union republic; no other products are listed

by union republic, and no data are available for the output of timber or wood products by major economic region or by oblast. Production data for the union republics must be obtained where possible from handbooks published in each republic. Apart from the RSFSR, the republics with important wood-processing industries are the Ukraine, Belorussia, Lithuania, Latvia and Estonia. Difficulty in obtaining ready access to these handbooks compounds the general scarcity of regional production data in the latest USSR and RSFSR handbooks.

The 1978 issue of *Narodnoye khozyaistvo RSFSR*[18] provides production figures only for lumber, plywood, paper, and paperboard in provinces of the Russian Republic, the most important major area for forest-based industries in the USSR. Comprehensive regional analysis of the timber and wood-processing industries, however, requires additional data on the output of commercial timber, roundwood substitutes, chemical and mechanical pulp, matches, particleboard, fiberboard, timber for export, and those items consumed in unprocessed form which constitute one-quarter of the Soviet demand for timber. Regional production of these items must be estimated from fugitive data, i.e., from data appearing incidentally in other sources, or from specific studies of individual industries or regions. Such data are fragmentary and incomplete; they are not subject to the same definitional and methodological rigor or control as those appearing in the official handbooks and are not always identified by year.

Soviet rail freight rates also are found in relatively few published sources; the rates used in this study are different from those previously used by Barr[19] and have been in effect since 1 January 1974.[20] The rail freight costs incurred by Soviet shippers of timber and wood products can be accurately determined for all shipments covered in this paper. The matrix of Soviet interregional rail distances employed in previous analyses[21] is used here and the advent of new feeder lines such as Ivdel-Sergino or Khrebtovaya—Ust-Ilimsk does not affect the accuracy of this matrix. No attempt has been made to forecast changes in the interregional distance matrix which might occur by 1990 following completion of the BAM.

Soviet foreign trade data are published annually and, although publication of some items ceased in the 1970s,[22] data pertaining to timber are adequate for this study. Because the regional origin of export-destined timber is not published in official statistical compilations, this study utilizes data from Kanevsky and Shaitanov[23] for the year 1972. The total amount of timber exported in 1970 and 1975 (the two basic dates used throughout this study) has been allocated among those regions cited by Kanevsky and Shaitanov as exporting timber in 1972. The total estimated amount of timber to be exported in 1990 has also been allocated according to Kanevsky and Shaitanov although the assumption of no change in the relative importance of regions exporting timber is tenuous.

## Methodology and Assumptions

The objectives of this paper require identification for the years 1970, 1975, and 1990 of (1) the regional production of roundwood (and roundwood substitutes) for export, processing, and unprocessed consumption, (2) the optimal interregional shipment patterns of commercial roundwood, and (3) the regional relationship between roundwood (or its equivalent) production and the potential supply of timber.

The first step in the analysis is to determine the volume of production in 87 basic regions of each primary component of the timber and wood-processing industries for 1970 and 1975, and to estimate expected volumes for 1990; for discussion, however, the basic regions (oblasts, krais and ASSRs) are aggregated into larger regional units (described in Barr[24]) whose composition (Fig. 1) differs from the official standard, multipurpose, major economic regions common to Soviet sources but corresponds to all previous work on Soviet forestry published by the author.

Comparability among sectors of the timber and wood-processing industries is achieved by converting all output figures of processed items into roundwood requirements, $m^3(r)$ (Table 1); when the sectors are combined in this form for major regions, they yield regional balances (Table 2) of production and consumption of timber and surplus or deficit in supply and demand.* The national importance of key items in 1979 and 1980 (commercial roundwood) for which data are available is also provided in Table 1. The conversion factors employed in this study have been used in previous works by the author[25] and help ensure that total annual supply equals annual demand. Estimation of the regional composition and distribution of the timber and wood-processing industries for 1990 assumes not only that conversion factors currently in effect will continue to be relevant, but that the Soviet economy will continue to consume and produce the same commodities in 1990 as in 1975.

Although many economic and social priorities ultimately determine the amount of wood which enters a host of manufactured items extending from lumber to pitprops, the demand for timber may, in this paper, be taken as the amount of wood utilized each year in the primary production of wood products and in the preparation of items for final-product use in unprocessed form. Some timber, usually less than five percent of total timber production, is exported as roundwood, and a small amount of wood material is exported in the form of wood chips to Finland and Japan; due to their long-term nature, these activities are assumed to exist through to 1990. The role of Japanese demand for timber and wood products in the development of Soviet Far Eastern forests is the subject of considerable debate, particularly in terms of the extent to which Far Eastern timber will be processed before sale to Japan, and the amount of larch which the Japanese are willing to import. The discussions of these and related topics by Braden[26] and Rodgers[27] are highly germane to the argument presented in the present chapter.

## Timber Production and Demand, 1990

This paper offers a scenario of the 1990 regional composition and distribution of Soviet timber and wood-pro-

cessing industries (Table 3) based on the assumption that the annual increment of growth in domestic supply and demand for roundwood from 1975 to 1990 will correspond to that recorded for the period 1970–75. This scenario envisions for 1990 an aggregate net production (i.e., one that excludes wood chips and mill waste equivalents) of all forms of timber (commercial roundwood, industrial *and household* fuelwood) of 425.16 million $m^3$ (Table 3), and an aggregate demand for commercial roundwood (and equivalent) and industrial fuelwood of 433.45 million $m^3(r)$ (Table 1).

If the annual increment in growth of demand for commercial roundwood (and equivalent) and industrial fuelwood, 1976–90, is assumed to correspond to that recorded in the USSR between 1964 and 1975, then the aggregate demand in 1990 is estimated to be 433.24 million $m^3$. The difference between the two 1990 estimates of demand is less than .05 percent. The 1990 estimate based on the annual increment 1970–75 is utilized here because some of the sectoral changes within the forest industry in this period appear more likely than changes from 1964–75 to extend into the near future.

The period 1970–75, for example, saw impressive increases in production of fiberboard and particleboard as replacements for lumber and plywood, and in consumption of mill residues and industrial fuelwood as substitutes for commercial roundwood in wood-processing. This period was associated with relatively small increases in the output of lumber, plywood, and wood pulp. Consequently, although the 1990 national aggregate demand by the timber and wood-processing industries can be estimated accurately on the basis of national change in each sector for either 1964–75 or 1970–75, different relative emphasis on the component sectors of the timber and wood-processing industries in each period affects the level of demand expected for each region in 1990. Those regions displaying the greatest increment 1970–75 feature most prominently in the estimates of regional change, 1975–90. Estimation of 1990 on the basis of the period 1964–75 instead of 1970–75, therefore, would have included major past changes in industries which are now receiving low investment priority.[28]

In the second stage of analysis, regional surpluses and deficits in timber supply are incorporated into the transportation problem of linear programming (Table 4) to obtain optimal flow patterns of roundwood for 1970, 1975, and 1990.[29] These optimal solutions serve a normative function for each year because they indicate how roundwood should move if there were no differences in the quality of wood, in the species of timber required by consumers, and in the agencies responsible for producing and consuming roundwood. This form of linear programming also assumes that the objective of the system is to optimize the flow of commodities by minimizing the total cost of transportation. The optimal patterns derived here assume that all roundwood moves by rail; in reality, however, of the timber hauled out of the forest by the Ministry of Timber and Wood Processing in 1974, 33 percent moved to the railway, 39 percent to waterways, and 28 percent directly to consumers (this form does not likely affect interregional shipments).[30] The relative importance, however, of hauls to the railway and directly to

---

*The sources employed to derive Tables 1 and 2 are listed in the appendix.

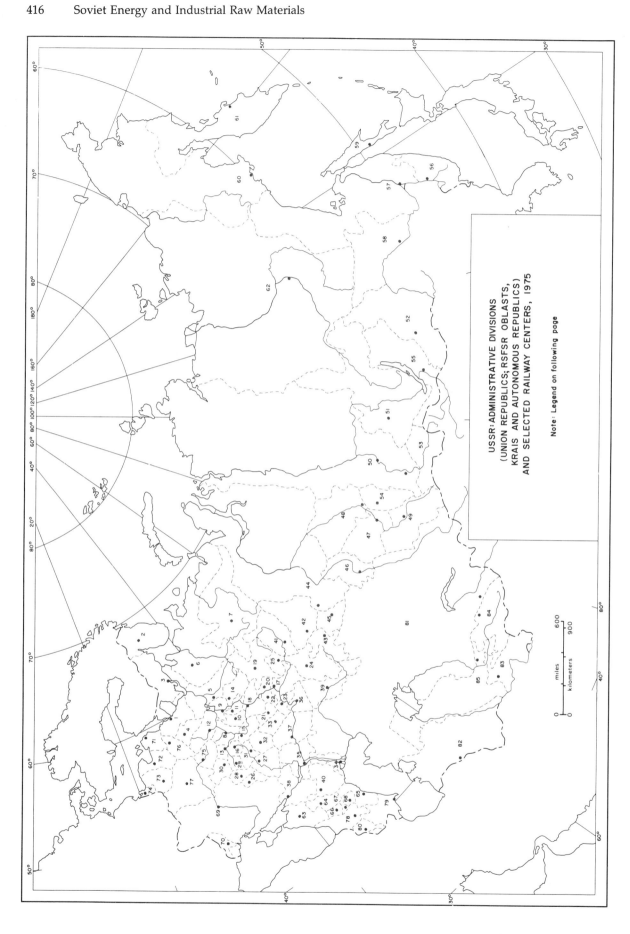

USSR: ADMINISTRATIVE DIVISIONS
(UNION REPUBLICS; RSFSR OBLASTS,
KRAIS AND AUTONOMOUS REPUBLICS)
AND SELECTED RAILWAY CENTERS, 1975

Note: Legend on following page

Figure 1
Regions, Republics, Administrative Divisions, and Centers Used for Measuring Rail Distances
(Numbers correspond to divisions on Figure 1. Names in bold face type are regional aggregations
used in the study.)

| Administrative Division | Number on Map | Rail Center | Administrative Division | Number on Map | Rail Center |
|---|---|---|---|---|---|
| **Northwest** | | | **West Siberia** | | |
| Leningrad Obl. | 1 | Leningrad | Omsk Obl. | 46 | Omsk |
| Murmansk Obl. | 2 | Kirovsk | Novosibirsk Obl. | 47 | Novosibirsk |
| Karelian ASSR | 3 | Medvezhegorsk | Tomsk Obl. | 48 | Tomsk |
| Novgorod Obl. | 4 | Novgorod | Altai Krai | 49 | Barnaul |
| Vologda Obl. | 5 | Vologda | **Central Siberia** | | |
| Arkhangelsk Obl. | 6 | Plesetsk | Krasnoyarsk Krai | 50 | Krasnoyarsk |
| Komi ASSR | 7 | Ukhta | Irkutsk Obl. | 51 | Taishet |
| Moscow Obl. | 8 | Moscow | Chita Obl. | 52 | Chita |
| Yaroslavl Obl. | 9 | Yaroslavl | Tuva ASSR | 53 | Abakan |
| Vladimir Obl. | 10 | Vladimir | Kemerovo Obl. | 54 | Kemerovo |
| Ivanovo Obl. | 11 | Ivanovo | Buryat ASSR | 55 | Ulan-Ude |
| Kalinin Obl. | 12 | Kalinin | **Far East** | | |
| Kaluga Obl. | 13 | Kaluga | Maritime Krai | 56 | Iman |
| Kostroma Obl. | 14 | Galich | Khabarovsk Krai | 57 | Khabarovsk |
| Ryazan Obl. | 15 | Ryazan | Amur Obl. | 58 | Belogorsk |
| Tula Obl. | 16 | Tula | Sakhalin Obl. | 59 | Uglegorsk |
| **Volga—West Urals** | | | **Siberian North** | | |
| Tatar ASSR | 17 | Kazan | Magadan Obl. | 60 | Magadan |
| Gorky Obl. | 18 | Gorky | Kamchatka Obl. | 61 | Ust-Kamchatsk |
| Kirov Obl. | 19 | Kirov | Yakut ASSR | 62 | Yakutsk |
| Mari ASSR | 20 | Ioshkar-Ola | **North Caucasus** | | |
| Mordvinian ASSR | 21 | Saransk | Krasnodar Krai | 63 | Krasnodar |
| Chuvash ASSR | 22 | Kanash | Stavropol Krai | 64 | Stavropol |
| Ulyanovsk Obl. | 23 | Ulyanovsk | Dagestan ASSR | 65 | Makhachkala |
| Bashkir ASSR | 24 | Ufa | Kabardinian-Balk. ASSR | 66 | Nalchik |
| Udmurt ASSR | 25 | Izhevsk | North Osetian ASSR | 67 | Ordzhonikidze |
| **Chernozem** | | | Chechen-Ingush ASSR | 68 | Grozny |
| Belgorod Obl. | 26 | Belgorod | **Southwest** | | |
| Voronezh Obl. | 27 | Voronezh | Ukraine | 69 | Kiev |
| Kursk Obl. | 28 | Kursk | Moldavia | 70 | Kishinev |
| Orel Obl. | 29 | Orel | **West** | | |
| Bryansk Obl. | 30 | Bryansk | Estonia | 71 | Tallinn |
| Lipetsk Obl. | 31 | Lipetsk | Latvia | 72 | Riga |
| Tambov Obl. | 32 | Tambov | Lithuania | 73 | Kaunas |
| Penza Obl. | 33 | Penza | Kaliningrad Obl. | 74 | Kaliningrad |
| **South Volga** | | | Smolensk Obl. | 75 | Smolensk |
| Astrakhan Obl. | 34 | Astrakhan | Pskov Obl. | 76 | Pskov |
| Volgograd Obl. | 35 | Volgograd | Belorussia | 77 | Minsk |
| Kuibyshev Obl. | 36 | Kuibyshev | **Caucasus** | | |
| Saratov Obl. | 37 | Saratov | Georgia | 78 | Tbilisi |
| Rostov Obl. | 38 | Rostov | Azerbaijan | 79 | Baku |
| Orenburg Obl. | 39 | Orenburg | Armenia | 80 | Yerevan |
| Kalmyk ASSR | 40 | Elista | **Central Asia** | | |
| **Urals** | | | Kazakhstan | 81 | Alma-Ata |
| Perm Obl. | 41 | Perm | Turkmenistan | 82 | Ashkhabad |
| Sverdlovsk Obl. | 42 | Sverdlovsk | Tadzhikistan | 83 | Dushanbe |
| Chelyabinsk Obl. | 43 | Chelyabinsk | Kirghizia | 84 | Frunze |
| Tyumen Obl. | 44 | Tyumen | Uzbekistan | 85 | Tashkent |
| Kurgan Obl. | 45 | Kurgan | | | |

consumers has increased since 1965 at the expense of hauls to waterways; in some eastern regions such as Tyumen Oblast where new railways have gone into operation (e.g., Ivdel-Sergino and Tavda-Sotnik), the proportion of timber hauled to the railway system by the Ministry was 47 percent in 1974, but that hauled to waterways was only 22 percent. These figures show that the relative importance of rail-borne timber movement varies among regions but that it seems to be increasing significantly as railways are extended into developing timber regions and as recent environmental protection legislation curtails the traditional forms of free-floating river drives of timber. Nevertheless, the optimal shipment patterns presented in this study differ considerably from reality by assuming that rail freight rates adequately reflect the cost of all interregional movement of roundwood.

The final stage of analysis compares estimated 1990 regional demand with potential regional ability to supply timber. Potential supply is deemed to be synonymous with mean annual increment of the growing stock reported for each basic region. Estimates of potential supply do not take account of variation in demand for particular species by domestic or international consumers of Soviet timber; data are not available on which to base realistic estimates of regional differences in the utilization of individual timber species, or the impact on wood-processing of variation in the locational characteristics of different species (Tables 5 and 6). This study assumes, therefore, that the general predominance of larch in East Siberian and Far Eastern forests will not adversely affect the general future utilization of these forests, that domestic utilization of larch for structural, pulping and peeling purposes will continue to expand in the USSR to offset shortfalls in the production of other coniferous species, and that coniferous species other than larch will dominate sales to such export markets as Japan.

Most of the stringent assumptions required in this study could be alleviated to some extent in future research if sufficient funds were made available to probe

TABLE 1
USSR Timber Supply and Demand

| Item | 1970 Volume (roundwood equivalent m³ (r) × 10³) | Percent of Total | 1975 Volume (roundwood equivalent m³ (r) × 10³) | Percent of Total | 1979 Volume (roundwood equivalent m³ (r) × 10³) | Percent of Total | Estimated 1990 Volume (roundwood equivalent m³ (r) × 10³) | Percent of Total |
|---|---|---|---|---|---|---|---|---|
| Supply | | | | | (1980: 275,000.00) | | | |
| Commercial roundwood | 298,548.00 | 93.1 | 312,902.00 | 89.7 | 273,000.00 | 82.9 | 355,964.00 | 82.1 |
| Industrial fuelwood | 12,600.00 | 3.9 | 22,200.00 | 6.4 | 56,000.00 | 17.0 | 51,000.00 | 11.8 |
| Wood chips and mill waste | 9,000.00 | 2.8 | 13,300.00 | 3.8 | | | 26,200.00 | 6.0 |
| Imported roundwood | 468.30 | .2 | 286.17 | .1 | 207.90 | .1 | 286.17 | .1 |
| Total supply | 320,616.30 | 100.0 | 348,688.17 | 100.0 | 329,207.90 | 100.0 | 433,450.17 | 100.0 |
| Total supply for domestic consumption | 305,316.30 | 95.2 | 331,819.17 | 95.1 | 313,982.90 | 95.4 | 411,327.78 | 94.9 |
| Demand | | | | | | | | |
| Lumber | 176,636.46 | 55.1 | 176,346.94 | 50.6 | 153,384.00 | 46.6 | 175,478.38 | 40.5 |
| Plywood | 6,462.20 | 2.0 | 6,950.10 | 2.0 | 6,282.10 | 1.9 | 8,413.80 | 1.9 |
| Chemical pulp | 25,036.55 | 7.8 | 33,516.00 | 9.6 | 34,530.30 | 10.5 | 58,954.35 | 13.6 |
| Groundwood pulp | 4,011.75 | 1.3 | 4,206.00 | 1.2 | — | — | 4,788.85 | 1.1 |
| Sleepers | 9,623.53 | 3.0 | 9,741.18 | 2.8 | — | — | 10,094.13 | 2.3 |
| Matches | 936.17 | .3 | 1,104.93 | .3 | — | — | 1,611.21 | .4 |
| Fiberboard | 395.77 | .1 | 779.00 | .2 | 893.00 | .3 | 1,928.69 | .4 |
| Particleboard | 2,592.72 | .8 | 5,144.10 | 1.5 | 6,103.50 | 1.9 | 12,798.24 | 3.0 |
| Subtotal: Major wood-processing industries | 225,695.15 | 70.4 | 237,788.25 | 68.2 | — | — | 274,067.55 | 63.2 |
| Tanning-extractive material | 900.00 | .3 | 1,012.50 | .3 | — | — | 1,350.00 | .3 |
| Material for processing acetic acid | 800.00 | .3 | 800.00 | .2 | — | — | 800.00 | .2 |
| Packing wood | 8,000.00 | 2.5 | 9,142.88 | 2.6 | — | — | 12,571.52 | 2.9 |
| Pitprops | 18,000.00 | 5.6 | 14,300.00 | 4.1 | — | — | 3,200.00 | .7 |
| Poles | 5,600.00 | 1.7 | 6,272.00 | 1.8 | — | — | 8,280.00 | 1.9 |
| Ship and marine timber | 2,400.00 | .7 | 2,400.00 | .7 | — | — | 2,400.00 | .6 |
| Construction and miscellaneous timber | 43,921.15 | 13.7 | 60,103.54 | 17.2 | — | — | 108,650.71 | 25.1 |
| Subtotal: Other uses | 79,621.15 | 24.8 | 94,030.92 | 26.9 | — | — | 137,260.23 | 31.7 |
| Roundwood export | 15,300.00 | 4.8 | 16,869.00 | 4.9 | 15,225.00 | 4.6 | 22,122.39 | 5.1 |
| Total demand | 320,616.30 | 100.0 | 348,688.17 | 100.0 | 329,207.90 | 100.0 | 433,450.17 | 100.0 |
| Total domestic demand | 305,316.30 | 95.2 | 331,819.17 | 95.1 | 313,982.90 | 95.4 | 411,327.78 | 94.9 |

Sources are listed in Appendix I.

into individual characteristics of the Soviet timber and wood-processing industries through case studies of regional variation in the relative importance of rail versus water shipment of timber or in the utilization of different timber species in particular industries (e.g., consumption of birch and poplar in the plywood industry). The general need for these assumptions—caused by the lack of sufficient data outside the Soviet Union to support penetrating analyses of regional variation in important phenomena throughout the country—likely will continue as long as Soviet authorities restrict the free dissemination of hard data related to the locational characteristics of the timber and wood-processing industries.

## Timber Supply

### Timber Reserves

Soviet timber reserves primarily consist of coniferous species (Table 5) and are predominantly located in the European Northwest and North, the Urals, Western and Eastern Siberia, and the Far East[31] (Table 6). Forests in the European Soviet Union have traditionally been overcut although they have the greatest amount of reforestation. Forests in Siberia are remote, relatively inaccessible, and dominated in the eastern districts by larch. Forests in the European USSR supported initial development of wood-processing and have continued to be associated with the greatest regional concentrations of wood-processing although development plans officially emphasize the gradual curtailment of some processing activity in European USSR and the expansion of large, capital-intensive operations closer to the location of untapped forest reserves in the North and Siberia. The accessible forests of European USSR are characterized by significant proportions of immature stands of conifers and of major stands of deciduous species. The deciduous species are frequently described as a hindrance to loggers and are abused on site or ignored although they represent significant raw materials for production of furniture, plywood, matches, and particleboard. Although deciduous species are currently disparaged by consumers of wood, they do comprise a significant potential source of wood material if tastes and technology change in the future. Nevertheless, many sites previously devoted to deciduous species are replanted after harvesting with coniferous seedlings.

Most of the demand for roundwood in the USSR is directed toward coniferous species which are primarily found in the taiga (Figures 2 and 3) extending across the northern regions of European USSR and diagonally toward the south across Siberia and the Far East. Most of the USSR's mature timber is concentrated in Siberia and the Far East. In the European-Uralian regions of the country, 80 percent of the mature timber is found in the European North and the Urals.[32] The western regions of the USSR, excluding the northern realm, have the highest growth rates in the country (approximately twice the national average of 1.35m$^3$/ha.) but have the lowest relative share of mature timber due to past and current heavy rates of utilization. The average age of all USSR stands is

101 years but that of coniferous species is 116 years.[33] The prevailing age of mature coniferous forests in the European north and Siberia is 150 to 250 years which attests to the decadence of many stands. This decadence is especially characterized by low annual growth increments and poor quality of timber containing serious defects.[34]

Changes in the utilization of forests and the manner of their regeneration are evident from comparison of the 1966 and 1973 forest inventories.[35] The volume of mature coniferous timber declined but that of deciduous stands increased; the forested area, however, increased mainly due to the expansion of coniferous forests of which one-third were comprised of pines. The volume of cutting in Group 1 forests (USSR forest groups are defined in Table 5) increased by 35 percent and now makes up approximately 15 percent of the total volume of timber supplied for domestic consumption; the volume of cutting in Group 2 forests declined in the 1970s but that in Group 3 forests remained practically unchanged. Group 2 and 3 forests, however, are not uniformly accessible and only 56 percent of their volume can be described as accessible or currently capable of exploitation.

Soviet forest resources are characterized by great regional disparities in composition, age, and volume and offer different possibilities and challenges for development. Northern and eastern forests are dominated by conifers and mature to overmature stands; they need to be cut and scientifically replanted to grow and to have future utility. European forests generally have been overcut, are dominated by juvenile and immature stands, contain important reserves of deciduous timber, and offer the best possibilities for rapid regeneration and improvement given good management. Soviet administrators in Karelia, for example, justify the relatively expensive harvesting of timber from thinnings and improvement cuttings for commercial use by saying that "this work is more costly than basic-use (mature trees) cutting but is much cheaper than it is to bring in wood from the country's eastern regions. It is urgently necessary that comprehensive enterprises operating on the principles of continuous forest use be set up in Karelia."[36] Most demand for Soviet timber is concentrated in forest-deficient European regions and beyond the western borders of the USSR; the Soviet Union is meeting this demand with active regeneration of European forests and shipments to these markets from the North and Siberia. If petroleum should decline in relative importance as an earner of foreign exchange by 1990, the Soviet Union could conceivably embark upon even greater efforts to regenerate European forests to support domestic and foreign demand for timber beyond 1990 but meet many of the needs for timber during the remainder of this century and in the early years of the next one with greater amounts of timber from the European North, Siberia, and the Far East.[37]

### Timber Import

Soviet imports of roundwood (Table 1) have traditionally consisted of exotic tropical hardwoods consumed in the specialized woodworking industries of industrial European USSR. Such wood is of no consequence to the estimates presented in this study. Recently, however, the Soviet Union has been purchasing coniferous round-wood from Mongolia[38] and this study assumed that Mongolian roundwood is consumed in Buryatia, the point of entry, and will reach approximately 107,000 m³ in 1990.

Soviet imports of roundwood, traditionally small, were estimated for 1990 in Table 1 to correspond to those recorded for 1975. Import of roundwood in the late 1970s declined temporarily, but rose again in the early 1980s.[39] Soviet purchases of roundwood from Mongolia appeared to stabilize in 1978;[40] the locational significance of these forests to the USSR is likely to be enhanced in the 1980s as the quality of timber harvested from accessible forests in southern Siberia declines. Other provinces in southern Siberia regularly obtain extra-regional roundwood— 200,000 m³ per annum in the 1970s, primarily pulpwood and pitprops—from the Soviet Far East.[41]

## Timber Consumption

### Policies and Practices

Utilization of Soviet forests appears foremost to be conditioned by the investment priorities and decisions associated with domestic timber consumption in the USSR. Utilization of timber in the USSR is not constrained by the physical availability of timber but rather by the ability of the domestic economy to absorb wood in manufacturing or in direct end-product consumption. Although many economic and social priorities ultimately determine the amount of wood which enters a host of

manufactured items extending from lumber to pitprops, the *demand* for timber may, in this paper, be taken as the amount of wood utilized each year in the primary production of wood products and in the preparation of items for final-product use in unprocessed form. Furthermore, some timber, usually less than 5 percent of total timber production, is exported as roundwood; a small amount of wood material is exported in the form of wood chips and other mill residues to Finland and Japan.[42] The sale of all forms of roundwood and mill residues to Finland declined in the late 1970s, recovering again in the 1980s[43] and the import of chemical pulp, papers and paperboards from Finland generally increased. These shifts in trade appear to reflect shortages of timber, wood fiber, and semi-manufactured paper products in the European USSR.

The sale of roundwood, including pulpwood, to Japan declined in the late 1970s and early 1980s, but the sale of Soviet lumber and mill residues to that country generally held steady or increased.[44] These changes in the mix of Soviet timber and wood products sold to Japan appear to reflect the ability of Soviet Far Eastern forests to meet the demand for timber in Pacific export markets, and year-to-year changes in the levels of foreign demand appear mainly to affect the volumes of specific types of timber and wood products. Further development of the timber and wood-processing industries of Siberia and the Soviet Far East is envisaged in the guidelines of the 11th Five-Year Plan although no specific projects are mentioned in it[45] or in a major review of projects slated to commence operation in 1981.[46]

Policies governing the utilization of timber in the Soviet Union seek to ensure conversion of an ever-increasing

TABLE 2
Regional Surpluses and Deficits of Timber for Domestic Consumption (m³ (r) × 10³)

| Regions | 1970 Timber Supply | Percent of Total | 1970 Timber Demand | Percent of Total | Surplus | Deficit | 1975 Timber Supply | Percent of Total | 1975 Timber Demand | Percent of Total | Surplus | Deficit |
|---|---|---|---|---|---|---|---|---|---|---|---|---|
| USSR | 305,316 | 100.0 | 305,316 | 100.0 | — | — | 331,819 | 100.0 | 331,819 | 100.0 | — | — |
| RSFSR | 282,688 | 92.6 | 238,168 | 78.0 | 44,519 | — | 309,420 | 93.2 | 262,463 | 79.1 | 46,956 | — |
| Northwest | 26,403 | 8.7 | 23,668 | 7.7 | 2,735 | — | 26,838 | 8.1 | 25,809 | 7.8 | 1,019 | — |
| European North | 59,876 | 19.6 | 27,108 | 8.9 | 32,768 | — | 68,903 | 20.8 | 32,407 | 9.7 | 36,497 | — |
| Central Russia | 16,172 | 5.3 | 20,349 | 6.6 | — | 4,178 | 17,528 | 5.3 | 21,814 | 6.6 | — | 4,286 |
| Volga-W. Urals | 31,692 | 10.4 | 33,854 | 11.1 | — | 2,162 | 33,690 | 10.2 | 36,504 | 11.0 | — | 2,814 |
| Chernozem | 2,900 | .9 | 5,846 | 1.9 | — | 2,946 | 3,143 | .9 | 5,974 | 1.8 | — | 2,831 |
| S. Volga | 1,005 | .3 | 11,822 | 3.9 | — | 10,817 | 996 | .3 | 12,447 | 3.8 | — | 11,451 |
| Urals | 54,570 | 17.9 | 35,584 | 11.7 | 18,986 | — | 58,352 | 17.6 | 40,688 | 12.2 | 17,664 | — |
| W. Siberia | 10,700 | 3.5 | 10,096 | 3.3 | 604 | — | 11,300 | 3.4 | 10,561 | 3.2 | 739 | — |
| C. Siberia | 57,289 | 18.8 | 42,474 | 13.9 | 14,815 | — | 64,590 | 19.5 | 47,986 | 14.5 | 16,605 | — |
| Far East | 14,161 | 4.6 | 14,544 | 4.8 | — | 383 | 16,676 | 5.0 | 15,373 | 4.6 | 1,302 | — |
| Siberian North | 2,469 | .8 | 2,156 | .7 | 313 | — | 2,242 | .6 | 2,239 | .7 | 3 | — |
| N. Caucasus | 2,605 | .8 | 6,295 | 2.1 | — | 3,689 | 2,117 | .6 | 6,185 | 1.9 | — | 4,069 |
| Southwest | 7,825 | 2.6 | 35,140 | 11.5 | — | 27,315 | 8,979 | 2.7 | 36,112 | 10.9 | — | 27,133 |
| West* | 15,606 | 5.1 | 21,686 | 7.1 | — | 6,080 | 13,990 | 4.2 | 22,716 | 6.8 | — | 8,726 |
| Caucasus | 513 | .2 | 3,099 | 1.0 | — | 2,586 | 452 | .1 | 3,062 | .9 | — | 2,610 |
| Central Asia | 1,530 | .5 | 11,595 | 3.8 | — | 10,065 | 2,033 | .6 | 11,942 | 3.6 | — | 9,909 |
| SUM of Regional Units | | | | | 70,221 | 70,221 | | | | | 73,829 | 73,829 |
| SUM of Regional Subunits (Oblasts, Krais, and ASSR's) | | | | | 94,161 | 94,161 | | | | | 96,782 | 96,782 |

*The West includes Kaliningrad, Pskov, and Smolensk oblasts of the RSFSR.
Sources are listed in Appendix I.

proportion of domestic roundwood production (commercial timber and fuelwood) into wood products or commercial end-products but also envisage that the total gross annual consumption of roundwood by the domestic economy will decrease. The annual output of roundwood steadily decreased after the early 1970s to a total of 354 million m$^3$ in 1979, a volume equal to that produced annually in the late 1950s. It recovered slightly to 357 million m$^3$ in 1980. The volume of commercial roundwood, 273 million m$^3$, in 1979 (Table 1) was equivalent to that of 1965, but the volume of fuelwood (78.1 million m$^3$) was similar to that reported in the early 1930s.[47] The general decline in output of roundwood reduces the volume of timber production estimated for 1990 in Table 1 but probably will affect to a lesser degree the increases expected in wood products as roundwood substitutes become more important in the USSR and as the efficiencies of roundwood conversion improve with the installation of more efficient equipment. A smaller gross output of roundwood, however, suggests that the pressure on Soviet reserves is decreasing and that many forces, both positive (technological change) and negative (labor shortages, managerial ineptitude, and transportation bottlenecks) are affecting the timber and wood-processing industries.

The forms of wood material being consumed by the processing industries increasingly reflect the desire by Soviet foresters to utilize mill residues in the form of wood chips and to divert usable forms of fuelwood into the industrial sector for processing. Consumption policies also emphasize the need to consume more deciduous softwoods and the major eastern conifer, larch, to relieve the pressure on the major commercial coniferous forests which are overcut in many regions. Consumption of wood in unprocessed form is presently in a state of flux. Furthermore, the 11th Five-Year Plan[48] calls for the increased production (output) of chemical pulp and other semi-manufactured forest products, presumably at the expense of unprocessed forms of timber consumption.

These policies governing the consumption of timber, of course, affect regional levels of timber harvesting in the USSR. By placing greater capital investment in the utilization of mill residues, Soviet foresters reduce the need to fell more roundwood in peripheral regions and can increase the amount of wood fiber recovered from existing logging operations. Greater utilization of mill residues and substandard sizes of timber (fuelwood) delays the advent of logging operations in presently inaccessible areas of the European North, Siberia and the Far East. More efficient use of timber supplies from present areas of timber harvesting also reduces the need to transfer greater amounts of roundwood over the major trunk railroad lines connecting regions of forest surplus with those having timber deficits. By alleviating the intensity of wood flows over major connecting railways in this manner, the Soviet Union reduces the need to divert capital into new settlements and infrastructure of all types in difficult northern and eastern environments. Furthermore, by increasing the efficiency of wood utilization in established regions of logging operations, capital can be diverted from high-cost greenfield wood-converting projects into more economical measures associated with expansion of existing manufacturing operations. The literature is replete with examples supporting the hypothesis that the pace of development of timber harvesting and wood conversion in northern and eastern regions is being held to manageable proportions by greater emphasis on comprehensive utilization of existing timber supplies in established regions.

Soviet policy-makers are also groping with the dilemma posed by large stocks of deciduous species in European forests and the great proportion of larch in eastern forests. More intensive use of birch, poplar and aspen, for example, could further obviate the need to harvest greater amounts of timber of all species in the north and Siberia. The direct impact of greater emphasis on deciduous species, however, can only be inferred from fragmentary data because statistics on the regional production of timber by species are not published in the USSR. Suggestions by leading Soviet forest specialists, however, indicate that investment planners and decision makers are increasingly becoming aware of the savings inherent in utilization of deciduous species in regions accessible to the existing transportation and settlement systems of the USSR. The 11th Five-Year Plan[49] emphasizes the need to make fuller use of the Soviet European growing stock and to carry out more comprehensive conversion of all roundwood and wood fiber.

Emphasis on European and accessible Asian regions, however, neatly sidesteps many problems and advantages associated with utilization of the predominantly larch forests of Eastern Siberia and the Far East. One of the major obstacles facing development of the larch forests is the propensity of larch to sink when rafted. On

| 1990 Timber Supply | Percent of Total | 1990 Timber Demand | Percent of Total | Surplus | Deficit |
|---|---|---|---|---|---|
| 411,328 | 100.0 | 411,328 | 100.0 | — | — |
| 389,386 | 94.7 | 335,375 | 81.5 | 54,011 | — |
| 27,956 | 6.8 | 32,230 | 7.8 | — | 4,274 |
| 95,906 | 23.3 | 48,303 | 11.7 | 47,603 | — |
| 21,581 | 5.3 | 26,209 | 6.4 | — | 4,629 |
| 39,646 | 9.6 | 44,453 | 10.8 | — | 4,807 |
| 3,874 | .9 | 6,359 | 1.5 | — | 2,486 |
| 967 | .2 | 14,320 | 3.5 | — | 13,353 |
| 69,676 | 16.9 | 56,001 | 13.6 | 13,676 | — |
| 13,100 | 3.2 | 11,959 | 2.9 | 1,141 | — |
| 86,196 | 21.0 | 64,521 | 15.7 | 21,675 | — |
| 25,100 | 6.1 | 17,862 | 4.4 | 7,238 | — |
| 1,556 | .4 | 2,488 | .6 | — | 931 |
| 617 | .2 | 5,858 | 1.4 | — | 5,242 |
| 12,319 | 3.0 | 39,028 | 9.5 | — | 26,709 |
| 9,024 | 2.2 | 25,806 | 6.3 | — | 16,782 |
| 269 | .1 | 2,950 | .7 | — | 2,681 |
| 3,541 | .8 | 12,981 | 3.2 | — | 9,439 |
| | | | | 91,333 | 91,333 |
| | | | | 115,184 | 115,184 |

the other hand, although larch is not a prime component in the manufacture of plywood, pulp or lumber, it is utilized in the production of railway sleepers, pitprops, poles, construction wood, and packing wood, and can be utilized in the production of wood pulp.

Furthermore, because most of the coniferous stands, dominated by larch, in eastern forests are mature and overmature (Table 6), timber development in these forests could disregard the general need to achieve a balance between annual increment and annual cut and could greatly exceed the constraints imposed by the need for sustained yield cutting in established forests. (This is already occurring along the Ivdel-Sergino and Tavda-Sotnik railways in Tyumen Oblast.)[50] The immediate advantage offered by these eastern forests is their heavy proportion of timber which needs to be cut now. Eastern forests have, therefore, a greater potential for development in the near and intermediate-term future than appears from the statistics on mean annual increment because so much of their actual growing stock is currently mature and overmature and is contributing very little to the annual growth of new wood fiber in the Soviet Union. These forests, therefore, can sustain cutting in this century at levels far surpassing their current mean annual increment and can play a significant role in the next century if they are replanted to ensure perpetual harvesting through the techniques of sustained-yield forest management.

The nature of present and future demand for larch by world and domestic markets, however, is far from certain and is beyond the scope of this paper. Development of the timber industries in these forests is limited by the low volume and annual increment per unit area of actual growing stock, the traditional preference of consumers for pine, spruce, and fir, the cost of overcoming environmental constraints, the existence of strong socio-perceptual biases toward the east by Soviet workers, the cost of shipping timber in raw or processed forms by land to market, the investment alternatives posed by other forest regions, and the competition for investment capital by other sectors of the Soviet economy. Most of these obstacles would still exist if eastern forests contained other coniferous species, and may be taken as general regional constraints rather than as limitations related specifically to larch.

Soviet wood utilization policies are, therefore, increasingly becoming more region-specific and reflect a growing awareness that wood consumption policies should take into account the different species and overall characteristics associated with the major regional forests. The acuity, impact, and authority of such wood-consumption policies, however, are reduced by continual shortages of investment capital in the timber and wood-processing industries which encourage a multitude of expedient measures designed to maintain timber production by overcutting accessible timber stands and by con-

TABLE 3

Estimated Net Regional Production of Timber, 1990 (excludes imported roundwood or domestic wood chips or millwaste but includes household fuelwood)

| Regions | (1) Total Commercial Timber Cut | | (2) Commercial Timber Cut for Export | | (3) Industrial and Household Fuelwood Cut | | (4) Total Annual Timber Cut (1) + (3) | |
|---|---|---|---|---|---|---|---|---|
| | $m^3 \times 10^3$ | % of Total | $m^3 \times 10^3$ | % of Total | $m^3 \times 10^3$ | % of Total | $m^3 \times 10^3$ | % of Total |
| USSR | 355,964 | 100.0 | 22,122 | 100.0 | 69,195 | 100.0 | 425,159 | 100.0 |
| RSFSR | 337,326 | 94.8 | 21,901 | 99.0 | 66,668 | 96.3 | 403,994 | 95.0 |
| Northwest | 16,900 | 4.7 | 3,252 | 14.7 | 10,020 | 14.5 | 26,920 | 6.3 |
| European North | 68,895 | 19.3 | 3,274 | 14.8 | 21,350 | 30.8 | 90,245 | 21.2 |
| Central Russia | 22,200 | 6.2 | 619 | 2.8 | 4,800 | 6.9 | 27,000 | 6.4 |
| Volga-W. Urals | 35,100 | 9.9 | 1,571 | 7.1 | 4,910 | 7.1 | 40,010 | 9.4 |
| Chernozem | 3,600 | 1.0 | | | 181 | .3 | 3,781 | .9 |
| S. Volga | 900 | .3 | | | 44 | .1 | 944 | .2 |
| Urals | 63,200 | 17.8 | 885 | 4.0 | 9,360 | 13.5 | 72,560 | 17.1 |
| W. Siberia | 13,100 | 3.7 | | | 2,900 | 4.2 | 16,000 | 3.8 |
| C. Siberia | 75,100 | 21.1 | 2,212 | 10.0 | 10,448 | 15.1 | 85,548 | 20.1 |
| Far East | 34,000 | 9.6 | 9,955 | 45.0 | 1,462 | 2.1 | 35,462 | 8.3 |
| Siberian North | 1,200 | .3 | 133 | .6 | 613 | .9 | 1,813 | .5 |
| N. Caucasus | 600 | .2 | | | | | 600 | .1 |
| Southwest | 9,828 | 2.8 | 44 | .2 | 1,728 | 2.5 | 11,556 | 2.7 |
| West[a] | 8,457 | 2.3 | 177 | .8 | 580 | .8 | 9,037 | 2.1 |
| Caucasus | 269 | .1 | | | 40 | .1 | 309 | .1 |
| Central Asia | 2,615 | .7 | | | 759 | 1.1 | 3,374 | .8 |

[a]The West includes Kaliningrad, Pskov, and Smolensk oblasts of the RSFSR.
[b]Includes forests of all forestry and non-forestry ministries and administrations.
SOURCES: The data in this table are derived from the sources listed in the Appendix for Tables 1 and 2.

tinuing to utilize inefficient and obsolete processing facilities in established regions. Policies which attempt to bring about improvement in timber utilization and the composition of species harvested often conflict with practices of expediency necessitated by shortages of investment capital and by the need to maintain current production levels despite the potential for more economical production in other regions and the possibility that continuation of numerous current practices may cause irreparable long-term damage to the forest resources of established regions.

Domestic Demand

This study derives the national structure of consumption of roundwood and mill residues for 1970 and 1975 from physical output data pertaining to each wood product and each form of roundwood consumed directly in unprocessed form, and estimates the national structure expected for 1990 (Table 1) on the basis of change in consumption of each wood product and final-demand item between 1970 and 1975 (discussed above). The data in these tables show that the Soviet Union is steadily increasing its substitution of mill residues and industrial fuelwood for commercial roundwood and that these two substitutes will account for nearly one-fifth of total wood supply by 1990. The net demand for commercial roundwood and both forms of fuelwood (Table 3) and the

decline of gross annual timber output in the 1970s strongly suggest that the total consumption of roundwood in the near future will remain substantially below the figures for mean annual increment of 520 million m$^3$ estimated by Solecki[51] or of 618 million m$^3$ estimated by Holowacz.[52]

The output mix of wood products and wood used directly by final consumers will change by 1990; the production of lumber and sleepers will decline relative to the output of particleboard, fiberboard, and chemical pulp. Of the roundwood used directly, only the consumption of construction wood (wood consumed during construction in unprocessed form) will increase substantially. Most other forms of roundwood used directly or in processed form will not change markedly in their relative national importance.

The output mix presented for 1990 contains subtle yet important changes from earlier years; many of these changes assume a special importance when based on the 1964 output mix[53] or when compared with estimates of the mix in 1956 and 1960.[54] The sheer size of the total demand for industrial roundwood, for example, ensures that change in demand for any item during any five-year period will not dramatically alter the relative importance of that item in the national consumption pattern. Nevertheless, steady overall change is underway in the USSR and clearly relates to the growing importance of commercial roundwood substitutes and substitutes for

| (5) Forested Area (1973) | | (6) Actual Growing Stock$^b$ (1973) | | (7) Annual Increment of Principal Species | | Total Annual Timber Cut as a Percent of Annual Increment of Principal Species |
|---|---|---|---|---|---|---|
| ha × 10$^6$ | % of Total | m$^3$ × 10$^6$ | % of Total | m$^3$ × 10$^3$ | % of Total | (4) as % of (7) |
| 769,800 | 100.0 | 81,780 | 100.0 | 1,023,379 | 100.0 | 42 |
| 728,000 | 94.6 | 78,510 | 96.0 | 940,527 | 91.9 | 43 |
| 20,577 | 2.7 | 2,058 | 2.5 | 27,858 | 2.7 | 97 |
| 60,940 | 7.9 | 6,431 | 7.9 | 64,580 | 6.3 | 140 |
| 15,385 | 2.0 | 1,721 | 2.1 | 45,077 | 4.4 | 60 |
| 21,199 | 2.8 | 2,450 | 3.0 | 51,627 | 5.0 | 77 |
| 3,488 | .5 | 386 | .5 | 11,232 | 1.1 | 34 |
| 2,468 | .3 | 178 | .2 | 6,492 | .6 | 15 |
| 73,468 | 9.5 | 8,532 | 10.5 | 98,925 | 9.7 | 73 |
| 33,803 | 4.4 | 4,431 | 5.4 | 55,893 | 5.5 | 29 |
| 232,617 | 30.2 | 29,213 | 35.7 | 331,015 | 32.4 | 26 |
| 83,189 | 10.8 | 9,726 | 11.9 | 104,865 | 10.3 | 34 |
| 174,011 | 22.6 | 12,614 | 15.4 | 125,008 | 12.2 | 2 |
| 3,535 | .5 | 523 | .7 | 9,456 | .9 | 6 |
| 9,500 | 1.2 | 1,030 | 1.2 | 27,349 | 2.7 | 42 |
| 16,890 | 2.2 | 1,577 | 1.9 | 38,800 | 3.8 | 23 |
| 4,130 | .5 | 550 | .7 | 7,361 | .7 | 4 |
| 14,600 | 1.9 | 360 | .4 | 17,841 | 1.7 | 19 |

TABLE 4
Summary Characteristics of Optimal Interregional
Shipments* of Commercial Roundwood
for Domestic Consumption

| Year | Matrix Size | Volume Shipped $m^3 \times 10^6$ | Total Shipping Cost (current rubles) $\times 10^6$ |
|---|---|---|---|
| 1970 | 22 origins, 62 destinations | 94.16 | 371.0 |
| 1975 | 24 origins 60 destinations | 96.78 | 411.6 |
| 1990 | 30 origins 54 destinations | 115.18 | 570.7 |

NOTE: Similar characteristics for 1964 are listed in Brenton M. Barr, *The Soviet Wood-Processing Industry: A Linear Programming Analysis of the Role of Transportation Costs in Location and Flow Patterns* (Toronto: University of Toronto Press, 1970), p. 84. These characteristics in addition to alternative optimal solutions and post-suboptimal solutions for Soviet roundwood flows are discussed in Brenton M. Barr and K. Smillie, "Some Spatial Interpretations of Alternative Optimal and Suboptimal Solutions to the Transportation Problem," *Canadian Geographer*, 16, no. 4 (1972): 356–64.

*The volumes of these shipments are contained in Brenton M. Barr, *Domestic and International Implications of Regional Change in the Soviet Timber and Wood-Processing Industries, 1970–1990*, Discussion Paper No. 4 (June 1978), Association of American Geographers, Project on Soviet Natural Resources in the World Economy, Tables 5, 6, and 7.

lumber and plywood in the construction and furniture industries. Unfortunately for those advocating overall increases in the comprehensive utilization of round-wood, the expected growth in demand for construction wood appears to offset the gains in productivity achieved by greater capital investment in the production of substitute items.

Estimates of timber consumption for 1990 assume that change in the relative importance of branches of the timber and wood-processing industries prior to 1975 will continue into the near future, and that the annual incremental changes in these industries in the near future will not exceed those achieved to date; a decline in these annual increments will not invalidate the scenario presented in this analysis but will likely reduce the competition in world markets by Soviet timber and related products otherwise expected in 1990. These assumptions across the spectrum of wood products and unprocessed items appear to be consistent with the apparently long periods required to change many general categories of phenomena in the USSR and yet they accept the ability of that country to focus special attention via various forms of "storming" on the output of specific commodities within any industrial sector. Most important to this study, however, is that the estimates of consumption for 1990

TABLE 5
Actual Growing Stock in Forests of State Significance (Principal Species)

| Species | 1966 Volume $m^3 \times 10^6$ | Percent of Total | 1973 Volume $m^3 \times 10^6$ | Percent of Total | Percent of Mature and Overmature Timber in Total Volume | Percent of 1973 Volume in European-Urals Regions |
|---|---|---|---|---|---|---|
| Larch | 26,664 | 35.8 | 26,600 | 35.2 | 75.6 | .4 |
| Pine | 14,292 | 19.2 | 14,500 | 19.2 | 60.0 | 33.1 |
| Spruce | 12,217 | 16.4 | 11,900 | 15.7 | 81.5 | 55.5 |
| Siberian stone pine | 6,655 | 8.9 | 7,000 | 9.3 | 65.7 | 1.4 |
| Fir and others | 2,707* | 3.6* | 2,500 | 3.3 | 68.0 | 8.0 |
| Total conifers | 62,535 | 83.9 | 62,500 | 82.7 | 71.7 | 18.9 |
| Oak | 871 | 1.2 | 1,000 | 1.3 | 30.0 | 70.0 |
| Beech | 510 | .7 | 500 | .7 | 40.0 | 100.0 |
| Others | 732 | 1.0 | 1,000 | 1.3 | 33.3 | 80.0 |
| Total tolerant[a] hardwoods | 2,113 | 2.9 | 2,500 | 3.3 | 52.0 | 56.0 |
| Birch | 7,100* | 9.5 | 7,400 | 9.8 | 55.4 | 36.5 |
| Aspen | 2,200 | 2.9 | 2,500 | 3.3 | 72.0 | 40.0 |
| Others | 590 | .8 | 700 | .9 | 42.9 | 57.1 |
| Total intolerant[b] hardwoods | 9,890 | 13.2 | 10,600 | 14.0 | 58.5 | 38.7 |
| TOTAL ALL SPECIES | 74,538 | 100.0 | 75,600 | 100.0 | 69.2 | 22.9 |

*Fir volume is 2,200 million m³, 2.9 percent of total USSR volume; data marked* have been derived from V. L. Dzhikovich, *Ekonomika lesnogo khozyaistva* (Moscow: Lesnaya promyshlennost, 1970), p. 36.

SOURCE: B. S. Petrov, *Spravochnik ekonomista derevoobrabatyvayushchei promyshlennosti*, 2nd ed. (Moscow: Lesnaya promyshlonnost, 1974), p. 6; species totals are taken from Table 6 of this report; V. A. Nikolayuk, "Changes in forest resources as a result of human activity," *Lesnoye khozyaistvo*, 1975, no. 7, pp. 2–6.

NOTE: Forests of State Significance exclude forests administered by nonforestry ministries and administrations including collective farms, state farms and nature preserves but comprise Group 1 forests (environmental protection forests, 13.3 percent of total volume), Group 2 forests (limited-cutting forests in forest-deficit regions, 6.5 percent of total volume), and Group 3 forests (major commercial forests, 80.2 percent of total volume). Forests in the European North, West and East Siberia, and the Far East are comprised almost entirely of Group 3 forests.

[a] = tverdolistvennye porody (shade-tolerant deciduous species), principally oak, beech, ash.

[b] = myagkolistvennye porody (shade-intolerant deciduous species), principally birch, aspen, poplar, basswood (linden).

demonstrate that the USSR can continue to change its output mix in the timber and wood-processing industries in the near future as it has in the recent past (or in line with the period 1975–80) and satisfy all demand for roundwood and mill residues from domestic timber reserves while still possessing significant volumes of unused timber. If the Soviet Union is assumed to effect greater efficiency in wood conversion and utilization after 1990,[55] to offset the increased cost of developing eastern and northern forests through greater efficiency in harvesting and processing operations,[56] and to receive higher real prices for timber and wood products on domestic and world markets, then its timber and wood-processing operations beyond 1990 should occur without seriously curtailing the supply of wood for production of any wood-based items now important to the national economy. The possibility that the USSR, to offset shortfalls in particular domestic regional markets, might become a major purchaser of a broad spectrum of forest products in world markets like other industrial nations, or a more significant importer of selected forest products such as chemical pulps, papers, and paperboards (currently imported in modest amounts from Finland) the costs of which are partially financed by exports of roundwood cannot be ruled out. Although well beyond the

scope of the present paper, the prospect of the USSR purchasing capital-intensive forest products abroad with surplus foreign exchange derived from petroleum exports, avoiding or postponing the costly development of remote forests and related infrastructure, and allocating scarce domestic investment energies to high-priority industries, is a subject which should be included in future analyses of the Soviet forest industries. The limitations inherent in the estimating technique employed in this paper, however, preclude making any general forecasts for the period following 1990.

### The Spatial Concurrence of Timber Supply and Demand, 1990

Regional Levels of Timber Harvest and Growth

Estimates of the 1990 total timber harvest (Table 3) reveal that the European North, Urals, Central Siberia, and Far East will account for two-thirds of the total. If the relatively small contributions of the Northwest and Western Siberia are added to this share, then nearly 78 percent of Soviet timber in 1990 will originate from these six regions which in 1973 accounted for 74 percent of the actual growing stock and 67 percent of the annual increment of principal forest species. The estimates of timber harvest for 1990 thus indicate that an approximate balance between the relative location of timber harvest and that of timber reserve will prevail by that date although the annual increment in the six regions—685 million m$^3$—will more than support their expected timber harvest of 347 million m$^3$. If only 56 percent—the share of all USSR commercial forest currently accessible—of the annual increment of these six regions is assumed to be available for harvesting in accessible stands, then the 384 million m$^3$ which can be cut in these regions is 37 million m$^3$ in excess of that predicted for 1990. Thus, without drawing extensively on the forests of the Siberian North—Yakutia, Magadan, and Kamchatka—the Soviet Union will be able to meet its incremental needs for timber by 1990 from the major accessible forests of the taiga extending from the White Sea to the Sea of Okhotsk.

The remaining regions, excluding the Siberian North, which is unlikely to become a significant timber harvesting region by 1990, account for approximately 22 percent of the expected 1990 timber harvest and approximately 21 percent of the annual increment of principal forest species. If the forests of the remaining regions are assumed (based on their proximity to railway and river transportation arteries) to be 80 percent accessible, then they could supply 172 million m$^3$ which is 74 million m$^3$ in excess of their expected harvest of approximately 98 million m$^3$. These regions also possess sufficient average-age, mature, and overmature timber to support their expected 1990 levels of cutting (regional figures are given in Table 5 and 6).

While the data presented in this report support the contention that the Soviet Union has sufficient reserves of timber to meet expected levels of demand in 1990 and possibly for several decades beyond that date, they do not reveal whether the USSR can meet future demand for

| Percent of Mature and Overmature Timber in European-Urals Forests | Mature and Overmature Forests in European/Urals Regions as Percent of USSR Mature and Overmature Forests |
|---|---|
| — | — |
| 37.5 | 20.7 |
| 75.8 | 51.5 |
| 100.0 | 2.2 |
| 100.0 | 11.8 |
| 60.2 | 15.8 |
| 28.6 | 66.7 |
| 40.0 | 100.0 |
| 33.3 | 80.0 |
| 28.6 | 30.8 |
| 37.0 | 24.4 |
| 60.0 | 33.3 |
| 25.0 | 33.3 |
| 41.5 | 27.4 |
| 53.2 | 17.6 |

TABLE 6
Age and Species Characteristics of Major USSR Forests[a]

| Region[b] | | USSR | | |
| Species | Conifers | Tolerant Hardwoods | Intolerant Hardwoods | Total[c] |
|---|---|---|---|---|
| **Actual Growing Stock** | | | | |
| Volume ($m^3 \times 10^6$) | 62,535 | 2,113 | 9,980 | 74,538 |
| Percent of total USSR volume | 83.9 | 2.8 | 13.3 | 100.0 |
| Percent of USSR total of each species | 100.0 | 100.0 | 100.0 | 100.0 |
| Percent of total regional volume | 83.9 | 2.8 | 13.3 | 100.0 |
| **Proportion of Actual Growing Stock in Stands Which Are** | | | | |
| Average age | 12.2 | 26.0 | 21.8 | 13.8 |
| Approaching maturity | 10.9 | 14.3 | 14.3 | 11.5 |
| Mature or overmature | 73.4 | 51.7 | 59.0 | 70.9 |
| Other | 3.5 | 8.0 | 4.9 | 3.8 |
| (Expressed as percent of total regional volume of each species; total = 100 percent) | | | | |

TABLE 6 (*cont.*)

| Region[b] | | Volga-Vyatka | | |
| Species | Conifers | Tolerant Hardwoods | Intolerant Hardwoods | Total |
|---|---|---|---|---|
| **Actual Growing Stock** | | | | |
| Volume ($m^3 \times 10^6$) | 1,284 | 41 | 483 | 1,808 |
| Percent of total USSR volume | 1.7 | — | .7 | 2.4 |
| Percent of USSR total of each species | 2.1 | 1.9 | 4.9 | 2.4 |
| Percent of total regional volume | 71.0 | 2.3 | 26.7 | 100.0 |
| **Proportion of Actual Growing Stock in Stands Which Are** | | | | |
| Average age | 23.0 | 43.9 | 26.3 | 24.3 |
| Approaching maturity | 16.8 | 12.2 | 12.2 | 15.5 |
| Mature or overmature | 48.8 | 26.8 | 52.6 | 49.3 |
| Other | 11.4 | 17.1 | 8.9 | 10.9 |
| (Expressed as percent of total regional volume of each species; total = 100 percent) | | | | |

TABLE 6 (*cont.*)

| Region[b] | | East Siberia | | |
| Species | Conifers | Tolerant Hardwoods | Intolerant Hardwoods | Total |
|---|---|---|---|---|
| **Actual Growing Stock** | | | | |
| Volume ($m^3 \times 10^6$) | 24,695 | — | 2,594 | 27,289 |
| Percent of total USSR volume | 33.2 | — | 3.5 | 36.7 |
| Percent of USSR total of each species | 39.5 | — | 26.2 | 36.7 |
| Percent of total regional volume | 90.5 | — | 9.5 | 100.0 |
| **Proportion of Actual Growing Stock in Stands Which Are** | | | | |
| Average age | 11.3 | — | 20.7 | 12.2 |
| Approaching maturity | 10.5 | — | 15.2 | 10.9 |
| Mature or overmature | 76.8 | — | 61.3 | 75.3 |
| Other | 1.4 | — | 2.8 | 1.6 |
| (Expressed as percent of total regional volume of each species; total = 100 percent) | | | | |

| | RSFSR | | | | Northwest | | |
|---|---|---|---|---|---|---|---|
| Conifers | Tolerant Hardwoods | Intolerant Hardwoods | Total | Conifers | Tolerant Hardwoods | Intolerant Hardwoods | Total |
| 61,234 | 1,453 | 9,525 | 72,212 | 6,536 | — | 1,068 | 7,604 |
| 82.2 | 2.0 | 12.8 | 96.9 | 8.8 | — | 1.4 | 10.2 |
| 97.9 | 68.8 | 96.3 | 96.9 | 10.5 | — | 10.8 | 10.2 |
| 84.8 | 2.0 | 13.2 | 100.0 | 86.0 | — | 14.0 | 100.0 |
| | | | | | | | |
| 11.8 | 22.4 | 21.0 | 13.2 | 11.6 | — | 26.8 | 9.8 |
| 10.7 | 13.2 | 14.1 | 11.2 | 6.7 | — | 9.8 | 7.1 |
| 75.4 | 57.9 | 60.3 | 72.2 | 78.6 | — | 57.4 | 75.6 |
| 2.1 | 6.5 | 4.6 | 3.4 | 3.1 | — | 6.0 | 7.5 |

| | Urals | | | | West Siberia | | |
|---|---|---|---|---|---|---|---|
| Conifers | Tolerant Hardwoods | Intolerant Hardwoods | Total | Conifers | Tolerant Hardwoods | Intolerant Hardwoods | Total |
| 2,183 | 17 | 780 | 2,980 | 6,244 | — | 2,491 | 8,735 |
| 2.9 | — | 1.1 | 4.0 | 8.4 | — | 3.3 | 11.7 |
| 3.5 | .8 | 7.9 | 4.0 | 10.0 | — | 25.2 | 11.7 |
| 73.2 | .6 | 26.2 | 100.0 | 71.5 | — | 28.5 | 100.0 |
| | | | | | | | |
| 11.8 | 58.8 | 19.4 | 14.0 | 10.6 | — | 11.2 | 10.8 |
| 13.0 | 11.8 | 11.7 | 12.7 | 13.2 | — | 12.8 | 13.1 |
| 71.1 | 17.6 | 61.0 | 68.1 | 75.0 | — | 74.3 | 74.8 |
| 4.1 | 11.8 | 7.9 | 5.2 | 1.2 | — | 1.7 | 1.3 |

| | Far East | | |
|---|---|---|---|
| Conifers | Tolerant Hardwoods | Intolerant Hardwoods | Total |
| 19,163 | 782 | 816 | 20,761 |
| 25.7 | 1.1 | 1.1 | 27.9 |
| 30.6 | 37.0 | 8.3 | 27.9 |
| 92.3 | 3.8 | 3.9 | 100.0 |
| | | | |
| 11.8 | 10.0 | 21.0 | 12.1 |
| 10.6 | 9.3 | 12.9 | 10.6 |
| 75.8 | 77.9 | 59.4 | 75.3 |
| 1.8 | 2.8 | 5.8 | 2.0 |

[a] = "Forests of state significance;" these forests exclude those administered by nonforestry ministries and administrations, collective farms, state farms, and nature preserves.

[b] = The composition of the major regions of the RSFSR differs from that of the RSFSR's regional units employed throughout the remainder of this study because of the form used to report the data in the source for this table. The total regional composition of the RSFSR, corresponds closely to that found throughout the report; Kaliningrad Oblast is included in the RSFSR.

[c] = Total refers to total of coniferous and deciduous species reported in this table; the total Actual Growing Stock of USSR forests reported in the source for this table includes willows, shrubs, and miscellaneous vegetation.

SOURCE: B. S. Petrov, *Spravochnik ekonomista derevoobrabatyvayushchei promyshlennosti*, 2d ed. (Moscow: Lesnaya promyshlennost, 1974), pp. 7–9.

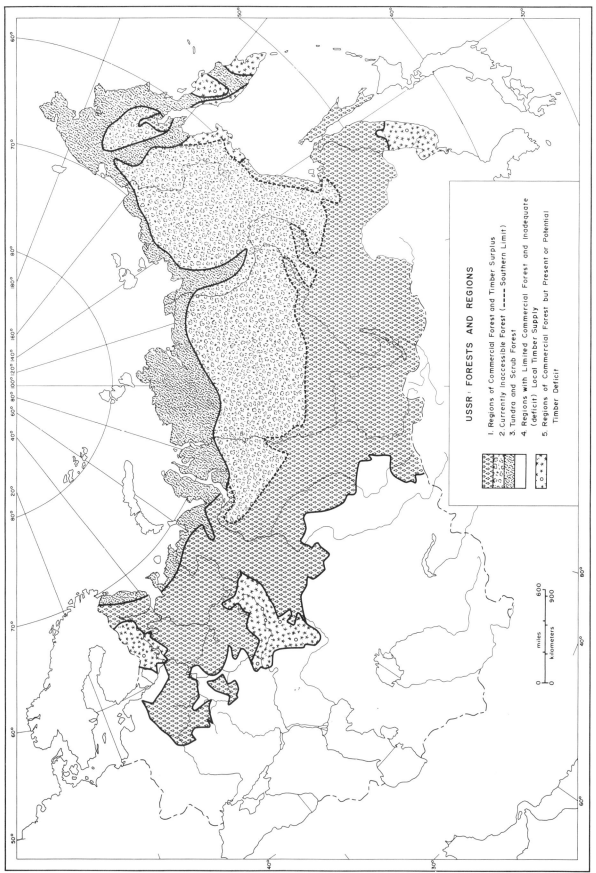

USSR: FORESTS AND REGIONS

1. Regions of Commercial Forest and Timber Surplus
2. Currently Inaccessible Forest (———— Southern Limit)
3. Tundra and Scrub Forest
4. Regions with Limited Commercial Forest and Inadequate (deficit) Local Timber Supply
5. Regions of Commercial Forest but Present or Potential Timber Deficit

Figure 2

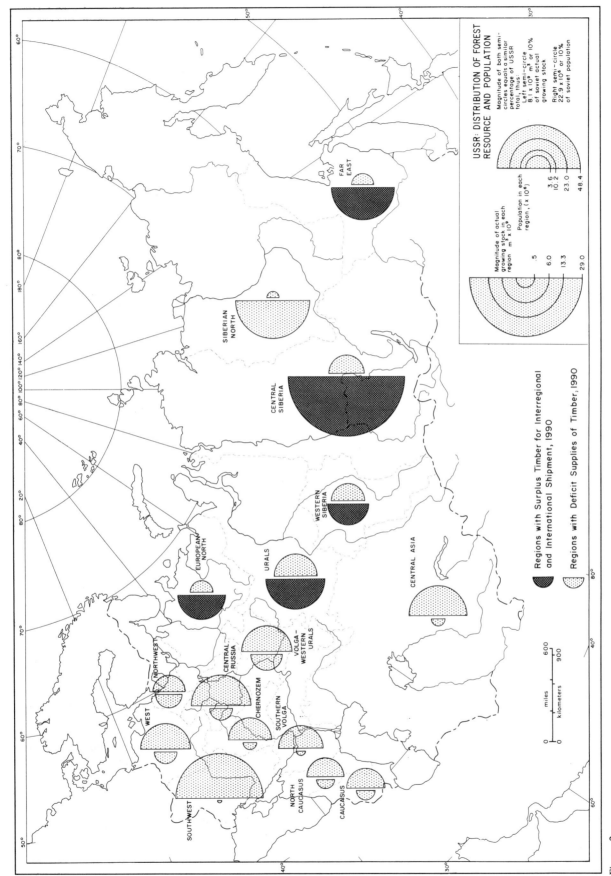

Figure 3

individual species of timber without making significant changes in the species allocated to wood processors. This problem requires extensive further investigation of the literature for clues as to the relative current importance of each species in the timber harvest of major forest regions, and the importance which demand for each species is likely to assume in the future. If Soviet foresters are able to substitute greater amounts of larch and deciduous species, for example, in the domestic consumption of pine, spruce, fir, and Siberian stone pine, then their ability to continue to supply these four species at least to foreign consumers is assured. Nevertheless, this issue requires careful investigation and evaluation of related, technological, economic and market forces excluded from the present geographical analysis.

## Optimal Patterns of Timber Shipped for Domestic Consumption

Previous analyses by the author[57] suggest that linear programming solutions of Soviet roundwood shipments differ in total cost from the actual patterns of such shipments by less than 20 percent; the greater economy evident in the linear programming solutions probably is due to the importance of established supplier-consumer relationships within Soviet industry, the importance of species differentiation (ignored here) and the significant amount of roundwood which actually moves cheaply by water rather than expensively by rail as assumed here. Nevertheless, if all Soviet roundwood did move interregionally by rail rather than by water, the correspondence in total cost between actual and optimal shipment patterns probably would be close; the patterns of shipment derived in the optimal solutions for 1970, 1975, and 1990, therefore, may be taken as instructive of the prevailing spatial shipment patterns which currently exist and which will occur if the levels of regional demand and supply expected in this study are achieved in 1990.

Improved management of Soviet forests and regional shifts in demand by wood processors are steadily increasing the number of forest-surplus regions within the USSR and are reducing the complexity of interregional flow patterns. The volume of roundwood to be shipped for domestic consumption is expected to increase by 22.3 percent between 1970 and 1990, but the cost of shipping that increment will increase total shipping cost by 53.8 percent, a reflection of the greater distances which are being incurred as wood deficits are supplied from increasingly peripheral or distant regions (Table 4, costs are in constant 1974 rubles).

If present trends continue in the spatial shifts of regional surpluses and deficits of timber for domestic consumption, then the USSR will have five major regions (but thirty provinces) supplying timber (Figure 3) interregionally to the domestic economy by 1990. These regions comprise large areas of the taiga and have been previously shown to be capable of meeting the total levels of harvesting likely to occur in them by 1990. Like the patterns of 1964, 1970, and 1975 flows produced by the author,[58] the major directions of wood shipment expected

for 1990 will continue to be north-south, east-west, and northeast-southwest vectors (Figure 4) with an economic rationale supported by the dual solution to the interregional transportation solutions of linear programming.[59] According to Abouchar[60] the "different rents" displayed for each surplus (shipper) region may be thought of as "reflecting producers' differential advantages *with respect to the existing demand and supply pattern*" because they indicate where an additional unit of capacity—in this case, an increment of surplus roundwood—will secure the greatest saving in shipment cost. These differential rents confirm that Soviet foresters should increase the amount of timber harvested in those regions closest to established areas of demand—European USSR—if traditional markets are to be satisfied with industrial roundwood. The differential rents also add justification to the Soviet practice of overcutting in European regions although the figures do not permit the long-term wisdom of such overcutting to be evaluated. On the other hand, the differential rent figures may be interpreted as demonstrating the disadvantage of harvesting geographically peripheral timber for interregional shipments to domestic markets. The rent figures inadvertently also comment on the folly of meeting foreign demand by rail shipments of timber from peripheral northern and eastern regions (advocated by Kanevsky and Shaitanov[61]), although the location and volume of foreign demand are not incorporated into these figures.

In regions of timber deficits, the dual solution to linear programming provides figures representing "zonal consumption surcharges" which reflect the cost—a penalty—of consuming roundwood in each region where insufficient local supplies exist. These figures suggest strongly the penalty that Soviet consumers of roundwood are paying by continuing to produce away from adequate timber supplies. The surcharges are greatest in those traditional areas of consumption and are least in those areas closest to northern and eastern suppliers. The zonal surcharges confirm the wisdom of policies to relocate timber consumption closer to the sources of supply although limitations in the data preclude acceptance of the zonal surcharges as complete statements of the economic advantage in shifting existing domestic consumers of interregional roundwood shipments to forest-surplus regions.[62]

The zonal surcharges may, however, be taken as important evidence of the transportation penalties being paid by supporting timber consumption in southern and western forest-deficit regions and those transportation disadvantages likely to be incurred if additional direct consumption of roundwood were encouraged in these regions. This additional consumption might be that associated with production in these regions of pulp, plywood or lumber, for example, for eastern and western European markets. The zonal consumption surcharges, however, do not affect the viability of suggesting that secondary manufacturing of wood products should be conducted in these regions on the basis of pulp or other relatively pure raw materials shipped from forest-deficit areas in a manner similar to the shipment of wood pulp

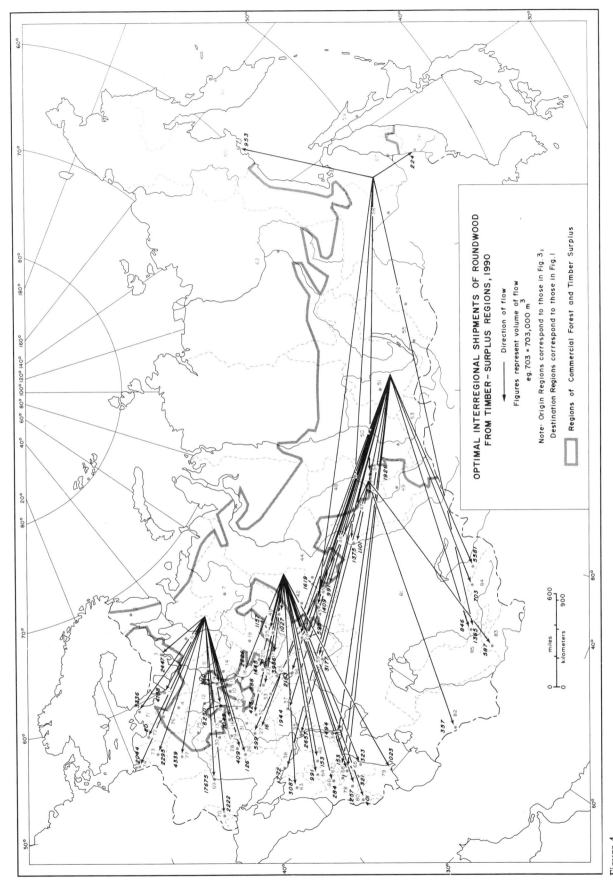

OPTIMAL INTERREGIONAL SHIPMENTS OF ROUNDWOOD
FROM TIMBER—SURPLUS REGIONS, 1990

⟶  Direction of flow

⟶  Figures represent volume of flow
    eg.703 = 703,000 m³

Note: Origin Regions correspond to those in Fig. 3;
      Destination Regions correspond to those in Fig. 1

☐  Regions of Commercial Forest and Timber Surplus

Figure 4

from the peripheral forests of Canada to the paper and
paperboard producers located in major North American
and world industrial markets.

Timber Export

Suggestions by knowledgeable Soviet writers[63] for development of the export side of the timber industry are
consistent with the export volume estimated for 1990
(Table 1). The calculations of total demand for wood
products in 1990 presented in this paper do not include
separate amounts of each product which might be destined for export—such calculations are beyond the scope
of this study and are discussed at length in Lenz and
Kravalis,[64] Brougher,[65] and North and Solecki.[66] This paper
assumes instead that the USSR will continue to develop
each sector of the forest-based economy in a manner
consistent with the recent past and will continue to allocate to foreign trade those amounts of each commodity
which can be spared from its domestic requirements and
which can be profitably marketed in the industrial west
and CMEA countries. The export of timber and wood
products through to 1990, however, may be adversely
affected by regional and national levels of timber harvesting if labor and transportation problems in the USSR are
exacerbated in the 1980s. The micro economics, however,
associated with production of each commodity, and the
profitability of particular export shipments cannot be
calculated outside the USSR and are not forthcoming
from Soviet sources.

Two sectors of the timber and wood-processing industries which have not had significant conflicts between
domestic and foreign demand are those associated with
roundwood and lumber production; traditionally they
also have been the two dominant export sectors of the
forest-based industries. Soviet export volumes of roundwood and most timber products, including lumber,
however, declined abruptly in the late 1970s although the
value of these exports increased.[67] The decline in timber
and forest-product exports, if not reversed, will further
reduce the demand for roundwood estimated in Table 1.
Furthermore, this decline suggests that the reduction in
Soviet roundwood production discussed above may
reflect not only a policy of more comprehensive conversion of roundwood for domestic and foreign consumption, but an economic and technological malaise in the
timber and wood-processing industry preventing both
the maintenance of previous levels of production and the
achievement of net increments to productive capacity in
the forest and in processing plants. As noted above, any
reduction in gross demand for timber will lower the pressure on the total Soviet resource although that registered
in developed and accessible regions may increase. The
Soviet need for foreign exchange will likely continue to
outpace its ability to sell abroad and will continue to
necessitate export sales of raw materials. Raw materials
such as timber, and relatively unsophisticated manufactured products such as lumber and related items—
even if dressed, kiln dried, and packaged—will also assume a greater relative importance in foreign exchange

accounts in future years if Soviet exports of petroleum
decline.

To support the increased export of roundwood and
lumber, the Soviet Union is planning to expand the felling of export timber and output of export lumber in the
European North, in Western and Eastern Siberia, and in
the Far East. In the North and Far East, forests are far
from domestic markets but are accessible to port-oriented
processing facilities geared to foreign demand. Furthermore, the high costs associated with development in all
four regions, plus the long overland hauls associated
with shipments of Siberian timber through Mediterranean and Baltic ports[68] apparently can be offset by the
value received for high-quality wood and products from
these regions in foreign markets. The Soviet domestic
demand for many wood products is not sufficiently differentiated or discriminating in quality to warrant the
construction of high-quality producing facilities in northern and eastern regions.

If Soviet planners are prepared to invest coherently in
high-quality processing operations in peripheral regions
to meet Western and CMEA demand for wood products,
and to continue the locational investment pattern undertaken in the 1960s to meet demand by Finland, Japan,
and the Eastern European members of CMEA, then the
timber reserves of northern European regions, Siberia,
and the Far East are more than sufficient to satisfy all
wood needs through to 1990 and for some time beyond. If
Soviet planners continue to engage in the "lumpiness of
investment in the industry" described by North and
Solecki,[69] and to export predominantly lumber and roundwood (see the penetrating discussion of this problem in
relation to Soviet Far Eastern exports to Japan by Allan
Rodgers),[70] thereby foregoing the opportunities locally to
engage in the integrated export-oriented processing
advocated by Kanevsky and Shaitanov, Soviet forests can
still provide adequate supplies of commercial roundwood. Export of finished products implies greater possible efficiency in the utilization of roundwood and associated mill residues, greater longevity of existing resources,
but greater present capital investment; by emphasizing
the export of lumber and roundwood, the Soviet Union
reduces the overall efficiency of roundwood utilization,
effectively shortens the life expectancy of existing accessible reserves but reduces the need for allocating scarce
investment capital to the wood-processing industries.

Soviet planners currently appear to favor a combination of both these alternatives but lay heavier stress on
continued export of roundwood and lumber than on the
rapid growth of wood-product export, although increasing cooperation within CMEA appears to oblige the
USSR to assign significant quantities of finished products
to its eastern European trading partners.[71] To support the
continued importance of lumber and timber export, the
USSR probably will continue to "highgrade" its selection
of coniferous species in northern and eastern forests by
emphasizing the harvest of pine, spruce and fir and by
downplaying the export possibilities inherent in the extensive stands of larch east of the Yenisei River.[72] Reports
in the Soviet press support speculation that excessive

reliance on harvesting pine, spruce and fir for export eventually will necessitate the assignment of greater supplies of larch to the domestic timber and wood-processing industries because previous overcutting of these more popular species has already seriously depleted their reserves in some key areas.[73] If Soviet foresters are forced to increase their domestic dependence on larch forests, then greater development can be expected in Eastern Siberia and the Far East; there is no doubt that these forests can fulfill the estimates presented in this study.

Larch already comprises a significant share of the total timber consumption in many large timber processing operations in Siberia: at Krasnoyarsk (45 percent), Ust-Ilimsk (25 percent), and Bratsk (15 to 25 percent). In 1977, larch comprised 35 percent of the volume of coniferous logs exported by the USSR to Japan although Japanese purchasers felt that this proportion was undesirable and that the volume of larch should not exceed 27 percent of future shipments. The volume of larch officially and covertly included in sales to Japan is thus a point of contention which is likely to become more acute when timber for Japan is harvested from the predominantly larch stands adjacent to the BAM.[74]

Export Impact on World Markets

Estimates in Table 1 suggest that the USSR may export approximately 22 million m³ of roundwood by 1990 if world markets continue to be satisfied by the USSR as they have been in the 1970s. Soviet exports to Japan, Finland and the CMEA countries are subject to long-term agreements and contain few sudden changes caused by market fluctuations although poor business conditions in Japan periodically cause cutbacks in the amount of roundwood and mill residues being shipped by the USSR to that country. *World Wood*[75] reported in late 1976, for example, that "reduction in the production of pulp and paper in Japan has induced the Japan Chip Trading Co., which is the sole importer of Siberian chips for pulp and paper manufacturers, to ask the Soviet Lumber Export Corporation to cut down its delivery of chips to 450,000 m³. This is 60 percent less than stipulated in their ten-year contract. American suppliers have been asked to make a similar reduction." If Sutton's prediction[76] is accepted, that timber deficits in the United States by the end of the century probably can be satisfied by surplus production shipped from Canada, then the major market area of uncertain but potentially great impact for Soviet timber sales must be the markets of Western Europe, where imports from Sweden and Finland may be negligible by the end of the century,[77] and Japan. Nearly 66 percent of the USSR's volume in roundwood equivalent units of principal forest-product exports in 1974 was directed to the countries of Europe (Eastern and Western Europe), 21 percent to Japan, and 13 percent to other nations.[78] Exports of all forest products from the USSR by the year 2000 are expected to make up 11 to 12 percent of the total volume of industrial roundwood removals and reach 55

to 65 million m³ (r), of which Europe may receive 30 to 35 million m³ (r).[79]

Soviet exports of timber have been estimated in the present study to be approximately 5 percent of domestic industrial timber supply by 1990; if the estimate of 65 million m³ (r) is accepted as being exportable to all markets as early as 1990, then approximately 27 million m³ of roundwood could be exported to all markets; acceptance of a total export volume of 55 million m³(r) also representing 12 percent of industrial roundwood removals and an export of timber composing 5 percent of industrial roundwood removals leads to a total export of timber in 1990 of 23 million m³. This lower estimate of 23 million m³ is close to the figure of 22 million m³ estimated in the present study. If expectations that European nations will be able to obtain only 55 percent of total Soviet forest product exports by the year 2000 are applied to Soviet timber exports, then Europe could receive 12.6 million to 14.8 million m³ of Soviet timber. These shipments could be achieved as early as 1990 and still conform to the general export volume of timber export estimated for that year in this study.

Given that the United Nations estimates pertain to the year 2000, then the estimate in this study confirms that European timber needs predicated upon Soviet supply can adequately be met in the year 1990, and probably for many years following 1990 in view of the large resource surpluses which the USSR clearly has when its forest resource is analyzed in terms of the regional characteristics of its expected supply and demand relationships.

If Europe's demand for Soviet timber were to expand more quickly than anticipated in the United Nations study, then the expanded demand in 1990 could still be easily met from Soviet timber reserves. If growth of European demand were to contract by 1990, then the Soviet Union might engage in excessively aggressive marketing tactics to ensure as much access as possible to European markets. The United Nations study noted that "it is difficult to find a rational basis on which to estimate future exports of forest products from North America";[80] it is difficult for any individual researcher, therefore, to predict the impact of Soviet timber on world or European markets in 1990 *if these markets should be depressed and encourage excessively aggressive competition from their traditional timber suppliers.* If the relative magnitude of Soviet timber exports to Europe, however, should be less important in 1990 than in 1974 but greater to Japan, then North American sales by 1990–2000 should increase slightly in Europe to pick up the shortfall in Soviet sales and should also increase in Japan as that country expands its total need for timber imports and is unable to account for its entire increment of demand from the USSR.[81]

If the USSR's real ability to export timber by 1990 is that estimated in this study, and if world demand, particularly in Europe, Japan, and North America, continues in the manner predicted by the United Nations, then Soviet timber is unlikely to be capable of dominating world markets by the last decade of this century. The likely significance of Soviet timber sales abroad by 1990 is that they will be insufficient to satisfy the potential world demand for Soviet timber and will, therefore, enable other timber-exporting nations such as the United States and Canada to sell timber on world markets.

## Discussion:
## Problems and Options in the Timber and Wood-Processing Industries

The immediate problem facing any observer of the USSR's forest economy is that of comprehending the sheer magnitude of timber resources in that country. Words such as "inexhaustible opportunities" and "uncounted riches," no longer fashionable in North America, still impress and awe audiences both in the USSR and abroad when they are applied by Soviet leaders to descriptions of Soviet resource potential.[82] When Soviet exploitable forests, however, are compared with the commercial timberlands of the United States and with the Canadian forest suitable for regular harvest, the area and maximum allowable cut of the North American forests are respectively 1.36 and 1.47 times greater than those of the USSR although the total volume of the Soviet forest exceeds that of North America by approximately one-third.[83] The most realistic estimate of Soviet annual allowable cut accepted by Sutton is almost identical to that of the United States.

Unlike those of either the United States or Canada, the Soviet Union's forests do not lie adjacent to established or relatively accessible areas of the country. The basic problem of the geography of Soviet forests is that all increments to the supply of roundwood in the near and intermediate-term future will have to originate in forests which are relatively inaccessible to existing interregional transportation facilities and to existing wood-processing centers. Furthermore, these geographically peripheral forests are heavily dominated by stands of larch. In some of the peripheral forests, such as in those of the European North and Western Siberia, the river systems facilitate rafting of logs but traditional forms of water-borne movement of logs now strongly conflict with the interests of many other groups, particularly with those of the fishing and conservation lobbies. The use of rivers to float logs in Siberia could theoretically obviate the need to invest in rail facilities except that increased use of Siberian forests will probably necessitate large movement of larch, a species which has a high propensity to sink.

In many of the remote forest stands, timber floating is the only way to move timber to market. At the present time, approximately 50 percent of all timber felled moves at least some distance by water but in the North, Siberia and the Far East, this figure exceeds 70 percent. Waterways suitable for timber floating, 140,000 km in length, support a timber throughput of 53 billion ton-kilometers per annum.[84]

The geographical distribution of timber reserves in the USSR thus does not coincide with the basic rail transportation system and is heavily characterized by a North/East-West/South dichotomy. The North and East of the USSR have most of the forest reserves but are characterized by inhospitable terrain, difficult physical environ-

ments for logging and living,[85] harsh climates and slow natural growth rates, and relative inaccessibility to the USSR's domestic and East European markets. The West and South, on the other hand, have environments conducive to human and plant communities, terrain that does not usually offer difficulties to forest-related equipment, relatively mild climates and fast growth rates, and are either synonymous with, or relatively accessible to, the major industrial consumers of roundwood in the USSR and Eastern Europe (the CMEA countries). All regions, however, are relatively far from world demand for roundwood although some of the river and port-oriented processing facilities of the North and East are economically accessible to European and Asian markets.

The basic dilemma caused by the spatial dichotomy of resource distribution in the USSR for Soviet foresters is compounded by the large amounts of mature and over-mature timber in the North and East and by the extensive overcutting of forests in the West and South. Although the West and South offer the greatest potential for regeneration of forests, they also have the greatest demands for agricultural land and for land related to urban and industrial growth. Furthermore, regeneration is expensive even when the supporting infrastructure is in place. In the North and East, however, the forests are old and can be cut greatly in excess of their current mean annual increment with consequent savings to the forest economy, although the relative absence of railways, settlements, and processing facilities means that development of forests in these regions places heavy demands on the investment capital of the USSR. Competing demand for capital is one of the reasons for the relatively slow development which northern and eastern forests have hitherto experienced.

The impact of the long-standing relative dearth of capital for development of northern and eastern forests has been compounded in the 1970s by the growing shortage of labor in these regions. Insufficient labor in the peripheral northern and eastern regions of the USSR thwarted plans for the development of manufacturing away from the heartland of the USSR as early as the late 1950s but its impact on the ability of Soviet leaders to develop natural resource sites has only become fully apparent in the 1970s. The problem in timber development, therefore, is that those areas synonymous with greatest potential are also those with the most severe labor problems. Although labor is relatively more available in the West and South, the demands by other industrial sectors, including agriculture, mean that labor for use in the forests and wood-processing mills of the heartland is also in short supply. In all regions, therefore, the shortage of labor is becoming more severe and requires attendant investments in capital equipment to increase productivity in the forests as well as capital investment in wood-processing.

Shortage of capital and labor are probably major factors leading the USSR to modernize many processing facilities in established centers of the West and South rather than to proceed as rapidly as possible with the creation of extensive new processing centers in the North and East. Shortages of labor in the North and East have not only influenced the growth of primary manufacturing facilities but have necessitated the import of labor from Bulgaria for the last ten years to harvest timber in the Komi ASSR; in the 10th Five-Year Plan, 1976–80, this activity of the Bulgarians in the Komi ASSR was matched by expansion of participation of North Korean labor in the logging industry of Khabarovsk Krai and Amur Oblast.[86] Soviet overtures to Japan, however, for the long-term commitment of Japanese labor to joint Siberian projects have so far not been successful. Shortage of capital and expertise has led the USSR to engage members of CMEA in joint manufacturing and processing ventures such as the Ust-Ilimsk wood-processing complex in which five East European nations are participating with the USSR. The Soviet Union carried out engineering preparation of the site and designed and constructed the pulp mill. Approximately 40 percent of the project's cost was met by Bulgaria, Hungary, East Germany, Poland and Rumania in the form of machinery, equipment, materials, and transportation and communication systems.[87]

Soviet planners and leaders obviously realize that, whatever their decisions concerning the amount of timber to be harvested, and the type of processing to be conducted, activities in the North and East will increasingly involve foreign participation in the form of labor,[88] capital, or both. Suggestion that the USSR may eventually become the destination of foreign workers in a manner similar to Western Europe in the 1960s may be premature, but the increasing attraction of CMEA, for example, for Mediterranean and other third-world nations may result in large-scale temporary enlistment of foreign labor to develop the timber and wood-processing industries of the North and the East by 1990.[89]

The relative difficulty of developing the infrastructure of peripheral regions is evident from reports on construction of the "project of the century," the BAM.[90] The BAM is placing inordinate demands on the USSR's labor and capital supply, and the traumas associated with the climate and living conditions throughout the BAM territory attest to the great difficulties of human habitation in the peripheral Soviet regions. (Alan Smith[91] referred to "geography and climate—a deterrent to overpopulation.") Furthermore, the BAM itself is dependent in many respects on foreign technology and equipment and its very economic viability may be a function of the USSR's ability to export raw materials to countries of the Pacific Basin. The BAM initially will facilitate the export of raw materials and throughout the rest of the 20th century probably will be heavily associated with movement of petroleum, timber and minerals for export. There is no indication to date that large shares of the total capital slated for investment in wood-processing in the near future, for example, will be marshaled into projects associated with the BAM[92] or other Siberian railways. In fact, if economic viability of the BAM were predicated on the generation of flows of high-value manufactured or semi-manufactured commodities such as lumber, pulp, and paper, then a significant share of capital invested in the timber and wood-processing industries during the 10th Five-Year Plan, 1976–80, should have been associated with projects located in the areas served by the BAM. Such an investment

pattern did not occur, and the current location of Soviet wood-processing investment is likely to be no different than if the BAM had never been conceived.

Further evidence that Soviet planners and leaders lean heavily toward development of the timber and wood-processing industries in established regions of the West and South is found in the current shifts toward greater use of wood waste and industrial fuelwood as substitutes for commercial roundwood. Mill waste is rapidly becoming the most significant ingredient in the production of wood pulp and particleboard, and is synonymous with a more comprehensive use of wood fiber in established timber-producing areas. Fuller use of roundwood delays the need to obtain substantial increments of fiber from northern and eastern forests. Similarly, the substitution of industrial fuelwood for distant supplies of commercial roundwood is increasing in the processing industry and reduces both the need for relocation of investment and labor to peripheral regions. All these substitutes for commercial roundwood appear to be significantly retarding the extent to which the Soviet timber and wood-processing industries need to relocate to the North and East by 1990.[93]

The regional location of these industries implies at first glance the existence of opposing "forces pushing development of the Soviet forest products industry in opposite directions."[94] The tendency for development of certain types of capital-intensive wood-processing in the North and East, and the continued growth of a broad spectrum of development in the West and South should not be taken as conclusive evidence of a conflict in development of timber and wood-processing industries but rather as complementary aspects of a general process of improvement in the spatial economy of the entire Soviet forest industry. This industry is complex and many of its subdivisions possess characteristics which differ from each other. Soviet planning directives increasingly recognize the need to develop capital-intensive projects for the manufacture of lumber, pulp, paperboard, and fiberboard in peripheral regions while facilities for the manufacture of paper, particleboard, plywood, etc., are expanded in the heartland. Soviet reluctance to abandon regeneration activity and to forego new investment in existing European facilities in favor of a wholesale movement to the North and East suggests that the latter regions will undergo development only to the extent that investment in the West and South cannot be carried out more profitably.

The nature of wood-processing itself suggests that the primary forms of wood conversion involving significant loss of weight will continue to be raw material oriented irrespective of the general locational forces being exerted on the spatial economy, and will continue being located in the North and East while secondary forms of conversion such as paper and fiberboard may be expanded near the western Soviet borders (for sales to CMEA and Western European markets) on the basis of in-transit processing of northern and eastern semi-manufactured inputs or near many of the existing wood-processing facilities and markets located in the major domestic European regions of the USSR.

Except for the upgrading of processing and related transport facilities in the small number of port complexes in the North and East, the pattern of development of Soviet timber and wood-processing industries evident today probably would not be different from that associated with a Soviet economy lacking a strong commitment to international trade. Forests of the European North, northern Urals, central Siberia and the Far East might not have undergone such significant development during the past six decades if the USSR did not ship timber abroad but the pattern of wood processing (excluding facilities located at Arkhangelsk and Igarka) which has developed during this period has chiefly been intended to satisfy domestic markets. Clearly, therefore, Soviet leaders have traditionally possessed options on the extent to which they are prepared to develop timber and wood-processing industries related to foreign trade. The option to export timber has been exercised for many reasons including the need to earn foreign exchange as quickly as possible. In the future, however, the ability to earn foreign exchange without substantial investments of capital, or capital substitutes such as foreign labor rather than conscripted labor, will be much less than in the past. Furthermore, that timber which can be harvested with available labor faces many competing demands within the domestic economy. Thus, on the one hand, shortages of capital and labor may force curtailment of significant exports of raw timber. On the other hand, export of timber constitutes the greatest source of foreign exchange from the Industrial West after the export of oil.

A major dilemma thus facing those Soviet leaders responsible for timber and wood processing, foreign trade, and general economic and industrial growth is that future growth of the Soviet industrial economy appears to be predicated on the import of Western technology and that the ability to pay for such technology rests to a significant degree on earnings from the Cinderella of Soviet industry, the forestry sector. Furthermore, sustained output and future growth of the timber and wood-processing industries cannot be achieved without these industries having extensive access to Western technology, i.e., to foreign-exchange funds. Soviet leaders do not appear to have any long-term option but to develop the timber industry in the future, to export timber, and to effect the necessary related changes in the geography of timber production. The scenario developed in this paper seems quite justified in assuming that the USSR will eventually develop its timber-export sector and will produce such timber from the traditional northern and eastern regions.

Other developments suggest that this expectation of export based on timber rather than on wood products may be somewhat circumvented by greater integration within CMEA whereby the Soviet Union will supply forest products in exchange for CMEA-developed or CMEA-purchased high-technology goods. Soviet leaders show increasing signs of a shift toward reliance on CMEA as a source of the items which convertible currency might purchase on world markets. If CMEA projects become more numerous in the USSR, and if these projects involve expansion of wood-processing either in the USSR or on the basis of USSR timber in the CMEA countries themselves, then Soviet timber supplies now exported to the Industrial West may increasingly become directed toward CMEA or toward CMEA-related projects within the Soviet Union. Whichever variant involving CMEA is adopted, the geography of timber and primary wood-processing industries associated with CMEA integration is unlikely to be substantially different from that inherent in current developments related to satisfying domestic Soviet demand.

Traditional export has been water-borne from the lumber and timber ports of the North and East. CMEA trade is likely to involve rail shipments from accessible Soviet regions to Eastern Europe. Wood-processing, never a major contributor to forest-based exports to the Industrial West, is likely to occur in those areas accessible to the Soviet rail network such as Ust-Ilimsk rather than at ports or in the forest-deficit regions of the West and South although the location of secondary processing facilities on the western border of the USSR would ensure the retention of political control over investment while maintaining direct access to the CMEA markets. Greater CMEA involvement in the Soviet timber and wood-processing industries, therefore, probably will not change the regions in which roundwood originates but may change the direction of roundwood flows and the extent to which integrated development of Soviet wood-processing occurs in the North and East.

Closer integration within CMEA is unlikely to affect the geography of Soviet wood-processing or to reduce the need of the USSR to produce timber or timber-related goods for many domestic and other international markets. Satisfaction of all these markets throughout the remaining decades of the twentieth century, however, will necessitate significant expansion of timber harvesting in the North and East but will also induce greater locational economies in wood-processing and resource management in the forests of the West and South. Soviet leaders may have several options open within their general need to develop international forest-based commercial relations but whatever paths are chosen, the ongoing international need for timber export will mean that the forests of the North and the East will play a significant role far into the future. Whatever the specific ultimate form of Soviet international trade in forest-based products, all general estimates of future development must incorporate careful analysis of the differential regional characteristics of the Soviet forest, timber, and wood-processing industries.

## Conclusions

This paper estimates the spatial implications in 1990 of anticipated domestic and foreign demand for Soviet timber, the ability of Soviet forests to sustain anticipated levels of timber harvesting, the optimal flow patterns likely to be associated with satisfaction of domestic regional demand, the economic advantages in terms of transportation cost savings attainable through redistribution of regional supply and demand patterns, and the ability of Soviet timber exports to satisfy and affect major world timber markets.

Analysis was conducted on the basis of forest-product data expressed in terms of roundwood equivalent, 1974 rail transportation freight rates, and on the expectation that the Soviet Union will engage in a level of timber harvesting and consumption in 1990 that is consistent with growth of its forest economy between 1970 and 1975. The estimates of timber available for export in 1990 concur with those of the United Nations for the year 2000 although the level of timber to be harvested and consumed in the USSR in 1990 estimated in this study is lower than that presented in all other Western estimates of future Soviet forest activity. No other Western study has estimated future timber supply and demand by examining the likely regional structure of the timber and wood-processing industries, or by measuring the critical physical increases in timber harvesting which can be realistically posited and achieved in the European North, in Western and Eastern Siberia, and in the Far East. The scenario presented for 1990 thus portrays the characteristics of the timber and wood-processing industries to be expected by 1990 if the USSR continues to change and develop in a manner consistent with most of its post–World War II development. Expectations of greatly expanded future performance in the Soviet forest industries during this century are clearly unfounded. If the USSR radically departs from past growth patterns it is likely to be in the form of stagnation or decline caused by reductions after 1976 in the allocation of capital to reforestation, manufacturing investment, and regional infrastructure, but not by the volume of timber available for harvesting. If future growth conforms to that recorded for the period 1970–1975, the timber and wood-processing industries will register modest increases but still will not be constrained by the physical volume of the timber resource. The USSR will record significant achievements indeed in the 1980s if it is able to expand and develop by 1990 in a manner consistent with that of the 1960s and early 1970s.

The present study was originally intended to complement the expected Soviet long-range forecasts to 1990. This plan apparently is not to be implemented as such and many of its objectives are now contained in the "General Outline for the Location of Productive Forces in the USSR for the Period Ending 1990."[95] Given the absence, therefore, of planning targets, the scenario presented in this study must be based on criteria other than those that were expected to emanate from the long-term plan. If Soviet planners are unsure that their priorities and abilities will achieve accelerated rates of growth in the future, then they could turn to past performance as a means of justifying their implicit future expectations. If planners and economic managers do strive to continue to extend the growth of the forest industry in a manner consistent with the past, then the scenario presented in this study can be taken as a guide to what may happen rather than what the forest economy could become if stringent assumptions were met.

The "General Outline" emphasizes that energy and material-intensive industries should be located in appropriate hinterland areas but also envisages in the European USSR a fuller utilization of low-quality deciduous timber in the production of particleboard and plywood, and modernization of existing plants and equipment. These suggestions reinforce trends evident in production statistics which indicate that Soviet planners are continuing to reassess the relative merits of development in that country's heartland and hinterland areas, and that different schools of thought within the Soviet leadership and administration have prevented the enunciation of definite national and regional economic objectives. The needs of individual sectors of the Soviet economy further reinforce the dilemma posed to those seeking unanimity and simplicity in planning by a large and diverse country with spatially differentiated demands and capabilities. The present study demonstrates how the needs of the lumber and pulp industry, for example, do not spatially coincide with those of the plywood or particleboard industry; each industry has different requirements for timber species and has different relationships with sectors of domestic and foreign demand. Apparently Soviet planners cannot reconcile the need to develop lumber and pulp in northern and eastern regions while simultaneously developing plywood and particleboard capacity in established European regions and still focus the nation's attention on such spectacular projects as the BAM or the Angara-Yenisei territorial-production complex.

The quality of resources and the influence of internal and external scale economies, including those associated with transportation costs, may preclude the promulgation by Soviet planners of relatively simple and clear-cut prognostications of future development. Furthermore, the greater integration or cooperation of the Soviet economy with economies of the CMEA and the Industrialized West acts to reduce the ability of Soviet planners to set forth immutable plans for the future. Soviet ability to earn foreign exchange, and foreign need for Soviet resources fluctuate with the world industrial economy and prevent the Soviet Union from ignoring the uncertain nature of world economic conditions when planning its own future development. So many components of the Soviet future now rest with the vagaries and complexities of that country's international economic relations rather than with relatively straight-forward rigid ideologically-based planning directives as in the past that prediction of the future development of even such seemingly unsophisticated industries as those associated with timber and wood-processing is a confusing and often bewildering assignment.

As the Soviet economy has matured and expanded in its international relations, Soviet planners and administrators have become more aware of the need to be conscious of the costs associated with regional development and resource utilization, and may have derived some measures for internal use in the calculation of the relationship between a unit of foreign exchange and domestic costs of development and production. Greater awareness of economic efficiency in the allocation of scarce resources has important implications for regional development and exploitation of such spatially-extensive resources as timber because it means that Soviet planners will be forced to stress the renewable aspects of timber resources by encouraging forest regeneration in existing regions of activity rather than by engaging in hit and run or "nomadic" cutting techniques which have been so noticeable in the northward and eastward movement of logging.[96] Future supplies of timber will emanate not only from the virgin forests of the north and east but also from better managed stands in European and Uralian regions. More emphasis will be placed on utilization of heretofore frequently ignored deciduous species in accessible regions of European USSR and in the planting of select timber species during the process of reforestation.

Soviet regional resource development also appears to be increasingly influenced not only by foreign markets but also by the changing availability of labor reserves within the USSR. The "General Outline," in its present form is unacceptable to Gosplan because it has omitted specific proposals for the supply of adequate labor resources to northern and eastern developments and for the full employment of Central Asian and Transcaucasian populations. The reluctance of young Soviet labor to remain in rural and peripheral regions is a common complaint of the Soviet press and is seriously hampering the USSR's ability to exploit peripheral resources—such as timber—without the expensive attendant amenities and infrastructure obviously now demanded by many Soviet workers. The environmental and social hardships associated with development in those regions coinciding with the location of the bulk of Soviet timber reserves further exacerbate the already short supply of labor available for many of the onerous and socially unrewarding jobs associated with the timber and wood-processing industries.

The Soviet Union obviously can overcome many of the obstacles it faces in development of timber and other resources in the peripheral regions of the European North, Siberia, and the Far East. More productive technology can reduce the need for labor but will require changes in the traditional priorities of Soviet planners who have downplayed the importance of foreign technology and domestic innovation in the resource-extractive sectors of the timber industry. Foreign technology for many of the branches of the wood-processing industry can enhance the economic viability of both resource extraction and conversion in peripheral regions and is now a common ingredient in most of the major operations of the pulp and paper industry.

Greater wage incentives for labor by themselves are unlikely to attract the necessary number of workers to developing forest regions as long as alternative forms of employment are available in the economies of heartland regions. Improvements in the quality of life, however, coupled with the techniques practiced in other regions of the world for moving labor to and from difficult areas on a rotational basis, plus real incentive wages could help the USSR overcome many of the current and anticipated labor shortages in northern and eastern regions. Greater use of foreign labor also cannot be dismissed as eventually becoming an important ingredient of Soviet labor and regional development policy, especially if the USSR continues to draw into its sphere of political and economic

influence countries with significant indigenous surpluses of labor and shortages of such raw materials as timber.

Many subjects related to forest-based regional economic development and international commodity sales require further analysis in terms of their possible association with regional timber reserves, international marketing patterns, foreign technology, domestic and international supplies of capital, and shortages of skilled and semi-skilled labor. The present study simply demonstrates that the Soviet Union has sufficient *quantities* of timber resources to sustain a large domestic forest-based industry and to participate in world timber markets to the year 1990; many of the *qualitative* dimensions of the Soviet 1990 timber industry will depend on the ultimate resolution of numerous, increasingly acute, but still poorly understood processes and influences affecting utilization of timber resources.

## NOTES

1. Brenton M. Barr, *The Soviet Wood-Processing Industry: A Linear Programming Analysis of the Role of Transportation Costs in Location and Flow Patterns* (Toronto: University of Toronto Press, 1970); Brenton Barr, "Regional Variation in Soviet Pulp and Paper Production," Association of American Geographers, *Annals*, 61 (March 1971): 45–64; Brenton Barr and K. Smillie, "Some Spatial Interpretations of Alternative Optimal and Suboptimal Solutions to the Transportation Problem," *Canadian Geographer*, 16, no. 4 (1972): 356–64.

2. *Soviet Geography: Review and Translation*, 18, no. 9 (November 1977): 699–700.

3. See Brenton M. Barr, "The Importance of Regions in Analyses of the Soviet Forest Resource: A Reply," *Canadian Geographer*, 10, no. 4 (1966): 234–37.

4. Barr, *Soviet Wood-Processing*; Barr, "Regional Variation"; Barr and Smillie, "Some Spatial Interpretations"; Barr, *Domestic and International Implications of Regional Change in the Soviet Timber and Wood-Processing Industries, 1970–1990*, Discussion Paper No. 4 (June 1978), Association of American Geographers, Project on Soviet Natural Resources in the World Economy; Barr, "Soviet Timber: Regional Supply and Demand, 1970–1990," *Arctic*, 32, no. 4 (1979): 308–28.

5. W. R. J. Sutton, "The Forest Resources of the USSR: Their Exploitation and Their Potential," *Commonwealth Forestry Review*, no. 160 (June 1975): 110–38.

6. Robert N. North and Jan J. Solecki, "The Soviet Forest Products Industry: Its Present and Potential Exports," *Canadian Slavonic Papers*, 19, no. 3 (September 1977): 281–311.

7. Sutton, "Forest Resources," p. 136.

8. North and Solecki, "Soviet Forest," pp. 310–11.

9. Sutton, "Forest Resources," p. 112.

10. Ibid.

11. Kathleen Braden, *The Role of Imported Technology in the Export Potential of Soviet Forest Products*, Discussion Paper No. 16 (November 1979), Association of American

Geographers, Project on Soviet Natural Resources in the World Economy.

12. R. L. Sopko, ed., *Special Report: Pulp and Paper Industry in the USSR* (Stockholm: Dirosab, Institute of East-European Market and Economic Research, 1976).

13. Jaakko Pöyry Consulting Oy, "Outlook for Forest Industries in the Comecon Countries—Prospects for Machinery Exports," (Helsinki, 8 February 1977). The cost of this report is $5,600; the cost of the subsection devoted to the USSR (about 100 pages and appendices) is $1,500 (personal communication, Kari Ramo, Jaakko Pöyry Consulting Oy, 27 February 1978).

14. United Nations, Economic Commission for Europe and FAO, *European Timber Trends and Prospects 1950 to 2000* (Geneva: Supplement 3 to vol. 29 of the *Timber Bulletin for Europe*, 1976).

15. Ibid., p. i.

16. Barr, *Soviet Wood-Processing*; Barr, "Regional Variation; Barr, *Domestic and International*.

17. *Narodnoye khozyaistvo SSR v 1979 g.* [Economy of the USSR in 1979] (Moscow: Statistika, 1980).

18. *Narodnoye khozyaistvo RSFSR v 1978 g.* [Economy of the RSFSR in 1978] (Moscow: Statistika, 1979).

19. Barr, *Soviet Wood-Processing*; Barr and Smillie, "Some Spatial Interpretations."

20. V. I. Melnikov et al., "Transport costs in rail hauls of wood products," *Ekonomika i upravleniye* 1977, no. 4 (Moscow): 45.

21. Barr, *Soviet Wood-Processing*; Barr and Smillie, "Some Spatial Interpretations."

22. Theodore Shabad, private observations, Washington, October 1977.

23. M. V. Kanevsky and G.Ya. Shaitanov, *Lesnoi eksport SSSR* [Wood exports of the USSR] (Moscow: Lesnaya promyshlennost, 1975), pp. 109–20.

24. Barr, *Soviet Wood-Processing*.

25. Barr, *Soviet Wood-Processing*; Barr and Smillie, "Some Spatial Interpretations."

26. Kathleen Braden, "Role of Imported."

27. Allan Rodgers, *Commodity Flows, Resource Potential and Regional Economic Development: The Example of the Soviet Far East*, Discussion Paper No. 27 (October 1980), Association of American Geographers, Project on Soviet Natural Resources in the World Economy.

28. J. Holowacz, *World Wood Review*, 18, no. 6 (May 1977): 20.

29. See Barr, *Domestic and International*, Tables 5, 6, and 7.

30. Melnikov, "Transport costs," p. 7.

31. Barr, *Soviet Wood-Processing*, pp. 44–48.

32. V. A. Nikolayuk, "Changes in forest resources as a result of human activity," *Lesnoye khozyaistvo*, 1975, no. 7, p. 4.

33. B. S. Petrov, *Spravochnik ekonomista derevoobrabatyvayushchei promyshlennosti* [Handbook of the woodworking industry economist] 2nd edition (Moscow: Lesnaya promyshlennost, 1974), p. 6.

34. V. L. Dzhikovich, *Ekonomika lesnogo khozyaistva* [Economics of the forest industry] (Moscow: Lesnaya promyshlennost, 1970), pp. 38–39.

35. See Nikolayuk, "Changes in forest resources," and G. I. Vorobyev et al., *Lesnoye khozyaistvo SSSR* [Forest economy of the USSR] (Moscow: Lesnaya promyshlennost, 1977), p. 129.

36. *Current Digest of the Soviet Press* (hereafter *CDSP*), 29, no. 6 (1977): 11.

37. The 10th Five-Year Plan said a basic task was "to expand logging and wood-processing in Siberia and the Far East and to make more rational use of timber resources, *especially* in the European part of the USSR," *CDSP*, 28, no. 16 (1976): 19. Phased development of European, Urals and Siberian forests and possible levels of harvesting in Siberia by 2000 is discussed in V. S. Belousova, I. N. Voyevoda, and N. G. Salatova, "Ways of enhancing the cost-effectiveness of wood production and the use of forest resources in Siberia," *Priroda lesov i povysheniye ikh produktivnosti* [The environment of forest and enhancement of productivity] (Novosibirsk: Nauka, 1973), pp. 243–58 (reference of p. 248).

38. *Vneshnyaya torgovlya SSSR v 1975 godu* [Foreign trade of the USSR in 1975] (Moscow, 1976).

39. *Vneshnyaya torgovlya SSSR v 1978 g.* (Moscow, 1979), p. 39; *Vneshnyaya torgovlya SSSR v 1981 g.* (Moscow, 1982), p. 39.

40. *Vneshnyaya torgovlya SSSR v 1978 g.*, p. 230. *Vneshnyaya torgovlya SSSR v 1981 g.*, p. 230.

41. *Ekonomicheskaya geografiya lesnykh resursov SSSR* [Economic geography of forest resources of the USSR] (Moscow: Lesnaya promyshlennost, 1979), p. 307.

42. *Pulp and Paper International*, Review Number, 1975, p. 84; J. Brougher, "USSR Foreign Trade: A Greater Role for Trade with the West," in U.S. Congress, Joint Economic Committee, *Soviet Economy in a New Perspective*, 94th Cong., 2nd sess., 1976, pp. 677–94.

43. *Vneshnyaya torgovlya SSSR v 1978 g.*, pp. 173–75; *Vneshnyaya torgovlya SSSR v 1981 g.*, p. 173.

44. *Vneshnyaya torgovlya SSSR v 1978 g.*, p. 241; *Vneshnyaya torgovlya SSSR v 1981 g.*, pp. 239–40.

45. *Pravda Ukrainy*, 2 December 1980, p. 6.

46. *Ekonomicheskaya gazeta*, 1981, no. 1, p. 11.

47. *Narodnoye khozyaistvo SSSR v 1979 g.*, p. 191. The volume of commercial roundwood recovered slightly in 1980, to 278 million m³, dropping again slightly to 277 million in 1981.

48. *Pravda Ukrainy*, 2 December 1980, p. 4.

49. Ibid.

50. *CDSP*, 29, no. 19 (1977): 17.

51. Reported in Sutton, "Forest Resources," p. 112.

52. Ibid.

53. Barr, *Soviet Wood-Processing*, p. 24.

54. Prepared as background material for Barr and Smillie, "Some Spatial Interpretations."

55. J. L. Keays and J. V. Hatton, "The Implications of full-forest Utilization and Worldwide Supplies of Wood by year 2000," *Pulp and Paper International* (June 1975): 49–52.

56. See P. Blandon, "Soviets Plan Greater Logging Productivity," *World Wood* (March 1977), pp. 18–19.

57. Barr, *Soviet Wood-Processing*.

58. Ibid.

59. See Barr, *Domestic and International*, Tables 5, 6, and 7.

60. Alan Abouchar, "The Transportation Dual and Economic Planning," *Annals of Regional Science* 3, no. 2 (1969): 181.

61. Kanevsky and Shaitanov, *Lesnoi eksport*, pp. 120–25.

62. This problem is discussed in *CDSP*, 29, no. 51 (1977): 7, 28.

63. For example, Kanevsky and Shaitanov, *Lesnoi eksport*.

64. Allen Lenz and Hediga Kravalis, "An Analysis of Recent and Potential Soviet and East European Exports to Fifteen Industrialized Western Countries," in U.S Congress, Joint Economic Committee, *East European Economies Post-Helsinki*, 95th Cong., 1st sess., 1977, pp. 1055–75; and "Soviet /EE Hard Currency Export Capabilities," mimeo, Office of East-West Policy and Planning, Bureau of East-West Trade, U.S. Dept. of Commerce, 11 October 1977.

65. Brougher, "USSR Foreign Trade."

66. North and Solecki, "Soviet Forest Products."

67. *Vneshnyaya torgovlya SSSR v 1978 g.*, pp. 27–28; *Vneshnyaya torgovlya SSSR v 1979 g.*, pp. 27–28.

68. Kanevsky and Shaitanov, *Lesnoi eksport*, pp. 120–25.

69. North and Solecki, "Soviet Forest Products," p. 288.

70. Allan Rodgers, *Commodity Flows*, pp. 68–70.

71. See Arthur J. Smith, "The Council of Mutual Economic Assistance in 1977: New Economic Power, New Political Perspectives and Some Old and New Problems," in *East European Economies Post-Helsinki*, pp. 152–73.

72. Kanevsky and Shaitanov, *Lesnoi eksport*, pp. 120–25.

73. See the discussion in *CDSP*, 28, no. 14 (1976): 21, 32.

74. Derived from: Kathleen Braden, "Role of Imported," p. 23; personal communications from Kathleen Braden, 31 May 1979, and 3 September 1979; visit to Bratsk by the author, July 1976.

75. *World Wood*, 17, no. 11 (October 1976): 5.

76. Sutton, "Forest Resources," p. 136.

77. Ibid.

78. United Nations, *European Timber Trends*, p. 148.

79. Ibid.

80. Ibid., p. 159.

81. Ibid., pp. 161, 163.

82. *Pravda*, 12 October 1974, p. 2.

83. Sutton, "Forest Resources," p. 113.

84. *Lesnaya promyshlennost*, 1977, no. 8, p. 7.

85. Discussed in P. Blandon, "Contemporary problems in the Soviet forest and wood economy," *Osteuropa*, 30, no. 4 (April 1980): 330–43.

86. *Lesnaya promyshlennost*, 1977, no. 10, pp. 1–3; *Lesnaya promyshlennost*, 1977, no. 11, pp. 3–8.

87. *CDSP*, 28, no. 11 (1976): 27.

88. See *CDSP*, 29, no. 52 (1977): 20.

89. See the general discussion of CMEA's expanding influence in Soviet and third-world development in A. J. Smith, "Council of Mutual Economic Assistance."

90. Many facets of the BAM's construction are discussed in *CDSP*, 28, no. 14 (1976): 21, 32; no. 19: 1–6, 27; no. 36: 9–11; 29, no. 28 (1977): 3–6, 8.

91. A. B. Smith, "Soviet Dependence on Siberian Resource Development," in *Soviet Economy in a New Perspective*, p. 481.

92. Plans for industrial projects related to the BAM are discussed in *CDSP*, 28, no. 48 (1976): 14, 18.

93. Soviet policies related to substitute forms of wood fiber, resolution of labor shortages, regional specialization in advanced forms of wood-processing, and many associated matters alluded to in the present study are cogently reviewed in "Matching Manpower and Industry Sites," *CDSP*, 29, no. 47 (1977): 1–4; "Process More Timber Near Cutting Sites," *CDSP*, 29, no. 41 (1977): 7, 28; *Lesnaya promyshlennost*, 1977, no. 1, pp. 1–3; no. 8, pp. 6–7; and no. 10, pp. 1–3; Yu. A. Kudryavtsev, "The forest industry of the land of the Soviets," *Lesnoi zhurnal*, 1972, no. 6, pp. 11–17.

94. North and Solecki, "Soviet Forest Products," p. 301.

95. *Soviet Geography: Review and Translation*, 18, no. 9 (November 1977): 699–700.

96. See the general dialogue between conservationists and lumbermen related to this problem in *CDSP*, 28, no. 32 (1976): 1–6.

## APPENDIX

*Sources for Tables 1 and 2*
Table 1

The basic sources of statistical material for 1970, 1975, 1979, and 1980 are: *Narodnoye khozyaistvo SSSR v 1970 godu* (Moscow, 1971), *Narodnoye khozyaistvo SSSR v 1975 godu* (Moscow, 1976), *Narodnoye khozyaistvo SSSR v 1979 godu* (Moscow, 1980), *Narodnoye khozyaistvo RSFSR v 1970 godu* (Moscow, 1971), *Narodnoye khozyaistvo RSFSR v 1975 godu* (Moscow, 1976), *Vneshnyaya torgovlya SSSR za 1970 godu* (Moscow, 1971), *Vneshnyaya torgovlya SSSR v 1975 godu* (Moscow, 1976), *Vneshnyaya torgovlya SSSR v 1979 godu* (Moscow, 1980), and personal communications, Mr. J. Holowacz.

Supporting sources and those containing fragmentary and fugitive data are I. S. Yarmola, *Voprosy lesosnabzheniya v SSSR* [Wood supply problems in the USSR] 2nd ed., (Moscow: Lesnaya promyshlennost, 1972); M. V. Kanevsky and G.Ya. Shaitanov, *Lesnoi eksport SSSR* [Wood exports of USSR] (Moscow: Lesnaya promyshlennost, 1975); *Narodnoye khozyaistvo Belorusskoi SSR 1976* [Economy of Belorussian SSR 1976] (Minsk, 1976); *Spravochnik ekonomista derevoobrabatyvayushchei promyshlennosti* [Handbook of the woodworking industry economist] 2nd ed. (Moscow: Lesnaya promyshlennost, 1974); *Ekonomika i kultura Litovskoi SSR v 1975 godu* [Economy and culture of Lithuanian SSR in 1975] (Vilnius, 1976); *Narodnoye khozyaistvo Latviiskoi SSR v 1973 godu* [Economy of Latvian SSR in 1973] (Riga, 1974); N. A. Medvedev, *Ekonomika lesnoi promyshlennosti* [Forest industry economics] 2nd ed. (Moscow, 1976); Z. V. Uchastkina et al., *Spravochnik po ekonomike dlya rabotnikov tsel-*

*lyulozno-bumazhnykh predpriyatii* [Economics handbook for workers in pulp and paper mills] (Moscow: Lesnaya promyshlennost, 1973); Z. V. Uchastkina, *Ekonomika tsellyulozno-bumazhnoi promyshlennosti* [Economics of pulp and paper industry] 2nd ed. (Moscow: Lesnaya promyshlennost, 1973); V. V. Glotov, *Lesnaya i lesopererabatyvayushchaya promyshlennost ekonomicheskikh rayonov* [Timber and woodworking industry by economic regions] (Moscow: Lesnaya promyshlennost, 1970); *Narodne gospodarstvo Ukrainskoi RSR u 1973 rotsi* [Economy of Ukrainian SSR in 1973; in Ukrainian] (Kiev, 1974); G. K. Stupnev, S. M. Khasdan and V. N. Plakhov, *Derevoobrabatyvayushchaya promyshlennost za gody devyatoi pyatiletki* [Woodworking industry in the 9th Five-Year Plan] (Moscow: Lesnaya promyshlennost, 1976); S. M. Khasdan, *Sostoyaniye i osnovnye napravleniya razvitiya derevoobrabatyvayushchikh proizvodstv* [Present state and basic trends of development of woodworking plants] (Moscow: Lesnaya promyshlennost, 1973); *Ekonomika i kultura Litovskoi SSR v 1974 g.* (Vilnius, 1975); *Narodnoye khozyaistvo Estonskoi SSR v 1969 g.* (Tallinn, 1970); *Ekonomicheskaya gazeta*, 1981, no. 5, p. 11.

Calculation of the 1980 values of imported roundwood and roundwood exports departs slightly from that used for the other categories to avoid the methodological problem of negative imports that would occur if the negative change, 1970–75, in imported roundwood were projected to 1990. Household fuelwood does not comprise part of interregional shipment of roundwood and is excluded from Table 1; household fuelwood is included in Table 3 to gauge the effect of all timber harvesting on the annual increment of principal species.

The terms employed by foresters to describe the USSR's forests are discussed in Barr, *Soviet Wood-Processing*, pp. 40–44, and Sutton, "Forest Resources," pp. 110–112.

Table 2

In addition to the sources for Table 1, Table 2 was compiled from data in Nikolayuk, "Changes in forest resources"; S. G. Sinitsyn, *Lesnoi fond i organizatsiya ispolzovaniya lesnykh resursov SSSR* [The forest resource and organization of forest resource use] (Moscow: Lesnaya promyshlennost, 1976); *Narodnoye khozyaistvo SSSR v 1973 g.* (Moscow, 1974); *Narodnoye khozyaistvo RSFSR v 1973 g.* (Moscow, 1974).

# 18

# THE ROLE OF IMPORTED TECHNOLOGY IN THE EXPORT POTENTIAL OF SOVIET FOREST PRODUCTS

KATHLEEN E. BRADEN
Seattle Pacific University

## Introduction

The forests of the Soviet Union contain approximately 82 billion cubic meters of wood, or 34 percent of world reserves, including 58 percent of the world's coniferous forests.[1] Yet the forest products sector of the Soviet economy has not traditionally performed well, both in terms of supplying domestic markets or realizing export potential.

Soviet planners are acknowledging the poor record of the forest products industry, particularly in light of the disappointing performance of the Bratsk forest products complex in East Siberia. The Ministry of Timber and Woodworking has often fallen short of planned output targets for production from commercial species, with shortfalls at times reaching more than 10 million cubic meters.[2] The Ministry of Pulp and Paper has been criticized in the Soviet press for paper shortages, which are blamed on factors ranging from lack of raw materials to organizational problems. In 1977 the pulp production plan was not fulfilled, and the pulp industry worked at only 89.6 percent capacity.[3]

The completion of the 10th Five-Year Plan (1976–80) witnessed a decline in output in the logging, sawnwood and plywood branches of the forest products industry from 1975 levels of production. No output targets for these three sectors were published in the guidelines of the 11th Five-Year Plan (1981–85).[4] Furthermore, dissatisfaction with administration in the forest products industries was reflected in the November 1980 reorganization of ministries, with the two major forest products administrations recombined, as they had been twelve years previously, into the single Ministry of Timber, Pulp, Paper, and Woodworking (abbreviated in Russian as *Minlesbumprom SSSR*).

One of the problems in the forest products industries has been the lack of investment attention by central planners. Technological levels in the industries remain

*The support of the International Research and Exchanges Board and the United States Office of Education (Fulbright-Hays Program) is gratefully acknowledged by the author.*

far behind those of Western forest products nations, and improvements in machinery are distributed unevenly throughout the sector. Equipment in many branches of the forest products sector, particularly sawnwood, is criticized as outdated and inefficient.[5] Forest products have grown unevenly, and are still dominated by lower value materials such as roundwood.

Despite poor performance, the Soviet forest products sector has a substantial potential for improvement in satisfying domestic needs and becoming a significant export force in the world market. Brenton Barr has suggested that the Soviet Union is capable of fulfilling world demand for its timber through 1990 and beyond, provided technological improvements in the comprehensive use of roundwood continue to be made. The findings in this chapter would temper that conclusion by pointing out changes that must occur before such a goal can be realized.

The USSR has traditionally imported much of the technology needed in its diverse forest products sector. World War II played an important role in improving Soviet technology as many factories were expropriated in Karelia or on Sakhalin Island and as the war reparations programs brought in European forest products equipment.

Beginning in the 1960s, the type and volume of foreign technology imports began a shift toward large-scale "turnkey" projects, integrating advanced technology from many nations. In some cases, this policy has been successful in enhancing output levels, but in other cases the resulting complexes have not operated satisfactorily.

A brief assessment of some characteristics of the Soviet forest products sector would be helpful in comprehending both the assets and problems of the industry. These characteristics can be summarized as follows:

1. *Heterogeneity of the Sector*

The Soviet forest products sector should not be viewed as a single industry within the USSR economy, but convenience of analysis frequently causes the sector to be treated as a unit. This report uses the term *forest products sector* to encompass logging (referred to as wood removals by Soviets), sawnwood, pulp and paper, composition board (fiberboard and particleboard), paperboard, wood chemicals, furniture, and miscellaneous wood products such as railroad ties or matches. Silvicultural activities are not within the scope of this report. Until the 1980 recombination of ministries, management of the forest products industry was the responsibility of two national administrations, the Ministry of Pulp and Paper and the Ministry of Timber and Woodworking. These administrations had been criticized for lack of interministry coordination, and reports in the Soviet press provided evidence of ministry rivalry.[6] Furthermore, some local autonomy is possible in the sector because small-scale, mobile logging operations in remote areas are often beyond ministry control. N. A. Medvedev, former director of the Economic Planning Administration in the Ministry of Timber and Woodworking, noted in 1978 that lumber was being produced by enterprises affiliated with more than seventy different ministries and departments. Enterprises under direct ministry control accounted for less than half of total output.[7]

Despite the sector's diversity, Soviet planners are aware that by-products of some processing methods can be used as inputs into other branches, such as sawmill chips for the pulp industry. More integration has been attempted among enterprises in new forest industry complexes.

## 2. Resource Stock Quantity and Quality

The distributional pattern and characteristics of the USSR's vast quantity of wood will be discussed later, with the aim of explaining the importance of these patterns to the Soviet export position. However, the drawbacks may be summarized as follows: much of the wood is in inaccessible areas, or at least in areas which would be expensive to harvest; the stock composition contains many less desirable commercial species; and a large portion of the resource requires long regrowth periods to maintain stocks.[8]

## 3. Resource Waste

Soviet forests have traditionally suffered from lack of sound cutting, replanting, and utilization measures. Selective cutting was not practiced in the past, and the less desirable species, particularly of the deciduous type, were left as waste or burned on site. Reforestation is still not widespread, although recent improvements have been attempted.

## 4. Spatial Imbalance of Resource and Markets

The heartland-hinterland development debate is keenly felt in the forest products sector, and will be a frequent theme in this report. Many of the remaining substantial stands of timber in the USSR are located east of the Urals, far from the main source of domestic demand. Stands closer to consumption points have been drawn down to the point of overutilization. However, some advantage is enjoyed in the location of export facilities for wood products along the Pacific coast or in the European Northwest. New timber and chip processing ports have been constructed in the Soviet Far East, and completion of the Baikal-Amur Mainline rail system should facilitate the export of wood from East Siberia to coastal ports.

## 5. Technology Imports

The forest products sector's capital stock has been dominated by foreign machinery and equipment. This characteristic is particularly true for sawnwood and fiberboard industries, less true for the logging or furniture sectors, and more recently true for pulp and paper and particleboard industries. The Soviets have expressed an interest not only in substituting foreign capital for domestic, but also in upgrading their management and innovation skills. Recent technical cooperation agreements with Western nations may advance Soviet engineering capabilities for plan design and maintenance. This report provides some details on these agreements.

## 6. Low-value Products

Soviet forest products are of lower value than in comparable Western nations. Even recently, a large portion of yearly wood removals still went for firewood. In 1980, for example, 22 percent of wood removals by cubic meter measure was counted as firewood. The United States, Canada, and Finland each produce five to ten times the amount of basic lumber products per tree felled than does the USSR.[9] Utilization of wood in the USSR follows a different pattern from that in Western nations. Less construction lumber and plywood is used, particularly since single family houses are not prevalent in Soviet urban areas. More Soviet composition board goes into the making of forms or furniture. The Soviet packaging industry consumes less paperboard and paper than that in the West. Wood exports from the USSR have also been dominated by low value products such as roundwood.

## 7. Poor Sector Performance and Large Growth Potential

As noted earlier, the Soviet forest products sector has often failed to fulfill planned output targets and has not received a high investment priority from Soviet planners. Solecki and North have suggested that domestic consumption has at times suffered so that export levels might be maintained. However, one must take into account the large resource stock and the potential world demand for Soviet forest products. Despite current shortcomings, the Soviet forest products sector has the potential for favorable growth rates both in domestic production and export-oriented activities, provided the sector's problems can be addressed by Soviet planning.

## The Current Export Position of the Soviet Forest Products Sector

Even the most positive predictions about the USSR's ability to meet world demand for Soviet forest products through 1990 note many conditions which must be satisfied before the Soviets can realize their potential. These conditions usually relate to problems of regional imbalances in timber supply, overcutting trends, quality drawbacks to the wood resource, lack of investment in new capacity, and the need to import much of the required capital. This section will examine briefly some of the spatial patterns which affect the Soviet forest products sector and have an impact on export potential. The geographic characteristics of the forest products sector are only summarized here, as they have been covered more fully elsewhere.[10]

## Distributional Patterns[11]

Most of the timber land in the Soviet Union is located within the RSFSR in the taiga forest zones. Table 1 presents a regional breakdown of selected RSFSR forest characteristics. Some important aspects of the stock's distribution include species mix, accessibility, age structure, and trunk diameter size.

The USSR is dominated by coniferous stands of larch, pine, spruce, fir and Siberian stone pine (see Table 2). Regions east of the Urals account for more than 75 percent of the coniferous forest area, and approximately 65 percent of the coniferous cutting area. The remaining deciduous stands, comprised primarily of birch, aspen and oak are found mainly in western areas of the USSR, in the Soviet Far East, and in mixed stands with conifers throughout river valleys of the RSFSR.[12]

About 73 percent of RSFSR timber is considered mature or overripe in age structure, particularly in eastern areas which have been underutilized. This "old age" characteristic represents costly foregone opportunity for consumers in the Soviet economy.

Table 2 presents the mix of commercial species in certain RSFSR regions and the regional breakdown of tree trunk diameter size. Larger diameter stocks are found in Tomsk and Irkutsk oblasts and Primorsky Krai. However, even virgin USSR timber is generally smaller in diameter than comparable original stocks in North America because of different growing environments. Rapid advances in international technology for efficient use of small diameter trees have made smaller trunk size less of a problem for the Soviets. Yet, differences in diameter

sizes are sometimes cited by Soviet authors as reasons for the lower productivity of timber stands, despite the now common use of small diameter, second-growth trees in the West.[13]

Table 3 shows a sample of the use of various species in a large Siberian forest products complex. One of the problems in the Siberian forest species mix is the prevalence of larch, a less desirable commercial tree. Larch logs tend to sink in water, limiting transport choices. Larch is also highly resinous and presents production problems as machinery becomes gummed up with resins. However, the large quantity of larch available to the Soviets suggests that the acquisition of technology for the efficient use of larch should be a high priority. One of the major problems facing the Soviet forest products industry has been the imbalance between resource location and processing facilities location. Before the 1960s, most of the processing facilities were heavily utilized, often to the point of severe overcutting. Furthermore, centers of Soviet final demand for wood products showed a similar orientation to processing centers. Long distance hauls of raw materials or intermediate products would be necessary as the focus of timber harvest migrated eastward and northward. Thus, the forest products sector is subject to the heartland-hinterland controversy which many resource-oriented sectors of the Soviet economy are experiencing.

Rather than increase expensive long-distance hauls of logs, Soviet planners would prefer to transport final products which could better withstand freight charges. In the last two decades, planners have chosen to begin the shift of processing centers to heavily forested sites in East Siberia and Northern European Russia (see Table 4), often through creation of large-scale forest products complexes, such as Bratsk and Ust-Ilimsk. The shift has been most pronounced in woodpulp and paperboard man-

## TABLE 1
Geographic Distribution of RSFSR Forest Resource and Cut, 1973 (in million cubic meters)

| Region | 1 Forest Covered Area | 2 Including Coniferous | 3 Cutting Area | 4 Including Coniferous | 5 Actual Cut | 6 Percent Mature and Overripe |
|---|---|---|---|---|---|---|
| Northwest | 7,605.0 | 6,536.1 | — | — | 96.9 (27%) | 75.6 |
| Central | 1,569.5 | 800.3 | — | — | 28.9 ( 8%) | 28.7 |
| Volga-Vyatka | 1,807.8 | 1,283.8 | — | — | 29.6 ( 8%) | 49.3 |
| Central Chernozem | 106.5 | 31.2 | — | — | 1.1 ( .3%) | 12.8 |
| Volga | 945.3 | 235.9 | 7.8 | 1.3 ( .3%) | 11.3 ( 3%) | 40.8 |
| North Caucasus | 402.9 | 49.7 | 4.0 | 0.5 ( .1%) | 3.5 ( 1%) | 48.3 |
| European RSFSR | 12,437.0 (16%) | 8,937.0 (15%) | 168.5 (28%) | 97.6 (28%) | 171.3 (47%) | 64.0 |
| Urals | 2,979.7 ( 4%) | 2,183.3 ( 4%) | 68.5 (11%) | 35.2 ( 9%) | 57.0 (16%) | 68.1 |
| West Siberia | 8,736.0 (12%) | 6,243.5 (10%) | 104.0 (17%) | 51.4 (13%) | 31.6 ( 9%) | 74.8 |
| East Siberia | 27,432.7 (38%) | 24,695.2 (40%) | 160.0 (27%) | 115.6 (30%) | 66.5 (19%) | 75.2 |
| Far East | 21,396.2 (29%) | 19,162.9 (31%) | 102.3 (17%) | 84.2 (22%) | 32.1 ( 9%) | 75.4 |
| Total RSFSR | 72,981.6 | 61,221.9 | 603.0 | 384.0 | 359.0 | 72.8 |

NOTE: Sources for this table used different regionalization schemes, and exact correspondence was not possible. Forest covered area includes Groups I, II and III of forest types. Cutting area includes only regions for industrial exploitation.
SOURCES: For columns 1, 2 and 6, *Spravochnik ekonomista derevoobrabatyvayushchei promyshlennosti* [Economist's handbook of the woodworking industry] (Moscow: Lesnaya promyshlennost, 1974), p. 7. For columns 3 and 4, V. V. Glotov, *Razmeshcheniye lesopromyshlennogo proizvodstva* [Location of the forest products industry] (Moscow: Lesnaya promyshlennost, 1977), p. 21. For column 5, *Narodnoye khozyaistvo RSFSR v 1975 godu* [The economy of the RSFSR in 1975] (Moscow: Statistika, 1976), pp. 86–89.

TABLE 2
Commercial Species Mix and Trunk Diameter by Selected Regions (by percent of total species in region)

| Region | Spruce-Fir | Larch | Other Conifer | Hardwood | Coniferous Species Trunk Diameter | | |
|---|---|---|---|---|---|---|---|
| | | | | | <14cm | 14–24cm | >14cm |
| Arkhangelsk Oblast | 62 | — | 32 | 6 | 45 | 49 | 6 |
| Komi ASSR | 67 | — | 22 | 11 | 16 | 54 | 30 |
| Kirov Oblast | 56 | — | 13 | 31 | 25 | 56 | 19 |
| Perm Oblast | 72 | — | 12 | 16 | 22 | 56 | 22 |
| Sverdlovsk Oblast | 24 | — | 58 | 18 | 26 | 60 | 14 |
| Tomsk Oblast | 12 | — | 70 | 18 | 17 | 43 | 40 |
| Tyumen Oblast | 13 | 11 | 58 | 18 | 25 | 55 | 20 |
| Krasnoyarsk Krai | 23 | 31 | 34 | 12 | 19 | 58 | 23 |
| Irkutsk Oblast | 13 | 10 | 67 | 10 | 19 | 51 | 30 |
| Chita Oblast | — | 71 | 23 | 6 | 29 | 53 | 18 |
| Yakut ASSR | — | 100 | — | — | 45 | 49 | 6 |
| Primorsky Krai | 44 | 11 | 20 | 25 | 21 | 43 | 36 |
| Khabarovsk Krai | 45 | 40 | 9 | 6 | 34 | 51 | 15 |
| RSFSR Total | 14 | 38 | 21 | 21 | — | — | — |

SOURCES: V. V. Glotov, *Effektivnost razmeshcheniya proizvodstva lesnoi promyshlennosti* [Cost-effectiveness of location of the forest industry] (Moscow: TsNIITEILesprom, 1968), pp. 31–32. *Lesnoi fond RSFSR* [The forest resource of the RSFSR] (Moscow: Goslesbumizdat, 1962). See also: V. L. Gorovoi and G. A. Privalovskaya, *Geografiya lesnoi promyshlennosti SSSR* [Geography of the forest industry of the USSR] (Moscow: Nauka, 1966); V. V. Varankin, *Metodologicheskiye voprosy regionalnoi otsenki prirodnykh resursov* [Methodological problems of regional evaluations of natural resources] (Moscow: Nauka, 1974).

ufacture, less so for labor-intensive or market-oriented forest products like plywood, paper and furniture. The recent literature suggests that Soviet planners are evaluating the desirability of large forest products centers with complex operational linkages. Shabad has suggested that the East-West development argument has been decided in favor of already-developed European regions.[14] In the case of the forest products sector, some evidence is available to support Shabad's suggestion. Many older and inefficient sawmills in the European USSR are under reconstruction to modernize their machinery and operations. The scale of construction at some Siberian sites has fallen under criticism as the Bratsk complex has performed below capacity. The planned Lesosibirsk complex has been temporarily slowed as engineering decisions are reviewed.

Bratsk may serve to illustrate some of the problems created by huge timber processing centers.

Construction at the Bratsk forest products complex began in 1962. By 1975, capital investment had reached 927 million rubles, and the 10th Five-Year Plan (1976–80)

TABLE 3
Species Use in the Ust-Ilimsk Complex
(drawing on 437 million cubic meters of stock)

| Species | Percent of Total Wood Inputs |
|---|---|
| Pine | 40.0 |
| Spruce | 8.6 |
| Fir | 5.9 |
| Larch | 25.0 |
| Stone Pine | 5.0 |
| Hardwoods | 15.5 |

SOURCE: A. P. Petrov, "Organizatsiya kompleksnogo ispolzovaniya lesnykh resursov" [Organization of the complex use of forest resources]. Unpublished manuscript, Leningrad Forestry Academy, 1978, p. 247.

called for 420 million rubles investment. Planned annual material consumption for the complex includes 8 million cubic meters of roundwood drawing on a raw-material base of 3.4 million hectares.[15]

Table 5 shows estimates of output from Bratsk for 1973–75. There is little evidence to suggest recent improvements in the utilization of capacity at Bratsk. A 1978 *Izvestiya* article criticized the pulp and paper industry for not operating to full capacity from 1976 through 1978, and noted that the Bratsk, Selenginsk, and Amursk mills were operating at a loss. The article said that Bratsk used only 75 percent of its pulp production capacity in 1977 and failed to meet planned targets for output, profit and unit cost.[16]

The Bratsk complex has suffered from many of the disadvantages that a pioneering facility experiences, and therefore some of the problems that have occurred are easy to understand. Labor supply has been a continuing source of difficulty for planners of Siberian facilities. While wages are substantially higher at Bratsk than in forest products enterprises of European Russia, the labor turnover rate is high. Lack of social infrastructure has been blamed for some of the dissatisfaction of the labor force. Construction costs are high not only for plant building, but also for worker facilities and housing.

At the beginning of operations, many start-up delays were experienced at the Bratsk complex, Finnish machinery manufacturers interviewed by the author (see Appendix A) reported that equipment was delivered to Bratsk in some cases 2 to 2½ years earlier than buildings were completed. Severe climatic conditions caused storage problems.

Much of the technology used at Bratsk was supplied by foreign companies, but the actual import arrangements were made by *Prommashimport*, the Soviet foreign trade agency dealing with heavy machinery. The industrial ministries had less direct control over delivery dates of imported equipment. A separate administration handles construction of actual plant buildings. Coordination problems among all agencies involved in Bratsk resulted from this division of responsibilities. Other large complexes, such as Ust-Ilimsk, experienced similar start-up delays.[17]

Soviet planners are noting that sheer size of operations alone may not guarantee superior production performance. The disappointments at Bratsk may serve those in the USSR who favor less complex facilities and the modernization of older plants in western regions of the Soviet Union. However, complete agreement has apparently not been reached regarding locational policy for industrial sites. Galanshin, the former Minister of Pulp and Paper, suggested in 1978 that planning priority be given to completion of the Lesosibirsk complex in Krasnoyarsk Krai and the Asino complex in Tomsk, coupled with expansion at Ust-Ilimsk and the Amursk complexes.[18]

On the other hand, Voyevoda and Glotov have suggested that forest-industry complexes should have a narrower specialization in Siberia and the Far East, thus reducing the intricate production linkages required in a Bratsk-type complex.[19] They suggest that Siberian locations are favorable for pulp and paperboard mills, which require heavy inputs of raw materials, fuel, energy, and water but comparably less labor than do other forest products industries. Capacity could be increased in the European USSR for production of composition boards which require relatively more labor and can use by-products for raw materials. Voyevoda and Glotov suggest further that commercial timber operations and composition board enterprises are efficient activities for the Urals and for Kirov and Vologda oblasts. They base these locational ideas on breakdowns of production costs by region. Table 6 shows regional indices of total costs by industry branch, and tends to support Voyevoda and Glotov's thesis.

The construction of the Baikal-Amur Mainline is un-

likely to have a major impact on the location of processing facilities for the Soviet domestic wood market, but may direct more East Siberian timber to the Pacific coast for export. Total roundwood removals for the BAM zone are projected to reach 30 to 35 million cubic meters, with logging taking place mainly in the Upper Lena and Komsomolsk districts.

### Current Export Position of Soviet Forest Products

Several factors affecting the significance of Soviet forest products exports on the world market may be noted: the relative autonomy of the export sector, the mix of products exported, the location of export markets, and the purpose of forest products exports from the point of view of Soviet planners. A further influence, technology requirements, has a direct bearing on market orientation and product mix of forest exports, but will be discussed fully later in this report.

A brief look at the capacity of the Soviet forest products sector to continue to expand export levels would first be useful. Table 7 presents some growth indicators for the sector. While growth rates in industrial wood harvested, value of output, and exports of roundwood and sawnwood are impressive for the 1964–80 period, a closer examination suggests that growth has not been continuous. Disaggregating the time frame shows that the most recent trends display declining rates in all growth indicators.[20] The SOVMOD model predicted a 23.5 percent growth in the forest products output for 1975–80, consistent with the 1964–68 and 1969–73 periods.[21]

Barr has suggested a scenario wherein, given continuation of recent trends, the USSR will be capable of meeting world demand for its forest products through 1990. This is likely to be the case, should growth rates continue to show the longer term upward trend, and should the Soviet forest products sector overcome the slump suggested by the 1974–80 period.

TABLE 4
Regional Shifts in the Forest Products Industry, 1960 and 1975 (by regional share of national output)[1]

| Region | Sawnwood | | | Plywood | | | Fiberboard | | | Particleboard | | | Woodpulp | | |
|---|---|---|---|---|---|---|---|---|---|---|---|---|---|---|---|
| | 1960 | 1975 | Share Shift | 1960 | 1975 | Share Shift | 1960 | 1975 | Share Shift | 1960 | 1975 | Share Shift | 1960 | 1975 | Share Shift |
| I. Heavily forested[2] | 48.0 | 55.5 | +7.5 | 38.9 | 41.7 | +2.8 | 48.5 | 56.4 | +7.9 | 5.0 | 27.7 | +22.7 | 53.1 | 73.5 | +20.4 |
| Northern Russia | 18.0 | 18.6 | +0.6 | 25.0 | 19.6 | −5.4 | 25.0 | 24.8 | −0.2 | 3.8 | 11.7 | +7.9 | 24.7 | 39.2 | +14.5 |
| Urals | 10.0 | 10.0 | 0 | 8.0 | 15.3 | +7.3 | 16.2 | 13.5 | −2.7 | 0.6 | 7.6 | +7.0 | 19.1 | 10.0 | −9.1 |
| West Siberia | 4.0 | 6.1 | +2.1 | 2.4 | 2.5 | +0.1 | — | 2.0 | +2.0 | 1.3 | 2.4 | +1.1 | — | — | — |
| East Siberia | 11.0 | 15.0 | +4.0 | 1.3 | 2.3 | +1.0 | — | 11.8 | +11.8 | — | 4.4 | +4.4 | 0.8 | 17.3 | +16.5 |
| Far East | 5.0 | 5.8 | +0.8 | 2.3 | 2.1 | −0.2 | 7.3 | 4.4 | −2.9 | 1.3 | 1.7 | +0.4 | 8.5 | 7.1 | −1.4 |
| II. Lightly forested | 52.0 | 44.5 | −7.5 | 61.1 | 58.3 | −2.8 | 51.5 | 43.6 | −7.9 | 95.0 | 72.3 | −22.7 | 46.9 | 26.5 | −20.4 |
| USSR total | 100.0 | 100.0 | | 100.0 | 100.0 | | 100.0 | 100.0 | | 100.0 | 100.0 | | 100.0 | 100.0 | |

[1]Physical units, except for furniture, which is in value units.
[2]According to Glotov, the heavily forested regions of the USSR include the following: Arkhangelsk, Kirov, Kostroma and Vologda oblasts and Karelian and Komi ASSRs in Northern European Russia; Perm and Sverdlovsk oblasts and Bashkir ASSR in the Urals; Kemerovo, Tomsk and Tyumen oblasts and Altai Krai in West Siberia; all of East Siberia; all of Far East.
SOURCES: V. V. Glotov, *Razmeshcheniye lesopromyshlennogo proizvodstva* [Location of forest products industries] (Moscow: Lesnaya promyshlennost, 1977), pp. 24, 27, 29, 33, 36, 37, with furniture allocated to heavily and lightly forested regions on the basis of oblast data in *Narodnoye khozyaistvo RSFSR v 1970* [The economy of the RSFSR in 1970], pp. 138–39 (for 1960) and *Narodnoye khozyaistvo RSFSR v 1975 godu*, pp. 127–28 (for 1975).

Estimates of the Food and Agriculture Organization for 1977 show the USSR ranking fourth in log export volumes after Indonesia, the United States and Malaysia. In veneer exports, the USSR ranks second after Canada; in particleboard exports, third after West Germany and the United States; in fiberboard, second after the United States; in plywood, fourth after the United States, Japan and Canada; and in industrial roundwood, second after the United States. The USSR ranks first in volume of sawnwood exports.[22]

The FAO predicts that Europe will continue to experience a wood deficit and rising consumption. The agency predicts that the USSR and Canada will be the principal sources of roundwood and sawnwood exports to Europe. A recent consulting study by Jaakko Pöyry of Finland predicts that Scandinavian nations will have a difficult time competing with North America for forest products markets because of high interest charges which have adversely affected profit levels in Scandinavian forest products companies, while North American companies have enjoyed high profitability.[23]

It appears that the ability of the USSR to step into the European and Asian forest products markets more extensively depends largely on its own domestic decisions, rather than on competition from other nations. Most authors allow the great potential of Soviet forest products to play a large role in world markets, but many feel that Soviet planners need to increase investment in forest utilization.[24]

The product mix of Soviet exports and the locations of export markets are two factors affecting the Soviet export position which bear examination.

Product Mix of Exports

Table 8 shows the 1964–81 mix of forest products exports by value from the USSR. Most of exports are comprised of relatively low value roundwood and sawnwood. The

TABLE 5
Output of Selected Products at Bratsk Forest Products Complex in 1973–75 Compared with Installed Capacity

| Product | Unit | Ca-pacity | Output 1973 | 1974 | 1975 |
|---|---|---|---|---|---|
| Sawnwood | Thous. Cu.M. | 750 | 237.4 | 299.0 | 326.7 |
| Fiberboard | Mill. Sq.M. | 40 | 11.0 | 27.3 | 34.0 |
| Pulp[1] | Thous. Tons | 700 | 183.2 | 220.3 | 374.0 |
| Colophony | Thous. Tons | 20 | 13.4 | 15.6 | 16.4 |
| Feed Yeasts | Thous. Tons | 90 | 17.8 | 18.6 | 20.0 |
| Plywood[2] | Thous. Cu.M. | 200 | — | — | — |

[1]This may vary depending on type of pulp produced. These figures are for merchant cellulose.
[2]Plywood operations began in 1977.
SOURCES: Petrov, "Organizatsiya"; V. V. Glotov, *Lesnaya i lesopererabatyvayushchaya promyshlennosti ekonomicheskikh rayonov* [The timber and wood-processing industries of economic regions] (Moscow: Lesnaya promyshlennost, 1970), p. 191.

share of these commodities has fluctuated between 83 and 66 percent over the fifteen-year period, but has been generally downward. The emphasis on primary products exports reflects the general orientation toward lower value forest products in the USSR. While Soviet planners have desired to shift to export commodities of higher value, the current structure seems likely to continue, at least through 1990 for several reasons: substantial investment is required to upgrade quality or create new production facilities; the location of export facilities as noted by Barr is commonly close to areas of timber exploitation or sawmilling centers, but less conveniently situated with respect to higher-value products enterprises; and finally, the Soviets may have to substitute lower grade deciduous wood or forest byproducts in domestic consumption to free higher quality and quantity wood for export.

Location of Export Markets

The 1981 share of European markets in Soviet forest products exports is shown in Table 9. Europe is the major destination of most Soviet forest products, although Japan has become a prime market for Siberian roundwood exports.

There is little reason to believe that this geographic pattern of export destinations will change substantially by 1990. Europe should continue to absorb a large percentage of Soviet forest products exports, with the CMEA nations perhaps accepting a lower share in favor of hardcurrency destinations for USSR output.[25]

The Soviet Union has, at times, been aggressive in meeting the targets of Exportles, the Soviet trade organization dealing with forest products exports. In 1978, for example, the USSR temporarily cut its prices of coniferous sawnwood by an average of 15 percent for the British market to remain competitive with Sweden. Soviet prices were also linked to the Swedish krona to insure no disadvantage from changes in Swedish currency.[26] Britain alone accounted for 12 percent of Soviet coniferous sawnwood sales abroad in 1981, second after East Germany, the principal buyer within the Soviet bloc.

| | Paper | | | Paperboard | | | Furniture | | |
|---|---|---|---|---|---|---|---|---|---|
| | 1960 | 1975 | Share Shift | 1960 | 1975 | Share Shift | 1960 | 1975 | Share Shift |
| | 47.1 | 56.7 | +9.6 | 14.4 | 41.3 | +26.9 | 14.3 | 14.0 | −0.3 |
| | 17.9 | 29.5 | +11.6 | 4.4 | 20.5 | +16.1 | 3.4 | 3.1 | −0.3 |
| | 21.9 | 20.2 | −1.7 | 2.1 | 4.6 | +2.5 | 4.3 | 3.6 | −0.7 |
| | 0.04 | — | 0 | — | 0.5 | +0.5 | 2.2 | 2.2 | 0 |
| | 0.43 | 2.6 | +2.2 | 0.3 | 11.7 | +11.4 | 2.4 | 2.3 | −0.1 |
| | 6.8 | 4.4 | −2.4 | 7.6 | 4.0 | −3.6 | 2.0 | 2.8 | +0.8 |
| | 52.9 | 43.3 | −9.6 | 85.6 | 58.7 | −26.9 | 85.7 | 86.0 | +0.3 |
| | 100.0 | 100.0 | | 100.0 | 100.0 | | 100.0 | 100.0 | |

TABLE 6
Regional Indices of Production Costs[1] by Forest Products Industry Branch

| Region | Logging | Sawnwood | Coniferous Plywood | Particle Board | Fiber Board | Pulp | Wood Chemicals |
|---|---|---|---|---|---|---|---|
| Arkhangelsk Oblast | 137 | 115 | 108 | 115 | 111 | 104 | 114 |
| Vologda Oblast | 118 | 104 | 100 | 105 | 102 | 102[3] | 108 |
| Karelian ASSR | 127 | 115 | 108 | 115 | 111 | 103 | 114 |
| Komi ASSR | 121 | 117 | 113 | 119 | 110 | 106 | 111 |
| Kostroma Oblast | 103 | 100 | — | 102 | 100 | — | 103 |
| Central Region | 109 | 101 | — | 100 | 100 | — | 104 |
| Kirov Oblast | 111 | 103 | — | 103 | 101 | 100 | 104 |
| Bashkir ASSR | 107 | 104 | — | 109 | 101 | 100 | 105 |
| Sverdlovsk Oblast | 100 | 108 | 101 | 110 | 102 | 102 | 105 |
| Perm Oblast | 106 | 108 | 104 | 111 | 103 | 101 | 110 |
| Tyumen Oblast | 119 | 118 | 112 | 119 | 110 | 107 | 106 |
| Tomsk Oblast | 125 | 108 | 104 | 113 | 105 | 103 | 102 |
| Krasnoyarsk Krai[2] | 104–109 | 103 | 107 | 116 | 103 | 104 | 100 |
| Irkutsk Oblast[2] | 109–127 | 102 | 109 | 113 | 104 | 106 | 101 |
| Chita Oblast and Buryat ASSR | 114 | 105 | 110 | 114 | 106 | 104 | 106 |
| Amur Oblast and Khabarovsk Krai | 133 | 121 | 119 | 129 | 119 | 111 | 119 |

[1]Costs include: Fuel, wages, amortization, capital investment, and transport of output but do not include raw materials costs. The index number 100 refers to the lowest cost area.
[2]The variation in the index numbers is due to the large geographic area covered by the region.
[3]The Vologda Oblast pulp index appears in the original source as 10 . . , with the last digit missing. Recomputation indicates that the value should be 102.
SOURCE: V. V. Glotov, *Razmeshcheniye lesopromyshlennogo proizvodstva* [Location of the forest products industry] (Moscow: Lesnaya promyshlennost, 1977), p. 177.

TABLE 7
Growth Indicators for Forest Products Industry

| Year | Roundwood Exports (Mill. Cu.M) | Yearly Growth | Roundwood and Sawnwood exports (Mill. Cu.M) | Yearly Growth | Total Harvest (Mill. Cu.M) | Yearly Growth |
|---|---|---|---|---|---|---|
| 1964 | 9.4 | — | 17.0 | — | 385.3 | — |
| 1965 | 11.1 | 18% | 19.1 | 12.3% | 378.9 | −1.6% |
| 1966 | 12.4 | 11.7% | 20.4 | 6.8% | 373.5 | −1.5% |
| 1967 | 12.4 | 0 | 19.8 | −3.0% | 383.0 | 2.5% |
| 1968 | 12.8 | 3.2% | 20.7 | 4.5% | 380.4 | −1.0% |
| 1969 | 13.6 | 6.3% | 21.5 | 3.9% | 374.2 | −1.7% |
| 1970 | 15.3 | 12.5% | 23.3 | 8.4% | 385.0 | 2.9% |
| 1971 | 14.6 | −4.6% | 22.5 | −3.0% | 384.7 | −1.0% |
| 1972 | 14.9 | 2% | 22.9 | 1.7% | 383.0 | −0.5% |
| 1973 | 18.7 | 25.5% | 26.9 | 17.5% | 387.8 | 1.3% |
| 1974 | 18.2 | −2.7% | 26.1 | −3.0% | 388.5 | 0.2% |
| 1975 | 16.9 | −7.1% | 24.7 | −5.0% | 395.0 | 1.7% |
| 1976 | 17.9 | 5.9% | 26.4 | 6.9% | 384.5 | −2.6% |
| 1977 | 17.8 | −0.5% | 26.1 | −1.1% | 376.8 | −2.0% |
| 1978 | 17.4 | −2.2% | 26.8 | 2.7% | 361.4 | −4.1% |
| 1979 | 15.2 | −12.7% | 22.9 | 14.6% | 354.0 | −2.0% |
| 1980 | 13.9 | −9.5% | 21.1 | −7.9% | 356.6 | +0.8% |
| 1964–68 growth | | 36.2% | | 21.8% | | −1.3% |
| 1969–73 growth | | 37.5% | | 25.1% | | 3.6% |
| 1974–80 growth | | −23.6% | | −19.2% | | −8.2% |
| 1964–80 growth | | 47.9% | | 24.1% | | −7.4% |

SOURCES: *Vneshnyaya torgovlya SSSR* [Foreign trade of the USSR] (Moscow: Statistika, 1965–81); *Narodnoye khozyaistvo SSSR* [The economy of the USSR] (Moscow: Statistika, 1965–80).

A small market for Soviet plywood and composition board exists in North America, but major Soviet competition for roundwood, pulp and paper, or sawnwood seems unlikely in American or Canadian markets. The USSR has yet to compete in South American markets, other than CMEA-related sales to Cuba.

Japan absorbs most of Soviet forest products exports to Asia, although a small percentage of some commodities, such as paper, is sold to North Korea, Thailand, India, Mongolia and the Middle East. The Soviets have not yet entered Pacific-rim markets for forest products on a large scale, and show little indication to do so in the future. Competition from developing local forest products industries in Pacific nations, as well as from the United States, Canada, and New Zealand would be formidable. However, the construction of the BAM, the abundance of Siberian raw materials, and the build-up of Soviet Far East port facilities suggest that the Pacific rim may be a future area for expansion of Soviet markets.

Japan is likely to continue its role as the USSR's major Pacific trading partner in forest products because of the availability of Japanese technological expertise, the desirability of a hard-currency market and the lack of domestic raw materials. The USSR currently supplies 17 to 20 percent of Japan's total wood products imports. However, there is a danger that Soviet planners may overestimate Japan's ability to absorb larger amounts of roundwood shipments from Siberia.

The mix of species exported to Japan from Siberia may be the key to understanding Japan's demand. The Soviets have encouraged Japanese import firms to accept a greater portion of larch in Siberian shipments than is desirable from the point of view of the Japanese market. Table 10 shows the share of larch in Japan's imports of Soviet roundwood.

Interviews with Japanese trading companies (see Appendix A) have revealed the desire of Japan to place ceilings on the amount of larch acceptable in future agreements with the USSR. Japanese import firms have set a 27 percent limit on the amount of larch to be purchased, with Exportles deciding the remaining species mix. However, the amount of larch shipped to Japan varies seasonally, with the largest larch share, 50 to 70 percent of timber exported from Siberia, occurring in February when southern areas in Siberia have better port accessibility but receive greater amounts of larch. Japanese firms have also expressed apprehension about the completion of BAM, feeling that the amount of larch shipped will increase. The new logging areas to be opened up by BAM are dominated by larch stands.

Japan and the USSR also have agreements for the sales of pulp chips from Siberia. Soviet trade planners hope future arrangements with Japan will include higher portions of finished or intermediate products, such as plywood, but Japanese buyers have resisted this pressure, saying that Soviet plywood is unsuitable in Japanese markets.

The future mix of forest products export to Japan from Siberia is likely to continue to be roundwood, sawnwood and pulp chips. The level of Soviet participation in the Japanese market should remain stable, unless competition from the United States or Canada is curtailed.

| Industrial Wood Harvest (Mill. Cu.M) | Yearly Growth | Output by Value 1964 = 100 | Yearly Growth |
|---|---|---|---|
| 276.9 | — | 100 | — |
| 272.8 | −1.5% | 102.7 | 2.7% |
| 270.7 | −1.0% | 107.7 | 4.9% |
| 286.9 | 6.0% | 115.8 | 7.5% |
| 289.9 | 1.0% | 122.2 | 5.5% |
| 286.3 | −1.2% | 128.6 | 5.2% |
| 298.6 | 4.3% | 136.1 | 5.8% |
| 298.4 | 0 | 143.0 | 5.0% |
| 297.6 | −1.0% | 149.4 | 4.5% |
| 304.2 | 2.2% | 157.5 | 6.1% |
| 303.7 | −0.2% | 164.7 | 4.6% |
| 312.9 | 3.0% | 175.0 | 6.3% |
| 302.9 | −3.2% | 177.7 | 1.5% |
| 296.1 | −2.2% | 183.0 | 3.0% |
| 283.6 | −4.2% | 185.7 | 1.5% |
| 273.0 | −3.7% | 182.9 | −1.5% |
| 277.7 | +1.7% | | |
| | 4.7% | | 22.2% |
| | 6.2% | | 22.5% |
| | −8.8% | | 16.1% |
| | 0.3% | | 83.0% |

## Technology Transfer to the USSR Forest Products Sector

The USSR forest products sector, historically a heavy consumer of foreign machinery and equipment, presents a good example for examining the impacts of technology transfer on a Soviet industry.

Philip Hanson has compared industry branch shares of Western machinery imports with industry branch shares of total production investment in the Soviet economy and judged timber, pulp and paper, light industry, and shipping to be above average users of Western technology.[27] Antony Sutton, in his review of Western technology transfer and Soviet economic development, showed that a large share of capacity in the pulp, paper, and sawmilling industries of the USSR is of foreign origin.

The USSR forest products sector has not produced many international innovations, and the technological level of the sector's machinery and equipment lags behind the most up-to-date machinery in Western nations. As seen in Table 11, the actual level of machinery and equipment imports in the Soviet forest products industry varies from year to year. However, the share of total stock attributable to foreign technology shows a steady growth, paralleling general growth of investment in the industry.

This section will review the changing patterns of technology imports and the direct benefits of technology transfer to the Soviet forest products sector.

The term "technology transfer" can take a wide variety of meanings.[28] Only embodied technology, the knowledge that is represented in actual products such as machinery and equipment, will be considered here. License arrangements, technology transfer through publications, or other forms of disembodied technology transfer will not be covered. However, some reference will be made to the transfer of knowledge inherent in technical cooperation agreements or training of personnel.

### Patterns of Technology Imports

Sutton has pointed out that much of present day Soviet capacity in the forest products sector originated after World War II. Expropriation by the Soviets of existing factories on Sakhalin Island from Japan or in the Karelian region from Finland resulted in an immediate addition to Soviet technical knowledge. Further enhancement of technological levels came from the movement of German woodworking machinery to the USSR after World War II and from the incorporation of the Baltic states into the Soviet Union.

Many Finnish companies that have continued to supply the USSR with forest products machinery and equipment originally expanded their own capacity to meet Soviet war reparations requirements, often with the help of United States loans.[29]

The importation of technology has taken many forms and has had separate effects on various branches of the forest products industry. For example, the Soviet fiberboard industry is almost exclusively dominated by Polish and Swedish plants. On the other hand, furniture enterprises in the USSR have relied most often on domestic machinery and equipment.

One can note an evolving pattern in the form of technology transfer to Soviet forest products industries. Each stage indicates a response by Soviet planners to unsatisfactory aspects of the prevailing form of technology absorption. The stages that will be discussed here are: (1) individual machinery imports and copying, (2) turnkey plant purchases, (3) technical cooperation agreements. Joint ventures for the construction of machinery plants are not yet important but may occur in the future. These stages do not exhibit distinct time boundaries and may occur simultaneously during overlapping periods. Barter or compensatory agreements, wherein technology is provided in exchange for a portion of industry output, will also be discussed.

1. *Individual Machinery Imports and Copying.* Machinery represents the embodiment of current and past knowledge about a technological process. For example, the sale of the latest model saw, debarker, or plywood press may be an indication of the engineering skill inherent in the invention. When the invention is successfully placed within a system of operations, one may term it an innovation. However, the technical skills embodied in the invention and the organizational skills needed to make a successful innovation, are not automatically transferred with the sale of a machine. Soviet planners have, at times, not been entirely successful in fitting an individual machine into their production systems or in reproducing the engineering skills necessary to copy or repair a machine.

Imitation is not always the most efficient form of technology absorption, but rather may represent a one-time technical boost to a particular enterprise, without necessarily advancing the technological frontier of a whole Soviet industry. Furthermore, even when imitation is successful, it is a time-consuming process which does not alleviate a temporary gap in industrial knowledge. By the time a machine is successfully reproduced and diffused throughout an industry, it may already be outdated by advanced standards.

Sales of individual machines to the USSR or of individual production lines have emphasized larger capacity designs and have shown a geographic trend eastward. For example, Sateko Oy of Finland has sold many lines of log and lumber handling equipment to the Arkhangelsk and Leningrad areas, but many of their lines are

TABLE 8
Selected USSR Forest Products Exports by Value 1964–81 (in million rubles)

| Product | 1964 | 1965 | 1966 | 1967 | 1968 | 1969 | 1970 | 1971 | 1972 | 1973 | 1974 | 1975 |
|---|---|---|---|---|---|---|---|---|---|---|---|---|
| All forest products | 455.7 | 528.3 | 559.9 | 563.7 | 614.9 | 652.0 | 749.1 | 778.2 | 776.7 | 1020.5 | 1438.5 | 1378.2 |
| Forest products share in total exports | 6.6% | 7.2% | 7.0% | 6.5% | 6.4% | 6.2% | 6.5% | 6.3% | 6.1% | 6.4% | 6.9% | 5.7% |
| Roundwood | 126.7 | 162.0 | 176.0 | 179.1 | 209.9 | 213.9 | 254.3 | 255.7 | 252.6 | 408.4 | 563.8 | 464.6 |
| Sawnwood | 253.6 | 275.0 | 276.9 | 254.4 | 263.1 | 275.9 | 300.0 | 317.5 | 308.2 | 372.7 | 566.3 | 561.5 |
| Plywood | 19.2 | 21.7 | 23.0 | 23.4 | 25.6 | 26.9 | 32.5 | 34.0 | 35.2 | 41.2 | 58.5 | 58.5 |
| Sulfite pulp | 22.2 | 23.2 | 21.9 | 26.2 | 31.1 | 35.2 | 38.9 | 41.4 | 42.7 | 42.3 | 44.0 | 49.3 |
| Sulfate pulp | 5.8 | 6.5 | 9.1 | 12.1 | 11.9 | 13.7 | 15.6 | 20.5 | 23.8 | 27.2 | 49.4 | 28.2 |
| Paper | 23.8 | 28.7 | 35.7 | 39.4 | 49.7 | 57.3 | 65.0 | 68.3 | 73.8 | 81.1 | 116.6 | 113.0 |
| Roundwood and sawnwood as percent of all forest products exports | 83 | 83 | 81 | 77 | 77 | 75 | 74 | 74 | 72 | 77 | 79 | 74 |

Source: *Vneshnyaya torgovlya SSSR* [Foreign trade of the USSR], various years.

apparently being used now in Siberia, particularly at Ust-Ilimsk and Bratsk.[30] Tampella of Finland increased its capacity after World War II to supply large Soviet orders for pulp, paper and paperboard lines. The regional destination of Tampella's sales have ranged from Bratsk and Krasnoyarsk in East Siberia to Koryazhma in the European Northwest, Astrakhan on the Volga River and Sakhalin Island off the Pacific coast. Some of these sales have been individual machinery lines, and some have been entire mills.

However, problems arose with Soviet purchases of individual equipment, even when involving large-capacity machinery lines, as destinations included areas with adverse environmental conditions and larger enterprises with intricate production linkages. Machines delivered by foreign suppliers would sometimes remain unused, awaiting construction of buildings. The Siberian climate could prove destructive to equipment left outdoors without protective enclosures. Most Finnish suppliers would guarantee their machinery only up to 12 months after the delivery date, whereas installation delays of up to 5 years were not uncommon at the Bratsk project. Some Finnish companies offered to hold machines in Finland until facilities at Siberian projects were completed, but Prommashimport desired delivery on original dates. Guarantees were extended in some cases, but delays in start-ups were still adverse for Soviet industry.

Copying individual machines or purchasing individual production lines did not automatically produce innovations or transfer technical skills to Soviet engineers. When technology adoption was not viewed within a total production system, the technical spurt sought by Soviet planners could be delayed or lost. The purchase of turnkey plants has therefore evolved as a second stage of technology transfer.

2. *Turnkey Plant Purchases.* The intricacies and engineering difficulties of ambitious Bratsk-type projects may have caused a subtle change in Soviet attitudes toward foreign technology supply. Information restrictions about plant locations, site conditions and engineering-technical specifications were eased for foreign companies. Administrative organization has changed slightly to reflect more divided responsibility for project start-up dates. While local construction administrations are still absorbing much of the blame for delays, Prommashimport is now required to attempt better synchronization with industry and construction organizations.

Technology transfer has now evolved toward turnkey plants, wherein suppliers assume responsibility for engineering and technical design, oversee construction, and guarantee a start-up date to the Soviets. In effect, the technology supplier builds the plant-system and "turns the key" over to the user.

Svetogorsk is a good example of a successful turnkey forest products project in the USSR. Tampella and Rauma-Repola were the main Finnish suppliers for this pulp and paper complex, originally located in Finnish territory, and now in the European RSFSR. Svetogorsk reached 100 percent capacity within six months of completion, as opposed to a two year average for other Soviet projects. Tampella began deliveries of pulp machinery to Svetogorsk in 1974, and a new production phase began in 1979. One further advantage of Svetogorsk is its proximity to Finland (two kilometers from the Finnish border), which allows Finnish engineers and technical advisers easier access to the complex.

Another Finnish company, Ahlström, supplied a complete diffuser-washer plant to the Syktyvkar pulp mill in the Komi ASSR with a guaranteed start-up date.[31] On the Yenisei River at Lesosibirsk, Plan-Sell Oy of Finland contracted in 1975 for a turnkey sawmill project worth $75 million, with a 1978–79 guaranteed start-up date.[32]

The composition board industry has had an even longer history of complete mill deliveries to the USSR. Poland and Sweden have supplied fiberboard mills since 1959. The mills have increased in capacity through the years to reflect changing levels of technology.

Poland and Finland have supplied whole particleboard mills to the USSR. Valmet, the state-owned Finnish machinery manufacturer, recently began selling 250,000 cubic meter capacity particleboard mills to the USSR.

TABLE 9
European and CMEA Share of Major Forest Product Exports from USSR, 1981 (in percent of total exports by quantity measure)

| Commodity | European Share[1] | CMEA Share[2] |
|---|---|---|
| Roundwood[3] | 57 | 19 |
| Coniferous Sawnwood | 77 | 39 |
| Plywood[4] | 74 | 40 |
| Sulfite pulp | 97 | 74 |
| Sulfate pulp | 89 | 48 |
| Paper | 70 | 69 |
| Fiberboard | 78 | 64 |
| Particleboard | 92 | 81 |

[1]Includes European nations of CMEA.
[2]Includes only the European members of CMEA.
[3]40 percent of roundwood was shipped to Japan.
[4]Canada, the United States, Cuba and Egypt were often major plywood purchasers.
SOURCE: *Vneshnyaya torgovlya SSSR v 1981 godu* [Foreign trade of the USSR in 1981] (Moscow: Finansy i Statistika, 1982).

| 1976 | 1977 | 1978 | 1979 | 1980 | 1981 |
|---|---|---|---|---|---|
| 1500.2 | 1690.0 | 1591.1 | 1742.7 | 2008.5 | 1893.4 |
| 5.3% | 5.1% | 4.5% | 4.1% | 4.1% | 3.3% |
| 472.2 | 546.0 | 479.9 | 586.9 | 614.8 | 531.8 |
| 613.9 | 687.3 | 637.1 | 673.8 | 783.8 | 712.0 |
| 59.1 | 59.4 | 62.9 | 66.9 | 79.3 | 80.7 |
| 49.5 | 47.6 | 47.0 | 44.1 | 55.2 | 49.3 |
| 81.3 | 104.5 | 117.6 | 117.6 | 165.6 | 192.8 |
| 124.7 | 139.1 | 143.8 | 145.3 | 171.6 | 187.8 |
| 72 | 72 | 70 | 72 | 70 | 66 |

TABLE 10
Japanese Imports of Soviet Roundwood and Sawnwood by Species Mix; Selected Years
(in percent share of total imports of the commodity from USSR)

| Item | Quantity Measure | | | | | U.S. Dollar Value Measure | | | | |
|---|---|---|---|---|---|---|---|---|---|---|
| | 1965 | 1968 | 1971 | 1974 | 1977 | 1965 | 1968 | 1971 | 1974 | 1977 |
| Roundwood | | | | | | | | | | |
| Pine | 24.34 | 37.47 | 29.02 | 26.46 | 28.99 | 25.47 | 38.34 | 30.11 | 28.76 | 32.99 |
| Sitka spruce | 0.02 | — | — | — | — | 0.02 | — | — | — | — |
| Fir and spruce | 51.31 | 34.34 | 37.92 | 36.02 | 36.29 | 51.98 | 37.31 | 41.33 | 37.83 | 38.44 |
| Larch | 19.67 | 27.47 | 33.00 | 37.42 | 34.69 | 17.79 | 23.57 | 28.50 | 33.31 | 28.54 |
| White and yellow cedar | 0.32 | 0.11 | — | — | — | 0.35 | 0.12 | — | — | — |
| Hemlock | — | — | — | 0.02 | — | — | — | — | 0.31 | — |
| Red cedar[1] | 0.17 | 0.18 | — | — | 0.01 | 0.19 | 0.19 | — | — | 0.01 |
| Other Coniferous | 4.12 | 0.41 | 0.03 | 0.05 | — | 4.16 | 0.44 | 0.03 | 0.04 | — |
| Sawnwood | | | | | | | | | | |
| Pine < 160mm thick | 2.25 | 21.42 | 3.83 | 6.23 | 3.19 | 2.14 | 19.19 | 1.70 | 3.17 | 2.15 |
| Pine > 160mm thick | 63.43 | 42.27 | 38.18 | 28.44 | 22.80 | 64.47 | 43.52 | 40.11 | 31.93 | 25.11 |
| Fir and spruce < 160mm thick | 6.37 | 6.12 | — | 6.64 | 0.83 | 6.15 | 6.31 | — | 4.10 | 0.92 |
| Fir and spruce > 160mm thick | 24.72 | 21.31 | 57.51 | 40.93 | 63.08 | 24.39 | 23.52 | 57.97 | 46.27 | 65.94 |
| Larch < 160mm thick | 2.20 | 6.35 | 0.45 | 15.71 | 9.41 | 1.93 | 4.60 | 0.20 | 12.74 | 5.23 |
| Larch > 160mm thick | 1.00 | — | — | — | 0.57 | 0.89 | — | — | — | 0.56 |
| White and yellow cedar | — | 1.60 | — | 1.26 | — | — | 1.80 | — | 1.57 | — |
| Other coniferous | — | 0.90 | — | 0.76 | 0.08 | — | 1.03 | — | 0.18 | 0.05 |

[1]Some difficulties in translation of tree species between Russian, Latin, English and Japanese are apparent. The Russian tree "kedr" is actually unlike Western red cedar found in the United States, and is properly translated as Siberian stone pine. However, Japanese trade statistics have noted the tree here as "red cedar."
SOURCE: Japan Ministry of Finance, *Import Statistical Schedule*, selected years.

Rauma-Repola of Finland has supplied 100,000 cubic meter capacity mills in the past.

While turnkey plants are expensive purchases for the Soviet forest products industry, they are expected to be money-saving in the long run as delays and technical problems are minimized. However, they do not represent the ultimate stage of technology transfer because the learning component of adopting new technology is not necessarily transferred to the labor sector. Actually, some of the design and administrative burden is merely transferred to the technology supplier. A further stage, tech-

nical cooperation agreements, has therefore evolved most recently in the transfer of technology to the USSR.

3. *Technical Cooperation.*[33] Many Finnish suppliers of forest products machinery and equipment to the USSR have entered into a new type of technical cooperation agreement. Wärtsilä and Valmet, for example, signed cooperative agreements with the USSR for delivery of paper machinery to the Syktyvkar complex, wherein 10 percent of the equipment would be supplied by the USSR machine building industry.

Some foreign companies have recently had a form of

TABLE 11
USSR Imports of Forest Products Machinery 1964–81 (in million rubles)

| Equipment | 1964 | 1965 | 1966 | 1967 | 1968 | 1969 | 1970 | 1971 | 1972 | 1973 | 1974 | 1975 | 1976 | 1977 | 1978 | 1979 | 1980 | 1981 |
|---|---|---|---|---|---|---|---|---|---|---|---|---|---|---|---|---|---|---|
| Forest products machinery and equipment* | 73.1 | 36.7 | 36.8 | 71.7 | 98.8 | 100.2 | 91.4 | 63.9 | 115.8 | 128.6 | 138.8 | 150.0 | 213.1 | 250.5 | 229.7 | 215.7 | 209.2 | 168.6 |
| Woodworking equipment | .6 | .5 | .7 | .4 | 2.0 | 4.1 | 2.0 | 2.8 | 3.5 | 6.0 | 3.3 | 10.2 | 7.7 | 6.4 | 3.9 | 7.3 | 8.0 | 15.7 |
| Total | 73.7 | 37.2 | 37.5 | 72.1 | 100.8 | 104.3 | 93.4 | 66.7 | 119.3 | 134.6 | 142.1 | 160.2 | 220.8 | 256.9 | 233.6 | 223.0 | 217.2 | 184.3 |
| Share in total value of imported machinery and equipment | 3.07 | 1.53 | 1.62 | 2.70 | 3.20 | 2.90 | 2.51 | 1.80 | 2.50 | 2.50 | 2.30 | 1.77 | 2.11 | 2.23 | 1.61 | 1.54 | 1.44 | 1.16 |

*Excluding woodworking; emphasizing paper, cellulose and composition board.
SOURCE: *Vneshnyaya torgovlya SSSR* [Foreign trade of the USSR], various years.

technical cooperation built into contracts with the USSR. Rauma-Repola has been including such clauses in its contracts with the Soviets since 1966.

Technical cooperation means that actual engineering and design information or training is shared with Soviet personnel. The learning component of technology itself is therefore directly transferred to the labor sector. The Finnish-Soviet Intergovernmental Commission for Economic Cooperation currently has scientific and technical committees which oversee working groups, including ones involved in paper, pulp and mechanical woodworking.[34] These groups allow Soviet representatives to have more direct contact with the foreign plants where the machinery is actually made. Finnish representatives are allowed reciprocal visits to Soviet enterprises.

In some areas of technical cooperation, the sharing of new information may be reciprocal between the USSR and Finland. This does not appear to be the situation for forest products, where even Soviet accounts admit to the relative backwardness of this USSR sector in terms of machine-building.[35] The benefits to Finland from such cooperative agreements include a continued strong position in the Soviet machinery market and an easier flow of information about Soviet plant specifications.

The trend toward Soviet purchases of turnkey plants and technical cooperation agreements results in some foreign technology being indirectly transferred to the USSR. The term "indirect" here refers to Soviet purchases of technology from nations which are not the primary contractors. For example, when it purchases Finnish machinery and equipment, the USSR may indirectly attain any foreign technology that has been adopted by Finland. In some cases, Western nations serve as intermediaries between the USSR and third-party technology suppliers, acting as funnels for some international best-practice techniques.

From the point of view of third-party technology suppliers, these intermediate agents may be a necessity if the supplier is small-scale, highly specialized, or unfamiliar with Soviet market conventions. Both Japanese and Finnish companies have included third-nation machinery components in some of their sales to the USSR. When turnkey plant sales are made, such inclusions are almost inevitable.[36]

Technology transfer to the Soviet forest products sector not only has shown stages of development toward more effective direct learning processes, but also has become more efficient in combining the best techniques from many sources.

Advantages of Soviet Technology Purchases

Soviet planners have in effect substituted foreign technology sources for ambitious domestic investment in machine building for the forest products sector. Although these purchases were not made in isolation from domestic capital stock, some substitution of foreign capital for Soviet capital has occurred, particularly since the industry has traditionally purchased technology. The specific advantages of imported technology can be seen by examining some industry goals and suggesting ways that foreign technology has contributed to their achievement.

1. *Development of Frontier Regions.* The adverse environmental conditions of new forest industry areas call for use of advanced technology. The large scale of enterprises in these regions and the severe shortage of labor increase the desirability of up-to-date production methods. The degree to which such new capital has been substituted for labor in these regions has not actually been measured, but there is reason to assume that labor-saving lines of machinery are preferable, especially in areas where wages and labor turnover rates are high. Much of the equipment delivered to new Siberian complexes, such as Ust-Ilimsk, include computer systems to control many of the sorting and processing procedures. The majority of computer systems in use appear to be of foreign make.[37]

However, the environmental conditions which call for advanced technology may discourage some potential foreign suppliers. Large-scale plants designed for Siberian sites may require technical concepts which cannot in turn be applied widely in other forest products regions of the world. Japanese firms have indicated that Soviet planners requested Japan to propose some turnkey pulp and paper projects in Siberia, but most Japanese companies declined, feeling that they had little experience in such extreme environments. Yet, many companies, particularly in Europe, have supplied new technology to Siberian complexes. Finland, France, Sweden and Eastern European nations have been the principal sellers of forest products machinery and equipment to Siberia.

2. *Efficient Resource Utilization and Environmental Protection.* The goal of Soviet forest products industry planners to utilize wood and wood by-products more efficiently was noted earlier. The technology to utilize wood waste products, wood chips, or to harvest whole trees more completely has not been available in the USSR to the degree that it has in Western nations. Imported technology, particularly in turnkey plants, has included measures for the most efficient use of forest resources as world technological levels respond to limitations on wood supply. For example, sawmill technology in Europe, the United States, and Canada employs computer systems to determine optimum cutting patterns to maximize lumber yield from logs. Soviet purchases of debarker units and computer-run sawmills allow fuller utilization of each log or cant.

The Soviet desire to minimize environmental pollution hazards from forest products industries, particularly water pollution from pulp facilities, requires waste treatment technology that has not yet been developed domestically by the USSR.[38] Thus, some Soviet purchases of Western forest products technology has been in the realm of anti-pollution equipment, often included in turnkey plant arrangements. The new Svetogorsk pulp mill includes a waste treatment plant supplied in 1975 by Oy Yleinen Insinööritoimisto of Finland.[39] Ahlström of Finland sold anti-water pollution equipment to the Syktyvkar pulp mill and the Ust-Ilimsk pulp mill includes a sludge treatment process provided by Japan.[40]

Technology Transfer and Export Potential

If performance in the forest products sector is benefited by technology transfer, the export position of the sector should be similarly influenced. Benefits to the export sector will be considered here in terms of product mix and Soviet ability to compete in the world market, wider use of larch, and the special case of compensatory or barter trade arrangements.

## Product Mix and Ability to Compete in the World Market

Soviet planners desire to maintain or expand current export levels but face a diminishing source of easily accessible wood supply. They must therefore turn to more efficient use of stocks or expand into new regions. Both supply alternatives require advanced technology inputs. Western forest products technology has been oriented toward more efficient utilization of trees, thinnings, and by-products, and this technology could be transferred to the USSR for use in traditional forest cutting areas. The second alternative, expansion into new regions, may prove more difficult because machinery inventions for forest exploitation under special Siberian conditions present a unique technological challenge. Some of the transportation technology needed for access to new stands of timber has already been developed for coincidental exploitation of other Siberian resources, but wood extraction and processing machinery that can efficiently operate under Siberian conditions creates new engineering problems.

The product mix and quality of forest products exports also may be affected by technology imports. As the Soviets attempt to upgrade the value of wood products exported, foreign technology inputs become increasingly important. The composition board industry, for example, has been more dependent on imported technology than the processes used to produce roundwood for export. The pulp and paper industry requires heavier inputs of advanced technology as the capacity and complexity of plants increase. Therefore, to achieve higher value wood products exports, it seems likely that the USSR will rely even further on imported machinery and equipment.

The quality of exported wood products may also be influenced by imported technology. Soviet demands for quality in wood products have generally been lower than those of Western countries, which have a longer history of finished products exports and presumably more experience in quality control. When urged by the Soviets to accept composition board, Japanese trading companies expressed concern that Soviet quality would not meet Japanese standards. One American firm which has been importing Soviet birch plywood had initial quality control problems, but is now satisfied with the quality of the board sent after the company provided the Soviet enterprises with Western-made sanders.[41]

To some degree, the Soviets may be able to substitute attractive prices for quality considerations, but if they move away from dependence on roundwood and sawnwood exports, some new technology will be required to maintain even minimal international standards. The new technology is most likely to come from abroad.

## Use of Larch

Efficient industrial use of larch is one key to maintaining long-term export levels of Soviet forest products, and

foreign technology may be important in developing the option to export larch. However, most Western forest products nations do not possess the extent of larch that is present in the USSR, and therefore the stock of existing knowledge about its use is limited.

The Soviets have some ongoing research projects for more comprehensive utilization of larch, and do use a high proportion of this wood in Siberian processing facilities. Foreign nations have also shown some interest in developing larch use technology. Japan, for instance, has not been eager to accept a high portion of larch in Soviet timber shipments and the uses of larch it does accept are mainly for foundations in house construction. However, the price for larch set by the USSR is so low compared to other wood that Japan has shown some interest in research and development for larch utilization.[42] Performance of samples of Soviet larch veneers has been disappointing thus far due to resin content and drying problems. However, Toyama of Japan has been conducting research to improve the quality of larch veneer as an overlay for tropical hardwoods or particleboard.

Technology for larch use has been limited, but more advanced, in interior regions of the United States and Canada where relatively small stands of similar larch grow. A United States group has approached the Soviets with proposals for constructing experimental larch plywood plants in the Soviet Far East.[43]

European technology suppliers such as Finland have had less experience in larch utilization and therefore have shown less interest in developing this technology for sale to the USSR. But, given the potential for both domestic larch use and export, particularly with the development of logging areas along the BAM, creation of technology for efficient larch utilization may prove to be the most important problem facing the USSR forest products sector in the future.

## Compensatory Trade Agreements: The Case of the Joint Development Projects with Japan[44]

Barter or compensatory trade agreements are those in which the Soviet Union is provided technology by a trading partner in exchange for a share of project output, most frequently in a natural resource industry. These arrangements have been used in the forest products sector, and are closely tied to exports of Soviet wood products.

Japan and the USSR have extensive barter arrangements for wood products and technology, and their joint projects provide good case studies of both the benefits and drawbacks to compensatory agreements.[45]

The first agreement began in 1969 and ended in 1973; the second ran from 1975 through 1979; a third was signed in March 1981 and is to run until 1986.[46] These agreements provide general guidelines for the amount of Soviet timber that is exported to Japan through Japanese timber importing companies, while bank credits are provided for the Soviets to purchase a set amount of Japanese machinery or products over the period of agreement. A variety of Soviet foreign trade agencies, including Prommashimport and Exportles, are involved in the general agreements. Japan formed the KS Industry Company to oversee the barter arrangements with the participation of many major Japanese trading companies.

Under the first agreement, approximately 8 million cubic meters of timber were purchased by Japan each year, and $163 million worth of machinery and equipment was sold by Japan to the USSR, including transportation machinery, road building equipment, bulldozers, and forest products machinery for use in Siberia and the Far East. Ten Japanese planers, for example, were sold to Krasnoyarsk and to other sawmills near Lake Baikal. Under the agreement with Prommashimport, Soviet engineers went to Japan to study the machinery beforehand but no Japanese advisers were sent to Siberia. Two plywood lines were sold for use around Lake Baikal and Irkutsk in 1973, partly using Finnish built veneer equipment. Japanese sawmill machinery was sold for use with small diameter logs at the Sovetskaya Gavan mill. Some United States headrig equipment was included, as well as Finnish kiln equipment. In this case Japanese supervisors were provided, but as often occurred with Siberian facilities, start-up delays hampered operations.

The second Soviet-Japanese agreement provided for similar levels of timber purchases by Japan and $550 million worth of bank loans to the USSR for technology purchases. General categories of Japanese items sold under the second agreement included: transportation machinery, timber processing machinery, log handling equipment, forestry machinery, paper and paperboard manufacturing machinery and equipment, spare parts, cables, consumer goods and small vessels. The second agreement also provided contracts for some pulp and paper technology transfer, including paper and paperboard machinery and repair of existing Siberian mills.

Separate from the project, further agreements were worked out for the pulp and paper sector. In December 1971, Japan and the USSR signed an agreement for deliveries of chips and pulpwood of leaf-bearing trees and deliveries from Japan of equipment for production of chips and pulpwood.[47] This agreement ran from 1972 through 1981 and provided a $45 million credit from Japan for Soviet purchases of machinery and equipment, with corresponding Japanese purchases of chips and pulpwood from Siberia. Several large Japanese paper companies have consumed 8 million cubic meters of chips and 4.7 million cubic meters of pulpwood. The Soviet port of Nakhodka-Vostochny has served as the main shipment point, with Japanese firms supplying some of the chip-carrying vessels.

Other separate pulp and paper projects are being discussed for the expansion of existing mills or construction of new facilities at Lesosibirsk, Amursk, Khabarovsk, and on Sakhalin Island.

A third forest products agreement was signed in 1981, but problems arose during negotiations. A recession in the Japanese timber market had reduced demand for Soviet roundwood and precluded an increase in the amount of timber Japan agreed to buy. The Soviets wanted Japan to purchase a higher amount of finished wood products, but Japanese firms resisted this suggestion because of quality problems with Soviet output. Under the terms of the third agreement, the USSR will export to Japan 12 million cubic meters of roundwood and 1.24 million cubic meters of sawnwood by 1986.[48] Another problem was that some technology the USSR wanted to purchase from Japan was beyond the scope of Japanese expertise, largely because of conflicting scales of production. Many Japanese forest products firms are geared to small-scale operations, while Soviet complexes in Siberia are of large capacity and set in entirely different environmental conditions.

Financial arrangements for the wood products projects have also been difficult. In both the first and second agreements the Soviet Union did not expend all the credits allowed for purchases of Japanese products. About 90 percent of the credit advanced by Japan in the first agreement was actually used, with the balance canceled by Japan at the end of the period. This problem was continued with the second project. As of 1978, 25 percent of the credit advanced still remained to be used by the Soviets. In some cases, the USSR requested extensions because Siberian facilities were not ready to order or install Japanese equipment. The chip and pulpwood agreement was also behind schedule in the amount of credit used by the USSR.

Rising prices have caused difficulties for both parties. The Soviets have faced higher machinery costs as a result of inflation in the Japanese economy. At the same time, the Soviets have raised prices on log exports in accord with rising world log prices and greater scarcities at home. The *Japan Lumber Journal* reports prices of Soviet timber on a quarterly basis. All Soviet logs have steadily increased in price, with the more desirable species going up at a faster rate than larch. Some speculative Japanese log importers are willing to pay higher prices, thereby causing internal conflict among Japanese companies. The seasonal fluctuation of log species mix in exports has also been upsetting to Japanese purchasers. In some quarters, larch has comprised up to 70 percent of log shipments, far above the 25 percent level the Japanese would prefer.[49]

Despite these difficulties, some benefits have occurred to the Soviet wood export sector through the agreements with Japan. First, the agreements have provided a lower cost method of obtaining needed technological improvements in the forest products sector. Second, they have improved Soviet access to the Japanese hard-currency wood market and have given Exportles experience in dealing with Japanese importing companies. Third, they have accelerated expansion or creation of port facilities for wood exports in the Soviet Far East. Finally, they have allowed an indirect flow of third-nation technology into Siberia as Japanese trading companies have, in effect, acted as intermediaries for Prommashimport.

On the whole, this type of barter arrangement is beneficial for the Soviet forest products sector, both in terms of improving technical efficiency and gaining access to Western markets. However, in the case of the forest product agreements, the benefits to Japan are more questionable. The Japanese demand for Soviet timber had leveled off, while Soviet demands for large scale technology have increased. The USSR must also make a strong attempt to fully use the bank credits provided by Japan to provide a steady market for Japanese machinery and products.

**Measuring the Productivity of
Foreign Capital**

Although the transfer of Western technology to the
Soviet Union is not a new phenomenon, econometric
methods have only recently been used to measure the
impacts of foreign technology on the Soviet economy.
This measurement process is still in an experimental
stage and has become the focus for much debate in economics literature.

This section presents preliminary results of the author's ongoing research in this area. The methodology
employed is based on work done by Green, Levine and
Jarsulic. The results, given the limitations of the econometric techniques, should not be taken as conclusive
statements about the impact of Western machinery on the
Soviet forest products sector.

Purpose of the Measurement

Purchases of Western machinery and equipment in the
forest products sector may be documented and performances of individual machines compared, but the
technological superiority of Western capital can only be
assumed without some form of econometric analysis. The
purpose of the measurement attempted here is to compare the marginal productivities of foreign technology
and Soviet domestic technology over time. If we can
suggest that the marginal productivity of foreign technology, embodied in imported capital stock, is significantly
higher than that embodied in domestic capital stock, we
can state with more assurance that foreign technology
should have definite beneficial impacts on the forest
products sector. We could also then suggest that the
export potential for Soviet forest products will be enhanced through further purchase of foreign capital. Provided that the knowledge inherent in foreign capital can
be diffused to other factors of production, domestic capital may be upgraded through direct or indirect absorption
of foreign technology.

The methods used here to measure the comparative
marginal productivities of foreign capital and domestic
capital in Soviet forest products are based on techniques
developed experimentally by Green and Jarsulic in a September 1975 SRI International working paper.[50] Since this
pioneering work appeared, other methods have been
developed for similar measurement exercises, but employing different production function specifications.[51]

To make the comparison of marginal products, a null
hypothesis is stated here as follows:

1) $$H_0 : \frac{\hat{a}^F}{\overline{K}^F} - \frac{\hat{a}^D}{\overline{K}^D} = 0$$

where: $\hat{a}^F$ = marginal productivity of foreign capital
stock in forest products derived through
the Cobb-Douglas production function specified below
$\overline{K}^F$ = mean value of foreign capital stock
$\hat{a}^D$ = marginal product of domestic capital stock
$\overline{K}^D$ = mean value of domestic capital stock

The alternate hypothesis is:

2) $$H_A : \frac{\hat{\alpha}^F}{\overline{K}^F} - \frac{\hat{\alpha}^D}{\overline{K}^D} > 0$$

Green and Jarsulic tested specific values of a variable
defined as $N$, the magnitude by which foreign capital's
marginal productivity exceeded that of domestic capital.
In this case, we only test for $N = 1$, that is, we desire to
show only that the marginal productivities of the two
stocks differ significantly, and that the marginal productivity of the foreign stock is greater than that of the
domestic stock.

The Regression Statement

To derive the marginal productivities of the two separate
capital stocks, a Cobb-Douglas production function is
specified:

3) $$Q = f(K^\alpha, L^\beta, M^\gamma)$$

where:  $Q$ = output
$K^\alpha$ = a capital component
$L^\beta$ = a labor component
$M^\gamma$ = a raw-material component

For the purpose of comparison, the capital component
must be further broken down to reflect the mix of foreign
and domestic capital in the total stock. Domestic stocks
are treated as a residual after the foreign capital series is
constructed:

4) $$K^D = K^T - K^F$$

where: $K^T$ = total capital stock in forest products.

The function is:

5) $$Q = AK^{F\alpha^F} + K^{D\alpha^D} + L^\beta + M^\gamma$$

Other production function forms have been suggested by
Green, Weitzman and Toda. The SOVMOD work has
often used a first-differences approach, wherein year-to-
year changes are used as the basis for specifying a production recipe, rather than utilizing a time series.[52] Toda
has discussed the empirical problem of determining the
elasticity of substitution between capital and labor and
between foreign and domestic capital. This determination implicitly affects the form of the function. Weitzman
has suggested that the elasticity of substitution between
capital and labor for Soviet cases should be less than that
between the two types of capital stock. He points out the
bias in favor of a higher marginal productivity for foreign
capital because it is so scarce relative to domestic capital.
However, in the forest products industry, the quantity of
foreign stock has historically been high in comparison to
other sectors of the Soviet economy. It is not clear that
Soviet planners could more easily substitute between
domestic and foreign capital than between capital and

labor. The technical differences between the two stocks and the engineering capabilities required could cause difficulties in substituting between the two types of capital.[53]

Other problems with the Cobb-Douglas function in this case study related to specification of trend; multicollinearity among the two capital stocks, output and time; and autocorrelation.

A cross-sectional production function could be a useful tool in separating the impacts of foreign and domestic capital. Rather than examining the relationship of the capital stocks to output over time, forest products regions of the USSR could be used as a basis for comparison. The cross-sectional approach may prove a good approach for future work, although data difficulties arise in allocating foreign stocks across regional breakdowns for other production factors.

The Data Base

A 22-year time series was constructed for the total forest products sector 1955–76. Since the sector is treated in aggregate form, very different results might be obtained by dealing with the pulp and paper industry separately.

*Output*: An index based on growth in total output was constructed from official Soviet data for the entire forest products sector. Output rises steadily over the time period.[54]

*Labor*: The labor series is based on thousands of workers per year in the total sector, and is taken from Feshbach and Rapawy through 1974 and official Soviet data for 1975 and 1976.[55] Labor rises steadily until 1970, then declines.

*Raw Materials*: Raw materials, in million cubic meters of wood removals per year, were taken from official Soviet data.[56] The amount of raw materials varies from year to year, but displays a slight upward trend over time.

*Total Capital Stocks*: Total capital stocks specification was formulated using official Soviet data on basic funds. The stocks were based on 1955 rubles, with a five percent retirement rate (a rate which approximates Soviet amortization/retirement of machinery) and new investment interjected only for nonstructures as follows:

6)              $K_t^T = (.95) K_{t-1}^T + I_{t-1}^{NS}$

where: $.95 = 1 - .05$ (retirement)
$I^{NS}$ = yearly basic fund investment less investment in structures.[57]

The initial level set for the stock in 1955 was based on total basic funds less that share of basic funds attributable to structures. Therefore, the total stock constructed does not include investments in structures, and allows a more direct comparison with foreign stocks which include only machinery and equipment.

Total stocks increase steadily over the time period.

*Foreign Stocks*: Specifications of foreign stocks presented a unique problem in the forest products sector because the post–World War II level of imports showed a peak because of the war reparations program. This peak has not again been reached in ruble value of yearly im-

ports. Therefore, we are faced with a decline in the *share* of foreign stock over the sample period, although the absolute amount of foreign stock declines until 1962 and then rises steadily. However, historic evidence suggests that foreign stock in forest products may be underestimated by the series constructed here. Sutton has suggested that levels of foreign stocks exceeded 65 percent of total stock for various sectors and periods of production in forest products industries.[58] Therefore, the 1955 foreign stock level here, 65 percent of total stocks, may be a conservative estimate. The underestimation can be seen particularly through closer examination of the Finnish contribution to post–World War II Soviet forest products capital. Finnish export statistics for the 1950–55 period show that by 1955, Finland's share alone could have accounted for 65 percent of Soviet forest products capital stock.[59] Thus, the estimate used here does not even include foreign capital from normal trade, expropriation of facilities during World War II, postwar transfer of capital from Germany, or historic foreign capital already on hand.

Accepting the conservative estimate of 998.4 million rubles foreign stock in 1955, the stock is built up as follows:

7)              $K_t^F = (.95) K_{t-1}^F + MI_{t-1}/P_{t-1}$

where:  $.95 = 1 - .05$ retirement rate
$MI_{t-1}$ = all forest products machinery imports in ruble values for period $t-1$[60]
$P$ = price deflator based on German export price index for machinery

The 5 percent retirement rate may be high for foreign capital due to its scarcity with respect to domestic capital and its probable superior technical level over domestic capital. However, foreign capital stocks based on lower retirement rates did not severely affect the data (see Table 12) except for a higher ending stock value and an earlier upturning in the series.

The share of foreign capital in total capital (using the 5 percent retirement rate) declined each year from the postwar peak to a level of 21 percent in 1976. This is still a substantial share of total stock attributable to foreign origin, but may actually represent an underestimation of the influence of foreign capital in the forest products sector. Table 13 shows the difference between estimating the weight of foreign capital based solely on yearly imports and estimating the weight of foreign capital based on total foreign capital stock. The share of imports in yearly machinery investment is also shown in Table 13.

The yearly influence of both foreign capital stock and machinery imports in forest products also depends upon specification of a lag structure, i.e., the amount of time it takes foreign technology to be assimilated into general Soviet technological levels. In this case, no lag structure is specified. Therefore, it is assumed that investment in new capacity and imports of foreign machinery are assigned to the year for which they are reported in official data. In reality, the impacts of new investment or of imports may not be felt until several time periods after

TABLE 12
Foreign Capital Series for Forest Products
Based on Various Retirement Rates 1955–76
(in million rubles with deflated import values)

| Year | Five Percent Retirement | Four Percent Retirement | Three Percent Retirement |
|------|------|------|------|
| 1955 | 998.4 | 998.4 | 998.4 |
| 1956 | 958.8 | 968.8 | 978.8 |
| 1957 | 927.9 | 947.1 | 966.5 |
| 1958 | 903.8 | 931.5 | 959.8 |
| 1959 | 878.9 | 914.6 | 951.3 |
| 1960 | 864.0 | 907.1 | 951.8* |
| 1961 | 853.5 | 903.4 | 955.9 |
| 1962 | 854.9* | 911.4* | 971.3 |
| 1963 | 946.6 | 1,009.4 | 1,076.7 |
| 1964 | 1,012.6 | 1,082.3 | 1,157.6 |
| 1965 | 1,034.9 | 1,111.9 | 1,195.9 |
| 1966 | 1,019.4 | 1,103.7 | 1,196.2 |
| 1967 | 1,003.8 | 1,094.9 | 1,195.7 |
| 1968 | 1,023.0 | 1,120.6 | 1,229.3 |
| 1969 | 1,068.8 | 1,172.6 | 1,289.3 |
| 1970 | 1,112.8 | 1,223.3 | 1,348.1 |
| 1971 | 1,144.4 | 1,261.5 | 1,394.8 |
| 1972 | 1,146.9 | 1,270.8 | 1,412.7 |
| 1973 | 1,188.9 | 1,319.4 | 1,469.8 |
| 1974 | 1,235.5 | 1,372.6 | 1,531.7 |
| 1975 | 1,295.2 | 1,419.2 | 1,587.2 |
| 1976 | 1,316.2 | 1,467.2 | 1,644.4 |

*End year for declining trend in foreign capital.

their reporting. For example, machinery imported in 1970 may not actually be placed into the production process until several years later. Green and others have noted this difficulty in specifying the proper lag structure, and future attempts at measuring foreign capital stock should take some lag periods into account.[61]

## Results

The data in log form were used to estimate the production function with the following results:

8)    $LQ = 3.93 + .596LK^F + .499LK^D - .626LL - .16LRM$
T-values    (1.10)    (7.70)    (14.26)    (1.50)    (.92)

S.e.  = .024
$R^2$  = .995
D.W. = .997

Only the two capital stocks appear significant in the equation, and the Durbin-Watson statistic, although it falls in the inconclusive range at the one percent confidence level, suggests an autocorrelation problem. Furthermore, multicollinearity difficulties are indicated, corresponding to those expressed by Green and Jarsulic, with trend, capital, and output. Other functions were attempted by this author to allow for a .02 trend in forest products, as well as weights of factor inputs by shares in total costs, but results are not yet conclusive.

To test the null hypothesis noted in equation (1), the following test statistic was employed:

TABLE 13
Share of Foreign Technology in Soviet
Forest Products Sectors 1955–76

| Year | Foreign Capital Stock[1] as Percent of Total Capital Stock | Yearly Machinery Imports as Percent of Total Capital Stock[2] | Yearly Machinery Imports as Percent of Total Machinery Investments[3] |
|------|------|------|------|
| 1955 | 65.0 | 0.70 | 5.0 |
| 1956 | 57.5 | 1.02 | 7.5 |
| 1957 | 51.2 | 1.23 | 9.6 |
| 1958 | 46.3 | 1.03 | 7.5 |
| 1959 | 41.3 | 1.36 | 10.8 |
| 1960 | 37.7 | 1.42 | 11.7 |
| 1961 | 34.7 | 1.79 | 13.9 |
| 1962 | 32.3 | 5.07 | 42.9 |
| 1963 | 33.4 | 4.00 | 35.7 |
| 1964 | 33.7 | 2.42 | 23.0 |
| 1965 | 32.6 | 1.14 | 10.7 |
| 1966 | 30.4 | 1.05 | 9.5 |
| 1967 | 28.2 | 1.95 | 18.3 |
| 1968 | 27.2 | 2.57 | 24.7 |
| 1969 | 26.9 | 2.45 | 22.2 |
| 1970 | 26.4 | 2.07 | 18.1 |
| 1971 | 25.5 | 1.33 | 10.9 |
| 1972 | 23.9 | 2.07 | 21.8 |
| 1973 | 23.7 | 2.11 | 18.8 |
| 1974 | 23.1 | 1.90 | 16.2 |
| 1975 | 22.4 | 1.84 | 14.5 |
| 1976 | 21.5 | 2.23 | — |

[1]Foreign capital stock using 5 percent retirement rate.
[2]Deflated value of forest products machinery imports.
[3]Estimates for 1962 and 1963 may be high due to underestimation of machinery investment for these years because of poor data availability.

9)    $$\dfrac{\dfrac{\hat{\alpha}^F}{\bar{K}^F} - \dfrac{\hat{\alpha}^D}{\bar{K}^D}}{S\left(\dfrac{\hat{\alpha}^F}{\bar{K}^F} - \dfrac{\hat{\alpha}^D}{\bar{K}^D}\right)}$$

where:

$$S\left(\frac{\hat{\alpha}^F}{\bar{K}^F} - \frac{\hat{\alpha}^D}{\bar{K}^D}\right) = \sqrt{\frac{1}{(\bar{K}^F)^2}S_{\hat{\alpha}F}^2 + \frac{N^2}{(\bar{K}^D)^2}S_{\hat{\alpha}D}^2 - \frac{2N}{\bar{K}^F\,\bar{K}^D}\text{cov.}(\hat{\alpha}^F, \hat{\alpha}^D)}$$

$N = 1$
$S^2$ = values from variance/covariance matrix

The resulting T value is 1.807. For 17 degrees of freedom, we can reject the null hypothesis that there is no difference in the marginal productivities of foreign and domestic forest products capital at the 95 percent confidence level.

However, further testing would show that we cannot push the N value much higher than 2 before we enter a range where:

$$\frac{\hat{\alpha}^F}{\bar{K}^F} - N\frac{\hat{\alpha}^D}{\bar{K}^D} \not> 0$$

Therefore, while foreign capital's marginal productivity in forest products may be significantly higher than that of domestic capital, it is well below the magnitude of superiority that Green and Jarsulic suggest for other industries. Subsequent analysis by this author employed a cross-sectional approach to compare the marginal productivities of foreign and domestic capital. Twenty-eight Soviet fiberboard complexes in a variety of regions were compared, representing approximately 50 percent of national output for the year 1972 (square meters measurement). Thirteen of the complexes used machinery of foreign origin; fifteen, of Soviet origin. A similar Cobb-Douglas specification was chosen, but rather than compare the marginal productivity of foreign and domestic stocks as two subsets of the same capital, the two groups of complexes were compared for the study year of 1972. The analysis showed that the marginal productivities of the capital variable in each group were not significantly different at the 95 percent confidence level.[62]

The time series approach to productivity comparisons for Soviet and foreign machinery has fundamental problems relating to the inseparabilities of the two capital stocks. Other factors such as price inflation and price index specification further weaken the methodology. The cross-sectional approach eliminates some of the problems with the time element, but depends to no less an extent on the reliability of determining the true stock origin. Both approaches discussed here did not demonstrate a clear superiority on the part of foreign machinery and equipment in place within the Soviet forest products industrial system. Given that the measurement techniques do not yet allow for full capture of the direct and indirect benefits of imported capital, foreign technology in Soviet forest products still does not appear to provide any strikingly different economic growth than would Soviet capital.

## Conclusions

The forest products industries of the USSR continue to be a severely depressed sector of the Soviet economy. The guidelines to the 11th Five-Year Plan released in 1981 did not specify quantitative growth goals for logging, sawnwood, or plywood, and the recombination of the forest products ministries in 1980 reflects continuing official dissatisfaction with the performance of the sector. Forest products would appear to be an investment-hungry sector which could stand to benefit highly from the import of foreign technology. Logging and sawn materials, in particular, remain undermechanized or burdened with outdated equipment. Imported machinery and equipment was shown to have played a continual and substantial role in forest products investment, yet growth continues to be disappointing for these industries. Finally, econometric comparisons of foreign and Soviet capital stock did not uncover any basic superiority of performance on the part of foreign capital, although further testing might reveal variations in results based on type of forest products industry considered, or modification of methodology.

At the same time, forest products were shown to be a sector of good potential for growth and expansion of exports, given that Soviet planners can achieve the improvements needed in the industries, and given a continued squeeze on domestic consumption.

Technology transfer alone cannot be regarded as a panacea for the ills affecting the Soviet forest products industry. We seem to accept the idea that Soviet purchases of foreign capital allow substitution for indigenous development of production techniques to spur economic growth. This conclusion is questionable for the forest products sector. The evidence presented in this study suggests that technology purchases by the USSR provide at best a short-term benefit. Foreign capital has traditionally made up a large percentage of Soviet investment in the sector, yet forest industries continue to perform below potential. While imported technology may be more productive or up-to-date than Soviet machinery and equipment, better machinery alone does not insure transfer of knowledge or skills, nor does it insure a more efficient production system.

The paper also indicated that the form of technology transfer is an important factor in providing longer term benefits to the industry. The evolution toward technical cooperation and more direct transfer of skills to the Soviet labor force should prove more effective than prototype copying in improving industry performance. Turnkey projects wherein Soviet engineers are directly involved in planning and design may be more beneficial than outright purchases of advising talents from abroad. The key to the most effective form of technology transfer for long-run economic growth may be the development of joint projects between Soviet and Western machinery manufacturers. Such projects, however, are still a long way from realization.

Despite the limitations on foreign technology's total benefits, there is no doubt that the USSR forest products industry has many areas in which imported machinery can make a significant contribution when efficiently incorporated into the domestic production system. This study has pointed out the importance of foreign technology in the use of small-diameter logs, in the efficient utilization of byproducts and thinnings, in the development of techniques for more comprehensive use of larch, in the upgradings of export products quality, in the availability of anti-pollution measures, and in the redesign of older plants. Some technology purchases have been less than successful, and the Bratsk forest products complex presents a case in which ambitious plans for a large scale complex may have outpaced the capability of the Soviet system to absorb or make full use of advanced foreign techniques. And, at times, lack of coordination among responsible agencies in the USSR has diminished the benefits of imported machinery.

The point to be stressed here is that foreign technology's success in improving Soviet forest products industry performance is more a function of proper incorporation of foreign capital into the Soviet planning and production scene, than a function of the higher efficiency of imported capital *per se*. Therefore, this study also presented a variety of other factors which affect the forest products industry and the potential for export level growth or change in the product make-up of wood exports. These factors, taken together with the impacts of foreign technology, provide the most complete picture of export potential in forest products.

For example, the distributional pattern of the resource stock and industrial centers was noted as a central influence on the performance of the sector, both in terms of domestic production and export levels. While Soviet planners apparently contemplated transfer of production centers to eastern complexes, evidence suggests that this pattern may be reevaluated in favor of upgrading older facilities in the western USSR. Foreign technology can play a role in both options. Many Siberian complexes have enjoyed high levels of imported equipment, but at the same time, foreign technology and advisers are aiding in the retooling of older plants.

It has been suggested that foreign technology purchases are a necessary prerequisite to the development of Siberian resources. While environmental conditions and the lack of infrastructure in Siberia do demand advanced techniques, other factors to consider include proper integration of facilities and determination of optimal complex size, methods to insure a stable labor force, and provision of markets for output. The joint projects with Japan point out not only the benefits of barter arrangements for attaining technology and providing a market for Siberian wood, but also the problems associated with log exports from Siberia. In this case the Soviets depend on Japan both as a supplier of technology and as a market for Siberian forest products.

The characteristics of the resource stock were also shown to be important in this study, with relatively less useful larch stands dominating Siberian forests, particularly in the new BAM zones. Indications are that foreign technology for larch use from Japan, the United States, and Canada may be influential in making fuller use of the USSR's vast larch resource.

The desire of Soviet planners to upgrade the product mix of wood exports is evident, and foreign technology may help improve the quality and sophistication of Soviet wood exports, but not without substantial readjustment and investment in the sector. Roundwood and sawnwood are thus likely to continue as the main wood products exported.

## NOTES

1. V. V. Glotov, *Lesnaya i lesopererabatyvayushchaya promyshlennosti ekonomicheskikh rayonov* [The timber and wood-processing industries of economic regions] (Moscow: Lesnaya promyshlennost, 1970), p. 280.

2. N. A. Medvedev, *Current Digest of the Soviet Press* 30, no. 17 (24 May 1978): 10. In 1978–79 major shortfalls in log deliveries were reported in Arkhangelsk Oblast, Karelian ASSR and Perm Oblast. In 1978, plan underfulfillment in Perm Oblast reached 3 million cubic meters. See: *World Wood*, June 1979, pp. 33–34.

3. *Current Digest of the Soviet Press* 30, no. 29 (16 August 1978): 8.

4. *Pravda*, 5 March 1981, pp. 1–7.

5. Medvedev, *Current Digest*, p. 9.

6. This intra-ministry conflict is described in *Current Digest of the Soviet Press* 30, no. 4: 20 and 30; no. 29: 7.

7. Medvedev, *Current Digest*, p. 9.

8. For comprehensive reports on forest stock characteristics, see: V. L. Gorovoi and G. A. Privalovskaya, *Geografiya lesnoi promyshlennosti SSSR* [Geography of the forest industry of the USSR] (Moscow: Nauka, 1966); A. A. Tsymek, *Lesoekonomicheskiye rayony SSSR* [Forest-economic regions of the USSR] (Moscow: Lesnaya promyshlennost, 1975); Jan J. Solecki, "USSR Forest Resources: Their Utilization and the Effect on the Soviet Environment." Paper read at Conference on Soviet Resource Management, June 1974, University of Washington; and Brenton Barr, *The Soviet Wood Processing Industry* (Toronto: University of Toronto Press, 1970), Chapter 3.

9. Medvedev, *Current Digest*, p. 9.

10. See for example, Gorovoi and Privalovskaya, *Geografiya lesnoi promyshlennosti*; Tsymek, *Lesoekonomicheskiye rayony*; Barr, *Soviet Wood*; and V. V. Varankin, *Metodologicheskiye voprosy regionalnoi otsenki prirodnykh resursov* [Methodological problems in regional evaluations of natural resources] (Moscow: Nauka, 1974), Chapter 2.

11. Maps showing the geographic distribution of forest characteristics may be found in Barr, *Soviet Wood*, and Gorovoi and Privalovskaya, *Geografiya lesnoi promyshlennosti*.

12. Forests are divided administratively in the USSR into: Group 1 (forests under complete protection, about 13.3 percent of all forests); Group 2 (forests in deficit regions where limited harvesting is allowed, about 6.5 percent); Group 3 (major commercial forests, about 80.2 percent). The Soviets classify tree species differently than Western foresters. The major Soviet divisions are: conifers (*khvoinye*), hardleafs (*tverdolistvennye*), and softleafs (*myakgolistvennye*). Conifers includes pine, spruce, larch, fir, and stone pine. Hardleafs include oak, beech, ash, maple, and elm. Softleafs include birch, aspen, and linden.

13. See, for example: A. A. Porokhin, *Umensheniye zatrat truda v proizvodstve fanery* [Labor cost reductions in plywood manufacture] (Moscow: TsNIIF, 1968), p. 4.

14. Theodore Shabad, "Some Geographic Aspects of the New Soviet Five-Year Plan." Paper read at 1976 St. Louis meetings of American Association for the Advancement of Slavic Studies, and printed in *Soviet Geography: Review and Translation* 19, no. 3 (March 1978): 202–05.

15. A. P. Petrov, "Organizatsiya kompleksnogo ispolzovaniya lesnykh resursov" [Organization of the complex use of forest resources], unpublished manuscript, Leningrad Forestry Academy, 1978.

16. *Current Digest of the Soviet Press* 30, no. 29 (16 August 1978): 8.

17. Ibid., 31, no. 7 (14 March 1978): 18.

18. Ibid., 30, no. 29 (16 August 1978): 8.

19. V. V. Glotov and I. N. Voyevoda in *Current Digest of the Soviet Press* 30, no. 17 (24 May 1978): 10–11.

20. Various opinions have been expressed on Soviet ability to expand exports of forest products. For contrasting views, see: Brenton Barr, *Domestic and International*

*Implications of Regional Change in the Soviet Timber and Wood Processing Industries, 1970–1990*, Discussion Paper No. 4 (June 1978), Association of American Geographers, Project on Soviet Natural Resources in the World Economy; R. N. North and J. J. Solecki, "The Soviet Forest Products Industry: Its Present and Potential Exports," *Canadian Slavonic Papers* 19, no. 3: 281–311; W. R. J. Sutton, "The Forest Resources of the USSR: Their Exploitation and Their Potential," *Commonwealth Forestry Review* 54, no. 160 (June 1975): 110–38; Irving Holland, "Comparative Advantage and Potentials for World Trade in Wood Products," *Forest Products Journal* 27, no. 10 (October 1977): 55–58; T. Ekstrom, *Development Trends and Export Potential of Soviet Forestry* (Stockholm: Royal College of Forestry, Department of Forest Economics, 1970).

21. Donald Green et al., *The SRI-WEFA Soviet Econometric Model: Phase Three Documentation* (Stanford Research Institute Technical Note SSC—TN—2970—5, May 1977), Vol. 1: 42. Also presented in Donald Green et al., "An Evaluation of the 10th Five-Year Plan Using the SRI-WEFA Econometric Model of the Soviet Union." In U.S., Congress, Joint Economic Committee, *Soviet Economy in a New Perspective*, 94th Congr., 2nd sess., 1976, pp. 301–31.

22. *World Wood Review 1979*, 4 July 1979.

23. See *World Wood*, May 1979, p. 65.

24. Holland, "Comparative Advantage"; Ekstrom, *Development Trends.*

25. Edward Hewett, *Soviet Primary Products Exports to CMEA and the West*, Discussion Paper No. 9 (May 1979), Association of American Geographers, Project on Soviet Natural Resources in the World Economy.

26. *World Wood*, March 1978, p. 29. According to Soviet foreign trade statistics, the price of a cubic meter of sawnwood for Britain declined from 85 rubles in 1977 to 72.60 rubles in 1978, rising again to 88 rubles in 1979.

27. Philip Hanson, "International Technology Transfer from the West to the U.S.S.R.." In U.S., Congress, Joint Economic Committee, *Soviet Economy in a New Perspective*, 94th Congr., 2nd sess., 1976, p. 801.

28. For a review of the meaning of technology transfer, see: Raymond Vernon, ed., *The Technology Factor in International Trade* (New York: Columbia University Press, 1970).

29. Antony C. Sutton, *Western Technology Transfer and Soviet Economic Development 1945 to 1965* (Stanford, Ca.: Hoover Institution Press, 1974), pp. 73–74.

30. Unless otherwise noted, the information presented on location of foreign technology in the USSR came from interviews conducted in Finland and Japan, February 1978. Appendix A presents a list of companies whose representatives agreed to interviews. Appendix B presents some sample sales of forest products technology to the USSR.

31. Some geographic relationships seem to have existed in the past between location of supplier nations and locations of technology use in the USSR. For example, Finnish machinery manufacturers often sold to plants in Leningrad or Arkhangelsk oblasts. Japan supplied technology to Siberia or the Soviet Far East. This relationship seems less marked now with sales of large turnkey plants. European nations such as Finland, Sweden, and France are providing technology to Siberian complexes. Mitsubishi of Japan supplied equipment to the Syktyvkar plant in the Komi ASSR.

32. *World Wood*, February 1978, p. 3.

33. Details on technical cooperation agreements were provided by Aaro Ikonen, Finnish-Soviet Commission for Economic Cooperation, Helsinki.

34. *Protocol—Long Term Program for the Development and Intensification of Economic, Commercial, Industrial, Scientific and Technical Cooperation Between Finland and the USSR Through 1990* (May 1977). Signed in Moscow, this agreement provides goals in various spheres, including forest products, industrial cooperation and specialization, joint research and development, and mutual exchange of scientific information. See also U.S., Congress, House of Representatives, Committee on Science and Technology, *Soviet Scientific and Technical Cooperation with Countries Other than the United States*, 96th Congr., 1st sess., 1979.

35. Medvedev, *Current Digest*, p. 9.

36. U.S. equipment is at times sold indirectly through Japan or Europe to the Soviet Union. American firms interviewed felt that the use of intermediary-nations as agents was beneficial in shortening the transaction period, because firms in Europe and Japan were often more experienced in negotiating with the Soviets. See Kathleen Braden, "The Role of Trade with the United States and Japan in the Development of Siberia's Forest Resources." Paper presented at the 72nd Annual Meeting of the Association of American Geographers, New York, 14 April 1976.

37. See, for example, *Finnish Trade Review*, June 1975, p. 37, for information on the computer systems purchased by the USSR for use at the Ust-Ilimsk complex.

38. For a case study of water pollution from the pulp and paper industry, see Craig ZumBrunnen, "The Lake Baikal Controversy: A Serious Water Pollution Threat or a Turning Point in Soviet Environmental Consciousness." In Ivan Volgyes, ed., *Environmental Deterioration in the Soviet Union and Eastern Europe* (New York: Praeger, 1974), pp. 80–122.

39. *Finnish Trade Review*, August 1976, p. 19.

40. Interview with Wako Koeki Company, Tokyo, February 1978.

41. Correspondence with Baltic Birch, Allied International, Inc., of Boston, Ma.

42. In 1980, for example, random length logs sold from the USSR to Japan listed FOB price per cubic meter as follows: larch, $58.80; fir, $90.50; pine and stone pine, $92.40. *Japan Lumber Journal* 31 May 1980, p. 12.

43. Interview with Alan Cole, of Premier Gear and Machine Works, Portland, Ore., 1977.

44. The projects are variously known as the Far East forest resource development projects and the KS projects, for the names of the negotiators of the first agreement, Kawai of Japan and Sedov of the Soviet Union.

45. Most of the material in this section, unless otherwise noted, came from interviews with representatives of Japanese trading companies in Tokyo, February 1978.

46. Compare with the five-year frame agreements be-

tween Finland and the USSR, *Finnish Trade Review*, July 1974, p. 6.

47. For Soviet responses, see: V. Spandaryan, "The Development of Soviet-Japanese Economic Relations," *Foreign Trade*, 1975, no. 4, p. 26. V. Spandaryan, "A New Development in Soviet-Japanese Trade," *Foreign Trade*, 1977, no. 12, pp. 14–19.

48. *Japan Lumber Journal*, 20 June 1981, p. 19.

49. Ibid., pp. 14–15. Also, Ibid., 30 December 1978, pp. 12–13 for report on November 1978 agreement with Exportles representative. This agreement updated some of the trade terms for Japanese imports of Soviet logs, including the specification of import quantities on a quarterly, rather than yearly basis.

50. Donald W. Green and Marc Jarsulic, "Imported Machinery and Soviet Industrial Production, 1969–1973: An Econometric Analysis," *Soviet Econometric Model Working Paper*, no. 39 (September 1975). Also see H. S. Levine and D. W. Green, "Implications of Technology Transfer for the USSR," *East-West Technological Cooperation* (Brussels: NATO, Directorate of Economic Affairs, 1976), pp. 43–78.

51. See the following articles in *Journal of Comparative Economics* 3, no. 2 (June 1979): Martin L. Weitzman, "Technology Transfer to the USSR: An Econometric Analysis," pp. 167–77; Donald Green, "Technology Transfer to the USSR: A Reply," pp. 178–80; Yasushi Toda, "Technology Transfer to the USSR: The Marginal Productivity Differential and the Elasticity of Intra-Capital Substitution in Soviet Industry," pp. 181–94.

52. Green *SRI-WEFA Econometric Model*. Also: Donald W. Green, "The Microfoundations of Soviet Production Functions: An Engineering Approach," *Soviet Econometric Working Paper*, no. 45 (April 1976).

53. Weitzman, "Technology Transfer," p. 174; Green, "A Reply," p. 179; Toda, "Marginal Productivity Differential," p. 182.

54. Based on *Narodnoye khozyaistvo SSSR* [The economy of the USSR], statistical yearbooks, table on rates of growth of industrial output. 1955–57 based on growth rates of forest products output in Rush V. Greenslade and Wade E. Robertson, "Industrial Production in the U.S.S.R.," U.S. Congress, Joint Economic Committee, *Soviet Economic Prospects for the Seventies*, 93rd Congr., 1st sess., 1973, p. 271.

55. Murray Feshbach and Stephen Rapawy, "Soviet Population and Manpower Trends and Policies," U.S. Congress, Joint Economic Committee, *Soviet Economy in a New Perspective*, 94th Congr., 2nd sess., 1976, p. 137.

56. *Narodnoye khozyaistvo SSSR*, various years, table on commercial timber removals.

57. Ibid., data on new basic funds investment less the basic funds share attributable to structures (in Russian, *zdaniya* and *sooruzheniya*).

58. See Antony Sutton, *Western Technology*, pp. 184–90.

59. Finnish trade statistics for the 1950–55 period from *Ulkomaankauppa, Suomen virallinen tilasto, Tullihallitas* [Foreign Trade, Official Statistics of Finland, Board of Customs].

60. USSR Ministry of Foreign Trade, *Vneshnyaya torgovlya SSSR* [Foreign trade of USSR], statistical yearbooks, various years.

61. For a discussion of lag structures, see Green and Jarsulic, "Imported Machinery."

62. Kathleen E. Braden, "Technology Transfer to the USSR Forest Products Sector." Ph.D. dissertation, Department of Geography, University of Washington, 1981, Chapter 6.

---

# APPENDIX A

Companies, Agencies and Individuals Interviewed

USSR

*I. N. Voyevoda*, Forestry Group. Institute of Economics and Organization of Industrial Production, Academy of Sciences USSR, Siberian Division, Novosibirsk.

*V. V. Glotov*, economist, All-Union Institute for Raising Qualifications of Leading Workers and Specialists of Forest and Woodworking Industries, Moscow.

*A. P. Petrov*, deputy rector, Leningrad Forestry Academy.

*S. V. Sorokin*, laboratory of Siberian Institute of the Forest Industry, Krasnoyarsk (re: use of larch).

*G. A. Privalovskaya*, Institute of Geography, Academy of Sciences USSR, Moscow.

FINLAND

*Sateko*, Logging and Sawn Timber Handling Equipment, Helsinki.

*Jaakko Pöyry and Co.*, consultants, Helsinki.

*Tampella Oy*, paper machinery, Tampere.

*A. Ahlström*, pulp and paper machinery, Karhula.

*Wärtsilä AB*, paper machinery, Helsinki.

*Valmet Oy*, sawmill and particleboard equipment, Helsinki.

*Rauma-Repola*, particleboard machinery, Helsinki.

*Finnish Foreign Trade Association*, Helsinki.

*Finnish-Soviet Commission for Economic Cooperation*, Helsinki.

JAPAN

*Japan Association for Trade with the Soviet Union and Socialist Countries of Eastern Europe*, Tokyo.

*Nissho-iwai Company*, Tokyo.

*Marubeni Corporation*, Tokyo.

*C. Itoh*, Tokyo.

*Mitsubishi Corporation*, Tokyo.

*Sumitomo*, Tokyo.

*Mitsui and Company*, Tokyo.

*Progress Trading Company*, Tokyo.

*Wako Koeki Company*, Tokyo.

UNITED STATES

*Nicholson Manufacturing Company*, Seattle, Wash.

*Norman Springate and Associates, Inc.* (consultants) Portland, Ore.

*Premier Gear and Machine Works*, Portland, Ore.

*Weyerhaeuser*, International Planning Department, Tacoma, Wash.

*Lamb-Grays Harbor Company*, Hoquiam, Wash.

*Stetson-Ross Company*, Seattle, Wash.

APPENDIX B*
SELECTED SALES OF FOREST PRODUCTS TECHNOLOGY
POST 1960 TO USSR FROM FINLAND, JAPAN AND U.S.

| Item | Value or Capacity | Year of Sale or Beginning of Operation | Selling Nation | Location of Use in USSR |
|---|---|---|---|---|
| Turnkey sawmill | $75.5 million | 1978 | Finland | Lesosibirsk |
| Log merchandiser | $43.5 million | 1980 | Finland | Ust-Ilimsk |
| Chipper-canter | $250,000 | 1973 | U.S. | Siberia |
| Chipper-edger | $ 70,000 | 1973 | U.S. | Arkhangelsk |
| Ring debarkers | $1 million | 1974 | U.S. | ? |
| Feed conveyors | ? | ? | U.S. | Siberia |
| Sawmill machinery | 300,000 cu. m. logs per year | 1977 | Japan | Sovetskaya Gavan |
| Planers | 150m. per minute | 1972–73 | Japan | Siberia and Far East |
| Debarkers | ? | mid-1970s | Japan | Khabarovsk, Far East |
| Sawngoods processor | 600,000 cu. m. per year | 1975 | Finland | Ust-Ilimsk |
| Pulp and paper waste treatment | ? | 1975 | Finland | Svetogorsk |
| Paper and paper-board machinery | ? | ? | Finland | ? |
| Washer-sulfate pulp mill | 500 tons/day | 1976 | Finland | Syktyvkar |
| Paper and paper machinery | ? | various | Finland | Bratsk, Baikalsk, Krasnoyarsk, Koryazhma, Astrakhan, Balakhna, Solikamsk, Segezha, Syasstroi, Dolinsk, Svetogorsk |
| Paper machinery | ? | 1961 | Finland | Riga |
| Paper machinery | ? | 1967 | Finland | Leningrad |
| Paper machinery | 8 mill. rubles | 1977 | Finland | Leningrad |
| Digesters and washers | ? | mid 1960s | Finland | Arkhangelsk, Koryazhma, Bratsk, Segezha |
| Paper plant modernization | ? | ? | Finland (and France) | Lesosibirsk |
| Paper machinery | ? | 1977 | Finland | Petrozavodsk, Izhevsk |
| Turnkey pulp and paper plant | ? | 1974–79 | Finland | Svetogorsk |
| Paper and paperboard machinery | 270 tons/day | 1970 | Finland | Syasstroi |
| " | 825 tons/day | 1977 | Finland | Bratsk |
| " | 610 tons/day | 1977 | Finland | Krasnoyarsk |
| " | 320 tons/day | 1977 | Finland | Stupino |
| " | 320 tons/day | 1978 | Finland | Stupino |
| Steam generating units | ? | 1969–70 | Finland | Bratsk |
| " | ? | 1961–65 | Finland | Dolinsk, Baikalsk, Balakhna, Koryazhma, Zhidachov, Astrakhan |
| Paper and cardboard machinery | $10 million | 2nd KS | Japan | Siberia |
| Pulp and papermill | 250,000 tons/year | Pulp and Chip Project | Japan | Lesosibirsk |
| Pulpmill expansion | 250,000 tons/year | Pulp and Chip Project | Japan | Amursk |
| Pulp and papermill | –500,000 tons per year of newspaper –150,000 tons per year of wrapping paper –$600–700 million | Pulp and Chip Project | Japan | Khabarovsk |
| Pulp and paper mill modernization | ? | Pulp and Chip Project | Japan | Sakhalin |
| Pulp sludge treatment | $8 million | 1977 | Japan | Ust-Ilimsk |
| Particleboard plants | 100,000 cu. m. per year | 1972–75 | Finland | Vologda, Syktyvkar, Ukraine, Belorussia, Sovetsk, Zheshart, Riga, Arkhangelsk |
| Particleboard plant | 250,000 cu. m. per year | 1976 | Finland | Zheshart |

*NOTE: These sales represent only a sample of total sales and are presented to give examples of types of equipment sold. Data were collected through interviews with companies listed in Appendix A and through industry journal reports. Some listings above may overlap within major sales. Other nations which have concluded major sales of forest products technology to the USSR include: France, West Germany, Poland, Sweden, Switzerland, Canada and Belgium.

# 19

# SOVIET IRON ORE: ITS DOMESTIC AND WORLD IMPLICATIONS

TONY MISKO
CRAIG ZUMBRUNNEN
University of Washington

## Introduction

Iron ore is one of the most abundant natural resources located on the earth. Although it is abundant, it is neither uniformly distributed nor concentrated. It is the basis of the world's iron and steel industry. The resultant production of pig iron, crude steel and steel products remains a key indicator of a nation's industrial development, prosperity, and position of power.

Over the past quarter century, global trade in iron ore has increased at an average annual rate of 10 percent.[1] The increased demand for ore by the industrial nations has resulted in a marked shift in the pattern of global import and export trade. Australia, Brazil, Canada, the Soviet Union, and Venezuela have emerged as the major exporting nations with Japan, Western Europe's Coal and Steel Community,[2] the United States, and the CMEA bloc of Eastern Europe[3] as the major importing nations. At present, the exporting nations are placing two-thirds of iron ore production onto the world market. All, with the exception of the Soviet Union, confine their exports primarily to the industrialized West. The Soviet Union exports are destined almost exclusively to its CMEA partners. The most significant change in the world trade pattern has been the rise of Japan as a major importer.[4]

The Soviet Union possesses the greatest iron ore reserves in the world, both proven and potential. Although exploration of its resources of iron ore has not been fully accomplished, the reserves of categories $A + B + C_1 + C_2$ (see Appendix I) as of 1 January 1975 were 107.1 billion tons, including 63.7 billion tons in the proven categories $A + B + C_1$.[5] As can be seen from Table 1, Soviet iron reserves far exceed those of any other nation. The USSR is also the greatest producer of both crude and marketable iron ore. With its present facilities, it has been able to increase annual crude ore production by an average of 17.5 million tons and marketable ore by an average of 6.9 million tons from 1960 to 1980[6] (see Table 2).

The European or western portion of the USSR has been extensively prospected and exploited. Its huge reserves more than meet the needs of the Soviet industrial heartland and adjacent hinterland. These deposits are within economic rail and water-shipping distance of all Europe. The Asian or eastern portion, in turn, has not been fully prospected and explored, accessible deposits appear to be of limited significance. But scattered reports indicate the existence of large remote deposits sufficient ultimately to supplement the needs of the European portion of the country, satisfy the proposed iron and steel developments in Siberia and the Far East, and still constitute great potential for foreign export. These Siberian deposits, when fully put into production on completion of the Baikal-Amur Mainline, should be in a position to penetrate the large Japanese market.

Although the Soviet Union's annual iron-ore exports since 1961 increased 2.7-fold, from 16.3 million to a high point of 43.6 million tons in 1975, they declined thereafter to 38.1 million tons in 1980.[7] Furthermore, despite a 14-fold absolute increase in exports since 1950, the Soviet Union's relative position has slipped from second to third among the ore-exporting nations, behind Australia and Brazil.[8] Over 95 percent of Soviet iron ore exports are bound for CMEA countries (in 1981, 33.0 million tons out of a total of 34.2 million tons exported).[9] Under 1974 agreements, annual Soviet exports to Eastern Europe were to have reached 48 million tons by 1980,[10] which now seems to have been far from realistic.

The present pattern of iron ore marketing could be altered dramatically if the Soviet Union should decide to undertake an energetic program to increase its iron ore production and compete fully in the world market. To fulfill the role of a major international supplier of iron ore, that is, greatly expand exports to non-CMEA countries, the USSR would have to further exploit proven deposits by opening up new mines, by upgrading mining and enrichment technology, and by improving domestic surface transportation infrastructure and maritime facilities. Yet despite the tremendous export potential manifested in vast iron ore reserves, there does not appear to be a shortage of iron ore on the world market for the Soviet Union to fill.[11]

This study seeks to systematically assess the Soviet Union's iron-ore potential to 1990. The first section presents a concise history of prerevolutionary Russian and Soviet iron ore exploration and development. The second

TABLE 1
Iron Ore Resources of the World (ca. 1970)
(millions of metric tons)

| Country | Reserves | Potential | Total Reserves |
|---|---|---|---|
| Australia | 16,165 | NA | 16,165 |
| Brazil | 30,050 | 10,164 | 40,214 |
| Canada | 33,628 | 86,389 | 120,017 |
| China | 5,882 | 24,751 | 30,633 |
| France | 6,525 | 4,500 | 11,025 |
| India | 8,646 | 20,406 | 29,052 |
| Sweden | 3,370 | NA | 3,370 |
| United States | 7,617 | 97,898 | 105,515 |
| Soviet Union | 107,100* | 193,800 | 305,300 |
| Venezuela | 2,097 | NA | 2,097 |

SOURCE: *Survey of World Iron Ore Resources* (New York: United Nations, Department of Economics and Social Affairs, 1970), pp. 169, 191, 233, 264, 288, 376, 377, 404, 467.
*P. A. Shiryayev, Ye. N. Yarkho and Yu. M. Borts, *Metallurgicheskaya i ekonomicheskaya otsenka zhelezorudnoy bazy SSSR* [Metallurgical and economic assessment of the iron-ore base of the USSR] (Moscow: Metallurgiya, 1978), p. 9.

TABLE 2
Soviet Crude and Marketable Iron Ore Production,
1960–85 (millions of metric tons)

| Year | Crude Ore | Marketable Ore | |
|---|---|---|---|
| | | Old series | New series |
| 1960 | 141.5 | 105.9 | 105.9 |
| 1965 | 237.5 | 153.4 | 153.5 |
| 1970 | 355.4 | 195.5 | 197.3 |
| 1975 | 441.5 | 232.8 | 235.0 |
| 1976 | 460.0 | 239.1 | 241.3 |
| 1977 | 477.0 | 239.7 | 242.0 |
| 1978 | 481.1 | 244.2 | 246.4 |
| 1979 | 481.0 | — | 241.7 |
| 1980 | 498.1 | — | 244.7 |
| 1981 | — | — | 242.4 |
| 1982 est. | — | — | 242.2 |
| 1985 plan | 600.0 | — | 262.4 |

SOURCES: *Narodnoye khozyaistvo SSSR v 1980 godu* [The economy of the USSR in 1980] (Moscow: Finansy i Statistika, 1981), p. 159; Theodore Shabad, "News Notes," *Soviet Geography: Review and Translation*, various issues. The offical Soviet time series for marketable iron ore production was revised in 1980 for the period 1970–78, adding 1.5 to 2 million tons a year, apparently as a result of a revision in the production series for the RSFSR; see Shabad, "News Notes," SGRT 22, no. 4 (April 1981): 288.

section reviews the central role that the Soviet iron and steel industry has played in regional economic planning since the beginning of the forced industrialization drive in 1928. The third section focuses on recent trends in the Soviet iron ore industry. The fourth section discusses the regional distribution of Soviet iron ore reserves. The fifth section explores in greater geographic detail the various iron ore districts, their principal reserves and production, and the domestic and foreign distribution patterns of the marketable ore. The sixth section speculates about production projections to 1990. A seventh section analyzes potential ore consumption in Siberia. The concluding section explores the past, present, and future prospects for Soviet iron-ore exports.

### Early Russian and Soviet Iron-Ore Production and Mineral Exploration and Development

The mineral exploration efforts under the czars can be classed as haphazard. Despite the fact that qualitative and quantitative knowledge about iron ore deposits was limited, Czarist Russia was using local charcoal reduction plants to smelt high-grade ore in central European Russia at Tula in the seventeenth century. During the eighteenth century the focus of Russian iron smelting switched to the Urals, where rich iron ore deposits were found beneath the charcoal-yielding forests. Expanding output rapidly in the Urals, Russia became the world's leading iron producer by the mid-eighteenth century. In the nineteenth century Russia's preeminence in ore and iron production was eclipsed by other European nations because of its lag in adopting the new coke-based smelting technology. The dawn of the Russian railroad era in the late nineteenth century stimulated a rapid shift away from charcoal-based smelting in the Urals to large, more efficient coke-fired blast furnaces in the southern European part of the country, where Donets Basin coking

coal and Krivoi Rog iron ore were found in close proximity. Having established its commanding role before the turn of the century, the Krivoi Rog ore district still maintains its positions as the Soviet Union's leading producing deposit, although its relative share has declined.[12]

Prior to the Bolshevik Revolution the country had not been explored systematically or extensively for minerals. The areas that showed promise of significant deposits then were not exploited efficiently to yield any great quantities. The policy toward exploring industrial raw materials is now systematic and deliberate. Thousands of geologists and technicians have been trained and are exploring the extensive land mass for new deposits of useful minerals.[13] The European portion of the Soviet Union has undergone extensive prospecting with significant increments in the overall iron ore reserves. The Asian portion, on the other hand, is practically virgin territory by comparison. If any new, large deposits of iron ore are to be uncovered, in all probability they will be discovered in Siberia and the Far East.

Since the beginning of centrally controlled economic development in 1928, a series of five-year plans has been initiated and implemented. Although these plans, in part, determine the goals for both the exploration and production of industrial raw materials, they have not always been fulfilled as planned. Nevertheless, the progress achieved has been greater than that under the czars. In 1929, the reserves of $A + B$ type ore (Appendix I for ore definitions) totaled 2.1 billion tons. By 1936, the reserves were 4.5 billion tons; by 1946, 5.2 billion, and by 1971, almost 20 billion tons.[14] Thus, since the end of World War II the reserves have increased very significantly. The continued exploration of known deposits and the development of new deposits have put the Soviet Union in the forefront as the major iron ore possessing and producing nation in the world today.

## The Role of Ferrous Metallurgy in Soviet Economic Development Policy

In general, the initial economic development policies of the Soviet Union according to Marxist-Leninist doctrine called for: (1) rapid industrialization, (2) development of the backward regions of the nation, (3) distribution of the economic activities as evenly as possible, and (4) location of the means of production close to natural resources and/or markets so as to minimize the combined costs of transportation and socially necessary labor.[15] The drive to industrialize rapidly took precedence over other aspects of the nation's economy. The early established industrial centers in the European part of Russia served as the basis for expansion of the iron, steel, and related industries. To reach the goal of increased iron and steel production, emphasis was placed on developing the nation's natural resources, especially iron ore and coal.[16] In essence, the iron and steel industry became the symbol as well as the physical linchpin of the forced industrialization campaign.

Soviet industrial location policies can be dichotomized temporally into the Stalinist "political" and the post-Stalinist "economic" eras. Under Stalin economic development decisions became the realm of the politician and defensive military strategist and hence, economic efficiency criteria were often neglected. Stalinist industrial location policies culminated geographically in a push eastward into the Urals and beyond. While such developments were consistent with the four Marxist-Leninist tenets cited above, the interior locations and dispersed pattern for the build-up of strategic industries, such as iron and steel, were also strongly motivated by military considerations. Of course, the discovery of rich iron deposits in the Urals and cheap coking coals in the Kuznetsk Basin were also strong locational attractions. Nothing more typified this eastward move toward resource sites than the long-distance marriage between Magnitogorsk's rich magnetite ore and Kuznetsk coal, which reinstated the Urals as a major iron and steel center focused on the new Magnitogorsk complex. Simultaneously, a Siberian iron and steel complex was built at Novokuznetsk, then known as Stalinsk. Although the 2,250-kilometer long-haul transport of the coal westward and ore eastward was not economic per se, the German invasion in June 1941 easily vindicated the long-term wisdom of the Urals-Kuznetsk project.[17]

These two regions are now far less dependent on each other for raw materials. The Urals iron and steel industry now receives coking coal from the Karaganda deposits of Kazakhstan in addition to that from the Kuznetsk Basin. As the rich local ores have been depleted, the Urals iron and steel plants have been forced to rely on the low-grade iron-vanadium deposit at Kachkanar and long-haul ores from Rudny in Kazakhstan, the Kola Peninsula ores, the Kursk Magnetic Anomaly and Krivoi Rog. In turn, Kuznetsk iron and steel production is now based on iron ore from the nearby deposits of Gornaya Shoriya, Teya, Abaza, and from the more distant Korshunovo deposit at Zheleznogorsk in Irkutsk Oblast. In the meantime, exploration and exploitation of the iron ore and coking coal

deposits of Kazakhstan led to the development of another iron and steel complex at Temirtau near Karaganda. This complex now competes with the Urals for Kazakhstan iron ore, some of which is also shipped to the Kuznetsk Basin to supplement its depleting ore sources.[18]

Despite Stalin's eastward development thrust, the Ukraine, throughout the Soviet era, has maintained its production dominance in ferrous metallurgy's quadruplet of coking coal, iron ore, pig iron and steel. The proximity of Krivoi Rog iron ore, Donets Basin coking coal, fluxing agents, and markets for iron and steel products led to a highly economically rational locational inertia in the Ukraine that was not deterred by Stalin's industrialization drive to the Urals and beyond.

After his death in 1953, cost consciousness began to receive higher priority in the economic-geographic development decision calculus used by central planners while the goal of spatially uniform development began to be viewed as less realistic. This policy shift was based on the pragmatic recognition of geographically uneven resource endowments, labor supply problems in the east, and high infrastructure and environment costs in the east. As high-grade, direct-shipment iron ore supplies began to be depleted in the 1950s at a rate faster than the introduction of ore enrichment technologies, the transport burden increased dramatically. Since, in percentage terms, iron ore is the greatest raw material input in pig iron and (nonscrap) steel smelting, the dwindling supplies of high grade ores increased the locational pull of ore sites. The Ukraine and the Central Industrial Region of European Russia received renewed attention as foci for iron and steel development. Unlike most other industrial raw materials, especially energy resources, which are concentrated in the north and east, over 60 percent of proven Soviet iron ore reserves are located in the European part of the USSR west of the Urals.[19] Over 33 percent of the proven reserves ($A + B + C_1$) are in the Ukraine, predominantly in the Krivoi Rog deposits, 26 percent are associated with the increasingly important Kursk Magnetic Anomaly deposits of south central European Russia, and 3.9 percent are in Karelia and the Kola Peninsula.[20] Based on the latter deposits and Pechora Basin coking coal, an integrated iron and steel complex was established at Cherepovets in 1955 to supply the steel needs of Leningrad and its hinterland.[21] The Lipetsk plant in Central Russia is becoming increasingly important, while the nearby Tula plant remains modest by comparison. The recent large-scale expansion of productive capacity at Lipetsk is predicated on KMA ores,[22] as are the Stary Oskol direct reduction plant, which is nearing completion, and a much larger proposed CMEA-oriented integrated steel complex, also slated for the Stary Oskol area.[23]

With the exception of Western Siberia (the Kuznetsk Basin area), iron and steel development, and economic development in general, has been slower in the Asian USSR. The region's remoteness from the developed western zone, lack of adequately trained manpower, limited market hinterland, insufficient infrastructure, and need for greater capital outlays have combined to slow exploitation and development. The recent emphasis has been on hydropower and coal energy resources, minerals, timber, other raw materials, planned nodal urban and industrial construction, and limited transport linkages. The potential for developing Siberia has been enhanced through the harnessing of the Angara and Yenisei rivers. The construction of huge hydroelectric power stations provides needed energy to industrialize the Krasnoyarsk and, potentially, the Transbaikal region along the Trans-Siberian Railroad and the BAM. Little has developed with regard to iron and steel production based on local raw materials. There have long been plans for building an iron and steel complex at Taishet at the junction of the Trans-Siberian and Taishet-Lena rail lines. Ground-clearing work in fact began in 1959 but was suspended after a couple of years. A linear programming model of the Soviet iron and steel industry indicates that Taishet is, indeed, an economically viable location for steel production.[24] Although construction of a similar integrated project has been proposed for the Aldan area of southern Yakutia based on Neryungri coking coal and Aldan ore, Svobodny or Komsomolsk seem to be preferred sites.[25] Two steel facilities, a one-million ton plant at Komsomolsk and a much smaller plant at Petrovsk-Zabaikalsky, consume long-haul pig iron and local scrap as the basis for their steel production, which is consumed exclusively in Eastern Siberia and the Far East. Another small steel-scrap plant is under construction at Komsomolsk, with a designed electric-furnace capacity of 500,000 tons.[26]

While a more detailed review of the Soviet iron and steel system is presented elsewhere,[27] some summary comments are appropriate here. First, despite recent disappointments arising from the failure to even approach the long-term goal of 250 million tons of steel annually by 1980[28] (actual 1980 production was 147.9 million tons, having declined from a 1978 high point of 151.5 million tons), the Soviet Union is the leading steel producing nation in the world.[29] Second, iron and steel have been both the workhorse and shining example of the forced industrialization campaign. Third, after an early Soviet push eastward, the preponderance of iron ore reserves in the European USSR is again determining the locational pattern of the industry, notwithstanding the reduced transport burden of enriched ores. For example, of the ten largest plants, three each are situated in the Ukraine and the Urals (Krivoi Rog and Magnitogorsk being the largest). Lipetsk and Cherepovets are the two largest plants in European Russia; Temirtau (Karaganda) and the West Siberian plant in the Kuznetsk Basin are in the east. Although pig iron and steel are produced in some forty other plants, the top ten account for 56 percent of all Soviet steel.[30] Fourth, ore demands in the Urals and West Siberia, combined with the relatively poor resource base in the east, are creating ever greater long-haul transport problems for the Soviet Union. Fifth, the Urals' continued high level of steel production can be attributed to locational inertia coupled with a heavy use of locally generated scrap, rather than the dictates of the current spatial economy. To a lesser extent the same can be said of West Siberian production. Sixth, allowing for the assumed European origin of most Soviet steel exports, systems mod-

eling suggests that the Soviets would be well advised to concentrate future iron and steel development mainly in the Ukraine and southern European Russia, and secondarily in Kazakhstan and, surprisingly perhaps, in East Siberia.[31] Indeed, for the most part, the Soviets seem to be proceeding along these directions.

These general spatial characteristics of the iron and steel system today are, of course, the culmination of the dynamic raw material supplies and costs, labor costs, transportation costs, market demands, the geographic legacy of Stalin's location policies, and technological changes. The vanguard role of iron and steel in the Soviet industrialization effort has resulted in prodigious increases in iron ore production, and as the supply of higher-grade, direct shipment ores has declined, increasing emphasis has been placed on the use of lower grade ores and the technology to enrich them. It is to these recent trends in Soviet iron ore production that we now turn.

## Trends in the Soviet Iron Ore Industry

Except for the severe dislocations associated with World War II and the leveling off in recent years, Soviet crude and marketable iron ore production has been trending monotonically upward. These upswings in crude and marketable iron ore tonnages were due, in part, to the opening of new mines, increased capacity of established mines, and increasing use and expansion of iron-ore enrichment facilities utilizing the latest in domestic and foreign technology.

The number of underground and surface mines has increased from 66 and 58 in 1968 to 71 and 64 in 1978 respectively.[32] Despite this small increase in the number of mines, their combined capacity of marketable ore increased significantly from 200 million tons in 1968 to 285 million tons in 1978, an average annual increase of 8.5 million tons.[33] During this period, actual production of crude ore increased from 307.6 million tons to some 480 million tons and marketable ore[34] from 175.7 million tons to some 245 million tons.[35]

More significant for the objectives of this research is the fact that the iron ore industry has essentially been stagnant since 1976 (Table 2). Marketable ore tonnage actually declined by 4.7 million tons in 1979 to a level of 241.7 million tons. Despite the rebound in 1980 to 244.7 million tons, actual production fell far short of the original planning target of 276 million tons.[36] The same was true with respect to crude ore with 1980 production at 498 million tons compared with an original five-year plan goal of 560 million tons for 1980.[37] The five-year plan goal for 1985 has now been set at 600 million tons of crude ore and 262.4 million tons of marketable ore.

These increasingly problematic shortfalls are due in part to the declining tenor of Soviet iron-ore workings. Because iron ore is not found in a pure state, its natural iron content can vary greatly within a given deposit as well as from deposit to deposit. For example, the Kachkanar deposit in the Urals averages 16.5 percent iron compared to that of the Dneprorudnoye mine in the Ukraine with 63.3 percent.[38] In addition, the ores contain various chemical components that may be either beneficial or detrimental in the production phases of iron and steel. The harmful impurities that pose the most important problems include silica, phosphorus, sulfur, alumina, arsenic, and hydrates. They must be reduced to acceptable levels for blast furnace use. These impurities affect the efficiency and life of smelting facilities. On the other hand, manganese, calcium, nickel, titanium, chromium, molybdenum, and vanadium can be beneficial in acceptable quantities. Such things as the kind of ore, its iron content, and impurities can have a deciding influence on both domestic and potential foreign markets for Soviet iron ore.

Profitable crude iron ore should possess an iron content in the vicinity of 30 percent or greater to render it economic for direct blast furnace charge. Ore of less than 30 percent Fe is generally considered uneconomical. The iron content of Soviet reserves has been on the downturn. In 1960, they averaged 44.5 percent iron. By 1970, this percentage decreased to 37.3 percent and by 1979 an average of 35.5 percent.[39] Simultaneously, through the implementation of various ore enrichment technologies, the average content of iron in the shipped ore increased from 54.3 to 59.6 percent.[40] About 41 percent of all concentrates produced have a metal content of 65 percent or more. In 1980, some 420 million tons of low-grade ore (16 percent to 35 percent metal content) was enriched to 60 percent or greater metal content before shipping and only about 70 million tons had a sufficiently high metal content to warrant direct shipping (see Table 3).[41]

The modern iron smelting industry demands high quality crude ore or increased iron content concentrates to cut the costs of transportation, smelting, and slag dis-posal, and to increase furnace efficiency and profits. These demands have resulted in the expenditure of huge sums of money, time, technology, and equipment to develop methods to concentrate the abundant reserves of average and low-grade iron ores. High-grade ores formerly fed directly to the blast furnace are now enriched also to produce a more nearly uniform (i.e., efficient) furnace charge and reduce raw-material assembly costs. In general, ore enrichment thus reduces iron and steel production costs and leads to greater profits. The industry objective seems to be to produce iron concentrates containing more than 60 percent Fe and 5 to 8 percent $SiO_2$.

The early enrichment techniques employed by the Soviet Union consisted of simple crushing, washing, and jiggling techniques.[42] Now the techniques include flotation, magnetic separation, electro-separation, roasting, and others. Technology is being researched for application to various complex ores, such as the extraction of iron concentrates from complex ferruginous quartzites and oxidized ores in nonmagnetic forms.[43]

In the Soviet period, iron ore preparation from 1917 to 1927 used simple washing and crushing techniques. From 1928 to 1949, dry and wet magnetic separation, magnetic-gravity, and flotation were introduced. During the period 1931–32, a three-stage crushing installation was perfected to enrich oxide ores through the use of gravity-magnetic methods. The dry magnetic separation method was used to enrich sulfurous ores. Experimental work was undertaken in 1933 to develop a means of enriching iron quartzites. As a result gravity, magnetic, and magnetic roasting techniques were introduced. In the 1950s, ore concentration was centered on the deposits of the Kursk Magnetic Anomaly where an experimental

TABLE 3
Trends of Soviet Iron Ore Production, Enrichment, and Export, 1968–85 (million metric tons)

| Year | Crude Ore Production | Marketable Ore Production* | Direct Shipping Ore | Concentrate Production | Pellet Production | Sinter Production | Marketable Ore Exported | Pellets Exported |
|---|---|---|---|---|---|---|---|---|
| 1968 | 307.6 | 175.7 | 73.0 | 102.7 | 7.2 | 128.2 | 32.2 | — |
| 1969 | 328.2 | 185.2 | 76.2 | 109.0 | 9.4 | 132.9 | 33.1 | — |
| 1970 | 355.4 | 196.2 | 69.2 | 127.0 | 10.6 | 138.2 | 36.1 | — |
| 1971 | 374.8 | 202.2 | 62.0 | 140.2 | 13.7 | 140.7 | 36.5 | — |
| 1972 | 388.5 | 207.3 | 65.1 | 142.2 | 18.1 | 143.0 | 38.4 | — |
| 1973 | 403.6 | 215.3 | 69.6 | 145.7 | 21.5 | 146.1 | 41.4 | — |
| 1974 | 421.8 | 224.8 | 76.9 | 147.9 | 23.3 | 148.7 | 43.3 | — |
| 1975 | 441.5 | 232.8 | 80.8 | 153.0 | 27.5 | 152.9 | 43.6 | — |
| 1976 | 460.0 | 239.1 | 80.1 | 159.0 | 31.4 | 152.1 | 43.1 | 2.4 |
| 1977 | 477.0 | 239.7 | 78.7 | 161.0 | 33.0 | 153.0 | 41.0 | 5.0 |
| 1978 | 481.1 | 244.2 | 75.0 | 169.0 | 35.0 | 155.0 | 40.6 | 5.5 |
| 1979 | 481.0 | 241.7 | c.73.0 | c.168.0 | 44.3 | 160.0 | 39.0 | 5.5 |
| 1980 | 498.1 | 244.7 | c.70.0 | c.175.0 | 50.9 | 158.0 | 38.1 | 8.8 |
| 1981 | | 242.4 | | | | | 34.2 | 9.2 |
| 1985 Plan | 600 | 262.4 | | | 68 | 164 | | |

*The marketable ore series through 1978 is presented as given in Soviet sources before the 1980 revision (see note in Table 2).

Sources: S. N. Shalayev and S. Ya. Arsenyev, "Ways of enhancing the cost-effectiveness of the iron-ore industry in the 10th Five-Year Plan," *Gorny zhurnal*, 1976, no. 3, p. 4; United States Department of the Interior, *Mineral Yearbook*, 3, Area Reports: International (Wahington: Government Printing Office, 1970, 1971, 1972, 1975), various pages; Theodore Shabad, "Soviet Regional Policy and CMEA Integration," *SGRT* 20, no. 4 (April 1979): 241; V. V. Strishkov, *Mineral Industries of the U.S.S.R.* (Washington: Department of the Interior, Bureau of Mines, 1979), pp. 13–14; *Vneshnyaya torgovlya SSSR v 1981 g.* [Foreign trade of the USSR in 1981] (Moscow: Finansy i Statistika, 1982), p. 25; Theodore Shabad, "News Notes," *SGRT* 19, no. 4 (April 1978): 290; Ibid., 22, no. 4 (April 1981): 287–88; Ibid., 23, no. 4 (April 1982): 294–95.

magnetic enrichment complex was constructed to upgrade the local ores. By 1959, facilities were under construction to process the ferruginous quartzites of the KMA. Magnetic-gravity methods were also employed at Olenegorsk in the Kola Peninsula to process the local magnetite-hematite ores. After 1958 more emphasis was given to iron ore deposits in the eastern regions. Accordingly the deposits at Rudny, Kachar, and Lisakovsk in Kazakhstan as well as Zheleznogorsk in East Siberia were to receive added investment funds for enrichment facilities.[44]

Due to the physical and chemical complexity of iron ore, it is necessary to develop specific means to enrich or prepare specific types of ore. Sintering is by far the most important method of upgrading ore in the Soviet Union today. Approximately 90 percent of all sinter is fluxed (Table 3). The goal is to produce only self-fluxing furnace burden. In the sintering process, the ore is mixed with coke breeze, ignited to drive off some of the undesirable content of the ore and produce a clinker of high quality furnace burden. Calcite or dolomite can be added to produce a self-fluxing furnace charge. The operation can be conducted at the concentrating site or at the blast furnace.

The most significant breakthrough in iron ore enrichment was perfecting the process of pelletizing iron concentrates. This was achieved in the United States after World War II. The first commercial pellet production in the Soviet Union did not occur until 1965. Since then pelletizing units have been installed at Rudny in Kazakhstan, Kachkanar in the Urals, the North and Central concentrators in the Krivoi Rog basin, the Komsomolsk mine near Kremenchug,[45] and at Gubkin and Zheleznogorsk in the Kursk Magnetic Anomaly.[46] In pelletizing, the fine iron particles are separated from the gangue by various means, such as grinding and flotation, and are balled into marble size pellets by either a rotary or disc machine. The fine iron particles are bound in the operation by a binding material, such as bentonite clay, hardened by firing in a kiln and then shipped. As in sintering, the pellets can be made self-fluxing. The operation is conducted at the mining site. Plans are to upgrade the total sinter and pellet production to self-fluxing blast furnace burden. This will improve blast furnace efficiency and reduction through the use of electric furnaces and lower transportation costs.

The iron ore enrichment facilities in the Soviet Union comprise 92 concentrating units of which 29 have sintering plants and 7 pelletizing facilities. During the 1968–80 period, the production of concentrates increased from 102.7 million tons to about 175 million tons, sinter from 128.2 million tons to 158 million tons, and pellets from 7.2 million tons to 50.9 million tons (Table 3).[47] About 85 percent of the ore is agglomerated by either sintering or pelletizing.[48] Introduced in 1954, the agglomeration plants were initially of small capacity, 3,000 to 5,000 tons per day.[49] Their capacities now range from 25,000 to 35,000 tons per day with larger capacity facilities under construction.[50]

The more modern pelletizing technique was not applied in the Soviet Union until 1965.[51] The Ukraine produced almost 60 percent of the total pellets in the nation

in 1976 (18 million metric tons of a total 31.4 million tons).[52] Pellet production in the Ukraine increased by 20 million tons after the installation of facilities employing American and CMEA technology.[53] In 1978, the Gubkin and Zheleznogorsk units combined produced about 10 million tons of pellets.[54] New and expanding pelletizing facilities coming on line in the KMA are to augment the region's output by 9 million tons.[55] The 1976–80 Plan called for the Soviet iron-ore industry to increase pellet production to 60 million tons by 1980,[56] a figure that was overly optimistic since actual 1980 output was 50.9 million tons.

Pellets possess several advantages over direct shipping crude and some forms of concentrate. They reduce cost of transportation, attrition during transportation and storage, and have desired physical and chemical characteristics and a high iron content of 60 to 68.5 percent. Accordingly, these characteristics give pellets the ideal qualities for competitive entry into the world iron-ore market.

The average iron content of concentrates has increased from 59 percent in 1965 to around 62 percent in 1980.[57] Simultaneously, the share of concentrate in total usable ore has steadily risen from only 10 percent in 1940, to 53 percent in 1965, 62 percent in 1970, 65 percent in 1975, and 72 percent in 1980.[58] In other words, whereas 18 percent of the total crude ore in 1940 received (or required) beneficiation, by 1980 the percentage had grown to nearly 85 percent. While much of this increase in enrichment has been dictated by dwindling reserves of high-grade, direct-shipment ore, part of it is, of course, the result of technological changes in iron and steel making processes. Accordingly, agglomerated and self-fluxing sinter and pellets perform more efficiently (and hence, economically) in modern blast furnaces.

At present, the enrichment of iron ore in the Soviet Union is thus being intensively pursued. Old concentrators are being improved through the upgrading of the technology employed and new, and larger facilities are being built, such as those in the Gubkin and Zheleznogorsk districts of the Kursk Mangetic Anomaly; Komsomolsk and the Northern and Central concentrators of the Krivoi Rog district in the Ukraine; Kachkanar in the Urals; and Kovdor and Olenegorsk in the Kola Peninsula.[59] Although some facilities still employ simple enrichment techniques, the newer facilities use more sophisticated methods to enhance the amount of recoverable iron from easily enriched magnetites and hematites.[60] Various flotation, magnetized roasting, high and low intensity separators, wet and dry magnetic separators, electro-static and others are now incorporated into the enrichment technology of the Soviet Union. Complex polymineralic ores and to a lesser extent ferruginous quartzites still present novel and difficult challenges.

Some of the techniques and technology employed are of Soviet origin, whereas others, such as pelletizing, originated in the West. Today the CMEA nations, Finland, West Germany and the United States are contributing their expertise and technology to the construction of Soviet iron-ore enrichment enterprises.[61] The increased adoption and utilization of both Soviet and foreign enrichment technology will not only improve the domestic quality and quantity of usable iron ore but also enhance the potential for future export beyond the CMEA countries.

Because the Soviet command economy is not geared to respond to price signals, it comes as no suprise that the Soviet iron-ore pricing structure has been sluggish in responding to the economic implications of dwindling high-grade reserves, on the one hand, and changing technological conditions within the iron and steel industry on the other. Shabad has documented in considerable detail the 1975 revisions in Soviet iron-ore prices.[62] By 1975, the old 1967 price structure was yielding steadily declining profit rates in the ore industry overall as well as significant distortions within the profit structure on a regional and/or iron-ore product basis.

Those 1975 revisions sought to align wholesale prices and production costs, especially with regard to high-value products, such as self-fluxing agglomerate and pellets. Accordingly, while prices for these ore products were increased, those for fine direct-shipping ores were reduced significantly. Except for the Kola Peninsula, where prices were reduced, the net effect of the price reform was to simultaneously raise the profit rates in all other ore-producing districts and reduce the regional disparities in the profit rates (see Table 4).[63]

Not surprisingly, trends in the real costs of ore production have continued to rise. As a result, another ore price revision was scheduled for implementation by 1 April 1981[64] as part of the Council of Ministers' resolution "On Improving Planning and Strengthening the Economic Mechanism's Influence in Enhancing Production Efficiency and Work Quality."[65] A cornerstone of this resolution is imbedded in its title, namely, to strengthen the role of economic levers and incentives.[66] Accordingly, the new wholesale prices are to improve "the role of prices in reducing the material-intensiveness of output and in expanding the use of inexpensive types of raw materials and other materials."[67] Also, an effort is to be made to better internalize the costs of geological prospecting for the extractive industries. At present only 40 percent of the total state prospecting outlays are reimbursed by the fixed ruble rates per unit of output (differentiated by type of mineral) paid by extractive enterprises. An increase in the number of enterprises subject to these payments and an increase in the rates charged is being planned in an effort to eliminate this state subsidy.[68]

According to N.T. Glushkov, Chairman of the State Price Committee USSR, new price lists for raw ores as well as refractory materials, coal, coke, petroleum and petroleum products, gas, electrical and thermal energy, and round timber have been developed and confirmed.[69] Mathematical programming models are being utilized to develop marginal or shadow prices for various commodities within the iron and steel industry.[70] Presumably, the Price Committee has been utilizing these various derived pricing data to establish the new iron-ore prices. Given the Soviet history of vascillation between periods of highly centralized planning and periods of more decentralized decision making, one must remain rather cautious about the long-term efficacy of these rather modest attempts at strengthening market forces in Soviet resource decision making.

## Distribution of Soviet Iron Ore Reserves

Overall Soviet reserves of iron ore in the $A + B + C_1 + C_2$ categories have ranged around 110 billion metric tons over the last decade and a half, with anywhere from 50 to 60 percent confirmed in the proven categories $A + B + C_1$. As of 1 January 1966, total reserves were 109.7 billion tons, including 56.1 billion proven;[71] as of January 1971, they were respectively 113.9 billion and 62.5 billion tons; as of January 1975, 107 billion and 63.7 billion tons; and as of January 1976, 111.1 billion and 67.3 billion tons. The tendency has been for an increasingly large share of the reserves to be confirmed in the proven categories: in 1966, the confirmed share was 51 percent, in 1976 it was 60 percent. By 1 January 1981, the $A + B + C_1$ reserves had risen to 77.6 billion tons.[72]

By far the largest share of the probable ($C_2$) reserves is found in the Kursk Magnetic Anomaly (KMA), the vast iron-ore basin of Central Russia, which accounted for 50 percent of the probable reserves in 1975, or 21.7 billion out of 43.4 billion tons (Table 5). The KMA thus represents the largest potential source of recoverable iron ore, although the overall reserve figure appears to have been adjusted downward over the last 15 years. It was 41.6 billion tons in 1966, 43.6 billion in 1971[73] (also cited as 43.4 billion tons[74]) and 38.4 billion tons in 1975.[75]

As of January 1975, the average iron content of the proven reserves in the USSR as a whole was 36.9 percent.[76] Of the total proven reserves of 63.7 billion tons, 9.3 billion tons (14 percent) was direct shipping ore and 46.6 billion tons (75 percent) was said to be easily dressed.[77] The rest was regarded as requiring more complex beneficiation procedures.[78] If probable reserves were to be included, the share of direct-shipping ores (mainly in the KMA) would rise to 25 percent.[79] At the current Soviet crude ore production level of some 490 million tons per annum (see Table 2), the 1975 $A + B + C_1$ reserves are sufficient for 130 years and the total reserves (107 billion

TABLE 4
Regional Impact of 1975 Iron-Ore Price Reform

| Ore district | Average price change (percent) | Profit rates (in relation to capital) (in percent) | |
|---|---|---|---|
| | | in 1967 prices | in 1975 prices |
| Kola Peninsula | −4.9 | 13 | 10.7 |
| Kursk Magnetic Anomaly | +23.1 | 2.3 | 7.8 |
| Ukraine | +7.7 | 7 | 9.7 |
| Transcaucasia | +10.6 | 6.8 | 10 |
| Urals | +13.7 | 5.4 | 9.9 |
| Siberia | +14.8 | 5.1 | 10 |
| Kazakhstan | +66.6 | −6.3 | 8.7 |
| USSR Average | +12.4 | 5.4 | 9.4 |

SOURCE: Theodore Shabad, "News Notes," SGRT 16, no. 6 (June 1975): 416.

TABLE 5
Soviet Iron Ore Reserves as of January 1, 1971
and January 1, 1975 (in billion metric tons)

| | 1971 Reserves | | 1975 Reserves | |
|---|---|---|---|---|
| | $A + B + C_1$ | $C_2$ | $A + B + C_1$ | $C_2$ |
| USSR | 62.5 | 51.4 | 63.7 | 43.4 |
| Western part | 39.4 | 33.6 | 40.9 | 26.7 |
| Northwest | 2.6 | 1.0 | 2.5 | 0.3 |
| Kursk Magnetic Anomaly | 16.8 | 26.8 | 16.7 | 21.7 |
| Ukraine | 19.8 | 5.8 | 21.4 | 4.7 |
| Transcaucasia | 0.33 | 0.01 | 0.27 | 0.01 |
| Urals | 8.4 | 6.7 | 8.4 | 6.8 |
| Eastern part | 14.7 | 11.0 | 14.4 | 9.9 |
| West Siberia | 1.2 | 0.3 | 1.3 | 0.3 |
| East Siberia | 3.6 | 1.3 | 3.6 | 1.1 |
| Far East | 1.6 | 0.9 | 1.8 | 1.0 |
| Kazakhstan | 8.3 | 8.4 | 7.6 | 7.6 |

SOURCES: 1971 reserves: N. D. Lelyukhina, *Ekonomicheskaya effektivnost razmeshcheniya chernoi metallurgii* [Cost-effectiveness of the location of the iron and steel industry] (Moscow: Nauka, 1973), p. 117; 1975 reserves: P. A. Shiryayev, Ye. N. Yarkho and Yu. M. Borts, *Metallurgicheskaya i ekonomicheskaya otsenka zhelezorudnoy bazy SSSR* [Metallurgical and economic assessment of the iron-ore base of the USSR] (Moscow: Metallurgiya, 1978), p. 9.

tons) for 218 years. As indicated by Table 1, the overall iron reserves of the Soviet Union greatly surpass the combined reserves of the United States and Canada. Thus, considering potential reserves, the Soviet Union has adequate reserves to meet current annual production levels for over 600 years!

Unlike many other industrial raw materials and energy resources, proven Soviet iron ore reserves are concentrated in the west with the European industrial heartland (including the Urals) possessing 77 percent of the reserves and the east possessing only 23 percent (see Table 5). Furthermore, half of the reserves are in the Krivoi Rog and Kursk Magnetic Anomaly deposits. In addition to the deposits of rich magnetite ($Fe_3O_4$), hematite ($Fe_2O_3$), siderite ($FeCO_3$), goethite ($FeO.OH$), titanomagnetite ($Fe_2TiO_4$), ilmenite ($FeTiO_3$), and magnesioferrite ($MgFe_2O_4$) ores, billions of tons of reserve ore consist of low iron content ferruginous quartzites, commonly referred to as taconite in the United States. These types of deposits are now being mined on a large scale in the Krivoi Rog and Kursk Magnetic Anomaly ore basins.[80]

Considering that large tracts of Soviet territory with potential iron-ore deposits have been explored only cursorily and that the actual definitions of reserves are subject to change because of their dependence on technological change and dynamic production costs, it seems likely that major additions to proven reserves will accrue over the next few decades. The most detailed and recent data on Soviet iron ore reserves appear in Table 6. Most of the reserve figures date from the middle 1970s. Appendix II, which consists of a genetic classification of Soviet iron ore deposits, lists some additional deposits.[81] It is now time to turn to a more geographically disaggregated discussion of the major Soviet iron ore reserves, producing districts, and ore transport flows.

## Major Soviet Iron Ore Producing Districts

Consistent with the geographical division utilized to construct Table 5, the Soviet Union can be separated into an European zone (including the Urals) and an Asian zone. This distinguishes between the highly developed industrial European portion of the country possessing upwards of 75 percent of the proven Soviet iron ore reserves, producing 83 percent of the marketable ore, and the less industrially developed Asian portion possessing 25 percent of the proven reserves and producing 17 percent of marketable ore. Table 7 provides a regional portrait of marketable ore production for the seventies. The increased restrictions on the official publication of spatially disaggregated production data since 1977 make a comprehensive and detailed discussion of reserves, production, and transport flows difficult. Nonetheless, some detailed discussion is possible. Before proceeding, Table 8 can be utilized to highlight the overall trends in ore production during the past decade.

The most striking feature of the Soviet iron extraction industry has been its stagnation since the mid-seventies. This deteriorating performance is apparently due to chronically inadequate investment, some raw-material shortages and declining ore quality. Because of spiraling construction costs, the modest increases in capital spending have yielded increasingly smaller increments to capacity.[82] Presumably, the rapid growth in Soviet military spending has siphoned off the needed investment funds, as well as "a large share of the economy's best scientific, technical, and managerial talent and large amounts of high-quality materials components and equipment."[83]

In terms of spatial-temporal changes in the relative share of total output during the seventies, the KMA district of Central Russia has been the shining star, increasing its share from 9 percent of output in 1970 to 16.3 percent in 1980. The KMA recorded the largest percentage growth rate (121 percent) as well as the largest absolute increase in output (21.5 million tons) during the same ten-year period. The second fastest growth rate occurred in Kazakhstan (39 percent), but its relative share increased only modestly from 9.2 percent in 1970 to 10.5 percent in 1980. Despite the fact that the Ukrainian ore output grew at a rate (13 percent) less than the national rate (24 percent), its output still dominates the industry at 51.3 percent of total production. Although this represents a relative decline from its 1970 share of 56.4 percent, the Ukraine's absolute increase of 14.3 million tons represented 30.0 percent of the country's total expanded output between 1970 and 1980. Again, the KMA dominated the overall growth picture accounting for 45 percent of the augmented production. In this category, Kazakhstan ranked third by contributing 16 percent of the additional ore. The big regional loser was the Urals region. From ranking second to the Ukraine in regional ore production in 1970, the Urals slipped to fourth in 1980 behind the KMA and Kazakhstan as well as the Ukraine. In fact, 1980 production was an estimated 1.5 million tons below that at the beginning of the decade. As cited previously, dwindling reserves of rich ores and construction lags and

TABLE 6
Selected Soviet Iron-Ore Deposits

| Region | Name of deposit (name of mining town if different) | Status | Reserves (bill. m.t.) $A+B+C_1$ | $C_2$ | Average Fe content | Main Fe minerals |
|---|---|---|---|---|---|---|
| Northwest | Olenegorsk | mined | 0.43 | 0.03 | 32.3 | M,H,FQ |
| | Kovdor | mined | 0.64 | 0.05 | 31.5 | M |
| | Kostomuksha | mined | 1.07 | 0.08 | 35.0 | M,H |
| KMA | Mikhailovka (Zheleznogorsk) | mined | 2.28 | 0.59 | 37.5; 58.5 | FQ,H,M,S |
| | Lebedi (Gubkin) | mined | 2.32 | 0.46 | 36.0; 56.9 | S |
| | Stoilo (Gubkin) | constr. | 2.48 | 0.26 | 35.2; 53.1 | FQ |
| | Yakovlevo | constr. | 1.87[a] | 8.19 | 60.5 | H,HG,HH,M |
| | Gostishchevo | not used | 2.59 | 7.83 | 61.5 | H,M |
| | Chernyanka | not used | 1.90 | 0.01 | 54.5 | H,FQ |
| | Pogromets | not used | 0.33 | 0.04 | 54.7 | H,M |
| Ukraine | Kremenchug (Komsomolsk) | mined | 2.22 | 0.83 | 38.1 | M,H |
| | Krivoi Rog | mined | 15.90 | 3.23 | 37.9; 57.6 | H,M,HH,HG,FQ |
| | Belozerka (Dneprorudnoye) | mined | 0.69 | 0.18 | 63.3 | H |
| | Kerch | mined | 1.69 | 0.39 | 37.7 | HG |
| Transcaucasia | Dashkesan | mined | 0.27 | 0.01 | 26.5 | M |
| Urals | Peschanka (Rudnichny) | mined | 0.17 | — | 54.5 | M |
| | Kachkanar | mined | 6.06 | 6.06 | 16.6 | TM |
| | Goroblagodat (Kushva) | mined | 0.14 | — | 36.8 | M |
| | Bakal | mined | 0.58 | 0.36 | 32.1 | S,HG,HH |
| | Magnitogorsk | mined | 0.17 | — | 44.9 | M,H |
| | Akkermanovka (Novotroitsk) | mined | 0.12 | — | 27.1–30.0 | HH,HG |
| Kazakhstan | Kachar | constr. | 1.14 | 0.31 | 44.9 | M |
| | Sarbai (Rudny) | mined | 0.68 | 0.14 | 45.6 | M |
| | Sokolovka (Rudny) | mined | 0.92 | 0.09 | 41.0 | M |
| | Ayat | not used | 1.70 | 5.00 | 37.1 | HG,S |
| | Lisakovsk | mined | 1.72 | 1.16 | 35.2 | HG,S |
| | Karazhal | mined | 0.31 | 0.06 | 55.6 | M,MH,H |
| | Ken-Tyube | not used | 0.11 | — | 52.0 | M |
| West Siberia | Bakchar group | not used | — | —[b] | under 30 | HG |
| | Sheregesh | mined | 0.23 | 0.05 | 35.0 | M |
| | Tashtagol | mined | 0.36 | 0.05 | 44.7 | M |
| | Abakan (Abaza) | mined | 0.70 | — | 45.3 | M |
| | Teya (Vershina Tei) | mined | 0.13 | 0.01 | 32.9 | M,H,MF |
| | Anzas | not used | 0.15 | 0.02 | 38.2 | M |
| East Siberia | Korshunovo (Zheleznogorsk) | mined | 0.33 | 0.01 | 34.4 | M,H |
| | Rudnogorsk | mined | 0.21 | 0.06 | 43.3 | MF |
| Far East | Chara-Tokko | not used | 2.00 | 3.00 | NA | FQ |
| | Tayezhnoye | not used | 0.71 | 0.58 | 42.0 | M |
| | Gar | not used | 0.21 | 0.18 | 41.7 | M |
| | Kimkan | not used | 0.19 | 0.03 | 35.6 | M,H |

[a]$B + C_1$ reserves only.

[b]Geological reserves, severe water-logging problems.

LETTER KEY FOR MAJOR MINERALS:

I: Ilmenite ($FeTiO_3$)  
G: Goethite ($\alpha FeO.OH$)  
H: Hematite ($\alpha Fe_2O_3$)  
M: Magnetite ($Fe^{+2}Fe_2^{+3}O_4$)  
S: Siderite ($FeCO_3$)  
MF: Magnesioferrite ($MgFe_2^{+3}O_4$)

TM: Titanomagnetite ($Fe_2TiO_4$)  
MH: Maghemite ($\alpha Fe_2^{+3}O_3$)  
FQ: Ferruginous quartzites  
HG: Hydrogoethite  
HH: Hydrohematite

SOURCES: P. A. Shiryayev, Ye. N. Yarkho and Yu. M. Borts, *Metallurgicheskaya i ekonomicheskaya otsenka zhelezorudnoy bazy SSSR* [Metallurgical and economic assessment of the iron-ore base of the USSR] (Moscow: Metallurgiya, 1978), pp. 11–19; G. A. Braun, *Zhelezorudnaya baza metallurgii SSSR* [The iron-ore base of the iron and steel industry of the USSR] (Moscow: Nedra, 1970), various pages; N. D. Lelyukhina, *Ekonomicheskaya effektivnost razmeshcheniya chernoi metallurgii* [The cost-effectiveness of location of the iron and steel industry] (Moscow: Nauka, 1973), various pages; V. I. Smirnov, ed., *Rudnye mestorozhdeniya SSSR* [Ore deposits of the USSR] Vol. 1 (Moscow: Nedra, 1974), various pages; A. T. Khrushchev, "The Formation of the Industrial Complex of the Kursk Magnetic Anomaly," *Soviet Geography: Review and Translation* 16, no. 4 (April 1975): 241; V. V. Strishkov, *Mineral Industries of the USSR* (Washington: Department of the Interior, Bureau of Mines, 1979), pp. 14–15; Theodore Shabad, "News Notes," *SGRT*, various issues 1970–82; and Theodore Shabad and Victor L. Mote, *Gateway to Siberian Resources (the BAM)* (Washington: Scripta, 1977), pp. 81, 149–50.

TABLE 7
Geographical Distribution of Soviet Iron Ore
Output 1970–85 (million tons usable ore)

| | 1970 | 1975 | 1978 | 1979 | 1980 | 1981 | 1985 Plan |
|---|---|---|---|---|---|---|---|
| USSR | 197.3 | 235.0 | 246.4 | 241.7 | 244.7 | 242.8 | 262.4 |
| RSFSR | 66.5 | 88.8 | 93.0 | 89.4 | 92.4 | 89.8 | 106 |
| Europe | 25.4 | 45.0 | 49.7 | 47.0* | 50.0* | — | — |
| KMA | 17.8 | 36.0 | 37.0* | 37.0* | 39.3* | — | 43 |
| Kola | 7.6 | 10.0 | 9.7 | 10.0* | 10.7* | — | — |
| Urals | 26.5 | 26.1 | 25.3 | 25.0* | 25* | — | — |
| Siberia | 12.9 | 15.5 | 15.8 | 16.0* | 17* | — | — |
| Ukraine | 111.2 | 123.3 | 127.3 | 126.0 | 125.5 | 126 | 128 |
| Kazakhstan | 18.2 | 21.4 | 24.9 | 25.3 | 25.8 | 25.6 | 27 |
| Rudny | 15.0 | 16.0 | 16.5* | 17.0 | 17.0* | — | — |
| Azerbaijan | 1.4 | 1.35 | 1.18 | 1.1 | 1.0 | 1 | 1 |

*Estimate.
SOURCES: USSR: *Narodnoye khozyaistvo SSSR v 1980 godu* [The economy of the USSR in 1980] (Moscow: Finansy i Statistika, 1981), p. 159; RSFSR: *Narodnoye khozyaistvo RSFSR v 1980 godu* (Moscow: Finansy i Statistika, 1981), p. 64; Ukraine: *Narodne gospodarstvo Ukrainskoi RSR v 1979 rotsi* (Kiev: Tekhnika, 1980), p. 95; Kazakhstan: *Narodnoye khozyaistvo Kazakhstana v 1978 godu* (Alma-Ata: Kazakhstan, 1979), p. 31. Other figures from various issues of *Soviet Geography: Review and Translation*. (The regional breakdown within the RSFSR is based on unrevised data and does not add up to the revised totals for the RSFSR.)

technological difficulties with problematic local ore bodies such as Kachkanar,[84] account for the Urals' declining output. The Azerbaijan republic is a second region experiencing an apparent slight absolute decline in output. The principal iron-ore deposits and ore flows to iron and steel centers are shown in Figure 1.

### The European Iron Regions

The European part of the Soviet Union is richly endowed with iron ore deposits of sufficient quality and quantity to sustain the domestic iron and steel industry far into the forseeable future. In some instances where high-grade ores are almost depleted, low-grade ores are being exploited and enriched through various technological pro-

cesses. The European region may be subdivided into five iron ore districts: (1) Northwest, (2) Central Russia, (3) Ukraine, (4) Transcaucasia, and (5) the Urals.

*The Northwest.* The iron ore deposits of the Northwest are located in the Karelian ASSR and the Kola Peninsula. The 1975 reserves are 2.8 billion tons, 2.6 percent of Soviet reserves (see Table 5). These reserves contain 2.5 billion tons of ore classified as $A + B + C_1$ and include magnetites, titanomagnetites, hematites, and ferruginous quartzites. About 588 million tons of recoverable iron.[85] The principal deposits being mined are Olenegorsk, Kovdor, and Kostomuksha.[86]

The deposits at Olenegorsk and Kovdor consist of low-grade, 20 to 40 percent iron (average 32 percent), titanomagnetites, magnetites, and ferruginous quartzites with a high silica content. Mining began at the first deposit in 1955 in phase with the completion of the first blast furnace at the Cherepovets iron and steel plant. The mining and concentrating complex at Kovdor lagged behind and was not commissioned until 1962. Since the Olenegorsk ores are acidic and the Kovdor ones basic, they must be blended at Cherepovets in a ratio of two tons of Olenegorsk ore to each ton of Kovdor ore to yield a neutralized and suitable furnace charge. The exclusive use of Olenegorsk in the early years necessitated the use of large quantities of limestone flux to neutralize the acidic ore. This requirement, in turn, increased the smelting costs and reduced blast furnace efficiency at Cherepovets.[87] The ores from both deposits are enriched to a 64 percent iron concentrate. By 1976 annual production of concentrate at Olenegorsk was about 6 million tons and at Kovdor about 4 million tons.[88] Expansion programs are under way at both of these Kola Peninsula mining complexes.[89] Their combined annual output reached about 11 million tons in 1980.[90] The Kirovogorsk open pit at Olenegorsk was opened in July 1978 and was supposed to reach its rated annual capacity of 5 million tons of crude ore by the end of 1980.[91]

As noted previously these two mines serve as the pri-

TABLE 8
Regional Trends in Marketable Iron Ore Production 1970–80

| Region | Share of total 1970 output (in percent) | Share of total 1980 output (in percent) | Index of production 1970 = 100 | Absolute growth in output (in $10^6$ tons) | Share of absolute growth (in percent) |
|---|---|---|---|---|---|
| USSR Total | 100.0 | 100.0 | 124 | 47.4 | 100.0 |
| RSFSR | 33.6 | 37.7 | 139 (+)* | 25.9 | 55 |
| Europe | 12.9 | 20.8 | 197 (+) | 24.6 | 52 |
| KMA | 9.0 | 16.3 | 221 (+) | 21.5 | 45 |
| Kola | 3.9 | 4.5 | 141 (+) | 3.1 | 6.5 |
| Urals | 13.4 | 9.8 | 94 (−) | −1.5 | −3 |
| Siberia | 6.5 | 6.5 | 132 (0) | 4 | 8 |
| Ukraine | 56.4 | 51.3 | 113 (−) | 14.3 | 30 |
| Kazakhstan | 9.2 | 10.5 | 139 (+) | 7.6 | 16 |
| Rudny | 7.6 | 6.9 | 113 (−) | 2.0 | 4 |
| Azerbaijan | 0.7 | 0.4 | 71 (−) | −0.4 | −0.8 |

*(+), (0), (−) represent growth rates above, equal to, or below the national average (124.2 percent), respectively.
SOURCE: Authors' calculations based on the data for Table 7.

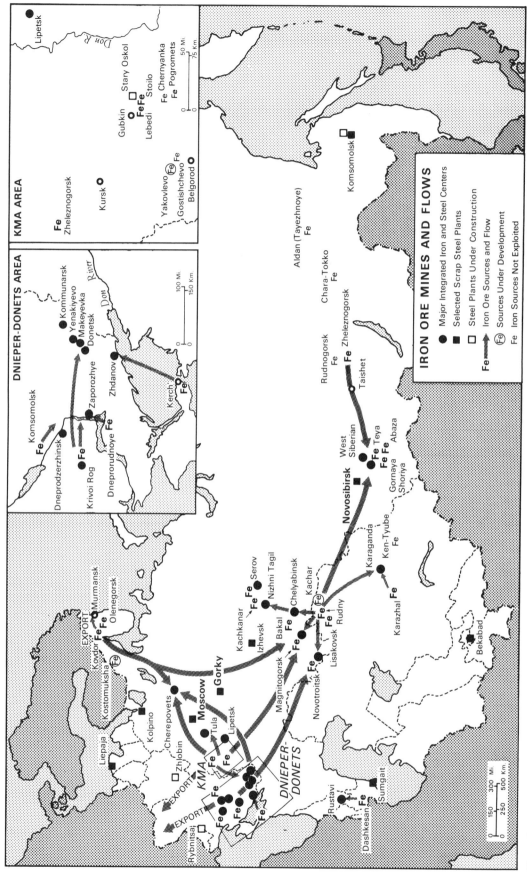

Figure 1

mary source of ore for the Cherepovets iron and steel plant (Fig. 1). About 8 million tons, or 70 percent of the output, is shipped to the Cherepovets plant with the remaining 3 million tons of output destined for export through Murmansk and some small long-haul shipments to Magnitogorsk in the Urals.[92] While the shipments to Murmansk are by rail, the flows to Cherepovets and Magnitogorsk are increasingly by combined rail-water-rail routes, by rail to Kandalaksha, by water through the White Sea-Baltic and Baltic-Volga waterways to Cherepovets or on through the Volga and then by rail from one of several Kama or Volga ports to Magnitogorsk. Such a multimodal route is said to save a 1,370 km rail haul in the case of Cherepovets and, depending on the transshipment node, 720 to 2,250 km in the case of Magnitogorsk. However, because of inadequate transport capacity and terminal bottlenecks, only 0.55 million tons were shipped to Magnitogorsk and 1.2 million tons to Cherepovets by the combined route in 1975. Although expanded water-terminal receiving capacities for both destinations have been recommended,[93] it seems likely that rail-only transit will continue to dominate. The Soviet transport system has been traditionally slow to shift freight flows from rail to alternate water routes. Linear programming runs of the Soviet iron and steel industry performed as part of the present research project indicated that Kovdor and Olenegorsk would be optimal sites for the origin of ore exports.[94]

A new development in the Northwest region is the Kostomuksha ore deposit. In October 1973, the Soviet and Finnish governments signed a joint venture agreement for the construction of a mining, concentrating and pelletizing complex at the ore site. A subsequent agreement concerning the first stages of construction during 1977–82 was initialed in May 1977. The deposit (35 percent ore Fe content) can be mined by surface techniques and is said to have reserves for 40 to 60 years of operation at a full annual capacity of 26.5 million tons of crude ore for conversion to 8.9 million tons of pellets. The first of three designed stages, placed in operation in 1982, will produce 2.96 million tons of pellets annually from 3.25 million tons of concentrate (8 million tons of crude ore). Finland is to receive about one-third of the output as compensation for constructing the complex.[95]

*Kursk Magnetic Anomaly.* This region in Central European Russia is considered to have the largest iron-ore deposits in the world, with reserves of 38.4 billion tons in 1975 in the $A + B + C_1 + C_2$ categories. Although the possible $C_2$ category was revised downward, from 26.8 billion tons in 1971 to 21.7 billion in 1975 (Table 5), it still represents one-half of the entire $C_2$ category in the Soviet Union.[96] Of the total KMA reserves, the rich ore, with 53 to 62 percent iron, amounts to some 26 billion tons, and the low-grade quartzites, of 35 to 37 percent iron, some 12 billion tons, having been the subject of downward revision from an estimate of 17 billion tons in 1971.[97] Table 9 illustrates the distribution of KMA reserves as of January 1975.

Not surprisingly, these vast reserves of the Kursk Magnetic Anomaly have dominated the iron ore scene in the Soviet Union for the last two decades. The KMA is estimated to extend over 200,000 km².[98] Essentially, there are two northwest-southwest trending magnetic-anomaly zones: a southwest belt through Lgov—Oboyan—Belgorod and a northeast belt through Shchigry—Tim—Stary Oskol—Valuiki.[99] Ferruginous quartzites associated with Precambrian metamorphic rocks are buried at great depths, and their lower contact or boundary has not been determined. The depth of the upper contact varies considerably. For example, in Kursk Oblast, the quartzite beds are within 30 to 170 meters of the surface, while in the south in Belgorod Oblast they are 300 to 700 meters below the surface. Outside this main section of the KMA the depth of burial is even greater.[100]

The central section is the most thoroughly investigated and many large ore deposits have been found. For instance, large deposits exist at Lebedi, Yakovlevo, Gostishchevo, Stoilo, Pogromets, and Chernyanka, in Belgorod Oblast (see Tables 6 and 9 and Fig. 1).[101]

The most interesting of these deposits are the high-

TABLE 9
Iron Ore Reserves in the Kursk Magnetic Anomaly ($A + B + C_1 + C_2$, as of 1 January 1975) (in billion metric tons)

|  | $A + B + C_1$ | $C_2$ | $A + B + C_1 + C_2$ |
|---|---|---|---|
| Total KMA | 16.73 | 21.66 | 38.39 |
| Kursk-Orel district | 2.49 | 0.80 | 3.29 |
|    Zheleznogorsk deposit | 2.28 | 0.59 | 2.87 |
| Stary Oskol district | 7.55 | 0.88 | 8.43 |
|    Lebedi deposit (Gubkin) | 2.32 | 0.46 | 2.78 |
|    Stoilo deposit (Gubkin) | 2.48 | 0.26 | 2.74 |
| Novy Oskol district | 2.23 | 0.05 | 2.28 |
|    Pogromets | 0.33 | 0.04 | 0.37 |
|    Chernyanka | 1.90 | 0.01 | 1.91 |
| Belgorod district | 4.46 | 19.93 | 24.39 |
|    Yakovlevo | 1.87 | 8.19 | 10.06 |
|    Gostishchevo | 2.59 | 7.83 | 10.42 |

SOURCE: P. A. Shiryayev, Ye. N. Yarkho, and Yu. M. Borts, *Metallurgicheskaya i ekonomicheskaya otsenka zhelezorudnoy bazy SSSR* [Metallurgical and economic assessment of the iron-ore base of the USSR] (Moscow: Metallurgiya, 1978), p. 12.

grade ores that contain from 53 to 62 percent iron. These hematite-martite and siderite-martite ores are associated with the upper weathered crust of the quartzites.[102] This crust is usually from 30 to 40 meters thick, but increases in some places in Belgorod Oblast to 300 meters or more. Unfortunately, the overburden consists of thick sedimentary rocks with aquifers. As a consequence, exploitation is often hampered by difficult hydrogeological conditions.[103] Nevertheless, the estimated size of the high-grade reserves, 26 billion metric tons, makes the deposits worthy of investigation and development.[104] The quartzite reserves have an iron content of 35 to 37 percent and need to be concentrated, to some 67 percent, before being utilized by blast furnaces.[105]

The first evidence of the magnetic anomaly was observed during a topographic survey in the late eighteenth century. This discovery was forgotten until 1874 when N. Smirnov of Kazan University identified the anomaly while making a geomagnetic survey of European Russia. From 1895 to 1918, Professor Ye. Ye. Leist of Moscow University studied the KMA.[106] He suggested that a large iron-ore deposit might be the cause of the magnetic anomaly. According to Kapitonov, it was only after the Bolshevik Revolution that the Kursk Magnetic Anomaly became a focus of attention.[107] Lenin appears to have been interested in it. In 1921 the Supreme Council of the National Economy, on Lenin's initiative, created a special commission for the study of the KMA. In July 1921, the first borehole was drilled near Shchigry in Kursk Oblast. Magnetic quartzites were reached at a depth of 167 meters.[108]

As a result of the commission's investigation of other borings, the general nature, genesis, grade and approximate reserves of several deposits were established. High-grade iron ore was discovered near Lebedi, Stoilo, Volokonovka and Novy Oskol.[109]

World War II halted the investigation, but after the war it was resumed on an enlarged scale. From 1948 to 1959, 1.4 million meters of boreholes were drilled, a detailed map of the KMA's magnetic field was compiled, and geological investigations confirmed that the KMA was associated with the Voronezh crystalline massif bordering on the Dnieper-Donets depression in the south and the Moscow basin in the north.[110]

Mining operations are now under way in two districts: Gubkin in Belgorod Oblast and Zheleznogorsk in Kursk Oblast. In July 1952, commercial exploitation officially began in the Gubkin district with the completion of an experimental quartzite shaft mine at Korobkovo.[111] However, most of the initial production, starting in 1959, was open-pit rich ore, supplemented after 1972 by the concentration of open-pit quartzite (taconite).[112] Currently several mines are operating in the Gubkin area: the Korobkovo quartzite mine, the South Korobkovo quartzite mine and concentrator, the Lebedi high-grade ore surface mine, quartzite mine and concentrator, the South Lebedi high-grade ore surface mine, and the Stoilo high-grade ore surface mine.[113]

At the Lebedi complex in the Gubkin district, the mining of rich direct-shipping ore began in 1959[114] and the first concentrating capacity to process the low-grade quartzite

followed in 1972.[115] By 1975 the concentrator was converting 14.7 million tons of quartzite into 5.7 million tons of concentrate.[116] An 8.6 million ton pelletizer plant went on stream in August 1975[117] and reached its designed capacity in 1978. Expansion of both the quartzite pit and the concentrator proceeded in the second half of the 1970s, reaching a total of 38 million tons of crude ore and 15 million tons of concentrate by 1980. Further doubling of output was envisaged by 1990.[118]

At Stoilo, the other major ore deposit in the Gubkin district, mining of the limited rich-ore reserves (some 120 million tons of 53.1 percent ore) began in 1968, and now runs around 4.6 million tons of direct-shipping ore a year. In 1976, construction began at Stoilo on a mine and concentrator to exploit the much larger reserves of quartzite (some 2.3 billion tons of 35.2 percent ore).[119] The open-pit quartzite mine is projected for an ultimate capacity of 40 million tons of crude ore a year. The first stage, with a capacity of 20 million tons of crude ore for conversion to some 8.5 million tons of 67 percent concentrate, was originally scheduled to go into operation in 1978, but has been carried over into the 11th Five-Year Plan (1981–85).[120]

The other major active ore-producing district of the KMA is the Mikhailovka deposit at Zheleznogorsk in Kursk Oblast. This deposit was first developed in the late 1950s, with first stage (2.5 million tons) of the rich-ore section being put into operation in 1962, a second stage (2.0 million tons annual ore capacity) in 1965,[121] and the quartzite mine and concentrator in 1973.[122] A second KMA pelletizer plant of 6 million tons capacity commenced operation at Zheleznogorsk in 1976 with a first-stage capacity of 3 million tons annually, and was doubled in 1977.[123]

The two current mining districts, the Mikhailovka deposit at Zheleznogorsk and the Lebedi and Stoilo deposits at Gubkin, are to be augmented by an underground mine under construction at the high-grade Yakovlevo deposit in the Belgorod district.[124]

A major expansion program in the Gubkin district is also designed to provide 4.3 million tons of high-grade concentrate (Fe content greater than 70 percent) for a direct reduction plant under construction at Stary Oskol.[125] This new steel-making complex brings up the topic of the role of foreign assistance in the development of the KMA. At the beginning of 1974, the Soviet Union and West Germany signed an agreement providing for the participation of three German concerns, Krupp, Salzgitter, and Korf Stahl, in the construction of a KMA direct-conversion steel plant at Stary Oskol.[126] The plant, which circumvents the blast furnace stage by proceeding from high-grade ore pellets through sponge iron to electric arc furnace, will have an ultimate capacity of 4 million tons of crude steel and 3 million tons of rolled products.[127] Kobe Steel of Tokyo is also a supplier of equipment and materials for the plant.[128] The complex will also include a pelletizing plant with a capacity of 5 million tons annually.[129] Allis-Chalmers has supplied the Soviets with pelletizing technology and Kobe Steel is actually building the plant.[130] About 2 million tons of these pellets a year will be used to recompense the West German participation in the joint venture.[131] The pellets are to be converted into sponge pellets by four Midrex direct reduction plants being built by two West German companies, Korf Stahl and Lurgi. Scheduled for completion in the early 1980s at a cost of $234 million, the four sponge iron facilities in the first stage of the project will have a combined annual capacity of 1.7 million tons.[132] The Soviet Union's CMEA partners have also been involved in KMA developments. For example, Bulgarian workers assisted in the construction of the first stage of the Zheleznogorsk pellet plant completed in 1976.[133]

Interestingly enough a least-cost linear-programming model has vindicated the Soviet decision to locate a new steel complex at Stary Oskol. Even with the constraint of 1970 total Soviet steel production (minus exports) of 108.9 million tons, the hypothetical Stary Oskol plant entered the solution with an optimal production of 5.5 million tons annually.[134] The locational pushes and pulls that have occurred in the Soviet steel manufacturing system since 1970 and the increased steel output (a high point of 151.5 million tons in 1978)[135] suggest that the much larger (10 to 12 million ton annual steel capacity) integrated iron and steel complex designed to serve the CMEA market from the Stary Oskol area[136] would also be economically justified.

The locational attractiveness of the KMA is derived from many factors. The most important of these are proximity to iron ore (the major weight-reducing steel input), coking coal, domestic and CMEA markets and skilled labor as well as developed transportation and social-economic infrastructures. The negative factors are environmental, especially water and the loss of productive chernozem farm land. Subsurface water creates costly and problematic underground ore mining, while relatively sparse surface water supplies could hinder conventional steel processes.[137] Soviet geographers have written about substantial environmental damage that has already occurred in connection with economic development in the KMA region.[138] They urge caution and recommend a centralized administrative body to insure prudent industrial development along with environmental protection.

By the mid-1960s, the KMA was producing 12 million tons of ore of which 10.5 million tons was direct-shipping ore and 1.5 million tons concentrate. Of this total output, the Gubkin complex was yielding 7.5 million tons and the Zheleznogorsk complex 4.5 million tons.[139] Total production of usable ore from all the KMA mines and concentrators was planned to be 18.1 million tons by 1970 and 40 million tons by 1975.[140] Thus, actual production for these two respective target years (17.8 million tons and 35.8 million tons)[141] failed to reach the plan targets. The 1975 planned production level was reached in 1980,[142] with 23 million tons originating in the Gubkin district and 16 million tons at Zheleznogorsk.[143] The 1980 goal for KMA of 47 million tons was not achieved.

The tentative 1990 marketable ore target for the KMA is 93 million tons.[144] This target also seems optimistic. For example, between 1970 and 1980 annual growth averaged 2.2 million tons. To achieve the tentative 1990 goal, usable KMA ore output would have to increase at an average rate of 5.3 million tons annually. While early production in the KMA consisted mainly of surface-mined, direct-shipping ores, capacity additions have been primarily from low-grade quartzites requiring concentration and pelletization.[145] Furthermore, underground mining will increasingly require costly technical solutions to the problematic hydrogeology of the KMA deposits.[146] As a result of these factors, future additions to the KMA's usable ore capacity seem likely to be ever more difficult to achieve. Finally, considering that the KMA region experienced both the highest relative regional growth rate and the largest absolute increase in annual output (21.5 million tons compared to 14.3 million tons for the second-place Ukraine)[147] during the seventies, the tentative 1990 target is likely to be underfulfilled by as much as 20 million tons.

The KMA ores have an ever increasing market range. At present, KMA ores are shipped to Tula, Lipetsk (about 14 million tons) and Cherepovets in European Russia, to Magnitogorsk, Chelyabinsk, Novotroitsk and possibly Nizhni Tagil in the Urals (combined about 14 million tons annually), to the Ukraine, and to Eastern Europe, especially to the Katowice iron and steel plant in Poland (see Fig. 1).[148] In the mid-seventies, 700,000 tons of ore from Zheleznogorsk traveled yearly by rail to the coal and ore terminal at Ust-Donetsky, then through the Volga-Don Canal and up the Volga and Kama to Perm for rail transshipment to Chelyabinsk and Nizhni Tagil. Although this quantity was to increase to 1.5 to 2 million tons by 1980, no recent citations were found.[149] Local KMA ore pellets will also supply the Stary Oskol direct-reduction steel plant. Modeling runs indicated that ore emanating from Zheleznogorsk in 1970 would optimally flow to Cherepovets and Moscow, while that from Gubkin would travel to Moscow, Kulebaki, Gorky and Lipetsk. With the inclusion of the Stary Oskol site, Zheleznogorsk supplied only Moscow, while Gubkin supplied only Moscow and Stary Oskol.[150] It must be noted that potential export flows were excluded from the model, and Moscow's model-indicated optimal steel production greatly exceeded its actual 1970 production figure. Constraining all steel production facilities to their actual 1970 capacities might well have extended the range of KMA ore flows. On the other hand, little if any KMA ore reached the Urals in 1970.

In summary, while we are more cautious than Soviet planners in our assessment of the growth potential of KMA ore production through 1990, this should not be construed to mean that the region's future prospects are bleak—far from it. Large investments in mine development, machinery, ore preparation facilities, transportation, and the addition of foreign labor, capital, and technology have transformed the KMA into the most rapidly growing iron ore producing region in the Soviet Union. Although it now produces only 38 percent of the marketable ore produced by Krivoi Rog,[151] the KMA should be able to more than offset any decreases that might occur as the Krivoi Rog deposits decline in their share of total ore produced in the Soviet Union. While we foresee slower KMA growth than do Soviet planners, we nonetheless still project that around the turn of the century the KMA could overtake Krivoi Rog as the principal iron ore producing district in the Soviet Union.

*The Ukraine.* This republic was the most important source of iron ore during the early Russian industrialization drive of the late nineteenth century and still maintains a similar position in the Soviet Union today. Its prominence is directly related to the concentration of vast reserves at Krivoi Rog, nearby Donbas coking coal, and historical inertia stemming from the early start the region had in the modern iron and steel industry. Although challenged by the KMA district, the Krivoi Rog area is still the heart of the Soviet iron-ore mining and preparatory industry, and the leading source of Soviet ore exports, chiefly to Eastern Europe. Since the end of World War II, huge investments have been channeled into the region to reconstruct, renovate, and expand the ore mining and enrichment facilities and transport network.

The reserves of $A + B + C_1$ grades of ore were 1.8 billion tons in 1940, 11.8 billion in 1965, 19.4 billion in 1969, and 19.8 billion in 1971.[152] Between 1971 and 1975 the overall reserves ($A + B + C_1 + C_2$) remained steady, with some $C_2$ reserves confirmed in the proven category, which rose to 21.4 billion tons.[153] In 1975, the Ukraine possessed 39 percent of the $A + B + C_1 + C_2$ ore reserves of the European USSR (west of the Urals), and 24 percent of overall Soviet reserves.[154] The rich ores range from 51 to 64 percent iron, while the overall average is 37.6 percent.[155] In 1940 the Ukraine accounted for 66.6 percent of total Soviet marketable ore production, dropping to 52.9 percent in 1950, before rebounding slightly to 55.8 percent in 1960, and 56.4 percent in 1970.[156] In 1980, Ukrainian mines supplied 125.5 million tons of marketable ore, or 51.3 percent of the total Soviet production of 244.7 million tons.[157] While the republic's relative share of Soviet ore output is now expected to continue to decline mainly because of the growth of the KMA's output, the Ukraine's deposits, especially Krivoi Rog, should still remain the largest center of ore production throughout the rest of the century. The Ukraine has four major iron ore mining regions: Krivoi Rog, the Dneprorudnoye deposit, the Kerch Peninsula, and the Komsomolsk deposits near Kremenchug.

The Krivoi Rog deposits alone were estimated at 15.9 billion tons of $A + B + C_1$ ore and an additional 3.2 billion tons of $C_2$ in 1975. Of this quantity, rich ores (57.6 percent Fe) account for 2 billion tons and quartzites (averaging 35.9 percent Fe) the remaining 17 billion tons.[158] This amounts to nearly 90 percent of the total $A + B + C_1$ reserves of the Ukraine. Second only to the KMA in Soviet ore reserves, the Krivoi Rog iron-ore basin extends in a northnortheasterly direction for about 100 km along the right bank of the Ingulets River and its tributaries, the Saksagan and Zheltaya. Because the Krivoi Rog geologic series forms a complex Precambrian synclinorium, ore-bearing structures have been segregated into a number of north to south ore fields, namely the Popelnastoye (not exploited), Zheltaya, Annovka, Pervomaisk, Saksagan, and Ingulets ore fields. The largest reserves of rich ores lie concentrated in the Saksagan area where the ore-bearing strata are up to 2,000 meters thick with up to eight seams of ferruginous quartzites. Four major rich ore types have been identified in the basin as illustrated in Table 10. The four types of ore exist only in the Zheltaya ore field where

TABLE 10
Rich Ore of the Krivoi Rog Basin
(important elements in percent weight)

| Type of Ore | Iron | Phosphorus | Sulfur |
|---|---|---|---|
| Martite and hematite-martite | 63.7 | 0.26 | 0.043 |
| Martite-hematite-hydrohematite | 62.3 | 0.08 | 0.03 |
| Hematite-hydrohematite-hydrogoethite | 57.5 | 0.088 | <0.01 |
| Magnetite and magnetite-specularite | 54.0 | 0.04 | 0.15 |

SOURCE: V. I. Smirnov, ed., and D. A. Brown, trans., *Ore Deposits of the USSR* 1 (London: Pitman, 1977), p. 106.

Proterozoic granitic intrusions have hydrothermally and metasomatically altered the iron quartzites and slates.[159]

Prior to World War II, Krivoi Rog produced 18.9 million tons of ore, exclusively direct-shipping ore. By 1965 total output had grown to 80 million tons of usable ore, but only 60 percent continued to be direct-shipping ore whereas 40 percent was concentrate or enriched low-grade ore.[160] Shabad reports that in 1980 the Krivoi Rog basin yielded 37 million tons of direct-shipping ore from deep underground mines and 70 million tons of concentrate derived from open-pit mines producing some 160 million tons of low-grade taconite ores. While the commissioning of the new deep 4-million-ton Yubileinaya high-grade ore mine in late 1980 offers the possibility of raising and maintaining the output of direct-shipping ore at 40 million tons per annum, further expansion of the basin's output seems destined to depend on *deep mining* and enrichment of low-grade iron quartzites. Accordingly, the first such mine and concentrator, the Pervomaisk complex, began operation in late 1980 with a designed first-stage capacity of 13.8 million tons of crude ore, to be converted ultimately to 6.3 million tons of concentrate when a concentrator is completed in the mid-1980s.[161]

For the present, open-pit mining of iron quartzites still predominates. The crude ore is enriched at five concentrators. The largest, the Northern concentrator, between Terny and Zheltye Vody, has an annual capacity of 48 to 50 million tons of crude ore, which yields 20 million tons of concentrate of which some 18 million tons is pelletized. The other enrichment facilities are the Central concentrator near Mirovskoye north of Krivoi Rog; the Southern concentrator and the new Krivoi Rog concentrator, just south of Krivoi Rog, and the Ingulets concentrator. All these complexes except the Ingulets facility either are being expanded or have recently been expanded.[162] With these added capacities and the planned deep mining of low-grade ores, Krivoi Rog is likely to remain the Soviet Union's largest producer of iron ore until the end of the century, with the KMA district constituting the only strong challenge.

To the north, along the left bank of the Dnieper, lies the Komsomolsk deposit. This deposit contains 2.22 million tons of $A + B + C_1$ reserves.[163] The mined ore (some 34 million tons) is enriched at the Dnieper concentrator, opened in 1970 at Komsomolsk east of Kremenchug, where 14 million tons of concentrate is produced annually. A pelletizing plant at Komsomolsk has been expanded to a capacity of 12 million tons, with the Allis-Chalmers Company, of West Allis, Wisconsin, providing the technical expertise and equipment.[164]

The Kerch Peninsula iron ore deposits are second to those of Krivoi Rog in the Ukraine. However, their total reserves, estimated at 2.1 billion tons, represent only a little over 11 percent of Krivoi Rog's total reserves. The $A + B + C_1$ reserves total 1.7 billion tons, with an average 37.7 percent iron and a high 18 percent silica content. The principal ore types are the "tobacco" and "brown" ores. Because an economically viable technology for enriching tobacco ores has not been developed, only the brown ores are being exploited by open-pit mining. One-third, or 570 million tons, of the $A + B + C_1$ reserves are of the brown type, composed chiefly of hydrogoethite and ferrimontmorillonite. The ores are of marine sedimentary oolitic origin with a fragmented to fine texture.[165] As a result, the ore is difficult to transport by rail in open ore cars. A high-phosphorus, enriched self-fluxing sinter is therefore shipped hot in covered barges plying the Sea of Azov between Kerch and the Azovstal plant at Zhdanov.[166] A small, uneconomic integrated iron and steel plant that existed at Kerch before World War II was destroyed during the war and has not been rebuilt. The production of usable ore appears to have peaked in the late sixties at 6 to 7 million tons annually.[167] Currently, the Kerch mines yield 4 million tons of ore concentrate.[168] We do not expect substantial expanded output in the coming decade.

The fourth and final ore district of the Ukraine is the Dneprorudnoye iron-ore mining complex on the Belozerka deposit southwest of Zaporozhye on the south shore of the Kakhovka reservoir on the Dnieper River. The deposit, with $A + B + C_1$ reserves of 0.69 billion tons, contains high-grade ores (66 percent Fe) suitable for direct use in open hearth steel furnaces and other direct-shipping ores (58 percent Fe) for direct charging of blast furnaces. Explored in the late fifties, the first stage of the underground mine began operation around 1970.[169] Although annual capacity was originally planned at 7 million tons, mine development has encountered groundwater problems and the production level in 1980 was only 3 million tons of high-grade ore.[170]

The known and presumed flows of Ukrainian iron ore are summarized in Figure 1. As is apparent, Krivoi Rog ores have the widest geographical market range. In addition to supplying ore to blast furnaces at Krivoi Rog, Cherepovets, Tula, Lipetsk, Zhdanov, the Urals, the Donbas and the Dnieper riverside iron and steel districts, the Krivoi Rog basin is still far ahead of the KMA as the largest source of ore exports to Eastern Europe.[171] The high-phosphorus Kerch ores, as previously noted, are shipped exclusively to the Azovstal plant at Zhdanov.[172] The direct-shipping ores from Dneprorudnoye and the pellets and ore concentrate from the Komsomolsk complex are consumed locally in the Dnieper Bend iron and steel district, mainly at Zaporozhye.

*Transcaucasia.* This region has only one commercially significant iron ore deposit, the Dashkesan magnetite deposit (see Fig. 1), 40 km southwest of Kirovabad in the Azerbaijan SSR. This ore deposit consists of volcanic-sedimentary rocks of Middle and Late Jurassic age forming a gentle syncline having four ore sectors. The northwestern sector, averaging 35.1 percent Fe, consists of a skarn-ore deposit resting on limestones or volcanic tuffs. The northeastern skarn-ore body, averaging 49.5 percent Fe, rests conformably between tuffites and a volcanic sequence. The 42.1 percent Fe grade skarn-ore of the southeastern sector rests on limestones, while the 49.4 percent Fe ore of the southwestern sector is composed of a layered series of skarn-ore lenses separated by nonore-bearing skarns. The combined $A + B + C_1$ reserves of the four sectors are 270 million tons.[173]

The Dashkesan deposit has been mined since 1954, yielding 2 million tons of crude ore during the sixties, or 1.4 million tons of usable concentrate from two open-cast mines.[174] Since 1970 the production of concentrate has been trending slightly downward, from 1.3 to 1.4 million tons annually to 1.1 million by 1979 and 1980. All of the concentrate is shipped to the nearby Rustavi iron and steel plant southeast of Tbilisi.[175] Production of usable ore should continue through 1990 at a level of 1.0 to 1.15 million tons yearly.

*Urals.* This region has dropped to fourth place among the major iron-ore producing regions of the Soviet Union behind the Ukraine, KMA, and Kazakhstan. The iron ore deposits are found throughout much of this ancient mountainous region. In 1975, the Urals contained 13.2 percent of all the $A + B + C_1$ categories of iron ore in the USSR, totaling 8.4 billion tons (see Table 5). The overall reserves as of 1975 were put at 15.2 billion tons.[176] Gradually, as other iron ore districts in the European part of the country have increased in importance, the Urals deposits have slowly been relegated to a secondary role as a result of the exhaustion of the richer reserves. Magnitogorsk especially has experienced a marked decrease in local iron-ore reserves.

Urals usable ore production reached a plateau of 27 to 28 million tons annually during the late fifties and throughout the sixties before declining slightly during the 1970s to 25 million tons in 1980.[177] The only hope for the Urals to expand its output lies with the Kachkanar deposit discussed below. But, even with Kachkanar expansion, the Soviet Union will be lucky to maintain a Urals usable ore production level of 20 to 26 million tons through 1990.

For the sake of discussion the Urals commercial ore deposits can be grouped into eight deposits: (1) Peschanka, (2) Kachkanar-Gusevogorsk, (3) Goroblagodat, (4) Alapayevsk, (5) Bakal, (6) Kusa, (7) Magnitogorsk, and (8) Akkermanovka.

The Peschanka deposit is situated 10 km south of Krasnoturinsk in Sverdlovsk Oblast. Although the northern sector has already been depleted, the western, southern and Novo-Peschanka sectors combined contained reserves of 173 million tons of $A + B + C_1$ ores and 24 million tons of $C_2$ category ore. The iron content is 48.5 to 54 percent.[178] Mining during the 1970s presumably has reduced these reserves perhaps to as little as 125 to 150 million tons. The commercial mineral is primarily magnetite in this sedimentary-volcanic sequence. While seventeen ore segregations have been explored, six contain most of the reserves. It seems likely that up to 4 million tons of concentrate are utilized annually in the Serov iron and steel mill. Several small mines to the north, around Ivdel, have been depleted.

The Kachkanar deposit (including both Gusevogorsk and Kachkanar proper) is in Sverdlovsk Oblast 30 km northwest of Nizhnyaya Tura, midway between the Serov and Nizhni Tagil iron and steel plants. The ore body consists of a gabbro-pyroxenite pluton occupying 110 square km. The principal iron ore mineral is titano-magnetite (15 to 18 percent Fe) with a solid solution of 2 to 18 percent ilmenite ($FeTiO_3$), 0.8 to 2.0 percent $TiO_2$, and 0.05 to 0.31 percent $V_2O_5$, and platinum metals measured in tenths of a gram per ton.[179] While the vanadium mineral helps make this low-grade ore (average of 16.6 percent Fe) economic, concentrating titanium and platinum ores would make the whole operation uneconomic. Commercial development of the Kachkanar deposit began in 1958[180] and Shabad's figure of 7 million tons of concentrate from around 40 million tons of crude ore in 1977[181] suggests that Kachkanar accounts for one-third of Urals production of usable ore. Kachkanar ore is shipped to Nizhni Tagil for conversion to steel with the resulting vanadium slag (15 percent vanadium) being moved to Chusovoi for processing into ferrovanadium and vanadium steels.[182] Although Kachkanar production could be expanded to reduce the Urals ore deficit, Soviet planners appear to prefer long-haul KMA ores to this local low-grade poly-mineralic ore. The availability of empty eastbound rail cars also tends to favor KMA over Kachkanar expansion.

Located 40 to 45 km northnortheast of Nizhni Tagil near Kushva, the Goroblagodat deposit consists of fifteen ore bodies associated with skarn formation. The dimensions of these bodies range from 200 to 930 meters in length and vary from 2 to 84 meters in thickness. Based on mineral composition these skarn ores can be classified as uniform magnetite, garnet-magnetite, magnetite-garnet, and magnetite-garnet skarns. Averaging 35.5 percent iron, the ores also contain currently uneconomic trace quantities of titanium, manganese, magnesium, vanadium, cobalt, copper and zinc. In 1971 the reserves of $A + B + C_1$ ores were estimated at 141 million tons and category $C_2$ at 16 million tons. Underground mining has been dominant, although, open-pit mining also is done.[183] Recent production data appear to be unavailable. Nonetheless, it is doubtful that Goroblagodat's output of marketable ore exceeds 3 to 4 million tons per annum.

The Alapayevsk group is 100 km east of Nizhni Tagil. The ore bodies are restricted to layers within Carboniferous age limestone. The commercial grade hydrogoethite and siderite ores range from 20 to 58 percent iron, with an average of 38.5 percent. The $A + B + C_1$ reserves totaled a modest 42 million tons in the early seventies.[184] Annual production is probably less than 2 million tons. Used locally at Alapayevsk, these ores will probably be depleted before 1990.

Until the early seventies, western Chelyabinsk Oblast had two major iron mining districts, Kusa and Bakal. While the former Kusa titanomagnetite deposit has

played out,[185] the Bakal deposit near Satka is today second only to Kachkanar in the Urals region. Encompassing an area of 150 square km of Upper Proterozoic sedimentary and metamorphic rocks, the Bakal group consists of at least 24 ore deposits.[186] Having been worked since the early Urals iron and charcoal smelter days, the surface-mined rich limonite ores were nearly exhausted by the early sixties. Therefore, more recent production has been from lower-grade (28 to 37.5 percent Fe), shaft-mined, siderite ores that require beneficiation by roasting before becoming part of a blast furnace charge.[187] In the early seventies, the reserves of $A + B + C_1$ siderite ores totaled 560 million tons and those of the brown-ironstone (limonite) 39 million tons.[188] The marketable ore, estimated at 8 million tons annually, flows mainly to Chelyabinsk.

As a result of lavish local consumption (over 15 million tons per year) since the fifties, the high-grade magnetite ores at Magnitogorsk are virtually exhausted. From a maximum production of 13.7 million tons of high-grade ore in 1957, Magnitogorsk's output plummeted by 1977 to 4 million tons of concentrate from lower-grade sulfurous ores.[189] It seems likely that output has continued to decline since then.

The Akkermanovka ores, situated near Novotroitsk in a Mesozoic depression filled with continental and marine sediments, consist primarily of hydrogoethite and hydro-hematite. The upper horizon ores average 32.0 percent iron, 0.4 percent nickel and greater than 1.0 percent chromium. The lower horizon ores are lower in iron (27.1 percent) and nickel (0.29 percent), but higher in chromium (1.43 percent). The $A + B + C_1$ reserves in the early seventies were 163 million tons and category $C_2$ ores 120 million tons.[190] We estimate usable ore production to be 1 million tons annually.

The Asian Iron-Ore Regions

The ore resources of the Asian regions have not been fully explored despite the discovery of large reserves. The overall reserves totaled 24.3 billion tons, comprising 22.7 percent of all Soviet reserves, as of 1975. Both of these measures have probably grown since then. The figures contained 14.4 billion tons of $A + B + C_1$ magnetite, hematite, siderite, ferruginous quartzite, and titano-magnetite averaging 39.7 percent iron (see Table 5).

From a mere 2.35 percent of total Soviet usable ore production in 1940, Asian production grew steadily to 21.6 percent in 1965 before European production reasserted itself, contracting Soviet Asia's share to 15.7 percent of total output in 1975. By 1980, Asia's relative share had again grown modestly to 17 percent, or some 42 million tons out of 244.7 million tons.[191] For discussion's sake, the ore deposits of Soviet Asia can be grouped into five regions: (1) Kazakhstan, (2) Central Asia, (3) West Siberia, (4) East Siberia, and (5) the Far East.

*Kazakhstan.* The exploitation of the iron ore deposits of Kazakhstan is of recent vintage when compared to those of the Northwest, the Ukraine, the Urals, Central Russia, and even West Siberia. The rapid development has thrust the region into the third position ahead of the Urals (see

Table 7). In 1946, iron ore reserves in Kazakhstan totaled only 100 million tons. By 1975, the reserves were 15.2 billion tons, including 7.6 billion tons of $A + B + C_1$ ores, or 14.2 percent of the Soviet total.[192]

The largest concentration is in Kustanai Oblast and totals 7.1 billion tons, or 93 percent of the $A + B + C_1$ reserves of Kazakhstan. The Lisakovsk deposit of high-phosphorus ore contains reserves of 1.72 billion tons. The Kachar deposit of magnetite ore holds 1.14 billion tons, while the two Rudny deposits, Sokolovka and Sarbai, contain 920 million and 680 million, respectively. The iron content varies from 35 to 46 percent. The $A + B + C_1$ reserves at the Karazhal deposit of high-grade (55.6 percent Fe), hematite and magnetite were 310 million tons in the 1970s. Karazhal is 270 km southwest of Karaganda. Approximately 370 km farther to the southwest lie the Balbraun and Kerege-Tas deposits of Proterozoic hematite quartzites. While the proven $A + B + C_1$ reserves of these two ore bodies are 77 million and 49 million tons of 40.4 percent iron content, respectively, prospective reserves have been estimated at 500 million tons.[193] The Taldy-Espe deposit, located 45 km southwest of Saksaulskaya railway station just north of the Aral Sea, encompasses $A + B + C_1$ reserves of 100 million tons of 35.3 percent iron. A final small Kazakhstan deposit is the Abail siderite and brown ironstone ore deposit in southern Kazakhstan (see Fig. 1). Ranging from 35.6 to 48.4 percent iron, the total $A + B + C_1$ siderite and ironstone ores amount to a meager 15 and 13 million tons respectively.[194] We do not anticipate this deposit being worked during this decade.

In 1970, Kazakhstan produced 18.2 million tons of marketable ore, 15 million tons from the Rudny mines, and about 3 million tons from the Karazhal deposit. The problematic high-phosphorus Lisakovsk mines began yielding about 1.5 million tons of low-grade (49 percent Fe) concentrate in 1975, by which time the output of Rudny and Karazhal had grown to 16 million tons and 4 million tons, respectively. Kazakhstan's 1980 output of usable ore, 25.8 million tons, was obtained as follows: Rudny, 17 million tons; Karazhal, 4 million tons, and Lisakovsk, 5 million tons, all concentrate except for Karazhal's contribution. The long delayed Kachar pit mine is planned to commence operation in the mid-1980s.[195] Except for Kachar's new output and hoped for improved technology at Lisakovsk's enrichment facilities, no major ore production expansion is anticipated in Kazakhstan in the short run.[196]

The Kazakhstan ores have a wide market range. For example, both Karazhal and Lisakovsk output goes to the Karaganda iron and steel plant. While most of the Rudny output, over 12 million tons, is transported to the Urals, a few million tons is being shipped to the two Kuznetsk iron and steel plants and a residual small quantity is consumed at Karaganda.[197] Kachar's future output seems destined for the Urals mills. There have also long been plans to expand the ore supply for the Karaganda iron and steel plant by developing the small, but high-grade surface deposit of Ken-Tyube, some 55 km east of Karkaralinsk. Reserve estimates of Ken-Tyube run 112 million tons of 52 percent direct-shipping ore.

*Central Asia.* The deposits of Central Asia are of minor importance. The reserves totaled 59.7 million tons or about 0.1 percent of Soviet reserves in the early seventies.[198] While further exploration could yield new deposits, the region's remoteness from iron and steel centers, and hence, both domestic and foreign markets, suggests that the region is not likely to receive a high priority for either prospecting or development.

*West Siberia.* The West Siberian iron and steel industry has been focused on the Kuznetsk Basin since the 1930s as part of the Urals-Kuzbas combine. Originally based on coking coal for iron-ore, long-haul trade with the Urals, the Kuzbas ties with the Urals were loosened by the development of Karaganda coking coal and a group of local iron ore deposits collectively referred to as Gornaya Shoriya, the Shor mountain country, named for a local ethnic group. Mines at Temirtau and Odrabash shipped their crude ore to a nearby enriching facility at Mundybash. Railroad construction during World War II allowed for the development of two other Kuzbas iron ore deposits, Tashtagol located 200 km southeast of Novokuznetsk and Sheregesh located 30 km northnortheast of Tashtagol.[199] The former deposits occur in a Middle Cambrian folded metamorphosed eruptive-sedimentary stratigraphic sequence. Within the sequence three ore types exist: (1) a rich magnetite ore with greater than 45 percent Fe content, (2) rich segregated skarn ore with a range of 30 to 45 percent Fe, and (3) leaner segregated skarn ores with 20 to 30 percent iron. Overall the ore averages 44.7 percent iron, 0.11 percent sulfur and 0.1 percent phosphorus. The $A + B + C_1$ reserves total 360 million tons and are supplemented by 50 million tons of $C_2$ category ore. The Tashtagol deposit is currently being shaft-mined.[200]

The Sheregesh deposit is also composed of Middle Cambrian volcanic and sedimentary rocks with some Ordovician terrigenous strata in the western part of the field. The principal ore mineral is magnetite. The deposit consists of three ore types and grades identical to the Tashtagol deposits. The $A + B + C_1$ reserves are also of similar size, 234 million tons; but of lower average grade, 35 percent iron. Similar, too, the deposit is currently being exploited by underground shaft mining.[201]

Since some of the ores from the Tashtagol and Sheregesh deposits require enrichment, a 5.8 million-ton concentrator was constructed at Abagur on the outskirts of Novokuznetsk.[202] Annual production from these various Kuznetsk mines peaked in the mid-1960s at 5.3 million tons, declined to 4.5 million tons in 1970 and has remained at that level.[203] These ores currently supply only about one-fourth of the 18 million tons of annual blast furnace demand generated by the West Siberian and Kuznetsk iron and steel plants.[204] We do not foresee any possible expansion of usable ore production within the immediate Kuzbas area.

Two hundred kilometers to the northwest of Tomsk lies the West Siberian iron ore basin. Having an areal extent of 66,000 square km of horizontal Cretaceous, Oligocene and Quaternary sedimentary deposits, the total reserves containing more than 30 percent iron have been estimated at 400 billion tons. Four main deposits have

been identified within this basin: the Narym, Kolpashevo, South Kolpashevo, and the Bakchar. The latter
deposit, considered to be the best, has geological reserves
calculated to be 28 billion tons.[205] Despite the vastness of
these West Siberian deposits, severe hydrogeologic problems are likely to prevent commercial development for
decades. These deposits are not mentioned in reserve
data for 1971 and 1975 (see Table 5).

In summary, in the early seventies the reserves of West
Siberia aggregated to 1.33 billion tons of $A + B + C_1$
categories having an average of 38.9 percent iron. This
total represented 2.1 percent of the Soviet total $A + B +
C_1$ reserves.[206]

*East Siberia.* This region had triple the $A + B + C_1$ reserves of West Siberia, 3.6 billion tons, or 5.7 percent of
the total Soviet reserves as catalogued in the seventies.
The region has not been thoroughly prospected; nonetheless, recent discoveries suggest iron ore reserves may
be greater than thought a few years ago.[207] The East Siberian region includes the Khakas-Sayan, Angara-Pit, Angara-Ilim and other smaller deposits.

The Khakas-Sayan deposits are in Krasnoyarsk Krai.
The Abakan deposit, at Abaza 176 km southwest of Abakan, consists of Lower Cambrian volcanic-sedimentary
rocks. The ores are magnetite types with estimated reserves of 700 million tons of 37.1 to 40.4 percent iron.[208]
Approximately 100 km southwest of the Abaza mine lies
the Anzas deposit, so far unexploited, whose magnetite
ores occur in metamorphosed sedimentary-volcanic
Cambrian rocks. The quality ores with an average iron
content of 38.2 percent include 151 million tons of $A + B
+ C_1$ and 16 million tons of $C_2$ category ores.[209] Exploita-
tion of direct-shipping ores (45 percent Fe) at Abaza to
serve the Kuzbas mills began in 1957 and production has
leveled off at about 2 million tons annually.[210] Production
at the Teya deposit located 183 km west of Abakan began
in 1966. The magnetite skarns are of relatively low-grade
(32.9 percent Fe) with a high aluminum and magnesium
content which requires beneficiation at the open-pit mine
site. Teya has 130 million tons of categories $A + B + C_1$
ores, while the directly adjacent Abagas magnetite
deposit has 73 million tons.[211] The Teya mine yields about
2 million tons of concentrate a year for the Kuzbas mills.[212]
During the 1970s two other small mines with 45 percent
ore were opened up farther to the east in Krasnoyarsk
Krai at Irba and Krasnokamensk (Kazyr area). While by
1975 they were extracting only 0.5 million tons of concentrate, each is planned to have an eventual annual
capacity of 2 million tons of concentrate.[213]

The Lower Angara deposit is found in the southern
part of the Angara-Pit iron ore basin (see Fig. 1). With $A +
B + C_1 + C_2$ reserves totaling 1.2 billion tons, the poten-
tial reserves may be over 5 billion tons. Averaging 40.4
percent iron, the hematite ores contain varying amounts
of other strategic minerals.[214] These ores are remote from
nonwater modes of transport and seem to be a decade or
two away from commercial exploitation.

To the east lies the Tagar deposit situated within Lower
Cambrian and Carboniferous sedimentary strata. Consisting of a series of magnetite ores, principally magno-

magnetite, which range from 28.9 to 39.5 percent iron,
they seem quite problematic for development because of
their remoteness as well as high sulfur content. Reported
reserves amount to 240 million tons in the $A + B + C_1$
categories.[215]

A more likely future commercial deposit appears to be
the Berezovo deposit, just south of Nerchinsky Zavod, in
eastern Transbaikalia (see Fig. 1). Located within a
Paleozoic-Mesozoic sedimentary basin, the deposit has
245 million tons of $A + B + C_1 + C_2$ reserves, including
high-grade (44.6 percent Fe) brown ironstones and sider-
ites and 200 million tons of lower-grade (35.7 percent Fe)
siderite ores.[216]

East Siberia has two commercially significant ore deposits, both within the Angara-Ilim iron ore region, the
Korshunovo and Rudnogorsk ores. The development of
Korshunovo has given rise to the mining town of
Zheleznogorsk in Irkutsk Oblast. The ore is part of metasomatically altered Upper Cambrian and Ordovician
sedimentary rocks. Reserves are significant, 330 million
tons and 95 million tons of $A + B + C_1$ and $C_2$ classes,
respectively. The low-grade ore (34.4 percent Fe) has
been quarried, enriched, and shipped to the Kuzbas mills
since 1965.[217] Current concentrate production appears to
be 6.2 to 6.5 million tons annually.[218] Northwest of
Zheleznogorsk some 125 km lies the Rudnogorsk deposit
associated with a volcanic pipe. The principal ore mineral
is magnomagnetite or magnesioferrite. Two kinds of ores
are present: (1) rich ores (53.1 percent Fe) totaling 66
million tons, and (2) segregated ores (39.8 percent Fe)
totaling 143 million tons. The remaining reserves, 60 million tons, are all $C_2$ category segregated ores.[219] Rudnogorsk yielded its first ore in late 1981 and further development may be expected in the current decade based on the
size of the reserves, their accessibility by rail, and their
quality.[220]

*The Far East.* The recent increased interest in the natural
resources of the Far East is related, in part, to the development of the BAM railroad as a means of transporting
them either to the west or east and the potential Pacific-
rim markets, especially Japan. The region contains potentially a tremendous storehouse of industrial raw materials. The region has at least three known major iron ore
districts: (1) Aldan of the Yakut ASSR, (2) Zeya-
Selemdzha in Amur Oblast, and (3) the Lesser Khingan in
the Jewish Autonomous Oblast. Total proven reserves
are continuing to grow dramatically, probably now being
double the 2,775 million tons recorded as of 1976 (see
Table 5).

Located 80 to 100 km north of the Neryungri coking
coal deposits, the Aldan iron ore deposits, mainly
Tayezhnoye, held 1.5 billion tons of reserves in 1975,
chiefly magnetite and martite ores. Total reserves may
climb to as high as 20 billion tons. The $A + B + C_1$ quality
ores at Tayezhnoye were 710 million tons with over 40
percent iron content.[221]

In recent years, geological exploration has centered on
the Chara-Tokko iron ore deposits in southwest Yakutia,
where reserves have been estimated at 5 billion tons,
including 2 billion in the $C_1$ category.[222] The ore, low in

sulfur and phosphorus, seems suitable for large-scale direct reduction steel making.[223]

To the southeast in the Zeya-Selemdzha area of Amur Oblast lies the Gar deposit containing 390 million tons of total reserves (averaging 41.7 percent Fe) accessible by open-pit mining.[224] The BAM's completion also holds open the prospect for exploitation of the reputed billions of tons of iron ore reserves of the Uda-Selemdzha district situated approximately 400 to 450 km northeast of Svobodny.[225] Finally, the Lesser Khingan Mountains in the Jewish Autonomous Oblast of Khabarovsk Krai is the location of the Kimkan ferruginous quartzite ore deposit containing 220 million tons of $A + B + C_1$ class ores. This deposit is in need of further investigation to determine its real economic potential.[226]

The iron ore deposits of East Siberia and the Far East clearly contain more than adequate reserves to meet the needs of any iron and steel making complexes when and if any are constructed to serve the needs of the region. An integrated iron and steel plant has been proposed for the Aldan district, Svobodny, Komsomolsk or Taishet. More important for òur purposes is the use of these deposits potentially as a basis for exporting crude and prepared ore to Japan and possibly other world markets. Inadequate surface transportation coupled with the usual host of infrastructure and amenity shortcomings in both East Siberia and the Far East serve as the major domestic obstacles to rapid expansion of Soviet Asia's ore production before the late 1980s at the earliest.[227] Other international obstacles also loom on the horizon, but will be dealt with later. The current distribution patterns of Urals, Kazakhstan, Siberian and Far Eastern iron ore is portrayed on Fig. 1.

**Projection of Soviet Iron Ore Production to 1990 and 2000**

Information in this chapter thus far clearly indicates that the Soviet Union has the largest known and potential iron ore reserves in the world. Many question marks appear, however, when one attempts to extrapolate future Soviet production performance based solely on physical potential. The chronic underfulfillment of production targets from both regional and aggregate perspectives suggests that growth of usable ore production during the remainder of this century will not keep pace with those of the sixties and early seventies. The implication of the data in Table 11 seems germane to any consideration of future Soviet iron-ore production performance. After peaking in 1970, the five-year moving average of annual ore increments has declined dramatically, especially since 1976. Given the host of technological, ore quality, accessibility, labor, management, and other problems previously mentioned in this chapter, the Soviet Union is not likely to significantly reverse this trend for over a decade. Except for the KMA and possibly Krivoi Rog workings, substantial expansion seems destined to depend on the development of the Siberian and Far Eastern reserves. Rational development of these reserves, however, appears to be dependent on many factors beyond purely Soviet domestic considerations as will be cited in the next section. In essence, based on our review of the literature, we project regional Soviet iron ore production by 1990 to be as indicated in Table 12.

During this decade the overall quality and quantity of the present deposits will gradually diminish as extraction continues on an increasing scale. This downward trend can be partly remedied through the discovery of new deposits of economic crude ore, the application of improved enrichment technology, a change in the definition of marketable ore (market forces), and an increase in the efficiency of the iron and steel industry. On the other hand, deposits of lesser quality, prohibitive economics of development, and the unavailability of suitable technology and foreign markets could further aggravate the overall iron ore outlook for a considerable time. As a result, our projections are significantly less than those derived from linear trend projections. Projections to the year 2000 are plagued even more by both domestic and international uncertainties. Nonetheless, we project Soviet marketable iron ore production, by the end of the century, to fall within the range of 300 to 325 million tons annually. Our estimates have been tempered by factors such as a possible future global "steel glut," resource substitutions, and increasing levels of scrap available for recycling.

TABLE 11

Five-Year Moving Average* of Annual Increments in Total Soviet Marketable Ore (in 1000's metric tons)

| Year | Increment | Year | Increment |
|------|-----------|------|-----------|
| 1965 | 8888.6 | 1973 | 7920.0 |
| 1966 | 7873.4 | 1974 | 7926.2 |
| 1967 | 7337.8 | 1975 | 7320.6 |
| 1968 | 7639.6 | 1976 | 7382.0 |
| 1969 | 7868.8 | 1977 | 6483.0 |
| 1970 | 9180.0 | 1978 | 5740.0 |
| 1971 | 9040.0 | 1979 | 3233.8 |
| 1972 | 8500.0 | 1980 | 2399.4 |

*Increment based on average of the increases over the previous five years.

SOURCE: Derived from the old-series data in Table 2 and other official Soviet sources.

TABLE 12

Projections of Soviet Usable Iron Ore Production to 1990 (in millions of metric tons)

|  | 1980 (Actual) | 1990 (Projected) |
|--|---------------|-------------------|
| Northwest Russia | 10.7 | 13–17 |
| KMA | 39.3 | 50–75* |
| Urals | 25 | 20–26 |
| Kazakhstan | 25.8 | 27–35 |
| Azerbaijan | 1.0 | 1.0–1.3 |
| Ukraine | 125.5 | 130–145 |
| Siberia | 17 | 18–30 |
| USSR Total | 247.7 | 260–290 |

*Soviet plans have called for up to 93 million metric tons.
SOURCE: Authors' estimates.

## Conclusion: Past, Present, and Future Soviet Iron Ore Exports

The most critical motivating factor behind this investigation of the Soviet iron ore industry has been an attempt to ascertain what role the Soviet Union will likely play in the international iron-ore market during the coming decade. Unlike some of the other industrial raw materials researched for this volume, we believe iron ore resources will have a low profile in any of the so-called impending "resource wars" between East and West, resource-rich and resource-poor nations, now being debated.[228] Despite the tremendous scale of global iron-ore trade,[229] we believe ore supply sources are diversified enough and ore demand is elastic enough to discount arguments about global resource wars concerning iron ore for decades!

At the present time the Soviet Union is not considered to be a major exporter of iron ore on the world market. Its past and present foreign markets are concentrated within the bordering CMEA nations. Because these nations are so inadequately endowed with indigenous iron reserves, there is no possibility of their meeting their own needs from domestic sources. For example, in 1981, East European countries produced only some 3 million tons of ore while importing some 33 million tons from the Soviet Union.[230] Table 13 reveals the quantity, total value, price per unit output, and the geographical distribution of

Soviet ore exports (direct-shipping and concentrates combined) for selected years from 1960 through 1981. Since 1972, Soviet exports to the six CMEA countries of Eastern Europe have been fairly stable.[231] According to 1974 trade agreements involving several cooperative measures between CMEA countries and the USSR, additional ore production and processing capacities at Krivoi Rog and Komsomolsk in the Ukraine, and the KMA deposits in Central Russia were to raise Soviet ore deliveries to these nations up to 48 million tons annually by 1980.[232] This goal was missed by a wide margin. Given the economic upheaval in Poland, the largest importer, and the Soviet ore industry's recent performance, we do not even foresee this target being surpassed by 1990, especially if the Soviets carry through with their plans to construct a large, 10 to 12 million ton iron and steel making complex (in addition to the Stary Oskol direct-reduction steel plant) in the KMA district oriented toward the CMEA market.[233] Such a plant would release much of the pressure to ship relatively low value ore to Eastern Europe. Furthermore, Table 13 illustrates that total Soviet ore exports have actually monotonically decreased since their peak in 1975. Similarly Table 14 indicates that the share of total marketable ore exported has also been declining, although the start of pellet exports (Table 3) has compensated somewhat for the downward trend in nonpelletized material.

TABLE 13
Soviet Iron-Ore Exports, 1960–81 (in 1000's of metric tons)

| | 1960 | 1965 | 1970 | 1975 | 1976 | 1977 | 1978 | 1979 | 1980 | 1981 |
|---|---|---|---|---|---|---|---|---|---|---|
| **CMEA** | | | | | | | | | | |
| Bulgaria | — | 842 | 1,029 | 1,679 | 1,638 | 1,682 | 1,636 | 2,150 | 2,176 | 2,279 |
| Czechoslovakia | 5,066 | 7,966 | 10,820 | 12,236 | 12,755 | 11,198 | 10,863 | 9,876 | 10,327 | 9,695 |
| East Germany | 2,003 | 2,610 | 2,687 | 2,730 | 2,397 | 2,772 | 2,529 | 2,771 | 3,201 | 2,964 |
| Hungary | 1,683 | 2,267 | 3,030 | 4,011 | 4,126 | 4,112 | 4,140 | 3,948 | 3,056 | 3,390 |
| Poland | 5,238 | 7,353 | 9,894 | 11,111 | 11,838 | 11,761 | 11,455 | 13,412 | 13,664 | 10,554 |
| Rumania | 851 | 1,714 | 4,245 | 6,288 | 5,135 | 4,599 | 4,373 | 4,221 | 4,198 | 4,074 |
| Total CMEA | 14,841 | 22,752 | 31,705 | 38,055 | 37,889 | 36,124 | 34,996 | 36,378 | 36,622 | 32,956 |
| **Non-CMEA** | | | | | | | | | | |
| Austria | 341 | 400 | 351 | 742 | 623 | 757 | 726 | 724 | 546 | 660 |
| Belgium | — | — | — | — | 225 | — | 37 | — | — | — |
| West Germany | — | 447 | 303 | 89 | 186 | 230 | 539 | 121 | — | — |
| Netherlands | — | — | — | — | — | 159 | 479 | — | — | — |
| Italy | — | — | 1,012 | 1,727 | 1,692 | 1,594 | 1,415 | 517 | 479 | 240 |
| Japan | — | — | 1,258 | 1,425 | 947 | 1,016 | 1,034 | 650 | 45 | — |
| Norway | — | — | — | — | 81 | 98 | 45 | 46 | — | — |
| Britain | — | 511 | 1,390 | 954 | 865 | 418 | 683 | — | — | — |
| United States | — | — | — | 205 | 132 | — | — | — | — | — |
| Total Non-CMEA | 341 | 1,358 | 4,314 | 5,142 | 4,751 | 4,272 | 4,958 | 2,058 | 1,070 | 900 |
| Residual not allocated in country tables | 0 | 28 | 81 | 429 | 486 | 550 | 651 | 576 | 416 | 382 |
| Total Exports (1000's tons) | 15,182 | 24,138 | 36,100 | 43,626 | 43,126 | 40,946 | 40,605 | 39,012 | 38,108 | 34,238 |
| Total Rubles (1000's rubles) | 157,536 | 224,293 | 292,404 | 498,152 | 472,881 | 440,706 | 427,462 | 426,385 | 422,827 | 471,959 |
| Average Price (rubles/ton) | 10.38 | 9.29 | 8.10 | 11.42 | 10.96 | 10.76 | 10.53 | 10.93 | 11.10 | 13.79 |

SOURCE: *Vneshnyaya torgovlya SSSR* for corresponding years.

TABLE 14
Share of Soviet Usable Iron Ore Production
Allocated to Export (1960–81)

| Year | Total Production (million tons) | Total Exports (million tons) | Exports as Share of Total Production (percent) |
|------|------|------|------|
| 1960 | 105.9 | 15.18 | 14.3 |
| 1965 | 153.5 | 24.14 | 15.7 |
| 1970 | 197.3 | 36.10 | 18.3 |
| 1975 | 235.0 | 43.63 | 18.6 |
| 1976 | 241.3 | 43.13 | 17.9 |
| 1977 | 242.0 | 40.95 | 16.9 |
| 1978 | 246.4 | 40.61 | 16.5 |
| 1979 | 241.7 | 39.01 | 16.1 |
| 1980 | 244.7 | 38.11 | 15.6 |
| 1981 | 242.4 | 34.24 | 14.1 |

SOURCES: Tables 2 and 13 and *Vneshnyaya torgovlya SSSR* for corresponding years.

Given the above facts and trends combined with our production projections, the Soviets would have to export between 16.5 and 18.5 percent of their total 1990 production just to satisfy the 1974 trading agreements with CMEA. Furthermore, to fulfill these CMEA agreements and to return to the 1975 level of non-CMEA exports, the Soviets will have to allocate between 18.2 and 20.4 percent of their production to the export market. Although the Soviet Union would prefer the CMEA countries to seek alternative non-Soviet sources to meet their future incremental needs for iron ore, there seems little likelihood that the hard currency and international debt problems of East European treasuries will allow this to happen. Then, too, the Soviet Union, perhaps motivated by political consideration, has expressed interest in importing low-grade iron ore from India on a long-term contract.[234] Thus, our most basic conclusion is that the USSR will not be able to offer more than 10 million tons annually for export to hard-currency markets by 1990; however, we expect the actual amount to be closer to 5 million metric tons.

This rather pessimistic assessment should be tempered by a number of more optimistic possibilities. First, Krivoi Rog will long remain a key factor in Soviet export performance, with vast reserves, a well developed modern infrastructure, and a convenient location for either rail or water transit to current and potential markets in East and West Europe, the United States, and the Middle East. The mathematical modeling in Chapter 20 supports this economic-geographic interpretation of Krivoi Rog. In the second half of the decade if the Soviets were forced to start importing oil, a barter trade of enriched iron ore concentrate (suitable for direct-reduction steel furnaces) in return for oil could become evident. Second, a concerted effort to expand KMA surplus production could also facilitate such a new trading pattern. Third, Kola and Karelian developments could modestly expand exports to Britain, northwest Europe, and Finland.

Finally, the Japanese market simultaneously holds out the greatest export promise and the most uncertainty. Soviet-Japanese cooperative efforts to develop Siberian resources have cooled in recent years and Soviet intransigence on negotiations over Japanese territorial claims in the Kuril Islands does not augur well for greatly expanded trade. Then, too, Japanese manufacturers are finding it increasingly difficult to market their current levels of steel production. Hence, while the East Siberian and Far Eastern ore reserves discussed previously are much in evidence, and the BAM and its associated spur lines make their large-scale exploitation feasible in the last half of the decade, we suspect that the Japanese market will not be significantly stronger than it is today. Furthermore, domestic demand in Siberia does not appear to warrant new large-scale ore development in East Siberia or the Far East.

In the final analysis, after distilling out the implications of a myriad of facts, trends, and possibilities, we conclude that the Soviet Union will not play a significantly enlarged role in international iron ore trade by 1990 compared with today. We foresee the absolute upper limit on Soviet exports to be 55 million tons at the end of the decade of which 80 to 90 percent will remain within the CMEA bloc. Exports to the West will range between 2 and 10 million tons, probably around 5 million tons. Actual total exports could be as low as 40 million tons, which would squeeze out nearly all trade with the West. Détente's demise could dictate this low level of East-West ore trade regardless of unforeseen Soviet efforts to produce ore surpluses. US-USSR ore trade is likely to be trivial to nonexistent through the eighties. Economic upheaval in Eastern Europe, ore-for-oil barter trade possibilities with the Middle East, the vagaries of Soviet-Japanese relations and vacillations in the world iron and steel markets make more precise predictions hazardous.

## NOTES

1. International Iron and Steel Institute, *Report on Iron Ore: Past Trends 1950 to 1974* (Brussels, 1974), p. 32.

2. The European Coal and Steel Community is composed of: Belgium, France, Italy, Luxembourg, the Netherlands and West Germany.

3. The East European members of Comecon (or CMEA) are: Bulgaria, Czechoslovakia, East Germany, Hungary, Poland, and Rumania.

4. Allan L. Kretz and Arthur W. Wright, *The World Market for Iron Ore and Scrap: A Background Study*, Discussion Paper No. 5 (September 1978), Association of American Geographers, Project on Soviet Natural Resources in the World Economy, pp. 2–10.

5. P. A. Shiryayev, Ye. N. Yarkho and Yu. M. Borts, *Metallurgicheskaya i ekonomicheskaya otsenka zhelezorudnoy bazy SSSR* [Metallurgical and economic assessment of the iron-ore base of the USSR] (Moscow: Metallurgiya, 1978), p. 9.

6. Hereafter, all metric iron ore tonnage will be expressed simply as tons.

7. *Minerals Yearbook, Area Reports: International* (Washington: Department of the Interior, Bureau of Mines, 1980), p. 759.

8. Kretz and Wright, *World Market for Iron Ore*, pp. 3–4.

9. *Vneshnyaya torgovlya SSSR v 1981 g.* [Foreign trade of the USSR in 1981] (Moscow: Finansy i Statistika, 1981).

10. Theodore Shabad, "Soviet Regional Policy and CMEA Integration," *Soviet Geography: Review and Translation* (hereafter, *SGRT*), 20, no. 4 (April 1979): 242.

11. Kretz and Wright, *World Market for Iron Ore*, pp. 2–10; Peter J. Kakela, "Iron Ore: From Depletion to Abundance," *Science* 212, no. 4491 (10 April 1981): 132–36.

12. Theodore Shabad, *Basic Industrial Resources of the USSR* (New York: Columbia University Press, 1969), pp. 35–37.

13. V. V. Strishkov, *Mineral Industries of the USSR* (Washington: Department of the Interior, Bureau of Mines, 1979), pp. 5–60.

14. N. D. Lelyukhina, *Ekonomicheskaya effektivnost razmeshcheniya chernoi metallurgii* [Cost-effectiveness of location of the iron and steel industry] (Moscow: Nauka, 1973), pp. 110–117.

15. N. N. Baransky, *Ekonomicheskaya geografiya SSSR* (Moscow: Ministerstvo kultury, 1956), pp. 14–17.

16. N. P. Leverov, "V. I. Lenin and the development of the iron-ore base," *Sovetskaya geologiya*, December 1969, pp. 3–9.

17. Craig ZumBrunnen, "The Soviet Union." In George Hoffman, ed. *A Geography of Europe: Problems and Prospects* (New York: Ronald Press, 1977), pp. 486–89.

18. Theodore Shabad, "News Notes," *SGRT* 21, no. 4 (April 1980): 252–54.

19. Shiryayev et al., *Metallurgicheskaya*, p. 9.

20. Ibid.

21. Shabad, *Basic Industrial Resources*, p. 39.

22. Shabad, "News Notes," 21, no. 4 (April 1980): 254.

23. Shabad, "Soviet Regional Policy," p. 243.

24. Craig ZumBrunnen, Jeffrey Osleeb, and Charles Morrow-Jones, *Modeling the Optimal Commodity Flow Patterns Within Soviet Ferrous Metallurgy: Implications for Soviet Iron Ore and Coking Coal Export*, Discussion Paper No. 14, (October 1979), Association of American Geographers, Project on Soviet Natural Resources in the World Economy, p. 32.

25. Victor L. Mote, "The Baikal-Amur Mainline: Catalyst for the Development of Pacific Siberia," in Theodore Shabad and Victor L. Mote, *Gateway to Siberian Resources (The BAM)* (Washington: Scripta, 1977), p. 86.

26. Shabad, *Basic Industrial Resources*, pp. 266, 269–71; Shabad, "News Notes," *SGRT* 22, no. 7 (September 1981): 448–52.

27. ZumBrunnen, Osleeb, and Morrow-Jones, *Modeling Soviet Metallurgy*, pp. 1–57.

28. Shabad, "News Notes," *SGRT* 15, no. 4 (April 1974): 240; V. P. Korostik, "Comparative Analysis of the Iron Ore Basins of Krivoi Rog and the Kursk Magnetic Anomaly," *SGRT* 20, no. 4 (April 1979): 228.

29. Shabad, "News Notes," *SGRT* 21, no. 4 (April 1980): 255; Ibid., 22, no. 4 (April 1981): 289.

30. Ibid., 20, no. 4 (April 1979): 272.

31. ZumBrunnen, Osleeb, and Morrow-Jones, *Modeling Soviet Metallurgy*, pp. 23–33.

32. Strishkov, *Mineral Industries* (1979), p. 14.

33. Ibid., pp. 13–14.

34. Marketable ore consists of two basic components:

direct-shipping ore and concentrate (enriched low-grade ore).

35. Strishkov, *Mineral Industries* (1979), pp. 13–14.

36. Shabad, "News Notes," 21, no. 4 (April 1980); 252; Ibid., 22, no. 4 (April 1981): 289; Strishkov, *Mineral Industries*, p. 14; "Plan and Fulfillment for the First Half of 1980," *Current Digest of the Soviet Press* (hereafter, *CDSP*) 32, no. 29 (20 August 1980): 7.

37. Shabad, "News Notes," *SGRT* 18, no. 4 (April 1977): 277; Ibid., 19, no. 4 (April 1978): 289–90; Ibid., 21, no. 4 (April 1980): 252; Ibid., 22, no. 4 (April 1981): 287; Strishkov, *Mineral Industries* (1979), p. 14.

38. G. A. Braun, *Zhelezorudnaya baza chernoi metallurgii SSSR* [The iron-ore base of the iron and steel industry of the USSR] (Moscow: Nedra, 1970), p. 95.

39. Strishkov, *Mineral Industries* (1979), p. 14; P. Kazanets, "The raw-material base of the iron and steel industry on the Lenin anniversary," *Gorny zhurnal*, no. 4 (April 1974): 19; *Gorny zhurnal*, 1980, no. 4.

40. *Gorny zhurnal*, 1980, no. 4.

41. Shabad, "News Notes," *SGRT* 22, no. 4 (April 1981): 287.

42. V. Yu. Grand, V. G. Derkach and P. B. Shapiro, in Nauchno-issledovatelsky i proyektny institut mekhanicheskoi obrabotki poleznykh iskopaemykh, *Trudy* 1, no. 113 (Leningrad, 1963): 78.

43. American Iron and Steel Institute, *Steel in the Soviet Union* (New York, 1959), pp. 53–54.

44. Grand et al., *Trudy*, pp. 8–12.

45. Shabad, "News Notes," *SGRT* 18, no. 8 (October 1977): 615.

46. Ibid., 20, no. 4 (April 1979): 270, Ibid., 21, no. 4 (April 1980): 253.

47. V. S. Strishkov, *Mineral Industries of the USSR* (Pittsburgh: Department of the Interior, Bureau of Mines, 1977), p. 9; Strishkov, *Mineral Industries* (1979), pp. 13–14.

48. Strishkov, *Mineral Industries* (1979), p. 13.

49. Shabad, "News Notes," *SGRT* 16, no. 6 (June 1975): 413.

50. Ibid., 19, no. 4 (April 1978): 289–92.

51. Ibid., 16, no. 6 (June 1975): 413.

52. Shabad, "Soviet Regional Policy," p. 242.

53. Shabad, "Soviet Regional Policy," pp. 240–44; Shabad, "News Notes," *SGRT* 19, no. 4 (April 1978): 290.

54. Shabad, "News Notes," *SGRT* 19, no. 4 (April 1978): 290.

55. *Vneshnyaya torgovlya*, 1976, no. 12, p. 8.

56. Shabad, "News Notes," *SGRT* 19, no. 4 (April 1978): 289.

57. Ibid., 16, no. 6 (June 1975): 413; *Gorny zhurnal*, 1981, no. 4.

58. Ibid., 19, no. 4 (April 1978): 289; Ibid., 21, no. 4 (April 1980); 252; *Gorny zhurnal*, 1981, no. 5.

59. Strishkov, *Mineral Industries* (1979), p. 14.

60. Shabad, "News Notes," *SGRT* 20, no. 4 (April 1979): 252–54; Shabad, *Basic Industrial Resources*, pp. 37–44.

61. Strishkov, *Mineral Industries* (1979), pp. 2–5, 14–15.

62. Shabad, "News Notes," *SGRT* 16, no. 6 (June 1975): 413–16.

63. Ibid.

64. N. T. Glushkov, "Improving the Economic Mechanism: On the Development of New Wholesale Prices," *CDSP* 22, no. 18 (4 June 1980): 1–5.

65. "In the Central Committee CPSU and the Council of Ministers USSR," *CDSP* 31, no. 30 (22 August 1979): 1–6, 14.

66. Ibid.: 5–6, 14.

67. Glushkov, "New Wholesale Prices," p. 4.

68. G. Bazarova, "Improving the Economic Mechanism: The Incentive Functions of Payments into the Budget," *CDSP* 32, no. 18 (4 June 1980): 13.

69. Glushkov, "New Wholesale Prices," p. 2.

70. For example, see, Kh. N. Gizatullin, "Marginal costs of iron-ore resources," *Ekonomika i matematicheskiye metody*, 14, no. 4 (July-August 1978): 700–08; Z. P. Tsimdina, T. Ya. Serezhenko, G. N. Bukina and N. S. Miter, *Modelirovaniye razvitiya i razmeshcheniya proizvodstva v chernoi metallurgii* [Modeling the development and location of the iron and steel industry] (Novosibirsk: Nauka, 1977).

71. Braun, *Zhelezorudnaya baza*, p. 29.

72. Lelyukhina, *Ekonomicheskaya effektivnost*, p. 117; Shiryayev et al., *Metallurgicheskaya*, pp. 8–9; *Razvedka i okhrana nedr*, 1981, no. 6, p. 15.

73. Lelyukhina, *Ekonomicheskaya effektivnost*, p. 117.

74. A. T. Khrushchev, "The Formation of the Industrial Complex of the Kursk Magnetic Anomaly," *SGRT* 16, no. 4 (April 1975): 241.

75. Shiryayev et al., *Metallurgicheskaya*, p. 9.

76. Ibid., p. 8.

77. Ibid., p. 10.

78. Ibid.

79. Ibid, p. 8.

80. Khrushchev, "Kursk Magnetic Anomaly," p. 246; Shabad, "News Notes," *SGRT* 19, no. 4 (April 1978): 289.

81. Also, a few discrepancies exist between the deposit names in Table 6 and those of Appendix II.

82. *The Soviet Economy in 1978–79 and Prospects for 1980* (Washington: Central Intelligence Agency, June 1980), pp. 7–8.

83. Ibid., p. 16.

84. Shabad, "News Notes," *SGRT* 19, no. 4 (April 1978): 291.

85. Lelyukhina, *Ekonomicheskaya effektivnost*, p. 117.

86. V. I. Smirnov, ed. and D. A. Brown, a trans., *Ore Deposits of the USSR*, Vol. 1 (London: Pitman, 1977), pp. 9–11, 35–109.

87. Shabad, *Basic Industrial Resources*, pp. 117–18.

88. Shabad, "News Notes," *SGRT* 19, no. 4 (April 1978): 291.

89. Strishkov, *Mineral Industries* (1979), p. 14.

90. Shabad, "News Notes," *SGRT* 23, no. 4 (April 1982): 295.

91. Strishkov, *Mineral Industries* (1979), p. 15.

92. Shabad, "News Notes," *SGRT* 22, no. 4 (April 1981): 289.

93. Shabad, "News Notes," *SGRT* 18, no. 6 (June 1977): 422.

94. ZumBrunnen, Osleeb and Morrow-Jones, *Modeling Soviet Metallurgy*, pp. 15–21.

95. Strishkov, *Mineral Industries* (1979), p. 15; and "Finish Group to Build Major Soviet Facilities for Iron Production," *Wall Street Journal*, 19 May 1977, p. 3; Shabad, "News Notes," *SGRT* 23, no. 7 (September 1982).

96. Khrushchev, "Kursk Magnetic Anomaly," p. 241; Shiryayev et al., *Metallurgicheskaya*, p. 12.

97. Shiryayev et al., *Metallurgicheskaya*, p. 12.

98. Khrushchev, "Kursk Magnetic Anomaly," p. 240.

99. Ye. I. Kapitonov, "The Kursk Magnetic Anomaly and its Development," *SGRT* 4, no. 5 (May 1963): 10–11.

100. Ibid., pp. 11–13

101. Ibid., p. 13.

102. V. Ya. Rom, "Geographical Problems in the Iron and Steel Industry of the USSR," *SGRT* 15, no. 3 (March 1974): 130.

103. Kapitonov, "Kursk Magnetic Anomaly," p. 13.

104. Khrushchev, "Kursk Magnetic Anomaly," p. 241.

105. Ibid., p. 240.

106. Kapitonov, "Kursk Magnetic Anomaly," p. 10.

107. Ibid., pp. 10–11.

108. Ibid.

109. Ibid., p. 11.

110. Ibid.

111. Kapitonov, "Kursk Magnetic Anomaly," pp. 13–14; V. P. Novikov, "The Kursk Magnetic Anomaly—A Promising Iron-Ore Base for the Iron and Steel Industry of the Urals," *SGRT* 10, no. 2 (February 1969): 76–77. A small quantity of high-grade ore was first extracted from a deep mine at Korobkovo in 1932; see: A. T. Khrushchev, "The Zheleznogorsk Mining Node as Part of the Industrial Complex of the Kursk Magnetic Anomaly," *SGRT* 21, no. 6 (June 1980); 370.

112. Shabad, "News Notes," *SGRT* 16, no. 5 (May 1975): 331.

113. Kapitonov, "Kursk Magnetic Anomaly," pp. 13–14.

114. Shabad, "News Notes," *SGRT* 17, no. 6 (June 1976): 427.

115. Ibid., 16, no. 10 (December 1975): 688.

116. Ibid., 18, no. 1 (January 1977): 76.

117. Ibid.

118. Shabad, "News Notes," *SGRT* 18, no. 4 (April 1977): 278.

119. Ibid., 17, no. 6 (June 1976): 427; *Gorny zhurnal*, 1981, no. 7, pp. 3–4.

120. *Gorny zhurnal*, 1981, no. 7, pp. 3–4.

121. Shabad, *Basic Industrial Resources*, p. 99.

122. Shabad, "News Notes," *SGRT* 17, no. 6 (June 1976): 427.

123. Ibid., 18, no. 4 (April 1977): 278.

124. Strishkov, *Mineral Industries* (1979), p. 14; Khrushchev, "Zheleznogorsk," p. 371.

125. Shabad, "News Notes," *SGRT* 18, no. 4 (April 1978): 278; Khrushchev, "Zheleznogorsk," p. 371.

126. Konstantin Kuznetsov, "The Kursk Magnetic Anomaly," *Culture and Life*, 1975. no. 11, p. 5.

127. Shabad, "News Notes," *SGRT* 18, no. 1 (January 1976): 60–61; Shabad, "Soviet Regional Policy," p. 243.

128. R. Mathieson, *Japan's Role in Soviet Economic Growth* (New York: Praeger, 1979), p. 131.

129. Kuznetsov, "Kursk Magnetic Anomaly," p. 5.

130. Mathieson, *Japan's Role*, p. 131.

131. Kuznetsov, "Kursk Magnetic Anomaly," p. 5.

132. "GRF Firms Win DM500 mn. Iron Sponge Order from the U.S.S.R.," *Financial Times*, 15 December 1977.

133. *Stroitelnaya gazeta*, 8 December, 1976.

134. ZumBrunnen, Osleeb, and Morrow-Jones, *Modeling Soviet Metallurgy*, p. 32.

135. Shabad, "New Notes," "*SGRT* 21, no. 4 (April 1980): 259; Khrushchev, "Zheleznogorsk," p. 374.

136. Shabad, "Soviet Regional Policy," pp. 243–44.

137. Shabad, "News Notes," *SGRT* 18, no. 1 (January 1975): 60–61; Kapitonov, "Kursk Magnetic Anomaly," p. 13; and Khrushchev, "Kursk Magnetic Anomaly," pp. 247–48; Khrushchev, "Zheleznogorsk," p. 374.

138. V. V. Andreyev, T. V. Zvonkova, N. V. Luzanov, and A. T. Khrushchev, "Problems of Environmental Protection in Connection with the Formation of the Industrial Complex of the Kursk Magnetic Anomaly," *SGRT* 20, no. 5 (May 1979): 291–96; V. I. Forafontova, "Economic Evaluation of the Damage Caused to Natural and Economic Features by the Iron Ore Industry of the KMA," *SGRT* 21, no. 6 (June 1980): 377–92, and Khrushchev, "Zheleznogorsk," pp. 374–75.

139. Shabad, *Basic Industrial Resources*, p. 99.

140. Rom, "Geographical Problems," p. 130.

141. See Table 8.

142. Shabad, "News Notes," *SGRT* 22, no. 4 (April 1981): 288–89.

143. Ibid., 21, no. 4 (April 1980): 254.

144. Ibid.

145. Ibid., 17, no. 6 (June 1976): 427; Ibid., 20, no. 4 (April 1979): 270.

146. Kapitonov, "Kursk Magnetic Anomaly," p. 13; Khrushchev, "Kursk Magnetic Anomaly," pp. 247–48.

147. See Table 8.

148. Shabad, "News Notes," *SGRT* 18, no. 6 (June 1977): 422; Ibid., 19, no. 4 (April 1978): 290; Ibid., 20, no. 4 (April 1979): 270; Ibid., 21, no. 4 (April 1980); 254.

149. Ibid., 18, no. 6 (June 1977): 422.

150. ZumBrunnen, Osleeb, and Morrow-Jones, *Modeling Soviet Metallurgy*, p. 42.

151. Shabad, "News Notes," *SGRT* 22, no. 4 (April 1981): 288.

152. Lelyukhina, *Ekonomicheskaya effektivnost*, p. 117.

153. Shiryayev et al., *Metallurgicheskaya*, p. 12.

154. Ibid., p. 9.

155. Ibid., p. 15.

156. Shabad, *Basic Industrial Resources*, p. 36; Shabad, "News Notes," *SGRT* 20, no. 4 (April 1979): 269.

157. Shabad, "News Notes," *SGRT* 23, no. 4 (April 1982): 295.

158. V. I. Smirnov, ed., *Rudnye mestorozhdeniya SSSR*, 1 (Moscow: Nedra, 1974) p. 104, Shiryayev et al., *Metallurgicheskaya*, p. 15.

159. V. I. Smirnov, ed., D. A. Brown, trans., *Ore Deposits of the USSR*, 1 (London: Pitman, 1977), pp. 102–6.

160. Shabad, *Basic Industrial Resources*, p. 37.

161. Shabad, "News Notes," *SGRT* 22, no. 4 (April 1981): 287–88; *Gorny zhurnal*, 1981, no. 3; *Sotsialisticheskaya industriya*, 15 June 1982.

162. Ibid., 21, no. 4 (April 1980): 253–54.

163. Shiryayev et al., *Metallurgicheskaya*, p. 120.

164. Shabad, "News Notes," *SGRT* 19, no. 4 (April 1978): 289; Ibid., 20, no. 4 (April 1979): 270; Ibid., 22, no. 4 (April 1981): 288; Strishkov, *Mineral Resources* (1979), pp. 14–15.

165. Smirnov, *Ore Deposits*, pp. 83–85.

166. Shabad, *Basic Industrial Resources*, pp. 179–80.

167. Ibid., pp. 36, 179–80.

168. Shabad, "New Notes," SGRT 22, no. 4 (April 1981): 288.

169. Shabad, *Basic Industrial Resources*, p. 186.

170. Shabad, "News Notes," *SGRT* 22, no. 4 (April 1981): 288.

171. Shabad, *Basic Industrial Resources*, pp. 35–44, 179-94; Shabad, "News Notes," *SGRT* 18, no. 4 (April 1977): 278.

172. Shabad, *Basic Industrial Resources*, p. 179.

173. Shiryayev et al., *Metallurgicheskaya*, p. 12.

174. Shabad, *Basic Industrial Resources*, pp. 155–56.

175. Ibid.; Shabad, "News Notes," *SGRT* 21, no. 4 (April 1980): 253; Shabad, "News Notes," *SGRT* 22, no. 4 (April 1981): 288.

176. Lelyukhina, *Ekonomicheskaya effektivnost*, pp. 113, 139; Shiryayev et al., *Metallurgicheskaya* p. 16.

177. Shabad, *Basic Industrial Resources*, p. 36, Shabad, "News Notes," *SGRT* 23, no. 4 (April 1982): 295.

178. Smirnov, *Ore Deposits*, pp. 38-40

179. Ibid, pp. 35–37.

180. Shabad, *Basic Industrial Resources*, p. 219.

181. Shabad, "News Notes," *SGRT* 19, no. 4 (April 1978): 291.

182. Shabad, *Basic Industrial Resources*, p. 219.

183. Smirnov, *Ore Deposits*, pp. 40-43.

184. Ibid., pp. 96–97.

185. Ibid., pp. 33–34.

186. Ibid., p. 76.

187. Shabad, *Basic Industrial Resources*, p. 224.

188. Smirnov, *Ore Deposits*, pp. 76–79.

189. Shabad, *Basic Industrial Resources*, pp. 226–27; Shabad, "News Notes," *SGRT* 19, no. 4 (April 1978): 291.

190. Smirnov, *Ore Deposits*, pp. 90–92.

191. See Table 7, and Shabad, *Basic Industrial Resources*, p. 36.

192. Shiryayev et al., *Metallurgicheskaya*, p. 19.

193. Smirnov, *Ore Deposits*, pp. 54–55, 85–88, 93–94.

194. Ibid., pp. 75, 81–83, 94–95, 108–9.

195. Shabad, "News Notes," *SGRT* 19, no. 4 (April 1978): 290–92; Ibid., 22, no. 4 (April 1981): 287–89.

196. Shabad, "News Notes," *SGRT* 20, no. 4 (April 1979): 270; Ibid., 19, no. 4 (April 1978): 291–92.

197. Shabad, "News Notes," *SGRT* 20, no. 4 (April 1979): 270; Ibid., 21, no. 4 (April 1980): 254.

198. See Table 5.

199. Shabad, *Basic Industrial Resources*, p. 235.

200. Smirnov, *Ore Deposits*, pp. 46–47.

201. Ibid., pp. 49–51.

202. Shabad, *Basic Industrial Resources*, p. 235.

203. Shabad and Mote, *Gateway to Siberian Resources*, p. 6; Shabad, "News Notes," *SGRT* 22, no. 4 (April 1981): 288.

204. Shabad, "News Notes," *SGRT* 19, no. 4 (April 1978): 292.

205. Smirnov, *Ore Deposits*, pp. 88–89.

206. Lelyukhina, *Ekonomicheskaya effektivnost*, p. 117; Shiryayev et al., *Metallurgicheskaya*, p. 18.

207. Mathieson, *Japan's Role*, p. 129; I. P. Bardin, *Chernaya metallurgiya: Razvitiye proizvoditelnykh sil Vostochnoi Sibiri* [Iron and steel industry. Development of productive forces of East Siberia] (Moscow: Academy of Sciences USSR, 1960), p. 136.

208. Smirnov, *Ore Deposits*, pp. 67–69.

209. Ibid., pp. 65–67.

210. Shabad, *Basic Industrial Resources*, pp. 250–51; Shabad and Mote, *Gateway to Siberian Resources*, pp. 6, 48.

211. Shabad, *Basic Industrial Resources*, pp. 250–51; Smirnov, *Ore Deposits*, pp. 47–49; Shiryayev et al., *Metallurgicheskaya*, p. 18.

212. Shabad and Mote, *Gateway to Siberian Resources*, pp. 6, 48.

213. Ibid.

214. Smirnov, *Ore Deposits*, pp. 79–81.

215. Shiryayev et al., *Metallurgicheskaya*, p. 18.

216. Ibid.

217. Ibid., pp. 69–71; Shabad, *Basic Industrial Resources*, p. 260.

218. Shabad and Mote, *Gateway to Siberian Resources*, p. 6.

219. Smirnov, *Ore Deposits*, pp. 71–72.

220. Shabad and Mote, *Gateway to Siberian Resources*, p. 48; Shabad, "News Notes," *SGRT* 23, no. 2 (February 1982): 121–23.

221. Shiryayev et al., *Metallurgicheskaya*, p. 18; Shabad, "News Notes," *SGRT* 21, no. 1 (January 1980): 54; P. G. Bunich, "The BAM and the Economic Development of the Soviet Far East," *SGRT* 16, no. 10 (December 1975): 647; O. A. Kibalchich, "The Baikal-Amur Mainline and the Integrated Economic Development of the Eastern Regions of the USSR," *SGRT* 17, no. 6 (June 1976): 389.

222. *Razvedka i okhrana nedr*, 1981, no. 6, p. 14.

223. V. S. Sidorova and A. A. Vadyukhin, "New Technology and the Location of the Iron and Steel Industry in the Eastern Portion of the USSR," *SGRT* 18, no. 1 (January 1977): 34.

224. Ibid., p. 35.

225. Shabad, "News Notes," *SGRT* 21, no. 1 (January 1980): 54–55.

226. Shabad and Mote, *Gateway to Siberian Resources*, p. 11; Mathieson, *Japan's Role*, p. 130.

227. "Baikal-Amur Mainline," *Rechnoi transport*, no. 1 (1976): 55.

228. For example, see: James Arnold Miller, Daniel I. Fine, and R. Daniel McMichael, *The Resource War in 3-D: Dependency, Diplomacy, Defense* (Pittsburgh: World Affairs Council of Pittsburgh, 1980).

229. Kretz and Wright, *The World Market for Iron Ore*, pp. 2–10.

230. Shabad, "Soviet Regional Policy," p. 241.

231. See Table 13, and *Vneshnyaya torgovlya SSSR* for corresponding years.

232. Shabad, "Soviet Regional Policy," p. 242.

233. Ibid., p. 243.

234. "Review of Trends and Policies in Trade Between Countries Having Different Economic and Social Systems," UNCTAD, TD/B/808 (16 July 1980).

## APPENDIX I
## THE CLASSIFICATION OF MINERAL RESERVES IN THE USSR

| Class | Degree of exploration of the deposit | Economic importance of the given class of reserves |
|---|---|---|
| A | Delineated by mine openings or boreholes; position, form and structure of the mineral body, distribution of the mineral by grades in different blocks and mining conditions are known. | May be used for planning and current production, mine designing and investment planning. |
| B | Delineated by mine openings, ore boreholes, the principal indicators: thickness of mineral bodies, mineral grade, position, mine engineering conditions are known for the deposits as a whole. The individual blocks of different characteristics are not outlined. In the case of deposits of sustained thickness and grade, a limited zone of extrapolation may be included. | May be used as a basis for detailed exploration. If some reserves are classed as A, the B reserves may be used as a basis for mine designing and investment planning. In the case of complex and variable deposits, where A reserves cannot be determined by exploration, mines are designed on the basis of B reserves. |
| $C_1$ | The main features of the deposit are known only in general terms. The deposit is outlined by exploratory openings and by extrapolation of geologic and geophysical data. | May be used for long-range production planning and as a basis for exploration. In the case of very complex and extremely variable deposits, in the absence of reserves classed as A and B, $C_1$ reserves are used as a basis for mine designing and investment planning. |
| $C_2$ | Reserves are estimated tentatively; the main features of a deposit are determined on the strength of geologic and geophysical data confirmed by few exploratory openings. | May be used as a basis for organization of exploration. |

## APPENDIX II
## CLASSIFICATION OF IRON-ORE DEPOSITS OF THE USSR

| Genetic Group | Class (Association) | Deposit[1] and Location |
|---|---|---|
| Magmatic | Low-titanium magnetite, in intrusives of the dunite-pyroxenite-dunite association | Kachkanar, Gusevogorsk, Pervouralsk (Urals); Lysansk (East Sayan) |
| | Titanomagnetite-ilmenite, in gabbroic and gabbro-amphibolitic intrusives | Kusa, Kopan (Southern Urals) |
| | High-titanium titanomagnetite, in gabbroic and gabbro-diabase intrusives | Pudozhgorsk (Karelia); Kharlovo (Altai) |
| | Perovskite-titanomagnetite and apatite-magnetite, in alkaline-ultramafic intrusives with carbonatites | Afrikanda, Kovdor (Kola Peninsula) |
| Contact-metasomatic | Magnetite calc-skarn | Magnitogorsk, Vysokogorsk, Lebyazhye, Goroblagodat, North Peschanka, etc. (Urals); Adayevo and other deposits of the southern half of the Turgai iron-ore province, Dashkesan (Azerbaijan), Atansor (Central Kazakhstan); Beloretsk and Kholzun (Gorny Altai); Tashtagol, etc. (Altai-Sayan district); Chokadam-Bulak (Tadzhikistan) |
| | Magnetite magnesian-skarn and magnesian-calc-skarn | Teya (Kuznetsk Alatau); Kaz, Sheregesh (Gornaya Shoriya); Zhelezny Kryazh (Eastern Transbaikalia); Tayezhnoye, Pionerskoye (South Yakutia) |
| | Scapolite-albite and scapolite-albite-skarn magnetite | Kachar, Sarbai, Sokolovka (Turgai province); Goroblagodat (Urals); Anzas (West Sayan) |
| | Magnetite and hematite, hydrosilicate | West Sarbai (Turgai province); Abaza (Khakasia); individual sectors of deposits of preceding classes |
| Metamorphic (metamorphosed) | Precambrian ferruginous quartzites | Krivoi Rog, Komsomolsk (Ukraine); Olenegorsk (Kola Peninsula); Kostamuksha (Karelia); Karsakpai (Central Kazakhstan); Lesser Khingan (Soviet Far East) |
| | Magnetite and magnetite-specularite contact-metamorphosed sedimentary (with relicts of sedimentary iron ores) | Kholzun (Gorny Altai) |
| Hydrothermal | Magnomagnetite, associated with traps | Korshunovo, Rudnogorsk, Tagar, Neryuda, etc. (Eastern Siberia) |
| | Magnetite specularite, intensely metasomatic | Paladauri (Georgia); Kutim (western slopes of the Northern Urals) |
| | Iron-carbonate vein-metasomatic | Bakal (Southern Urals); Abail (Southern Kazakhstan) |
| Marine sedimentary (weakly metamorphosed and unmetamorphosed) | Sideritic (brown-ironstone in the zone of oxidation) layered, in marine terrigenous-carbonate sediments | Komarovo-Zigazinsk, Katav-Ivanovsk, and other groups (Southern Urals) |
| | Hematitic, in marine carbonate-terrigenous sediments | Lower Angara (Eastern Siberia) |

APPENDIX II *(cont.)*

| Genetic Group | Class (Association) | Deposit[1] and Location |
|---|---|---|
| | Hematitic and magnetite-hematitic, in eruptive-sedimentary sequences | Karazhal group (Central Kazakhstan); Kholzun (Gorny Altai) |
| | Siderite-leptochlorite-hydrogoethite, pisolite-oolitic, in marine carbonate-terrigenous sediments | Kerch (Crimea); Ayat (Turgai province); Bakchar (Western Siberia) |
| | Magnetite, partially titaniferous marine placers | Recent "black" beach sands of the coasts of the Black, Caspian, and Japan seas; fossil beach sands in Azerbaijan, etc. |
| Continental sedimentary | Hydrogoethite, pisolite-oolite, lacustrine-paludal | Large number of small deposits on the Russian Platform and other parts of the Soviet Union |
| | Siderite-leptochlorite-hydrogoethite, pisolite-oolite, naturally alloyed with chromium and nickel, lacustrine-paludal, associated with weathering crust of ultramafic rocks | Akkermanovka group (Southern Urals); Serov (Northern Urals); Malka (North Caucasus) |
| | Siderite (brown-ironstone in zone of oxidation) hypergene-metasomatic, in littoral-lacustrine coarsely-clastic, predominantly carbonate sediments | Berezovo (Eastern Transbaikalia) |
| | Siderite-leptochlorite-hydrogoethite, in ancient fluvial sediments | Lisakovsk (Turgai province); Taldy-Espe (Northern Aral region) |
| | Predominantly martite eluvial-deluvial (cobbly) | Vysokogorsk (Central Urals) |
| Weathering crusts (residual and infiltration) | Goethite-hydrogoethite (brown-ironstone) and martite-hydrogoethite zones of oxidation of deposits of sideritic and skarn-magnetite ores | Bakal (Southern Urals); Berezovo (Eastern Transbaikalia); Vysokogorsk (Urals) |
| | Goethite-hydrogoethite, ocherous, naturally alloyed with chromium and nickel, in weathering crust of ultramafic rocks | Yelizavetinsk (Central Urals) |
| | Hydrogoethite, in eluvial-deluvial sediments in karst limestones | Alapayevsk (eastern slopes of Urals) |
| | Martite and hydrohematite, in ferrugenous quartzites | Yakovlevo, Zheleznogorsk, (KMA); Saksagan group (Krivoi Rog) |

[1]In this table, almost all the significant deposits are shown that possess proved reserves of over 100,000 tons. Smaller deposits are indicated in those cases when significant deposits are not known for comparison.

Source: Adapted from V. I. Smirnov, ed. D. A. Brown, trans., *Ore Deposits of the USSR*, Vol. 1 (London: Pitman, 1977), pp. 9–11.

# 20

# MODELING THE OPTIMAL COMMODITY FLOW PATTERNS WITHIN SOVIET FERROUS METALLURGY: IMPLICATIONS FOR SOVIET IRON ORE AND COKING COAL EXPORTS

CRAIG ZUMBRUNNEN
University of Washington

JEFFREY OSLEEB
Boston University

CHARLES MORROW-JONES
Ohio State University

Cartography by
KARL JOHANSEN
University of Washington

## Introduction

Since the industrialization debates of the 1920s, Soviet economic development strategies can fairly be characterized as strongly favoring investment in heavy industrial sectors while slighting both the agricultural and consumer-service sectors of the economy. Within this context, the Soviet iron and steel industry represents the premier success story emanating from the unbalanced development policies. While the iron and steel industries of the West, with the possible exception of the Japanese, have lost much of their romantic national aura first to the petrochemical and more recently to the innovative aerospace, electronics, and data processing industries, the chauvinistic marriage between the Soviet iron and steel industry and the "motherland" has remained intimate and enduring. Stripping away its nationalist glamour, the iron and steel industry has in fact long been a most crucial sector of the Soviet economy. The situation can be interpreted as arising concomitantly with Soviet autarkic development policies, regardless of whether one perceives these economic policies as having been self-initiated or invoked in response to exogenous political and economic factors.[1]

Over the last decade or so, however, the world has witnessed increasing Soviet interest in relaxing autarkic policies in favor of greater participation in international trade. In essence, Western observers discern two primary categories of motivating factors for this turn of events: (1) political and (2) economic. With much qualification one can conceive of Soviet foreign trade with (nonsocialist) developing nations as being primarily politically moti-

vated, trade with CMEA as being both politically and economically motivated, and trade with the industrialized West as being economically motivated. More specifically the latter trading patterns can plausibly be interpreted as attempts by the Soviet leadership to redress chronic economic efficiency and labor productivity problems with an infusion of modern technology for the lagging industrial sectors and to diffuse consumer pressures resulting from decades of relative neglect of the agricultural sector with the purchases of wheat and corn primarily for food-grain usage. Although the commodity structure of Soviet foreign trade has evolved substantially over the years, trade statistics indicate that even with CMEA countries the USSR still possesses characteristics more commonly associated with those of a developing nation than a first-order industrial power.[2] In other words, the emerging pattern of import motivated trade coupled with the ruble's lack of convertibility and United States restrictions on Export-Import Bank credits has precipitated a severe balance-of-payment problem for the Soviet Union. Hence, like a developing country the USSR has been forced to export raw materials to the West (as well as CMEA) to earn hard currency to offset its rising hard-currency trade deficit.

While in recent years petroleum exports have dominated Soviet hard-currency earnings, reaching 51 percent in 1977,[3] the ability of the Soviets to maintain such export levels has been the subject of much discussion and debate.[4] On the other hand, no one seriously questions the vastness of Soviet iron ore[5] or coking coal reserves.[6] Both of these raw materials, especially the former, have long played a role in Soviet exports, but mainly to CMEA countries.[7] The question thus arises as to the potential role that these two Soviet primary products may play in the international commodity arena.

More specifically, within the limitations of the data (1970) and model used, this study seeks to throw some light on the following questions. First, assuming that the Soviets are optimizers, what would the commodity flow patterns for 1970 steel production and distribution look like? Second, assuming that the Soviets place highest priority on producing steel for domestic consumption, where do the iron ore and coking coal reserves appear? Third, and more important for our purposes, are these "optimal" reserve locations accessible to or remote from current or potential foreign markets? Fourth, what locational changes may be in the offing in the iron and steel industry in view of the increasingly expensive underground Donets coking coals compared to the cheaper, but remote, Kuznetsk coals? Similarly, what regional steel production changes may be economically warranted as a result of both the depletion of the Urals coking coal[8] and iron-ore deposits[9] on the one hand, and the rapid development of the massive, but hydrogeologically problematic KMA (Kursk Magnetic Anomaly) iron-ore deposits in market-oriented European Russia, on the other? Over the years the Soviets have proposed a number of new steel producing centers. Accordingly, which, if any, of them appear to be economically viable locations? Simultaneously, which, if any, of the current (1970) steel production sites are uneconomic? Are there strong economic arguments for expanding the output of some steel complexes while reducing or even dismantling others?[10] Finally, in what ways may these various model-indicated geographical changes be relevant to the future prospects of Soviet exports of iron ore and coking coal? Thus, in several ways this spatial analysis of the Soviet iron and steel industry augments the value of the iron ore commodity study in the previous chapter.

## Raw Data and Initial Assumptions

Several sets and types of raw data were collected and utilized for this investigation. First, the Soviet railroad system, selected major inland and coastal waterways, and selected pertinent surface roads were encoded to form a transportation network consisting of 914 nodes and internodal distances.[11] The overwhelming tonnage of both Soviet iron ore and coke was transported by rail in 1970 and it is safe to assume that the same was true of steel.[12] Second, three (linear and commodity undifferentiated) modal transport rates were employed:

(1) 0.4 kopecks per metric-ton kilometer for rail;
(2) 0.2 kopecks per metric-ton kilometer for water; and
(3) 0.8 kopecks per metric-ton kilometer for surface road transit.[13]

The internodal distances were all multiplied by their appropriate modal rates and the resulting transformed data were then processed by a minimum distance algorithm to yield a minimum-cost-distance matrix connecting all raw-material sites to all steel production sites, both existing (in 1970) and proposed, as well as the production sites to all demand points.

Third, raw-material and steel production information were assembled. Reasonably good estimates of 1970 Soviet iron ore production and extraction costs at 25 sites (see Table 1) and coking coal output and extraction costs at 16 sites (see Table 2) were gleaned and compiled from a host of sources. Similarly, estimates of 1970 location-specific steel production figures for 43 plants were collected (see Table 3). The data year (1970) was selected due both to the low level of aggregation of the raw-material input and steel production data compared with more recent Soviet figures and with the idea in mind of using

TABLE 1
Iron Ore Inputs

| Location (node number)* | Estimated Production (1970) ($10^3$ metric tons) | Extraction Costs (rubles per ton) |
|---|---|---|
| Kovdor (50) | 2,900 | 3.00 |
| Olenegorsk (51) | 5,100 | 3.00 |
| Tula (8) | 200 | 3.00 |
| Lipetsk (12) | 200 | 3.00 |
| Zheleznogorsk (52) (KMA) | 5,600 | 2.40 |
| Gubkin (53) (KMA) | 12,000 | 2.40 |
| Kremenchug (54) | 2,600 | 2.40 |
| Krivoi Rog (15) | 102,800 | 2.40 |
| Dneprorudnoye (55) | 200 | 2.40 |
| Kerch (56) | 4,600 | 2.40 |
| Dashkesan (57) | 1,400 | 3.00 |
| Ivdel (58) | 200 | 4.75 |
| Kachkanar (59) | 2,300 | 5.00 |
| Kushva-Blagodat (60) | 5,900 | 4.75 |
| Vysokaya (61) | 2,500 | 4.75 |
| Alapayevsk (32) | 400 | 4.75 |
| Bakal (62) | 4,500 | 4.75 |
| Magnitogorsk (36) | 9,000 | 1.00 |
| Rudny (63) | 15,000 | 3.65 |
| Lisakovsk (64) | 200 | 3.65 |
| Novotroitsk (65) | 800 | 4.75 |
| Karazhal (66) | 3,000 | 3.65 |
| Gornaya Shoriya (67) | 5,000 | 3.31 |
| Abaza (68) | 2,000 | 3.31 |
| Zheleznogorsk-Ilimsky (69) | 6,000 | 3.38 |

*Numbers in parentheses refer to node numbers on Figures 1 and 3.
SOURCES: Theodore Shabad, *Basic Industrial Resources of the USSR* (New York: Columbia University Press, 1969), p. 36; Shabad, "News Notes," *Soviet Geography: Review and Translation*, scattered references over past several years; *Narodnoye khozyaistvo SSSR v 1970 g.* (Moscow, 1971), p. 193; Paul Lydolph, *Geography of the U.S.S.R.*, 2nd ed. (New York: John Wiley and Sons Inc., 1970), p. 509; *Gorny zhurnal* December 1972, p. 12; V. P. Novikov, "The Kursk Magnetic Anomaly—A Promising Iron-Ore Base for the Iron and Steel Industry of the Urals," *Soviet Geography: Review and Translation*, 10, no. 2 (February 1969): 70–71.

1970 as a baseline against which to assess the economic rationale of subsequent possible locational shifts within the industry. In addition to these 43 existing steel centers, 7 locations which have been suggested in the Soviet literature as potential foci for future integrated iron and steel centers—namely, Taishet (44), Barnaul (45), Gorky (11), Kostroma (47), Rzhev (48), Kursk (49), and Stary Oskol (46)—were selected for inclusion in a second 50-plant model run.[14] While the first two sites represent on-again off-again Siberian locations, the latter five all represent market-oriented European sites predicated on the expanding iron ore production from the KMA. Interestingly enough, a steel plant using the so-called direct conversion process and with an initial capacity of 1.8 million tons of steel annually is currently under construction with West German financial and technical help at Stary Oskol (46).[15] A prodigious iron and steel complex with a projected capacity of 10 to 12 million tons of steel, essentially for serving the CMEA market, has long been planned for KMA region,[16] and Shabad[17] reports it was still in the offing as recently as 1976. Thus, this investigation will provide an ex post facto evaluation of these two steps.

TABLE 2
Coke Inputs

| Location (node number)* | Estimated Coke Production (1970)[a] ($10^3$ metric tons) | Extraction Costs (rubles per ton) |
|---|---|---|
| Vorkuta (80) | 6,100 | 6.00 |
| Pavlograd (70) | 1,900 | 19.00 |
| Krasnoarmeisk (71) | 4,400 | 19.00 |
| Donetsk-Makeyevka (22) | 13,400 | 19.00 |
| Shakhtersk (74) | 100 | 19.00 |
| Artemovsk (72) | 5,400 | 19.00 |
| Stakhanov (73) | 5,900 | 19.00 |
| Voroshilovgrad (75) | 1,400 | 19.00 |
| Shakhty (77) | 3,600 | 19.00 |
| Krasnodon (76) | 2,400 | 19.00 |
| Tkvarcheli (78) | 400 | 10.00 |
| Tkibuli (79) | 400 | 10.00 |
| Kizel (81) | 1,100 | 10.00 |
| Karaganda (38) | 8,200 | 4.10 |
| Kemerovo (82) | 5,000 | 6.00 |
| Novokuznetsk (41) | 17,500 | 6.00 |

*Numbers in parentheses refer to node numbers on Figures 1 and 3.
[a]Production values are deflated to represent coke rather than coking coal because for this analysis coking is presumed to take place at the minehead.
SOURCES: *Narodnoye khozyaistvo SSSR v 1970 g.*, (Moscow, 1971), p. 188; A. S. Romanuk and I. Slovikovsky, "The Nonrenewable Resources of the Ukraine," mimeographed paper (data based originally on *Ugol Ukrainy*, no. 5 (May 1974), p. 51), p. 19; Theodore Shabad, "News Notes," *Soviet Geography: Review and Translation*, scattered references over past several years; Ian F. Elliott, *The Soviet Energy Balance* (New York: Praeger, 1974), pp. 122–76, 269–70.

Fourth, since linear programming does not allow for the imbedding of nonlinear production cost functions, estimated Soviet steel production data for 1970 from Table 3 were multiplied by the appropriate steel cost data from Table 4 resulting in a production-scale weighted average cost of 35.44 rubles per ton of steel.[18] In the actual computed runs the rounded value of 35.0 rubles per ton was used.

Fifth, the weakest portion of the data set is the point source estimates of steel demand for all Soviet cities equal to or greater than 65,000 inhabitants in 1970. Total Soviet domestic steel consumption thus had to be allocated to a total of 304 demand nodes. As previously stated in the introduction, the objective in this analysis was to determine the optimal geographical flow patterns in the Soviet steel industry which satisfy *domestic* steel demand. Accordingly, the 7.0 million tons of steel which were exported in 1970 were subtracted from the actual 115.9 million tons produced to arrive at the assumed aggregate domestic steel demand of 108.9 million tons.[19]

This quantity was disaggregated by the following procedure. First, good 1970 Soviet regional steel demand data[20] allowed for the allocation of the 108.9 million to 19 economic regions. Within each of these regions, the regional demand was assigned to individual nodes (i.e. all cities $\geq$ 65,000 population within a given region) proportional to a city's population size[21] weighted by the summed fraction of the city's labor force engaged in industry, construction, and transportation.[22] Although less than wholly reliable, such a disaggregation procedure

seems to us to be about the best estimating method one could hope for given the complete lack of actual point-source demand data for the Soviet Union. Furthermore, since the location of steel production is more sensitive to pull of raw material inputs than markets, the use of these

TABLE 3
Steel Production for Existing Plants (1970)

| Location (node number)* | Quantity[a] ($10^3$ metric tons) |
|---|---|
| Liepaja (1) | 400 |
| Leningrad (2) | 1,000 |
| Kolpino (3) | <1,000 |
| Mogilev (4) | 200 |
| Cherepovets (5) | 5,500 |
| Moscow (6) | 1,000 |
| Elektrostal (7) | 1,000 |
| Tula (8) | 1,000 |
| Vyksa (9) | <1,000 |
| Kulebaki (10) | <1,000 |
| Gorky (11) | 1,000 |
| Lipetsk (12) | 3,000 |
| Dneprodzerzhinsk (13) | 5,000 |
| Dnepropetrovsk (14) | 5,000 |
| Krivoi Rog (15) | 8,800 |
| Zaporozhye (16) | 5,000 |
| Kramatorsk (17) | 1,000 |
| Konstantinovka (18) | 1,000 |
| Kommunarsk (19) | 1,000 |
| Yenakiyevo (20) | 1,000 |
| Makeyevka (21) | 5,000 |
| Donetsk (22) | 5,000 |
| Taganrog (23) | 1,000 |
| Zhdanov (24)[b] | 10,600 |
| Volgograd (25) | 1,900 |
| Rustavi (26) | 1,400 |
| Sumgait (27) | 700 |
| Izhevsk (28) | 1,000 |
| Serov (29) | 1,000 |
| Chusovoi (30) | 1,000 |
| Nizhni Tagil (31) | 6,100 |
| Alapayevsk (32) | 1,000 |
| Zlatoust (33) | 2,000 |
| Chelyabinsk (34) | 4,800 |
| Beloretsk (35) | 1,000 |
| Magnitogorsk (36) | 12,300 |
| Novotroitsk (37) | 3,000 |
| Temirtau (38) | 100 |
| Karaganda (39) | 2,100 |
| Bekabad (40) | 1,000 |
| Novokuznetsk (41)[c] | 7,400 |
| Petrovsk-Zabaikalsky (42) | 1,000 |
| Komsomolsk-na-Amure (43) | 1,000 |

*Numbers in parentheses refer to location numbers on Figures 1 and 3.
[a]Because of the crude estimates for many of these sites the estimated total production, 116.3 million tons, is slightly more than the actual total of 115.9 million tons. Also regional totals for European Russia, the Urals and the Ukraine vary slightly from actual regional data as a result of this obligatory estimating effort.
[b]Combined for both plants at the Zhdanov node.
[c]For this study the newer West Siberian plant, located a mere 16 kilometers northeast of Novokuznetsk is considered to be situated at Novokuznetsk, thus here and in the two computer runs node 41 will represent both, combined production sites.
SOURCES: A. T. Khrushchev, *Geografiya promyshlennosti SSSR* [Geography of industry of the USSR] (Moscow, 1969), pp. 253–72; Theodore Shabad, *Basic Industrial Resources of the USSR* (New York: Columbia University Press, 1969), pp. 35–44; *Atlas SSSR*, 2nd ed. (Moscow, 1969), pp. 107, 124–47; *Oxford Economic Atlas of the World*, 4th ed. (Oxford: Oxford University Press, 1972), pp. 42–43; Theodore Shabad, "News Notes," *Soviet Geography: Review and Translation*, scattered references over the past several years.

TABLE 4
The Relationship between Steel Costs
and the Production Capacity of Plants

| Production Capacity (million metric tons) | Mean Production Cost (rubles per ton) |
|---|---|
| | Steel |
| 10 | 25.60 |
| 5 to 7 | — |
| 4 to 5 | 35.00 |
| 3 to 4 | 38.50 |
| 2 to 3 | — |
| 1 to 2 | 42.16 |
| 0.5 to 1 | 45.00 |
| 0.3 to 0.5 | 46.70 |
| 0.2 to 0.3 | 49.00 |
| 0.1 to 0.2 | 56.90 |

SOURCE: V. Ya. Rom, "Geographical Problems in the Iron and Steel Industry of the USSR," *Soviet Geography: Review and Translation*, 15, no. 3 (March 1974): 126.

estimates seems warranted given the broad general spatial insights hoped for from the analyses.

Finally, some additional simplifying assumptions need to be explicitly stated. First, all steel production was assumed to involve a uniform technology using the direct inputs of both iron ore and coke. Therefore, constant and spatially homogeneous raw material input ratios were utilized, namely 1.35 units of iron ore and 0.63 units of coke per 1.00 units of steel.[23] After the analyses were completed, another Soviet source was found which cites values of 1.67 for iron ore and 1.30 for coking coal for 1969.[24]

Actually this *coking coal* value of 1.30 is very close to our *coke* coefficient of 0.63 for, as previously stated in Table 2, we have assumed that the coking process takes place at the minehead and have deflated the coking coal production values to yield coke production equivalent.[25] Fluxing inputs, water, scrap steel, and alloy ores were assumed to be ubiquitous.[26] In order to make the model runs conform to the 1970 Soviet steel production ranges, both threshold (50,000 metric tons) and ceiling (12 million metric tons) steel production output constraints were included. The implications of these operationally simplifying assumptions will be noted in the discussion of the analysis.

**The Model**

A variant of the Beckmann-Marschak linear programming model was employed in this investigation.[27] The objective, thus, is to minimize total system costs, $Z$, that is input extraction costs, assembly costs, (average) production costs and distribution costs (see Appendix I). While this model is straightforward and simplified compared to recent Soviet spatial system modeling of the iron and steel industry,[28] our objectives do not warrant such a detailed and complex effort. Nonetheless, the approach taken here allows for the simultaneous determination of input sites, allocations, market areas and steel plant sizes for the entire Soviet steel producing system which minimizes total system costs. Thus, this model is a location

model to the extent that some established steel production sites in both the 43-plant and 50-plant run may (do) not enter and therefore are not included in the final "optimal" solution. Furthermore, some potential plants (50-plant run) not presently in existence may (do) produce a positive level of output in the final solution of the second run. The results of the two computed simulation runs are discussed in the following section.

**Results of the Analysis**

Detailed results of the two simulations are included in a number of figures and tables. The geography of the 43-plant run is displayed in Figures 1 and 2 and that of the 50-plant run in Figures 3 and 4. Summary data on raw material reserves and optimal plant sizes are listed in Tables 5 through 7, while the internodal commodity flows are enumerated in Appendices II and III.

For the purposes of the AAG project the most important geographical results, of course, are the size and location of the model-predicted slack activity for iron ore and coke production. Figures 1 and 3 illustrate not only the relative quantities and distribution of these underutilized raw-material inputs, but the optimal assembly flow patterns as well (see Appendices II and III for quantitative flow data). In 1970 the Soviet Union exported 36.1 million tons of iron ore, of which 32.9 million tons was destined for Eastern Europe. These exported ores originated almost exclusively from the Krivoi Rog and the KMA deposits.[29] As shown in Table 5, both of our model runs yield surplus iron ore of 47,373 million metric tons, or an excess of 11.27 million tons over the total of actual 1970 exports. This discrepancy arises from three sources: (1) our use of a possibly low iron ore input coefficient as previously noted, (2) production uses not accounted for such as wrought iron, and most importantly (3) our decision to delete from the analysis the 7 million metric tons of steel (equivalent to 9.45 million tons of iron ore) produced for export.

Nonetheless, a comparison between the model-predicted unutilized iron ore production and the actual Soviet production surpluses and export patterns is quite interesting. Similar to the actual situation, Krivoi Rog possesses the overwhelming fraction of the surpluses in both of the model runs (see Table 5). However, the KMA workings are completely allocated to five steel plants within the Central Russian region of the country (see Appendix II) in the 43-plant run and simply to Moscow and the proposed Stary Oskol steel site in the 50-plant run. In essence, the two actual surplus iron ore producing centers in the KMA district are replaced in both computer runs by the two Kola Peninsula ore mines at Olenegorsk and Kovdor. These latter two mining centers, of course, ship their actual production to the admittedly expensive Cherepovets steel works, which in both the 43-plant run and the 50-plant run produces sufficient steel only to satisfy its own endogenous demand. In effect, the very large expansion of steel production at Moscow indicated by the model supplants the role of Cherepovets and other small northwestern steel plants. Furthermore, it also

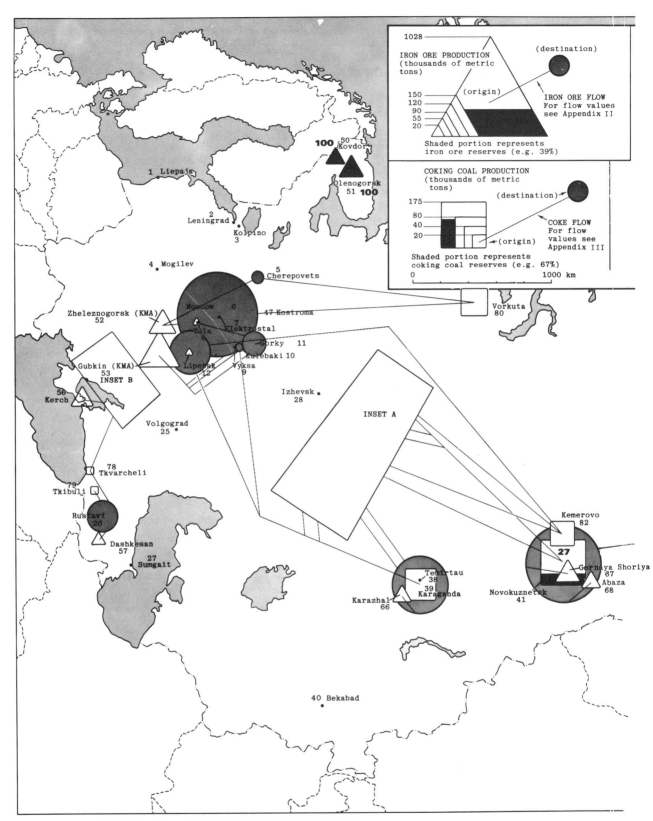

# RAW MATERIAL ASSEMBLY FLOWS
## Existing Plants (43)

Figure 1

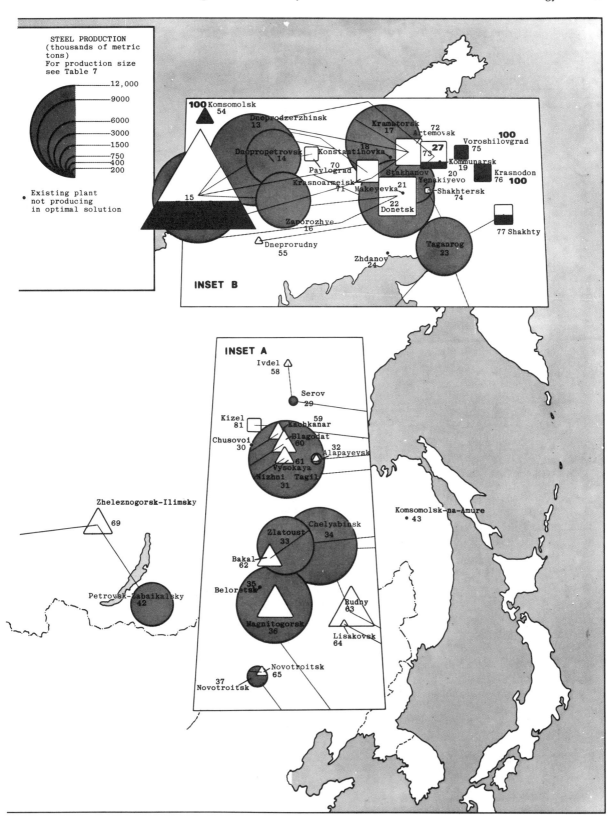

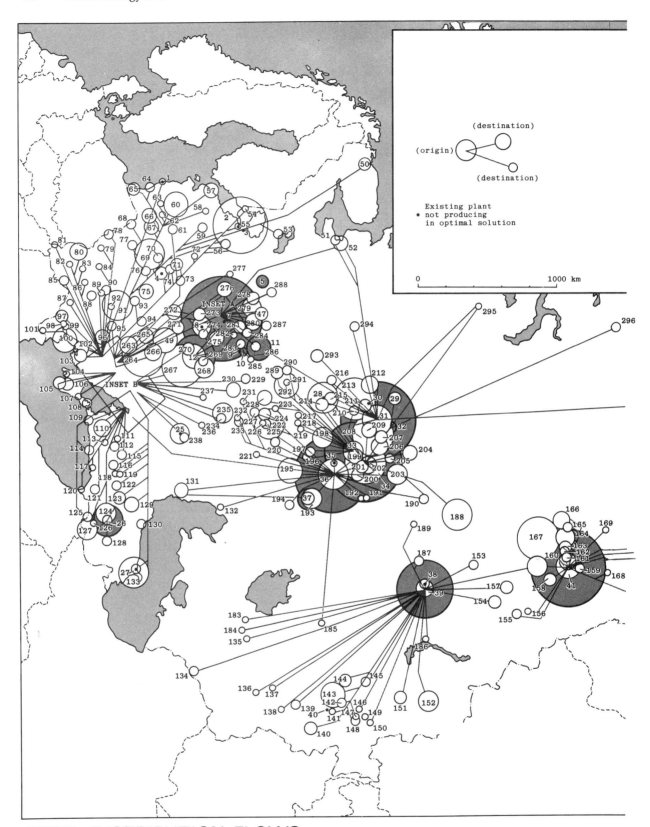

# STEEL DISTRIBUTION FLOWS
## Existing Plants (43)

Figure 2

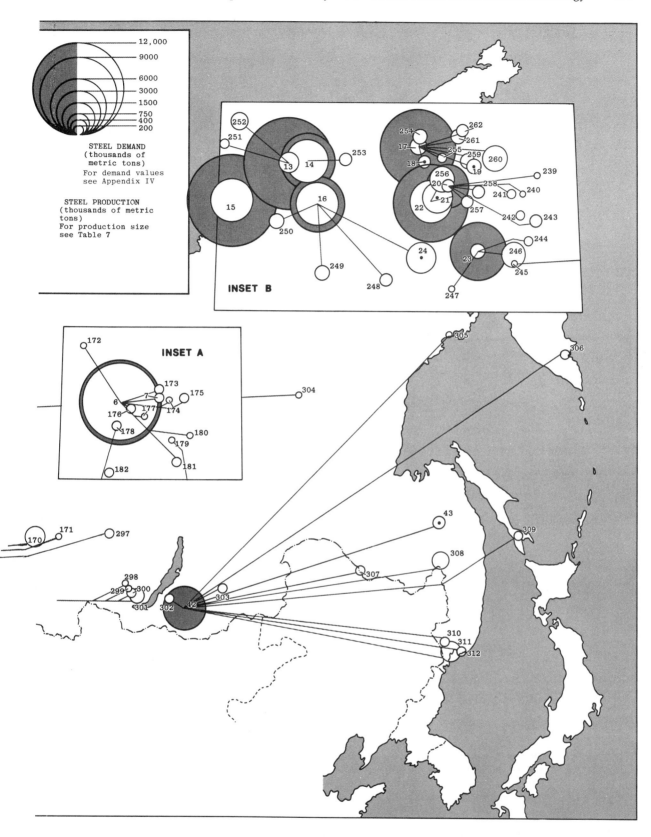

STEEL DEMAND
(thousands of
metric tons)
For demand values
see Appendix IV

STEEL PRODUCTION
(thousands of metric
tons)
For production size
see Table 7

INSET B

INSET A

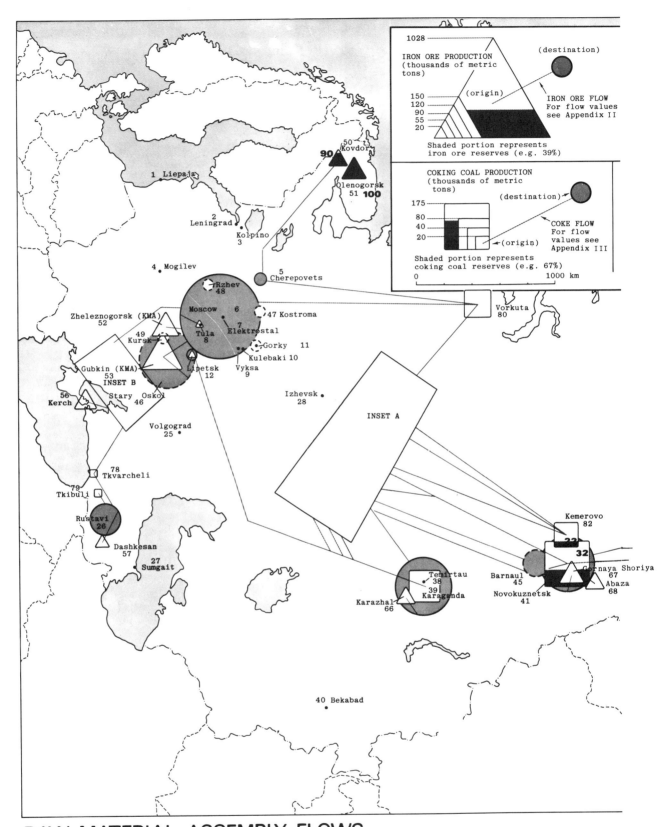

RAW MATERIAL ASSEMBLY FLOWS
Existing and Proposed Plants (50)

Figure 3

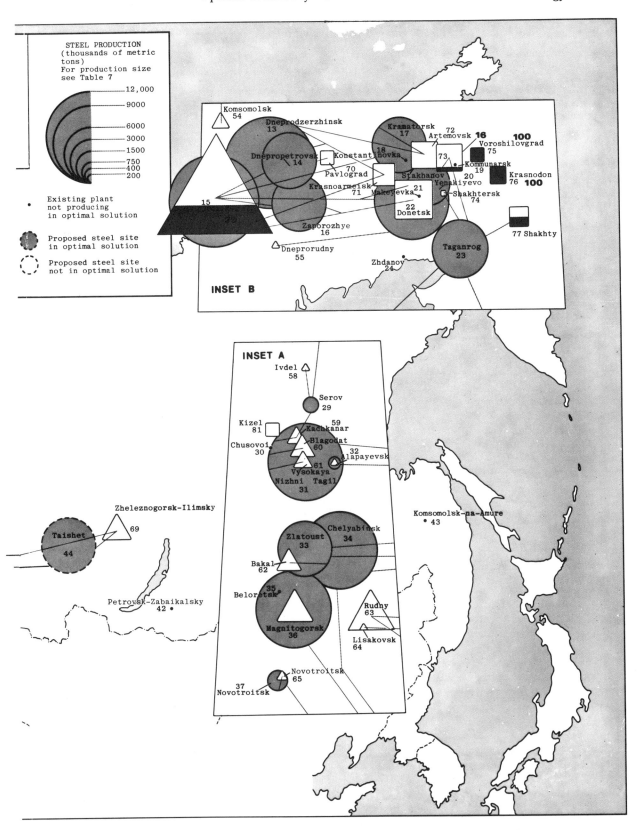

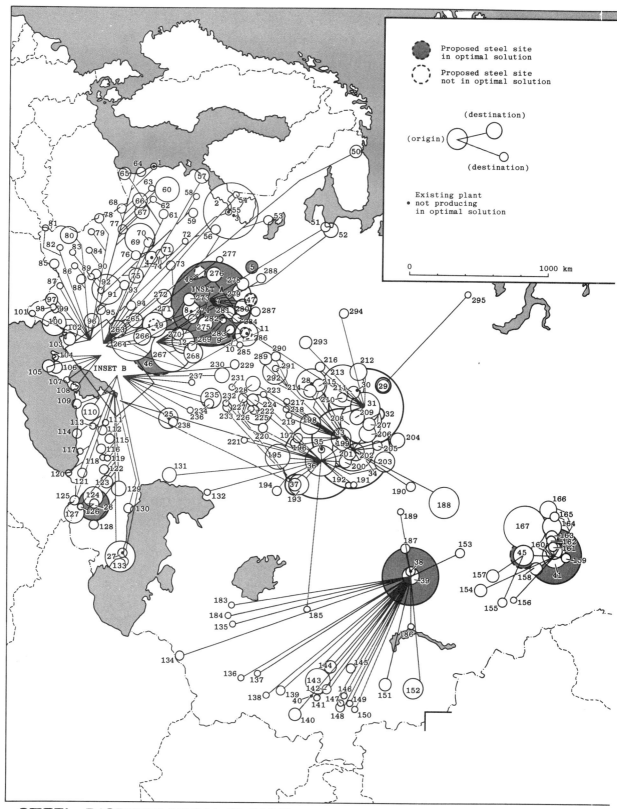

# STEEL DISTRIBUTION FLOWS
## Existing and Proposed Plants (50)

Figure 4

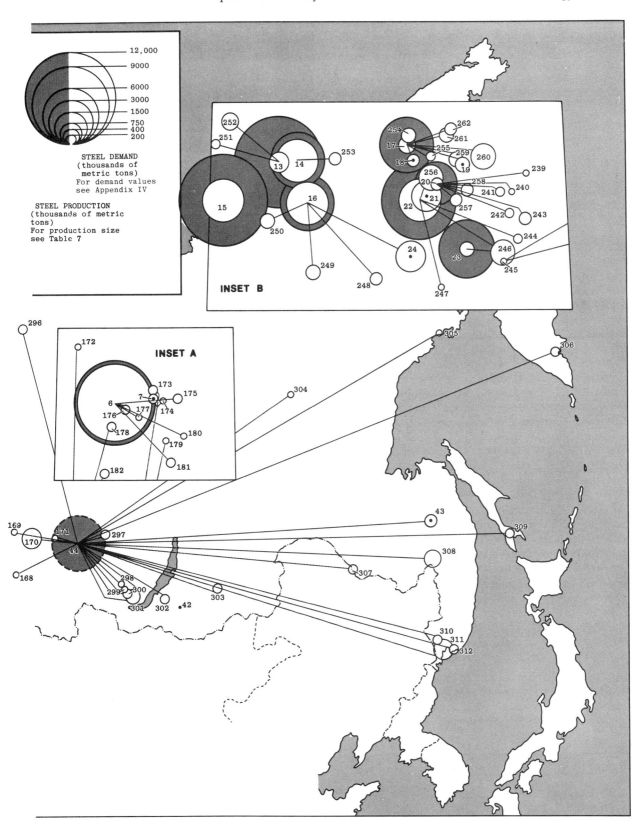

STEEL DEMAND
(thousands of
metric tons)
For demand values
see Appendix IV

STEEL PRODUCTION
(thousands of metric
tons)
For production size
see Table 7

INSET B

INSET A

TABLE 5
Model-Predicted Slack Activity: For Iron Ore

| Location (node number) | Unutilized Iron Ore Production ($10^3$ metric tons)[a] | |
| --- | --- | --- |
| | 43-node run[b] | 50-node run[c] |
| Kovdor (50) | 2,900* | 2,623 |
| Olenegorsk (51) | 5,100* | 5,100* |
| Komsomolsk (Ukr.) (54) | 2,600* | 0 |
| Krivoi Rog (15) | 36,773 | 39,650 |

*This quantity represents 100 percent of the 1970 ore production at this node.
[a]Model estimated production for all of the other 22 ore deposits is equal to their respective upper limits as shown in Table 1.
[b]See Figure 1.
[c]See Figure 3.

absorbs the surplus KMA production, thus precluding the present export shipments to CMEA countries and the three large Urals plants at Magnitogorsk, Chelyabinsk, and Novotroitsk.[30] Concurrently, then, Kola deposits are freed for possible export. Certainly surplus production in the Kola region would be conducive for the USSR's ore exports to Britain by sea through Murmansk.

With regard to coking coal and coke, the agreement between actual patterns of surplus production and exports is even closer. Similar to the case of iron ore, the constraint equating steel production with 1970 presumed domestic demand, the possible use of a high coking coal to coke conversion coefficient, and unaccounted for smelting uses at pig-iron-only furnaces and in nonferrous metallurgy combine to bring about coke surpluses which exceed the actual quantity exported in 1970. Nevertheless, the 43-node run suggests that the actual pattern of Soviet surpluses and exports tends strongly toward optimality. More specifically, as Table 6 reveals, approximately 60 percent of the optimal surpluses occur in the Donets Basin, the present source of virtually all Soviet coking coal and coke exports.[31] The model-predicted surplus at Novokuznetsk in reality is probably consumed by greater long-haul shipments to European steel centers plus use at pig-iron-only sites and nonferrous metallurgical sites in the Urals, Kuznetsk Basin, and Kazakhstan.

Interestingly enough, the 43-plant model indicates that the relatively cheap coke of Karaganda and Novokuznetsk can economically withstand long-haul shipping to

TABLE 6
Model-Predicted Slack Activity: For Coke

| Location (node number) | Unutilized Coke Production ($10^3$ metric tons)[a] | |
| --- | --- | --- |
| | 43-node run[b] | 50-node run[c] |
| Stakhanov (73) | 1,566 | 928 |
| Voroshilovgrad (75) | 1,400* | 0 |
| Shakhty (77) | 1,833 | 1,833 |
| Krasnodon (76) | 2,400* | 2,400* |
| Kemerovo (82) | 0 | 1,100 |
| Novokuznetsk (41) | 4,656 | 5,594 |

*This quantity represents 100 percent of the 1970 coke production at this node.
[a]Model estimated coke production for all of the other ten sites is equal to their respective upper limits as shown in Table 2.
[b]See Figure 1.
[c]See Figure 3.

Central Russia. However, in the 50-plant iteration which yields an overall system cost savings of 24.7 million rubles annually over the 43-plant run, only Karaganda coke remains competitive in European Russia west of the Urals. Concomitantly, the regional pattern of surplus coking coal (coke) production shifts eastward with the Kuznetsk Basin's share increasing from 40 to 56.5 percent while the Donets Basin's share is shown declining according to 43.5 percent. These regional shifts are congruent with Shabad's reasoned assessment that expanded Soviet coal and coking coal exports would have to be obtained from long-haul coals ". . . either directly for export or to compensate in the European USSR for any rise in coal shipments from the Donets Basin."[32] Furthermore, remembering that we have specified in the models that coking takes place at the minehead lends even more weight to the argument that if the Soviet steel industry were to tend toward greater optimality (from the perspective of satisfying domestic steel demand most cheaply), then a larger portion of the Donets Basin's coking coal and coke production would be utilized domestically.

This observation follows necessarily from two facts. First, while the assumption of coking at the minehead is by and large valid for the Donets region, it is less valid for the Karaganda and Kuznetsk basins and not true at all for the Pechora Basin (Vorkuta). Extensive coke batteries exist in the Urals (and at Moscow, Lipetsk, and Cherepovets) which means coking coal rather than coke must be shipped there, resulting in nearly double the transport costs calculated by the computer runs for flows originating in the Pechora, Karaganda, and Kuznetsk basins and destined for the Urals. Second, the backhaul cost savings once derived from the symbiotic transport relationship between surplus Urals iron ore moving to the Kuznetsk Basin in return for surplus Kuznetsk coking coal no longer exist as the Urals has both coking coal and iron ore deficits while the Karaganda and Kuznetsk plants still have inadequate local iron ore supplies.[33] Thus, if the actual Soviet logistics of the intermediate coking process had been imbedded into the model, then the economic-geographic range of Donets coking coal would have expanded and those of the other three basins would have been contracted.

An unequivocal decision as to whether or not the Soviets should expand their coking operations in the Karaganda and Kuznetsk basins relative to the Urals awaits a thorough investigation of the tradeoffs between potential transport savings and the sum of the required capital expenditures in the two eastern basins and the possible writeoff of some of the sunk costs of the large coke-chemical facilities operating in the Urals. Nonetheless, the "coke" production surpluses which eminate from our 50-plant run would be consistent with expanded exports to Japan provided Chinese-Japanese trade does not steal some of Siberia's and the BAM's thunder![34] At the same time, a comparison of the coking coal output performance between the Kuznetsk and Donets basins since 1970, and especially in light of the presumed absolute decline in the Donets output in 1978,[35] certainly agrees with the eastward shift indicated by the 50-plant run. Thus, the linear programming results as well as post-1970 Soviet performance both corroborate the Shabad citation that an eastward shift in Soviet coking coal is almost inevitable.

Although of less direct interest to this study, some discussion of the optimal steel production pattern is warranted because future industrial location developments manifested by the model runs would necessarily affect the spatial pattern of potential iron ore and coking coal export origins. Crude comparisons between the optimal locations and quantities of steel output calculated by the programming algorithm and the plant-by-plant estimates of actual steel production for 1970 are available in Table 7, final demand amounts in Appendix IV, and both on Figures 2 and 4. It should be noted that the 43 steel production sites chosen include only sites which produce steel. Thus, small ferrous metallurgy centers such as

TABLE 7
Model Predicted Optimal Steel Production (in $10^3$ metric tons)

| Location and Node Numbers on Maps 1–4 | 43-Plant Run | Estimated Difference between 43-Plant Run & Estimated Actual 1970 Production | 50-Plant Run | Estimated Difference between 50-Plant Run & Estimated Actual 1970 Production |
|---|---|---|---|---|
| Liepaja (1) | 0 | −400 | 0 | −400 |
| Leningrad (2) | 0 | −1,000 | 0 | −1,000 |
| Kolpino (3) | 0 | −1,000 | 0 | −1,000 |
| Mogilev (4) | 0 | −200 | 0 | −200 |
| Cherepovets (5) | 205 | −5,295 | 205 | −5,295 |
| Moscow (6) | 9,961 | +8,961 | 9,582 | +8,582 |
| Elektrostal (7) | 0 | −1,000 | 0 | −1,000 |
| Tula (8) | 0 | −1,000 | 0 | −1,000 |
| Vyksa (9) | 0 | −1,000 | 0 | −1,000 |
| Kulebaki (10) | 160 | −840 | 0 | −1,000 |
| Gorky (11) | 894 | −106 | 0 | −1,000 |
| Lipetsk (12) | 2,112 | −888 | 148 | −2,852 |
| Dneprodzerzhinsk (13) | 12,000 | +7,000 | 12,000 | +7,000 |
| Dnepropetrovsk (14) | 3,935 | −1,065 | 4,043 | −957 |
| Krivoi Rog (15) | 12,000 | +3,200 | 12,000 | +3,200 |
| Zaporozhye (16) | 4,558 | −442 | 4,558 | −442 |
| Kramatorsk (17) | 7,042 | +6,042 | 4,803 | +3,803 |
| Konstantinovka (18) | 0 | −1,000 | 0 | −1,000 |
| Kommunarsk (19) | 0 | −1,000 | 0 | −1,000 |
| Yenakiyevo (20) | 2,498 | +1,498 | 2,498 | +1,498 |
| Makeyevka (21) | 0 | −5,000 | 0 | −5,000 |
| Donetsk (22) | 7,022 | +2,022 | 7,022 | +2,022 |
| Taganrog (23) | 3,407 | +2,407 | 3,407 | +2,407 |
| Zhdanov (24)* | 0 | −10,600 | 0 | −10,600 |
| Volgograd (25) | 0 | −1,900 | 0 | −1,900 |
| Rustavi (26) | 1,037 | −363 | 1,037 | −363 |
| Sumgait (27) | 0 | −700 | 0 | −700 |
| Izhevsk (28) | 0 | −1,000 | 0 | −1,000 |
| Serov (29) | 148 | −852 | 379 | −621 |
| Chusovoi (30) | 0 | −1,000 | 0 | −1,000 |
| Nizhni Tagil (31) | 7,925 | +1,825 | 7,695 | +1,595 |
| Alapayevsk (32) | 296 | −704 | 296 | −704 |
| Zlatoust (33) | 3,333 | +1,333 | 3,333 | +1,333 |
| Chelyabinsk (34) | 8,024 | +3,224 | 7,815 | +3,015 |
| Beloretsk (35) | 0 | −1,000 | 0 | −1,000 |
| Magnitogorsk (36) | 6,666 | −5,634 | 6,666 | −5,634 |
| Novotroitsk (37) | 593 | −2,407 | 593 | −2,407 |
| Temirtau (38) | 0 | −100 | 0 | −100 |
| Karaganda (39) | 5,457 | +3,357 | 4,687 | +2,587 |
| Bekabad (40) | 0 | −1,000 | 0 | −1,000 |
| Novokuznetsk (41)* | 7,288 | −1,112 | 5,479 | −1,921 |
| Petrovsk-Zabaikalsky (42) | 2,341 | +1,341 | 0 | −1,000 |
| Komsomolsk-na-Amure (43) | 0 | −1,000 | 0 | −1,000 |
| Taishet (44) | NA | NA | 4,150 | +4,150 |
| Barnaul (45) | NA | NA | 979 | +979 |
| Stary Oskol (46) | NA | NA | 5,528 | +5,528 |
| Kostroma (47) | NA | NA | 0 | 0 |
| Rzhev (48) | NA | NA | 0 | 0 |
| Kursk (49) | NA | NA | 0 | 0 |
| Gorky (11) | NA | NA | 0 | 0 |

*Two plants.

Kosaya Gora (at Tula), Asha, and Almaznaya (at Stakhanov), which produce pig-iron only, were omitted from this preliminary study. In any subsequent investigation we would hope to be able to include explicitly not only the intermediate coking, enrichment, and pig-iron stages, but also technical input coefficients appropriate for the four different steel making processes used in the USSR, namely, open hearth, oxygen converter, electric arc, and the new direct reduction method.[36]

Because our computer simulations do not include the 7.0 million tons of steel exported, a column-by-column comparison of the regional steel production data contained in Table 8 is not straightforward. On the other hand, it seems quite reasonable to assume that the overwhelming fraction of Soviet steel exports originated at European Russian, Ukrainian, and Urals mills. Hence, assuming the Soviets are optimizers, production in these three regions should exceed that predicated by the L-P package, at least in the 43-plant run. This situation is true except for the Ukraine. Then, too, one must keep in mind that the high level of the Urals' actual steel production results from very sizable scrap steel contributions.[37]

Remaining cognizant of these qualifications, the correspondence between the actual regional production values and the predicted ones for the 43-node steel production system is quite good (see Table 8). These results lead us to conclude that on a broad regional scale the distribution of steel production in the Soviet Union tends towards optimality. Of course, our assumption of a uniform product means that the computer optimal transport costs are less than the real costs, even allowing for a minimum of cross-hauling resulting from different steel mill specializations and locational differences in final demand by product type. Again, such added model complexity is neither warranted by the nature of this study nor possible to operationalize due to data and cost con-

straints. Returning to the comparison, we also believe that the correspondence supports our method of arriving at point source demand figures for internal steel consumption.[38] The two notable discrepancies are European Russia and the Urals, but each has a plausible explanation.

By referring to Tables 3 and 7, one may discern that with the exception of Lipetsk and Cherepovets, all of the European plants outside the Ukraine are small. In addition, they are dependent on either long-haul coking coal from the north or east or expensive Donets coke. These plants serve relatively small markets except for Moscow, Leningrad, Gorky, and Minsk. The close proximity of the two weight-losing inputs, iron ore and coking coal, in the Ukraine could thus possibly yield additional net system transport savings. Accordingly, the model indicated that it would be cheaper to close most of these small plants in favor of large-scale output expansion at Moscow and long-haul steel distribution flows essentially from expanded Ukrainian production (see Table 7 and Figures 2 and 4). These implicit cost savings are evident despite the fact that the average production cost figure of 35 rubles per ton was used. In other words, the iterative or initial inclusion of values from the curvilinear production cost schedule of Table 4 according to the estimated size of existing plants in 1970 should have indicated even more strongly the weak competitive position of many of these small European installations. Their continued operation can only be justified by locational inertia, abundance of local scrap steel, and/or production of specialty steels. These are all factors not captured by our analysis. On the other hand, in an earlier and simpler programming analysis[39] in which Soviet coke imports from Poland were assigned to Grodno's node, Mogilev and Leningrad entered the final solution with outputs of 1.12 and 1.68 million metric tons, respectively. This assumption which better reflects the reality of 1970 would very likely have again produced a closer correlation between the actual and predicted spatial pattern of steel production than our current analyses do.

The discrepancy in the Urals, we believe, arises for two reasons. First, as previously mentioned, the Urals region makes considerable and, compared with the rest of the country, a disproportionate use of scrap steel inputs. As a result the region is able to smelt greater amounts of steel than our optimality models compute without resorting to as large volumes of distant iron ore and coking coal (coke) as our uniform technical production function would require. The size of the disparity and the admitted availability of scrap might hint that our demand estimating procedure underestimates demand in the Urals, especially because of the presumed high level of military goods manufactured in the area. While this may in fact be true, one must remember that we had available to us good Soviet regional steel consumption data.[40] Therefore, unless these Soviet demand data were deliberately falsified, we maintain that the discrepancy can be accounted for by the role of scrap and industrial inertia. More specifically, both computer iterations support the supposition that increasing iron ore deficits in the Urals concomitant with the loss of possible backhaul savings from the Urals-

TABLE 8
Regional Comparisons Between Optimal and (Estimated) Actual 1970 Steel Production (in $10^3$ metric tons)

| Region | Estimated Actual* | 43-plant run | 50-plant run |
|---|---|---|---|
| Baltic | 400 | 0 | 0 |
| Belorussia | 200 | 0 | 0 |
| European Russia | 18,400 | 13,332 | 15,463 |
| Ukraine[a] | 49,400[b] | 52,462 | 50,631 |
| Transcaucasia | 2,100 | 1,037 | 1,037 |
| Urals | 33,200[c] | 26,985 | 26,777 |
| Kazakhstan | 2,200 | 5,457 | 4,687 |
| Central Asia | 1,000 | 0 | 0 |
| West Siberia | 7,400 | 7,288 | 6,458 |
| East Siberia | 1,000 | 2,341 | 4,150 |
| Far East | 1,000 | 0 | 0 |
| Total | 116,300* | 108,902[†] | 108,902[†] |

*Column values were obtained by simply aggregating the crude nodal estimates from Table 3. Thus, the column sum exceeds the actual 1970 production by approximately 400,000 metric tons.
[†]Excludes steel exports.
[a]Includes the Taganrog steel mill.
[b]This estimate is approximately 2.8 million tons over 1970 regional data.
[c]This estimate is approximately 2.8 million tons under 1970 regional data.

Kuznetsk Combine have made Urals' steel relatively more expensive over time. Nonetheless, industrial inertia—the material, labor and time costs of building new complexes or expanding existing ones possessing locational advantages combined with overall costs of scaling down or closing steel-making facilities—may for extended periods of time overshadow the potential transport savings generated by the modified spatial pattern of our essentially static model. Certainly the previously mentioned cost savings of 24.7 million rubles annually of the 50-plant solution over the 43-plant one are relatively small in comparison to the conversion costs which would be involved.[41] On the other hand, the question for Soviet planners is not really a static one of how to most cheaply produce 108.9 million tons (or 115.9 million tons) of steel annually, but rather the dynamic question of how to most cost-effectively and rapidly expand Soviet steel production. The optimistic assessments of the early seventies had steel targets as high as 275 million tons of steel annually by 1980.[42] However, the actual 1980 production of 147.9 million tons was 3.6 million tons less than the 1978 peak production year level of 151.5 million metric tons. Output recovered slightly to 148.6 million tons in 1981, but dropped off again in 1982 to some 147 million tons.[43] Within the context of determining sites for such possible expansion to take place, even our static models can be useful. Reference back to Table 7 and Figures 2 and 4 will assist us in this task of shedding some light on possible future Soviet geographic development policies in the iron and steel industry.

Taking heed of the various qualifications we have advanced, we would cautiously argue that Soviet regional steel production in 1970 tends toward optimality. Disaggregating to the scale of individual plants, however, leads one to conclude that production within regions tends to suboptimality. Comparisons on a plant-by-plant basis reveal considerable correspondence between the model results and the estimated 1970 production figures. For example, with three exceptions, Volgograd, Makeyevka, and Zhdanov, actual plants which drop out of the analysis are of relatively small capacity, equal to or less than 1 million metric tons. Our contention is that the consistent deletion of these small plants from both runs suggests they are uneconomical, and hence, unreaped economies of scale still exist within the production system, especially at the *within* region scale. Consideration of curvilinear production costs would, of course, strengthen our argument even more.

The failure of the intermediate-sized Volgograd plant (1.9 million tons actual production) to enter either of the solutions is not terribly surprising considering its geographical situation distant from both raw materials and large markets. More noteworthy are the absences of Makeyevka (5.0 million tons in 1970) and the two Zhdanov mills (combined production 10.6 million tons in 1970) in both of the optimal solutions. These outcomes seem rather odd given the fact that both sites are located in the southeast Ukraine where both computer runs indicate optimal regional values exceeding the actual one for 1970. Closer inspection of Table 7, and Figures 2 and 4, however, reveals that expanded production at nearby Yena-

kiyevo and Donetsk offsets 70 percent of the implied loss of Makeyevka. Also, more distant Kramatorsk's expansion may be both a cause of as well as an effect of Makeyevka's disappearance.

The demise of the Zhdanov mills is more problematic. The coastal Taganrog plant makes up for slightly less than one-fourth of the Zhdanov losses. Two other explanations seem to have merit. First, considering the regional demand structure, other locations such as Taganrog and Zaporozhye are better situated. Apparently when assembly costs are also taken into account Zhdanov loses out to several other Ukrainian plants. Second, the port of Zhdanov quite plausibly would have appeared in an optimal solution which included both steel produced for exports and export destinations.

There are two additional big losers, Cherepovets and Magnitogorsk. The Cherepovets case has already been explored, while the huge indicated reduction at the latter Urals' giant merely reflects the economic reality of increased long-haul costs of coking coal and Kazakh ores to replace locally depleted raw materials. The economic rationale for continued expansion of the increasingly obsolete Magnitogorsk location (15.8 million tons for the 1979 plant)[44] is certainly not obvious. Again, possibly industrial inertia, growth in local demand, scale economies and/or agglomeration economies not accounted for in our model formulation can explain the continued Soviet love affair with Magnitogorsk.

It seems quite easy to account for all the indicated foci of expanded output. The Moscow case as already cited is clearly an example of market-pull, while Krivoi Rog and Karaganda expansions represent raw-materials pulls. The other potentially large expansions—Kramatorsk, Nizhni Tagil, Chelyabinsk, Taganrog, Donetsk, and Dneprodzerzhinsk—seem based on varying combinations of extractive, assembly, and distribution cost advantages.

A concise comparison between the predicted plant sizes and market areas of the two optimal solutions is all that remains on the discussion agenda (see Table 7 and Appendix IV).[45] Overall the stability and congruence between both computed plant sizes and market regions are striking. The nineteen sites which fail to enter the 43-plant solution also fail to produce in the 50-plant solution. In the 50-plant run production at three additional plants disappears—Kulebaki, Gorky, and Petrovsk-Zabaikalsky. What happens to the proposed sites is, of course, of greater relevance.

Of the seven proposed sites three emerge as producing centers in the 50-plant optimal solution. Most significant, Stary Oskol, the location of the direct-reduction method steel mill currently under construction, enters the solution in a very substantial way—5.5 million metric tons making it the eighth largest producing facility in the optimal system. Barnaul in West Siberia and Taishet in East Siberia also appear as optimal locations for steel centers. These additions naturally are the ultimate cause of changes in the commodity flow patterns of final steel demand between the two simulations. Kulebaki's and Gorky's markets are subsumed by Moscow's and Nizhni Tagil's. Stary Oskol's market impinges on Kramatorsk's to the south and Moscow's and Lipetsk's to the north and northeast, respectively. In the east Taishet completely absorbs Petrovsk-Zabaikalsky's role, while making inroads into the markets of the two West Siberian mills and releasing pressure on the Urals to supply Norilsk and Yakutsk. The Novokuznetsk and Karaganda plants all have their outputs reduced and their market areas contracted by the interstitial location of Barnaul between them. Nonetheless, Karaganda's indicated production is still 2.6 million tons above its actual one in 1970, thereby strengthening its position as an economically rational site for expanded steel production.

## Summary and Conclusions

Reflecting back on our stated objectives, what tentative conclusions can be drawn from this investigation? We are interested in what the Soviets can, should and likely will do under their modus operandi of ever greater concern for cost effectiveness. While the linear programming model can yield results of the "should" type, other descriptive empirical evidence must be brought to bear on the "can" and "likely will do" questions. Without undue repetition from the forthcoming iron ore and coking coal commodity studies,[46] it is critical to place our results against the background of major Soviet developments in the iron and steel industry which either have occurred since 1970 or are now planned for the future.

Because our model is static and we are really interested in a dynamic process, it is far more appealing from a practical point of view to focus attention on locations, especially the optimal plant locations and sizes, where expansions are predicted than on these where closures are indicated. This is true because expanding demand for steel and the historic Soviet policy of excessively long capital depreciation policies augur strongly for continued production at plants which are economically obsolete. Accordingly, we will first review the regional changes in actual Soviet steel production since 1970 against the results of our model run and use this information in turn to aid in our interpretation of the actual post-1970 changes in the pattern of Soviet iron ore and coking coal production against those suggested by our simulations.

The 43-plant model predicated larger steel output increases for Moscow, Dneprodzerzhinsk, Krivoi Rog, Kramatorsk, Chelyabinsk, and Karaganda, and large decreases for Cherepovets, Makeyevka, Zhdanov, and Magnitogorsk. The 50-plant run was very close except for Moscow and Kramatorsk where increases were smaller than expected as a result of the entry of the Stary Oskol site. Similarly the indicated increase at Karaganda was dampened by new production at Barnaul, while optimal West Siberian production was diminished still further by the theoretical production at Barnaul and Taishet. In point of fact, steel production has expanded significantly, not only at Dneprodzerzhinsk, Krivoi Rog, Chelyabinsk, Karaganda, and Nizhni Tagil, but at Cherepovets, Lipetsk, Zhdanov, Magnitogorsk, and the West Siberian plant as well. It is these latter five expansions that merit cursory discussion.

To really understand these departures from the linear programming results, one has to consider, of course, changes during the seventies in the distribution of Soviet iron ore and coking coal production. The major stories in the iron ore industry have been the 2.2-fold increase in KMA production between 1970 and 1980 (Chapter 19, Table 7) and the large absolute increase in the Ukraine. Meanwhile, growth has been slow in the Kola district, modest in Kazakhstan, and stagnant in the Urals and Siberia.[47] Although still dominant, Donets coking coal production has been essentially static. The largest increases have been in the Kuznetsk Basin which implicitly agrees nicely with our simulation results. Small increases have occurred in Kazakhstan and the Pechora Basin.[48]

Accordingly, then, the KMA ore and Pechora coking coal expansion have permitted the expanded production at both Cherepovets and Lipetsk. Since it appears very unlikely to us that the Soviets will expand the steelmaking role of Moscow due to concerns over environmental quality and "excessive" urban growth, we perceive the growth at Cherepovets and Lipetsk as clear examples of second-best choices. We are confident that, had we built in low output constraints on the Moscow and Elektrostal plants, Moscow's large predicted expansion would have shifted to these two other European steel centers.

Furthermore, the large KMA expansion has been directly instrumental in the expanded steel production in the Urals, especially at Magnitogorsk, Chelyabinsk, and Novotroitsk and possibly even indirectly at the West Siberian mill by freeing up some of the Rudny ores for shipment to the Kuznetsk mills.[49] On the other hand, the Zhdanov expansions are more difficult to reconcile with our model results. Perhaps, the answer lies in a scarcity of steel plate,[50] the export market, and expanded Krivoi Rog ore production.

In summary, then, the modeling results either explicitly or implicitly contain significant ex post facto explanations for most of the geographical changes in the Soviet iron and steel industry which have occurred during the seventies. Iron ore exports will continue to originate from the European USSR for a long time, while coking coal production and export potential will continue to shift eastward.[51] During the eighties we expect to see expanded coking facilities in the Asiatic USSR in order to reduce the large westward coking coal flows.[52] The soundness of the Soviet decision to develop a major steelmaking complex at Stary Oskol clearly seems above reproach. While the Barnaul site may remain dormant, we fully expect to see construction activity revived in Taishet during the eighties. Of final interest is the fact that the 24.7 million rubles net savings of the 50-plant run over the 43-plant run were achieved despite 166,000 rubles higher iron ore extraction costs and 26,600,200 rubles higher coke costs. Implicit in this result is the economic reality of the Soviet Union's vastness and its chronic long-haul transportation problems. More interesting, perhaps, is the real albeit modest hidden Soviet subsidy of the East European iron and steel industry implicit in this result. In other words, if the Soviet Union were to produce steel for its own domestic consumption in the cheapest manner, (i.e., defined here as the mode exemplified by the 50-plant rather than the 43-plant simulation) then its predicted coking coal reserves (see Table 6) would not be located as close to the CMEA coking coal export markets. In fact, if our model had been formulated to minimize the total cost of Soviet steel production (i.e., domestic plus export demand), the increases in steel production presumably would have occurred primarily in the European part of the Soviet Union. As a result, the relative share of the predicted coking coal reserves in the CMEA adjacent areas would have declined even more.

Although it would be interesting to update[53] and expand this study, much more important is the fact that the results of these linear programming models both corroborate and extend the implications drawn from a host of less formal, but nonetheless empirically based, research efforts in this volume.

## NOTES

1. For a concise review of the Soviet debate over interdependence versus autarky see Marshall I. Goldman, "Autarky or Integration—the USSR and the World Economy," in U.S. Congress, Joint Economic Committee, *Soviet Economy in a New Perspective*, 94th Cong., 2nd sess., 1976, pp. 81–96; and Marshall I. Goldman, *The Changing Role of Raw Material Exports and Soviet Foreign Trade*, Discussion Paper No. 8 (June 1979), Association of American Geographers, Project on Soviet Natural Resources in the World Economy, pp. 44–52.

2. For example, see Goldman, *Raw Material Exports*, pp. 1–44, and Edward H. Hewett, *Soviet Primary Product Exports to CMEA and the West*, Discussion Paper No. 9 (May 1979), Association of American Geographers, Project on Soviet Natural Resources in the World Economy, pp. 1–46.

3. Goldman, *Raw Material Exports*, p. 17.

4. For example, see Goldman, *Raw Material Exports*, pp. 30–43; Leslie Dienes and Theodore Shabad, *The Soviet Energy System* (Washington: Scripta, 1979), pp. 217–94; Leslie Dienes, *Soviet Energy Policy and the Hydrocarbons*, Discussion Paper No. 2 (April 1978), Association of American Geographers, Project on Soviet Natural Resources in the World Economy; Leslie Dienes, "The Soviet Union: An Energy Crunch Ahead?," *Problems of Communism*, 26, no. 5 (September-October 1977): 41–60; Leslie Dienes, "Soviet Energy Resources and Prospects," *Current History*, March 1978; Robert Campbell, "Implications for the Soviet Economy of Soviet Energy Prospects," *The ACES Bulletin*, Spring 1978, pp. 37–52; Robert Campbell, *Soviet Energy R & D: Goals, Planning and Organization* (Rand Corporation: R-2253-DOE, May 1978); Robert Campbell, *Soviet Energy Balances* (Rand Corporation: R-2257-DOE, October 1978); Arthur W. Wright, "The Soviet Union in World Energy Markets," in Edward W. Erickson and Leonard Waserman, eds., *The Energy Question: An International Failure of Policy*, 1 (Toronto: University of Toronto Press, 1974); *Prospects for Soviet Oil Production*, ER-77-10270 (Washington: U.S. CIA, April 1977); *Prospects for Soviet Oil Production: A Supplementary*

*Analysis*, ER-77-10425 (Washington: U.S. CIA, June 1977); and U.S. Congress, Senate, Select Committee on Intelligence, *The Soviet Oil Situation: An Evaluation of CIA Analyses of Soviet Oil Production*, 95th Cong., 2nd sess., 1978, p. 15.

5. For reserve figures of KMA (Kursk Magnetic Anomaly), see Ye. I. Kapitonov, "The Kursk Magnetic Anomaly and Its Development," *Soviet Geography: Review and Translation* (hereafter *SGRT*), 4, no. 5 (May 1963): 10–15; and V. P. Korostik, "Comparative Analysis of the Iron-Ore Basins of Krivoi Rog and the Kursk Magnetic Anomaly," *SGRT*, 20, no. 4 (April 1979): 225–30.

6. For examples of coal and especially coking coal reserves, see Dienes and Shabad, *Soviet Energy System*, pp. 106, 121–24; and Ian F. Elliot, *The Soviet Energy Balance* (New York: Praeger Publishers, 1974), pp. 122–75.

7. Hewett, *Soviet Primary Product Exports*, p. 55, and Theodore Shabad, "Soviet Regional Policy and CMEA Integration," *SGRT*, 20, no. 4 (April 1979): 237, 240–44.

8. Dienes and Shabad, *Soviet Energy System*, p. 123.

9. *Pravda*, 3 April 1978, p. 2.

10. Because our model only utilizes average steel production costs rather than using a nonlinear production function combined with the fact that this Soviet value (35 rubles per metric ton) may not incorporate all amortization costs of these hypothetical new plants, the model-predicted closures, expansions, contractions, and additions must be considered suggestive rather than definitive.

11. Primary sources for this transport system were *Skhema zheleznykh dorog SSSR* [Railroad atlas of USSR] (Moscow: Ministerstvo putei soobshcheniya SSSR, 1972) and *Atlas SSSR* (Moscow: Glavnoye upravleniye geodezii i kartografii pri Sovete Ministrov SSSR, 1969), pp. 102–03. Surface routes were included only to link cities over 65,000 in 1970 not having railroad connections.

12. *Transport i svyaz SSSR* [Transport and communications of the USSR] (Moscow: Transport, 1972), pp. 50–51, 58–59, 96–97, 144–45.

13. *Transport i svyaz SSSR*, pp. 111, 151, and 187. The 0.2 rate for waterborne transit essentially amounts to the average of the 0.245 k/t-km for river transit and 0.146 k/t-km for sea transit. The 0.8 k/t-km is a reasonably assumed figure which has essentially no impact on the outcome of the analysis because of the small number of links involved (k/t-km—kopecks/ton-kilometer).

14. The numbers in parentheses refer to these plant locations on Figures 3 and 4.

15. Shabad, "Soviet Regional Policy," p. 243, and *Pravda*, 31 January 1975.

16. A. T. Khrushchev, "The Formation of the Industrial Complex of the Kursk Magnetic Anomaly," *SGRT*, 16, no. 4 (April 1975): 247.

17. Shabad, "Soviet Regional Policy," p. 243.

18. Although these data are a bit old (1964) for 1970 application, they represent the most recent cost data that we found.

19. *Narodnoye khozyaistvo SSSR v 1970 g.* [Economy of the USSR in 1970] (Moscow: Statistika, 1971), pp. 191 and 616.

20. N. D. Lelyukhina, *Ekonomicheskaya effektivnost raz-*

*meshcheniya chernoi metallurgii* [Cost-effectiveness of location of the iron and steel industry] (Moscow: Nauka, 1973), p. 22.

21. For city sizes, see *Narodnoye khozyaistvo SSSR v 1970 g.*, pp. 37–45. Cities over 65,000 in the Moscow conurbation not included as demand nodes in Appendix IV have had their population added to that of Moscow city proper.

22. For urban employment data by sectors, see Chauncy Harris, *Cities of the Soviet Union* (Chicago: Rand McNally and Co., 1970), pp. 70–78.

23. V. V. Kistanov and A. A. Epshtein, "Problem of Optimal Location of an Industrial Complex," *SGRT*, 13, no. 3 (March 1972): 144.

24. M. Kh. Gankin, V. A. Petruchik, and V. M. Fomin, eds., *Perevozki gruzov* [Freight hauls] (Moscow: Transport, 1972), p. 120.

25. To be specific, the actual 1970 Soviet coking coal production of 164.8 million metric tons was deflated to yield 76.8 million tons of coke. Thus, point-source coking coal figures were multiplied by 46.6 percent to obtain the corresponding coke figures. Accordingly, $0.466 \times 1.30 = 0.606$, which is quite close to our value of 0.63. At this point, we would probably have to argue that the larger iron ore coefficient should be used in any subsequent analyses and sensitivity runs. The net result of having used the smaller coefficient, of course, is that iron ore reserves are larger; however, the distribution patterns of reserves remain unchanged.

26. For the argument justifying the ubiquitousness and/or minor cost differential significance of these raw materials, see Allan Rodgers, "Industrial Inertia: A Major Factor in the Location of the Steel Industry in the U.S.," *Geographical Review*, 42 (January 1952): 57.

27. See Martin J. Beckmann and Thomas Marschak, "An Activity Analysis Approach to Location Theory," *Kyklos*, 8 (1955): 125–43.

28. For example, see Z. P. Tsimdina, T. Ya. Serezhenko, G. H. Bukina and N. S. Miter, *Modelirovaniye razvitiya i razmeshcheniya proizvodstva v chernoi metallurgii* [Modeling of the development and location of production in the iron and steel industry] (Novosibirsk: Nauka, 1977).

29. Shabad, "Soviet Regional Policy," p. 241.

30. Shabad, "News Notes," *SGRT*, 20, no. 4 (April 1979): 270; and V. P. Korostik, "Comparative Analysis," p. 228.

31. Shabad, "Soviet Regional Policy," p. 237.

32. Ibid., p. 237.

33. Shabad, "News Notes," *SGRT*, 20, no. 4 (April 1979): 261–65, 269–72.

34. "We Won't Be Shanghaied," *The Economist*, 21 July 1979, p. 81; and Shabad, "News Notes," *SGRT*, 16, no. 2 (February 1975): 124.

35. Shabad, "News Notes," *SGRT*, 20, no. 4 (April 1979): 262.

36. Other modeling goals would include back-hauling commodity differentiated transport rates, piece-wise linear approximations of the different Soviet steel production functions, addition of alloying raw material inputs, etc. Although laudable, such sophistication seems unwarranted except for systematic investment planning studies initiated within the Ministry of Ferrous Metallurgy USSR.

37. Shabad, "News Notes," *SGRT*, 20, no. 4 (April 1979): 272.

38. The decision to include only cities equal to or greater than 65,000 was predicated first on the availability of sectoral employment data for these size cities (see Harris, *Cities of Soviet Union*, pp. 70–78) and second on computer costs.

39. Craig ZumBrunnen, Jeffrey Osleeb and Charles Morrow-Jones, "West Versus East: The KMA and an Evaluation of the Possible Future Geographical Distribution of Soviet Steel Production" (Paper presented at Annual Meeting, Association of American Geographers, New York, April 1976), pp. 21–22.

40. Lelyukhina, *Ekonomicheskaya effektivnost*, p. 22.

41. Computer costs and time prevented us from doing a third run in which the 43 plant sites would have been assigned individual production values equal to the estimates of their respective 1970 outputs. Such a sensitivity analysis would have allowed us to make a comparison of the total system costs of a system similar to the Soviet Union's actual 1970 pattern minus the cross-hauls, etc., with that of our two optimal solutions.

42. Shabad, "News Notes," *SGRT*, 21, no. 4 (April 1980): 252.

43. Ibid., p. 255 and Shabad, "News Notes," *SGRT*, 22, no. 4 (April 1981): 289; also *SGRT*, 23, no. 4 (April 1982): 296.

44. Shabad, "News Notes," *SGRT*, 20, no. 4 (April 1979): 271.

45. Appendix IV includes only the demand nodes and their amounts. The model-predicted final demand flow data are available in Craig ZumBrunnen, Jeffrey Osleeb, and Charles Morrow-Jones, *Modeling the Optimal Commodity Flow Within Soviet Ferrous Metallurgy: Implications for Soviet Iron Ore and Coking Coal Exports*, Discussion Paper No. 14 (October 1979), Association of American Geographers, Project on Soviet Natural Resources in the World Economy, pp. 46–57.

46. Shabad, "News Notes," *SGRT*, 20, no. 4 (April 1979): 271–72; Shabad, "News Notes," *SGRT*, 17, no. 5 (May 1976): 347–48; 18, no. 4 (April 1977): 280–81; and 18, no. 9 (November 1977): 703.

47. Shabad, "News Notes," *SGRT*, 20, no. 4 (April 1979): 269–70.

48. Ibid., pp. 261–65.

49. Ibid., p. 270.

50. Shabad, "News Notes," *SGRT*, 18, no. 4 (April 1977): 280–81.

51. Shabad, "News Notes," *SGRT*, 20, no. 4 (April 1979): 265.

52. Dienes and Shabad, *Soviet Energy System*, pp. 123–24; Shabad, "News Notes," *SGRT*, 18, no. 9 (November 1977): 703.

53. For example, see Shabad's discussion of revised Soviet iron ore pricing, "News Notes," *SGRT*, 16, no. (June 1975): 413–16.

# APPENDIX I

$$\min Z = \sum_{i=1}^{n} \sum_{j=1}^{m} (C_i^I + t_{ij}^I) X_{ij}^I + \sum_{k=1}^{p} \sum_{j=1}^{m} (C_k^c + t_{kj}^c) X_{kj}^c +$$

$$\sum_{j=1}^{m} \sum_{d=1}^{q} C_j^* X_{jd}^* + \sum_{j=1}^{m} \sum_{d=1}^{q} t_{jd}^* X_{jd}^* \qquad (1)$$

Subject to:

$$\sum_{j=1}^{m} X_{ij}^I \le S_i^I \quad v_i \qquad (2)$$

$$\sum_{j=1}^{m} X_{kj}^c \le \Sigma S_k^c \quad v_k \qquad (3)$$

$$\sum_{j=1}^{m} \sum_{d=1}^{q} X_{jd}^* = \sum_{d=1}^{q} D_d \qquad (4)$$

$$\sum_{i=1}^{n} X_{ij}^I - \alpha_j^I \sum_{d=1}^{q} X_{jd}^* = 0, \ \sum_{k=1}^{p} X_{kj}^c - \alpha_j^c \sum_{d=1}^{q} X_{jd}^* = 0 \qquad (5 \ \& \ 6)$$

$$x_j^* \ge K_j^L \quad v_j \qquad (7)$$

$$x_j^* \le K_j^U \quad v_j \qquad (8)$$

$$x_{ij}^I, X_{kj}^c, X_{jd}^* \ge 0 \quad v_{i,j,k,d} \qquad (9)$$

Where:

$C_i^I$ = the extraction cost of iron ore at the $i^{th}$ location

$t_{ij}^I$ = the transportation cost for iron ore between the $i^{th}$ iron ore site and the $j^{th}$ steel plant

$X_{ij}^I$ = the quantity of iron ore shipped between the $i^{th}$ iron ore site and the $j^{th}$ steel plant

$C_k^c$ = the extraction cost of coal at the $k^{th}$ location

$t_{kj}^c$ = the transportation cost for coal between the $k^{th}$ coal site and the $j^{th}$ steel plant

$X_{kj}^c$ = the quantity of coal shipped between the $k^{th}$ coal site and the $j^{th}$ steel plant

$C_j^*$ = production costs at the $j^{th}$ steel plant

$X_{jd}^*$ = the quantity of steel shipped from the $j^{th}$ steel plant to the $d^{th}$ demand point

$t_{jd}^*$ = the transportation cost between the $j^{th}$ steel plant and the $d^{th}$ demand point

$S_i^I$ = the supply of iron ore at the $i^{th}$ iron ore site

$S_k^c$ = the supply of coal at the $k^{th}$ coal site

$D_d$ = the total demand for steel at the $d^{th}$ demand point

$\alpha_j^I$ = the input coefficient for iron ore at the $j^{th}$ steel plant = 1.35

$\alpha_j^c$ = the input coefficient for coal at the $j^{th}$ steel plant = 0.63

$K_j^L$ = the lower limit or threshold size of the $j^{th}$ steel plant = 50 thousand metric tons

$K_j^U$ = the upper limit of the size of the $j^{th}$ steel plant = 12 million metric tons

# APPENDIX II
## IRON ORE FLOWS

| From: Iron Ore Site (Node #)* | 43 Plant Run | | 50 Plant Run | |
|---|---|---|---|---|
| | To: Steel Plant (Node #)* | Quantity ($10^3$ metric tons) | To: Steel Plant (Node #) | Quantity ($10^3$ metric tons) |
| Kovdor (50) | — | — | Cherepovets (5) | 277 |
| Olenegorsk (51) | — | — | — | — |
| Tula (8) | — | — | Moscow (6) | 200 |
| | Gorky (11) | 200 | — | — |
| Lipetsk (12) | Lipetsk (12) | 200 | Lipetsk (12) | 200 |
| Zheleznogorsk (52) | Cherepovets (5) | 277 | — | — |
| | Moscow (6) | 5,323 | Moscow (6) | 5,600 |
| Gubkin (53) | Moscow (6) | 8,125 | Moscow (6) | 4,537 |
| | Kulebaki (10) | 216 | — | — |
| | Gorky (11) | 1,007 | — | — |
| | Lipetsk (12) | 2,651 | — | — |
| | — | — | Stary Oskol (46) | 7,463 |
| Komsomolsk (Ukr.) (54) | — | — | Moscow (6) | 2,600 |
| Krivoi Rog (15) | Krivoi Rog (15) | 16,201 | Krivoi Rog (15) | 16,201 |
| | Dneprodzerzhinsk (13) | 16,201 | Dneprodzerzhinsk (13) | 16,201 |
| | Dnepropetrovsk (14) | 5,312 | Dnepropetrovsk (14) | 5,458 |
| | Zaporozhye (16) | 6,154 | Zaporozhye (16) | 6,154 |
| | Kramatorsk (17) | 9,507 | Kramatorsk (17) | 6,484 |
| | Yenakiyevo (20) | 3,372 | Yenakiyevo (20) | 3,372 |
| | Donetsk (22) | 9,280 | Donetsk (22) | 9,280 |
| Dneprorudnoye (55) | Donetsk (22) | 200 | Donetsk (22) | 200 |
| Kerch (56) | Taganrog (23) | 4,600 | Taganrog (23) | 4,600 |
| Dashkesan (57) | Rustavi (26) | 1,400 | Rustavi (26) | 1,400 |
| Ivdel (58) | Serov (29) | 200 | Serov (29) | 200 |
| Kachkanar (59) | — | — | Serov (29) | 312 |
| | Nizhni Tagil (31) | 2,300 | Nizhni Tagil (31) | 1,988 |
| Kushva-Blagodat (60) | Nizhni Tagil (31) | 5,900 | Nizhni Tagil (31) | 5,900 |
| Vysokaya (61) | Nizhni Tagil (31) | 2,500 | Nizhni Tagil (31) | 2,500 |
| Alapayevsk (32) | Alapayevsk (32) | 400 | Alapayevsk (32) | 400 |
| Bakal (62) | Zlatoust (33) | 4,500 | Zlatoust (33) | 4,500 |
| Magnitogorsk (36) | Magnitogorsk (36) | 9,000 | Magnitogorsk (36) | 9,000 |

## APPENDIX II (*cont.*)

| From: Iron Ore Site (Node #)* | 43 Plant Run | | 50 Plant Run | |
|---|---|---|---|---|
| | To: Steel Plant (Node #)* | Quantity ($10^3$ metric tons) | To: Steel Plant (Node #) | Quantity ($10^3$ metric tons) |
| Rudny (63) | Chelyabinsk (34) | 10,833 | Chelyabinsk (34) | 10,551 |
| | Karaganda (38) | 4,167 | Karaganda (38) | 3,328 |
| | — | — | Barnaul (45) | 1,122 |
| Lisakovsk (64) | Karaganda (38) | 200 | — | — |
| | — | — | Barnaul (45) | 200 |
| Novotroitsk (65) | Novotroitsk (37) | 800 | Novotroitsk (37) | 800 |
| Karazhal (66) | Karaganda (38) | 3,000 | Karaganda (38) | 3,000 |
| Gornaya Shoriya (67) | Novokuznetsk (41) | 5,000 | Novokuznetsk (41) | 5,000 |
| Abaza (68) | Novokuznetsk (41) | 2,000 | Novokuznetsk (41) | 2,000 |
| Zheleznogorsk-Ilimsky (69) | Novokuznetsk (41) | 2,839 | Novokuznetsk (41) | 397 |
| | Petrovsk-Zabaikalsky (42) | 3,161 | — | — |
| | — | — | Taishet (44) | 5,603 |

*Node numbers refer to Figures 1 and 3.

## APPENDIX III
## COKE FLOWS

| From: Coke Site (Node #)* | 43 Plant Run | | 50 Plant Run | |
|---|---|---|---|---|
| | To: Steel Plant (Node #)* | Quantity ($10^3$ metric tons) | To: Steel Plant (Node #) | Quantity ($10^3$ metric tons) |
| Vorkuta (80) | Cherepovets (5) | 123 | Cherepovets (5) | 123 |
| | Moscow (6) | 5,977 | Moscow (6) | 5,750 |
| | — | — | Serov (29) | 227 |
| Pavlograd (70) | Dnepropetrovsk (14) | 1,900 | Dnepropetrovsk (14) | 1,900 |
| Krasnoarmeisk (71) | Dneprodzerzhinsk (13) | 3,939 | Dneprodzerzhinsk (13) | 3,126 |
| | Dnepropetrovsk (14) | 461 | Dnepropetrovsk (14) | 526 |
| | — | — | Krivoi Rog (15) | 748 |
| Donetsk-Makeyevka (22) | Donetsk (22) | 4,213 | Donetsk (22) | 4,213 |
| | Krivoi Rog (15) | 6,452 | Krivoi Rog (15) | 6,452 |
| | Zaporozhye (16) | 2,739 | Zaporozhye (18) | 2,735 |
| Shakhtersk (74) | Taganrog (23) | 100 | Taganrog (23) | 100 |
| Artemovsk (72) | Dneprodzerzhinsk (13) | 426 | Dneprodzerzhinsk (13) | 2,518 |
| | Krivoi Rog (15) | 748 | — | — |
| | Kramatorsk (17) | 4,225 | Kramatorsk (17) | 2,882 |
| Stakhanov (73) | Dneprodzerzhinsk (13) | 2,835 | Dneprodzerzhinsk (13) | 1,556 |
| | Yenakiyevo (20) | 1,499 | Yenakiyevo (20) | 1,499 |
| | — | — | Stary Oskol (46) | 1,917 |
| Voroshilovgrad (75) | — | — | Stary Oskol (46) | 1,400 |
| Shakhty (77) | Taganrog (23) | 1,767 | Taganrog (23) | 1,767 |
| Krasnodon (76) | — | — | — | — |
| Tkvarcheli (78) | Taganrog (23) | 178 | Taganrog (23) | 178 |
| | Rustavi (26) | 222 | Rustavi (26) | 222 |
| Tkibuli (79) | Rustavi (26) | 400 | Rustavi (26) | 400 |
| Kizel (81) | Nizhni Tagil (31) | 1,100 | Nizhni Tagil (31) | 1,100 |
| Karaganda (38) | Karaganda (38) | 3,274 | Karaganda (38) | 3,274 |
| | Lipetsk (12) | 570 | Lipetsk (12) | 89 |
| | — | — | Chelyabinsk (34) | 943 |
| | Magnitogorsk (36) | 4,000 | Magnitogorsk (36) | 4,000 |
| | Novotroitsk (37) | 356 | Novotroitsk (37) | 356 |
| Kemerovo (82) | Nizhni Tagil (31) | 2,303 | Nizhni Tagil (31) | 3,517 |
| | Lipetsk (12) | 697 | — | — |
| | — | — | Alapayevsk (32) | 178 |
| | Zlatoust (33) | 2,000 | Zlatoust (33) | 205 |

## APPENDIX III (cont.)

| From: Iron Ore Site (Node #)* | 43 Plant Run | | | 50 Plant Run | |
|---|---|---|---|---|---|
| | To: Steel Plant (Node #)* | Quantity ($10^3$ metric tons) | | To: Steel Plant (Node #) | Quantity ($10^3$ metric tons) |
| Novokuznetsk (41) | Novokuznetsk (41) | 4,373 | | Novokuznetsk (41) | 3,288 |
| | Kulebaki (10) | 96 | | — | — |
| | Gorky (11) | 537 | | — | — |
| | Serov (29) | 89 | | — | — |
| | Nizhni Tagil (31) | 1,352 | | — | — |
| | Alapayevsk (32) | 178 | | — | — |
| | — | — | | Zlatoust (33) | 1,795 |
| | Chelyabinsk (34) | 4,814 | | Chelyabinsk (34) | 3,746 |
| | Petrovsk-Zabaikalsky (42) | 1,409 | | — | — |
| | — | — | | Taishet (44) | 2,490 |
| | — | — | | Barnaul (45) | 587 |

*Node numbers refer to Figures 1 and 3.

## APPENDIX IV
## STEEL DEMAND NODES AND QUANTITIES

| Node Number* | Location | Quantity ($10^3$ metric tons) | Node Number* | Location | Quantity ($10^3$ metric tons) |
|---|---|---|---|---|---|
| 1. | Liepaja | 96 | 37. | Novotroitsk | 239 |
| 2. | Leningrad | 3,731 | 38. | Temirtau | 166 |
| 3. | Kolpino | NA* | 39. | Karaganda | 451 |
| 4. | Mogilev | 242 | 40. | Bekabad | NA |
| 5. | Cherepovets | 205 | 41. | Novokuznetsk | 785 |
| 6. | Moscow | 6,322 | 42. | Petrovsk-Zabaikalsky | 181 |
| 7. | Elektrostal | 143 | 43. | Komsomolsk-na-Amure | 297 |
| 8. | Tula | 527 | 44. | Taishet | NA |
| 9. | Vyksa | NA | 45. | Barnaul | 598 |
| 10. | Kulebaki | NA | 46. | Stary Oskol | NA |
| 11. | Gorky | 959 | 47. | Kostroma | 220 |
| 12. | Lipetsk | 885 | 48. | Rzhev | NA |
| 13. | Dneprodzerzhinsk | 634 | 49. | Kursk | 837 |
| 14. | Dnepropetrovsk | 2,087 | 50. | Murmansk | 292 |
| 15. | Krivoi Rog | 1,603 | 51. | Severodvinsk | 158 |
| 16. | Zaporozhye | 1,841 | 52. | Arkhangelsk | 324 |
| 17. | Kramatorsk | 421 | 53. | Petrozavodsk | 148 |
| 18. | Konstantinovka | 294 | 54. | Vyborg | 61 |
| 19. | Kommunarsk | 343 | 55. | Pushkin | 77 |
| 20. | Yenakiyevo | 257 | 56. | Novgorod | 121 |
| 21. | Makeyevka | 1,096 | 57. | Tallinn | 378 |
| 22. | Donetsk | 2,456 | 58. | Tartu | 80 |
| 23. | Taganrog | 306 | 59. | Pskov | 108 |
| 24. | Zhdanov | 1,167 | 60. | Riga | 763 |
| 25. | Volgograd | 716 | 61. | Daugavpils | 104 |
| 26. | Rustavi | 107 | 62. | Panevezys | 71 |
| 27. | Sumgait | 152 | 63. | Siauliai | 96 |
| 28. | Izhevsk | 1,224 | 64. | Klaipeda | 168 |
| 29. | Serov | 193 | 65. | Kaliningrad | 280 |
| 30. | Chusovoi | NA | 66. | Kaunas | 317 |
| 31. | Nizhni Tagil | 1,097 | 67. | Vilnius | 329 |
| 32. | Alapayevsk | NA | 68. | Grodno | 135 |
| 33. | Zlatoust | 521 | 69. | Minsk | 1,099 |
| 34. | Chelyabinsk | 2,533 | 70. | Borisov | 101 |
| 35. | Beloretsk | 67 | 71. | Vitebsk | 277 |
| 36. | Magnitogorsk | 1,054 | 72. | Velikiye Luki | 80 |

APPENDIX IV (*cont.*)

| Node Number* | Location | Quantity (10³ metric tons) | Node Number* | Location | Quantity (10³ metric tons) |
|---|---|---|---|---|---|
| 73. | Smolensk | 176 | 139. | Samarkand | 164 |
| 74. | Orsha | 140 | 140. | Dushanbe | 229 |
| 75. | Gomel | 326 | 141. | Leninabad | 75 |
| 76. | Bobruisk | 166 | 142. | Angren | 122 |
| 77. | Baranovichi | 122 | 143. | Tashkent | 937 |
| 78. | Brest | 124 | 144. | Chimkent | 214 |
| 79. | Lutsk | 60 | 145. | Dzhambul | 137 |
| 80. | Lvov | 436 | 146. | Namangan | 88 |
| 81. | Uzhgorod | 52 | 147. | Margelan | 79 |
| 82. | Ivano-Frankovsk | 67 | 148. | Fergana | 161 |
| 83. | Ternopol | 54 | 149. | Andizhan | 95 |
| 84. | Rovno | 75 | 150. | Osh | 73 |
| 85. | Chernovtsy | 148 | 151. | Frunze | 264 |
| 86. | Khmelnitsky | 73 | 152. | Alma-Ata | 534 |
| 87. | Beltsy | 68 | 153. | Balkhash | 76 |
| 88. | Vinnitsa | 168 | 154. | Semipalatinsk | 203 |
| 89. | Berdichev | 66 | 155. | Ust-Kamenogorsk | 199 |
| 90. | Zhitomir | 128 | 156. | Leninogorsk | 72 |
| 91. | Kiev | 1,287 | 157. | Rubtsovsk | 229 |
| 92. | Belaya Tserkov | 86 | 158. | Biisk | 254 |
| 93. | Chernigov | 125 | 159. | Mezhdurechensk | 130 |
| 94. | Konotop | 164 | 160. | Prokopyevsk | 433 |
| 95. | Cherkassy | 125 | 161. | Kiselevsk | 199 |
| 96. | Kirovograd | 388 | 162. | Belovo | 170 |
| 97. | Kishinev | 238 | 163. | Leninsk-Kuznetsky | 202 |
| 98. | Bendery | 49 | 164. | Kemerovo | 525 |
| 99. | Tiraspol | 82 | 165. | Anzhero-Sudzhensk | 168 |
| 100. | Izmail | 63 | 166. | Tomsk | 462 |
| 101. | Odessa | 936 | 167. | Novosibirsk | 1,829 |
| 102. | Nikolayev | 347 | 168. | Abakan | 60 |
| 103. | Kherson | 274 | 169. | Achinsk | 63 |
| 104. | Yevpatoriya | 58 | 170. | Krasnoyarsk | 578 |
| 105. | Sevastopol | 203 | 171. | Kansk | 74 |
| 106. | Simferopol | 221 | 172. | Klin | 93 |
| 107. | Feodosiya | 58 | 173. | Noginsk | 120 |
| 108. | Kerch | 134 | 174. | Pavlovsky Posad | 76 |
| 109. | Novorossiisk | 138 | 175. | Orekhovo-Zuyevo | 137 |
| 110. | Krasnodar | 484 | 176. | Lyubertsy | 137 |
| 111. | Kropotkin | 71 | 177. | Zhukovsky | 73 |
| 112. | Armavir | 151 | 178. | Podolsk | 193 |
| 113. | Maikop | 98 | 179. | Voskresensk | 67 |
| 114. | Sochi | 162 | 180. | Yegoryevsk | 76 |
| 115. | Stavropol | 143 | 181. | Kolomna | 155 |
| 116. | Cherkessk | 176 | 182. | Serpukhov | 141 |
| 117. | Sukhumi | 66 | 183. | Nukus | 41 |
| 118. | Kislovodsk | 66 | 184. | Tashauz | 38 |
| 119. | Pyatigorsk | 67 | 185. | Kyzl-Orda | 89 |
| 120. | Batumi | 81 | 186. | Pavlodar | 162 |
| 121. | Kutaisi | 152 | 187. | Tselinograd | 156 |
| 122. | Nalchik | 128 | 188. | Omsk | 1,294 |
| 123. | Ordzhonikidze | 208 | 189. | Kokchetav | 61 |
| 124. | Tbilisi | 706 | 190. | Petropavlovsk | 149 |
| 125. | Leninakan | 155 | 191. | Kustanai | 90 |
| 126. | Kirovakan | 92 | 192. | Rudny | 96 |
| 127. | Yerevan | 609 | 193. | Orsk | 653 |
| 128. | Kirovabad | 152 | 194. | Aktyubinsk | 130 |
| 129. | Grozny | 301 | 195. | Orenburg | 865 |
| 130. | Makhachkala | 163 | 196. | Salavat | 115 |
| 131. | Astrakhan | 359 | 197. | Sterlitamak | 187 |
| 132. | Guryev | 84 | 198. | Ufa | 674 |
| 133. | Baku | 1,005 | 199. | Miass | 378 |
| 134. | Ashkhabad | 155 | 200. | Troitsk | 212 |
| 135. | Urgench | 38 | 201. | Korkino | 205 |
| 136. | Chardzhou | 59 | 202. | Kopeisk | 452 |
| 137. | Bukhara | 69 | 203. | Kurgan | 614 |
| 138. | Karshi | 43 | 204. | Tyumen | 367 |

APPENDIX IV (*cont.*)

| Node Number* | Location | Quantity (10³ metric tons) | Node Number* | Location | Quantity (10³ metric tons) |
|---|---|---|---|---|---|
| 205. | Shadrinsk | 181 | 260. | Voroshilovgrad | 924 |
| 206. | Kamensk-Uralsky | 490 | 261. | Lisichansk | 332 |
| 207. | Asbest | 220 | 262. | Severodonetsk | 253 |
| 208. | Sverdlovsk | 2,572 | 263. | Poltava | 451 |
| 209. | Pervouralsk | 340 | 264. | Kharkov | 2,963 |
| 210. | Kungur | 185 | 265. | Sumy | 384 |
| 211. | Lysva | 212 | 266. | Belgorod | 443 |
| 212. | Berezniki | 425 | 267. | Voronezh | 1,940 |
| 213. | Perm | 2,464 | 268. | Tambov | 570 |
| 214. | Sarapul | 263 | 269. | Michurinsk | 190 |
| 215. | Votkinsk | 216 | 270. | Yelets | 299 |
| 216. | Glazov | 170 | 271. | Orel | 229 |
| 217. | Almetyevsk | 77 | 272. | Bryansk | 315 |
| 218. | Bugulma | 54 | 273. | Kaluga | 208 |
| 219. | Oktyabrsky | 67 | 274. | Novomoskovsk | 153 |
| 220. | Buzuluk | 143 | 275. | Ryazan | 346 |
| 221. | Uralsk | 98 | 276. | Kalinin | 340 |
| 222. | Kuibyshev | 1,055 | 277. | Vyshni Volochek | 85 |
| 223. | Dimitrovgrad | 71 | 278. | Rybinsk | 249 |
| 224. | Togliatti | 253 | 279. | Yaroslavl | 590 |
| 225. | Novokuibyshevsk | 105 | 280. | Ivanovo | 494 |
| 226. | Chapayevsk | 87 | 281. | Vladimir | 231 |
| 227. | Syzran | 151 | 282. | Gus-Khrustalny | 84 |
| 228. | Ulyanovsk | 307 | 283. | Murom | 112 |
| 229. | Saransk | 135 | 284. | Kovrov | 140 |
| 230. | Penza | 378 | 285. | Arzamas | 48 |
| 231. | Kuznetsk | 74 | 286. | Dzerzhinsk | 181 |
| 232. | Volsk | 61 | 287. | Kineshma | 109 |
| 233. | Balakovo | 104 | 288. | Vologda | 169 |
| 234. | Engels | 144 | 289. | Cheboksary | 288 |
| 235. | Saratov | 622 | 290. | Ioshkar-Ola | 118 |
| 236. | Kamyshin | 98 | 291. | Zelenodolsk | 78 |
| 237. | Balashov | 62 | 292. | Kazan | 760 |
| 238. | Volzhsky | 144 | 293. | Kirov | 236 |
| 239. | Kamensk-Shakhtinsky | 82 | 294. | Syktyvkar | 100 |
| 240. | Gukovo | 93 | 295. | Vorkuta | 86 |
| 241. | Sverdlovsk (Ukr.) | 190 | 296. | Norilsk | 120 |
| 242. | Novoshakhtinsk | 123 | 297. | Bratsk | 138 |
| 243. | Shakhty | 247 | 298. | Cheremkhovo | 89 |
| 244. | Novocherkassk | 143 | 299. | Usolye-Sibirskoye | 68 |
| 245. | Bataisk | 88 | 300. | Angarsk | 181 |
| 246. | Rostov-na-Donu | 822 | 301. | Irkutsk | 349 |
| 247. | Yeisk | 74 | 302. | Ulan-Ude | 196 |
| 248. | Berdyansk | 242 | 303. | Chita | 158 |
| 249. | Melitopol | 332 | 304. | Yakutsk | 89 |
| 250. | Nikopol | 302 | 305. | Magadan | 74 |
| 251. | Aleksandriya | 168 | 306. | Petropavlovsk-Kamchatsky | 181 |
| 252. | Kremenchug | 414 | | | |
| 253. | Pavlograd | 209 | 307. | Blagoveshchensk | 127 |
| 254. | Slavyansk | 302 | 308. | Khabarovsk | 434 |
| 255. | Artemovsk | 198 | 309. | Yuzhno-Sakhalinsk | 105 |
| 256. | Gorlovka | 936 | 310. | Ussuriisk | 127 |
| 257. | Thorez | 261 | 311. | Vladivostok | 519 |
| 258. | Krasny Luch | 287 | 312. | Nakhodka | 123 |
| 259. | Stakhanov | 384 | | | |

*NA (not applicable) refers to nodes which are either ore, coke, or plant sites in the model, but too small to satisfy the operational definition of a demand node.

# 21

# SOVIET MANGANESE ORES: OUTPUT AND EXPORT

W. A. DOUGLAS JACKSON
University of Washington

## Introduction

Manganese (Mn), a metallic element, is widely distributed in nature where it appears mainly in the form of oxides, silicates, or carbonates.[1] Manganese-ore bodies, on the other hand, are considerably more restricted geographically. Of the world's producing countries, the Soviet Union has long held a commanding position (Table 1). Soviet reserves of manganese ore, moreover, are extensive, matched in size and quality by no other country with the possible exception of the Republic of South Africa.

## The Problem of Estimating Reserves

Precise estimates of Soviet reserves are difficult, if not impossible, to achieve. Apart from the general shroud of secrecy that tends to envelop Soviet discussion of ore bodies, the very nature of the ore bodies themselves poses a problem. As of January 1976, the Soviet Union estimated its reserves (of ore containing 23 to 28 percent manganese) at 2.565 billion metric tons.[2] This amount is said to represent 74 percent of world reserves, the world total being 3.56 billion tons.[3] The 1976 Soviet reserve estimate includes refractory and/or lower-grade materials and draws on geological inference.[4] Some evidence of the latter is afforded by data cited in a study by V. A. Boyarsky published in 1975 (Table 2).

Boyarsky gives total Soviet reserves at 2.5 billion metric tons (1971 data), a phenomenal increase of almost 2 billion since 1950. However, only 0.9 billion metric tons fall within the realm of studied reserves $(A + B)$,[5] while the balance (some 1.6 billion metric tons) is based substantially on geological testing and inference. Boyarsky claims 74 percent of world reserves in his assessment.

Western estimates reduce the size of the Soviet reserve. The U.S. Bureau of Mines in 1975 suggested that *identified world manganese reserves* might total only 2 billion short tons, or 1.8 billion metric tons. Of the latter, the bureau attributed 37.5 percent (about 675 million) to the USSR and 45 percent to South Africa. The Bureau of Mines also estimated that *identified world resources other than reserves* amounted to 1.6 billion short tons (1.45 billion metric tons), of which the USSR accounted for 37 percent and South Africa 48.7 percent. The estimates of the bureau are restricted, moreover, to those manganese deposits deemed "to have reasonable prospects of availability at a cost within the next 25 years."

Whatever the ultimate size, the Soviet Union has led the world in manganese output over the past century. Production in 1980 amounted to 9.75 million metric tons, which greatly exceeded that of South Africa, the nearest rival.[6]

In addition to the Soviet Union and South Africa, other important producers (as shown in Table 1) include Gabon, Brazil, India, and Australia. The United States, like the industrialized countries of Western Europe and Japan, remains highly dependent on imports. The lack of significant output in the United States has necessitated a long-standing program of stockpiling, the main suppliers in recent years being South Africa, Brazil, and India.

## The Form of Manganese Ores

Manganese deposits vary substantially.[7] Generally they are found in the form of secondary deposits, the manganese having been dissolved out of primary rock, of crystalline or metamorphic nature. Thus, as in the Soviet Union, the most extensive ore bodies are found as sediments or residuals. Oxides of manganese (in hydrated or dehydrated forms) consitute the major ore minerals. The lesser ore-bearing bodies are composed of silicates or carbonates. However, the mixed composition of the ore makes specific determination of their quality difficult leading to considerable confusion even among geologists.

The most common mode of occurrence, as evident in the major Soviet deposits, is pyrolusite ($MnO_2$), one of the mineral associations of manganese dioxide, providing manganese in one of its purest forms. *Psilomelane*, thought to be a colloidal form of $MnO_2$ but which has absorbed impurities, is a variant. Of the manganese carbonates, *rhodochrosite or diagolite* is the principal one, containing variable amounts of iron, calcium and magnesium carbonates. The manganese content of the ore can be considerably enriched by roasting which leads to the

TABLE 1
World Production of Manganese[1]
(thousand metric tons)

|  | 1960 | 1965 | 1970 | 1975 | 1980 |
|---|---|---|---|---|---|
| **OECD** | | | | | |
| United States[2] | 73 | 27 | 4 | 0 | 0 |
| Australia | 62 | 102 | 751 | 1,560 | 1,961 |
| Italy | 49 | 48 | 50 | 0 | 9 |
| Japan | 324 | 303 | 270 | 158 | 80 |
| **Other Countries** | | | | | |
| Brazil | 999 | 1,400 | 1,880 | 2,160 | 2,360 |
| Gabon | 0 | 1,280 | 1,450 | 2,240 | 2,147 |
| Ghana[3] | 545 | 604 | 405 | 409 | 252 |
| India | 1,200 | 1,650 | 1,650 | 1,580 | 1,645 |
| South Africa | 1,190 | 1,570 | 2,680 | 5,770 | 4,743 |
| **Soviet-bloc Countries** | | | | | |
| USSR | 5,872 | 7,576 | 6,841 | 8,459 | 9,750 |
| Eastern Europe | 477 | 461 | 390 | 278 | 187 |
| Bulgaria | 25 | 42 | 33 | 35 | 49 |
| Hungary | 123 | 213 | 169 | 131 | 90 |
| Rumania | 175 | 126 | 102 | 112 | 48 |
| **Other[4]** | | | | | |
| Yugoslavia | 13 | 8 | 15 | 17 | 30 |

[1]The metal content of the ore of various countries is as follows: the United States, more than 35 percent; other noncommunist countries and Cuba, 25–53 percent; the USSR, about 35 percent; Yugoslavia, about 35 percent; Rumania, 30 percent; Bulgaria, about 27 percent; and Hungary, 26 percent.
[2]Shipments.
[3]Dry weight.
[4]Estimates for China are not shown. Output may have amounted to 1 million metric tons in 1974. Mexico accounted for 403,000 tons and Morocco, 175,000 tons.
SOURCE: Adapted from *Handbook of Economic Statistics, 1982* (CIA, Directorate of Intelligence, Washington, September 1982), p. 133; *Minerals Yearbook 1974*, vol. 3, Area Reports: International (Bureau of Mines, U.S. Department of Interior, Washington, 1977), p. 53.

decomposition of the latter carbonates. *Rhodonite* is a manganese silicate ($MnSiO_3$), containing 42 percent manganese; however, *braunite* ($3 Mn_2O_3.MnSiO_3$) is the only silicate manganese ore mineral. Because the more extensive deposits of manganese ore are found as sediments, much of the mining in the Soviet Union today is carried out by open-pit or open-cast methods although underground mining also occurs.

## The Importance of Manganese to Modern Industry

Since the middle of the 19th century manganese has constituted a major component of the metallurgical industry. Identified as an entirely new and separate element in the latter decades of the 18th century, manganese nevertheless assumed no commercial significance until the Industrial Revolution was well under way. Since 1856 when Sir Henry Bessemer first used the metal successfully as an addition to steel, the practice of requiring manganese for metallurgical purposes has become a world-wide phenomenon.[8] Normally for each ton of steel produced, 13 to 14 pounds of manganese metal are consumed. If consumption levels have on average run higher in the Soviet Union, the higher rates may in large measure be attributed to the low manganese content of Soviet iron ores, the high sulfur content of Donets coke, and the

abundance and availability of the ore. In any event the vital importance of manganese to an industrialized or industrializing economy is established.

The application of manganese to steel has at least two major functions. First, the addition of manganese serves as a purifier. It helps to correct the effects of sulfur in steel which would remain brittle. Hot rolling or forging would otherwise result in cracking. Manganese also leads to the removal of oxygen from steel since the presence of oxygen also produces a brittle steel.

Second, manganese has an alloying effect. It improves the physical strenth of steel and enhances ductility, hardness, and abrasion-resisting properties.

Of the ferroalloys, two are of principal importance: ferromanganese and spiegeleisen. The latter, which means literally "mirror-iron", derives its names from the shiny appearance of its fractures. Spiegeleisen, as an alloy of iron and manganese, contains up to 30 percent manganese. Spiegeleisen is in less demand generally than ferromanganese whose manganese content greatly exceeds that of the former. The ferromanganese most commonly used possesses up to 80 percent manganese. Some use of manganese ore is made in the production of pig iron but by far the greatest demand is in the steel industry.

Since World War II the range and scope of other uses of manganese have expanded, though the volumes are minimal. Small quantities of manganese are employed in the chemical industry and in the manufacture of dry-cell batteries (usually high-grade pyrolusite). Manganese is also used in glass-making and in the ceramic industry where manganese reduces the effects of iron in the sand. The paint and varnish industry also requires some manganese as do fertilizer producers which utilize the sulfate form. For metallurgical purposes, however, a higher manganese content is generally employed.

## The Distribution of Soviet Ore Bodies

Soviet reserves of manganese are found in numerous deposits widely scattered throughout the country[9] (Table 2). As of the early 1970s, however, only 20 of these were actually mined. Quality manganese ores are even more restricted geographically (Figure 1). Indeed, most, over 90 percent, of Soviet reserves of high or commercial quality (in the category $A + B + C_1$) are concentrated in three locations, all in the western part of the country. Two of these are found within the Ukrainian manganese basin: near the city of Nikopol on the Kakhovka Reservoir of the Dnieper River in Dnepropetrovsk Oblast and, to the east, the newer Bolshoi Tokmak deposit in Zaporozhye Oblast. The Nikopol deposits are estimated to contain less than 40 percent of the ores of workable quality, the Bolshoi Tokmak 44 to 45 percent. The third deposit of significance is located in western Georgia, at Chiatura. Although Chiatura ores were once regarded as the richest and largest deposit under Russian control, capable of supplying nearly half the world's requirements, the Chiatura deposit today contains less than 8 percent of the Soviet reserves of metallurgical value.[10]

TABLE 2
Distribution of Reserves of Manganese Ores in the USSR (1 January 1971)

| Region | Number of Deposits | $A + B$ million metric tons | By Category $A + B + C_1$ million metric tons | By Category $A + B + C_1$ percent of Soviet reserves | $C_2$ million metric tons |
|---|---|---|---|---|---|
| RSFSR | 14 | 46.7 | 155.1 | 6.1 | 2.5 |
| Urals (Sverdlovsk Oblast) | 12 | 15.7 | 50.2 | 2.0 | — |
| Western Siberia (Kemerovo Oblast) | 1 | 29.1 | 98.5 | 3.8 | — |
| Far East (Khabarovsk Krai) | 1 | 1.9 | 6.4 | 0.3 | 2.5 |
| Ukraine | 16 | 779.5 | 2,094.6 | 82.4 | 313.9 |
| Dnepropetrovsk Oblast (Nikopol) | 15 | 629.6 | 985.1 | 38.8 | 6.8 |
| Zaporozhye Oblast (Bolshoi Tokmak) | 1 | 149.9 | 1,109.5 | 43.6 | 307.1 |
| Georgia | 16 | 54.8 | 227.5 | 8.9 | 15.2 |
| Chiatura | 14 | 54.3 | 218.3 | 8.6 | 13.0 |
| Kazakhstan (Karaganda Oblast) | 6 | 11.2 | 66.9 | 2.6 | 6.5 |
| Total | 52 | 892.2 | 2,544.1 | 100.0 | 395.1 |

SOURCE: V. A. Boyarsky, *Razvitiye otkrytoi dobychi rud 1950–1970 gg.* [The development of the open extraction of ore, 1950–70] (Moscow: Nauka, 1975), p. 34.

Lesser deposits of ore, differing in geologic form, are found in the Urals, in Kazakhstan, and in several regions of Siberia and the Soviet Far East. Some of the deposits, though varying greatly in size and quality, nevertheless have had considerable local significance. They represent about 9 percent or less of the known workable ores.[11]

The Ukrainian Manganese Basin:
Nikopol and Bolshoi Tokmak Deposits

The manganese deposits of the Ukraine, estimated at more than 82 percent of the Soviet total (category $A + B + C_1$), extend over a large area. The ores lie principally within a band approximately 25 km wide stretching a distance of some 240 km from near the iron-mining and steel center of Krivoi Rog in the west to Orekhov in the east. For much of its extent the belt parallels the north shore of the Kakhovka Reservoir. To the north, upstream on the Dnieper River, are the steel manufacturing cities of Zaporozhye, Dnepropetrovsk and Dneprodzerzhinsk. To the east lies the industrial complex of the Donets Basin.

Within this belt lie the West Nikopol and East Nikopol ore areas. At the eastern end of the reservoir is the Bolshoi Tokmak deposit. Other occurrences of manganese are scattered throughout the belt.[12]

These Ukrainian ores for the most part occur in recent (Lower Oligocene) sand-clay sediments. The beds tend to be horizontal and of a thickness of up to 30 meters. Generally they rest under an overburden whose depth ranges from 480 to 790 meters. Approximately 37 percent of the Ukrainian deposits fall with the $A + B$ category, while Ukrainian mines have yielded 76 percent of the commercial ore.

The ores produced at Nikopol have been in the past mainly pyrolusite, that is oxides whose color varies from relatively soft grey to black.[13] Average manganese content has ranged form 25 to 30 percent (Table 3). The latter is raised to 40 to 50 percent or more, after the ore is sorted, crushed, washed and concentrated.

Banny et al. described the Nikopol ores as consisting of three types of ore: (1) 54 to 45 percent manganese; (2) 44 to 40 percent manganese; and (3) 39 to 29 percent manganese. The iron content was said to be 0.7 to 3.5 percent, phosphorus 0.17 to 0.23 percent, and silica 9.0 percent.[14]

The beneficiation of Nikopol ores has yielded two products for shipment.[15] Class I, with a manganese content of 45 to 50 percent, has been consigned to the production of ferroalloys. The other, Class II, with a 35 to 40 percent manganese concentrate, has moved to blast furnaces.

Lelyukhina notes that scattered through the Nikopol reserves are manganese ores low in phosphorus.[16] Although the latter constitute only about 2 percent of the total, they are suitable for ferromanganese after concentration.

The more recent references to the Nikopol deposits suggest that the oxide ores are being depleted. Lelyukhina, for example, estimates that the carbonate and oxide-carbonate ores of Nikopol represent about half the deposits of the Nikopol Basin. They are capable of producing, however, a high quality concentrate with a manganese content of 27.7 to 44.8 percent.

Traditionally, Class I concentrates of Nikopol have been high in silica and phosphorus, higher than those produced at Chiatura. However, the Nikopol concentrates have been more suitable for metallurgical purposes because they are both coarser and cleaner. Moreover, the Ukrainian manganese deposits, situated within a short distance of the iron and steel mills of the South, have afforded an economic advantage that has contributed substantially to growth and expansion of the prime Soviet metallurgical base.

Most of the increase in production in the Nikopol Basin

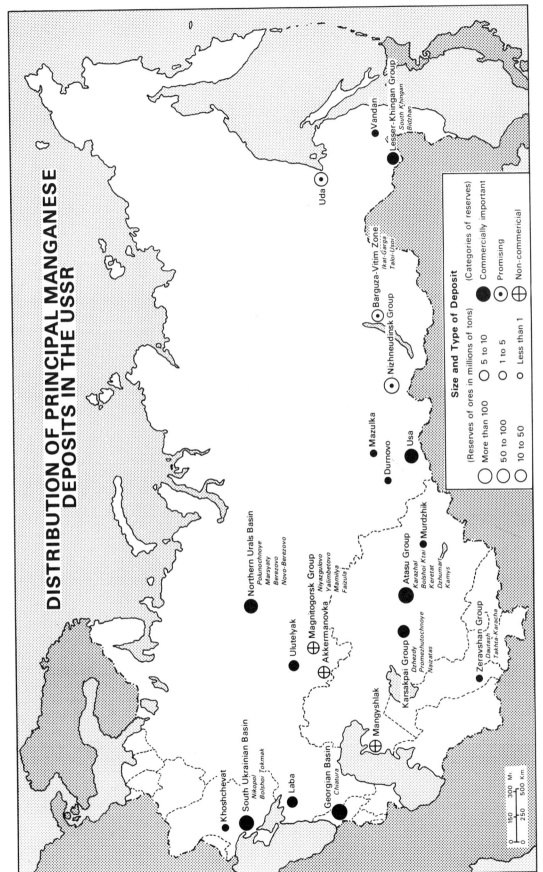

Figure 1

TABLE 3
Distribution of Reserves of Manganese Ores in the Soviet Union (1970)

| | Total | | A + B | | 1970 output percent | Production cost (percent of average Soviet cost) | |
|---|---|---|---|---|---|---|---|
| | percent of total | Average Mn content percent | percent of reserves | percent of total | | crude ore | marketed ore |
| USSR | 100.0 | 23.6 | 35.2 | 100.0 | 100.0 | 100.0 | 100.0 |
| Western USSR | 93.3 | 23.7 | 36.0 | 95.3 | 99.0 | 100.2 | 98.2 |
| Volga | 0.3 | 10.0 | 80.0 | 0.7 | — | — | — |
| Ukraine | 82.1 | 24.2 | 37.2 | 86.8 | 76.0 | 104.5 | 103.7 |
| Transcaucasia | 8.9 | 20.6 | 24.1 | 6.1 | 23.0 | 90.4 | 79.8 |
| Urals | 2.0 | 21.2 | 31.3 | 1.7 | — | — | — |
| Eastern USSR | | | | | | | |
| W. Siberia | 3.9 | 19.6 | 29.6 | 3.3 | — | — | — |
| Far East | 0.2 | 20.8 | 29.0 | 0.2 | — | — | — |
| Kazakhstan | 2.6 | 22.9 | 16.7 | 1.2 | 1.0 | 93.1 | 275.3 |

SOURCE: N. D. Lelyukhina, *Ekonomicheskaya effektivnost razmeshcheniya chernoi metallurgii* [The cost-effectiveness of the distribution of the iron and steel industry] (Moscow: Nauka, 1973), p. 229.

has been from open-pit operations. In 1977, the last year for which detailed figures are available, the basin yielded 15 million tons of crude ore, including 3 million tons (20 percent) from the basin's 7 shaft mines, and 12 million tons (80 percent) from the basin's 9 open pits. The crude ore, which averaged 26 percent metal content, was converted into 6.6 million tons of concentrate with an average metal content of 40.6 percent at 5 concentrators, clustered in the western part of the basin around Ordzhonikidze and in the eastern part around Marganets. The concentrators at Marganets have been undergoing expansion, which necessitates the mining of rather hard or lumpy carbonate ores from the southern edge of the main zone of oxide ores. Nikopol and Zaporozhye are major centers for the production of ferromanganese alloys.[17]

In contrast to Nikopol, the Bolshoi Tokmak deposit is characterized by a somewhat steeper gradient on the surface of the crystalline basement rock in the northern sector and by a more gently sloping southward continuation. This trend has caused a relatively narrow development of the zones of oxide and mixed ores compared to the Nikopol deposit. There is also a rather extensive distribution of carbonate ores, which increases the need for washing. The development of the zones of the Bolshoi Tokmak deposit began in 1979 with the start of excavation of the first shaft mine at Lukyanovka, some 20 miles southeast of Zaporozhye. It was planned to go into operation in 1983 with a first stage capacity of 9 million tons of crude ore, to be concentrated in the proposed Tauric Concentrator at the mine.[18]

The Western Georgian Manganese Basin:
The Chiatura Deposit

The manganese deposit at Chiatura is one of the largest in the world. However, its reserves of high-grade ore are no longer extensive, being greatly exceeded by the deposits at Nikopol and possibly Bolshoi Tokmak.[19] Georgian reserves are placed at about 9 percent of the Soviet total.

The deposit at Chiatura, of Lower Oligocene origin, is located within the Kvirila valley about 25 km east of Kutaisi. The ore basin is said to comprise an area of up to 21 square km. About 85 percent of Chiatura ores have been residuals, but metamorphosed and other complex forms are found as well.[20]

The deposit consists of a number of manganese ore-bearing strata. The latter, like those in the Ukrainian basin, are horizontal and continuous, alough there is a vaguely defined easterly dip. In places the number of ore-bearing strata vary, numbering from 3 to 18 and reaching even 25. The beds rest gently on limestone rock of Upper Cretaceous origin. On the margins of the deposit the level sedimentary nature of the ore strata is broken by faulting and steep dipping.[21]

Open-pit mining is carried on, but there are at least 23 underground mines and adits in hillsides. Still 1,417,000 metric tons were produced by open-pit methods in 1969 compared with 396,000 tons in 1958, a factor leading to a reduction in the overall cost of mining. In 1969, for example, a ton of ore produced from underground mines cost 84 percent more than a ton obtained from open-pit methods.[22] The superior quality Chiatura ores have come historically from the lower part of the manganese horizon.[23] The upper part, on the other hand, has been relatively poor. At present, the most valuable ores, mainly pyrolusite, are obtained in the western and especially central parts of the Chiatura deposit, i.e., at Perevisi, Shukruti, Zeda-Rgani, and other sites.[24] To the east carbonate ores tend to dominate (about 39 percent of the reserves in the deposit) and substantial impoverishment occurs. In the eastern and northern parts of the basin, the ore horizon completely thins out.

In the past, according to Nalivkin, the Chiatura ores rarely were enriched since they possessed up to 52 to 58 percent of manganese, a raw material that was the finest in the world.[25] Banny[26] estimated that the best Chiatura ores contained 50 to 57 percent manganese, 0.4 to 1.5 percent iron, 0.1 to 0.25 percent phosphorus, and 3.5 to

8.5 percent silica. The ordinary ores contained 25 to 47 percent manganese. On the whole, however, the impression left by Soviet writers is one of a steady decline in the manganese content of Chiatura ores. Kandelaki, in a study of the problems of the iron and steel industry in the Georgian republic, reports that as the mining of manganese moved from the central and richest part of the Chiatura deposit to the periphery, the manganese content fell from 43.5 percent in 1934 to 33.3 percent in 1946 and to 27.95 percent in 1958.[27] Ores of first quality have diminished substantially—a decline from 36.1 percent in 1947 to 19.4 percent in 1965. With this has come an increasing use of carbonate ores, which nonetheless have produced, after washing, a material with 43 percent manganese content.[28]

As of 1 January 1970, more than 94 percent of the Transcaucasian ores fell within the category $A + B + C_1$ (of which 26.6 percent were $A + B$) and only 5.8 percent were in category $C_2$.[29] Lelyukhina describes the Chiatura ores as primary oxides, carbonates and silicates.[30] The first represents 37 percent of all the deposits in category $A + B + C_1$, the carbonates 45.6 percent, and the silicates 17.3 percent. The manganese content of the oxides is given at 30 percent, with 0.02 to 0.4 percent phosphorus and a silica content of 8 to 50 percent. The average manganese content of the carbonate ores is 26.1 percent, with a phosphorus content of 0.15 to 0.18 percent and a silica content of 20.2 to 24.1 percent. The silicate ores, on the other hand, have a manganese content of 27.2 percent, a phosphorus content of 0.1 to 0.2 percent, with more than 30 percent silica.

Because of the physical nature of the oxide ores, disintegrating readily into fines, concentration was always a difficult task. Still, concentration has yielded a product of exceptional purity, that has contained up to 80 to 90 percent manganese dioxide. Even so the nature of the ores has made the Chiatura product unsuited to blast furnace use unless mixed with other ores. Of the beneficiated ore, two-thirds contains about 48.7 percent manganese. The remaining third, Class II, has a manganese content of 25.6 percent. Expansion of concentrating facilities has been under way since 1974.[31] Chiatura manganese is processed into ferromanganese at Zestafoni, but most of it is shipped from the Caucasus in the form of enriched ores.[32]

## The Urals Deposits

The deposits of manganese in the Urals are relatively small, though numerous. Among the better quality ores, certainly possessing some further value in the future, are those on the eastern slope of the northern Urals.[33] There, in the Serov and Ivdel regions, is a narrow discontinuous belt of ore-bearing sediments stretching from north to south for more than 150 miles.

Oxidation produced pyrolusite and psilomelane, especially at Polunochnoye and Berezovo,[34] but these forms have had limited distribution and must be assumed to be worked out.[35] Carbonate ores are also present with an average manganese content of 17.8 to 27.2 percent. Attempts at enrichment have revealed the possibility of

obtaining quality manganese concentrates for the production of ferromanganese and silico-manganese. Reserves are estimated at 50 million metric tons, with prospective reserves set at 100 million metric tons. Mining has been carried out in the past at Polunochnoye and Marsyaty.

Small deposits of manganese are also found in the Middle Urals, in the Sverdlovsk, Miass, Magnitogorsk and Baimak areas.[36] Here the appearance of manganese has been in the rhodonite form. Braunite also occurs and, where oxidation occurred, psilomelane and pyrolusite developed. Such ores as the latter, near Magnitogorsk, were worked out during World War II.[37] The silicate ores have a manganese content of 15 to 25 percent, although in places it may reach 30 to 35 percent. The total reserves of semi-oxidized and primary sedimentary metamorphosed ores (mainly silicates) have been estimated at 3 million metric tons.[38] Commercial exploitation of these deposits has been slow.

## The Kazakhstan Deposits

The ores of Central Kazakhstan have been estimated at about 100 million metric tons; however the deposits tend to be relatively small.[39] The ores are sedimentary, but a geologic period of violent volcanic activity accounts for the presence of manganese.

The Karazhal deposits, in the Atasu region of Karaganda Oblast, lie within an ore field that is oriented east-west and extends a distance of 11 km. It consists of 5 deposits, representing independent segregations of iron and manganese ores (i.e., Bolshoi Ktai, East Karazhal, West Karazhal, etc.). The best ores are of the psilomelane and semi-oxidized braunitic types, with a manganese content reaching up to 40 to 50 percent. These ores are firm, and low in iron, phosphorus and silica. On average, however, the manganese content ranges from 19 to 30 percent, depending on form.[40]

The Karsakpai group of deposits lies almost due west of Karazhal, somewhat to the northwest of Dzhezkazgan. The principal mining center is Dzhezdy, formerly Marganets, but reserves are small and the average ore content is between 11 and 17 percent.[41] Dzhezdy ores were shipped to Magnitogorsk during World War II, a journey that entailed considerable overland hauling. The average manganese content of enriched ores is about 27 percent. The cost of a ton of concentrate is said to be very high[42] (Table 3). Accordingly, the ore production from the Kazakhstan deposits has been negligible (less than 100,000 tons a year).

In the Mangyshlak Peninsula, a large deposit of very low-grade ore has long been known and studied. The quantity of carbonate ores with a manganese content of from 5 to 10 percent exceeds some 30 million metric tons.[43]

## The Siberian Deposits

The largest deposit of manganese ore in Siberia is the Usa deposit, discovered during World War II. It lies in Kemerovo Oblast, in the Kuznetsk Alatau, near the middle course of the Usa River, a right-bank tributary of the Tom.

The deposit lies on the steep western limb of a syncline, much disturbed by fracturing and folding.[44] The greater portion of the manganese and much of the iron in the Usa deposit are present in the form of carbonate minerals with a manganese content of 20 percent. Manganese in silicate form amounts to about 30 percent of the bulk composition with a manganese content of 26.7 percent.[45]

The Mazulka deposit, located southwest of Achinsk on the Trans-Siberian Railway, was a minor source of manganese of local significance in World War II. Soviet writers indicate that the better ores have been worked out.[46] Of sedimentary-metamorphic origin, the oxidized ore was mainly pyrolusite, with the manganese content running as high as 47 percent.[47] However, although the ore beds were said to be as much as 120 feet thick in places, the quality was not uniform. In 1936, reserves were estimated at 1.6 million tons.[48] Some of the manganese was used at the steel mill at Novokuznetsk.

Mention might also be made of the Nikolayevka deposit in the Nizhneudinsk group (Sayan region) in Eastern Siberia.[49] This deposit is the largest and most studied ore body within the group, but average manganese content is only about 16.6 percent, with a phosphorus content of 0.19 percent.

## The Soviet Far East Deposit

The principal deposit of manganese in the Soviet Far East is found in the southern part of the Lesser Khingan Mountains, not far from the Kimkan railway station on the Trans-Siberian Railway in Khabarovsk Krai. The geological associations characteristic of the Khingan ores have led to the formation of comparatively large manganese deposits in Brazil, South Africa and other parts of the world. But in the Soviet Far East this association has produced a relatively modest scale of ore occurrence. The deposit is characterized by a mixed iron-manganese mineralization. Studies, however, continue.[50] Reserves are said to be about 10 million metric tons of manganese oxide ores (35 percent manganese) and manganese silicates (21 percent).

## History of Russian Manganese Ore Production

### Czarist Russia

The mining of manganese in the Soviet Union predates World War I and the Bolshevik Revolution. Although the Chiatura deposit was known in 1848, operations did not get under way until 1879.[51] Manganese was produced in the Urals in 1882, but output in the years ahead remained small though steady. The growth of the iron and steel industry in the southern Ukraine in the 1880s led to the development of the Nikopol deposits, beginning in 1886.[52]

In the ensuing decades to World War I, Russia emerged as and remained (except for the short period 1908–11 when its output was exceeded by that of India) the world's leading producer and exporter of manganese ore. From the 1880s to 1913, Russian production aggregated

12.5 million metric tons, which annually accounted for 40 to 53 percent of world output. Since the output of the mines vastly exceeded the requirements of Russia's fledgling iron and steel industry, anywhere from 80 to 90 percent or more was exported. In 1913, when Russian manganese output reached its maximum in the pre-World War I period, 1,245,000 metric tons was mined.

Since the diffusion of iron and steel production through Europe and elsewhere had occurred rapidly in the latter half of the 19th century and early 20th century, foreign demand and competition for Russian manganese increased, especially in the years immediately preceding the outbreak of World War I. Moreover, by the turn of the century the United States had become a major consumer of manganese, in which imports were to play an increasingly important role. Still on the eve of World War I, Imperial Germany was the world's leading consumer and importer of manganese, and Imperial Russia was the principal source of supply.

From the very beginning of operations, the Chiatura ore body propelled Russia into a position of preeminence in the world manganese trade. The high quality of Chiatura ores was quickly recognized. Early estimates of reserves ran as high as 40 million tons of 52 percent ore or 80 million tons of 42 to 47 percent manganese.[53] In 1913 the output of the Georgian deposit reached almost a million metric tons, from 303 mines comprising 437 galleries. Over 90 percent of the tonnage was regularly exported.

The Nikopol deposit, oriented toward the new iron and steel base in the Donets Basin, produced less than a third of Russian manganese. In 1913, it yielded about 276,000 metric tons. Still about 20 percent of its production was exported, primarily by rail, to Germany.[54] Estimates of Nikopol reserves ran, in the prerevolutionary period, to about 7.4 million metric tons.[55]

The Urals deposit yielded from 3,000 to 4,000 tons, most of the ore coming from the mines at Marsyaty, Sapalskoye, Urazov and Faizula. It was consumed locally.

The Chiatura operations were dominated by foreign capital, mainly German, British, Belgian, French, and American. The Schalker Gruben and Hütten Company of Gelsenkirchen, Germany, took all of its own output, helping Germany to become the major foreign consumer of Chiatura ores.[56] The British firm, Forward Brothers, and the Industrial and Commercial Company of Antwerp also accounted for a sizeable portion of the output, followed in last place by Panassie of France. Immediately prior to the outbreak of the war, Germany took over 37 percent of Chiatura exports, followed by Britain (22.9), Belgium (19), and the United States (12). France imported only 5 percent.

### The Interwar Period

During the war and revolution, Russian output and export of manganese declined as the socioeconomic turmoil of the period intensified. Russian production in 1914 was about 700,000 metric tons, a figure nearer the long-term prewar pattern. However, in 1915 the mines yielded only about 50,000 tons and, in 1916, no more than 150,000 tons.[57] Chiatura shipped at least 30,000 tons in 1915, but movements of Caucasian ore in 1916 drew on stocks on hand at the port of Poti on the Black Sea.[58] Since the war brought exports through the Dardanelles to a standstill, Chiatura shipments were principally destined for the Donets region where demand for manganese exceeded the output of the Nikopol mines at the time.

The year 1922 brought the beginning of the restoration of the manganese industry, now in Soviet hands. During the war, much of the Chiatura concentrate had been insufficiently washed. During the civil war period, the local Caucasian government had taken over the operation of the mines although prices were regulated through an association comprising British and indigenous mine owners.[59] Chiatura, too, had always suffered from poor transport facilities and the capacity of the port of Poti for moving manganese had been affected by shallow water.

In 1923 a branch railway line was constructed to link some of the Chiatura mines with Shorapani, a station on the Transcaucasian railway.[60] At Shorapani the ore was then reloaded from narrow-gauge cars to the broad gauge of the main line. Facilities for handling the ore at Poti, 120 miles to the west, and as well at the port of Batumi, an additional 20 miles to the southwest, were expanded and improved. In the latter part of the 1920s greater use was made at Chiatura of aerial ropeways for moving the ores, since even the rail connection proved insufficient.[61]

Comparable improvements were made at Nikopol and at Marsyaty (Urals). The work carried out at Nikopol brought substantial success. Even by the 1st Five-Year Plan period (1928–32), output at Nikopol had climbed significantly. In some years Nikopol produced more ore than Chiatura, i.e., 1926–27, 1928, and 1921–33. At Nikopol ore was sorted by hand before going to the concentrating plant where it was crushed, washed in log washers and jigs, and concentrated with jigs and tables or by flotation. About 3 tons of Nikopol crude ore was required to make a ton of concentrate.[62]

As a result of these improvements, Soviet output of manganese regained prewar levels. From 223,500 metric tons in 1923, production climbed to over 1 million tons by 1926, although the latter represented 83 percent of the 1913 record year. By 1929 output had surpassed even 1913.

Russian manganese reserves in 1917 had been estimated at 168 million metric tons.[63] Geological research and study in the late 1920s had increased the reserves so that by 1934 the Soviet Union claimed some 650 million metric tons. New deposits had been discovered, especially east of the Urals. By 1 January 1938, Soviet reserves had reached 786 million metric tons, including 230 million of measured reserves.[64]

By 1934, it was clear that Nikopol had the larger deposit, although the Chiatura ores were touted for their high manganese content. Deposits other than Nikopol and Chiatura then accounted for about 7 percent of Soviet production. Mazulka, because of its nearness to the Trans-Siberian Railway, yielded 131,000 metric tons, the

ore serving the needs of the newly developing Novokuznetsk iron and steel plant. Urals output, accounting for about 29,000 tons, went to local blast furnaces. The rest originated in Kazakhstan.

During the 1930s, Chiatura continued to supply most of the export ores, although even as late as 1935 Nikopol shipped 67,000 tons abroad. However, despite the continued increase in total Soviet output, exports began to decline. Whereas much of total Russian production was exported in 1913, the ratio of exports to output fell to 41 percent in 1934 and to only 20 percent in 1936. The USSR continued as the world's leading producer, but India now assumed the role of major world exporter. In the early 1930s, Germany had regained its leading position in Russian exports, but that abruptly declined in 1936 as Nazi aggressiveness surfaced. At that point, the United States became the major consumer of Soviet manganese.

The Postwar Period

Recovery from the ravages of World War II took several forms. Above all there was an effort to uncover new ore bodies, especially in regions east of the Urals, and to enlarge the manganese reserves of the country as a whole.[65]

The search was a substantial one and it was rewarded with a certain degree of success. Boyarsky notes that reserves, rated at 578 million metric tons in 1951, grew to 2,544 million in 1971 (Table 4). Of the latter, 892.2 million was regarded as falling in the category $A + B$ (Table 2). Such estimates affirmed the Soviet world position; the USSR claimed to have 74 percent of world reserves of manganese. However, despite these claims (noted at the beginning of this paper), the tempo of discovery slackened near the end of the 1950s (Figure 2). Whatever claims are made for the Soviet resource base, estimates of total manganese reserves have not changed significantly since the early 1960s. Moreover, the geographic imbalance caused by the disparate distribution of ore bodies has imposed costly restraints in view of the dispersal of the iron and steel industry.

The Performance of Nikopol and Chiatura

The German occupation of the Ukraine had for the most part taken the Nikopol mines out of operation. The recovery there, necessitated too by the demands of postwar

TABLE 4
Increase in Soviet Manganese Reserves
(million metric tons)

| Year | Volume | Year | Volume |
|------|--------|------|--------|
| 1951 | 578    | 1971 | 2,544  |
| 1956 | 1,658  | 1972 | 2,549  |
| 1961 | 2,592  | 1976 | 2,565  |
| 1966 | 2,565  |      |        |

Source: Boyarsky, *Razvitiye*, p. 24. Data for 1976 from Strishkov, "Mineral Industries."

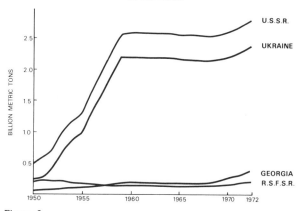

Figure 2
SOURCE: V. A. Boyarsky, *Razvitiye otkrytoi dobychi rud, 1950–1970 g.* (Moscow: Nauka, 1975).

expansion of the iron and steel industry in the Donets Basin, the Urals and elsewhere, entailed the opening up of lower-grade deposits and, associated with that, a long-term program of construction of additional beneficiation plants. (It was estimated in 1972 that when the new concentrators were completed, they would have a capacity to handle more than 15 million tons of crude ore per year.)[66]

The program of expansion at Nikopol led to a substantial increase in output. By the first half of the 1960s, Nikopol had overtaken Chiatura as the leading producer of manganese in the Soviet Union (Table 5). Whereas in 1950, Ukrainian output had amounted to 903,000 metric tons, by 1965 it had climbed to 4,651,000 metric tons. The upward trend continued through the 1970s, reaching

TABLE 5
Soviet Regional Output of Manganese
(thousand metric tons)

|  | Total | Ukraine | Georgia | Others |
|---|---|---|---|---|
| 1913 | 1,245 | 276 | 966 | 3 |
| 1928 | 702 | 531 | 172 | 0 |
| 1932 | 832 | 443 | 389 | 0 |
| 1937 | 2,752 | 957 | 1,650 | 145 |
| 1940 | 2,557 | 893 | 1,449 | 215 |
| 1945 | 1,470 | 206 | 850 | 414 |
| 1950 | 3,377 | 903 | 1,837 | 637 |
| 1955 | 4,743 | 1,620 | 2,900 | 223 |
| 1960 | 5,872 | 2,725 | 3,036 | 111 |
| 1965 | 7,576 | 4,651 | 2,873 | 52 |
| 1970 | 6,841 | 5,202 | 1,569 | 70 |
| 1975 | 8,459 | 6,537 | 1,835 | 87 |
| 1980 | 9,750 | 6,920 | 2,779 | 51 |
| 1981 | (9,300) | (6,500) | 2,734 | (50) |
| 1982 est. | (9,700) | (6,900) | (2,800) | |
| 1985 Plan | 10,100 | | | |

SOURCES: *Narodnoye khozyaistvo SSSR v 1980 g.* [The economy of the USSR in 1980] (Moscow: Finansy i Statistika, 1981), p. 159; *Narodne gospodarstvo Ukrainskoi RSR u 1980 rotsi* [The economy of the Ukrainian SSR in 1980; in Ukrainian] (Kiev: Tekhnika, 1981), p. 110; *Narodnoye khozyaistvo Gruzinskoi SSR v 1973 godu* [The economy of the Georgian SSR in 1973] (Tbilisi: Sabchota Sakartvelo, 1974), pp. 68–69; *Zarya Vostoka*, 7 February 1976, 3 February 1980, 5 February 1981, 31 January 1982; *Gorny zhurnal*, 1982, no. 1 and no. 3.

7,428,000 in 1979, but dropped off somewhat thereafter. Moreover, increasing amounts of ore were obtained by open-pit methods, 80 percent in 1977 compared with 69 percent in 1965 (see Table 6).[67]

Output at Chiatura, by contrast, having reached over 3 million metric tons in the late 1950s, declined to half of that level by 1970. Despite the continued overall increase in Soviet manganese production (Table 5), the changing relationship between Nikopol and Chiatura reflected significant resource trends as well. The absolute decline at Chiatura was accounted for by the depletion of higher-grade oxide ores, and with it the growing cost of underground mining.[68] By 1970, Georgia contributed 1.6 million tons, or 23 percent of total Soviet output. During the ensuing decade, the increase in the capacity of Georgian beneficiation plants, brought Chiatura output up to 29 percent of the total by 1980.[69] Lower-grade carbonates, obtained mainly through surface mining, account for over 20 percent of Chiatura's ore output.[70] Such ores, of course, required concentration. The remaining 80 percent is produced from underground mines.

## Quality and Geographic Problems

A long-term deficiency in Soviet manganese ores in the category $A + B + C$ was observed by Feitelman in 1969 when he stated that, of the reserves *in that category*, 70 percent were represented by low-grade carbonate ores.[71] Boyarsky (1975) recognized that carbonate ores account for about 60 percent of the usable ores, but that ores suitable for ferromanganese and the chemical industry constitute no more than 30 percent.[72] Lelyukhina noted that high quality ores not requiring enrichment had sharply declined.[73]

As the Bolshoi Tokmak ores are increasingly utilized during the 1980s, Soviet manganese production will compel widespread mining of carbonate ores. Though the cost of producing 1 ton of crude ore may be less at Bolshoi Tokmak than at Nikopol because of surface mining, the cost of concentration will run 1.5 to 2 times more than with Nikopol ores.[74]

The increasing reliance on lower-grade manganese ores is evident from the ratio of crude ore mined to usable ore. In 1950, 4.7 million tons of crude manganese ore yielded 3.4 million tons of concentrate.[75] In 1965, it required 16.3 million tons of crude to produce 7.6 million tons of concentrate. In 1976, 20 million tons produced 8.4 million tons of marketable ore.[76] The Ukraine, until 1971, fared better than the country as a whole. In that year 12.8 million tons of crude yielded 5.6 million tons of concentrate.[77] Since then the ratio has undoubtedly worsened. Still, Nikopol ores are deemed "adequate for the foreseeable future."[78] And, with the utilization of Bolshoi Tokmak ores, it is expected that Ukrainian output over the next two decades will rise from 7.4 million metric tons to at least 25 to 26 million.[79]

The decline in usable ores is clearly evident in the fields in the eastern regions. There the manganese base is regarded by Soviet writers as "unsatisfactory." Output at Urals, Siberian and Kazakhstan mines has never contrib-

TABLE 6
Indices of Output of Nikopol Enterprises, 1965

| Enterprise | Output percent | Of which by open pit | Manganese content in marketed ore, percent | Production cost of marketed ore, ruble/ton |
|---|---|---|---|---|
| Nikopol Manganese Trust | 43.1 | 52.4 | 28.5–54.4 | 14.90 |
| Ordzhonikidze Manganese Trust | 46.1 | 76.6 | 27.7–55.28 | 13.31 |
| Chkalov Mine-Concentrator Combine | 10.8 | 100.0 | 30.96–48.32 | 17.37 |
| Nikopol Basin Total | 100.0 | 68.8 | 39.62 | — |

SOURCE: *Ukraina i Moldaviya*, in the series *Prirodnye usloviya i yestestvennye resursy SSSR* (Moscow: Nauka, 1972), p. 380.

uted more than a fraction of total Soviet production (Table 5), but these scattered deposits have played a role in regional iron and steel production. Although output from these eastern mines exceeded 200,000 tons in the 1940s and 1950s, it appears to have leveled off at around 50,000 tons in recent years (Table 5). Virtually all of this is attributed to the mines in Kazakhstan, which have sent manganese to the ferroalloy plants at Yermak (opened 1968) and Nikopol, the Kazakhstan ores being sulfur-free and free of impurities.[80] In any event the future prospects for manganese production in the eastern regions, according to Boyarsky, are not favorable.[81]

Approximately 95 percent of the "active" deposits of commercial or industrial quality are to be found in the western regions of the country, in the Ukraine and Georgia.[82] The Ukraine alone possesses more than 82 percent of the ores of the USSR falling within the superior quality range, whatever their deficiencies may be.

## Exports

Soviet exports of manganese in recent decades have been largely to the Comecon countries in Eastern Europe. Prior to World War II, imports of manganese ore from the Soviet Union represented approximately one-third of all

manganese imported by the United States, but, with the onset of the cold war, the trade came to an end. In view of the Soviet Union's large domestic consumption of manganese for its iron and steel industry, it is no longer the world's largest exporter, having been exceeded by South Africa, Brazil, and India (Table 7), and since 1970 also by Gabon and Australia.

After the early 1950s, Soviet exports of manganese steadily increased, reaching a peak of 1.48 million metric tons in 1974, when some 17 percent of production was exported (Table 8). Thereafter growing domestic needs

TABLE 7
World Exports of Manganese Ores

| | 1965 | | 1970 | |
|---|---|---|---|---|
| | thousand metric tons | percent | thousand metric tons | percent |
| Total | 8,008 | 100.0 | 8,818 | 100.0 |
| South Africa | 1,054 | 13.2 | 2,040 | 23.2 |
| Brazil | 1,068 | 13.3 | 1,588 | 18.0 |
| India | 1,580 | 19.7 | 1,580 | 17.9 |
| USSR | 1,020 | 12.7 | 1,200 | 13.6 |
| Gabon | 1,147 | 14.3 | 825 | 9.4 |
| Australia | 46 | 0.7 | 625 | 7.1 |
| Zaire | 406 | 5.1 | 330 | 3.7 |
| Ghana | 574 | 7.2 | 250 | 2.8 |
| Morocco | 321 | 4.0 | 105 | 1.2 |
| Ivory Coast | 171 | 2.1 | 45 | 0.5 |
| Guinea | 158 | 2.0 | — | — |
| Others | 451 | 5.7 | 230 | 2.6 |

SOURCE: *Zakavkazsky ekonomichesky rayon*, in the series *Razvitiye i razmeshcheniye proizvoditelnykh sil SSSR* (Moscow: Nauka, 1973), p. 57.

TABLE 8
Soviet Exports of Manganese

| | Manganese ore (thousand metric tons) | Dioxide (metric tons) | Ferromanganese (metric tons) |
|---|---|---|---|
| 1940 | 263 | — | — |
| 1946 | 281 | — | — |
| 1950 | 277 | — | — |
| 1955 | 852 | — | — |
| 1958 | 833 | 7,400 | 45,700 |
| 1959 | 979 | 8,600 | 50,300 |
| 1960 | 973 | 9,000 | 50,800 |
| 1961 | 896 | 9,200 | 51,600 |
| 1962 | 963 | 11,500 | 55,700 |
| 1963 | 986 | 8,900 | 58,900 |
| 1964 | 979 | 13,100 | 59,600 |
| 1965 | 1,020 | 15,800 | 67,300 |
| 1966 | 1,218 | 16,900 | 87,400 |
| 1967 | 1,250 | 17,000 | 87,000 |
| 1968 | 1,150 | 19,000 | 97,200 |
| 1969 | 1,197 | 18,200 | 107,500 |
| 1970 | (1,200) | 15,900 | 118,500 |
| 1971 | (1,200) | 16,800 | 124,800 |
| 1972 | (1,300) | 13,900 | 129,700 |
| 1973 | (1,300) | 8,700 | 135,000 |
| 1974 | 1,482 | — | — |
| 1975 | 1,411 | — | — |
| 1976 | 1,342 | — | — |
| 1977 | 1,352 | — | — |
| 1978 | 1,186 | — | — |
| 1979 | 1,317 | — | — |
| 1980 | 1,255 | — | — |
| 1981 | 1,194 | — | — |

SOURCES: *Vneshnyaya torgovlya SSSR* [Foreign trade of the USSR], statistical yearbooks, various years. From 1970 through 1973, total manganese exports were rounded to the nearest hundred thousand tons; exports of manganese dioxide and ferromanganese were last reported in 1973.

and a loss of Western markets led to a decline of exports, which were down to 13 percent of production by 1981.

Most Soviet manganese exports have gone to Czechoslovakia and Poland, two countries with large iron and steel industries (Table 9). Until the early 1970s, a substantial share of Soviet manganese exports also went to the developed industrial countries of Western Europe and Japan, but most of these exports were phased out during the 1970s. In 1970, the four principal customers in Eastern Europe (Bulgaria, Czechoslovakia, East Germany, Poland) took about 63 percent of Soviet exports; by 1981, the share of these countries had risen to 93 percent (Table 9).

Soviet exports of manganese ore have also included dioxide, suitable for batteries and the chemical industry, but volumes are modest (Table 8). Eastern Europe has been the principal destination, notably East Germany, Poland, and Czechoslovakia. The East European countries took as well a significant portion of the Soviet exports of ferromanganese and silicomanganese. This volume should increase in the years ahead as a result of a contract awarded to Japan in 1976 for a new high carbon ferromanganese plant. The new plant was scheduled for completion in 1980, with an output of 1.1 million tons per year.

Chiatura continues to account for over half the Soviet exports of manganese which now is principally in the form of concentrates. The rest originates at Nikopol, although exports from the Ukraine represent only about 10 percent of its concentrate. The detemination of the quality of Chiatura ores and the need for concentration has led to a Soviet recommendation that in future *all*

manganese concentrate be converted into ferromanganese (at the Zestafoni ferroalloy plant) for export. Presumably the Japanese contract will help achieve this goal.

---

## NOTES

1. An excellent, but brief, discussion of the mode of occurrence is found in A. H. Sully, *Manganese* (London: Butterworths Scientific Publications, 1955), pp. 3–5.

2. V. V. Strishkov, "Mineral Industries of the USSR." Report originally published in *Mining Annual Review*, *1979*, reprinted by Bureau of Mines, U.S. Department of Interior, Washington, 1979, p. 16. According to Strishkov, reserves of manganese ore in categories $A + B + C_1$ were estimated at the end of 1969 by the Soviets at 2.5 billion tons, with an average manganese content of 23 to 26.4 percent. Personal correspondence from Strishkov, dated 20 June 1978, confirmed the estimate. Strishkov wrote that Soviet manganese reserves in place as of January 1976 totalled 2.565 billion tons, with a metal content of 23 to 28 percent.

See also George Markon et al., *Mineral Industries of Eastern Europe and the USSR* (Bureau of Mines, U.S. Department of Interior, Washington, 1978), p. 27. *Ukraina i Moldaviya*, in the series *Prirodnye usloviya i yestestvennye resursy SSSR* [Natural conditions and natural resources of the USSR] (Moscow: Nauka, 1972), p. 72, estimates the total reserves in the Ukraine at 2.408 billion tons (as of 1 January 1971), of which 2.094 billion tons fall within the categories $A + B + C_1$. This estimate would give the Ukraine 94 percent of reserves in those categories.

3. Gilbert L. DeHuff, "Manganese," *Mineral Facts and Problems*, 1975 edition (Bureau of Mines Bulletin 667, U.S. Department of Interior, Washington, 1975), p. 658.

4. DeHuff, "Manganese," p. 659.

5. The mineral reserves of the Soviet Union have been classified according to $A + B + C_1$ categories since 1933. In short, the categories refer to the following levels:

$A$ -fully studied and surveyed (operating reserves)
$B$ -geologically studied (total reserves)
$C_1$-geologically established, confirmed by scattered testing and ore sampling (indicated reserves)
$C_2$-hypothesized (inferred reserves).

See Demitri B. Shimkin, *Minerals. A Key to Soviet Power* (Cambridge: Harvard University Press, 1953), pp. 19–20.

6. V. V. Strishkov, "Mineral Industries of the USSR," p. 16; *Soviet Geography: Review and Translation* (hereafter *SGRT*), vo. 21, no. 4 (April 1980): 255.

7. For a detailed geological assessment of the occurrence of manganese in the Soviet Union, see V. I. Smirnov, ed., *Ore Deposits of the USSR*, vol. 1 (London: Pitman Publishing Ltd., 1977): 114–78.

8. Sully, *Manganese*, pp. 103, gives a brief account of the history of manganese as a recognized metal. For a discussion of modern uses of manganese, see *The Making of Steel* (New York: American Iron and Steel Institute, 1951), pp. 76 ff.

9. Smirnov, *Ore Deposits*, p. 115 ff. See also D. V. Naliv-

---

TABLE 9
Soviet Exports of Manganese Ore by Country
(1970, 1975, 1980, 1981) (thousand metric tons)

|  | 1970 | 1975 | 1980 | 1981 |
|---|---|---|---|---|
| Total | (1,200) | 1,411 | 1,255 | 1,194 |
| Comecon |  |  |  |  |
|   Bulgaria | 80 | 126 | 125 | 117 |
|   Czechoslovakia | 153 | 341 | 397 | 372 |
|   East Germany | 175 | 179 | 135 | 130 |
|   Poland | 365 | 484 | 490 | 493 |
| Other Centrally Planned Economies |  |  |  |  |
|   North Korea | 21 | 20 | 29 | 15 |
|   Yugoslavia | 31 | 30 | 36 | 38 |
| Developed Market Economies |  |  |  |  |
|   Britain | 42 | — | — | — |
|   Canada | 11 | — | — | — |
|   France | 109 | — | — | — |
|   Japan | 96 | 112 | — | — |
|   Norway | 37 | 57 | — | — |
|   Sweden | 47 | 26 | — | — |
|   West Germany | 43 | — | — | — |
| Not identified | — | 36 | 43 | 29 |

SOURCES: *Vneshnyaya torgovlya v 1970 g.* [Foreign trade of the USSR in 1970] (Moscow, 1971); *Vneshnyaya torgovlya v 1975 g.* (Moscow, 1976); *Vneshnyaya torgovlya v 1981 g.* (Moscow, 1982). The 1970 export total is rounded in the source to 1.2 million tons.

kin, *Geology of the USSR* (Toronto: University of Toronto Press, 1973), pp. 371–72; N. P. Banny et al., *Ekonomika chernoi metallurgii SSSR* [Economics of the iron and steel industry in the USSR] (Moscow: Metallurgiya, 1960), p. 207 ff.; I. M. Varentsov, *Sedimentary Manganese Ores* (Amsterdam: Elsevier Publishing Co., 1964), p. 7 ff.; D. M. Korulin, *Geologiya i iskopayemye SSSR* [Geology and minerals of the USSR] (Minsk: Vysshaya Shkola, 1965), p. 67 ff.; V. A. Boyarsky, *Razvitiye otkrytoi dobychi rud, 1950–1970 g.* [The development of the open extraction of ore, 1950–1970] (Moscow: Nauka, 1975), p. 23 ff.; N. D. Lelyukhina, *Ekonomicheskaya effektivnost razmeshcheniya chernoi metallurgii* [The cost-effectiveness of the distribution of the iron and steel industry] (Moscow: Nauka, 1973), p. 228 ff.

10. Lelyukhina states that the Georgian deposits have 8.9 percent of Soviet reserves in categories $A + B + C_1$, as does Boyarsky. However, Feitelman indicates that Chiatura has only 6.5 percent of the manganese in those categories. See N. G. Feitelman, *Ekonomicheskaya effektivnost zatrat na podgotovku mineralno-syryevoi bazy SSSR* [Cost-effectivess of investment in the mineral resource base of the USSR] (Moscow: Nauka, 1969), p. 38.

11. Lelyukhina, *Effektivnost*, p. 228; Feitelman, *Effektivnost*, p. 38.

12. Smirnov, *Ore Deposits*, pp. 119–37. See also *Ukraina i Moldaviya*, pp. 379–82.

13. Sully, *Manganese*, pp. 26–27.

14. Banny, *Ekonomika*, p. 208; A. S. Osintsev, *Ekonomika chernoi metallurgii SSSR* [Economics of the iron and steel industry in the USSR] (Moscow: Metallurgiya, 1969), p. 56.

15. Sully, *Manganese*, p. 26; A. W. Groves, *Manganese*, 2nd ed. (London: Imperial Institute, Mineral Resources Department, 1938), p. 101. For an up-to-date evaluation see Gilbert L. DeHuff, "Manganese," in *Minerals Yearbook, 1976* (Bureau of Mines, U.S. Department of Interior, Washington, 1977), p. 812.

16. Lelyukhina, *Effektivnost*, p. 229.

17. *Razvitiye metallurgii v Ukrainskoi SSR* [Development of the iron and steel industry in the Ukrainian SSR] (Kiev: Naukova dumka, 1980), pp. 406–07; *Gorny zhurnal*, 1978, no. 5; V. V. Strishkov, "Mineral Industries of the USSR." Report originally published in *Mining Annual Review, 1977*, reprinted by Bureau of Mines, U.S. Department of Interior, Washington, 1977, p. 13.

18. *Ukraina i Moldaviya*, p. 381; Smirnov, *Ore Deposits*, p. 137; Varentsov, *Sedimentary Manganese*, pp. 7–8; *Pravda Ukrainy*, 6 July 1979, 13 March 1980; *Sotsialisticheskaya industriya*, 26 October 1979.

19. An elaborate discussion of the Georgian manganese deposits is given in *Metallicheskiye poleznye iskopayemye* [Metallic mineral deposits], vol. 1, in the series *Prirodnye resursy Gruzinskoi SSR* [Natural resources of the Georgian SSR] (Moscow: Akademiya nauk SSSR, 1958), pp. 48–76. See Smirnov, *Ore Deposits*, pp. 137–43, where the Laba deposit in the North Caucasus is also discussed, pp. 149–50; Lelyukhina, *Effektivnost*, pp. 231–32; Boyarsky, *Razvitiye*, p. 33.

20. Groves, *Manganese*, pp. 98–101; Sully, *Manganese*,

pp. 24–26; Nalivkin, *Geology*, pp. 676–77; Smirnov, *Ore Deposits*, pp. 137–43; Theodore Shabad, *Basic Industrial Resources of the USSR* (New York: Columbia University Press, 1969), p. 158; see also D. Ghambashidze, *Mineral Resources of Georgia and Caucasia* (London: George Allen & Unwin Ltd., 1919), pp. 21–22.

21. Smirnov, *Ore Deposits*, pp. 137–38.

22. *Zakavkazsky ekonomichesky rayon* [Transcaucasian economic region], in the series *Razvitiye i razmeshcheniye proizvoditelnykh sil SSSR* [Development and distribution of the productive forces of the USSR] (Moscow: Nauka, 1973), pp. 55–56.

23. Smirnov, *Ore Deposits*, p. 140.

24. Ibid., pp. 140–41.

25. Nalivkin, *Geology*, p. 677.

26. Banny, *Ekonomika*, p. 207.

27. E. Ya. Kandelaki, *Ekonomicheskiye problemy chernoi metallurgii Gruzinskoi SSR* [Economic problems of the iron and steel industry in the Georgian SSR], vol. 1 (Tbilisi, 1968), p. 202.

28. Nalivkin, *Geology*, p. 677.

29. *Zakavkazsky ekonomichesky rayon*, pp. 55–56.

30. Lelyukhina, *Effektivnost*, p. 230.

31. "The Mineral Industry of the USSR." *Minerals Yearbook, 1974*, vol. 3 (Bureau of Mines, U.S. Department of Interior, Washington, 1977), p. 955.

32. DeHuff, "Manganese 1975," p. 660.

33. Smirnov, *Ore Deposits*, pp. 143–148; 166–68.

34. Ibid., p. 147.

35. P. Ya. Antropov, *Bogatstva nedr nashei rodiny* [The mineral wealth of our country] (Moscow: Gospolitizdat, 1956), p. 28; P. Ya. Antropov, *Perspektivy osvoyeniya prirodnykh bogatstv SSSR 1959–1965* [Prospects of the development of the natural wealth of the USSR 1959–1965] (Moscow: Gosplanizdat, 1959), p. 50; Smirnov, *Ore Deposits*, p. 148.

36. Groves, *Manganese*, p. 103. Reserves of manganese in the Sverdlovsk area were estimated in 1934 at about 8 million tons. Smirnov, *Ore Deposits*, p. 167.

37. Lelyukhina, *Effektivnost*, p. 232; Smirnov, *Ore Deposits*, p. 167.

38. Smirnov, *Ore Deposits*, p.167.

39. There is a brief reference to manganese ore bodies in *Kazakhstan* in the series *Prirodnye usloviya i yestestvennye resursy SSSR* (Moscow: Nauka, 1969), pp. 60–61. See also Smirnov, *Ore Deposits*, pp. 148–149; 160–65.

40. Smirnov, *Ore Deposits*, p. 164.

41. Lelyukhina, *Effektivnost*, p. 234; *Kazakhstan*, p. 60.

42. Lelyukhina, *Effektivnost*, p. 234.

43. Smirnov, *Ore Deposits*, pp. 148–49.

44. Ibid., p. 153.

45. Ibid., p. 153.

46. Banny, *Ekonomika*, p. 208; see also Nalivkin, *Geology*, p. 469. See reference in *Zapadnaya Sibir* [Western Siberia], in the series *Prirodnye usloviya i yestestvennye resursy SSSR* (Moscow: AN SSSR, 1963), p. 56.

47. Sully, *Manganese*, p. 27; Groves, *Manganese*, p. 102.

48. Sully, *Manganese*, p. 27.

49. Smirnov, *Ore Deposits*, pp. 150–51.

50. Ibid., pp. 171–72.

51. A. H. Curtis, *Manganese Ores*. Monographs on Mineral Resources with Special Reference to the British Empire. Imperial Institute (London: John Murray, 1919), p. 74; *50 let Sovetskoi geologii* [50 years of Soviet geology] (Moscow: Nedra, 1968), p. 268.

52. Curtis, *Manganese Ores*, p. 74.

53. Ghambashidze, *Mineral Resources*, pp. 21–23; Groves, *Manganese*, p. 99; *The Marketing of Manganese Ores*. Trade Information Bulletin No. 599. (Bureau of Foreign and Domestic Commerce, U.S. Department of Commerce, Washington, 1929), p. 16.

54. Curtis, *Manganese Ores*, p. 76.

55. Ibid., p. 76.

56. Ibid., pp. 78–79.

57. Ibid., p. 75.

58. Ibid., p. 76.

59. *Industrial Readjustments of Certain Mineral Industries Affected by the War*. Tariff Information Series No. 21 (U.S. Tariff Commission, Washington, 1920), p. 133.

60. Groves, *Manganese*, p. 99.

61. Ibid., p. 99.

62. Ibid., p. 101.

63. Ibid., p. 103, citing Gubkin, 1936.

64. Shimkin, *Minerals*, p. 65.

65. *50 let Sovetskoi geologii*, pp. 270–71.

66. *Ukraina i Moldaviya*, p. 381.

67. Osintsev, *Ekonomika*, p. 56; Boyarsky, *Razvitiye*, p. 19.

68. See Shabad, *Industrial Resources*, pp. 45, 158; Shabad, "News Notes," *SGRT*, vol. 12, no. 9 (November 1971): 624.

69. Shabad, "News Notes," *SGRT*, vol. 20, no. 4 (April 1979): 271; see also Ye. D. Kobakhidze, *Promyshlenny kompleks Gruzinskoi SSR* [Industrial complex of the Georgian SSR] (Tbilisi, 1974), p. 41.

70. Strishkov, "Mineral Industries," p. 16.

71. Feitelman, *Effektivnost*, p. 38.

72. Boyarsky, *Razvitiye*, p. 33.

73. Lelyukhina, *Effektivnost*, pp. 228 ff.

74. *Ukraina i Moldaviya*, p. 381.

75. Shabad, *Industrial Resources*, p. 45.

76. Strishkov, "Mineral Industries," p. 13.

77. Shabad, "News Notes," *SGRT*, vol. 14, no. 3 (March 1973): 209; see also Kandelaki, *Problemy*, p. 223.

78. Boyarsky, *Razvitiye*, p. 33.

79. *Ukraina i Moldaviya* p. 381.

80. Lelyukhina, *Effektivnost*, pp. 229, 234.

81. Boyarsky, *Razvitiye*, p. 33.

82. Feitelman, *Effektivnost*, p. 38.

# 22

# SOVIET CHROMITE ORES: OUTPUT AND EXPORT

W. A. DOUGLAS JACKSON
University of Washington

The Soviet Union, which has long held a commanding world position as a producer and exporter of chromite, appears to have been forced in recent years to reevaluate its situation as exports declined after having reached a peak in the early 1970s and production began to stagnate. The difficulties stem from a decline in readily accessible open-pit mining of high-grade ore in the Soviet Union's chromite district and the need for beginning the use of lower-grade ores through beneficiation and the exploitation of deeper ore bodies through the time-consuming and costly excavation of large shaft mines. The deteriorating chromite position has been responsible for widespread prospecting and exploration for additional chromite sources in the USSR.[1] It has also prompted speculation in some quarters in the West that the Soviet Union may be displaying interest in gaining access to foreign chromite sources and might eventually turn from exporter to a potential net importer.[2] For this reason, a review of Soviet chromite ores, the history of development and export, is warranted.

## The Nature and Uses of Chromite Ores

The geologic origins, formations, and chemical composition of chromite ores as a rule are diverse and complex.[3] Although Soviet commercial ores are highly concentrated geographically, they are no exception to the rule. It is because of this diversity and complexity that generalizations concerning Soviet chromite ores cannot be discussed here in any detail.

Spatially and genetically, according to Smirnov, chromite deposits are associated with complexes of ultramafic rocks and belong to the group of magmatic formations.[4] As a result, chromite ores are found in intrusives. Such intrusives or ultramafic massifs are distributed in geosynclinal areas, in zones where the geosynclines and platform rock meet, and on platforms. The period of formation of such massifs extends from the pre-Paleozoic to the Mesozoic, inclusively.

In these massifs, the ore bodies are usually arranged in the form of belts, and are connected with deep-seated localized faulting. However, the degree of saturation of geosynclinal areas with ultramafic rocks is uneven, and the dimensions of the outcrops of such massifs vary greatly. In the Soviet Union chromite deposits and ore-shows occur at various depths.

Chromite, a mineral element ($FeO.Cr_2O_3$), is the principal source of chromium, a very hard, whitish metal with a number of significant and vital uses.[5] Like manganese, chromite serves as an alloy in the iron and steel industry. Small amounts of chromium add strength and hardness to steel; larger amounts turn iron into stainless steel. In addition, chromium is used for electro-plating nickel to provide a hard, shiny, nontarnishable coating.[6] Historically, chromite was first used in the making of pigments and chemicals for leather tanning. Its other uses, i.e., in the iron and steel industry, were not developed until late in the nineteenth century.

Chromite, by its composition a ferrous chromate, may contain as much as 68 percent chromic oxide and 32 percent ferrous oxide. In some pure chromites, a certain proportion of chromic oxide has been replaced by ferrous oxide. It is possible to have chromite ores that contain as little as 30 percent chromic oxide, but are nevertheless free from waste materials.

Depending on their use, chromite ores are divided into three categories: metallurgical, refractory, and chemical. The metallurgical ores must contain a chromium-to-iron ratio of up to 3 to 1 for maximum usefulness; they should, therefore, possess no less than 48 percent chromic oxide. A high-chromium iron alloy known as ferrochromium carries 65 to 72 percent chromium, less than 2.5 percent silicon, and minor amounts of manganese and carbon. The United States iron and steel industry long used a high-grade chromite, containing 45 to 55 percent chromic oxide, or 30 to 36 percent chromium. Since much of the chromite mined in the United States belongs to the high-iron category, American ores remain unsatisfactory as a metallurgical resource.[7] For this reason, the United States has remained almost totally dependent on foreign quality imports, a dependency all the more critical since chromium is one of the most indispensable of the ferroalloy metals.

For refractory purposes, the chromite ores should be low in iron, but high in chromic oxide, and possess as well aluminum oxide ($Al_2O_3$). On firing, magnesium oxide (MgO) is added to form magnesium silicates. In the chemical industry, chromite ores should be high also in chromic oxide, but low in both aluminum oxide and silica ($SiO_2$).

**Soviet Chromite Ores**

In the Soviet Union, chromite ore deposits and ore-shows are found in many regions of the country, including the Urals, the Caucasus, Central and Eastern Siberia, Eastern and Southern Kazakhstan, and the Far East.[8] As in the case of commercial manganese output, Soviet chromite ores and production are highly localized in the central and southern Urals. In the central Urals, mining at one time or another has been reported from 25 sites, including Sarany (Perm Oblast), Klyuchi (Sverdlovsk Oblast), Verblyuzhegorsk (Chelyabinsk Oblast), Khalilovo (Orenburg Oblast).[9] These are for the most part older mining sites on which Soviet industry and the export trade drew in the past. Except for Sarany, these older sites ceased operation with the discovery in the late 1930s of the great South Kempirsai massif in the Mugodzhar Hills of the southern Urals, in Aktyubinsk Oblast of northwest Kazakhstan. The Sarany ores, now mined in a single shaft mine, are of low grade, suitable only for refractory and chemical uses, and contributed only 6 percent of Soviet chromite output in 1975, or about 240,000 metric tons out of a total production of 3.4 million. The Kempirsai massif, centered on the chromite mining center of Khromtau, has been exploited since the late 1930s by the Donskoye mining administration, named for a village on the site. The Khromtau operation became the basis of Soviet self-sufficiency and expanding export trade. In 1965, about 40 percent of the Khromtau output, then totaling about 2.4 million tons, went to the Soviet ferroalloy plants, of which one is near by at Aktyubinsk, for conversion into ferrochromium for the domestic iron and steel industry, while 31 percent went for export. The rest went for refractory and chemical uses in Soviet industry.[10]

Deposits of the Central Urals

*Sarany.* The Sarany deposit is located on the western slope of the Urals in Perm Oblast, some 60 km east of the ferroalloy city of Chusovoi.[11] Here ultramafic rocks have been intruded into metamorphosed Paleozoic beds. The

TABLE 1
Analysis of the Crude Ores of Sarany Deposit
(average content, in percent)

| Ore Body | $Cr_2O_3$ | FeO | $SiO_2$ | CaO | $Al_2O_3$ | MgO |
|----------|-----------|-------|---------|------|-----------|-------|
| Western  | 35.86     | 17.68 | 6.25    | 0.24 | 15.11     | 16.85 |
| Central  | 38.24     | 18.53 | 5.00    | 1.36 | 18.80     | 15.16 |
| Eastern  | 33.17     | 20.05 | 5.14    | —    | 20.35     | 16.20 |

SOURCE: V. I. Smirnov, ed., *Ore Deposits of the USSR*, vol. 1 (London: Pitman Publishing Co., 1977), p. 231.

intrusive rock is strongly serpentinized peridotite, and several bands of ore are found in it. In addition the stream beds draining the area contain deposits of placer chromite. A rough estimate dating to the 1930s placed total reserves at nearly 7 million tons.[12] However, the ores contain 35 percent chromic oxide, making them suitable only for the production of refractories (Table 1). Annual output averages 200,000 tons. The only mining is carried on at the main Sarany mine in the northern part of the ore area, around the urban settlement of Sarany, founded in 1940.

*Klyuchi.* On the eastern slopes of the Urals, 35 km southeast of Sverdlovsk, on the left bank of the Iset River, is a cluster of 200 small deposits and ore-shows.[13] The age of the massif is believed to be Carboniferous, displaying ultramafic rocks and other complexes. The chromites are found principally in peridotites and dunites, as elongated ore bodies. Reserves in the 1930s were estimated at 600,000 tons of ore carrying 17 percent oxide, and are no longer being used.

*Verblyuzhegorsk.* These ores, together with the deposits at Sarany and Klyuchi, formed the basis of the Russian chromite industry from around 1930 until the discovery of the Kempirsai massif.[14] The Verblyuzhegorsk ores are located on the eastern slope of the Urals in southern Chelyabinsk Oblast not far from Kartaly. Reserves were estimated at 170,000 tons in the 1930s.

*Khalilovo.* Although these ore bodies lie in the southern section of the Urals, they are included here because in geologic origins they are closer to the ores referred to above, and have little or no connection with the Kempirsai massif. Mining began in 1926 and, prior to World War II, Orenburg Oblast, in which the ores were located, produced about a fifth of Soviet output.[15] The chief deposits were around Khalilovo, near Orsk. The ores carried an average grade of 50 percent $Cr_2O_3$. Output was exported via Novorossiisk on the Black Sea, some 700 km away. Later, there was also some mining, especially in World War II, at the Akkarga site, on the border between Orenburg Oblast and Kazakhstan.

Deposits of the Southern Urals in Northwest Kazakhstan

*South Kempirsai Massif (Khromtau).* Discoveries of chromite were first recorded as early as 1920.[16] But it was not until 1936 that small chromite outcrops were identified in the southern part of the Kempirsai massif of deep-seated volcanic rocks, which had already been yielding nickel-cobalt ores in its northern portion, around the mining settlement of Batamshinsky. In 1937, an exploration party located the main deposits of high-grade chromite at the village of Donskoye, which was to give its name to the new mining administration as well as to the railroad station at the end of a 25-km spur. However the mining settlement itself, which began operations in 1938, was named Khromtau (chrome mountain). It was raised to the urban status of workers settlement in 1943 and had a population of 7,672 in the 1959 census. Further growth resulted in its being raised to city status in 1967, and its population in the 1970 census appears to have been between 10,000 and 15,000.

Four ore fields have been identified in the South Kempirsai massif, and within them are concentrated about 160 deposits and ore-shows. All the commercial deposits of high quality chromite ore are concentrated in the southeast, in the Donskoye ore field, around Khromtau.

The structures of the chromite ores in the massif are complex and varied. Chemical composition of the raw chromite, too, is subject to considerable fluctuation. In some deposits, such as the Almaz-Zhemchuzhina, the amount of chromic oxide rises to 58–59 percent, but in other formations it is lower. The amount of iron oxide present also varies throughout the Donskoye field but within narrower limits. The average for the latter is about 12.5 percent (Table 2).

Soviet geologists recognize two ore zones in the Kempirsai massif—a western and eastern zone (Figure 1). The two zones, extending roughly 23 km NNE, are joined at the southern end forming a cluster of deposits just south and east of the town of Khromtau. This is the area where the first open pits were initially excavated, starting with the Gigant pit east of Khromtau in 1938 and the Almaz-Zhemchuzhina, now called the Obyedinenny (United) pit, in 1940. In the western zone, some 9 km north of Khromtau, another major cluster of deposits known as 20 Years of the Kazakh SSR was developed starting in the middle 1950s, when chromite production accelerated its rate of growth. Another major development began in 1973 in the area of the adjoining deposits known as 40 Years of the Kazakh SSR and Molodezhnoye, which are situated in the eastern ore zone, 4 km northeast of the 20 Years deposit. The development in the eastern ore zone involved the excavation of an open pit in the 40 Years deposit, starting operations in 1978, and the first major deep shaft mine in the Molodezhnoye deposit, which yielded its first ore in 1981. Data on the reserves contained within the various deposits of the western and eastern zones are not available; they have long been recognized as extensive, especially in the 40 Years—Molodezhnoye deposit.[17] This important deposit as well as the 20 Years deposit in the western zone have been used by Smirnov for analysis[18] (Table 3).

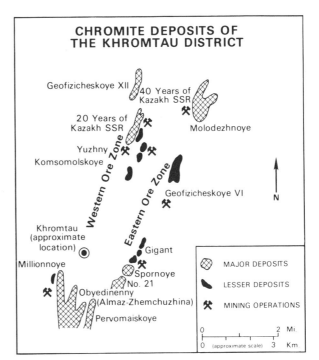

**CHROMITE DEPOSITS OF THE KHROMTAU DISTRICT**

Figure 1
Source: "Chromite deposits of the Khromtau district," *Gorny zhurnal*, 1978, no. 7, p. 7.

## Other Soviet Deposits

*Caucasus.* The chromite ores of the Caucasus are located in the Armenian SSR on the northeastern shore of Lake Sevan near Shorzha.[19] The ultramafic massif, stretching for some 80 km to the southeast, crosses into the Azerbaijan SSR. Some ten small deposits and ore-shows falling primarily within serpentinized dunite and peridotite, have been discovered. In addition to the Shorzha, deposits at Geidara, Ipyag and other sites have been worked, but the quality of the ores varies. Reserves, in any case, are not large.

*Siberia.* Of the reserves and quality of the ore-shows in Siberia, for example in the Kuznetsk Alatau and in the Tuvinian ASSR, little is known.

### Early Development of Russian-Soviet Ores

The chromite ores of Russia were first identified in the early 19th century.[20] Sarany was know in the 1830s, but mining in the Urals did not get under way until after mid-century. Though the agency of foreign companies, most of the output was exported. From about 1830 to 1870, the United States was the leading producer of chromite in the world, with mines in Pennsylvania and Maryland. From then until near the end of the century, first place shifted to Turkey. Thereafter, Russia advanced to first place, a position held for the next five years. For 1901, output amounted to 22,169 metric tons, or 47 percent of total world output.[21] Although Russian mines yielded

TABLE 2
Analysis of Principal Components in Deposits
of the Khromtau Area (percent)

| Deposit | Cr$_2$O$_3$ | FeO | S$_1$O$_2$ | CaO | P |
|---|---|---|---|---|---|
| Obyedinenny (Almaz-Zhemchuzhina) | 49.05 | 12.5 | 8.1 | 0.42 | 0.002 |
| Millionnoye | 49.5 | 12.3 | 8.2 | — | 0.008 |
| Pervomaiskoye | 46.0 | 14.8 | 9.4 | 0.3 | 0.001 |
| Geofizicheskoye VI | 55.0 | 12.2 | 4.9 | — | 0.020 |
| Komsomolskoye | 49.6 | 11.6 | 7.8 | — | 0.012 |
| Geofizicheskoye XII | 10.5 | 8.4 | 29.2 | 0.23 | 0.001 |

Source: V. I. Smirnov, ed., *Ore Deposits of the USSR* vol. 1 (London: Pitman Publishing Co., 1977), p. 200.

TABLE 3
Analysis of the Principal Components in the Ores of Selected Deposits of the Khromtau Area

| Ore Deposit | $Cr_2O_3$ | FeO | $SiO_2$ | CaO | P |
|---|---|---|---|---|---|
| 20 Years of Kazakh SSR | 22.3–62.1 | 9.2–15.1 | 1.3–21.7 | 0.22–1.3 | 0.03 |
| 40 Years of Kazakh SSR— | | | | | |
| Molodezhnoye | 19.3–58.95 | 9–14.5 | 0.3–30.0 | 0.84 | 0.005 |

SOURCE: V. I. Smirnov, ed., *Ore Deposits of the USSR* vol. 1 (London: Pitman Publishing Co., 1977), pp. 206, 207.

26,217 metric tons of chromite in 1913, a goal recovered by 1925 (30,111 tons),[22] primacy was surrendered to New Caledonia, whose shallow, easily worked deposits were substantially mined by 1920. For the 1920s, Southern Rhodesia (the present Zimbabwe) dominated the world markets, but with the discovery of the Kempirsai field, the Soviet Union assumed a commanding position. In 1935, Soviet production amounted to 217,000 metric tons, with Southern Rhodesia in second place. Throughout the interwar period, world production of chromite was dominated by the Soviet Union, Britain (through its African and Indian dependencies) and the United States, principally through its Philippine mines. United States needs were supplied by the Philippines, Cuba, New Caledonia and Britain.[23]

A major exporter prior to the revolution, Russia found its sales abroad collapse with the upheaval, and they resumed only in 1926. In 1936, exports ceased altogether, by which time the country was consuming the output of its own mines. The discovery and development of the Kempirsai deposits changed the Soviet Union's world status, as the only major industrial state totally self-sufficient in chromite and chromium.[24]

During the 1950s continued exploratory work in the Kempirsai massif, especially in the Donskoye field around Khromtau, raised Soviet estimates of total chromite reserves. Shimkin in 1953 assumed that Soviet reserves in the aggregate were 25 million to 30 million metric tons.[25] But, in the light of Soviet geological exploration, these estimates were soon rendered obsolete. Chromite reserves in the USSR were said to have risen sevenfold during the postwar period, from more than 35 million tons to some 270 million tons, of which 95 percent were in the Khromtau district. The reserve base was said to have been enhanced particularly by the discovery in 1960 of the 40 Years of the Kazakh SSR—Molodezhnoye deposits in the eastern ore zone and by the exploration of deeper portions of the older Almaz-

Zhemchuzhina (now Obyedinenny) deposit in 1955 and of the Millionnoye deposit in 1961. These discoveries alone were said to have added some 80 million metric tons to the reserves.[26]

Both the rapid postwar expansion of the iron and steel industry and the additional geological discoveries led to an enlargement of processing capacity. Electric furnaces for the production of ferrochromium at the Aktyubinsk ferroalloys plant were enlarged, and ferroalloy capacity elsewhere was also expanded.[27]

### Recent Status of Soviet Chromite Reserves, Output and Export

According to Boyarsky, the Soviet Union in early 1971 had a total of 28 chromite deposits, of which 26 had been explored to the extent of having explored reserves in the categories $A + B + C_1$ (Table 4). About 95 percent of these reserves, involving a total of 17 deposits, are concentrated in the Khromtau district of northwest Kazakhstan, the only supplier of high-grade metallurgical chromite. The other deposits are of lower grade and are situated in the Sarany district of Perm Oblast in the Urals. About 40 percent of the explored reserves, or 111 million metric tons out of 271 million, were within the $A + B$ category of industrial reserves ready for mining, with nearly 99 percent of the $A + B$ reserves concentrated in the Khromtau district. According to the Soviet estimate, the Soviet Union had 18 percent of world chromite reserves.[28]

While some of the smaller, easily accessible surface deposits of high-grade ore in operation since the later 1930s became depleted, new surface deposits continued to be developed, especially after 1955, when production began to surge. For example, the Yuzhny open pit on the 20 Years of the Kazakh SSR site began operations in 1974, the Geofizicheskoye I pit on the Obyedinenny site followed in 1976, and the 40 Years of the Kazakh SSR pit in

TABLE 4
Classification of Soviet Chromite Reserves (1971)

| | Number of Deposits | Deposits by Category | | |
|---|---|---|---|---|
| | | $A + B$ (000 tons) | $A + B + C_1$ (000 tons) | Percent of USSR total |
| Perm Oblast (Sarany) | 9 | 2,765 | 13,794 | 5.1 |
| Aktyubinsk Oblast (Khromtau) | 17 | 108,585 | 257,432 | 94.9 |
| Total | 26 | 111,350 | 271,226 | 100.0 |

SOURCE: V. A. Boyarsky, *Razvitiye otkrytoi dobychi rud, 1950–1970 gg.* (Moscow: Nauka, 1975), pp. 34–38.

1978.[29] By that year, in 40 years of operation, the Khromtau district had mined 63.1 million metric tons of crude ore in open-pit operations, yielding 54.1 percent of marketable ore after washing and sorting operations.[30]

It became apparent, however, that the exploitation of high-grade ore in open pits was beginning to approach a limit. A Western source, seeking to demonstrate that the Soviet Union would have to turn abroad for future supplies of chromite, said that the content of chromic oxide in some ores mined in the Khromtau district had dropped as low as 28 percent by the mid-1970s.[31] Soviet data continued to show a high average $Cr_2O_3$ content (Table 5).

The Soviet Union decided on a two-pronged approach to maintain its level of chromite production: first, through the construction of concentrators that would upgrade some of the poorer ores to marketable quality; second, through the tapping of deeper ore bodies by the costly and time-consuming construction of shaft mines.

The first concentrator, designed for the beneficiation of one million tons a year of ore with less than 45 percent chromic oxide, went into operation in 1973. By the late 1970s, it was turning out more than 500,000 tons of concentrate with a $Cr_2O_3$ content of 50 percent. A second concentrator was reported under construction.[32]

In an effort to tap some of the deeper high-grade ores, plans were announced in the 1970s for the construction of two large shaft mines. One, the Molodezhnoye mine, with a designed capacity of about 2 million tons, was to tap the deeper ore bodies in the large deposit of 40 Years of the Kazakh SSR—Molodezhnoye, in the eastern ore zone. The other, the Tsentralnaya (Central) mine, with a designed capacity of 4 million tons of ore, was to be built in the southern cluster of deposits, just south of Khromtau, including the Millionnoye, Almaz-Zhemchuzhina (now Obyedinenny), Pervomaiskoye and No. 21 deposits. After eight years of construction, the Molodezhnoye deep mine opened its first stage of 800,000 tons to production in May 1981. Under an apparently upgraded design, the second and third stages of the new mine were to raise its final capacity to 3 million tons instead of the 2 million originally announced. If the two huge underground mines are completed, the designed combined capacity would be 7 million tons, or double the 1980 Khromtau output of 3.4 million tons.[33]

The history of Soviet production and exports of chromite can be divided into three periods since World War II: (1) slow growth and low exports from 1945 to 1955; (2)

rapid growth of production and exports from 1955 to the early 1970s; (3) stagnating production and declining exports since 1975 (Table 6).

During the immediate postwar period, the Khromtau operation was still in a developing stage, and Soviet chromite production was widely scattered as a result of the wartime exploitation of a number of small deposits in the Urals on an emergency basis. As late as 1955, Khromtau contributed only 70 percent of Soviet output, or some 500,000 metric tons out of 700,000, with the rest coming from the Sarany deposit of the Urals.[34] Exports in the immediate postwar period had gone mainly to the United States, which took around 90 percent of Soviet chromite exports. But Soviet chromite shipments to the United States were suspended around 1950, at the height of the cold war, and Soviet exports dropped as a result to their lowest level in the early 1950s before a new market could be built up both in Western Europe and Japan and in Eastern Europe.

In the period of rapid growth of the Soviet chromite industry after 1955, production soared to the 3 million ton mark by 1970 as the development of the Khromtau district was intensified. The Khromtau operations accounted for 93–94 percent of all Soviet production, with the Sarany mine contributing 6–7 percent. This surge of production was accompanied by a rapid growth of exports, from 158,000 tons in 1955 to 1.2 million tons in 1970. The Soviet Union built up an export market in Western Europe and Japan, and shipments to the United States resumed around 1960. The expansion of the Soviet export market was further enhanced in the late 1960s as a result of United Nations economic sanctions against Rhodesia, the other major producer of metallurgical grade chromite, after its unilateral declaration of independence from Brit-

TABLE 5
Chemical Composition of Chromite Ores at
Five Open-pit Mines in the Khromtau Area (1974)

| Mines | $Cr_2O_3$ | FeO | $SiO_2$ | MgO | $Al_2O_3$ | CaO |
|---|---|---|---|---|---|---|
| Yuzhny | 51.5 | 13.5 | 6.53 | 15.6 | 7.8 | 0.84 |
| Millionnoye | 52.5 | 13.2 | 4.70 | 17.8 | 8.7 | 0.40 |
| Geofizicheskoye III | 44.5 | 10.2 | 9.86 | 22.1 | 6.06 | 2.56 |
| Geofizicheskoye VI | 52.8 | 11.4 | 5.30 | 17.7 | 6.83 | 2.90 |
| Obyedinenny (formerly Almaz-Zhemchuzhina) | 56.0 | 15.4 | 1.82 | 13.0 | 10.30 | 1.10 |

SOURCE: Stal, 1974, no. 10, p. 911.

TABLE 6
Output and Export of Soviet Chromite (1945–81)
(million metric tons)

| | Output | Exports | | Apparent consumption and stocks |
|---|---|---|---|---|
| | | Total | U.S. | |
| 1945 | 0.3 | 0.122 (1946) | 0.103 (1946) | 0.2 |
| 1950 | 0.42 | 0.096 | 0.063 | 0.32 |
| 1955 | 0.71 | 0.158 | — | 0.55 |
| 1960 | 1.45 | 0.427 | — | 1.0 |
| 1965 | 2.45 | 0.748 | 0.223 | 1.7 |
| 1970 | 2.95 | 1.2 | 0.410 | 1.8 |
| 1975 | 3.4 | 1.171 | 0.270 | 2.2 |
| 1977 | 3.0 | 0.673 | 0.077 | 2.3 |
| 1979 | 3.2 | 0.775 | 0.134 | 2.4 |
| 1980 | 3.4 | 0.567 | 0.099 | 2.8 |
| 1981 | 3.3 | 0.567 | 0.076 | 2.7 |
| 1985 Plan | 3.8 | | | |

SOURCES: Output based on Central Intelligence Agency, Handbook of Economic Statistics 1981 (NF HES 81-001, November 1981), p. 121, adjusted on basis of Khromtau production graph in Gorny zhurnal, 1978, no. 7, inside front cover; 1980 output from Gorny zhurnal, 1981, no. 1; 1981 output from Gorny zhurnal, 1982, no. 1; 1985 plan from Gorny zhurnal, 1982, no. 3. Vneshnyaya torgovlya SSSR, foreign trade statistical yearbooks (various years). Apparent consumption and stocks as a residual.

ain in 1965. By 1970, 80 percent of the Soviet Union's exports were going to the developed industrial countries.

The situation changed radically in the 1970s. Growth of the Soviet industry slowed in the first half of the 1970s and then began to stagnate as Soviet planners began to cope with the gradual depletion of easily accessible surface deposits of high-grade material by moving to the concentration of lower-grade material and the development of underground mines to tap deeper deposits. For the first time in the history of the Soviet chromite industry, production levels declined, from 3.4 million tons in 1975 to 3.0 million in 1977, recovering only after the first stage of the new open pit at the 40 Years of Kazakh SSR deposit was put into operation. By 1980, output levels were back to 3.4 million tons, but slipped again in 1981, to 3.3 million tons. The 1985 plan was set at 3.8 million tons.

While total exports held more or less steady during the first half of the 1970s, it became evident that the Soviet Union was losing its Western markets, and this trend became accentuated in the second half of the 1970s as total exports declined from some 1.17 million tons in 1975 to a range of 500,000 to 600,000 tons. By 1981, United States imports from the Soviet Union were at one fifth the 1970 level, Japanese and West German imports had been phased out altogether and far smaller amounts went to other traditional customers in Western Europe (Table 7). In 1981, Soviet exports totaling 567,000 metric tons went predominantly to the centrally planned economies in Eastern Europe (some 70 percent of the total).

A major factor in the deterioration of the Soviet export position in Western markets was a technological development involving a shift from high-grade metallurgical ore, containing at least 48 percent $Cr_2O_3$, to lower-priced

chemical-grade chromite in the iron and steel industry. For years, the electric furnace had been the standard process for reduction of chromite, requiring the high-grade material for the production of ferrochromium alloys. In the late 1960s, a newly developed process made it possible to produce chromium-containing metal from the lower-priced chemical-grade chromite for direct use in making stainless steel, bypassing the chromium alloy addition as a separate intermediate product. The principal beneficiary of this technological shift was the South African industry, which had long been a leading producer of chemical-grade chromite. South African chromite production more than doubled during the 1970s as the lower-priced chemical-grade material replaced part of the higher-priced metallurgical chromite in world markets (Table 8).

## The Prospects

A combination of a deteriorating Soviet raw-material position and technological change in the use of chromite have combined to mark the end of an era in which the Soviet Union dominated the world chromium market with its exports of relatively low-priced metallurgical-grade material. Although chromite reserves in the Khromtau district of the Soviet Union appear ample, the need for concentration of lower-grade material and the construction of costly deep mines have had an impact on Soviet chromite prices putting Soviet exports at a disadvantage in relation to the cheaper South African product.

Although the recent developments appear to affect mainly the Soviet export position and the nation's reserves for domestic consumption appear adequate, it has been suggested that the Soviet Union may begin to look abroad for access to chromite sources at costs below those imposed by the deteriorating resource situation at home. Since the largest reserves are now said to be in South Africa and Zimbabwe, some quarters in the West have interpreted Soviet interest in southern Africa as being motivated at least in part by the potential need for chromite from abroad, posing a potential threat to the West-

TABLE 7
Soviet Chromite Exports by Destinations
(thousand metric tons)

|  | 1960 | 1965 | 1970 | 1975 | 1980 | 1981 |
|---|---|---|---|---|---|---|
| TOTAL | 427 | 748 | (1,200)[1] | 1,171 | 567 | 567 |
| Western countries |  |  |  |  |  |  |
| United States | — | 223 | 410 | 270 | 99 | 76 |
| Japan | 61 | 123 | 124 | 95 | — | — |
| France | 48 | 88 | 114 | 95 | 23 | 8 |
| West Germany | 77 | 76 | 131 | 156 | — | — |
| Sweden | 58 | 67 | 133 | 140 | 10 | 30 |
| Italy | 4 | 45 | 33 | 27 | — | — |
| Subtotal | 248 | 622 | 945 | 783 | 132 | 114 |
| Eastern Europe |  |  |  |  |  |  |
| Poland | 54 | 58 | 76 | 109 | 128 | 140 |
| Czechoslovakia | 53 | 33 | 89 | 131 | 131 | 130 |
| East Germany | 9 | 21 | 25 | 40 | 33 | 32 |
| Hungary | — | 11 | 13 | 17 | 15 | 15 |
| Yugoslavia | — | — | — | 61 | 64 | 88 |
| Subtotal | 116 | 123 | 203 | 358 | 371 | 405 |
| Others | 65 | 3 | (−)[1] | 30 | 64 | 48 |

[1]Soviet total is rounded, making it impossible to determine the precise residual for the "Others" category.
SOURCE: *Vneshnyaya torgovlya SSSR*, Soviet statistical foreign trade yearbooks (various years).

TABLE 8
Soviet Chromite Production in World Perspective
(thousand metric tons)

|  | 1960 | 1965 | 1970 | 1975 | 1980 | 1981 |
|---|---|---|---|---|---|---|
| USSR | 1,450 | 2,450 | 2,950 | 3,400 | 3,400 | 3,300 |
| South Africa | 772 | 942 | 1,427 | 2,078 | 3,414 | 2,870 |
| Albania | 289 | 312 | 466 | 779 | 1,020 | NA |
| Zimbabwe | 606 | 586 | 363 | 590 | 552 | 530 |
| Philippines | 735 | 555 | 566 | 520 | 525 | 500 |
| Brazil | 5 | 24 | 28 | 173 | 287 | 410 |
| Turkey | 481 | 567 | 519 | 717 | 400 | 400 |
| Finland | 0 | 0 | 121 | 331 | 341 | 341 |
| India | 101 | 60 | 271 | 500 | 320 | 325 |

SOURCE: For USSR, see Table 6; for other producers, Central Intelligence Agency, *Handbook of Economic Statistics 1982* (CPAS 82-10006, September 1982), p. 135.

ern economies.[35] Since there is no known substitute for chromium in stainless steel, and the use of other metals such as nickel, cobalt, etc. in lieu of chrome alloys, would entail a greater cost factor, chromite ores have now gained a strategic significance to which future world power relationships may testify.

## NOTES

1. *Khromity Urala, Kazakhstana, Sibiri i Dalnego Vostoka* [Chromites of the Urals, Kazakhstan, Siberia and the Far East] (Moscow, 1974).

2. James Arnold Miller, Daniel I. Fine, and R. Daniel McMichael, eds., *The Resource War in 3-D—Dependency, Diplomacy, Defense.* World Affairs Council of Pittsburgh. Pittsburgh 1980; Amos A. Jordan and Robert A. Kilmarx, *70: Strategic Mineral Dependence: The Stockpile Dilemma* (Beverly Hills: Sage Publications, 1979); *Mineral Facts and Problems. 1975 Edition.* Bulletin 667 (Washington: Department of the Interior, Bureau of Mines, 1976).

3. According to the Soviet geologist V.I. Smirnov, the only commercially important chromium-bearing minerals are the chrome-spinels (MgFe) $(Cr,Al,Fe)_2O_4$, of which the most significant are magnochromite (MgFe) $Cr_2O_4$; alumochromite (MgFe) $(CrAl)_2O_2O$. See V.I. Smirnov, ed., *Ore Deposits of the USSR* Vol. 1 (London: Pitman Publishing Co., 1977), pp. 179 ff.

4. Ibid., p. 179.

5. Thomas S. Lovering, *Minerals in World Affairs* (New York: Prentice-Hall, 1944), p. 220 ff; James T. McDivitt, *Minerals and Men. An Exploration of the World of Minerals and its Effect on the World We Live In* (Baltimore: Johns Hopkins Press, 1965), pp. 56–57.

6. *The Making of Steel* (New York: American Iron and Steel Institute, 1951), pp. 76 ff.

7. Lovering, *Minerals*, p. 221.

8. Smirnov, *Ore Deposits*, p. 181.

9. Ibid., p. 181.

10. Theodore Shabad, *Basic Industrial Resources of the USSR* (New York: Columbia University Press, 1969), pp. 45, 307; *Nedra Kazakhstana* [Minerals of Kazakhstan] (Alma-Ata: Kazakhstan Publishers, 1968), pp. 204–05.

11. Smirnov, *Ore Deposits* p. 225; P. Ya. Antropov, *Perspektivy osvoyeniya prirodnykh bogatstv SSSR, 1959–65* [Prospects of development of the mineral wealth of the USSR, 1959–65] (Moscow, 1959), p. 53.

12. A.H. Sully, *Chromium* (London: Butterworth Scientific Publications, 1954), pp. 8–9.

13. Smirnov, *Ore Deposits*, pp. 215 ff.; Sully, *Chromium*, p. 73.

14. Smirnov, *Ore Deposits*, pp. 220 ff.; Sully, *Chromium*, p. 73.

15. Smirnov, *Ore Deposits*, p. 214; Sully, *Chromium*, p. 73.

16. Smirnov, *Ore Deposits*, p. 182; *50 Let Sovetskoi geologii* [50 Years of Soviet geology] (Moscow, 1965), p. 275.

17. D.M. Komlin, *Geologiya i poleznye iskopayemye SSSR* [Geology and minerals of the USSR] (Minsk: Vysshaya Shkola, 1965), p. 121. Smirnov states that the number of ore bodies comprising a particular deposit is varied. The

Molodezhnoye deposit consists of only one large ore body, the Almaz-Zhemchuzhina of 5, the 40 Years of the Kazakh SSR of 15, and the Millionnoye of 99! The bodies are separated by segregations of dunites, pyroxene dunites, and less frequently peridotites. Smirnov, *Ore Deposits*, pp. 195, 197; *Gorny zhurnal*, 1976, no. 3 and 1978, no. 7; also *Kazakhstanskaya pravda*, 17 May 1981.

18. Smirnov, *Ore Deposits*, pp. 204–10. The Molodezhnoye deposit consists of a compact ore body. Along the strike, it extends for 1,540 meters with a width in plan of 200 to 300 meters, and a maximum thickness of 140 meters. The body does not crop out on the present surface, but occurs at depths of 422 to 600 meters and sinks evenly in a southerly direction. The ore body is cut by tectonic fractures. See especially p. 207.

19. Komlin, *Geologiya*, p. 267; Smirnov, *Ore Deposits*, pp. 210–14; Sully, *Chromium*, p. 74.

20. *50 Let Sovetskoi geologii*, p. 272; Robert Allen and G.E. Howling, *Chrome Ore and Chromium* (London: Imperial Institute, 1940), p. 73.

21. *50 Let Sovetskoi geologii*, p. 272.

22. *Godovoi obzor mineralnykh resersov SSSR za 1926/27 g.* [Annual survey of mineral resources of the USSR for 1926–27] (Leningrad, 1928), pp. 1052, 1056; H.M. Hoar, *World Trade in Chromite.* Trade Information Bulletin No. 252 (Washington: Department of Commerce, 1924), p. 8.

23. Sully, *Chromium*, pp. 8–9.

24. Komlin, *Geologiya*, p. 121; Antropov, *Perspektivy*, p. 52.

25. Demitri B. Shimkin, *Minerals. A Key to Soviet Power* (Cambridge: Harvard University Press, 1953), p. 55.

26. N.G. Feitelman, *Ekonomicheskaya effektivnost zatrat no podgotovku mineralno-syryevoi bazy SSSR* [Cost-effectiveness of investment in the mineral raw material base of the USSR] (Moscow: Nauka, 1969), p. 40; Komlin, *Geologiya*, p. 121; V.A. Boyarsky, *Razvitiye otkrytoi dobychi rud, 1950–1970 gg.* [Development of open-pit mining of ores, 1950–70] (Moscow: Nauka, 1975), pp. 24, 35.

27. M. Gardner Clark, *The Economics of Soviet Steel* (Cambridge: Harvard University Press, 1956), p. 307.

28. Boyarsky, *Razvitiye*, p. 35.

29. Theodore Shabad, "News Notes," *Soviet Geography: Review and Translation* vol. 15, no. 6 (June 1974): 346; *Kazakhstanskaya pravda*, 15 February 1976; *Gorny zhurnal* 1976, no. 3, and 1978, no. 7.

30. V.V. Strishkov, "Soviet Union," in *Mineral Industries of the USSR* (Washington: Department of the Interior. Bureau of Mines, 1979), p. 12; also *Gorny zhurnal*, 1978, no. 7.

31. Miller, Fine and McMichael, *Resource War*, p. 42.

32. *Gorny zhurnal*, 1976, no. 3 and 1978, no. 7.

33. *Kazakhstanskaya pravda*, 5 September 1980 and 17 May 1980; *Gorny zhurnal*, 1976, no. 3 and 1979, no. 8.

34. *Ugol*, 1977, no. 11, states that 70 percent of 1955 chromite production was surfaced-mined, meaning in the Khromtau district.

35. For a review of the United States' dependency on imported chromium and recommendations as to how this dependency can be lessened, see *Contingency Plans for Chromium Utilization* (Washington: National Academy of Science, 1978).

# 23

# NICKEL AND PLATINUM IN THE SOVIET UNION

RUSSELL B. ADAMS
University of Minnesota

## Introduction

Russia and the Soviet Union have long been recognized for their mineral wealth, in particular Siberia, as a "treasure-house" of valuable metals, ostensibly waiting to be developed. Diverse deposits of common and rare metallic ores were known and mined as early as the seventeenth century when Czarist expeditions reached the Urals Mountains, where gold, silver and gemstones were taken for the royal family and lesser nobility.[1] In Peter the Great's reign (1682–1725), interest in mineral exploitation accelerated because of the Czar's obsession with Western technology and industry, and a similar spirit exists today. However, the principal minerals extracted for most of the eighteenth and early nineteenth centuries were coal, iron ore, precious metals, selected nonferrous ores, e.g., lead, zinc and copper, and nonmetallic minerals for construciton. Imperial Russia had not reached the stage of ferrous alloys, although abundant manganese deposits were known and coming into use on the eve of World War I. Russia's metallurgical industry was concerned mainly with producing pig iron and steel, first on the basis of Urals charcoal and ores and, after the introduction of coke metallurgy, on the basis of Krivoi Rog ore and Donets Basin coking coal in the Ukraine.

This prerevolutionary activity did stimulate exploration for a wide variety of ores which were already important in the industrial economies of Europe and the United States. Undoubtedly, Mendeleyev's work on the periodic table of elements played a role in the stimulus to catalogue resources. Also, the work of N.S. Kurnakov and his students during the years 1890 to 1920 provided a theoretical base for thermometallurgy in equilibrium diagrams and phase transformation in the heat treatment of metals.[2] Thus, there was some carry-over effect of pre-Soviet efforts, but disruption of the Bolshevik Revolution, Civil War and the power struggle of the 1920s necessitated virtually a fresh start in metallurgical progress which can be dated from the early 1930s to the present. Targets for the first five-years plans, beginning in 1928, augmented by wartime exigencies (1941–45), strongly sparked mining and metallurgical advances for nearly all the ferrous alloys, including nickel. Among the precious metals, attention to the platinum group has been mainly a post-World War II phenomenon, although platinum itself and palladium were recovered for their high value before 1900.

The main purpose of this paper, in keeping with the theme of other chapters in this book are: (1) to examine the conditions for exploitation of nickel and platinum within the USSR; (2) to evaluate the importance and direction of Soviet use and exports of the two metals; and, (3) to present a prospective outlook for the short-run future of nickel and platinum on world markets, within a framework of Soviet policies and global demand.

## Nickel

Nickel is a scarce and increasingly costly metal. Several former common uses, such as coinage, have been sacrificed or reduced in favor of more vital or nonsubstitutable uses. Because of its strategic value, nickel is produced and allocated in most countries under some degree of governmental control. This is clearly the case in the USSR, which has promoted exploration, mining, and distribution to various economic sectors, notably the steel and defense industries, as well as absolute control of exports. The Soviet Union has been a leading producer and exporter of nickel since World War II and the prospects for continuation are propitious in light of rising price levels and sluggish output in some countries.

*Without the assistance of a number of persons, this project would have been immeasurably more difficult. I wish to acknowledge special gratitude to members of the team, particularly Robert G. Jensen and Theodore Shabad, and to Hedija Kravalis of the Department of Commerce and to Joseph Filner of Noblemet, New York, for encouragement, suggestions and information. Also, I appreciate the bibliographical aid of Dr. Robert Britton of the Science Museum of Minnesota; cartographic service of the Department of Geography; and typing service of Rebecca Himango of the Department.*

General Properties

Nickel is a metal of antiquity, known and used before its identification as a metallic element, as early as the fourth millennium B.C. at Ur of the Chaldees.[3] Its alloying value with iron and copper was known in the Middle East, where coins and utensils were made with nickel compositions of 3 to 25 percent. It was first identified as an element in 1751 and confirmed by purification by Richter in Europe a few years later.[4] Thus, precise knowledge of the metal and its varied uses are a relatively modern discovery.

Nickel belongs to the transition group, along with iron and cobalt, in the fourth series of the periodic table. It has an average atomic weight of 58.7 among five stable isotopes, which are found under a wide range of depositional conditions. Nickel is actually abundant, more so than copper, zinc or lead, constituting an estimated 0.008 percent of the earth's upper crust to rank it twenty-third among all elements, while the earth's core may be 7 percent nickel.[5] But there are not many localized concentrations in the igneous rocks in which it occurs since they are not readily susceptible to weathering. Nickel is also found in sea water but not at an economically recoverable rate, as well as in meteorites; the chief minerals that are commercially mined are the sulfides and oxides, while the arsenides are of minor importance today. In the USSR, sulfide nickel ores are the richest source but oxides are also fairly widespread.

The properties of nickel that render it of high value are the following:[6] (1) crystal form and lattice constant, which promote alloying and closely-packed films; (2) density (8.9 g/cm²), which affects heating, annealing, and sound conduction; (3) optical properties of high reflectivity; (4) high melting point and heat capacity; (5) high thermal conductivity; (6) very low electrical resistivity; (7) thermal electromotive force, with which it is negative to platinum, for thermocoupling; (8) magnetic strength; (9) chemical properties, such as resistance to corrosion and alkali solutions; and, (10) mechanical properties of tensile strength, extreme hardness, durability, ductility, and creep resistance. Nickel can be purified to 99.99 percent and, if not, is subject to loss in value, but impurities such as cobalt and manganese may enhance its efficacy for given purposes. Nickel is also amenable to many treatments, viz., melting and casting, forging, welding, soldering, annealing, machining, grinding, and above all, electroplating. There are at least ten commercially used nickel alloys which may be electrodeposited. Finally, for structural materials, nickel alloys with copper, chromium, iron, and a legion of other metals in superalloys. The Monel alloys with copper are the most important and may be produced without separation of the two components. Nickel is indeed one of the most versatile of all metals and therefore has a universal and durable demand. Not unexpectedly, Soviet metallurgy and technology have reached levels of sophistication in nickel which are tantamount, or sometimes even superior, to those in the West, although most techniques were developed before 1940 in Europe and the United States.[7]

Uses and Changing Demand

Although nickel has a wide range of uses, about 90 percent of it goes into alloys along with chromium, molybdenum, cobalt, aluminum, titanium, and others in varying proportions. The USSR has adequate reserves of these minerals, such that future production of nickel steel, alloy steel and superalloys is not threatened. The Soviet pattern of nickel use cannot be precisely determined, but it probably parallels that of the United States which, in addition to alloys, uses nickel in batteries, dyes, pigments, and insecticides.[8] Chemicals, oil refining, electrical equipment, machinery, aircraft, motor vehicles, and machinery, in roughly that order of importance, are leading sectors for nickel consumption in the United States. They are also prominent in the USSR and growing at generally higher rates than in the United States, so the Soviet domestic demand for nickel may constrain future exports. Some of the specialty uses of nickel which indicate a continuing and probably increasing demand, within the USSR and worldwide, are the following: for alloys in manufacturing equipment exposed to corrosive chemicals; in wrought and cast alloys of 95 to 99 percent nickel to resist caustic solutions; in metal products such as cutlery, tools, boilers, and hospital equipment; in superalloys for aircraft, turbines, and jet engines; for stainless steels in vehicle bodies and trim; in nearly all alloys for electrical equipment, using up to 80 percent nickel in them; for household appliances; and in boats to resist salt water.[9] Few, if any, of these applications are apt to decline in demand, but there are possible substitutes and opportunities for higher rates of recycling and recovery of nickel.

Primary nickel is produced in various forms—powder, briquets, ingots, cathodes, and, prominently in the USSR, ferronickel, which contains up to 50 percent nickel. Most of these forms can yield a significant supply of scrap, especially in shaping operations. Scrap brokers are key figures in raising the percentage of recovered scrap, even at the international level. With nickel prices steadily rising, scrap is becoming increasingly important, varying in quantity between 20 and 60 percent of the primary metal. More efficient recovery will, of course, suppress growth in primary production and exports, but not necessarily total consumption. Soviet scrap is also reused domestically at a high rate while United States high-nickel alloy scrap usually goes to West Germany or Japan for reuse. Such trade channels impinge upon the global supply-demand equation and thereby affect nickel exporters such as the USSR.

Nickel is not an irreplaceable metal, but substitutes in most cases are more costly or inferior to high-quality nickel. Chromium, manganese, molybdenum, and copper are partly substitutable in alloy steels and iron castings, while cobalt and platinum may replace nickel in some catalysts.[10] The USSR produces most of these substitute materials, but some of its potential markets also have them, e.g., the United States molybdenum. More promising to substitute for nickel are titanium and numerous plastics to intensify corrosion resistance; they are not necessarily cheaper, but in some cases are more available and superior to nickel.

## World Reserves of Nickel

Despite the abundance of nickel in the earth's crust, the available reserves for commercial extraction are fairly modest. Reserves estimates vary, but generally range around 60 to 70 million metric tons of nickel content.[11] Almost all the present recoverable reserves are the two basic types: (1) nickel-copper sulfides associated with cobalt and platinum-group metals, which are found mainly in the Soviet Union and Canada; (2) nickel silicates associated with weathered lateritic material in tropical and subtropical regions. The surface laterites, which are found mainly in New Caledonia, Cuba, Indonesia and the Philippines, may ultimately become more important as a source of nickel than the deeper sulfide deposits, which now account for most of the nickel mine production. Seabed nodules represent another potential future source.

The ranking of the Soviet Union in world nickel reserves is unclear because of the secrecy imposed by the Soviet authorities on reserves and output figures for virtually all metals, except for iron ore, manganese and chrome. Soviet nickel reserves are known to have risen substantially in the 1960s with the discovery of vast new sulfide deposits in the Norilsk area of northern Siberia, now the principal Soviet producing district. Among the last published statements on Soviet reserves, published in the late 1960s, was one to the effect that nickel reserves in 1965 where 60 percent over the 1955 level and 40 percent over the 1958 level,[12] presumably as a result of the northern Siberian discoveries, which also continued after 1965. These discoveries were said to have moved the Soviet Union into first place among the reserve holdings of the world nickel countries. A Soviet source in the late 1960s, without stating a Soviet reserve figure, ranked the USSR first, ahead of Canada, for which the source listed reserves of 5.7 million tons; New Caledonia, with 4.2 million tons, and Cuba with 4 million tons.[13] The implication was that the USSR, according to Soviet estimates, had at least 6 million tons of reserves in the middle 1960s.

Before the expansion of the reserve base in northern Siberia, sulfide ores were said to represent two-thirds of both Soviet reserves and production of nickel, and silicate ores one third.[14] However, the discovery of the additional Siberian sulfide reserves appears to have shifted the sulfide-silicate ratio further in favor of the sulfides, and a later Soviet source gave it as 3:1 instead of 2:1.[15]

The United States Bureau of Mines, in its latest estimates, places the USSR in third place among reserves, with 8.1 million tons, or 13 percent of the world total, behind New Caledonia and Canada, which are said to account for nearly one-half of world reserves.[16] Other reserve leaders are Indonesia, the Philippines, Australia, Cuba and the Dominican Republic, each with over one million tons of reserves in terms of metal content.

## Deposits and Mining of Nickel in the USSR[17] (Fig. 1)

The initial discoveries of nickel in prerevolutionary Russia and the USSR were silicate ores in the Urals, and these deposits represented the basis of the early Soviet nickel industry until the discovery of sulfide deposits in the Kola Peninsula of northern European Russia and especially in the Norilsk area of northern Siberia, which have now eclipsed the Urals silicates in importance.

Nickel was first discovered in Russia in the Urals in the 1820s, but the initial finds in the Revda area, west of the present Sverdlovsk, were taken to be copper ores and were identified as nickel only in 1854. The ores were first used in 1874 in the Revda iron-smelting furnace to make ferronickel, containing 70 percent nickel and 23 percent iron, but Russian nickel production soon ceased when the discovery of the large nickel deposits of New Caledonia led to a fall in nickel prices and made the Urals operations uneconomical. Czarist Russia depended on nickel imports, which amounted to 1,300 tons in 1917.

Interest in a domestic nickel industry revived after the Bolshevik Revolution, and the discovery of additional nickel silicate deposits in the central Urals led to the construction of the first smelter at Verkhni Ufalei, which opened in 1933 with a capacity of 3,000 tons of nickel a year. It was followed by a second smelter at Rezh, northeast of Sverdlovsk. The early surface silicate mines near these smelters soon exhausted their small reserves, and in the late 1930s, the center of the Urals nickel industry moved southward to Orsk, where a larger smelter, the South Urals Nickel Plant, was to be based on a series of deposits around Orsk. The Orsk smelter, initially designed to process 1 million to 1.3 million tons of silicate ore, with a metal content of around 1 percent, was to produce 10,000 tons of metal. It yielded its first matte, an intermediate product with 20 to 25 percent nickel, in December 1938, and its first electrolytic nickel in February 1939.[18]

The Orsk smelter used ore from four silicate deposits discovered during the 1930s. They were the Aidarbak deposit near Khalilovo, some 25 miles northwest of Orsk; Akkermanovka, 15 miles west, and Aidyrlinsky (Aidyrlya, 80 miles to the northeast). A fourth mine was developed on the Kempirsai deposit, in Kazakhstan, 45 miles south of Orsk, giving rise to the mining settlement of Batamshinsky. The Orsk nickel industry and its supporting mines played a key role in World War II in supplying material for tough armor plates for tanks and other military uses. The Orsk smelter also derived cobalt as a coproduct in the treatment of the nickel ores. The nickel raw-material base was further expanded in the 1960s with the development of the Buruktal deposit, 100 miles east of Orsk. The site was reached by railroad in 1961 and the mining settlement of Svetly (Cleartown) arose next to the railroad station known as Rudny Klad (Mineral Trove). However, the treatment of the local ore appeared to pose problems, and pilot plant tests to make ferronickel in an electric furnace were still reported under way at Svetly in the mid-1970s.[19]

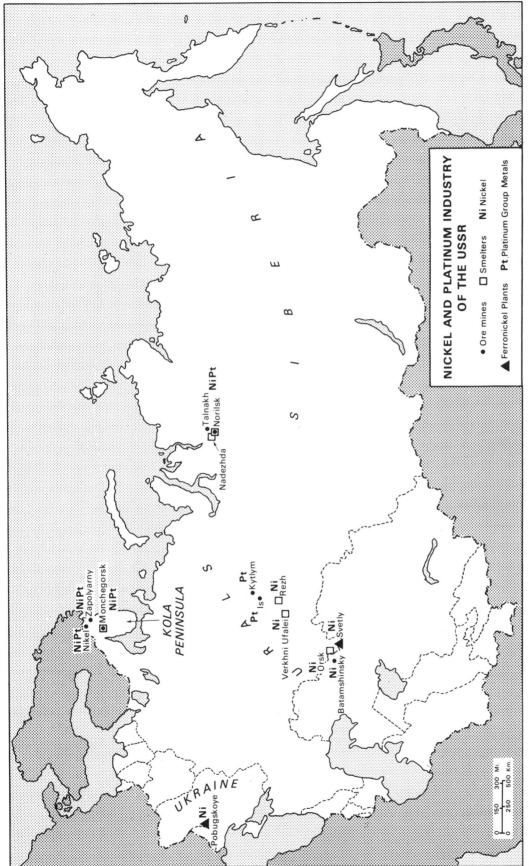

Figure 1

Another ferronickel project using silicate ores, at Pobugskoye in Kirovograd Oblast of the Ukraine, appears to have been more successful. Although the settlement of Pobugskoye, 15 miles northwest of Pervomaisk, was inaugurated in 1961, technical development proved difficult, and the first ferronickel was produced in local electric furnaces only in 1973.[20]

The early Soviet development of a nickel industry based on the silicate ores of the southern Urals has been eclipsed since World War II by the sulfide-based nickel industry of the Kola Peninsula and especially of the Norilsk district in northern Siberia. The importance of the northern operations can be gauged in part by the fact that it stimulated the development of an unusual Arctic shipping service aided by the development of nuclear-powered icebreakers.

The first copper-sulfide ores in the Kola Peninsula were found by the Russians in 1931 on the slopes of the Nittis and Kumuzhye hills in the Monchetundra area, just to the west of the rich apatite deposits of the Khibiny Mountains. The development of mines and a smelter gave rise to the settlement of Monchegorsk, which was raised to the status of a city in 1937. The Monchegorsk smelter, which became known as Severonikel (North Nickel), yielded its first matte in 1939, its first electrolytic nickel in 1940, and its first cobalt coproduct in 1941, just before the German attack on the Soviet Union in World War II. With the Monchegorsk nickel plant in the zone of military operations, its equipment was promptly dismantled and evacuated to safer locations in the interior of the Soviet Union, including Orsk and Norilsk.

Although the Monchegorsk smelter was restored after the war, the local Nittis-Kumuzhye mines proved too small in reserves to sustain a long-term operation, and Monchegorsk shifted to other ore sources. The first supplementary source was the Kaula deposit in Finland's Petsamo (Pechenga) district, which passed to Soviet control at the end of World War II. The deposit was developed on the eve of the war by the International Nickel Company of Canada (Inco), which also built a smelter designed to produce 7,000 tons of matte from 200,000 tons of ore. The Russians named the mining settlement Nikel, rebuilt its mine and smelter, and the entire undertaking, known as Pechenganikel, was back in operation by the end of 1946. The Kola raw-material base was further expanded by the development of the Zhdanov deposit, northeast of Nikel. A mining settlement named Zapolyarny was established on the site in 1957, and it was raised to the status of city in 1963, reflecting the magnitude of the operation. The first stage of the large open-pit mine, which yields low-grade copper-nickel sulfide ore, went into operation in the summer of 1965, together with a concentrator that supplies pelletized concentrate to both Nikel and Monchegorsk for further processing. The latest addition to mining capacity in the Kola Peninsula was the opening of the Severny (North) mine in the Pechenga district at the end of 1975.

Despite the development of the new mining capacity, the nickel industry in the Kola Peninsula became increasingly dependent on concentrate and intermediate products from Norilsk, where a major expansion in min-

ing capacity starting in the mid-1960s was not matched by a corresponding expansion of metallurgical capacity. Surplus concentrates from Norilsk began moving to Monchegorsk via the Northern Sea Route and through the port of Murmansk, and led in turn to a major expansion of smelting capacity at Monchegorsk. The expansion program included a copper electrolysis plant, which started operation in 1978. Previously the copper cycle at Monchegorsk ended with the production of blister copper, which was then sent for refining elsewhere in the Soviet Union. The construction of nickel refining capacity at Monchegorsk was completed in early 1982. The expansion program was designed to raise nickel and copper smelter output at Monchegorsk by 50 percent.[21]

The development of the Norilsk district in northern Siberia, which has become the principal center of Soviet nickel, has gone through several distinctive stages.[22] Although its development began in the 1930s, it proceeded slowly because of the isolation of the area and its harsh Arctic environment, and was not given impetus until the emergency years of World War II. However the present significance of nickel and associated platinum-group metals in the Norilsk district did not emerge until the discovery of vast new reserves in the 1960s.

Although the decision to proceed with Norilsk development was taken in 1935 after the initial mineral wealth of the area had been established, it was not given high priority at first because the more accessible Monchegorsk area in the Kola Peninsula and the silicate deposits in the relatively well settled Orsk district of the southern Urals were being developed at the same time. Because of the difficulty of drawing labor to the remote and hostile Norilsk project, it was placed from the very beginning under the People's Commissariat of Internal Affairs (NKVD), which ran the Soviet Union's prison camps. The initial approach to Norilsk was by water during the brief summer shipping season, with barges moving up the Pyasina River from the Kara Sea to the trading post of Valek, from which a primitive, narrow-gauge railroad covering the 8 miles to Norilsk was built in early 1936. However, the principal approach to Norilsk was to be from the Yenisei River port of Dudinka, and the first 70-mile narrow-gauge rail link from Dudinka was opened to traffic in 1937. It was modernized and converted to wide gauge in 1952, and ultimately electrified to handle the growing volume of heavy ore trains.

The initial mining operations focused on rich vein ore, which was extracted from the so-called Norilsk-1 deposit in Rudnaya Mountain (ore mountain) and did not require concentration. A pilot plant went into operation in 1938 and the first, small smelter yielded its first nickel matte for refining at Monchegorsk in early 1939. The census in that year gave Norilsk a population of 13,886. However refined electrolytic nickel at the small smelter did not follow until three years later. In the meantime, construction got under way in 1939 on a second and larger smelter, and work was accelerated when the German invasion of the Soviet Union started in the summer of 1941. With the help of equipment evacuated from the newly completed Monchegorsk smelter in the war zone, the large Norilsk smelter yielded its first nickel matte in 1942 and refined electrolytic nickel the following year. A cobalt plant followed in 1944, by which time the population of Norilsk had risen to 30,000. Part of the Norilsk metals output was flown out by air and made contributions to the Soviet war effort.

After the initial exploitation of rich vein ore, mining operations expanded through the development of open pit mines that made use of disseminated ores. The first open pit mine, Ugolny Ruchei (Coal Creek), started production in 1940, and excavation of the larger Medvezhi Ruchei (Bear Creek) pit began in 1945. A large concentrator to beneficiate the growing volume of lower-grade disseminated ore was put on stream in 1948, and by 1950 as much as 90 percent of the ore was surface-mined. The disseminated ore at greater depths was tapped by a new shaft mine, Zapolyarny, which raised the proportion of deep-mined ore to one-third by the middle 1960s. Other postwar developments included the opening of a separate copper smelter in 1950 (expanded in 1967) and the closing of the first, small wartime nickel smelter as uneconomical in 1952. The abolition of the institution of forced labor on a mass scale after Stalin's death lead to a temporary decline of Norilsk operations in the middle 1950s as rehabilitated prisoners were released and gradually replaced by free workers who had been commandeered to the area. In 1955 alone, 26,000 workers arrived to replace departing prisoners. As evidence of the institutional shift from a virtual prison camp to a civilian enterprise, Norilsk was officially granted the status of city in 1953, and the economic management transferred the following year from the Interior Ministry to the Ministry of Nonferrous Metallurgy. After the deterioration of performance associated with the upheaval of the middle 1950s, the Norilsk operation was said to have become a profit-making enterprise by Soviet cost-benefit calculations in 1958.

Until 1965, mining operations had been confined to the deposits initially discovered in the 1930s on the southwest outskirts of Norilsk. The gradual depletion of these deposits led to an intensive exploration effort elsewhere in the area. High-grade, but deep additional deposits were identified in 1961 at Talnakh, some 15 miles north-northeast of Norilsk, and in 1966 in the Oktyabr area, 4 miles northwest of Talnakh. The prospects appeared so promising that a series of large underground mines of increasing depth and size was projected. The first and shallowest mine, extending to some 570 feet, was the Mayak (Lighthouse) mine, which went into operation in 1965. The significance of this first mine alone became evident when it was disclosed in 1970 that it contributed 50 to 60 percent of the entire Norilsk output. The second new mine, Komsomol, went into operation in 1971 after 6 years of construction and extended to a depth of 1,500 to 2,000 feet. It was said to have three times the capacity of Mayak. The third mine, Oktyabr, went into operation in 1974 after 5 years of construction, extending to a depth of 3,000 to 4,000 feet, with a designed capacity of six times that of Mayak. Its sixth and seventh stages were completed in 1980. Since 1973, construction has been under way on an even deeper mine, Taimyr (initially called the Gluboky or Deep mine), extending to 5,000 feet. The

Taimyr mine, the deepest in the Soviet Union, was scheduled to yield its first ore by 1983.

The tenfold expansion of mining capacity, from some 20,000 tons of nickel metal content in 1965 to perhaps 200,000 tons in the early 1980s, created a surplus of concentrate that began to be shipped to Monchegorsk for smelting starting in the late 1960s. The growing ore traffic, in turn, stimulated expansion of the ore-carrying fleet plying the Northern Sea Route from Dudinka to Murmansk, and of a fleet of icebreakers, including nuclear icebreakers, to keep the sea lanes open during the winter season. Since 1978, virtually year-round service has been assured.

The smelting potential in the Norilsk district itself was further enhanced in the 1970s by the construction of a huge smelter, with a capacity of 550,000 tons of nickel matte (100,000 tons of nickel content) at Nadezhda, some 10 miles west of Norilsk. The Nadezhda smelter, using Finnish technology, was designed to use high-sulfur iron containing tailings left from the beneficiation operations in the Talnakh district for the extraction of nickel and copper matte and merchantable sulfur, with the iron content of the tailings being discarded. Construction of the Nadezhda smelter began in 1970, sulfur recovery started in 1979, and the nickel and copper matte were first produced in 1981. The raw material for the Nadezhda plant is supplied from the Talnakh concentrators via a system of 20-mile-long slurry pipelines.

World Production Trends

As a result of the development of the Talnakh deposits and the construction of the associated Nadezhda smelter, the Soviet Union has begun to rival Canada as the leading world producer of nickel. Canada has been the principal producer since the late 19th century, mainly from the Sudbury area in Ontario and Thompson in Manitoba. Along with New Caledonia, Canada has supplied most of the Western markets. World nickel production did not reach 10,000 tons annually until 1900. Output spurted briefly to 45,000 tons during World War I but subsequently declined until the late 1930s. Prices fluctuated during this period between 60 cents and $1.40 per pound, but there was no strong demand pressure on other sources. The sharp rise in world output was activated by the onset of World War II, when production reached 180,000 tons in 1941. The Soviet share at the time was about 20,000 tons but newly opened mines in the 1930s undoubtedly contributed to the growth. A brief postwar slump until the early 1950s was then followed by a phenomenal increase, nearly doubling every seven years, to 500,000 tons in 1965. Concomitantly, the USSR increased its percentage of world output and began to enter world markets in earnest in the late 1950s, as nickel prices began to rise past the $1.00 per pound level by the late 1960s.[23] Search and discovery and expansion of existing deposits brought onto the scene a number of new significant producers, e.g., Australia, Cuba and the Philippines. Thus, the three leaders—Canada, the USSR and New Caledonia—do not command as high a market share today as they did twenty years ago.

Table 1 reports production of leading nickel producers for intermittent years during the 1970s and an estimate of capacity for 1985.[24] Except for the USSR, the figures are derived from publications of the United States Bureau of Mines giving the nickel content of mine output. Statistics are also available for smelter output, but they differ markedly from mine output. Nickel-mining countries such as Canada and New Caledonia export some of their mined nickel in the form of intermediate products and do not smelt their entire mine output. Other countries, without nickel mines, import large amounts of intermediate products for smelting and report large amounts of smelter output of nickel, for example, Japan. For the USSR, because of the secrecy surrounding official output figures of nickel, there is a wide spread of Western estimates, ranging in 1977 from 159,000 short tons (Bureau of Mines) to 242,000 short tons (Central Intelligence Agency). Bureau of Mines estimates for the USSR do not appear to reflect scattered Soviet data, notably the remarkable rise of production in the Norilsk-Talnakh district in the late 1960s and early 1970s. CIA estimates are consistent with the little information available from Soviet sources, and have therefore been used in Table 1 for the USSR. It is presumed that mine output and smelter output in the USSR are identical because of negligible trade in intermediate products.

Supply-demand relationships between developing countries with weak domestic markets and the industrialized West affect Soviet production and potential exports. New Caledonia is a sizable reserve and production source from open-pit mines of lateritic ores operated mainly by the French conglomerate Société le Nickel (SLN), which is undergoing expansion to new sites and a smelter.[25] Amax of the United States and Inco of Canada, in addition to Japanese interests, indicate that more New Caledonia nickel will be on world markets in the 1980s. Production has fluctuated in the past decade, but New Caledonia still ranks third with 15 percent of world output, most of which is destined for the industrialized West. The Australian mineral boom of the 1970s is reflected in threefold expansion of nickel output from 1970 to 1977. The Western Mining Corporation, at Kalgoorlie, in addition to foreign concerns, is expected to raise Australian nickel production to nearly 10 percent of world production by 1985 and to pose therefore as a major force on world nickel markets.[26]

Despite a sluggish performance in the 1970s, Canadian nickel is still crucial to world supplies, accounting for one-forth of the total in the late 1970s. Depletion along with higher costs, labor problems, and inventory build-ups have resulted in actual decline of Canadian output from an apparent peak in 1970. Projected capacity of Canadian nickel to 1985 is modest, but Canada should retain its leading position with about the same level of production as the USSR, each roughly one-fifth of world output. Other countries among the leaders (Table 1) have generally recorded higher growth rates than the Soviet Union in recent years. Cuba has emerged during the Castro era, along with Soviet economic and technological assistance, as the fifth nickel producer. Cuban growth prospects are propitious; further expansion is slated as part of integrated Comecon projects. The Dominican Republic follows Cuba in production from rapid expansion during the 1970s by American and West European investors. South Africa, which has been a long-term producer, has also increased its output of byproduct nickel from platinum mining, but prospects for further growth are not auspicious. Greece and the Philippines, which are also tied into Western trade channels, have expanded their nickel output, as has Indonesia which is expected to attain sixth rank among producers by 1985. The United States, eleventh among producers in 1978, has had static to declining nickel production since the 1960s from a single mine in Oregon. Despite research effort and investment in a pilot plant in the Duluth gabbro complex, United States nickel output is constrained by high costs of mining and lower copper prices. Very little of the big American demand is apt to be met by even an appreciable expansion of United States nickel production.

A number of other countries have become nickel pro-

TABLE 1
World Mine Production of Nickel[a] (1,000 short tons)

|  | 1970 | 1975 | 1977 | 1985[b] (capacity) |
|---|---|---|---|---|
| 1. Canada (all forms) | 305.9 | 267.0 | 259.4 | 275.0 |
| 2. USSR[c] (content of ore) | 150.0 | 215.0 | 242.0 | 300.0 |
| 3. New Caledonia (recoverable) | 116.1 | 146.9 | 120.2 | 140.0 |
| 4. Australia (content of conc.) | 32.8 | 83.6 | 94.6 | 115.0 |
| 5. Cuba (oxide-sulfide content) | 38.8 | 40.3 | 40.8 | 75.0 |
| 6. Dominican Republic[d] | — | 29.7 | 26.7 | 37.0 |
| 7. South Africa | 12.7[e] | 22.9 | 25.4 | 28.0 |
| 8. Greece (recoverable) | 9.5 | 31.0 | 21.0 | 40.0 |
| 9. Philippines | ? | 10.5 | 16.5 | 55.0 |
| 10. Indonesia (content of ore) | 17.2 | 21.2 | 15.4 | 70.0 |
| 11. United States (content of ore) | 15.9 | 17.0 | 14.3 | 16.0 |

[a]Selected and calculated from *Minerals Yearbook*, Vol. 1, 1977 Edition, Table 12, p. 664, and 1972 Edition, Table 11, p. 877 (Washington: Department of the Interior, 1980).
[b]*Mineral Facts and Figures*, 1980 Edition, "Nickel," Bulletin 671 (Washington: Department of the Interior, 1980), Table 2, p. 3.
[c]Central Intelligence Agency, *Handbook of Economic Statistics, 1980* (ER 80-10452), October 1980, p. 147.
[d]Nickel content of ferronickel only.
[e]Refined metal only.

ducers of note in recent years; some of their output may have an effect on Soviet production and exports, because of trade agreements, common markets, and differential cost-price levels. Poland and China are ostensibly self-sufficient in nickel; Albania and Finland have exportable surpluses; Botswana has appeared on the list of the top ten producers in the last few years; and Brazil and Guatemala are now among the minor producers.[27] No attempt is made here to forecast what impacts, direct or indirect, there may be on USSR output and trade from the diffusion of nickel production into the developing countries; but the data on hand suggest that production trends are not so favorable for the USSR to compete in nickel sales as effectively as it did in the 1970s.

In the USSR, the start of operations in the Norilsk-Talnakh district of northern Siberia fostered a very rapid rise of production, with an officially reported 94 percent increase in the 10-year period 1965–75, from 110,000 short tons to 215,000. However, in the period 1976–80, because of delays in the expansion of mining capacity and in the construction of the Nadezhda smelter (originally scheduled for completion in 1977), output growth was only 8.8 percent, or to about 258,000 short tons in 1980. With the completion of the large new smelter and the start of mining operations in the Taimyr mine, rapid growth is planned to resume in the first half of the 1980s, with a targeted increase of about 15 percent, to around 300,000 short tons by 1985.

## International Trade in Nickel

Nickel is a relatively low-volume commodity that is actively traded on world markets. Most of the surplus-ore countries have weak markets, while few of the industrialized markets have significant domestic production of nickel. The striking exception is the USSR, since Canada, Australia and South Africa are not high-demand economies, although they are using increasing amounts of their own nickel. It is not feasible, if at all possible, to construct a matrix of nickel flows between all countries because of the diverse forms of products, including scrap, and also because of nondisclosure by most Soviet-bloc countries, as well as incomplete data from Western nations. However, it is estimated from market-country imports that about 70 percent of all smelter nickel enters into world trade channels. For example, United States imports of 240,000 tons in 1977 were 28 percent of world smelter production.[28] West Germany typically imports about one-third as much as the United States, France and Britain about 15 percent each, while Japan, Italy, the Netherlands, and most other West European countries import lesser but significant amounts, most of it being unwrought nickel. There is a great deal of processing and reexport of finished products, as in the case of Norway, the United States, Britain, and West Germany. This obscures the net trade picture so that simple summation of the data would overestimate world trade volumes. These counterflows also exist among the nonmarket countries, although probably to a lesser extent. Exported Soviet nickel products are presumed to have been processed almost entirely from domestic ores.

Table 2 reports the *value* of nickel imports for the leading market economies in 1975 and 1979.[29] United States imports of $513 million represented 36 percent of the total in 1979, the main supplier being Canada (57 percent), followed by Norway and Britain, and to an increasing extent from New Caledonia, the Philippines, and the Dominican Republic as either ferronickel or concentrates.

Direct United States imports from the USSR in 1978 were 6,800 short tons, or 2.7 percent of the total.[30] The dependency is certainly greater if indirect trade channels via West European processors are included, possibly as high as 10 percent. West Germany, as the second ranked importer, obtains most of its unwrought nickel from West European trading partners, South Africa, the USSR, and some developing countries. This is the general pattern for the major nickel-importing countries, with special cases such as the French linkage with New Caledonia and Japanese interests in Australia and Southeast Asia. In general, the industrialized West as a bloc is not highly dependent on Soviet nickel, although some members individually rely on it for substantial portions of their imports.

## Soviet Nickel Exports

The USSR is established as one of the leading exporters of nickel in both unwrought and fabricated forms. The infant Soviet nickel industry before World War II was unable to generate surpluses, and the growth of domestic demand through most of the 1950s precluded any substantial export. In the last two decades, however, with the development of the Norilsk-Talnakh resources, Soviet nickel production has exceeded national needs by increasing margins. In the last few years, the Soviet industrial growth rate has been decelerating, particularly in heavy industry such as steel, which is a main demand sector for nickel. Assuming that nickel production continues to expand at past rates, a potential for more exports should be generated, although there is no firm evidence to indicate this trend. A determinant as important as supply-demand relationships is *price* on world markets, which is essentially exogenous to the Soviet economy. It is quite possible that the USSR has been building up inventories of nickel, and other marketable metals, during the last 3 to 5 years, awaiting higher price levels.

Soviet sources do not publish the volumes and destinations of specific commodities that have military or industrial uses. Group categories, such as "Ferrous metals" have shown rapid growth in export value since 1974.[31] Chromium, manganese, cobalt and nickel constitute important members of this group, which recorded $3 billion worth of exports in 1978, an increase of 67 percent, which was nevertheless lower than the general growth in total exports due to the phenomenal increase in oil shipments. The value of exports has continued to climb, but the proportion that is "ferrous metals," and specifically nickel, cannot be closely estimated. Over the 1974–76 period, exports of Soviet nickel alloys (unwrought) to the industrialized West averaged about $68 million per year.[32] At existing price levels, this amounted to approximately 30,000 tons a year, which was about 14 percent of USSR

TABLE 2
Nickel Imports and Exports: World Market Economy[a]
(unwrought, in million U.S. dollars)

|  | 1975 | 1979 |
|---|---|---|
| Imports |  |  |
| United States | 412.7 | 512.7 |
| West Germany | 159.2 | 215.8 |
| France | 76.4 | 113.6 |
| Japan | 36.3 | 101.2 |
| Britain | 90.7 | 98.1 |
| Italy | 30.4 | 83.0 |
| Sweden | 60.9 | 59.6 |
| Spain | 19.4 | 28.0 |
| Netherlands | 18.2 | 27.1 |
| Belgium-Luxembourg | 14.9 | 22.2 |
| Brazil | 7.0 | 16.5 |
| Austria | 8.4 | 14.7 |
| Finland | 0.8 | 14.2 |
| World Market Economy | 1,036.2 | 1,440.2 |
| Exports |  |  |
| Canada | 406.4 | 426.5 |
| Norway | 132.4 | 172.1 |
| United States | 25.7 | 119.2 |
| Britain | 38.7 | 88.0 |
| West Germany | 9.4 | 64.2 |
| New Caledonia | 58.5 | 50.9 |
| Philippines | 29.6 | 50.2[b] |
| Finland | 24.4 | 49.3 |
| Australia | 52.4 | 38.2[b] |
| South Africa | 43.7 | 38.2[b] |
| France | 24.1 | 26.3 |
| Netherlands | 12.0 | 20.7 |
| World Market Economy | 991.8 | 1,218.3 |

[a]Selected from data in the *United Nations Yearbook of International Trade Statistics, 1979* (United Nations, New York, 1980), p. 369.
[b]For 1978.

smelter output and roughly 5 percent of the international trade in nickel. To this tonnage must be added exports outside of the West, which are estimated to be about one-third of Soviet nickel exports, for a total of 45,000 tons during that period. This would leave a reasonable share of about 170,000 tons per year for domestic consumption, which is about two-thirds that of the United States. The total Soviet nickel exports constitute about 8 percent of the world trade in nickel, a considerably smaller share than the USSR production percentage (20 percent or more) in view of large Soviet demand. Most of the other major mining countries (Table 1) export most of their nickel because of weak internal demand.

Because of Soviet secrecy on nickel exports, destinations can be obtained only from trade-partner statistics. Processing and reexport trade further complicate the analysis. However, known imports, demand approximations, trade ties and general influence of market access provide a general regional allocation of Soviet nickel exports.

1. *Western Europe* is the USSR's largest nickel market and it will probably remain so for some time. Of the West European countries, West Germany has been fairly consistently the principal buyer of Soviet nickel, with Britain and France being less dependent on Soviet nickel because of imports from New Caledonia, Canada and Australia.

Italy is the fourth West European customer, followed by the Netherlands, Belgium and Luxembourg. Norway is a special case of large-scale refining of nickel, some of which may originate in the USSR. West European demand for nickel, judging from industrial structure and gross national product, is parallel to that of the United States. The author's estimate is that 50 to 60 percent of Soviet nickel exports to the West are destined for Western Europe, but this amount satisfies no more than one-fourth of the region's consumption. Thus, the USSR is relatively more market-dependent on Western Europe than, conversely, Western Europe is on the USSR for supply; but the mutual dependency is strong and should persist since none of the West European countries mine any significant amount of nickel. In potential terms, Western Europe may not be so promising: economic growth rates in nickel-using industries have been generally slow, recycling is on the upswing, price inflation, substitutes, and distance of sources all militate against a large increase in nickel imports from the Soviet Union.

2. *Eastern Europe*, with the exception of Poland, is dependent on Soviet nickel because of steady growth in steel and other industries as well as the trade commitments of CMEA. Czechoslovakia and East Germany are good markets, but the region as a whole is not a big market for nickel. The estimate is that 10 to 15 percent of Soviet nickel exports go to Eastern Europe and that, given stable trade relations, the share will be maintained since there are few attractive alternatives. The USSR has virtually a captive market in Eastern Europe and is likely to match price competition from future cheaper sources. Exceptions may be Yugoslavia and Rumania, but these are minor markets.

3. *The United States*, which consumes nearly one-third of the world's nickel, relies principally on Canada (about half of U.S. imports), Norway, the USSR, Australia, the Philippines, and Botswana. The Soviet direct shipments are about 6 percent of American imports and not likely to increase under present conditions. But the huge American market may be viewed by the USSR as having future growth potential for exports, if Canadian nickel continues to become scarcer and higher-priced. The United States has options in developing tropical laterites in source countries and perhaps domestically as well. The present dependency of the United States on Soviet nickel is not likely to increase much in percentages; but in absolute terms, including indirect imports, the hard currency value to the USSR is considerable.

4. *Japan* is a good prospect for expanded Soviet nickel exports. It ranks third in smelter output, demand is high and still rising, and trade ties with the USSR seem likely to intensify. In the 1970s, Japan ranked behind West Germany and ahead of the United States in imports of Soviet nickel. However, Japan has alternative sources of mineral supplies, including nickel. Trade and development agreements between Japan and the Soviet Union may improve prospects of nickel exports from Siberian deposits in connection with construction of the Baikal-Amur Mainline.[33]

5. *Other Markets*. An estimated 10 to 15 percent of Soviet nickel exports finds its way in smaller volumes to

trading partners under bilateral agreements or on the market for special order. South Asia (India, in particular), selected Middle East and African countries, Brazil and others in Latin America buy limited amounts of nickel. Also Finland imports some Kola Peninsula concentrates for smeltering. Some of these markets have considerable potential, but the Soviet role in their future nickel needs is uncertain and may hinge more on political relations than on economic grounds.

## Prices

The price of nickel has vacillated widely, i.e., by a ten-to-one ratio between its highest and lowest levels over the last sixty years. From peaks in the mid-nineteenth century of over $3.00 per pound the secular trend was downward, irregularly, to 25 cents in the early 1920s on world markets.[34] Subsequently, nickel prices have advanced quite steadily, with the exception of cyclical drops, to recent (1980–81) levels of $2.00 to $2.40 per pound. On the New York Metals Exchange, 1982 nickel futures were being quoted as $2.50 to $2.70 per pound.[35] Thus, nickel has been alternately costly, if not scarce, and moderately priced. The inflationary trend was upward until early 1980 but then fell off so that a 4 percent decline in Western world consumption was predicted for 1981.[36] Until the entry of the USSR and newer larger producers, nickel prices were essentially controlled by costs and policies of the major Canadian companies, which supplied well over half of the nickel to market economies. They no longer enjoy such direct monopolistic power, but nickel output and pricing is still in the hands of a relatively small number of producing firms and governments. Private capital has financed most of the development in the non-Communist world, but governmental regulation and partial ownership has rendered the industry quasi-public in many cases, e.g., in Indonesia and Botswana.[37] Soviet production has of course been entirely under state control, but global market prices are still largely determined in the West, so that the USSR has had to contend with competition to market its nickel. Internally, the Soviet Union has been facing an increasing cost situation of higher extraction and labor costs, coupled with inert copper prices, which render decreasing marginal returns from the Norilsk operation. Thus, the USSR has little control over nickel prices, even though its production and market share rivals that of Canada.

Soviet nickel production and world price levels (Fig. 2) have taken divergent paths since the late 1960s. Nickel prices were quite stable during the 1960–66 period while Soviet production rose steadily and has continued to do so to the present. In 1969, nickel prices jumped abruptly, then began to increase slowly in the early 1970s and rapidly since 1973 to the present, with the salient but brief decline from 1976 to 1978. Over this two-decade period, the USSR has built up its markets with little apparent relationship to world nickel prices. A time series correlation coefficient, based on yearly percentage changes, is low positive ($r_p = 0.38$); it is lowered by the slow response of Soviet producton during the 1970–76 period to rapid price growth. However, if *sales* rather than production

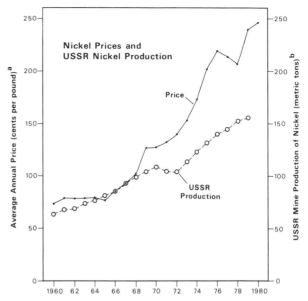

Figure 2
a. From *Mineral Facts and Problems*, 1980 ed., "Nickel" (Washington: U.S. Department of the Interior, Bureau of Mines, 1980), Table 6, p. 12.
b. *United Nations Statistical Yearbook*, 1968, 1975, 1978 (New York: United Nations).

were available for the time span, the correlation would undoubtedly be higher, because the USSR evidently has released from stocks large volumes of nickel in selected years, such as 1974 when it sold $106 million of unwrought nickel alloys to the West; this was 1.6 percent of all such Soviet exports for fourteenth rank among commodities.[38] Nickel prices did increase sharply that year to $1.72 per pound for an estimated Soviet export of 61,600 tons to the West, at least twice the average annual volume during the 1970s. But 1974 was not typical; the volatility of nickel prices, along with the steady USSR production curve, if not annual sales, suggest low elasticity for two principal reasons: (1) the USSR has limited production capacity, as is the case anywhere for heavily capitalized industries, to expand rapidly output to meet external market demand; and, (2) the USSR has a more rigid marketing structure, i.e., buyer-seller connectivity, than many nickel producers which have more immediate access to buyers, for example, on the spot market.

## Strategic Aspects and Stockpiling

Nickel has not been classified as a "strategic" metal by the United States government, chiefly because of access to Canadian supplies, but the United States does depend to an increasing degree on overseas sources, in particular Britain and Norway.[39] Other West European countries and Japan, which import Soviet nickel, also ship nickel in finished or unwrought form to the United States. Nickel is one of four materials in the Defense Materials System; this means that defense contractors can obtain preference ratings to insure supplies during acute shortages. The increased military budget of the Reagan administration implies a strengthening of these governmental commitments. Since imports account for 60 to 70 percent of the domestic demand (production and scrap for the balance), the United States Government has stockpiled nickel for most of the post-World War II period. The strategic stockpile has been reduced to zero at various times (in 1971 and early 1980), but the goal set in April 1980 was 200,000 tons, somewhat less than consumption for one year. Governments in other large nickel-using countries have adopted similar and even more controlled measures to insure nickel supplies during emergencies or short supplies.

The USSR clearly plays a role in contributing to national supplies of importing countries, principally Japan and West European buyers. Concomitantly, the Soviet Union seeks hard-currency credits for nickel sales; these would presumably be sacrificed by restricted exports in times of emergency. The "resource war," which might be dated from Soviet purchases of chromite a decade ago, now involves a wide range of strategic metals. Investors and the military of Western countries are keenly interested in buying up supplies of high-priced metals, including nickel, for fear of cutoffs.[40] This effort to build up both governmental and private stockpiles has been particularly intense for nickel because of its relatively low price. As demand pressure accumulates, price rises are nearly certain. The USSR and other suppliers may be expected to respond to more profits from the inflation by accelerating production efforts and releasing stockpile supplies.

An opposing view to the foregoing is expressed by experts writing for the World Affairs Council in Pittsburgh.[41] The USSR imported chrome ore from Iran in 1980, despite difficulties with the Khomeini government. This may presage a drastic reduction in mineral exports by USSR and other Warsaw Pact countries, as well as the bartering and buying up of minerals on open markets. Simultaneously, it is believed that the Eastern bloc is developing a negative minerals balance. Nickel may be one of the shortfalls, along with oil, although it is reported that Siberian projects, which include Norilsk, have top priority. There are both political and military implications as well. East European buyers would have to pay much higher prices for Soviet minerals, perhaps the prevailing world price. Also, according to the World Affairs Council, there has been a decline in Soviet ore quality and a lag in new discoveries. It also seems likely that the USSR is increasing its strategic mineral stockpiles for the military, titanium being specifically cited; if the policy is as broad as implied, a wide range of ferroalloys, light materials, and rare earths are almost certain to be included. The impact of this cutoff of Soviet exports would mean a substantial reduction in both nickel and platinum on world markets, from 15 percent and 25 percent of global supplies, respectively. It is doubtful that alternative sources for Western markets could be developed within the decade to offset these losses and, in any case, rapid price inflation would ensue. Thus, the Soviet leadership may have some ability to influence world supplies of key minerals and thereby economic and technologic development in the West and the third world.

## Platinum-Group Metals

Because of the rarity and strategic nature of platinum-group metals in military-industrial uses, reserves and production are not known in detail for a number of countries, including the Soviet Union, which has released only gross and irregular information since the 1920s. Localization of the volume mined and refined in the USSR is often uncertain although the limited areas of main activity are described in published works with respect to the geology and technology of platinum metals. In terms of trade, it cannot be assumed that exports from the USSR reflect surplus production in a given year, since the national policy of stockpiling platinum may mean addition or depletion from refined reserves. Also, world price levels and the chronic Soviet need for foreign exchange influence exports of the metals. At times of peak prices in the 1970s, and in years of large imports by the Soviet Union, its platinum exports exceeded any surplus over domestic demand, thus depleting the stockpile. In general, fluctuations from year to year are considerable, not only because of policies and prices, but also because of the variable yields from existing and newly opened mines. The following discussion of Soviet platinum, therefore, must be viewed in the context of a metallic resource that has special physical and economic characteristics.

### General Properties and Uses[42]

Platinum (Pt) is the most important element and metal of the platinum group, which also includes palladium, iridium, osmium, rhodium and ruthenium. Most mining operations extract two or more of these metals jointly because of their common association and high value. Platinum is the heaviest in Group VIII of the periodic table; it has density, thermal conductivity, and acid resistivity. Platinum has a moderately high melting point (1774° C.), tensile strength, and coefficient of hardness (in annealed form, which can be upgraded by electrodepositing). Platinum's natural form is cubic with crystal lattices but these are modifiable by processing to render it versatile for a variety of uses. Physically, platinum is gray-white, lustrous, ductile, and resistant to corrosion and oxidation, thus having characteristics similar to gold, while palladium, the other important metal in the platinum group, resembles silver in many respects. But platinum's nonpareil property is its electrical conductivity, especially at lower temperatures, the highest of any metal.

The uses of platinum have steadily expanded since its discovery and principal original value in jewelry and decorative artwork. As the "queen of metals," it is still highly prized for its reflectivity in diamond settings and in dentistry to harden gold and to reduce discoloration. Also, platinum-iridium alloys are used medically in hypodermic needles and cautery points. However, the growth in demand for platinum has occurred chiefly from industrial applications, which have nearly doubled its comsumption every decade since 1940.

When platinum was found to be a catalyst in promoting

electrical reactions, in addition to being noncorrosive, its industrial era began. It was used in the nineteenth century in boiler fabrication to produce sulfuric acid by the contact process, thereby establishing its role in the growing chemical industries of Europe and the United States. However, platinum's dominant use remained in jewelry and art objects until the onset of World War II when industrial demand enhanced its position to that of a strategic material for war-related chemical and electrical applications. Nevertheless, the volume consumed was not great enough to cause shortages, due to American stockpiling and Canadian supplies, since nonessential uses were sacrificed in the early 1940s.

## Platinum in Russia: Background[43]

Platinum (from platina, "little silver," in Spanish) was discovered in the sixteenth century in South America along with placer gold, but it was not until the latter eighteenth century that crude platinum was melted in laboratories, prior to any particular application. European chemists isolated other metals in the platinum group, the last being ruthenium (after *Ruthenia*, an old name for Russia) in 1845. Colombia's Choco Province was the only minable world source until 1819 when platinum was first found in gold-bearing river gravels in the Upper Iset district of the Urals, near Yekaterinburg (the present Sverdlovsk). The first Urals deposits were found to be similar to those of Colombian osmiridium, containing 2 percent platinum, and were regarded as more promising for exploitation and access to European markets. The first virtually pure platinum placer deposit, in which gold was only a coproduct, was found in 1824 farther north in the basin of the Is River, a tributary of the Tura, with alluvial deposits of high platinum content (65 to 87 percent). This was followed by the discovery of even richer ore along the Sukhoi Visim River, southwest of Nizhni Tagil.

It was the discovery of the latter deposit that became the basis for platinum mining in Russia, which soon became a major supplier to world markets. In 1825, the first year of commercial exploitation, the Urals placer yielded 87 kilograms (2,800 troy ounces) and in 1831 production was up to 1,750 kg (56,000 troy ounces).

Czarist Russia declared platinum to be a state monopoly, issuing private mining licenses, but controlling refining, storage and exporting under the care of the St. Petersburg Mint. It was then determined that Russian platinum was purer than the Colombian metal for alloying in rings, coins, and art objects. This period established platinum's principal uses, and Russia's premier position, for the most of the nineteenth century, including research into chemical and industrial applications. Also, the role of platinum in coinage was promoted by the Czarist Government to strengthen the national currency. Assays found that the ruble coins were impure, i.e. 97 percent platinum, but the output was substantial and coins circulated widely. Colombian platinum declined as a result, but counterfeiting, hoarding and smuggling devalued the Russian coins to end the early period of the Russian platinum industry. Yield from the Urals dropped to less than 10,000 ounces annually until revival, predi-

cated on a broader base, began in the 1860s. Russian platinum satisfied domestic demand and part of the European market, thus activating further search for deposits although most mining was still confined to the Urals. New mines were opened but they could no longer keep pace with world demand, as competitive and cheaper foreign sources were found to terminate what had been a near-Russian monopoly for seventy years. However, the establishment of the basic geology and metallurgy of platinum before the Bolshevik Revolution served as a foundation for advancement during the Soviet era. Mining was limited to the Urals, but knowledge of platinum's depositional conditions and potential reserves had provided Soviet geologists and mining engineers with a sound base for further exploration.

## Occurrence and Mining of Platinum in the USSR

Under Soviet rule, the discovery of platinum deposits has accompanied that of other metalliferous ores since the late 1920s. Soviet mining geology began intensive prospecting from the prerevolutionary base and started to pay dividends during the first two five-year plans (1928–32 and 1933–37) with the discovery of the nickel-copper-cobalt ores of the Kola Peninsula and the Norilsk district, which yielded platinum-group metals as coproducts. The Norilsk deposits were particularly rich in platinum-group metals, especially palladium, and the potential of the Norilsk district was further expanded in the 1960s with the discovery of the nearby Talnakh deposits. Since the 1940s the Norilsk district has become by far the principal producer of platinum-group metals in the Soviet Union, replacing the old Urals deposits.

The Urals deposits are associated with ultrabasic dunite in small oval intrusive bodies surrounded by peridotite and pyroxenite with gabbro formations. These dunite masses of 0.3 to 10 square miles are rich in platinum, but Soviet efforts at lode mining in the 1920s were not economic.[44] The commercial mining operations are concentrated in rich platinum-bearing gravels found in old river beds, on river terraces and in present-day streams. The weight of the platinum results in concentrations of pay streaks of up to five-foot thickness on stream bottoms. The richer and coarser deposits are found adjacent to the dunite source, with platinum grains becoming finer and fewer farther downstream. The original dunite sources extended in a north-south belt just east of the Urals divide, with platinum deposits intermittent in a belt 200 miles long from the Nizhni Tagil district northward. The principal concentrations of dunite intrusions occur near two mountain peaks, Veresovy Bor and Denezhkin Kamen. The original placer mines southwest of Nizhni Tagil have been replaced by newer and more productive areas farther north. These producing areas are clustered along the Is River, around the mining settlements of Malomalsk, Artelny, Valerianovsk and Is, and to the north around Kytlym. Judging from the fact that some of these places were given the urban status of workers settlement in 1933, they probably reached the peak of activity in the 1930s, when they were the Soviet Union's sole suppliers of platinum-group metals until the discovery and development of the now far more significant nickel-associated northern deposits. Only 2 percent of the nation's commercial concentrations of platinum-group metals are now found in placer deposits of the Urals. In terms of metals distribution in the Urals deposits, platinum is by far the most significant, with osmium and iridium predominating among the associated metals; rhodium and ruthenium account for less than 2 percent of the total.

The Norilsk-Talnakh resources of platinum-group metals differ sharply from the Urals resources because of their high content of palladium. The Norilsk ore distribution of platinum-group metals is 70 to 75 percent palladium, 22 to 26 percent platinum, 1.6 to 3.75 percent rhodium, 0.3 to 0.6 percent ruthenium and 0.15 to 0.43 percent iridium. In contrast to the Urals placer deposits, which are naturally concentrated and can be recovered by gravity separation, the Norilsk-type platinum resources are disseminated widely through the complex nickel-copper-cobalt ore and can be recovered only as a byproduct of nickel and copper smelting. Because of the high value-to-weight ratio of platinum-group metals, they are usually flown out of Norilsk, which has direct air service to Moscow.[45]

It is the high value of the platinum-group metals in the Norilsk operation that explains in part the tremendous investment put, by the Soviet authorities, into the development of that remote area of northern Siberia, including some of the world's deepest mines in the Talnakh district, and the provision of the costly icebreaker route between Dudinka, the port of Norilsk and Murmansk. The continuing high-cost development of the Norilsk-Talnakh area[46] and the prospect of further recoverable deposits northeast beyond Talnakh[47] suggest that Norilsk is likely to remain the prime source of Soviet platinum for an indefinite period of time.

Although the nickel-copper industry based on the resources of the Kola Peninsula also yields platinum-group metals,[48] this area does not have the potential of the Norilsk district, both because of a growing depletion of nickel reserves and because the platinum-group metal content of the ores has been substantially lower than at Norilsk-Talnakh.

A potential platinum region is Yakutia, where ores have been found in association with gold placers both in the Vilyui River basin of western Yakutia and in the Aldan region of southern Yakutia. These deposits are in many ways similar to those of the Urals. However, in view of the large resources of the Norilsk-Talnakh district, virtually all the development effort has been concentrated in northern Siberia and little has been done to determine the potential of other regions.

Other Producers

Since Soviet platinum competes on world metal markets, a cursory look at other sources is relevant. The first priority of the USSR platinum industry is satisfaction of its own demand, which accounts for an estimated 40 to 60 percent of production in a given year.[49] Exports to the industrialized West must meet prevailing price levels, while a variable proportion of output is sent to Soviet-bloc countries and the developing nations, in aid or exchange agreements, perhaps at underpriced levels.

Although Russia produced most of the world's platinum during the nineteenth century, the Soviet Union today probably incurs higher real production costs than do several other producers. Canada became Russia's first commercial competitor in the 1890s from the Sudbury, Ont., mines of the International Nickel Company.[50] Sudbury sperryolite yields primary platinum, as do several other Canadian mines in Manitoba and the Northwest Territories, chiefly from nickel ore. Canadian production has been impressive during war periods when it has exceeded Soviet output, but mines have been shut down since the 1950s, so that Canada has typically produced less than half the Soviet amount in recent years. Canadian platinum is refined in Western Europe and the United States and appears to be in a steadily declining and unreliable position for supplying future markets.

South Africa is clearly the coleader along with the USSR in producing and selling platinum, as well as rhodium, ruthenium and osmium. Three horizons in the Bushveld Complex alone, from dunite pipes, produce in a concentrated area nearly as much platinum as the USSR and, because of lower domestic demand, South Africa exports a great deal more. The Merensky Reef reserves are large and possibly greater than once expected.[51] South Africa has integrated operations on site, as well as superior infrastructure and marketing connections, and a reputation for prompt delivery of flawless metal. Rustenburg platinum, which greatly expanded operations of mining, smelting and refining in the 1950s and 1960s west of Pretoria, is the best-known name on world platinum markets. It controls output and sets prices which most other producers, including the Soviet Union, must competitively meet. South Africa has also been in the research forefront of mining and refining methods, e.g., smelting concentrates from chromite-rich ores by using a stable gas plasma at very high temperatures.[52] This technique may have implications for Soviet platinum which could be extracted from chromite mines in Kazakhstan.

The world's other platinum sources have a spotty distribution. Colombian alluvial platinum on the west side of the Andes is associated with chromite, dunite and pyroxenite from which it is concentrated out of river gravels of tertiary conglomerates. Colombia, however, has not kept pace in exploration and mining since about 1910. The United States was a small producer of primary platinum from the Goodnews Bay district (Platinum Creek), Alaska; but this mine closed in 1976 and most of the small output has been a byproduct of copper or gold-placer operations in the Sierra Nevada, Oregon, Washington and Utah, in addition to secondary recovery.[53] Ethiopia is known to have platinum placer deposits in dunite cores in the drainage area of the Blue and White Nile.[54] USSR aid and presence in Ethiopia since the 1960s may be an incentive to mine these dormant deposits and contribute to an enhanced role of Soviet-developed platinum. Japanese deposits are associated with gold placers in Hokkaido and Honshu, but reserve estimates are modest. Similarly, Sierra Leone has small alluvial placer deposits from weathered gabbro. More promising are Australian deposits associated with gold placers in New South Wales, new polymetallic discoveries in the Northwest, and with lateritic serpentine in Tasmania. However, none of these minor foreign deposits, with the possible exception of Australia, is likely to have any appreciable effect on world supplies in the near future.[55]

Reserves of Platinum

As is the case with many mineral resources, the estimation of platinum reserves is speculative. This uncertainty is compounded in the case of platinum because of co-deposition and variable richness of known reserves and outdated or nonexistent surveys in prospective areas. World reserves of platinum are generally judged to be substantial and adequate to meet demand well into the twenty-first century. By the year 2000, global demand is predicted to reach 5.5 million ounces, of which 27 percent will be required by the United States, for an annual growth rate of 3.2 percent.[56] The major deterrents to marketing will be production costs and free trade barriers, not resources *per se*. In Table 3, the dominant reserve position of South Africa and the second rank of the USSR are evident for the platinum-group metals. The United States appears to have considerable potential in "other platinum-group resources," mainly from the Montana-Stillwater Complex and the Duluth Gabbro, but they are believed to be predominantly palladium. The Soviet figure of 200 million ounces of platinum-group resources, as of 1978, is roughly a 60-year reserve at present rates of production. This projection is probably conservative. South Africa appears to be in a stronger reserve position.[57]

The USSR's reserves of palladium are reportedly twice those of platinum, which in turn are estimated to be about 12 percent of the world total. For the total potential resources, the Soviet share is roughly the same, but this estimate of 400 million ounces is probably low and likely to increase in the future from further exploration. The USSR's largest reserves in the Norilsk area are distinctive in that palladium accounts for three-fourths of the group composition and platinum for about one-fourth, in contrast to the predominance or equality of platinum in South Africa, Canada and Colombia. The Urals placers also contain mainly platinum.

Technological Implications

The process of mining, extraction, refining and fabrication of platinum metals is complex and capital-intensive. Few metals require so much specialized equipment and power consumption relative to amount of the finished product. The technology employed in the USSR is an amalgam of older Russian methods and those developed in Canada (Falconbridge), South Africa (Rustenburg), and Soviet adaptations. A Bessemer matte of nickel-copper sulfides and alloys is slowly cooled, crushed, ground, and magnetically separated into nickel-copper sulfides and alloys; the latter are then electrolytically broken down into copper, nickel and precious metals. Platinum-group concentrates are separated, by aqua regia, into platinum, palladium and gold from the others, followed by two filtration processes which yield platinum salts and sponges that must be further purified by acids and ignition up to 99.5 percent for most commercial uses.[58] Gold and rhodium accompany platinum to the final separation stage by this technique, but at Norilsk, palladium and nickel along with platinum are the main products of final refining. The heavy power requirements to operate the smelter and refinery are variously estimated at 15 to 25 percent of total production costs. At Norilsk, a 500-MW thermal power station, originally burning local coal, was converted to natural gas brought in by pipeline from the Messoyakha field in the 1970s. It has been suggested that gas from the giant fields in the Lower Ob basin (Urengoi and others) might also be utilized at Norilsk.[59]

On the research frontier, information regarding Soviet technological progress in platinum is available, and publications in the West are evaluated and applied in the USSR. Development of processes to utilize low-grade ores by the U.S. Bureau of Mines may be of interest to Soviet mining engineers in the future as depletion sets in. Electrodeposition techniques, although long known, are being improved to protect high-strength metals and to coat various shapes with platinum-group metals. Thus, platinum is a high-technology industry undergoing continuous research. The USSR is not disadvantaged in this respect, while capital, power and personnel requirements may restrict development in some countries that have the ore but not the technology.

TABLE 3
World Platinum-Group Metals Resources[1] (million troy ounces)

|  | Platinum | Palladium | Platinum Group | Other Platinum-Group Resources | Total |
|---|---|---|---|---|---|
| USSR | 60 | 120 | 200 | 200 | 400 |
| United States | NA | NA | 1 | 299 | 300 |
| Canada | 4 | 4 | 9 | 7 | 16 |
| Colombia | 1(?) | — | 1 | 4 | 4(?) |
| South Africa, Rep. | 456 | 310 | 970 | 1,430 | 2,400 |
| Rhodesia | NA | NA | NA | 100 | 100 |
| World totals | 520 | 434 | 1,180 | 2,040 | 3,220 |

[1]Mineral Facts and Problems, 1980 Edition, "Platinum-Group Metals," Bulletin 671 (Washington, Dept. of the Interior, 1980), p. 4.
[2]Australia, Ethiopia, Finland and the Philippines have reserves but they are not estimated.

National Production Trends

Although Russia lost its preeminence in platinum by the
end of the last century, and the Bolshevik Revolution and
Civil War crippled the industry after World War I, the
USSR has regained a prominent role on the world scene.
The Soviet platinum industry is fully integrated and
self-sufficient, in that all stages from mining through
fabrication are domestically performed. Finished metal is
exported for further processing abroad at the buyer's
option, but the USSR exercises its capability to market
fabricated products. This is not generally true for other
countries where market pull and trade agreements have
separated various stages.

Because of secrecy and disclosure regulations, it is difficult to compare volumes of mined platinum among all
countries. For the platinum group as a whole, the USSR
rapidly expanded its output since the opening of Norilsk
to a level of 250,000 troy ounces in 1955, to surpass Canada at roughly 23 percent of the world total.[60] However,
the Soviet platinum proportion in the group is low (about
one-fourth) compared with other countries since palladium is dominant (about three-fourths) in the Norilsk
deposits. For the remainder of the 1950s the USSR reported no appreciable change in output around a fluctuating world total. Since the 1960s, when the expansion
program began in the Talnakh district near Norilsk,
Soviet production of the platinum-group has registered
steady growth to 3.05 million ounces in 1978 for an estimated 48 percent of the world group output and 763,000
ounces, or 28 percent, of the platinum alone.[61] The Canadian share has declined to 5 percent, while South Africa
accounted for 45 percent of the group total and an estimated 65 percent of the world's platinum. Colombia,
Japan, the United States and Australia, in that order,
follow as minor producers, each with less than 1 percent.
Projections to 1985 indicate a growth in world capacity to
8.7 million ounces for the group total and a similar Soviet
share. Thus, it appears that the USSR platinum industry
is still growing but at no more than the world rate.
Assuming that domestic rquirements will continue to
increase, Soviet platinum can be expected to maintain,
but not significantly increase, its relative role in world
markets during the 1980s. Two conditions might change
the prospects: (1) new or greatly expanded production
sites, as at Talnakh, or, (2) a policy change by the government that would vary the amount of primary platinum
released from stocks.

Changing Consumption Patterns

Since the 1930s, platinum has experienced a proliferation
of new uses and a spatial dispersion of markets. This is
also true for palladium, in which the USSR is the production leader. Platinum may be used in pure form, in alloys
with other metals of the group, or with silver, gold and
other metals. Platinum's principal uses, which have
shifted considerably in recent years, may be summarized
as follows:
1. *Chemical* industries, where the catalytic activity of
   platinum and its resistance to corrosion and oxida-

tion have rendered it essential to the reduction of
organic compounds, especially in the catalytic
cracking of oil to raise octane ratings; other uses are
in the manufacture of nitric acid, oleum, hydrocy-
anic acid, vitamins, and a wide range of antibiotics;
also, along with rhodium or iridium, platinum is
utilized in jet engines for reignition, in laboratory
vessels, for valves, nozzles and high-quality glass,
and most importantly in recent years with palladium for exhaust catalysts to reduce the emission of
carbon monoxide and hydrocarbons from motor vehicle engines.
2. *Electrical* industries are the second largest user of
   platinum, although palladium is cheaper and substitutable for many applications; platinum alloys are
   important components of telephone circuits, voltage regulators, clocks, sparkplugs, and thermocou-
   ples in ferrous metallurgy; also, platinum along
   with rhodium is the standard alloy for electroplating; these applications have remained fairly stable
   in demand in the past decade. But the forthcoming
   demand for platinum should expand rapidly in electronic devices with growth in computer and high-
   technology devices.
3. *Dental and medical* uses have increased briskly to
   replace gold.
4. *Jewelry* and art consumption of platinum is the only
   major use that has had a static or declining demand
   in recent years, but a variety of miscellaneous applications, as in ceramic glass, have more than
   compensated.

Table 4 reports biennially for 1969–79 world mine production of platinum, exclusive of other metals in the
groups, the USSR output and share, and United States
imports and demand pattern, as representative of growth
and sectoral shift. Changes in the United States do not
necessarily reflect world trends, but they are a large part
of them and have in the past been forerunners of change
in other industrialized economies. Even under limited
trade with the United States, the Soviet Union's platinum
industry is affected because of similar structural changes
in other countries. While world platinum output increased over the decade by some 70 percent, the USSR
expanded its production over 2.5-fold to 28 percent of the
global total; the United States imports nearly tripled from
a burst at the end of the 1970s. Total United States demand, which is now back up to 50 percent of the world
mine output, has undergone important shifts. The striking addition to demand has been by automotive industries, which account for over half of the American consumption, nearly all of this attributable to environmental
requirements on emission controls. Some of the reported
decline by chemical industries is the result of reclassification to automotives. The West European and Japanese
markets are also responding to this demand sector,
although at a slower pace. However, by the year 2000
alternatives to platinum for emission controls are
anticipated.[62]
Catalytic cracking of petroleum is now standard in
refinery construction, so platinum demand has greatly
enlarged on a world scale, but only modestly in the

TABLE 4
Platinum Production and U.S. Demand, 1969–79[1] (1,000 troy ounces)

| | 1969 | 1971 | 1973 | 1975 | 1977 | 1979 | 1969/79 |
|---|---|---|---|---|---|---|---|
| World Mine Output | 1,403 | 1,708 | 2,365 | 2,613 | 2,705 | 2,858 | 1.71 |
| USSR Output (est.)[2] | 309 | 393 | 520 | 663 | 698 | 800 | 2.67 |
| percent of world | 22% | 23% | 22% | 25% | 26% | 28% | — |
| U.S. Imports, Refined | 379 | 492 | 886 | 980 | 931 | 1,482 | 2.98 |
| U.S. Demand pattern: | | | | | | | |
| Automotive | — | — | — | 273 | 354 | 803 | — |
| Chemicals | 175 | 135 | 239 | 149 | 84 | 99 | 0.77 |
| Oil refining | 62 | 137 | 124 | 108 | 75 | 170 | 1.34 |
| Ceramics and glass | 63 | 41 | 72 | 34 | 60 | 88 | 1.69 |
| Electrical | 112 | 52 | 117 | 74 | 90 | 116 | 1.05 |
| Dental supplies | 22 | 23 | 28 | 17 | 27 | 27 | 1.78 |
| Jewelry and arts | 36 | 19 | 22 | 23 | 35 | 28 | 0.83 |
| Other | 47 | 20 | 56 | 21 | 65 | 78 | 2.18 |
| Total U.S. demand | 517 | 427 | 658 | 699 | 790 | 1,409 | 2.54 |
| Percent of world mined output | 36.8% | 25.0% | 27.8% | 26.8% | 29.2% | 49.3% | — |

[1]Selected and computed from Mineral Facts and Figures, 1980 Edition, "Platinum-Group Metals," Bulletin 671 (Washington, Department of the Interior, 1980), Table 7, p. 11.
[2]Author's estimate by a factor of 0.25 (Norilsk platinum percentage) applied to USSR platinum-group totals.

United States. This is also the case in electrical industries, but dental, ceramic and glass uses have had a lively and general demand growth and should continue to expand.

Demand shifts in the USSR, which have direct impact upon exports and therefore world supplies, must be inferred from internal economic change because they are not reported in Soviet sources. Given the high priority accorded to chemical and electrical industries, and their rapid growth, it seems safe to assign an increasing share of platinum consumption to them, very likely over 60 percent. Soviet oil production is probably the third consumer with 15 to 20 percent of domestic demand. Soviet automotives are also growing demand sectors, but they are not so subject to the emission control problem as in the United States. Other Soviet uses are minor, except for ceramics which are vital in space industries. Dental uses of platinum have never been important, since palladium is cheaper, and platinum prices for jewelry have skyrocketed to prohibitive levels.[63]

Marketing and World Trade

Platinum takes various channels from mine to market, in general from a few producing countries via processing centers to most of the developed economies. Concentrates are shipped from mining countries, such as Colombia and Canada, to refining countries such as Britain and the United States for consumption and reexport. South Africa, which dominates world marketing, refines platinum but also exports about 35 percent of its mined platinum for refining abroad. The United States imports chiefly from South Africa and the USSR, while its exports are about one-third of refined output (as of the late 1970s); Britain has a similar supply-demand pattern. There are no tariffs on United States imports of platinum-group metals or scrap for either Most Favored Nations or non-MFN, but there is a 65 percent ad valorem duty on alloys from non-MFN exporters.[64] This practically dictates

Soviet exports to the United States in unwrought or semi-manufactured form, while other countries do not normally impose tariffs on Soviet platinum in any form.

The USSR is not in a strong competitive position vis-a-vis South Africa in world platinum markets, but its production in most years exceeds domestic demand. Thus, Soviet exports are significant in a number of markets. The United States, Britain and the East European countries are destinations for the bulk of Soviet platinum exports, and some of the latter is reexported to the West, including the United States. Other buyers of Soviet platinum and palladium are Switzerland, Norway, Sweden, West Germany, Japan, France, the Netherlands, and India.

The USSR entered world platinum markets in the late 1950s on a small scale to earn hard-currency credits, and also to promote trade. Domestic production, however, could barely keep pace with demand in the 1960s, so exports shrunk to zero in some years. Not until the early 1970s, when Soviet platinum production passed the 500,000-ounce level (Table 4), did exports regularly begin to have a significant influence on international markets. In 1974 platinum exports to the industrialized West were valued at $371 million.[65] At prevailing prices of $150 per ounce, this represented about 250,000 ounces of exported platinum (unwrought, partly worked), or 42 percent of the Soviet production in that year, and roughly one-third of all world exports. Large withdrawals from stocks were undoubtedly necessary, indicating an ability and inclination to earn foreign exchange (for grain imports), and to serve political goals, e.g., détente, under appropriate conditions. Platinum exports declined sharply the next year and also changed in direction. By 1976 Japan became the leading buyer with 48 percent of Soviet platinum sales, followed by the United States (30 percent), West Germany (9 percent), Britain, and Switzerland. But export destinations to the West should be viewed as a whole since platinum, like gold, is readily redistributable among trading partners.

By the 1970s, then, the USSR became the second-ranked platinum exporter, behind South Africa and far ahead of Canada. Estimates for 1980 (not yet verified) indicate that Soviet production capacity will continue to expand to about 900,000 ounces by 1985, and that export potential may reach 100,000 ounces, or 25 to 30 percent of world exports.[66] Equally noteworthy is the wider distribution of Soviet exports as new buyers are added. Despite deteriorating political relations, the United States has continued to import Soviet platinum, either directly or via Western Europe and Japan, in sponge or semi-manufactured form. Platinum imports vary widely from year to year, while the platinum-group totals are more stable. For all members of the group, mainly because of palladium, United States dependence upon the USSR is in the 25 to 30 percent range.

Soviet platinum has arrived on world markets through contractual agreements with the East European governments, Western buyers, both public and private, and with some less developed countries. Not much is sold on the spot market because of currency problems and the Soviet Ministry of Foreign Trade, which cannot easily execute short-term sales and purchases. Most of the growth in exports in the past decade has occurred in Western Europe, the United States, and Japan; the latter may be the best prospect because of need and purchasing power. Japan has been the largest buyer of finished platinum (rolled and unrolled) from the United States but this might be short-circuited by direct purchase from the USSR with which Japan has had a sharp increase in general trade since the mid-1960s. There is not assurance, however, that the present and planned mining activity in the USSR, even with expansion at Norilsk-Talnakh, can appreciably increase surpluses at costs that are competitive with new finds in South Africa and some of the smaller producers. Indeed, Soviet export gains during the 1970s, designed to earn hard currency, may have strained capacity beyond economic limits.

## Strategic Aspects and Stockpiling

Since its initial recognition as a valuable industrial metal with military implications, platinum has been designated as a "strategic," "guarded," or "critical" material. Scarcity, high prices, and general nonsubstitutability underlie the concern of government, investors, and industrial users with the maintenance of platinum supplies. Since 1940, platinum has consistently been on the United States list of strategic metals, i.e., those vital to defense and industry but available in large quantities only from foreign sources. Every government of platinum-using countries exercises some degree of import control, price regulation, or stockpiling, but the United States is particularly concerned because of its high consumption and dependence on foreign resources. According to some sources, the USSR has been engaging in a "resource war" since it purchased Rhodesian chromite in the early 1970s.[67] More recently, the Soviet Union is said to have purchased cobalt and even metals in the platinum-group from Africa and European countries to secure larger

supplies, to release exports at high prices and, according to some, to threaten future Western access to them.[68]

Among the five most strategic materials—the others being titanium, manganese, chromium and cobalt—platinum is in the shortest supply. In January 1981 the United States stockpile was only a five-month supply to back up the eleven-week supply in the industrial pipeline, far short of the fourteen-month stockpile goals which would cost about $400 million to reach at current prices.[69] Measures which may be taken to alleviate the shortage are underway; the recycling of spent automobile exhaust catalysts, payment of a conversion fee by certain industries to the refiner, reallocation of the platinum pool to strategic industries, scrap recovery, and substitution, e.g., rhenium for platinum in petroleum-reforming catalysts. But these methods incur cost and are anticipated to save no more than the demand increase in the United States. The decline of Canadian production and the high demand for South Africa platinum in all Western markets suggest a small U.S. stockpile, unless domestic reserves in Montana can be developed. The problem is also political. Although stockpile quotas were resumed in 1976, Congress did not appropriate funds for acquisitions. Under the Reagan administration, the Defense Department's enlarged budget may assist the platinum industry with contracts to buy and process more of the metal for stockpiling.[70]

In any case, the USSR cannot be viewed as a dependable supplier of more platinum, particularly at present price levels.

### Prices

Platinum commands one of the highest price levels of any metal, being exceeded normally by only a few rare materials, such as rhodium and osmium in its own group.[71] Since the costs of recovery and processing are shared by other members of the platinum group, there is a joint supply and demand which is affected by price changes among them; these may be more important determinants of output and price than the inherent scarcity of the metal itself. Platinum sales may be quite elastic with respect to short-term price changes which are mainly a function of Western demand. However, over the longer run production has been rather inelastic, e.g., world output increased by approximately 25 percent while prices rose nearly sixfold. USSR production has been less responsive to price fluctuations than that of South Africa and Canada. Soviet platinum exports act somewhat as a stabilizer to satisfy demand which cannot be fully met by market economy producers. At the same time, contractual obligations may result in short-term losses when platinum prices decline, or conversely, in large profits with sharp price increases.

During the 1970s platinum prices first rose gradually and then dramatically, paralleling and usually staying ahead of gold. Platinum's spot price in 1972 was in the range of $105 to $106 per troy ounce while gold was selling in London and New York at $50 to $70 per ounce. Prices continued on an upward trend throughout the decade, although dealer prices remained below producers prices for much of the time, thus placing a strain on reserve stocks and activating Western demand on controlled sources such as the Soviet Union. By 1977 platinum had risen only moderately into the $160 to $190 range, while gold narrowed the differential at $140 to $170 per ounce.[72] These were the last days of relatively cheap precious metals, since both gold and platinum prices have more than quadrupled during the past four years. Platinum peaked in late 1979 at $905 per ounce, along with gold at $840, but there has been a significant decline and levelling off, particularly for platinum, in the past eighteen months. In March 1981, platinum's price on the New York Metal Exchange was $450 per ounce (with 1982 futures at $540), while gold prices on world markets are $510 to $520 (with 1982 futures over $650).[73] The Soviet response to platinum prices that are only one-half that of their peak is not clear. USSR data are not yet available for 1980–81, but it seems certain that "profits" are now low and that Soviet platinum exports may be restricted until Western price levels rise toward their former levels.

USSR Prospects

The USSR typically retains less than half of its mined and refined platinum for domestic use. During the four-year period, 1975–78, exports are estimated to have been on the order of 350,000 to 450,000 ounces annually. Production figures of the past few years suggest a levelling off or slight decline. Dealer speculation and record prices in 1979–80 caused uncertainty in world markets. Precise allocation of Soviet exports is difficult to determine but the trade commitments to CMEA are assumed to be modest. Japan, Western Europe, and the United States account for the bulk (at least 75 percent) of Soviet platinum sales in most years. The Japanese share is rising, Britain's levelling off, and the United States' fluctuating according to government stockpiling and industrial purchases by importers who redistribute from their supplies.[74]

However, the USSR is displaying increased interest in the larger, developing economies, such as Brazil and India, which have propsects for demand growth in platinum-using sectors, notably in oil refining and electrical industries. Economic growth projections indicate that the less developed countries could take up slack in demand for platinum by Western markets, although they are not likely to buy large quantities. In short, if trade relations do not deteriorate and the reputed "resource war" does not intensify, Soviet platinum is expected to continue to play a vital role, and possibly a slightly larger one than in the 1970s. If, for example, world demand again doubles decennially until the year 2000, Soviet platinum exports would probably exceed a million ounces per year and thus be greater than the current South African figure. But there are contingencies: (1) does the USSR have the production capability to expand that rapidly? (2) will the lower-cost Bushveld and Merensky Reef operations fulfill expectations? and (3) what new or presently minor sources of platinum will appear as competitors?

Additional uncertainties are governmental policy and domestic demand within the USSR. The Soviet leadership may pursue a path of conservation, although the need for hard-currency credits has prevailed in the past, and platinum is highly marketable. It is essentially like gold in international trade. Also, the growth dynamics of the Soviet economy imply an increasing domestic demand—in all the leading sectors of use—which will exert a downward pressure on export potential. The ultimate answer lies in the rate of discovery and output of new finds in the Norilsk area, other metalliferous Siberian zones, and possibly the Kola Peninsula. Unquestionably, the expansion of platinum production in the USSR has a high priority because of both internal and external forces.

## Conclusion

The Soviet Union has good geologic potential for expanding its nickel and platinum production. The Norilsk-Talnakh district is the dominant source and despite the harsh environment and high operation costs, plans call for future expansion in the region. The Urals and the Kola Peninsula will only make minor contributions to total Soviet production.

The USSR has equaled Canada in nickel output, but the prospects for increased Soviet exports may encounter increased competition from other sources such as Australia, Indonesia, and Botswana. Scrap recovery and the development of nickel substitutes may also constrain Soviet export potential in nickel. Soviet platinum and palladium are likely to continue challenging South Africa on the world market. Platinum exports to the United States and other Western economies will most certainly continue, but with fluctuations in amount in response to price changes and the Soviet need for hard currency. The currently depressed price of platinum has reduced sales, but when the price rebounds increased exports from the USSR and South Africa may be expected.

## NOTES

1. James S. Gregory, *Russian Land, Soviet People* (New York: Pegasus, 1968), pp. 504–07.

2. Michael T. Florinsky, ed. *Encyclopedia of Russia and the Soviet Union* (New York: McGraw-Hill, 1961), p. 350.

3. Samuel J. Rosenberg, *Nickel and Its Alloys*, National Bureau of Standards Monograph 106 (Washington: Government Printing Office, May 1968), p. 1.

4. Ibid., pp. 1–2.

5. Ibid., p. 3.

6. Ibid., pp. 9–40.

7. For a technical treatment of nickel metallurgy in the USSR, see V.I. Smirnov, *Metallurgiya nikelya* [Nickel metallurgy] (Moscow: Metallurgizdat, 1950).

8. Norman A. Matthews and Scott F. Sibley, "Nickel." In *Mineral Facts and Problems 1980 Edition* Bulletin 671 (Washington: Department of the Interior, Bureau of Mines, 1980), p. 4.

9. Ibid., p. 5.

10. Ibid., p. 11.

11. H. R. Cornwall, "Nickel." In *U.S. Mineral Reserves,*

U.S. Geological Survey Professional Paper 280, 1973, pp. 437–42.

12. M. N. Godlevsky, "Preparation of the raw material base for the nickel industry and associated geological problems," *Razvedka i okhrana nedr*, 1967, no. 10–11, p. 53; *50 let Sovetskoi geologii* [50 years of Soviet geology] (Moscow: Nedra, 1968), p. 298.

13. Sh. Yesenov, D. Kunayev and S. Mukhamedzhanov, *Nedra Kazakhstana* [Minerals of Kazakhstan] (Alma-Ata: Kazakhstan Publishers, 1968), p. 209.

14. N. A. Bykhover, *Ekonomika mineralnogo syrya* [Mineral economics] (Moscow: Nedra, 1967), p. 298.

15. *50 let Sovetskoi geologii*, pp. 298–99.

16. Matthews and Sibley, "Nickel," p. 6.

17. Most of the following discussion is based on Godlevsky, "Raw material base," and *50 let Sovetskoi geologii*.

18. V. G. Altov, *Goroda Orenburgskoi oblasti* [Cities of Orenburg Oblast] (Chelyabinsk, 1974), pp. 83–86.

19. *Tsvetnye metally*, 1975, no. 1; 1976, no. 6; 1976, no. 11; *Stroitelnaya gazeta*, 20 February 1976.

20. *Pravda*, 12 November 1970; *Stroitelnaya gazeta*, 23 November 1973; *Tsvetnye metally*, 1974, no. 4.

21. *Sovetskaya Rossiya*, 13 November 1977; *Stroitelnaya gazeta*, 7 November 1978 and 15 March 1981.

22. The discussion of the development of Norilsk is based on the following sources: *Gorny zhurnal*, 1970, no. 7 and 1975, no. 8; V. N. Lebedinsky and P. I. Melnikov, *Zvezda Zapolyarya* [Stars of the Arctic] (Moscow: Profizdat, 1971); N. N. Urvantsev, *Norilsk* (Moscow: Nedra, 1969); V. P. Dunayev, *Samy severny* [The northernmost] (Moscow: Geografgiz, 1960).

23. Rosenberg, *Nickel and Its Alloys*, pp. 6–7.

24. *Minerals Yearbook*, Vol. 1, 1972, 1977 (Washington: Department of the Interior, Bureau of Mines), "Nickel" chapters; and Matthews and Sibley, "Nickel," Table 2, p. 3.

25. *Minerals Yearbook*, Vol. 1, 1977, p. 668.

26. Ibid., pp. 662–69.

27. *Mining Annual Review*, 1979, p. 17.

28. *Minerals Yearbook*, Vol. 1, 1977, pp. 662 and 664.

29. *United Nations Yearbook of International Trade Statistics, 1979* (United Nations, New York: 1980), p. 369 and pp. 732–33 calculated from data therein).

30. Matthews and Sibley, "Nickel," p. 9 (from flow chart).

31. Central Intelligence Agency, *Handbook of Economic Statistics, 1980* (ER 80-10452), October 1980, Table 59, p. 88.

32. *USSR 1976 Hard Currency Exports to the Industrialized West* (Washington: Department of Commerce, 1978), Table 3.

33. Several papers of the AAG Project on Soviet Natural Resources in the World Economy deal with these prospects. For a detailed discussion, see chapter 7 in this volume.

34. Rosenberg, *Nickel and Its Alloys*, p. 6.

35. *The Wall Street Journal*, issues of March 1981.

36. *Barclays Commodities Survey* (London: January 1981), p. 3.

37. *Minerals Yearbook*, Vol. 1, 1977, pp. 663–64 and 667.

38. *USSR 1976 Hard Currency Exports*, Table 3.

39. Matthews and Sibley, "Nickel," p. 11.

40. *The Wall Street Journal*, 15 April 1981, p. 1.

41. D. Fine, *Business Week*, 8 September 1980, review of *Resource Wars* (Pittsburgh: World Affairs Council), p. 58.

42. Most of the following material is from: C. C. Allen, *The Platinum Metals* (Ottawa: Mineral Resources Division, Department of Mines and Technical Surveys, 1961), Chapter 2 and 5, pp. 3–19 and 34–51.

43. Selected from Donald McDonald, *A History of Platinum* (London: Johnson Matthey, 1960), Chapter 12 (Platinum in Russia), pp. 156–68; *50 let Sovetskoi geologii*, pp. 339–42.

44. Allen, *Platinum Metals*, pp. 14 and 17.

45. The amount transported in this manner is not known but is assumed to be a large share of production.

46. *Minerals Yearbook*, Vol. 1, 1977, pp. 735–36.

47. L. V. Razin, "Geologic and Genetic Features of Forsterite Dunites and Their Platinum-Group Mineralization," *Economic Geology* 71 (1976), pp. 1371–76.

48. V. V. Strishkov, "The Minerals Industry of the USSR," in *Minerals Yearbook 1974*, Vol. 3, Area Reports International (Washington: Department of the Interior, Bureau of Mines, 1977), pp. 920, 926, 934–50.

49. Estimated by the author from average value of exports in mid-1970s and production volumes.

50. Allen, *Platinum Metals*, pp. 1–2, and 7–11.

51. G. von Gruenwaldt, "The Mineral Resources of the Bushveld Complex," *Minerals Science and Engineering*, 9, no. 2 (April 1977): 83–90.

52. J. H. Jolly, "Platinum-Group Metals," *Mineral Facts and Problems, 1980 Edition* (Washington: Department of the Interior, Bureau of Mines, 1980), pp. 5–7.

53. *Minerals Yearbook*, Vol. 1, 1972, p. 1044; Jolly, "Platinum-Group Metals," p. 2.

54. Allen, *Platinum Metals*, pp. 19–20.

55. G. J. S. Govett and M. H. Govett, eds., *World Mineral Supplies: Assessment and Perspective* (Amsterdam: Elsevier, 1976).

56. Jolly, "Platinum-Group Metals," from Table 16, p. 18.

57. "Platinum—Great Importance of the Bushveld Complex," *World Mining*, August 1980, pp. 56–59.

58. Allen, *Platinum Metals*, pp. 20–26.

59. N. S. Uspenskiy, "Use of Natural Gas in the Nickel and Tin Industries of the USSR," *Tsvetnye Metally*, 16, no. 4 (April 1975): 27.

60. Allen, *Platinum Metals*, p. 56.

61. Jolly, "Platinum-Group Metals," from Fig. 3, p. 10. The Central Intelligence Agency estimate for Soviet production of platinum-group metals has been running about 15 percent higher than the U.S. Bureau of Mines estimate, or 3.5 million ounces in 1978.

62. Ibid., p. 17.

63. Author's observation on a trip to Moscow in 1978 and report by a tourist in 1980.

64. Jolly, "Platinum-Group Metals," Table 14, p. 13.

65. *USSR 1976 Hard Currency Exports*, Tables 3 and 4.

66. Based on a constant percentage (25 percent) of estimated platinum-group export by the USSR for 1985, as reported in: Jolly, "Platinum-Group Metals," p. 3.

67. Fine, *Business Week*.

68. "Russia's Sudden Reach for Raw Materials," *Fortune*, 28 July 1980.

69. "How We're Fixed for Strategic Minerals," *Fortune*, 29 February 1981, p. 70.

70. *The Wall Street Journal*, 15 April 1981, p. 9.

71. Rhodium prices have typically been 2.5 times higher than platinum, while osmium has averaged 40 to 70 percent higher.

72. *Minerals Yearbook*, Vol. 1, 1977, p. 1047.

73. *The Wall Street Journal*, 2 February 1981, p. 26.

74. Courtesy of Joseph Filner, president of Noblemet, New York, in Minneapolis, in the spring of 1979.

# 24

# THE SOVIET GOLD-MINING INDUSTRY

MICHAEL KASER
Oxford University

## Sources of Information

"One cannot help feeling that, in playing the guessing game, the government offices with access to sources of special information do not necessarily score better than academic scholars . . . The Bureau of Mines went far off the mark. It is also evident that estimates made by technical experts on the basis of some technical indicators are usually less reliable than those made by economists."[1]

The reference is to a comparison of estimates on the Chinese economy during the statistical blackout of 1959–76 with the official data released after the Cultural Revolution, but it is not without relevance to the study of Soviet gold production. The actors are the same—United States government bodies, the Bureau of Mines and the Central Intelligence Agency, at least one technical expert,[2] and a certain number of economists.[3] The only detailed field-by-field description at the time of writing are those of the present writer in 1971,[4] and with Dowie in 1974,[5] but in 1978 Consolidated Gold Fields (which had sponsored the studies just mentioned) published the first findings of a new field-by-field examination, reviewing the Muruntau deposit in Uzbekistan.[6] The following year the same source covered the Zod mine in Armenia,[7] and in 1980 byproduct gold.[8] All are drawn upon in the regional analysis that follows and, in the aggregate summary presented further below, the company's forecast of the Soviet total expected is also noted; these were announced by an executive director of the company, M.E. Becket, in January 1980.[9]

For this new study the present writer has used the journal of the Ministry of Nonferrous Metallurgy USSR, *Tsvetnye metally*, reports from Soviet newspapers and radio, and books published in Moscow or in the regional centers of gold production. None of these refer to production by forced labor and to establish an historical series—only one reference has been found to such gold mining today—a detailed search has been made of accounts by former workers in and around the camps of the Northeast and of Yakutia. In his two previous field-by-field studies, the writer was able to find statistical abstracts that published index numbers that could indicate, albeit very indirectly and imperfectly, a time series of gold production. No such help was afforded by the Central Statistical Administration USSR or its regional bodies for the period after 1974: the publication of oblast abstracts has virtually ceased and oblast breakdowns in the national or union-republic abstracts have been sharply thinned.

## Administration of the Industry

The Soviet government's development of gold mining dates from the appointment, in February 1924, of Feliks Dzerzhinsky, from the Revolution until then the chief of the secret police (Cheka to 1923, then OGPU), as chairman of the Supreme Council of the National Economy. A protagonist of self-sufficiency for the USSR in metals production (policies confirmed at the 14th Party Conference in April 1925 and at the 14th Party Congress in December 1925), he convened a first national conference on nonferrous metals at the Businessmen's Club, Moscow, in late March 1925.[10] He conveyed a resolution by the party's Central Committee of January 1925 that the country should seek to become self-sufficient in nonferrous metals. Lenzoloto, the state trust that had operated the country's biggest goldfield since 1921, was handed over to a British company within a general policy of granting foreign concessions in industries where technical re-equipment was crucial to development. Lena Goldfields Company operated the workings until 1928. A Main Administration for the Gold and Platinum Industry (Glav-*noye upravleniye* zoloto-*platinovoi promyshlennosti*, abbreviated Glavzoloto), was established in September 1927 as a company with the state as sole shareholder. In August 1928 it was placed under the supervision of the People's Commissariat of Finance. Mining operations were conducted by the Tsvetmetzoloto Corporation, which was placed under the People's Commissariat of Nonferrous Metallurgy on its estalishment in March 1939.[11] Like all People's Commissariats it was redesignated a Ministry in March 1946.[12] By World War II, the Commissariat had added two trusts to the original Lenzoloto: Amurzoloto for the workings in the Amur Basin and Dzhugdzhurzoloto in Yakutia.[13] By that time, however, output by forced labor in the prison camps of the People's

Commissariat of Internal Affairs (NKVD, later MVD) substantially surpassed that of all the civilian enterprises, in which, even so, quite large contingents of prison labor were used.[14]

As is described in greater detail in the section on the Northeast (in Russian, *Severovostok*), the principal gold production zone employing prisoners was Dalstroi. Forced labor also opened up the nickel deposits of Norilsk (which began deliveries in May 1942)[15] and all nonferrous metals output from prison camps was administered by a Main Administration for the Special Production of Nonferrous Metals (Glavspetstsvetmet).[16] The Ministry of Nonferrous Metallurgy took over all such operations when the camps were closed in 1956–57;[17] probably to facilitate their absorption, Glavzoloto was divided into Glavvostokzoloto (Main Administration for the Gold and Platinum Industries of the Far East and East Siberia) and Glavzapadzoloto (Main Administration for the Gold and Platinum Industries of West Siberia, the Urals and Kazakhstan). This may also have been in response to the devolution of mining and manufacturing to the regional economic councils (sovnarkhozy) during 1957–65. The ministry was abolished in those years; its existence had not in fact been continuous, for it was merged in large ministries in 1948–50 and 1953–54.

Reestablished in 1965 after the reversal of Khrushchev's devolution, the union-republic Ministry of Nonferrous Metallurgy reconstituted Glavzoloto and confirmed its operation through regional agencies (in alphabetical order): Altaizoloto, Amurzoloto, Kazzoloto, Lenzoloto, Primorzoloto, Severovostokzoloto, Uralzoloto, Uzbekzoloto, Yakutzoloto, Yeniseizoloto, Zabaikalzoloto and Zapsibzoloto. These were state corporations, trusts or combines according to their importance; one for Armenia, Armzoloto, was later set up to replace an enterprise, the lowest entity with an autonomous balance sheet, and one enterprise, Tadzhikzoloto, was directly subordinate to Glavzoloto. All other gold industry combines (kombinaty) and enterprises (predpriyatiya) were run by the regional agencies.

The industry was reorganized during the 9th Five-Year Plan 1971–75. The Minister, P. F. Lomako, wrote in 1976 that the mergers in that reorganization were pursuant to a decree of 13 October 1969 on "Measures to Improve Management and to Reduce Expenditure on Managerial Staff."[18] The form that the upper echelons took in the Ministry was, however, more dictated by the General Statute for National and Republic Industrial Corporations of 2 March 1973. Glavzoloto, which since the beginning of the exploitation of diamonds in Yakutia had become the Main Administration of the Gold, Platinum and Diamond Industries, convened a meeting of activists in Irkutsk on 27–28 February 1975 to report "decisions of the December plenum of the party's Central Committee."[19] It is likely that the changes were reported to that meeting. By the start of 1976 , Soyuzzoloto, a national industrial administration, had been established to run the gold industry. A central apparatus remained in the Ministry, for the Minister noted that "the national industrial corporation, will continue to use the nonferrous metallurgical administrations as links."[20] Soyuzzoloto is a profit-and-

loss agency, in contrast to Glavzoloto, which was carried on the Ministry's budget. At the bottom end of the administrative scale, mergers of enterprises under the Ministry reduced the total from 360 in 1968 to 266 in 1977, mainly by the demotion of 101 enterprises with fewer than 1,000 staff; between them and the 10 national industrial administrations (of which Yakutalmaz took over those in diamonds) were production corporations.[21] Of the latter no list for the gold industry seems to have been published but, as the following sections by corporation indicate, nine have been identified in Soviet journals and media reports during 1976–80 (alphabetical order): Armzoloto for the Armenian SSR, Kazmintsvetmet, for all nonferrous metallurgy in the Kazakh SSR (absorbing, it would appear, both Altaizoloto and Kazzoloto), Lenzoloto, Primorzoloto (which seems to have incorporated Amurzoloto), Severovostokzoloto for Magadan Oblast, Uralzoloto, Uzbekzoloto for the Uzbek SSR, Yakutzoloto for the Yakut ASSR and Zabaikalzoloto; those without a territorial indication cover more than one administrative region of the Russian Federation. The absence of references to Yeniseizoloto and Zapsibzoloto may indicate demotion in the light of their relatively small production: in the text which follows they are discussed under "Other Siberia." Tadzhikzoloto is probably a combine (kombinat) for the Tadzhik SSR and a corresponding combine, putatively "Kirgizzoloto," must have been established for the new lode mining operations in the Kirghiz SSR. The existence of such combines may be inferred from the Minister's observation that by 1976 "almost all gold ore was utilized within the ore-dressing (*gorno-obogatitelny*) and mining-metallurgical production corporations and combines."[22]

As a further phase in the rationalization the Ministry handed over, in 1980, its repair and reconstruction service, Soyuztsvetmetremont Production Corporation to the Building and Repair Trust, Stroimontazh, of the Ministry of Assembly and Special Construction USSR (a ministry which usually concerns itself with the installation of imported or new technology); in announcing this, a senior official of the Ministry of Nonferrous Metallurgy forecast that from 1981 the ratio of repair-work to installed capital assets would substantially increase in Soyuzzoloto.[23]

The order used in the following field-by-field description is east-to-west (see Figure 1 for field locations): the Northeast, Maritime Region, Yakutia, Transbaikalia, Lena, West Siberia, Kazakhstan (including all byproduct output), Kirghizia, Tadzhikistan, Uzbekistan, the Urals and Armenia; a note on the production section ends with discussions of other gold-bearing areas and the prospects for gold extraction from marine sands and the use of private prospectors. The order has the advantage (as Table 1 shows) of starting with the Soviet Union's principal production zone. The Northeast has been the leading production zone since 1934, when the opening (in late 1933) of the Bilibino deposit raised output above the Aldan fields. The latter had only briefly held the production lead from the Lena district. The lead of the Northeast is being challenged only in the current five-year plan, 1981–85, during which Uzbekistan output, principally

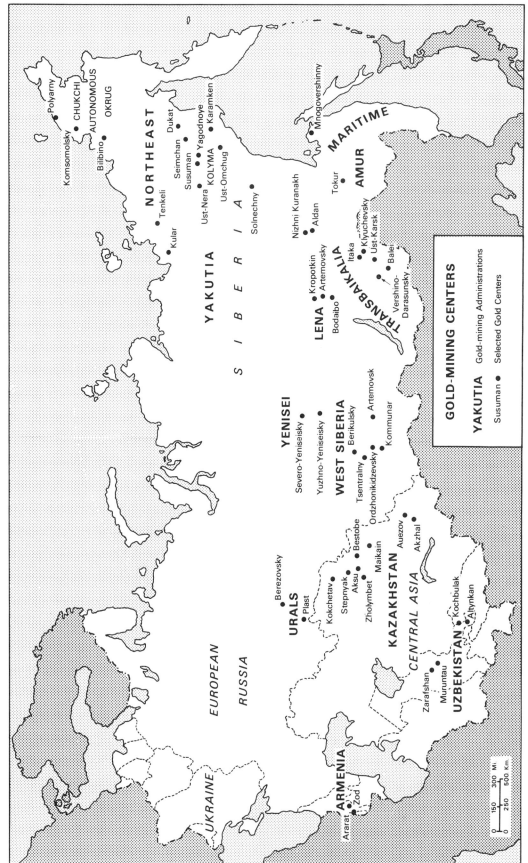

Figure 1

TABLE 1
Soviet Gold Production by Field (metric tons)

|  | 1970 | 1980 | 1990 Projection |
|---|---|---|---|
| Severovostokzoloto (Northeast Gold Production Corporation) | 82 | 85 | 72 |
| Primorzoloto (Maritime Gold Production Corporation) | 14 | 17 | 22 |
| Yakutzoloto (Yakutian Gold Production Corporation) | 40 | 49 | 68 |
| Zabaikalzoloto (Transbaikal Gold Production Corporation) | 17 | 28 | 43 |
| Lenzoloto (Lena Gold Production Corporation) | 15 | 16 | 18 |
| Other Siberian producers | 13 | 14 | 10 |
| Byproduct gold | 48 | 61 | 91 |
| Main product gold in Kazakhstan | 9 | 9 | 6 |
| Central Asian producers | 16 | 44 | 94 |
| — Kirghizia | — | — | 5 |
| — Tadzhikistan | 1 | 1 | 4 |
| — Uzbekistan | 15 | 43 | 85 |
| Uralzoloto (Urals Gold Production Corporation) | 9 | 11 | 13 |
| Armzoloto (Armenian Gold Production Corporation) | 1 | 10 | 20 |
| Other | — | — | 2 |
| Total | 264 | 344 | 459 |

SOURCES: Tables 2 to 12 for 1970 and 1980; see text for 1990 projections.

from Muruntau and Mardzhanbulak, will exceed that of the Northeast.

## Northeast Siberia

Conquest's collation of reports by former forced and free laborers and by other witnesses of "this horrible piece of history"[24] states that the first gold in Kolyma seems to have been found in 1910 when a fugitive convict sold some to a trader. His name, or diminutive, survives—Boriska—and the first gold mine was called Boriskin.[25] After the Bolshevik Revolution, systematic exploration was conducted between 1926 and 1934 from the Central Geological Research Institute at Aldanzoloto, chiefly by Yuri Bilibin (1901–52), who is honored in the names of two mines, a town and a local mineral, bilibinite.[26] Private prospectors (the subject of a separate entry below following the field descriptions) began gold extraction in 1927 but were barred from the area between 1932 and 1957. The latter dates embrace the operation of the Main Administration for Construction in the Far North (*Glavnoye upravleniye stroitelstva Dalnego Severa*, abbreviated Dalstroi),[27] created as an agency of the People's Commissariat of Internal Affairs (NKVD) in December 1931, and closed by the successor Ministry of Internal Affairs (MVD) in 1957. Dalstroi should be confused neither with Glavdalstroi, which was concerned with construction in the area to the south of Dalstroi (*Glavnoye upravleniye po stroitelstvu predpriyatii v rayonakh Dalnego Vostoka*)[28] nor with Dalstroiproyekt, an agency for town planning and civil engineering design that was in existence in 1968[29] (and may still continue).

Dalstroi effectively supplanted the civil administration and acted as an economic ministry. At the time of its creation, the entire territory along the Pacific littoral from the Chukchi and Kamchatka peninsulas to Vladivostok formed part of the Far Eastern Krai and its western border with the Yakut ASSR ran through virtually uninhabited taiga. No precise delimitation of Dalstroi territory seems to have been laid down: it certainly took in from the Yakut ASSR the lower reaches of the Kolyma and all of the Indigirka. Its southern boundary was, however, delimited on 22 July 1934, when a Lower Amur Oblast was separated from the Far Eastern Krai, and on 20 October 1938, the krai was transformed into Khabarovsk Krai. The area of Dalstroi and that to the south of the Lower Amur Oblast were designated "rayons directly subordinated to the Krai Executive Committee." The Far Eastern Krai was abolished at the same time, the southern extremity becoming the Maritime Krai; Amur Oblast (created in 1932) remained within Khabarovsk Krai until 1948, when it was made a separate oblast, and the "direct subordination" was an administrative anomaly (though it was also used in Central Asia). During the period when prison labor was most brutally used and punitive discipline was at its most severe, the chairman of the Khabarovsk Krai Executive Committee was S.A. Goglidze. Henry Wallace, who, as Vice President of the United States, made a wartime visit to Magadan and the Dalstroi goldfields, correctly described him as "an intimate friend of Stalin,"[30] but did not appreciate that until 1938 he had been Minister of Internal Affairs in Stalin's own repubic of Georgia. When Goglidze was executed, on 23 December 1953, with Beria and other secret police chiefs, he was described as "recently chief of one of the administrations of the Ministry of Internal Affairs USSR," and convicted of "exterminating honorable cadres devoted to the cause of the Communist Party and the Soviet regime."[31] The civil administration was wholly in the hands of the secret police.

As an agency thereof, the head of Dalstroi was also an official of the People's Commissariat for Internal Affairs and a dictator subject only to the policy laid down from Moscow. Even so the first incumbent, E.P. Berzin (December 1931 to October 1937), a Latvian, treated the masses of forced labor shipped to Magadan with a considerable degree of decency and efficiency, which enabled him "in such a comparatively short period, to achieve such significant results—to organize and launch the greatest gold-production trust in the Soviet Union and in an almost deserted, wild and severe region."[32] Such testimony, by a prisoner who was in Dalstroi from 1936 unil 1941, is amply confirmed.[33] The successors, K.A. Pavlov (1937–40) and I.F. Nikishov (1940–46), were required to give priority to the punitive at the expense of the productive and, as indicated below, gold output leveled off. Even to Vice President Wallace, whose naive belief in the total normality of the administration must have amazed him, Goglidze spoke of Nikishov's all-embracing power: "He runs everything around here. With Dalstroi's resources at his command, he's a millionaire." He also spoke, without Wallace realizing, of the "aristocracy" of the free workers in contrast to the serfdom of the prisoners.[34] The Dalstroi head from 1946 until Stalin's death, P.P. Derevenko, was even more like certain gentry of pre-emancipation times; he selected actors and artists among prisoners for what was nothing but a serf theater.[35]

The passing of Stalin in March 1953 and the arrest (June 1953) and execution of the Minister of Internal Affairs, L.P. Beria, began a return to more normal administration. Dalstroi's territory was made into an ordinary civil division (Magadan Oblast) and Khabarovsk Krai was transformed into the area it has today (Kamchatka was separated and Lower Amur reincorporated; the gold deposits of both areas remained under Primorzoloto). Dalstroi was liquidated in 1957 after a succession of amnesties had largely cleared the camps. A number of survivors among the older prisoners stayed on in the area, presumably with nowhere else to go after long incarceration and a special pension plan was introduced for them in 1956; in 1957 there were 11,000 such pensioners, of 45 and over, in Magadan Oblast.[36]

Gold mining in Magadan Oblast was separated from the dissolved Dalstroi into the Northeastern Gold Mining Trust (Severovostokzoloto) in 1957, while workings on the territory of the Yakut ASSR formed part of Yakutzoloto, both, like other regional gold-mining agencies subordinated to the Ministry of Nonferrous Metallurgy. Severovostokzoloto was converted into a state corporation in January 1971.[37]

Stalin's objectives in opening up the Northeast during the 1st Five-Year Plan (October 1928 to December 1932) may be seen as threefold. The first was put to the then director of Glavzoloto, A.P. Serebrovsky, in the following way: "This process must be applied to our outlying regions of Russia. At the beginning we will mine gold, then gradually change over to the mining and working of other

minerals, such as coal and iron."[38] In other words, the policy was to develop a hitherto virgin area for a product of high value-to-weight ratio and, once the infrastructure was provided, to go on to extract minerals with a lower ratio. A second reason was to replace grain by gold as a Soviet export: collectivization had prejudiced future grain output at a time when urban requirements for foodstuffs were rapidly increasing with forced industrialization. The confiscation (or acquisition otherwise) of gold from private holders then being conducted was a finite source. Solzhenitsyn describes the position: "The state needed property and gold and there was as yet no Kolyma. The famous 'gold fever' began at the end of 1929; only the fever gripped not those looking for gold but those from whom it was being shaken loose."[39] A third factor was the sudden availability of forced labor in the persons of the peasantry imprisoned or exiled for resistance to collectivization. One estimate puts at 5 million the number of kulaks and other peasants who were killed or died of starvation and 3.5 million those who were imprisoned. When the lives of class enemies were so cheap, they could readily be expended in a vast pioneering and risky venture.[40]

Use of that forced labor in Dalstroi until the end of 1937 was nevertheless reasonably efficient; compared with the later period it was described as Kolyma's "golden age."[41] Furthermore, since the rivers had never previously been panned and placers would have been located at the most accessible deposits, the early results must have been good; commercial panning by private prospectors had begun in 1927 but fewer than 200 men seem to have been involved. According to contemporary Western estimates, total Soviet gold output rose from 53 metric tons in 1931 to either 124 or 131 tons in 1934.[42] The lower estimates for the period carry greater conviction, having been issued by the United States Mint and, until that for 1938, down to the last fine ounce. On that basis, the increment during the first three years of Dalstroi was 71 tons. This is the order of magnitude of an estimate for 1936 made by a former prisoner, 4,000 wooden cases containing 20 kg of gold in double leather bags,[43] that is, some 80 tons.

Other estimates by former prisoners must be judged exaggerations, even at a time when nuggets could be picked up at random and the richest sands washed, for the manpower and infrastructure were simply not there to handle the volume of "ground" (the general term for both overburden, termed in Russia *torf*, "peat," and auriferous burden, *pesok*, "sand"). A group of 62 Polish former prisoners put output at 20 tons in 1932, 70 in 1933 and 150 in 1934[44] and a Russian prisoner, Petrov, understood the 1939 plan to be 250 tons,[45] though the group's estimate, for that year, was the astronomical 325 tons (with 400 as an all-time record in 1940).[46]

A further development program was formulated at a Kolyma geological conference in November 1936,[47] and Pavlov, the head of Dalstroi who took over in late 1937, was reportedly given orders to double gold output in 1938, by increasing the prison population by 30,000 to 60,000. A Swiss woman prisoner remarks that this was as much a question of supply as of demand for manpower: "All existing camps in Siberia were so overcrowded with prisoners that it became necessary to relieve the over-flow" by extending the shipping season from Vladivostok-Nakhodka to Magadan-Nagayevo by means of icebreakers. This was, of course, the peak year of the Terror, and she estimates that about 100,000 prisoners were brought in. While the latter must be too large, calculation of the net available manpower must take account of the high mortality—26,000 executions by shooting alone in 1938—and a derived output must allow for declining productivity (ground shifted per man), since the punishment and death of prisoners had become at least as important an objective as production.[48] The mining population is estimated in 1938 at 150,000 by Conquest,[49] of whom half may have been actually mining. For 1940 an official figure of free employment is available—68,000 in all occupations and 30,000 in occupations not specified in the returns, and hence a maximum of gold mining.[50] Estimates of output per person at the time vary widely—from 2 kg per year[51] down to 0.5 kg,[52] and Petrov suggests something like 1.2 kg per man-year.[53]

If the output and manpower figures quoted by former prisoners are anywhere near correct, output (80 tons) from 30,000 men would yield 2.7 kg per worker in 1936. An estimate for that year has its importance because, by 1950, ten times as much ground had to be washed per unit of gold extracted as in 1936;[54] since there had been no mechanization between those dates, each man would, by 1950, have been producing only 0.27 kg of gold for the same volume of ground shifted. In 1945 the ground shifted per man was 8 cu. meters (cu.m.) per day, or, if 100 days were worked, 800 cu.m. There is evidence, summarized by Dowie[55] that gold content is 0.35g per cu.m. which would mean 0.28 kg per year per man. If the estimate of 35 tons annually in 1951–57 (discussed below) is accurate, an output of 0.28 kg per man would have required 125,000 miners. This is by no means out of line with populations of upwards of 300,000 indicated by Wallace and by Conquest.[56]

Nevertheless, a decline from 2.7 kg per year in 1936 to 1.2 kg two years later is considerable, but it is not unreasonable in the light of the change to penal priority and the extension of the fields, which yield less metal per cu.m. of ground shifted (the richest placers must have been worked first and the volume of overburden per cu.m. of auriferous ground would have been greater). At the 75,000 employment roughly estimated for 1938, 90 tons would have been produced, which is consistent with the United States Mint estimate of a total Soviet main-product output of 163 tons.[57] Jasny, whose estimates of contemporary farm production were recognized to be remarkably accurate when Stalin's statistical secrecy was lifted, puts 1940 output also at 100 tons, but a Polish economist, a prisoner himself in the USSR at the time, though never incarcerated in Kolyma, judges there to be "a certain exaggeration in this estimate."[58]

A Dalstroi output of some 90 tons in 1938 implies 73 tons in other areas of the USSR, a reasonable increment in output during the 1930s if the United States Mint's estimates are near the truth.

Prisoners continued to pour in during 1939 and 1940 but mortality rose and productivity continued to fall.

More mines were developed but this is not to say that net gold output increased: the prisoners were sent into new regions where there would be a period of gestation—or disaster, as in the case of the expedition to Pestraya Dresva Bay in 1940–41[59]—and then free workers moved into the existing workings.[60] Output in 1940 was from 66 mines,[61] average employment in which was at least 2,000,[62] viz., 132,000. Because Petrov, in citing that figure, pointed out that his mine was small, one could roughly allow 160,000, of whom perhaps 90,000 were extracting ground. At a further decline to 0.8 kg per man, output in 1940 would have been 72 tons. This again is consistent with the United States Mint estimate—a rounded 4 million ounces, or 125 tons; it is too approximate to attach much importance to the residual implied for areas other than Dalstroi, but it would be 53 tons, compared with the 73 tons in 1938. War preparations were generally reducing output in those sectors not devoted to armaments, and yields per man would have been declining elsewhere also.

During World War II, output was not pressed as urgently as beforehand, for the availability of Lend-Lease from the United States diminished the need for gold to pay for imports and the invasion had halted a heavy Soviet export balance to Nazi Germany (a drain which Stalin tolerated in the vain expectation of averting Hitler's enmity). But even in 1944, there were 300,000 persons in the Dalstroi "community" and 1,000 mines (doubtless individual placers, not administrative mining enterprises) were in operation.[63]

Identification of a 1940 output and productivity is important in the light of two official index numbers relating that year to postwar performance. The indexes have (with difficulty, according to the Soviet sources) been amended to allow for the transfer of the Indigirka mines from Dalstroi to Yakutzoloto, leaving only Magadan Oblast in Severovostokzoloto.[64] In 1958, gold output was 56 percent of that in 1940,[65] and productivity (ground shifted per man) on the same base year was 430 in 1950, 2,450 in 1960 and 6,120 in 1965;[66] compared with 1940, triple the auriferous ground was needed per unit of gold in 1950.

The link between Dalstroi output of an estimated 72 tons in 1940 and Severovostokzoloto output of 1958 must allow for the transfer of the Indigirka mines to Yakutzoloto in 1957. In 1953, there were 144 placers in the Indigirka.[67] Wallace's '1000' of 1944 indicates roughly the number in Dalstroi, of which, say, 900 were for gold. On the tentative assumption that proportions did not much change, and that average output per placer was the same in Indigirka as elsewhere in Dalstroi, 16 percent must be deducted for the transferred area. Heroic as such assumptions are, they can be accepted only if other indicators confirm the results.

Table 2, therefore, adapts 1940 output to the Severovostokzoloto area, viz. 60.5 tons, whence 1958 output is shown as 34 tons. Other index numbers relate 1958 to 1965 (a 96 percent increase[68]), 1965 to 1970 (24 percent increase[69]) and annually for those years:[70] production in 1970 would thus be 82 tons. Interpolating for 1959 at 36.7 tons, productivity in metal per worker may be approxi-

TABLE 2
Gold Production in the Northeast Gold Corporation (Severovostokzoloto)

| Tonnage of Metal Produced | | | | | | | |
|---|---|---|---|---|---|---|---|
| 1940 | 60.5 | 1960 | (40.0) | 1971 | (77.6) | | |
| 1950 | (52.6) | 1961 | (44.0) | 1972 | (81.5) | | |
| 1951 | (54.4) | 1962 | (48.5) | 1973 | (80.7) | | |
| 1952 | (56.3) | 1963 | (53.2) | 1974 | 79.9 | | |
| 1953 | (58.1) | 1964 | (58.5) | 1975 | 77.3 | | |
| 1954 | (50.8) | 1965 | 66.4 | 1976 | (78.8) | | |
| 1955 | (41.7) | 1966 | 70.0 | 1977 | (79.3) | | |
| 1956 | (36.9) | 1967 | 73.1 | 1978 | (80.0) | | |
| 1957 | (34.5) | 1968 | 75.4 | 1979 | (81.3) | | |
| 1958 | 33.9 | 1969 | 79.1 | 1980 | 84.8 | | |
| 1959 | (36.7) | 1970 | 82.3 | 1990 | (72) | | |

| Administration | | | |
|---|---|---|---|
| Mining and Concentrating Combine[a] | Administrative Center[b] (founding date) | Administrative Rayon | Main Metal |
| (a) Chukchi Autonomous Okrug | | | |
| Bilibino | Bilibino (1958) | Bilibino | Gold |
| Iultin | Iultin (1954) | Iultin | Tungsten |
| Komsomolsky | Komsomolsky (1959) | Chaun | Gold |
| Pevek | Pevek (1950; town 1967) | Chaun | Tin |
| Polyarny | Polyarny (1973) | Shmidt | Gold |
| East Chukchi | (?) Provideniya | (?) Provideniya | Gold |
| (b) Magadan Oblast proper | | | |
| Dukat | Dukat (1976) | Omsukchan | Gold |
| Karamken | Karamken (1974) | Khasyn | Gold |
| Orotukan | Orotukan (1953) | Yagodnoye | Gold |
| Srednekan | Seimchan (1953) | Srednekan | Gold |
| Susuman | Susuman (1953; town 1964) | Susuman | Gold |
| Tenke | Ust-Omchug (1953) | Tenke | Gold |
| Yagodnoye | Yagodnoye (1953) | Yagodnoye | Gold |

| Enterprises | |
|---|---|
| (a) Placers | |
| Adygalakh | Krasnoarmeisky |
| Aliskerovo | Kurchatovsky |
| Anyui | Leningradsky |
| Baranikha | Maldyak |
| Berelekh | Mandrikovo |
| Berzin | Omchak |
| Bolshevik | Otrozhny |
| Burkandya | Pyatiletka |
| Dalny | Semiletka |
| Debin | Shiroki |
| Dvadtsatpervogo Syezda KPSS | Shturmovoi |
| Dvadtsatvtorogo Syezda KPSS | Sorok Let Oktyabrya |
| Dvadtsat Pyat Let Oktyabrya | Sorok Pyat Let Oktyabrya |
| Eksperimentalny | Sorok Pyat Let VLKSM |
| Frunze | Topoliny |
| Gastello | Udarnik |
| Gorky | Ust-Omchug |
| Gorny | Vostochny |
| Gygychan | |
| | (b) Ore Mines |
| Dukat | Matrosov (in Tenke combine) |
| Karamken | Polyarny |
| | (c) Artels |
| | Enterprise with which the artel has operated |
| Arktika | Burkhala |
| Avangard | — |
| Bilibino | Bilibino |
| Chukotka | Komsomolsky |
| Druzhba | Gorky; Orotukan |
| Dvadtsattretego Syezda KPSS | — |

TABLE 2 (*cont.*)

| Enterprises | |
|---|---|
| Gornaya | Gastello |
| Gornyak | Burkhala; Dvadtsat Pyat Let Oktyabrya |
| Iskra | Eksperimentalny |
| Kolyma | — |
| Luch | Orotukan |
| Maiskaya | Orotukan |
| Mekhanizator | Orotukan |
| Mir | Orotukan |
| Oktyabr | — |
| Perspektivnaya | Iultin |
| Podvig | Bilibino |
| Raduga | Sorok Let Oktyabrya |
| Rassvet | Bilibino |
| Razvedchik | Kurchatovsky |
| Romashka | Bilibino |
| Salyut | Orotukan |
| Sever | Orotukan |
| Soyuz | Maldyak |
| Svetlaya | Frunze |
| Tayezhnaya | Kurchatovsky |
| Vympel | Sorok Let Oktyabrya |
| Vostok | Komsomolsky |
| Znamya | — |
| Zvezda | Sorok Pyat Let VLKSM; Srednekan |

[a]Berelekh has been described as a GOK (Magadan Radio, 23 May 1979) and Orotukan as an enterprise (Magadan Radio, 12 March 1980).
[b]Date is of designation as workers' settlement.
SOURCE: For production, see text. List of GOK in 1973 from Seletsky, *Gody*, p. 9, supplemented by later designation as GOK confirmed by the Magadan Radio, 11 February 1975 (Iultin), 5 June 1978 (Orotukan), 30 August 1979 (Karamken), 12 January 1980 (Dukat), 12 March 1980 (Pevek) and 24 September 1980 (Komsomolsky). Territorial locations from *SSSR: Administrativno-territorialnoye deleniye soyuznykh respublik na 1 yanvarya 1980*, pp. 166–69. Names of placers and artels from Magadan Radio 1971–80. Names of placers previously worked may be found in Conquest, *Kolyma*, pp. 234–41 and Kaser, "Regional Time Series," p. 69. The production series for 1951–58 applies to the estimated output for 1958, an index of industrial employment in Magadan Oblast in *Narodnoye khozyaistvo Magadana*, 1960, p. 71; 1951 is extrapolated from the rate of growth 1951–53.

mated from manpower figures for Magadan Oblast, some 57,000 assumed in mining,[71] or, say, 50,000 in gold mining, viz. 0.73 kg per worker.

It was earlier estimated that prison labor in 1950 yielded only 0.28 kg per worker and an index of productivity in ground shifted, also quoted, put 1960 at 5.7 times 1950. Since the deduced rise in productivity per unit of metal was 2.6-fold (from 0.28 kg per worker in 1950 to 0.73 kg in 1959), the ratio of ground to metal would have been doubled (2.2 times). The most that can be said is that this is reasonable in light of deeper workings, viz. more overburden to be cleared to reach auriferous ground. Dowie finds that the proportion of overburden (waste) to auriferous ground varies from less than 1:1 to 5:1 (with some evidence of an average of 2:1).[72] A doubling of the ratio of ground to metal could also include a reduction in the gold content per cu.m. of auriferous ground.

A final check on the postwar series to 1970 is furnished by a Soviet statement that gold production in 1966–70 exceeded both that of 1959–65 and of 1951–60 (though by a small margin).[73] Table 2 shows 1966–70 to aggregate 379 tons; 1959–65, 347 tons (on freehand interpolation), and 1951–60, 356 tons, if 1951 to 1957 averaged 35 tons. The estimates can thus satisfy the excess of 1966–70 over each preceding period, and 1951–60 over 1959–65, but would indicate a much lower output than previously estimated for the final years of the prison-camp period.[74] None of the Soviet prisoners' statements were available to authors compiling estimates soon after the war (on the basis of

postwar releases, mainly of foreigners held in the camps). It is, if true, a striking testimony to the inefficiency of forced labor. If the present estimates are correct the only economically justifiable periods of gold mining in the Northeast were 1932–38, before the punitive regime began, and after 1956, when the prison camps were almost all disbanded.

From that date, placers requiring a high labor input per gram because of inaccessibility to machinery or power or because of the configuration of the terrain were increasingly turned over to teams of private prospectors (artels). Doubtless some of the freed prisoners remained in the area in such a capacity. In parallel, mechanization was introduced in the placers that stayed under state administration and the lode mines began to be exploited (they contributed 2.6 percent of Upper Kolyma output in 1959[75]). The response of increasing capital intensity to the declining availability of manpower was rational, the more so as free labor became relatively more costly as conditions improved elsewhere in the USSR.

The relativity of Magadan with respect to the long-settled parts of the country worsened in two respects. After the execution of Beria in 1953 and especially after Khrushchev's secret speech to the 20th Party Congress in 1956, the fear of arbitrary arrest by either the ordinary citizen or the professional could subside. By contrast, while the secret police ruled, "probably the biggest attraction" to free work in Dalstroi was that "the NKVD had no right to arrest a voluntary Kolyma worker without personal permission from Berzin in every individual case. And he very seldom granted such permission."[76] Secondly, financial rewards were high in Dalstroi in relation to pay elsewhere and, during wartime and postwar rationing, "commercial shops" (selling off-ration products at higher prices) were not required because rations for volunteer workers seem generally to have been honored. Food and other consumer goods became more generally available throughout the USSR in the 1960s (though preferential access by the privileged persisted in what remained a shortage economy) and money wages rose substantially. As part of a general codification of wage rates initiated in 1957, there was a reduction in 1960 of the supplements payable in the Far North (which includes the entirety of Magadan Oblast) and the remotest areas (which include nearly all the goldfields of the Northeast); it was not until 1 January 1968 that the various northern increments (*severnye nadbavki*) were enhanced.[77]

More capital-intensive methods were required not only to substitute for labor but because the further deposits needed exploitation much beyond the simple manual stage. In general, the provisioning of Magadan Oblast was much facilitated from 1964 by the year-round operation of a shipping service to Nagayevo, the port for Magadan; the icebreakers *Admiral Makarov, Yermak, Leningrad* and *Vladivostok* maintained a 700-mile channel through the ice-bound Okhotsk Sea from December to May.[78] The metaled all-weather road system was substantially developed in the later 1960s and the 1970s.

The factors specific to gold mining are three. First, lodes began to be seriously exploited. There was only one mine at that time in the Northeast in operation, Matrosov (*imeni Matrosova*), which was noted as one of the five major lode workings in the USSR in a study of the preparations for the 1971–75 five-year plan;[79] explorations of lodes with possibly some commercial extraction had been undertaken at Mandrikovo and Neva. The 750 m deep Matrosov mine was a relatively simple operation—loading of blasted rock being onto hand-trolleys—and both the 1971 and 1974 studies assumed it to have produced 2.5 tons in 1970.[80] The statement, already noted, that in 1959 lode mining contributed 2.6 percent of Northeast output (estimated at 36.7 tons) would show production then of 0.95 tons. A lode mine named Polyarny was opened in 1969 in the extreme north on the Arctic littoral, 60 miles to the west of Mys Shmidta (Chukchi Autonomous Okrug).[81] Since it accounted for a 30 percent rise in lode output that year[82] and Matrosov is believed to have then been running at 2.4 tons, a production of 0.7 tons is indicated.

The 1971–75 plan forecast the development of two other and apparently much larger lodes—one deep-mined, the other strip-mined. A rich gold and silver deposit had been discovered at Karamken in the 1960s and was scheduled to go into operation in 1974.[83] Construction in the event lagged (the five-year plan is shown below to have been underfulfilled) and Prime Minister Aleksei N. Kosygin visited the site in March 1974[84] to stress its importance. The mine began production in early 1978.[85] A tin area around Omsukchan, opened during World War II, was found to contain gold and silver in the 1960s and was ranked after Karamken in developmental

importance.[86] Named the Dukat mining and concentration combine, it began open-cast mining and milling in January 1980. The Omsukchan area, which was originally linked to the coast at Pestraya Dresva (to which, after the ill-fated expedition of 1940–41, a road was built during the war), is now accessible from the main Kolyma Highway by a road built in the late 1940s.[87]

Second, underground placer mining declined. In 1960, its share was 13 percent compared to 30 to 45 percent only a few years previously. More powerful equipment (bulldozers, scrapers and long excavators) permitted the stripping of overburden, exposing the so-called buried placers. Earlier undermining had been carried out when the overburden was as little as 4 m thick, but from this time overburdens of 10 to 12 m began to be stripped. Whereas with abundant manual labor clearing the overburden had been by drilling and explosives during the winter, by 1959, 85 percent (19 million cu.m.) of overburden was being cleared by bulldozers and excavators. The first (small) dredge had been installed on the Kolyma only in 1950; but by 1963 there were 17 electric-powered dredges of 210 liters bucket capacity. Even so the use of dredges on permafrost required heavy expenditure on thawing out: between 5 and 6 million cu.m. of ground had annually to be thawed around 1963 and the costs of thawing represented 40 percent of the value of gold gained in Upper Kolyma.[88] Hydraulic jet mining of deposits became widespread after 1961, but only after heavy investment to supply electricity.

Finally, a number of tailings were reexploited because the rough and ready panning of the Dalstroi period had left a great deal of metal unextracted. Some of the tailings and many new deposits where a team and a bulldozer were adequate remained manually worked. The head of Glavzoloto observed, in 1958, when private prospectors had just been readmitted to the Northeast region: "There are always small deposits where the organization of state mining is inexpedient. I am myself all for private prospecting. Some gold-diggers can find gold in places where it is not expected to occur."[89] As is described in the section on private prospectors, below, the number of such teams became particularly significant in the Northeast in the post-Dalstroi period and it is important to decide whether the output indexes for government corporations include the metal sold by them. The two previous papers prepared by the present writer assumed that the private and public output were separate but new evidence and a consequential review of the old suggests that corporation reports include production of the artels in the area.

The new evidence is contained in the decree of the Council of Ministers USSR of 10 March 1975, "On the Confirmation of a Model Statute for Prospecting Teams."[90] Among the list of previous decrees repealed are those "On the Confirmation of a Model Statute for Prospecting Teams in the System of the Ministry of Nonferrous Metallurgy USSR" of 23 December 1947, and "On the Confirmation of Rules for Accounts with Prospectors and the Use of Pay-Books in the System of the Ministry of Nonferrous Metallurgy USSR" of 15 February 1948; decrees of 1 July 1947 and of 29 April 1949 made corresponding provisions for the system of the Main Administration of Special Nonferrous Metals (Glavspetstsvetmet) of the Ministry of Internal Affairs USSR. The titles of these decrees, incidentally, suggest that private prospectors, even if barred from the Dalstroi area, were allowed in other regions mined by prison labor (a fact confirmed by interview material on Yakutzoloto), but the aspect relevant here is the assimilation of prospectors' accounts with the pay-books of regular state employees, and the place of prospectors "in the system of" the state agency. The decree itself requires "systematic surveillance (kontrol) of the productive-economic and financial performance of prospectors' teams and forbids the concealment of gold excavated, transport out of the area of discovery and its sale to private citizens." The production of any prospectors' team must, therefore, be sold to the government corporation in whose territory it operates.

The second group of evidence is statements that artels are given production plans by the relevant corporation and that the latter raises goals in the same way that it does for its own enterprises. Thus, within Severovostokzoloto, the Kolyma and Gornaya artels were reported to have "fulfilled their monthly plan for May 1979."[91] The Romashka artel did the same for May 1980, but "the May target for artels in Severovostokzoloto was not met. The Ministry of Nonferrous Metals USSR set the panwashers of Magadan Oblast additional tasks."[92]

The year 1970 was selected for intensive investigation in the two previous studies. The present writer in 1971 estimated (on much slighter evidence than marshaled for the present study) Northeast output as 65 tons by the Ministry and 10 tons by artels, viz. 75 tons[93] compared with the 82 tons now assessed. Dowie, in 1974, put the Northeast Corporation at 98 tons but he and the present writer assumed artels to be in addition to this output.[94] This accounts for part of the excess of those estimates over the figures put forward (without regional breakdown) by the Central Intelligence Agency. Other elements in the disparity were the high estimate for lode mining (7.5 tons in the 1974 study compared with 2 in the 1971 study; no information on the subsumption made by the CIA) and the assumptions on the productivity of placer mine equipment, which yielded an output of 91 tons[95] (72 tons in the 1971 study; no information on that subsumed in the CIA estimates). It might be mentioned that attention was concentrated on 1970 because the terminal year of a five-year plan and the base year of the next tend to evoke more quantitative comment in the Soviet media than a mid-plan year.

The revised 1970 output estimate is used in the present chapter as the basis for the estimates to 1980* and the

projection to 1990. The five-year plan target for 1971–75, a 7.8 percent increment, was made public,[96] but not apparently those for 1976–80 or 1981–85.[97] The increment planned for 1971–75 was well below the reported increase of 23.9 percent for the previous quinquennium, and a number of possible causes may be suggested. On the operational side the opening of the Polyarny lode mining complex in 1969, and the work scheduled for the two other big lode deposits, Karamken and Dukat, may have taken labor, power, materials and transport that otherwise would have been made available for placers; of those four inputs, labor and power were probably the most crucial. For only one of the five years does an annual plan appear to have been made public—1975, expressed in percentage changes over 1974—but it is revealing in scheduling a cut in manpower. The published targets for the Northeast Corporation were increases of 25 to 27 percent in ground shifted, 15 to 18 percent in auriferous ground washed and 7 to 9.8 percent in labor productivity (a term which, as noted earlier, can apply to outputs of metal, of auriferous ground washed or of ground shifted) and a reduction in employment of 1,200.[98] An order of magnitude of the absolute volume of employment to which that cut was applied is available in Dowie, who estimates (from the equipment available and the volume of ground moved) that 47,500 workers were accountable to gold production in the Northeast Corporation in 1970 out of a reported workforce of 183,000 in Magadan Oblast in all employment.[99] This is in line with ratios estimated for earlier years and, if correct, would suggest a reduction of 2.5 percent if manpower had stayed constant since 1970, or of 9.5 percent in 1970 if cuts of 2.5 percent had been applied in each of the intervening years. If the cuts had all been of 2.5 percent in each year of the five-year plan, the reduction of the workforce by some 12 percent would have, with the 7.8 percent output increase, shown a productivity gain of 21 percent, although the 4 percent it represents annually is not necessarily either the 7 percent or the 9.8 percent in the plan for the single year 1975.

The other shortage must have been of electricity. A 20 MW floating coal-fired generating station had been anchored at Zeleny Mys (at the mouth of the Kolyma River) and supplied power from 4 November 1970,[100] and at Bilibino, a nuclear-power plant operated its first 12 MW generating unit in December 1973, and its second on the last day of 1974, with the fourth and final one in 1976.[101] These supplied the Chukchi district rather than the Upper Kolyma, where the earliest site for a nuclear plant had been envisaged—a project reportedly conceived in 1952.[102] The central districts of Magadan Oblast, that is the Upper Kolyma, were not linked in a grid until the beginning of 1980,[103] though its main power source, the Kolyma hydroelectric plant, had not begun to operate and it was fed from a coal-fired thermal electric station at Arkagala. The Kolyma plant (900 MW) was due to generate power at the end of 1980[104] and the startup was announced in February 1981.[105] The First Secretary of the Magadan Oblast party committee, S. Shaidurov, writing in late 1978, had said that the Magadan power grid was no longer equal to the demand for power by the energy-intensive mining of the region.[106] An example of energy intensity is the practice of keeping truck engines running

---

*For which the present writer acknowledges with great appreciation the detailed examination of Soviet media reports on mines in the Northeast in 1975–79 by Dr. Renfrew Christie during the Long Vacation, 1979. He was unable to see the results of his research for this chapter because in 1980 he was sentenced to ten years' imprisonment following conviction by a court in South Africa (of which he is a national) for activity prejudicial to the state. His doctoral dissertation at the University of Oxford, "The Electrification of South Africa," is forthcoming (London: Macmillan).

continuously in winter, even at night when the driver is asleep, because of the difficulty of starting in the cold and the absence of heated garages. New vehicles from the KamAZ truck plant, with a separate heating system that will permit engines to be switched off, were tested on the Kolyma Highway in 1978.[107]

An altogether different set of reasons may have argued for a deceleration of gold output in the 9th Five-Year Plan 1971–75. The USSR had sold no gold in the West since 1965, and reserves were mounting; the Soviet Government may well have judged the world price insufficient to justify a high priority for production for export.

Although a two-tier world market had opened in March 1968, the peaks of 1968 ($42.60 per ounce) and of 1969 ($43.82) were not very much above the price of $35 at which central banks continued to deal. Indeed, throughout 1970, when the 9th Five-Year Plan was being drafted, the price only briefly exceeded $38, and in January 1970 was below the central bankers' price. The arrangement between the United States and South African authorities of December 1969 on a floor of $35 per ounce, and the introduction of Special Drawing Rights (SDRs) on 1 January 1970, checked the expectation that gold would fall below $35, but gave no grounds for belief in a rise.

That the State Planning Committee and the Ministry of Finance USSR took into account the bleak prospect of profit on bullion sales may be indirectly inferred from the introduction of an augmented plan in 1972[108] and a plenary meeting of the Magadan Oblast party committee (attended by a Deputy Minister of Nonferrous Metallurgy) in 1973 to stimulate output.[109] The price rise that reached nearly $200 in 1974 began in mid-1972, the year in which the USSR, after an absence of six years, returned to sell on Western markets. On a formal calculation, the domestic price at which Glavzoloto then sold to the State Bank, 2 rubles per gram,[110] was equivalent at the official exchange rate to $68.42 per ounce; such a price ruled for the entire second half of 1972 and was comfortably exceeded from February 1973 onward.

In any event the mid-period increment in the target was not met. The original goal for 1975 was, on the reports available, reached by only two combines, Bilibino and Tenke,[111] of seven then operating[112] and by only half the placers known to the present writer (some 20 out of 40).[113] The annual plan for 1975, which need not have been the five-year goal if revisions had been made in the latter, was underfulfilled by 12 percent.[114] On the assumption that the annual plan did coincide with the five-year target, an 88 percent fulfillment of a planned 7.8 percent rise indicates a 1975 output 6.1 percent below that of 1970, or 77.3 tons. On the same assumption, because the 1975 plan was 10 to 12.5 percent above 1974, the latter would have been a little above 1975 actual, namely 77.9 tons. Other, tenuous evidence that output declined over the 1971–75 plan is that 1971 output failed to reach the rate required for the five-year plan[115] and that the augmented plan for 1972 was only 5 percent above 1971.[116]

The base-year output for the ensuing five-year plan, 1975, is estimated to have been reached from 73 tons by placer-mining and 4.3 tons from the two lode-ore mines then in operation, Matrosov and Polyarny. If there were

some 40 placers and 30 artels (the list is compiled from those that were mentioned on the Magadan Radio during 1971–80), the average output per placer enterprise or artel would have been 1 ton. The only evidence of a placer enterprise's output is that Shturmovoi was to wash 0.9 million cu.m. of sand in 1975.[117] At Dowie's estimate of gold per cu.m. of washed ground in the Northeast,[118] that volume would yield 0.7 tons, but that particular mine is one of the oldest in Dalstroi and could be below the average. The only evidence of an artel's production is a statement that 250 private prospectors working with 56 bulldozers at the Pyatiletka placer deposit in 1971 earned 5,000 to 6,000 rubles apiece.[119] Since gold was then bought from them at 1 ruble per gram, their takings indicate 5.5 kg each, or 1.4 tons for the artel. A rough mean of 1 ton per enterprise or artel shows a Northeast placer output in excess of 70 tons. Of the lode output, Matrosov is estimated to have produced 2.3 tons and Polyarny 2 tons.

In the absence, already noted, of a published goal for 1976–80, it is possible to assume that only a modest increment in placer output was envisaged—say a goal of 75 tons for 1980—with the principal increase coming from the two lode-mining combines scheduled to begin operation in the quinquennium. Work had begun on the construction of Karamken in 1972[120] and a large contingent of demobilized soldiers had been brought to work on the Dukat site in 1975.[121]

The Karamken plant went into operation in November 1978 and attained full capacity in June 1979.[122] From its photograph it is approximately one quarter the size of the Muruntau plant,[123] which, as shown in the Uzbek section of this chapter, is estimated then at 20 tons (i.e., 5 tons for Karamken). Dukat produced its first output only in January 1980,[124] and may be bigger than Karamken, for it was stated that "it is second to none among the enterprises in the Northeast of the USSR as regards the automation of production processes."[125] Karamken was important enough to be visited during construction (as noted above) by Prime Minister Kosygin, in 1974,[126] and, if Dukat is bigger, a capacity of 6 tons reached probably in 1981 could be tentatively suggested.

The text of the five-year plan 1976–80 for the USSR as a whole spoke of increasing the output of precious metals and of accelerating the development of the gold-mining industry: Uzbekistan and the Far East were mentioned as centers for the growth of the output of precious metals. The only figure quoted for the entire nonferrous metals industry was a planned growth of 23 to 25 percent.[127] In introducing the plan to the 25th Party Congress, Kosygin made no mention of precious metals.[128] In the course of the plan period, the Chairman of the Presidium of the Far East Research Center of the Academy of Sciences USSR, Academician Nikolai A. Shilo, criticized the development of nonferrous metals in the Far East Economic Region (which includes Magadan Oblast[129]) as not rational and stated that his research center had elaborated a suitable program.[130]

The Northeast Gold Corporation was among the selected mining agencies of the Ministry to be endowed with its own research or design organization in 1977; an administrative reorganization took place in that year and its director general, D. Ye. Ustinov, was commended by the Minister.[131] Two years later, nevertheless, a new director general, A.V. Pogrebny, was installed, took part in an expanded collegium session of the Ministry on 10 January 1980, and was among those exercising "self-criticism": Severovostokzoloto was stated not to have fulfilled its 1979 plan for mining work, to have utilized bulldozers only 58 percent of the time (against 63 percent planned) and to have shifted only 50,000 cu.m. per year per bulldozer. Finally, the same session, which was attended by Vladimir I. Dolgikh, the national party secretary responsible for industry, noted that the Karamken mill was overstaffed (in 1979 by 400 more than the Dalstroiproyekt design).[132]

There were only two years in which Severovostokzoloto came reportedly close to fulfilling its annual plan, viz. 1976[133] (89 percent by 17 September) and 1980 (99.5 percent by 1 December);[134] plans may have been achieved on such bases. The sole report of completion of a gold production target for the entire five-year plan 1976–80 was for the Chukchi Autonomous Okrug,[135] which contains two combines, Bilibino and Polyarny, and at least four placer enterprises, Aliskerovo, Leningradsky, Komsomolsky and Krasnoarmeisky, which are big enough to have workers' settlements designated;[136] there were eight such placer enterprises with workers' settlements in Magadan Oblast.[137] The two long-established lode mines, Polyarny and Matrosov, were given public praise for their operation in 1979 and 1980 respectively;[138] the former was running 3 percent above its five-year plan rate.[139]

The estimates for 1976–80 in Table 2 assume a modest rise in placer output, from 73 tons in 1975 to 75 tons in 1980, and of lode output from 4.3 to 10.3 tons (Polyarny 2, Matrosov 2.3, and Karamken 5, all at capacity, Dukat only 0.5 tons), viz. to 84.8 tons.

The 11th Five-Year Plan for 1981–85 for the USSR as a whole observes only that the output of precious metals will rise, but, whereas the previous plan had specified growth in the Far East, no mention is made of precious metals in the RSFSR. This is an indication, though a weak one, of no planned growth; the only area where a gold mining expansion is specified is the Kirghiz SSR.[140]

The signs are of a substitution between 1981 and 1985 of lode ore for placer output. The latter is labor-intensive and the Soviet economy as a whole is running into a severe manpower shortage. The need to exploit deeper and more remote sites would require more electric power and more capital for what are probably deposits with a lower metal content per cu.m. How far the fall will go through the 1980s is a decision that depends on Moscow, but placer reserves are poor: it was written of the 1976–80 survey that "an alarming situation exists as regards fulfillment of the plan for increasing placer gold in the Anyui, Chaun and Omsukchan expeditions."[141] One could hazard a forecast that placer output would be down to 50 tons in 1990.[142] By contrast the capacity of the four major lode-mining plants, some 16 tons, could be doubled, given that the two (of an estimated 11 tons) were actually built in a decade and that there seem to be deposits still to exploit. Severovostokgeologiya, the Northeastern geological exploration agency, had "large collectives of geolo-

gical prospectors" in Magadan Oblast and Yakutia in 1980, but since the terrain they were in was free of snow cover for only 60 days, they needed more suitable transport: there were insufficient MI-4 and MI-5 helicopters (in summer one day in three is unsuitable for flying in them) and only 25 to 30 of the 160 teams have all-terrain vehicles.[143] There were nearly 100 prospecting geologists in the Chukchi district in the same year.[144] With 22 tons produced from lodes and 50 from placers, the 1990 output could thus be 72 tons in the Northeast, which would thus lose its primacy to the projected output of Uzbekistan.

### Maritime Region

Although other goldfields than Kolyma received forced labor under Stalin's rule, there is nothing like the flood of former prisoners' reports that could be drawn upon for the previous section. Solzhenitsyn notices this difference and observes: "How is it that there is such a concentration of Kolyma memoirs while the non-Kolyma memoirs are almost nonexistent? Was this because they really hauled the cream of the crop to Kolyma? Or was it, no matter how strange this may seem, that in the nearby camps they died off more rapidly?"[145] Since the goldfields of Siberia other than the Northeast produced, on this writer's estimates, 124 tons in 1980, it is unfortunate that such sources cannot be used for the detail of history or locations.

The area covered comprises the Maritime (Primorsky) Krai, Khabarovsk Krai, Sakhalin Oblast, Kamchatka Oblast and Amur Oblast. The area of the Amurzoloto combine has been exploited longer than those of the Pacific littoral; although some gold has been extracted, Kamchatka and Sakhalin are not yet of commercial significance.

The placers discovered around 1850 along the Zeya and Bureya rivers were important before the Revolution and the first gold concession of the post-revolutionary government (then the independent but Soviet-oriented Far Eastern Republic) was to authorize a United States concessionaire, J.C. Vint, to exploit for twenty years the existing placers of Beregovoi, Blagoveshchensky, Kodachny, Novopokrovsky, Petrovsky, Vtoroi, Yevdokiyevsky and Zakharovsky and part of those in the Smirtak River valley; the increases in taxation as the New Economic Policy was terminated compelled him to relinquish the concession in 1928. Two prospecting licences, neither of which lasted more than two years, were issued to United States companies.

Gold mining in Amur Oblast was subsequently neglected, though in 1928 the trust, then named Dalzol, unsuccessfully tried to recruit Chinese laborers to work the Amur River deposits. The creating of the Jewish Autonomous Oblast led to some sporadic workings in Birobidzhan.

Six districts were distinguished in the Amur region,[146] along and among the tributaries of the Zeya, the upper Amur, the Selemdzha and the Niman rivers and in the Khingan and the Unya-Bomnak districts. The placers generally were heavily worked and, since "the majority of settlements of Amur Oblast had been founded as centers of gold mining,'' the area became one of ghost towns.[147] Placer depletions were also indicated at the administrative level by the loss of urban status of four workers' settlements in the late 1960s and in the 1970s. Kirovsky, founded in 1940 near Solovyevsk, was reduced to rural status in 1968; Gluboki, founded in 1957 on the upper Mamyn River, a tributary of the Selemdzha, was also made a village in 1968. They were followed in 1974 by Lukachek, on the upper Selemdzha, which had gained urban status in 1942, and in 1979 by Yasny, on the upper Gar River (a tributary of the Selemdzha); Yasny had been listed as an urban workers' settlement since 1936.

A commentary of 1965 "refuted the opinion that the Amur goldfields were exhausted"; although dating from the mid-nineteenth century, it said, they had been merely neglected under previous five-year plans,[148] and it was reported that Amurzoloto would double its production by 1970.[149] This was not, however, due to a revival of placer production but to the opening of an ore-dressing plant at Tokur in 1966, using electricity from a small local coal-fired power station at Ogodzha. The availability of electric power in Amur Oblast has subsequently been much increased. A hydroelectric station on the Zeya, a major tributary of the Amur, reached its designed capacity of 1,290 MW in June 1980, having been under construction since 1964.[150] A still larger plant, of 2,000 MW, has been planned on the Bureya River since 1973 and should reach capacity by the mid-1980s.[151]

Amur Oblast was part of Khabarovsk Krai until 1948, and, together with Maritime Krai was operated for gold mining by the Primorzoloto combine.[152] From administrative changes in 1975 emerged a Primorzoloto Corporation.[153] Gold mining in the region goes back to half a century before the Revolution at Nikolayevsk and near Vladivostok and in discoveries in the Kamchatka peninsula. As part of the settlement between Japan and the USSR, whereby Japan recognized the Soviet incorporation of the Far Eastern Republic, the Japanese-Soviet Treaty of 1925 provided for Japanese gold-mining concessions in the area. These were taken by two companies, but only for a short time.[154]

Like other industries in the Soviet Far East, gold mining was little developed in the interwar period and no substantial transfer of capital resources was envisaged until the Seven-Year Plan (1959–65), drafted under the influence of the Chinese-Soviet dispute, which forced on the Soviet Government's attention the contrast of an empty region claimed by the Chinese to populous and industrialized Manchuria.

The tempering effect of the Pacific allows an earlier start and a later end to the season than in the rest of Siberia, viz. mid-March to mid-December; at least one placer, Tumnin, works all year round. Test drillings in 1968 indicated the presence of gold in Kiyevka Bay (Sea of Japan), on the shore of the Tatar Gulf, and at the estuary of the Oblukovina in Kamchatka. Experimental extraction of auriferous sand by suction pump began at Tinkan Bay in 1969. In 1966, only five deposits were being worked, but the 1966–70 plan laid down an output increment of nearly 20 percent. During that period new mines began in the Sikhote-Alin Mountains in 1969, three plac-

ers started (in 1968) in Kamchatka, on the three Goltsovka rivers (Dalnyaya, Srednyaya and Blizhnyaya) and the Kamenisti placer in 1966; a new dredge was installed at the Milkan placer in lower Amur Oblast in 1970. More intensive prospecting yielded discoveries in the Tugur-Chumikan district on the shores of the Okhotsk Sea, in the Iman area and on the upper Bikin River.

Some placer gold exists in the territory of the former Lower Amur Oblast, that is to the north of the locations currently worked and to the south of the Northeast zone, but most placer deposits were exhausted between the 1850s and the Revolution.[155]

Although the number of alluvial deposits known in Kamchatka now exceeds one hundred, future policy for the peninsula is intended to concentrate on fisheries. The first nugget found in Kamchatka was flown to Moscow in 1963, but the Ogancha deposit has not yet been commercially assessed. A road was completed to the site in 1968 but similar access to the known lodes of the Sredinny Range is as yet considered uneconomic. Some operations have been reported at Goltsovka and Kamenisti, but their output is assumed still to be negligible.

There are small placers in South Sakhalin, which were worked under Japanese administration before World War II, and further geological survey has been in progress since 1968. A reference to them in 1976 notes only that there are deposits in the Langeri River district[156] and a specialist visit of Western geologists to the island in 1979 mentioned no gold.[157]

The only lode currently exploited in Khabarovsk Krai is at Mnogovershinny, but for the first time in the Soviet Far East gold has been discovered in the igneous rocks of volcanic mounds (sopki).

There are no indications of output in absolute values for any mine in Primorzoloto. If Tokur is among the second ranking group of mines described in 1968,[158] it could then have been producing 1.6 tons per year. The other ore mine in Amurzoloto, Kharga,[159] is small, as is Mnogovershinny in Primorzoloto and could then, together, have supplied about 1.5 to 2 tons.

As Table 3 shows, 17 placers have been identified in Amurzoloto and 11 in Primorzoloto. Western sources spoke of 12 dredges working in the former in 1968 and of 40 in the latter in 1969.[160] Dowie's estimate of the output of a small dredge, 0.15 tons per year, multiplied by 40 yields 6 tons or precisely the plan for 1963 for Amurzoloto.[161] The opening of the Tokur dressing plant in 1966 would have added some 3 tons, on the assumption that it took ore also from Kharga, and an increment of 3 tons from placers by 1970 would satisfy the five-year plan target for 1970 of double 1965—an assumed 12 tons. Some further expansion in the 1970s can be attributed to the introduction of larger dredges[162] but in the absence of any major development Amurzoloto output in 1975 and 1980 is estimated at 10 tons from placers and 3 tons from ore. The new Zeya hydro station and the Baikal-Amur Mainline are expected to foster both lode mining and placer dredging. A dredge was assembled in 1982 on the Urkima, a right tributary of the Nyukzha, near the BAM's Larba station.[163] A forecast of 16 tons in 1990 may not be unrealistic (Table 3).

If the dredges in Primorzoloto were roughly of the

TABLE 3
Gold Production in the Maritime Gold Corporation
(Primorzoloto)

| | Tonnage of Metal Produced | | |
|---|---|---|---|
| | Amurzoloto | Primorzoloto | Total |
| 1960 | (6) | (2) | (8) |
| 1963 | (6) | (2) | (8) |
| 1965 | 6 | 2 | 8 |
| 1966 | 9 | 3 | 12 |
| 1970 | 12 | 3 | 15 |
| 1975 | (13) | (3) | (16) |
| 1980 | (13) | (4) | (17) |
| 1990 | (16) | (6) | (22) |

| Administration and Enterprise | |
|---|---|
| Under Amurzoloto (with date designated as town or settlement) | Under Primorzoloto |
| (a) Placers | (a) Placers |
| Beregovoi | Armu-Iman |
| Blagoveshchensky | Blagodatny |
| Ekimchan (1961) | Birakan |
| Koboldo (1958) | Glavsat |
| Kodachny | Kherpuchi |
| Novopokrovsky | Kolchan |
| Oktyabrsky (1939) | Milkan |
| Petrovsky | Polina Osipenko |
| Smirtak | (formerly Kerbi) |
| Solovyevsk (1934) | Semenovsky |
| Stoiba (1942) | Sofiisky |
| Ugochan | Tumnin |
| Urkima | |
| Vtoroi | |
| Yevdokiyevsky | |
| Zakharovsky | |
| Zlatoustovsk (1942) | |
| (b) Lode | (b) Lode |
| Kharga | Mnogovershinny (1974) |
| Tokur (1949) | |

SOURCE: For production and administration see text. Names of places from Blagoveshchensk and Khabarovsk Radios and "Far Eastern Economic Region," BSE, 3rd ed., 7 (Moscow, 1972): 517. Designation dates from SSSR: deleniye, pp. 86–88, 91–93 (none in Maritime Krai).

same capacity as those in Amurzoloto 1970 output, placer output was barely 2 tons and Mnogovershinny ore could have brought no more than 1 ton. Output at the time was described as "small"[164] although increasing yearly to 1968.[165] Table 3, therefore, shows output moving up from 2 tons in the 1960s. In 1966 five deposits were being worked (which would agree with half a ton apiece, or about 2.5 tons output) and two others were in preparation,[166] and the 1966–70 target for gold output was a "nearly 20 percent increment."[167]

Some expansion took place in the second half of the 1970s. Scholarly literature argued for renewed development[168] and in the 1976–80 period, industrial production in Khabarovsk Krai rose by 26.5 percent.[169] The major development in the goldfields was a valiant transfer overland through an area devoid of roads to the Kerbi placer at Polina Osipenko in 1976, thereby prolonging the washing season where only a dredge had previously

worked.[170] In 1979 the mine was described as "leading in socialist competition"[171] and one of its dredges, by shifting 1 million cu.m. of auriferous ground in 1979, was likely to exceed its five-year plan goal by one fifth.[172] The same report spoke of sound development at Tumnin and another reported that Sofiisky, by reason of "automation, telemechanics and industrial television," had raised labor productivity by 50 percent over 1976–80.[173] An output of 4 tons is estimated for 1980 and descriptions of capital investment suggest that output could rise to 6 tons by 1990 (Table 3).

Yakutia

After a strike by a private prospector in 1923 and a veritable gold rush (the only unorganized one of Soviet times), a national mining trust, Aldanzoloto, was established in 1925. It undertook no mining itself but sponsored the continued work of private prospectors and the creation of cooperatives among the 13,000 mines already there; the territory was not made, like the Lena fields, available to concessionaires from abroad. Gold prospectors in the 1920s and 1930s wastefully worked only the high-grade deposits, abandoning a settlement as those grades were worked out. A study of that period[174] noted, in 1973, that a score of abandoned settlements were to be found in the Aldan and another report speaks of considerable quantities of gold then being obtained by the mechanized reworking of placers.

The introduction of machinery was first constrained by distance from the Aldan placers to the Trans-Siberian railway, but a road was built in 1931 to Never, a railroad station just east of Skovorodino. The highway allowed equipment to be shipped and resulted in output soon exceeding that of the Lena-Vitim fields, when it contributed between 20 and 25 percent of total Soviet production. On the eve of World War II, the population of the mining settlements within the Aldanzoloto area was 50,000;[175] the Aldan district, as a whole, had a 1939 population of 53,000 and eventually reached around 1960 some 64,000.[176] The ore of Nizhni Kuranakh began to be opened up in 1945, a concentration plant at Lebediny dates from the 1950s, a lode mine at 50-letiye Oktyabrya from 1969. The modest fall in population—to 60,900 at the 1970 census—was partly due to a cutback in placer mining, but also to a fall in mica production in the area.

On the administrative level, the cutback in placer mining was evident in the conversion of a cluster of workers' settlements south of Aldan from urban to rural status in the 1950s and 1960s. They were Vtoroy Orochen and Verkhne-Stalinsk (in 1956), Usmun in 1958, Dzhekonda in 1962 and Orochen in 1969. Another settlement, Spokoiny, farther to the southeast, was also demoted in 1956.

The four main mining towns in the 1970 census had 55 percent of the district's population, the gold centers being Aldan (17,700), Tommot (8,000) and Nizhni Kuranakh (6,400). The fourth was the coal-mining town of Chulman, which has since then been supplanted by the larger coal city of Neryungri, developed in the 1970s.[177] The name of one of its satellite settlements, Zolotinka, recalls the possibility of gold even there.

The principal placers of the Aldanzoloto combine are located along the rivers Orto-Sala, Kuranakh, Yakokut, Dzhekonda, Kurochan and Tommot, with the richest around Kurochan and Tyrkanda. Operations in the 1960s were "highly mechanized, above all by dredges."[178] In 1956 "powerful electric dredges of 210-liter bucket capacity (80 meters long and weighing 1,200 tons)" were in operation.[179] Although the placers of central Aldan are characterized by a high metal content, an average of 420 to 500 mg per cu.m., the richest deposits have already been worked out, with the exception of Tyrkanda. Reworking areas considered to have too low a metal content for the previous extraction methods has given a new lease of life to the area. Nevertheless the main thrust of development is the ore in the Kuranakh Basin, which has "long-term prospects."[180] The first ore mine to be operated was at Lebediny in 1934: in 1937 it was supplying 27 percent of all the gold produced by the Yakutzoloto trust. Nizhni Kuranakh was opened up in 1945 and the following year up to a thousand private prospectors were working at the site; the state mine was begun in 1947.[181]

The favorable prospects of the Aldan gold fields were singled out by the First Secretary of the Yakut Republic Communist Party, G.I. Chiryayev, in an article in 1974 perceiving their further development with the iron-ore and coking-coal deposits, respectively, at Aldan and at Neryungri.[182] The development of this region has also been fostered by the mining of phlogopite (a magnesia mica). The deposits were opened up during World War II; output rose from 1942 to 1951, but then declined. It was revived in the 1960s.[183]

The placer enterprises identified in the Aldanzoloto combine probably aggregate no more than 3 tons but the Nizhni Kuranakh ore mine and dressing plant under it,[184] from a photograph of 1974 and its description in 1968,[185] could be producing 15 tons from open-cast mining, viz. 18 tons in all, as it probably did in 1970.

Chronologically, the Dzhugdzhur fields along the Allakh-Yun River, were the next to be opened up after Aldan. Placers began to be worked in 1932, and, when large drafts of prison labor were brought in, the Dzhugdzhurzoloto trust was established (1939), later redesignated a combine. The prisoners worked at the Ynykchansky placers while free workers were at the small deposits of Minor and the still smaller Yur.[186] Free workers at the state enterprises were encouraged by the provision of a special gold voucher (zolotoi bon) to work as independent prospectors during the winter, access to the well-stocked shops to exchange vouchers being subject to a daily average of 2 grams of gold. Since there were over 10,000 at the mines (free and forced) and 350 days would be worked at that minimum, output must have been at least 7 tons. One advantage to sheer production of having a prison camp under the NKVD in the trust was that "the rich uncle, Dalstroi" could be called upon for equipment and goods in wartime short supply. Dzhugdzhurzoloto was liquidated in 1956 when the prison camps were closed, having "opened up over sixty placers, of which the majority produced gold." At its closure it ran six placer administrations from its headquarters in Allakh-Yun.[187] The degree of shrinkage can be seen by the

demotion of the whole to a single Ynykchansky placer administration (priiskovoye upravleniye)[188] but by 1971 redevelopment allowed it to be promoted back to the Dzhugdzhurzoloto combine.[189] In 1957 placers produced 94.8 percent of output and lode only 5.2 percent. About 58 percent of the placer gold in that district came from open workings, 19.5 percent from underground deposits and 22.5 percent came from prospectors in 1957.[190] The future of the Allakh-Yun region, however, "lies not only in placers but in the exploration and exploitation of lode deposits."[191]

The resurgence of the Dzhugdzhur gold district was associated in part with the discovery of a major lode ore deposit in the 1960s[192] and a mine and mill went into operation at Solnechny in the early 1970s.[193] The large electric power requirements of the new mill were met by a floating power station of 20 MW that was anchored on the Aldan River at Eldikan and transmitted its electricity to Solnechny over a 110-mile line.[194]

Judging from the administrative status of settlements, placer activities continue around Allakh-Yun (founded in 1937), Ynykchansky (1940) and Brindakit (1947), and a new placer settlement was founded in 1978 at Yugorenok, on the Yudoma River. But two others, dating from the 1940s, were demoted to rural status in the 1970s—Ogonek in 1972 after 23 years' existence and Yur in 1978, after 36 years.

Because, in 1955, output in Indigirka was administered separately (by Dalstroi) and because the Yana River deposits had not then been opened up, an implicit index of a 3.9-fold rise for Yakut gold and mica output between 1940 and 1955[195] helps to illustrate the scale of expansion at Aldan and Dzhugdzhur in parallel with Dalstroi. In the first five years, i.e. by about 1944, the production in the Dzhugdzhur district reached 40 to 45 percent of Yakut output.[196] The year 1955 was the last full year before the camps were closed. There was certainly a decline in the Dzhugdzhur district before the revival began around 1970, and while the lode workings could have been running at 2 tons, the placers may have halved (i.e., from 7 to at most 4 tons). An estimate for 1980 suggests that output might return to its previous levels, substituting dredges for manual labor, say 8 tons.

For an assessment of Yakutian gold output today, as already noted, the Indigirka and Yana mines must also be considered. The fact that Yakutzoloto raised its output by 23.6 percent between 1955 and 1958, i.e. when Indigirka was absorbed, and by 65.5 percent between 1950 and 1959[197] without allowing for Indigirka and that by 1964 the latter was the biggest gold producer of Yakutia[198] indicates the rate of development without, however, furnishing an absolute level.

Supplying gold in commercial quantities first in 1937, the Indigirka mines operated under Dalstroi, until the dissolution of the organization in 1957, partly because of the inaccessibility of the region, administered from Ust-Nera, from the Lena basin. By 1953, 144 placers and 11 lode deposits "had been opened in the upper Indigirka basin, and by 1964 they numbered over 280," thereby reaching first place for output among the gold-bearing areas of Yakutia.[199] In 1957, all gold was placer, 54.2 percent being underground, 31.8 percent open and 14 percent from prospectors.[200] Ore deposits were known, but not worked, and as late as 1962 it was still being stated that all Indigirka gold was from placers.[201] Substantial ore working was not begun until the opening of a concentration mill at Pobeda in 1969. The latter does not seem to be a large mine and is roughly put at producing 1 ton in 1970 and 2 tons in 1980. There were, on the other hand, rich placers in exploitation through this period. A Western visitor to the Marshalsky placer enterprise in 1973 observed from a notice board that it comprised 15 mines totaling some 1.5 tons output. He also met an artel of some 12 men that another member of the visiting party thought could produce 100 kg per year.[202] Marshalsky may have been somewhat bigger, but seven enterprises at 1.5 tons would show 10.5 tons and (on a rough ratio of artels to enterprises, as in the Northeast) another 1.5 tons from private prospectors. That relationship would fit a statement relating to 1957 where 14 percent of Indigirka output came from prospectors compared to 22.5 percent in the Dzhugdzhur area.[203] Twelve tons from placers in 1970, plus 1 from ore shows an Indigirka total of 13 tons. Nothing seems to have been reported about trends in the 1970s but it is likely to have been upward and placers could be on the order of 15 tons in 1980, viz. 17 tons in all.

Finally, placers on the lower reaches of the Yana, which flows into the Arctic Ocean between the Lena and the Indigirka, began to be exploited only in 1958. The season there is as late and short as that on the Indigirka. Its recent mining development, especially of its boom town, Deputatsky, owes more to tin (since 1936) than to gold, but Deputatsky is the administrative center for the Yana gold-mining combine, whose operations extend to the Verkhoyansk Range, where gold is found in the valleys of the Tompo, Kele and Sobopola and in the Kular Ridge. In the Kular Ridge, the damming of the Drugaya Klep River in the 1970s remedied a shortage of water in the washing season. Placer production in 1980 was located at Kular (including Vlasovo) and Tenkeli, and the installation of a mobile power unit at Tenkeli in 1977 (dragged on skis from Nizhneyansk at the mouth of the Yana)[204] will have augmented gold production. No indication of output size or trends has been discovered and it is assumed that these placer enterprises produced 3 tons in 1970 and 5 tons in 1980.

In looking to the future, deposits are being explored, but not apparently yet exploited, in northwest Yakutia. The most active site appears to be the coastal alluvial plain where the Anabar River reaches the Laptev Sea and its upper reaches, in the Anabar Massif. The headquarters for the geological parties is the settlement of Yurung-Khaya, on the lower Anabar River, and the exploration effort appears to be concentrated around the geological field settlement of Amakinsky, on the Ebelyakh, a right tributary of the Anabar (Lat. 71°N Long. 114°E).

Well to the south, near the long-worked Vitim deposits (worked by Lenzoloto, and discussed below), gold is found along the left-bank tributary of the Lena, the Vilyui, where the placer deposits also contain platinum. Although mentioned as long ago as 1940 as gold-platinum sands,[205] no gold mines were marked along the

entire course of the Vilyui in a map of 1969.[206] The installation of a hydroelectric plant on the Vilyui would promote such exploitation, although in the 1970s the power was consumed by the dynamic diamond industry. A station at Chernyshevsky, rated at 648 MW, began to supply at a first stage in 1967 to the original mines at Mirny and from 1969 the Aykhal-Udachny diamond district.[207] But the generation at full capacity is such that some would be likely to be available for other consumers.

Tables 4 and 5 summarize the estimates made in the foregoing paragraphs and extrapolate to 1990. On such a projection the rise from a roughly estimated 40 to 49 tons in 1970–80 of 22.5 percent, would be exceeded by that of 49 to 68 tons in 1980–90 (39 percent). In effect what would happen would be a transfer of placer mining from the Northeast where deposits are declining to the less exploited fields of Yakutia. That Yakutia is a likely candidate for expansion is possibly shown by the commendation of its chief gold administrator in each of the last two five-year plans.[208] It has also been promoting new technology in prospecting (computer analysis of geological, geophysical, geochemical and radiation data[209]), in placer mining (a remote controlled bulldozer operation[210]) and in lode mining, by sinking inclined mine shafts.[211] It ranks on these projections only just behind the Northeast in the output estimates for 1990. The new estimates revise downward those of Dowie and Kaser of 48.8 tons in 1970.[212]

Transbaikalia

The Transbaikal Gold Corporation, promoted from a trust during the 1973–75 reorganization,[213] covers Chita Oblast and the Buryat ASSR. In Chita Oblast, gold has been continuously mined since a discovery in 1777 at Nerchinsk on the Shilka, a tributary of the upper Amur, and in the Buryat ASSR since placers were worked around Lake Baunt, in the Lena Basin, in the 1840s. The Klyuchevsky and Davenda placers in the south were worked by a British firm before the Revolution and revived in the 1930s. Most deposits were quickly exhausted and it is a feature of the area that placers are small and relatively short-lived. The "expeditionary method" (use of excavators with mobile gold-washing devices or bulldozers with hydraulic lifters and washing attach-

TABLE 4
Yakutian Gold Production by Mining Mode and by Districts (in metric tons)

|  | 1940 | | 1970 | | 1980 | | 1990 | |
|---|---|---|---|---|---|---|---|---|
|  | Placer | Lode | Placer | Lode | Placer | Lode | Placer | Lode |
| Aldan | 5 | 4 | 3 | 15 | 3 | 15 | 3 | 20 |
| Dzhugdzhur | 3 | — | 4 | 2 | 6 | 3 | 8 | 7 |
| Indigirka | 1 | — | 12 | 1 | 15 | 2 | 17 | 3 |
| Yana | — | — | 3 | — | 5 | — | 7 | — |
| Vilyui | — | — | — | — | — | — | 3 | — |
| Total | 9 | 4 | 22 | 18 | 29 | 20 | 38 | 30 |

SOURCE: See discussion in text.

ments) is hence employed in preference to permanent installations, and it appears to be the objective to establish many small placers. The dredges at Ust-Karsk and on the Cherny Uryum River (at Ksenevka, Itaka, Mostovka and Chaldonka) are all reportedly small (though with technology at Mogocha on the same river that includes closed circuit television). A placer technique that was pioneered in Transbaikalia is the experimental covering of alluvial deposits with polyvinyl chloride sheeting so as to thaw the sand earlier; in the normal way the season begins in mid-April. This and other improved techniques have added a month to the placer season, which now averages 255 days (March-November). The standard method of opening a new field is for bulldozers to clear the gravel and sand from the permafrost layer,

which is left to thaw for two years; the excavator or dredge arrives only in the third year. The season starts rather later in the Cherny Uryum River (April) and on the Unda (late March).

Placers on the Chikoi River were first exploited in 1844 but only small workings continued as interest shifted to molybdenum mining.[214] There was, however, considerable revival in the late 1960s.

An assessment of eastern Transbaikal workable reserves in 1967 showed that only 19.4 percent were in placers; 30.0 percent of lode ore could be strip-mined and 50.6 percent had to be extracted underground.[215] There has, in fact, been reef-working since 1929 and the Balei combine comprises one of the larger gold mines in the USSR, Taseyevo (which reached capacity of nearly 4 tons

TABLE 5
Gold Production of the Yakutian Gold Corporation (Yakutzoloto)

| Tonnage of Metal Produced | | | | | | | |
|---|---|---|---|---|---|---|---|
| 1940 | 13 | 1959 | (23) | 1970 | 40 | | |
| 1942 | 12 | 1960 | 23 | 1971 | (40) | | |
| 1950 | 20 | 1961 | (25) | 1972 | (40) | | |
| 1951 | 21 | 1962 | (26) | 1973 | (42) | | |
| 1952 | 22 | 1963 | (27) | 1974 | (43) | | |
| 1953 | 23 | 1964 | (28) | 1975 | (44) | | |
| 1954 | 24 | 1965 | 30 | 1976 | (45) | | |
| 1955 | 25 | 1966 | 32 | 1977 | (46) | | |
| 1956 | 21 | 1967 | (34) | 1978 | (47) | | |
| 1957 | 21 | 1968 | (36) | 1979 | (48) | | |
| 1958 | 22 | 1969 | (38) | 1980 | 49 | | |
| | | | | 1990 | (68) | | |

| Administration and Enterprises | | | |
|---|---|---|---|
| Enterprise | Designation as town or settlement | Enterprise | Designation as town or settlement |
| Aldanzoloto Combine (administered from Aldan) | | Indigirzoloto Combine (administered from Ust-Nera) | |
| (a) Placers | | (a) Placers | |
| Aldan | 1939 (town) | Marshalsky | — |
| Leninsky | 1932 | Nelkan | 1964 |
| Pyatidesyatiletka Oktyabrya | 1932 | Olchan | 1977 |
| | | Razvedchik | — |
| Tommot | 1923 (town) | Ust-Nera | 1950 |
| Yakokut | 1962 | | |
| (b) Lode | | (b) Lode | |
| Lebediny | 1969 | Pobeda | — |
| Nizhni Kuranakh | 1950 | | |
| Dzhugdzhurzoloto Combine (administered from Eldikan) | | Yanzoloto Combine (administered from Deputatsky) | |
| (a) Placers | | (a) Placers | |
| Allakh-Yun | 1937 | Kular | 1965 |
| Brindakit | 1947 | Tenkeli | 1973 |
| Eldikan | 1948 | Vlasovo | 1973 |
| Ynykchansky | 1940 | | |
| Yugorenok | 1978 | | |
| (b) Lode | | | |
| Solnechny | 1972 | | |

SOURCE: For production in 1940, 1970 and 1980 see text. 1970 was 35 percent over 1965 (*Tsvetnye metally*, 1971, no. 1) and on index 1942 = 1, 1950 was 1.7, 1960 1.9, 1965 2.5 and 1966 2.7 (*Yakutiya za 50 let v tsifrakh* (Yakutsk, 1967), p. 26). Administrative enterprises from text, with dates of towns or workers' settlements from *SSSR: deleniye*, pp. 57–60. Estimate for 1955 from statement that Yakutian output then was about one-fifth of the Soviet total (Pokshishevsky, *Yakutiya*, p. 105).

TABLE 6
Gold Production in the Transbaikal
Gold Corporation (Zabaikalzoloto)

### Tonnage of Metal Produced

| 1940 | 5.1 | 1960 | 11.9 | 1971 | (19.0) |
|---|---|---|---|---|---|
| 1950 | 6.0 | 1961 | 13.0 | 1972 | (20.0) |
| 1951 | 6.7 | 1962 | 13.9 | 1973 | (21.0) |
| 1952 | 7.0 | 1963 | 14.0 | 1974 | (22.0) |
| 1953 | 7.6 | 1964 | 15.0 | 1975 | (23.0) |
| 1954 | 8.1 | 1965 | 16.0 | 1976 | (24.0) |
| 1955 | 8.4 | 1966 | (16.2) | 1977 | (25.0) |
| 1956 | 8.8 | 1967 | (16.4) | 1978 | (26.0) |
| 1957 | (9.5) | 1968 | (16.6) | 1979 | (27.0) |
| 1958 | 10.0 | 1969 | (16.8) | 1980 | 28.0 |
| 1959 | (11.0) | 1970 | 17.0 | 1990 | (43) |

### Administration and Enterprises

| Enterprise | Designation as town or settlement | Administrative Division |
|---|---|---|
| (a) Placers | | |
| Chikoi | 1938 | Buryat ASSR |
| Davenda | 1951 | Chita Oblast |
| Itaka | 1938 | Chita Oblast |
| Ksenyevka | 1939 | Chita Oblast |
| Mogocha | 1950 (town) | Chita Oblast |
| Mostovka | — | Chita Oblast |
| Tsipikan | — | Buryat ASSR |
| Ust-Karsk | 1934 | Chita Oblast |
| (b) Lode | | |
| Baleizoloto Combine (Lyubov, Sosnovsky, Taseyevo, Unda) | Balei (town) | Chita Oblast |
| Vershino-Darasun ore-mining administration | Vershino-Darasunsky, 1932 | Chita Oblast |
| (?) Baunt ore-mining administration | Bagdarin, 1973 | Buryat ASSR |

SOURCE: For production, see text: the decimals given in tonnages are spurious accuracy, since the application of the index itself is speculative. Administrative locations and dates from SSSR: deleniye, pp. 23–25 and 246–48.

a year in 1966) and the deepest, Darasun, one shaft of which goes to 630 m and which, as a group of three neighboring workings together, produced around 1970 another 4 tons[216] (Table 6).

Alluvial gold had been extracted at Balei for half a century before gold-bearing quartz was discovered in 1928; the first ore was recovered the following year, when the Balei gold administration was set up. A dressing plant was built in 1935 (the Ordzhonikidze works); another was established later for the Lyubov and Khaverga ore mines.[217] Ore is blasted, shipped on trolleys hauled by electric locomotives to a cylindrical dumper which lifts it to the surface bunker, whence it is discharged into tip lorries for the dressing plant. Reserves currently equal ten years' production, but, even in the unlikely event of no new veins being located, the Balei field has a further life of five years to sort its tailings. The Maiskoye deposits were discovered in the 1930s and placers were worked on the northern slopes; a number of quartz veins were found there after World War II, and self-grinding of

the primary ore was introduced into the Klyuchevsky mill during 1976–80;[218] the process employs the force of larger pieces of ore to grind the smaller, without the need to insert grinding balls.

In the Buryat ASSR, gold mining, long practiced at the Baunt and upper Vitim placers, developed to lodes in the early 1960s. The major placers of Baunt are Tsipikan, Fedorovsky and Kedrova, all mechanized, either by dredges or bulldozers.[219] There are numerous polymetallic mines in the area—Akatui and Novoshirokinsk are among those where gold is specified as a byproduct; a prewar survey notes gold in other polymetallic mines.[220]

The big reef mine at Taseyevo was reequipped with self-grinding mills before that (already noted) at Klyuchevsky: indeed the Taseyevo mill was the test-ground for this equipment. Its installation raised output of finished material from 0.53 to 0.60 tons per cu.m. per hour and reduced electricity consumption without significant change in grinding quality.[221] Furthermore, sublevel cutting with single-stage extraction at Taseyevo in 1971–75 reduced losses from 21.7 to 13.3 percent and ore impoverishment from 20.8 to 17.5 percent.[222] No indication other than these has been given of the effect of reequipment but it is suggested that Taseyevo output could have doubled from 4 tons in 1970 to 8 in 1980 and that Klyuchevsky could have risen from 2 to 3 tons. The three other mines under the Balei administration may have produced a ton apiece by 1980 and talk in 1974 of developing two new lode deposits at Balei, Sverdlovskoye and Srednegolybtaiskoye,[223] could be linked with the award of orders and medals to workers and engineers of the combine in 1979 for the mining and processing of gold ores:[224] another two tons of lode-mined ore could have resulted. It may also be relevant to the expected expansion that the 1976–80 plan for Transbaikalia was fulfilled well ahead of time (on 22 April 1980).[225]

On the basis of the existence of 50 dredges in the goldfields of Chita Oblast, Dowie estimated placer output in Transbaikalia in 1970 at 8 tons. The implied output of 1 ton per placer (6 in Chita Oblast, 2 in the Buryat ASSR) seems high and the revised estimate is 6 tons; further mechanization in the 1970s may be assumed to have offset a decline in metal per cu.m. and output in 1980 is assumed to have remained at the same level. Lode-mining estimates as set out above may be summarized as follows (in tons):

| | | 1970 | 1980 |
|---|---|---|---|
| Baleizoloto: | Taseyevo | 4 | 8 |
| | Sverdlovskoye | – | 1 |
| | Srednegolybtaiskoye | – | 1 |
| Darasun | | 4 | 6 |
| Klyuchevsky | | 2 | 3 |
| Lyubov | | 0.5 | 1 |
| Sosnovsky | | – | 1 |
| Unda | | 0.5 | 1 |
| TOTAL | | 11 | 22 |

Production, as expected, changed in favor of lodes—from just under two-thirds in 1970 to nearly four-fifths in 1980. In the light of the statement already quoted that placers constituted only 14.4 percent of Chita Oblast reserves in 1967, they are assumed to be capable of contributing only 2 tons by 1990. Potential remains in the Buryat ASSR, however, where placer deposits are still apparently unexploited in the Dzhida, Kurba and upper Angara basins.[226] If they were developed as the existing Baunt deposits were exhausted, output could perhaps be 3 tons in 1990.

With respect to lodes, a 1974 survey was described as "deciding the fate of the raw materials base of the Balei combine"[227] and the installation of new equipment then and soon after suggests that the results were favorable. Moreover, it had previously been claimed that the cost of Balei ore was the lowest in the USSR.[228] Some expansion from the estimated 22 tons of lode-mined ore in 1980 could be projected to 1990, possibly by developing the Lyubov, Sosnovsky and Unda mines to 4 tons apiece. The activation of the third mine at Darasun (2 tons) and an increase at Balei of 4 tons, cumulates to an estimate of 15 tons of new capacity, i.e. to a total output from placers and lodes in Transbaikalia of 43 tons.

An attempt is also made to trace output back to 1940, even though the only statement on gold output is that the five-year plan target for 1966–70 was a 6 percent rise from existing enterprises.[229] It is assumed above that Sosnovsky (the main new capacity of 1966–70) did not operate until the end of the plan period, and a 1965 output of 16 tons could be estimated. The rough surrogate of Chita Oblast mining and metallurgical output was used by the present writer in a previous study[230] and is applied again to obtain an approximation to a time series for gold output in Table 6. The 5 tons thus derived, in a highly speculative manner, would not be inconsistent with the operation of three long-established placers (as shown by the dates of workers' settlements there) and of a lode mine at Balei.

## Lena District

It was from the Tikhon-Zada goldfields that Prince Peter Kropotkin set out on 2 July (O.S.) 1866 on his Olekma-Vitim Expedition. He wrote:

> I remain firmly convinced that in time, when this land has been visited by more teams of prospectors, it will turn out that there are numerous other and probably more convenient trails linking the Olekma and Nerchinsk districts. Should gold deposits be found in these areas, they will undoubtably be criss-crossed within a few decades by trails leading in every direction.[231]

His expedition reached Chita on 8 September (O.S.) and by 1913 over 10,000 workers were employed in 770 workings along the Lena, Vitim, Olekma, Patom, Khomolkho and Bodaibo rivers. Almost 40 Russian and foreign companies were engaged in goldmining, and after expropriation following the Revolution, their property was made available to a state goldmining trust, Lenzoloto [Lena Gold], on the right bank of the Lena, and to private Soviet prospectors on the left bank.

TABLE 7
Gold Production in the Lena
Gold Corporation (Lenzoloto)

| Tonnage of Metal Produced | | | | | |
|------|--------|------|--------|------|--------|
| 1940 | (8.1) | 1960 | (11.1) | 1971 | (15.4) |
| 1950 | (9.7) | 1961 | (11.3) | 1972 | (15.5) |
| 1951 | (9.8) | 1962 | (11.4) | 1973 | (15.6) |
| 1952 | (10.0) | 1963 | (11.6) | 1974 | (15.7) |
| 1953 | (10.2) | 1964 | (11.8) | 1975 | (15.8) |
| 1954 | (10.0) | 1965 | (12.1) | 1976 | (16.0) |
| 1955 | (9.5) | 1966 | (12.7) | 1977 | (16.1) |
| 1956 | (9.0) | 1967 | (13.3) | 1978 | (16.2) |
| 1957 | (9.6) | 1968 | (13.9) | 1979 | (16.3) |
| 1958 | (10.2) | 1969 | (14.6) | 1980 | (16.4) |
| 1959 | (10.9) | 1970 | (15.3) | 1990 | (18) |

Urban Places in Lena District Associated with Gold Mining

| Place | Date of designation as settlement or town |
|-------|------------------------|
| Bodaibo (headquarters of gold operations) | 1925 (town) |
| Artemovsky | 1929 |
| Balakhninsky | 1976 |
| Kropotkin | 1938 |
| Marakan | 1960 |

A number of places have lost their urban status, suggesting exhaustion of the placer operations that they served. These settlements and their years of urban status are:

| | |
|---|---|
| Andreyevsk | (1933–76) |
| Aprelsk | (1932–70) |
| Svetly | (1935–69) |

Source: For production, see text. Urban centers and dates from *SSSR: deleniye*, pp. 124–27.

One of the prerevolutionary concessionaires, the Lena Goldfields Company, was allowed in 1925 to reactivate its contract of 1908 over a large area of territory for a 30-year lease in the main mining area, and a 50-year lease for subsidiary enterprises. Of the gold and silver extracted 25 percent could be exported and the remainder sold to the Soviet government at the world price. The British company raised additional capital for the venture from United States interests, but saw scant return, for the concession was unilaterally cancelled in 1928. The workings, like all others in the country, were thereupon absorbed into the Main Gold Administration, which at approximately the same time (1 August 1928) was in turn taken over by the People's Commissariat of Finance.[232] The property expropriated comprised a very large dredge and other assets which cost the company $17.5 million at contemporary prices.

As already noted, the Lena fields soon lost their lead to the Aldan operations, but they have remained the most highly mechanized among placer workings: in 1969 over 70 percent of extraction was by fully mechanized opencast stripping or dredging (methods which accounted for over 90 percent of production). They are notable also for the world's biggest dredge (weight 10,300 tons with 600 liter scoops, 230 m. long, 40 m. above the water at its highest), built by the Kuibyshev Heavy Engineering

Plant, Irkutsk, and installed in 1969 on the Marakan River near the Bolshoi Patom. The placer is described as the richest in reserves of the USSR and the new dredge has by itself doubled production from the entire Bodaibo area. The placer is said to be "saturated like a sponge" and a smaller dredge would not excavate to the required depth of 50 m. For the installation (by Dragstroimash, the dredge assembly trust for Siberia and the Far East, founded in 1947) a 150-km road was completed from Bodaibo north to Marakan. The Marakan dredge and other gold-mining facilities in the Bodaibo district receive electric power from a 86-megawatt hydroelectric station at Mamakan, southwest of Bodaibo. Construction on the station began in 1956, and the four 21.5-megawatt generating units were installed in 1961–62.

The center of the Lena gold-mining district in northeastern Irkutsk Oblast is the town of Bodaibo, on the Vitim River (a Lena tributary). The mining operations extend upstream along the small Bodaibo River toward the northeast and then, beyond the Kropotkin Mountains, along the Vacha and Zhuya rivers, which are part of the Olekma drainage basin (another Lena tributary). The oldest mining settlement in the upper reaches of the Bodaibo River is Artemovsky, which dates from 1929. Shifts in mining operations over the years can be inferred from the changing urban status of mining settlements. Two settlements near Artemovsky—Aprelsk and Andreyevsk—lost their urban status after some 40 years of operations (Table 7) suggesting depletion of deposits. At the same time the growth of a new mining site was suggested in 1976, when the settlement of Balakhninsky, between Bodaibo and Artemovsky, was granted urban status. In the upper reaches of the Vacha and Zhuya rivers, the longest standing urban settlement is Kropotkin, dating from 1938. Another, known as Svetly, was phased out in 1969 after some 34 years of urban status.

Lode deposits have been worked since well before World War II in the Vacha basin at Atyrkan-Birikan (Innokentyev and Tikhon-Zada mines). The Birikan mine was accorded publicity in 1973 when a nugget weighing 3,190 g in a curious shape (a roe antler, according to a Tass report of 5 August 1973) was unearthed.[233] The mine at Artemovsky appears the most important: it was reported in 1967 as using new high-speed drilling techniques[234] and in 1980 to be performing well.[235]

Ore mining began in the mid-1960s in the Bodaibo basin (probably at Vodyanisty, where a 1940 survey recorded quartz veins in metamorphosed sandstone, though with gold of low finesse, mixed with silver).[236] The relative poorness of that lode could well account for the comment in 1962 that the mine would show a high current cost. Nevertheless, it was added, the capital recoupment would be better than at placers, where dredges had to be moved as deposits were exhausted. Since the Artemovsky and Bodaibo placers are (in that order, followed by the Vacha placer) the most profitable of the group, the contrast in current cost could be considerable. The combine has deposits sufficient for 30 to 50 years, mostly in deep-lying placers, but also as ore.[237]

The five-year plan of 1966–70 envisaged the installation of 7 new dredges (including the 600-liter unit just de-

scribed) and a production increase of 60 percent (1970 over 1965). The trust had prepared 17 new deposits, 4 mines and 3 open-cast hydraulic sites in the previous seven-year plan period, 1959–65, and the reworking of old sites was being undertaken in the mid-1970s in the Lena basin.

Expansion under the 1966–70 plan was large enough for the Lena district to be ranked second of those mentioned by the Minister of Nonferrous Metallurgy, who stated the production increment to be 26 percent. This was achieved by a major increase in labor productivity, since Lenzoloto underwent the greatest reduction of personnel of any Glavzoloto division, i.e. by 1,300 people (labor productivity had increased 66 percent while wage outlays had risen only 23 percent).[238] However, no statement seems to have been published on either the 1971–75 or the 1976–80 five-year plans. The dredges installed in the area are continuing to provide rapid increments of throughput of sand and gravel with lower labor intensity. Production with smaller dredges over the previous twenty years is assumed to have grown only slowly (1.5 percent a year on average), with a decline as labor at the placers was withdrawn in the mid-1950s. The rate overall would have been nothing like the mining and manufacturing production index for Irkutsk Oblast as a whole (18.3 times increase between 1950 and 1970 and 1.6 times between 1945 and 1950), but the 20 percent increase in the oblast's output between 1940 and 1945 is of the order of magnitude one might expect for the decade 1940–50 as a whole. These very tentative estimates of trend were applied to Dowie's calculations[239] and conform to a Soviet statement that the 1940 output was below that of Yakutzoloto.

Dowie's 1970 estimate shows 14 tons from placers and 1 from lode and the remarkable paucity of references to the Lena district in the journal of the Nonferrous Metallurgy Ministry suggests lack of development. On the other hand, Lenzoloto was promoted from trust to combine in the 1960s[240] and to corporation in the 1970s.[241] It is suggested that output was fairly constant in the 1970s (Table 7 shows a modest rise due to reequipment) but that development of lode mining is envisaged for the 1980s. On so uncertain a basis, figures are no more than guesses but a projection is nevertheless made of a rise from 16 to 18 tons.

## Other Siberian Gold Districts

Two mining districts are of note in the western part of Siberia, both within Krasnoyarsk Krai. One is the Yenisei district (Yeniseizoloto) on the right bank of the Yenisei River in the Yenisei Ridge; the other is the so-called West Siberian district (Zapsibzoloto), centered in Khakas Autonomous Oblast and in Kemerovo Oblast in the mountains of the Kuznetsk Alatau.

In the Yenisei district, known historically as the Yenisei taiga, placers were first discovered in the 1820s and were exploited by individual panning in a gold rush of the 1840s. By the middle of the 19th century, this area was one of Russia's principal gold-producing districts. Virtually all the placers are now operated by dredges and,

TABLE 8
Gold Production in Other Siberian Areas

Tonnage of Metal Produced

| 1940 | 8 | 1970 | 13 |
|---|---|---|---|
| 1950 | 9 | 1980 | 14 |
| 1960 | 10 | 1990 | (10) |

Urban Places in Western Siberia Associated with Gold Mining

| Place | Date of designation as settlement or town |
|---|---|
| *Yenisei District* | |
| Motygino | 1960 |
| Novo-Yerudinsky | 1939–80 |
| Severo-Yeniseisky | 1928 |
| Teya | 1957 |
| Yuzhno-Yeniseisky | 1928 |

(Two other places, Ayakhta, founded in 1933, and Pit-Gorodok, founded in 1939, lost their urban status in the 1950s.)

| *Khakas Autonomous Oblast* | |
|---|---|
| Balakhchin | 1934–67 |
| Balyksa | 1932 |
| Kommunar | 1932 |
| Kyzas | 1932–67 |
| Ordzhonikidzevsky | 1940 |
| Priiskovy | 1940 |
| Znamenity | 1934 to mid-1950s |
| Zolotogorsky | 1940 to mid-1950s |
| *Other Krasnoyarsk Krai* | |
| Artemovsk | 1939 (town) |
| Chibizhek | 1941 |
| *Kemerovo Oblast* | |
| Berikulsky | 1931 |
| Komsomolsk | 1952 |
| Kundat | 1957–78 |
| Makaraksky | 1943 |
| Pervomaisky | 1931 to mid-1950s |
| Spassk | 1949 |
| Tsentralny | 1929 |
| Ursk | 1935 |

SOURCE: For production and administration, see text. Dates and locations from *SSSR: deleniye*, pp. 71–78 and 140–43.

despite more than a century of operations, the Yenisei district remains one of the richest producing areas in the western part of Siberia.

The placer mines extend over an area of around 200 miles between the Angara River in the south and the Stony Tunguska in the north. The southern portion was originally centered along the Uderei River at the settlement of Yuzhno-Yeniseisky (1959 population: 2,500), which was given urban status in 1928, but placer mining in the area became depleted, and the center of operations moved southward to Motygino in the 1950s. Motygino is the supply port on the Angara River, and placer operations are being conducted nearby along the Rybnaya and Bolshaya Murozhnaya rivers, right tributaries of the Angara.

The northern portion of the Yenisei gold district is centered on the settlement of Severo-Yeniseisky, which also gained urban status in 1928, and recorded a 1959 population of 6,200, suggesting the greater significance

compared with Yuzhno-Yeniseisky. On the northern outskirts of Severo-Yeniseisky is the Sovetskoye lode mine and mill, the only lode mine in the Yenisei district. Another urban settlement is Teya, founded in 1957, which serves as the center of dredging operations along the Teya and Noiba rivers. Both Severo-Yeniseisky and Teya are supplied by a 100-mile highway from Bryanka, the shipping head on the Bolshoi Pit River to the south, a right tributary of the Yenisei. In the 1930s and 1940s, there was mining activity farther upstream on the Bolshoi Pit around the settlements of Pit-Gorodok and Ayakhta, but they were abandoned by the mid-1950s. Another mining settlement that appears to have exhausted its nearby placers is Novo-Yerudinsky, on the Yeruda River, which functioned for more than 40 years, from 1939, when it was granted urban status, until its demotion to rural status in 1980.[242]

On the border between Krasnoyarsk Krai and Irkutsk Oblast, in the Eastern Sayan Mountains, there had been small-scale panning for gold in the upper reaches of the Gutara, Bolshaya Biryusa and Malaya Biryusa rivers in the 19th century. The placers were later abandoned, but efforts were made sporadically to reopen them and to prospect for additional gold-bearing deposits in the area.[243]

A more permanent gold-mining center in the Eastern Sayans is the town of Artemovsk, farther west within Krasnoyarsk Krai. Mining on the site dates from 1911, when the Olkhovsky settlement was founded on a rich lode deposit. In 1939, the workers' settlement was raised in urban status to town, indicating the importance of the operation, and it was renamed Artemovsk.[244] Access to the mining town was improved in the mid-1960s with the completion of the Abakan-Taishet railroad, but the significance of the operation appears to have been slowly declining, judging from population trends. Artemovsk had a population of 13,000 in the 1959 census, and 10,500 in 1970. Among a number of satellite placer settlements in the Artemovsk area (Kuzmovka, Georgiyevka, Tinsuk) the most important appears to be Chibizhek, which has had urban settlement status since 1941.[245]

The Zapsibzoloto (West Siberian Gold Administration) in the mountains of the Kuznetsk Alatau falls into two clusters, in Kemerovo Oblast on the western slopes and in Khakas Autonomous Oblast on the eastern slopes. Placer deposits have been worked since the 1830s, and the exploitation of lodes began early in the 20th century. Labor unrest before the Bolshevik Revolution led to a decline in production, but gold mining was redeveloped in the 1920s, and by 1931 was double that of 1913.

In Kemerovo Oblast, the gold-mining cluster is situated south of the city of Mariinsk along the Kiya River and its tributaries in what has been known historically as the Mariinsk taiga. The earliest Soviet mining settlements are Tsentralny (founded in 1929) and Berikulsky (founded in 1931), where facilities were rebuilt and expanded in the late 1920s and early 1930s.[246] The renovation at Tsentralny (1959 population: 6,100) involved introduction of the separate cyanation of crushed ores and silts, and resulted in the doubling of production at Tsentralny. At Berikulsky (1959 population: 6,500), an ore-crushing mill was rebuilt, followed by an extraction mill employing both flotation and settling processes.[247] An expansion of operations was evident during World War II, with the creation of the urban settlment of Makaraksky (1943; 1959 population: 3,200) and in the 1950s when two more settlements received urban status, Komsomolsk in 1952 (1959 population: 5,100) and Kundat in 1957 (1959 population: 1,500). The latter apparently depleted its resources within a period of some 20 years, and was deprived of urban standing in 1978. Another settlement that has been abandoned is Pervomaisky, which dated from 1931 and was phased out in the mid-1950s.

On the eastern slopes of the Kuznetsk Alatau, in Khakas Autonomous Oblast, both placers and lodes have been mined along three headstreams of the Chulym River—the Sarala, Cherny Iyus and Bely Iyus.[248] The two urban settlements in the Sarala basin, both dating from 1940, are Ordzhonikidzevsky (1959 population: 4,500), with lode production, and Priiskovy (from the Russian word *priisk*, meaning "placer"). Also suggestive of the economic activity in the area is the name of a satellite mining place, Transvaal, near Priiskovy. Another urban settlement, Zolotogorsky (meaning "gold mountain"), which also dated from 1940, was deprived of urban status in the mid-1950s, suggesting depletion of resources and abandonment. Another old mining place that was phased out at the same time was Znamenity, on the Cherny Iyus River, which had been given urban status in 1934. Nearby, in the watershed between the two Iyus rivers, is the urban settlement of Kommunar, which was founded in 1932 and had a population of 7,000 in 1959.[249] Farther south is the depleted mining site of Balakhchin, where a settlement had urban status from 1934 to 1967.

Farther south in Khakas Autonomous Oblast, placer deposits in the Kuznetsk Alatau and the Western Sayan Mountains gave rise to two urban settlements in 1932. One, in the upper reaches of the Tom River, Balyksa, was originally in Kemerovo Oblast, but was later transferred to Khakas Autonomous Oblast. The construction of a railroad from the Kuznetsk Basin across the Kuznetsk Alatau into Khakas Autonomous Oblast (completed in 1959) provided easy access to Balyksa and maintained its existence. The second gold-mining settlement, Kyzas, which is situated farther south in the Western Sayan Mountains, lost its urban status in 1967 after 35 years.[250]

Elsewhere in Kemerovo Oblast, gold placers have been reported in operation in the Salair Mountains, on the western side of the Kuznetsk Basin,[251] and in the Shor mountain country, south of the basin. In the Salair Mountains, the urban settlement of Ursk, founded in 1935, appears to be in a placer mining area. In the Shor mountain country, the urban settlement of Spassk, founded in 1949, is the center of dredging operations in the so-called Altai placer.[252] Gold has been discovered in the Tuva ASSR, chiefly in the Todzha area, but costs were reported to be prohibitive.[253]

Before World War II, West Siberian output seems to have been considerable and with at least fourteen placer areas and the same number of lode mines at 0.3 tons each (a rough approximation to an average), 8 tons could have been produced. There is every indication of a subsequent decline: the placers that seemed to be operating around 1970 could still show a 0.4 ton average, but two lode mines were substantial—the Sovetskoye of Severo-Yeniseisky at, say, 2 tons, and the Sarala lode mine (Ordzhonikidzevsky) 2.5 tons—and the other ten mines could, with improvements, be running at 0.5 tons each. Thus, 1970 output on this speculative basis could be 3 tons from placers and nearly 10 tons from lodes, or 13 tons in all. There seemed to be a certain revival in the 1960s in what was otherwise a depleting area, and 1960 output is put as low as 10 tons, and 1950 at 9 tons. Prospects are poor and the forecast for 1990 is 10 tons (Table 8).

A rough verification that 3 tons might be the right order of magnitude for placer output can be obtained from a statement that around 1960 Yakutia accounted for "up to 53.5 percent of placer gold in the Siberian economic regions."[254] On the 1970 estimates made in the foregoing sections, Yakutia accounted for 49 percent (in tons):

| | |
|---|---|
| Chita Oblast, Buryat ASSR | 6 |
| Irkutsk Oblast | 14 |
| Kemerovo Oblast and Krasnoyarsk Krai | 3 |
| Yakut ASSR | 22 |
| TOTAL | 45 |

### Kazakhstan Gold Mines and USSR Byproduct Gold

A reorganization undertaken during the 10th Five-Year Plan (1976–80) introduced an industrial corporation coterminous with the Ministry of Nonferrous Metallurgy of the Kazakh SSR and designated by the ministry's acronym Kazmintsvetmet.[255] It apparently absorbed three gold-mining trusts. One, Altaizoloto, which had been set up either during World War II or soon afterward, operated in the Altai Mountians of eastern Kazakhstan. The two others, Kazzoloto, established before the war, and Maikainzoloto, operated in the northern regions of the republic.[256]

Since virtually all gold extracted in Kazakhstan is byproduct gold of the important base metals industry, all byproduct suppliers are discussed in this section, which draws on Consolidated Gold Fields' analysis of 1980.[257] Kazakhstan's role in byproduct gold production is evident from the fact that it accounts for some 73 percent of the Soviet Union's lead smelter output, 46 percent of the zinc and 33 percent of the copper (as of 1975).

The oldest mine from which gold was extracted was the Ridder mine in the Altai, started in 1794: it is hence appropriate to begin with a survey of lead-zinc ores. Ridder was flooded in 1916 and reactivation was delayed until 1928, partly because it became a pawn in Anglo-Soviet relations. The chairman of its pre-nationalization owners, Russo-Asiatic Consolidated, Leslie Urquhart, a mining engineer who had long worked at Ridder, proposed to the Soviet Government in June 1921 that his company's compensation be in the form of a concession to operate the mine for 99 years. The Government initially rejected the proposal but by September 1922 it had modified its concessions policy to the point that it signed an agreement (Krupp and the Mendelssohn Bank of Berlin now having taken shares in the company), only to be overruled by Lenin personally in October, almost his last political act before his eventually fatal stroke. Had he not been so opposed, an Anglo-German concern would have run Ridder.[258] The Ridder mine and a lead smelter were reactivated under Soviet control, and the entire complex was renamed Leninogorsk in 1940. Mining operations in the original Leninogorsk and Sokolny mines were supplemented in 1965 by a huge open pit excavated on the Tishinka deposit (discovered in 1958). The open-pit operation ceased in 1976 because of great depth, and exploitation of deeper ore bodies was taken over by shaft mining. The recovery of gold from the lead-zinc ores at Leninogorsk was estimated in the Gold Fields study to have been 2.7 tons in 1977. Nearby, the Zyryanovsk lead-zinc deposit is estimated to have produced 1.8 tons of gold in 1980; Belousovka half a ton, and Verkhne-berezovsky a third of a ton. Gold is also being recovered from complex ores on the border between Kazakhstan and Altai Krai, where the older Zolotukha operation at Gornyak on the Altai side of the border was supplemented in the 1970s by the Orlovka mine at Zhezkent on the Kazakhstan side. In 1981, a long delayed concentrator also began processing the ores of the nearby Nikolayevka open-pit mine at Ust-Talovka.[259] In southern Kazakhstan, the Achisai mine and other operations at the town of Kentau supply enough lead-zinc ore to furnish 2 tons of gold annually.[260]

Byproduct gold from all these deposits is extracted mainly by mills and smelters at Leninogorsk and Zyryanovsk and by the Irtysh smelter at Glubokoye, all in eastern Kazakhstan.

Outside Kazakhstan byproduct gold from lead-zinc ores is obtained at Almalyk in Uzbekistan, from ores mined just across the border with Tadzhikistan at Altyn-Topkan (designated a settlement in 1951 with extraction beginning in 1954) at an estimated 1977 production rate of 4 tons, in the Far East, at mines of the Dalnegorsk (formerly Tetyukhe) lead mill, which the Gold Fields estimate puts at 1.1 tons for 1976 and, by implication, 1.6 tons in 1980.[261]

Kazakhstan is also important in copper ores from which gold is derived although more byproduct gold from this metal is obtained from Urals ores. The Kounrad deposit at Balkhash in Kazakhstan was opened in 1934 and redeveloped between 1958 and 1968: Gold Fields estimates gold output since the reconstruction to be 8.4 tons annually. No less than eight copper deposits are worked in the Urals and furnish byproduct gold: a detailed description is made by Gold Fields with the following gold outputs (tons per year): Mednogorsk (Orenburg Oblast) 0.7; Buribai (Bashkir ASSR) 0.3; Degtyarsk (Sverdlovsk Oblast) 1.47; Gai (Orenburg Oblast) 5.04; Levikha (Sverdlovsk Oblast) 0.56; Pyshma (Sverdlovsk Oblast) 2.45; Sibai (Bashkir ASSR) 2.24; and Krasnoturinsk (Sverdlovsk Oblast) 0.77. Production from Kalmakyr at Almalyk in Uzbekistan, however, is assessed by Gold Fields as outweighing either the Urals or Kazakhstan in gold derived—an annual out-turn of 17.25 tons is estimated. Kadzharan in Armenia is put at supplying 2.52 tons, but rising to 4.2 tons in 1985; two other Armenian copper deposits (Kafan and Dastakert) add 0.3 tons.

Finally, the Norilsk complex in the far north of Krasnoyarsk Krai is believed to provide some 0.7 tons as byproduct.[262]

In sum, the estimates put 16.0 tons of gold as derived from lead-zinc ores (of which 7.6 tons in Kazakhstan) and 44.1 tons from copper ores (of which 8.4 tons from Kazakhstan) in 1977; of the aggregate 60 tons Kazakhstan furnished 16, or 27 percent. In the ordinary course of events an approximate time series could be worked back on a ratio to outputs of lead, zinc and copper, but the USSR has published no statistics of their production since before World War II, either in absolute quantities or in index number form. A series could, nevertheless, be constructed from two sets of Western estimates, those of Zaleski for 1940 and 1951–52, and of *Metal Statistics* (Frankfurt) for 1957–79.[263] No production goals were published for nonferrous metals in the 10th Five-Year Plan (1976–80) and it was therefore not possible to apply the ratios to targets for the output of lead, zinc and copper. The original goal of the 5th Five-Year Plan (1951–55) may

TABLE 9
Output as Byproduct Gold (metric tons)

| | From lead-zinc ores | From copper ores | Total |
|---|---|---|---|
| 1940 | 1.8 | 6.4 | 8.2 |
| 1950 | 2.5 | 9.8 | 12.3 |
| 1951 | 3.0 | 11.1 | 14.2 |
| 1952 | 3.6 | 12.9 | 16.5 |
| 1953 | (4.2) | (13.6) | (17.8) |
| 1954 | (4.8) | (14.3) | (19.1) |
| 1955 Plan | 6.5 | 19.4 | 25.9 |
| 1955 | 5.4 | 15.0 | 20.4 |
| 1956 | (5.5) | (15.5) | (21.0) |
| 1957 | 5.6 | 16.1 | 21.7 |
| 1958 | 6.4 | 16.7 | 23.1 |
| 1959 | 6.8 | 17.5 | 24.3 |
| 1960 | 7.3 | 19.8 | 27.1 |
| 1961 | 7.7 | 21.8 | 29.5 |
| 1962 | 8.1 | 23.9 | 32.0 |
| 1963 | 8.3 | 25.8 | 34.1 |
| 1964 | 9.0 | 27.8 | 36.8 |
| 1965 | 9.2 | 29.8 | 37.0 |
| 1966 | 9.8 | 31.8 | 41.6 |
| 1967 | 9.9 | 32.8 | 33.7 |
| 1968 | 10.4 | 33.8 | 44.2 |
| 1969 | 10.7 | 34.8 | 45.5 |
| 1970 | 11.3 | 36.7 | 48.0 |
| 1971 | 12.0 | 39.3 | 51.3 |
| 1972 | 12.8 | 40.9 | 52.1 |
| 1973 | 14.2 | 42.1 | 56.3 |
| 1974 | 14.6 | 42.1 | 56.7 |
| 1975 | 15.5 | 44.1 | 59.6 |
| 1976 | 15.6 | 44.9 | 60.5 |
| 1977 | 16.0 | 44.1 | 60.1 |
| 1978 | 15.7 | 45.3 | 61.0 |
| 1979 | 15.5 | 45.7 | 61.2 |
| 1980 | (15.0) | (46.0) | (61.0) |
| 1990 | | | (91.0) |

SOURCE: See text.

not have been reached because of the closure in 1954–56 of prison camps attached to mines in Kazakhstan.[264]

A single target in the 1981–85 plan of "20 to 25 percent" for copper, is relevant to byproduct gold. This would indicate, on unchanged extraction rates, a 1985 byproduct yield of 55 to 57.5 tons, say 56.5 tons. On the other hand, no data are cited for lead or zinc, but aluminum (15 to 20 percent), and nickel and cobalt (1.3 times) are listed. *Metal Statistics*, from which the estimates in Table 9 are drawn, suggests a decline in 1978 and 1979, on which some corroboration can possibly be found in the low increments for the combined output of the ferrous and nonferrous metals industry (mining, concentration and manufacture) of 2.0 percent in 1978 and 0.2 percent in 1979. If byproduct gold from lead-zinc ores were just 15 tons in 1980, the proposed expansion of lead-zinc mining in Siberia (see below) might raise gold recovery to 19.5 tons in 1985. Together byproduct output in 1985 seems likely at around 76 tons, or 15 tons above 1980. To project the same growth for 1986–90 is hazardous, but, if done, shows 91 tons.

The Gold Fields study has some concrete examples of new projects in the 1980s. It notes plans for the development of lead-zinc deposits at Gorevka, on the lower Angara River in Krasnoyarsk Krai, and at Ozerny, in Buryat ASSR. These may ultimately yield 4.5 tons. The study also suggests that expansion at the Kadzharan copper deposit in Armenia will add 7.5 tons by 1985 to the 2.5 tons estimated for 1980 and at the Kentau lead-zinc complex in Kazakhstan will add another ton during 1981–85.[265] If 13 to 15 tons are to be added in the first half of the 1980s, it is not unreasonable to postulate 91 tons in 1990.

As stated at the beginning of the chapter, primary gold production in Kazakhstan is far less significant than byproduct recovery from complex ores of the lead, zinc and copper industry. Moreover, whatever small placers were worked in Kazakhstan have been exhausted, and virtually all primary gold production is from lode mines. Two principal gold-mining areas must be distinguished: Eastern Kazakhstan, where the Altaizoloto trust operated before the reorganization of the 1970s, and northern Kazakhstan, with the Kazzoloto and Maikainzoloto trusts (Table 10).

By far the largest gold-lode operation is the Bakyrchik mine at Auezov in the Kalba Mountains of Semipalatinsk Oblast. Gold was first reported on the site in 1944–45, and fuller exploration in the middle 1950s identified a major deposit, on which a dressing plant went into operation in 1970.[266] The urban settlement on the site was established in 1962 under the name Bakyrchik, and was renamed Auezov in 1967. Other gold-mining places associated with lodes, are in operation, judging from their continuing urban status. They are Oktyabrsky (an urban settlement since 1951) to the northwest of Auezov, and Boko (1954) and Akzhal (1934) to the south. A number of mines that operated in World War II southeast of Auezov in the Kalba Mountains appear to have become depleted and closed down. They include Baladzholsky and Sentas, established in 1941, and Kazan-Shunkur, established in 1945. All were phased out by the 1950s as urban settle-

TABLE 10
Primary Gold Production in Kazakhstan (metric tons)

| 1940 | (0.6) | 1961 | (4.3) |
|------|-------|------|-------|
| 1950 | (1.3) | 1962 | (4.7) |
| 1951 | (1.5) | 1963 | (5.1) |
| 1952 | (1.8) | 1964 | (5.5) |
| 1953 | (2.0) | 1965 | (5.9) |
| 1954 | (2.3) | 1966 | (6.4) |
| 1955 | (2.8) | 1967 | (6.9) |
| 1956 | (3.0) | 1968 | (7.4) |
| 1957 | (3.2) | 1969 | (8.0) |
| 1958 | (3.5) | 1970 | 9.0 |
| 1959 | (3.8) | 1980 | (9.0) |
| 1960 | (4.0) | 1990 | (13.0) |

Urban places associated with primary gold-lode production

| | Designation as urban settlement or town |
|---|---|
| Altaizoloto (Semipalatinsk Oblast) | |
| Akzhal | 1934 |
| Auezov (until 1967, Bakyrchik) | 1962 |
| Boko | 1954 |
| Oktyabrsky | 1951 |
| Kazzoloto | |
| (Tselinograd and Kokchetav oblasts) | |
| Akbeit | 1957 |
| Aksu (until 1961, Stalinsky) | 1940 |
| Bestobe | 1940 |
| Birlestik (possible association with Vasilkovka lode deposit) | 1978 |
| Stepnyak | 1937 (town) |
| Zholymbet | 1940 |
| Maikainzoloto (Pavlodar Oblast) | |
| Maikain | 1937 |

SOURCE: For production see text. Dates of designation from *SSSR: deleniye*, pp. 385–422.

ments, although Kazan-Shunkur was still referred to as a mine in a 1970 source.[267]

In northern Kazakhstan, a cluster of gold-lode settlements arose in the 1930s, and have remained urban places since that time although reserves may be on the way to depletion. These places are Stepnyak in Kokchetav Oblast, with the status of town since 1937, and three urban settlements in Tselinograd Oblast—Aksu, Bestobe, and Zholymbet—all founded in 1940. A fourth place, Akbeit, farther west in Tselinograd Oblast, was given urban status in 1957. Stepnyak was reported, in the 1950s, to have a mill that served the other mining settlements. But its decline is shown by a drop in population from 23,000 in the 1939 census to 13,000 in the 1959 census and a mere 8,800 in 1975.[268] Zholymbet served as the headquarters of the Kazzoloto trust.[269] The significance of gold mining in northern Kazakhstan was further enhanced in the middle 1960s with the discovery in 1965 of a major new lode deposit in the Vasilkovka area, 12 miles north of the city of Kokchetav. The creation of the urban settlement of Birlestik in 1978, northwest of the reported lode find, may have been associated with its development.

Finally, there is the mining town of Maikain, southeast

of Ekibastuz in Pavlodar Oblast, where complex, polymetallic ores appear to be worked mainly for their gold content. Maikain has had the status of urban settlement since 1937. Its continuing significance was suggested by the opening of a new concentrator in 1962, yielding copper, zinc, barite and pyrites in addition to gold, and by the construction of a rail spur that reached Maikain in 1969.[270]

In seeking to estimate the primary gold production of Kazakhstan, Dowie finds Auezov likely to have produced 2 tons in 1970 and Bestobe and Zholymbet 1.6 apiece. If the other northern Kazakhstan sites produced only a ton each, a total of some 9 tons appears indicated and no expansion is envisaged in estimates through the decade to 1980. In the absence of any better measure to run a time series back to 1940, the official index of nonferrous production in Kazakhstan is used for 1940 to 1971.[271]

The projection of depletion by 1990 reflects warnings in 1978 from, for example, the editor of the newspaper *Rudny Altai* that because geological prospecting was reduced "the lost years cannot be recovered," up to the Minister of Nonferrous Metallurgy of the Kazakh SSR, V. Grebenyuk, that "not until recently did capital investment in nonferrous metallurgy in Kazakhstan reach the 1965 level."[272]

## Central Asia

Some half million tons of auriferous ore was mined in the nineth to twelfth centuries at Kyzylalma on the Angren River in what is today the Uzbek SSR[273] but only in very recent times has the wealth of gold and the ease of its extraction there been realized. Prospecting trusts, Tadzhikzoloto and Uzbekzoloto, were set up in the 1930s, leading to the exploitation of placers on the Yakh-Su in Tadzhikistan and the Sarta-Butkan lode in Uzbekistan. In the early 1940s, A.V. Korolev established the presence of gold in the copper ores of Kalmakyr at Almalyk (discussed under byproduct gold) and described a rich gold-bearing belt in the Kyzyl Kum desert. However, not until 1957 did an intensive exploration effort begin in Uzbekistan, culminating in the discovery of the important Muruntau lode deposit in the Kyzyl Kum in 1958.[274]

As a result of these and other major discoveries, the Uzbekzoloto trust was promoted in late 1965 to the rank of a corporation.[275] As of the mid-1970s, it administered three major ore-treatment plants and associated mines based on the Muruntau deposit in the Kyzyl Kum, the Chadak deposit on the northwest side of the Fergana Valley, and the Kochbulak deposit near Angren.[276] In 1980, a fourth major gold-mining complex went into operation at Mardzhanbulak, northeast of Samarkand.[277]

The development of the Muruntau deposit in the Kyzyl Kum desert was probably one of the most important events in the Soviet gold-mining industry in the 1960s. It called for the provision of a vast array of infrastructure, including the construction of a highway and railroad from the base town of Navoi, some 150 miles to the southeast, a 48-inch aqueduct from the Amudarya, 150 miles to the west, and the construction of a new town of Zarafshan, some 15 miles west of the actual mine and mill

at Muruntau. The new town arose in the early 1960s as the settlement of Surgali, was renamed Zarafshan and raised to the status of urban settlement in 1967. The first gold was produced in 1969 from an open-cast mine, said to be the biggest in the world. As an indication of the importance of the gold operation, the settlement of Zarafshan was raised to city status in 1972; it was given directly the higher rank of city under oblast jurisdiction instead of passing first through the intermediate rank of city under rayon jurisdiction. The following year, the second stage of the gold operation was completed with some shaft mines, and full capacity was to have been achieved in 1975.[278] Zarafshan, originally designed to become a city of 40,000 population, was reported to have 18,000 in 1974. Muruntau itself, situated at the south foot of the gold-bearing Tamdy-Tau hills, was made an urban settlement in 1976.

The Zarafshan-Muruntau complex has been closely investigated in a Gold Fields study, both from Soviet technical publications and from satellite imagery.[279] The mill was the first in the world to employ the resin-in-pulp extraction process, a method which Gold Fields state eliminates the requirement to filter the cyanide pulp and thereby saves on capital cost.[280] A note of caution must be sounded on the use of Soviet technical studies, for with respect to Uzbekistan, exact reference is not normally made to the refinery in which the process described is installed. It is, in fact, possible that some of the references are to the smaller Chadak-Altynkan operation and that Gold Fields have, by a confusion, been misled into attributing 80 tons a year to Muruntau-Zarafshan and terming it "the largest gold mine in the world."[281]

Certainly it was a substantial refinery from the start. In its first year there is indirect evidence that it was producing gold at the rate of 4.3 tons a year.[282] Output certainly expanded and ten years after starting up, that is by 1978, an output of some 30 tons is estimated.[283]

The Muruntau-Zarafshan operation has eclipsed an earlier gold mine in the Kyzyl Kum, the Kokpatas mine some 60 miles northwest of Zarafshan. The Kokpatas mine, which began to be exploited a few years before Muruntau, is in the vicinity of the town of Uchkuduk, which is believed to be associated with uranium production.[284] The Kokpatas gold deposit also contains quartz, pyrite and arsenic, and the ore is treated in a local concentrator.[285]

In the Samarkand region of central Uzbekistan, two other small lode mines were being explored or went into operation about the same time as Kokpatas; they are Charmitan and Karakutan.[286] But their secondary significance is evident from the fact that they have not given rise to urban mining settlements. The major development in the region was the construction of the gold-mining center of Mardzhanbulak, which is some 30 miles northeast of Samarkand, just across the border within neighboring Dzhizak Oblast. The development of Mardzhanbulak was given wide publicity, with the Uzbek party leader, Sh. R. Rashidov, taking part in groundbreaking ceremonies.[287] Mardzhanbulak was given urban status as a workers' settlement in 1977, and was raised to the next urban rank of city under rayon jurisdiction in 1980. In that year the first of several shaft mines started production, yielding a complex gold-bearing ore of a quartz-pyrite-arsenopyrite-polymetallic association.[288] Mill output at Mardzhanbulak is estimated at 6 tons a year.

In eastern Uzbekistan, gold mining is significant in the Chatkal and Kurama mountains. The most important lode center is the Chadak deposit on the south slopes of the Kurama Mountains, where the Guzaksai open-cast mine and the Pirmirab shaft mine are in operation, and a concentrator began to treat the ore in late 1969 after four years of construction. The settlement of Altynkan, associated with this operation, was given urban status in 1966 within Namangan Oblast of the Fergana Valley.[289] Production is estimated at 1 ton a year.

Across the Kurama Mountains, in the Angren River valley, two additional gold centers are Angren and Almalyk. At Angren, a gold-treatment mill began operations in 1973, at an assumed rate of 2 tons a year. It is being supplied mainly by nearby mines, notably the Kochbulak mine, on the north slope of the Kurama Mountains, which has been producing since 1968. Another supplier may be the old Kyzylalma lode deposit on the right bank of the Angren River, where exploration was reported under way in 1968.

At Almalyk, in addition to the gold from the copper-molybdenum mine at Kalmakyr (discussed in the section on byproduct gold), there appears to be lode gold mining in nearby deposits, notably Kauldy, on the north slope of the Kurama Mountains.

In Tadzhikistan, production continues to be limited to placer exploitation, notably in the Darvaza district, where the placers of the Yakh-Su have long been mined. A small dredge was put on the Yakh-Su in 1967, when the Tadzhikzoloto production corporation was formed, and the larger one (with 380-liter scoops) was installed in 1968-69 at 1,800 meter elevation near Siofark. There have long been plans for developing a major lode deposit at Taror (Toror), some 20 miles south of Pendzhikent in the Zeravshan Mountains. Pending that development, Tadzhik gold output was estimated by Dowie at around 1 ton a year.[290]

The increment between 1970 and 1975, on the above estimates, conforms to that planned for Uzbekzoloto, viz. 2.3 times,[291] as indicated in Table 11. For the period after 1975, the small increases shown for total ferrous and nonferrous metallurgy in Uzbekistan are applied to the 1975 estimates up to 1979.[292] The slow rise is possibly borne out by the diminution of news in Soviet media

about Uzbek gold, especially about Muruntau, over these four years. In 1980 the estimated 6 tons yielded by Mardzhanbulak is added in (Table 12).

The prospects remain sizable for Zarafshan-Muruntau and the enlargement of capacity was likely to be completed at the start of the 1980s, adding 25 or so tons. The little exploited Chatkal-Kurama and Angren regions will doubtless be utilized and could readily supply a further 5 tons each. The five-year plan for 1981-85 provides for an unspecified increment in Uzbek precious metals, a continuation of the rise shown over recent years.[293] A gold-lode project is to be brought into use in Kirghizia during 1981-85 at Dzheru (Talas Oblast) and could also be in the 5 ton range, and Tadzhikzoloto may only add, say, 3 tons. A total of 85 tons for Uzbekzoloto would bring it well ahead of Northeast Siberia or Yakutia by 1990; Kirghiz output at 5 and Tadzhik at 4 would give Central Asia 94 tons in that year.

## Urals

If Uzbekistan bids to have the biggest gold mine in the world in Zarafshan-Muruntau, the Urals may claim the longest-running. A report of 1940 described Berezovsky, where gold was first mined in 1745 as "still one of the largest lodes in the country."[294] On the eve of World War I, in 1913, the Urals contributed 5.2 tons of gold, or 18 to 20 percent of the national production, although by the 1930s the deposits were "poor" and "almost exhausted."[295] Even so, the 1940 survey observed that "lode production in the Urals continues to play a leading role among the country's gold districts."[296] The long-established Berezovsky and Plast mines were reconstructed in the 1920s, and even today Berezovsky is one of the leaders among the enterprises that make up the Uralzoloto Production Corporation.

The 1940 survey classified no less than 32 lode districts in the Urals, running in an almost continuous zone from the Arctic Urals to the southern extremity across the frontier in Kazakhstan. By that time Uralzoloto had been moved up from a trust to a combine but the cost effectiveness of its contribution to the war effort must have been judged low, because it and three others under the People's Commissariat of Nonferrous Metals lost 17,000 skilled workers to the armed forces. It remained important enough to be promoted to a corporation in 1970, and a report of 1972 stated that it comprised nine mining administrations.[297] One very rough procedure to estimate

TABLE 11
Regional Estimates of Central Asian Gold Production (metric tons)

|  | 1967 | 1968 | 1969 | 1970 | 1971 | 1972 | 1973 | 1974 | 1975 |
|---|---|---|---|---|---|---|---|---|---|
| Zarafshan-Muruntau | | | 4 | 13 | 18 | 23 | 28 | 28 | 31 |
| Altynkan-Chadak | | | | 1 | 1 | 1 | 1 | 1 | 1 |
| Angren | | | | | | | 3 | 3 | 3 |
| Almalyk | | 1 | 1 | 1 | 1 | 1 | 1 | 1 | 1 |
| Tadzhik | 0.3 | 1 | 1 | 1 | 1 | 1 | 1 | 1 | 1 |
| Total | 0.3 | 2 | 6 | 16 | 21 | 26 | 34 | 34 | 37 |

Source: See discussion in text.

TABLE 12
Gold Production in Soviet Central Asia (metric tons)

| | | | |
|---|---|---|---|
| 1967 | 0.3 | 1974 | 34 |
| 1968 | 2 | 1975 | 37 |
| 1969 | 6 | 1976 | 38 |
| 1970 | 16 | 1977 | 39 |
| 1971 | 21 | 1978 | 40 |
| 1972 | 26 | 1979 | 41 |
| 1973 | 34 | 1980 | 44 |

Gold Mining Places and Administrative Status in Uzbek SSR

| Oblast | Date of establishment as workers' settlement or town |
|---|---|
| Navoi Oblast | |
| Zarafshan | settlement (1967); town (1972) |
| Muruntau | settlement (1976) |
| Samarkand Oblast | |
| Charmitan | |
| Karakutan | |
| Dzhizak Oblast | |
| Mardzhanbulak | settlement (1977); town (1980) |
| Namangan Oblast | |
| Altynkan (Chadak deposit) | settlement (1966) |
| Tashkent Oblast | |
| Kokpatas (near Angren) | |
| Kauldy (near Almalyk) | |

SOURCE: For production, see text. Administrative status from *SSSR: deleniye*, pp. 359–82.

output is to assume that at the time an administration could not be established if its output were below 1 ton annually.[298] The other method, used by Dowie,[299] is to estimate 2 tons for each major lode mine (Berezovsky and Plast), a little under 1 ton apiece to four smaller lode mines (3 tons in all) and 2 tons from the 13 placer workings identified as in operation. This also shows 9 tons around 1970, which is used in the present study as a base year (Table 13) and applied to the two revealed index numbers of growth.[300] Since 1972 nothing indicative of output has been published but qualitative evidence suggests that new workings have been opened.[301]

In any event, Berezovsky and Plast would appear to be by far the most important gold-mining centers in the Urals. At Berezovsky, gold mining dates from the mid-18th century, first from lode ore and starting with the early nineteenth century from surface placers. The Berezovsky operation moved Russia into first place among world gold producers by 1845, accounting for 47 percent of world gold output. From the inception of the operation until World War I, Berezovsky yielded 57.4 tons, of which 45 percent was lode gold. Under Soviet rule, the old mines were modernized, and in 1938 the town of Berezovsky (under direct oblast jurisdiction, the highest urban rank) was formally established on the northeast outskirts of Sverdlovsk. Its population, which had declined from a prerevolutionary level of 11,200 in 1897 to 8,000 in 1926, rose to 25,600 in the 1939 census, 30,600 in 1959, and 38,400 in 1970.[302] The gold-bearing quartz ore, which occurs in the form of veins within some 350 granitoid dikes, is being mined in several underground mines,

of which the Yuzhnaya (Southern) mine is the largest. A mill recovers the gold from the quartz ore. Some of the ore is also being sent to copper smelters in the Urals, where the quartz serves as a flux and the gold is recovered as part of the metallurgical process.[303] A new deep mining complex, the Severnaya-Tsentralnaya (North Central) mine, was reported under construction in the early 1970s to tap the northern portion of the deposit and was scheduled for operation in the early years of the 10th Five-Year Plan (1976–80).[304]

The other major Urals gold-lode center is Plast in Chelyabinsk Oblast, associated with the Kochkar lode deposit. This site was discovered in 1844, and its development began in the 1860s.[305] Like Berezovsky, the Kochkar operation was modernized under Soviet rule and in 1940 gave rise to the city of Plast under oblast jurisdiction. In the mid-1960s, the Plast-Kochkar operation was said to consist of three underground mining sectors—North, South and Novo-Troitsky—totaling 12 shaft mines.[306] In contrast to Berezovsky, which has been slowly growing in population (probably because of the addition of manufacturing industries), Plast has been declining: its population, recorded at 31,000 in the 1939 census, was 26,000 in 1959 and 23,000 in 1970.

Outside of these two Urals gold centers, there are small lode operations and placers along the entire eastern slopes of the Urals, with concentrations in the upper reaches of the Lozva, Sosva, Tura, Neiva, Pyshma, Miass, and Ui rivers. Only a few gold operations appear to have been significant enough to give rise to separate urban workers' settlements. In Sverdlovsk Oblast, the settlement of Kytlym, southwest of Karpinsk, and the settlements of Valerianovsk, Is and Kosya, north of Kachkanar, combined the working of platinum placers with gold placers. In Bashkir Oblast, the settlement of Mindyak, formed in 1938 northeast of Beloretsk, has long been associated with gold placer operations. And in eastern Orenburg Oblast, the settlement of Kumak, which was given urban status in 1936, arose on the basis of a gold deposit.

In projecting Urals production beyond 1970, there seemed evidence enough for putting 1980 Urals output at 2 tons more than in 1970 and forecasting an addition of 2 tons during the 1980s.

Some Urals gold is accounted for as byproduct. Thus the Uchaly, Baimak and Sibai deposits are mined mainly for copper and zinc, and 2.2 tons of gold from them has been included in the estimates derived from the Gold Fields study. The latter records that the copper deposits assume output at that rate to 1992 and there is no doubt that the Urals is now more important for byproduct than for primary gold (an estimated 13.5 tons in 1978 against 10.6 tons).

## Armenia

Alexander the Great's conquest of Armenia was intended, according to Strabo, to assure the supply of gold for his vast empire; the Roman Empire, too, minted coins from Armenian gold. It is in the same area, the Zod Pass, below Mount Bezyrnyan, that the Soviet Union's latest gold production association, Armzoloto, has been established. Its origin is in an expedition of the Caucasus Trust for Nonferrous Metals Prospecting in 1951, but with no immediate success.[307] Eventually quartz gold of "semicommercial ore" (with a content not far short of the minimum) was discovered; despite the poor prognosis, a mine was sunk and a concentrating plant built. The optimism (doubtless more indulged in during 1957–65, when the regional economic councils then extant had greater powers of local investment) was justified by finding ores "with a very high content" in the mountains behind Zod. By March 1966, if not previously, a combine had been set up[308] and an experimental concentrator then completed, produced "several dozen kilograms of gold" in 1961; a larger pilot plant began operation at the end of 1971.[309] The completion of the Zod gold project was delayed for many years by changes in design. It was originally planned to develop the lode deposits only through underground mines, but in the course of the development it was decided to have both open-cut and shaft mining. The excavation of the open-cast mine began only in 1973. In another design change, the gold-treatment mill, originally planned for the vicinity of the mill, was to be relocated because of fears that mill wastes would pollute nearby Lake Sevan. The new mill site was the town of Ararat, in the Araks River plain southeast of Yerevan. The relocation of the treatment mill, on which construction began in 1969, called for the building of a 122-kilometer railroad linking the Zod mine to the existing rail system. The entire complex project, including mine, railroad and mill, was finally completed in 1976.[310] In order to reduce transport costs self-grinding installations for the primary ore were put in at Zod during 1976–80.[311] A sign of efficient mining technique at Zod was a report of 1980 (which, incidentally, confirmed the promotion of Armzoloto to Production Corporation) showing that self-propelled mining equipment there in 1979 was utilized 74 to 100 percent of working time compared with 37.5 percent for the Ministry of Nonferrous Metallurgy as a whole; on the other hand, employment in the Zod mine was 220 staff above that planned in the design.[312] At Ararat, a pilot plant tested the electrosmelting of the concentrate (the ores sampled showed 19 to 86 grams per ton) in 1973.[313] The Gold Fields study finds that the original plan called for the traditional application of gold precipitation from the cyanide solution with zinc dust (as in the Zod experimental plant) but the success of the resin-in-pulp process at Zarafshan led to its adoption at Ararat.[314]

Unlike many other Soviet mineral development projects, the Zod gold-lode development did not give rise to any new urban centers. The work force for the Zod mines was accommodated in the existing rayon seat of Vardenis, 8 miles west of Zod. Vardenis, known as Basargechar until 1969, was given the status of workers' settlement in that year, possibly in connection with the Zod project. As for Ararat, the site of the ore-treatment plant for Zod, it had been an industrial town in its own right, having arisen in conjunction with the construction of a cement plant in the 1930s. Ararat was promoted from workers' settlement to town in 1962, as a result of expan-

sion of production of cement and other building materials, and the location of the gold mill nearby stimulated further expansion in the late 1960s and early 1970s.

The estimate of Gold Fields for Armenian output in 1978 is 10 tons:[315] the time series shown in Table 14 takes this as the output from 1977, because the plant opened in February 1976,[316] with 9 tons in 1976. The history of Zod throws some light on the apparent acceleration of gold projects in 1972 (as discussed in connection with Northeast Siberia), in that work on the railroad connecting Zod with the line to Ararat "did not advance significantly until an acceleration order was issued in 1973."[317] This is slight evidence that the Soviet authorities did not judge investment in gold to be of high priority while the world gold price for free sales was close to the central bankers' price, but that the ending of the two-tier system induced a change of view.

The experimental plant in operation from 1966 to 1970 and the pilot plant of 1971–76 are assumed respectively to have yielded half a ton and 1.5 tons annually. The three placers that seem to have been operating throughout the period and the probable opening of a fourth in the 1970s[318] justify rounding these quantities up to the nearest ton.

With ample deposits still available for exploitation, it would seem reasonable to project a 1990 output of 20 tons in Armenia.

Private Producers

Mention has been made above of the role of private artels, teams of prospectors operating under contract to the gold-mining corporation in the area of which they work, and of the contention in this study (as opposed to the

TABLE 13
Gold Production in the Urals Production Corporation (Uralzoloto) (metric tons)

| | | | | | |
|---|---|---|---|---|---|
| 1940 | (9.0) | 1960 | (6.0) | 1971 | (9.2) |
| 1950 | (6.9) | 1961 | (6.3) | 1972 | (9.4) |
| 1951 | (6.7) | 1962 | (6.7) | 1973 | (9.6) |
| 1952 | (6.6) | 1963 | (7.0) | 1974 | (9.8) |
| 1953 | (6.5) | 1964 | (7.4) | 1975 | (10.0) |
| 1954 | (6.3) | 1965 | 7.8 | 1976 | (10.2) |
| 1955 | (6.3) | 1966 | 8.1 | 1977 | (10.4) |
| 1956 | (6.1) | 1967 | (8.3) | 1978 | (10.6) |
| 1957 | (6.0) | 1968 | (8.5) | 1979 | (10.8) |
| 1958 | (5.9) | 1969 | (8.8) | 1980 | (11.0) |
| 1959 | 5.7 | 1970 | 9.0 | 1990 | (13) |

Urban Places Associated with Gold Production

| Name | Oblast | Urban Designation | Date of Formation |
|---|---|---|---|
| Berezovsky | Sverdlovsk | town | 1938 |
| Is | Sverdlovsk | settlement | 1933 |
| Kosya | Sverdlovsk | settlement | 1933 |
| Kumak | Orenburg | settlement | 1936 |
| Kytlym | Sverdlovsk | settlement | 1933 |
| Mindyak | Bashkir ASSR | settlement | 1938 |
| Plast (Kochkar deposit) | Chelyabinsk | town | 1940 |

Source: For production and administration, see text. Dates of designation from *SSSR: deleniye*, pp. 19–32, 188–90, 217–22, 242–45.

TABLE 14
Gold Production in the Armenian Production
Corporation (Armzoloto) (metric tons)

| 1966 | 1 | 1974 | 2 |
|---|---|---|---|
| 1967 | 1 | 1975 | 2 |
| 1968 | 1 | 1976 | 9 |
| 1969 | 1 | 1977 | 10 |
| 1970 | 1 | 1978 | 10 |
| 1971 | 2 | 1979 | 10 |
| 1972 | 2 | 1980 | 10 |
| 1973 | 2 | 1990 | (20) |

Urban Centers Associated with the Zod Project

| Vardenis (former Basargechar; serves Zod mines) | settlement (1969) |
|---|---|
| Ararat (cement center; serves gold ore mill) | settlement (1938); town (1962) |

SOURCE: For production and administration, see text. Dates of designation from *SSSR: deleniye*, pp. 491–94.

writer's previous papers on gold) that their output is reported by the corporation concerned and should not be separately accounted. Not only, as explained above, do artels have "pay-book" and plan-target relations with their corporation (and its divisions) but they participate in socialist competition in exactly the same way as state employees do on placers.[319]

In consideration of future prospects, it is likely that the role of artels will increase to slow down the decline of placer production in areas where this cannot be done by mechanization. The decree of 1975, already noted, provides for the State Bank of the USSR to accord artels credit for up to 12 months so that they may pay their members advance dividends and to cover their production costs; for the Ministry of Nonferrous Metallurgy to establish lists of mines (other than diamond mines) that can be worked by artels, to cover some of the costs of artels in certain circumstances, and both to assist and control their operations; and for state trade agencies to supply food without requiring cash payment (i.e. to run an account like any state enterprise).[320] Artels or private citizens finding precious metals or diamonds may not take them out of the area of discovery and must deliver them to the appropriate "receiving points." The reliance on private initiative in the extraction of precious metals is in line with more recent policies to promote the private sector in agriculture and hence seems likely to continue.

Other Sources of Primary Gold

A rough estimate is included in Table 1 of 2 tons by 1990 from sources other than the corporations listed. Output from such areas is believed to have been negligible in both 1970 and 1980.

Small placers have been found in the Ukraine. In the Carpathian Mountains, some in the upper reaches of the Cheremosh River and near Kolomyya on the Prut were said to merit evaluation; a prospecting dredge was dispatched under a program of the Ukrainian State Planning Committee to increase prospecting outlays by 50 percent

during 1969 and 1970. Prut placers, discovered in 1963 on the west bank, were said to be worthy of commercial extraction because there was surplus manpower in the region and a good road network in Ivano-Frankovsk Oblast, which would partly at least offset the relatively low gold content. Surveys on the east bank of the Dnieper in Dnepropetrovsk Oblast have shown gold with nickel sulfide and with silver; one selected sample showed 36.7 grams of gold and 55.9 grams of silver per ton. Eight test drillings were made, of which two yielded a commercial ratio.

In European Russia, gold is known to exist in Yaroslavl, Vladimir and Tula oblasts; some, in upland sedimentary deposits, was found in 1967, in Voronezh Oblast. Gold of up to 0.6 grams per ton has been found in quartz veins in the Kursk Magnetic Anomaly iron-ore deposits. The first gold discovered in Russia was in Arkhangelsk province, a mine at Voitsa being worked between 1745 and 1784.

Placer deposits have been found at Inguri in Georgia and lodes in the Nakhichevan ASSR, and the substantial exploitation in Armenia suggests that the Caucasus may hold promise.

If any of this potential is to be exploited in the 1980s the price of gold on world markets (or Soviet expectations of the price) will have to remain high, and probably higher than at present with respect to other tradable goods. The Soviet Union may not entirely offset its loss of foreign earnings on oil exports by an increase in those from natural gas during the 1980s, and hence may expand high-cost sources of gold production to provide external purchasing power.

A wholly new area from which such extraction may take place is offshore. The Geological Institute of the Far East Center of the Academy of Sciences USSR drew up in 1974 a metallogenic map of a sub-Pacific ore belt along the Soviet littoral that showed both gold and tin,[321] and in 1980 an enterprise, Northern Maritime Tin (Sevmorolovo), was set up to mine tin from the Arctic continental shelf. A suction dredge with its own electric motor was tested for operation up to 100 meters below the ice and in 1981 was to be worked all the year round.[322] A study of four samples of marine sands in 1976 showed that centrifugal concentration permitted almost complete extraction of gold in two cases (94 to 97 percent) but low extraction in the others (not exceeding 52 percent) and there are undoubtedly technical difficulties to overcome before commercial utilization of offshore deposits is undertaken. Within a decade, that would be possible.

**Comparisons with Other Estimates**

The various regional estimates compiled in this study are brought together in Table 15. The estimates compiled in this study accord with the two others to which reference was made in the opening paragraphs. That for 1978 is 330 tons, and Gold Fields put for 1977–78 a range of 280 to 350 tons.[323] The Central Intelligence Agency's unclassified compendium of statistics gives 296 tons in its 1980 issue,[324] which represented an increase on the 1978 estimate published of 275 tons in the previous year's issue.[325]

TABLE 15
Summary of Gold Production Estimates 1940–80 (metric tons)

| Gold Producer | 1940 | 1950 | 1951 | 1952 | 1953 | 1954 | 1955 | 1956 | 1957 | 1958 | 1959 | 1960 | 1961 | 1962 | 1963 |
|---|---|---|---|---|---|---|---|---|---|---|---|---|---|---|---|
| Northeast Siberia | 61 | 53 | 54 | 56 | 58 | 51 | 42 | 37 | 35 | 34 | 37 | 40 | 44 | 49 | 53 |
| Maritime | 4 | 6 | 6 | 6 | 6 | 6 | 7 | 7 | 7 | 7 | 7 | 8 | 8 | 8 | 8 |
| Yakutia | 13 | 20 | 21 | 22 | 23 | 24 | 25 | 21 | 21 | 22 | 23 | 23 | 25 | 26 | 27 |
| Transbaikalia | 5 | 6 | 7 | 7 | 8 | 8 | 8 | 9 | 9 | 10 | 11 | 12 | 13 | 14 | 14 |
| Lena | 8 | 10 | 10 | 10 | 10 | 10 | 10 | 9 | 10 | 10 | 11 | 11 | 11 | 11 | 12 |
| Other Siberian Producers | 8 | 9 | 9 | 9 | 9 | 9 | 9 | 9 | 9 | 9 | 10 | 10 | 10 | 10 | 11 |
| Kazakhstan | 1 | 1 | 2 | 2 | 2 | 2 | 3 | 3 | 3 | 4 | 4 | 4 | 4 | 5 | 5 |
| Byproduct Suppliers | 8 | 12 | 14 | 17 | 18 | 19 | 20 | 21 | 22 | 23 | 24 | 27 | 30 | 32 | 34 |
| Tadzhik SSR | | | | | | | | | | | | | | | |
| Uzbek SSR | | | | | | | | | | | | | | | |
| Urals | 9 | 7 | 7 | 7 | 7 | 6 | 6 | 6 | 6 | 6 | 6 | 6 | 6 | 7 | 7 |
| Armenian SSR | | | | | | | | | | | | | | | |
| TOTAL | 117 | 124 | 130 | 136 | 141 | 135 | 130 | 122 | 122 | 125 | 133 | 141 | 151 | 162 | 171 |
| CIA ESTIMATES | | | | | | | | | | | | | | | |

Source: Tables 2 to 12; CIA, *Handbook of Economic Statistics, 1982*, p. 77.

| 1964 | 1965 | 1966 | 1967 | 1968 | 1969 | 1970 | 1971 | 1972 | 1973 | 1974 | 1975 | 1976 | 1977 | 1978 | 1979 | 1980 |
|---|---|---|---|---|---|---|---|---|---|---|---|---|---|---|---|---|
| 59 | 66 | 70 | 73 | 75 | 79 | 82 | 78 | 82 | 81 | 80 | 77 | 79 | 79 | 80 | 81 | 85 |
| 8 | 8 | 12 | 13 | 13 | 13 | 14 | 14 | 15 | 15 | 15 | 16 | 16 | 16 | 16 | 17 | 17 |
| 28 | 30 | 32 | 34 | 36 | 38 | 40 | 40 | 41 | 42 | 43 | 44 | 45 | 46 | 47 | 48 | 49 |
| 15 | 16 | 16 | 16 | 17 | 17 | 17 | 19 | 20 | 21 | 22 | 23 | 24 | 25 | 26 | 27 | 28 |
| 12 | 12 | 13 | 13 | 14 | 15 | 15 | 15 | 16 | 16 | 16 | 16 | 16 | 16 | 16 | 16 | 16 |
| 11 | 11 | 12 | 12 | 12 | 12 | 13 | 13 | 13 | 13 | 13 | 14 | 14 | 14 | 14 | 14 | 14 |
| 6 | 6 | 6 | 7 | 7 | 8 | 9 | 9 | 9 | 9 | 9 | 9 | 9 | 9 | 9 | 9 | 9 |
| 37 | 37 | 42 | 43 | 44 | 46 | 48 | 51 | 52 | 56 | 57 | 60 | 61 | 61 | 61 | 61 | 61 |
| | | | | 1 | 1 | 1 | 1 | 1 | 1 | 1 | 1 | 1 | 1 | 1 | 1 | 1 |
| | | | | 1 | 5 | 15 | 20 | 25 | 33 | 33 | 36 | 37 | 38 | 39 | 40 | 43 |
| 7 | 8 | 8 | 8 | 9 | 9 | 9 | 9 | 9 | 9 | 10 | 10 | 10 | 10 | 11 | 11 | 11 |
| | | 1 | 1 | 1 | 1 | 1 | 2 | 2 | 2 | 2 | 2 | 9 | 10 | 10 | 10 | 10 |
| 183 | 194 | 212 | 220 | 230 | 244 | 264 | 271 | 285 | 298 | 301 | 308 | 321 | 325 | 330 | 335 | 344 |
| | 166 | 177 | 185 | 193 | 205 | 218 | 224 | 243 | 250 | 262 | 258 | 276 | 285 | 296 | 307 | 317 |

The convergence of the three sets of estimates draws to a close a period of considerable controversy. No official Soviet statistics have appeared other than those for 1928, but the external estimates for the ensuing decade brought together in Table 16 carried credence. It is of interest that the U.S. Mint's estimate, in very rounded figures for 1939

TABLE 16
Soviet Gold Production, 1922–40 (metric tons)

| 1922/23 | 11 | 1930 | 45 | 1936 | 161 |
|---|---|---|---|---|---|
| 1923/24 | 20 | 1931 | 53 | 1937 | 167 |
| 1924/25 | 25 | 1932 | 62 | 1938 | 163 |
| 1926/27 | 23 | 1933 | 77 | 1939 | 155 |
| 1928 | 28 | 1934 | 120 | 1940 | 117–125 |
| 1929 | 33 | 1935 | 149 | | |

Source: 1922/23 to 1928 from Amtorg, *Economic Review of the Soviet Union*, III, cited by A. C. Sutton, *Western Technology and Soviet Economic Development 1917–1930* (Stanford, Ca.: Hoover Institution, 1968), p. 96; 1929–33 from A. Z. Arnold, *Banks, Credit and Money in Soviet Russia* (New York: Columbia University Press, 1938, p. 416); 1934–40, estimates of the United States Mint cited by H. Schwartz, *Russia's Soviet Economy*, 2nd edn. (Englewood Cliffs, N.J.: Prentice-Hall, 1954), p. 484 (upper figure of 1940 range); Table 15 (lower figure of 1940 range).

and 1940, of a sharp decline in Soviet gold production are borne out by those in the present study: 117 tons (3.76 million ounces) here compared with 4 million ounces, implying (if the estimate for Dalstroi is correct), a fall (to 56 tons) of gold produced by other fields (which, by difference, the present writer estimates above as 73 tons in 1938). On these estimates, Dalstroi just topped 60 tons both before World War II and after it, but never could have reached the 400 tons in 1940 or 300 tons in 1946 attributed on the basis of reports from former prisoners in 1947.[326] Such magnitudes led Western commentators to place high totals on aggregate Soviet output: a postwar peak of 300 tons in 1945 was succeeded by a nadir of 150 tons in 1950, whereafter a steady rise took place to 240 tons in 1964.[327] In 1964, however, the CIA put out a revised estimate of as low as 135 to 155 tons (which compares with 171 tons here estimated for 1963). By 1970 the CIA series showed 203 tons[328] but was reduced to a slightly lower level in 1978, in which the revised 1970 figure, for example, became 199 tons.[329] For subsequent years the disparity was wider: thus the former series showed 308 tons for 1975, but the revised series only 255 tons. The present writer notes, with considerable interest, that his present series yields 308 tons for 1975 or virtually the same as the early CIA series.

Meanwhile he had contributed to the 1971 study, estimating 208 tons for 1970;[330] with Dowie in 1974, levels were revised to 346 tons for that year.[331] For reasons explained above (some double-counting and excessive assessments of certain fields) an output of some 344 tons seems justified for 1980.[332]

### Reserves and Sales

The difference between estimates of Soviet gold reserves at the end of 1935 and at the end of 1960 can be used as a rough verification of the output series and an indication

that, if the reserve estimates are correct, a higher output series for 1936–60 is preferable to the lower estimates of the CIA.

Before stating that case, two other procedures that serve to verify the estimates for 1960 may be mentioned. First, a Soviet textbook of economic geography stated in 1963 that "Eastern Siberia is at present the biggest supplier of gold in the country."[333] The book went to press in December 1962 and statistics cited in it refer to 1961 at the latest. If the statement refers to 1961, the estimates of this study show 51 tons output, which is greater than that for Northeast Siberia, the next biggest production area, 44 tons.[334] Second, a book of 1961 stated that "whereas the major proportion of Magadan Oblast output is from placers, elsewhere about half the production is from ores and half from placers."[335] This statement is taken to refer to

TABLE 17
Soviet Gold Reserves (metric tons at 31 December)

| | Official State Bank Returns | |
|---|---|---|
| | | Total |
| 1913 | | 1,183[a] |
| 1917[b] | | 1,000[c] |
| 1927 | | 146 |
| 1935 | | 247[d] |

| | CIA Estimates | | | | | |
|---|---|---|---|---|---|---|
| | First Estimate | | Second Estimate | Latest Estimate | | |
| | Total | Yearly Change | Total | Total | Yearly Change | Disposals[e] |
| 1960 | 2,270 | — | — | — | — | — |
| 1961 | 2,100 | −170 | — | — | — | — |
| 1962 | 2,000 | −100 | — | — | — | — |
| 1963 | 1,600 | −400 | — | — | — | — |
| 1964 | 1,330 | −270 | — | — | — | — |
| 1965 | 975 | −355 | 903 | 921 | — | — |
| 1966 | 1,125 | +150 | 1,036 | 1,027 | +106 | −71 |
| 1967 | 1,265 | +140 | 1,176 | 1,146 | +119 | −66 |
| 1968 | 1,415 | +150 | 1,324 | 1,287 | +141 | −52 |
| 1969 | 1,570 | +155 | 1,478 | 1,455 | +168 | −37 |
| 1970 | 1,730 | +160 | 1,638 | 1,631 | +176 | −42 |
| 1971 | 1,895 | +165 | 1,746 | 1,797 | +166 | −58 |
| 1972 | 1,950 | +55 | 1,729 | 1,842 | +45 | −198 |
| 1973 | 1,850[f] | −100 | 1,647 | 1,747 | −195 | −445 |
| 1974 | — | — | 1,704 | 1,836 | +89 | −173 |
| 1975 | — | — | 1,776 | 1,899 | +63 | −195 |
| 1976 | — | — | 1,642 | 1,797 | −102 | −378 |
| 1977 | — | — | 1,536 | 1,702 | −95 | −380 |
| 1978 | — | — | 1,389 | 1,527 | −175 | −471 |
| 1979 | — | — | — | 1,581 | +54 | −253 |
| 1980 | — | — | — | 1,811 | +230 | −87 |
| 1981 | — | — | — | 1,889 | +78 | −248 |

[a]Plus 130 held abroad and 383 circulating as gold coin.
[b]1 November.
[c]Plus 1,789 held abroad.
[d]Plus an undisclosed stock held "for emergency purposes" by the People's Commissariat of Finance (see Arnold, *Banks, Credit and Money*, p. 414).
[e]From CIA estimates of output and annual change.
[f]NATO estimate approximately 2,000 (quoted *Financial Times*, 12 July 1974, citing *NATO Review*).
Source: 1914–36 balance sheets of the State Bank cited in gold rubles in A. Z. Arnold, *Banks, Credit and Money in the Soviet Union* (New York, 1937) Tables 1, 7 and 60 at 1.29 rubles per gram, except in 1936 when the content had become 5.67 rubles per gram of fine gold. First CIA estimates for 1961–74 *USSR: Long-Range Prospects for Hard Currency Trade* (Washington: January 1975), Table 1; second CIA estimates from CIA, *Handbook of Economic Statistics 1979*, p. 69; latest CIA estimates from CIA, *Handbook of Economic Statistics 1982*, p. 77.

1960, when this study finds about 30 lode mines in operation. If each produced between 1.5 and 2 tons, output from lodes would have been 45 to 60 tons; half of this study's estimate for the USSR, less Northeast Siberia (Table 15) is 50 tons. It may also be recalled that two statements relating Yakutia to total output have been reconciled with the estimates for that area, namely that it represented about one-fifth of the Soviet total[336] and that it accounted for 53.5 percent of all Siberian placer production.[337]

Table 17 shows the official returns of Russian and Soviet gold reserves in 1913, 1917, 1927 and 1935. It is of some historical interest that (if the CIA estimates for the end of 1979 are correct) the stock on the eve of World War I, to which one would add gold rubles in circulation and a little bullion held abroad (1,696 tons in all), was less than that at the end of 1979 (1,581 tons), for external trade (imports plus exports) in gold rubles represented a value of 2,241 tons in 1913, and 79,279 tons in 1979.[338] The official return for the end of 1935 is incomplete because bullion was also held by the Commissariat of Finance "for emergency purposes." For the purposes of the calculation in Table 18 it is assumed that such a reserve would not have exceeded half the State Bank's reserve (247 tons) and the total availability is put at 350 tons. Gold had been disbursed heavily under the 1st Five-Year Plan (1928–32) for equipment purchases and under the 2nd (1933–37) the commercial credits incurred under the 1st were being repaid: a high gold reserve is most unlikely. Between 1936 and 1960, both years inclusive, some industrial use must have taken place. As already noted, the CIA does not specify its consumption estimates, but for 1966–70, when virtually no sales for convertible currency took place (see Table 19), its implied allowance (output increment less rise in reserves) varies between 37 and 71 tons, or about

### TABLE 18
Reconciliation of Gold Reserves 1935 and 1960
(metric tons)

| | | |
|---|---|---|
| 1. Cumulative production | 1936 to 1940 | 763 |
| 2. Cumulative production | 1941 to 1949 | 1,080 |
| 3. Cumulative production | 1950 to 1960 | 1,439 |
| 4. Total | 1936 to 1960 | 3,282 |
| 5. *Less* industrial use | 1936 to 1969 | −210 |
| 6. *Less* sales to West | 1936 to 1960 | −1,281 |
| 7. Net addition to reserves | | 1,791 |
| 8. Reserves 31 December 1960 | | 2,270 |
| 9. *Less* reserves 31 December 1935 | | −350 |
| 10. Net addition to reserves | | 1,920 |

NOTE: This calculation serves to verify the orders of magnitude of the estimates made in this study from the known 1935 and the estimated 1960 reserve and could indicate that either the cumulative output less disposals is 130 tons too low or 1960 reserves are 130 tons too high.

SOURCE:
Row 1: Table 16
Row 2: estimated roughly at 120 tons per year
Row 3: Table 15
Row 5: 6 tons for 1935–50, 11 tons for 1950–60 (which compares with an average estimated by the CIA of 54 tons in 1966–71) for industrial uses
Row 6: sales for convertible currency of 1,105 tons in 1953–60 from Table 19
Rows 8 and 9: from Table 17 (assuming 100 tons in Commissariat of Finance in 1935).

### TABLE 19
Soviet Gold Sales for Convertible Currency
(metric tons)

| | | | | | |
|---|---|---|---|---|---|
| 1953 | 75 | 1963 | 500 | 1973 | 280 |
| 1954 | 75 | 1964 | 410 | 1974 | 227 |
| 1955 | 75 | 1965 | 487 | 1975 | 141 |
| 1956 | 150 | 1966 | — | 1976 | 341 |
| 1957 | 260 | 1967 | 14 | 1977 | 338 |
| 1958 | 220 | 1968 | 11 | 1978 | 422 |
| 1959 | 250 | 1969 | — | 1979 | 223 |
| 1960 | 176 | 1970 | — | 1980 | 70 |
| 1961 | 270 | 1971 | — | 1981 | 290 |
| 1962 | 195 | 1972 | 150 | | |

SOURCE: 1953–59, Kaser, "Soviet Gold," p. 229; 1960, 1965 and 1973–79 from proceeds of gold sales and mean gold price in CIA, *Handbook 1979*, pp. 67 and 41, and CIA, *Handbook 1980*, pp. 61 and 40; 1961–64 and 1966–72 from CIA, *USSR: Long-Range Prospects for Hard Currency Trade* (Washington: January 1975), p. 2; 1980–81, *Economic Survey of Europe* (New York: United Nations), p. 311, and *Gold 1981*, p. 18, less estimate for sales by other Communist countries (verified from other sources).

one-third of production. By that time, however, gold was in demand for electronics, whereas in the 1930s and 1940s it was used industrially only in chemical and electrical engineering and in photography.[339] Little decorative or dental use was authorized and it is believed that the jewelry trade was exclusively supplied from recycled gold (purchased or confiscated from private citizens). As an absolute minimum an allocation of 6 tons annually is put for 1935 to 1950 and 11 tons annually thereafter (a higher allowance on the assumption of increased allotments to industry and to decorative uses once postwar reconstruction was complete.[340] Sales for convertible currency were, it seems, stopped once the economy was self-sufficient (exports were down to 0.5 percent of gross national product[341]), and resumed only in 1953. Sales from 1953 to 1960 were some 1,281 tons.

Thus the present writer's output series (Table 15 with an estimate for 1941–49 at the average of 1940 and 1950) cumulates to 3,282 tons, from which at least 1,491 tons were withdrawn, leaving 1,791 tons to add to reserves. The increment between the 350 tons reserve of 1935 and the 2,270 tons of 1960 estimated by the CIA is 1,920 tons. Output should be higher (rather than lower) than the estimates shown in this study; the CIA output series is lower than those shown here.

The political controversy over the CIA series arises because the USSR would patently have been depleting stocks (on known sales to the West) more rapidly than on any higher series. On the estimates made here, deducting 50 tons rising to 60 tons annually for disposals other than such sales,[342] stocks would have been reduced in 1976–78 (Table 20). Of the 1990 projected output of some 470 tons (Table 1), 70 tons could be deducted for disposals other than sales to the West, leaving 400 tons as a discretionary volume for sale without affecting stocks. Whether those sales are made (or more or less is sold by depletion or accretion to reserve) depends on the world price and the Soviet need for convertible currency.

Of these two, the incentive to sell at the world price depends on its relationship to the domestic cost price and the domestic retail price.

Between July 1967 and January 1976, wholesale prices

TABLE 20
Output and Disposals 1975–80 (metric tons)

|  | 1975 | 1976 | 1977 | 1978 | 1979 | 1980 |
|---|---|---|---|---|---|---|
| Output | 308 | 321 | 325 | 330 | 335 | 344 |
| Sales to West | 141 | 341 | 338 | 422 | 223 | 70 |
| Other disposals | 50 | 52 | 54 | 56 | 58 | 60 |
| Net change in reserves | +117 | −72 | −67 | −148 | +54 | +214 |

SOURCE: Tables 15 and 19 and estimate of other disposals (see note 342).

(which are cost prices plus a profit mark-up that has to include a 6 percent charge on capital assets) for nonferrous metals were virtually unchanged: for the Ministry as a whole the profit mark-up was 11 to 13 percent of the sum of labor materials and depreciation.[343] According to the Minister of Nonferrous Metallurgy USSR, the changes introduced in 1976–80 "should insure that all normally operating enterprises are profitable . . . Wholesale prices for nonferrous ores and concentrates are linked in most cases to their metallurgical value."[344] Gold of 583 fineness (14 carats) was sold between 1967 and 1976 to industrial users at 3.804 rubles per gram; in 1,000 fineness (24 carats), it was 6.42 rubles per gram. Gold bought from the general public was being bought in 1978 at 11.65 rubles per gram of 1,000 fineness (24 carats)[345] or 362 rubles per ounce. Two court cases have indicated still higher prices for illegal sales. A miner at the Sarala mine in Ordzhonikidzevsky (Khakas Autonomous Oblast) tried to sell stolen gold in Alma-Ata for 18,000 rubles:[346] nuggets of 516 and 106 grams were mentioned. If that was the sum total, then the black market price for 622 grams would have been 28.93 rubles per gram, but would have been lower if more was at stake. Another theft by a gold miner the following year revealed a black market price of 16 rubles per gram.[347]

A study by an official of the Ministry of Nonferrous Metals used in 1977 an exchange rate of one dollar to one ruble in comparing Soviet wholesale prices of nonferrous metals with those on the world market[348] and the above ruble prices may thus approximately be taken as dollars. Thus at world prices in excess of $200 per ounce, sales were acceptable on profitability grounds.

The Soviet authorities sell gold jewelry in foreign-currency shops at prices that are not aligned to the world price at the official rate. In October 1979, the unit price of 14 carats (in a ring) was 8.74 rubles per gram, the equivalent of 15 rubles per gram of 24 carats, or 466 rubles per ounce.[349] Because the ruble is exchanged in such shops at the official parity, the dollar equivalent was $724 per ounce; the world price was in fact $400 per ounce at the time, and an exchange rate of nearly twice the official would seem relevant, as indicated in the next paragraph.

Domestic retail prices are still higher. In April 1969, the price was 5.647 rubles per gram[350] for 583 fineness (14 carats), or 9.686 rubles for 24 carats, that is 301 rubles per ounce. Retail prices of gold and silver jewelry were raised by 60 percent in March 1978[351] and by a further 50 percent in July 1979,[352] and reached 45 rubles (14 carats) per gram by November 1981, or 1,400 rubles per ounce. The Comecon rate of 2.30 Soviet rubles to the transferable ruble,[353]

equivalent to the ruble-dollar rate, is the best conversion factor, putting 14 carat gold at $795 per ounce. The retail price in dollar terms thus appears to be double the wholesale price, but it is the latter, estimated at least as $660 per ounce, that determines whether exports are profitable.

Soviet willingness to sell gold at prices below that floor depends on the need for foreign currency to pay for imports. In the context of gold production, continued sales can be expected within a range determined by world prices and by the accounting loss suffered for gold compared with the loss (or profit) for alternative exports.

## NOTES

1. Kang Chao, "The China-Watchers Tested," *The China Quarterly*, 81 (March 1980): 97.

2. David Dowie, "The Production of Primary Gold during 1970 by the Soviet Union," in *A Methodological Study of the Production of Primary Gold by the Soviet Union* (London: Privately circulated by Consolidated Gold Fields, 1974), pp. 1–46.

3. The present writer's first examination of Soviet gold production was "Soviet Gold Production and Use" in D. Lloyd-Jacobs, P. Fells, et. al., *Gold 1971* (New York: Walker, 1971), pp. 146–216. Previous Western estimates are collated by Diethard Stelzl, "Aspekte der Produktion; des Verkaufs und der Reserven von Gold in den osteuropäischen Ländern," *Jahrbuch der Wirtschaft Osteuropas*, 1973, no. 4, pp. 397–421; the principal later studies are Richard Rockingham Gill, "Impact of Price Movements on Soviet Gold Reserves and Foreign Trade Debt," *Osteuropa Wirtschaft*, 1974, no. 2, pp. 112–19; the annual studies of Consolidated Gold Fields (London), *Gold 1972* to *Gold 1980* (privately circulated) and the present writer's "Soviet Gold Production," in United States Congress Joint Economic Committee, *The Soviet Economy in a Time of Change* 2, (Washington: United States Government Printing Office, 1979): 290–96.

4. Kaser, "Soviet Gold," pp. 160–93.

5. Dowie, "Production," and Kaser, "Regional Time-Series for Gold Production," in *A Methodological Study of the Production of Primary Gold by the Soviet Union* (London: Privately circulated by Consolidated Gold Fields, 1974), pp. 55–115.

6. Christopher Glynn, *Gold 1978* (London: Privately circulated by Consolidated Gold Fields, 1978), pp. 45–51.

7. Christopher Glynn, *Gold 1979* (London: Privately circulated by Consolidated Gold Fields, 1979), pp. 48–50.

8. David Potts, *Gold 1980* (London: Privately circulated by Consolidated Gold Fields, 1980), pp. 50–58.

9. Michael Beckett, *Financial Post*, Conference, Toronto, 24 January 1980. The text of the speech was kindly furnished to the present writer by the author, but was widely reported in financial newspapers at the time.

10. I. A. Strigin (Chief Editor) and A. V. Troitsky, "Pages from the past (the years of the first five-year plans)," *Tsvetnye metally*, 1976, no. 9, p. 15.

11. On the 1925 concession, E. H. Carr, *Socialism in One Country 1924–1926*, 3 (London: Macmillan, 1964): 414; on

the 1928 abrogation, E. H. Carr and R. W. Davies, *Foundations of a Planned Economy 1926–1929*, 1–2 (London: Macmillan, 1969): 715; on the discussions within the parent company, A. P. Cartwright, *Gold Paved the Way: the Story of the Gold Fields Group of Companies* (London: Macmillan, 1967), p. 180; and on the operations in the USSR, J. Littlepage and D. Bess, *In Search of Soviet Gold* (New York, 1937). Tsvetmetzoloto closed in 1930 the central laboratories of its Mining Chemical Trust (reportedly well-equipped and with a staff of 50, headed by a foreign specialist); the premises were apparently needed by the state corporation (*obyedineniye*) to accommodate its tariffs and rates department. See *Vtoroi plenum komiteta po khimizatsii narodnogo khozyaistva SSSR 28 V-2 VI 1930 g.*, (Leningrad, 1932), p. 306, cited in R. Lewis, *Science and Industrialization in the USSR* (London: Macmillan, 1979), p. 112.

12. The acronym is Mintsvetmet; the acronym Mintsvetmetzoloto stands for the Moscow Institute of Nonferrous Metals and Gold named after M. I. Kalinin. See *Slovar sokrashchenii russkogo yazyka* [Dictionary of Russian language abbreviations] (Moscow, 1963), p. 259, for the expansion of the acronym; Mintsvetmetzoloto in the 1930s is noted in *Tsvetnye metally*, 1976, no. 9, p. 19.

13. P.F. Lomako (Minister of Nonferrous Metallurgy of the USSR), "Nonferrous metallurgy during the Great Patriotic War," *Tsvetnye metally*, 1974, no. 4, pp. 1–27.

14. Thus in Dzhugdzhurzoloto, Ynykchansky was worked by "thousands" of convicts whereas the free workers were at the smaller Minor. One of those free workers of 1940–42, now Professor Israel Getzler, senior associate member of St. Antony's College, Oxford (to whom the author is indebted for this information) was a *spetspereselenets* ("special settler"), compulsorily removed from that part of Poland annexed by the USSR for declining Soviet citizenship. The so-called free workers were not necessarily there of their own volition. An oblique public reference by the Minister of Nonferrous Metallurgy recently appeared. In Kolyma, he wrote, "at the start of February 1943, a universal recruiting drive was launched to provide a tank column named after Feliks Dzerzhinsky (evidently for NKVD workers). Those who volunteered for the army to join that column were numerous. It was not possible to satisfy all such requests." P. F. Lomako, "In mortal combat with the aggressors," *Tsvetnye metally*, 1980, no. 5, p. 12.

15. *Tsvetnye metally*, 1980, no. 5, p. 7. In accordance with what must be a censorship requirement on silence about forced labor, the workers are called "men of Norilsk" (norilchane) and the head of the enterprise, A. A. Panykov, "director of the combine."

16. Mentioned in *Sobraniye postanovlenii Pravitelstva SSSR*, 1975, no. 9, p. 181.

17. Prison labor has been reported as still used at Korkino (Chelyabinsk Oblast) and in the Lena fields (Nikolai Scharegin, a former prisoner, *Now*, London: 12 December 1980, p. 64).

18. P. F. Lomako, "The nonferrous metallurgy of the USSR at a new stage," *Tsvetnye metally*, 1976, no. 5, p. 5.

19. Magadan Radio, 27 February 1975. These and subsequent monitored reports are reproduced from the summaries published by the British Broadcasting Corporation (by permission).

20. Lomako, "Nonferrous metallurgy," (1976), p. 5.

21. P. F. Lomako, "On the road set out by Great October," *Tsvetnye metally*, 1977, no. 10, pp. 4, 11; all main administrations (*glavki*) were stated to have been liquidated.

22. Lomako, "Nonferrous metallurgy," (1976), p. 5.

23. F. P. Yeltsev, "Improve the exploitation and repair of technical equipment in nonferrous metallurgical enterprises," *Tsvetnye metally*, 1980, no. 6, pp. 5 and 7. The corporations correspondingly handed over their building agencies: thus Severovostoksantekhmash was put under Minmontazhspetsstroi, *Stroitelnaya gazeta*, 17 September 1980, p. 2.

24. Robert Conquest, *Kolyma. The Arctic Death Camps* (London: Macmillan, 1978), p. 231. The principal reports had been employed by the present writer for Kaser, "Regional Time-Series."

25. Conquest, *Kolyma*, pp. 38–39.

26. For a biography obscuring most of his relevant work, because it was published when Kolyma was being exploited by forced labor, see *Bolshaya sovetskaya entsiklopediya* [Great Soviet Encyclopedia], 5, 2nd ed., (Moscow, 1950): 167 (hereafter *BSE*); for a fuller biography see the same, 3, 3rd. ed., (Moscow, 1970): 320, which also gives the chemical composition of bilibinite.

27. *Slovar sokrashchenii*, p. 157.

28. Ibid., p. 122.

29. It is mentioned by S. M. Navasardov and V. L. Svechinsky, *Bioklimaticheskiye i gigiyenicheskiye aspekty arkhitekturnoplanirovochnogo resheniya zhilogo kompleksa na Severe* (Magadan, 1968) and by V.V. Yanovsky, Ye. M. Kokorev and Ye. M. Shershakova, *Demografosotsiologicheskiye obosnovaniya dlya proyektirovanii tipovykh priiskovykh kompleksov Severo-Vostoka* (Magadan, 1968), cited by V. V. Yanovsky, *Chelovek i sever* [Man and the north] (Magadan, 1969), pp. 119 and 113, respectively.

30. Henry A. Wallace, *Soviet Asia Mission* (New York: Reynal and Hitchcock, 1946), p. 32. The description of him as chairman of the Executive Committee is from the same.

31. Indictment in the Beria case, *Pravda*, 17 December 1953, and court decision, *Pravda*, 24 December 1953, both translated in R. Conquest, *Power and Policy in the USSR* (London: Macmillan, 1961), pp. 441 and 446 respectively.

32. Vladimir Petrov, *Escape from the Future* (Bloomington, Ind.: Indiana University Press, 1973), pp. 124, 129–31.

33. See Conquest, *Kolyma*, esp. pp. 43–46; Yanovsky, *Chelovek*, p. 16.

34. Wallace, *Soviet Asia*, quotations from pp. 33 and 134 respectively.

35. Michael Solomon, *Magadan* (Toronto, 1971), cited by Conquest, *Kolyma*, p. 70.

36. Yanovsky, *Chelovek*, p. 59.

37. P. F. Lomako, *Tsvetnye metally*, 1971, no. 1.

38. Stalin's words are cited in A.P. Serebrovsky, *On the Gold Front*, quoted by Timothy Green, *The World of Gold Today*, 2nd ed., (Harmondsworth: Penguin, 1973), pp. 84–85.

39. Alexander Solzhenitsyn, *The Gulag Archipelago*, 1 (London: Collins/Harvill Press, 1974): 52.

40. Conquest, *Kolyma*, p. 41.

41. "Golden age" for the period under Berzin is from Varlam Shalamov, *Récits de Kolyma* (Paris, 1969), cited by Conquest, *Kolyma*, p. 43, who (pp. 44–47) quotes confirmation by other former prisoners, who term the period from late 1937 as the "tempest" (p. 49). At that later time, intellectuals were herded with the rest and even particularly humiliated, but under Berzin their expertise was usefully employed. Thus A.Ye. Khodorov, formerly of the Bureau of Scientific Agricultural Literature, "was in 1936 subject to lawless reprisals on a slanderous denunciation. . . (He) managed in the Far North to apply his knowledge of geobotany. His manuscripts, "The Vegetation Resources of the Coast of the Sea of Okhotsk," and "Fodder Resources and Reindeer Pastures" were handed over to the Department of Reindeer Breeding of Dalstroi" (from an article rehabilitating him by V. N. Nikiforov, "Abram Yevseyevich Khodorov (on his 80th birthday)," *Narody Azii i Afriki*, 1966, no. 5, pp. 219–23, cited by Ines Rubin, *Approach to Factual Material in Recent Soviet Bibliographical and Biobibliographical Publications*, Research Paper no. 41, Soviet and East European Research Centre of the Hebrew University of Jerusalem (Jerusalem, 1981), p. 30. Berzin, shot on 11 November 1939, apparently as a Japanese spy (Conquest, *Kolyma*, p. 46), has been rehabilitated and a mine is named after him (Magadan Radio, 22 April 1977, as reported by the BBC monitoring service).

42. Arthur Z. Arnold, *Banks, Credit and Money in Soviet Russia* (New York: Columbia University Press, 1937), p. 416 gives 52.8 to 130.6 metric tons. Estimates of the United States Mint, cited by Harry Schwartz, *Russia's Soviet Economy*, 2nd ed., (Englewood Cliffs, N.J.: Prentice-Hall, 1954), p. 484, range in fine ounces from 1,655,725 (53.2 tons) to 3,858,089 (124.1 tons).

43. Petrov, *Escape*, p. 158.

44. Silvester Mora (pseudonym of Kazimierz Zamorski) *Kolyma—Gold and Forced Labor in the USSR* (Washington and New York, 1947), p. 10, cited by Stelzl, "Aspekte der Produktion," p. 406.

45. Petrov, *Escape*, p. 240.

46. Stelzl, "Aspekte der Produktion," p. 406.

47. K. I. Vronsky, *Na zolotoi Kolyme* [In golden Kolyma] (Moscow, 1965).

48. The estimate of arrivals and of executions is from Elinor Lipper, *Eleven Years in Soviet Prison Camps* (London and Chicago, 1951), pp. 172 and 107 respectively. Reports of declining productivity abound. Thus Solzhenitsyn, *Gulag*, 2 (1975): 567, writes of 500 miners sent to drive shafts in March 1938 at Zarosshi Spring (Shturmovoi mines); initial metal content was found to be low, the working was abandoned and, in the thaw, the shafts collapsed. But the whole effort was repeated in March 1939 at the same spot.

49. Conquest, *Kolyma*, pp. 105–06.

50. *Narodnoye khozyaistvo Magadanskoi oblasti* [The economy of Magadan Oblast] (Magadan, 1960), p. 71.

51. Lipper, *Eleven Years*, pp. 102–03.

52. Naum Jasny, "Labour and Output in Soviet Concentration Camps," *Journal of Political Economy*, 59 (October 1951), pp. 405–19.

53. Petrov, *Escape*, p. 201; his mine produced 5 tons with 2,000 men (2.5 kg per man), but this was "hardly one-half of what others delivered."

54. Kaser, "Soviet Gold," p. 164.

55. Dowie, "Production," p. 14.

56. Conquest, *Kolyma*, p. 227, estimates an average prisoner population during 1944–53 of 300,000 to 500,000 compared with 400,000 in 1940. On p. 65 he points out that only prisoners sentenced to less than 5 years benefited from the 1953 amnesty; most of the releases (those sentenced for 15 to 25 years) came in 1955 and 1956. Hence manpower was probably constant to 1955.

57. Schwartz, *Soviet Economy*, p. 484: 5,235,909 ounces. The Mint's estimates for 1939 and 1940 (5 and 4 million ounces) are confirmed by the present study (see Table 16).

58. Stanislaw Swaniewicz, *Forced Labour and Economic Development. An Enquiry into the Experience of Soviet Industrialization* (London: Oxford University Press, 1965), p. 292.

59. Lipper, *Eleven Years*, p. 108. Conquest, *Kolyma*, p. 106 notes that "of several thousand prisoners and 800 free citizens" embarked in the summer of 1940 only 150 prisoners and 200 free citizens survived to return to Magadan after a winter there. The area was eventually opened up and he estimates 20,000 prisoners to have been working at four mines at Omsukchan in 1949. The tin lodes were becoming exhausted in the 1970s but a major gold mine, named Dukat (described below), opened in 1970.

60. Lipper, *Eleven Years*, p. 277.

61. Conquest, *Kolyma* p. 105.

62. Petrov, *Escape*, p. 187.

63. Wallace, *Soviet Asia*, p. 35. The word "community" is his.

64. *Problemy razvitiya proizvoditelnykh sil Magadanskoi oblasti* [Development problems of Magadan Oblast] (Moscow, 1961).

65. *Ekonomicheskaya geografiya SSSR: Dalni Vostok* [Economic geography of the USSR: the Far East] (Moscow, 1966), p. 448 (one of a 22-volume economic geography of the USSR).

66. *Izvestiya Sibirskogo Otdeleniya Akademii Nauk SSSR*, 1967, no. 11.

67. S. S. Korzhuyev, ed., *Yakutiya* (Moscow, 1965), p. 60.

68. *Ekonomicheskaya gazeta*, 1966, no. 31.

69. *Partiinaya zhizn*, 1979, no. 14.

70. V. F. Seletsky, *Gody rosta* [Years of growth] (Magadan, 1971), p. 9, 1968, 113.6; 1969, 119.2; and 1970, 123.9.

71. Employment in branches not otherwise specified was in Magadan Oblast as follows (in thousands): 30 in 1940, 120 in 1950, 69 in 1955 and 57 in 1959 (*Narodnoye khozyaistvo Magadana*, 1960, p. 71); *Problemy* gives total Dalstroi employment in 1952 as 233,000.

72. Dowie, "Production," p. 8.

73. Seletsky, *Gody*, p. 5.

74. Mora, in Stelzl, "Aspekte der Produktion," p. 406 gives 300 tons for 1946.

75. *Dalni Vostok*, p. 449.

76. Petrov, *Escape*, p. 130; he also describes the considerable emoluments of the volunteer worker in Dalstroi.

77. For details and figures of the regions affected, see Terence Armstrong, *Soviet Northern Development, With Some Alaskan Parallels and Contrasts*, Occassional Paper no. 2 of the Institute of Social, Economic and Government Research (Fairbanks, Alaska: University of Alaska, 1970), esp. pp. 24–27, and Armstrong, "The Boundaries of the 'Far North'" and "Localities Equated to the 'Far North' in the USSR," *Polar Record*, 14, no. 93 (1969): 836–40.

78. Theodore Shabad, "Trip Reports: Magadan and the Upper Kolyma Country," *Soviet Geography: Review and Translation* (hereafter *SGRT*) 21, no. 2 (February 1980): 100.

79. "A Discussion of the 1971–75 Five-Year Plan," *Tsvetnye metally*, 1968, no. 7, p. 2. The qualifying noun *imeni* ("in the name of" or "named for") is omitted in this text (Matrosov and Gastello are the relevant names of the Northeast).

80. Kaser, "Soviet Gold," p. 153 puts 3 tons for the Northeast (which, as shown below, can break down into 2.4 tons from Matrosov and 0.7 tons from Polyarny); Dowie, "Production," p. 34, estimated 2.4 tons, but both he and Kaser, "Regional Time-Series," p. 69, attached importance to Mandrikovo and Neva, leading the former to attribute to three mines 2.5 tons apiece (i.e. 7.5 tons in the Northeast, Dowie, p. 37).

81. Theodore Shabad, "News Notes," *SGRT* 15, no. 6 (June 1974): 385 and 20, no. 2 (February 1979): 125.

82. Seletsky, *Gody*, pp. 1 and 12.

83. *Sovetskaya Rossiya*, 3 March 1972, and *Sotsialisticheskaya industriya*, 13 November 1979, cited by Shabad in "News Notes," *SGRT* 21, no. 3 (March 1980): 185.

84. *Pravda*, 12 March 1974.

85. *Na stroikakh Rossii*, 1978, no. 8, p. 5 with an illustration of the mill buildings cited and reproduced by Shabad in *SGRT*, 21, no. 3 (March 1980): 185.

86. Seletsky, *Gody*, pp. 15–16 and Shabad, "News Notes," *SGRT* 19, no. 3 (March 1978): 215.

87. Shabad, "New Notes," *SGRT* 21, no. 5 (May 1980): 323.

88. *Dalni Vostok*, p. 450.

89. *Trud*, 5 March 1958.

90. *Sobraniye postanovlenii Pravitelstva SSSR*, 1975, no. 9, pp. 163–81 (decree no. 47 of 1975).

91. Magadan Radio, 21 May 1979.

92. Ibid., 5 June 1980 (the quotation, which may not be verbatim, is from *BBC Summary of World Broadcasts*, Part 1, *USSR: Weekly Economic Report*, Second series, SO/W 1092, 18 July 1980, p. A17).

93. Kaser, "Soviet Gold," p. 153.

94. Dowie, "Production," p. 43 and Kaser, "Regional Time-Series," p. 116.

95. Dowie, "Production," p .15.

96. Seletsky, *Gody*, p. 71.

97. The search for a published target included Dr. Christie's examination of Soviet media and the writers' perusal of *BBC Summary of World Broadcasts*, Part I, *USSR: Weekly Economic Report*, the *Current Digest of the Soviet Press, Extracts from the Soviet Press of the Soviet North*, and *Tsvetnye metally*, all for 1975–80.

98. Magadan Radio, 23 January and 28 February 1975 (the latter cited the 9.8 percent productivity plan).

99. Dowie, "Production" p. 12.

100. *Yezhegodnik Bolshoi Sovetskoi Entsiklopedii* [Annual of the Great Soviet Encyclopedia] (hereafter *Yezhegodnik BSE*), 1971, p. 51; see also Shabad, "News Notes," *SGRT* 12, no. 3 (March 1971): 178, and John Sallnow, "Cherskiy and the Lower Kolyma Valley," (Trip Report), *SGRT* 21, no. 2 (February 1980): 105.

101. *Yezhegodnik BSE*, 1975, p. 40, *Izvestia*, 24 June 1976; see also Shabad, "News Notes," *SGRT* 15, no. 4 (April 1974): 247 and 27, no. 8 (October 1976): 572.

102. Conquest, *Kolyma*, p. 111 "Site D–2, 754 km from Magadan"; the technology had been mastered in 1947 (communication from Dr. David Holloway, University of Edinburgh, author of "Innovation in the Defense Sector," in: R. Amann and J. M. Cooper (eds.), *Industrial Innovation in the Soviet Union* (New Haven, CT: Yale University Press, 1982), pp. 276–366.

103. *Stroitelnaya gazeta*, 1 February 1980, p. 2.

104. Ibid., 24 September 1980, p. 1; see also Theodore Shabad, "Magadan and the Upper Kolyma Country," *SGRT* 21, no. 2 (February 1980): 103.

105. Shabad, "News Notes," *SGRT* 22, no. 5 (May 1981): 343–44. The unit later proved defective.

106. *Pravda*, 13 December 1978, p. 2.

107. *Izvestiya*, 27 February 1978; some trucks were actually driven directly over winter roads across most of the Arctic USSR from the KamAZ plant at Naberezhnye Chelny (renamed Brezhnev in 1982).

108. Magadan Radio, 7 January 1972.

109. Ibid., 27 September 1973.

110. See Kaser, "Soviet Gold," pp. 215–16.

111. Lomako, "Nonferrous metallurgy," (1976), p. 5 and Magadan Radio, 27 October 1975, repectively.

112. Listed in Seletsky, *Gody*, p. 9.

113. Magadan Radio, 30 July; 11, 12, 22, and 29 August; 4, 11, 17, 22, 23, 24, and 25 September; 20, 22, and 24 October; and 3, 20, and 27 November 1975.

114. 87.14 percent fulfillment by 7 December (Magadan Radio, 8 December 1975).

115. Magadan Radio, 28 October 1971.

116. Ibid., 7 January 1972.

117. Ibid., 26 March 1975.

118. Dowie, "Production," p. 15.

119. A. Levikov et al., *Kolyma i Kolymchane* [Kolyma and its people] (Moscow, 1971).

120. *Sovetskaya Rossiya*, 3 March 1972.

121. Magadan Radio, 17 November 1975.

122. Ibid., 2 April 1979, *Sotsialisticheskaya industriya*, 13 November 1979; Shabad, "News Notes," *SGRT* 21, no. 3 (March 1980): 185, which also has the photograph referred to in the text (from *Na stroikakh Rossii*, 1978, no. 8, p. 55).

123. Photograph in *Ogonek*, 23 January 1971.

124. *Pravda*, 7 March 1980.

125. Moscow Radio, 12 January 1980 (the quotation, from *BBC Summary of World Broadcasts*, Part 1, *USSR: Weekly Economic Report*, 18 January 1980, may not be verbatim).

126. *Pravda*, 12 March 1974.

127. *Pravda*, 7 March 1976.

128. Ibid., 2 March 1976.

129. For article on the Far East Economic Region and figure see *BSE*, 7, 3rd ed.,: 516–17.

130. *Pravda*, 8 August 1978, p. 3.

131. *Tsvetnye metally*, 1977, no. 10, pp. 11–12.

132. Ibid., 1980, no. 3, pp. 5, 9, and 14.

133. Magadan Radio, 17 September 1976.

134. Ibid., 1 December 1980.

135. Ibid., 7 December 1980.

136. From location of workers' settlements by those names in *SSSR: Administrativno-territorialnoye deleniye soyuznykh respublik 1980* [USSR: Administrative-territorial divisions of union republics] (hereafter *SSSR: deleniye*) (Moscow, 1980), p. 169.

137. *SSSR: deleniye*, p. 167.

138. Magadan Radio, 2 August 1979 and 28 March 1980.

139. Ibid., 4 June 1979.

140. "Five-year plan directives of the 26th party congress," *Pravda*, 5 March 1981, pp. 3 and 6.

141. Magadan Radio, 3 December 1979.

142. Information on trends in placer production is sparse in the extreme and this conclusion is of course inductive. Of the three placer enterprises for which any index has been published (1965 = 100), Eksperimentalny showed a rise in 1970 (133.5) while Komsomolsky (47.5) and Dvadtsatvtorogo Syezda KPSS (49.6) more than halved their output (Seletsky, *Gody*, p. 9).

143. *Izvestiya*, 16 July 1980, p. 2.

144. *Trud*, 18 June 1980, p. 2.

145. Solzhenitsyn, *Gulag* 2, p. 116.

146. A. A. Smirnov, "Minerals of the native gold group," *Mineraly SSSR*, 1 (Moscow-Leningrad, 1940): 101–78.

147. *Dalni Vostok*, pp. 262–63.

148. Moscow Radio, 6 March 1965.

149. Russo-British Chamber of Commerce, London, circular to members, 5 December 1968.

150. *Pravda*, 26 June 1980; for description, see Shabad, "News Notes," *SGRT* 21, no. 8 (October 1980): 547.

151. *Sotsialisticheskaya industriya*, 19 October 1973; see Shabad, "News Notes," *SGRT* 15, no. 2 (February 1974): 119 and 21, no. 8 (October 1980): 547.

152. It was a "trust" in the 1950s: "Khabarovsk Krai," *BSE*, 46, 2nd ed., (Moscow, 1957): 17, and a "combine" according to Khabarovsk Radio, 19 October 1973.

153. P. F. Lomako, "New frontiers for nonferrous metallurgy," *Tsvetnye metally*, 1975, no. 3, pp. 1–15. The first mention of Primorzoloto as a state corporation seen by the writer was in Khabarovsk Radio, 24 October 1979.

154. A. C. Sutton, *Western Technology and Soviet Economic Development* (Stanford, Ca.: Hoover Institution, 1968), p. 10.

155. "The Lower Amur Oblast," *BSE*, 2, 2nd ed., (Moscow, 1954): 597.

156. "Sakhalin," *BSE*, 23, 3rd ed., (Moscow, 1976): 6.

157. Hiroshi Kimura, "Southern Sakhalin," *SGRT* 21, no. 2 (February 1980): 110–13.

158. Dowie, "Production," p. 34, referring to the editorial in *Tsvetnye metally*, 1968, no. 7, already mentioned.

159. Both listed in *Tsvetnye metally*, 1967, no. 10.

160. Russo-British Chamber of Commerce, circular to members, 5 December 1968, and Dowie, "Production," pp. 18 and 20 (his latter reference seems a misprint).

161. Khabarovsk Radio, 22 May 1963.

162. For references, see Kaser, "Regional Time-Series," p. 111.

163. See Theodore Shabad and Victor L. Mote, *Gateway to Siberian Resources (the BAM)* (New York: Wiley, 1977), passim, for the BAM; also Moscow radio, 3 July 1982.

164. *Dalni Vostok*, p. 329.

165. *Gudok*, 9 February 1968.

166. *Pravda*, 8 December 1966.

167. Kaser, "Regional Time-Series," p. 118.

168. See I. M. Mayergoiz (Moscow University) "The Unique Economic-Geographic Situation of the Soviet Far East and Some Problems of Using It over the Long-Term," *Vestnik Moskovskogo Universiteta, geografiya*, 1974, no. 4, pp. 3–9 (translated, *SGRT* 16, no. 9 (November 1975): 428–34).

169. Khabarovsk Radio, 1 December 1980.

170. *Sotsialisticheskaya industriya*, 24 November 1976, p. 2.

171. Khabarovsk Radio, 17 October 1979.

172. Ibid., 5 November and 23 may 1979, respectively.

173. Ibid., 23 June 1980. The citation, from *BBC Summary of World Broadcasts*, Part 1, *USSR: Weekly Economy Report*, 1 August 1980, p. A17, may not be verbatim.

174. V. M. Khodachek, "On the formation of population in regions of the Far North of the USSR," in *Severo-Zapad yevropeyskoi chasti SSSR* [The northeast of the European part of the USSR] 9, (Leningrad, 1973): 44–57 (translated in *SGRT* 15, no. 5 (May 1974): 288–98). On the "gold rush" of 1923–25 and a Western reporter's impressions of 1975, see Christopher S. Wren, "Siberian Gold-Mining Country," *International Herald Tribune*, 3 April 1975.

175. R. A. Davies and A. J. Steigler, *Soviet Asia* (London, 1944), p. 98.

176. Khodachek, *Severo-Zapad*, pp. 44–57.

177. Shabad and Mote, *Gateway*, pp. 78–79.

178. Korzhuyev, *Yakutiya*, p. 21; see also p. 396.

179. V. V. Pokshishevsky, *Yakutiya: priroda, lyudi, khozyaistvo* [Yakutia: environment, people, economy] (Moscow, 1957), p. 99.

180. Korzhuyev, *Yakutiya*, pp. 396–97.

181. V. V. Mityushkin, *Sotsialisticheskaya Yakutiya* [Socialist Yakutia] (Yakutsk, 1960), p. 109.

182. *Ekonomicheskaya gazeta*, 1974, no. 32, p. 5.

183. N. A. Solovyev, *Sorok let Yakutskoi ASSR* [Forty years of the Yakut ASSR] (Yakutsk, 1962), cited in Korzhuyev, *Yakutiya*, p. 398.

184. As confirmed by the description of the employment of a deputy elected to the Soviet of Nationalities in 1979, as on the staff of the Nizhni Kuranakh Gold Extraction Plant of the Aldanzoloto Combine (*Tsvetnye metally*, 1979, no. 6, p. 2).

185. *Gorny zhurnal*, 1974, no. 4, which Dowie, "Production," pp. 29–30 identifies with a large mine requiring

30 to 41 MW of electricity capacity and 40,800 to 68,000 square m. of buildings described in *Tsvetnye metally*, 1968, no. 7.

186. Information (as acknowledged in note 14) from Professor Getzler; the same source for the further assessment of the placers when he was there in 1940–42.

187. Mityushkin, *Yakutiya*, pp. 109 and 112.

188. Ibid., pp. 105–12.

189. Yakutsk Radio, 24 November 1971; the designation may have been earlier.

190. Mityushkin, *Yakutiya*, p. 112.

191. Korzhuyev, *Yakutiya*, p. 398.

192. *RSFSR: Vostochnaya Sibir* [East Siberia] (Moscow, 1969), p. 436; N. V. Chersky, *Bogatstva nedr Yakutii* [Mineral resources of Yakutia] (Yakutsk, 1971), p. 135.

193. *Stroitelnaya gazeta*, 22 July 1970; *Komsomolskaya pravda*, 12 November 1972.

194. *Sotsialisticheskaya industriya*, 28 January 1975; see Shabad, "News Notes," *SGRT* 16, no. 5 (May 1975): 343 for detail and background.

195. From *BSE*, 49, 2nd ed. (Moscow, 1957): 542 and Korzhuyev, *Yakutiya*, p. 21; for detail, see Kaser, "Regional Time-Series," p. 80.

196. Pokshishevsky, *Yakutiya*, p. 166.

197. Mityushkin, *Yakutiya*, pp. 38 and 112.

198. Korzhuyev, *Yakutiya*, p. 60.

199. Ibid.

200. Mityushkin, *Yakutiya*, p. 114.

201. *Vostochnaya Sibir*, p. 253.

202. Communication to the present writer from Terence Armstrong, deputy director of the Scott Polar Research Institute, Cambridge, England, after a visit in connection with the Second International Permafrost Conference, Yakutsk.

203. Mityushkin, *Yakutiya*, pp. 112–14.

204. Shabad, "News Notes," *SGRT* 18, no. 10 (December 1977): 613.

205. Smirnov, "Minerals," pp. 101–78.

206. *Vostochnaya Sibir*, p. 241.

207. Shabad, "News Notes," *SGRT* 17, no. 3 (March 1976): 211–12.

208. T. G. Desyatkin, for "outstanding success in the 1971–75 plan" and in 1977 (*Tsvetnye metally*, 1976, no. 5, p. 7 and 1977, no. 10, p. 11).

209. *Soviet News* (London), 4 April 1967, p. 8.

210. Magadan Radio, 17 January 1975.

211. *Pravda*, 5 February 1979, p. 6.

212. Dowie, "Production," p. 44; Kaser, "Regional Time-Series," p. 80.

213. It was a "trust" according to the Chita Radio, 7 February 1968, and a corporation according to the Moscow Radio, 9 September 1979, and *Tsvetnye metally*, 1980, no. 4, p. 7.

214. *Vostochnaya Sibir*, p. 766.

215. F. F. Bybin and B. N. Miloslavsky, "Some characteristics of the development of the mining industry in eastern Transbaikalia," *Izvestiya Sibirskogo otdeleniya akademii nauk SSSR*, 1968, no. 1, p. 21.

216. Dowie, "Production," p. 31, based on analysis of reports on both mines in *Tsvetnye metally*, 1967, no. 8, p. 3.

217. *Vostochnaya Sibir*, p. 791.

218. V. I. Revnivtsev, "Problems of the tenth five-year plan," *Tsvetnye metally*, 1977, no. 3, p. 2.

219. *Vostochnaya Sibir*, pp. 737–38.

220. Smirnov, "Minerals," pp. 101–78.

221. Ye. Ye. Andreyev, P. V. Kuznetsov, A. V. Bortnikov and V. S. Kizei, "Industrial tests on automatic control systems for a self-grinding mill at the Taseyevo plant," *Tsvetnye metally*, 1976, no. 6, p. 85.

222. A. P. Shurnikov, "Ways of making full use of ore material," *Tsvetnye metally*, 1976, no. 4, p. 2.

223. Chita Radio, 27 December 1974.

224. Moscow Radio, 9 September 1979.

225. *Tsvetnye metally*, 1980, no. 4, p. 7.

226. *Vostochnaya Sibir*, p. 685.

227. Chita Radio, 28 February 1974.

228. *Izvestiya*, 28 June 1966.

229. Chita Radio, 26 April 1966.

230. Kaser, "Regional Time-Series," p. 88, citing *Promyshlennost SSSR*, 1957, p. 53; *Narodnoye khozyaistvo RSFSR v 1957 godu*, pp. 45 and 47.

231. From Report on the Olekma-Vitim Expedition as quoted by S. Bogatko in *The Great Baikal-Amur Railway* (Moscow: Progress Publishers, 1977), p. 95 (original *Magistral veka*). The expedition reached Chita on 8 September 1866 (old calendar style).

232. See note 11 for sources.

233. Tass, 5 August 1973.

234. *Tsvetnye metally*, 1967, no. 10.

235. Ibid., 1980, no. 4, pp. 9–19.

236. Smirnov, "Minerals."

237. *Vostochnaya Sibir*, p. 253.

238. P. F. Lomako, *Tsvetnye metally*, 1971, no. 1.

239. Dowie, "Production," p. 44.

240. *Tsvetnye metally*, 1971, no. 1.

241. Moscow Radio, 7 March 1980.

242. *Vostochnaya Sibir*, p. 537.

243. Ibid., p. 659; *Tsvetnye metally*, 1976, no. 11, p. 12.

244. *Vostochnaya Sibir*, pp. 533–34.

245. *Sovetsky Soyuz* [Soviet Union] East Siberia volume (Moscow: Mysl, 1969), p. 230 (part of a 22-volume regional geography of the Soviet Union).

246. *Tsvetnye metally*, 1967, no. 10.

247. Smirnov, "Minerals"; *Tsvetnye metally*, 1966, no. 12, p. 15.

248. *Vostochnaya Sibir*, p. 510.

249. Ibid., p. 519.

250. Ibid., p. 511.

251. *Sovetsky Soyuz* [The Soviet Union] West Siberia volume (Moscow: Mysl, 1971), pp. 318–19; Revnivtsev, "Problems," p. 2.

252. *Zapadno-Sibirsky ekonomichesky rayon* [West Siberian economic region] (Moscow: Nauka, 1967), p. 32; *Sovetsky Soyuz*, West Siberia volume. p. 322.

253. G. N. Cherdantsev et. al., *Ekonomicheskaya geografiya SSSR: RSFSR* [Economic Geography of the USSR: The RSFSR] (Moscow, 1956), p. 412.

254. Mityushkin, *Yakutiya*, p. 116.

255. *Tsvetnye metally*, 1980, no. 3, p. 6.

256. Kazzoloto is mentioned, but Altaizoloto is not in a book of 1940 (Smirnov, "Minerals").

257. *Gold 1980*, pp. 50–58.

258. For details on the Urquhart negotiations see E. H. Carr, *The Bolshevik Revolution 1917–1923* (London: Macmillan, 1953), pp. 354–44, 431–33 and 477. The account in *BSE* 24, 2nd edn., (Moscow, 1953) is misleading. On the Soviet concessions policy as it eventuated (the first beneficiary being Sinclair Oil on Sakhalin), see E. H. Carr, *The Interregnum 1923–1924* (London: Macmillan, 1954), pp. 245–57.

259. *BSE* 9, 3rd edn., (Moscow, 1972): 612; 3 (Moscow, 1970): 161; *Gold 1980*, pp. 56–57; Shabad, "News Notes," *SGRT* 18, no. 8 (October 1977): 614; 22, no. 6 (June 1981): 397–98.

260. *Gold 1980*, p. 57; *SSSR: deleniye*, p. 422.

261. *Gold 1980*, pp. 57–58.

262. Ibid., pp. 50–55; administrative locations from *SSSR: deleniye*, passim.

263. E. Zaleski, *Stalinist Planning for Economic Growth 1933–1952* (London: Macmillan, 1980 and Chapel Hill, N.C.: University of North Carolina Press, 1980), pp. 581–627; *Metal Statistics, 1957–66*, pp. 123, 173, 230 and 261, *1960–69*, pp. 131, 181, 238 and 169; *1969–79*, pp. 177, 240, 306, and 345. The latter's zinc estimates were increased in later editions of the yearbook and the previous, lower, series was adjusted upward by the margin shown for 1969. The lead-zinc index is the aggregate of the tonnages of each. The *Metals Statistics* series agrees broadly with that of the U.S. Bureau of Mines (according to *Mineral Yearbook 1964*, lead output was 7 percent higher, zinc 5 percent higher and copper output as shown).

264. See Solzhenitsyn, *Gulag* 1, p. 124; *Gulag* 3, pp. 372–74, 436–39.

265. *Gold 1980*, pp. 54, 57, 58.

266. Most information from Smirnov, "Minerals"; Bakyrchik from *Yezhegodnik BSE, 1971*, p. 48.

267. *Pravda*, 22 February 1970.

268. *Kazakhskaya SSR* (Moscow: Geografgiz, 1957), p. 307; *BSE* 24, 3rd edn., p. 494.

269. Sh. Yesenov, D. Kunayev, S. Mukhamedzhanov, *Nedra Kazakhstana* [Minerals of Kazakhstan] (Alma-Ata: Kazakhstan Publishers, 1968), p. 342.

270. *Kazakhstanskaya Pravda*, 1 December 1956 and 20 June 1969; *Tsvetnye metally*, 1975, no. 11.

271. Index 1940–50 from *Promyshlennost SSSR*, 1957, p. 79; from *Narodnoye khozyaistvo Kazakhskoi SSR* (Alma-Ata, 1957); 1958 was 264 percent of 1950, 1965 plan was 1.7 times 1958 and the 1970 plan was 1.68 times 1965 according to *Razvitiye narodnogo khozyaistva Kazakhstana za 50 let Sovetskoi vlasti* (Alma-Ata, 1967), pp. 102–30; 1960, 1965 and 1971 were linked by an index cited in *BSE* 11, 3rd ed. (Moscow, 1973): 156; *Yezhegodnik BSE, 1973*, p. 124 combined results for 1972 for ferrous and nonferrous metallurgy as 5 percent over 1971.

272. Respectively Yu. Razgulyayev, *Pravda*, 4 October 1978, p. 2 and V. Grebenyuk, *Pravda*, 3 December 1978, p. 2.

273. *Mineralno-syryevye resursy Uzbekistana*, Part I (Tashkent, 1976), p. 93.

274. Ibid., pp. 93–94.

275. Ibid., p. 23.

276. Ibid.

277. Shabad, "News Notes," *SGRT* 22, no. 2 (February 1981): 128.

278. *Pravda*, 4 July 1969 and 26 May 1970; *Pravda Vostoka*, 31 May 1967; 8 July 1972; 4 October 1973; 26 December 1973.

279. Soviet sources are reticent about naming Muruntau in technical papers, possibly because of the size and novelty of the facilities. The Gold Fields study, like its companion statements on Armenian and byproduct gold, does not state sources. The following appear to be among the relevant Soviet papers, judging both from content and the overlapping authorship (Druzhina and Mineyev): "Recovery of gold from pulps by means of pore carrier extraction," *Tsvetnye metally*, 1975, no. 1, p. 81; G. Ya. Druzhina, A. A. Batsuyev and V. A. Khomutnikov, "Redex sorption of gold and silver from cyanide waste effluents, *Tsvetnye metally*, 1976, no. 5, p. 85; G. G. Mineyev, G. Ya. Druzhina and G. A. Stroganov, "Sorption of gold from ore heap leaching solutions using activated carbon," *Tsvetnye metally*, 1976, no. 12, p. 68; "Economics of heap leaching from poor quartz ores," *Tsvetnye metally*, 1976, no. 12, p. 14. But, as explained in the text, these and other papers may not refer to Muruntau.

280. *Gold 1978*, pp. 46–51; *Gold 1980*, p. 49.

281. *Gold 1980*, p. 49.

282. *Ogonek*, 23 January 1971, showed a photograph of the storeroom at Muruntau a few months after the mill started up, showing 36 ingots of 10 kg each; the photographer was assumed to have selected an image which gave the best impression, suggesting that this was the total stock at the time; Dowie postulated that gold would be stripped once a month and a rate of 4.3 tons a year was derived.

283. This is based on estimates of ore supplied and of its metal content; Dowie, "Production," p. 32, calculated 28 tons from employment, a derived wage bill and the receipts from gold sold that would cover such outlay (but without knowledge whether a profit or a subsidized loss was made). If the estimate is wrong, the Karamken estimate would also be affected (see note 122).

284. *Pravda*, 8 April 1968; *Pravda Vostoka*, 14 May 1968; Leslie Dienes and Theodore Shabad, *The Soviet Energy System* (New York: Wiley, 1979), p. 178.

285. *Tsvetnye metally*, 1969, no. 7.

286. *Pravda Vostoka*, 11 September 1969.

287. Ibid., 25 March 1976.

288. Ibid., 12 November 1980; Shabad, "News Notes," *SGRT* 22, no. 2 (February 1981): 128.

289. *Pravda Vostoka*, 28 April 1967; 28 June 1967; 24 December 1969.

290. Dowie, "Production," p. 21: 0.33 tons from the small dredge installed in 1967 and 0.51 from the large dredge; he assumes the operation of two other small dredges from the early period.

291. Tashkent Radio, 12 December 1972.

292. As cited in successive issues of *Yezhegodnik BSE*: percentage increments over preceding year: 1976, 4.0; 1977, 1.4; 1978, 2.2; and 1979, 3.9. The 1976–80 Five-Year Plan spoke of an increase in precious metals in Uzbekistan without a figure (*Pravda*, 7 March 1976).

293. T. N. Osetrov, Deputy to the Soviet of Nationalities from the Karshi constituency (*Izvestiya*, 2 December 1978).

294. Smirnov, "Minerals."

295. *Money, Prices and Gold in the Soviet Union*, Monograph no. 3, School of Slavonic and East European Studies (London: School of Slavonic and East European Studies, 1934), p. 23; the 1913 figure is from *Razrabotka mestorozhdenii poleznykh iskopayemykh Urala* [Exploitation of mineral deposits in the Urals] (Moscow: Nedra, 1967), p. 13.

296. Smirnov, "Minerals."

297. *Dengi i kredit*, 1972, no. 4, p. 33.

298. Kaser, "Regional Time Series," pp. 108–09.

299. Dowie, "Production," pp. 19, 21, 35 and 37.

300. 1965 output was 36 percent above 1959 (*Kommunist Tadzhikistana*, 21 July 1955) and 1966, 3 percent above 1965 (Tass, 5 February 1968). The use of 1959 rather than 1958 (the base-year of the Seven-Year Plan) suggests that 1958 output was in fact higher than 1959 and it is therefore assumed that production was declining until 1959. A total decline of 20 percent between 1950 and 1959 and a rise of 2.7 percent between 1966 and 1973 was assumed. It was further assumed that 1940 was about the 1970 level, because Smirnov, "Minerals" in that year listed no fewer than 32 lode deposits and 24 placer workings (list in Kaser, "Regional Time Series," pp. 108–09). It was judged that two thirds of the 56 were actually operating in 1940 (38 operations) each producing a quarter of a ton (9 tons).

301. Such obscurity is nothing new. I. I. Komar, *Geografiya khozyaistva Urala* [Economic geography of the Urals] (Moscow, 1964) mentions gold in his detailed district-by-district survey but without indication of actual activity.

302. Ye. Animitsa, *Goroda srednego Urala* [Cities of the Middle Urals] (Sverdlovsk: Middle Urals Publishers, 1975), pp. 31–40 (detailed account of the history and economy of Berezovsky).

303. *Razrabotka mestorozhdenii*, p. 359.

304. Animitsa, *Goroda*, p. 35.

305. *Razrabotka mestorozhdenii*, p. 388.

306. Ibid.

307. *Gudok*, 24 March 1968.

308. *Stroitelnaya gazeta*, 23 March 1966.

309. *Kommunist*, 13 January 1972; Shabad, "News Notes," SGRT 13, no. 5 (May 1972): 329.

310. *Gold 1979*, pp. 48–49.

311. Revnivtsev, "Problems," p. 2.

312. *Tsvetnye metally*, 1980, no. 3, pp. 4, 9.

313. G. B. Grigoryan, F. G. Arutunyan and Yu. G. Petrosyan, "Pilot plant tests of high temperature electrosmelting of gold-bearing concentrates," *Tsvetnye metally*, 1973, no. 10, pp. 17–19.

314. *Gold 1979*, p. 49.

315. Ibid.

316. *Sotsialisticheskaya industriya*, 22 February 1976; Shabad, "News Notes," SGRT 17, no. 6 (June 1976): 428.

317. Shabad, "News Notes," SGRT 15, no. 1 (January 1974): 50; 15, no. 10 (December 1974): 669.

318. Kaser, "Regional Time Series," pp. 124–25.

319. Kolyma and Gornaya artels pledged fulfillment of two monthly plans in May 1979; artels of the Srednekan concentrator decided to support the initiative of the Chukchi artel of the Komsomolsky concentrator to extract specified additional quantities in 1979; the Arktika artel of the Polyarny concentrator initiated an oblast competition to extract 5 percent more gold than planned in 1980 (Magadan Radio, 21 May and 28 May 1979, 5 June 1980). Reference is made above to the imposition of additional targets on artels (Magadan Radio, 5 June and 6 June 1980).

320. Decree of the Council of Ministers of the USSR "On confirmation of the model statute for prospectors' artels," *Sobraniye postanovlenii pravitelstva SSSR*, 1975, no. 9, pp. 163–64.

321. Tass, 26 December 1974.

322. Moscow Radio, 26 October 1980.

323. *Gold 1980*, p. 49.

324. CIA, *Handbook of Economic Statistics 1980* (Washington: National Foreign Assessment Center, October 1980), p. 63.

325. CIA, *Handbook 1979*.

326. Mora, cited in Stelzl, "Aspekte der Produktion," p. 406.

327. Stelzl, "Aspekte der Produktion," pp. 406–07.

328. CIA, *Handbook 1976*.

329. CIA, *Handbook 1978*. The U.S. Bureau of Mines, *Mining Annual Review 1978*, p. 571, gives a lower series (245 tons compared to the CIA's 270) but excludes byproduct output and is hence not comparable.

330. Kaser, "Soviet Gold," p. 153.

331. Kaser, "Regional Time Series," p. 47; Dowie, "Production," p. 44.

332. Since this research was completed, *Gold 1981* has appeared, with descriptions of Severovostokzoloto and Primorzoloto (pp. 58–64); no regional output estimates were, however, proffered and the aggregate output estimate was put at 300 tons.

333. *Vostochnaya Sibir*, p. 253.

334. See Table 15 for Yakutia (25 tons), Transbaikalia (13 tons) and Lena (11 tons); Yenisei is estimated at 2 to 3 tons (see Kaser, "Regional Time Series," p. 115).

335. *Problemy*.

336. Pokshishevsky, *Yakutiya*, p. 105, says that Yakutia produces one-fifth.

337. Mityushkin, *Yakutiya*, p. 116 (as note 254).

338. *Narodnoye khozyaistvo SSSR v 1979 g* (Moscow, 1980), p. 567, converts current priced trade into gold rubles of 0.987412 grams of gold and shows 2,270 million rubles in 1913 and 80,290 million rubles in 1979.

339. BSE 17, 2nd edn., (Moscow, 1952): 154.

340. A notable use that began in the 1950s was regilding of church cupolas.

341. F. D. Holzman, "Foreign Trade," in A. Bergson and S. Kuznets (eds.), *Economic Trends in the Soviet Union* (Cambridge, Ma: Harvard University Press, 1963), p. 290; he also quotes Soviet gold exports at 110 million rubles in 1930–31 but cannot say at what exchange rate the estimate was made.

342. CIA estimate for 1966–71 averaged 54 tons; Kaser,

"Soviet Gold," p. 228, 1969–71 averaged 42 tons. Sales of jewelry and to industrial users would have increased during the 1970s.

343. G. T. Kuznetsov, *Tsenoobrazovaniye v tsvetnoi metallurgii* [Price formation in nonferrous metallurgy] (Moscow, 1977), pp. 29, 85, 86.

344. Lomako, *Tsvetnye metally*, 1977, no. 4, pp. 1–11.

345. E. Andres, "On the characteristic of the assurance of monetary stability under socialism," *Ekonomicheskiye nauki*, 1978, no. 12, p. 46.

346. *Kazakhstanskaya Pravda*, 2 March 1978, p. 4.

347. *Trud*, 15 February 1979, p. 6.

348. Kuznetsov, *Tsenoobrazovaniye*, p. 84. At that exchange rate, he shows, domestic wholesale prices in the USSR were lower than world prices in 1972 for copper, magnesium and titanium but little difference for aluminum, but they were lower also for aluminum, nickel, lead, zinc and antimony in 1974. That the exchange rate is not too erroneous for nonferrous metals is shown on p. 83, where Soviet cobalt, cadmium, bismuth and mercury prices at that rate are well above world prices.

349. Observation by the present writer in Moscow.

350. *Finansy SSSR*, 1969, no. 4, pp. 80–85: made up of wholesale price 3.804, fee for assay and hallmarking, 0.125, tax 1.178 and retail mark-up 0.540.

351. *Trud*, 1 March 1978, p. 3.

352. *Pravda*, 1 July 1979, p. 3.

353. Michael Kaser, "The Hungarian Forint," *International Currency Review*, 9, no. 6: 155.

# 25

# RESOURCE VALUATION AND THE EFFICIENCY OF SOVIET RESOURCE PRODUCTION AND USE

JUDITH THORNTON
University of Washington

The fundamental determinants of Soviet natural-resource exports are the domestic production and use of natural resources. At any given world price, the greater is the output of a good and the smaller its use, the greater will tend to be the amount of the good exported. Further, the more efficiently the good can be produced and used at home, the more of the good will tend to be exported.

This chapter analyzes the efficiency of Soviet production and use of natural resources. It presents and discusses some data on production costs and prices for the major natural resources. Then it turns to a detailed examination of Soviet resource valuation—a central element in determining production costs and a source of both analytical and practical difficulty for Soviet decision-makers. Finally, it discusses Soviet material balances for natural resources and recent attempts to apply optimizing models to the allocation of natural resources.

## Costs and Prices of Natural Resources

Unlike a market economy, Soviet central planning relegates costs and prices to a subordinate role—merely facilitating the formulation and implementation of plans—in the allocation of scarce inputs and outputs. Still, Soviet planners are not indifferent to costs and prices; indeed, much is made of these bourgeois vestiges in both scholarly and practical analyses of Soviet economic problems. If anything, costs and prices have increased in importance in recent years, with the economic reforms that began in the mid-1960s and the major expansion of foreign trade since 1970.

There is a marked contrast between the time patterns of Soviet user prices of raw materials and fuels on the one hand and the time patterns of production costs and producer prices for those goods on the other hand. Prices paid by users—so-called industrial prices—have remained relatively fixed for long periods of time, with infrequent major revisions (1955, 1967). A revision was scheduled to take effect in January 1982; however, the official date for publication of the new price schedules (1 April 1981) passed without news, amid signs of regional

discord over the proposed changes. The 1967 revision included substantial increases for fuels and raw materials. Given events since 1967, the next revision will likely include similar increases. While user prices have remained remarkably stable, unit production costs and prices paid to producers—so-called enterprise prices—have been subject to significant changes. Tables 1 and 2 illustrate the movements of costs and enterprise prices for selected years since 1950. Note that the data show rapid rises for all the major natural resources except oil and gas, for which costs fell during the 1950s before leveling off in the early 1960s and then beginning to rise in the late 1960s.

The average production cost of fuel in the Soviet economy rose about two and one-half times during the postwar period. Time-series for coal show steadily rising costs of production from the early 1950s on; in 1975, the figure was more than 2.6 times its level in 1955. For oil and natural gas, unit costs fell between 1950 and 1965 and then began to increase. Between 1965 and 1975, the average cost of oil extraction rose by a factor of 2.4, and the average cost of natural gas more than tripled.

Soviet fuel production costs are, of course, far from uniform, as Tables 3 through 5 show. For coal, the interbasin range of extraction costs is enormous, even correcting for heat value (Table 3); costs range widely within basins as well.[1] For broad regions, the variation is somewhat less; for instance, Dienes and Shabad estimate regional average costs for 1973 as follows:[2]

| Central Russia | 18.2 rubles/ton of standard fuel |
| Ukraine | 11–13 |
| Siberia | 8.6–9.5 |
| Central Asia | 15.0 |
| Kazakhstan | 14.0 |
| Urals | 15.4 |

Oil and gas costs show even more regional variation than coal (see Tables 4 and 5). In 1971, the ratio of highest to lowest-cost region for oil (Sakhalin/Western Siberia) was 5.29. In 1975, the similar ratio for gas (Kuban/Krestishche) was 13.02. Only Kazakhstan and Western Siberia experienced persistently falling oil production costs into the 1970s (the latter became a major oil producer only in the late 1960s). The regional pattern of cost *increases* is varied and complex; noteworthy are the ap-

TABLE 1
Average Cost and Price Data for Fuels, Selected Years (rubles per metric ton of coal and oil, per 1,000 cubic meters of gas)

| | (1) Coal | (2) | (3) Crude Oil | (4) | (5) | (6) Natural Gas | (7) | (8) |
|---|---|---|---|---|---|---|---|---|
| | Production Cost | Cost and Profit | Production Cost | Value of Output | Campbell Estimates | Production Cost | Enterprise Price | Industry Price |
| 1950 | 6.73 | N.A. | 8.56 | 9.53 | 6.24 | N.A. | N.A. | N.A. |
| 1955 | 6.34 | 6.29 | 5.91 | 6.89 | 4.92 | 1.48 | N.A. | N.A. |
| 1960 | 9.19 | 7.60 | 3.26 | 4.27 | 3.30 | 0.59 | 1.02 | 12.30[e] |
| 1965 | 11.41 | 8.52 | 3.03 | 4.40 | 2.99 | 0.44[a] | 1.03[b,c] | 12.30[a,e] |
| 1970 | 15.48 | 16.94 | 3.91 | 10.74 | 4.29 | 0.66[b] | 5.80[b,d] | 17.99[b,e] |
| 1975 | 16.79 | 17.16 | 7.31 | 12.61 | N.A. | 1.27 | 5.55[d] | 17.59[e] |

N.A. = not available
[a]1966
[b]1971
[c]Production cost + profit
[d]Production cost + and geological prospecting + profit
[e]Enterprise price + (transport cost + profit) + turnover taxes
SOURCES: Columns (1)–(4), Judith Thornton, *Cost Account Estimates* (unpublished manuscript); Column (5), R. W. Campbell, *Trends in the Soviet Oil and Gas Industry* (Baltimore: Johns Hopkins Press, 1976); Columns (6)–(8), estimates supplied by Albina Tretyakova.

proximate doublings of costs, in the five years 1966–71, in Tataria, Bashkiria, Kuibyshev, Sakhalin, and the Ukraine. Some of the regional cost increases are even larger for natural gas for the five years 1966–71; those doubling or more include the Ukraine, the Kuban, Stavropol, Uzbekistan, and Turkmenia.

In the face of changing production costs, the Soviet Government has sought to maintain stable fuel prices to users. Fuel prices are differentiated regionally to reflect transport costs and the scarcity value of "deficit" fuels. Within a given region, the structure of relative user prices is designed to reflect possibilities for substitution among fuels, on a caloric-equivalent basis (but generally disregarding differences in the handling costs of using different fuels).

TABLE 2
Prices of Ores and Metals (rubles per metric ton)

| | 1955 | 1964 | 1967 | 1975 |
|---|---|---|---|---|
| Aluminum | 476 | 498 | 660 | — |
| Cobalt | N.A. | 24,461 | 24,449 | — |
| Copper | 660 | 672 | 846 | — |
| Titanium | N.A. | 3,078 | 2,961 | — |
| Iron Ore | N.A. | 3.37 | 7.65 | 8.60 |
| Pig Iron: Kuznetsk | 22.8 | 27.0 | 41.2 | — |
| Manganese Ore | N.A. | 9.68 | 23.79 | — |
| Molybdenum | N.A. | 20,644 | 17,258 | — |
| Magnesium | 720 | 720 | 761 | — |
| Nickel | N.A. | 2,420 | 3,705 | — |
| Lead | 715 | 706 | 643 | — |
| Mercury | N.A. | 9,643 | 19,966 | — |
| Zinc | 315 | 329 | 541 | — |
| Vanadium | N.A. | 69,686 | 49,914 | — |
| Tin | 10,300 | 10,214 | 10,280 | — |
| Tungsten | N.A. | 13,440 | 14,467 | — |

SOURCES: K. N. Plotnikov and A. S. Gusarov, *Sovremennye problemy teorii i praktiki tsenoobrazovaniya pri sotsializme* [Contemporary problems in the theory and practice of price formation under socialism] (Moscow: Nauka, 1971); and V. I. Shkatov and B. S. Suponitsky, *Optovye tseny na produktsiyu tyazheloi promyshlennosti* [Wholesale prices for the products of heavy industry] (Moscow: Ekonomika, 1969).

In the early 1960s, all fuels were badly underpriced compared with either cost or productivity. The coal industry persistently suffered large losses, and the profits of oil and natural gas extraction were well below industry averages. In 1965, profit rates on the value of fixed capital stock were − 17.4 percent in coal, 6.0 percent in oil extraction, and 6.9 percent in natural gas.[3]

The price reform of 1967 had a greater impact on fuel prices than on any other sector of industry. The average price increase between 1966 and 1967 for all of heavy industry was 18 percent; for coal, however, the new enterprise prices were 81 percent higher, while in oil extraction they were 230 percent higher.[4] Since 1967, both oil and natural gas have borne sizable charges for geological prospecting; in the case of natural gas, these charges amount to more than direct production cost (see Table 1, column 7). Field prices were set to include both large profit margins and rental charges, the latter levied at a fixed rate per unit of output. The difference between industry prices charged to users and field prices paid to suppliers exceeded transport costs, indicating that the transport sector was to collect at least part of the rent earned. Campbell has argued that the field prices paid to

TABLE 3
Production Costs of Coal by Basin, Selected Years (rubles per metric ton of standard fuel[a])

| Basin | 1960 | 1965 | 1970 | 1975 | 1977 |
|---|---|---|---|---|---|
| Donets | 12.7 | 14.4 | 15.4 | 17.0 | 17.7 |
| Kuznetsk | 5.5 | 6.2 | 6.6 | 8.6 | 9.0 |
| Pechora | 14.3 | 16.5 | 15.5 | N.A. | N.A. |
| Moscow | N.A. | N.A. | N.A. | 24.1 | 25.0 |
| Karaganda | 8.2 | 10.8 | 10.9 | 12.8 | 13.0 |
| Ekibastuz | N.A. | N.A. | N.A. | 2.5 | 2.5 |
| Kansk-Achinsk | N.A. | N.A. | N.A. | 2.4 | 2.9 |

[a]One ton of standard fuel has a heat value of 7 million kilocalories.
SOURCE: Central Intelligence Agency, *USSR: Coal Industry, Problems and Prospects* (ER 80-10154, March 1980).

TABLE 4
Production Cost of Crude Oil for Major Regions, Selected Years (rubles per metric ton)

| Region | (1) 1950 | (2) 1955 | (3) 1960 | (4) 1966 | (5) 1970 | (6) 1971 | (7) 1975 |
|---|---|---|---|---|---|---|---|
| USSR Average | 6.24 | 4.92 | 3.30 | 3.03 | 4.29 | 4.37 | 7.31 |
| RSFSR Average | 4.58 | 2.84 | N.A. | 2.19 | N.A. | 3.73 | — |
| Volga-Urals | N.A. | 2.06 | 1.64 | N.A. | 3.30 | N.A. | — |
| Tatar ASSR | 3.39 | 1.57 | 1.37 | 1.55* | 2.70 | 2.88 | — |
| Bashkir ASSR | 2.97 | 1.97 | 2.10 | 2.63* | 4.98 | N.A. | — |
| Kuibyshev Oblast | 2.68 | 2.21 | 1.34 | 1.79* | 2.87 | 3.00 | — |
| Volgograd Oblast | 9.62 | 1.53 | 1.46 | N.A. | N.A. | N.A. | — |
| West Siberia | N.A. | N.A. | N.A. | 10.30*c | 3.54 | 3.40 | — |
| North Caucasus | 4.70a | 5.35 | 6.04 | 4.89*b | 3.82 | 4.05 | — |
| Sakhalin | 15.24 | 14.76 | 11.19 | 8.43* | N.A. | 18.00 | — |
| Azerbaijan | 6.85 | 8.86 | 7.17 | 7.70* | 10.72 | 11.80 | — |
| Kazakhstan | 11.21 | 9.55 | 8.84 | 8.57 | 5.32 | 5.42 | — |
| Turkmenia | 5.30 | 6.19 | 4.93 | 3.33* | 4.38* | 5.72d | — |
| Uzbekistan | 3.50 | 5.44 | 6.47 | 10.13 | 13.28*e | N.A. | — |
| Ukraine | 23.70 | 12.21 | 4.32 | 2.55* | 4.85 | 5.03 | — |

*Official figures.
aKrasnodar Krai
bDagestan
c1965
dCentral Asia
e1968
SOURCE: Campbell, *Trends in Soviet Oil and Gas*, pp. 34, 103; for column (7), see Table 1 (column 3).

suppliers after the price reform were set too low (and with too much differentiation among fields) to be efficient.[5] The planners' goal of capturing rents centrally thus conflicted with incentives to expand output.

There are also serious defects in the marginal valuations (*zamykayushchiye zatraty*, literally "closing outlays") used in drawing up long-term plans. Although the academics who developed procedures for estimating the marginal values were quite clear that only variable costs should be used in costing the output from established

TABLE 5
Production Cost of Natural Gas for Major Regions, Selected Years (rubles per 1,000 cubic meters)

| Region | (1) 1950 | (2) 1955 | (3) 1960 | (4) 1965 | (5) 1970 | (6) 1975 |
|---|---|---|---|---|---|---|
| Ukraine | — | — | — | — | 0.48 | 1.07 |
| Shebelinka | — | — | 0.28 | 0.26 | 0.36 | 0.99 |
| Krestishche | — | — | — | N.A. | 1.48 | 0.42 |
| Western Ukraine | — | — | 0.26 | 0.25 | 0.35 | N.A. |
| Krasnodar Krai (Kuban) | — | — | 0.80 | 0.31 | 0.91 | 5.47 |
| Saratov Oblast | 1.74 | 2.23 | 1.02 | — | — | — |
| Stavropol Oblast | — | 18.67 | 0.16 | 0.21 | 0.44 | 1.54 |
| Volgograd Oblast | — | — | 0.59 | 0.23 | — | — |
| Lvov Oblast | 1.43 | 0.68 | 0.44 | — | — | — |
| Kuibyshev Oblast | 1.42 | 1.71 | 1.53 | — | — | — |
| Komi ASSR | — | 1.58 | 2.66 | — | 1.17 | 1.70 |
| Uzbekistan (Gazli) | — | — | 2.94 | 0.16 | 0.16 | 1.08a |
| Turkmenia | — | — | — | — | 0.35 | 0.73 |
| Tyumen Oblast | — | — | — | — | 0.95 | 1.46 |
| Orenburg Oblast | — | — | — | — | 1.29 | 1.59 |

aUzbekistan (1970: 0.23 for comparison).
SOURCES: R. W. Campbell, *The Economics of Soviet Oil and Gas* (Baltimore: Johns Hopkins Press, 1968) and R. D. Margulov, Ye. K. Selikhova, and I. Ya. Furman, *Razvitiye gazovoi promyshlennosti i analiz tekhnoekonomicheskikh pokazatelei* [Development of the gas industry and analysis of technical-economic indicators] (Moscow, 1976).

sites, industry planners have acted otherwise. In most plans for expansion of capacity, coal is treated as the marginal fuel, and its cost at the margin includes a 15 percent return on the replacement value of the associated capital stock.[6]

Prices charged to fuel users after the economic reform showed substantial uniformity. For example, fuel oil prices to users were virtually identical throughout the USSR, west and south of Siberia.[7] Calculated in terms of standard fuel, the prices of coal, oil, and gas were similar, although user prices of coal still showed local cost variations attributable to transport charges.

Since 1967, prices paid by energy users have remained nearly constant while the world price of oil has first quadrupled, then doubled again. The potential value of Soviet petroleum exports has risen apace. Soviet domestic use of hydrocarbons faces competition both from the opportunity to sell oil and gas for hard currency and from the desire to continue sending energy supplies to its Comecon allies (although the price realized on such supplies has lagged behind the world price). However, these competing uses of energy products have not been reflected in the domestic prices charged for fuel. Data in Table 6 show that world prices of oil rose by 540 percent between 1970 and 1975, that Soviet contract prices in Comecon trade more than doubled, but that domestic wholesale prices rose only 1 percent. Wholesale prices of coal actually declined. Thus, whatever increase in the efficiency of fuel use has been achieved since 1970 has been due largely to planners' mandates, not to increased user prices.

Tables 7 through 9 summarize Soviet export prices for coal, oil, and natural gas to Comecon and the West. In trade with the West, Soviet oil prices have followed world prices, albeit with some lag. By 1975, the Soviet hard-currency oil price was more than four times its 1970

TABLE 6
Soviet Domestic and Export Price Indexes for
Primary Products, Selected Years (1970 = 100)

| Commodity | Price Index | 1960 | 1966 | 1971 | 1972 | 1973 | 1974 | 1975 |
|---|---|---|---|---|---|---|---|---|
| Coal | Contract[a] | 115 | 98 | 101 | 120 | 107 | 108 | 230 |
| | World | 82 | 80 | 109 | 115 | 120 | 152 | 193 |
| | Wholesale[b] | 70 | 65 | 98 | 96 | 95 | 94 | 95 |
| Oil | Contract | 133 | 97 | 101 | 102 | 104 | 117 | 216 |
| | World | 103 | 100 | 122 | 138 | 182 | 643 | 640 |
| | Wholesale | 36 | 42 | 101 | 101 | 101 | 100 | 101 |
| Iron ore | Contract | 121 | 101 | 101 | 102 | 103 | 105 | 138 |
| | World | 123 | 106 | 112 | 107 | 91 | 118 | 166 |
| | Wholesale | 37 | 41 | 99 | 98 | 99 | 99 | 100 |
| Manganese | Contract | 220 | 97 | 100 | 90 | 99 | 103 | 99 |
| ore | World | 152 | 152 | 122 | 117 | 150 | 220 | 264 |
| | Wholesale | 30 | 34 | 98 | 95 | 96 | 96 | 97 |
| Pig iron | Contract | 144 | 102 | 99 | 100 | 100 | 99 | 152 |
| | World | 101 | 89 | 110 | 112 | 115 | 155 | 186 |
| | Wholesale | 56 | 56 | 100 | 100 | 100 | 99 | 101 |
| Zinc | Contract | 93 | 98 | 111 | 121 | 132 | 129 | 270 |
| | World | 72 | 83 | 103 | 123 | 282 | 428 | 272 |
| | Wholesale | 61 | 61 | 100 | 100 | 100 | 100 | 100 |
| Lead | Contract | 134 | 104 | 119 | 135 | 141 | 173 | 190 |
| | World | 58 | 75 | 83 | 97 | 140 | 203 | 149 |
| | Wholesale | 111 | 107 | 100 | 100 | 100 | 100 | 100 |
| Aluminum | Contract | 110 | 100 | 102 | 109 | 100 | 110 | 120 |
| | World | 93 | 88 | 98 | 84 | 84 | 109 | 109 |
| | Wholesale | 74 | 74 | 100 | 100 | 101 | 101 | 101 |
| Cellulose | Contract | 111 | 111 | 107 | 114 | 119 | 123 | 158 |
| | World | 63 | 65 | 113 | 106 | 113 | 161 | 244 |
| | Wholesale | 47 | 60 | 98 | 101 | 97 | 71 | 71 |

[a]For sales to Comecon.
[b]Domestic wholesale price.
SOURCE: N. M. Mitrofanova, *Tseny v mekhanizme ekonomicheskogo sotrudnichestva stran-chlenov SEV* [Prices in the economic cooperation mechanism of the member-countries of Comecon] (Moscow: Nauka, 1978).

TABLE 7
Soviet Export Prices of Oil, Selected Years
(rubles per metric ton)

| | (1) 1955 | (2) 1960 | (3) 1965 | (4) 1970 | (5) 1975 | (6) 1980 |
|---|---|---|---|---|---|---|
| 1. To Comecon: Crude oil + products | 29.9 | 19.8 | 17.1 | 15.3 (15.5) [33.53] | 33.5 (33.5) | N.A. (70.9) N.A. |
| 2. To Western Europe: Crude oil + products | 13.0 | 10.3 | 9.1 | 11.9 (14.8) [10.41] | 60.5 (63.5) [60.49] | N.A. (85.4) N.A. |
| 3. Total exports: Crude oil only [Crude oil + products] | 19.8 | 13.9 | 12.7 | 12.3 [13.26] | 43.4 [43.37] | N.A. N.A. |

SOURCES: 1955–75 (no parentheses or brackets): Campbell, *Trends in Soviet Oil and Gas*; (1970–80): Raimund Deitz, "Price Changes in Soviet Trade with CMEA and the Rest of the World," in U.S., Congress, Joint Economic Committee, *Soviet Economy in a Time of Change* (Washington: Government Printing Office, 1979); [1970, 1975]: unit value indices supplied by Edward Hewett.

age, and these sectors are slated for new increases in the 1981 revision of prices.[9]

The data in Table 6 for the nonfuel minerals (plus cellulose) show the same general pattern between domestic, Comecon, and world prices as was noted above for the fuels. World prices generally rise (the least for aluminum). Comecon prices generally tag along behind world prices. Domestic wholesale prices, however, remain virtually constant (except for cellulose, which saw a 30 percent price reduction between 1973 and 1975, at the same time that world prices were rising by a like amount, with a further 50 percent rise due the following year). Thus, we again conclude that domestic users' incentives to economize on these goods, to free them up for export where it is worthwhile, had to come by fiat—they could not have come from price signals.

**Soviet Resource Valuation**

Costs of production underlie the economist's concept of supply—the different levels of output that are economical to produce at different prices. Supply in turn determines transaction prices, given demand. These propositions hold not only for market but also for centrally planned economies, so long as scarcity persists. Enterprises, socialist as well as capitalist, combine scarce inputs into outputs. Which outputs? Those demanded by the planners, as agents of the party. At the outset of this chapter, it was noted that Soviet planners seem to care about costs and prices, and in fact have to use them in their work, even though they are subordinate to the quantity indicators of the plans.

The calculation of production costs in natural-resource industries involves a special problem: the valuation of

level, and by 1980 almost six times the 1970 level. In trade with the Comecon countries, however, the 1975 average price of 33.5 rubles per ton was well below world prices and only some two times greater than the 1970 level. The disparity between prices charged to Comecon and world prices diminished in the late 1970s, but in 1980, at an average price of 70.9 rubles per ton, prices to Comecon were still nearly 20 percent below prices to the West.

Soviet export prices of natural gas have risen steadily, doubling between 1960 and 1970, then doubling again between 1970 and 1976. Coal prices, too, have responded to the increases for oil and natural gas, rising for West European purchasers in 1974 and for Comecon in 1975.

Like fuels, most metal ores and other primary products were badly underpriced on the eve of the 1965 economic reform. One source reports the following profit rates on fixed capital in 1965: iron ore, −5.8 percent; manganese ore, −8.4 percent; chrome ore, 20.3 percent.[8] As Table 2 shows, the 1967 price reform more than doubled the enterprise prices of iron and manganese ores and mercury, and provided substantial increases in the prices of aluminum, copper, nickel, tungsten, and zinc. (Note that the prices of titanium, molybdenum, lead, and vanadium were reduced in 1967, and the prices of magnesium and tin hardly changed.) Again today, however, profit rates in the extractive industries are reported to be below aver-

TABLE 8
Soviet Export Prices of Natural Gas, Selected Years
(rubles per 1,000 cubic meters)

| Year | (1)<br>To Comecon | (2)<br>To Western Europe | (3)<br>Total |
|------|-------------------|--------------------------|--------------|
| 1950–55 | 6.75 | — | 6.75 |
| 1956–66 | 6.88 | — | 6.88 |
| 1967 | 14.02 | — | 14.02 |
| 1970 | 14.36 | — | 13.88 |
| 1973 | 14.37 | 14.62 | 13.33 |
| 1974 | 14.86 | 12.42 | 15.20 |
| 1975 | 23.65 | 17.20 | 23.35 |
| 1976 | 32.10 | 19.32 | 28.45 |

SOURCE: Unit values supplied by Edward Hewett.

resource stocks. In natural-resource production, stocks of potential goods—e.g., timber on the stump, or coal reserves in the ground—have to be present for production to take place. No matter how much capital and labor one applies, there has to be a stock of crude oil present to produce crude oil.

Just having a stock handy, or suspecting one will be found if a well is sunk, is not enough, of course. So long as resource stocks, and the other inputs required technically to produce from it, are scarce, it is necessary to be able to place a value on a given stock at a given time, and to know when that value will change, by how much (or at least in what direction), and why. Without a method of valuation, it is not possible to make decisions such as the best rate at which to deplete a given stock, the right quantities of other inputs to combine with the stock, or the optimal amounts to invest in new stocks. To put it differently, to make such decisions is to place values on resource stocks, whether or not one likes or intends it.

Markets afford one method of assigning values (prices) to resource stocks or (what is the same thing) to flows of resources from the stocks. Those values result from the aggregation of managers' decisions about the various resources—rates of depletion, inputs combined in production, or investments in new stocks. Provided property rights to all scarce inputs (including natural resources) are well-defined and enforced, competitive markets will yield the efficient acquisition, holding, and use of natural-resource stocks. Those whose decisions are

at variance with the market's aggregate of decisions will suffer losses, and either learn to avoid them in the future or get out of the business.

Soviet planners, like their capitalist counterparts, face scarcity and thus have an incentive to manage their natural resources efficiently. In contrast to a market economy, however, under central planning the requisite values of resource stocks and flows do not form as a result of the functioning of the system. Rather, if they are to be used explicitly, values must be deliberately formulated and introduced into the planning and management process. If that is not done, the resource values will still form but only implicitly, as shadow prices resulting from the priorities contained in the quantity allocations so familiar in Soviet planning practice. There can be no guarantee, of course, that the *de facto* shadow values will be those the planners would have intended, had they calculated them out in advance.

Until the 1960s, resource valuation was seldom recognized in the USSR as an aspect of efficient planning warranting explicit treatment. In recent years, though, the problem has received increasing attention in the Soviet economic and planning literatures. In this section, I examine in detail recent developments in the Soviet methodology for valuing natural resources.

### A "Standard Methodology" for Natural Resources

As argued earlier, unrealistically low prices for natural-resource products have impeded the expansion of supply and provide little incentive for users to economize. Under the chronic excess demand that has characterized the Soviet natural-resource sector, users have scant influence on the quality of deliveries. Complaints in the press about coal shipments adulterated with stones, metal, and sand, or about coal that will not burn,[10] are typical. The impending general price reform (now overdue) is supposed to address the problems created by the low natural-resource prices.

Meanwhile, Soviet planners have been taking major administrative measures for more than a decade to attempt to deal with the wasteful use of natural resources. Between 1968 and 1975, the Supreme Soviet passed legal codes spelling out the rights and obligations of resource managers with respect to land, water, and forest resources; a draft code for the administration of mineral resources was published in January 1975.[11] More significantly, between 1973 and 1976, the State Committee on Science and Technology undertook a review of price-setting and use for natural resources. An Acting Scientific-Technical Commission on Economic Valuation of Minerals, headed by N. P. Fedorenko, was named to prepare a *Standard Methodology for the Monetary Valuation of Natural Resources in the National Economy*.[12] The actual task of preparing the draft document was turned over to the Central Economic-Mathematical Institute (TsEMI). The *Methodology* was to set up procedures for determining the economic value of mineral deposits and for choosing parameters that would secure the more efficient use of natural resources both in current and in perspective (long-run) planning.

TABLE 9
Soviet Export Prices of Coal, Selected Years
(rubles per metric ton)

| Year | (1)<br>To Comecon | (2)<br>To Western Europe | (3)<br>Total |
|------|-------------------|--------------------------|--------------|
| 1950 | 9.74 | — | 9.12 |
| 1955 | 13.64 | — | 12.77 |
| 1960 | 14.23 | 12.60 | 13.32 |
| 1965 | 12.76 | 12.08 | 12.19 |
| 1970 | 12.17 | 9.71 | 11.27 |
| 1974 | 13.40 | 18.93 | 16.14 |
| 1975 | 28.27 | 31.61 | 29.81 |
| 1976 | 28.67 | 27.80 | 29.47 |

SOURCE: Unit values supplied by Edward Hewett.

Attempts to develop improved measures for the valuation of natural resources followed logically from the revision of the *Standard Methodology for Determining the Economic Efficiency of Capital Investment and New Technology in the Economy*, published in 1969.[13] Following the publication of that document, a series of methodologies were worked out by committees of economists and published for the use of planners in various agencies: one for setting the wholesale prices of new products (1974), one for evaluating the economic efficiency of new technology (1977), and one for calculating optimal growth and location of production in perspective planning (1977).[14]

All of these methodologies took as their basis an approach to the problem of optimizing resource allocation in the Soviet economy derived from the work of L. V. Kantorovich.[15] Kantorovich derived the efficient pattern of resource allocation from an optimizing model, based on solving an objective function that minimized the cost of output, subject to constraints reflecting limited resources, given technologies, and the levels of output set by the center. This was, of course, optimizing in the most limited sense, since the central plan specified targets for inputs as well as outputs. But there was still some opportunity to improve both the regional dimension of supply and the structure of demand.

Kantorovich was clear that the main purpose of this analysis was the development of marginal-cost shadow prices, and that these prices would generate resource rents:

> The incorrect relationship of prices of the products of various branches of industry results from the fact that price formation gives insufficient weight to differential rent, especially in mining and timber. As a result, the effect and advantages of using rich natural resources are not fully disclosed (p. 214).

The Kantorovich model was fully in the tradition of Western microeconomic theory in treating time-discount rates and even such sophisticated measures as differentiated marginal prices for peak and off-peak use of electricity. He also raised the issue that was administratively the most difficult—the effect that the substitution of rents for differentiated purchase prices would have on the distribution of revenues among tax-collecting units. Improved measures of economic rent would make it harder for resource-producing units to conceal and retain rents. Furthermore, tax revenues from rents were likely to shift away from manufacturing regions and toward regions of primary-resource supply.

Following Kantorovich's proposals, scholars in the laboratory of K. G. Gofman at TsEMI put forward a series of proposals that applied a Kantorovich-type model, first, to the estimation of the structure of differential rents for land and, second, to the estimation of marginal-cost prices for natural resource products.[16] On the basis of its past work, Gofman's laboratory at TsEMI was assigned the task of drafting the tentative *Methodology for the Valuation of Natural Resources*.[17]

The resulting *Draft Methodology*, first circulated in 1975, consisted of six proposals:

1. Differential rent should be the sole basis of the economic value of all types of natural resource stocks.
2. Differential rent should be calculated as the difference between the value of the "first final output" of an exploiting industry and the total cost of variable inputs and movable capital employed in resource extraction and exploitation.
3. The cost of output at a specific site should be based on the actual prices of variable inputs and the actual technical constraints and norms in use in the industry.
4. The cadastral values of resource stocks at a particular site should be calculated as the capitalized value of the maximum differential rents earned by exploiting the site.
5. The discount rate to be used in capitalizing rents should be established centrally for each industry.
6. When costs of extraction differ at different sites, supply plans should be adjusted toward low-cost sites in order to maximize rents.

The *Methodology* underwent certain changes between its drafting and its adoption as a political document. The interest rate for capitalization of rents, set at 12 percent in early versions, was reduced to 8 percent for land and ore deposits and to 2 percent for standing timber in the final version.[18] More significantly, the sphere of the *Methodology* was restricted to use only in perspective (not current) planning. The marginal-cost values were to be used to measure the expected rate of return to alternative capital investments, to evaluate the productivity of geological prospecting work, and to establish the estimated values of resource stocks in the records of resource cadasters.[19] But they were *not* to be used for determining actual accounting costs, actual transfer prices, or the amounts of actual rental charges or taxes. The old system of differentiated accounting prices was to continue unchanged for current planning and management.

This essentially political (not economic) decision effectively severed the information and incentive functions of the price system. While marginal-cost prices were to provide the information for drawing up natural resource development plans, another quite different set of historical prices would still underlie the accounting costs paid by firms and the accounting revenues and profits earned by firms. Thus, there was no place in the final document for Gofman's proposal that the Council of Ministers should establish a resource management agency in each region empowered to exercise the rights of ownership over the natural resources of the region—that is, to lease those resources to enterprises and industry associations for extraction, to define the terms of extraction, and to levy monetary rental charges on the extracting agencies.[20]

As the basic principles of the new methodology emerged, branch research institutes in the extractive industries were assigned the task of working out individual branch methodologies for the valuation of their resource stocks. Use of these branch methodologies, too, was restricted to the evaluation of resource stocks in the State Resource Balances.

The restriction placed on the sphere of application of the valuation methodology points up the difficulty of introducing efficiency measures into an administrative environment. If resource rents can be concealed and captured by decision-makers at various levels in the ministerial hierarchies when information measures are poor, then these same officials will have little incentive to improve the measurement of their resource stocks or of their economic values. Gofman and the members of his laboratory clearly see the need to extend the use of marginal-cost prices to actual financial transactions; they address an even more fundamental problem with the proposal for creation of regional resource administrations for more effective monitoring and exercise of ownership rights over resources. But, to the extent that such efficiency proposals threaten the traditional functioning of the bureaucracies, they are likely to be sidelined or eviscerated.

### Valuing Resource Deposits

As noted, the value of resource deposits is derived from the value of the differential rent earned by the site. Soviet economists develop the theory of differential rent in much the same way that Western microeconomic theory does. In Western theory, the demand for resources is derived from their use value in the production of final products, called their "value of marginal product." In a world where production and consumption adjust to market-clearing price signals, the prices of ores and fuels will tend to reflect both their contribution to output and also the cost at the margin of expanding their production. The term "at the margin" is deceptively simple, considering the manifold possibilities of adjustment open to any decision maker. The margins of adjustment include all the alternative ways of expanding output at each point in time and over time. Of course, when the production and consumption of a good have not adjusted fully to a market-clearing price, then the resource can have many different use values and many different marginal costs. There will be gains in efficiency from transferring the resource from lower- to higher-value uses, and from transferring its production from higher- to lower-cost suppliers.

Good theoretical treatments of differential rent appear in several recent Soviet sources.[21] Gofman and Tsvetkov describe the application of the theory to perspective planning.[22] According to Gofman, while current practice still bases the value of natural resource products on the average costs of extraction, the goal of the new branch methodologies is to establish natural resource values based on "effectiveness in use at the margin." "Effectiveness" is defined as the benefit from having an extra unit of resource; it equals the shadow price of the supply constraint on that resource, since changes in the availability of an unconstrained resource have no effect on output. Differential rent earned by a resource deposit is measured as the difference between the value of the resource product evaluated at its marginal cost (*zamykayushchiye zatraty*) and the direct, local costs of the variable inputs used in extracting the resource, discounted over the life of the site. It may be expressed as

$$R = \sum_{t=1}^{T} \left[ \frac{Z_t - S_t}{(1 + E)^t} \right]$$

where $R$ is the economic value of a deposit, $Z$ is the marginal cost of the resource product produced, $S$ is the total annualized cost at that site, and $E$ is the interest rate.[23]

The process of establishing the value of resource deposits involves an interaction between regional or local decision-makers and the center. Deposits are valued at the same time that estimates are made of the sizes of stocks in the State Resource Balance. First, marginal-cost values of the final resource products ($Z_t$) are worked out and approved by the center. (Although the branch methodologies use the term "marginal-cost values" to refer to the prices of final resource products, the estimation procedures described derive the "value of marginal product," or marginal benefit from an additional unit of resource, rather than the cost of expanding resource output an additional unit in cases where the two measures differ.) Then, using information from sites with similar geological characteristics, a number of alternative technological variants for developing a site are spelled out. Each variant specifies the total amount of resource product that would be extracted from a deposit, the time path of extraction, the investment and direct costs of extraction ($S_t$), and their time path. All these values are discounted back to a single point in time, yielding a monetary net value of the deposit ($R$) for each of the technological variants.

All past outlays (sunk costs) are ignored (as they should be) in estimating the differential rent of an established site. For established sites, accounting deductions to cover geological-prospecting outlays as well as amortization charges to replace immobile capital are excluded from the calculation of cost. Thus, many mines or wells that are making accounting losses under current Soviet practice would earn positive rents (and thus have positive values) under the proposed new system. The only mines or wells that would make losses (and hence have negative values) would be those not covering their variable costs. These, presumably, would be candidates for closure. For new mines or wells, in contrast, the full cost of future geological work and capital investment would be included in the estimate of total cost, since before the fact all resources except the deposit itself are mobile.

Because the new branch methodologies are to be used only for perspective planning and not for current accounting, financial valuation, or taxation, their use would not deal directly with two of the most serious sources of inefficiency in resource use—a cost structure for inputs that rewards the wasteful drawdown of stocks, and a price structure for output that encourages underexploitation of superior sites. When the resource manager is rewarded for reducing the measured cost of output, he frequently finds it in his interest to substitute unpriced resource stocks for priced labor and capital. His financial incentives encourage consumption of stocks to the point where their net contribution to his reward function is zero. His superiors attempt to control stock drawdown by specifying extraction norms, but the application of the norms is policed badly, judging from reports in the press.

When the government collects resource rents in the form of a charge on output—whether as a charge on units of output produced, as in the case of oil, or as a lower differentiated price on the output of superior deposits, as in the case of mineral deposits—the lower net revenue received by the firm reduces the quantity of variable inputs the firm would choose to apply. In the absence of offsetting output targets, there will be underexploitation of superior deposits.[24]

In Figure 1, the function ABC shows the value of a resource extracted from a superior deposit by variable inputs when output is measured at the price paid by a user. The function DEC measures the same resource valued at the lower, differentiated price paid to this firm or valued at the net price $(l - r)$ that the firm receives after extraction of a rental charge of $r$ per unit output. The line FEBH represents the cost of producing the resource (assumed constant for convenience). A manager whose reward function depends on profit and who receives the lower net price would choose to employ $V_0$ of his (priced) variable inputs. Although at that level of activity the value to society of having an extra unit of production is $GV_0$, the return to the enterprise is only $EV_0$—just equal to the cost. Society would gain output $(V_1 - V_0)$ worth $GBV_1V_0$ and costing only $EBV_1V_0$ if the firm could be induced to expand output.

Soviet managerial rewards are not, of course, based on total profits but rather on achieving output targets.[25] A reward function that depended on extra output could lead a manager to expand output and thus offset the distortion caused by a tax on output or by too low a price. The problem is, though, to induce the manager to hire just the right amount of variable inputs and not too many—in effect, dipping into the rents to pay for extra inputs whose cost exceeds their price. In the figure, the manager should hire $V_1$, but might hire $V_2$, thereby reducing the total rents to society by the amount BJK.

Nothing in the Soviet output-based managerial reward function ensures that it will be $V_1$ instead of $V_2$—or $V_0$.

Neither output-maximizing rewards nor rental charges on output affect the firm's incentive to substitute unpriced resource stocks for priced variable inputs at each level of output. Ministries do attempt to reduce this form of waste by specifying and enforcing "coefficients of extraction" for resource stocks and by monitoring stock drawdown by means of the State Resource Balances. But ministry officials, too, face short-run targets for output and for nominal costs. Since no one "owns" resource stocks, no one may gain from actions that conserve stocks. Soviet economists have commented on the need to shift rental charges from output to resource stocks for some time. For example,[26]

> In our economic practice, rent is deducted from output rather than being charged against resource stock (taking into account conditions of use). Thus, the worse the work of an enterprise and the lower its output, the less rent it has to pay.

If the new *Methodology* were actually applied to the financial accounts of the enterprises, it could improve the financial basis for both input choice and output choice. The rental charge would be levied as a charge on units of resource stock consumed. The enterprise would receive the marginal-cost price for output and would pay the differential rental value of units of stock consumed. Of course, problems could still arise in measuring the actual stock remaining in a deposit. And, in negotiating the original rental charges, resource managers would have incentives to overestimate the costs of extraction and to underestimate the possible yield from stocks so that they could capture resulting slack in some manner by local personnel.

## Estimation of the Marginal-Cost Value of Resource Products

The new methodology would derive measures of differential rent from estimates made by central planners of the marginal-cost value of units of resource product. As in the case of differential rents, the sphere of use of the marginal-cost unit values would be limited to perspective planning. They would be used for projecting the social returns to capital investments and for setting the cadastral valuation of resource stocks in the State Resource Balances.[27]

In practice, the marginal unit values are derived as the shadow prices of fixed resource constraints in large linear programming models. (Examples of some of these models are discussed below.) The typical model poses the optimizing problem in the following manner: minimize the cost of producing a fixed mix of final outputs, valued at centrally set prices, subject to constraints on the supplies of a set of natural resource inputs, fixed prices for other variable inputs (that are thus assumed to be available in unlimited quantities), and technological coefficients relating the constrained and unconstrained inputs to the desired outputs.[28]

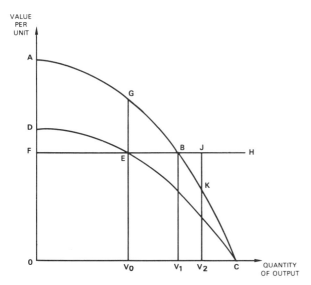

Figure 1

Gofman describes an approximate method of calculating the marginal unit value of a scarce metal as follows: in each possible use of the metal, calculate an incremental value, $z_i$, as[29]

$$z_i = \frac{c_i - p_i}{q_i},$$

where $c_i$ is the cost of a unit of final output using the nearest substitute metal; $p_i$ is the cost of a unit of final output using this metal, excluding any rental value for the metal in question; and $q_i$ is the per unit consumption (*udelny raskhod*) of this metal per unit of final output. When one of the possible uses of a resource is export, the incremental value in that use is taken to be the foreign exchange earned through export.

All possible uses of the ore would be ranked and the most profitable uses would be satisfied first, up to the point where supply was exhausted. On the supply side, too, deposits would be ranked by cost, with output coming from the lowest-cost sites first. Thus, the shadow unit value of the ore would be bounded by the unit cost of the last deposit in use and the unit cost of the next deposit held in reserve.

Gofman minimizes the difficulties in applying the methodology to current Soviet planning, even though the actual structure of Soviet output in the resource industries is almost certainly far from optimal and existing wholesale prices far from the marginal unit values. For so-called deficit commodities, the marginal unit value used in Soviet planning would still equal the shadow price of the scarce input, which price would exceed the marginal cost of expanding supply. For non-deficit resource products, including those in excess supply, the marginal unit value would "establish the maximum permissible level of incremental unit cost of any output of an extractive branch in a particular period."[30]

Just as future output of the extractive braches would be adjusted toward the optimal output, wholesale prices (gross of rents or taxes on the resource) would move toward the optimal marginal unit values:[31]

The primary principles of contemporary practice in price formation are: a single price for a single product irrespective of individual differences in costs of production, interregional differences in prices that reflect differences in costs of transport, price differentials for substitute products that reflect differences in effectiveness, and increases in the prices of deficit commodities . . .

The estimation of marginal unit values for the products of extractive industries is intended to give planners more and better information about the economy than they get from existing wholesale prices, costs, norms, and performance indicators. Nevertheless, since the shadow unit values estimated are only as good as the information used in the model, the planners are substituting one kind of information problem for another. Martin Weitzman, John Bonin, and Alan Marcus have proposed interesting incentive structures for planned systems that would, in essence, reward producers for the provision of accurate information as well as for the production of output.[32] In current Soviet practice, however, producers lack effective incentives to provide accurate information to the planners.

Even if an optimizing model were capable of providing the planners with reliable shadow prices for use in perspective planning, the decision-makers responsible for executing current plans still would likely find it in their own self-interest to keep current wholesale prices below marginal levels. Current wholesale prices for extractive products, which are set on the basis of average cost, tend to generate excess demands for extractive inputs. With excess demands for the inputs that are under their control, allocators of extractive products enjoy considerable power through their ability to assign things of value to some individuals and to withhold them from others. Inputs do, in fact, tend to move toward higher-valued uses under current Soviet arrangements, but mainly because enterprises and ministries spend real resources trying to get access to allocations, and it pays higher-value users to spend more. Activity directed at acquiring raw materials that are in excess demand employs inputs that could produce other goods. Thus, rents are dissipated that could have been collected if shadow price unit values were applied in current production decisions as well as in perspective planning.

If we use Soviet practice in the pricing of capital investment during the last decade as our model, we would predict that the impending revisions of accounting prices (originally due to be announced in April 1981 but now delayed) will show only a partial adjustment in the prices of extractive products toward efficient levels. If so, those responsible for allocating those products will continue to enjoy the private benefits of excess demand.

## Taking Account of Time

Like the rest of the new valuation methodology, the underlying theory for comparing the flow of resource services over time could have come straight from a Western economics text. There is, however, one difference, and it is the avenue by which the political element in Soviet investment allocation asserts itself in practice: the setting of differentiated interest rates for different sectors—much like the subsidized low interest rates charged to irrigation and hydroelectric power projects in our own economy.

Gofman's book on the methodology of resource valuation presents the basics of capital theory, including the treatment of expected changes in price level and differences in risk, but then proceeds to list the different discount rates to be charged in practice in different industries. He ignores the inconsistency between his recommended theory and this practical departure from it. No mention is made of the cost to the Soviet economy if the flow of benefits from investment in one type of resource deposit really is much lower than the flow of benefits from investment in another type.[33]

In the new methodology, future returns from a present investment are brought back to a current value using the present-value coefficient (*koeffitsient privedeniya*), $V_t = 1/(1 + E)^t$, where $E$ is the discount rate and $t$ refers to the time periods over which discounting is to occur. There are four different formulas used in different situations for summing the annual differential rents earned, $r$, to derive the total rental value, $R$, of a resource deposit.[34] There is the basic present value equation:

$$R = r \sum_{t=1}^{n} V_t = \frac{r}{1 + E} + \frac{r}{(1 + E)^2} + \ldots + \frac{r}{(1 + E)^n},$$

which reduces to $R = r/E$ for a permanent stream; in this latter case, $E$ is termed the capitalization coefficient in Western fashion. When branches are estimating the value of a project that begins to yield a return after a gestation period of $y$ years, they are directed to use:

$$R = r \sum_{y=1}^{n} V_y = \frac{r}{(1 + E)^{y-1}}$$

When a project has a limited life of $T$ years, the appropriate calculation is:

$$R = r \sum_{t=1}^{T} V_t = \frac{r[(1 + E)^T - 1]}{E(1 + E)^T}$$

And, when the expected return on a project is expected to rise or fall at some rate, $k$:

$$R = r \sum_{t=1}^{T} \frac{(1 + k)^{t-1}}{(1 + E)^t}$$

If Soviet resource branches are making their calculations from the above equations, then American and Soviet accountants must be making their investment calculations from the same compound interest tables.

Estimates of the expected change of annual differential rent earned—the coefficient $k$ above—are based on estimates of change in the expected value of output and change in local costs of extraction. These are codified as industry coefficients of change, which are estimated from expert evaluations.[35]

The final version of *Methodological Basis for Valuation of Mineral Deposits* is far more terse on the question of time discount than the draft versions. Early versions of the draft methodology refer to discount rates of 8 and 12 percent. However, the final methodology for mineral deposits uses discount rates of 8 and 5 percent "in cases where changes over time in marginal costs used in calculation can be reliably estimated only for the first years in which a deposit is worked."[36]

In his book on the methodology of valuation, Gofman writes: "The normative efficiency of investment in immobile natural resources should, as a rule, be lower than norms of efficiency of capital investment. The discount rate should be no higher than 14 to 17 percent. In forestry, rates of return should be lower. The maximum discount rates should be 0.022 for pine, 0.024 for fir, and 0.023 for oak."[37]

A discount rate of 14 to 17 percent would imply a time horizon for investment of approximately 15 years. However, Gofman writes that the actual payback lifetimes of various investments in resource deposits are as follows: for coal mines, 40 to 60 years; for oil and gas, 15 to 30 years; for precious rare metals, 5 to 10 years; and for forest stands, 60 to 120.[38] According to Gofman, the low rates of return to forestry are an attempt to substitute for the inability to place a positive valuation on the environmental and hydrological services of standing timber. However, the long time horizons for coal and some oil and gas imply that economists expect larger increases in prices and rents for resources than are now specified in the valuation variables of perspective plans.

Property Rights in Resources

Even if the forthcoming new price system results in a substantial improvement in the accounting prices for natural-resource products, the Soviet system, like other large bureaucratic organizations, will face difficulties in enforcing the propery rights in socialist resources effectively. To assess how well the new arrangements will work, we must ask what decision-makers will gain from improving the efficiency of resource use and whether the gains from improved resource use will outweigh the costs of measuring, policing, and enforcing the desired changes.

It is clear that planners and managers do not always gain from avoiding inefficiency under present arrangements. Planners and officials of the Ministry of Finance can expect to gain from the introduction of charges for resource deposits if the charges increase budget revenues and the state's discretionary share of national income. It is doubtful, though, that the planners and financial officials of every region would benefit. A shift from output charges to rental charges would transfer tax revenues away from processing regions and toward extractive regions; such a shift would therefore be a subject of bitter dispute.

Leslie Dienes has argued persuasively that the relative underpricing of Siberian natural resources has tended to give unwarranted impetus to the location of industry in Eastern regions, presumably benefiting these regions.[39] The opposite case, that these regions have, on net, been hurt by the underpricing of their resources has been made by Bogachev. His view is that the underpricing of natural-resource products deprives the Eastern regions of the tax revenue for social overhead expenditures; this in turn raises the costs of labor and, thus, the construction costs of projects in these regions.[40]

The central planners will gain if the new pricing arrangements improve current economic performance. But the planners have no formal mechanism for profiting from conservation of resource stocks. They cannot collect a reward from their successors if they leave them with larger resource stocks. So we would not be surprised if the time horizon of the planners were short.

To the extent that official incentives measure and reward such activity, enterprise officials may have incentives to increase the efficiency of their use of resource deposits. Or they may have incentives to save resources without reporting such activity, if they can conceal and capture such savings in the form of private benefits. It appears that the Soviet bureaucratic environment allows some informal (if illegal) transfers of wealth from the state treasury to various levels of the bureaucracy, both to allow some limited management appropriability of gains to efficiency and perhaps to purchase bureaucratic loyalty.

The authors of the valuation methodology appear unconvinced that the existing institutional arrangements will provide adequate incentives to exercise property rights in resources efficiently. Instead, they propose that each region should establish a resource-owning organization. This organization would receive income from enterprises in the form of rental payments for the right to exploit resources (*platy za pravo raskhoda*). It might also engage in activities to reduce environmental pollution, which activities would be supported by special payments for conservation (*platy za pravo sberezheniya*). Associated with the resource-owning administration would be a new financial agency, called the "Bank of the Biosphere." The Bank would be financed by special charges on enterprises which would be placed in the Bank's "fund for the reproduction of natural resources" (*fond vosproizvodstva prirodnoi sredy*). The Bank could make loans for conservation projects either to the resource-owning organization or to the enterprises themselves, and it would collect interest on its loans. (It is not clear what incentive enterprises would have to borrow for conservation activities.) Under this plan, enterprises would pay two charges: one to the resource-owning organization for the right to extract resources, and the other into the conservation fund of the Bank of the Biosphere.[41]

Far-fetched as the above proposals may sound, it is clear that property rights in resources are not defined and enforced efficiently now. And marginal cost prices alone will not guarantee efficient resource allocation unless individual decision-makers share in the benefits and costs that result from their actions.

One last concern of the economists is the possibility that the government would allocate monopoly returns to itself as sole owner of resource deposits. In my view, however, it is unlikely that allocators would favor charging the full monopoly price for socialist resources as long as they can transfer benefits from the treasury to themselves by underpricing things of value.

## The State Resource Balances

A major use of the branch methodologies is supposed to be in the construction of inventories of natural-resource stocks in value terms. These inventories, patterned on the Soviet land cadaster, are characterized by a degree of detail that is an obsessive-compulsive's dream. All the physical, value, and locational characteristics of land and extractive stocks are said to be coded and stored in computer data banks, although how the data are actually used in the planning process is not altogether clear.

The State Land Fund has a venerable tradition, dating from the emancipation of the serfs and the institution of land redemption payments in 1861. Although scholars frequently complain that the measures of land quality are poorly related to actual tax payments, their use is widely

accepted.[42] In contrast, estimates of physical reserves of extractive products have often proved inaccurate. For example, one source estimates that 40 percent of $C_1$-category oil reserves have to be written off.[43] The planners' estimates of the size of resource stocks are the subject of frequent complaint by industry specialists. For example, Zhavoronkova complains that the "coefficient of complexity" measuring the share of valuable components extracted from a multi-metal ore is expressed for planning purposes as the ratio of the price-weighted materials actually extracted to the estimated total quantity of all valuable materials in the ore, without regard to whether it is actually cost-effective to attempt to extract every last unit of every component.[44]

Recently, estimates of the value of resource stocks based on the capitalization of differential rents have become the subject of similar dispute, because the estimates of quantity and of extraction cost threaten to become standards against which later enterprise performance is to be judged. This may be one reason why ministry officials appear adamant in wanting to keep the marginal valuations separate from actual costs and prices used in current accounting. One writer complains that estimates of the economic value of oil reserves overstate both the physical amount of extractable resource and the number of years over which any operating well can be expected to earn net rents over and above the capital and current costs of extraction. He contends that, at current prices, most wells earn rents for, at most, the first 5 years of operation. For the balance of their 15 to 20 year operating life, wells just cover operating costs, including the charges to amortize capital.[45]

The rules for registering land call for an inventory of the land fund on the basis of size, user, administrative and territorial division, physical quality, and economic use. The draft land legislation, adopted in 1969, provides for inventorying land into 6 main divisions: agricultural land, urban land, land devoted to non-agricultural production, forest land, land devoted to water resources, and unused land. Registration is carried out separately for 15 zones, including 42 provinces.

Within each category, land is rated on a 100 point system to establish indices of qualitative factors. The data bearing on economic value recorded on each piece of land include gross output and net income in present use, yield in present cultivation, potential yield under optimal cropping and technology, and rate of return to current and capital expenditures.[46]

The compilation of all this information provides detailed data on differential rents earned by land according to microzone. Recently, Soviet scholars who have had access to this information have applied cost-minimizing linear programs to estimate the potential differential rents that could be earned by land under optimal assignments at prices of an optimal plan. Smirnov presents a comparison of differential rents with taxes paid for 43 microregions of the Gorky Oblast in 1965 and 1966; his comparison shows a variation of differential rent from approximately plus 40 rubles per hectare to minus 15 rubles.[47] Fedorenko compares the differential rents actually earned in 16 microregions of the Moscow Oblast with the potential differential rents that these same regions would earn according to the calculations of an optimal plan; he concludes that the rents under an optimal plan would be anywhere from 22 to 400 percent higher than the rents currently earned.[48]

For mineral resources, separate valuations are made for deposits that have been explored in a preliminary way (*poiskovo-razvedochnaya stadiya*) and for deposits whose characteristics have been investigated in detail (*detalnaya razvedka*). The first valuation procedure includes all reserves, including $C_2$; the second set of values are estimates of reserves in categories $A$, $B$, and $C_1$.[49]

The cadastral valuation of preliminary resource stocks, including the $C_2$ category, is used in planning subsequent geological exploration and in setting temporary norms for ores of economic worth; it also determines which deposits are investigated further. At this stage, estimates are made of the size of the deposits, ore concentration, projected costs of extraction, and projected capital investment—although all of these numbers must be highly tentative at this stage as a deposit has had little real investigation.[50] For example, in the case of oil, if the presence of oil has been demonstrated by even one successful prospecting well, the deposit may be transferred to category $C_1$.[51] For certain resources, such as coal, there is an intermediate stage of exploration (*predvaritelnaya razvedka*) to establish the physical characteristics of the deposit—its structure, depth, and width of vein.[52]

The cadastral valuation of deposits that have been surveyed in detail is used to estimate the size of the resource stock in physical units and in comparable (quality-adjusted) physical units. It serves as the basis for segregating resources into those included in and those excluded from the State Resource Balances. It is used, as well, in drawing up precise extraction plans and technical and economic norms in the five-year plans.[53] The cadastral valuations are used to assign monetary values to resources in the state cadaster of mineral deposits, which underlies decisions for the establishment of new production facilities.

Both the preliminary and detailed valuations are used to reward geological prospecting work. The output measures for geological prospecting are simple indicators of activity or gross output. The main output index is the plan for growth of proven reserves by type of mineral. The use of simple, gross planning indicators allows prospecting organizations to compensate for incomplete or unsatisfactory work on sites of immediate relevance with growth of reserves at other sites of no current economic interest.[54] Procedures for awarding bonuses exacerbate the tendency toward the dispersion of effort—what is called "over-prospecting." Members of geological prospecting teams may also be awarded large bonus payments for the discovery of resource deposits of potential economic value. The Basic Principles of Oil Law for the USSR and Soviet Republics, dated 9 July 1975, state:[55]

Individuals who discover a previously unidentified deposit having industrial value and also individuals who uncover additional or new resource stocks at known sites which offer substantial increments of

industrial value are designated as primary discoverers.

Primary discoverers have the right to remuneration. Rights of discoverers and procedures for compensating them are determined in accordance with Soviet law.

In theory, the cadastral valuation of resources that have been surveyed in detail is supposed to be adjusted systematically to record additions to and withdrawals from stocks as a result of production experience. But there is still no item on the balance sheet of mining enterprises that measures or amortizes stocks of proven reserves.[56] Indeed, since the cadastral valuations are supposed to be derived from the marginal valuations of an optimal plan, they may be quite unrelated to the partial (*chastnye*) measures based on current wholesale prices.

Calculations of the cadastral valuation of state resource stocks have been presented by a number of Soviet specialists. Some calculations are based on current imputed resource rentals and others on the differential rents of optimal plans. Silayev and Shemov present estimates of the value of natural-resource stocks, based on imputed rents, that value agricultural land at 320 billion rubles, the total flow of water in the rivers at 85 billion rubles, standing timber at 100 to 175 billion rubles, and oil at 70 to 100 billion rubles. In their methodology, the capitalized rental value, $R$, is expressed as the present value of an expected future income flow, $r$, capitalized at an interest rate, $E$, of 12 percent (less an expected rate of price change, $a$, of 2 percent per year). For forestry, the interest rate is taken to be 1 percent and the expected price change to be 3 percent.[57] These valuations contrast with the assessment of Kassirov, who values the resource stocks of the extractive industries at 132.5 billion rubles and agricultural resources at only 156.5 billion rubles for 1970.[58]

Shifting the cadastral values of resource stocks to the firm basis of the differential rents of an optimal plan would do much to clarify issues that are currently in dispute, such as which deposits to include in the State Resource Balances. The branch methodologies are clear that the standard is now a value based on the differential rents of the optimal plan. But descriptions of the mineral balances stored in computer data banks suggest considerable confusion as to what resources are included at what values. It appears that the criteria for registering resources as "on balance" are only weakly related to the potential costs of extraction of these resources.[59]

## Estimation of Optimizing Models

Soviet planners recognize that the information coming from operating units in the economic system does not provide them with the basis for efficient decision-making. Thus, they have pushed valuations derived from optimizing models to serve as surrogate prices. Then, the planners can use their synthetic indicators to test information coming from enterprises and for negotiating with their ministries. Nevertheless, the values derived from optimizing calculations are still dependent on information supplied by firms and ministries themselves, and the resulting estimates of shadow prices and output allocations are only as good as the initial assumptions about the technology and resource constraints.

Because they must meet the needs of planners, Soviet models of resource use differ from typical Western models. A representative U.S. model consists of behavioral equations describing how decentralized economic agents will respond to changes in the incentives and constraints that they face. Concern is directed toward deriving the testable implications of the model and then testing these implications econometrically. The econometric results yield estimates of the parameters of behavioral equations—for example, price and income elasticities of demand.

Soviet models lack behavioral equations. Since they cannot assume maximizing behavior on the part of decentralized agents, they have to simulate optimizing behavior by including explicit optimizing computations.

A Soviet model starts with a set of plans. The main task of the economist is to derive from the desired plan a program of outputs of final and intermediate products that will meet the plan efficiently according to some specified goal function. So the model is concerned only with underlying technologies—with what can be done, rather than with what will be done by decentralized units. Thus, the parameters that emerge from a Soviet optimizing model are technological—the effect that relaxation of a constraint would have on the goal function.

In the models surveyed here, desired final outputs, available resource supplies, and feasible technologies were all specified in the initial assumptions. The economist estimated the plan that would minimize the cost of constrained inputs from the assumptions given. Most of the Soviet models consist of large systems of equations. Hence one interesting aspect of their work has been the development of iterative algorithms for the solution of large programming problems and the elaboration of procedures for decomposing large, complex problems into several hierarchical subproblems.

Soviet economists are open about the problems that they face in using cost-minimizing linear programs to estimate parameters for the Soviet economy.[60] Since the requirements for computer capacity rise rapidly with the number of constraints imposed in the problem, many of the models described in the resource literature cannot be estimated at Soviet research facilities. The shadow prices that are used in perspective planning seem frequently to have been estimated from approximate, hand calculations, and many of the values that are supposed to be derived endogenously seem actually to have been prespecified.

Another problem is the instability of the estimated shadow prices in the models. Since only a few technologies can be considered, small changes in the output plans generate large changes in the input coefficients and shadow prices of constrained inputs. Further, since the economists have to take as givens the output targets of the official annual plans—in which one industry's output is another industry's input—there is little room for actual

cost-minimizing adjustment in the models. The structure of demand is improved, but the level of supply is constrained at the outset.

Not the least of the problems is the lack of data on industry costs and technologies. Since aggregate data are subject to tight departmental controls, most economists have better access to information on individual economic units than to aggregate data. Apparently, the assumptions of the economists have to be "adjusted" until a desired result is generated by the model.

Gofman and other members of his laboratory at TsEMI have developed linear programming models to estimate optimal plans for agricultural products and for the cutting of timber.[61] Their agricultural model considers the possibilities for shifting land between crops across regions. The program minimizes the cost of producing and transporting crops and animal products. Costs are minimized subject to constraints on each of the following in each region: quantities of variable inputs, quantities of fertilizer, specified minima for the consumption of each product in each region, transport constraints, and national constraints for the minimum total output of each product.

As described, the model has the problem that some of the costs to be minimized are, in fact, shadow prices that are supposed to be estimated by the model itself. In fact, the actual estimation procedure proceeds by stages. First, shadow prices are estimated for land, animal stocks, and variable inputs from the output constraints of the output plans, the resource constraints given to the regions, and the costs of priced inputs. Then the resource (value of marginal product) shadow prices are treated as costs in the solution to a cost-minimizing problem that estimates the marginal cost of providing the guaranteed level of consumption of the $i$th product in the national total and in each regional plan. There appears to be little room for actual adjustment in a model that is so heavily constrained.

The authors derive the following minimum and maximum marginal values for agricultural products in their model:[62]

| | |
|---|---|
| Wheat | 146–158 rubles/ton |
| Rye | 149–161 |
| Barley | 145–157 |
| Corn | 173–188 |
| Potatoes | 138–154 |
| Buckwheat | 322–338 |
| Millet | 128–144 |

In a similar model for the timber industry, they estimate that the marginal value of sawn timber varies from 32 rubles per cubic meter in the Baltic region to 14 rubles in the Far East, because the cost of transport is so much higher for wood than for agricultural products.[63] In Table 10, their estimates of the marginal values of wood by region are compared with the estimates of differential rent derived by Brenton Barr.[64] Although their regionalizations differ, the structure of shadow prices is similar.

An article that appeared shortly after publication of the methodology for valuation of mineral deposits presents

TABLE 10
Marginal Values for Wood Products

| Oblasts and Economic Regions | Gofman: Marginal Value (Rubles per cubic meter) | Barr: Differential Rent (Rubles per cubic meter) | |
|---|---|---|---|
| Arkhangelsk Oblast | 24 | | 16.60 |
| Vologda Oblast | 22 | | 17.35 |
| Karelian ASSR and Murmansk Oblast | 24 | | 17.00 |
| Komi ASSR | 23 | | 15.26 |
| Leningrad Oblast | 26 | | — |
| Kostroma Oblast | 24 | | 17.31 |
| Central Russian Economic Region | 28 | | — |
| Bashkir ASSR | 24 | | — |
| Volga Economic Region | 26 | | — |
| Kirov Oblast | 22 | | 16.66 |
| Volga-Vyatka Economic Region | 26 | | — |
| North Caucasus Economic Region | 32 | | — |
| Sverdlovsk Oblast | 20 | | 15.04 |
| Perm Oblast and Udmurt ASSR | 22 | | — |
| Tyumen Oblast | 22 | | 14.48 |
| Tomsk Oblast | 22 | | 11.92 |
| Novosibirsk, Omsk, Irkutsk, Kemerovo oblasts and Altai Krai | 19 | Irkutsk | 9.58 |
| | | Altai | 12.82 |
| Krasnoyarsk Krai | 17 | | 11.01 |
| Chita Oblast, Khabarovsk Krai, Buryat ASSR | 16 | Chita | 6.82 |
| | | Khabarovsk | 2.16 |
| | | Buryat | 7.93 |
| Far East | 14 | | — |
| Baltic Republics | 32 | | — |
| Ukraine and Moldavia | 31 | | — |
| Belorussia | 30 | | — |

the results of an attempt to apply the new procedures to the estimation of marginal values for iron ore and iron production.[65] The author, Kh. N. Gizatullin, estimates the marginal value of ore deposits from the dual to a cost-minimizing linear program. Then he demonstrates how the valuation of resource sites can be used by industrial planners to choose the optimal investment program and time path of extraction of a mining enterprise. Furthermore, the shadow values of iron production and iron ores can be linked: the shadow value of iron *production* at enterprise $i$ $(u_i)$ is equal to the quantity, the shadow valuation of iron *ore* from deposit $j$ $(v_j)$ divided by the technical coefficient of iron production at $i$ per unit of ore of type $j$ $(w_{ji})$, minus the unit cost of making iron at $i$ from ore of type $j$ $(c_{ji})$:

$$u_i = \frac{v_j}{w_{ji}} - c_{ji}.$$

Some of the problems in applying the valuation methodology show up in the Gizatullin example. The optimizing model makes use of actual accounting prices for priced variable inputs, including standard normative charges for capital investment. In this, it violates the (correct) prescription in the valuation methodology that all normative charges assigned to sunk capital should be excluded from the estimation of cost.

Interestingly enough, a Western optimizing model of the Soviet iron and steel industry shares similar data problems.[66] The authors are forced to rely on Soviet mea-

sures of extraction and production cost that are based on average industry costs, including normative charges for sunk capital. Including such charges will make production from new facilities look unrealistically attractive relative to continuing production at existing facilities.

Many of the optimizing models used in planning are characterized by mind-boggling detail and size. Such a model for the valuation of mineral sites is described by Tsvetkov.[67] This model contains 5 different sets of constraints: one for resource supplies to the extractive branches; another for the fuel and energy branches; a third for construction; a fourth for repair and equipment; and a fifth for aggregate resource limits.

Most of these large, detailed models are solved in a series of hierarchical, disaggregated steps. A model estimated by Antsyshkin and Polyanskaya uses 5 stages of iteration to generate regionally-differentiated prices for energy coal.[68] Vaik uses a 3-stage iterative approximation to the results of a full optimizing model.[69]

A not insignificant advantage of resource valuation by means of optimizing models is the opportunity it provides for valuation of environmental resources on a par with other traditionally-priced inputs. Some interesting examples are a model for pricing water resources by Ushakov,[70] and the costing of environmental damage by Bagrinovsky and Lemeshev.[71]

The most important disadvantage of the reliance on optimizing models is their bias toward static analysis. Although the estimation of the present values of deposits provides a framework for considering the full dynamic path of extraction, the static linear programs estimate a single annual rental value for a single site, and this one-period shadow price is applied for the duration of the planning period. Varshavsky and Varshavsky have published an interesting dynamic model for the development of the crude oil and natural gas industries; this model fits production and cost functions and estimates a distributed lag for capital investment.[72] Rayatskas and Sutkaitis have estimated a dynamic model that incorporates capital expenditures for the reduction of environmental pollution.[73]

## Conclusions

The upcoming industrial price revision will serve as a test of sorts of the Soviet economy's ability to adjust to external and internal changes in circumstance. It is important to the long-term functioning of the Soviet system that accounting prices and planning prices should correspond. In order for incentive mechanisms to function at all, social costs must be reflected not just in design calculations but also in real operating prices. But improved prices are a necessary, not a sufficient condition for improved use of resource deposits. When (as now) the manager of a resource has control over it only in its present use, he has no incentive to generate the information that would reveal its best possible long-term use.

Any shift of accounting prices toward market-clearing values will generate groups of losers and gainers. Rental charges will increase the incomes and taxes of extractive regions like Siberia. For petroleum, which is already highly profitable, revenues could be shifted from refining to extraction. For coal, an industry that now barely covers cost, the addition of rental charges will force large increases in the production costs of users such as electric power and metallurgy.

Supplementing the regional tensions are reformist pressures from the proponents of economic decentralization. These voices have been submerged since the failure of the 1965 Kosygin reforms. At present, the vertical organization of the branch ministries is as strong as it has ever been, and there are frequent reports of lack of interbranch coordination in the territorial-production administrations.[74]

In the absence of functioning markets, the only successful way to achieve coordination beyond branch and regional boundaries seems to be to internalize all activities under a single administrative head. Thus, scholars who have been close to the large Siberian development efforts are calling for a new organizational unit organized on the program principle.[75] These scholars seem to have in mind an organization something like an American corporation. However, the only existing institution in the Soviet system that is able to cut across branch and territorial boundaries is the military—a very nonreformist institution.

Two questions seem important for the future. First, how far will the price revision go towards matching the operating prices used in current planning and management with the marginal values being developed for use in perspective planning? We cannot know for sure, but past experience would suggest at most a partial match up, a set of half measures that strike a compromise of some sort. Soviet politicians no less than their Western counterparts deal in compromises among competing claims.

Second, what impact will the price changes have on the efficiency of Soviet production and use of natural resources? If the changes are substantial (as they ought to be), there would also be substantial effects on output and use decisions. The effects are not, though, likely to be so profound as to engender major shifts in trade patterns, either within the USSR or at its borders. The 1967 price revision made sizable changes but caused no about-faces. This time, of course, there is a robust Soviet modeling industry to trace through the effects of any revisions; one place to look for effects of the price revision will be in the publications of the large-scale modelers. One certainty midst all the guessing is that these scholars will still find operating costs and prices of natural resources wanting in terms of overall economic efficiency.

## NOTES

1. For example, Torbin reports a range within the Donets Basin in 1970 of 5.63–47.96 rubles per ton of coal of given quality (V. I. Torbin, *Territorialnaya differentsiatsiya tsen v tyazheloi promyshlennosti* [Territorial differentiation of prices in heavy industry] (Moscow, 1974), p. 232. In 1977, coal production costs unadjusted for heat values ranged from 1.5 (Ekibastuz) to 25 rubles per ton (Moscow).

2. Leslie Dienes and Theodore Shabad, *The Soviet Energy System* (Washington: V. H. Winston, 1979), p. 74.

3. V. I. Shkatov and B. S. Suponitsky, *Optovye tseny na produktsiyu tyazheloi promyshlennosti* [Wholesale prices for the products of heavy industry] (Moscow: Ekonomika, 1969), p. 4.

4. S. G. Stolyarov, *O tsenakh i tsenoobrazovanii v. SSSR* [On prices and price formation in the USSR] (Moscow: Statistika, 1969).

5. R. W. Campbell, "Prices, Rent, and Decision Making: The Economic Reform in Soviet Oil and Gas Production," *Jahrbuch der Wirtschaft Osteuropas* 2 (1971): 291–313.

6. Examples of such procedures are reported in Institut Ekonomiki, AN SSSR, *Problemy ekonomicheskoi effektivnosti razmeshcheniya sotsialisticheskogo proizvodstva v SSSR* [Problems of cost-effectiveness of the location of socialist production in the USSR] (Moscow, 1968).

7. Shkatov and Suponitsky, *Optovye tseny.*

8. Ibid.

9. K. G. Gofman, *Ekonomicheskaya otsenka prirodnykh resursov v usloviyakh sotsialisticheskoi ekonomiki* [Economic evaluation of natural resources under conditions of socialist economics] (Moscow: Nauka, 1977).

10. See Yu. Semyonov, "Increase the Donets Basin's potential," *Izvestiya*, 8 December 1979, p. 2; and L. Kaibysheva and Ye. Manucharova, "Why Power Stations Stand Idle," *Izvestiya*, 24 April 1980, cited in *Current Digest of the Soviet Press* 32 (28 May 1980): 12.

11. "Draft Principles on Mineral Resources," *Current*

*Digest of the Soviet Press* 27 (12 February 1975): 8–14 (from *Izvestiya*, 18 January 1975). See the codes on land, forest, and water in *Vedomosti Verkhovnogo Soveta SSSR*, 1968, no. 23, item 435; 1970, no. 50, item 566; and 1975, no. 23, item 435.

12. For a list of the members of that commission, see "Methodological principles for an economic valuation of mineral deposits," *Ekonomika i matematicheskiye metody* 14 (May–June 1978): 405.

13. "A Standard method for determining the cost-effectiveness of investment in new technology for the economy," *Ekonomicheskaya gazeta*, 1969, no. 39; English translation in *MATEKON* 8 (1970): 3–52.

14. Respectively, *Metodika opredeleniya optovykh tsen na novuyu produktsiyu proizvodstvenno-tekhnicheskogo naznacheniya* [Methodology for determining the wholesale prices of new products for productive-technical purposes] (Moscow: Preiskurantizdat, 1974); "Methodology for determining the cost-effectiveness of using new technology inventions, and rationalizers' proposals in the economy," *Ekonomicheskaya gazeta*, 1977, no. 10; and "Standard methodology for calculating the optimization of growth and location of production over the long term," *Ekonomika i matematicheskiye metody* 13 (November-December 1977): 1137–50.

15. L. V. Kantorovich, "On Prices, Norms, and Economic Efficiency," *Problems of Economics*, August-September-October 1976, pp. 212–21 (from *Ekonomika i organizatsiya promyshlennogo proizvodstva*, January 1971); also in L. V. Kantorovich: *Essays in Optimal Planning* (White Plains, N.Y.: International Arts and Sciences Press, 1976), pp. 212–21.

16. K. G. Gofman, I. M. Khrabrov, A. A. Gusev, A. F. Mudretsov, and G. V. Pronin, "Optimal Land Management," *Ekonomika i matematicheskiye metody*, 1971, no. 6; translated in *MATEKON* 9 (Spring 1973): 71–89. Also, K. G. Gofman, A. A. Gusev, and A. F. Mudretsov, "Determination of marginal costs on the production of extractive industries," *Ekonomika i matematicheskiye metody* 11 (1975): 695–706.

17. K. G. Gofman, I. M. Khabrov, B. S. Verkhovsky, V. I. Denisova, A. F. Mudretsov, G. V. Pronin, A. A. Gusev, and I. I. Stanov, *Izkhodnye polozheniya metodiki ekonomicheskoi otsenki prirodnykh resursov* [Basic propositions of methods for the economic evaluation of natural resources] (Moscow: TsEMI, 1975).

18. Gofman, *Ekonomicheskaya otsenka*, pp. 220–21.

19. See "Methodological principles," p. 406. The last application of marginal cost has become a matter of dispute.

20. Gofman, *Ekonomicheskaya otsenka*, p. 64.

21. V. Bogachev, "On mineral rent and the valuation of raw-material and fuel deposits," *Voprosy ekonomiki*, 1974, no. 9, pp. 25–38; P. G. Bunich, "Payments for working captial and natural resources in the system of administration of socialist social production," *Ekonomika i matematicheskiye metody* 12 (November-December 1976): 1057–70; Yu. V. Sukhotin, "Socially necessary outlays and rent evaluations," *Ekonomika i matematicheskiye metody* 12 (September-October 1976): 850–63; and idem, "On prices and rent payments," *Ekonomika i matematicheskiye metody* 12 (November-December 1976): 1071–81.

22. Gofman, *Ekonomicheskaya otsenka*; N. I. Tsvetkov, *Voprosy ekonomicheskogo izucheniya i otsenki mestorozhdenii mineralnogo syrya* [Problems of economic analysis and valuation of mineral-resource deposits] (Moscow: Nauka, 1977).

23. Gofman, *Ekonomicheskaya otsenka*, p. 27; also "Methdological principles," p. 410.

24. For the case of natural gas, see Campbell, "Prices, Rent, and Decision Making," pp. 295–96.

25. The 1965 reform of planning and management did introduce a profit *rate* on capital as a success indicator, alongside the traditional output target. The profit-rate target, however, does not affect the management decision at issue here.

26. Bunich, "Payments," p. 1065.

27. Gofman, *Ekonomicheskaya otsenka*, pp. 82–84.

28. Gofman et al., "Determination of marginal costs," pp. 695–706. Problems arose in some of the early attempts to estimate marginal unit values from linear programs because the authors posited the maximization of a total cost function based on the full cost of all inputs including the constrained inputs, the latter to be valued at the shadow prices emerging from the solution. This was a nonsensical statement of the problem, since each possible extremum would generate a different set of values for the constrained inputs and, thus, a different cost function.

29. Gofman, *Ekonomicheskaya otsenka*, p. 103.

30. "Methodological principles," p. 407.

31. Gofman, *Ekonomicheskaya otsenka*, p. 80.

32. Martin Weitzman, "The 'Ratchet Principle' and Performance Incentives," *Bell Journal of Economics* 2 (Spring 1980): 302–08; John Bonin and Alan Marcus, "Information, Motivation, and Control in Discretionary Managerial Behavior," *Journal of Comparative Economics* 3 (September 1979): 235–52.

33. Gofman, *Ekonomicheskaya otsenka*, pp. 105–15.

34. Ibid., pp. 105–08.

35. Ibid., p. 108.

36. Compare Gofman et al., *Izkhodnye polozheniya*, with "Methodological principles," p. 411.

37. Gofman, *Ekonomicheskaya otsenka*, p. 124.

38. Ibid., p. 121.

39. See Chapter 16 in this volume.

40. V. Bogachev, "On the question of intensifying the development of Siberia's natural resources," *Kommunist*, 1980, no. 3, pp. 89–100.

41. Gofman, *Ekonomicheskaya otsenka*, pp. 66–67.

42. See, for example, I. K. Smirnov, *Sotsialno-ekonomicheskiye osnovy otsenki zemli v sotsialisticheskom obshchestve* [Socio-economic bases of land valuation in a socialist society] (Leningrad University, 1975), pp. 27–29.

43. Cited in Robert W. Campbell, *Trends in the Soviet Oil and Gas Industry* (Baltimore: Johns Hopkins, 1976), p. 12.

44. I. P. Zhavoronkova, *Ekonomicheskiye voprosy uluchsheniya ispolzovaniya mineralno-syryevykh resursov SSSR* [Economic problems of improving the use of mineral raw-material resources in the USSR] (Moscow: Nauka, 1973), pp. 67–71.

45. A. I. Bozhedomov, "On the problem of economic valuation of oil fields," *Izvestiya akademii nauk, seriya ekonomicheskaya*, 1979, no. 5 (September-October), p. 71.

46. N. V. Degtyarev and L. I. Osipov, *Zemelnoye pravo i zemelny kadastr* [Land law and the land cadaster] (Moscow: Yuridicheskaya literatura, 1975), pp. 176–77, 195–96, 207.

47. Smirnov, *Sotsialno-ekonomicheskiye osnovy*, p. 28.

48. N. P. Fedorenko, ed., *Ekonomicheskiye problemy optimizatsii prirodopolzovaniya* [Economic problems of optimizing nature management] (Moscow: Nauka, 1973), p. 32.

49. "Methodological principles," p. 409.

50. Tsvetkov, *Voprosy ekonomicheskogo izucheniya*, p. 13.

51. Campbell, *Trends in Soviet Oil and Gas*, p. 13.

52. Tsvetkov, *Voprosy ekonomicheskogo izucheniya*, p. 14.

53. "Methodological principles," p. 410.

54. T. S. Khachaturov, "Natural resources and national economic planning," *Voprosy ekonomiki*, 1973, no. 8; translated in *Problems of Economics*, March 1974, pp. 1–17.

55. *Osnovy zakonodatelstva neftyanoi promyshlennosti SSSR* [Fundamentals of legislations in the oil industry of the USSR] (Moscow: Gosyurizdat, 1976), pp. 14–15.

56. Khachaturov, "Natural Resources," p. 15.

57. Ye. D. Silayev and V. N. Shemov, "Economic valuation of the natural-resource potential of a region," *Izvestiya akademii nauk, seriya ekonomicheskaya*, 1977, no. 2, pp. 20–23.

58. O. Kassirov, "Rental relations and the development of economic methods of management," *Ekonomicheskiye nauki*, 1974, no. 5; translated in *Problems of Economics*, January 1975, pp. 55–73.

59. I. I. Stanov, "The content of an information system about nature management," *Ekonomicheskaya otsenka i ratsionalnoye ispolzovaniye prirodnykh resursov* [Economic valuation and rational use of natural resources] (Moscow: TsEMI, 1975), pp. 3–19.

60. For an excellent discussion of the problems, see L. V. Kantorovich, Ye. G. Golshtein, V. L. Makarov, and I. V. Romanovsky, "A contemporary mathematical system for economic management," *Izvestiya akademii nauk SSSR, seriya ekonomicheskaya*, October 1972.

61. Gofman et al., "Determination of marginal costs."

62. K. G. Gofman et al., "Optimal planning and management of the economy," *Ekonomicheskaya otsenka*, p. 100.

63. Ibid., p. 102.

64. See Chapter 17 in this volume, Table 7.

65. Kh. N. Gizatullin, "Marginal costs of iron ore resources," *Ekonomika i matematicheskiye metody* 14 (July-August 1978): 700–08. He notes that the methodology described in the article was used to calculate the marginal values of iron ore deposits in the Urals and Kazakhstan for the period 1976 to 1980.

66. See Chapter 20 in this volume.

67. Tsvetkov, *Voprosy ekonomicheskogo izucheniya*, pp. 45–106.

68. S. V. Antsyshkin and T. M. Polyanskaya, "On possible ways of improving the system of prices on the basis of optimal sectoral plans (with particular reference to steam coal)" *Ekonomika i matematicheskiye metody* 14 (May-June 1978): 518–30.

69. L. Ye. Vaik, "On an integrated optimization of regional fuel and energy balances," *Ekonomika i matematicheskiye metody* 12 (November-December 1976): 1032–91.

70. Ye. P. Ushakov, "Optimization of the development and location of production in a region in light of the replenishment of water resources," *Ekonomika i matematicheskiye metody* 14 (January-February 1978): 78–86.

71. K. A. Bagrinovsky and M. Ya. Lemeshev, "On the planning of economic development in light of ecological needs," *Ekonomika i matematicheskiye metody* 12 (July-August 1976): 681–91.

72. A. Ye. Varshavsky and L. Ye. Varshavsky, "Modeling the economic development of the oil and gas industry," *Ekonomika i matematicheskiye metody* 13 (September-October 1977).

73. R. L. Rayatskas and V. P. Sutkaitis, "Modeling economic dynamics in light of pollution of the environment," *Ekonomika i matematicheskiye metody* 15 (January-February 1979): 45–57.

74. For example, A. P. Krylov, "Concerning rates of exploitation of oil fields," *Ekonomika i organizatsiya promyshlennogo proizvodstva*, January 1980, pp. 66–74.

75. For instance, ibid., and Bogachev, "On mineral rent."

# IV

## THE ROLE OF RAW MATERIALS
## IN SOVIET FOREIGN TRADE

# 26

# SOVIET NATURAL RESOURCE EXPORTS
# AND THE WORLD MARKET

ARTHUR W. WRIGHT
University of Connecticut

In the economist's paradigm, economic activities are typically the joint outcome of supply-side and demand-side forces. The first three parts of this book have examined the supply-side forces bearing upon Soviet exports of natural resources—the regional dimension, reserves, production, costs, and so on. In this final part of the volume we turn our attention to the demand-side forces. The Soviets cannot, of course, export natural resources in a vacuum. They must find markets for their exports in the other countries making up the world economy. How the USSR deals with the rest of world economy, and vice versa, will therefore be one of the key factors that determine the volumes of Soviet natural resource exports and their significance in various world markets.

## The Soviet Role in the World Economy
## in Broad Terms

Historically the Soviet Union has played only a limited role in the world economy, and in statistical terms this remains true today. Exports account for a relatively small proportion of Soviet gross national product—5 to 10 percent. In part this limited role reflects the continent-size scale of the Soviet economy: what would be export (and import) flows in economies of the geographic size of Britain or Hungary are domestic product flows in the USSR. It is for this same reason that the United States' role in the world economy appears smaller than it otherwise might.

The Soviets' international economic role has also been limited out of deliberate choice. A high degree of autarky was a policy goal under Stalin, both for its own sake and in response to foreign hostility toward trading with the upstart Communist government. The Soviet Union has also followed protectionist policies toward specific categories of goods, for example, many agricultural and metal products, including strategic goods.

For more than a decade now, the attitude of Soviet political leaders toward international trade has been evolving away from autarky for its own sake, with a matching change in foreign attitudes. While statistically exports may still be only a tiny fraction of GNP—the USSR is still a large and growing continental economy—there has been a pronounced shift in policy toward the vigorous if selective use of trade as an integral part of overall Soviet economic strategy. This shift has little to do with a desire for greater contacts with the outside world per se. Rather, it seems to stem from attempts to cope with lagging labor force growth, capital-goods saturation in many industries, and the continued domestic inability to develop and introduce improved methods of production. One way to acquire modern technology is to import it. To do that, of course, a nation must export domestically produced goods to obtain the necessary foreign exchange.

For the Soviet Union, paying for imported modern technology means exporting natural resource products. In spite of Russian industrialization dating back more than a century, the USSR today does not have a comparative advantage in many lines of manufacturing that are regularly traded on world markets. Indeed, the very technological backwardness that motivates the import policy is a barrier to exporting manufactured goods. (Weapons and some space-derived products are notable exceptions here, of course.) Thus (as Edward Hewett has aptly remarked) primary products are virtually the only export industry in the USSR.

It is not a serious exaggeration to say that the Soviet Union has the international trade pattern of a developing country. By Marshall Goldman's reckoning, raw-material exports generate more than 80 percent of Soviet hard-currency earnings; the proportion is still above a half when we add "soft-currency" earnings (from barter and trade with other Communist countries within the Council of Mutual Economic Assistance, or Comecon). Judith Thornton estimates that, in 1979, the extractive industries accounted for only 7.5 percent of Soviet industrial output, but for 52.5 percent of the total value of Soviet exports. In an as yet unpublished statistical compendium, she presents data showing that Soviet net exports as a share of total production have, since 1960, risen for many products (crude oil and refined products, natural gas, aluminum, copper, gold, potash, magnesium, roundwood and sawnwood) and remained roughly constant for others (chromite, coal, zinc, iron ore, and manganese).

The Soviet resemblance to a developing country extends beyond the heavy dependence on natural resource exports for most of the nation's foreign-exchange earnings. Imported capital goods are an important input into the very expansion of the natural resource industries themselves. Attention has focused on oil and gas equipment, but they are by no means the sole example. To pay for the capital goods, the Soviets have in effect made use of foreign investment. This is most clear in the case of East European contributions of manpower and other inputs to help construct pipelines destined to carry exports to Comecon countries. But the large credits obtained from hard-currency countries, especially where all or part of the repayment is in kind and price is not preset (so that the lender assumes an *equity* risk, can also be viewed as foreign investment. The acceptance of foreign investment, of course, carries with it a commitment to paying back the investors by achieving the necessary level of exports.

It is eminently reasonable to expect, then, that the Soviet Union will continue its efforts to export natural resource products for many years to come. The composition of those exports may change over time, but the total level of effort will doubtless remain high. For example, if oil export proceeds do in fact decline, we should look for Soviet attempts to increase export revenues from other natural resource industries, perhaps natural gas, but also nonfuel minerals as well. After all, with a strategy based on importing advanced technologies, the major export sector must bear most of the burden of paying for the imports.

## Soviet Conduct in World Markets

With the Soviets playing a small but determined role in the world economy, it is of interest to examine how they conduct themselves in world markets. How is their foreign trade policy set? What is their position in world markets? And how do they behave in response to those conditions—by trying to manipulate the markets or merely by taking maximum advantage of the opportunities presented?

It is not uncommon to encounter references to Soviet export "surpluses," especially applied to a general commodity such as a raw material (as opposed to a specific item like a custom-made machine tool). It is important in thinking about Soviet foreign trade conduct to be clear about what is meant by a "surplus." It should *not* be interpreted as a quantity of a good available for export because it is left over after domestic "requirements" are met, perhaps the result of an accidental production overrun, or an amount not needed by domestic producers for some reason. Rather, it should be seen as an amount expressly produced or made available from stocks for export.

This point is easily illustrated by examining the following identity:

$$Q_p + M = Q_u + X,$$

where $Q_p$ is the quantity produced, $M$ is the quantity imported, $Q_u$ is the quantity used domestically, and $X$ is the quantity exported. In the Soviet centrally planned economy, all four quantities are decision variables set in advance by the central planning authorities, with appropriate rewards and penalties tied to achievement of the targets that, taken together, add up to the planned totals. An export "surplus" will show up as "net exports," $X - M$, obtained by regrouping the terms in the identity:

$$X - M = Q_p - Q_u.$$

The surplus is, of course, equal to production less domestic use, but it does not just happen; it is the result of deliberate decisions on all four variables.

We can think of the decisions on the export surplus variables as issuing from a process by which objectives are pursued subject to certain constraints. The objectives may be political or strategic as well as the more traditional economic gains from international trade. On occasion the Soviets have used trade to gain favor with particular nations (e.g., buying sugar from Cuba and oil from Iraq). Strategically, they clearly set great store by having economically viable Communist allies in Eastern Europe. And Moscow's possible manipulation of world markets for political or strategic purposes has received considerable attention of late. (More on the last two topics below.) But as a general rule, for a broad range of products and for the vast majority of transactions, the economic objective appears to be paramount.

The constraints limiting the attainment of the objectives include all the factors that determine supply (marginal costs at different places, at different times): reserves, capital outlays and interest, wages, weather, transport charges, etc. Also a constraint are Soviet central planning institutions. It is widely acknowledged (at least outside the USSR) that those institutions are a clumsy, slow-moving way of allocating resources, and that they probably raise the overall level of production costs somewhat compared with decentralized institutions.

More to the present point, however, the Soviet-type central planning system operates with aggregate, economy-wide plans that are equal to the sum of their enterprise-levels parts. (In contrast, "indicative" planning, at least in principle, operates with aggregate figures based only on estimates of firm-level decisions.) Moreover, in a complex industrial economy, the plans for the various individual goods interlock in such a way that the effects of a change in any single plan ramify throughout the economy. A further feature of Soviet planning is that plans are "taut"—that is, output targets tend to be based on optimistically lower input coefficients—so that the entire plan has a small tolerance for failure in any of its components. A significant shortfall in the production of a key primary input can disrupt the plans of many industries.

In such a system, foreign trade cannot operate on an *ad hoc*, casual basis any more than can the much larger domestic component of the economy. Many production plans depend on imported inputs, which must be paid for with foreign exchange or with its barter equivalent in goods. Either way, it is necessary to plan for the exports that will cover the foreign-exchange bill.

The overall foreign trade plan in a centrally planned economy will be reflected in the planned change in the state's foreign-exchange balances for a given period. This change need not be zero in every period; in fact, it is possible to run a growing balance-of-payments deficit over time, provided that exports are growing and expected to continue to do so. It should be added that, if Soviet leaders choose to pursue political rather than economic ends through trade, any foreign-exchange cost of the politicking must be covered by exports as well. An example here is the extraordinary Soviet aid supplied to Poland in 1981 and 1982, in the form of both exports diverted from other Comecon countries (which thus shared in the cost) and extra hard-currency imports.

The foregoing analysis does not mean that the USSR can never make short-run, "unplanned" changes in exports (or imports). Indeed, as we shall see, there is considerable evidence that such changes occur and not infrequently. In comparison with long-run, "planned" changes, however, short-run shifts are harder to effect and entail higher costs. (Soviet central planning is no different in essence in this respect from any other allocation mechanism: the faster the adjustment, the higher the cost.) When the Soviets make short-run changes in foreign trade, we should expect to find compelling reasons—sharply higher export prices, for instance, or a perceived strategic threat of some kind.

One important element in Soviet foreign-trade conduct is the degree to which Soviet exports affect the world-market prices of the various export goods. The overall international role of the USSR may be relatively small, but an increase or decrease in Soviet sales can reduce or raise the price in a given market. To the extent the Soviets are "perfect competitors" or "price takers," so that changes in their export decisions have only negligible effects on the market price, their foreign-trade behavior will be more opportunistic and hence more easily understood and predicted. If they have some monopoly power, so that their decisions do affect market prices, their behavior will be more cautious, more concerned with learning "where the demand curve is" and, for outsiders, less easily read and predicted.

The consensus among students of the Soviet economy is that the USSR is a price taker in many markets, including most of those with which this book is concerned. In the focal oil market, the structure of world prices for different kinds of crude oil is determined by the large Persian Gulf producing countries; hence declines in Soviet oil exports, or even oil imports by the USSR, will have little impact on world oil prices (despite fears to the contrary in some quarters). In natural gas, the price in any particular market is governed by world oil prices. (Imperfect substitutability with oil and the national-security concerns of importing countries may give the USSR some spatial monopoly in the West European gas market, but it is probably limited and of little significance.) In the markets for wood products, most metals, and the major traded minerals, the Soviet Union is best viewed as a price taker.

Two important exceptions may be chromite and gold. Along with South Africa (both) and Zimbabwe (chromite), the USSR is one of the world's few major producers and exporters of these metals. The secrecy that often surrounds their activities in the gold and occasionally the chromite markets is commonly confused with their secrecy on domestic oil reserves. The latter is almost certainly motivated by national-security concerns. The former is better understood as arising from the effects of Soviet decisions on world prices. If it becomes known that the Soviets are going to increase sales, world market prices will decline in anticipation. Obviously, the USSR would like to minimize the anticipated price declines, enabling them to sell more before prices fall. If this argument is correct, we should observe less concern for secrecy when sales are being reduced, which seems consistent with causal, circumstantial evidence.

Does the Soviet Union try to manipulate world markets or merely to take the fullest advantage of market opportunities? Clearly, in markets where they are price takers, the Soviets' choices are restricted to the latter. But even where they are price searchers, their ability to "manipulate" the market is not necessarily very great.

The ability of large firms or national trading monopolies to push world markets around is greatly exaggerated. Apart from natural disaster (floods, droughts, volcanoes) and wars (Japan's cut-off of natural rubber supplies in World War II), the sole success in recent memory has been Saudi Arabia's oil production cutbacks, and those were abetted by the Arab-Israeli War of 1973 and the Iranian revolution (1979–80); witness the Saudis' difficulties with other oil producing nations' price demands the rest of the time. The exaggeration is due to a series of popular misconceptions about monopoly power. (One is that it means, literally, "sole supplier," a condition that holds in actuality only for living artists of the stature of Picasso.) It does *not* convey the ability to set price at arbitrarily high levels; "what the traffic will bear" is determined by market demand. It seldom leads to cartel behavior—the joint monopolization of a market. And it does not by itself provide the means of enforcing an embargo, selective or total.

The Soviet Union doubtless enjoys considerable monopoly power within Comecon, although it is difficult to gauge the extent of it because (as we argue below) intrabloc trade is insulated from outside market forces and internal bloc prices are negotiated at length and in great detail. (Martin Kohn, an American economist, has quipped that Eastern Europe enjoys the "leverage of weakness" *vis-à-vis* the USSR.) The Soviets have also been known to participate in international cartels (e.g., that for wooden matches led by Sweden in the 1930s). The late Alexander Gerschenkron of Harvard University, has shown, however, that they played the classically duplicitous role of the price cheat.

It is doubtful that the Soviet Union could manipulate the world gold market. At least the American "gold bugs," who favor a return to the gold standard in monetary policy and who are not known to think the USSR especially friendly to the United States, are not worried about it; indeed, one of them took pains to scotch the notion in a 1981 *Wall Street Journal* OpEd article. Manipulation could have a chance of success in the chromite market, but the reason might be the potential political instability in Zimbabwe and the diplomatic vulnerability of South Africa, not the Soviet Union's position in that market *per se*.

The concept of the "resource war" is a logically extreme form of market manipulation. (This concept, discussed in Chapter 1 above, reminds one of the ideology sometimes attributed to the leaders of the Central Powers in World War I.) The idea is that a major power (e.g., the USSR) would secure control of a large share of world supplies of a vital commodity, and then exact a tribute in the form of strategic concessions from other powers (e.g., the United States) that wish to buy the commodity. Stated so baldly, the prospect of a resource war raises a haunting specter of craven economic dependence on the triumphant warrior-nation. Fortunately, the realistic prospect is not nearly so stark.

First, getting the requisite stranglehold on supply would require truly extraordinary measures. To cut off Western rubber supplies, the Japanese Navy had to close the Pacific Ocean to trade, and the Japanese Army had to seize control of a number of countries. Those measures and, of course, Pearl Harbor ultimately provoked the United States to wage a full-scale war against Japan. Even if military retaliation could be avoided, the warrior-nation would have to make sure its own supplies of other commodities were not vulnerable to "resource-war" retaliation by the intended victim-nations. Thus, whole groups of commodities, not just one or two, would have to be brought under secure control.

Second, a resource war could be won only if there were few if any substitutes for the target commodities. We know, of course, that even in the short run there are many substitutes for any commodity. An important one is simply doing without nonessential goods that require it for their manufacture or use. A second substitute is a strategic stockpile to tide the nation over the short run. In the long run, of course, all manner of substitution possibilities become available, for example, synthetics (as in rubber); more costly sources (lower-grade ores such as taconite iron ore and dawsonite alumina ore, smaller or deeper oil and gas wells, and heavy crudes); redesigned production and consumption processes (nylon bushings and motor mounts, and new forms of alloy steel); new consumption habits (nylon-less legs, and moving from suburbs back to urban cores); and so on.

In short, the prospect of a resource war, while terrifying at first glance, takes on a much more manageable aspect once one reflects on the necessary and sufficient conditions for winning such a war. Those conditions appear arduous indeed. It may be prudent to take certain insurance measures, such as building a strategic stockpile; in fact, analyses of market disruptions, sparked by the Arab oil embargo of 1973 have found that the mere existence of a stockpile reduces the chances of deliberate disruptions by reducing the payoff to the would-be perpetrator. With even minimal prudence by the United States, the USSR could be deterred from waging a resource war.

## The Comecon Connection

To this point, we have neglected one fundamental determinant of Soviet conduct in world foreign trade: its membership in, and leadership of, the Comecon trading bloc. The relationship between the USSR and the other members of Comecon (the East European Six, on which we shall focus—Bulgaria, Czechoslovakia, East Germany, Hungary, Poland, and Rumania—plus Cuba, Mongolia, and Vietnam) is complex and imperfectly understood by outsiders. This is due in part to the inherently politico-strategic as well as economic nature of Comecon. Also, information on its detailed inner workings is hard to come by in the West. Without some grasp of Comecon, though, our understanding of Soviet foreign-trade conduct would be incomplete.

Comecon is at bottom a customs union, not unlike that of Western Europe's Common Market. (Indeed, Comecon was initially formed after World War II in response to the Marshall Plan and the accompanying institutions that gradually evolved into the Common Market.) Like any other customs union, Comecon members trade preferentially with one another, reaping gains from so doing that presumably outweigh the opportunity costs from foregoing trade with outsiders. In Comecon, the distribution of benefits and costs—that is, the distribution of net benefits—among the members is largely implicit in form, deriving from the interlocked, bilateral trade agreements that add up to total intrabloc trade. (Despite attempts to devise and use special "clearing rubles," multilateral clearing among national trade balances in common financial units is basically lacking within Comecon.)

As a result, it is not easy to calculate either the distribution of net benefits in any given year, or the impact on that distribution of changes in the prices of major categories of goods. After a spate of controversy over whether the USSR exploited Eastern Europe, or vice versa, the Western literature left the matter as containing a large, irreducible area of uncertainty. The actual process of arriving at the bilateral trade agreement is even more difficult, of course, and requires long and involved negotiations; similarly, implementing the agreements frequently entails making numerous adjustments.

Interestingly, the broad role of the USSR in the world economy is replicated within Comecon. The Soviets specialize in exporting raw materials to Eastern Europe, and the East Europeans export manufactures to the Soviet Union. The degree of Soviet specialization in raw-material exports is somewhat less pronounced in Comecon trade than in world trade, but it is evident nonetheless.

The implication of the foregoing discussion is that the Soviet Union's exports of natural resources to the West depend on its Comecon connection as well as the world prices it can obtain for its exports. Because of the complexity of the Comecon connection, a straightforward statement of the nature of the dependence is not possible. Two points may be helpful here:

(1) For some purposes, Comecon trade—Soviet exports to and imports from Eastern Europe—can be separated from other world trade flows. In the overall sense,

however, Comecon trade is an integral part of the world trade pattern. For example, a reduction in Soviet shipments of a good outside Comecon in order to increase shipments to Eastern Europe does not necessarily represent a net reduction in total world shipments. While the relation may not be exactly one to one, we still have to consider the corresponding reduction in East European purchases of the good on the world market as a result of the additional Soviet shipments.

The key variable on which to focus attention is not the physical quantities of goods going to Comecon or non-Comecon countries, but rather the differential in the terms on which the goods are traded. Such a differential is part of the implicit distribution of the net benefits of membership in the Comecon customs union. To the extent the world-maket price of a good is higher than the price in Comecon, the customs union buyer gains and the seller bears a cost; and vice versa.

(2) The existence of differentials in the terms of trade between Comecon and the world market—inevitable in any customs union—means that there will be constant tension between sales inside and sales outside Comecon. The tension will be most severe for goods like oil that are heavily in demand on the world market and that experience sudden sharp increases in world prices. There will be a strong incentive to sellers to shift the good in question out of Comecon and onto the world market, and a like incentive for buyers to try to keep the good within the bloc, at the protected price. (An instructive analogy here is United States domestic pressures to prohibit exports of commodities the prices of which suddenly jump on world markets, for example, oil.) The effect of the custom union is to slow down the adjustments of both sellers (increasing sales) and buyers (reducing use) to the new, higher price.

A sharp change in the world price of a heavily traded good radically alters the distribution of net benefits within the customs union. Thus, part of the adjustment process must be renegotiation of the internal terms of trade within Comecon. In the short run, the seller, facing a surge in demand for the good from buyer-members of the customs union, may simply limit the quantities it will sell at the favorable internal price; of course, the precise distribution of the limited amounts will then become an internal political issue. This is what happened within Comecon in the case of oil; the Soviets have limited quantities sold at the Comecon price to those "planned" (i.e., negotiated); "above-plan" deliveries fetch the world price—and in hard currency. In the longer term, the intrabloc price (along with the prices of many other goods as well) will be revised to bring the entire price structure into line with the relative prices on the world market. This also has been happening in the case of oil.

Note that, on grounds of economic efficiency for the entire trading bloc, the internal price should be adjusted immediately upon the increase in the world-market price. Otherwise, both producer and user will be receiving incorrect signals about what to invest in and produce or use. Efficiency is, of course, only one of the goals of customs unions; hence we do not expect there to be such rapid adjustment.

There is, then, a Soviet "commitment" to its East European allies in Comecon with respect to exports of natural resources. That commitment is one determinant of Soviet exports of natural resources to countries outside Comecon: the stronger the commitment, the smaller the quantities of natural-resource exports shipped outside the bloc, other things remaining the same. But the commitment is not an absolute one; the USSR will not meet Eastern Europe's "needs" at any cost. Rather, it is a relative commitment in which noneconomic criteria play a role but economic considerations create a constant tension between sales within and outside the bloc. Other things typically do not remain the same, either; for instance, as world prices shift, Soviet exports of natural resources will shift, both the total exports to all countries and the mix of those exports between Comecon and the rest of the world.

## Soviet Natural Resource Exports in Historical Perspective

We noted earlier in this chapter that the USSR has the trade pattern of a developing country. In fact, this is not a new trade pattern of Russia. The composition of primary-product exports may have changed over time—agriculture has changed from an export sector to an import sector—but their predominance as a group in total exports has not. Thus, it is appropriate to begin this final section of the book, on international trade, by putting Soviet natural resource exports in historical perspective. Marshall Goldman does so in Chapter 27.

Goldman's paper sets out how, in a setting of rapid, even urgent industrialization, the Soviet economy has nevertheless continued to specialize in the export of raw materials to pay for imports. He identifies a set of internal forces that have shaped and will continue to shape Soviet export potentials in natural resources, such as the internal management of resource production (surprisingly inefficient) and the ambivalence of many Soviet decision makers even today toward the outside world. Goldman also documents the manner in which the Soviets have made use of world markets to pursue their broader goals by means of raw-material exports. The latter discussion illuminates with telling detail a number of points in our general characterization of Soviet export behavior.

## Determining the Mix of Soviet Natural Resource Exports

One implication of our earlier discussion is that Soviet export behavior can be represented as a balance-of-payments adjustment mechanism. Slack in the hard-currency account should permit the USSR to shift emphasis to objectives having to do with its Comecon partners. In contrast, hard-currency deficits should force Soviet planners to pay more attention to export sales on world markets.

Western scholars largely lack access to the institutional details that would allow a direct empirical test of the above implication. It is thus necessary to fall back on indirect tests. The second paper in this section, Chapter 28 by Edward Hewett, presents the results of such tests. Hewett finds evidence for the hypothesis of an adjustment mechanism using primary products. Interestingly, he also finds that the mechanism is not bipolar (i.e., between Comecon and the OECD countries) as is often thought, but rather tripolar (with the developing countries providing an alternative outlet for Soviet hard-currency exports). This finding illustrates clearly the dangers of not looking at the world economy as a whole in attempting to assess the impact of Soviet natural resource exports on world markets.

### East European Energy Dependence and Policy Options

The world oil-price shocks of 1973 and 1979–80 forced Western scholars to look more closely at the nature and significance of the Comecon connection in Soviet foreign trade conduct. Eastern Europe is energy-poor, the USSR energy-rich by comparison. The tension between exporting oil to Comecon and exporting it to non-Comecon customers was referred to earlier. How Moscow responds to that tension has profound implications for living standards and growth rates in Eastern Europe. At the same time, the East European countries must work out their own responses.

The East European responses constitute the topic of the third chapter in this section of the book, Chapter 29 by George Hoffman. Noting the high degree of East European dependence on the USSR for high-grade fuels, Hoffman explores by turns the various options the fuel importers in Comecon have for adjusting to sharply higher energy prices—reducing planned increases in energy use, raising domestic energy production, increasing hard-currency inports, or persuading the Soviet Union to be more liberal on intra-Comecon terms for energy shipments. He finds no good options, plus a number of reasons to expect the last one to be best. The implications of that assessment, if it is accurate, for Soviet energy and other primary-product exports outside Comecon are well worth pondering.

### Foreign Economic Constraints on Soviet Resource Development

Earlier, we stressed that the USSR's resemblance to a developing country in its pattern of foreign trade extended beyond merely a high share of raw-material exports to the actual use of foreign investment to develop new export supplies of natural resources. This feature of Soviet foreign trade conduct opens up the possibility that external constraints may place bounds on the Soviet potential for maintaining or expanding exports of natural resources. The final paper in this section, Chapter 30 by Lawrence Brainard, addresses that possibility. Brainard explores the possible effects of conditions in world financial and goods markets on Soviet export potentials in the natural-resource industries. His conclusions throw the issue back to the conditions explored in the first three sections of the book—to the Soviets' abilities to respond to the opportunities afforded by the world markets, and thus to such variables as reserves, development plans and management, and regional policies. The binding constraints, then, appear to be domestic, not foreign.

# 27

# THE CHANGING ROLE OF RAW-MATERIAL EXPORTS AND SOVIET FOREIGN TRADE

MARSHALL I. GOLDMAN
Wellesley College and
Russian Research Center
Harvard University

## Introduction

One of the lessons of the sharp increases in energy and raw-material prices of 1973–74 was that the past is not a reliable guide to the future. Before October 1973, few people accurately predicted the dramatic success of the OPEC (Organization of Petroleum Exporting Countries) cartel in effecting a traumatic increase in oil prices. Similarly, until 1974, not many observers thought that the raw-material producing nations would be anything but supplicants at the table of world power. There seemed to be no chance that the less developed countries (LDCs) of the world would threaten the dominance of the OECD (Organization for Economic Cooperation and Development) nations.

Then in late 1973 it appeared that a fundamental, perhaps permanent, change had taken place. Led by OPEC, the poor of the world began to assert themselves. Awed by the change, the OECD countries began to fear not only for the maintenance of their dominant position, but in some cases for their very existence as democratic and economically viable states. Would they be able to continue paying their bills to raw-material producers, and if not, would this generate a world-wide recession and a collapse of the rich?

Before long it became clear that the world economic order was not about to disintegrate completely. The dominance of the raw-material producers over the industrialized countries was short-lived, at least for the time being. An exception was the oil producers, whose power is real and persists. But on the whole, the power of the OECD countries has not been surrendered to the raw-material producers among the LDCs.

The USSR has not been an unaffected bystander in all of this. Although the Soviet Union has long been regarded as the world's second largest industrial power, from the perspective of foreign trade, the Soviet Union is more of a raw-material exporter than an industrial power. As indicated in Table 1, in 1980, 84 percent of all the Soviet Union's hard-currency earnings were derived from the export of raw materials. True, the Soviet Union is the world's largest exporter of various types of machinery and machine tools, but these go predominantly to either the other members of the Council of Mutual Economic Assistance (CMEA) or to the LDCs. Soviet machinery has almost no market in the OECD countries. As indicated in Table 2, whereas the Soviet Union may sell $29 million worth of machinery a year to a country like West Germany, it buys in return $1,764 million, 60 times more (1980 data). The same vast disparities exist in Soviet trade with Japan, the United States, Italy, France and Britain.

In contrast, the Soviet role as a raw-material producer and exporter in both soft- and hard-currency countries is an important one. After Saudi Arabia, the Soviet Union is the world's second largest oil exporter. After the Netherlands, the Soviet Union is the world's second largest exporter of natural gas, having moved up from third place in 1976.[1] As has been shown elsewhere in this volume, it is also a major factor in the timber, iron ore, manganese, chrome, asbestos, apatite, potash, nickel and precious metals markets as well. Moreover, if the Soviet Union chooses to, it could be a major factor in several of these raw-material markets for years to come. While its oil reserves are a state secret and therefore much disputed, it is readily agreed that the Soviet Union has enormous deposits of a variety of other resources, and in several cases it leads the world.[2] For example, according to one Soviet economic geographer, it has 59 percent of the world's coal reserves, 41 percent of its iron ore, 37 percent of its natural gas, 80 percent of its manganese and 54 percent of its potash.[3] The USSR also has substantial deposits of apatite and asbestos.

Given such resources, it is clear that Soviet interests are very much linked to those of the raw-material exporting countries. Not only do the Soviets increase their prices (now even to Eastern Europe) along with anyone else when OPEC does, but also the Soviet Union is not constrained to withhold production and exports as Saudi Arabia and occasionally some of the others have been in order to assure the continued effectiveness of OPEC. It is not surprising, therefore, that when raw-material prices soared in 1973 and 1974, the Soviet Union benefited enormously. As shown in Table 3, the Soviets recorded one of their best trade balances in years in 1974.

TABLE 1
Exports of Major Soviet Commodities to Hard-Currency Countries in 1980 ($ Millions)

| | Austria | Belgium | Denmark | France | Great Britain | Greece | Italy | Japan | Netherlands |
|---|---|---|---|---|---|---|---|---|---|
| Coal | 45 | 23 | 19 | 56 | — | 2 | 61 | 105 | — |
| Oil and refined products | 358 | 731 | 332 | 2,336 | 247 | 504 | 1,814 | 163 | 1,046 |
| Natural gas | 324 | — | — | 447 | — | — | 768 | — | — |
| Metallic ores | 6 | — | — | 1 | — | — | 9 | — | — |
| Nonmetallic minerals | 3 | 11 | — | 7 | — | — | 3 | 15 | 1 |
| Iron and steel | 9 | — | 5 | — | 3 | 1 | 113 | 23 | — |
| Chemicals | 11 | — | 6 | 26 | 26 | 11 | 26 | 20 | 65 |
| Potash | 5 | 24 | 2 | — | 9 | — | 18 | 30 | — |
| Ammonia | — | — | — | — | — | — | 45 | — | — |
| Wood and wood products | 38 | 45 | 14 | 105 | 221 | 9 | 118 | 604 | 53 |
| Cotton | 8 | 11 | — | 127 | 23 | — | 9 | 115 | 3 |
| Furs | 1 | 1 | 1 | 3 | 80 | 2 | 8 | 6 | 1 |
| Misc. | 3 | 4 | — | 5 | 8 | — | 2 | 8 | 4 |
| Products Total | 811 | 850 | 379 | 3,113 | 617 | 529 | 2,994 | 1,089 | 1,173 |
| Machinery | 9 | 35 | 6 | 41 | 45 | 64 | 32 | 9 | 14 |
| Export Total | 870 | 1,263 | 392 | 3,364 | 1,289 | 614 | 3,150 | 1,425 | 1,541 |
| Automobiles (units) | | | | | | | | | |
| 1980 | 2,221 | 17,036 | 3,361 | 12,358 | 19,309 | 6 | 3,106 | — | 7,010 |
| 1979 | 3,819 | 15,952 | 4,597 | 18,161 | 22,423 | 5,538 | 2,182 | — | 7,039 |
| 1978 | 1,765 | 13,475 | 4,916 | 13,865 | 19,416 | 3,106 | 2,774 | — | 5,374 |
| 1977 | 3,886 | 10,043 | 4,099 | 12,946 | 14,921 | 2,536 | 2,538 | — | 8,814 |
| 1976 | 3,184 | 14,635 | 5,833 | 12,584 | 9,498 | 2,688 | 2,106 | — | 6,154 |

*Includes West Berlin
NOTE: 1 ruble = $1.50
SOURCE: *Vneshnyaya torgovlya SSSR*, 1980.

If the Soviets thought that a new era had arrived, they soon found out that the changes were not all permanent. The lesson was learned in 1975, when the high prices of 1973 and 1974 precipitated the recession of 1975. In an abrupt reversal of 1974, the Soviet Union found many of its raw-material markets had collapsed. According to Soviet statistics, their exports to the OECD countries in 1975 actually fell from the previous year (see Table 3).

The about-faces of these momentous years make it difficult for anyone who attempts to project the role of the Soviet Union in world raw-material markets. This includes those who have now gone to the other extreme and argue that, instead of exporting, the Soviet Union has embarked on a course of importing coupled with political encroachment in an effort to gain a stranglehold on the world's strategic reserves.[4] We should realize by now that what often appears to be inevitable in the light of present developments may never come to pass. For that reason there are often sharp differences of opinion about what Soviet policy will be in the years ahead. It is hard enough to anticipate Soviet chances for fulfilling an annual production plan, let alone to anticipate their position in 1985, as the Central Intelligence Agency has tried to do. The attempt, by the contributors to this volume, to project natural resource development in the Soviet Union through the 1980s to 1990 is even more of a challenge. This paper is part of the same project and faces the same pitfalls. Even the Soviets themselves have been unable to reach agreement on what the future holds. For several

years, foreign observers have been waiting for the promised 15-year economic projections to 1990. They have not been forthcoming, apparently because Soviet economic officials have been unable to agree on the long-run prospects for the Soviet economy.[5]

Rather than attempting an overall prognosis for the period to 1990, this paper will try instead to trace the past export patterns of some of the more important Soviet raw materials down to the present. I will begin with an historical perspective on the role of raw-material exports in prerevolutionary Russia. An effort will be made to discern trends and responses by the USSR to changes in political and economic developments. How have the patterns varied over the years? How does the existing planning and production system in the USSR affect the availability of Soviet exports? What role does CMEA play in Soviet trade priorities? What are the future prospects for the export of specific commodities and what will be the overall trade level? Will the Soviet Union really attempt to corner the market for strategic raw materials and refuse to export such items?

### History: The Prerevolutionary and Pre-World War II Era

In view of its relatively underdeveloped industry, it was to be expected that industrial exports from prerevolutionary Russia would be almost nonexistent. As officially

| Spain | Sweden | Switzer-land | U.S.A. | West Germany* | Others | Total | Finland |
|---|---|---|---|---|---|---|---|
| 4 | 27 | — | — | 12 | — | 354 | 139 |
| 245 | 402 | 418 | 20 | 2,739 | 262 | 11,617 | 2,215 |
| — | — | — | — | 1,093 | 2 | 2,634 | 143 |
| — | — | — | 5 | 1 | 2 | 24 | — |
| 1 | 15 | 2 | 2 | 36 | 7 | 103 | 7 |
| 18 | 9 | — | — | 20 | 2 | 203 | 25 |
| — | 5 | 24 | 5 | 159 | 3 | 387 | 37 |
| — | 5 | — | — | — | 4 | 97 | 11 |
| — | — | — | 105 | — | 14 | 164 | — |
| 16 | 12 | — | 1 | 133 | 7 | 1,376 | 101 |
| 1 | — | — | — | 21 | 6 | 324 | 15 |
| — | 4 | 11 | 6 | 18 | 1 | 143 | 2 |
| — | 4 | — | 3 | 7 | 2 | 50 | 33 |
| 285 | 483 | 455 | 147 | 4,239 | 312 | 17,476 | 2,728 |
| 10 | 10 | 2 | 7 | 31 | 38 | 353 | 90 |
| 377 | 532 | 668 | 227 | 4,643 | 402 | 20,757 | 3,035 |
| — | 3,919 | 393 | — | 3,421 | 10,992 | 83,132 | 9,762 |
| — | 2,284 | 4,693 | — | 7,104 | 12,000 | 105,792 | 10,935 |
| — | 3,535 | 2,267 | — | 11,312 | 4,471 | 86,276 | 9,697 |
| — | 3,047 | 588 | — | 12,056 | 3,615 | 79,089 | 9,061 |
| — | 2,708 | 1,818 | — | 15,828 | 4,134 | 81,170 | 11,817 |

classified by Soviet statistical authorities, earnings from machinery exports in 1913 amounted to less than 0.3 percent of total export revenue.[6] In contrast, industrial imports constituted 17 percent of ruble imports.

Given its reputation as the bread basket of Europe, it should come as no surprise that grain (first wheat and then barley) was the largest single export. It provided one-third of all foreign-exchange earnings. Next in importance was timber, which accounted for 11 percent. Linen, leather, and fats were other important earners of foreign exchange.

Perhaps more surprising is Russia's position, prior to the Revolution, as the world's leading exporter of petroleum. Russia was the world's largest producer of petroleum until 1902, when it was surpassed by the United States. Russian oil exports fluctuated considerably (e.g., they accounted for only 3 percent of export earnings in 1913), but Russia led the world in this department right up to World War I.[7] Coincidentally, in the early nineteenth century, Russia was also the world's largest producer of iron and steel.[8] However, Russia failed to keep up with the rest of the world in the production of both petroleum and steel. Now, interestingly enough, it again produces more petroleum and steel than anyone else.

The year 1913 was the last substantial export year for Russia until the late 1920s. World War I, the Revolution, and the Civil War that followed wrought enormous damage on the economy. Foreign trade virtually ceased after 1919. It was not until the 1960s that the ruble value of

Soviet exports exceeded the level recorded in 1913. The pre-World War II peak in the Soviet period was reached in 1930, and even then trade volume was only about two-thirds of the 1913 ruble value. The makeup of exports in 1930 had changed a bit from 1913. In the more recent year, grain exports accounted for 20 percent of total earnings, timber earned 17 percent, and petroleum 15 percent. The main difference was that the importance of grain had diminished. Indeed, in 1929, because of a drop in the harvest, virtually no grain was exported, although exports resumed in 1930. Several decades later, Khrushchev criticized Stalin because he had exported grain during this period of collectivization. These exports increased the suffering and brought death from starvation to millions of peasants.

Before moving to the post-World War II era, it is necessary to say a special word about petroleum. Although wheat and timber generally brought in more revenue, petroleum exports continued to be an important source of income throughout the 1930s. Only in 1939 did petroleum exports virtually cease. Moreover, exports of crude oil and refined products frequently amounted to over 25 percent of the total production of the country's crude oil, a figure which is nearly identical with similar comparisons in the 1970s.

After World War II the geographic pattern of Soviet trade changed rapidly. Soviet officials diverted almost all trade to the nearby Communist countries of Eastern Europe, and in 1949 to China. Throughout this period the

TABLE 2
Soviet Machinery Trade with Selected Countries ($ Millions)

| | Britain | | France | | West Germany | | Italy | | Japan | | United States | |
|---|---|---|---|---|---|---|---|---|---|---|---|---|
| | Exports | Imports | Exports | Imports | Exports | Imports | Exports | Imports | Exports | Imports | Exports | Imports |
| 1958 | — | 18 | — | 13 | — | 41 | — | 7 | — | 3 | — | 1 |
| 1959 | — | 44 | — | 39 | — | 39 | 1 | 11 | — | 11 | — | 7 |
| 1960 | — | 58 | 1 | 63 | 1 | 96 | 1 | 30 | — | 19 | — | 28 |
| 1961 | — | 77 | 1 | 69 | 1 | 91 | 1 | 43 | 1 | 29 | — | 16 |
| 1962 | — | 62 | 1 | 88 | — | 59 | 1 | 33 | 2 | 77 | — | 20 |
| 1963 | 1 | 64 | 1 | 33 | 1 | 73 | 1 | 80 | 2 | 86 | — | 1 |
| 1964 | 1 | 47 | 2 | 42 | 2 | 134 | 1 | 52 | 3 | 133 | — | 4 |
| 1965 | 1 | 70 | 2 | 28 | 2 | 71 | 1 | 39 | 2 | 73 | — | 6 |
| 1966 | 2 | 102 | 3 | 55 | 2 | 98 | 1 | 38 | 1 | 106 | — | 7 |
| 1967 | 3 | 93 | 5 | 101 | 5 | 60 | 4 | 83 | 2 | 66 | — | 8 |
| 1968 | 7 | 134 | 5 | 193 | 9 | 103 | 6 | 110 | 2 | 65 | — | 9 |
| 1969 | 2 | 125 | 5 | 183 | 5 | 172 | 4 | 200 | 4 | 75 | — | 38 |
| 1970 | 5 | 110 | 7 | 174 | 28 | 136 | 5 | 196 | 3 | 122 | — | 24 |
| 1971 | 5 | 95 | 7 | 173 | 15 | 182 | 3 | 151 | 6 | 140 | — | 29 |
| 1972 | 10 | 108 | 10 | 160 | 20 | 367 | 6 | 146 | 6 | 241 | 1 | 58 |
| 1973 | 17 | 121 | 18 | 189 | 17 | 513 | 12 | 197 | 5 | 214 | 1 | 226 |
| 1974 | 29 | 76 | 20 | 362 | 19 | 736 | 18 | 210 | 6 | 251 | 2 | 253 |
| 1975 | 29 | 198 | 25 | 561 | 34 | 1,332 | 19 | 412 | 4 | 583 | 5 | 600 |
| 1976 | 28 | 229 | 44 | 674 | 59 | 1,470 | 15 | 425 | 6 | 659 | 4 | 820 |
| 1977 | 34 | 135 | 39 | 776 | 40 | 1,449 | 21 | 669 | 8 | 938 | 3 | 481 |
| 1978 | 48 | 346 | 47 | 1,032 | 51 | 1,506 | 36 | 715 | 3 | 1,245 | 3 | 410 |
| 1979 | 81 | 399 | 54 | 1,044 | 37 | 1,465 | 36 | 606 | 6 | 973 | 15 | 513 |
| 1980 | 45 | 406 | 41 | 947 | 29 | 1,764 | 32 | 611 | 9 | 862 | 7 | 467 |

SOURCE: From annual issues of *Vneshnyaya torgovlya SSSR*. (Rate of exchange before 1972 was $1.11 = 1 ruble. In 1972 it was $1.213 to 1 ruble; in 1973 and 1974, $1.34 = 1 ruble; in 1975, $1.32 = 1 ruble; 1976, $1.34 = 1 ruble; 1977, $1.37 = 1 ruble; in 1978, 1979, and 1980, $1.50 = 1 ruble.)

Soviets continued to export small amounts of petroleum to such traditional customers as Britain, Italy, and Sweden. But most Soviet exports were rerouted from the West to the East, and trade volume rose rapidly almost every year.[9]

While much of the prewar composition of Soviet trade, such as the export of timber and petroleum, carried over into the post-World War II era, there were some differences. One of the most notable was the increase in machinery exports. At their peak, machinery exports in 1938 amounted to only 5 percent of total earnings.[10] In contrast, in 1950, they accounted for 12 percent, and by 1960, for 21 percent of all earnings.[11] As noted earlier, little of this machinery went to hard-currency countries.

Since World War II, as before the Revolution, the burden of earning hard currency for Russia has fallen on raw materials. One notable change from the earlier period is that grain, at least since 1963, is now more likely to be an import rather than an export commodity. As indicated in Table 1, the main hard-currency income earner is now petroleum: it already accounted for 20 percent of hard-currency earnings in 1972, just before the fourfold increase in world oil prices, and for 30 percent in 1973; in 1980, petroleum exports accounted for 56 percent of hard-currency earnings and 34 percent of total earnings. Until 1977 timber was consistently the second most important hard-currency product. Now it is third after natural gas. Cotton is the fourth largest export earner.

The makeup of the raw-material export package and the composition of the importers has varied from year to year, but certain patterns do persist. Like the United States, the Soviet Union not only supplies many of its domestic needs, but has a large export capacity as well. But in contrast to the USSR, since World War II, the United States has become more dependent on imports for many raw materials. Whereas the United States now finds itself importing major commodities such as potash, manganese, chromium, asbestos, nickel, platinum-group metals, gas, and some 40 percent of its petroleum, the Soviet Union exports all these items. In the extreme case of petroleum, the Soviet Union had net exports of as much as 27 percent of its production in recent years. It has sustained oil exports of about a quarter of production since 1965. Coincidentally, this is about the same percentage of production that was exported in 1932.

Iron ore is also a major Soviet export commodity, with exports running about one-sixth of production. Manganese exports take almost one-seventh of production. Ginned-cotton exports amount to 30 to 31 percent of production. Most other exports, such as coal, pig iron, rolled steel, and timber account for less than 10 percent of total production. Although net natural gas exports in 1977 were only 6 percent of production, the percentage increased significantly to almost double that after the opening of the Orenburg pipeline in 1979.

Even though Soviet domestic consumption of these raw materials has grown steadily, the Soviets have been able just as steadily to increase the share of exports of many of them. Most of the increase in the percentage of goods exported has occurred since 1955. It has been par-

TABLE 3
Soviet Trade Balances with Hard-Currency Countries ($ million)

|  | 1971 | 1972 | 1973 | 1974 | 1975 | 1976 | 1977 |
|---|---|---|---|---|---|---|---|
| Western data | | | | | | | |
| Imports from USSR | 2,553 | 2,915 | 4,561 | 6,839 | 7,166 | 8,803 | 10,548 |
| Exports to USSR | 2,251 | 3,328 | 4,894 | 6,258 | 11,086 | 12,106 | 12,112 |
| Balance for USSR | + 302 | − 413 | − 333 | + 581 | −3,920 | −3,303 | −1,564 |
| Soviet data | | | | | | | |
| Exports to West | 2,319 | 2,491 | 4,327 | 6,739 | 6,346 | 8,420 | 10,187 |
| Imports from West | 2,429 | 3,565 | 5,254 | 6,910 | 11,419 | 12,574 | 11,845 |
| Balance | − 110 | −1,074 | − 927 | − 171 | −5,073 | −4,154 | −1,658 |

Exchange rate: 1971, 1 ruble = $1.11
                1972, 1 ruble =  1.21
                1973, 1 ruble =  1.34
                1974, 1 ruble =  1.34
                1975, 1 ruble =  1.32
                1976, 1 ruble =  1.34
                1977, 1 ruble =  1.37

SOURCE: Soviet data from *Vneshnyaya torgovlya SSSR*. Western data from *Annual Issues of Directions of Trade*, published by the International Monetary Fund.

ticularly noticeable in petroleum and petroleum products, for which net exports as a percentage of production have moved from 5 percent in 1955 to 27 or 28 percent in 1980. For gas, the share increased from a negative value in 1972 to 12 percent in 1980. The comparable figure for timber is 2 percent of production exported in 1960 and 5 percent in 1980; for cotton 25 percent in 1960, and 30 percent in 1980. Manganese is an exception to this trend. The share of coal, iron ore, pig iron, and rolled steel production exported increased, then decreased, compared with 1960, although the percentage generally remains higher for most of these items in 1980 than it was in 1960.

There is less of a clear pattern in the breakdown of exports between hard-currency (or OECD) countries and members of CMEA. The share of timber going to OECD countries has remained high, and the share of gas, iron ore, and cotton exports has increased sharply in recent years. In the extreme cases of timber and natural gas, over half of Soviet exports go to Western Europe. The percentage of paper and manganese exports destined for the OECD bloc has decreased. The comparable percentage of coal, petroleum, and petroleum products has fluctuated. In recent years the share of exports going to the OECD countries has increased sharply, but much of the increase has come at the expense of LDCs rather than the CMEA bloc.

In sum, raw materials have consistently been an important component of Russian exports, pre-Soviet as well as Soviet. In the prerevolutionary period grain constituted as much as one-third of Russia's export earnings. Timber and timber products were the largest export earners. Prior to 1902, Russia was the world's largest petroleum producer, although by 1914 petroleum exports accounted for only 3 percent of total export earnings.

The 1917 Revolution and ensuing Civil War brought enormous disruption to the Soviet economy. Following collectivization, grain exports fell sharply and never reattained the prewar level. The Soviet Union was no longer the bread basket of Europe.

To take up the slack in export earnings, the Soviets increased their export of timber and petroleum, which in the late 1920s and early 1930s accounted for about 17 percent and 15 percent respectively of their export earnings. In the latter part of the 1930s, the relative importance of timber increased slightly to 20 percent, while petroleum fell to a little under 10 percent.

In the years immediately after World War II, the flow of Soviet exports was shifted to Eastern Europe and China, the Soviet Union's new Communist allies. Grain continued to be an important export commodity for a time, and exports reached a peak of 7.8 million tons in 1962. However, total exports never reached the 9 million ton level of 1914 or the 33 percent prewar share of total export earnings. Indeed, beginning in 1963, the Soviet Union became a major grain importer. While timber continued to be a consistent export-earning commodity, the most important change was the ever increasing importance of petroleum, particularly after the petroleum price increases of 1973–74. By 1980, all raw-material exports accounted for 84 percent of total Soviet hard-currency earnings.

## Can the USSR Maintain Raw-Material Production?

An important question for the future development of the Soviet Union is whether the Soviets will be able to increase their raw-material production so as to sustain or raise exports and at the same time meet domestic needs. While we in the United States worry about whether production itself will diminish, for the Soviets the question goes beyond that to whether the *rate of increase* in production will cease. It has been suggested that, at least for some raw materials such as petroleum and perhaps strategic metals, Soviet production will soon level off and may even diminish.[12] If this should happen, it would have serious ramifications for Soviet export earnings and thus for the import of technology.

There is one advantage that comes to the Soviets from being a late developer. The Soviets have only belatedly begun the intense development of their resources. In addition, the Soviets can draw upon a vast land mass, much of which still has not been adequately prospected and which may yet prove to hold rich deposits.

In the past, the Russians (both Czarist and Soviet) have developed most of the existing deposits themselves. Frequently, foreign technology has been used in the initial stages of development. But the Russians have usually managed soon after to take over and carry through on their own.[13] This is not to deny that the Soviets are often inefficient in their work, but generally they have managed to expand their production base on their own.

A prime example of this is the development of the Tyumen oil fields in Western Siberia. The first petroleum discovery in this desolate, remote area was made only in 1959.[14] The first exploitation of the fields took place only in 1964, when a mere 200,000 tons of oil was extracted. Yet by 1980, despite the mosquitos, swamps, permafrost, and difficult supply conditions, production was 312 million tons, or slightly over half of all Soviet oil production. Moreover, virtually the entire effort was carried out with existing Soviet labor and technology.

The Soviets have been equally impressive in exploiting the natural gas fields, which are located in even more desolate, inaccessible regions. Unlike petroleum, which if need be can be transported in a variety of ways, natural gas can be moved only by pipeline. This means the Soviets must build not only roads to the production sites, but pipelines to get the gas out. And unlike a road (which need not be in perfect repair at all times), a pipeline must be built so that it can withstand extreme changes in weather without sustaining so much as a crack. This has been difficult to achieve, and the Soviets have been slow in fulfilling all of their pipeline construction plans. But sooner or later they complete their projects, and they have managed to ship gas from some of the most hostile areas of the world, whether Arctic tundra or Central Asian desert.

The pattern of irrepressible (if erratic) progress is repeated in almost all fields of Soviet resource development. The Soviets have managed to tap vast quantities of natural wealth with only modest outside help. True, most of the earlier exploration and development took place in more readily accessible areas. As these fields become depleted, it becomes necessary to move increasingly to the North or the East or to adopt more advanced extraction techniques. There is little sign that this tendency will reverse itself.[15]

The decision to build the costly Baikal-Amur Mainline (BAM) was made in large part to open up the vast quantities of raw materials located along the route for export to the Pacific Basin. To undertake such projects, however, the Soviets have often had to turn to the capitalist world for equipment and technology. Thus a large proportion of the exploration and secondary recovery equipment being used in new petroleum areas is imported from outside the Soviet bloc. Similarly much of the machinery being used to build the BAM railroad is foreign. But the basic effort itself is being carried out almost exclusively by Soviet engineers and workers. The few exceptions to this include Japanese contributions to develop and export Siberian coal and timber, a West German effort to build a direct-conversion steel plant in the Kursk Magnetic Anomaly, a joint Japanese-U.S. endeavor off Sakhalin to drill for oil and gas, a Finnish venture in Karelia to develop iron ore and timber, and Bulgarian and North Korean concessions to cut and process timber.

On occasion the Soviets have asked their East European allies to help finance the development of mineral reserves and pipelines from which a large portion of the intended output is destined for Eastern Europe. A recent example of this is the assignment of responsibility for building specific links of the Orenburg pipeline to the East European members of CMEA, except for Rumania, which has financed the purchase of imported compressors and other pipeline equipment. In other instances, the East European countries have provided the Soviet Union with loans for the development of raw-material production.[16] Yet in the total picture, these efforts account for a relatively small portion of Soviet activity. The Soviets are remarkably self-reliant.

Soviet officials are, of course, sometimes confronted with difficult challenges, as older deposits become depleted. At Magnitogorsk, the site of the largest iron and steel plant, for example, the local source of iron ore is now depleted.[17] This necessitates a search for new sources of supply, which are farther from existing processing centers, raising shipping costs and requiring major capital expenditures. With few exceptions, the result is higher unit costs of production.

The progressive depletion of resources is well illustrated in the case of petroleum. The CIA has documented the recent declines in output from what once were the main sources of supply.[18] As a result, in 1980 the European portion of the USSR (including the Urals) supplied only 43 percent of the country's oil, 37 percent of the gas, and some 46 percent of the coal, while the eastern part of the Soviet Union supplied well over half of those resources.[19] With 75 percent of Soviet population and 83 percent of the industrial production located west of the Urals, there is a clear disparity between population and industrial production, on the one hand, and resource availability, on the other. This disparity will in all likelihood continue to grow.[20]

The Soviets are pursuing several different strategies to cope with the growing distance between population and raw materials. First, they are trying to increase their transportation capacity. This involves the construction of new and supplemental pipelines as well as highways and railroads. During the 10th Five-Year Plan (1976–80), for example, the Soviets built some 45,000 kilometers of pipelines, including 30,000 km for natural gas and 14,900 for crude oil and refined products.[21] Leslie Dienes has calculated that, based on the recent rate of pipeline activity, the Soviets have been laying the equivalent of an Alaska pipeline every four to five weeks.[22] In addition to increasing the capacity to ship raw materials, new pipelines and especially railroads also open up new areas of the country for exploration and ultimate production. The best example is the Baikal-Amur Mainline, but the laying of new pipeline can have the same result. Such efforts are expensive, but there are times when the resource deposits unearthed are so large that unit costs of production actually fall. The opening of the Tyumen oil deposits is one such example.

Soviet planners have to cope not only with moving more raw materials to the western USSR, but also with moving workers to the north and east. Inevitably, labor turnover is enormous. At a number of remote sites, the Soviets have resorted to flying in and out entire shifts of workers, so that the workers do not have to stay on the site for a prolonged period of time.[23] Compared with the traditional Soviet practice of relocating workers and their families in new towns, this was considered wasteful, but in many ways it is the best solution to the Soviets' problem. Coincidentally, some Canadian firms have recently found that this rotating policy is also the best method for holding on to workers in similarly remote areas of Canada,[24] and it is widely used in offshore drilling around the world.

The Soviets also plan to increase the amount of industrial processing in the eastern regions. This will eliminate some of the transportation volume that now includes large amounts of dirt and other waste along with the desired minerals. It will also make it possible to utilize some raw materials that in the past were simply discarded. A good illustration of this effort is the current construction of a major petrochemical complex at Tobolsk. Located near the Tyumen field, the Tobolsk operation will also provide a ready market for much of the natural gas associated with petroleum extraction. As recently as 1979, as much as 11 billion cubic meters of this gas (or 79 percent of all the associated gas flared in the Soviet Union) was lost in the West Siberian oil fields.[25] However, the situation was being remedied by an intensive program of gas-plant construction, and by 1982 the flaring of West Siberian gas was reported down to some 5 billion cubic meters.

Developments such as the petrochemical complex at Tobolsk, and another at Tomsk, as well as energy-intensive industries like aluminum reduction near some of the Siberian hydroelectric stations have a plausible rationale. They utilize valuable raw materials that would otherwise be discarded or emitted into the atmosphere, and they also transform those raw materials into a more valuable commodity. The value of associated gas is increased by as much as 10 times per cubic meter when it is processed into petrochemical products such as fertilizer or plastic. Some of these products will be exported. This was also the reason for the construction of the 1,000-mile ammonia pipeline from Togliatti to the new chemical export terminal of Yuzhny, near Odessa, as part of the swap of American superphosphoric acid for Soviet ammonia and urea. Whenever the Soviets export such energy-intensive products as gas-based ammonia or power-intensive aluminum, they are in effect exporting

energy as well. But the exports and the markets are diversified and the value added increases, thereby enhancing the overall economic benefit to the USSR.

Another way for the Soviets to increase the export yield from their raw materials is to reduce waste at both the extraction and manufacturing stages. Rationalization will, however, require basic changes in the Soviet planning system, particularly in incentives.

While raw-material waste has always been a feature of the Soviet system, the degree of concern increased sharply in the mid-1970s when the Soviet Union, along with the rest of the world, was confronted with higher prices of raw materials. Until then, the Soviets treated minerals in the ground as free goods; a law passed in 1930 abolished payments of rent on land to be mined.[26] By contrast, Soviet managers have had to pay for the labor and capital goods they use. The predictable result is that, in the words of Academician Khachaturov, the enterprise "prefers to make more economical use of its capital even if it means neglecting natural resources."[27]

This result can be understood as the consequence of not charging the Soviet mining enterprise the full replacement cost of mineral reserves. All miners everywhere tend to take out the best (most accessible, richest) minerals first. As those minerals are depleted, costs per ton of additional output rise. At some point, the variable cost per ton at the working mine will exceed the total cost per ton at a new mine, and it will pay to abandon the old mine for the new mine.

It is here that Soviet and capitalist practices diverge. The Soviet miner faces a lower effective cost of replacing the spent reserves, by moving to a new mine, than does his capitalist counterpart.[28] This is because the cost of the new mine site and much of the geological prospecting and exploration costs are not charged to the Soviet mining enterprise.[29] Hence, a Soviet miner is less apt to dig or drill in the harder-to-reach corners of a deposit than is a capitalist miner. Moreover, in shaft mining the Soviet manager is more likely to leave behind pillars of coal or potash, used to support the ceiling, instead of replacing them with an artificial support before moving on.[30] Recognizing these tendencies, Soviet economists have been arguing for the introduction of a rent or raw-material charge. As Khachaturov sees it, "If the enterprise has to pay for natural resources, it will treat them as carefully and economically as productive capital."[31]

To the extent that reserve replacement costs are not charged to Soviet mining enterprises, Soviet pricing practices are such that raw materials tend to be underpriced in the USSR. Underpricing in turn induces consumers of raw materials to use more of them than they otherwise would. This helps to explain why the Soviet Union expends more fuel per kilowatt of electric power and per ton of open hearth steel smelted, and more metal per unit of engine power, than the United States does. In the Soviet machine tool industry, for example, over 25 percent of all the rolled steel used is discarded as scrap.[32] Given the planning system with its emphasis on output targets and the tendency to understate or ignore the true costs involved, it was inevitable that there would be waste in Soviet mining practices.

This waste is translated into Soviet extraction ratios that are very much lower than those that prevail in the non-Communist world. Soviet economists and geologists constantly complain that Soviet mining and drilling practices are needlessly wasteful. In contrast to the American experience where recovery rates in coal mines, particularly strip mines, are often 90 to 100 percent, in the Soviet Union the figure is frequently only 70 percent.[33] The recovery rate of mica is as low as 10 percent, while the recovery of potassium salts and petroleum reportedly is 40 to 50 percent of that which can be extracted. Normally the extraction rate of ferrous and nonferrous metals in the Soviet Union is about 80 percent, but at the Krivoi Rog mines it is only 54 percent.[34] The respected economist, Tigran Khachaturov, reports that often 40 to 50 percent of the solid minerals which can be mined are left in the ground.[35]

The flaring of natural gas produced as a byproduct of petroleum extraction has been of special concern to Soviet economists. For a time as much as 40 percent of this gas was flared.[36] In fairness, it should be pointed out that, for many years, gas was similarly flared in Iran and Saudi Arabia. The issue is whether the cost of recovering and using the byproduct natural gas (including shipping costs) is matched or outweighed by the value of the gas in use. Industrial development tends to make gas more valuable and to reduce shipping costs as the spatial density of production increases. Iran and Saudi Arabia have both harnessed increasing amounts of byproduct natural gas for use or export as they have become increasingly industrialized. With the longstanding Soviet emphasis on industrialization, many Soviet economists have argued that the Soviet Union should be recovering and using more of its byproduct gas.

The planning system is also ill-suited to locating new deposits. Remember that planning targets are usually spelled out in terms of some physical measure. For those in agencies like the Ministry of Geology whose work involves drilling, the most reasonable index seemed to be the number of meters drilled. The more meters drilled, the better the performance, or at least so one might think. Unfortunately, Soviet geological crews soon discovered that, the deeper they dug, the longer it took them and the less likely it was that they would fulfill their plans. As a result the crews have tended to prefer to drill shallower holes. As an article in *Pravda* put it, "Deep drilling means reducing the speed of the work and reducing the group's bonuses." As a result, "In some places the land is becoming increasingly pitted with shallow exploratory holes drilled in incessant pursuit of a larger number of total meters drilled." Further, "There are geological expeditions in the Kazakh Republic that have not discovered a valuable deposit for many years but are nonetheless counted among the successful expeditions because they fulfill their assignments in terms of meters."[37] It would be far more efficient to base the compensation of drilling teams on the amounts of raw material actually discovered.

Moreover, even when a deposit is found, the drillers from the Ministry of Geology bear no responsibility for determining the size of the deposit. Consequently, the

actual producing ministries must also maintain their own drilling units. In some instances as many as three separate drilling agencies may be involved in preparing a single deposit, duplicating one another's work and moving three rigs in and out instead of just one.[38]

Another institutional block to the efficient use of mineral deposits is the division of responsibility for mining in the Soviet Union among several large ministries or state committees. For instance, there are the Ministry of Ferrous Metallurgy, the Ministry of Nonferrous Metallurgy, the Ministry of the Coal Industry, the Ministry of the Chemical Industry, the Ministry of the Gas Industry, the Ministry of the Petroleum Industry and the Ministry of Construction Materials Industry. Unfortunately, nature does not always break herself up into the same neat, precisely defined categories. For example, a valuable mineral such as apatite is often mixed in with iron ore in the same deposit. Yet, because the Ministry of Ferrous Metallurgy is only accountable for iron ore output, a million tons a year of apatite was discarded at the Kovdor mine by the agencies of the Ministry of Ferrous Metallurgy rather than used for fertilizer.[39] Similarly, the gravel extracted with iron ore at Krivoi Rog and Kursk is also tossed aside as waste instead of being used for construction. In the same way, the Ministry of Ferrous Metallurgy also rejects as slag significant quantities of valuable minerals such as vanadium, titanium, nickel, chrome, cobalt and copper, and even platinum.[40] In its turn, the Ministry of Nonferrous Metallurgy discards valuable quantities of ferrous metals.[41] Some of this waste might be eliminated by more coordinated planning, but complete elimination would require a drastic revision of economic incentives.

The failure of the Soviet bureaucracy to divide itself up in the same way as nature also helps to explain the flaring of so much natural gas. Until recently, virtually none of the flaring was done by the Ministry of the Gas Industry. Most of it was done by the Ministry of the Petroleum Industry, which produced the gas as a byproduct but had petroleum as its main concern.[42] Therefore, the plan fulfillment efforts of the Ministry of Petroleum Industry were little affected by what happened to the byproduct natural gas it ended up with.

## The Special Role of Energy

How much will the shortcomings in the Soviet planning system act to hamper the fulfillment of Soviet output and export targets? There is no doubt that there has been a fall in the rate of growth of production of most Soviet raw materials in the last few years. The growth rate for petroleum fell from an annual increase of 7 percent or more in the early 1970s to about 1 percent in 1981. Even more striking, absolute coal production, not just the rate of growth, has been declining steadily since 1978, and iron ore extraction has been virtually stagnant since the late 1970s. Natural gas is one of the few products whose rate of growth has increased in recent years. Whereas natural gas output increased by only 4 percent in 1972, in 1980 and 1981 it increased by about 7 percent. It should be remembered, of course, that it is the *rate of growth* that is falling, not (except for coal) the actual amount produced. In principle this is a good sign. If there are to be increased exports, Soviet officials must first of all insure that output increases. If output falls, the Soviets may still be able to raise exports if they decide to divert supplies from domestic uses to export markets. But that would require severe readjustments, with the risk of dislocations, in the Soviet economy. Clearly, the Soviets would prefer to increase output. Let us consider, therefore, what the output potential of the various raw materials might be.

From the standpoint of export earnings, the most important commodity is petroleum. Since petroleum accounted for over $20.8 billion in Soviet hard-currency earnings in 1980, any reduction in petroleum exports would pose a serious balance-of-trade problem. As it is, in recent years they have had trade deficits of up to $4 billion.

While Soviet petroleum has always been an important foreign-exchange earner, its really significant impact dates from the fourfold price increase of 1973–74. Thus, while petroleum accounted for only 22 percent of hard-currency earnings and 13 percent of all Soviet export revenues in 1972, by 1974 the figure had soared to almost 40 percent of hard-currency earnings and 21 percent of total export revenues. In 1980, when Soviet petroleum prices to Eastern Europe were almost at world price levels, petroleum was a source of 56 percent of Soviet hard-currency earnings and 34 percent of its overall earnings. In many ways, therefore, the USSR is like a nation with a one-crop economy.

If the CIA is correct, Soviet petroleum production will start to level off in the early 1980s, as will exports.[43] In the CIAs more pessimistic estimate, production was supposed to fall as early as 1979. Equally important, based on its April 1977 calculations, the CIA projected that the drop in production would necessitate not only a corresponding drop in exports, but the actual importation of oil, so that by 1985 the Soviet bloc would be importing 3.5 to 4.5 million barrels a day.

The transformation from a net exporter of petroleum to a net importer would cause a crisis in Soviet foreign trade. At current world petroleum prices, importing 3.5 to 4.5 mbd would cost $37 to $45 billion a year. If to that are added nonpetroleum Soviet hard-currency imports for $24 billion (as of 1980), the Soviet Union would have an overall import bill of some $60 billion to $70 billion a year. At the same time, the loss of over one-half of its $20.8 billion earnings from petroleum exports, in the absence of substantial new exports, would leave the Soviets with only $9 billion of exports. The result would be annual trade deficits of $50 billion to $60 billion.

Of course, much of that deficit would have to be carried by the Soviet Union's East European allies, who produce little petroleum of their own. Moreover, in addition to the Soviet Union's visible trade exports, the Soviets also have hard-currency earnings from the sale of gold, diamonds and military equipment. The Soviets hope that by 1985 they will be able to expand some of their other exports, especially machinery and natural gas. To be realistic, though, it is unlikely that export earnings will increase

much, since even if hard-currency natural gas exports double, gas will still bring in only about $1 billion. Moreover, the East Europeans already have a hard-currency trade deficit each year. Finally, if the Soviet bloc buys that much petroleum, the price could go up, causing the import bill to be even higher.

Recognizing these criticisms, the CIA belatedly reduced its estimates of the bloc's 1985 imports.[44] In its more recent forecast, it predicted that the bloc would have to import only 2.7 mbd, none of which would be required by the Soviet Union itself, and production would fall to only 10 to 11 mbd, not the 8 to 10 originally forecast. But even this seems to be too extreme a situation. Petroleum exports are obviously vital for Soviet export earnings. Moreover, the Soviets seem determined to insure there will be petroleum available to export. What are they doing to bring that about?

The first step is to eliminate certain wasteful domestic consumption habits. The decision to double the retail price of gasoline in early 1978 was a step in that direction. However, the total motor vehicle stock in the Soviet Union is small to begin with, so that the curtailed use of gasoline will not be all that important. In addition, the decision to buy gasoline is generally more dependent on access to ration coupons than on price.

Yet there remains much the Soviets can do, especially in industry, electricity generation and household heating.[45] For example, building insulation is poor, and drafts are omnipresent. More important, the Soviets have been seeking to reduce their heavy use of petroleum in electricity generation and central heating. This has been more difficult than expected. In the 10th Five-Year Plan, the objective was to reverse the rising trend in oil consumption by electric power stations by reducing the share of oil in the fuel mix from 29.5 percent in 1975 to 28 percent in 1980. But, as shown in Table 4, this goal could not be achieved. In fact, the share of oil increased even further, to 35.2 percent, by 1980. In the current, 11th Five-Year Plan, another attempt is to be made to reverse the trend.

In the natural-resource-poor European part of the

TABLE 4
Fuel Mix of Thermal Power Stations (under Electric Power Ministry USSR) (in percent)

|  | 1970 | 1975 | 1980 Plan | 1980 Actual | 1985 Plan |
|---|---|---|---|---|---|
| Oil | 23.5 | 29.5 | 28.0 | 35.2 | 25.9 |
| Gas | 23.8 | 22.0 | 22.0 | 24.2 | 31.5 |
| Coal | 47.5 | 44.5 | 45.8 | 37.9 | 39.6 |
| Peat | 3.4 | 2.1 | 2.6 | 1.0 | 1.5 |
| Oil shale | 1.8 | 1.9 | 1.6 | 1.7 | 1.5 |

SOURCE: Theodore Shabad, "News Notes," *Soviet Geography: Review and Translation* 22, no. 7 (September 1981): 448.
NOTE: Thermal power stations under the jurisdiction of the Electric Power Ministry USSR use roughly one-fourth of all the fossil fuels consumed in the Soviet Union. They generate about three-fourths of the electricity, with the rest of the electric power produced by hydroelectric and nuclear stations and by power-generating facilities under other jurisdictions.

632  The Role of Raw Materials in Soviet Foreign Trade

Soviet Union, the Soviets have been pursuing an aggressive program to increase their atomic energy capacity. Although their plans are behind schedule, they seek to increase the amount of power generated by nuclear reactors from 2 percent in 1975 to 14 percent in 1985.[46] The Soviets are also making an effort to increase the use of coal, but because of the problems in the coal industry, this has been as difficult as reducing the share of oil (Table 4).[47] The Soviets have also improved the overall efficiency of their use of energy: the ratio of energy consumed to GNP produced has started to decline.[48]

The Soviets are trying to rationalize not only their consumption patterns, but production procedures as well. Although a radical shakeup of the existing planning system would be required to solve many of the basic problems, there is still room for improvement within the existing framework. Rates of recovery in the Soviet oil fields, as we saw, are quite low; with improved incentives, the Soviets could increase the rate of extraction considerably. The expectation that they will in fact do so is the basis for the report by PetroStudies Company of Sweden that the Soviets, by 1985, will be exporting, not importing, about 3.7 mbd. While the PetroStudies report goes to the other extreme from the CIA prediction, there is no doubt that the Soviets can increase their production in existing fields, in many instances merely by increasing the number of wells in existing fields. The Soviets are in the process of changing their incentive system so that the main criterion of oil development becomes the maximization of differential rent instead of the present system of minimizing development costs.[49]

If they are to be effective, the Soviets will also have to improve the quality of their drill pipe and drill bits. With the main success indicator for Soviet pipe manufacturers not the durability of the pipe or even the length but the tonnage,[50] it is not surprising that Soviet drill pipe often has threading defects. Thus, as little as 15 percent of a driller's time is actually spent on drilling. The remainder is spent on taking out and reinserting the drill pipe to attach new drill bits and replace the pipe.

The Soviets are trying to solve these problems with both their own and foreign resources. For example, to improve their offshore exploration efforts in the Caspian Sea, they have combined all offshore drilling efforts under the Ministry of Gas Industry. Now the gas industry will presumably focus on the discovery and ultimate extraction of fuel deposits instead of countenancing an indicator that stresses only meters drilled. At the same time, the Soviets have decided to buy an American drill bit plant in the hope of improving the quality of their own drill bits. They are also considering the use of foreign technology in order to produce better pipe and secondary recovery equipment. Such measures could go a long way toward sustaining, if not increasing, production in old wells and increasing output in new wells.

Still, it is unlikely that under the present system the Soviets will be able to solve all their problems. Even if the Soviets were to convert to a market system, they might not be able to adopt an efficient energy policy. After all, even we in the United States have had difficulty adopting such a policy. The problem in the Soviet Union, just as in the United States, is that consumer interests do not coin-

cide with those of the producers or the conservationists. A rational policy would probably call for a sharp increase in energy prices. However, Soviet authorities, just as many American senators, are reluctant to push up consumer prices. The 1978 increase in retail gasoline prices (the first increase since 1972) is an exception, but the household prices of gas and electricity have been unchanged for decades. In the coal and peat industries, state enterprises have usually run at a loss and a subsidy has been necessary, particularly when production costs rise as a consequence of moving out to the far north and east for reserves.[51] After a wholesale and retail price increase in 1967, profits as a percentage of working and fixed capital in the coal industry, which ran at a loss of 17 percent in 1965, increased to 7.3 percent in 1970.[52] But this was short-lived. With no further price increase, the profit rate has fallen continuously, so that in 1980 the coal industry had a loss of 7.5 percent, and the peat industry 1.7 percent. The same trend has affected the petroleum and gas industries. The profit rate for petroleum, which was 5.7 percent in 1965 rose to 27.8 percent in 1970 and fell to 8.6 percent in 1980. The figures for gas were 9.3 percent in 1965, 64.5 percent in 1970, and 15.2 percent in 1980.[53]

That profit rates fluctuate so in the energy industry is an inherent disadvantage of the Soviet economic system. Ironically, the Soviets have long said that one advantage of their foreign trade system is that Soviet prices and currency are insulated from world market forces. In principle that should pose no problem, since the proportion of exports to GNP is not much more than 8 percent. In specific sectors, however, particularly those discussed in this paper, such a policy is bound to create distortions. In industries such as petroleum, iron ore and manganese ore, where exports amount to 15 percent or more of total production, world prices cannot be ignored, especially in the wake of the major price increase that took place in the years after 1973.

The decision in 1977 to increase significantly the importation of petroleum exploration and drilling equipment suggests that the Soviets have come to recognize the role of world prices in making decisions about domestic production. The evident change in attitudes in the petroleum industry may some day be repeated in other Soviet raw-material producing ministries. If the overdue wholesale price reform for the whole economy causes Soviet domestic prices to reflect more accurately world prices and export opportunities, it could lead to the commitment of even more investment resources to the development of natural resource production.

To compensate for the lack of market clearing prices, as signals leading to efficient resource use, the Soviets have had to resort to other methods. One of their favorite techniques is to enact laws or resolutions calling for improved efficiency. These techniques invariably produce less than fully satisfactory results. One of the laws, enacted by the Supreme Soviet in 1975, was titled "On Measures for Further Strengthening the Protection of Natural Resources and Improving the Use of Raw Materials."[54] This law is not much different from earlier laws, including a decree on raw materials adopted in 1972 titled, "On More Intensive Protection of Nature."[55] Predictably, neither of these measures has been any more effective than those enacted in an earlier era.[56] The lack of impact can be seen in the fact that it is necessary to keep enacting new laws.

## Raw Materials and the Balance of Trade

One of the remarkable features about the trade figures presented earlier in this paper was that in recent years the Soviets have increased not only the absolute export volumes of several commodities, but also the relative shares of total production exported. Given the increased cost of finding new raw-material reserves and then of mining and shipping the materials, this process might have been expected to come to a halt; indeed, a few years ago it did look as if the percentage being exported was diminishing. What explains the recent increase?

While it is hard to judge precisely what determines Soviet actions, there is good reason to believe that the volume of Soviet raw-material exports is dependent at least in part on a Soviet desire to reduce its trade deficits. There are significant exceptions to the trend (e.g., iron ore and manganese). Yet despite these exceptions, since 1972 Soviet trading patterns have changed markedly and there is reason to believe that Soviet officials have used raw-material exports to hard-currency markets as a balancing mechanism, even if it has meant sacrificing some of the needs of the domestic economy.

The most striking example of hard-currency balancing is in petroleum exports. The total volume of exports as well as the total volume to the OECD countries rose continuously until 1974. Then, because world prices increased fourfold, hard-currency petroleum earnings, which had doubled from 1972 to 1973, doubled again in 1974. This left the USSR with one of its most favorable trade balances in years, and there was no need to export as much as they had in 1973. Thus hard-currency oil exports fell from 36 million tons in 1973 to 31 million tons in 1974. In 1975, however, the Soviets failed to anticipate the effect on oil demand of the world-wide recession, and they allowed their imports nearly to double. The result was a record deficit of $4 billion to $5 billion (see Table 3).

The deficit was caused in part by the serious crop failure, which necessitated larger than expected grain imports. In addition, Soviet imports had been predicated on the assumption that export earnings would continue to grow as they had in 1974. However, the world recession reduced both raw-material demand and prices, and as a result Soviet hard-currency receipts fell. For example, timber sales (which totaled about $1 billion in 1974) fell to $700 million in 1975. Similarly, sales of cotton fell from $360 million to $274 million. The demand for energy products remained relatively strong, however, so that (even though prices dropped a bit) the Soviets were able to offset their shortfall in the other markets with an increase in the absolute volume of energy products sold for hard currency. Hard-currency coal revenues rose from $230 million in 1974 to $371 million in 1975. Natural gas exports to hard-currency customers rose from 5 billion cubic meters to 7 billion cubic meters, and more importantly revenue more than doubled from $87 million to

about $200 million in 1975. However, increased petroleum sales provided the biggest supplement. Hard-currency exports of oil rose from 31 million to 38 million tons, and earnings rose from $2.6 billion to $3 billion. They would have risen even more if petroleum prices had not weakened. Without the increase in earnings from energy, Soviet hard-currency receipts would have been about $700 million less than they were.

While the Soviets tried to reduce their imports in 1976, they again found it necessary to import large quantities of grain. Thus, it was necessary to increase exports again. The timber and cotton markets firmed a bit, and so the Soviets grossed $200 million more than the previous year. Hard-currency coal exports actually diminished, but this was more than compensated for by a dramatic increase in petroleum and natural-gas exports. Hard-currency gas exports increased by 40 million cubic meters, or by about 60 percent, and revenues rose about 70 percent. Petroleum exports jumped by 11 million tons (or 30 percent), and revenues rose by $1.5 billion (or 50 percent). Because the accumulated debt was still large, the extra effort to export raw materials was continued into 1977. This time export earnings of all the major commodities increased, with hard-currency petroleum revenue jumping the most by $800 million. The jump was not as large as previous increases, because of mounting pressures to retain some raw materials for domestic use, and because the trade deficit was no longer so large.

That Gosplan and Ministry of Foreign Trade officials consciously pursued the course of action just described was acknowledged in an interview held at Gosplan in December 1978. At this meeting, a deputy chairman of Gosplan, N.N. Inozemtsev, and several of his colleagues acknowledged that an explicit decision was made to export $1.5 billion worth of petroleum beyond what was originally intended, in order to reduce the trade deficit.

It seems clear, therefore, that Soviet officials are prepared to adjust their raw-material export flows to pay for their imports. It will be interesting to see what will happen to raw-material exports if and when the Soviets manage to solve their balance-of-trade problem. What, for example, will happen if their wheat harvest should improve significantly, and if they also manage to increase their non-raw-material exports? The implication is that the Soviets will reduce exports of their raw materials, particularly petroleum and coal. The reduction will affect mostly customers who do not have long-term contracts. This should mean that East European customers will continue to receive their allocations, as will those who are engaged in joint ventures. Such a policy satisfies not only the general desire to conserve nonrenewable raw materials where possible, but (as we shall see) some strong Russian nationalist sentiments as well.

## Interdependence or Autarky

If Soviet goods continue to flow onto the world market, it could have ramifications beyond the mere increase of raw-material production. The Soviets could find themselves becoming increasingly dependent on the world market, and vice-versa. That could have both positive and negative consequences.

One Western perspective is that, the more the Soviets become a part of the world trading pattern, the greater the likelihood that they may some day be drawn out of their isolation. There is a danger in overstating this possibility, since foreign trade is not necessarily a guarantee of lasting peace and friendship. If anything, it is as much a source of animosity and conflict as love and harmony. But given the size of the Soviet Union and its historic fear and distrust of foreigners, anything that can be done to draw the Soviets out is generally to be welcomed rather than dreaded.

Foreign trade, particularly of raw materials, seems a particularly suitable means for bringing this about. As we saw, given the opportunity, the Soviets would gladly cut back on some of their exports, particularly petroleum and coal. But in the absence of some dire political development, it seems clear that the Soviets are planning to engage in long-term export arrangements.

They have begun investing in facilities that are intended only to enhance export opportunities. The best example of this is the network of natural-gas pipelines. The Soviets have borrowed billions of dollars to build a series of pipelines through Eastern Europe to Western Europe, and (prior to the Iranian revolution of 1979) they were ready to commit themselves to billions more for a new project involving the flow of gas from Iran to the Soviet Union and from the Soviet Union to Western Europe.

During the first few years of such projects, it might be in the Soviet interest to abrogate their debt commitments and then to suspend the barter payments of natural gas. After all, the pipelines are located for the most part in the Soviet Union or Eastern Europe, and Western lenders would have a hard time repossessing their collateral. But after a time, when more and more of the debt is repaid, and as Soviet equity in the pipeline increases, presumably the Soviets will have less incentive to default. Indeed, it is in the Soviet interest to sustain the flow of product until little of the revenue is required for repayment. That should already be the case in the Soviet gas pipeline to Austria, which has been shipping Soviet gas for better than 10 years.

Moreover, while the Soviet system may not seem subject to the same profit considerations that we face in the West, no doubt the Soviets recognize the consequences of abandoning or idling a billion dollar investment. The pressure may not be as great to maintain the flow of oil, since oil can be stored for a longer period of time. In addition, pipeline transmission is not the sole means of transporting petroleum; thus, if the Soviets decide to curtail their petroleum exports, they could continue to use the petroleum pipeline to obtain income from its use, but merely reduce their use of other transportation facilities, such as ships and railroads. And these ships and trains can then be diverted to other uses. Yet an ammonia pipeline and an electrical transmission grid, particularly if extended to Western Europe, would be economic burdens if exports were to be cut off. Once in operation,

such projects, just as with gas pipelines, must be kept in use. This is a factor tending to promote a steady flow of exports.

Gradually the Soviets seem to be building an ever increasing number of investment projects designed in large part to serve the foreign market. One example is the new $300 million alumina plant at Nikolayev on the Black Sea. This plant processes bauxite imported from Guinea and it will ultimately send the reduced alumina to a new aluminum plant at Sayanogorsk in Siberia for further refining. Similarly, to serve Occidental Petroleum's ammonia import project, the Soviets expanded their ammonia-manufacturing capacity and other service facilities. Since the domestic Soviet market is already well supplied with ammonia, if the Soviets stopped exporting, not only to Occidental, but also to others in Italy, West Germany and France, they would be forced to close down their operations. A curtailment or reduction in foreign trade would similarly affect their Siberian container land bridge and merchant marine operations.

Of course, if the Soviets should ever decide to curb their foreign trade activity, they would not be the only ones affected. Obviously, their customers risk serious disruption, particularly if they allow themselves to become overly dependent on Soviet raw materials. For example, Soviet exports already make up about 20 percent of West Germany's imports of diesel fuel and apatite concentrate, 30 percent of the asbestos, and a growing share of the crude oil and natural gas.[57] Extension of the Soviet electrical grid to West Germany and other countries could further jeopardize West European economic independence.

But the Soviets are not the only ones with leverage; importers of Soviet goods can also inflict disruption on the Soviet economy. Thus, the increasing flow of Soviet petrochemicals, such as plastics, synthetic fibers and fertilizers, can work its way into Western markets only if Soviet exporters drastically cut prices. This is happening now, and the cries of dumping are accompanied by pleas for import curbs. Western manufacturers and trade unions are already mounting intensive campaigns to curb Soviet sales. If Soviet exports are cut off, though, the Soviets will be hard pressed to find ways to earn the hard currency necessary to repay the debt incurred to import the factories that now produce these petrochemicals. Moreover, a cut-off could drive the Soviets back into isolationism.

That the Soviet Union now finds itself increasingly dependent on foreigners for inputs and markets is regarded with considerable distaste by some in the USSR. Such sentiments are not necessarily limited to just a few planners. Resentment is particularly widespread when, in order to expand exports, domestic consumption is reduced. The sharp increases in the export of petroleum in 1975 and 1976 had an acute impact in the growth of domestic consumption. Whereas until 1974 domestic consumption never increased by less than 7 percent a year, in 1975 it increased by only 5.8 percent—a figure still large enough to be accommodated without much difficulty. In 1976, however, domestic consumption increased by only 2.9 percent and in 1977 by 3.6 percent to 4.7 percent. In both instances there were reports of shortages of gasoline that seemed to transcend the usual complaints of inept planning procedures.[58]

Reacting to such developments, some in the Soviet Union have warned about the danger of too much interchange with the West. Some even go so far as to seek a cessation of most, if not all, trading relationships. For those familiar with Russian history, much of the present debate will seem like nothing more than a continuation of the old argument between the Slavophiles and the Westernizers. The Slavophiles of the nineteenth century urged that Russia turn its back on the West. Failure to do so, they argued, would open Russia's borders not only to Western goods but Western ideas and ways of doing things. That would mean slums and strikes as well as degradation and disruption and ultimately social unrest. Instead, they argued, Russia with its great population and natural wealth would be better advised to follow its own path and pace of development. Russia should adhere to the traditional Russian way of doing things, looking for guidance to such indigenous institutions as the Russian rural commune and the Russian church. The Westernizers, by contrast, saw things Russian as obstacles to be overcome in the necessary process of opening Russia up to modernity and progress.

The modern-day version of the debate is most eloquently reflected in exchanges between Alexander Solzhenitsyn and Andrei Sakharov. Obviously neither one can be considered an official spokesman for anything in the Soviet Union, but their views nonetheless find support throughout the country. Solzhenitsyn, in a letter dated 5 September 1973, resurrected the banner of the Slavophiles. He urged Soviet leaders to turn their backs on the outside world and concentrate on internal Soviet development. He called for an end to the stress on rapid industrialization and urged a halt to further sales to the West of Russia's natural resources, such as Siberian natural gas, oil, and timber. As he put it: "We, a great industrial superpower, behave like the most backward country, by inviting foreigners to dig our earth and then offer them in exchange our priceless treasure—Siberian natural gas." In fact, he wants a "Russia first" policy to "save our raw material patrimony for future Russian generations." The raw materials will always be valuable, but the Western technology will soon become obsolete. Why give up something timeless and valuable for something ephemeral? In response, Sakharov argued that such a policy would be isolationist. As Sakharov put it: "Our country cannot exist in economic and scientific isolation without world trade, including trade in the country's natural resources, or divorced from the world scientific technical progress—a condition that holds not only danger, but at the same time the only real chance of saving mankind."[59]

Besides Sakharov and Solzhenitsyn, others reflecting the same clash of opinions represent more official points of view. In one extreme case, Professor K. Suvorov, in his request for economic independence of the USSR, seemed to go beyond urging economic autarky for the CMEA, to a return to Stalin's version of socialism in one country.[60] He even cited Stalin as the originator of such an idea. The reference to Stalin which originally was printed in *Pravda* was thoughtfully omitted in an otherwise fairly complete report of the article in *Soviet News* (the news bulletin of the Soviet Embassy in London).[61] As Suvorov saw it, Stalin wanted the Soviet Union "to steer the course towards the country's industrialization, the development of production of the means of production, and the formation of reserves for economic maneuvering," to insure the Soviet Union's economic independence from the world's capitalist economy and to achieve the complete triumph of socialism. This "industrialization of the USSR would insure the economic independence of the country and the ousting of capitalist elements from all the sectors of the national economy, consolidate the Soviet Union's economic and defense potential and strengthen friendship among the people's." This advocacy of autarky by Suvorov was opposed by those who seemed undisturbed that the country would continue to be dependent on "the world's capitalist economy."

Without taking such an extreme stand, there are others who nonetheless worry that the Soviet Union may be overexploiting its natural resources and that foreigners may be benefiting at the expense of future Russians. The emphasis on future generations is a recurrent theme of both politicians and economists.[62] Even those who accept the need to exploit Soviet raw materials because they want Western technology warn that such a policy is not always as simple as it seems and that it necessitates ever increasing expenses because of the need to go off farther into the North and the East.[63]

There is even some reason to believe that the debate extends into the Politburo itself. Of course, there is a danger in placing too much emphasis on the slightly different utterances that were made one day by Party Secretary Brezhnev and a few days later by Prime Minister Kosygin. Nonetheless, in October 1974, Brezhnev is reported as having said: "The natural resources of our country allow us to look to the future without danger. To make a long story short, our country is a country with uncounted riches and *inexhaustible* opportunities. It is our job to use these riches and opportunities properly and economically."[64]

In contrast, three weeks later, Kosygin seemed to view the situation in a different perspective. As he put it when covering the same subject, "Our country is provided with everything necessary so that the Soviet economy can develop dynamically. Our resources are great. But they are *not inexhaustible*. They belong not only to the present but to the future generation of Soviet people. Therefore it is our task to use them intelligently, carefully and in the most rational way possible so that each kilogram of fuel, metal, cement, cotton, fertilizer, synthetic material—so that all of these serve the socialist economy as effectively as the most advanced raw-material technology permits."[65]

Even more fascinating, it was not long before Brezhnev changed his attitude and came to the realization that more care was required in the exploitation of raw materials. "The demand of the country for energy and raw materials grows increasingly and therefore production becomes all the more costly," he later said. "Consequently, if we are to avoid an extraordinary increase in capital investments, it is necessary to use raw materials more effectively."[66]

Finally, those who justify the continuation of raw-material exports sometimes adopt a novel (for the USSR) rationale. A. A. Trofimuk, deputy head of the Siberian Division of the Soviet Academy of Sciences, urged an even faster exploitation of oil and gas.[67] He is concerned that it is only a matter of time before new energy substitutes are found. Therefore the Soviet Union had better use its reserves now before they become valueless.

## An Attempt to Corner the Market?

Recently some observers outside the Soviet Union have begun to warn that focusing too much on Soviet raw-material exports as a hard-currency balancer overlooks the strategic use to which raw materials can be put.[68] As they see it, it is the strategic planners, not the romantic nationalists or the foreign trade officials, whom we should pay attention to. They warn of growing Soviet efforts to gain control of a large percentage of strategic materials that are essential for the conduct of modern day economic and military life. These materials include commodities such as cobalt, titanium, chromite, platinum and manganese. Thus, instead of using raw-material exports to generate hard-currency resources to pay for imports, the Soviets will use these minerals to force political concessions. According to such theories, not only will the Soviets curb their imports, but in their reach for raw-material control, the Soviets are also attempting to foment political takeovers in some of the resource-rich countries of Africa.

Undoubtedly the Soviets would like some day to be in the position where they can impose hurtful embargoes on countries like the United States, just as the United States has tried to do to them. The best defense against such embargoes, however, is for the United States to find alternative sources of supply both at home and abroad, including the maintenance of stockpiles. However grave the possible threat, these concerns seem premature. Short of war, the strong likelihood is that the Soviet Union will continue to export rather than hoard raw materials. This reflects not altruism but necessity. The Soviets have no other way to pay for their imports.

Admittedly it is difficult to know exactly when the Soviet Union is doing something for political reasons and when the motivation is economic. Given the unpredictable working of the Soviet economy, it is all but impossible to know when the Soviet switch from an export to an import posture is a sign of a basic shortage rather than a temporary bottleneck, a supply breakdown, a regional problem, a political gesture to help some developing country, or an attempt to corner the market. In some instances the Soviets have switched from a selling to a buying posture almost overnight, and then back to an exporting position again. Inevitably this causes confusion among would-be analysts.

When attempting to analyze what the Soviets are up to, the observer must use caution. For example, in 1970–73, when Soviet imports of 12 billion cubic meters of natural gas into the Caucasus and Central Asia exceeded Soviet exports of 5 to 7 billion cubic meters to Eastern and Western Europe, at least one writer took this as a sign of an imminent Soviet energy shortage.[69] That this was instead a way of increasing economic efficiency and reducing the transportation of natural gas within the Soviet Union was ignored, as was the fact that the Soviet Union has the world's largest deposits of natural gas—albeit in regions that are remote from most of the Soviet population. Admittedly, the termination of about 10 billion cubic meters of these imports when the Shah of Iran was overthrown did cause disruption in Armenia and Georgia, but with time, natural gas from inside the Soviet Union was rerouted to these Caucasian republics without seriously affecting the supply of natural gas to the Soviet Union's other external and internal consumers.

On occasion, the misinterpretation of the Soviet switch from exports to imports has led some to attach sinister motives to such an act. Granted that the Soviets have at least their share of sinister motivations. It is nonetheless important that analysts not be misled, particularly if they tend to generalize from the examples they find. Thus, Daniel I. Fine, who has argued that the Soviets have begun a campaign to corner the supply of the world's strategic reserves, predicates at least part of his analysis on the Soviet need to import natural gas. As he sees it, the cessation of natural-gas imports from Iran after the Shah's overthrow was a major stimulus to the subsequent invasion of Afghanistan:[70]

"Since 1970 the Soviet Union has been increasingly dependent on gas from Iran. Its limited access under the previous regime has been uncertain since late 1979. With further supplies reduced over the Iranian insistence for higher prices, the Soviet Union has partially compensated for this short-fall by *additional imports* from occupied Afghanistan, a supply strategy dependent upon military and political control over Kabul."

While the Soviets may indeed be seeking to seize or influence the control of valuable minerals, such behavior cannot be extrapolated from Fine's analysis of what he implies is a natural-gas emergency in the Soviet Union. First, Iranian natural-gas imports never totaled more than 4 percent of total Soviet production. Second, Afghanistan was supplying only one-fifth of what Iran was. Third, despite a possible increase in Afghan gas deliveries to the Soviet Union in 1980,[71] Soviet exports of natural gas to Western and Eastern Europe exceeded by 20 times the amount imported from Afghanistan. In sum, just as there is a danger of overemphasizing the role of economics in Soviet behavior, so there is a danger of overemphasizing politics and strategy.

## Conclusion

Sooner or later the Soviets will deplete their raw-material deposits. Notwithstanding the Bolshevik Revolution, this holds for the Soviet Union as well as everybody else.

But given the problems the Soviet Union has had in converting its now massive but still unsophisticated industry to world standards, it is unlikely that the Soviet quest for advanced technology from outside its borders will soon abate. And since the Soviet Union is unable to pay for this technology with fabricated goods, in all likelihood it will have to continue to rely on the exportation of raw materials and semi-fabricates. In a time of intense political and military confrontation, it may attempt to use control of those resources for strategic ends, but the greater likelihood is that it will find itself selling more raw materials than many in the Soviet Union might prefer simply because it is unable to sell anything else on the world market.

Fortunately for the Soviet Union, its reserves are extensive. Thus, although its mining procedures are inefficient and it is necessary to reduce the amount of waste, the prospects for continued production and exploitation are good. Unlike so much of the world, the constraint on the Soviet Union is not so much nature as it is Soviet man and his incentive system. While nature's limitations cannot be neglected, the challenge is to improve the system so as to extract efficiently more of what is there. Because of the importance of raw materials, the Soviets will in all probability find some way to meet this challenge, even if they have to bring in foreign help to do so.

---

## NOTES

1. *Petroleum Economist*, September 1978, pp. 362–63.
2. Ibid., p. 362.
3. G. I. Martsinkevich, *Ispolzovaniye prirodnykh resursov i okhrana prirody* [Resource use and environmental protection] (Minsk: BGU, 1977), p. 64.
4. Daniel I. Fine, "Mineral Resource, Dependency Crisis: the Soviet Union and the United States," in James Arnold Miller, Daniel I. Fine, and R. Daniel McMichael, eds., *The Resource War in Three-D—Dependency, Diplomacy, Defense* (Pittsburgh: World Affairs Council of Pittsburgh, 18th World Affairs Forum, 1980), p. 37.
5. This is based on interviews in the Ministry of Petroleum in December 1977, and in Gosplan in December 1978; and on the failure of the 1990 projections to appear as of this writing.
6. Ministerstvo vneshnei torgovli SSSR (hereafter MVT SSSR), *Vneshnyaya torgovlya SSSR za 1918–1940* (Moscow: Vneshtorgizdat, 1960), p. 45.
7. Tsentralnoye statisticheskoye upravleniye, *Narodnoye khozyaistvo SSSR v 1958 godu* (hereafter *Narkhoz*) (Moscow: Gosstatizdat, 1959), p. 208.
8. Marshall I. Goldman, "The Relocation and Growth of the Prerevolutionary Russian Ferrous Metals Industry," *Explorations in Entrepreneurial History* 9, no. 1 (October 1954): 19.
9. *Vneshnyaya torgovlya SSSR 1918–66*, p. 64–65.
10. Ibid., p. 17.
11. Ibid., p. 73.
12. Central Intelligence Agency, *Prospects for Soviet Oil Production*, ER-77-10270, Washington, April 1977. See also Fine, "Mineral Resource."

13. Robert W. Tolf, *The Russian Rockefellers* (Stanford: Hoover Institution Press, 1976). See also Goldman, "Relocation and Growth."
14. *Review of Sino-Soviet Oil*, May 1977, p. 21.
15. *Foreign Trade*, February 1977, p. 15.
16. A. I. Zubov, "The USSR and the resolution of the fuels-energy and raw material problem in the CMEA countries," *Istoriya SSSR*, 1976, no. 1, p. 60.
17. *Pravda*, 3 April 1978, p. 2.
18. CIA, *Prospects for Soviet Oil Production*.
19. A. M. Nekrasov and M. G. Pervukhin, *Energetika SSSR v 1976–1980 godakh* [Electric power of the USSR in 1976–80] (Moscow: Energiya, 1977), p. 149; Theodore Shabad, "News Notes," *Soviet Geography: Review and Translation* 22, no. 4 (April 1981): 273, 276, 280.
20. Nekrasov and Pervukhin, *Energetika*, p. 144.
21. *Narkhoz 1980*, p. 330.
22. Leslie Dienes, "The Soviet Union: An Energy Crunch Ahead?" *Problems of Communism*, September-December 1977, p. 48.
23. *Current Digest of the Soviet Press* (hereafter *CDSP*), 16 November 1977, p. 18; *Sotsialisticheskaya industriya*, April 1978, p. 3; *Pravda*, 20 April 1978, p. 2.
24. *The Wall Street Journal*, 26 October 1978, p. 48.
25. Central Intelligence Agency, *USSR: Development of the Gas Industry*, ER78-10393, Washington, July 1978, p. 48; *CDSP*, 8 February 1978, p. 2; *Izvestiya*, 12 March 1980; *Neftyanik*, 1981, no. 3; Leslie Dienes and Theodore Shabad, *The Soviet Energy System* (New York: John Wiley, 1979), pp. 95–97.
26. *Voprosy geografii*, vol. 78: Natural Resource Evaluation, 1968, p. 47.
27. T. Khachaturov, "Natural resources and economic planning," *Voprosy ekonomiki*, August 1973, p. 17.
28. Marshall I. Goldman, *The Spoils of Progress* (Cambridge: MIT Press, 1972), p. 49.
29. N. K. Feitelman, "Economic evaluation of mineral resources," *Voprosy ekonomiki*, November 1968, p. 110.
30. Natural pillars left behind often contain more than 20 percent of a mine's ore or coal (*Trud*, 12 August 1967, p. 2). Potash salt pillars often amount to as much as 50 percent of a mine's potential output (*Literaturnaya gazeta*, 1 February 1975, p. 10).
31. Khachaturov, "Natural resources," pp. 20–21.
32. Ibid., p. 26; *Sotsialisticheskaya industriya*, 3 March 1978, p. 2.
33. K. Ye. Gabyshev, "Economic evaluation of natural resources and rent payments," *Vestnik Moskovskogo universiteta, ekonomika*, 1969, p. 17.
34. Ibid., p. 18; *Sotsialisticheskaya industriya*, 8 January 1971, p. 2.
35. Khachaturov, "Natural resources," p. 17; Martsinkevich, *Ispolzovaniye*, p. 65.
36. G. Mirlin, "Cost-effectiveness of mineral resource use," *Planovoye khozyaistvo*, 1973, no. 6, p. 32; *Review of Sino-Soviet Oil*, May 1976, p. 23.
37. *Pravda*, 27 January 1978, p. 2.
38. *Turkmenskaya iskra*, 6 December 1977, p. 2; *Literaturnaya gazeta*, 18 January 1978, p. 10.
39. Khachaturov, "Natural resources," p. 27.
40. Ibid.; *Trud*, 12 August 1967, p. 2; *Sotsialisticheskaya*

*industriya*, 24 March 1978, p. 1; *CDSP*, 5 November 1977, p. 1.

41. "Conserve and multiply natural resources," *Planovoye khozyaistvo*, no. 6, June 1973, p. 5.

42. Central Intelligence Agency, *USSR: Development of the Gas Industry*, p. 47.

43. Central Intelligence Agency, *Prospects for Soviet Oil Production*, p. 1.

44. Central Intelligence Agency, *Soviet Economic Problems and Prospects*, ER77-10436U, Washington, July 1977, p. 22.

45. *Izvestiya*, 10 September 1978, p. 2; *Petroleum Economist*, September 1978.

46. Nekrasov and Pervukhin, *Energetika*, p. 114; Theodore Shabad, "News Notes," *Soviet Geography: Review and Translation* 22, no. 7 (September 1981): 447.

47. Nekrasov and Pervukhin, *Energetika*, p. 153; Shabad, "News Notes," *Soviet Geography: Review and Translation* 22, no. 7 (September 1981): 448.

48. Central Intelligence Agency, *The Soviet Economy in 1976–77, An Outlook for 1978*, ER78-10512, Washington, August 1978, p. 6.

49. PetroStudies Report GOP-782, *Soviet Preparations for Major Boost of Oil Exports* (Malmo, Sweden, 1978), pp. 3, 13–17.

50. *Pravda*, 28 February 1978, p. 2.

51. Yu. Yakovets, "Economic levers and enhancing the cost-effectiveness of the mineral raw material complex," *Planovoye khozyaistvo*, January 1978, pp. 69–70; *Narkhoz 1964*, p. 749; *Narkhoz 1965*, p. 759.

52. *Narkhoz 1977*, p. 638; *Narkhoz 1978*, p. 544.

53. Ibid., 1980, p. 506.

54. *Pravda*, 9 July 1975, p. 1.

55. Decree of the Council of Ministers USSR and the Central Committee of the Communist Party of the Soviet Union, 29 December 1972.

56. Goldman, *Spoils of Progress*, pp. 294–99.

57. *Ekonomicheskaya gazeta*, 1978, no. 17, p. 22.

58. *Sotsialisticheskaya industriya*, 24 August 1978, p. 1; 22 September 1978, p. 1.

59. *New York Times*, 15 April 1974, p. 1; *The New York Review of Books*, 13 January 1974, pp. 3–4.

60. *Pravda*, 18 December 1975, p. 2.

61. *Soviet News*, 13 January 1976, p. 15.

62. *Soviet News*, 15 July 1975, p. 242; Yakovets, "Economic levers," p. 77.

63. Yu. Yakovets, "Mineral price movements," *Voprosy ekonomiki*, June 1975, p. 3.

64. *Pravda*, 12 October 1974, p. 2 (emphasis added).

65. *Pravda*, 3 November 1974, p. 2 (emphasis added).

66. *Sotsialisticheskaya industriya*, 24 March 1978, p. 1.

67. Dienes, "Soviet Union," pp. 57–58.

68. Fine, "Mineral Resource," p. 37.

69. *The Wall Street Journal*, 18 June 1973, p. 20.

70. Fine, "Mineral Resource," p. 38 (emphasis added).

71. Theodore Shabad, "The Soviet Union and Afghanistan: Some Economic Aspects," (Paper delivered at the 13th National Convention of the American Association for the Advancement of Slavic Studies, Pacific Grove, Ca., 20–23 September 1981), p. 4.

# 28

# SOVIET PRIMARY PRODUCT EXPORTS
# TO CMEA AND THE WEST

EDWARD A. HEWETT
Brookings Institution

## I. Introduction

This paper analyzes Soviet decisions concerning primary product exports, focusing in particular on the division of exports between the Soviet-bloc countries (CMEA[1]) and the developed West. Primary products shall be defined here to include not only unprocessed raw materials (for example, crude oil) but also raw materials after initial processing (for example, oil products and steel products). In terms of the commodity classification used in Soviet trade statistics, primary products so defined include most of groups 2 (Fuels, Minerals and Metals) and 5 (Agricultural Raw Materials, except for Food Products). These two commodity groups (in particular, 2) have been, and are likely to continue to be, the major sources of Soviet export proceeds.

Table 1 shows the share of these two product groups in total Soviet exports and in their exports to countries for two years, one before and one after the price explosion of 1973–74. Even before the price explosion, 45 percent of all Soviet exports, and 63 percent of the exports to bloc countries, were in these two groups. Later 56 percent of Soviet exports to all countries fell in these two groups. For bloc countries, the 1976 share of the two groups was 52 percent, reflecting in part (as shall be shown below) that prices in Soviet trade with the bloc did not rise as rapidly as those in Soviet trade with the West, but also reflecting the relatively slower growth rate of real primary product shipments to the bloc in comparison with shipments to the West.

Since 1970, the Soviets have shown increasing reluctance to supply primary products to Eastern Europe, mainly because Soviet planners would much prefer to supply machinery and equipment, far more profitable (at bloc prices) than primary products. The price changes in world markets in 1973–74 were only faintly echoed in the bloc, which increased Soviet pressure for Eastern Europe to look elsewhere for primary products.

*The author is grateful to Lawrence Brainard, Marshall Goldman and Arthur Wright for their helpful comments on a previous draft.*

The data generally available on Soviet primary product exports commingle the effects of price and quantity increases, and consequently they are virtually useless in their present state for conveying information on how much real Soviet primary product shipments to Eastern Europe have grown relative to shipments to the West. Section II addresses that issue, separating out price and quantity changes in Soviet exports of major primary products to the bloc and the West.

Having reconstructed the record, the next logical step is to try to explain it. If we can find some stable relationship between variables that matter to Soviet planners (e.g., the balance of payments in hard currency, terms of trade, domestic shortages) and primary product shipments to the bloc and the West, then we have formed the foundation for predicting future Soviet decisions on primary product exports. Sections III and IV address this issue. Section III discusses the institutions which determine Soviet primary product exports, focusing on Soviet planning institutions and the major institutions determining intrabloc trade flows. Section IV estimates a model of primary product exports, using the information on planning institutions in Section III and the data developed in Section II. Section V contains a summary, conclusions, and a discussion of possible future directions for research on this problem.

## II. Reconstructing the Record on Soviet Primary Product Exports

The problem is to assemble a data set useful in studying Soviet planners' decisions on the level of primary product exports to bloc countries and to the developed West. In constructing plans on primary product exports, Soviet planners determine the physical quantities available for export, and the division of those quantities among bloc countries, the West, and other countries. Therefore to study those decisions one must have quantities or quantity indices for Soviet primary product exports to these country groups.

Summary statistics available in Soviet foreign trade yearbooks neither report such indices, nor lend themselves to their construction.[2] Consequently, it was necessary to build up the primary product export data set directly from data on exports to the individual countries

TABLE 1
The Share of Primary Products in All Soviet
Exports and in Soviet Exports to Bloc
Countries 1970 and 1976

| | Percent of total value of exports to: | | | |
| | All Countries | | Bloc Countries | |
| --- | --- | --- | --- | --- |
| | 1970 | 1976 | 1970 | 1976 |
| Fuels, Minerals and Metals (Group 2) of which: | 35.4 | 47.5 | 50.0 | 45.7 |
| Fuels and Electricity | 15.6 | 34.3 | n.d. | 27.3 |
| Ores and Metals | 19.8* | 13.2 | n.d. | 18.4 |
| Agricultural Raw Materials (except Food Products) (Group 5) of which: | 10.3 | 8.5 | 13.0 | 6.7 |
| Forestry and Cellulose-Paper Products | 6.5 | 5.3 | n.d. | 4.0 |
| Total (Groups 2 and 5) | 45.7 | 56.0 | 63.0 | 52.4 |

*There are relatively minor differences in the commodities included in Group 2 in 1970 and in 1976 because of modifications in the classification in 1971; for example, cable was in Group 2 in the old version, but is now in Group 1 (machinery and equipment), but these changes should have no noticeable effect on the overall figures.
SOURCES: 1970 data for all countries are from USSR, Ministry of Foreign Trade, *Vneshnyaya torgovlya SSSR za 1970 god* [Foreign trade of the USSR for 1970], p. 18. 1970 data for the CMEA countries are from E. Hewett, *Foreign Trade Prices in the Council for Mutual Economic Assistance* (Cambridge: Cambridge University Press, 1974), p. 79. All 1976 data are from *Vneshnyaya torgovlya,* 1976, p. 18.

within the bloc and the West. To simplify considerably the data collection task at no great cost to the information obtained, data were assembled for only the nine key product groups that dominate Soviet primary product exports to the West and to the bloc:

| 1976 Total Value of Soviet exports | Product Group | Commodity Designation |
| --- | --- | --- |
| 27.3% | Oil and oil products | 21–22 |
| 2.9 | Coal | 200 |
| 2.6 | Natural gas | 23001 |
| 1.7 | Iron ore | 24001 |
| 4.3 | Rolled steel | 264 |
| 2.6 | Nonferrous metals | 270 |
| 1.7 | Roundwood | 500 |
| 2.2 | Sawnwood | 501 |
| 2.7 | Cotton fibers | 51001 |
| 39.0 | | |

These nine primary products account for 39 percent of the total value of Soviet exports, and about 80 percent of all exports in Groups 2 and 5.

The level of aggregation in several of these product groups is higher than one would like, in particular for oil and nonferrous metals, but more disaggregated data were not available for all the years covered in the sample. Nevertheless it seems reasonable to assume for these

relatively homogeneous products that this level of aggregation will still allow meaningful statements on prices and quantities.

Annual data for these nine primary products for 1959–76 were obtained from the Soviet foreign trade statistical yearbooks (*Vneshnyaya torgovlya SSSR*) for various years. For each product group, Soviet exports to individual countries were aggregated into one of three series: exports to the bloc (excluding Vietnam);[3] to the West (eight of the nine European Economic Community countries—Belgium, Britain, Denmark, West Germany, Ireland, Italy, Netherlands, and France—plus Finland, West Berlin, Austria, Australia, Canada, New Zealand, Norway, United States, Switzerland, Sweden, and Japan); and to other countries. The resulting data give the detailed geographical distribution of the quantities and values of exports to these three destinations, and to a subdivision of the West category into EEC and other West; these data are available on request from the author.

The geographical division of the data roughly corresponds to a division by currency area. Exports to the West are almost all for hard currency; those to the bloc are almost all for nonconvertible currency (the Transferable Ruble), although recently there have been primary product sales within the bloc for hard currency. Sales to other countries, mainly to less developed countries, are sometimes in hard currency, sometimes in clearing currencies, but are generally insignificant for primary products.

Table 2 presents summary data for selected years on each of the nine product groups aggregated into three destinations, West, bloc, and other. For all products except gas, an average was computed. Gas was excluded from the average because, as a new entrant into the primary product export group, gas exports are growing at an astronomical pace.

Columns (1) to (3) present indices of change in quantities exported for each product group, 1970 = 100. Within each product group the quantities are assumed to be homogeneous. For example, the tonnages of rolled steel products exported to each Western country were added up for each year, then divided by 1970 tonnage, to obtain the quantity index;[4] for that commodity group the index shows that 1976 Soviet exports to the bloc were only 1 percent above the 1970 level, while exports to the West had fallen 70 percent. The average quantity indices in Columns (1) to (3) are a weighted sum of the eight quantity indices. The weights are the values of 1970 exports of each product group to the West, to the bloc and to other countries. For example, for these eight primary products, the average quantity index shows that the physical volume of Soviet primary product exports to the West in 1976 was 46 percent above 1970.[5]

Columns (4) to (6) report unit value indices obtained by dividing total values of exports in each product group to each region by total quantities exported in each product group to that region. For example, Column (4) shows that unit values of oil exports to the West rose more than sixfold over the 1970–76 period. The weighted averages in Columns (4) to (6) are computed in the same way as the average quantity indices, using 1970 values. For example, the weighted average unit value for exports of the eight products to the West rose by more than three and a half times over the 1970–76 period.

Columns (7) and (8) show, respectively, the quantity of exports to the West divided by the quantity of all exports, and the value of exports to the West divided by the value of all exports. Minor differences between these two ratios are unimportant, given possible differences in product composition between exports to different currency areas, but major differences (say, more than 3 or 4 percent) indicate differences in relative prices. The most obvious case is oil. In 1976, 37 percent of the tonnage of oil exports went to the West, yet the West accounted for 49 percent of the value.[6] Columns (9) and (10) provide the same data for exports to the bloc. The residual for other countries is not shown. The averages for Columns (7) to (10) are unweighted.

Column (11) reports estimates of the ratio between the quantity of net exports in each group and total production in that group. The average here is, again, unweighted.

Columns (12) and (13) show for each product group the ratio of the value of exports of that product group to the bloc and the West, respectively. For example, in 1976, nonferrous metals accounted for 2.9 percent of the value of all Soviet exports to the West. The "average" here is a sum of the percentages for the eight product groups. For example, by 1976 these eight primary products accounted for 38.8 percent of the value of all Soviet exports to the bloc, and 66.5 percent of the value of all exports to the West.

Several major points emerge from Table 2:

1. In the 1960s, the eight primary products in this sample accounted equally for about 40 percent of the value of Soviet exports to the bloc and the West. By 1976, mainly because of the price explosion, the eight primary product groups accounted for over 65 percent (70 percent, including gas) of the value of Soviet exports to the West, and still only 40 percent of the value to the bloc.

2. On average, net exports are about one-fifth of the production of these eight primary products, although there is a good deal of variation around that average.

3. In value terms, the share of these eight primary products going to either the bloc or the West was about 90 percent in the 1960s, moving down to 80 percent in the 1970s, and within that share there was a definite shift toward the West. In terms of physical quantities, the share has been a relatively constant 90 percent, but with a somewhat less pronounced shift toward the West (reflecting higher relative prices in trade with the West).

4. Net exports of gas became positive only in 1974, but they are growing at a phenomenal pace. By 1976 they accounted for 4 percent of the value of exports to the West, and 3.9 percent of exports to the bloc.

Figure 1 shows unit value indices (uvi) and quantity indices for Soviet exports to the bloc and the West for all years 1959–76; these indices are the weighted averages reported for selected years in Columns (1) to (6) of Table 2. Through 1970 the quantity indices show rather similar movements, although the quantities of exports to the

West rose more rapidly than those destined for bloc countries. There is a striking decrease in exports to the West in 1974–75, coinciding with the increase in export prices. In 1976, the quantity of Soviet exports to the West moved back on trend.

The drop in 1974–75 is intriguing. It suggests that the Soviets may have withheld primary products from Western markets, because (even with restricted deliveries) foreign currency targets were overfulfilled. Note that the drop is not confined to oil, but also shows up in nonferrous metals, roundwood and sawnwood. This suggests a rapid response in several primary products to the improved terms of trade. An analysis of this response will be discussed later.

The quantity indices show that exports to the bloc have grown much more slowly than those to the West. They grew almost not at all in 1970–72, increased at a relatively rapid pace in 1973–75, then totally stagnated in 1976 as (presumably) Soviet planners diverted primary products to the West. Ignoring short-term trends, the general movement of the index suggests that the Soviets were very serious when they told the bloc, as they did repeatedly in the 1970s, that increased shipments of Soviet primary products will be hard to get and will involve substantial East European investments in the USSR.

The unit value indices in Figure 1 show that the Soviets benefited greatly from the world price movements *in trade with the West*. Energy products led the price increases, but prices rose for all primary products. Bloc prices responded with a lag, and quite moderately. In fact, so far intrabloc trade has been insulated from the dramatic changes in the relative world market prices of primary products of recent years, this despite the announced intentions of planners to use a five-year "sliding average price basis" to smoothly introduce those price changes into intrabloc trade. This is all to Eastern Europe's advantage, at a substantial cost to the USSR in terms of foregone export proceeds. The pricing system in intrabloc trade is discussed in more detail in Section III.[7]

The data in Table 2 indicate some significant differences among product groups—for example, in price and physical output trends, and in the share of exports in production. The two key variables are the share of net exports in total output and the division of those net exports between the bloc and the West. Prices are essentially outside planners' control; thus, quantity movements reflect decisions on planned net exports and their division, i.e., decisions on the two key variables. Figure 2 plots data for each of the nine product groups for these two variables. The horizontal axis measures the share of net exports in total output of each product and, the vertical axis measures the quantity of total exports of each product to the West divided by the quantity of exports of that product to all destinations. For each product group, two points are plotted depicting the earliest and latest date for which data are available in this sample. Beside each point the number in parentheses shows the value of exports of that product to the West in the given year, divided by total exports to the West. For any individual product, a movement to the northeast between two years means that both the share of net exports in production

TABLE 2
Soviet Exports of Selected Primary Products: Summary Statistics*

| | Changes in Quantities Exported To: | | | Unit Values | | | Exports to West[b] of this product as percent of Total Exports | | Exports to Bloc[a] of this product as percent of Total Exports | |
|---|---|---|---|---|---|---|---|---|---|---|
| | West[b] | Bloc[a] (1970 = 100) | Other | West[b] | Bloc[a] (1970 = 100) | Other | Quantity | Value | Quantity | Value |
| | (1) | (2) | (3) | (4) | (5) | (6) | (7) | (8) | (9) | (10) |
| Coal | | | | | | | | | | |
| 1959 | 36 | 53 | 41 | 133 | 117 | 92 | 30 | 29 | 62 | 65 |
| 1965 | 74 | 107 | 70 | 110 | 105 | 87 | 32 | 28 | 63 | 67 |
| 1970 | 100 | 100 | 100 | 100 | 100 | 100 | 37 | 33 | 53 | 57 |
| 1973 | 91 | 109 | 87 | 119 | 109 | 117 | 34 | 31 | 58 | 60 |
| 1974 | 101 | 113 | 99 | 205 | 110 | 197 | 35 | 43 | 56 | 45 |
| 1975 | 97 | 116 | 92 | 325 | 232 | 320 | 34 | 36 | 58 | 54 |
| 1976 | 101 | 115 | 113 | 308 | 235 | 291 | 34 | 35 | 56 | 53 |
| Oil | | | | | | | | | | |
| 1959 | 24 | 16 | 86 | 127 | 155 | 128 | 28 | 27 | 30 | 34 |
| 1965 | 65 | 59 | 118 | 88 | 119 | 131 | 40 | 28 | 43 | 54 |
| 1970 | 100 | 100 | 100 | 100 | 100 | 100 | 41 | 34 | 49 | 53 |
| 1973 | 115 | 136 | 100 | 226 | 107 | 133 | 39 | 48 | 53 | 42 |
| 1974 | 94 | 143 | 127 | 572 | 121 | 328 | 32 | 55 | 57 | 28 |
| 1975 | 108 | 154 | 166 | 535 | 223 | 315 | 33 | 43 | 55 | 41 |
| 1976 | 137 | 167 | 171 | 613 | 245 | 349 | 37 | 49 | 52 | 37 |
| Iron Ore | | | | | | | | | | |
| 1959 | 6 | 42 | n.d. | 252 | 120 | n.d. | 2 | 2 | 99 | 98 |
| 1965 | 31 | 72 | n.d. | 118 | 110 | n.d. | 6 | 3 | 94 | 97 |
| 1970 | 100 | 100 | n.d. | 100 | 100 | n.d. | 12 | 7 | 88 | 93 |
| 1973 | 114 | 115 | n.d. | 93 | 98 | n.d. | 12 | 6 | 88 | 89 |
| 1974 | 127 | 118 | n.d. | 114 | 107 | n.d. | 13 | 7 | 86 | 92 |
| 1975 | 121 | 120 | n.d. | 184 | 138 | n.d. | 12 | 9 | 87 | 91 |
| 1976 | 110 | 120 | n.d. | 193 | 131 | n.d. | 11 | 9 | 88 | 90 |
| Rolled Steel | | | | | | | | | | |
| 1959 | 54 | 32 | n.d. | 66 | 126 | n.d. | 6 | 3 | 75 | 78 |
| 1965 | 102 | 64 | n.d. | 81 | 117 | n.d. | 6 | 4 | 81 | 83 |
| 1970 | 100 | 100 | n.d. | 100 | 100 | n.d. | 4 | 4 | 82 | 81 |
| 1973 | 54 | 95 | n.d. | 108 | 99 | n.d. | 2 | 2 | 84 | 82 |
| 1974 | 25 | 96 | n.d. | 119 | 102 | n.d. | 1 | 2 | 86 | 80 |
| 1975 | 8 | 98 | n.d. | 132 | 169 | n.d. | 0 | 0 | 88 | 90 |
| 1976 | 31 | 101 | n.d. | 122 | 150 | n.d. | 1 | 1 | 86 | 79 |
| Nonferrous Metals | | | | | | | | | | |
| 1959 | 69 | 42 | 12 | 83 | 122 | 41 | 27 | 27 | 67 | 65 |
| 1965 | 153 | 75 | 28 | 62 | 111 | 33 | 32 | 29 | 62 | 64 |
| 1970 | 100 | 100 | 100 | 100 | 100 | 100 | 16 | 17 | 65 | 43 |
| 1973 | 224 | 125 | 149 | 120 | 138 | 82 | 25 | 27 | 56 | 44 |
| 1974 | 217 | 127 | 147 | 165 | 132 | 115 | 24 | 31 | 57 | 36 |
| 1975 | 157 | 139 | 71 | 158 | 170 | 47 | 20 | 26 | 70 | 66 |
| 1976 | 178 | 136 | 108 | 169 | 173 | 31 | 21 | 31 | 65 | 62 |
| Roundwood | | | | | | | | | | |
| 1959 | 17 | 42 | 45 | 66 | 84 | 96 | 56 | 45 | 40 | 50 |
| 1965 | 60 | 71 | 470 | 82 | 88 | 114 | 63 | 57 | 21 | 25 |
| 1970 | 100 | 100 | 100 | 100 | 100 | 100 | 76 | 72 | 22 | 25 |
| 1973 | 123 | 98 | 324 | 142 | 106 | 116 | 76 | 79 | 17 | 16 |
| 1974 | 115 | 102 | 386 | 206 | 133 | 175 | 74 | 78 | 19 | 16 |
| 1975 | 110 | 95 | 249 | 175 | 127 | 206 | 76 | 77 | 19 | 17 |
| 1976 | 118 | 92 | 317 | 163 | 138 | 205 | 76 | 75 | 17 | 17 |
| Sawnwood | | | | | | | | | | |
| 1959 | 78 | 37 | 34 | 77 | 96 | 95 | 63 | 56 | 28 | 33 |
| 1965 | 113 | 80 | 120 | 97 | 98 | 66 | 50 | 50 | 33 | 36 |
| 1970 | 100 | 100 | 100 | 100 | 100 | 100 | 44 | 42 | 42 | 43 |
| 1973 | 117 | 91 | 101 | 136 | 113 | 89 | 50 | 54 | 37 | 35 |
| 1974 | 82 | 113 | 109 | 258 | 117 | 261 | 37 | 47 | 48 | 30 |
| 1975 | 80 | 115 | 100 | 166 | 204 | 201 | 36 | 30 | 49 | 54 |
| 1976 | 120 | 90 | 113 | 184 | 206 | 189 | 50 | 45 | 35 | 39 |

*Cont. pp. 644–45.*

| Net Export[c] as percent of Total Output | Value of Exports of this product as percent of Total Exports to: | |
|---|---|---|
| | Bloc[a] | West[b] |
| (11) | (12) | (13) |
| 1.4 | 3.6 | 3.7 |
| 2.7 | 4.2 | 5.5 |
| 2.8 | 2.5 | 2.4 |
| 2.2 | 2.3 | 2.6 |
| 2.4 | 2.0 | 3.0 |
| n.d.[d] | 3.2 | 4.7 |
| n.d.[d] | 2.9 | 3.6 |
| 16.2 | 6.4 | 11.6 |
| 25.7 | 11.6 | 19.0 |
| 26.8 | 11.1 | 20.7 |
| 24.1 | 12.1 | 30.7 |
| 24.1 | 12.2 | 38.2 |
| 25.0 | 18.0 | 41.7 |
| 27.2 | 19.1 | 47.8 |
| 6.9[e] | 5.0 | .2 |
| 15.7[e] | 5.2 | .5 |
| 18.5[e] | 4.4 | .9 |
| 19.2[e] | 3.7 | .5 |
| 19.3[e] | 3.5 | .4 |
| 18.7[e] | 3.4 | .5 |
| 18.0[e] | 2.9 | .5 |
| 4.3 | 9.1 | 0.8 |
| 6.0 | 11.2 | 1.9 |
| 6.8 | 10.0 | 1.4 |
| 4.0 | 7.1 | 0.5 |
| 1.5 | 6.2 | 0.3 |
| 2.5 | 7.8 | 0.1 |
| 2.3 | 6.4 | 0.1 |
| 4.4[f] | 3.7 | 3.5 |
| 17.0 | 3.9 | 5.5 |
| 15.3 | 3.1 | 3.6 |
| 19.4 | 4.1 | 5.6 |
| 17.9 | 3.3 | 4.5 |
| 15.1 | 3.5 | 3.0 |
| n.d. | 3.3 | 2.9 |
| 0.8 | 0.8 | 1.7 |
| 2.9 | 0.9 | 6.9 |
| 3.9 | 1.0 | 8.6 |
| 4.8 | 0.8 | 8.6 |
| 4.6 | 0.9 | 7.0 |
| 4.2 | 0.6 | 5.8 |
| 4.6 | 0.5 | 4.5 |
| 4.0 | 1.6 | 6.3 |
| 7.1 | 2.3 | 10.2 |
| 6.8 | 2.0 | 5.8 |
| 7.1 | 1.6 | 5.3 |
| 6.8 | 1.7 | 4.2 |
| 6.6 | 2.2 | 3.7 |
| 7.4 | 1.6 | 3.5 |

and the share of total exports going to the West increased, and vice versa for a movement to the southwest. Movements to the northwest or southeast mean that one variable increased while the other decreased.

On the basis of the net export/output ratios, oil, nonferrous metals, and iron ore stand out as major export industries. Oil leads the group, but exports in the other two product groups have also risen much faster than output over the last 15 years, bringing them into the ranks of respectable export industries. What is unique about oil among these three is the high and steady share of exports to the West, close to one-half over the entire period. Almost all of the iron ore and much of the nonferrous metals go to the bloc, although the share of total exports going to the West was rising for iron ore but falling for nonferrous metals.

Cotton and gas appear to be on their way to joining these three as major export-oriented product groups; as yet, though, they still account for relatively small percentages of Soviet exports to the West (see numbers in parentheses). Large growth of gas exports is planned, and most likely during the 1980s the gas point will move east toward that for oil (perhaps moving west to meet it).

The remaining primary product groups share the common characteristic of low export/output ratios. Rolled steel exports account for a small and dwindling share of total output, reflecting problems in that industry in the USSR.[8] Almost all those exports go to the bloc, but shipments there did not increase in the 1970s. Export ratios, while still low, are increasing for roundwood and sawnwood. Roundwood is becoming the major hard-currency earner (mainly to Japan) in wood exports, while sawnwood exports are shifting toward the bloc. Coal shows little change.

Figure 2 suggests that Soviet planners have decided to exploit their abundant resource endowments and create export industries for key primary products. This is not a surprising conclusion, but it is nevertheless at variance with the conventional view that Soviet foreign trade planners use surpluses wherever they arise to finance needed imports, rather than consciously developing export industries. The primary products sector is an exception (and it is just that) in which Soviet planners appear determined to develop strong export capabilities. The interesting question is how Soviet planners make decisions on which industries to push as exporters and on dividing the resulting exportable surpluses between the bloc and the West. The next two sections address this question.

## III. The Institutional Setting

This section discusses Soviet decision-making processes on primary product exports. Soviet planning institutions are the most important actors here, but they are not alone, since bloc institutions and East European planners exert some influence on the share of Soviet primary products going to the bloc and on the exportable surplus itself. The object of this section is to try to understand how

TABLE 2 (*cont.*)

| | Changes in Quantities Exported To: | | | Unit Values | | | Exports to West[b] of this product as percent of Total Exports | | Exports to Bloc[a] of this product as percent of Total Exports | |
|---|---|---|---|---|---|---|---|---|---|---|
| | West[b] | Bloc[a] (1970=100) | Other | West[b] | Bloc[a] (1970=100) | Other | Quantity | Value | Quantity | Value |
| | (1) | (2) | (3) | (4) | (5) | (6) | (7) | (8) | (9) | (10) |
| Cotton | | | | | | | | | | |
| 1959 | 119 | 64 | 20 | 89 | 103 | 99 | 20 | 16 | 78 | 82 |
| 1965 | 171 | 83 | 30 | 94 | 104 | 123 | 22 | 18 | 76 | 80 |
| 1970 | 100 | 100 | 100 | 100 | 100 | 100 | 11 | 10 | 81 | 83 |
| 1973 | 481 | 87 | 215 | 106 | 101 | 104 | 38 | 36 | 50 | 52 |
| 1974 | 426 | 101 | 175 | 196 | 105 | 178 | 33 | 43 | 57 | 46 |
| 1975 | 472 | 99 | 275 | 134 | 132 | 127 | 34 | 32 | 52 | 55 |
| 1976 | 581 | 93 | 380 | 147 | 134 | 147 | 38 | 37 | 44 | 46 |
| Weighted Average, 8 Commodities | | | | | | | | | | |
| 1959 | 37 | 36 | 25 | 106 | 127 | 104 | 30 | 26 | 57 | 60 |
| 1965 | 84 | 71 | 66 | 87 | 112 | 85 | 30 | 27 | 60 | 65 |
| 1970 | 100 | 100 | 100 | 100 | 100 | 100 | 30 | 29 | 61 | 60 |
| 1973 | 135 | 110 | 118 | 176 | 107 | 118 | 35 | 35 | 56 | 50 |
| 1974 | 118 | 116 | 118 | 366 | 113 | 249 | 31 | 38 | 58 | 38 |
| 1975 | 119 | 120 | 94 | 339 | 180 | 215 | 31 | 34 | 59 | 52 |
| 1976 | 147 | 121 | 108 | 368 | 181 | 252 | 34 | 35 | 54 | 44 |
| Gas | | | | | | | | | | |
| 1959 | 0 | 0 | n.d. | n.d. | n.d. | n.d. | 0 | 0 | 0 | 0 |
| 1965 | 0 | 17 | n.d. | n.d. | 46 | n.d. | 0 | 0 | 98 | 100 |
| 1970 | 100 | 100 | n.d. | 100 | 100 | n.d. | 29 | 27 | 71 | 74 |
| 1973 | 207 | 173 | n.d. | 88 | 100 | n.d. | 29 | 24 | 60 | 64 |
| 1974 | 574 | 365 | n.d. | 125 | 103 | n.d. | 39 | 40 | 61 | 60 |
| 1975 | 841 | 482 | n.d. | 181 | 165 | n.d. | 42 | 41 | 59 | 59 |
| 1976 | 1,291 | 573 | n.d. | 193 | 224 | n.d. | 48 | 41 | 52 | 52 |

*Sources are discussed in the detailed tables from which these summary data are taken.

[a]CMEA bloc here excludes Vietnam, which only joined in 1978.

[b]"West" means the EEC, except Luxembourg, plus Austria, Australia, Canada, Finland, Japan, New Zealand, Norway, U.S., Switzerland, Sweden and West Berlin.

[c]Both numerator and denominator are quantities. Production data for all commodities except nonferrous metals are taken from various issues of USSR Central Statistical Administration, *Narodnoye khozyaistvo SSSR: statisticheskiy yezhegodnik* [The economy of the USSR: statistical yearbook] Nonferrous metals production data, which are not reported in Soviet data, are the sum of CIA estimates for outputs of major nonferrous metals reported in CIA, *Handbook of Economic Statistics, 1976* ER 76–10481 (September 1976).

[d]Imports were reported only by value for 1975–76; consequently the quantity of net exports could not be computed.

[e]These are gross export/production ratios, since no data are available on imports of iron ore, either in quantities or value. If there are imports they are probably negligible.

[f]1960 data.

[g]Excludes coal.

[h]Excludes coal and nonferrous metals.

decisions come about on the exportable surplus of primary products and the division of those exports between the bloc and the West. What are the important variables for Soviet planners, and how do they take them into account in the planning process? How, for example, do Soviet planners reconcile the needs of domestic producers, the needs of the bloc countries and the potential for hard-currency proceeds in making their decision on the size and division of the exportable surplus of key products?

Soviet planners make both short- and long-term decisions about primary products. The long-term decisions concern the general trends for exportable surpluses and their division. Over the next decade or so, how fast should exports of gas or oil grow? Should there be a secular increase in the share of gas or oil exports to the West?

Short-term decisions, in contrast, concern the exported surplus of primary products and its division for next year. Here many factors properly regarded as transitory may exert considerable influence, even inducing planners to move away temporarily from the long-term targets. For example, unexpected and severe balance-of-payment problems in Eastern Europe may cause planners temporarily to ship more oil than planned to allow East European planners to save on hard-currency costs of oil imports. Unexpected delays in opening a new steel rolling mill may cause a temporary decrease in the exportable surplus. And an unexpected improvement in primary product prices to the West (for example, in 1973–74) may

| Net Export[c] as percent of Total Output | Value of Exports of this product as percent of Total Exports to: | |
|---|---|---|
| | Bloc[a] | West[b] |
| (11) | (12) | (13) |
| 3.3 | 6.7 | 3.0 |
| 4.9 | 5.7 | 4.0 |
| 3.8 | 4.4 | 1.5 |
| 7.8 | 2.9 | 4.5 |
| 7.1 | 2.0 | 4.4 |
| 8.4 | 2.7 | 3.4 |
| 9.2 | 2.3 | 3.6 |
| 7.6 | 36.9 | 30.8 |
| 12.8 | 45.0 | 53.5 |
| 14.5 | 38.5 | 44.9 |
| 15.7 | 34.6 | 58.3 |
| 16.4 | 32.8 | 62.0 |
| 18.3[g] | 41.4 | 65.9 |
| 20.9[h] | 38.8 | 66.5 |
| n.d. | 0.0 | 0.0 |
| n.d. | 0.0 | 0.0 |
| n.d. | 0.5 | 1.0 |
| 1.9 | 0.6 | 1.0 |
| 0.8 | 1.0 | 1.0 |
| 2.4 | 2.5 | 3.0 |
| 4.4 | 3.3 | 4.0 |

allow Soviet planners to reduce quantities shipped to the West below planned values, using the savings to break bottlenecks elsewhere or to build up stocks, at the same time still meeting targets for hard currencies.

The Soviets have revealed very little about the operation of their foreign trade planning process. This section presents the information that is available, filling in the gaps with conjectures on how the process probably operates. Section IV attempts to go further by using econometric techniques to explore behavioral regularities in the data on exports of primary products.

### Soviet Institutions Involved in Primary Product Exports

Primary products destined for export move from the field or factory to the borders in response to decisions made and executed by many Soviet organizations familiar to students of the Soviet economy. But it is useful to consider how those organizations are related to each other just for primary product exports, and in particular precisely how central planners control the process.

Figure 3 presents a picture of the key institutions involved in primary product export decisions. Abstracting from the pervasive influence of the Politburo in all eco-

nomic decisions in the USSR, the pinnacle of the hierarchy pictured in Figure 3 is occupied by the Council of Ministers. Seven ministries within the Council of Ministers control the production of the nine primary products. Almost as important is Gosplan, within which there are divisions that closely parallel those in the ministries.[9] Also important is the division in Gosplan charged with balancing sources and uses for important product groups ("Material Balances . . .").

The Ministry of Foreign Trade, although part of the Council of Ministers, is in fact subordinate to Gosplan. Its main function in the planning process is to provide information to Gosplan concerning export and import possibilities. It supervises something over 40 foreign trade organizations (FTOs), each of which has a monopoly in the export and import of narrowly specified product groups.[10] As Figure 3 shows, seven FTOs are empowered to export the nine primary products. Each FTO is under the direct supervision of one or more directorates. All the primary product FTOs, with the exception of Exportlen (cotten), are supervised by the Directorate for the Export of Primary Products; Exportlen is supervised by the Directorate for the Export of End Products and Consumer Goods. There are also, within the Foreign Trade Ministry, directorates concerned with geographic areas and functional matters (e.g., currency); however, they do not directly supervise the FTOs, and the only importance they might have here is their participation in decisions concerning the geographic composition of exports.

The actual flow of primary products is from Enterprises through the State Committee on Material-Technical Supply (Gossnab) to the FTOs, and then on to foreign purchasers. Enterprises receive domestic wholesale prices for their shipments; therefore, exports and domestic sales are financially identical for them. FTOs pay the domestic wholesale price, but receive the foreign currency price. The domestic price multiplied by the official exchange rate is virtually certain to differ from the world price, since the official rate is not determined by markets, and domestic prices in the USSR do not include import costs computed with a market equilibrium exchange rate. For primary products in recent years, the foreign currency price has surely risen far above the domestic wholesale price, since the latter has not changed in the 1970s. Thus, the FTOs stand to make a profit out of price differences, although it is a profit they never actually see as it is confiscated.

Because industrial wholesale prices for fuels in the USSR remained constant throughout the 1970s, domestic producers have not seen their prices and profits rise along with the price increases on world markets. The state budget has captured all of the resulting gains. For producers to know that oil had suddenly become a highly profitable export for the USSR, they would have to be told by planners. Furthermore, the enterprises which explore and drill for oil, and those which refine it would need special prodding by planners to search for ways to increase the exportable surplus.

As the price relations between enterprises and FTOs

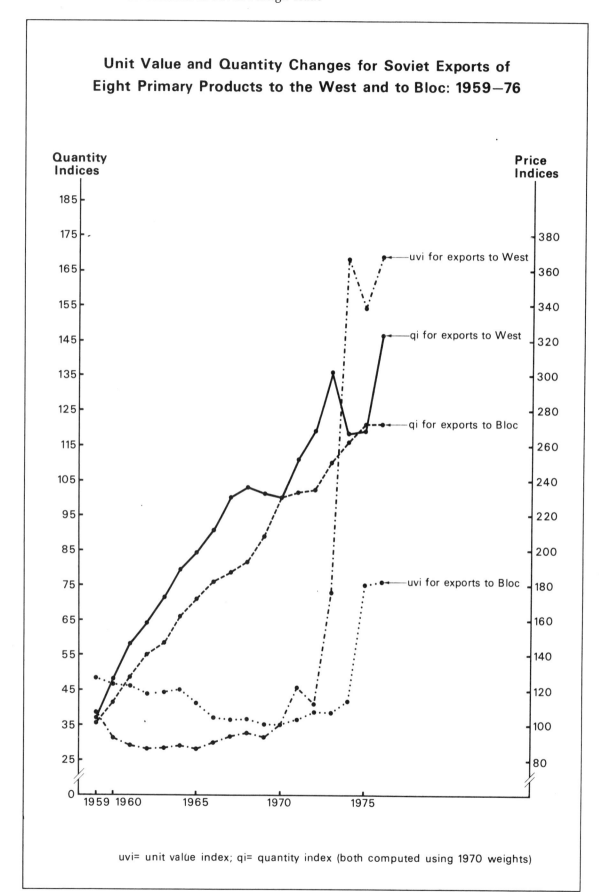

**Unit Value and Quantity Changes for Soviet Exports of Eight Primary Products to the West and to Bloc: 1959–76**

uvi= unit value index; qi= quantity index (both computed using 1970 weights)

Figure 1

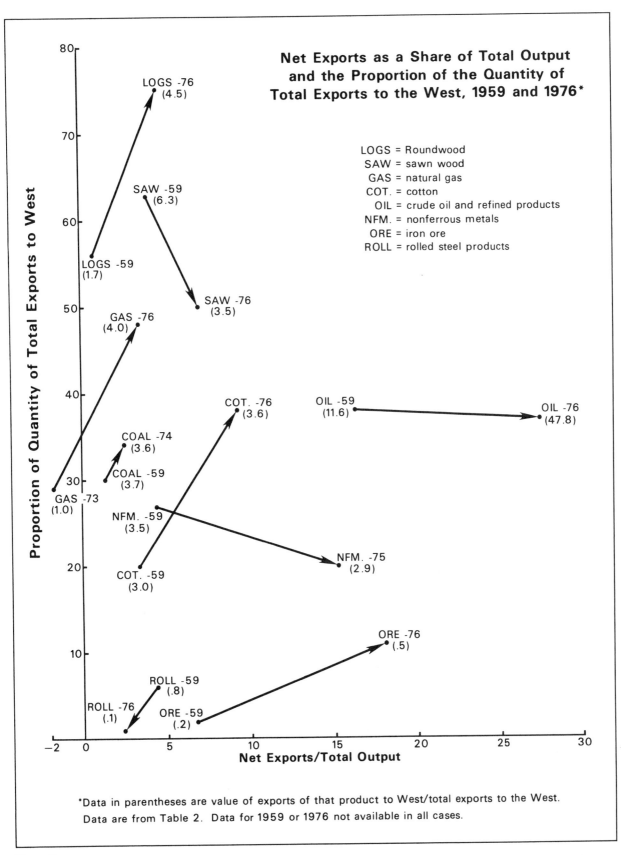

Figure 2

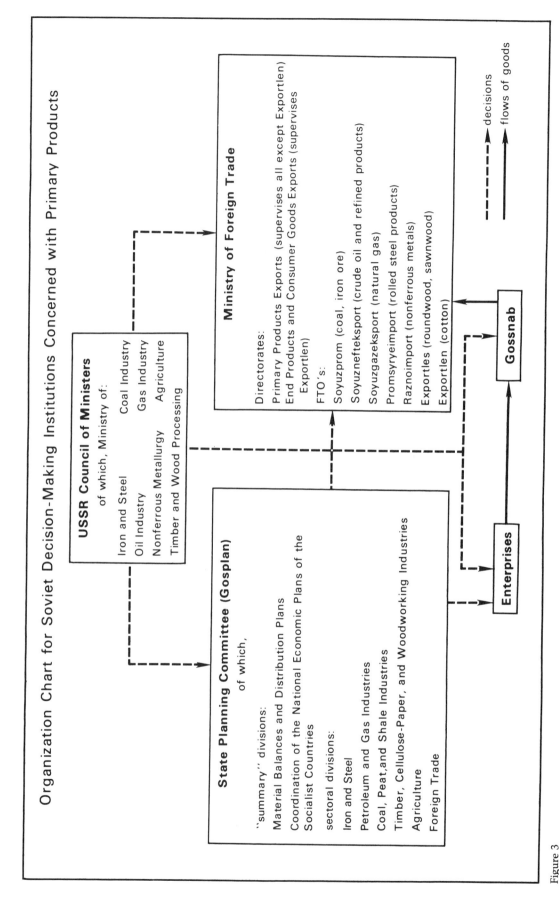

Organization Chart for Soviet Decision-Making Institutions Concerned with Primary Products

**USSR Council of Ministers**

of which, Ministry of:

Iron and Steel          Coal Industry
Oil Industry            Gas Industry
Nonferrous Metallurgy   Agriculture
Timber and Wood Processing

**Ministry of Foreign Trade**

Directorates:
Primary Products Exports (supervises all except Exportlen)
End Products and Consumer Goods Exports (supervises Exportlen)

FTO's:
Soyuzprom (coal, iron ore)
Soyuznefteksport (crude oil and refined products)
Soyuzgazeksport (natural gas)
Promsyryeimport (rolled steel products)
Raznoimport (nonferrous metals)
Exportles (roundwood, sawnwood)
Exportlen (cotton)

**State Planning Committee (Gosplan)**

of which,

"summary" divisions:
Material Balances and Distribution Plans
Coordination of the National Economic Plans of the Socialist Countries

sectoral divisions:
Iron and Steel
Petroleum and Gas Industries
Coal, Peat, and Shale Industries
Timber, Cellulose-Paper, and Woodworking Industries
Agriculture
Foreign Trade

**Gossnab**

**Enterprises**

- - - → decisions
——→ flows of goods

Figure 3

SOURCES: USSR Council of Ministers: Paul K. Cook, "The Political Setting," in U.S. Joint Economic Committee, *Soviet Economy in a New Perspective* (Washington, 1976), facing p. 16; Ministry of Foreign Trade: V. P. Gruzinov, *Upravleniye torgovli* [The management of foreign trade] (Moscow: 1975), p. 75, and Bureau of International Commerce, U.S. Department of Commerce, "State Trading and Other Organizations: USSR" (Washington, May 1975); State Planning Committee (Gosplan): V. S. Dadayan, *Ocherki o nashei ekonomike* [Essays on our economy] (Moscow: 1974), p. 84 (I am grateful to Murray Feshbach for this citation).

suggest neither plays an important role in determining the level of exports of individual primary products. FTOs and enterprises do no more than they are told, if that. Actual export decisions on these products are made high in the hierarchy, the major participants being Gosplan, the Council of Ministers, and the central administration of the Foreign Trade Ministry, with Gosplan in fact playing the central role. The planning process that occurs among these agents has been adequately described in detail elsewhere. I will confine my attention here to two areas of key interest: (1) the determination of exportable surpluses for individual primary products, and (2) the East-West division of exports.[11]

### Setting Long-Term Policy on Primary Product Exports

I define "long-term" policy to include the five-year plans as well as what are called in the USSR "long-term" plans, which usually cover 15 years. The five-year plans contain the most detailed published versions of Soviet planners' intentions for the development of the Soviet economy. The five-year plan law itself is usually rather brief, but it is always published. For 1971–75, relatively detailed information was available because the Soviets published a fuller, though still "sanitized" version.[12]

What is most striking about this document from the point of view of primary product exports is the absence of an explicit discussion of the exportable surplus or its divisions. One would expect that, at least for the major primary product export industries—oil, iron ore, and nonferrous metals—there would be some discussion of the projected portion of production available for export. Instead, the discussion is limited to output projections, projections for new capital investments, and discussions of particular themes for the five-year period (modernization of certain processes, more surface mining, and so on). A separate section on foreign trade is too general to be of any use whatsoever.

It is possible that unpublished long-term plans exist for the exportable surplus in key primary product industries, but it seems more likely that there is no explicit treatment of commodity-specific exportable surpluses in the five-year planning process. Although a few of the primary product industries are major exporters, most of the industry's sales are to the domestic economy, and the planning apparatus as a whole may focus on that, giving less emphasis to foreign sales.

This interpretation seems to contradict the conclusion in the preceding section that certain industries in the USSR have been developed as exporting industries. But when one thinks about how long-term planning processes must operate for these industries, it is apparent that this interpretation may fit the facts quite well.

Planners' control over increases in the outputs of particular products begins with their influence over the allocation of new capital investments; that influence gives them control over the expansion of productive capacity. Planners' control over the allocation of labor among industries (for example, through special wage rates for work on oil wells in Siberia) is of secondary importance, because capital, not labor, is the major determinant of capacity expansion in the Soviet economy. Given available information on the Soviet planning process and well-known characteristics of bureaucracies' budget-making processes, it seems likely that the planning process, both for annual and for five-year plans, is essentially a bargaining process among ministries for new capital. For many industries, material allocations are also of crucial importance, but that is not so much the case for the primary product industries. There the problem is to obtain capital in order to find the raw materials, to get them out of the ground, to ship them, and, where necessary, to process them. The primary product ministries compete for capital with other ministries, but also among themselves. The ability of a particular primary product ministry to defend or increase its share of the increment to the capital stock is believed to be a function of the following:

1. The political and economic power of the ministry, which is determined by its history, and the importance of the product it produces to the economy; therefore, past allocations to that sector determine how many supporters it has within the core of the planning hierarchy.
2. The history of domestic and foreign demand for the product. For example, have there been unusual excess demands for the product in recent years, or is the demand for the product likely to rise in the near future?
3. Proved or probable reserves of the necessary raw materials. A ministry bargaining for capital in order to work low-grade deposits of a raw material will, *other things equal*, probably encounter difficulties competing with a different ministry asking for more capital to exploit a high-grade raw material.
4. The relative world market price of the ministry's products. For large and easily visible increases (decreases) in the world market price of a product, ministries probably find it easier (harder) to obtain more capital, other things being equal.[13]

For the primary product industries the third factor is probably the most important, followed by the fourth. The Soviet system has a strong tendency to maximize growth rates of output. As long as a ministry can prove that the raw-material reserves are available, and if there is no visible problem in marketing excess output abroad, then that ministry has a strong position in the bargaining process. Increasing difficulty in finding new reserves will weaken the bargaining position of a ministry.

An alternative hypothesis is that Soviet planners allocate capital to try to maintain production, so that, as raw-material deposits diminish in quality and the cost of their exploitation increases, they would allocate more capital, not less, to the relevant ministries. This would be suicide and could hardly serve as a viable long-term policy for any planned economy, but it is certainly a conceivable policy for planners preoccupied with material balances to follow in the short run.

The available data on shares of new capital going to the primary product industries would seem to bear out the former hypothesis. As Table 3 shows, the share of capital to the fuel industries has been relatively stable between 18.0 and 20.0 percent, but within that there has been a

TABLE 3
The Share of Selected Primary Product Industries
in Total Capital Expenditures of State and
Cooperative Enterprise in the USSR, 1965–76
(in constant prices)

| | 1965 | 1970 | 1975 | 1976 |
|---|---|---|---|---|
| Fuel Industries | 20.0 | 18.0 | 18.8 | 19.1 |
| of which: | | | | |
|   Coal | 6.9 | 5.4 | 4.4 | 4.4 |
|   Oil | 10.1 | 8.9 | 9.8 | 10.1 |
|   Natural Gas | 3.0 | 3.7 | 4.6 | 4.6 |
| Iron and steel | 8.8 | 7.2 | 7.2 | 7.2 |
| Forest and woodworking industry | 3.4 | 3.5 | 3.0 | 3.0 |

SOURCE: Central Statistical Administration, *Narodnoye khozyaistvo SSSR
za 60 let* [The economy of the USSR over the last 60 years] (Moscow:
Statistika, 1977), p. 438.

shift away from coal and toward natural gas. The share
going to the oil industry shows no significant change.
This suggests the availabilities of high-grade raw materials are important to planners, and that the discovery of
natural gas deposits (combined with the well-known
high efficiency of that fuel) has provided the Ministry of
the Gas Industry with a strong bargaining position relative to the coal industry.

If these conjectures about the planning process are
correct, they suggest that the allocation of investment
funds among primary product industries will change for
some of the right reasons. Planned primary product output will respond in important part to changes in raw
material availabilities and perceived changes in relative
world market prices. Domestic demand develops independently, a function of choices concerning the technology embodied in primary product using sectors. And
for primary product sectors which win large infusions of
capital due to a combination of relatively favorable circumstances concerning the four factors listed above, the
supply will probably grow faster than domestic demand,
resulting in additional capacity that can be used to produce for export.

Therefore, while planners may not explicitly plan exportable surpluses, their decision process has the effect of
creating large and growing surpluses where raw-material
reserves permit it, and where world market prices suggest it. This is not altogether different from the workings
of market economies, where primary product industries
compete for capital on the basis of the rates of return they
can offer, which in turn are a function of world market
prices, domestic and foreign demand (related to prices),
and the availability of proved and probable reserves.
There are, nevertheless, major differences. First, the
Soviet planning process is incapable of the relatively fine
calculations typical of a price system. Only the dramatic
shifts in world market prices or raw material availabilities
will catch the attention of planners and provide useful
weapons to ministries in their competition for capital.
Second, if my conjecture is correct, the ability of ministries to obtain new investments on noneconomic grounds
is a feature of the Soviet and East European economies

that is for the most part absent from private sectors in the
West (albeit a far too familiar phenomenon in budget
allocations among government departments in the
West).

East European needs have always been an important
determinant of long-term plans for primary product outputs. The shift to hydrocarbons in several of the East
European countries following World War II was a shift
to imports from the USSR. Soviet nonferrous metal and
iron ore shipments provide important inputs for East
European industry. As the quantity indices so clearly
showed, the Soviets have in recent years begun to significantly reduce the growth rates in their shipments of primary products to Eastern Europe, as such shipments
have become less profitable at intrabloc prices. It is now
accepted practice that East European planners can only
request increments in primary product shipments from
the USSR if they are willing to pay dollars, or to provide
part of the capital necessary to expand output, process it
where necessary, and then ship it to the border. A good
example of this is the Orenburg gas pipeline, for which
Eastern Europe provided capital and labor to construct it,
with repayment in gas shipments.[14]

In addition, bloc cooperation in Soviet primary product
development has been formalized through institutions
within CMEA for coordinating member-countries' plans.
There is now an important committee within CMEA,
consisting of the heads of the national planning departments, which is empowered to handle the problems
of plan coordination; in addition, this committee is beginning to construct its own blocwide plans for key primary products. Within each five-year plan for each country, there is now a section listing cooperative projects,
which for the USSR means the primary product projects
for which there are joint investments.[15]

Consequently, East European planners are being
drawn into the bargaining process which goes on among
Soviet ministries. The primary product industries are
capital-hungry, in part because they are moving to more
inaccessible and less-promising locations for raw-
material extraction, and as a consequence it is becoming
increasingly difficult to defend their proportion of
domestic capital. Yet they can argue that Eastern Europe
needs the primary products for their industries, and the
USSR will only be in a position to meet those needs if
there are large increments to the capital stocks of the key
primary product sectors. Soviet planners then turn to
Eastern Europe with an increasingly clear ultimatum:
Eastern Europe must invest in the Soviet primary product
industries if it wants additional primary product shipments.

These propositions concerning the determinants of primary product outputs and exports are difficult to verify in
any precise way. One could envision an equation in
which the dependent variable is a ministry's share of total
new capital, and the independent variables are past investment allocations to that ministry (a proxy for the
power of the ministry), past and future demands for the
product (obtained possibly through input-output techniques), estimated increases in proved and probable reserves (for which data are scarce but estimatable in the

Soviet case), and relative world market prices. Nevertheless, while the hypothesis is conceivably testable, and the equation if estimated could be used for predictive purposes, there have been too few five-year plans in the postwar period to provide the degrees of freedom required to estimate coefficients. For the present, therefore, the hypothesized determinants of capital allocations to the primary product ministries must remain potentially useful but unverified propositions concerning developments in the primary product industries.

## Setting Short-Term Policy for Primary Product Exports

In theory, and to some extent in fact, short-term policy in the USSR is represented by a set of annual targets in the five-year plan. From the planners' point of view, the annual planning process differs from the five-year planning process because the constraints are far more confining in the short run. Allocating additional capital or labor to the primary product industries this year will have little effect on next year's output, which (for the primary product industries) has already been determined by the cumulation of planners' decisions over the previous five years; thus, as far as this year is concerned, next year's output is essentially a given.

Even if production next year is fixed, planners can still decide on the size of next year's exports and their division. Because these decisions are in the short run virtually independent of decisions on output, hence also capital, the primary product ministries have very little interest in the process. The main actors here would seem to be the Foreign Trade Ministry, particularly the Directorate for the Exports of Primary Products, and Gosplan. As the discussion in Section II showed, here the Soviet system is primed to respond rapidly to changes in world conditions. If Gosplan perceives that a major change in exogenous factors (for example, a change in the terms of trade, or in the balance of trade) requires changes in policies on the quantity of exports or the portion going for hard currency, it can implement those changes rather quickly through the Directorate for Exports of Primary Products, which controls all the FTOs except Exportlen. And, Soviet exports make up such a minor share of total trade in world markets for most of these products that they can export whatever quantities they want, over the range likely to be available, without much affecting the price. Primary products are, then, something like gold for Soviet planners; that is, they are commodities which, when necessary, can be diverted to world markets for relatively certain prices to earn hard currency with which to finance hard-currency imports.

To summarize, (1) Soviet planning institutions are set up so that, at least in the short run, primary products can be dealt with uniformly as a product; and (2) in fact primary products are in one sense a single product in that they all can be sold quickly on world markets for a fixed price.

What in fact are the factors that influence Soviet short-run decisions on the exportable surplus and its division? My hypothesis, based partly on casual observation, is

that Soviet planners will deviate substantially from long-term targets for the division of the exportable surplus in response to changes in one or a combination of several variables (in order of their importance):

1. Changes in hard-currency balance of trade. If hard-currency imports surge unexpectedly, primary product shipments are temporarily diverted from the bloc to the West.
2. Problems in Eastern Europe. Adverse shifts in the terms of trade in Eastern Europe, which could translate into decreases in real national income and the standard of living, may cause Soviet planners to step up deliveries of key primary products to hold down the hard-currency costs to Eastern Europe of primary product imports.
3. Changes in the Soviet terms of trade. Dramatic changes in their own terms of trade would cause hard-currency targets to be violated (either over- or underfulfilled), and Soviet planners can be expected to react with offsetting changes in primary product shipments.

These are testable propositions, and unlike the hypothesis on long-term policies, the data are sufficient to test them. The next section reports on tests of a model that incorporates some of these hypotheses.

## IV. Econometric Estimates of the Determinants of Primary Product Shipments to the Bloc and the West

This section specifies and estimates equations designed to explain the variance in the quantities of the eight primary products exported in significant quantities to the West and the bloc. Explaining this variance also explains changes in the division of shipments between the bloc and the West.

Equations for the individual product groups were not estimated separately because it seems most sensible to view these primary products as a group for reasons explained in Section III. Experiments with several of the individual product groups—oil and nonferrous metals—indicated that the results for individual products would not differ significantly from the overall results.[16]

The discussion in the last section points to the hard-currency balance of trade as a key independent variable. To introduce that variable in the equations that follow, it was necessary to resolve several issues concerning the most appropriate measure for our purposes. First, it is becoming increasingly difficult to measure the true hard-currency balance of trade using Soviet data on trade with various groups of countries. The Soviets now buy and sell in hard currency with a wide variety of countries, including (for some primary products) the bloc countries (still, I suspect, a small proportion of the total) and many developing countries. Without specific information on just what proportion of Soviet trade with non-Western countries is settled in hard currency, it is impossible to measure with complete accuracy the true hard-currency trade balance. I have used the trade balance reported in the Soviet trade data for "Developed Capitalist Countries" as an indicator of the overall hard-currency trade balance, and I suspect it is a fairly good indicator.

Another problem with the trade balance, however measured, is that prices have increased dramatically in recent years. Thus, at 1978 world market prices a ruble's worth of deficit means far less in terms of commodities than a ruble's worth of deficit meant 10 or 20 years ago. Because it seems unlikely that Soviet planners have "money illusion" about their deficits, I hypothesize that the important variable is not the nominal deficit, but the deficit relative to exports. This variable effectively takes out the influence of inflation on the size of the deficit, simultaneously normalizing the trade deficit for changes in the scale of Soviet foreign trade. Therefore, instead of using the hard-currency balance of payments per se as an explanatory variable, I shall use the "relative hard-currency balance of trade" (RELHCBOT), which is the balance of trade each year divided by exports that year. As figures 4 and 5 show, the hard-currency balance of trade (HCBOT) and therefore the RELHCBOT fluctuate cyclically about zero. Figure 4 suggests that the 1975–76 deficits in hard-currency trade were unprecedented in the time period covered by this sample. The RELHCBOT variable provides a somewhat different picture, suggesting that the 1975–76 deficits, while large, repeat similar deficits in 1972 and 1964 (both due to grain purchases). Although one cannot place much importance on it for such a small sample, it is interesting to note that the three peaks in these data series are increasingly far apart (first three, then five, then seven years apart, if we do not treat 1971 as a peak).

Even if one could satisfactorily resolve the problems of finding complete data for the hard-currency balance of trade and then deflating them, there remains at least one other problem. Some changes in the balance of trade are planned, reflecting the real-good inflow resulting from the use of a long-term loan; and some changes are unplanned, resulting, for example, from a need to use hard-currency imports to supplement a poor grain harvest. Planners presumably react much more quickly to the unplanned than the planned changes in the balance of trade, since only for the latter are there long-term plans to generate exports to pay for the imports. It would be useful, therefore, to divide the deficit into those parts covered by long-term capital flows and those by short-term capital flows, the latter presumably being the more important for explaining the variance in primary product exports going to the bloc and the West. It may be possible to develop data making that distinction, but it was not attempted for this paper.

## Soviet Primary Product Shipments to the Bloc

In specifying the equation explaining primary product shipments to the bloc, the hypothesis was that in the long run primary product shipments would be demand-related, i.e., closely linked to GNP growth rates; and that, in the short run an increase (decrease) in the Soviet hard-currency deficit would cause a decrease (increase) in exports to the bloc. If, for example, the hard-currency bal-

ance of payments deteriorated in year $t$, one would expect Soviet planners in year $t + 1$ to cut back on primary product shipments to the bloc, diverting those products to Western markets. It seems reasonable to expect a lag in planners' response to changes in the hard-currency balance of trade for several reasons:

1. long-term and short-term commitments exist for shipments of primary products to bloc countries;
2. the planning process is not continuous, but rather occurs at discrete intervals;
3. there is probably a recognition lag for all activity variables important to planners.

It is not clear how long that lag might be, so the equation is specified with a polynomial distributed lag designed to allow the data to set the length of the lag.

After experimenting with the length of the lag on RELHCBOT, the best specification turned out to be a four-period lag, specified as a third-degree polynomial. The resulting equation is:[17]

$$(1) \quad \text{LQCMEA70} = -2.963 + 1.571 \text{ LEEGNP}$$
$$(-9.013) \quad (22.078)$$
$$+ .104 \text{ RELHCBOT } (-1) + .153 \text{ RELHCBOT } (-2)$$
$$(2.169) \quad (2.448)$$
$$+ .278 \text{ RELHCBOT } (-3) + .204 \text{ RELHCBOT } (-4)$$
$$(5.050) \quad (3.523)$$

R-Squared: .989          Durbin-Watson Statistic = 2.419
(Corrected)
Data time period: 1963–76
Variables:

LQCMEA70 = Log of the 1970 weighted quantity index for Soviet exports of primary products to the bloc.

LEEGNP = Log of an index of East European GNP

RELHCBOT $(-t)$ = (hard-currency exports—h.c. imports)/h.c. exports, $t$ years back

The coefficient on LEEGNP is the elasticity of primary product shipments with respect to changes in East European GNP; it is very large relative to its standard error and hence is highly statistically significant. Thus, the true elasticity would appear to be almost certainly greater than unity, meaning that every 10 percent increase in East European GNP brings forth about a 15 percent increase in Soviet primary product exports to the bloc.

The coefficients on the RELHCBOT terms are all positive and two or more times their standard errors, tending to confirm the initial hypothesis that changes in primary product shipments to the bloc are positively correlated with lagged changes in the state of the hard-currency balance. A four-period lag does not seem unreasonable in light of the five-year length of typical Soviet-bloc trade agreements for primary product shipments; in the interim, of course, above-plan shipments can be negotiated, which is where some of this effect surely comes from. What is particularly interesting here is the result that the biggest effect of changes in RELHCBOT comes three years later, which suggests that Soviet export contracts are in fact binding.

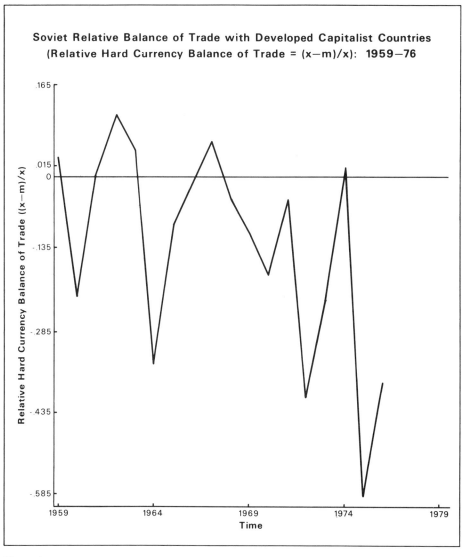

Figure 4

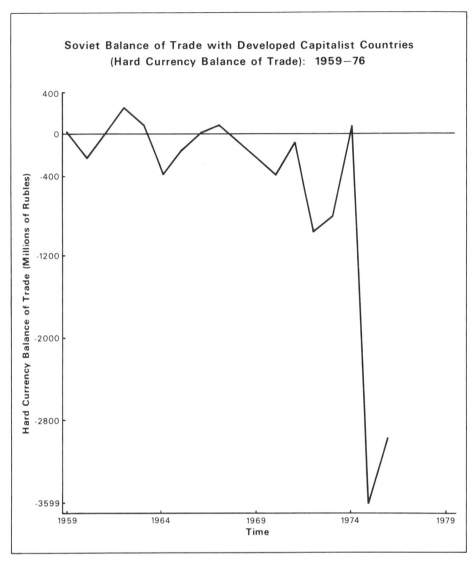

Figure 5

The RELHCBOT coefficients themselves relate changes in the *log* of the quantity index for primary product exports to the bloc to changes in net exports as a proportion of total exports. The sum of the weights, .739, suggests that a change of .01 in RELHCBOT (say from .11 to .12) will eventually (within 4 years) change LQCMEA by .0074, which means (taking the anit-log) a total change of about .74 percent in the quantity index.

The structure of the lagged effect of RELHCBOT, combined with cyclical characteristics of that variable, suggests that when the cycles are short the effect on primary product shipments to the bloc will be minimal. For example, when RELHCBOT is negative for several years, then positive for a couple of years, then negative again, the typical situation will be to have two positive and two negative years affecting current shipments, in which case they would roughly cancel each other out. But if the peaks in RELHCBOT are drawing farther apart, then the equations suggest that shipments to the bloc of primary products will begin to exhibit more marked fluctuations. If, for example, HCBOT did not improve markedly in 1977–78, exports of primary products to the bloc would probably stagnate, of which more in the next section.

## Soviet Primary Product Shipments to the West

I turn now to primary product exports to the West, the dependent variable being the 1970-weighted quantity index, QWEST70. The long-term trend here is depicted with a second-order polynomial in time (i.e., time, and time$^2$), which allows for the possibility that the growth rate of primary product exports is changing within the sample. These variables act as indicators of the strong upward trend in Soviet primary product output and the transmission of that trend to hard-currency exports. Western demand factors are not considered in this equation, under the assumption that the USSR does not significantly affect prices in world primary product markets, so that the elasticity of demand for Soviet primary products as a group is very large.

Again, the lagged values of RELHCBOT are introduced as the key variable to explain short-term fluctuations in QWEST70. The theory here is that a given change in RELHCBOT will cause planners to change exports in the opposite direction; for example, an increase in RELHCBOT will cause QWEST70 to fall. It seems reasonable to expect lags here for much the same reasons as before, albeit with somewhat different emphasis. There are long-term contracts for some Soviet exports to the West (especially in energy), but the contracts are not as all-pervasive as in intrabloc trade. The planning process and the recognition lag would be expected to operate here just as in Soviet exports to the bloc.

Again, after experimenting with various lag structures, the equation which appears to best explain the dependent variable is:

$$(2) \quad \text{LQWEST70} = 3.679 + .128 \text{ TIME} - .004 \text{ TIME}^2$$
$$\qquad\qquad (60.606) \quad (9.249) \qquad (-5.25)$$
$$- .227 \text{ RELHCBOT } (-1)$$
$$(-2.455)$$

R-Squared: .965          Durbin-Watson Statistic = 1.568
(Corrected)
Data time period: 1960–76
New Variable:

    LQWEST70 = The log of the 1970-weighted quantity index for Soviet exports to the West.

In this equation, the coefficient on TIME implies a time trend of 12.8 percent compound growth rate in primary product exports to the West. But the growth rate is decreasing, as indicated by the coefficient on the second term. Both of these coefficients are healthy multiples of their standard errors, and together they capture what casual observation of the data suggests; the strong upsurge in Soviet exports to the West is abating somewhat.[18]

Experiments with the lag structure on RELHCBOT settled on a one-period lag; there was no evidence of a longer lag in operation. This is a shorter lag than expected; however, there is much more freedom of maneuver in East-West trade than in intrabloc trade. Many of the primary products the Soviets sell to the West are not governed by long-term agreements, so that the Soviets can put them on the market or take them off at will.

What is more surprising and not so easy to explain is an apparent contradiction between equations (1) and (2). Equation (1) suggests that, when the hard-currency balance of trade deteriorates, Soviet primary product exports to the bloc fall and shipments are diverted to the West; and vice versa. If Equation (1) is to be believed, Equation (2) should show a similar lag structure between RELHCBOT and QWEST70: if it takes 4 years for changes in the RELHCBOT to work through exports to the bloc, then it should take 4 years for changes in RELHCBOT to work through exports to the West. Yet Equation (2) shows a much shorter lag than 4 years. Some exports appear to have been "lost." After several unsuccessful attempts to eliminate the inconsistency by respecifying and reestimating equations (1) and (2), I decided the only place the "lost" exports could be was in exports to other countries.

## Soviet Primary Product Exports to Other Countries

The dependent variable here is the quantity index of Soviet primary product exports to other countries (QRESID70), which means exports to countries other than the bloc and the developed West; these are the developing countries, some of which are Communist but not members of the Soviet bloc. QRESID70 is an index with no apparent pattern. The quantities are relatively small; there is no apparent time trend (which a regression against TIME confirmed); rather, there are wide fluctuations.

We do know that, in Soviet trade with many developing countries (including presumably all of the Communist countries outside CMEA), settlements on trade flows are in hard currency. Therefore it is conceivable that the Soviets are using these countries to increase or decrease sales of small quantities of primary products as their needs for hard currency change. Equation (3) suggests that is precisely what is occurring:

(3) LQRESID70 = 4.163 − .704 RELHCBOT (−1)
                (47.534)   (−2.328)
−1.930 RELHCBOT (−2) + .569 RELHCBOT (−3)
(−4.923)                (1.508)
−1.795 RELHCBOT (−4)
(−4.351)
R-Squared: .777        Durbin-Watson Statistic = 2.068
(Corrected)
Date time period: 1963–76
New Variable:
    LQRESID70 = The log of the 1970-weighted quantity
                 index of Soviet exports to other coun-
                 tries.

All the coefficients on RELHCBOT that are statistically significant (i.e., are two or more times their standard errors) have the expected negative sign, indicating that an improvement in RELHCBOT (which according to Equation (1) increases primary product exports to CMEA) decreases primary product exports to other countries. The lag is four periods long. The coefficients here are larger than those for Equation (1). This is to be expected since the amount of primary products freed up by a one percent drop in primary product shipments to the bloc will bring about a far greater percentage change in the smaller QRESID trade flows.

While these are rather strong results, and they are plausible, they still should be regarded as tentative. There is always the possibility that some spurious correlation is working in the background. To be sure this indeed does describe Soviet behavior, one would need to build a plausible case for where the primary products are being sold for hard currency, and which ones are being sold. This would require a more careful and detailed look at the "other" countries than I was able to give for this study.

### Estimates Using Time Trend Only

Soviet primary product exports to the Soviet bloc and to the West both exhibit strong time trends. (This is not, however, true of exports to other countries.) An interesting question, then, is how much of Soviet primary product export behavior could be explained solely by time-trend variables.

Table 4 reports the results of regressions of the dependent variables in each of equations (1) through (3) against a constant term, time, and (to capture possible changes in time-rates of growth) time-squared. As expected, the second-degree polynomial time trend "explains" virtually all of the variation in Soviet primary product exports to both the bloc and the West (corrected $R^2$ equals .992 and .955, respectively); also as expected, the time-trend results for other countries (column 3) are poor. Growth rates in shipments to both the bloc and the West are declining somewhat (viz., the negative coefficients on time-squared); and, while the growth rate is higher for the West than for the bloc (.143 vs. .123), it is also declining somewhat more rapidly (−.004 vs. −.003).

Equation (1) provides a better economic explanation of Soviet primary product exports to the Soviet bloc than column 1 of Table 4. The log of an East European GNP index (LEEGNP) probably picks up the first-degree time trend. The coefficients on the distributed-lag terms are sufficiently robust to suggest that the 4-year lagged adjustment describes actual Soviet behavior reasonably well. The significant deterioration of the Durbin-Watson statistic in Table 4 relative to Equation (1) further corroborates the preference for Equation (1) on economic grounds. Nevertheless, the strong trend for the bloc is readily evident.

Comparison of Equation (2) with column 2 of Table 4 clearly shows the effect of adding the economic variable for the relative hard-currency balance of trade. Compared with the purely time-trend results, those with the economic variable added show a slightly higher corrected $R^2$, a somewhat smaller coefficient on the first-degree time variable, and (most important) an improvement in the Durbin-Watson statistic. The coefficient on RELHCBOT lagged one period is sufficiently significant to suggest its explanatory power. Again, though, the importance of the time trend is clearly evident.

## V. Summary and Conclusions

Primary products remain the linchpin of Soviet exports to the West and the Soviet bloc. Soviet institutions appear to have good control over these exports, with an ability to

TABLE 4
Time Trends for Soviet Primary Product Exports to the Soviet Bloc, the West and Other Countries: 1959–76

|  | (1) | (2) | (3) |
|---|---|---|---|
| Dependent Variables: | LQCMEA70 | LQWEST70 | LQRESID70 |
| Independent Variables: |  |  |  |
| Constant | 3.517 | 3.600 | 3.853 |
|  | (136.760) | (57.957) | (13.470) |
| TIME | .123 | .143 | .043 |
|  | (19.787) | (9.469) | (0.633) |
| TIME$^2$ | −.003 | −.004 | .001 |
|  | (−9.178) | (−5.275) | (0.332) |
| R$^2$ (corrected) | .992 | .955 | .454 |
| Durbin-Watson statistic | 1.117 | 1.398 | 3.185 |

direct them to one market or another, including home users rather than exports, when the needs arise. There is strong empirical evidence that in recent years, the Soviets have used primary products as a balance of trade adjustment mechanism, pulling them out of or putting them back into the Soviet-bloc flows depending on their balance of trade in hard currency. Interestingly, it would not appear to be traditional Western markets, but rather smaller markets in developing countries, that take the brunt of the adjustment, although there is also evidence of adjustments (with a short lag) in Western trade flows.

It is important to keep in mind, however, that the adjustments in primary product shipments to the Soviet bloc and to the West involve for the most part only one or two percentage points shaved off or added to the growth rate. Most of the trade flows continue to grow in strong upward trends, a point emphasized by the regressions reported in Table 4.

Data for the years up to 1976 suggest, therefore, a very strong stability in the growth rates of primary product shipments to both the Soviet bloc and the West. But the recent deficits in Soviet-West trade have begun to take their toll. Equation (2) suggests that the big deficits of 1975–76 should have caused a big increase in primary product shipments to the West in 1976–77; indeed, there was a big jump in the 1976 shipments. Equation (1) suggests for the same reason that primary product shipments to the Soviet bloc should slow down for the same reasons, and that they should continue to be affected into the late 1970s. Indeed, primary product shipments to the bloc stagnated in 1976.

In 1977, the Soviet hard-currency trade deficit was 1,112 million rubles; in the first half of 1978 it was already nearly twice that large, at 1,907 million rubles.[19] Unless Soviet planners substantially changed the way they have behaved in similar circumstances, for the years 1979–81 or so we should have seen very slow growth in Soviet primary product shipments to the bloc, and continued high growth in these shipments to the West. Thus the bloc's share in primary product shipments should have continued its secular decline of recent years.

An additional consideration that strengthens this prediction is that the opportunity costs to the Soviets of exporting to the bloc have risen dramatically with the rapid rise in world market prices for primary products, especially energy. In the regressions reported in the last section, terms reflecting the growing products (not reported) never added significantly to an explanation of the variance. That is not surprising since only in the last three years of the sample did relative prices undergo an enormous transformation. For changes such as that, econometrics can offer no help. But these price changes can only put further downward pressure on primary product exports to the bloc, as the Soviets seek to free those products for more lucrative hard-currency markets.

Going beyond these qualitative predictions to quantitative predictions for future exports would require a model far beyond the scope of this paper. It would be necessary to model the determinants of the output of primary products, the determinants of the Soviet hard-currency balance of trade, and the effects on East European GNP of

changes in Soviet primary product shipments to them. Only in the context of relatively large macro models for the USSR (such as SOVMOD) and macro models for Eastern Europe could one begin to fully understand all of the interrelationships, and therefore to make useful predictions.

Aside from that, the one important unanswered question is how far the Soviets are willing to push East European austerity for the sake of hard-currency receipts. It would appear that the Soviets have a stake in political stability in Eastern Europe. It is quite conceivable that, at some point, they will ignore the economic signals, alter their past behavior, and push primary product shipments to Eastern Europe to avoid economic and political dislocations there.

## NOTES

1. The CMEA (Council for Mutual Economic Assistance) is the Soviet bloc's economic union of centrally-planned economies, including in its membership Bulgaria, Cuba, Czechoslovakia, East Germany, Hungary, Mongolia, Poland, Rumania, the USSR and Vietnam.

2. Data on the exports of important products to various countries are incomplete. Summary statistics on total exports to the world and to socialist countries are reported for the nine Soviet commodity groups, but only for recent years. Even were these data available for a long time period, they would be too aggregated to be useful for my purpose.

3. Vietnam did not join CMEA until 1978, and therefore is excluded from this data sample.

4. Even for these primary products, there are most likely problems arising from different product qualities within each product group. An obvious example is crude oil and refined products where a ton of crude oil is obviously not the same thing as a ton of refined products. The significance of that for the data used here is that if, say, relatively low priced products are the ones whose quantities are increasing relatively fast, a true quantity index (which weighted each individual product's quantity increase by its true relative price) would show a smaller increase than the quantity index here (which implicitly weights the increase in the ton of relatively low priced products as if they were average priced products). I suspect the resulting bias in the quantity (and unit value) indices used here is not great, but I have no way to prove it.

5. Experiments indicated that this index is insensitive to the weights used, if those weights come from the 1959–72 period. Obviously from 1973 on, oil prices rose dramatically and the weight on oil quantity increases rises correspondingly, so that a 1975-weighted index will differ from the 1970-weighted index. In this case the 1970-weighted index seems the best choice for depicting quantity movements over the entire period 1959–76.

6. Actually, there is more going on here than is apparent at first glance. At the official ruble-dollar exchange rate, ruble prices in intrabloc trade lie above those implied by comparable dollar prices multiplied times the

official exchange rate; in other words, the official exchange rate is overvalued, at least for the Transferable Ruble used in intrabloc trade. This means that, normally, even if prices in intrabloc trade were identical to world market prices, at official exchange rates the value of intrabloc trade would be inflated relative to East-West trade, and therefore the quantity shares of exports to the West would exceed the value shares. Indeed, as these data show, that is exactly what was happening in the 1960s. It was the mid-1973 price changes which, for this group of primary products, in effect devalued the Transferable Ruble.

7. For evidence on recent price changes in intrabloc trade, see my paper, "The Impact of the World Economic Crises on Intra-CMEA Trade," in E. Neuberger and L. Tyson (eds.) *Transmission and Response: Impact of International Economic Disturbances on the Soviet Union and Eastern Europe* (New York: Pergamon Press, 1980), pp. 323–48.

8. For a brief discussion of problems in the Soviet steel industry, see U.S. Congress, Joint Economic Committee, Subcommittee on Priorities and Economy in Government, *Allocation of Resources in the Soviet Union and China— 1978: Hearings, Part 4—Soviet Union* (Washington, 1978), pp. 1 and 153.

9. The divisions in Gosplan are more compact. Notice that nonferrous metallurgy is not mentioned. It is probably handled in the iron and steel division, since one state committee handled ferrous and nonferrous metallurgy until the two ministries were created in 1965.

10. There are a number of FTOs under other ministries, but none is involved in major commodity trade flows. For details, see John Quigley, *The Soviet Foreign Trade Monopoly: Institutions and Laws* (Columbus: Ohio State University Press, 1974). A few FTOs that deal in border trade in small amounts of products also handled by other FTOs, for example, Dalintorg and Lenfintorg, are of no importance in primary products.

11. For further information on the foreign trade planning process, see my "Most Favored Nation Treatment in Trade Under Central Planning," *Slavic Review* 37, no. 1 (March 1978): 25–39.

12. *Gosudarstvenny pyatiletni plan razvitiya narodnogo khozyaistva SSSR na 1971–75 gody* [The state five-year plan of the development of the economy of USSR in 1971–75] (Moscow: Politizdat, 1972).

13. If foreign trade efficiency indicators have any substantive influence on decisions concerning Soviet exports, this is where it probably occurs. For a discussion of these indicators, see my *Foreign Trade Prices in the CMEA* (Cambridge: Cambridge University Press, 1974), Chapter 4. For a recent treatment of the indicators in Soviet foreign trade decision making, see Steven H. Gardner, *Efficiency and Optimality Criteria in Soviet Foreign Trade Planning*, Ph.D. dissertation, University of California at Berkeley, 1978.

14. For information on these and similar projects, see my "Recent Developments in East-West European Eco-

nomic Relations, and Their Implications for U.S.-East European Economic Relations," in U.S. Congress, Joint Economic Committee, *East European Economies Post Helsinki* (Washington, 1977), pp. 174–98.

15. The Joint Committee on Planning and its projects are discussed in my 'Recent Developments. . . .''

16. Data on the hard-currency balance of trade were derived from official Soviet time series on exports to and imports from the developed capitalist countries (*Vneshnyaya torgovlya SSSR*, various years). The index of East European GNP, which were aggregated using 1972 GNPs as weights, were obtained from Thad Alton, "Economic Growth and Resource Allocation in Eastern Europe," in U.S. Congress, Joint Economic Committee, *Reorientation and Commercial Relations of the Economies of Eastern Europe* (Washington, 1974), p. 270; and Thad Alton, "Comparative Structure and Growth of Economic Activity in Eastern Europe," in U.S. Congress, Joint Economic Committee, *East European Economies Post Helsinki*, p. 229.

17. The choice of this lag structure came about by experimenting with various lengths for the lags, and various degrees for the polynomial. Four periods was the maximum number of periods for which each coefficient was at least twice its standard error, and for which $R^2$ was very high. This admittedly ad hoc approach is the best one I can do in the absence of an a priori case for a particular lag structure. For a brief discussion of polynomial distributed lags, see Jan Kmenta, *Elements of Econometrics* (New York: Macmillan, 1971), pp. 492–95.

The numbers in parentheses are the ratios of the estimated coefficients to their standard errors; a rule of thumb is that ratios greater than about 2.000 mean the estimated coefficient is significant at the 5 percent level or better. *R*-Squared is a measure of the percentage of the total variation in the dependent variable explained by the independent variables; the figures reported are all corrected for the reduction in degrees of freedom due to the number of independent variables used in the estimation. The Durbin-Watson statistic is a measure of the degree of serial correlation in the unexplained residual values of the dependent variable after the explanation provided by the independent variables has been taken into account; the value of the statistic, under the null hypothesis of zero correlation is 2.000.

18. An alternative form of this equation was tested, which used an index of Developed Market Economy GNPs instead of time as the independent variable. That equation explains only slightly less of the variance than Equation (2), which is to be expected given the strong time trend built into West European GNP. When the time trend was taken out of West European GNP, there was no indication of a significant relationship between deviations from trend in that variable and deviations from trend of Soviet primary product exports to the West. This corroborates the hypothesis of the small role Soviet primary products play on Western markets.

19. *Vneshnyaya torgovlya*, 1978, nos. 4 and 9.

# 29

# ENERGY DEPENDENCE AND POLICY OPTIONS IN EASTERN EUROPE

GEORGE W. HOFFMAN
The University of Texas

## Introduction

A critical factor in Soviet participation in world resource markets is its trade in resources with the six East European Communist countries in the Council of Mutual Economic Assistance (CMEA)—Bulgaria, Czechoslovakia, East Germany, Hungary, Poland and Rumania. In choosing between trade with the six, on the one hand, and the rest of the world, on the other, the USSR must continually weigh hard-currency earnings (and perhaps third-world diplomatic gains) against intrabloc gains and the stability of the Soviet-bloc alliance. Where the balance is struck for the various resources traded will clearly affect the Soviet presence in the world markets for those resources.

Since the 1950s, the East European allies have come to rely heavily on the USSR for deliveries of energy goods, especially oil but increasingly other forms (such as natural gas and electric power) as well.[1] Those deliveries were crucial to the growth of modern industry in Eastern Europe. Developments in world energy markets in the past decade have radically altered energy trade relationships between the Soviet Union and its allies. Rising prices threaten to undercut the already tenuous development efforts of the East European countries. At the same time the price structure has raised the cost to the USSR of exporting energy to Eastern Europe instead of selling it on world markets. Yet the Soviets are constrained in raising energy prices to East European buyers, both economically (because the allies are major trading partners) and politically (because an "oil shock" could destabilize the entire alliance).

*Research support from the Office of International Studies, U.S. Department of Energy, and from the Center for Energy Studies, University of Texas at Austin, is acknowledged. Appreciation is extended to several U.S. government agencies and to the United Nations Economic Commission for Europe, Geneva, for statistical and background data. I am also grateful to my colleagues Leslie Dienes, Edward Hewett, and Theodore Shabad for their helpful comments on a previous draft.*

This paper examines the problem of East European dependence on Soviet energy supplies, the possible solutions to that problem, and the impact of those solutions. The analysis falls into three sections: (1) regional disparities in resource endowments; (2) the impacts of the world market developments of the 1970s; and (3) Eastern Europe's policy options for dealing with their problems in the 1980s.

## Regional Disparities and Resource Endowment[2]

### Developments to 1945

Most of the countries of Eastern Europe were economically backward before World War I, and with few exceptions this situation continued during the interwar years. Apart from some mineral extraction and a few industries, the area was predominantly agricultural. Before 1918, the minerals were shipped to industrial centers in the Vienna Basin; in the interwar period, they were exported to pay for imports of manufactured goods. In both periods, a large percentage of the population depended upon agriculture, and the population was increasing rapidly, at a rate roughly three times that of Western Europe.

With the exception of Czechoslovakia, the new, heterogeneous national states created after World War I lacked a satisfactory basis for the development of their industry. With the loss of the old Austro-Hungarian market, industrial development in the interwar years was based on unsound principles: local raw materials which might have laid the foundation for a prospering industry were sold abroad, and finished products were imported. Economic development was often thwarted by divergent nationalist aspirations. In retrospect, it is surprising how much progress was made, since the region actually had only about ten years of peaceful independent development, from 1919 to the onset of the world depression. The economic devastation wrought by the depression lasted until the beginning of World War II.

### Postwar Changes

The end of World War II brought changes in the political geography of Eastern Europe, and with them a complete restructuring of the economic life of these countries by their new master, the Soviet Union. Early on, Moscow imposed Stalinist central planning in Eastern Europe, with only slight variations between the individual countries. It also discouraged economic and political cooperation with Western industrialized states. Through these measures, the Soviet Union attempted to implement in Eastern Europe a rapid industrialization modeled after its own development. The industries given priority were all energy-intensive—iron and steel, light metals, chemicals, and engineering.

The Soviet-enforced industrialization programs emphasized high rates of investment, abundant labor, and cheap raw materials. The latter had largely to be imported from the Soviet Union into the resource-poor East European countries. Agriculture, the largest sector of the East European economy, was neglected. The decision to rely on imported natural resources for industrialization was to have consequences in the 1970s, particularly in the case of energy.

### Resource Endowment

The countries of Eastern Europe possess natural resources that are mostly of limited quality and quantity. Until the early 1960s and the rapid growth of imports of Soviet oil and gas, the restrictions on imports resulted in overdiversification and uneconomical investments in expensive raw-materials production. Within the Soviet-bloc alliance, it was also difficult for Eastern Europe to develop exports of manufactures with which to earn hard currencies to finance imports from Western Europe and the United States.

Coal is the foremost available fuel resource in the East European countries, but (with the exception of bituminous coal in Poland) most of it is lignite (brown coal).[3] The lack of trading opportunities made coal the most important resource of the first five-year plans. With the exception of Rumania, all the East European countries had to rely on coal for their domestic industries. Signifi-

cant changes in the energy mix started only in the 1960s, and even in the late 1970s, Poland, East Germany, and Czechoslovakia still relied heavily on coal. All countries deficient in high-grade coal resources (particularly East Germany and Bulgaria) have imported Soviet anthracite, coking coal and high-grade steam coal. Poland, East Europe's sole coal exporter, has supplied several million tons to the Soviet Union's fuel-deficient western border provinces.

Generally speaking, the entire structure of industrial production in Eastern Europe is oriented toward imports of almost every basic metal and mineral from the Soviet Union. East European dependence on energy imports from the Soviet Union (Table 1) traces in large part to trying to produce too many products (especially machinery in too small quantities), the unbalanced development of its industrial production, and the building of energy-intensive industries. The entire bloc is now paying the price for the priorities established by Soviet as well as East European leadership during the early postwar economic development.

### The Impact of the Energy Crisis of the 1970s

The intensive industrialization drives in Eastern Europe in the first twenty-five years after World War II yielded high economic growth rates. It also added economic strength to Soviet-East European political ties. These achievements came about through high rates of investment and large-scale labor migration from agriculture to industry. They also carried with them the neglect of consumption, services and infrastructure.

Throughout the period to 1970, little investment went into modernizing raw-material production. This was a rational policy, given the low qualities and quantities of most of the region's raw-material resources. In the 1960s the Soviet Union was able to substantially increase its natural-resource exports to Eastern Europe, which in turn paid for the imports with manufactured goods. In

TABLE 1
Eastern Europe Energy Imports, 1970, 1977

|  | Energy imports as a share of energy consumption | | Energy imports from USSR as a share of energy consumption | | Energy imports from USSR as a share of total energy imports | |
|---|---|---|---|---|---|---|
|  | 1970 | 1977 | 1970 | 1977 | 1970 | 1977 |
| Bulgaria | 63 | 75 | 54 | 70 | 86 | 93 |
| Czechoslovakia | 29 | 42 | 23 | 35 | 80 | 85 |
| East Germany | 26 | 35 | 17 | 28 | 66 | 80 |
| Hungary | 43 | 54 | 28 | 44 | 66 | 82 |
| Poland | 14 | 20 | 12 | 15 | 87 | 75 |
| Rumania | 11 | 21 | 2 | 2 | 19 | 9 |

|  | 1970 | 1975 | 1978 |
|---|---|---|---|
| Soviet Share of Total Eastern Europe Oil Supply | 87 | 83 | 75 |
| (Excluding Rumania) | 92 | 90 | 88 |

Source: Central Intelligence Agency, *Energy Supplies in Eastern Europe. A Statistical Compilation* (ER 79–10624, December 1979), Tables 15, 17, 18.

the 1950s Soviet and East European trade in fuel and raw materials was nearly balanced, but by the mid-1960s the East European countries imported almost four times as much of these primary products as they exported to the USSR.

Average per capita energy consumption in the East European countries increased substantially after 1960. This was largely due to the industrial structures of these states, their energy utilization processes, relatively low fuel prices, and the continued use of low-grade coal, "resulting in low rates of heat capture (and) relatively high energy input to the energy industries themselves."[4] The especially high per capita energy consumption in the three northern countries—Poland, Czechoslovakia, and East Germany—was the result of their large iron-steel and chemical industries. Lignite was heavily used in some countries for generating power and for domestic heating (e.g., Czechoslovakia, Bulgaria and East Germany). These low-grade fuels were even used in some countries for chemical raw materials. In 1960, the proportion of solid fuels in the energy balances of all East European countries except Rumania ranged upward from more than 80 percent.

By 1960, then, modernization of the energy sector had become imperative, and that meant switching to hydrocarbons. Eastern Europe's own reserves of oil and gas were, however, inadequate to meet its growing needs. Thus, the bulk of their oil and gas had to be imported. With its limited ability to sell manufactures on the world market for hard currency, Eastern Europe had to import most of its hydrocarbons from the USSR.

East European imports of crude oil and refined products from the Soviet Union were 11.5 million metric tons in 1960. By 1973, the total exceeded 50 million tons, and by the late 1970s it stood at some 70 million tons. (As a share of Soviet oil exports, these totals rose from a third in 1960 to nearly half in the late 1970s.)[5] Even though, in the course of the 1970s, the Soviets grew increasingly reluctant to increase oil deliveries to Eastern Europe, the increases that occurred indicate some success in restructuring the East European fuel mix. Oil and gas accounted for 14.7 percent of energy use in 1960, 29.4 percent in 1970, and 41.2 percent in 1978. The share of coal had dropped to 56 percent in 1978 compared with 69 percent in 1970 (Tables 2 and 3).

Two factors stand out in the developments since the late 1960s. First, Eastern Europe has greatly increased its energy dependence on the Soviet Union. Second, the East European countries have steadily shifted from being an economic asset to being an economic burden to the Soviet Union. It is a burden which the Soviet Union, for political reasons, can hardly shed.[6]

The drastic changes in the world oil market since the early 1970s have posed serious problems for Eastern Europe. The USSR has stiffened its terms for oil exports to its allies, raising prices or requiring cooperative participation in energy-development projects. With the intrabloc prices still below world market levels, it has also limited increases in its deliveries of oil to those countries. While Moscow apparently is willing to cushion the impact of the oil price increases on its allies, it apparently also wants to

TABLE 2
Eastern Europe: Energy Consumption by Fuel Type, 1970, 1978 (percent of total consumption)

| | 1970 | | | |
| --- | --- | --- | --- | --- |
| | Coal | Oil | Gas | Primary Electricity |
| Bulgaria | 50.9 | 44.4 | 2.0 | 2.8 |
| Czechoslovakia | 74.6 | 18.1 | 3.4 | 3.9 |
| East Germany | 86.0 | 12.3 | 0.7 | 1.0 |
| Hungary | 53.1 | 28.0 | 13.8 | 5.1 |
| Poland | 82.7 | 10.4 | 6.3 | 0.7 |
| Rumania | 19.9 | 25.8 | 54.0 | 0.2 |
| Eastern Europe | 68.8 | 18.0 | 11.4 | 1.8 |

| | 1978 | | | |
| --- | --- | --- | --- | --- |
| | Coal | Oil | Gas | Primary Electricity |
| Bulgaria | 30.6 | 49.1 | 9.1 | 11.3 |
| Czechoslovakia | 61.4 | 26.4 | 9.2 | 3.0 |
| East Germany | 68.9 | 21.3 | 6.6 | 3.2 |
| Hungary | 30.5 | 41.6 | 23.4 | 4.4 |
| Poland | 76.4 | 15.6 | 7.5 | 0.5 |
| Rumania | 18.1 | 30.0 | 48.9 | 3.1 |
| Eastern Europe | 55.8 | 25.6 | 15.6 | 3.0 |

SOURCE: Central Intelligence Agency, *Energy Supplies in Eastern Europe. A Statistical Compilation* (ER 79–10624, December 1979). Attention is drawn to the data in United Nations, *World Energy Supplies 1973–78* (New York, 1979), which differ from the above for 1978. Total Eastern Europe figures for coal are 65.3 percent, oil 19.4 percent, natural gas 14.6 percent and primary electricity (hydro and nuclear) 0.7 percent.

force them to economize on oil use and not become addicted to subsidized oil imports.

The choices confronting the East European countries are not easy ones. The Communist planning system is notoriously rigid and slow to adapt to changing relative scarcities; only Hungary has had even moderate success in reforming the system to make it more flexible. At the same time, the East European countries have run up enormous hard-currency debts which can only be paid back by the proceeds from hard-curency exports. To the extent that stiffer terms on Soviet oil deliveries raise production costs and siphon off East European export goods, the hard-currency debt problem will be all the harder to solve. The stagnation of living standards in Eastern Europe since the mid-1970s, with its impact on political stability, cannot be ignored, either.

While energy policies would have to vary from country to country, depending upon resource endowments and specific industrial requirements, certain basic elements are common to the energy policies of the East European countries. Those elements include increasing domestic energy production, negotiation of energy trade agreements with nonbloc countries, improving energy efficiency (especially reducing the consumption of energy per unit of national product), and reduction of energy use through conservation measures. In the past, energy consumption has consistently increased more

TABLE 3
Eastern Europe: Energy Consumption by Source and Country, 1970, 1978 (million metric tons)

| | Domestic Production | Imports from Communist Countries | Imports from the West | Exports | Consumption* |
|---|---|---|---|---|---|
| | | 1970 | | | |
| Bulgaria | 20.54 | 31.01 | 2.58 | 0.95 | 53.18 |
| Czechoslovakia | 123.22 | 44.06 | 1.09 | 13.74 | 154.50 |
| East Germany | 159.39 | 49.64 | 2.99 | 9.25 | 202.78 |
| Hungary | 37.67 | 23.92 | 1.09 | 3.94 | 58.62 |
| Poland | 257.72 | 31.55 | — | 64.46 | 224.81 |
| Rumania | 119.54 | 5.85 | 6.26 | 16.86 | 114.78 |
| Eastern Europe | 718.08 | 186.055 | 13.87 | 109.48 | 808.66 |
| | | 1978 | | | |
| Bulgaria | 20.67 | 60.52 | 3.67 | 0.54 | 84.32 |
| Czechoslovakia | 129.06 | 81.60 | 2.31 | 14.14 | 198.83 |
| East Germany | 159.66 | 77.66 | 5.98 | 11.15 | 232.15 |
| Hungary | 41.34 | 41.48 | 3.94 | 6.26 | 80.51 |
| Poland | 344.08 | 55.76 | 10.34 | 86.90 | 323.27 |
| Rumania | 153.27 | 12.51 | 35.22 | 22.44 | 178.57 |
| Eastern Europe | 848.09 | 329.53 | 61.47 | 141.44 | 1,097.66 |

*These figures represent apparent consumption defined as domestic production plus total imports minus total exports.
SOURCE: Central Intelligence Agency, *Energy Supplies in Eastern Europe. A Statistical Compilation* (ER 79–10624, December 1979) modified.

rapidly than domestic energy production, resulting in greater dependence on imported energy. In addition, during the 1970s all of the East European countries increased their purchases of Western technology, for hard currency, of course.[7]

Before discussing the options available to the East European countries, it is appropriate to analyze their relations in the 1970s with the Soviet Union, the Western industrialized countries, and the Organization of Petroleum Exporting Countries (OPEC).

Eastern Europe and the Soviet Union

Eastern Europe as a whole imports close to one-third of the energy it consumes. Excluding Poland and Rumania,

the figure is 50 percent; for Bulgaria and Hungary alone, it is more than 50 percent. The share of oil produced for its own consumption, however, is only 4 percent (including Rumania, 20 percent). The Soviet Union provided (at lower than world market prices) 75 percent of Eastern Europe's oil imports in 1978 (excluding Rumania, 88 percent), with natural gas increasing in importance (see Table 4). Note that the share of Soviet oil deliveries grew less rapidly in the latter part of the 1970s than before. The East European countries themselves produced 82 percent of their consumption of natural gas in 1975; however, dwindling reserves will result in a drastic reduction of gas production after 1980, with the Soviet Union becoming the sole supplier of the expected deficit.[8]

For most of the energy imports from the USSR, pay-

TABLE 4
Eastern Europe: Imports of Crude Oil, 1973, 1978 (thousand metric tons)

| | Total | | USSR | | Percent of total oil import supplies by the USSR | | Iran and Iraq | | Other OPEC Countries | | Non-OPEC | |
|---|---|---|---|---|---|---|---|---|---|---|---|---|
| | 1973 | 1978* | 1973 | 1978 | 1973 | 1978 | 1973 | 1978 | 1973 | 1978 | 1973 | 1978 |
| Bulgaria | 9,652 | 12,600 | 7,513 | 11,300 | 82 | 89 | 606 | 890 | 1,164 | 400 | — | — |
| Czechoslovakia | 14,176 | 18,517 | 13,046 | 17,712 | 92 | 98 | — | 314 | 1,130 | — | — | 551 |
| East Germany | 16,045 | 19,600 | 13,025 | 17,760 | 92 | 77 | — | 1,057 | 145 | 840 | 2,875 | — |
| Hungary | 6,555 | 9,960 | 5,763 | 8,497 | 89 | 95 | 730 | 1,463 | — | — | — | — |
| Poland | 11,140 | 16,615 | 10,570 | 13,368 | 82 | 95 | — | 1,930 | 291 | — | 279 | 1,317 |
| Rumania | 4,143 | 12,937 | — | — | — | — | 2,600 | 8,500 | 1,600 | 3,250 | — | — |

*Figures for 1978 are estimates.
SOURCE: Foreign trade book of East European countries; *Statistisches Jahrbuch der Deutschen Demokratischen Republik* [Statistical Yearbook of the German Democratic Republic] Berlin, 1978 and 1979. Rumania from miscellaneous sources.

ments were made in soft currencies through intrabloc arrangements during the 1970s. There was also a considerable infusion of Western credits, with which the East European countries paid for much needed technology, incremental oil needs, and food products.

Soviet policy toward energy exports to the East European countries during the next decade will play an important role in the region's economic growth. Unchanged oil deliveries (80 million tons in 1980, including Cuba), as promised at the 34th Comecon Council session in June 1980 for the five-year plan period 1981–85, could force a retrenchment in the economic growth of the East European countries, in view of their projected growth in energy consumption of between 2 and 5 percent annually.[9] Increased natural gas exports will, of course, make up part of the difference. The alternatives are imports of oil from the world market, with payments in hard currencies, or payment with goods for Soviet incremental oil supplies that otherwise could be sold to the Western industrialized countries.

The East European countries have been forewarned by Moscow that major changes—closer integration in planning, investment contributions, greater internal efficiency, and eventually world market prices—will be expected in return for additional resource exports. The recent emphasis has been on a series of joint development projects, many of which were first proposed in the early 1970s. As envisioned by the Soviet Union, these projects are situated in Soviet territory, many in the western border areas, and after completion will benefit both the Soviet Union and the East European countries. The gas pipeline from Orenburg is a well known example. Another is the 750-kV electric power transmission line (the first of several projected Soviet-East European interties) between Vinnitsa (western Ukraine) and Albertirsa (Hungary), which raised Soviet electricity deliveries to Hungary from 4.4 billion KWH in 1978 to 7.5 billion in 1980. The integration of the Soviet electricity network with that of the East European countries will ultimately reduce the need for shipping fuels for power-generating purposes. Large nuclear power stations (several million kW capacity each) are being built or planned in the Soviet Union's western border areas for transmission of electricity into the common grid. Soviet electricity transmission met 16 percent of Hungary's needs and 14 percent of Bulgaria's needs in 1977,[10] and the Hungarian share increased by 1980 to 23 percent as a result of the completion of the 750-kV intertie. Finally, there is "Petrobaltic," an offshore oil exploration project in the Baltic Sea jointly financed by Poland, East Germany, and the Soviet Union.[11]

It is easy to understand why the Soviet Union is demanding cooperative investments, higher prices, and hard-currency payment for incremental resource sales within the bloc. For example, its allies (with the exception of Rumania) have been paying only about $15 per barrel for Soviet oil, roughly half its value at world prices. Thus, the USSR is bearing the burden of a subsidy not only in foregone revenues but also in investing in additions to capacity to meet growing demands.

At the same time, price increases on Soviet raw-material shipments will have deleterious effects on the economies of the East European countries. The diversion of manufactured goods, especially those of higher quality usually sold to the West, demanded by the Soviet Union in exchange for its fuels and raw materials is impeding Eastern Europe's efforts to supply hard-currency markets. "Rising Soviet raw material prices require the transfer of exportables from the West to the Soviet Union at the very time when high debt burdens require the maximization of exports to the West."[12]

Thus, both the Soviet Union and its East European partners face a real dilemma. Eastern Europe's economic well being, its economic and political stability, clearly depend on reliable supplies of imported energy and key raw materials for its expanding industrial production. With the Soviet promise at a CMEA council meeting to continue supplies in the 11th Five-Year Plan (1981–85) at the 1980 level, the East European countries will have to import any increases from nonbloc sources, paying world prices in hard currencies (or their real equivalents in goods). Measures for energy-savings, increased indigenous production and greater efficiencies in the use of energy will not noticeably improve the East European energy situation before the end of the 1980s. The East European countries are stuck with an inefficient capital stock and an inflexible economic system, with no easy way to change either. This puts the Soviet Union in a precarious situation. It should have considerable leverage, but because of the threat to East European economic and political stability, the USSR is in no position to cut oil shipments or raise prices much—it has even delayed further contemplated price increases for its oil exports.[13]

Eastern Europe and the West

Several factors have contributed to reestablishing trade between Eastern and Western Europe since the mid-1960s. The modernization of Eastern Europe's industries required high technology. Soviet reluctance to sell increasing quantities of oil forced the East European countries to look for export opportunities to earn foreign exchange with which to buy oil and advanced technology on the world markets. Perhaps more than anything else, there was the shift in bloc trading policies summed up in the slogan of "consumerism, integration and Western trade." The Western trade component became essential to Eastern Europe's fuel supply, technology, and to an extent food supply. A large part of the trade was based on borrowing sizable sums from Western commercial lenders, mostly private banks and government agencies who were anxious to develop new export markets.[14] An important factor in the expansion of this trade was that West European governments relaxed their restrictions on loans to Communist countries. United States trade has increased with the depreciation of the dollar, Export-Import credits and the lowering of United States tariffs on goods to Poland, Hungary and Rumania, but it is still well below that of most West European countries. One consequence of expanded trade with the East is that a significant part of East European plants built by Western countries are based on agreements to "buy back" some of the output as partial payment.

The infusion of Western credits resulted in a rapid growth of Eastern Europe's hard-currency debts, which by the end of 1979 amounted to close to $40 billion (compared with $10 billion in 1973).[15] Some $19.5 billion of the debt is held by Poland; better than 90 percent of Poland's hard-currency export earnings now go for debt service, and only Western willingness to continue debts avoid disaster. The other East European countries have by no means exhausted their borrowing capabilities, and credits continue to be available on the Western markets. Ultimately, of course, their imports will have to be paid for by exports to the West. In 1979, the difference between the hard-currency import bill plus interest-on-debt and hard-currency earnings totalled $8.4 billion, about 33 percent of 1979 hard-currency exports.[16]

The increase in energy prices may well have a depressing effect on East-West trade. Some believe that East European governments will impose import controls.[17] They may also divert exports originally designated for the West to the Soviet Union and the Middle East. Imports from the West are mainly energy-related capital goods such as turbines, offshore drilling rigs, and large-diameter pipe. Long range plans to upgrade the quality of manufacturing exports from Eastern to Western Europe certainly will be affected by a slowdown of Western equipment and technology imports. The reluctance of East European countries to become more heavily indebted also will act as a constraint to the expansion of East-West trade.

## Eastern Europe's Options in the 1980s: Toward a Viable Energy Policy

As was pointed out earlier, in the 1960s Eastern Europe shifted from a reliance on domestic coal for its primary energy supply to an energy mix relying heavily on imported hydrocarbons. While the rapid transition to a hydrocarbon base permitted modernization and rationalization, and with them faster economic growth, the imports of hydrocarbons also increased Eastern Europe's economic dependence on the Soviet Union. That dependence is now at the heart of East European energy policies, because of the fundamental change in the world oil market in the 1970s. In this last section, we consider East European energy policy options for the 1980s, and in particular the role of dependence on the USSR.

In the short run the East European countries can depend on a continuing supply of oil at current levels and an increased supply of natural gas from the Soviet Union. While Eastern Europe may be a liability to the Soviet Union, there is little danger of a drastic, sudden reduction in imports of essential resources so long as political and strategic considerations outweigh economic considerations. On the other hand, the price increases on oil and other raw materials that will eventually occur mean that Eastern Europe cannot count on Soviet solicitude for the long run. For one thing, the price increases reduce the value and raise the cost of their dependence on Soviet

energy deliveries. The most important of the East Europeans' policy options will be briefly analyzed in the following pages under two headings: domestic options and foreign options.

### Domestic Options

The East European countries face four domestic possibilities for coping with their energy problems. They can (1) produce more energy themselves; (2) export more goods to finance energy imports; (3) use less energy themselves; and (4) curtail the growth of output and living standards. All the possible outcomes over the coming decade can be described as combinations of these four possibilities.

There is every indication that the East European countries will rely heavily on the first option—increased production from domestically available energy resources. In 1980 coal still supplied close to 60 percent of Eastern Europe's energy consumption. Poland, with its exportable high-quality coal, experienced a 7.6 percent increase in production between 1974 and 1978, but a 9.5 percent increase in consumption during the same period. The consumption growth has now been arrested and increased attention has been given to lignite.[18] Modern machinery is the main hope for the low-calorific lignite, increasingly expensive to produce, of Bulgaria, Czechoslovakia, East Germany, Hungary, and Rumania. Lignite production is increasing (mainly from open-pit mines), but only small production increases have occurred in most of the countries during the last few years.[19] Oil production and reserves are generally meager in the East European countries, although offshore drilling in several countries could have some impact on increased production in the long run. Hungary supplies about 15 percent and Rumania 25 percent of needs from domestic oil, but both countries show a decline in the rate of production. East Germany and Poland produce small amounts of natural gas that perhaps could be increased slightly by greater investments. In Hungary natural gas accounts for one-third, in Rumania for 60 percent of domestic energy supplies, but production is declining in both countries.

Increasing nuclear power production has top priority in every East European country. It is already being felt in Bulgaria and East Germany, but drastic increases can not be expected much before the end of the 1980s. Construction of standardized nuclear power plants is proceeding everywhere in Eastern Europe. Standardization of equipment is moving at a rapid pace with plans for a 1990 capacity of 37,000 MW. Cooperation in fuel economy systems and manufacture of installations for the utilization of steam, heat and industrial waste are rapidly progressing. Uranium is mined under strict Soviet control in Czechoslovakia and Hungary. While nuclear power could be a possible long-term answer to Eastern Europe's energy problems, not much is expected before the 1990s when it will contribute 5 to 10 percent of the energy mix of individual countries. Still, in Bulgaria atomic power plants accounted for 62 percent of the increment in electricity output during 1974–78 and in East Germany 40 percent for the same period.[20]

The East European countries have vast potential for reducing energy use. According to Hewett, "there is abundant evidence that almost all of the East European countries consume far more energy per capita than one would expect of countries at their level of economic development."[21] Table 5 shows comparative data for per capita energy consumption; these data must be adjusted for differences in standards of living and climate, among other factors. While all East European countries have taken conservation measures (ranging from increased prices to administrative controls), a recent study by the United Nations Economic Commission of Europe concluded that "these measures were reported to have successfully reduced energy requirements on a microeconomic level. But the absence of any visible improvement in the utilization of energy materials on the overall level is to be noted."[22]

The efficiency of energy use—energy input per unit of output—differs considerably across the East European countries. While Eastern Europe shows a better record than Western Europe in particular applications (such as the consumption of fuel per kilowatt hour of electricity output), overall the East European countries rank among the highest energy consumers per unit of national product.[23] Unfortunately, the structural changes in the central planning system that many Western observers see as vital to the rationalization of the East European economies do not appear in prospect. To date, political inhibitions have outweighed the possible economic gains from adopting real reforms (with the partial exception of Hungary).

Reducing economic growth is not an option the East European countries would voluntarily accept, although it is a real possibility for the 1980s. The first signs appeared already toward the end of the 1970s. Whether this option comes to pass will depend on a number of developments, many of them beyond the control of individual governments; hard-currency debts and repayment policies, availability of credits from the West, trading opportunities with Western and OPEC countries, and the East Europeans' ability to restructure their now energy-intensive industries. The last is a slow development at

TABLE 5
Per Capita Consumption of Energy in Eastern Europe and Selected Other Countries and Regions, 1973, 1975, 1978 (kg per capita coal equivalent)

| Country or Region | 1973 | 1975 | 1978 |
|---|---|---|---|
| Bulgaria | 4,264 | 4,695 | 5,020 |
| Czechoslovakia | 6,607 | 6,925 | 7,531 |
| East Germany | 6,308 | 6,623 | 7,121 |
| Hungary | 3,024 | 3,233 | 3,451 |
| Poland | 4,551 | 4,989 | 5,596 |
| Rumania | 3,533 | 3,762 | 4,042 |
| Eastern Europe (excluding USSR) | 4,715 | 5,038 | 5,460 |
| Soviet Union | 4,705 | 5,087 | 6,510. |
| Western Europe | 4,230 | 3,990 | 4,245 |
| United States | 11,789 | 10,874 | 11,374 |
| Canada | 9,660 | 9,802 | 9,930 |

SOURCE: Adapted from United Nations, *World Energy Supplies 1973–1978* (New York, 1979).

best, and in view of the past emphasis on steel and chemical industries is probably not a realistic expectation.

Foreign Options

Eastern Europe faces foreign options chiefly in increased intrabloc cooperation and in increased trade with the rest of the world. Much has been made of the first option, but the actual degree of integration within the bloc has so far been quite limited. We have already mentioned the East European participation in Soviet energy development, which has been part of the price of obtaining increments to current Soviet oil shipments. Plans are also afoot for the joint development and financing of energy-related machinery, particularly in nuclear power. The actual integration of national plans, however, has not progressed very far towards significant levels, at least in energy production or use. Rumania has, of course, remained aloof from many of the integration efforts, including (and perhaps particularly) in energy.

Trade with the rest of the world is important to Eastern Europe for advanced technology and incremental oil imports. Inasmuch as Western commercial banks and government agencies are eager to promote trade with Eastern Europe, obtaining additional credits should not pose an insurmountable problem (except for Poland, a special case). Of course, any Western credits must eventually be repaid with foreign currencies or (what amounts to the same thing) quality manufactured goods.

An interesting twist here is that the USSR is now also demanding hard currencies or quality goods for extra energy and other raw-material exports to Eastern Europe. Demands by the Soviet Union for an increased share of East European exports to the Western industrialized countries would necessarily mean a reduction in imports from the West. Such demands thus would mean that East-West trade would be confined to essentials such as high priority technology and oil.[24]

Eastern Europe's trade with the OPEC countries must also be emphasized.[25] Current trade levels are relatively small, about 3 percent of East European trade turnover is with OPEC countries, and none of the latter receives more than 5 percent of its imports from Eastern Europe. But oil imports from OPEC quadrupled in 1978, reaching nearly 25 percent of all East European oil imports (see Table 4). Iran was the leading OPEC trading partner before 1979; between 1975 and 1978, Iran accounted for 29 percent of the total OPEC exports to the East European countries. In the same period, Iraq accounted for another 11 percent. East European governments had hoped to find OPEC-nation markets for their less sophisticated goods to pay for the much-needed oil.

Unfortunately, such markets have not materialized to any significant degree. First, whereas East European exports consist heavily of primary and intermediate goods (some two-thirds to three-quarters during 1970–76), the OPEC countries have shown a preference for Western technology, industrial goods, and real or financial assets. Thus, in spite of some growth in the volume of East European exports to OPEC during the 1970s, "in the region as a whole, the East European market share dropped from a peak of 3.2 percent in 1971 to only 1.9 percent in 1978."[26] Second, sizable trade deficits with hard-currency countries and the USSR have forced the East European countries to concentrate on export sales to the West and the Soviet Union.

## Summary

In the mid-1960s, East European energy policies shifted from reliance on domestic coal to the use of imported hydrocarbons. The shift permitted modernization and rationalization, and thus generated faster economic growth. But it also increased Eastern Europe's economic dependence on the Soviet Union, which was and still is the main source of the oil imports. This dependence on the USSR, at a time when Soviet oil production may be reaching its peak, poses fundamental problems for the future economic growth and political stability of every one of the East European countries.

The options available to the East European countries are, for the most part, of a long-term nature. Eastern Europe's requirements for oil and natural gas will increase in the next few years simply to satisfy present plans for continued economic growth. Most of these fuels must come from the Soviet Union. How long the Soviet Union will be able or willing to supply the increments, especially of oil, and on what terms, is hard to say. In case of an actual decline—as against a slowdown—in Soviet oil production, Soviet leaders will have a difficult choice: cut exports of oil to Western Europe, with a consequent decline in hard-currency earnings, or cut oil shipments to the East European allies.

The first is the more likely choice due to the danger of economic and political instability among the East European countries—a situation Soviet leaders are obviously trying to avoid. Since World War II, the region has been viewed as a "buffer against military and ideological challenges from the West and also as a possible base for extending Soviet influence into Western Europe."[27] So long as this remains true, the importance of regional stability insures Eastern Europe's well-being, thus making a dependable supply of fuel and raw materials for the USSR's East European partners a necessity.

While dependence on Soviet supplies will remain in the foreseeable future the most likely option, other options—increased intrabloc cooperation; increased trade with the rest of the world, including the OPEC countries; and joint development and financing of energy-related manufactures, especially in nuclear and computer related items—will become absolute necessities. While much has been written about integration within the Soviet bloc, in actuality very little has been accomplished thus far. Arranging barter agreements with certain OPEC countries—oil in exchange for industrial development aid—is another possibility, but thus far the OPEC countries have shown little interest in that type of trade.

What are the Western options with respect to these developments? The high net dollar debt owed by Eastern Europe, particularly Poland, has created mutual interest in successfully resolving the issues, among both banks and government officials in the West and economic and political officials in Eastern Europe and the Soviet Union. This situation obviously raises the intriguing question of whether the West will end up having to cooperate with the Soviet Union in resolving some of the problems of the weak East European countries. Poland, for instance, has recently received aid from the United States, West Germany, and the Soviet Union. Perhaps Eastern Europe can now exercise Martin Kohn's "leverage of weakness" upon the West as well as the USSR.[28]

## NOTES

1. Rumania, at least until 1980, has been an exception and will be omitted from the analysis except for passing references. Yugoslavia and Albania, sometimes considered part of Eastern Europe, are not members of CMEA and are therefore excluded from the discussions. They are not heavily dependent on the Soviet Union for fuels, although Yugoslavia bought (for hard currency) 5 million metric tons of crude oil and refined products in 1979 and approximately 4.5 million mt in 1980; planned deliveries of Soviet natural gas amounted to 2 to 3 billion cubic meters in 1980. On Yugoslavia's energy outlook, see George W. Hoffman, *Yugoslavia's Energy Supplies: Constraints and Outlook* Center for Energy Studies, The University of Texas at Austin, Policy Study no. 8, 1979.

2. This section draws on the author's paper, "Eastern Europe—Economic Growth and Resource Dependence," in George W. Hoffman, ed. *A Geography of Europe. Problems and Prospects* 4th edition (New York: John Wiley, 1977), pp. 436–51.

3. Central Intelligence Agency, *Energy Supplies in Eastern Europe: A Statistical Compilation* (ER 79–10624, December 1979); also *Handbook of Economic Statistics 1979* (ER 79–10724, August 1979).

4. Leslie Dienes, "Energy Prospects for Eastern Europe," *Energy Policy* 4 (June 1976): 120.

5. Edward A. Hewett, *Soviet Primary Product Exports to CMEA and the West* Discussion Paper No. 9 (May 1979), Association of American Geographers, Project on Soviet Natural Resources in the World Economy; J. R. Lee, "Petroleum Supply Problems in Eastern Europe," in U.S. Congress, Joint Economic Committee, *Reorientation and Commercial Relations of the Economies of Eastern Europe*, 93rd Congress, 2nd session, 1974, pp. 418–19 for 1960 and 1973 data.

6. A. Ross Johnson, *Eastern Europe Looks West* (Rand Corporation, Santa Monica, Ca., P–6032, November 1977).

7. The above paragraph draws on Cam Hudson, *Eastern Europe and the Energy Crisis: An Overview*, Radio Free Europe Research, RAD Background Report/136 (Eastern Europe), 10 June 1980.

8. The main factor here was the completion of the 1,700-mile Soyuz (Alliance) gas pipeline from the Orenburg field in the southern Urals to the East European countries. Those countries provided capital and labor to help construct this 56-inch pipeline, which has a total capacity of 28 billion cubic meters per year. Repayment

will take the form of natural gas shipments of 15.5 billion cubic meters a year over a 12-year period. Some natural gas from this pipeline is also going to Yugoslavia, Italy, Austria, and Western Europe.

9. Cam Hudson, *The 34th Comecon Council Session Ends*. Radio Free Europe Research, RAD Background Report/ 151 (Eastern Europe), 20 June 1980; "Mother Russia, give us more," *The Economist*, 28 June 1980; "Comecon gets a 5-year promise on oil," *The Economist*, 20 June 1980. Reports have been unclear as to whether the 400 million tons of oil for 1981–85 are total CMEA supplies or for the East European countries only.

10. Theodore Shabad, "Soviet Regional Policy and CMEA Integration," *Soviet Geography: Review and Translation* 20, no. 4 (April 1979): Table 4 and pp. 237–240.

11. *New York Times*, 24 January 1978. The joint ventures are not confined to energy, and some of the larger ones have involved Western participation. Nonenergy projects include the asbestos facility at Yasny in the southern Urals; a cellulose plant at Ust-Ilimsk; a nickel project in Cuba; iron-ore projects in the Ukraine and the KMA district; and ferroalloy projects at Nikopol in the Ukraine and in northeast Kazakhstan. Morris Bornstein has emphasized that "without Western equipment, licensing of technology, technical assistance and financing, these 'CMEA joint investments' would be impossible. Thus, Western participation has contributed decisively to one of the most prominently cited examples of CMEA 'integration,' "—Morris Bornstein, in U.S. Congress, Joint Economic Committee, *Soviet Economy in a Time of Change*, vol. 1, 96th Congress, 1st session, 1979, p. 308. For additional details of the joint development projects, see Shabad, "Soviet Regional Policy."

12. Cam Hudson, *The 34th Comecon Council Session: No Major Initiatives on the Horizon*, Radio Free Europe Research, RAD Background Report/147 (Eastern Europe), 16 June 1980, p. 5.

13. Martin Kohn put this point succinctly at a conference in April 1980: "Eastern Europe enjoys the leverage of weakness . . . it cannot be pushed too hard." See Robert Jensen, ed., *Conference on Soviet Natural Resources in the World Economy*, Discussion Paper No. 24 (October 1980), Association of American Geographers, Project on Soviet Natural Resources in the World Economy, p. 87.

14. During the last two election campaigns in West Germany, "Ostpolitik" has been sold by pointing to the advantages of trade with the East European countries and the Soviet Union and specifically its beneficial impact on West German employment opportunities. Other links consist of compensation and licensing agreements and a variety of joint ventures. A plant in Poland, for example, is wholly owned by Westerners and trades with the Soviet Union and Eastern Europe. Some of the products are marketed by agreement in West Germany.

15. Not counting debt in hard currency by CMEA's International Investment Bank and its International Bank for Economic Cooperation of about $5.5 billion. Allen J. Lenz, "Projected CMEA Hard-Currency Debt Levels Un-der Selected Trade Growth Assumptions," U.S. Department of Commerce, International Trade Administration, Office of East-West Policy and Planning, Program D–03–80, Staff Research Note, 20 May 1980; and United Nations, ECE, *Economic Survey of Europe in 1979*, pp. 157–65; "Doubts Plague West German Bankers on East Bloc's Ability to Pay Its Debts," *New York Times*, 2 September 1980.

16. Lenz, "CMEA Hard-Currency Debt," p. 5.

17. Edward A. Hewett, *The Soviet and East European Energy Crisis: Its Dimensions and Implications for East-West Trade*, Center for Energy Studies, The University of Texas at Austin, Policy Study no. 2, (August 1978), p. 26.

18. The domestic turmoil in Poland since 1980 has meant a steep decline in coal production, among many other goods and services. Until that turmoil is quieted, analysis of Poland's economic prospects will be a precarious exercise.

19. Czechoslovakia, for example, is making a major effort to increase production by moving a city with a population of 70,000 (Most), built on top of a major deposit.

20. United Nations, Economic Commission for Europe, *Economic Survey of Europe in 1979* (Geneva, 1980), p. 99; Leslie Colitt, "Czechs exporting nuclear reactors," *Financial Times*, 8 August 1980. Czechoslovakia plans to produce 17 reactors of 440 MW each by 1985 as part of an ambitious CMEA program to install 37,000 MW of nuclear generating capacity by 1990 in the East European countries. Each reactor is estimated to bring the equivalent of $35 million in sales to the producing Skoda enterprise.

21. Hewett, *Soviet and East European Energy Crisis*, pp. 12–15; see also Benedikt Korda, *Energy Consumption in the Soviet Bloc*, Forschungsberichte Wiener Institut für Internationale Wirtschaftsvergleiche, 41 (August 1977), and various reports by the Economic Commission of Europe, United Nations.

22. *Economic Survey of Europe in 1979*, p. 94.

23. John R. Haberstroh, "Eastern Europe: Growing Energy Problems," in U.S. Congress, Joint Economic Committee, *East European Economies: Post Helsinki* 95th Congress, 1st session, 1977, p. 393.

24. See Hewett, *The Soviet and East European Energy Crisis*, pp. 17–20.

25. This draws upon several recent studies analyzing East European relations with the OPEC countries and data published in the *Handbook of Economic Statistics 1979* and *Energy Supplies in Eastern Europe*.

26. Ronald G. Oechsler and John A. Martens, "East European Trade with OPEC," mimeo, p. 17.

27. U.S. Congress, Senate, Committee on Foreign Relations, *Perceptions: Relations Between the United States and the Soviet Union*, 95th Congress, 2nd session, December 1978, p. 10; also, J. F. Brown, *Relations Between the Soviet Union and Its Eastern European Allies: A Survey* (Rand Corporation, Santa Monica, Ca., R–1742–PR, November 1975).

28. Jensen, *Conference on Soviet Natural Resources*, p. 87.

# 30

# FOREIGN ECONOMIC CONSTRAINTS ON SOVIET RAW MATERIAL DEVELOPMENT IN THE 1980s

LAWRENCE J. BRAINARD
Bankers Trust Company

## Introduction

Soviet economic strategies for the 1980s include a major role for the development of raw materials. Natural resources have a key role in supporting projected growth rates in the Soviet Union and Eastern Europe. These growth rates are highly dependent on exports of raw materials to earn the foreign exchange necessary to pay for essential imports from the West. Although Soviet exports of manufactured goods to the West have received substantial official attention in recent years, there is little prospect that such exports will account for more than the 15 to 20 percent share of exports they represent at present.[1]

In drawing up economic plans for the coming years, Soviet planners face a number of emerging problems that were less troublesome in earlier years. One is the sharp slowdown and probable leveling off in oil production. More generally, the output of many raw materials is confronting sharply rising unit costs as more distant and less productive deposits of natural resources are developed. Labor, capital and infrastructure are generally lacking where the raw materials are located and must be supplied at substantial cost. Transport of raw materials also involves rising costs due to energy scarcities and bottlenecks encountered in the transport system. Another problem is lagging technological change and a retardation in the rate of increase in the labor force projected for the 1980s. There are prospects as well of a rising military burden in coming years owing to deteriorating relations with the United States.

Soviet planners have a number of options in dealing with these problems. Policy options in foreign trade are of particular interest. They may have significant effects—positive and negative—on Western governments through trade and credit policies. Two key issues are whether foreign trade options will bring significant benefits to the Soviet economy and whether they also impose constraints on Soviet economic development policy. Related to these issues is the question of whether the access to such foreign trade options should be restricted or controlled as a matter of Western policy.

Soviet imports of Western capital goods will depend importantly on the future growth of Soviet exports to the West. These exports, in turn, consist largely of raw materials (80 to 85 percent). Hence, the potential of raw-material exports to the West—a primary concern of this study—will largely determine the amount of foreign exchange available for imports of Western plant and equipment in the 1980s. An important aspect of that potential is the foreign economic constraints, including the availability of Western credit, facing Soviet planners in developing their natural resources. These constraints are the subject of this paper.

## Western Trade and Credit Options

Soviet trade and financial ties with the West augment domestic capital resources, thus providing a stimulus to economic growth. At present, Western capital imports are small relative to Soviet investment and are unlikely to grow much in the future. Imports of machinery and transport equipment from the West accounted for only about 5.5 percent of domestic machinery investment in 1975–76. This was up from a 3 percent share in the 1960s.[2]

More important is the qualitative contribution of Western capital to Soviet growth. Capital imports are typically allocated to priority sectors where their contribution to relieving critical bottlenecks yields high returns. Western capital may also help to raise the technological level of specific industrial sectors; the mineral fertilizer industry is a case in point. Though limited, these cases illustrate the significant, if selective, role that Western capital may play.

Potential benefits of foreign economic options in developing raw materials should thus be assessed in terms of relieving critical bottlenecks. Such bottlenecks may derive from the nature of Soviet economic priorities, the economic system, and the timing of major projects. Soviet resources, for example, might be available, but foreign capital might allow a job to be done more quickly and efficiently. The Soviet Union both produces and imports large diameter steel pipe for oil and gas pipelines; the domestic production capacity is insufficient to meet ambitious pipeline construction targets. Bottlenecks may also arise from lagging rates of technical change in certain economic sectors. Included in this category are backward technological processes, management, and production know-how for large, complex industrial units. A final aspect is that Soviet planners accept obligations in using these foreign options. Capital imports require credit, and credits must be repaid by future exports.

How might these foreign options act as constraints? Foreign borrowing makes sense when a country is able to invest the borrowed resources to obtain an acceptable rate of return after the repayments necessary to amortize the credit have been made. There are two aspects of this process: (1) the efficient use of the foreign capital goods being financed to manufacture the product; and (2) the sale of the product abroad to generate foreign exchange revenues. Constraints may be said to exist if prospective investment projects are postponed or cancelled. There are three possible cases:

(1) A country having profitable investment opportunities may be unable to secure the necessary credits to implement such projects. In this case, credit is the constraining factor.

(2) A country is able to use foreign capital efficiently to produce a given output, but sales prospects in foreign markets are unfavorable or sufficiently uncertain to cause postponement or cancellation of the project. In this case trade is the constraining factor.

(3) A country has profitable investment opportunities involving foreign trade and credit but is unable to implement them efficiently due to constraints of a domestic nature, such as shortages of labor, domestic capital (infrastructure) and inadequacies of management. In this case domestic factors are the constraining elements.

The task here is to determine whether Soviet planners face significant constraints in developing prospective raw-material projects. The next step is to identify situations where trade and credit are constraining factors and to distinguish them from cases where domestic factors may be more important. There may be multiple constraints in some cases.

## Prospective Raw-Material Projects

Before looking in more detail at the nature of trade and credit constraints on Soviet policy, a brief description is needed of major raw-material projects that have been discussed with Western companies. The size and costs of the projects mentioned should be viewed as order-of-magnitude estimates, since few parameters have as yet been fixed.[3]

*Oil and Natural Gas.* Western companies have made a number of proposals for exploration and development of new oil deposits, primarily in offshore waters in the Caspian Sea, Arctic and Pacific oceans. So far the only project to move ahead is a joint agreement made with Japan in 1974 to explore and develop oil deposits offshore from Sakhalin Island in the Sea of Okhotsk, north of Japan. Japanese credits for the current exploration phase are projected at about $225 million. Provided that reserves

justify full development, additional credits of $2.5 billion are to be provided by the Japanese. Repayment is to be made by oil deliveries to Japan (50 percent of production) over a ten-year period. Results of exploratory drilling, however, do not as yet justify further development of the area's oil potential. Discussions between the partners started in late 1980 concerning the feasibility of developing reserves of natural gas discovered in project drilling.[4]

Discussions with Western companies on other major oil projects are at various stages, but none of them appears near finalization. Major capital-goods imports for the oil industry, such as drilling rigs and gas injection equipment, are continuing. But, with the exception of the Sakhalin project, Western companies have not become involved directly in oil exploration and development projects.

A series of discussions had been held with Western companies regarding the development of natural gas deposits in the Urengoi area of northwest Siberia and in Yakutia in eastern Siberia.[5] The Western companies were to play a major role in supplying production equipment and building pipelines to transport the gas to liquefaction facilities for LNG exports or to existing pipeline systems for export to Western Europe. In both cases initial proposals in the early 1970s involved LNG exports.

In the Urengoi project, the LNG option has been dropped in favor of building a new pipeline that will permit additional gas exports to Western Europe from the area starting in 1984. The project involves the construction of a 4,500 km., large-diameter pipeline and over 50 compressor stations, stretching from the huge Urengoi field in northwest Siberia to the West German border with Czechoslovakia. Upon completion, approximately 40 billion cubic meters of gas is to be supplied annually over a twenty-year period. The project is estimated at $15 billion, and the Soviet Union was reported to be seeking about $10 billion in export financing for the purchase of pipe and other equipment from Western Europe and Japan. Additional bank credits were also to be arranged in the Eurodollar market. Prospective purchasers of the gas include West Germany (11 billion cubic meters) and France (8 billion cubic meters).[6]

The size of this project is huge by any standard. The total cost, $15 billion, is nearly equal to the Soviet Union's total foreign indebtedness of $16 billion at year-end 1980, and it is 60 percent of the level of Soviet exports to Western industrial countries in 1980.

The Soviet interest in this project reflects a desire to accelerate the development of natural gas production in the Urengoi area and speed its delivery to energy deficient regions in the European USSR, where it can be substituted for oil. Some Urengoi gas has been supplied to the Soviet transmission network since 1978. The long-term Soviet commitments to export some of the Urengoi gas to Western Europe are necessitated by the critical bottleneck posed by insufficient pipeline capacity to bring this gas in large quantities to Soviet consumers. Export earnings from gas sales would also act to offset probable declines in Soviet oil sales to the West.

The Yakutian LNG project would involve a pipeline of some 4,000 kilometers and a gas liquefaction facility for

LNG exports to Japan and the United States. A small credit of $50 million was agreed upon in 1974 for exploration activities. No further progress on the project has been made. The project would require credits at current costs of over $10 billion for full development.

*Forest Products.* In 1969, Japan signed the first of a series of agreements to develop timber resources in Siberia—the Forest Resource Development Project. A second agreement (1974), provided Japanese credits of $550 million in return for deliveries of logs and wood products during 1975–79. A third agreement for the period 1980–84 was delayed following the Soviet intervention in Afghanistan in 1979, but some $1 billion in credit from the Japanese Export-Import Bank was approved in December 1980.[7] Also, discussions have been held with U.S. and Japanese companies for several years regarding a major pulp and paper project at Lesosibirsk on the Yenisei River, costing more than $1 billion.

*Coal.* In 1974, Japan agreed to supply a credit of $450 million for equipment purchases for the development of the Neryungri coal deposits in southern Yakutia. Scheduled deliveries from the project are to begin in 1983. Total annual output from the project is projected at 13 million tons of crude coal, and exports of up to 5 million tons of coking coal concentrate are possible by 1985.[8] Efforts to increase coal exports from Neryungri beyond this volume are probable, and Western companies, probably Japanese, are likely to be invited to participate.

*Aluminum and Copper.* Soviet plans call for the construction of an aluminum smelter with an annual capacity of 500,000 tons at Sayanogorsk on the Yenisei River, where the large Sayan hydroelectric station went on stream in 1978. The contract for Western deliveries of machinery and equipment calls for credits projected at $500 to 600 million. Repayment of these credits would involve exports of about 100,000 tons of aluminum bars to Western Europe and the United States,[9] after the aluminum plant goes into operation, now expected in 1984.

Discussions with Western companies on developing copper deposits located at Udokan in Siberia, with estimated reserves of 1 billion tons, have taken place since the mid-1960s. These talks have proved inconclusive, probably because of the remote location of the site. The completion of the Baikal-Amur Mainline in the mid-1980s is expected to ease problems of access to the project, the cost of which is estimated to be in excess of $2.5 billion.[10] Discussions about the project were held with Japanese companies.[11]

*Asbestos.* The development of large asbestos deposits (long-staple fibers) located at Molodezhny in Siberia is projected following the completion of the BAM railway. The estimated cost of this project is about $150 million.

*Iron Ore.* Soviet planners project the construction of an integrated iron and steel complex to be located at a site yet to be determined in the Far East. Several iron-ore deposits of sufficient size are already known in eastern Siberia.

Part of the output would be designated for export markets.[12]

*Chemicals.* A large refinery-petrochemical project is underway at Tomsk in Siberia. Projected Western purchases of plant and equipment are some $2 billion. Repayments are being offered in the form of bulk chemical products such as methanol, synthetic fibers, raw plastics, and rubber.

## Credit as a Constraint

The main question is to identify which of these major projects, if any, may be constrained by trade or credit, or by a combination of the two. We first look at possible credit constraints.

There are two notable features in the Soviet use of Western credit. One is the importance of credit support from Western governmental agencies; such support may involve direct credits or guarantees on credits from private banks. The other is the major role of "compensation" or product-buy-back agreements. By securing commitments for long-term export sales, these agreements provide an assured repayment of the credits used.

Official financing from Western countries is provided by specialized agencies such as the U.S. Export-Import Bank, Coface in France, Hermes in Germany, and the Export Credits Guarantee Department in Britain. Government credit support was involved in about 50 percent of the estimated $16 billion Soviet gross foreign debt at the end of 1979. This proportion is the highest of any country in Eastern Europe. The Soviets prefer official financing to bank loans because of low, fixed rates of interest and generally longer loan maturities. Fixed interest rates on official credits average about 7.5 percent. In contrast, commercial bank credits are typically based on floating market rates of interest, which for dollar loans rose from about 8.5 percent in 1978 to over 15 percent by early 1980.

A second reason for preferring official financing is political. The Soviet Union has sought to expand commercial relations with the West primarily on the basis of government-to-government agreements. Such agreements help reduce the risks that would normally be associated with expanded commercial ties with market economies. If problems arise, the political agreement provides an assurance that the matter will be viewed in the context of government-to-government bilateral relations. As part of the agreement, the Western country normally commits to provide official export financing for Soviet purchases of capital goods up to a stated total amount.

The failure to reach a U.S.-Soviet trade agreement in 1975, after the passage of the Trade Act of 1974, was a major stumbling block to improved U.S.-Soviet commercial relations. Lacking the political assurances of such an agreement, Soviet leaders have been unwilling to develop closer commercial ties with U.S. companies since that time. Their reluctance appears in retrospect to have been wise. The economic sanctions announced by President Carter in January 1980 after the Soviet intervention in Afghanistan affected only about $150 million in U.S. technology exports. The major compensation project between the two countries, based on U.S. imports of ammonia in return for phosphates was sharply curtailed until the sanctions were lifted by President Reagan in 1981.

Commercial bank credit accounts for most of the remaining Soviet debt. There is an interesting contrast in Soviet practice here. On the one hand, wholly owned Soviet banks are active in the major financial centers in Europe, especially in Paris and London. An extensive network of interbank relationships with Western banks has also been built up over time. Bank-to-bank activities in money market deposits, foreign exchange dealings, and in short- and long-term borrowing are actively pursued. On the other hand, the Soviets have made only sparing use of the syndicated Eurocurrency loan market. This market offers borrowers the possibility of raising much larger sums of cash than through bank-to-bank credits. During the four years 1974–77, the Soviet Union borrowed $1.3 billion in syndicated loans. A further $650 million was added in 1978, but a large part of this sum was used to repay several of the earlier credits.[13] No further credits were negotiated during 1979–80. Up to now, the Soviet Union evidently has not felt the need to expand borrowing possibilities in this market.

Compensation agreements provide secure long-term export commitments, thus insuring that revenues will be generated to repay the credits taken. These agreements are, however, frequently misunderstood. Compensation typically involves two separate contracts, one for the sale of technology by the Western company and another for the sales by the Soviet agency which will supply the resultant product, usually raw materials. In order for the Soviet capital imports to be financed, the two contracts must be legally independent. Commercial banks are willing to assume only the credit risk of the Soviet borrower, the Bank for Foreign Trade. Repayment is therefore guaranteed and is not contingent on whether either side meets the contract provisions. The repayment of credits granted for Soviet imports of capital goods is not contingent on the fulfillment of the parallel contract for sales of the Soviet output from the project. Hence, the compensation agreement by itself does not give a Western bank any additional incentive to lend, since the bank receives the guarantee of the Soviet state in any case.

The link of compensation with credit is made on the Soviet side; it reflects the planners' concerns that a portion of future production be explicitly earmarked for exports. Soviet planners have placed priority on compensation agreements because the long-term purchase commitment by the Western firm provides an assured revenue source for servicing the project's debt. The risk that market prices could fall in the future is therefore borne by the Western partner, as is the risk that prices could rise. Obviously, the Western partner will be willing to accept this risk only if justified by the expected profits from its participation in a project. Pricing agreements for Soviet products to be supplied under compensation agreements are typically calculated with discounts from world market prices, presumably to compensate the

Western partner for perceived added risks in dealing with the USSR.

The compensation agreement has also been linked to government-to-government agreements for large resource projects, such as the export of natural gas to Germany in return for large-diameter pipe. This helps reduce risk to the Soviet side: by offering long-term supply commitments of needed raw materials, official financing can usually be secured for the entire package on advantageous terms.

There are two situations where credit could be a constraining factor in Soviet economic policy decisions. First, total debt could become large enough to cause banks to curtail further lending. Second, the specific form of credits for deals could pose problems, owing, for example, to the large size of individual projects or the desired maturity of the credit.

Size of Debt as a Constraint

Soviet debt could rise to very high levels either from the large credits needed for new development projects, or because exports (say, of oil) decline in the future, causing a fall-off in export revenue. As outlined above, credit makes sense if the associated investment yields an acceptable rate of return net of repayment through export sales. Hence, the level of debt is constrained by a country's present and future export capabilities. One projection of the level of Soviet credit requirements for probable and possible major development projects arrives at a figure of $30 to 35 billion.[14] This is a very large sum; but if the projects are economically viable in the sense noted above, there should be no cause for concern about creditworthiness. The debt will be large, but so will the associated exports.

There would be a problem, of course, if Western credits were used to develop non-viable projects. The evidence to date indicates that Soviet planners are taking a cautious approach to the use of credit. As already mentioned, a large portion of Soviet debt is explicitly linked to future export contracts. Further, the size of the future exports guaranteed by these contracts exceeds, in some cases substantially, the debt repayment obligations of the projects. There appears to be a dedication to export of a certain portion of the output of virtually all major projects, whether or not they are based on compensation.

There is also evidence that a major reassessment by Soviet planners of their borrowing policy has resulted in a more cautious approach to new projects. New orders for plant and equipment from the West rose from $1.7 billion in 1972 to a peak of $6.0 billion in 1976, but then fell to $2.8 billion by 1978; only one new compensation agreement was signed in 1978 and none in 1979.[15] Soviet borrowing from Western banks has also tapered off. Soviet net liabilities to Western banks declined from about $2.3 billion at the end of 1976 to an estimated $1.2 billion in June 1979; a year later the Soviet Union had achieved overall balance with assets and liabilities to Western banks of about $5.6 billion.

The source of this shift in Soviet credit policy is a serious "indigestion" problem in absorbing the Western capital already purchased. The indigestion is caused by shortages of complementary domestic labor and capital and by inadequacies of planning and management. An example of the indigestion problem, discussed in the Soviet press, concerned an ammonia plant being constructed under a compensation agreement with an unidentified Western company. Even though the project had been assigned high priority, the plant was brought on stream behind schedule. The article noted: "The delay was in fact foreordained since the volume of work to be undertaken was not backed up with the necessary resources." There were frequent interruptions in deliveries of materials and equipment, many design errors, and delays in technical documentation. The value of machinery waiting to be installed reached 23 million rubles, half of it accounted for by imported equipment.[16]

Problems such as these appear to be part of the cause of the postponement of major priority projects beyond 1980. The costs to the economy of these deferrals are enormous:[17]

> The costs are high indeed if the expensive multi-billion ruble projects, in some cases well under way, are not brought to a level of effective production in the Fifteen-Year Plan (1976–90). The gestation periods for these major projects, so central to improved future Soviet economic performance, are long in any event, but the possibility for converting facilities, or utilizing partially completed facilities, once the commitments are made, is very small. Regional energy, metal and transportation facilities are sunk costs. The returns come only after completing the economic complexes which provide them.

One example of such costs is illustrated by the delays and indecision in the development of the resource projects located along the BAM. The railroad promises to be underutilized for some time after completion in the mid-1980s because it will take years to bring these projects on stream even if they are started in the near future. The same is true for the new Sayan dam on the Yenisei. When the dam is completed in the early 1980s, there will be a significant lag before its power can be fully used because of delays in developing the associated aluminum smelter. The constraints that have led to these delays are not due to the level of Soviet debt.

On balance, Soviet borrowing policy to date has been conservative. There will undoubtedly be an increase in credits for new projects in the 1980s. But there is little to suggest that Soviet planners will change their views about how credit ought to be used. Despite the slowing of the economy's growth rate, credit use will likely be closely linked to projects with assured export prospects.

One remaining question is whether credit will be used to compensate for a fall-off in oil exports in the future. In a 1977 study the CIA projected a substantial deterioration in the Soviet balance of payments by the mid-1980s. The shift from current oil exports of 1 million barrels a day to the West, to imports projected at 2.7 million barrels a day by 1985 would cost $17 billion in 1977 prices.[18] It is not my purpose here to assess these projections, but to point out

that credit does not offer a solution to the Soviet oil problem.

Credit can play a role in bridging unexpected or temporary balance-of-payments shortfalls, but it is no substitute for the necessary real adjustment to the causes of these shortfalls. Soviet planners are undoubtedly aware of this fact. In 1975, for example, the Soviet hard-currency balance of trade worsened by $6 billion, moving from a surplus of $1.5 billion in 1974 to a deficit of $4.5 billion. Credit was used to cover the deficit, but policy changes were introduced to correct the imbalance. By 1977, the trade balance moved back into a $1.7 billion surplus. Judging by this example it is unlikely that Soviet planners foresee using credit to compensate for a fall-off in oil revenue, except to aid temporarily in facilitating the real adjustment process in the economy.

Form of Credit as a Constraint

The form of credit for specific projects may also impose a constraint. Some of the resource projects discussed above would require very large credits and long repayment terms. The Urengoi natural gas project, for example, will cost well over $10 billion at current prices, and require 10–15 years to be amortized. The maximum term on official and bank credits is currently only 10 years. The proposed Yakutian gas project, of comparable size, is further handicapped by the need for substantial credits from U.S. sources, including the U.S. Export-Import Bank.

Next in line in terms of total credits are the Sakhalin oil and Udokan copper projects, each requiring about $2 to 3 billion. The Sakhalin project is unique in that repayments will be in the form of oil deliveries; the Soviet Union has otherwise been reluctant to agree to such long-term oil delivery contracts to Western buyers. Given Japan's concern about the stability of future oil supplies, there is considerable official interest in seeing that the project moves ahead to the development stage. Credit is not likely to be a problem, although political problems as a result of Afghanistan may slow progress on the project—if sufficient oil reserves are discovered.

The Udokan copper project faces greater problems, because there is much less concern in Japan about future supplies of copper than of energy. Most of the copper to be exported in repayment for the credits would have to be sold on world markets. A major concern of the Japanese companies approached to participate in the project is the risk that world copper prices in the future might fall, causing losses from such sales. Hence, the major constraint on this project is not likely to be credit availability.

Credit arrangements pose obstacles to the implementation of these projects, but so does almost every other aspect of the projects: they are large; their locations are unfavorable; investment commitments are closely interrelated with other major investments in infrastructure; coordination and management tasks are formidable; and export commitments will be huge. In planning for these projects, Soviet planners face a complex set of constraints. Credit is an important constraint, but not the most important.

Another potential constraint from the form of credit relates to interest rates and disclosure. A Soviet decision to increase significantly its Euromarket borrowings from banks would require higher interest rate margins and better economic data. The interest rate on a Soviet syndicated credit in December 1978 was a fixed five-eighths percentage point over the banks' reference lending rate, the London Interbank Rate (LIBOR). The actual interest rate is set every six months at the prevailing LIBOR rate, which approximates the banks' cost. After tax, using the 46 percent U.S. corporate tax rate, a profit margin of five-eights of a point translates into a return on each dollar of credit extended of 0.35 percent. This is well below U.S. banks' desired return on assets in international lending; these targets are not known in detail, but they most likely exceed 0.75 percent on each dollar of loan assets.

The concern of U.S. banks for better economic information is frequently misunderstood. Unlike many West European and Japanese companies, American companies in trade with the Soviet Union do not operate under the umbrella of government-to-government agreements, nor do they enjoy the support of their government to the extent that foreign companies do. This factor, reflected in the 1980–81 embargo on most U.S. exports to the Soviet Union, acts to increase risks for American banks. Economic information is requested, not because the banks expect to find skeletons in the closet, but because information is an essential element of the banks' risk management. It is a factor that helps reduce uncertainty and builds confidence. Better information is necessary if U.S. banks are to be willing to support a significant expansion of lending above the current levels.

There are, therefore, real constraints concerning the form of credit for specific projects. These constraints, however, could effectively be relaxed by changes in Soviet policy and practice. Some of the largest projects could be split up into a sequential or stage-by-stage patterns of development. The Tomsk petrochemical complex, for example, was split into a number of separate plants for purposes of negotiating with Western companies. Modified policies regarding interest rate margins and information disclosure would also relax credit constraints.

Western techniques of project finance could be applied to some very large projects. One technique is production payments, which have been used extensively in oil and gas projects in the West. This is a secured form of financing in which borrowers assign to the lenders part of the rights to the revenues from the sale of the product. A recent example using this approach is a $10 billion LNG project in Nigeria.[19] This project was a potential competitor to the Soviet Urengoi natural gas project, because one of the major partners was Ruhrgas (West Germany), the largest foreign purchaser of Soviet gas. The financing package, which is not yet final, will be based on official export credits for machinery and equipment from the importing countries (the United States and eight West European countries) and project credits from commercial banks. Thus, greater Soviet flexibility in agreeing to financing arrangements may be a factor influencing the ultimate viability of projects.

Even though the obstacles to financing a very large project such as the Urengoi pipeline were ultimately surmounted, there would be constraints to undertaking other large Siberian resource projects. The decision to proceed with the Urengoi pipeline may effectively rule out other multibillion-dollar projects during the 11th Five-Year Plan (1981–85). The constraints would include the inevitable shortages of Soviet domestic capital and labor caused by the priority allocation of resources to the pipeline. Official Western credit agencies would be reluctant to increase their exposure much further due to their budgetary and per-country limits. Another worry is created by the concentration of risk in a single project. Any unforeseen delay in bringing the project on stream or difficulty in operating it according to plan would have serious consequences for Soviet creditworthiness and the institutions that put up the money. This is a reason why practically all of the financing for the project will be provided or guaranteed by Western governments.

Summary

Credit appears neither to offer much help nor to pose much of a constraint to solving the general economic policy problems that face Soviet planners in the 1980s. Solutions to these problems involve real adjustments in the economy, not more credits. Credit may facilitate such adjustments, as in 1975–76, by temporarily bridging unexpected balance-of-payments shortfalls. But the Soviet Union, unlike some of the East European countries, gave top priority to rapidly adjusting to the balance-of-payments problems that followed the 1974–75 world recession. Soviet borrowing policy is likely to remain conservative in the future, with attention paid both to rapid adjustment to balance-of-payments problems and to exports by means of compensation agreements. Soviet planners face a set of complex problems; credit is one of the constraints they face, but it is not at the top of the list.

**Trade as a Constraint**

The major foreign trade issues to examine concern the demand and price outlook for goods the Soviet Union will be exporting and the geographic locations of this demand. This involves an assessment of future demand for Soviet raw materials and the location of these resources relative to major consuming markets.

Prospects for new compensation deals involving raw materials are not promising at present. One factor limiting Western companies' interest in compensation is the current excess world capacity in many industries producing products the Soviet Union would like to export, such as basic chemicals, iron and steel, copper, and wood and pulp products. The depressed chemicals market in Western Europe has already been hard hit by Soviet and East European exports. The volume of imports from the East is still relatively small, no more than 5 percent of total supply;[20] however, the effect of this volume on prices at the margin has been significant. Soviet exports will increase sharply in the next few years as the plants now under construction are finished. The weak market has been a major concern of the Western companies negotiating compensation deals for the Tomsk chemical complex. In this circumstance, the companies do not want the chemical products, or compensation for their involvement, on the terms offered by the Soviets.

Similar concerns are evident in other major resource projects. The Japanese, for example, are reluctant to get involved in taking products from the projected Far Eastern iron and steel mill, given the substantial excess capacity in their domestic steel industry. The large size of the buy-back provisions of the aluminum deal and uncertain future market trends have been a stumbling block to progress in the negotiations with U.S., French and German concerns. A similar problem exists with the Udokan copper project. Firms negotiating on the Lesosibirsk pulp and paper mill have expressed worries about their ability to find outlets at satisfactory prices for paper and pulp products taken as compensation, because of weak markets in Western Europe and Japan.

External demand appears promising only in the cases of oil, natural gas, coal, asbestos, and lumber. All of the projects involving these commodities, with the exception of the new Urengoi natural gas pipeline, are primarily targeted on the Japanese market. The Yakutian LNG project is unlikely to see further development in the next decade because of its large size, complexity, and dependence on U.S. credits and LNG sales at steep prices. The remaining projects—Sakhalin oil, Neryungri coal, Molodezhny asbestos, and the third phase of the Forest Resource Development Project—all have good prospects for export demand. However, there are other problems.

Soviet planners face perhaps a unique set of restrictions in the geographic locations of demands for future exports. The basic thrust of Soviet resource development is toward the east (Siberia and the Far East), where the resources are located. The bulk of existing Soviet export commitments, however, are toward the west, primarily the CMEA countries in Eastern Europe and, to a lesser extent, Western Europe. The increasing cost of transporting resources westward from Siberia, deriving from rising energy costs, is a strong argument for redirecting trade toward the Pacific Basin, particularly Japan. The Pacific Basin option has gained in importance with the construction of the BAM railroad, and the best prospects for new resource projects are in the Japanese market.[21]

Prospects for trade with Japan, however, worsened markedly following the signing of the Japan-China peace and friendship treaty in 1978. One reason for the Japanese decision to tilt toward China in this way was frustration in negotiating the return to Japan of disputed islands north of Hokkaido. In turn, the Soviet Union is said to have threatened retaliatory action against the signing of the Japan-China treaty. Military bases have since been built on two of the islands.[22]

Japanese observers noticed a change in Soviet attitudes at the Tokyo meeting of the Japan-Soviet Business Cooperation Committee in February 1979. According to the Japanese press, the Soviet side indicated a strong desire to obtain Japan's cooperation in Siberian resource development. The Japanese reaction was straightforward:[23]

The Japanese side turned a cold shoulder to new Soviet overtures for participation in big development projects, such as construction of an integrated steel mill, and development of copper at Udokan and asbestos at Molodezhny. Japanese businessmen at the conference told their Soviet counterparts that they would carefully study the proposals which called for Japan's purchase of resources developed and products manufactured. This amounted to shelving the proposals.

The development of the China market in the next few years may hinder Soviet efforts to attract Western companies to Siberian projects. This is particularly true for Japanese companies. Large Soviet and Chinese projects will be competing for the same Western partners, for credits, and also for Western markets. Both China and the Soviet Union have publicized coal and copper projects, and both will be seeking help in developing offshore oil fields. The Chinese coal projects involve steam coal; this is likely to limit Japanese interest in Soviet coal to the special-purpose coking coal from the Neryungri project in Siberia. The Chinese are seeking Japanese participation in developing two copper mines in Anhui and Hubei provinces in China. Both mines are more easily accessible than the Udokan project.[24]

The Soviet Union's trade relations with Eastern Europe are another major factor in the geographic pattern of Soviet trade in the 1980s. Eastern Europe's stake in Soviet oil and other raw materials will continue throughout this period. The Soviet Union may not be able to meet the increments in East European demand to the same extent as in the past, but political considerations suggest that the continuation of raw-material supplies to Eastern Europe will remain a top priority. Given their debt problems, though, Eastern Europe will not be able to contribute much capital for new Soviet raw-material projects. Hence, export commitments to Eastern Europe will restrain efforts to increase exports to the West. And though the Soviet Union gains substantially from CMEA trade, the benefits are largely in the form of consumer rather than investment goods.[25]

In summary, the foreign trade constraints on Soviet resource development are varied and significant. The Soviet insistence on large buy-back provisions is a major stumbling block to the Lesosibirsk pulp and paper project, Udokan copper and the Far East iron and steel mill. Projects with the best prospects include the third phase of the Forest Resource Development Project, Neryungri coking coal, and Molodezhny asbestos. Constraints on projected Soviet resource development from competing resource projects in other countries are evident in natural gas, copper, and, to a lesser extent, coal and oil.

These trade constraints are primarily external, outside the control of Soviet policy. But their influence on Soviet priorities in the context of the long-term plan appear significant. The options that Soviet policymakers may consider using focus primarily on changes in the domestic constraints that limit the effectiveness of imported technology and, to a lesser extent, on changes in credit policy. Given the foreign-market and geographic constraints and the huge costs of deferring priority projects, experimenting with changes in both areas may become more desirable. For such options to have much impact in the period to 1990, however, major decisions would be necessary in the near future. There are no signs at present that such decisions are being contemplated.

## Conclusions

Among the foreign economic options constraining Soviet resource development in the coming decade, those in trade pose the greatest problems and challenges. Market demand and location represent significant constraints on future Soviet resource policy. Soviet planners possess little scope for a flexible adaptation to these constraints. At the same time, prospects for altering domestic constraints to a more efficient utilization of Western technology are dim. These domestic constraints have proven in the past to be very resistant to change, either by economic reform or by greater efficiency with existing institutions. By contrast, constraints on long-term plans for resource development related to credit appear much less important and more susceptible to modification through changes in Soviet policy. The major credit problem stems from the very large size of some of the projects.

In terms of relative importance, the following ranking of constraints on Soviet resource development is suggested:

(1) domestic factors limiting the effectiveness of imported technology, including shortages of domestic capital and labor for use in combination with foreign technology;
(2) foreign market demand and location factors limiting the access of Soviet raw materials; and
(3) factors relating to credit availability.

The ranking points to several conclusions for Western policy. First, the most important limitation on the use of foreign economic options by Soviet policymakers is a domestic one and is not, therefore, under the influence of Western policy. Secondly, the importance of credit availability as a constraining factor on Soviet policy is probably overestimated. Soviet credit policy appears cautious and conservative. For this reason, restrictions by Western governments on lending to the Soviet Union promise little in the way of political leverage. The most important issues for Western policy lie in the trade area, particularly conditions for market access of Soviet raw materials. These issues involve questions of market disruption, fair trade practices, and the regulation of trade in high-technology goods.

The political reaction in the West to the Soviet military involvement in Afghanistan has further limited the Soviet use of foreign economic options, It is difficult to judge how long-lasting and comprehensive the reaction is likely to be in individual countries. It is clear, however, that the response of Japan will be critical for future Soviet resource development plans, since the most promising projects are targeted on the Japanese market. Japan's initial reaction was to postpone decisions on several major project credits that had been under discussion, including the third phase of the Forest Resource Development Project. Another implication of recent political developments is that Western companies, already hesitant, will be even more reluctant to enter into large compensation projects. The risks associated with large buy-back obligations for both the Soviet and Western partners have been clearly illustrated by these political developments.

In light of these conclusions, the Soviet decision to proceed with the Urengoi pipeline project and to accept the substantial risks that it creates may be seen as a critical, even monumental, decision. It provides a reflection of the critical nature of the energy crisis as now perceived by Moscow's decision-makers. It also provides a reflection of the enormous costs that will now have to be borne by the rest of the economy as a result of the country's past inability to cope with its energy problems. It means that the accelerated development of other priority Siberian resource projects will effectively have to be deferred for the better part of the 1980s.

## NOTES

1. The role of Soviet raw-material exports is analyzed in Marshall I. Goldman, *The Changing Role of Raw Material Exports and Soviet Foreign Trade*, Discussion Paper No. 8 (June 1979), Association of American Geographers, Project on Soviet Natural Resources in the World Economy (chapter 27 of this volume).

2. Philip Hanson, "Western Technology in the Soviet Economy," *Problems of Communism* (November-December 1978), p. 22.

3. In addition to previous chapters in this volume, detail on major Soviet resource development projects can be found in Theodore Shabad, "Siberian Resource Development in the Soviet Period," in Theodore Shabad and Victor Mote, *Gateway to Siberian Resources (The BAM)* (New York: Halsted Press, 1977), pp. 1–61; and Dennis J. Barclay, "USSR: The Role of Compensation Agreements in Trade with the West," in U.S. Congress, Joint Economic Committee, *Soviet Economy in a Time of Change*, vol. 2, 96th Congress, 1st session, (Washington, 1979): 462–81; and on a continuing current basis in Shabad's "News Notes," in *Soviet Geography: Review and Translation*.

4. Interview data.

5. For details and history, see Jonathan P. Stern, *Soviet Natural Gas in the World Economy*, Discussion Paper No. 11 (June 1979), Association of American Geographers, Project on Soviet Natural Resources in the World Economy (chapter 15 of this volume).

6. "A Big Gas Deal Strains the U.S. Embargo," *Business Week*, 15 December 1980, p. 41. An agreement on this project was signed in November 1981.

7. *The Japanese Economic Journal*, 30 December 1980, p. 1. The credit also covered imports for several other small projects.

8. Theodore Shabad, "The BAM, Project of the Century," in U.S. Congress, Joint Economic Committee, *Soviet Economy in a Time of Change*, vol. 1 (1979): 173–74.

9. Barclay, "Role of Compensation Agreements," p. 476.

10. Barclay, "Role of Compensation Agreements," p. 478.

11. *The Japanese Economic Journal*, 30 October 1979, p. 12.

12. Shabad, "Siberian Resource Development," p. 174.

13. *Euromoney*, March 1979, p. 12.

14. Barclay, "Role of Compensation Agreements," pp. 473–74.

15. Barclay, "Role of Compensation Agreements," Appendix B; and Paul G. Erikson and Ronald S. Miller, "Soviet Foreign Economic Behavior: A Balance of Payments Perspective," U.S. Congress, Joint Economic Committee, *Soviet Economy in a Time of Change*, vol. 2 (1979): 243.

16. *Stroitelnaya gazeta*, 3 October 1979, p. 1.

17. John P. Hardt, "Military or Economic Superpower: A Soviet Choice." (Paper presented at the U.S. Military Academy, West Point, N.Y., 15–17 June 1978) p. 14.

18. Central Intelligence Agency, *Soviet Economic Problems and Prospects* (June 1977), p. 22. The CIA subsequently modified its forecast of major Soviet oil imports by the mid-1980s.

19. *New York Times*, 5 March 1980, p. D5; and *Financial Times* (London), 5 March 1980, p. 6.

20. "Chemicals in the East Explode West," *The Economist*, 10 February 1979, p. 84.

21. A thorough assessment of Japanese views toward Siberian development can be found in Richard L. Edmonds, *Siberian Resource Development and the Japanese Economy: The Japanese Perspective*, Discussion Paper No. 12 (August 1979), Association of American Geographers, Project on Soviet Natural Resources in the World Economy (chapter 9 of this volume).

22. "Changes in Soviet Stance," *The Japanese Economic Journal*, 27 February 1979, p. 10.

23. Ibid.

24. *The Japanese Economic Journal*, 30 October 1979, p. 18.

25. Paul Marer, "The Soviet Union and Eastern Europe: Economic Dimensions." (Paper presented to the American Political Science Association Convention, Washington, 31 August 1979), pp. 12–14.

# V

# IMPLICATIONS

# 31

# THE IMPLICATIONS OF SOVIET RAW MATERIALS FOR THE WORLD ECONOMY

ROBERT G. JENSEN
THEODORE SHABAD
ARTHUR W. WRIGHT

The primary objective of this volume has been to analyze the Soviet resource potential in energy and industrial raw materials with attention to possible implications for the world economy in the period to 1990. With that aim in mind, the contributors to the volume explored three broad but closely related dimensions of the problem. Part II of the book analyzes the challenge to resource development posed by the continental scale of the Soviet economy and by the striking spatial maldistribution of resource supplies and demands—problems that are exacerbated by inhospitable natural environments and lack of infrastructure in much of the area targeted for resource development. Part III examines in detail the development patterns and prospects of energy goods and industrial raw materials that might have long-term potential as exports and therefore, perhaps, some special significance in terms of world markets and Western policy concerns. Finally, in Part IV, we consider the crucial role of raw materials in Soviet foreign trade with attention to the policy dilemma that faces the USSR in dividing exports between its allies in the Soviet bloc and the Western nations including Japan. It remains now to summarize our findings and to assess the implications of the Soviet potential in energy and industrial raw materials in the broader context of Soviet relations with the world economy.

## Summary of Findings

Despite its position as a major industrial power, the Soviet Union has played a surprisingly limited role in the rapid expansion of world trade that took place after World War II. By 1980 the Soviet Union ranked only seventh in value of exports, just ahead of the Netherlands. In part, of course, the limited role of the Soviet Union in the world economy simply reflects the enormous geographic scale of its economy along with its diversified resource base and large domestic market. These features have enabled the USSR to reap benefits from interregional domestic trade that would be possible for countries with much smaller area or population only through international trade. The limited role of the USSR in the world economy also reflects the traditional desire of Soviet leaders for a high degree of self-sufficiency, to insulate domestic planning from the vagaries of international market forces and from the political hostility of capitalist trading-partner nations.

It is by no means certain that the Soviet Union has abandoned its *long-term* goal of maintaining a high degree of economic self-sufficiency, but there is no question in the short term that there has been a pronounced shift in policy toward the use of international trade as an integral part of Soviet economic strategy. This shift, as we suggest in Chapter 26, has little to do with a desire for greater integration in the world economy *per se* but instead represents a perception that trade can alleviate a number of critical problems in the domestic economy—declining rates of growth in the labor force, capital goods saturation in many industries, and above all an apparent lag in developing and introducing advanced technology and improved methods of production at a pace sufficient to offset reduced capital effectiveness and to meet new economic challenges.

Despite more than a century of industrialization, Soviet efforts during the 1970s to expand international trade, in order to alleviate domestic economic problems, followed the traditional Russian pattern of exporting natural-resource products to pay for imports of manufactured goods and modern technology. In recent years, raw-material exports have accounted for more than 50 percent of total Soviet exports and more than 80 percent of hard-currency earnings. Thus, as we have argued, the Soviet Union has a pattern of international trade more akin to a developing country than a modern, industrial superpower. This feature of Soviet trade is more than statistical in that imported capital goods are a significant input into the expansion of the very raw-material production itself that must sustain the exports. Although the Soviet Union has been able to reap substantial profits from energy products and some other raw-material exports over the past decade, its reliance on resource exports is not viewed with enthusiasm by the leadership. But efforts to change the export mix by increasing the share of manufactured goods or even by upgrading raw-material products have not met with significant success because the relative technological backwardness that called for expanded trade in the first place remains a barrier to the export of higher value-added items.

Because the Soviet Union is not likely to improve its competitive position in world markets for manufactured goods in the foreseeable future, we conclude that it will continue to depend heavily on the export of natural-resource products through the present decade if not well into the 21st century. The composition of these exports may change (e.g., from oil to natural gas, or from energy products to nonfuel resources) depending on domestic requirements and international markets, but the evidence presented in this volume suggests that the share of raw materials in total exports will remain high.

For the above reasons, Soviet resource development should no longer be viewed in isolation from the global economy. Despite current economic and political problems, the Soviet Union not only will continue to be virtually self-sufficient in energy and industrial resources, but has the potential, in terms of its resource base, to become more important in world markets for a number of raw materials. The extent to which that potential is realized will depend on the success and timing of complex regional development programs, the particular problems of individual resource projects, and a variety of domestic and international factors that will determine the volume and direction of Soviet foreign trade. Having examined each of these dimensions, we conclude that the period to 1990 is too short a time span for Soviet resource potential to be significantly realized and that, with some exceptions (notably natural gas), Soviet natural resources will play no more important a role in foreign trade or in world commodity markets than at present. In the longer term, after 1990, given current and prospective development efforts, Soviet natural resources could conceivably be more important in the world economy—or less.

## Resource Development in a Regional Context

One of the central arguments of this book is that Soviet resource potential must be evaluated in its regional context. Limited data notwithstanding, there is little doubt that the Soviet Union is basically self-sufficient in energy and industrial raw materials with a potentially large "surplus" that may be made available to the world economy. But, in the Soviet case especially, the simple existence of an enormous and varied resource base does not necessarily equate with the potential availability of resources. The latter, in any given period of time, will depend on relative location, environmental conditions, and the ability to provide labor, capital, and technology appropriate to the situation. Our investigation along these lines suggested that Soviet resource potential is likely to be more limited in the period to 1990 than previously thought.

The energy, mineral and forest resouces of the USSR are overwhelmingly concentrated in Soviet Asia, which contains most of the proven energy reserves, 70 percent of all standing timber and, except for iron ore and manganese, most of the nonfuel minerals as well. For the most part this vast area is relatively underdeveloped,

sparsely populated, and characterized by some of the most challenging physical environments to be found anywhere. In contrast, the European USSR, with a population of some 200 million, is faced with rising resource costs and serious deficits in basic energy supplies as local sources are becoming depleted. Thus, as we have shown, the Soviet Union must obtain increasing shares of most of its raw-material supplies from its vast Asian regions. Thus current and future development east of the Urals will be the key not only to the Soviet Union's domestic supplies but also to its potential as a raw-material exporter.

The economic development of Siberia is a classic example of heartland-hinterland relationships—capital and technology flow from the west to east and raw materials from east to west. A similar relationship applies to Soviet trade with Western Europe and the bloc countries, for example, in the development and flow of West Siberian oil and gas resources. Farther eastward in Siberia, the same kind of relationship may be suggested but it is oriented differently, toward the Pacific basin.

The concept of an economic north-south watershed dividing Siberia in accord with the flow of raw materials to the east or to the west (see Chapter 10) is important to our understanding of Soviet resource development and export potential. The overriding aim of resource development in the Soviet Far East, for example, appears to be exports to markets in the Pacific Basin rather than supplies of raw-material inputs for Soviet industry in the nation's distant western regions. Such an aim was dramatically illustrated by the Soviet decision in 1974 to go ahead with the construction of the Baikal-Amur Mainline (BAM) railroad, which is supposed to open up a vast new resource area in East Siberia and the Far East (see chapter 7).

The potential impact of the BAM and its resource hinterland are carefully evaluated in this book. In general, we conclude that initial Soviet enthusiasm for the project may have led to a somewhat overoptimistic assessment over the short term. By 1990 only one or two BAM area resources (coal and timber) are likely candidates for export. After that time, depending on foreign demand, additional commodities (asbestos, copper) could be exported but not to such an extent that they would be a decisive factor in Pacific markets. Even in a military-strategic perspective the BAM appears to have only limited significance for the Soviet position in East Asia beyond that which already exists (see Chapter 10). The BAM will, of course, have considerable impact in its immediate hinterland, focusing on certain nodes of development and territorial-production complexes, but even when these domestic benefits are added, the short-term benefits of the project do not seem to be what must have been hoped for, given the magnitude of Soviet investment. Long-term benefits may justify the project, but these are difficult to assess with any precision.

## Soviet Resource Potential

This volume documents the well known fact that the Soviet Union has one of the world's largest resource bases by virtue of its large size—nearly one-sixth of the earth's inhabited land area, not counting Antarctica—and diversified geological setting. As a result of the development of that potential to date, the USSR has become one of the largest producers of energy and raw materials in the world. Its domestic economy, among the two or three largest, consumes much of the output, but, in many cases, production in excess of consumption has made significant exports available to the rest of the world.

The Soviet Union's position in world resource markets has been affected over the years by two contrasting policies. Until the early to middle 1950s, the stress was on a policy of self-sufficiency aimed at insuring domestic supplies and avoiding dependence on imports from what Soviet policy-makers general regarded as a hostile world. The self-sufficiency policy was pursued even if the Soviet resource base in particular minerals was inadequate and their development incurred substantial costs, for example, in nonbauxitic ores for the aluminum industry. Since the late 1950s, and particularly during what has become known as the period of détente starting in the early 1970s, the Soviet Union has relaxed its past concern for self-sufficiency and has become willing to rely increasingly on interaction with the world economy. The new willingness to participate in the "international division of labor" has manifested itself not only in increased volumes of mineral exports, but in surprising dependence on imports of raw materials for industries that are considered strategic, notably bauxite ore for the aluminum industry.

The assessment of future trends in Soviet resource development has been hampered by the statistical secrecy that has traditionally veiled a large sector of Soviet economic activity. Reserves data have been made public for coal and natural gas, but not for oil, and for iron ore, manganese and chromium ore among the metals. Neither reserves nor production figures are being made available for the nonferrous metals. However, the Soviet reserves position alone, even if it were known in all cases, would not suffice to determine the likelihood of future developments. Since much of the resource base is found in uninhabited and undeveloped regions of Siberia, far from population and consumption centers and under severe climatic and environmental conditions, the opening up of newly identified deposits will often depend on the commitment of labor, capital and advanced technology and equipment. In most cases, new projects are dependent on the provision of new transportation routes and other infrastructure. The Soviet planners have seen a graphic illustration of the Marxist proposition that man, not nature, produces raw materials.

Our findings regarding Soviet resource potential and prospects of development through 1990 can best be summarized for two broad categories of products—the fossil fuels and the nonfuel minerals.

*Fossil Fuels.* The USSR is the world's largest producer of oil, the second largest producer of coal (after the United States) and is likely to surpass the United States in the production of natural gas in the mid-1980s. Nevertheless, the Soviet position in these energy goods is not equally promising in all cases. In coal, a period of stagnation has set in since the late 1970s as old deposits have gradually approached depletion and the development of new deposits has lagged. Although the resource base in coal is ample in sheer tonnage, about one-fifth of Soviet coal output is low-calorific brown coal or lignite, which is economically best used for power generation near mines and does not figure in world trade. Moreover, large domestic demands of the Soviet economy on the relatively more limited high-grade coal resources (anthracite and bituminous coking and steam coals) severely limit prospects for significant growth of coal exports through the 1980s. The principal exception is the development of the Neryungri bituminous coal deposit in southern Yakutia for export to Japan. Over the long term, the magnitude of Soviet coal exports will turn on world market demand and domestic extraction costs, both highly uncertain at this point.

In the case of oil, a once-mighty growth industry and still a key source of export earnings now faces uncertain prospects for the future. Total Soviet oil production has entered a period of stagnation or even possible decline through the 1980s as efforts are being made to develop the remote new West Siberian fields at a rate matching declines in older oil fields, notably the Volga-Urals. Although the Soviet planners have projected a slight growth in oil production in the first half of the 1980s, from 603 million metric tons in 1980 to 630 million in 1985, some Western specialists expect a gradual decline to set in. West Siberia is the last major oil-bearing province that has been identified in the Soviet Union. Judging from current exploration and development efforts, West Siberia is expected to engage the attention of the Soviet oil industry at least through the 1980s. Where it can or will turn next is not clear. With the leveling off of oil production and the continuing importance of oil exports as a source of foreign exchange for the Soviet Union, efforts are under way to achieve economies in domestic consumption of oil. The success of these efforts, on which the Soviet Union's ability to continue exports will depend, remains to be seen.

Natural gas offers the brightest outlook for the period through 1990 and beyond. Ambitious current development efforts are focusing on the Arctic gas fields of West Siberia (Chapter 15). In contrast to oil, where new reserves are scattered in medium and small-size fields, the West Siberian gas reserves are in supergiant deposits that enable concentrated development within a relatively limited area. The principal constraint in natural gas is not field development, but the laying of thousands of miles of large-diameter pipelines needed to transmit the gas to markets in the European USSR and for export to Eastern and Western Europe.

The West Siberian gas fields are so large that virtually the entire development effort during the first half of the 1980s is focused on the single field of Urengoi; the more northerly Yamburg field is scheduled to become the center of development in the second half of the 1980s. Soviet planners apparently view natural gas both as a substitute for crude oil in domestic consumption and as a partial replacement for declining hard-currency exports of oil to

Western Europe. While West Siberian gas development for overland pipeline transmission to Europe proceeds, the long-projected development of Far Eastern (Yakutian) gas reserves for exports as liquefied natural gas to Japan and possibly the West Coast of the United States is now in abeyance.

Aside from the fossil fuels, the Soviet Union has been building up a potential for energy exports in the form of nuclear-generated electricity. The nuclear power program, which is concentrated in the energy-short European USSR, envisages a series of large nuclear stations in the western border regions adjoining Eastern Europe. Nuclear generating capacity already in place supported electricity exports of 20 billion kilowatt-hours in 1981, and increases in both capacity and exports are planned for the 1980s. There have been discussions of a high-voltage intertie between the Soviet Union and West European power grids, taking advantage of time-zone differences to shift electricity back and forth according to periods of peak demand, but no concrete plans for such an exchange of electricity have been announced. Indirectly related to the energy picture are the Soviet Union's uranium enrichment services, which have become an increasingly important part of the international nuclear fuel cycle. These services involve the enrichment and re-export of uranium supplied by nuclear power utilities in Western Europe and elsewhere.

*Nonfuel Minerals.* These minerals can be divided into three categories in terms of Soviet resource potential and possible impact on world markets: (1) those produced well in excess of domestic consumption; (2) those for which production and consumption have been roughly balanced; and (3) those for which the Soviet Union has relied on imports for a substantial part of its consumption.

Among the export-oriented minerals, the Soviet Union is the world's largest producer of iron ore and manganese and is second only to South Africa in chromite production. The USSR has maintained its leading position in iron ore despite a deterioration in the quality of the resource base, as high-grade direct-shipping ores have become depleted and the emphasis has shifted to the use of lower-grade ores requiring beneficiation (Chapter 19). Of the roughly 500 million metric tons of crude ore mined in the USSR, more than 85 percent must be enriched, yielding about 180 million tons of usable ore in addition to some 70 million tons of direct-shipping ore. Virtually the entire Soviet iron ore output is either consumed by the domestic iron and steel industry or supplied to the steel industries of Eastern Europe, mainly Poland and Czechoslovakia. The potential for Soviet iron-ore exports outside the bloc appears to be limited. The start of production at the Finnish-assisted ore project of Kostomuksha in Karelia will make some ore available to the small Finnish steel industry and, over the longer term, the Baikal-Amur Mainline may open up East Siberian ore deposits in the Chara-Tokko and Aldan districts of Yakutia, either for export or as a basis for a projected iron and steel industry in the Soviet Far East, or both.

Manganese and chromite used to be important Soviet

mineral exports. But over the years the USSR has lost its share of the world market to competitive producing countries like South Africa, Gabon, Brazil and Australia, and it now supplies mainly the East European allies (Chapter 21). In chromite, the traditional advantage that the Soviet Union has enjoyed in its large high-grade ore deposit at Khromtau in northwest Kazakhstan has been eroded by technological change (Chapter 22). The development of a process in the early 1970s making it possible to use lower-grade chromite ores in stainless steel manufacture has worked to the benefit of South Africa, which has large reserves of the cheaper, lower-quality material.

While these traditional exports have lost their past positions in the world market, other minerals have become more significant. These include titanium and nickel and such high-value minerals as the platinum-group metals, diamonds and gold.

The development of the USSR into the world's largest producer of titanium, a strategic metal with military as well as industrial applications, dates from the late 1950s, when major deposits began to be developed in the Ukraine. Although much of current output is used at home, Soviet exports of titanium are expected to continue through the 1980s. The increasingly strong Soviet export position in nickel has been made possible by the development of the rich minerals complex at Norilsk in northern Siberia (Chapter 23). The importance of Norilsk, which yields not only nickel, but also copper, cobalt and platinum-group metals, can be judged from the large investment that Soviet planners have allocated to the construction of some of the deepest of Soviet mines to reach the rich ore bodies in the area, the development of a large city and other infrastructure under Arctic conditions, and the construction of a fleet of nuclear-powered icebreakers to insure the year-round delivery of Norilsk minerals output through the Arctic Ocean.

Little information is available on prospects in such high-value minerals as the platinum-group metals, diamonds and gold. However, the emphasis on the development of Norilsk, the main source of platinum and allied metals, suggests continued strength in Soviet exports. Diamond production appears to be holding steady or increasing in the principal production centers of Yakutia (Mirny, Udachny, and Aikhal). And the detailed study of gold included this volume (Chapter 24) documents the growth of Soviet gold production as the traditional center of production in northeast Siberia was supplemented in the 1960s by new mining centers in Uzbekistan and in the 1970s in Armenia.

Among nonmetallics, the Soviet Union has developed and is expected to maintain a strong export position in potash, a key input for agricultural fertilizer, and in asbestos, a traditional export. Soviet asbestos exports to Pacific Basin markets are expected to expand eventually as a result of the development of the Molodezhny deposit in Siberia's Buryat ASSR after the BAM provides access to the area in the mid-1980s. Mention should also be made of the buildup of the Soviet Union's ammonia industry, partly as a result of the barter deal with Occidental Petroleum Corporation signed in 1973. This deal, which calls for the exchange of Soviet ammonia, urea (another nitrogenous fertilizer) and potash for superphosphoric acid from the United States, stimulated not only the development of the world's largest ammonia industry, but the construction of two specialized chemical ports to handle the shipments—Yuzhny near Odessa and Ventspils in Latvia.

A rough balance between production and consumption appears to have been achieved in the Soviet Union in most other minerals, notably the base metals (copper, lead, zinc). Though first in the world in lead and zinc refining and second in refined copper production (after the United States), the Soviet Union has been hard pressed to maintain growth in these metals, mainly because of a lag in the development of additional ore resources. Its situation is probably strongest in copper, and exports are likely to increase once a decision is made to develop the large Udokan copper deposit in Siberia's Chita Oblast, another key mineral site that is to be made accessible by construction of the BAM.

Finally, there is the interesting group of minerals in which the Soviet Union, either out of choice or out of necessity, has become dependent on imports for part of its supplies. Most significant in this group is the heavy dependency on imports of bauxite, the aluminum ore, which is coming mainly from Guinea, and of alumina, the intermediate product, resulting from a paucity of high-grade bauxite resources within the Soviet Union. Among minerals that the USSR imports from allied countries are cobalt and nickel from Cuba, and fluorspar and molybdenum from Mongolia. Soviet domestic production of tin and tungsten, most of it in remote Siberian regions, is also supplemented by imports. Finally, there is the dependency on phosphate fertilizer materials, which involves not only the American shipments of superphosphoric acid from Florida, but also imports of phosphate from Morocco.

Foreign Trade Policy and Constraints

Since the late 1960s, the USSR has deliberately increased the use of hard-currency imports to improve its domestic performance. The increased hard-currency exports required to pay for those imports have consisted heavily of natural resources. As Marshall Goldman shows in Chapter 27, the heavy reliance on primary-product exports perpetuates a longstanding feature of Russian foreign trade behavior. As in the past, this reliance appears to make sense in terms of comparative advantage and will likely continue to do so for the foreseeable future. At the same time, it is important to recognize that the bias toward raw-material exports cannot be explained solely by comparative advantage. The Soviet institutional and planning system, not prices, almost guarantees a comparative inability to sell products to the West, *except* for relatively homogeneous raw materials.

Goldman sees continued pursuit of a raw-material export strategy as posing several challenges to Soviet decision-makers. The challenge of overcoming hostile climate and terrain and then of transporting goods thousands of miles is amply documented in parts I and II

of this volume. Another challenge that Goldman treats at some length is the planning and management of natural-resource development. Past practices, while workable, have not been overly efficient. Indeed, Soviet successes in developing natural resources for export can almost be said to have been achieved in spite of planning and management techniques that reward the wrong things and punish the right ones. Yet a third challenge analyzed by Goldman is responding in a timely way to shifts in relative world prices. The experience during the two previous world oil shocks shows that Moscow is willing and (despite lame institutions) able to swing oil supplies from domestic uses to exports, and from Comecon to the hard-currency countries, and then back again, within a relatively short time. That experience also demonstrates, though, that the planned change in foreign exchange balances for a given plan year acts as a brake on shifts of goods between domestic and world market uses. Thus, following sudden increases in world prices the Soviets have temporarily cut back oil export volumes, using the extra slack thus provided for domestic purposes; and with the softness in world oil prices of 1982 Soviet planners were able to raise export volumes somewhat to help offset the unexpected drop in hard-currency earnings.

Edward Hewett in Chapter 28 demonstrates that the Soviet use of primary products as a balance-of-payments adjustment mechanism is not confined to oil. Hewett finds systematic evidence, for a group of raw materials, of shifts in the regional pattern of exports—among Western, Comecon, and less developed countries—in response to movements over time in the terms of trade, both for all raw materials relative to other goods and within the group of raw materials itself. His finding that developing countries play an important role in Soviet hard-currency balance-of-payments adjustments is surprising but (once we have seen it) quite comprehensible. Overall, Hewett's results lend support to the view that one cannot fully understand Soviet foreign-trade behavior without looking at the world market; and conversely, the "non-Communist world market" is a potentially serious distortion of reality in studying foreign trade patterns.

In Chapter 26, we analyzed the complex interaction between Soviet trade with the Comecon countries of Eastern Europe and Soviet exports of natural resources. We spoke of a constant "tension" between shipments to Comecon countries and shipments to hard-currency countries, arising from the customs-union differential in intra- and extra-bloc terms of trade. George Hoffman's analysis, in Chapter 29, provides a detailed illustration of that tension for the crucially important case of energy. Hoffman shows that Eastern Europe has no really good options—given a bloc goal of maintaining minimum economic growth performance—except for the Soviet Union to provide liberal terms of trade on energy shipments within Comecon. Such terms of course translate into the USSR subsidizing its smaller allies and thereby forgoing part of its potential gains from exporting energy goods. In effect, liberal terms of trade in energy heighten the tension cited above. One implication of some consequence for Western energy importers is that Soviet energy exports may be less reliable than past Soviet performance would indicate. When the chips are down, curtailments of exports (even if temporary) to the West may be necessary to permit Moscow to fulfill its obligations to its East European allies. The analyses by Goldman and Hewett support this view.

The use of foreign trade to spur domestic economic performance opens the Soviet economy up to events in world markets. In particular, the use of a form of foreign investment to develop new export capacities in natural-resource industries means that the Soviets may face foreign as opposed to domestic constraints on the exportation of natural resources. Lawrence Brainard in Chapter 30 demonstrates, however, that domestic constraints, related to systemic failures of the command economy, are much more likely to be binding on Soviet decision-makers than foreign constraints. Provided they have sound projects, financial capital will be available to the Soviets. There is no getting around the possibility of price declines for Soviet export goods, but even there a variety of institutional arrangements can be and indeed have been used to share or diversify the risks.

### The Implications of Soviet Resource Export Potentials

We noted at the outset of this work that Soviet resource potential and strategy and the implications of expanded or reduced exports of energy and industrial raw materials from the USSR were likely to be of increasing international interest in the years ahead. That observation, if one judges it by the attention such questions have had in the press and in government-commissioned studies, has so far proved to be remarkably correct.

Soviet foreign trade in general and exports of natural resources in particular have become especially topical, indeed, even controversial. The Reagan administration has adopted a stiffer position toward Moscow than previous administrations on a broad range of issues—military expenditures, the crisis in Poland, continued fighting in Afghanistan, support for insurgencies in the developing world, and so on. Soviet natural resource potential figures directly in the debates over what United States and Western policy should be toward the USSR, because exports of energy and other strategic raw materials raise questions about economic dependence and the use of the latter for political leverage. Expanded exports of natural gas to Western Europe and the broader issues of "resource wars" are two examples. Thus, attempts to constrain natural-resource exports (and technology imports) are a possible focus for United States and Western policy aimed at hindering Soviet domestic development and foreign policy.

It is difficult, many would say not possible or even desirable, to separate the political and strategic aspect of East-West trade from the narrower issue of the mutual economic benefits that can be derived from trade. Questions about who may be dependent on whom, who has leverage over whom, and whether the results of sanctions merit the associated costs must therefore be addressed. The United States and its Western allies are divided on these questions and they are likely to remain

contentious issues in the years ahead. This is especially true if the West continues to be plagued by sluggish economic growth and high unemployment.

Running controversies concerning Soviet trade are difficult to keep in perspective and, to evaluate the different positions governments take, one must have a firm grasp of the underlying substance on which Soviet decisions are likely to be based in both the short and long term. We want to emphasize that the purpose of this book has been to reveal the substance on which Soviet decisions will be based, not to provide ammunition for the various sides of controversies.

A major contribution of this volume is to bring out the forces that underlie Soviet decisions on natural-resource production, consumption, and export or import. Any two of these three decisions imply the third. But one point brought out clearly is that export-import decisions need not always be the mere result of production and consumption decisions—i.e., a "surplus" left over out of domestic output after domestic "needs" are met. For commodities like oil and gas or gold, and for complex regional-resource development projects like the BAM, export-import decisions may be based on special considerations (such as how to raise hard currency to purchase advanced equipment and technology) that may determine the pace of development or changes in policy regarding domestic use of any particular resource. Thus, while it is important to comprehend the extent of reserves and costs of extraction, processing, and transportation, it is equally necessary to consider Soviet regional policy and foreign trade strategy to understand the likely impact of Soviet natural resources on world markets. This book does so in each of its major parts.

The Soviet Union apparently made a conscious decision in the late 1960s to abandon its exclusive reliance on self-sufficiency and to make greater use of world markets. The hoped-for gains would come in the form of imports, especially of goods embodying advanced technology, most of which had to be paid for in convertible or "hard" currencies. The necessary costs would be exports of domestic production for hard currencies. Given comparative advantage as it then stood and still does today, most of these exports had to be raw materials, whether primary or processed.

Part of the cost of the Soviet decision to make more use of world markets was to make the USSR more sensitive to the shifts and turns to which those markets are susceptible. Changes in world prices of traded goods affect a centrally planned economy no less than a market economy. Indeed, the centrally planned economy may be *more* vulnerable to changes in market conditions than a market economy because of the rigidities inherent in command planning. Once a plan (in all its full, interlocking complexity) is set, it is not easy to alter individual components of it, whether inputs or outputs, without risking harm to other, interdependent components. This is true of hard-currency imports and exports as well as their soft-currency or domestic counterparts. For this reason, any plan must contain at least an implicit planned change in hard-currency balances.

Enter unexpected changes in world prices. An increase

in import prices or a decrease in export prices will throw off hard-currency planning, necessitating some adjustment. Possibilities include: doing nothing for now, mortgaging the hard-currency reserves of future periods; increasing exports (difficult in the short term for reasons cited above); reducing imports (also difficult); or obtaining additional foreign credits, again mortgaging future hard-currency reserves for repayment of the debts. The opposite price change—a decrease in import prices or an increase in export prices—poses less of a challenge. Even here, though, the centrally planned economy may have more difficulty than a market economy in making effective use of the increase in purchasing power that such a change makes possible.

With the rapid changes (up *and* down) in world natural-resource prices of the 1970s and early 1980s, the USSR (like other industrial powers) has been confronted with the necessity of making a series of adjustments. When prices rise, the Soviets reap windfalls on existing production, but they must make major investments to expand capacity to take maximum advantage of the higher prices. By the same token, when prices fall, they must absorb windfall losses on existing production and face the prospect of idle or underutilized production capacity—and a *de facto* write-down of the value of part of their capital stock. Oil and gold are the most conspicuous examples of world market instability since the early 1970s, but they are by no means the only examples. Virtually every major metal and most of the minor ones have been subjected to sharp price run-ups followed by sudden declines and subsequent price volatility since the early 1970s.

The Soviets are well aware of the double-edged nature of market risks. This is clearly evidenced by the variety of institutional arrangements they have used for natural-resource projects geared to long-term commitments. Depending on the identity of the project partner (capitalist firm, socialist government, and so on), they have used joint ventures, contributed inputs, and long-term contracts with floating price terms. All of these arrangements include a large element of sharing of equity risks.

The position of the Soviet Union in world markets is by and large that of a price taker. That is, it cannot export enough of most products to significantly affect world prices. Thus, Moscow is limited to responding to changes in prices and to forming expectations about future price movements in determining the best responses. This is the situation, for instance, in oil, iron ore and copper. The situation is unclear for natural gas, because of the relatively great importance of spatial factors in gas markets. The West European gas market, for instance, has only three viable sources of supply—northern Europe, Algeria, and the USSR—with an upper limit placed on price by LNG imports. An obvious exception is gold, for which the Soviet Union appears to possess substantial market power and hence the ability to manipulate price.

But we should be cautious about leaping to conclusions here. What will govern *how* exactly the Soviets will manipulate price? If the USSR wants hard-currency imports (as we assume), they will behave as monopolists and set the monopoly rate of exports. Monopolists are constrained by demand; they cannot raise prices at will. In particular, the behavior of monopolies does not include denying access to products for political gain. At most, it implies a greater ability to threaten a punitive cutoff, because of their large relative size in the market.

This discussion has some bearing on the issue of whether the Soviets are positioning themselves in natural-resource markets to be able to engage in "resource wars." (The notion itself goes back at least to the 18th century, but more recently to some of the rhetoric before World War I. It is one of those concepts—another is "administered pricing"—that survives despite the virtual absence of empirical evidence for it.) In order to be able to conduct a resource war successfully, one must control enough of each product involved to create widespread disruption in the world market, *and* one must have such control over a number of different resources. In addition, it is necessary to stockpile products in which one might be vulnerable to retaliation. We are talking here not about mere monopoly power in one or two world markets, but about significant monopoly strength in a fairly large number of markets. Given what we know about world natural-resource markets, such strength is inconceivable for the Soviet Union.

A further factor in understanding the likelihood of a Soviet resource war against the West is to note that, while the USSR is an exporter of many different natural resources, it is also a high-cost producer of many of them, e.g., oil, gas, iron ore, etc. This would make it expensive to establish the necessary monopoly strength for a resource war.

Proponents of the "resource wars" argument (discussed in Chapter 1) have cited Soviet imports of chromite from Iran in 1979 as evidence in support of their position. But we suggest (Chapter 27) that this is hardly a sign that the Soviets are attempting to corner the market. More likely that deal, and similar ones, represent a simple attempt to overcome some kind of bottleneck in meeting plan commitments. In looking ahead it will not be surprising if the Soviets import modest quantities of a number of nonfuel minerals from time to time along with bauxite and alumina, which have become regular imports. But we think it is even more likely that on balance the Soviets will be exporting raw materials (perhaps more than they might like) because they have little else to sell in hard-currency markets.

The East European connection is undoubtedly very important to Moscow. In interpreting its impact on Soviet natural-resource exports, though, several points should be kept in mind. One is that the USSR would export many raw materials to Eastern Europe, even if the only factor considered were comparative advantage and relative transport costs. A second point is that, to a large extent, whatever the Soviets ship to Eastern Europe displaces trade on the world market. That is, East European demands are in fact part of world demand, and Soviet supplies are in fact part of world supply, even if the USSR and its allies trade among themselves within Comecon. The displacement is not 1-to-1, necessarily, because of the customs-union effect and its distortion of relative prices within and without the borders of the customs union. A third point is that, in trying to understand how the USSR and Eastern Europe will adjust to changes in market prices for natural resources, account must be taken of that customs-union effect. It is not unusual, for example, that the USSR would hold down the price of oil to Eastern Europe temporarily, following a world-price increase, to permit the East Europeans time to adjust. The Soviets are, of course, providing a subsidy by holding the price down; when prices eventually rise, therefore, it should not be taken as a sign that Moscow is working against the interest of its allies. Nor can one tell how fast Moscow is reducing the subsidy merely by looking at increases in oil prices; we should try to look at other changes in intra-Comecon terms of trade as well.

The bloc countries are, of course, a kind of "spatial sponge" soaking up Soviet raw-material exports that might otherwise be made available to other world markets. We conclude that East European dependence on the Soviet Union, combined with Soviet responsibility for sustaining the bloc economies (and maintaining a high degree of political control), will be a limiting factor for raw-material exports to the West. The Soviets, as we have shown, may shift exports from the bloc to the West to earn hard currency, but only within limits. Even though the need for hard currency and the technology it buys may be great, the Soviet Union cannot suddenly abandon Eastern Europe.

With only a few exceptions, then, Soviet raw-material exports do not and will not directly play a decisive role in world markets. We find no evidence to suggest their overall position will change significantly in the period to 1990. However, during that time the Soviets will continue to make vigorous efforts to expand production and to export raw materials outside the Soviet bloc, because it is only by doing so that imports of grain and technology can be continued. But the volume of trade, measured in terms of the size of the Soviet economy and the economies of major trading partners, is not likely to be large enough to result in significant or unequal dependence in either direction. This is not to say that trade is unimportant. The kind of sanctions that have been urged by some officials in the United States government, if supported by Western Europe, would no doubt hurt the Soviet economy. But they would not lead to total collapse or necessarily cause the Soviets to modify their foreign policy. Instead, in a more isolated and autarkic fashion, the Soviets would probably tighten their belts and "muddle through." Although Western economic sanctions against the Soviet Union have not worked well, Soviet leaders are well aware of the costs of dependency, and like Japan they may well seek to keep a healthy diversity among trading partners.

Certain individual commodities may be exceptions to this overall view in the years ahead. Before 1990, for example, natural gas exports to Western Europe could rise to 70 billion cubic meters, with West Germany, France, and Italy obtaining as much as one-third to one-half of their gas imports from the USSR. This prospect has been of concern to the United States government. But the West Europeans have apparently decided that the benefits of more diversified energy supplies outweigh any potential risk. It can even be argued that the foremost concern of the West Europeans is no longer natural gas but rather pipe *exports* to the USSR and the jobs dependent on them. Large natural gas exports could provide the Soviet Union with some additional leverage in Europe but only if we assume that supplies might be cut before European investments and credits are made good. After that time, unless we assume that Soviet needs for imported technology, equipment and agricultural products will no longer exist, one could argue that any political leverage will be more or less equally divided if not actually in favor of Europe.

Given its size, population, and relatively advanced stage of development, the Soviet Union (along with Eastern Europe) is an important component of the world economy, even more so of the world *political* economy. But the USSR is certainly not yet a major factor in international trade in any very direct sense. And international trade, we should remember, is still relatively unimportant in terms of Soviet gross national product, although it might be argued that foreign trade is more important to the economy in a qualitative sense than the volume might suggest. As an exporter of raw materials and as a country largely self-sufficient in natural resources, the Soviet Union can provide an additional source of supply in energy and industrial raw-material markets. Seen in this light, it would seem to make sense not to discourage the Soviet Union from expanding raw-material production both for domestic needs and for export. This does not mean that the Soviet Union should receive "foreign aid" as if it were a developing country or that credit should be provided at less than commercial market rates and tied to specific and deserving projects. But from the global economic perspective, it does suggest that normal commercial relations in this regard would result in more benefits than costs, especially as the strategic implications of Soviet natural resources and related regional development do not appear to be at all overwhelming.

# CONTRIBUTORS

Russell B. Adams, Associate Professor of Geography, University of Minnesota, Minneapolis, Minnesota.

Lawrence J. Brainard, Vice-President and Senior International Economist, Bankers Trust Co., New York, New York.

Brenton M. Barr, Professor of Geography, University of Calgary, Calgary, Alberta.

Kathleen Braden, Assistant Professor of Geography, Seattle Pacific University, Seattle, Washington.

Leslie Dienes, Professor of Geography, University of Kansas, Lawrence, Kansas.

Richard L. Edmonds, Lecturer, Department of Geography and Geology, University of Hong Kong, Hong Kong.

Marshall I. Goldman, Professor of Economics, Wellesley College, and Associate Director, Russian Research Center, Harvard University, Cambridge, Massachusetts.

Edward A. Hewett, Senior Fellow, Brookings Institution, Washington, D.C.

George W. Hoffman, Professor of Geography, University of Texas, Austin, Texas.

George A. Huzinec, Associate Research Director, Dancer Fitzgerald and Sample, Inc., New York, New York.

W. A. Douglas Jackson, Professor of Geography and International Studies, University of Washington, Seattle, Washington.

Robert G. Jensen, Chariman, Department of Geography, and Professor of Geography, Syracuse University, Syracuse, New York.

Karl Johansen, Staff Cartographer, Department of Geography, University of Washington, Seattle, Washington.

Michael Kaser, Professorial Fellow, St. Antony's College, and Reader in Economics, University of Oxford, Oxford, England.

Robert A. Lewis, Professor of Geography, Columbia University, New York, New York.

Arthur A. Meyerhoff, President, Meyerhoff and Cox, Inc., Tulsa, Oklahoma.

Tony Misko, Ph.D., Geography, Kent State University, Kent, Ohio.

Charles Morrow-Jones, Doctoral Candidate, Department of Geography, Ohio State University, Columbus, Ohio.

Victor L. Mote, Associate Professor of Geography, University of Houston, Houston, Texas.

Robert N. North, Associate Professor of Geography, University of British Columbia, Vancouver, British Columbia.

Jeffrey Osleeb, Associate Professor of Geography, and Senior Research Associate, Center for Energy and Environmental Studies, Boston University, Boston, Massachusetts.

Allan L. Rodgers, Professor of Geography, Pennsylvania State University, University Park, Pennsylvania.

Theodore Shabad, Editor, *Soviet Geography: Review and Translation*, and Lecturer in Geography, Columbia University, New York, New York.

Jonathan P. Stern, Energy Consultant, Conant & Associates, Ltd., London, England.

Judith Thornton, Professor of Economics, University of Washington, Seattle, Washington.

Allen S. Whiting, Professor of Political Science, University of Arizona, Tucson, Arizona.

Arthur W. Wright, Chairman, Department of Economics, and Professor of Economics, University of Connecticut, Storrs, Connecticut.

Craig ZumBrunnen, Associate Professor of Geography, University of Washington, Seattle, Washington.

# INDEX

Abakan, 482 (iron ore deposit)
Abaza, 482 (iron ore deposit)
Abrasives: in BAM service area, 164
Academy of Sciences USSR, 52–53
Achak, 366 (gas field)
Achinsk, 257
Achisai, 578 (byproduct gold)
Acrylonitrile, exports, 271
Administrative divisions, USSR, 416–17 (map)
Advanced support bases, 18. See also Territorial-production complexes
Afghanistan: Soviet imports of natural gas from, 102, 372, 373 (table), 376–77; Soviet incursion in, and Soviet-Japanese trade, 225, 675
Agriculture: exports and regional development of, 109; Japanese imports of, 218. See also Grain
Aidarbak, 538 (nickel deposit)
Aidyrlinsky, 538 (nickel deposit)
Aikhal, 270 (diamonds)
Air pollution, 50–51
Air pressure, 23, 25 (table)
Akatui, 573 (byproduct gold)
Akbeit, 579
Ak-Dovurak, 106, 269 (asbestos mine)
Akkermanovka, 480 (iron ore), 538 (nickel)
Aksu, 579
Akzhal, 579
Alampiyev, P. M., 111
Alapayevsk, 480 (iron ore deposit)
Aldan (town), 177, 179, 569
Aldan Upland: cobalt, 163; iron ore, 155–56, 482; mica, 163; titanium, 163
Aldanzoloto combine, 569–70
Alekseyev, V. R., 62
Algerian gas exports to Western Europe, 378
Aliskerovo, 567 (gold placer)
Alisov, N. V., 113
Allakh-Yun, 570
Almalyk (Uzbek SSR), 581 (byproduct gold)
Almaz-Zhemchuzhina, 531–33
Altai, 577 (gold placer)
Altaizoloto trust, 577, 579
Altunin, Ye. G., 404
Altynkan, 581

Altyn-Topkan, 578
Alumina: in BAM service area, 146; imports, 106
Aluminum: exports, 267; exports to Japan, 221; exports and regional development, 106; joint development projects, 670; production of, 267
Amakinsky, 571
American Petroleum Institute (API), 351–52
Ammonia: exports of, 270–71; production of, 271; specialization agreement on, with the West, 104, 271
Amu Darya, 335
Amur basin, 339
Amur Oblast: gold, 567–68
Amursk, 180, 208
Amurstal, 179
Amurzoloto combine, 556, 567–68, 569 (table)
Anabar River, 571 (gold)
Anadyr basin, 341
Andreyevsk, 575
Angara-Ilim, 482
Angara-Pit basin, 482
Angara River: Lower, 482 (iron ore); Upper, 159 (nickel)
Angren, 581
Aniva Gulf basin, 340
Annovka, 478 (iron ore field)
Anthracite, 252–53
Antimony: in BAM service area, 164
Anzas, 482 (iron ore deposit)
Apatite, 103, 268
API. See American Petroleum Institute
Aprelsk, 575
Aral Sea basin, 336–37
Ararat, 583
"Arctic hysteria," 21
Argun, 156 (iron ore deposit)
Arlan, 335 (oil field)
Armenia: gold, 582–83, 584 (table)
Armzoloto, 583, 584 (table)
Artelny, 547 (platinum)
Artels: in gold production, 564–65, 583–84
Artem (Maritime Krai), 201 (lignite)
Artemovsk (Krasnoyarsk Krai), 576 (gold)
Artemovsky (Irkutsk Oblast), 575 (gold)

Asbest, 106, 269
Asbestos: in BAM service area, 145; exports of, 268–69, 268 (table); exports to Japan, 219, 221; exports and regional development, 106–07; and joint development projects, 217, 230, 670; production of, 268–69
Associated gas: flaring of, 322, 371, 630; production of, 366–67, 367 (table)
Association of American Geographers, 4
Astrakhan, 259, 336
Atomic energy. See Nuclear electric power
Auezov, 579–80
Autarky, 3–4, 492, 617, 633–37
Avalanches, 45–46, 47 (map)
Ayakhta, 576
Azerbaijan: iron ore, 473; oil, 308

Badzhal, 163
Baibakov, Nikolai K., 261
Baikal-Amur Mainline. See BAM
Baikal Lake, 32, 141; mica, 163
Baikal, North, 173–76
Baikal Tunnel, 141
Baimak, 582 (byproduct gold)
Bakal, 480
Bakchar, 482 (iron ore deposit)
Baku district, 335, 307 (map), 312 (map)
Bakyrchik, 579–80
Baladzholsky, 579
Balakhany, 306, 308 (oil field)
Balakhchin, 577
Balakhninsky, 575
Balance of payments, hard-currency: and credit, 672; and gold, 268. See also Balance of trade
Balance of trade, hard-currency, 627 (table); for Eastern Europe, 664; and foreign trade policy, 619, 683–85; and petroleum, 631, 633; and primary product exports, 651–52, 655–57, 653 (fig.), 654 (fig.); and raw material resource exports, 633. See also Hard-currency exports
Balbraun, 481
Balei, 573–74
Baleizoloto combine, 572–74
Baltic Syneclise, 330
Balyksa, 577

East-West trade (*cont.*)
(tables), 601 (tables); and implications of Soviet resource potential for the world economy, 684–86; and implications for the USSR, 633–34. *See also* Foreign trade; Foreign trade policy

Economic development: and energy consumption, 276–78; and iron and steel, 466–67; and regional development, 11–12; and Siberian development, 11–12; in Stalinist period, 125, 466; and the world economy, 3–4, 617, 679–80. *See also* Regional development; Resource development; Siberian resource development

Economic regionalization: principles of, 129–30

Economic regions: of the USSR, 73 (map); "complex" development of, 129–30

Economic sanctions, U.S.: and credit, 670–71

Ekibastuz basin, 253, 288 (coal)

Elasticity of demand: for energy products in the centrally planned economies, 296–304

Electric power: and elasticities of demand in the centrally planned economies, 302–03, 303 (table); exports, 260, 261 (table); export and regional development, 102–03; 11th Five-Year Plan, 261; and fuel consumption in electric power stations, 281–83, 281 (table), 282–83 (table); and joint development project, 663; and nuclear power, 260–61, 261 (table)

Electric Power Ministry, 50

El Paso Gas, 151, 204, 217

Emba basin. *See* Caspian basin, North

Energy balance, 290–91 (table)

Energy consumption, 279–80, 280 (table), 385–89, 386 (table); in boiler and furnace, 280–83, 389–91, 391 (table), 392 (table), 393 (table); and economic development, 276–78, 276 (table); and elasticities of demand for energy products in the centrally planned economies, 296–304, 299 (table); in electric power stations, 281–83, 281 (table), 282 (table); in the Soviet Far East, 387; and GNP, 296–97, 304; and Siberian development, 387

Energy crisis: debates on, 346–56; impact of, on oil and gas industry, 343–56, 358

Energy industry: and exports, 252–61; and exports to Eastern Europe, 662–63, 660 (table); and exports and regional development, 100–03; and Japanese imports, 218–19; prices in, 598–600, 598 (table), 600 (table); production in, 252–61; production costs in, 597–98; and substitution possibilities, 279–84; and supplies, 285–89; and supplies in the Soviet Far East, 199, 201–04; transport, 397–401, 398 (table), 399 (table), 403–04; and the world economy, 5–7. *See also* Coal; Electric power; Natural gas; Oil

Energy intensiveness: of the Soviet economy, 277–78, 277 (table), 278 table); of industry, 387, 388–89 (table), 390 (table)

Energy mix, regional, 349–50, 350 (table), 389–93, 397; in thermal power stations, 631 (table)

Energy policy, 278–85, 632–33; and Comecon, 379–80; and Eastern Europe, 663; and energy exports, 379–80; and modeling, 284–85; and prices, 632; and substitution possibilities, 279–84; and the 10th Five-Year Plan, 281

Engineering-geographic regions, 39–40, 40–41 (table), 42 (map), 60–62, 61 (map)

Environmental constraints to Siberian development, 15–60, 58 (map); costs of, 58, 60; and human activity, 60 (map); and macroscale physical limitations, 20–42; and microscale physical limitations (natural hazards), 42–49; technogenic hazards, 49–56, 64–66, 65 (map); and TPCs and industrial nodes, 56–57, 59 (table). *See also* individual hazards

Environmental protection, 52–53, 56, 54–55 (table); and the 11th Five-Year Plan, 53; and forest products industry, 453; during Leninist phase (1917–24), 52; during neo-Leninist phase (1961–75), 53; and planning, 18, 20; during rational-growth phase (1976 to present), 53, 56; during Stalinist phase (1925–60), 52–53; and the 10th Five-Year Plan, 53

European USSR: fuel demand and supply of, 282–83, 390, 398–400; gold, 584; impact of foreign trade on, 111–12; iron ore, 473, 475–80; and the population/resource dichotomy, 11, 628–29, 680; and Soviet regional development policy, 117–18; steel, 506

Export-Import Bank of Japan, 216–17

Export-Import Bank, U.S., 375

Exportlen, 645

Exportles, 447, 449, 455

Exports. *See* BAM service area resources; Hard-currency exports; Natural resource exports; Primary product exports; Raw material resource exports

Extractive industries: exports and regional development of, 103–07

Far East, Soviet, 188–211, 189 (map); administrative divisions, 190 (table); and the BAM, 199; and Little BAM, 199; capital investment in, 190–91, 193, 190 (table), 193 (table); characteristics of, 188; coal, 199, 201–03, 201 (tables); energy consumption in, 387; and forest product exports, 208–09, 209 (table); and forest products industry, 206–08, 207 (table); and forest resources, 204–09, 205 (table), 206 (table); freight turnover of, 146 (map), 147 (map); and historical development, 190–91; impact

of foreign trade on, 112–13; and industrial production, 193–95, 193 (table), 194 (table); and industrial structure and development, 193–95, 191 (table), 193 (table); interregional commodity flows of, 146 (map), 147 (map), 195–98, 192 (table), 195 (table), 196 (tables), 197 (tables); iron ore, 482–83; labor supply and problems of, 85, 88–91, 89, 88 (tables), 192–93; natural gas, 203–04; oil, 203–04; population by region of, 190 (table); and Soviet regional development policy, 90–91, 191–95, 198; steel plant joint development project for, 210, 217, 229–30, 670; and TPCs, 178 (map); and Soviet trade with Japan, 209; and Soviet trade in the Pacific Basin, 209–10, 210 (table); and the Trans-Siberian Railroad, 190

Far East forest resource project with Japan: First, 208, 216, 670; Second, 217, 670; Third, 217, 670

Fedorovsk, 337–38, 349 (oil field)

Fedorovsky, 573 (gold placer)

Fergana depression, 308, 337

Ferroalloys: exports, 105, 266

Ferrous metallurgy. *See* Iron and steel industry

Ferrous ores. *See* Chromite; Iron ore; Manganese

Fevralsk, 180

Fifteen-Year Plan (1976–90), 4, 251, 411, 437, 624

Fine, Daniel I., 7, 636

Finland: and forest product trade with the Soviet Union, 420; and joint development project, 475; and technology transfer in the Soviet forest products industry, 450–53, 463 (table)

Five-Year Plans, 649–51; First (1928–32), 190 (Far East), 308 (oil), 310 (oil), 560 (gold); Second (1933–37), 310 (oil); Third (1938–42), 191 (Far East), 310 (oil); Sixth (1956–59), 216 (eastern regions); Eighth (1966–70), 198 (Far East), 367 (gas); Ninth (1971–75), 198 (Far East), 258 (gas pipelines), 367 (gas), 557 (gold), 565–66 (gold), 649 (primary product exports); Tenth (1976–80), 53 (environmental protection), 142 (the BAM), 198 (Far East), 199 (the BAM), 256 (oil), 258 (gas pipelines), 262 (forest products), 281 (fuel for electric stations), 344–45 (oil), 367–68 (gas), 379 (oil), 404 (gas), 442 (forest products), 445 (Bratsk forest product complex), 469 (iron ore pellets), 566–67 (gold), 631 (oil); Eleventh (1981–85), 53 (environmental protection), 131 (Siberian development), 147 (Neryungri coal), 148 (Udokan copper), 156 (railroad construction), 199 (the BAM), 251 (resource development), 252 (coal), 256 (oil), 257–58 (gas), 261 (nuclear power), 261–62 (forest products), 271 (chemicals), 369 (gas pipelines), 379 (oil), 404 (gas), 420